Forensic Nursing

KELLY M. PYREK

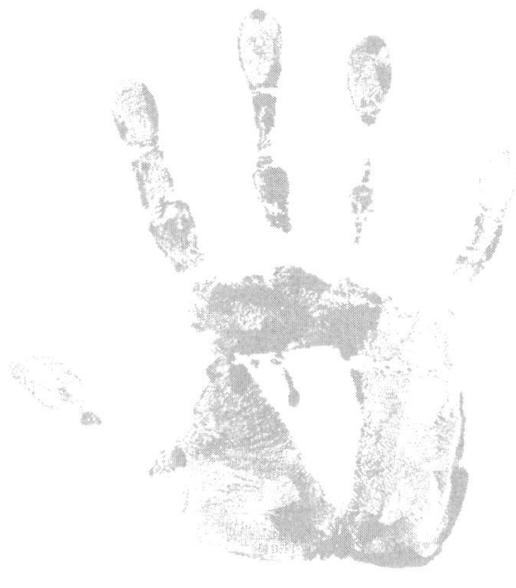

Taylor & Francis
Taylor & Francis Group
Boca Raton London New York

A CRC title, part of the Taylor & Francis imprint, a member of the Taylor & Francis Group, the academic division of T&F Informa plc.

Published in 2006 by
CRC Press
Taylor & Francis Group
6000 Broken Sound Parkway NW, Suite 300
Boca Raton, FL 33487-2742

Printed in the United States of America on acid-free paper
10 9 8 7 6 5 4 3 2 1

International Standard Book Number-10: 0-8493-3540-X (Hardcover)
International Standard Book Number-13: 978-0-8493-3540-2 (Hardcover)
Library of Congress Card Number 2005017336

Library of Congress Cataloging-in-Publication Data

Pyrek, Kelly.
Forensic nursing / Kelly Pyrek.
p. ; cm.
Includes bibliographical references and index.
ISBN-13: 978-0-8493-3540-2 (hardcover : alk. paper)
ISBN-10: 0-8493-3540-X (hardcover : alk. paper)
1. Forensic nursing. [DNLM: 1. Emergency Nursing-United States. 2. Forensic Medicine-methods--United States. 3. Crime Victims--rehabilitation--United States. 4. Mandatory Reporting--United States. 5. Nurse-Patient Relations--United States. WY 154 P998f 2006] I. Title.

RA1155.P97 2006
614'.1--dc22 2005017336

informa
Taylor & Francis Group is the Academic Division of Informa plc.

Visit the Taylor & Francis Web site at
http://www.taylorandfrancis.com

and the CRC Press Web site at
http://www.crcpress.com

Foreword

Principles of forensic nursing are being utilized in all aspects of nursing. Originally designed as healthcare's direct response to violence, this new discipline is now recognized as one of the most basic elements in the scientific and legal approach to the clinical investigation of trauma. By combining the forensic aspects of healthcare with the forensic services afforded to victims and offenders of abuse, neglect, and intentional and nonintentional injury, one can best approach nursing's holistic care of body, mind, spirit, and now the law, required in a culture of global violence.

Elements of daily nursing care are essential to every nurse in every hospital worldwide; however, the laws governing human injury will define the boundaries of forensic nursing practice. The role of the forensic nurse examiner (FNE) and those who will teach, develop, and promote change in antiquated health and justice systems will be recognized as leaders in a contemporary scientific world. The lack of qualified forensic clinicians and forensic pathologists has left a void between critical clinical intervention and the criminal investigation processing of forensic evidence, accurate documentation, and skilled testimony in courts of law.

For far too long, these essential services were relegated to physicians alone. With the advent of forensic nursing science, however, a new perspective in the medico-legal case management of victims of crime and those who commit criminal acts was accorded to protect their legal and human rights. This includes both the living and dead who require forensic interventions of doctors, nurses, police, social services, and the forensic sciences. Previously in the United States, those who survived criminal assaults, abuse, neglect, and liability-related injuries were not provided the quality forensic assessment and protection of their legal rights as were those who died. Due to the lack of skilled forensic clinicians in the clinical environs, only the deceased were properly evaluated by the forensic pathologist.

However, in other countries where forensic clinical intervention is managed by physicians known as forensic medical examiners (FMEs), there often remains a void in immediate response and state-of-the art skills. Because the FME is not in residence at the clinical facility, he or she must be located and respond to the emergency department, and it is not uncommon for all medical services, including life-saving interventions, to be withheld until the FME has arrived and collected evidence. In some countries, the patient is transferred to other hospitals and to different cities in search of clinical forensic services. On occasion, the patient dies during the interval between transfers, a situation referred to as "death by red tape."

Where the forensic nurse examiner is on staff on each shift, immediate forensic services can be provided without delay. Critical forensic evidence requiring timely recovery and preservation is collected and secured without interfering with urgent medical care. Because the forensic investigation of trauma and the collection of evidence are not considered medical treatment, the FNE can provide forensic services within the boundaries of nursing practice, which includes documentation of trauma and collection of specimens. Specialized education and training are required along with essential continuing education, peer review, credentials, and professional organization membership. Thus, the FNE is qualified as an expert witness in courts of law.

With the advances in contemporary medical and scientific technology, the need for victims to be provided with superior forensic services is central to the administration of justice. This text has outlined and identified the most significant fundamental knowledge for nurses who engage in clinical intervention and the scientific investigation of death in the clinical or community environs. This includes cases of sexual assault, child and elder abuse, domestic violence, motor vehicle trauma, gunshot and stab wounds, as well as neglect and violations of individual human rights; also included are the basics of evidence collection and preservation, photo documentation, legal aspects of forensic practice, and the application of nursing principles and philosophy to the law: forensic nursing science.

There is no better way to appreciate the unique contributions of forensic nurses to the healthcare and the social justice systems than to walk among them and to relive their experiences. The reader of this book has the opportunity to take such a vicarious adventure with a journalist who has compiled the chronicles of pioneers and leaders of forensic nursing. Kelly M. Pyrek is neither a nurse nor a forensic scientist, but she made it a priority to learn almost everything about nursing's newest specialty. She aptly demonstrates how forensic nurses work among law enforcement, legal, and forensic personnel, and what they bring to the table that is unique, socially relevant, and valuable. The author has immersed herself in educational ventures and stepped into the trenches with the best forensic nurse clinicians. Her findings, gleaned from interviews, observations, and journalistic investigations of actual cases, permit a glimpse into the virtual world of forensic nursing, replete with triumphs and tragedies that are typically associated with an emerging discipline.

—Virginia A. Lynch, MSN, RN, FAAFS, FAAN
International Consultant in Forensic Nursing Science
Faculty of Forensic Nursing and Forensic Health Sciences
Beth El College of Nursing and Health Sciences
University of Colorado, Colorado Springs

Preface

Forensic science might be at the apex of its popularity among members of the general public who have demonstrated a keen curiosity, satiated by a growing amount of forensic-related television programming. At the time of writing in 2005, no less than half a dozen forensic-themed shows appeared on network and cable television. The studious *Forensic Files* shares space and time in America's living rooms with the three "Hollywoodized" permutations of *CSI: Crime Scene Investigation,* and millions of people are tuned in to the exploits of the men and women who work as investigators, forensic scientists, and crime scene and lab technicians. From gritty to glamorous, from realistic to ridiculous, these shows have raised significant awareness of forensic science. Articles in the lay press have documented the "CSI factor," in which an increasing number of juries know about and expect to examine the forensic evidence involved in criminal and even some civil cases; think *Twelve Angry Men* of today. This is a *Law & Order* generation; undergraduate and graduate programs are filled to capacity with eager young people dreaming of an exciting career in forensic science or criminal justice. Are expectations of the field romanticized and unrealistic? Yes, but big dreams and high hopes can turn into the next big theories that continue to propel forensic science from the rudimentary to the refined, as history has already demonstrated. There is a significant dearth of forensic practitioners to keep pace with growing investigative demands on the criminal justice system stemming from criminal activity, violence, injury, and death, so we must grow a new crop of highly trained, astute professionals versed in medico-legal principles and practices.

It is this heavy investigative workload that, in part, opens the door for the heroes and heroines of forensic nursing. Nurses are not detectives, yet they possess an investigator's sense of curiosity and intuition, as well as keen observation and analytical skills. Nurses are not forensic laboratory technicians, but they execute evidence collection and preservation with impeccable precision. Nurses are not scientists per se, but they endeavor to meet the same exacting standards, and to satisfy the rigors of science-based study within the confines of nursing practice. Nurses are not prosecutors, yet in some small way they share a desire to see justice served. Conversely, investigators, forensic scientists, lab technicians, and prosecutors do not have the in-depth medical knowledge and psychosocial skills inherent to nursing. However, with increasing admiration of the contributions forensic nurses are making, these professionals appreciate nurses' ability to understand and integrate nursing practice into medico-legal cases.

Forensic nursing is the intersection of nursing and medical practice as applied to the law, hence it is very much a medico-legal discipline. In their forensic capacities, nurses assess, treat, and refer victims and perpetrators of violence, whose situations define the very essence of medico-legal investigation. These acts of violence include sexual assault, interpersonal violence, child and elder abuse, and assault of just about every sociodemographic group; they also see victims of motor vehicle accidents, product tampering, acts of terrorism, and other types of trauma. When serving as medico-legal death investigators, forensic nurses extend the nursing purview from the living to the dead, in investigating natural and suspicious or sudden death. Forensic pathologist Michael Baden, MD, once said to me, "Forensic nursing is a discipline whose time has come," and forensic scientist Henry C. Lee once told me that forensic nurses were "absolutely essential." Additionally, forensic laboratory directors Paul Ferrara and Barry Fisher have long respected forensic nurses for their professional prowess. These are noted and famed individuals whose opinions carry weight in the forensic science community; nurses must embrace these words of encouragement and cling to them as they continue to navigate uncharted territory in the clinical realm and bring their forensic skills to bear on health care cases of all dispositions.

Besides championing forensic nurses, this book is designed to make a strong case for the important emerging specialty of forensic nursing and its contributions to the medico-legal community. The preponderance of violence and trauma, both accidental and intentional, issues new clinical mandates for the health care industry as these medico-legal cases present in increasing numbers. The World Health Organization (WHO) defines violence as "the intentional use of physical force or power, threatened or actual, against oneself, another person, or against a group or community that either results in or has a high likelihood of resulting in injury, death, psychological harm, maldevelopment or deprivation" (Krug et al., 2002). In a 1996 resolution declaring violence a leading public health problem, the World Health Assembly called on the WHO to develop a typology of violence that characterized the different types of violence and the links between them (WHO, 1996). This typology divides violence into three broad categories according to characteristics of those committing the violent act: self-directed violence, interpersonal violence, and collective violence. This categorization differentiates between violence a person inflicts on himself or herself, violence inflicted by another individual or by a small group of individuals, and violence inflicted by larger groups such as states, organized political groups, militia groups, and terrorist organizations. In addition, the nature of violent acts can be physical, sexual, psychological, or involve deprivation or neglect. Forensic nursing is the most appropriate response to the challenge of violence and its impact on public health, and its practitioners are in an ideal position to not only treat its victims and perpetrators, but also to assist in the collection and cataloguing of data. The government is recognizing that it needs to track epidemiologic information related to violent deaths. In fact, the federal Centers for Disease Control and Prevention (CDC) are calling violence—including the approximately 50,000 homicide and suicide deaths annually—a significant public health issue (CDC, 2004a). According to the CDC's National Vital Statistics System, in 2001, almost 21,000 homicides and 31,000 suicides occurred, and almost 1.8 million people were assaulted. About 323,000 harmed themselves and were treated in hospital emergency departments. Additionally, in 2001, homicide was the second leading cause of death for people ages 10 to 24, and suicide was the third leading cause of death for people ages 10 to 24.

The challenge is that current data do not provide all the information needed to accurately assess the factors surrounding violent deaths. Death certificates, for example, cannot link victim and suspect information. The CDC recognized that local, state, and national policymakers and program developers did not have comprehensive information about violent deaths, and that although state and local agencies have detailed information that answers fundamental questions about patterns and trends in violence, this information is fragmented and inaccessible. Creating a system to pool these valuable data would help answer such fundamental questions:

- Are violent deaths in schools increasing or decreasing?
- What proportion of homicides result from illicit drug deals?
- How often do murder–suicides occur?
- How frequently are homicides associated with child maltreatment?
- How serious a threat are mass killings?

To better develop answers to these questions, the CDC created the National Violent Death Reporting System (NVDRS), a state-based violent death reporting system designed to provide accurate and timely information to inform decision makers about the magnitude, trends, and characteristics of violent deaths, and evaluate and continue to improve state-based violence prevention policies and programs. The goals of the NVDRS are to do the following:

- Link records from violent deaths that occurred in the same incident, which help identify risk factors for multiple homicides or homicide–suicides.
- Provide timely information through faster data retrieval. Currently, vital statistics data are not available until two years after the death.
- Describe in detail the circumstances that might have contributed to the violent death.
- Better characterize perpetrators, including their relationship to the victim(s).

Using these objectives, NVDRS illustrates a more comprehensive picture of violent incidents. The linked data provide law enforcement officials and death investigators a clearer picture of violent activity in their jurisdictions and will aid program operators to design and implement potentially successful prevention plans.

Since August 2004, the CDC has been funding 17 states (Alaska, California, Colorado, Georgia, Kentucky, Maryland, Massachusetts, New Jersey, New Mexico, North Carolina, Oklahoma, Oregon, Rhode Island, South Carolina, Utah, Virginia, and Wisconsin) to implement the NVDRS, and has also piloted the collection of data from state child fatality review teams in four of the states to better understand the value it adds to NVDRS.

In late April 2005, the CDC released the first data from the NVDRS. Data reported by the first six participating states (Maryland, Massachusetts, New Jersey, Oregon, South Carolina, and Virginia) show increases in suicide and homicide rates for the years 2000 through 2003. These data are in contrast to decreases in violent deaths reported in these states and nationwide from 1993 through 2000. Because this system only contains the first year of data in a small number of states, CDC officials say it is too early to determine how risk factors and trends might have changed in recent years. In 2003, homicide increased 4 percent and suicide increased 5 percent above 2002 rates in the six reporting states. Homicide rates among males under age 25 increased 18 percent in those states.

"NVDRS puts us on the front line to collect rapid, reliable data to better inform our prevention strategies," says CDC Director Julie Gerberding, MD, MPH. "With NVDRS, we can spot early warning trends for violent deaths and modify our prevention efforts. Among those warning signs are the role of alcohol and drugs in violent deaths, and how often a homicide is followed by a suicide."

The CDC established NVDRS in 2003 to address a crucial gap in understanding national and regional trends in violent deaths by combining relevant records into one repository of state-specific data. "This system provides states and communities valuable information that can be used to develop and implement tailored violence prevention efforts," says Ileana Arias, acting director of CDC's National Center for Injury Prevention and Control. "The data help to identify potential strategies and also allow us to evaluate our current violence prevention efforts and determine if they are saving lives."

The NVDRS will document the circumstances of suicides and homicides to help identify and evaluate prevention opportunities. Each state collects detailed information about a violent death directly from the records of state health departments, medical examiners and coroners, and law enforcement, providing a clearer picture of the circumstances surrounding violent deaths at the national, regional, and state levels. Information such as a history of depression or a family dispute, gang activity, drugs, and other circumstances surrounding the violent death are recorded.

Currently, 17 states participate in this state-based surveillance system. The next report expected late in 2005 will include the data from the initial six states as well as seven additional states (Alaska, Colorado, Georgia, North Carolina, Oklahoma, Rhode Island, and Wisconsin) that began collecting data in 2004. The final four states (California, Connecticut, New Mexico, and Utah), which began data collection in 2005, will not release any data until 2006. The CDC hopes to expand NVDRS to all 50 states so data can be compared across states and regions of the country, and to establish national violence-related data. Forensic nurses might one day become instrumental in assisting local jurisdictions in this data-collection process, especially as they continue to investigate regional and national violence-related trends, apply forensic nursing-driven knowledge to their interpretation of these data, and research and publish their findings for the benefit of the entire public health, forensic science, and criminal justice communities.

Colleagues who knew I was writing a book about forensic nursing had expressed joy that, finally, someone was going to chronicle this exceptional nursing specialty in a more personal way than a traditional textbook, without sacrificing any of the studious thought and research on the subject. They also pointed to the fact that I am neither a nurse nor a scholar. True. I am an old-school journalist with more than 20 years of award-winning editorial investigatory experience backing my byline. I know how to research, how to ask the right questions and elicit truthful answers, and how to get to the heart of the matter. In regional and national newspapers, magazines, and trade journals, I have interviewed hundreds and hundreds of people, both laypersons and experts, in dozens of different fields. I have written perhaps a million or more words as I pursued the stories that made readers laugh, cry, think, act, and react. Telling the stories that no one else does is important to me, and that desire is the impetus for this project.

I discovered forensic nursing in 2001. It was late at night, without fanfare or any indication of the treasure trove that was about to yield its incredible wonders to me. I was researching via the Internet an article about the hottest nursing specialties when the term *forensic nursing* leaped from the screen of my computer monitor. OK, I thought to myself, I certainly know what forensic means, having nurtured an interest in this field for the past decade. I knew nursing quite well, having grown up as the daughter of a career nurse. What marvelous things, I contemplated, could happen when the two words were fused together? Hours passed as I searched for every shred of information I could find on the subject. Back then, there wasn't much to be gleaned (today, however, an Internet search yields far greater and more current results, reflected in the fact more people are discovering forensic nursing for themselves), but I could fill in the blanks. I discovered that forensic nurses could, indeed, investigate medico-legal cases, and that they embraced the concept of living forensics, quickly dispelling the myth that forensic science is in the purview of the dead only. I discovered that a small, stalwart group of forensic nurses were making significant contributions to health care, law enforcement, death investigation, nursing jurisprudence, and criminal justice, to name just a few fields, and yet these nurses seemed to be the best-kept secret of the medico-legal world.

The journey began in 2002 when I launched *Forensic Nurse* magazine; along the way, I met some amazing individuals whose passion for and dedication to the specialty were unrivaled. If there is one thing I know, besides journalism and publishing, it's what makes nurses tick; after all, I grew up around nurses, and had a short stint in health care myself during high school and college. I know that nurses are traditionally overworked, underpaid, and continue to battle the "just-a-nurse" syndrome in their quest for personal and professional respect. They are breaking free of these stereotypical shackles, embracing the prestige of higher education and increased opportunities, demanding interesting assignments with impact, and tackling the difficult issues previously untouched by their medical and health care (and forensic!) colleagues. I know that nurses take every success and every failure very personally, and that they care very much about helping those in need, often at the expense of their own welfare. These nurses' devotion to their practice, and particularly to the unique medical needs of the forensic patient, is manifested in how hard they work on behalf of their patients, and to a large degree, how much these nurses put their own needs behind everyone else's. To this day, I can recognize a nurse from 100 paces away by that determined look on his or her face as he or she tries to make everything in the world right again.

I don't know if forensic nursing creates a new breed of supernurses, or whether these characteristics are already inherent in the nurses attracted to this specialty; whether it's nature or nurture, forensic nurses are extraordinary for several reasons. First, they continue to champion nursing at a time when nurses are stretched thin, underutilized, not given credit for their accomplishments, or abused by health care colleagues who are still not convinced of nurses' unimpeachable status. The nursing shortage is happening for a reason, and although the majority of forensic nurses are veterans, the field is attracting a new generation of nurses. Only time will tell if they have the maturity, stamina, and skills of this specialty's pioneers. Nursing is the oldest of all professions, yet many continue to take these special health care providers for granted. Imagine the Help Wanted ads for nurses: low pay, long hours, little respect. Who would still apply? The answer is more than ever, especially with the promise of change as forensic nursing science takes hold and changes minds.

Second, these nurses are entering a specialty that is still considered to constitute vast stretches of health care frontier. Those in the know realize that all nurses are forensic nurses, and that nurses have been unwittingly practicing forensics all of their careers. Progressive thought has finally given forensic nursing a name and an identity that is still being tested, scrutinized, and questioned. Forensic nurses must consistently validate what they do and what they contribute to the health care and medico-legal communities. They are still perfecting their practice, identifying and filling voids in practice, defining and pushing the parameters of that scope of practice, and blazing new trails. It's what they do best.

Third, forensic nurses face a practice that is only for those with a strong stomach, a pure heart, and a quick mind. Daily, they face the ugliness of society, the monstrous acts humans inflict on each other, and the inconceivable actions that most see only in their nightmares. These nurses know they are speaking for the injured, the traumatized, and the dead in a time when there is an overwhelming need for the proper medico-legal process and for its most necessary by-product, justice; if not justice, at the very least, a structured, scientific approach to understanding the medico-legal aspects of the adverse, the unexpected, and the hard-to-contemplate.

The cliché of nurses as part Sherlock Holmes, part Florence Nightingale is tiring because it suggests a vaguely cartoon-like depiction of a process that is very real and very serious to these nurses. It's not a hobby or a fleeting interest; it's a vocation worthy of the same respect as any other in the medico-legal community. These nurses mean business; they are on a never-ending quest to be science-based and taken seriously. They face enormous challenges in the future, even after overcoming significant barriers to practice. They face budget crunches and funding obstacles, questions of standardization of protocol and practice, quality issues, and gaps in training and education, among other important matters central to their effective practice. They lack a clearly defined career path, and they are knocking on doors for jobs until their knuckles are battered and bloody. They also can be their own worst enemies if they allow themselves to be; nurses are said to eat their young, so even as the specialty struggles for acceptance and recognition, nurses must take great care not to internalize these struggles in the face of doubt or discrimination, or lack of leadership and vision both within and outside of the field.

One would think this would be enough to scare off even the most determined of nurses, but they have a secret... they are addicted to the work, addicted to advocating through science for their patients, both living and deceased, because they know that no one else is as prepared and equipped to do so as they are. I should know. These nurses have welcomed this outsider journalist into their fold, and explained and discussed what they do for my professional edification and so I could better tell their stories to the world. They have taken me into their confidences, sharing their joys, their sorrows, their grievances, their worries, and their hopes for the field of forensic nursing. We have broken bread together, laughed and cried together, commiserated about the days that it felt too hard to proceed, and celebrated the times when it was easy and they could conquer the world. We have attended conferences together, enjoying a forum in which we could discuss, debate, and dream, all for the sake of advancing this wondrous nursing specialty.

Detractors of forensic nursing are as plentiful as its supporters. Forensic nurses have as their champions their patients, family members, and an increasing number of enlightened members of the law enforcement, forensic laboratory, and legal communities, a trend that is hard-won and by no means complete or widespread. Until there is a forensic nurse in every health care facility, school, prison, and medical examiner's office, and until the concept of living forensics is fully understood and accepted, there is much work to be done. It is the responsibility of every forensic nurse to tell his or her story, but better yet, to demonstrate his or her capacities and capabilities. That requires getting a foot in the door, and in many cases for these nurses, continually proving their mettle once they gain that coveted entry. Until it's no longer lip service on the part of prospective employers, forensic nurses must push for equity, parity, and greater purpose and relevance in their work, seizing every opportunity to make a case for their presence.

Through speaking with hundreds of nurses since 2001, and interviewing more than two dozen forensic nursing practitioners and other professionals for this book, I am convinced that this specialty will survive, thrive, and change for the better the way medicine interacts with the law. There is no limit to what forensic nurses can achieve, but they must be willing to jump those hurdles and break down those doors themselves. Arguably, in some places in this country, breaking through will be more difficult, as stereotypes, gender biases, and lack of comprehension of the importance of forensic science principles in health care delivery continue to challenge these nurses. As many nurses have revealed in one form or another, the good days are very, very good, but the bad days are enough to make you want to turn and run. May every forensic nurse who reads this book have feet of stone, not clay, and may every forensic and medical professional come to appreciate nurses' worth. Follow your convictions, and the respect will follow.

REFERENCES

Centers for Disease Control and Prevention. National Center for Health Statistics. National Vital Statistics System. 2004a.

Centers for Disease Control and Prevention. National Center for Injury Prevention and Control. Web-based Injury Statistics Query and Reporting System. 2004b.

Krug, E. G., Dahlberg, L. L., Mercy, J. A., Zwi, A. B., & Lozano, R., Eds. *World Report on Violence and Health.* New York: World Health Organization. 2002.

World Health Organization. *Global Consultation on Violence and Health. Violence: A Public Health Priority.* New York: World Health Organization. 1996.

Acknowledgments

The forensic nursing and forensic science communities are graced by the presence of numerous exceptional individuals who give freely of their time and considerable expertise. I have the continued privilege of interacting with many of these people both professionally and personally, and I am indebted to them for sharing their wise and wonderful perspectives, their good humor, and most of all, their unsurpassed dedication to the kind of work that separates swiftly the weak from the strong.

I wish to recognize the following people who have yielded gladly and enthusiastically their immense knowledge to me during the writing of this book, and during the past few years as the seeds for this project were being planted: Janet Barber, Virginia Lynch, Mary Dudley, Barry Fisher, Paul Ferrara, Georgia Pasqualone, Sharon Crowley, Nancy Cabelus, Diana Faugno, Candice DeLong, Meliss Vessier-Batchen, Melissa Becker, Bobbi Jo O'Neal, Rae Wooten, Susan Chewning, Patty Taylor, Mitch and Tascha Spears, Robert and Debbie Smith, Mary Sullivan, Barbara O'Donnell, Cari Caruso, Linda McCracken, Cathy O'Brien, Constance Morrison, Joanne Archambault, Donna Bader, Linda Ledray, Colleen Carney Love, Prudence Schifley, Tara Ferguson, Kathy Delaney, Faye Batiste Otto, Gail Lindsey, Joyce Williams, Valerie Sievers, Jackie Palmer, Margaret Whelan, Maureen Jones, Sheryl Gordon, Rita Hammer, Julie Jervis, Yvonne McKoy, Barbara Cammuso, Katherine Ramsland, Mary Muscari, Mary Fran Ernst, Jim Hurley, Bruce Sackman, Brian Donnelly, Charles Wetli, Patrick Besant-Matthews, William Smock, Vincent DiMaio, Henry Lee, and Michael Baden. Thank you for sharing your brilliance with me.

Having worked in publishing my entire life, I understand the significant effort required to escort a manuscript from concept to completion. I wish to express my heartfelt appreciation to the talented team at Taylor & Francis for believing in this project and making it happen.

Table of Contents

Dedication

To my mother Judi Pyrek, who, as a parent and a nurse, taught me the meaning and value of hard work, dedication, and integrity; and to Tony Hettinger, who, as my best friend and soul mate, keeps me balanced personally and professionally. Life would have no meaning without you both. Thanks for always believing in me.

With gratitude to Becky McEldowney Masterman for her support and encouragement, and for helping make a dream come true.

This book is also dedicated to forensic nurses everywhere for their remarkable courage, their unsinkable convictions, and for their uncommon valor in the face of personal and professional duress, as well as to the patient populations they serve in the name of justice.

1 Introduction to Forensic Nursing

CONTENTS

1.1 WHO NEEDS A FORENSIC NURSE?

An 81-year-old woman resides in a nursing home. She has mild dementia and suffers occasional spells of disorientation to time and place. While administering a shower, the woman's caregiver notices contusions on her inner and outer thighs, and redness in her perineal area. She initially attributes the redness to irritation caused by the woman's incontinence, but is puzzled by the bruise patterns. She searches the patient's medical record, scanning for previous entries that document the bruises, but finds no explanation for the injuries or the redness. The caregiver decides that if no one else mentioned these findings, neither should she. How could she know that a male nurse on the night shift had been fired from his previous job for sexually fondling elderly female residents?

A badly injured 58-year-old male victim of a motor vehicle accident lies unconscious in the intensive care unit of a 500-bed teaching hospital. The steady drip of the IV and the constant whoosh of the respirator are drowned out by the sounds of the chaotic shift change. While her incoming and outgoing colleagues engage in the end-of-shift report, the nurse slips into the patient's room and sidles up to the IV pole. She removes a syringe and a small vial from her pocket and injects its contents into the IV port. She tosses the syringe, the vial, and her disposable medical gloves into the trash can by the bed, and leaves the room silently and swiftly. How could the patient, immobile and sedated, know that the nurse had a penchant for mercy killing?

A mother brings her 2-year-old boy into the emergency room of a busy metropolitan hospital one night. The boy's face is flushed from crying and an elevated temperature, and the distraught woman is frantically trying to calm the youngster as she rushes toward a technician. As she shifts her child to her other hip and brushes the hair out of her eyes, she reveals a swollen lip and a pattern of red, blue, and purple bruising across her cheek. She catches the ER technician's gaze and looks down, mumbling something about her son spiking a fever. She tugs at her son's sleeve to hide the now-faint marks along the child's forearm. Will the technician realize the woman's fresh injuries and the boy's healing injuries are classic indications of abuse?

A body is discovered under some bushes by an early-morning jogger. The partially clad young woman had been raped, strangled, and left for dead in a quiet wooded area thick with underbrush. Police officers scurry around the body in their haste to set up a command post, and one patrol officer didn't notice that lodged in the sole of his boot is a small piece of cloth, matted with blood and hairs. He lumbers up a small incline to the squad car parked on a gravel road, where he absentmindedly proceeds to scrape mud off his shoes as he calls for the coroner.

Different patients, different injuries, different environments; what all of these fictional yet representative scenarios have in common is the need for a nurse who is specifically trained to recognize and respond to potential medico-legal cases. Who needs a forensic nurse? As we will see throughout this book, any individual who is a victim of trauma, accident, abuse, or other malicious intent, needs a forensic nurse.

1.2 INTRODUCTION TO FORENSIC NURSING

Until the last decade or so, forensic science had long been the exclusive domain of scientists, technicians, laboratory directors, members of law enforcement, and prosecutors, creating a medico-legal continuum that traditionally excluded health care in general and nursing in particular. Although not an intentional act of exclusion by the forensic science and criminal justice communities, inclusion of nursing was not considered to be an imperative, nor was it perceived as desired by clinicians. Medical practitioners, including nurses, have been characterized as being preoccupied with the living patient and disinterested in matters pertaining to the investigation of suspicious trauma and sudden or unexpected deaths, even in the clinical setting and elsewhere.

Traditionally, health care providers have been responsible for assessing, diagnosing, and treating patients; in no way have they been expected to also investigate suspected or alleged criminal acts because that was within the purview of law enforcement only. More progressive thought in subsequent decades convinced select medical personnel to contemplate medicine and health care's inherent role in medico-legal investigations. In many instances involving traumatic events, medical practitioners serve as first responders to individuals who are ill or have been wounded in some way. Frequently they are first to observe the presentation of injury, and during the administration of clinical interventions, they are able to further document signs, symptoms, and other physical, mental, and emotional manifestations of the patient in their care. These observations, documented in the patient's official medical record, become part of the medico-legal process as soon as health care practitioners put pen to paper. Therefore, some astute clinicians wondered, why aren't medicine and health care more closely aligned with law enforcement and criminal justice? The answer was, simply, that this alignment always has existed, but practitioners needed to understand and claim their medico-legal heritage to participate more fully.

The application of forensic science to nursing, although considered still to be quite new and contemporary, has deep roots within the more traditional health care delivery model. For as long as victims of violence have reported to the nation's emergency rooms, the health care system has required a method to treat and document these patients' injuries. Although proper acknowledgment and handling of these medico-legal cases were lacking in the past, in the 1980s and 1990s, forward-thinking individuals recognized that forensic nursing is an important facilitator of medico-legal investigation. Lynch (1995, 1997) has described the highly competent, comprehensive approach forensic nursing provides to the equal treatment of the victim and the perpetrator of the pervasive violence, trauma, terrorism, neglect, abuse, and other forms of malfeasance encountered in 21st-century society.

Sullivan (2005) says that clinical forensic nursing is one forensic nursing subspecialty that is underrepresented and not yet formally recognized within the general hospital setting. This subspecialty encompasses "a broad range of forensic knowledge and skills that may be applied to any patient care area within a health care facility." She writes:

> The clinical forensic nurse serves as a role model in clinical situations by increasing staff awareness of the potential for forensic implications in everyday patient care as well as working hand in hand with those charged with investigating patient complaints, suspicious patient events, unexpected death, questionable trends, and emergency/traumatic patient admissions. In addition to fulfilling another critical link between the clinical arena and the judicial system, the clinical forensic nurse is in a position to provide vital protection to victims of foul play when they are at their most vulnerable. The importance of evidence recognition, collection, and accurate documentation is a means to an end for giving patients who are victims of violence, true holistic care, all of which are components of forensic nursing.

1.3 CLINICAL FORENSIC MEDICINE AND "LIVING FORENSICS"

Smock (2003) states that forensic emergency medicine, also known as clinical forensic medicine, is "the application of forensic medical knowledge and appropriate techniques to living patients in the emergency department." He explains that most trauma patients seen in today's emergency department (ED) are not the victims of happenstance or accident, but of "malice and intent at the hands of assailants." Clinicians must now consider the many details they once overlooked as vital evidence in these medico-legal cases. Smock, Nichols, and Fuller (1993) write, "What was once considered confounding clutter that gets in the way of patient care (such as clothing and surface dirt) takes on a whole new significance when recognized for what it really is—evidence." They add:

> Traditionally, the emergency physician has been trained in the provision of emergency medical care without regard for forensic issues. In the process of providing patient care, critical evidence can be lost, discarded, or inadvertently washed away. Patients then lose access to information that can be of critical significance when criminal or civil proceedings arise secondary to their injuries.

Forensic nursing takes its cue from clinical forensic medicine, first embodied within the concept of a "police surgeon" and now more commonly referred to as a forensic physician, which has its origins in the United Kingdom. The profession is supported by the Association of Forensic Physicians, which states that forensic physicians must be registered medical practitioners and, ideally, should have a higher qualification such as the diploma in medical jurisprudence. These physicians promote the discipline and knowledge of clinical forensic medicine and advancement in medico-legal knowledge in all its aspects as applied to the work of police surgeons. Eckert et al. (1986) defined clinical forensic medicine as the application of the principles and practices of medicine to the elucidation of questions in judicial proceedings for the prosecution of the individual's legal rights prior to death.

Smock points to a void in clinical forensic medicine in the United States, citing the work of early pioneers such as John Smialek, MD, and William Eckert, MD, who documented the lack of such forensic practice here when a successful system was blooming in the United Kingdom. In 1986, medico-legal expert Cyril Wecht, MD, JD, stated, "It's a great shame and a source of much puzzlement why a group similar to police surgeons hasn't developed here... I believe those persons with both medical and forensic training could remove much of the guesswork, speculation, and hypotheses from the disposition of accident or assault cases involving living persons" (Smock et al., 1993).

In the United States, the first formal postgraduate program to educate the equivalent of the United Kingdom's forensic physicians was held in 1990 as a two-day seminar sponsored by the Illinois chapter of the American College of Emergency Physicians (ACEP). Although this program did not take hold, another postgraduate training seminar was established in 1994 by the Kentucky chapter of the ACEP and continued through 1998. In "Development and Implementation of the First Clinical Forensic Medicine Training Program," published in the *Journal of Forensic Science,* Smock et al. (1993) describe the creation of this first residency-based clinical forensic medicine training program and fellowship designed to address the unmet forensic needs of victims who are survivors of violent crimes and trauma. The Kentucky Medical Examiner's Office and the Department of Emergency Medicine at the University of Louisville began training physicians to provide clinical forensic evaluations. The clinical forensic physicians evaluate adult and pediatric victims of blunt and penetrating trauma, as well as sexual and physical abuse, and collect evidentiary material when indicated. The development of a clinical forensic medicine training program and fellowship at the resident physician level is internationally unique, the authors say.

Clinical forensic medicine is principally concerned with the provision of forensic medical services to the living and medical advice in the investigation of crimes. In other words, clinical forensic medicine is the branch of medicine that deals specifically with cases involving both legal and medical aspects of patient care. A forensic evaluation refers to the detection, collection, and preservation of evidence. Pattern-injury recognition, interpretation of injuries, documentation of testimony and injuries (including photography), reporting requirements, and regulations are all vital components of a forensic evaluation, but these issues are rarely discussed in most hospitals. Medical professionals working in prehospital care and acute-care settings are likely to encounter perplexing forensic issues related to child abuse, sexual assault, or unexpected child or adult death in their practice, so medical practitioners increasingly are being trained to handle these special cases.

William S. Smock, MD, MS, FACEP, FAAEM, knows clinical forensic medicine. Not only is he the author of the definitive text on the subject, *Forensic Emergency Medicine,* but he wears many hats, including serving as associate professor of emergency medicine and director of the Clinical Forensic Medicine Training Program at the University of Louisville in Kentucky; serving as a police surgeon for the Louisville Metro Police Department; working as a forensic consultant for the Office of the Chief Medical Examiner; serving as tactical physician for the Louisville Metro Police Department and the Floyd County Police Department; and working as the medical director of the Sexual Assault Nursing Program at his university. Smock, whose interests include domestic violence, forensic reconstruction of injuries, gunshot wound injuries, and tactical emergency medicine, believes that clinical forensic medicine should be at the forefront of the attention of every medical practitioner at every health care institution across the country. Much the same can be said for forensic nurses.

Smock says that emergency personnel, both by design and by default, evaluate and treat victims of violence, and that all of these kinds of patients "have injuries or conditions that have criminal or civil forensic medical implications and the prospect or specter of courtroom sequelae."

Forensic nursing is built on "living forensics," a concept steeped in clinical forensic medicine. In 1987, Harry

C. McNamara, then the chief medical examiner for Ulster County, New York, defined it as the "application of clinical forensic medicine to victims of trauma involving the proper processing of forensic evidence" (Lynch, 1995). Essentially, forensic nurses are trained to identify, document, collect, and preserve physical evidence from victims of trauma presenting to the health care setting.

Lynch (1997) explains that clinical forensic practice derives from the broader field of forensic medicine and is defined as "the application of clinical and scientific knowledge to questions of law and the civil or criminal investigation of survivors of traumatic injury and/or patient treatment involving court-related issues." She adds that living forensic patients are the survivors of criminal or liability-related injuries that result in an investigation by a legal entity. Lynch adds, "No longer can health care providers work in isolation from the legal issues previously delegated to law enforcement. It is the responsibility of health care professionals to maintain a high index of suspicion and to protect victims." Lynch states that nurses should provide leadership by routinely identifying, treating, and referring victims of abuse to the appropriate authorities. "To this end," Lynch wrote, "it is necessary to establish and train professionals in the philosophy of living forensics, beginning with emergency intervention." She adds, "Forensic nursing can provide an appropriate health care response to the sequelae of criminal and interpersonal violence."

Linda McCracken, RN, a nurse clinician and forensic nursing consultant in the emergency department of the Foothills Medical Centre in Calgary, Alberta, Canada, states:

> Health care and the law often become enmeshed during the critical moments when patient care supersedes the concern for social justice. Physicians, though supportive of the patient, focus their interventions on immediate life-saving measures and in doing so often unwittingly destroy crucial evidence. Due to the nature of emergency clientele and the emergency care setting, there is a forensic opportunity for the emergency nurse to play an important role in the pursuit of justice in areas of crime and victimization.

She adds that the emergency nurse is usually the first to see the patient, first to talk with the family, first to handle the patient's property, and first to deal with specimens and evidence. She adds, "The emergency nurse must be proactive in recognizing that any patient admitted to the emergency room with potential liability-related injuries, whether victim or victimizer, living or dead, is a clinical forensic patient."

McCracken, who is an active member of a number of trauma nursing associations and holds a certificate in forensic studies from Mount Royal College in Calgary, Alberta, Canada, says, "First and foremost, the emergency care provider must recognize that a potential forensic issue exists." She adds that potential forensic cases seen in the emergency room include individuals involved in motor vehicle accidents; attempted homicide or suicide; injuries involving firearms, knives, or other weapons; accidents (including fires, falls, or electrocution); work-related accidents; poisonings; overdoses or illegal drug use; sexual or nonsexual assaults; anyone in police custody for any circumstance; and sudden, unexpected death within or outside the health care institution. In the white paper, "Saving Lives, Saving Evidence," McCracken writes:

> When we as emergency-care providers deal with the injured from car collisions, domestic/physical abuse, sexual assault, child or elder abuse or neglect, work-related injuries and/or the families of them all, we are practicing clinical forensic medicine. What is done, what is saved, what is charted, are all important and can make the difference in the end results of litigation/conviction, long after the patient has left the ER domain.

McCracken says that she saw other members of the multidisciplinary team "fumbling as to their roles when we all came together over one case. It was time for emergency-care providers, and other health disciplines, to do their part in narrowing the gap in the medico-legal process." She adds:

> One way was to assure that we were not the cause of a miscarriage of justice because of what we documented, what we threw away or what we did with the patient's belongings that could potentially destroy the evidence. I learned the importance of evidence: gross, transient, trace and informational, and the first step in learning how to keep evidence from being destroyed.

McCracken devised a mnemonic, the ABCs of clinical forensic nursing, to assist nurses with their medico-legal responsibilities:

A = Assessment of the victim
B = Bridge the gap; liaison with outside agencies such as law enforcement and the medical examiner
C = Chain of custody; know the methods of evidence collection and establish continuity of evidence possession and disposition
D = Documentation of findings
E = Evidence
F = Families; keep them informed
G = Going to court; be prepared to provide written or oral testimony
H = Hospital policies; know where and how to access your institution's forensic protocols
I = Index of suspicion; be aware of signs of abuse and violence

McCracken says:

> Trauma-care providers are very good at finding out what is injured. We excel in the "E" part of the mnemonic of trauma care: "Expose" the patient to see what is hurt. Unfortunately, we are also skilled at throwing the soiled clothing away, washing the wounds, applying our magic ointments, and making judgments and suppositions when we are not expertly trained in that field. There were no guidelines for us to follow regarding basic forensic evidence collection in the trauma room, no clear direction in the forensic aspect of care other than those involving sexual assault or child abuse. I saw first-hand the need for a collaborative, consistent approach, between all disciplines when dealing with victims/victimizers in the health care setting. First of all, I knew health care providers thrived on mnemonics, so why not put together another one, that being "The Forensic ABCs of Trauma Care."

McCracken's dedication to promoting forensic issues among nurses lies deep within her passion for the field. "Forensic nursing seemed to be a natural evolution in my practice as an emergency nurse," she explains, "because I dealt constantly with victims of violence, work-related injuries, overdoses, organ donation cases, etc." She says what prepared her best for the rigors of her work was early exposure to the courtroom:

> Having been subpoenaed to court on cases in which I was the nurse attending the client while in the emergency room, I learned the hard way, by experience, how my role had to expand. I saw the importance of thorough and concise documentation of patients' statements and injuries. I developed a keen sense of intuition with each new case and recognized that critical thinking in the trauma setting included that "suspiciousness factor" when what I saw just didn't match with what I was being told.

McCracken has worked as a nurse for more than 31 years and says:

> Experience has been my best educator. No courses existed in forensic nursing in my training days. After 24 years of working as an RN (at that time 19 years in the emergency setting), I piloted the first forensic health studies distance program at our local community college. I received a certificate of achievement in forensic studies from Mt. Royal College in Calgary, Alberta, Canada. Most additional aspects (especially forensic education within the trauma science) were self-taught through literature searches and forensic workshops. Basic nursing curriculums didn't cover the forensic aspects of patient care. Forensic nursing is now an option in the nursing degree program and is not mandatory. I wasn't prepared for my role as witness in court testimony, so I learned by repeated experiences in that arena. I didn't understand injury patterns from a forensic standpoint other than those sustained from a medical standpoint, so I think nurses can be better prepared by incorporating forensic aspects of care within the trauma-care regimen, as well as have more in-service training as to the role of the bedside nurse in the court system.

McCracken believes that forensic nursing expands the traditional role of nursing by incorporating the forensic aspect of care into patients' care plans. "I am really giving holistic care to my patients and assuring justice for society." She adds:

> I feel as though my work is a vital link in the chain of justice, a member of a multidisciplinary team assuring that justice is served and those that cannot speak for themselves (like the children or the victims of domestic violence who are too afraid to report the abuse) are heard. My documentation, both written and photographic, tell the story and show the injuries. Even though by the time some cases finally get to court those injuries are healed, my written word is legal testimony for my patient.

1.4 THE DEVELOPMENT OF THE FORENSIC ANTENNA AND CULTIVATION OF THE INDEX OF SUSPICION

Most nurses believe they are born with an antenna of sorts, which is able to guide them through clinical practice and help them determine what is right and what is not, whether it's a decision, an action, a medical presentation, or a patient interview. Nurses have an uncanny ability to discern when something is not quite right; it's a skill that serves them particularly well in the application of forensic nursing.

Astute, well-trained nurses can identify suspicious situations that might fly under other health care professionals' radar. Winfrey and Smith (1999) say, "When an individual nurse masters forensic content and incorporates it into clinical practice, forensic science can also serve as a framework for honing intuition by increasing the suspiciousness factor."

The intuition of an experienced, seasoned clinician, coupled with accurate assessment, is a powerful combination. Paul and Heaslip (1995) say that the practice of "critically noticing" on the part of health care practitioners is essential. Intuition is second nature to nurses, who instinctively know when something is amiss. Eason and Wilcockson (1996) say that intuition is a rational knowledge base from which appropriate action is taken.

Mary K. Sullivan, RNC, CARN, MSN, BSN, says that nurses develop their forensic antennae as they mature in their nursing practice:

> First and foremost, the nurse must be comfortable and competent in his or her area of expertise, having a solid base of experience from which to draw. In order to know when something is not right, the nurse must first know when something is right. And that definitely comes with experience. Over time, every nurse gradually develops a sense of what's right and what's not right with patients, or with the routine in any given area of nursing practice. If a nurse is able to tune out the white noise, and tune in to what is happening with the patient, he or she can pick up an incredible amount of information.

McCracken explains that a nurse's index of suspicion is one's intuitive, "gut" feeling based on a health care provider's experience, education, and speed of reasoning. "This intuition signals that a particular patient or situation has potential forensic consequences," she says.

McCracken adds that the suspiciousness factor is a nurse's "little voice inside his or her head." She recalls a case that might never have been solved correctly had her forensic antenna not told her something wasn't adding up. It demonstrated the lesson of not taking things at face value, especially when they tie into cultural biases.

> This particular case involved a Native American individual, and it was assumed that all Native Americans are drunks. Unfortunately, that's the way people think. He was found in the downtown train station, lying at the bottom of the steps, with severe head trauma. He was brought in intubated and unconscious. Police weren't dispatched to the scene, as the paramedics and the train system security staff deemed that this was just another drunk Indian that fell down 30 cement steps. Well, the suspiciousness factor arose in me. I was the documenting nurse for the case and I said to myself, "Well, isn't that strange that the patient's shoes are tied?" I had already saved all the clothing—I am known as the "bag lady" by police services. I considered the mechanism of injury and saw that there was no cement anywhere on the body or on the clothing, and his pants weren't ripped; all of his injuries were from the neck up. I thought, "What did he do, bounce down the stairs on his head?" It didn't add up. I knew something was wrong.

McCracken says a little bit of sleuthing was in order:

> I thought, "I don't know who this man is, so I will play the role of the nurse and contact the police; I'll say he is an unidentified person and family members need to know he has life-threatening injuries. So let's call dispatch at the police and see if they will assist us in identifying this person." I always emphasize to other nurses to identify the unknown, as you never know what other illnesses they may have, so it was a plausible excuse. I phoned the police dispatch, and it just so happened that the dispatcher was a woman who used to be a unit clerk at the hospital with whom I used to work. I said, "I am calling because we don't know who this person is and wondered if the police would have the time to come to the hospital. He has some identifiable tattoos, so maybe they can figure out who he is." I said, "You're not hearing this from me, but I don't think he fell down the stairs." So she dispatched police and I said to them, "At all of the train stations there are video cameras; maybe we can see something—did he trip and fall or was he assaulted?" They played back the videotape and it showed two guys hitting the patient's head with baseball bats. And, he was already at the bottom of the stairs when he was assaulted. The case turned in an instant.

McCracken recalls another case in which experience and intuition kicked in.

> A man was found lying on a fresh grave in a cemetery, apparently the victim of a gunshot wound to the head. There again, suspicion kicked in because this guy had all of these lesions on his right arm that looked like skin-popping lesions, as if someone had been shooting up. I was assuming that he was left-handed because the lesions were up and down his right arm. But why is the gunshot wound on the right side of his head? It comes down to that forensic mindset. The police officer said that the man shot himself and they figured this was the grave of his girlfriend who had committed suicide. I said, "Out of interest, I lecture on forensic issues and I talk about bagging people's hands to protect possible gunshot residue, and I didn't see blood spatter or gunshot residue on his hand—has he got any?" He had nothing on either hand. The police officer insisted that the wound was self-inflicted. But even the physician said, "I am just charting one wound to the head—not even self-inflicted." It must have been a half-hour later that the police officer was bragging to others that he used to be a paramedic and how he knew what he was talking about. He was bragging about how smart he was on medical aspects, and I caught him hovering over the right hand of the victim, sniffing his hand for GSR after all.

> Suspiciousness is a mindset that nursing practitioners have, that others do not. Fortunately, I think a lot more people are questioning what they see these days. They don't have to become paranoid, but a little bit of forensic thought process is a very good thing. Having the suspiciousness factor is great, but health care personnel need to know what to do with it. They need guidelines to follow so that in the end, justice to the patient will be served, whether the person is the victim or the victimizer—it doesn't matter, we must be able to assist in justice.

Georgia Pasqualone, MSN, MSFS, RN, CEN, DABFN, a clinical forensic nurse specialist in Massachusetts, is the personification of the modern forensic nurse who wears many hats within her health care institution and her community. Several years ago she was designated as the hospital's forensic nurse consultant. She carries a pager and is on call 24/7 for the ED and for the rest of the hospital when potential forensic cases present. She reports that her colleagues in the ED are starting to recognize possible forensic situations and are becoming comfortable with summoning her for consultation.

> At first, they were not recognizing things like child or elder abuse; in our community, things like that just didn't happen. But after working with them and teaching them about forensic principles, they started recognizing that something was wrong. So they would call me and say, "This person has bruises all over and their story isn't making sense." I'd come down and take a look. I remember one time a novice nurse had a patient who had bruises. He called for me and said that something didn't feel right; he wanted to file an elder abuse report but he wasn't sure how to document his suspicions in the medical record. I took a look at the woman and I asked about the nurse's findings. He told me about the bruises, and I said, "But you've missed one of the most important things." He said, "What did I miss?" and I replied, "Look at her face very carefully." He studied her for about five minutes; he didn't see it immediately, but then bingo, he noticed that her eyebrows and her eyelashes were singed. So not only was it abuse, it was neglect because she had been smoking with the oxygen cannula in her nose and her son was allowing her to do this. She could have lit herself on fire. So I am there to help nurses recognize some of the minute details their inexperienced eyes haven't picked up yet. But they are learning to look a little more closely at what is in front of them and slowly they are feeling more proficient at noticing the little things.

Pasqualone says that part of her responsibilities include educating colleagues in the ED about forensic principles. She says that in Massachusetts, there are not enough sexual assault nurse examiners (SANEs) to go around, so she has taken it upon herself to train ED nurses in how to perform a sexual assault examination:

> I've taught them how to do the rape kit, how to fill out the paperwork properly, and I wrote up a two-and-a-half-hour continuing education program for all of the ED nurses in my hospital and made it a competency. Everyone viewed a training video, and they all had to practice with the rape kit, and now, if they have any questions, I leave the training video in the ED; all they have to do is throw it into the VCR and they can follow along with the videotape when performing the sexual assault kit.

With each bit of training, Pasqualone says, ED personnel are becoming more cognizant of medico-legal issues. "Little by little, they started recognizing forensic cases," she confirms.

> We don't take gunshot wounds here, as they are automatically routed into Boston, but we do get cases such as burns and stab wounds. ED personnel are becoming more aware of the statements which they need to document in the medical record, as well as the evidence which they need to collect and package. But it's been a very slow process due to the nature of the ED. It's a difficult crowd to get all in one spot at any one time. You have to catch them for 10 or 15 minutes at a time because they won't sit still. They are way too tired and too busy to come in before work or to stay after work and they are so exhausted.

Pasqualone plans to hold a forensic skills fair sometime in 2005 to reach these busy health care professionals:

> They will be able to learn how to recognize evidence, how to bag it, label it, and photo-document it. My other goal for the year is to initiate a comprehensive photo-documentation policy and protocol in the ED along with teaching them how to use a digital camera. I think I have figured out how to get past the question of manipulation; a new generation of printers allows the user to simply lock the camera on top of the printer, push a button, and there's your 4-by-6 print which can go right into the medical record.

She says that anything that makes medico-legal documentation easier for rushed ED personnel will benefit patients, health care providers, and the institution itself. She includes on the list addressing any forensic-related protocols that might be out of date, incomplete, or nonexistent:

> Prior to my arrival, our hospital had what they called a forensic policy, but it's not what you think. This policy only involved patients who came into the ED in police custody. That was then; with greater forensic awareness and training among personnel in the ED, now, if you ask nurses and physicians what our forensic policy is, they'll say excitedly, "That's the part about sticking evidence in a bag and sealing it!" And that tells me we're making real progress.

One of the basic tenets of the concept of living forensics, especially in the ED, is the "body as the crime scene"; that is, any injury suspected to have been caused by violence, abuse, neglect, assault, accidents, work-related injuries, or other circumstances of a medico-legal nature.

William Smock says there are a few simple steps clinicians can take to ascertain if an injury is accidental or inflicted. They should first determine if the injury is consistent with the history supplied by the patient. If the patient says she fell, do her injuries suggest a defensive posture or signs of a struggle instead? Clinicians should also be aware of pattern injuries, which are epithelial imprints of weapons that are consistently reproducible.

For example, an injury produced by a linear object such as a baseball bat or a broomstick will generally produce a distinctive mark with central clearing surrounded by parallel linear contusions, essentially an outline of the shape of the weapon. These contusions are created when blood beneath the object creating the impact is pushed up and out. In suspected domestic violence cases, clinicians might see marks made by a common linear object, the human hand. A victim who might have been grabbed forcefully might exhibit oval clustered contusions representing fingertips, usually found on normally protected parts of the body such as the inner arm or the inner thigh. Ropes, cords, belts, shoe soles, and the like will also leave distinctive patterns on the skin. One of the most celebrated cases of pattern injury was a partial license plate number imprinted on the legs of a victim of a hit-and-run motor vehicle accident. Burns from a cigarette, a curling iron, water splash, or immersion can cause thermal injuries. For instance, an immersion burn features a sharp line of demarcation between unburned and burned flesh. These kinds of injuries are particularly suspicious when seen in the very young or in the elderly.

Janet Barber, MSN, RN, a clinical nurse specialist in Indiana, says it takes discernment to be able to pick up on the clinical subtleties that separate suspicious situations from natural circumstances:

> Some nurses really want to develop that kind of a forensic antenna, while others don't want to think that every death or injury occurred because of malfeasance or intent to harm. There are some nurses who cannot accept as an operating principle that there is no such thing as a natural death. Nurses must question everything they take in with their five senses, and if they don't, they will miss something critical. I believe that some nurses are better than others at developing a forensic intuition or instinct. They are constantly on the uptake of everything around them. Those individuals who are good forensic nurses are the individuals who are good psych nurses or good ICU nurses or good ER nurses—these are people who don't miss very much. They take in information with their eyes, their ears, their nose, their sense of touch . . . they are constantly pulling in information. There are some nurses who are content to simply go through the motions of passing out meds, doing treatments, reading data off of monitors and putting it in the chart, and that's it. Forensic nurses are not content with that. They have to be the ones who raise the extra questions, who go the extra mile to solve a problem, and who don't take anything at face value. They are the ones who say to themselves, "I have to gather more data, I have to understand this, I have to be able to put it all together." Why do some people have that and others don't? I think forensic nurses do what they do, knowing that they, and their patients, are on the edge between life and death; that everything matters, and every little detail requires scrutiny. They don't take anything for granted, and they accept a higher level of responsibility in doing so. If you notice the kind of people who are attracted to forensic nursing, you'll see that they are not people who are just willing to grind through the day. Most of them are pretty extraordinary.

Barber emphasizes that even forensic nurses in training display a curiously perceptive sense of intuition. Barber, who teaches an online forensic nursing program, says she sees promise in young nurses who are beginning to sharpen their instincts.

> I have people from all over the world in this course, individuals of all ages and all specialties, and one of the common threads is their resourcefulness. I give them case studies involving various forensic nursing scenarios, and while my students don't necessarily have education about all of these elements, they are consistently able to think through the scenarios based on their gut instincts. I'll say, "You are planted in this particular scene. What would you be concerned about, what things would automatically be there, and how would you approach the circumstances?" and they are able to think through the exercise and come up with some amazing ideas that made me think to myself, "Wow, I wouldn't have thought of that."
>
> This kind of critical thinking and problem solving is essential to forensic nursing. This discipline requires nurses to function way beyond the basic level of nursing practice. If you want to be a nurse who functions at the basic level, you will not be a good forensic nurse; forensic nurses must delve below the surface, they have to ask the hard questions, they have to go where no one would go ordinarily. They really have to push the envelope. Some nurses are willing to do that, and if they are, they're great forensic nurses, but if not, they lack the drive needed in this challenging nursing discipline.

This zeal will propel a forensic nurse forward along a professional path that might invite criticism or cynicism from medical colleagues who understand neither the tenets of forensic nursing nor the mandate for its existence. Says Barber:

> I believe there are situations where forensic nurses are ostracized or labeled as a nut case by their co-workers who haven't bought into clinical forensic nursing. When forensic nurses say, "I'm sorry, I simply cannot take that at face value," other nurses may be thinking, "Why are they splitting hairs?" Or they may think the forensic nurse is casting some kind of doubt on their performance or their word, and they get defensive. The forensic nurse was simply being thorough in an assessment of the situation, for the patient's sake.

As a retired colonel in the nursing corps of the U.S. Air Force, Barber draws on a tactical allegory to illustrate her point:

It's simply good science to question everything. In every aircraft incident in the Air Force, there is an investigative team that combs through the wreckage and goes through every detail for reconstruction purposes; no one thinks anything about that because it's automatic, standard, everyday practice. But in hospitals, it has not become everyday practice; when somebody dies suddenly in the intensive care unit (ICU), nurses say, "Well, we just had a sudden death, that's the way it goes." But if they don't investigate it, they'll never know that the patient was electrocuted by their monitor, or a family member poisoned the patient, or someone plugged their trach tube, or whether their ventilator malfunctioned... it's never been popular to even ask these kinds of questions. It's usually a matter of, "Well, the patient died, let's get them ready for their family to come and see them," or "Let's prepare them for the morgue and move on." When clinicians start dealing with death scenes in a new way, that's anxiety provoking for nurses who are not open to forensic nursing concepts.

Barber points to a nurse who traveled to Southeast Asia to assist with humanitarian and medical efforts in the wake of the tsunami that struck in December 2004:

She's operating as usual, when suddenly she starts noticing that there is trafficking in children, orphans are disappearing from what everyone felt were safe havens, that people were stealing rationed items and selling them... suddenly the nurse realizes the forensic implications, and her role changes. It's the same in any hospital. You become a detective of sorts, and you begin looking for any irregularities. In cases of potential bioterrorism, for instance, the first patient who comes into the ER who has trouble breathing and has a weird rash, says, "I was walking down the street and having trouble breathing and I noticed my arms breaking out and I am coughing like crazy." The first patient who comes in with those signs and symptoms is an isolated incident and you don't think anything about it. But when the second and third patients come in with the same complaints, you begin to say, "Wait a minute, this is a pattern." The difference between a forensic nurse and other nurses is that with the very first patient, they begin to say, "Wait a minute, this is a highly irregular presentation without any provocation. I wonder if..." and so they begin to initiate better surveillance early because they have that sixth sense telling them something might be amiss. They don't assume anything, but if they can't account for why something is occurring, there might be something highly irregular they need to deal with. In cases of possible terrorism, there is a huge opportunity for forensic nurses because of their powers of intuition and observation. When a patient who has been in a bomb blast presents to an ER, how do you know from which direction the blast came? Well, if you do irrigations of the ears, nose, and mouth, and you notice there are more chemical materials returning from the right ear canal than the left ear canal, chances are the bomb was to the right of the patient when it blew up. Forensic nurses are constantly thinking about these kinds of variables because they have been well indoctrinated into such details. I think other nurses go through the motions and they don't necessarily put the pieces together. It's not only the clinical procedure, it's a different thought process entirely.

Barber says she believes awareness of forensic protocol on the part of nurses is improving, due in part to the saturation of forensic science in the popular culture.

It is beginning to sink in and influence nurses very subtly to the point they may say, "Wait a minute, I am in a position to be the key person in recognizing a potential forensic case and I'm on the first line of defense." I think the media has done a great job in helping to zoom in on the fact that it was a nurse that discovered this irregularity, or it was a nurse that put two and two together and got this information and began to develop suspiciousness about it. I think nursing organizations like the Emergency Nurses Association (ENA), the American Association of Critical Care Nurses (AACN), and the International Association of Forensic Nurses (IAFN) have continued to send the message about forensic protocol and little by little it's taking hold. I teach an online course for the University of California and in the last two or three courses, most of the students have not been ER, trauma, or ICU nurses per se, but they have been labor and delivery or pediatric nurses; they are seeing the need to understand forensic-related issues such as infant abduction, or why people abuse their children. They are saying to themselves, "I have to get a handle on how would I recognize an unhealthy family situation that might signify that this child is very likely an abuse case." I think these nurses are beginning to see that they have a key role in protecting patients by being educated, because the more they know, the more savvy they are going to be about seeing unusual things. Several of these nurses have said things like, "I would never forgive myself if I missed a case of infant abduction that was occurring right in front of me," or "I would never forgive myself if I sent a patient home from the ER after which the parent killed the child." I think they feel an intense responsibility to get educated so they don't inadvertently allow or facilitate wrongdoing. That's very important to most nurses. Students repeatedly tell me, "I used to not believe that things like infant abductions and elder abuse happened, but now, I want to know how I can help prevent it." They want to become better educated about these medico-legal issues.

Connecticut forensic nursing educator Barbara Moynihan, RN, PhD, APRN, associate professor of nursing at Quinnipiac University, suggests that nurses need to pay attention to their intuition:

They need to learn it's OK to trust their gut feelings or follow an educated hunch. If something just doesn't seem right, you're probably on track because there may be cause to be concerned. Forensic nurses are trained to look at every situation through a forensic lens; they will identify

> situations they might not have identified had they not looked through that lens. Potential forensic cases can be subtle, so nurses need experience in diverse areas of forensic theory and practice so that clinical experiences are consistent with and integrate didactic knowledge. To better understand law enforcement issues, clinical experiences should include time with law enforcement in a variety of settings. To better understand death investigation, the medical examiner's office is a valuable site in which to gain this critical knowledge. To better understand elder abuse, experiences are planned with adult protective services and the state's attorney's office. These experiences facilitate a better understanding of forensic concepts and practice.

Moynihan adds that her students embrace quickly the concept of living forensics and hone their skills at looking through the forensic lens. "They enjoy the challenge of examining and reviewing clinical cases. If they miss something, we research the situation, and frequently that 'Aha!' moment is experienced. Student nurses are eager to absorb and assimilate new knowledge and integrate this knowledge into practice."

1.5 INVESTIGATION OF SUSPICIOUS INJURY OR DEATH

Suspicious injury or sudden death cases are like jigsaw puzzles to forensic practitioners eager to connect what they hear from patients to what they visualize. "The responsibility of the forensic nurse is to use all senses when examining injuries," says Mary Dudley, MD, MSN, RN, chief medical examiner/forensic pathologist and district coroner for the Sedgwick County Regional Forensic Science Center in Wichita, Kansas. "What they have, what they see, documenting it very carefully, listening to what the individual has to say, listening to what is said from all different aspects, observing body language." Dudley says that at least 80 percent to 90 percent of cases that present have some forensic implication, or any case where clinical medicine would interface with the law. "I think it's very important... that the emergency room nurses have forensic training, so that they are able to identify and know what to look for on these different types of injuries that they may see," Dudley says.

"The interview process is really powerful because you can read people as to what they might be trying to mislead you on," says Bobbi Jo O'Neal, RN, BSN, F-ABMDI, deputy coroner at the Charleston County, South Carolina Coroner's Office:

> Most people aren't trying to do that; most cases that we do are natural cases, they're not the traumatic homicides that make the paper. But the ones that are the traumatic homicides are the ones where they're trying to mislead you. If you've done lots of interviews where they're natural and you see how people act when they're not trying to hide something, you can pick up when people are misleading you.
>
> As a death investigator, the first thing that I'm going to do is look at the body and make my own assessment of what I'm seeing. Then we talk with the family, or whoever those individuals may be. From our perspective, we're not going to tell them what we've found. We want them to say it to us. We want them to tell us what happened and then compare the two.

Charles Wetli, MD, chief medical examiner in the division of medical-legal investigations and forensic sciences in the Sidney B. Weinberg Center for Forensic Sciences, advises clinicians to be open to alternate explanations for injury when assessing a potential forensic case. "Make sure you keep an open mind, and don't become prejudiced about things." Wetli says:

> Sometimes the cause of a car crash is a bullet in the chest. Or the fire is started to cover up a homicide. Those kinds of things have to be kept in mind. You have to think dirty in these situations. Everything must correlate. If not, then you have to go back and start putting the pieces together and continue your investigation.
>
> You must approach the autopsy with much more intelligence, to answer questions that are going to be asked anywhere from the next day to five years later. I think the art of forensic pathology or forensic nursing is going to be to document things now in anticipation of questions that won't be asked for maybe three or four years down the road. It's your one chance to document everything. If questions do come up, you can go back to the file and look at the photographs and the diagrams and answer those particular questions that you have.

1.6 INVESTIGATING UNDIAGNOSED TRAUMA

Lynch (1995) advocates a systematic approach to investigating undiagnosed trauma. The first step, she says, is the evaluation of wound pattern characteristics, a process aided by detailed documentation of the appearance of the wound, followed by determination of the type of weapon used to inflict the injury. These wound characteristics, however, Lynch says, constitute evidence that might be obscured by emergency trauma care, so nurses should take great care to differentiate the two. Documentation should include a description of the injury, the location of the injury, and approximate measurements of wounds, supplemented by diagrams, body maps, or photography to assist in reconstruction of injury patterns if the case goes to court. "For patients who survive, or whose wound is excised or extended surgically, later reconstruction of the injury is not possible," Lynch writes, explaining that reconstruction becomes especially important when the patient lives for an indefinite period and later dies as a result of the injury. "Treatment procedures and the natural healing process alter the condition of the wound, thus eliminating the possibility of determining if the wound was inflicted with a single or double edged blade knife, an entrance or exit gunshot wound and so forth."

Lynch adds:

> Nurses should have an accurate knowledge of the types of injuries generally resulting in medico-legal patients and should be familiar with the appropriate terminology. Failure to recognize and describe injuries has confounded the testimony of victim and perpetrator as a defense strategy in the courtroom. The nurse not only appears unprofessional, but a serious crime may go unpunished.

Lynch believes that nurses' involvement in medico-legal investigations extends beyond the ED management of the patient, and that their responsibilities encompass physical evidence documentation and collection, and maintenance of the evidentiary chain of custody. "By implementing forensic protocol that emphasizes cooperation with the criminal justice sector, nurses are initiating a critical link in trauma systems that will provide for improved medico-legal outcomes," she writes.

1.7 A NEW NURSING SPECIALTY EMERGES

If physicians can engage in clinical forensic medicine, so too can nurses demonstrate their medico-legal capacities and expertise, for the benefit of living patients and decedents. It is this latter patient population, however, that has generated much speculation and surprise on the part of medical colleagues and uninformed laypersons. A very small number of nurses recognized this unparalleled opportunity for service to an unmet clinical need, and began to propose and describe the practice of clinical forensic nursing. In 1992, the IAFN was created to help support this newborn nursing specialty; today, the IAFN represents approximately 2,500 forensic nurses.

Virginia A. Lynch, MSN, RN, a founding member of the IAFN and one of the first nurses to use the term *forensic nursing*, defines it as "the application of clinical nursing practice to the assessment and care of trauma survivors, or those whose death is pronounced in the clinical setting, including the identification of previously unrecognized or unidentified injuries, as well as the proper collection, processing, and preservation of forensic evidence."

Lynch (1995) writes, "Forensics traditionally was associated with death and homicide. Today, trends in hospital and community health care have broadened this specialty to include identification of previously unidentified trauma and the collection of evidence from living patients." Lynch explains, "Violence and its associated trauma are widely recognized as a critical health problem . . . Forensic nursing represents a new era of nursing practice that is evolving in direct response to the sequelae of criminal and interpersonal violence." She writes, "The application of the principles and standards of the forensic specialist in nursing has been recognized as a vital new role in trauma care in the 1990s," and adds that every day, nurses encounter "the results of human behavior extremes" such as abused children; individuals suffering from blatant neglect and maltreatment or self-inflicted injury; and victims of firearm injuries, knife wounds, and other assaults. "As trends in crime and violence change, new antiviolence legislation is being implemented; consequently, new personnel resources are required to ensure that these legislative mandates are effectively meeting the needs of society."

Lynch describes the role nurses play in the medico-legal process: "Nurses have been challenged to share responsibility with the legal system to augment the resources available to patients with liability-related injuries, crime victims, and perpetrators or suspects in police custody." She describes a mutual responsibility concept that represents a new perspective in the holistic approach to legal issues in patient care. "There has been strong support for this concept from those who recognize the amount of knowledge required to go beyond the traditional treatment of crime victims and fill a greater role through forensic expertise in health care."

Forensic nurses say the general public and the majority of health care professionals misinterpret the meaning of the term *forensic*. *Taber's Cyclopedic Medical Dictionary* defines the term, stemming from the Latin word *forensic,* meaning "a forum," as "pertaining to the law," specifically, to public debate in courts of law. *Black's Law Dictionary* (Garner, 2001) defines forensic as "used in or suitable to courts of law or public debate."

Supporting the concept of living forensics, Lynch (1995) writes, "Any subdiscipline of science that practices its specialty within the arena of the law is practicing the principle of forensic science. Anywhere the world of law and the world of medicine collide, a medico-legal or forensic case occurs." She explains that traditionally, the term *forensic* carried with it a connotation of death or homicide, an association made in medical practitioners' and laypersons' minds due to pervasive attention to forensic pathology, the medico-legal investigation of death. Contrasted with forensic pathology, or a concern with the dead, is the aforementioned concept of living forensics, which Lynch describes as "a new trend in clinical and community health care that involves the awareness and recognition of unidentified or previously unrecognized trauma and the collection of evidence from living patients." Lynch adds, "Survivors of trauma requiring the investigation of injuries are the concern of the clinician, not the pathologist, although well-trained and experienced forensic pathologists are often willing to assist. Clinical forensic practice is becoming recognized as an essential component of health care in the United States and Canada. Indeed, it has been a respected discipline in public health for 200 years in other parts of the world."

If one accepts these definitions, one must therefore see that living forensics encompasses clinical forensic nursing. In 1992, the IAFN stated:

> Forensic nursing is the application of the forensic aspects of health care combined with the bio/psycho/social education of the registered nurse in the scientific investigation and treatment of trauma and/or death of victims and perpetrators of violence, criminal activity, and traumatic accidents. The forensic nurse provides direct services to individual clients, consultation services to nursing, medical and law-related agencies, as well as providing expert court testimony in areas dealing with questioned death investigative processes, adequacy of services delivery, and specialized diagnoses of specific conditions as related to nursing.

In several books and white papers, Lynch has outlined her vision of forensic nursing, which she sees as a natural progression of a nurse's education, training, and deep perception of how nursing and health care intersect squarely with the law, hence the use of the term *medico-legal investigation,* which is synonymous with clinical forensic nursing and related activities of trauma, accident, and death investigation. Lynch has pointed out that in a traditional nursing role, nurses care for patients from birth through their life span, and in the medico-legal role, nurses follow the continuum all the way to the patient's last chapter, death. Lynch writes, "When one considers the many cases of death that occur in the clinical setting that fall within the jurisdiction of the medical examiner or coroner, it is vital that clinicians are skilled in the documentation and preservation of evidence related to those cases." She explains that nurses are frontline health care providers who are usually the first to interact with a patient and the corresponding evidence, even before law enforcement becomes involved in the case. She further asserts that forensic nurses have earned their rightful place in the medico-legal community. Lynch (1997) writes, "Criminalists and pathologists alike have identified nurses as a previously untapped resource to the forensic sciences, particularly in the investigation of injury and death. With the evolution of this new practice arena in clinical nursing, the role of the forensic clinical nurse specialist is emerging." She adds that these nurses work in the clinical setting as well as in the community, and that "these individuals will become the designated clinicians in the assessment, treatment and referral in cases of physical assault, homicide or catastrophic accidents."

Canadian forensic nursing educator Arlene Kent-Wilkinson, RN, BSN, MN, has assembled the definitions of a number of forensic nursing specialties, including clinical forensic nursing, forensic correctional nursing, forensic ER nursing, forensic geriatric nursing, forensic legal nurse consulting, forensic mental health nursing, forensic investigator nursing, forensic examiner nursing, forensic occupational therapy, forensic pediatric nursing, forensic psychiatric nursing, and sexual assault nursing.

1.7.1 What's in a Name?

Forensic nursing is a broad term with which medical colleagues and laypersons alike still struggle to capture the full essence of the inherent responsibilities and roles. It is a collective noun that encompasses a multitude of nursing subspecialties in a variety of clinical and institutional settings. The degree to which persons try to comprehend the breadth and depth of forensic nursing is reflected in the field's equally difficult struggle to adopt uniform occupational titles. Until laypersons, health care professionals, and colleagues in the forensic community recognize, understand, and embrace the meaning of forensic nursing, the title of forensic nurse is not entirely meaningful. Until forensic nursing titles become more than just words on paper and reflect a critical mass of evidence-based practice, they will not be given credit where it is long overdue. In the meantime, however, individuals in the forensic nursing community are eager to define themselves with titles that accurately reflect their clinical responsibilities and their passion for their unique and challenging profession.

As will be explored in Chapter 6, one of the earliest incarnations of forensic nursing is the SANE. According to various members of the IAFN, before the organization's creation in 1992, forensic nurse examiner programs were developed independently, operated autonomously, and used different terminology to define this new nursing role. One of the earliest programs in Minneapolis used the title of sexual assault nurse clinician (SANC) to denote a clinical nursing role that surpassed examination of the sexual assault victim. The SANC broadened the continuum of services provided to sexual assault victims, emphasizing crisis intervention and supportive counseling in the ED environment and continuing with follow-up counseling by nurse counselors. Another early program in Memphis used the SANE acronym. Other, newer programs have adopted the title of sexual assault/forensic examiner (SAFE) or forensic nurse examiner (FNE). According to the IAFN, a program in Minnesota selected the title of SAFE because it desired to move beyond examination of sexual assault victims exclusively to the completion of evidentiary exams on domestic abuse victims, accident victims, and other populations where forensic evidence collection could be critical to the medico-legal process. At the October 1996 IAFN annual meeting, the council representing SANEs voted on the terminology it wanted to use in the standards to define this new position. Although there were some dissenting votes, the overwhelming decision was to use the title of SANE.

Forensic nurse specialist. Forensic nurse investigator. Clinical forensic nurse specialist. Forensic nurse examiner. It might be a matter of semantics to members of the larger health care and scientific communities, but these distinctions are important to the men and women proudly fulfilling these roles. Sullivan (2005) writes:

> As this specialty continues to evolve within hospital and clinical settings, the impact of clinical forensic nursing practice is being felt in many of the patient care areas to which nurses are routinely assigned. These nurses put on their "forensic caps" and apply this expertise to a practice that might have become routine or second nature. They now see routine patient care assessment and health care delivery in a whole new way. A nurse does not have to leave the bedside, the outpatient clinic, the nursery, or nursing home care unit to be a legitimate forensic nurse. Although specific titles and position descriptions have not been established, several roles appear to be emerging that constitute specific forensic nursing responsibilities. Some of these roles overlap.

Forensic nursing encompasses the subspecialties of clinical forensic nurse specialist, SANE, forensic nurse death investigator, correctional nurse, forensic psychiatric nurse, and many other disciplines that fall under the umbrella of forensic nursing. Sullivan adds, "There are as many combinations of how nurses fulfill their traditional and forensic nursing practices as there are individual nurses."

Sullivan (2005) writes:

> The clinical forensic nurse (CFN) who chooses to practice exclusively in the patient care setting brings together a combination of expertise that includes traditional nursing knowledge as well as skill sets that borrow from the SANE, death investigator, and legal nurse consultant. Skill sets include specific techniques for evidence collection and safeguarding as well as an understanding of the essential steps for maintenance of the chain of custody. There are also documentation requirements that include fundamentals of forensic photography. Forensic personnel must also be facile in the use of medical records and other source documents and may need to interpret their relevance to nonmedical personnel involved in the investigation.

Sullivan observes that four distinct roles are evolving: the clinical forensic nurse provider, the clinical forensic nurse examiner, the clinical forensic nurse specialist, and the clinical forensic nurse investigator.

Sullivan explains that while the clinical forensic nurse provider primarily serves in a caregiver role, "this nurse has obtained education and training in the forensic science disciplines and applies this expertise in patient-care scenarios." Sullivan writes:

> Forensic science principles and the art of "critically noticing" is applied to every patient encountered, whether it be in the emergency department, operating room, outpatient clinic, or an inpatient unit such as geriatric care, psychiatric, critical care, pediatric or obstetrics and gynecology. At this point it is very important to note that simply providing patient care and having the ability to recognize a potential forensic implication does not make one a clinical forensic nurse. The CFN not only recognizes what constitutes a medico-legal case, but knows what chain of events need to be set in motion and is able to do so. The CFN keeps current on rules and regulation for reporting, evidence collection techniques, and legal requirements of the justice system.

Sullivan says that the CFN is "forensically influenced" in all patient assessments and documentation of findings. She adds, "While the 'forensic antennae' are up, this nurse serves as an ideal role model for other staff in detecting inconsistencies and identifying what is potential forensic evidence in day-to-day patient-care activities."

The clinical forensic nurse examiner, Sullivan explains, frequently overlaps with the responsibilities of the CFN, although this nurse might also serve as a SANE or a medico-legal death investigator. Sullivan notes:

> The forensic nurse provider, if trained appropriately, may now wear the nurse examiner hat. Ideally, however, and depending on the circumstances, the forensic nurse examiner is not involved in providing patient care, unless perhaps it is in the emergency department and evidence is being collected during the course of providing treatment (removing a bullet; photographing a stab wound and then removing the clothing without cutting through the hole made by the wounding instrument). The forensic nurse examiner is called onto the scene and focuses completely on identifying, collecting, preserving, and documenting the evidence. This is a completely unbiased approach, whereas in the traditional nursing role, the caregiver is often viewed as the patient advocate. This approach would apply especially in an unexpected patient death or serious adverse patient events. It would not be appropriate for the same nurse involved in the care of the patient who expires unexpectedly to be evaluating the circumstances. Forensic nurse examiners are trained to conduct evidentiary examinations of victims of violence in and out of the hospital setting and are knowledgeable about preservation techniques when it comes to physical, medical, or trace evidence. These nurses have expertise in a specialty area such as sexual assault or death investigation and responding to crime scenes. These nurses can be qualified as fact or expert witnesses in a court of law.

The CFN specialists may work in a variety of health care settings, and commonly serve as scientists, educators, researchers, and consultants. Sullivan believes, "Within the hospital or clinical setting, the forensic nurse specialist has a broad range of nursing knowledge and can analyze patient-care events in a variety of specialty areas." The CFN investigator evaluates, reviews, or otherwise investigates patient care programs, patient care delivery systems, and patient complaints, according to Sullivan.

Sullivan believes that despite some surmountable current barriers to role implementation within the clinical setting, the CFN is a pivotal member of any institution's response to medico-legal cases. She writes:

> The clinical forensic nurse is an essential part of the continuous efforts to improve health care delivery. The CFN role is crucial in all dimensions of patient care including the frontline, hands-on care of all patient groups in all specialty areas as well as after the fact, when the quality of care is evaluated or investigated. In addition, the CFN is in an ideal position to ensure that the rights of victims of foul play are protected within the domain of the hospital or clinical setting. As the specialty continues to evolve, roles and responsibilities are becoming more defined and essential competencies more clearly identified. However, several important questions must be confronted before the CFN can be comfortably established within the health care arena, and many of the answers will depend on the jurisdiction in which the CFN wishes to practice. There must be a standardized way of handling suspicious patient events and managing medical evidence. The pioneers of this specialty will most likely find themselves in the center of patient care events, which will benchmark future nursing practice.

1.7.2 Every Nurse's Heritage as a Forensic Nurse

It is a conundrum because all nurses are essentially forensic nurses, yet this heritage is largely misunderstood, ignored, or not embraced by nurses. A CFN is any seasoned nurse who, through education and experience, has developed a unique set of skills encompassing medico-legal investigation, criminal justice, forensic psychology, forensic photography, or any other areas of advanced study and practice. Even though nursing's roots in clinical forensic medicine reach back for decades, it is only recently that the discipline of forensic nursing has struggled to make a name for itself, as well as achieve formal recognition and earn validation from the health care and scientific communities.

Interestingly enough, forensic scientists and pathologists first acknowledged forensic nursing; acceptance from the national nursing association would come a few years later. The American Academy of Forensic Sciences (AAFS) recognized forensic nursing as a scientific discipline at its 43rd annual meeting in 1991. The field was further validated in 1992 by the formation of the IAFN. It wasn't until 1995 when the ANA Congress of Nursing Practice granted formal recognition to the field as an official nursing specialty. Two years later, the ANA and the IAFN jointly produced the *Standards and Scope of Forensic Nursing Practice* to further guide practice and dispel doubts about the legitimacy of forensic nursing.

Bell and Benak (2001) write, "Every nurse encounters opportunities in his or her practice to apply principles of forensics." They point to cases of elder abuse and neglect that are seen daily in hospitals and nursing homes; victims of trauma and violence who are treated in emergency departments, operating rooms, and ICUs; and nurses working in psychiatric and correctional facilities that care for the mentally ill and the incarcerated who have experienced both roles of victim and offender. They add, "As nurses, and with diverse experience with humanity, it is possible to learn to recognize the many applications of this role . . . As a forensic clinical nurse consultant for hospitals, one can effectively intervene on behalf of clinical presentations that might include sexual assault, child/elder abuse and/or neglect, trauma, interpersonal violence and even death."

Pasqualone believes that nursing skills and medico-legal investigation abilities are complementary, parallel skill sets with immense opportunity for cross-application. She notes:

> My forensic training has made me a better nurse, but my nursing skills have helped me be a good investigator. As a nurse, I was taught to be a fact finder. There is no one in the world better at getting the facts than a nurse. We can ask people questions they don't realize they are answering. I have been able to develop these psychosocial skills even more with my forensic training. I am much more aware of what I am looking at; what I am smelling on someone's clothing, on their breath or about their person; I am more aware of what they are wearing, if there is foreign debris on their clothing or under their fingernails; I am better at looking for injuries and trying to detect a pattern; so forensic science education is critical. It has developed my nursing skills so that I am better attuned to my patients. I'm not sure I would be half as good a forensic investigator if I didn't have the nursing background.

Pasqualone likes to describe forensic nursing as a state of mind, a detective process, and an analytical way of thinking that kicks into high gear when a potential forensic case presents. "Unless you are employed in a job where you can be called a forensic nurse consultant, a sexual assault nurse examiner, or a legal nurse consultant and are doing that 40 hours a week, forensic nursing is something that is incorporated into your practice." She explains:

> You can be an ER nurse and suddenly a child comes in and you suspect child abuse, or an elder comes in and you suspect elder abuse. Something should click in your head and suddenly you are wearing the hat of a forensic nurse; all the things you learned about being a forensic specialist now kick in and you think about injury patterns, photo documentation and evidence collection. It may not be a hat you wear all the time, but it is a sense of knowing that exists below the surface.

Pasqualone points to home health as an example of a nursing specialty that deals with potential forensic patients. "Home health nurses would not describe themselves as forensic nurses yet they are the nurses going to what could be a primary crime scene. They are the ones who first see the environment, the people in it, and they are the first to see if there has been neglect or mistreatment in the home." Pasqualone adds the ED or the ICU also are prime arenas in which forensic cases present. "A nurse may be caring for a patient in the ICU and discover she has been sexually assaulted; or a child is brought into the ED for a tonsillectomy, but the nurse sees bruises and isn't sure what to make of them. That's when forensic training kicks in. Forensic nursing isn't necessarily one hat you put on continuously; it's a role you fall into when the moment presents itself."

Pasqualone says that at her hospital, "nurses have not identified themselves as forensic nurses nor have they recognized what the ED nurses have done over the years because they have never really given much thought to it." She adds:

> They never thought they worked in conjunction with the police. The police were always in the way; they were seen as an obstruction, so there was never anything collegial. The only occasional collegial relationship would be with the paramedics who would bring in patients from an accident scene; but then again, the paramedics weren't educated as to what information to give the nurses and the physicians, since what they said was extremely important in reconstructing the crime. On the other hand, nurses didn't know what to ask; maybe the paramedics had made observations at the scene and the clinicians didn't know what to ask for, so they weren't putting all the pieces together. Here's a person involved in an automobile accident, and the paramedics saw something but didn't give the right information to the nurse, and the nurse didn't know what to ask, so perhaps she couldn't figure out the true mechanism of injury. Luckily, some of the newer, younger doctors have begun to recognize the importance of mechanisms of injury and the fact that these telltale marks should go into the medical record. Because eventually, the case might go to court.

Pasqualone, who also teaches forensic nursing classes, adds there is hope that new generations of nurses will embrace firmly their heritage as forensic nurses:

> Some of the index of suspicion is teachable, but you acquire it over the years, too. I had five novice nurses in my last class, and they got a large dose of forensics. As fledgling nurses trying to absorb all of these principles, when they were out on the floor, they knew only enough about forensics to identify something questionable, and they knew enough to call me for consultation—and that's good. They didn't know what to do with the information they were looking at, but they knew to call me—something had stuck forensically. Older forensic nurses who have been around the block a time or two have seen and heard it all. They know when patients are lying, they know when the injuries aren't matching up with the story being told, and that's when their forensic instincts kick in. It's something you acquire over the years, but at least with this group of young nurses, they knew when something wasn't right. They couldn't quite put their finger on it; while they were in the general vicinity of having something bother them, something that just didn't make sense, they recognized it, and that's the first step. Forensic principles have started to take root, and we just have to nurture that.

Pasqualone recalls a time when a mother brought her young son to the hospital; the boy was covered with bruises.

> The mother was saying that the kid was accident prone and the feelings of the nurses that day were split down the middle. A couple of the nurses believed the mother, again because child abuse just doesn't happen in certain affluent communities, and the other nurses were upset because they believed the kid was being beaten. The nurses were at odds with each other. One nurse who felt that the mother was telling the truth became irate by the fact that we suspected her or someone in the family of child abuse. The injuries were there . . . could the kid be accident prone? Sure. Could he be so hyperactive that he bangs into things? Of course. But that's for child protective services (CPS) to sort out. Sometimes there is no definitive reason for the injuries we see in the ER; we see the injuries but we can't definitively say that it is or is not child abuse. If there is the least bit of suspicion, we have to report it, and let CPS make an assessment of the home and the family. What we see isn't always the truth, so we shouldn't push the panic button. It's the same with elders who are black and blue with their tissue-paper skin peeling off. Is that elder abuse? Well no, not all the time. I end my elder abuse lecture with a picture of a little old lady who is black and blue from head to toe and her skin is peeling off and she's oozing. But she's the happiest little lady you could ever meet. She is diabetic and she says that the slightest little whack causes a boo-boo, and it's not elder abuse. After my lecture I show a picture of this lady and I ask students, "Is this abuse?" and they are all ready to say in unison, "Yeah!" And then I say "Wrong! It's not elder abuse." I tell my students that you must sort it out, you have to get the whole story, and if the story doesn't make sense, that's when the hairs on the back of

your neck go up. But all of the pieces of the puzzle must fit into place. If you have one piece of the puzzle that is aggravating you and doesn't want to fit into place, it's better to err on the side of caution and call Protective Services. You can get all kinds of injuries in the ED and you don't know for sure what caused them, but you call the authorities because you don't want to be responsible for someone's death the next time something happens.

Doing what is right by the patient, even though it might appear contrary at the time, is the advisable path to take, experts say. Pasqualone says she recalls the reactions from colleagues when she pursued not only the correct forensic protocol, but pursued an advanced education to further give her clinical actions credence:

> I was ridiculed for getting my two master's degrees in forensic science. They told me I was too old, that I was being foolish, that nothing would ever come from it. I heard it all. Funny how these nurse naysayers are still working the night shift and weekends and they are miserable. In my position as clinical forensic nurse in the ED, if I collect evidence or if I ask all of the hard questions, I am modeling for others; they are watching me, they know that I am going to be fulfilling my responsibilities correctly in my role as a forensic nurse. I will not be ridiculed for my work, nor do I need to feel paranoid about what I do. That was well established about two years ago when I got called in for a case where an elderly woman had been sexually assaulted and had sustained major internal injuries. It wasn't until they got her to the OR that they realized she had been sexually assaulted, and by that time, much of the evidence had been washed away because she had been prepped for surgery. The staff didn't know what to do, so they called me. I very carefully took fingernail scrapings, did hair combings, and collected the clothing she had been wearing when she came into the ED. The other nurses were standing there, watching every little move I made, so I led by example. Awareness of forensic principles is growing, so forensic nurses need not feel self-conscious about their roles or their duties. They are there for a reason, and a critical one at that.
>
> It was with a great sense of pride that I collected my first piece of evidence, right after I had graduated from the University of New Haven. A stabbing victim came to the ED and I collected the T-shirt he was wearing. The cops didn't seem to want it, but I still knew that I needed to preserve it. So I jelly-rolled it carefully, making sure not to shake any trace evidence loose, put it in its own paper bag, put my seal on it, labeled it. About a year later, the case went to court and from underneath the table, the DA pulled out a shopping bag. My face lit up, and I thought to myself, "I know that bag!" That T-shirt turned out to be one of the key pieces of evidence in that case. I remember running out of the ED door and down the driveway, screaming, screaming for the two detectives to take the T-shirt. At least they didn't throw it out; they processed it correctly and it was a pivotal piece of evidence. Maybe at that time my colleagues were saying, "What the heck is she doing with that T-shirt? That's stupid," and even the cops didn't give it credence, but as it turns out, it was a good thing to do. So forensic nurses should never be apologetic about what they do and why they do it.

California forensic examiner Cari Caruso, RN, SANE-A, recalls a time when "nursing was just nursing." She adds:

> When I began to perform sexual assault examinations, we didn't call ourselves forensic nurses. We were just nurses who performed specific tasks according to protocol. I started doing the exams in 1990 and it wasn't until 1993 that I took a training class in sexual assault nurse examination. It wasn't so much that I was doing everything wrong, in fact, I was doing things right. After all, I can follow directions listed on a sheet of paper; however, it was in this course that I learned about the science behind the evidentiary examination, and I relished knowing where my rape kits go and how they are processed. I liken the experience to a bracelet that you have been wearing every day for a couple of years. You never paid much attention to it until you cleaned and polished it, and then all of a sudden, it really shines and you see the beauty in the bracelet anew. That's the way forensic nursing can be, and discovering that you work in a medicolegal environment.

In "Forensic Techniques" (2004), author Mary E. Muscari, PhD, a psychiatric-mental health nurse practitioner, pediatric nurse practitioner, and forensic nurse specialist, writes, "Nurses have long worked with forensic patients, particularly victims and perpetrators of violence. And while it is common to link the field of forensic nursing with death investigations or emergency department and correctional health settings, a significant amount of forensic nursing takes place within primary-care settings." Muscari adds, "Primary-care nurse practitioners are in an ideal position to identify victims and perpetrators of violence and to prevent future episodes of violence. To accomplish this, nurse practitioners need to screen all patients for potential victimization or offending behavior—and document their findings appropriately."

According to the IAFN, forensic nursing encompasses the following:

- The application of the nursing-related sciences to public or legal proceedings
- The application of the forensic aspects of health care in the scientific investigation
- The treatment of trauma or death of victims and perpetrators of abuse, violence, criminal activity, traumatic accidents, and environmental hazards

Muscari (2004) writes, "Nurses share responsibility with the legal system to augment the resources available to patients with liability-related injuries, crime victims and perpetrators or suspects in police custody. This mutual responsibility represents a new perspective in the holistic approach to legal issues surrounding patient care in clinical and community-based institutions."

If U.S. nurses haven't yet discovered their heritage, McCracken says that in her experience, Canadian nurses already have embraced this special heritage. "The nurses I meet do recognize that they are working in the trenches as forensic nurses." McCracken works 12-hour shifts, both days and nights, helps educate ED teams, and takes the opportunity to explain why their regular work encompasses forensic imperatives:

> The majority of the nurses are part of Generation X and are coming from another viewpoint altogether. These new nurses definitely will grasp their forensic responsibilities. However, the Baby Boomers, the ones I trained with, are a little harder to convince that they truly are engaging in forensic practice by working in the ED. They don't necessarily use the term "living forensics," but they are talking about recognizing abuse and assisting people, and these are the kinds of things that we have responsibility and accountability for in our standards of care.

McCracken explains that Canadian provinces are conducting universal screening for domestic violence, a practice that is seen as being on the cutting edge, but also as an essential component of ED intervention and a natural extension of nursing practice. "It has now been mandated by our regional nursing directors that all emergency nurses must screen, universally, for domestic violence," she explains.

> They view this forensic issue, domestic violence, as a health issue. It has become a standard of practice, and failing to do so is a breach of practice. After a media blitz and posters in every emergency department in the city telling patients who come into our facility that their nurse will be asking them about abuse in their life, the feedback we got was positive. Generally, the public supports our role in breaking the silence about family violence and bullying. It has also become the mandate of our provincial legislature that all agencies work together, from the courts to the shelters, from the emergency room to community and aboriginal agencies to set up a framework of action to allow all families and all individuals to live free of violence and abuse.
>
> Any time a patient comes into the ED, they are asked about their exposure to domestic violence. There has been a lot of resistance, especially coming from the older nurses who see it as a social issue, not a medical or health care issue, and it is none of their business. I am struggling to get them to understand that the process of asking is intervention, so I've planted a seed in their minds at the very least. I have tried to explain to them that this screening is now looked upon not as an option, but as a standard of practice that must be met just as you do vital signs. Our nursing managers are realizing the importance of the screening by nurses and they are on board, but we still need to get nurses to understand that the very act of asking is important—whether you disclose or not is not the issue. You have planted the seed that being beaten by an intimate partner is wrong.

McCracken says she has given much thought to the idea of expanding her nursing role in the field of domestic violence:

> Our city is a leader in the country in dealing with this issue, with its domestic violence conflict units, court system, and multiagency support groups. It is looking to house all these resources in one big center, something like the Family Justice Concept in San Diego. What they are missing on their team is a nurse who is part of the intake team assessing the victim for injuries, and photographing and documenting those injuries, and then linking the victim to the support agencies. I would like to be that nurse, and I am putting together a job proposal.

Forensic nurses in clinical settings recognize the forensic implications of every case that presents to the health care facility. They serve as the bridge between health care and the medico-legal community. Forensic nurses recognize forensic implications in even the most routine patient care situations and in health care worker interactions, as well as suspicious injuries, adverse events, and unexpected death. The forensic nurse is involved in all aspects of patient care, along the entire patient care continuum, from admission (traumatic or not), in triage in the ER, admission for a violent event, chronic disease, ICU, acute care, subacute care, long-term care and hospice, to homehealth care.

Sullivan (2002) states:

> The clinical forensic nurse is an essential part of any hospital team with the responsibility to evaluate and perform the root cause analyses (RCAs) of adverse patient events. Adverse patient events range from those causing minimal concern, to extremely serious action, but the vast majority of these are not criminal in nature. Regardless, the precise identification, collection, and management of facts, data, and medical evidence are critical, criminal or not. It is the duty of every health care provider to ensure a high level of quality patient care and accurate delivery of such services. This means all health care providers must

> have some level of awareness of what constitutes medico-legal significance. In addition, our patients deserve a safe environment in which to receive health care and health care providers deserve a safe place to practice.

In the clinical arena, forensic issues range from trauma and wound pattern evaluation to proper evidence collection and management and even to the evaluation of the level of care provided and timeliness of treatment. The role of the CFN is critical in each area of patient care delivery in that the nurse is most often the first to see the patient, whether in triage, as first responder in a code arrest, before the patient sees the primary care provider in a clinic, or before the elderly patient is formally admitted into the nursing home. Recognition of overt and subclinical abuse and neglect, as well as situations in which artificial means are used to create illnesses is often obscured by the mindset of the health care provider who is focused on natural illnesses (Anderson, 1998).

> The astute forensic nurse practicing in a clinical setting is able to maintain a professional balance between nursing assessments of natural illness while considering all possibilities, no matter how distasteful. Consideration of all angles and maintenance of a heightened awareness does not mean the clinical forensic nurse focuses only on the next investigation, but instead, a more thorough assessment of any given patient situation. (Sullivan, 2002)

Health care professionals traditionally have been trained to identify natural causes of injury and disease; however, overt as well as covert situations and manifestations relating to violence and neglect are in the purview of the forensic nurse.

1.7.3 Clinical Forensic Nursing Practice

Lynch (1995) writes, "In a comprehensive approach to the unmet needs of forensic victims who survive violent crimes and traumatic injuries, enhanced involvement in assisting the living is being explored through new roles for the emerging clinical forensic medical and nursing specialist." Previously, a patient had to die under extraordinary circumstances to be examined by an expert in forensic issues. New forensic specialists will become the designated clinicians who will evaluate and assess surviving victims of rape, drug and alcohol addiction, domestic violence (including abuse of spouse, children, elderly), assaults, automobile and pedestrian accidents, suicide attempts, occupation-related injuries, incest, medical malpractice and the injuries sustained therefrom, and food and drug tampering. Their injuries are the concern of society as a whole and require a combination of social systems interfacing with health care and the law to provide solutions. Contemporary roles require new responsibilities, including the determination of the circumstances surrounding trauma and the mechanism of injury, the identification of human rights violations (e.g., physical torture as well as neglect while in custody, during institutionalized or protective care, or in private homes), and determination of unsafe conditions and products (e.g., workplace hazards, injuries from toys, exposure to toxins, vehicular accidents).

Any patient admitted to the hospital with liability-related traumatic injuries is considered a clinical forensic patient. The case must be reported to a legal agency to ensure that proper investigation and follow-up action will ensue. The hospital staff most often comes in contact with police, victims, and perpetrators of violence and crime in the ED. Protection of the patient's rights remains the common goal of police officers and trauma nurses. Every hospital, regardless of its size and location, must eventually address problems of conflict with law enforcement agencies. Most often, these conflicts concern patients in legal custody and perpetrators of crime, as well as the confidentiality of victims' medical records. Policies that increase mutual understanding, define responsibilities, and promote coordination contribute to multidisciplinary, multiagency cooperation. The nurse's role as a clinical investigator provides a vital liaison between the investigative process and courts of law.

Although there are numerous subspecialties of forensic nursing, Mary K. Sullivan, RNC, CARN, MSN, BSN, forensic nurse examiner team coordinator for the U.S. Department of Veterans Affairs in Phoenix, asserts that one such forensic niche that has experienced difficulty in achieving traction is clinical forensic nursing, which she characterizes as "under-represented and difficult to implement... within the general hospital setting." She writes, "Nurses who possess forensic expertise have not been formally recognized or utilized in their hospital or clinical settings. In my opinion, using a clinical forensic nurse examiner (CFNE) would be a reasonable approach for several problems that health care facilities face today. Such a role requires nurses with a broad range of forensic knowledge and skills."

Sullivan enumerates the responsibilities of a CFNE. One important duty, she says, is ensuring that "trauma patients receive systematic assessments and that the findings are precisely documented. Identification, collection, and preservation of evidence in suspicious patient events or unexpected patient death are equally important functions." The CFNE would also function as a staff educator, raising awareness of forensic protocols as well for the potential for forensic cases to present in everyday patient care situations. "An extant member of the hospital staff who can work hand-in-hand with law enforcement agencies is vital to protect victims of foul play when they are at their most vulnerable," Sullivan writes.

Lynch (1997) says that CFN specialists are properly trained to identify, save, and preserve key pieces of physical evidence that might have been ordinarily destroyed. Lynch writes, "Complaints by law enforcement officers concerning nurses and EMTs refer to their constant struggle to save evidence from the well-meaning hands of uninformed emergency department practitioners and first responders." She adds, "Among the most important requests by police officers is for health care providers to preserve clothing removed from injured people in one piece; for example, cutting through a bullet hole may destroy its potential as evidence." Lynch says a forensic clinical nurse specialist can resolve these issues in the ED.

Sullivan advocates for the 24/7 presence of a CFNE in every health care institution, explaining that "these nurses would continue to meet whatever their usual position responsibilities might be, but be on call for forensic consultation when other health care staff perceived a need." This might not be a realistic plan for most health care facilities to implement, so Sullivan suggests that one CFNE could be scheduled 24/7 in the emergency department and one CFNE could cover the rest of the facility, similar to the way nurses function on code teams. "Forensic nurses as an integral part of the hospital's health care team would seem to be more accepted by peers than someone 'coming in from the outside,'" Sullivan notes, adding, "although this dual role has inherent challenges, no one knows more about the inner workings of a hospital and what it takes to deliver quality patient care than a nurse."

Lynch (1995) maintains that implementation of the role of CFN would provide "a uniquely skilled and qualified forensic professional" whose responsibilities would be to develop the appropriate forensic protocols in compliance with accreditation standards; triage patients at risk for forensic injuries; report to proper legal agencies; document, collect, and preserve evidence; secure evidence and maintain the chain of custody; and serve as liaison between the health care institution, law enforcement agencies, and the medical examiner or coroner and make referrals when medical treatment or crisis intervention is required.

1.7.4 The Role of Screening in Clinical Forensic Nursing

Forensic nurses serve a critical function by screening for potential forensic cases as they enter the health care system, whether it is through the ER, the ICU, the OR, or other inpatient or outpatient hospital departments.

Lynch (1995) cites a 1992 study conducted by the Family Violence Prevention Fund in San Francisco and the San Francisco Injury Center for Research and Prevention that evaluated the circumstances of victims of domestic violence admitted to 397 emergency departments in California. Researchers discovered that only 5 percent of adult victims of domestic violence were identified, due to time constraints, lack of training, and reluctance by health care professionals and patients to discuss domestic violence. Only 59 EDs surveyed had specific forensic policies, and only eight were adequately addressing identification, treatment, and intervention. Although response rate indicated that health care professionals were enthusiastic about helping these victims, few had developed programs to do so.

Lynch (1995) writes, "California is not alone in facing violence and its associated trauma. If time constraints interfere with the ideal clinical intervention in such cases, the presence of forensic specialists in nursing can ease the workload of the physician and better meet the needs of the victim of domestic violence, the criminal justice system, and other medico-legal agencies."

If the American Trauma Society is correct in its report that victims of domestic violence present to the hospital ED six times more often than members of the general population, the presence of CFNs as uniquely skilled and qualified forensic professionals could ensure health care facilities meet their responsibility of addressing interpersonal violence. Lynch (1995) envisions the nurse's responsibilities as developing the appropriate forensic protocols in compliance with accreditation standards; triaging patients at risk for forensic injuries; reporting to proper legal agencies; documenting, collecting, and preserving evidence; securing evidence and maintaining the chain of custody; and serving as a liaison between all relevant parties in the medico-legal community—the health care institution, law enforcement agencies, and the medical examiner or coroner.

Muscari (2004) advocates:

> Screen all patients for signs of victimization and violent offending, and be sure to screen across patient populations. Thus, pediatric nurse practitioners (NPs) should screen patients for partner violence, adult NPs should screen patients for child and elder abuse, and so on. All NPs should screen for animal cruelty, which has been associated with numerous forms of violence, as well as the presence of weapons in the household.

1.7.4.1 Screening for Interpersonal Violence

Screening for interpersonal violence (IPV) or intimate partner violence is within the realm of the forensic nurse's responsibilities as a frontline health care professional. Muscari (2004) writes, "IPV affects women and men in both heterosexual and same-sex relationships, and it can occur in teens through older adults." She points to a study of 149 abused women presenting to the justice system for protection orders or to file assault charges showing that only 24 percent of the 126 (86 percent) who had sought health care in the previous year had been assessed for IPV (Willson et al., 2001). Abuse of men has received little attention, but does exist, and the rate of domestic violence in the gay community is similar to that in the heterosexual community (Dalsheimer, 1998). Muscari writes, "Between 8 percent and 53 percent of adolescents report a history of being physically assaulted by an intimate partner, and unlike abuse in adult relationships, studies find similar rates of victimization among boys and girls." The American Medical Association (AMA) and other organizations recommend screening for IPV, and several clinically useful, valid screening tools are available, including the Partner Violence Screen, the HITS (Hurt, Insulted, Threatened, Screamed), and the WAST (Women Abuse Screening Tool). Positive results from these tools should be followed by use of the Danger Assessment and the HARASS (Harassment in Abusive Relationships: A Self-Report Scale) questionnaires to assess for domestic homicide risk. Risk factors for this include the victim leaving for another partner, the perpetrator's use of a gun, stalking, forced sex, and abuse during pregnancy (Campbell et al., 2003; Sheridan, 2003).

1.7.4.2 Screening for Child Abuse

Muscari (2004) writes, "The behavioral and physical signs of child abuse and neglect have been well documented. Nurse practitioners should become familiar with them." The U.S. Department of Justice's *Portable Guides to Investigating Child Abuse* is available online at http://www.ncjrs.org/html/ojjdp/portable_guides/abuse_02/contents.html.

According to Muscari, risk factors for child abuse include prematurity and low birth weight; being perceived as "different" or "unusual"; congenital anomalies; disabilities or chronic illness; and living in families with poverty, substance abuse, unemployment, high crime, or violence. She writes, "Histories tend to reveal clues such as multiple admissions or emergency department visits, 'doctor shopping,' and domestic violence. Parents may be reluctant to provide an account of the injury, may give conflicting histories, or may provide a history inconsistent with the injury (a 4-year-old with a bilateral fractured mandible who 'fell off a five-story fire escape')."

1.7.4.3 Screening for Elder Abuse

According to the National Center on Elder Abuse, any knowing, intentional, or negligent act that causes harm or serious risk of harm to a vulnerable adult constitutes elder abuse. Laws vary by state, but abuse can be categorized as physical, emotional, sexual, exploitative, neglect or abandonment. Risk factors for abuse are social isolation, mental impairment, a history of domestic violence, and, in some situations, simply living with someone else, such as a friend or caregiver. "All older adults should be screened for abuse, despite the paucity of appropriate screening tools," according to Muscari (2004). Nurse practitioners can use the Elder Assessment Instrument (EAI), a 41-item scale that reviews symptoms and subjective complaints of elder abuse, neglect, exploitation, and abandonment. Muscari advises nurses to "refer patients if there is any evidence of mistreatment without sufficient clinical explanation; the patient voices a subjective complaint of mistreatment; or you believe there is high risk for or probable elder abuse."

1.7.4.4 Screening for Rape

Muscari (2004) explains, "Nurse practitioners should also assess patients for violence outside the home, including the workplace, school and community. Violent acts can also occur in nursing homes and residential facilities, and assault and rape can take place anywhere. Many rapes go unreported—for reasons such as humiliation, shame, fear and denial—yet only a small percentage of health care providers routinely screen their patients for physical or sexual assault." When screening patients for sexual assault, Muscari advises that it is best not to use the word *rape,* as patients might not define rape in the same manner. "Instead, ask patients if anyone has ever forced them to have sex or to perform a sexual act. Screening during primary care visits is critical because some victims develop a silent reaction to rape, never telling anyone about the incident. These patients may exhibit signs of distress during the interview, such as poor self-esteem, lack of self-confidence, paranoia, dissociation, prolonged periods of silence and stuttering."

1.7.4.5 Screening for Offenders

"Violence is any assault that causes or intends to cause serious harm to other people. Health care providers should know that stress does not directly cause violence, but the probability of aggression in response to stress increases when certain conditions, such as lower socioeconomic status, early socialization to violence and lack of social integration, are present," Muscari (2004) writes. She says that substance abuse and schizophrenia have also been associated with aggression, and the most predictable risk factor for violence is previous commission of a violent act.

Regarding batterers, Muscari says, "No consistent psychiatric disorders have been noted among batterers, but abusive men share similar characteristics, such as low self-esteem, rigid sex-role stereotypes, depression, an intense need for power and control, a tendency to minimize the extent of their violence, a tendency to blame others for their behavior, violence in their family of origin, and substance abuse." Studies have shown that women batterers typically are young, anxious, emotionally excitable, worrisome, prone to substance abuse, tough-minded, uncaring, insensitive to others, and antisocial. They also have a history of family violence. Muscari notes that several researchers have recommended using the funneling technique to assess battering behavior, a technique that moves from general, open-ended questions to specific, direct questions that assess violent behavior. "Batterers tend to minimize their behavior, so questions may elicit euphemisms such as 'had a bad day,' 'lost my temper,' or 'self-defense' to refer to their own violent behavior," Muscari says.

Child abusers might be attempting to cope with personal attributes such as detection of immaturity, adolescent parenting, lack of parenting skills, unrealistic expectations of the child, unmet needs, isolation, poor impulse control, life crises, physical or mental health problems, and substance abuse, Muscari observes. "Parental demeanor during the interview can be quite revealing . . . Signs that a woman may be reaching her coping limit include claims that the baby is too difficult or heavy, thoughts of harming herself, or bizarre thoughts about the baby. Thoughts of self-harm or harm toward the baby require immediate attention." Elder abusers might be persons out for financial or personal gain, or caregivers who have difficulty coping with the demands of caring for an elderly parent. Finally, individuals who commit sexual violence might be looking for sexual expression of power and anger, motivated by retaliatory and compensatory intent, Muscari says.

Health care providers are challenged by the need to identify potential offenders based on the evidence of injury or information collected through a patient interview and history. "Offenders are not likely to voluntarily discuss their violent acts. Thus, alternate interviewing techniques are necessary," Muscari says. She explains that one method, known as the forensic genogram, provides information about the transmission of family patterns (including violence) that assist health care providers and the court in understanding offenders. Individual and family patterns of victimization, substance abuse, suicide attempts, and criminal activity can be mapped. Muscari writes, "Since offenders often present with extreme behaviors, genogram patterns are often profound. Understanding family influences ultimately assists in understanding the events that may have led to the offender's behavior. The genogram often reveals an upbringing of abuse, ineffective communication patterns and substance use. Average families have one or two members with maladaptive functioning; forensic families possess numerous dysfunctions."

Lynch (1997) says that health care providers have a duty to not only screen patients for signs of trauma of medico-legal significance, but to be familiar with their state's reporting requirements. She writes, "State reporting statutes specifically mandate that health care professionals who have cause to believe that an individual is being abused or neglected must report that suspicion to the proper authorities." States vary as to what must be reported, who should receive the report, and what degree of protection from liability the law offers to the person making the report. In general, Lynch says, cases that require reporting by health care providers include injuries caused by a lethal weapon, certain kinds of motor vehicle trauma, self-inflicted injuries, drug overdoses and poisoning, suspected criminal abortions, animal bites, child and elder abuse, sexual assault, individuals determined to be "dead-on-arrival," and individuals who have been treated in a hospital for wounds that could have been inflicted as a result of violence.

REFERENCES

Anderson, W. R. Medicolegal implications in clinical patient evaluation and treatment. In *Forensic Science in Clinical Medicine: A Case Study Approach* (pp. 223–234). Philadelphia: Lippincott-Raven. 1998.

Bell, K., & Benak, L. D. Forensic nursing: The fastest growing discipline of nursing for the 21st century. Available online at: www.iafn.org. 2001.

Campbell, J., Webster, D., Koziol-McLain, J., & Block, C. Risk factors for femicide in abusive relationships: Results from a multi-site case control study. *Am J Public Health. 93*, 7, 1089–1092, 2003.

Dalsheimer, J. Battered men: A silent epidemic. *Top Emerg Med. 20*, 4, 52–59, 1998.

Easen, P., & Wilcockson, J. Intuition and rational decision making in professional thinking: A false dichotomy? *J Adv Nurs. 24*, 4, 667–673, 1996.

Eckert, W., et. al. Clinical forensic medicine. *Amer J Forensic Med Path. 7*, 3, 101, 1986.

Garner, B. *Black's Law Dictionary* (Second Pocket Edition). St. Paul, MN: West Group. 2001.

Lynch, V. A. Clinical forensic nursing: A new perspective in the management of crime victims from trauma to trial. *Critical Care Nursing Clinics of North America. 7*, 3, 489–507, 1995.

Lynch, V. A. *Clinical forensic nursing: A new perspective in trauma.* Collins: Bearhawk Consulting Group. 1997.

McCracken, L. M. Living forensics: A natural evolution in emergency care. *Accident and Emergency Nursing. 7*, 211–216, 1999.

Muscari, M. E. Forensic techniques. Advance for Nurses Online. Sept. 2004.

Paul, R. W., & Heaslip, P. Critical thinking and intuitive nursing practice. *J Adv Nurs. 22*, 1, 44–47, 1995.

Sheridan, D. Forensic identification and documentation of patients experiencing intimate partner violence. *Family and Community Violence. 5*, 1, 113–141, 2003.

Smock, W. S. Forensic emergency medicine. Presentation at Forensic Focus conference, Scottsdale, AZ. June 2003.

Smock, W. S., Nichols, G. R., & Fuller, P. M. Development and implementation of the first clinical forensic medicine training program. *J Forensic Sci. 38*, 4, 835–839, 1993.

Sullivan, M. K. Clinical forensic nursing: A higher standard of care. *Forensic Nurse, 1*, 1, 4, 2002.

Sullivan, M. K. Opportunities and challenges in forensic nursing. In V. A. Lynch, Ed., *Forensic Nursing in the Hospital Setting*. In press, 2005.

Willson, P., Cesario, S., Fredland, N., & Walsh, T. Primary health care providers' lost opportunity to help abused women. *J Am Acad Nurse Pract. 13*, 12, 565–570, 2001.

Winfrey, M. E., & Smith, A. R. The suspiciousness factor: Critical care nursing and forensics. *Crit Care Nurs Q. 22*, 1, 1–7, 1999.

RECOMMENDED READINGS

Barber, J. Frontiers and challenges in critical care: Foreword. *Crit Care Nurs Q. 14*, 3, 1991.

Brenner, P., Tanner, C., & Chesla, C. From beginner to expert: Gaining a differentiated clinical world in critical care nursing. *Adv Nurs Sci. 14*, 3, 13–28, 1992.

Burgess, A. W. *Violence Through a Forensic Lens* (Second Edition). King of Prussia, PA: Nursing Spectrum Publishers. 2002.

Butt, J. *Sudden Death and Police Investigations* (Second Edition). Calgary. 1993.

Courson, S. The investigative specialty of forensic nursing. Pennsylvania State Nurses Association Career Center. Available online at http://www.psna.org/Career/forensic.htm.

Duval, J. Role of the forensic nursing specialist in an urban trauma center. In *Proceedings of the 47th Annual Meeting of the American Academy of Forensic Sciences*. Seattle. 1995.

Eyler, A., & Cohen, M. Case studies in partner violence. *Am Fam Physician. 60*, 2568–2576, 1999.

Hamberger, L., & Lahti, J. The family peace project: A model for training health care professionals to identify, treat and prevent partner violence. *J Aggression. 1*, 55–81, 1997.

International Association of Forensic Nurses. Available online at http://www.forensicnurse.org/about/default.html.

Kent-Wilkinson, A. Forensic family genogram: An assessment and intervention tool. *J Psychoso Nurs and Ment Health Serv. 37*, 9, 52–56, 1999.

Lynch, V. A. Forensic nursing in the emergency department: A new role for the 1990s. *Crit Care Nurs Q. 14*, 3, 69–86, 1991.

Lynch, V. A. Forensic aspects of health care: New roles, new responsibilities. *J Psychosoc Nurs and Ment Health Serv. 31*, 11, 5–6, 1993.

MacNamara, H. Living forensics (seminar brochure). Office of the Medical Examiner, Ulster County, New York. 1988.

Marsh, T. A nurse's guide to sleuthing. *RN. 41*, 8, 48–50, 1978.

McCracken, L. A link in the chain in the medico-legal process of evidence. *NENA Outlook Magazine. 21*, 1997.

McCracken, L. Living forensics: A natural evolution in emergency care. *Accident and Emerg Nurs J. 7*, 4, 211–216, 1999.

McCracken, L. The forensic ABC's of trauma care. *Canadian Nurse. 97*, 3, 30–33, 2001.

Mittleman, R., Goldberg, H., and Waksman, D. Preserving evidence in the emergency department. *AJN. 83*, 12, 1652–1656, 1983.

Sanders, C. The world of forensic nursing (Course No. 241). Available online at http://www.OnlineCE.net.

Smock, W., Ross, C., & Hamilton, F. Clinical forensic medicine: How ED physicians can help with the sleuthing. *American Health Consultants. 5*, 1, 1–8, 1994.

Stea, J. Behavioral health force protection: Optimizing injury prevention by identifying shared risk factors for suicide, unintentional injury, and violence. *Mil Med. 167*, 11, 944–950, 2002.

Taylor, W. Sexual assault: Identification, treatment and referral in the emergency department. *Top Emerg Med. 20*, 4, 4–11, 1998.

2 Forensic Nursing as Part of the Nursing Process

CONTENTS

2.1 THE NURSING PROCESS

At its core, nursing is the symbiotic relationship of art and science applied within the context of interpersonal relationships for the purpose of promoting wellness, preventing illness, and restoring health. The American Nurses Association (ANA) defines nursing as the "diagnosis and treatment of human responses to actual or potential health problems." The nursing process was established in 1973 through the formalization of the ANA's standards of practice, and it functions as a nurse's own "scientific method" for patient-care delivery.

The nursing process is an elemental framework on which basic tenets of nursing rest. It is a systematic problem-solving approach used to identify, prevent, and treat actual or potential health problems and promote wellness. Elements of the nursing process are the essential building blocks with which nurses of all specialties—including forensic nursing—build their respective practices. Forensic nurses base their specialized practice on these core values, adapting them to fit the unique aspects of their medico-legal work. It should be of some comfort, both to the uninitiated forensic nurse and to the colleague in the greater forensic science community, that the nursing process is predicated on an orderly, scientific, medico-legal approach. Like forensic nursing itself, the nursing process is dynamic, client oriented, goal directed, universally applicable, and most important, problem and solution oriented.

Many forensic cases present first in the emergency room, a place where the nursing process is most readily put to the test. Patricia Ann Bemis, RN, CEN, author of *Clinical Practice Guide of Emergency Care: The Ultimate Core Curriculum,* says that the structure of the nursing process lends organization to a tumultuous health care environment in which emphasis on a team approach is critical. Bemis (2003) writes:

> Organized chaos describes the emergency room. The nine steps of the emergency care process . . . are the organized part of the chaos. By using the same care process, all members of the emergency team can anticipate the care of the other and interrelate as a team. A team approach leads to stronger professional practices and improved patient outcomes. During a true emergency, it may be necessary to perform the steps simultaneously or out of sequence. When the care process is known and the same for all team members, the ability to adapt to change during a true emergency is easy.

Bemis explains that each team member must do the following:

- Perform a quick ABC (airway, breathing, circulation) assessment.
- Identify the patient.
- Use the patient's words for the chief complaint.
- Ask relevant questions to develop a history of the present illness.
- Develop nursing diagnoses related to the nature of the emergency.
- Plan by anticipating the medical care.
- Identify and perform initial assessments and interventions.
- Identify and perform ongoing evaluations and interventions.
- Provide discharge instructions.

Particularly in the ER setting, a nurse must quickly evaluate the patient with the AVPU mnemonic: A for alert signifies the patient is alert, awake, responsive to voice, and oriented to person, time, and place. V for verbal signifies the patient responds to voice, but is not fully oriented to person, time, or place. P for pain signifies the patient does not respond to voice, but does respond to painful stimulus such as a squeeze to the hand. U for unresponsive signifies the patient does not respond to painful stimulus.

The first step in the nursing process is assessment, steeped in data collection, or a systematic gathering of information about the patient that incorporates observation, interview, consultation, and examination. The patient is the primary source of both objective and subjective information, and secondary sources include the patient chart, family members, and health care colleagues. Subjective data—commonly called symptoms—is the information the patient or the caretaker tells the nurse during the nursing assessment. Objective data—commonly called signs—is information collected by using the senses, collecting information that can be seen (observation), felt (palpation), heard (auscultation or percussion), or smelled.

A patient's health history consists of biographical data, chief complaint, present illness and health status, past history, current health information, and family history. According to Bemis,

> The patient's identity, chief complaint, and history of present illness are developed by interview. The standard questions are who, what, when, where, why, how, and how much. "Who" identifies the patient by demographics, age, sex, and lifestyle. "What" develops the chief complaint that prompted the patient to seek medical advice. "When" determines the onset of the symptom. "Where" identifies the body system or part that is involved and any associated symptoms. "Why" identifies precipitating factors or events. "How" describes how the symptom affects normal function and describes the severity of the affect. The chief complaint is a direct quote, from the patient or other, stating the main symptom that prompted the patient to seek medical attention. A symptom is a change from normal body function, sensation, or appearance. A chief complaint is usually three words or less and not necessarily the first words of the patient. Some investigation may be needed to determine the symptom that prompted the patient to come to the ER. When the patient, or other, gives a lengthy monologue, a part of the whole is quoted.

Bemis advises nurses to use direct quotes to document the chief complaint, as well as to attribute the source of the quote, such as "the patient states..." or "John Smith, the husband, states...."

When taking the history of the present illness or injury, Bemis says nurses must ask themselves a multitude of probative questions, such as:

- If a weapon was involved, where is the weapon?
- When did the symptoms begin?
- If the symptoms are no longer active, how long did they last?
- If the symptoms were intermittent, how long did each episode last and how frequent were they?
- Where are the physical injuries and what body system is involved?
- Are any other symptoms associated with the chief complaint, such as drug or alcohol intoxication, nausea, vomiting, headache, sweating, or irregular or fast heartbeat?

With answers to these questions, nurses then should reconsider the nature of the emergency and consider whether a clinical presentation is masking for another medical condition such as:

- Overdose and poisoning for an overdose
- Carbon monoxide inhalation for carbon monoxide poisoning
- Stabbing, gunshot, and penetrating injury for injuries from a weapon
- Laceration for a laceration
- Hemorrhage for a laceration with hemorrhage

Bemis says nurses must then ask the hard questions, such as:

- Did an emotional crisis, such as a relationship crisis, disagreement, confrontation, or situational conflict, precede the symptoms?
- Is unlawful activity suspected?
- Was law enforcement at the scene? Which agency might have been present? (This question must be considered, as medical personnel are obligated to notify law enforcement if unlawful activity is suspected.)
- Has any treatment been initiated? Has it helped?
- Has the patient had similar problems before? When?
- What was the diagnosis and treatment?
- Does the patient have any pertinent past history?
- Does the patient take any routine medications? If so, what is the name, dosage, route, and frequency of the medication and when was the last dose taken?
- Does the patient have allergies to drugs or foods? What was the reaction?

In the nursing assessment, the patient's biophysical and psychosocial status is observed. Biophysical components are

- Integument
- Head and neck

- Respiratory
- Cardiovascular
- Musculoskeletal
- Neurological
- Genito-urinary
- Reproductive

The psychosocial components are

- Psychological
- Spiritual
- Social
- Developmental

Lynch (1997) writes, "In performing a forensic assessment, the forensic nurse specialist (as a clinical investigator or emergency clinician) is required to maintain an objective evaluation of the account provided in incidents of abuse." She outlines this list of factors that might assist nurses in confirming a suspicion of abuse:

- Multiple hematomas or scars in various stages of healing
- Concurrent injuries or evidence of neglect
- History of previous hospitalization for "accidental" trauma that is not explained fully or substantiated by the evidence
- Delay in the patient seeking medical attention and treatment
- Injuries appearing to be older than the alleged time or day of the accident
- An account of the injury that is incompatible with the age or ability of the patient, as in the instance of pediatric patients
- The patient appears to be excessively withdrawn or submissive
- Pattern injuries are indicative of suspicious or inflicted—not accidental—trauma

The second step in the nursing process is the nursing diagnosis. According to Carroll-Johnson and Paquette (1994), nursing diagnosis is defined as "a clinical judgment about individual, family, or community responses to actual or potential health problems/life processes. Nursing diagnoses provide the basis for selection of nursing interventions to achieve outcomes for which the nurse is accountable."

The nursing diagnostic statement is comprised of three elements:

1. The nursing diagnosis statement describes alterations in the patient's health status and ability to function.
2. The etiologies are those factors contributing to the existence or maintenance of the patient's health problem. These factors can be pathophysiological, psychosocial, situational, developmental, cultural, and environmental.
3. The defining characteristics are a cluster of subjective and objective signs and symptoms that represent a nursing diagnosis. The defining characteristics, gathered during the assessment phase, provide evidence that a health problem exists. The symptoms (subjective data) are changes that the patient feels and expresses verbally to the nurse. The signs (objective data) are observable changes in the patient's health status. Nurses are advised to use the phrase "as evidenced by" (AEB) to connect the etiology and defining characteristic statement. The nursing diagnoses are arranged and presented in the order of priority according to urgency and importance.

The third step in the nursing process is planning, which documents the characteristics of patient outcomes and goals, such as being

- Patient-centered
- Specific and measurable
- Realistic for the individual patient
- Of a limited time frame, with a target date and time for achievement

The fourth step in the nursing process is implementation of nursing intervention, which is defined as "any treatment, based upon clinical judgment and knowledge that a nurse performs to enhance patient/client outcomes. Nursing interventions include both direct and indirect care; nurse-initiated, physician-initiated, and other provider-initiated treatments" (McCloskey & Bulechek, 2000). Nursing activities are defined as "the specific behaviors or actions that nurses do to implement an intervention and which assist patients/clients to move toward a desired outcome" (McCloskey & Bulechek, 2000). When selecting an intervention, nurses must consider the following factors:

- Characteristics of the nursing diagnosis
- Research base for the intervention
- Feasibility of performing the intervention
- Acceptability to the patient
- Capability of the nurse

The fifth step in the nursing process is evaluation. The patient care plan is reviewed to determine if the patient's needs are being met and whether or not the stated goals are being achieved. The care plan can then be revised, continued, or discontinued based on its effectiveness.

In the ER environment, Bemis says initial assessments and interventions include the following:

- Considering where the patient is placed within the ER, as the goal is to provide a safe, harmless, and nonhostile environment.
- Communicating in short, concise statements while establishing rapport and trust.
- Encouraging the patient to verbalize.
- Getting vital signs.
- Performing a focused physical assessment of any areas of injury.
- Informing the patient, family, and caregivers of the usual plan of care and the expected overall time in the ER.
- Providing the patient with a device to reach someone for assistance and explaining how to use it.
- Establishing a set of rules for movement about the department and asking the patient to agree with the rules.

Ongoing evaluations and interventions include the following:

- Monitoring temperature, heart rate, blood pressure, and effectiveness of breathing.
- Monitoring therapy closely for the patient's therapeutic response.
- Informing the physician of adverse changes noted during ongoing evaluation.
- Documenting that the physician was notified of the adverse change and what orders, if any, were received.
- Monitoring closely for the development of adverse reactions to therapy and performing interventions to relieve the adverse reaction; asking the physician for a remedy.
- Keeping the patient, family, and caregivers well informed of the plan of care and the remaining time anticipated before disposition.
- Monitoring the patient's laboratory and X-ray results and notifying the physician of critical abnormalities; remedy abnormalities as ordered.
- Notifying the physician when all diagnostic results are available for review.
- Asking for establishment of a medical diagnosis and disposition.

2.2 THE FORENSIC NURSING SCOPE OF PRACTICE

In each step of the nursing process, forensic nurses plug into this formula the specific bits of data pertinent to a forensic case. The steps along this path are the same in forensic nursing as they are in any other nursing specialty, where the forensic nurse provides continuity of individualized care at the same time as preventing omissions and duplications in care. Throughout the nursing process, forensic nurses employ critical thinking skills that encompass:

- Reasoning
- Conceptualization
- Reflection
- Autonomous thinking
- Impartial decision making
- Problem solving
- Intuition
- Inductive and deductive reasoning

Says clinical nurse specialist Janet Barber, MSN, RN:

> There are many people raising the question about where forensic nursing fits within the scope of nursing. However, I think that since the American Academy of Nursing has inducted nurses into the academy based on their work in forensic nursing, and the ANA has endorsed the forensic nursing scope and standards of practice, all of these things point to the fact that the barriers are coming down and the wider field of nursing science is beginning to say yes, forensic nursing does fit, yes, it is a nursing role and responsibility. They are saying, "It is a specialty with which we are going to have to reckon." I think many are still trying to figure out how forensic nursing logically fits into the overall nursing framework and how it interfaces with other disciplines, but I don't think there is any question anymore about whether or not it fits. I would say that yes, there is increasing evidence in the nursing literature that the application of the nursing process is being made to various steps in forensic nursing. I think that whatever they are doing, forensic nurses always perform the various steps in the nursing process, conducting thorough data collection, assessments, planning, interventions, and evaluations. They consult each step of the nursing process and ask themselves, "Have I considered all of these elements?" and "How do they fit into forensic practice?"

2.3 THE SCIENTIFIC METHOD

What's more, both the nursing process, and especially the forensic nursing scope of practice, embrace the use of the scientific method, especially in the medico-legal arena. It is the process by which scientists, collectively and over time, endeavor to construct an accurate, reliable, consistent, and nonarbitrary representation of the world. In the recognition of the influence that cultural and societal beliefs have on an individual's perceptions, the use of standard procedures and criteria minimizes those influences and eradicates bias when a theory is being developed.

According to Bright (1952), the four steps of the scientific method are:

1. Observation and description of a phenomenon
2. Formulation of a hypothesis to explain the phenomenon
3. Use of the hypothesis to predict the existence of other phenomena, or to predict quantitatively the results of new observations
4. Performance of experimental tests of the predictions by several independent experimenters and properly performed experiments

If the experiments bear out the hypothesis it might come to be regarded as a theory or law of nature; however, if the experiments do not bear out the hypothesis, it must be rejected or modified. Key to the scientific method, experts say, is the predictive power of the hypothesis or theory, as tested by the experiment (Barrow, 1991). It is often said in science that theories can never be proved, only disproved, as there is always the possibility that a new observation will conflict with a long-standing theory. The scientific method requires that a hypothesis be ruled out or modified if its predictions are clearly and repeatedly incompatible with experimental tests. Further, its predictions must agree with experimental results if it is a valid description of nature. Experiments can test the theory directly or can test for consequences derived from the theory using mathematics and logic.

2.4 FORENSIC NURSING SCIENCE: A LOGICAL NEXT STEP?

Virginia A. Lynch, MSN, RN, is among a growing number of leaders in forensic nursing thought who embrace the relatively new term of *forensic nursing science* as a way to elevate this specialty of nursing practice and to celebrate its roots in science. Lynch says:

> To establish the foundation upon which forensic nursing is designed, it is necessary to examine the history of clinical forensic medicine, or living forensics, as it is sometimes called. This is a new field of inquiry brought to the attention of clinical nursing through an integrative practice model that unites the disciplines of nursing science, forensic science, and criminal justice in the common goal of protection of the victim's legal, civil, and human rights. As greater numbers of nurses are involved in the investigation process requiring the application of forensic science to nursing practice, increased collaboration with the criminal justice system is required. Forensic nursing's scientific knowledge base emerges from theories of nursing, forensic science, criminal justice, police science, and legal studies.

To demonstrate its roots in science, Lynch (1995) explains that the theoretical model of forensic nursing evolved from the role of the police surgeon in the United Kingdom, a practitioner of clinical forensic medicine hired by the police department and responsible for facilitating the management of the crime victim from the scene of the incident through the legal process. She writes:

> Forensic nursing, a clinical subspecialty, is complementary to clinical forensic medicine as it evolves in response to society's changing demands. In the past, medicine has had a working relationship with nursing, except in forensic medicine. The time has come to extend the interdisciplinary support and assistance to include the forensic physician and forensic nurse as a cooperative unit.

Forensic nursing is the application of the nursing process to public or legal proceedings, the application of the forensic aspects of health care to the scientific investigation of trauma. Clinical forensic nursing is defined as the application of clinical nursing practice to trauma survivors or to those whose death is pronounced in the clinical environs, involving the identification of unrecognized, unidentified injuries and the proper processing of forensic evidence. Lynch writes, "A serious gap in the criminal justice system has either been left open or partially filled by health (nurses, hospital physicians, emergency medical technicians, paramedics) and justice practitioners (police officials and attorneys) who essentially lack a forensic background. These individuals must be able to recognize problems in the existing system and raise the awareness of potential solutions."

"The concept of forensic nursing science has a familiar ring to it these days, now that everybody is saying it's not just forensic nursing, it's forensic nursing *science*," Janet Barber, MSN, FN, says:

> Virginia Lynch and I have heated discussions about this regularly. I tell her that nursing *is* a science and to say "forensic nursing science" is being somewhat redundant. Already, science is a purview of nursing, so I don't think it adds anything more to the equation. Virginia's idea is that the phrase addresses the scientific method and that it indicates the forensic nurse is guided by important principles of the scientific method. From that vantage point, I think it does have some validity. If using the word "science" helps nurses see the validity of the scientific processes, then I don't have any quarrel with that. Personally, I don't think it's necessary, but if that word helps nurses focus on objectivity and a systematic way of gathering data, evaluating it, and drawing conclusions, then so be it.

Meliss Vessier-Batchen, RN, MSN, a nurse death investigator in Louisiana, believes the term lends added credibility at a time when forensic nursing is still proving itself. "If you look at Virginia Lynch's earliest framework, nursing science is one of the three areas of the triangle created among forensic science and criminal justice," she says.

> Virginia has begun using that term which I am now perpetuating because I agree with the idea—it's not just forensic nursing, it is forensic nursing science. As forensic nurses, we bring a very scientific base to nursing. I feel strongly that forensic nursing is a science because it is based on scientific and criminal justice disciplines. That term will become more known in the future among all nurses. Forensic nursing is a science, not just a whim. It's more than a specialty, it's a science, growing in and of itself.

Vessier-Batchen says that it is essential for forensic nurses to conduct research and be published in respectable science-based journals to have their work taken seriously. "It's not enough to work hard; we must produce the research that will support the claims we are making. While these claims are honest and true, there is nothing out there to support them. If we want to be considered as a true science, we must provide empirical data, and get this data out into the scientific community."

California forensic examiner Cari Caruso, RN, SANE-A, says she recognizes a dichotomy between advocacy and science. "There is a way to accomplish both, but some nurse examiners find it easier to see themselves as a support person for the patient. Although I think there is a way to help patients, including referring them to victim-advocacy resources, we must keep our boundaries and be professional and highly scientific." For example, Caruso says:

> If the patient is not forthcoming, or needs special attention, he or she may skew the truth; they may be covering for someone even though they are reporting the sexual assault. If the nurse examiner sides with the patient, or if the nurse sees her role as supporting the patient and their history, they are crossing a boundary line. We, as examiners, weren't there at the time of the event, so we don't really know what happened. We serve the patient best by maintaining our objectivity, collecting the evidence, and making sure that we don't go overboard in our feelings. We have feelings about whether or not something is a bona fide event or not, but on the other hand, you shouldn't go overboard, regardless. There are times when I have examined the suspect and the victim in the same case, and there are times when I find that one side or the other appears to be more credible or the retelling of the events may be more consistent, but you must maintain objectivity at all times. Recently I saw a patient who gave me kind of a quirky story about her assault that allegedly happened on a cement patio. The detective called me from the scene and told me where the assault happened; he said it was very dirty and that the cement was covered with dirt and sand. This young lady was wearing a white shirt that didn't have a speck of dirt on it. Now that's not very consistent. She was having some difficulty and later on it came out that there were family problems involved; the mother told the detective that they were going to back off from the investigation. You have to let the evidence tell the story, and not be taken in by siding with the victim simply because they are the victim.

Caruso also detests the notion that forensic nurses are a bunch of bleeding hearts who do not traffic in science. "I don't want anyone to confuse us with victim advocates," she says. "Some people are trying to pigeon-hole forensic nurses as advocates, and while I am always an advocate for my patients' health, we as forensic nurses should never be confused with individuals whose job it is to work purely on behalf of the victim."

A major pitfall for nurses to avoid is allowing personal beliefs to interfere with the administration of science-based clinical practice. Caruso says she has seen instances in which forensic nurses have withheld emergency contraception from victims due to their religious beliefs:

> It's difficult for me to believe that people are still so old-fashioned or out of touch that they don't agree with providing emergency contraception to sexual assault victims. On a SANE-hosted Web site, there was a letter from a nurse saying, "I am a Christian and I have a problem with giving emergency contraception, what should I do?" I thought to myself, "First you need to understand that it's not an abortion; it's emergency contraception that prevents implantation." The bigger issue is that nurses like this need to examine whether or not their own beliefs spill over into their practice. Nurses must not push their beliefs on their patients; their job is to give them the options. A nurse would be remiss if he or she did not discuss emergency contraception with the victim. As a SANE, if you can't objectively discuss those kinds of issues with your patients, you are doing them a disservice.

In a similar vein, Caruso frets about nurses losing their scientific sensibilities if they identify too closely with victims due to a personal history of abuse of their own:

> I suspect that a private history of sexual assault or abuse is the reason why a lot of nurses get into an advocacy role. I have known nurses who have been assaulted and who have entered the field of forensic nursing because of it. That can be a very real danger zone, depending on how much you are thinking of your experiences when you are dealing with your patient. That will create boundary issues, especially if a patient's experience hits so close to home that you are going to be lost in the gray area between being a professional and relating too much to the patient's story. There are nurses who experience vicarious trauma and burnout from becoming too involved in their patients' situations. They must remember that they are there in a forensic capacity, a scientific capacity, not as a counselor. That's what victim advocates are for.

Another pitfall related to nurses' adherence to professionalism and science is the refusal or the reluctance to perform examinations of suspects or perpetrators of violence, again, due to a need to always support the victim. Caruso continues:

> Some nurses balk at examining suspects, but I have always cared for suspects and victims in the same way. I don't treat suspects any differently than I do victims, because it is not my place to pass judgment. I don't make the suspects tell me a history per se, but sometimes I get the feeling from them that maybe they have been victimized themselves. They are all my patients and they all need a fair shake. I have had a couple of cases of really terrible child abuse and sexual abuse. I saw one suspect who just about killed a 6-year-old; there was no question whether or not he had done it, as he had been caught doing it. However, he still is my patient and I didn't treat him any differently than anyone else who would walk through my door.

Barber urges forensic nurses not to engage in undue victimology in profiling their victims or perpetrators:

> I think many forensic nurses started in the field as being victim oriented, but as a discipline we are trying to move away from the idea of forensic patients as being victims only; in some cases they certainly are, but in other cases they are the perpetrator of the violent act. There are many nurses who want to get into someone's head to learn the underlying factors that would help explain why an act of violence occurred. What factors resulted in the perpetrator's violent act? What factors contributed to the victimization of the injured? This may be important, but if it consumes the forensic investigator's thought processes it is likely to interfere with their ability to accomplish an unbiased, complete evidentiary examination. In a one-car accident, these nurses are trying to figure out, "Were they really trying to kill themselves?" instead of noting the forensic details of the case. Instead of playing psychologist, forensic nurses should be asking themselves, "What am I seeing, what evidence do I need to collect for the experts who are going to do the analysis?" . . . That's what forensic nursing is truly about. I think that when you start diverting your attention from documentation and evidence collection to victimology, and trying to figure out why people victimize themselves, that detracts from the goals and purpose of forensic nursing. There are many nurses who would disagree with me, but that's OK; I would rather remain grounded in science. The difficult thing is that in the beginning, forensic nursing was based on helping people in need. We were looking at people who had been wronged, abused, neglected, assaulted, hurt in some way by an outside force, and nurses thought, "These poor people, something bad happened to them and we have to go pick up their shattered bodies and lives and get them back on the road." Now, forensic nursing has evolved to where we must compartmentalize our desire to care for, nurture, console—any nurse would do that, forensic nurse or not, because caring for and protecting human beings is instinctive. The forensic component of nursing comes to the forefront, the science of identifying, gathering, managing, preserving, and documenting evidence properly for others to analyze. The advocacy component is not unique to forensic nursing; it is within every nurse's purview, but the forensic nurse really cannot get overtly involved in advocacy. This nurse must stay within an objective, scientific framework, because if a nurse allows advocacy to supersede concern about the evidence, he or she will become diverted from the purpose of forensic nursing. Some nurses cannot function well in a forensic capacity because they become emotionally overwrought by the cases they see, and their objectivity is compromised. They have such an emotional reaction to patients that they forget what they are there for, and what they are there for is to gather scientific evidence and other objective information from which analytical experts can interpret and draw conclusions.

Arizona forensic nurse Mary Sullivan, MSN, RNC, CARN, a strong proponent of science-based nursing practice, concurs. "The forensic nurse must operate from a base of science at all times," she emphasizes.

> We can do victims a better service by putting on our forensic caps and being unbiased in our work. If not, we do the entire forensic nursing community a disservice. The forensic community is all about science. We will gain greater recognition as a nursing specialty through continued good performance, leading by good example, and through patience and tenacity. I think nurses must stay scientific and not align themselves with victims' organizations or advocacy roles. We will do more for the patients by being scientific and approaching our work as a forensic scientist would approach his or her work. In our hearts we can be pleading for the patient and doing our work for them, but as a forensic scientist, we must be unbiased and careful in our work. I think, in the long run, that will achieve greater recognition and results for victims and for our profession, and the rest of the scientific community would respect us for it.
>
> When you put on your forensic hat, you are not an advocate for the patient, you are an advocate for truth and justice. When I took the SANE training, for example, I was taught that you are there to collect the evidence. You are not there to make the case for the victim. You are there to gather the facts as professionally and accurately as you can, and to follow forensic protocol. You are not there to support the victim or hold her hand, as there are advocates expressly to fill that role. It is this way because when a forensic nurse goes to court, he or she must be scientific and be above reproach.

California forensic examiner Sharon Crowley, MN, RN, also believes nurses must approach their work from a strong grounding in science:

> I feel that as a nurse, as a person, as whatever I am, I feel that my biggest contribution to the victim's cause is to do the best job I can in the world of forensics. It's a scientific

endeavor, period. There's nothing to argue about. What I do as a forensic nurse is going to be dissected in a court of law, or dissected in a crime lab, and that's fine. Labs need science, courts like science, and we know juries admire science. My biggest contribution as an individual who happens to be a nurse is that I can make my best advocacy through scientific work. If I chose to be an advocate as a rape crisis counselor, that would be my best contribution, and I think there should be that distinction. I don't have a problem with it because I see my advocacy come through science. It's not personal. I have had feedback from victims who say they appreciate that approach, because it's what they need to help prosecute their case. I think there are others who can fill the advocacy role very well. If a nurse chooses to be an advocate, God bless him or her, but I don't think that nurse should consider himself or herself to be operating in a medico-legal capacity, because it's no longer science. Forensic nursing practice is not mandated by advocacy, it is mandated by science. While crimes such as sexual assault are interpersonal cases, the outcome and the way they are handled are based on scientific evidence. How victims recover is an issue separate from forensic nursing's goal to document injury and collect evidence. The best thing I can do for the patient is do my scientific work and still provide them with warmth, caring, and nurturing; that's the nurse part of me, and nurses do that best. But I am also a scientist. We have this unique capability to combine the best of both approaches in a service to victims.

Crowley says she struggles with the advocacy versus science dilemma in her work in sexual-homicide cases:

I know what I am attempting to prove is valuable to the scientific community, to the courts, and to law enforcement, but what is it doing for the victim's family? Who in their right mind would want to know, "By the way, not only has your loved one been murdered, but they have been sexually molested, too"? But then a victim's mother once thanked me for being able to offer the courts scientific evidence. To me, that answered my question without a doubt, and it gave me permission to pursue my work because I could still feel like I am advocating in my own way, through science. I don't think we, as forensic nurses, do people any favors by saying "Everything's going to be OK," because that's what a victim advocate is there to do. We are there to be scientific.

The AAFS has been open to the development of a forensic nursing section, overseen by at least a dozen designated fellows who have the credentials, the experience, and the requisite credibility as mandated by the academy. Many nurses, like Sullivan, see membership and fellowship in the academy as a sign that forensic nurses have arrived and are accorded the same level of professional respect afforded to other members of the forensic science community. It is a validation that has been a long time in coming, nurses say, but there has been a lack of nurses who have what it takes to reach this professional peak. Sullivan observes:

It's simply a matter of nurses doing the work it takes to achieve that level in the academy. Yes, it can take as long as eight, nine, 10 years. Nurses need to get busy and take care of business, and work the various levels in the academy. They must present, participate, attend meetings, and do whatever it takes to show the academy that they take their work seriously. Nurses must continually improve their skills, and be aware of how they are perceived by the general forensic science community.

As a whole, the forensic nursing community has not yet achieved consensus on everything it believes. And it will never gain the credibility and respect in the academy until it does. The nurses who are going to be accepted into the academy will play by the academy's rules, and they will prove themselves by the academy standards; those nurses will gain credibility and respect. Very simply, being a victim is not going to cut it with the academy. If we call our conferences scientific assemblies, they better be scientific. The same goes for our practice.

Crowley believes that nurses must continually work on raising their credibility quotient. "As nurses, we have always had to work harder to prove our mettle. I don't have a problem with that, as I think it's kind of fun to be challenged and rise to the occasion. Who wouldn't want to rise to excellence and do awesome things? As forensic nurses, that's our birthright." Crowley says she still laughs when she faces the absurdity of old issues of gender or occupational discrimination:

Nurses today still deal with feminist-like issues that were raging 30 years ago. We are still fighting the same battles of equity and competence, but that means we have to be better than we ever think we can be. It means excelling in nursing practice and being the very best that we can be, because we face enormous scrutiny. To get to the next level, forensic nurses must conduct research to thoroughly understand the issues. To play with the big boys, you have to hold your own. You have to do your homework, you have to keep up with the literature, and gee, maybe even contribute to the literature! The take-home message is, because forensic nurses are relatively new, we stand out, and we are being watched. So we must be prepared, and we must be impeccable in our practice.

As someone who has been published in prestigious scientific journals and has presented her research to numerous important scientific gatherings, Crowley knows the importance of nurses contributing science-based, evidence-based material to the current body of forensic science thought. Although they might not represent all of the goals of forensic nurses, these professional accomplishments propel the collective discipline forward, and help it create traction among the other sciences. Crowley emphasizes the importance of buy-in from the scientific community:

> None of us works in a vacuum. Forensic nurses need the greater forensic science community to help validate and recognize our work and our contributions. Once you get through the barrier of "you're just a nurse," which you can refute by your professional integrity and your performance, they will come around. Sometimes nurses are too busy trying to impress each other, when we need to concentrate on impressing the larger scientific community. When I wrote my book, when I submitted my research for publication . . . each time I had to prove myself. And that's OK, because it makes you reach inside yourself and want to show them what you can do. We need to prove to the scientists that we can be scientific, too. That's why I chose to publish in the *Journal of Forensic Science*. I think I am the first nurse to be a solo author in the *JFS*, and that's fun. But I had to fight some battles along the way, just like I did as a young nurse in my 20s. Once I wrote the article, it was time to work through the acceptance process. I could see from the beginning that the editor was in my court, but when it went out for blind peer review, some of their comments were the same I'd heard all my life about nurses. One of the reviewers said, "I could see where nurses should be allowed to examine living victims but I don't know if they should be examining post-mortem cases." I had to laugh, because SANEs fought this battle 15 years ago to examine living victims, and here I am hearing the same argument now. Another reviewer said, "Maybe you should have a physician as a co-author," and I thought, that's not going to happen—I'd rather not be published. I went through this with my book, too. It was the same old issue of yes, I'm "just" a nurse, and I'm happy with that, and yes, we can do things like publish our research, and then suddenly, "Wow, I've been published!" But it was a proving ground. I had to continually explain why nurses are qualified to do what they do, and that no, we're not trying to step on the toes of forensic pathologists or anybody else—we are simply trying to live up to our capacities as nurses.
>
> Some have asked, "How could a nurse be the one to go to a crime scene?" You can attend the annual AAFS meeting and you'll hear nurses say how they essentially do the entire crime scene, or the entire forensic protocol, and here I am writing a protocol and I've been criticized because I want to publish something that says a nurse should be able to collect the clothing as evidence . . . it can be unbelievable how many times we have to defend what we have a right to do, but then again, that has always been the nurse's burden. You have to reassure them, and catch flies with honey, not vinegar. I've done it as a nurse for more than 30 years, and even more so in forensics, but when you get those flies, believe me, they stick with you. They may be slow to come on board, but once they're on your side, they'll back you. For that reason, science is so very important. It's a scientific field, and forensic nurses must see themselves in that light. That's an awesome responsibility, but I think we're up to it. I know of a pathologist now who thinks forensic nursing is awesome, but I had a hard time convincing him in the beginning. It was probably all of my sweet talking and convincing and demonstrating my abilities. I'll go to my grave never knowing exactly what worked, but as long as it worked, I'm good with it. And hopefully, if we all make these kinds of inroads into the scientific community, future generations of forensic nurses will have it easier than we did.

Crowley recalls a moment in her life when she realized she had "arrived." She says,

> The academy has been so supportive and really wonderful to me as a nurse and as a member. At one of the meetings, my book was there, and I was walking along the vendor's booth, peeking at it . . . this was just after it had come out and I was so excited. I overheard two forensic pathologists talking; one of them said, "Yeah, that's such and such a book, it was written by a nurse, but she really knows what she is talking about." And I thought, "Oh my God, that's it in a nutshell." That's what you deal with daily . . . yeah, you're a nurse, and wow, you happen to be good at it. You can't let those kinds of comments bother you; you must be able to say, "That's cool, I'm just a nurse." And deep down you know your own worth. Or when you're on the witness stand in court and they try to attack you by saying "You're just a nurse," you have to be able to embrace that moment and say, "Yeah, isn't that cool?" And then show them your stuff.

REFERENCES

Barrow, J. *Theories of Everything*. New York: Oxford University Press, 1991.

Bemis, P. A. *Psychiatric Emergency and Suicide Attempt*. NursingCEU.com. 2003.

Bright, W. E. *An Introduction to Scientific Research*. McGraw-Hill, 1952.

Carroll-Johnson, R. M., & Paquette, M., Eds. *Classification of Nursing Diagnoses: Proceedings of the 10th Conference*. Philadelphia: J. B. Lippincott. 1994.

Lynch, V. A. Clinical forensic nursing: A new perspective in the management of crime victims from trauma to trial. *Critical Care Nursing Clinics of North America. 7*, 3, 489–507, 1995.

Lynch, V. A. *Clinical Forensic Nursing: A New Perspective in Trauma*. Collins: Bearhawk Consulting Group. 1997.

McCloskey, J. C., & Bulechek, G. M., Eds. *Nursing Interventions Classification* (Third Edition). St. Louis, MO: Mosby. 2000.

3 The Mandate for Forensic Nursing

CONTENTS

Although nurses are not crime fighters or armchair detectives, they play an important role in the criminal justice system by assessing, treating, and documenting injuries of victims and perpetrators of crime. Few would argue the fact that crime is a by-product of modern life, and the potential for new ways to inflict harm grows with the times. Bioterrorism, escalating conflict, and immigrant influxes all contribute aggravating factors to crime-rate escalation. Additional factors that influence crime rates include the strength of law enforcement agencies and other components of the criminal justice systems (prosecutorial, judicial, correctional), as well as citizens' attitudes toward crime, population density and degree of urbanization, and economic conditions, including income, poverty level, job availability, and education of its citizens.

Health care facilities are the frontline recipients of both victims and perpetrators of crime. It only stands to reason that reinforcing a facility's infrastructure to handle an increasing number of these individuals begins with the presence of an individual or team of individuals thoroughly and firmly entrenched in forensic principles. Lynch (1997) writes, "Due to the vast number of crime victims presenting in acute-care settings, the need for forensic specialists has been recognized. Forensic nurses do not compete with, replace, or supplant other practitioners; rather, they fill voids by accomplishing selected forensic tasks concurrently with other human-caring measures."

Bell and Benak (2000) say that violence is defined as any human action resulting in injury or abuse, and generally of the interpersonal variety rather than acts resulting from war or natural disaster; it is a pervasive, deceptive force that destroys the basic human foundation in society. They point to a greater awakening in 1985, when then-Surgeon General C. Everett Koop identified the impact of violence as a health care issue, calling for new public attitudes and programs addressing the needs of victim survivors. Bell and Benak write, "Victims of violence most often present to a public servant (including police, fire, emergency medical services, and health care personnel) for intervention and/or medical treatment. Violence crosses all economic and cultural boundaries and presents an unprecedented challenge to the public servant, as the public expects professionals to be well-prepared to manage forensic issues, the resultant outcome of violence." They reason that forensic nursing is a logical way to address violence and its by-products. They add:

> Traditionally, forensic content has not been included in the basic education of public servants. The unfortunate reality is that these professionals are not adequately prepared to manage the results of violent situations. The forensic evidence that is associated with an act of violence often goes unrecognized by health-care providers and is therefore lost. Successful prosecution of perpetrators of violence becomes difficult without physical evidence to corroborate a victim's story and circumstance.

3.1 THE SCOPE OF THE PROBLEM: 2002 AND 2004 CRIME REPORTS

The *Criminal Victimization, 2002* report of the U.S. Department of Justice's Office of Justice Programs in the Bureau of Justice Statistics (BJS) was released in August 2003. This National Crime Victimization Survey (NCVS), compiled by BJS statisticians Callie Marie Rennison, PhD, and Michael R. Rand, revealed long-term declines in victimization to the lowest per-capita rates in nearly 30 years. Overall violent victimization rates in 2002 were the lowest recorded since the inception of the NCVS in 1973.

In 2002, U.S. residents age 12 or older experienced about 23 million violent and property victimizations, according to the NCVS, including 5.3 million violent crimes (rape, sexual assault, robbery, aggravated assault, and simple assault), which continued a downward trend that began in 1994. Between 1993 and 2002, the violent crime rate decreased 54 percent, from 50 to 23 victimizations per 1,000 persons age 12 or older. In 2002, victims reported to police 49 percent of the violent crime they experienced, up from 43 percent of crimes reported since 1993. The NCVS collects data on nonfatal crimes against persons age 12 or older, reported and not reported to the police, from a nationally representative sample of U.S. households. Information on homicide comes from the Uniform Crime Reporting (UCR) program of the FBI.

The violent crime rate declined somewhat from 25 to 23 victimizations per 1,000 persons from 2001 to 2002. Aggravated assault rates fell significantly, and rape and sexual assault rates did not change from 2001 to 2002. Based on preliminary 2002 data from the FBI, the number of persons murdered in the United States increased 0.8 percent between 2001 and 2002. In 2001, 15,980 persons were murdered; the estimate for 2002 was about 16,110 murder victims. Preliminary data suggested that increases in the number of murders occurred in the south (+2.1 percent) and the west (+5.2 percent). Declines in the number of murders were measured in the northeast (–4.8 percent) and the Midwest (–2.8 percent).

In 2001, the year in which the most recent comprehensive data was available, the FBI reported a total of 15,980 murders or nonnegligent homicides. That total represents a 1.3 percent increase from the 15,586 murders recorded in 2000. The FBI defines murder in its annual *Crime in the United States* report as the willful (nonnegligent) killing of one human being by another. Not included are deaths caused by negligence, suicide, or accident; justifiable homicides; and attempts to murder or assaults to murder, which are scored as aggravated assaults. The FBI's UCR program gathers murder statistics from more than 17,000 city, county, and state law enforcement agencies.

Although the rate and level of homicide changes year to year, the relationship between victim characteristics and homicide tends to remain the same. For example, as in previous years, in 2001:

- Most murder victims were male (76 percent).
- When the race of the murder victim was known, about half were White (49.1 percent), and about half were Black (46.9 percent).
- When information on the victim–offender relationship was available, 76 percent of the offenders were known to the victim, and strangers murdered 24 percent of victims.
- Firearms were used in the majority of murders (63 percent).
- Offenders were most often male (90 percent), and most often adults (92 percent).
- Homicide generally is intraracial.
- Arguments were the most often cited circumstance leading to murder (28 percent).
- Homicides occurred in connection with another felony (e.g., robbery or narcotics) in 17 percent of incidents.

Comparing two-year average annual rates showed that for every category of crime except rape and sexual assault, the average annual rates were significantly lower in 2001–2002 than in 1999–2000. The average annual rate of rape and sexual assault was slightly lower in 2001–2002 than in 1999–2000. The average annual overall violent victimization rate declined 21 percent from 30 to 24 victimizations per 1,000 persons per year from 1999–2000 to 2001–2002. During the same time, aggravated assault rates fell 23 percent.

The rate of violent crime experienced by males, females, Whites, Blacks, and non-Hispanics fell significantly from 1999–2000 to 2001–2002. The rate of violence against Hispanics fell somewhat during the same period. Rates of violent victimization remained statistically similar between 1999–2000 and 2001–2002 for persons of "other" races. Violence against never married, married, and divorced or separated persons fell in 2001–2002 compared to 1999–2000. For persons under age 35 and those between ages 50 and 64, violent crime fell significantly from 1999–2000 to 2001–2002. A slight decline was measured for persons between ages 35 and 49. No change in the rate of violent victimization against persons age 65 or older was measured between 1999–2000 and 2001–2002. Violent crime decreased in every region and type of area of the nation over the same time period.

The rate of every major violent and property crime measured in the NCVS—rape and sexual assault, robbery, aggravated assault, simple assault, burglary, theft, and motor vehicle theft—fell significantly between 1993 and 2002. The overall violent crime rate fell 54 percent from 50 to 23 violent victimizations per 1,000 persons age 12 or older between 1993 and 2002. Other significant declines were measured in rates of rape and sexual assault (down 56 percent), aggravated assault (down 64 percent), and simple assault (down 47 percent).

Females were most often victimized by someone they knew, whereas males were more likely to be victimized by strangers during 2002. Of those offenders victimizing females, 40 percent were described as friends or acquaintances, 20 percent as intimates, and 7 percent as some other relative. Strangers to the victim committed 31 percent of the violence against females. In contrast, of those offenders victimizing males, 37 percent were described as friends or acquaintances, 3 percent as intimates, and 4 percent as some other relative. Strangers committed 56 percent of the violence against males.

During 2002, 71 percent of all violent crime victims did not face an armed offender. However, the presence of a weapon during a violent crime was related to the type of crime. For example, rape and sexual assault victims were the least likely (7 percent) and robbery victims the most likely (46 percent) to face an armed offender. The type of weapon also varied according to the type of violence. Four percent of victims of rape and sexual assault faced an offender armed with a firearm, compared to 25 percent of robbery victims. An offender brandishing a knife confronted 2 percent of rape and sexual assault victims and 12 percent of robbery victims. During 2002, 49 percent of all violent victimizations were reported to the police. The violent victimization of a female was more likely to be reported to the police than was the victimization of a male during 2002.

In October 2004, the FBI released crime figures for 2003—the latest data available at the time of writing—that showed that violent crime in the United States declined 3 percent from the estimated volume in 2002. Further, the five- and 10-year trend data indicated that the volume of violent crime declined 3.1 percent from the 1999 estimate and 25.6 percent from the 1994 estimate. A comparison of 2002 data to 2003 data showed that the rate of violent crime, estimated at 475 violent crimes per 100,000 inhabitants, decreased 3.9 percent in 2003. These results are from the FBI report, *Crime in the United States, 2003.*

At nearly 1.4 million offenses, the estimated volume of violent crime in the United States in 2003 declined 3 percent from the 2002 figure. In 2003, the offense of murder was the only violent crime to show an increase in volume (1.7 percent) compared to the 2002 data. Collectively, U.S. cities experienced a 3.9 percent decrease in violent crime in comparison to the 2002 figure. Violent crime decreased 3.7 percent in the nation's nonmetropolitan counties and 1 percent in metropolitan counties. Approximately 30.7 percent of violent crimes were committed with personal weapons such as hands, fists, feet, and so on. Perpetrators used firearms in 26.9 percent and knives or cutting instruments in 15.2 percent of violent crimes. Other weapons were used in 27.3 percent of violent offenses during 2003.

The UCR Program estimated that in 2003 law enforcement agencies nationwide made 597,026 arrests for violent crime, accounting for 4.4 percent of the estimated number of all arrests. Law enforcement agencies nationwide solved 46.5 percent of violent crimes in 2003. By offense type, agencies cleared 62.4 percent of murders, 55.9 percent of aggravated assaults, and 44 percent of forcible rapes.

Nationally in 2003, 12.2 percent of violent crime clearances involved only juveniles. Among the population groups, 12.2 percent of violent crime clearances in cities collectively involved only juveniles; 12.7 percent of violent crime clearances in metropolitan counties and 9.8 percent in nonmetropolitan counties involved only juveniles.

In 2003, law enforcement collectively reported an arrest rate of 5,109.3 arrests per 100,000 inhabitants. Law enforcement agencies in U.S. metropolitan counties made 3,731 arrests per 100,000 in population; law enforcement agencies in nonmetropolitan counties made 3,961.2 arrests per 100,000 in population. Compared to the data from 2002, the number of arrests in 2003 showed a slight increase (0.2 percent). The number of arrests for violent crime in 2003 decreased 2.3 percent; the number of arrests for property crime increased 0.7 percent.

Adults comprised 83.7 percent of all arrestees in 2003. By gender, 76.8 percent of those arrested in the United States were male. Compared to the 2002 data, the number of males arrested in 2003 declined 0.4 percent, whereas the number of females arrested in 2003 increased 1.9 percent. An examination of arrestee data by race indicated that 70.6 percent of those arrested in the United States in 2003 were White.

The UCR Program estimated that 16,503 murders occurred in the United States in 2003, representing a 1.7 percent increase from the 2002 estimate. Law enforcement agencies provided the UCR Program with supplementary data for 14,408 murders in 2003 showing that most murder victims (90.6 percent) were adults and most were males (77.6 percent). Of the male murder victims, 8.2 percent were juveniles (persons under the age of 18). Juvenile females comprised 13.5 percent of female murder victims nationwide. By race, 48.7 percent of murder victims were White, 48.5 percent were Black, and the remainder was of other races.

In 44.5 percent of murders, the relationship of the murder victim to the offender was unknown. Of the 55.5 percent of murders in which the victim–offender relationship was known, 77.6 percent of the victims knew their assailants. In those murders for which law enforcement personnel reported victim and offender relationship data, 32.3 percent of females were killed by their husbands or boyfriends, and 2.5 percent of males were killed by their wives or girlfriends.

Of the murders involving a single victim and a single offender, 92.4 percent of Black victims were killed by Black offenders; 84.7 percent of White victims were killed by White offenders. Of the murders in 2003 for which law enforcement identified the type of weapon, nearly 70.9 percent involved firearms. Offenders used knives or cutting instruments in 13.4 percent of murders; personal weapons such as hands, fists, and feet in 7.0 percent of murders; and blunt objects in 4.8 percent of murders. Four percent of murders were committed with other types of weapons.

In 2003, law enforcement investigation was unable to determine the circumstances in 33.9 percent of murders in the nation. The supplementary data also showed that 16.4 of murders were committed during the commission of another felony, such as during a robbery or a violation of a narcotic drug law.

An estimated 93,433 forcible rapes occurred in the United States in 2003, representing a 1.9 percent decrease from the 2002 estimate. The UCR estimated that 63.2 of every 100,000 females in the United States were victims of forcible rape in 2003. This rate represented a 2.7 percent decrease from the 2002 rate. By community type, the rate of forcible rape in the U.S. Metropolitan Statistical Areas (MSAs) was estimated at 64.5 forcible rapes per 100,000 females. There were an estimated 75.1 forcible rapes per 100,000 females in cities outside MSAs and 45.7 forcible rapes per 100,000 females in the nation's nonmetropolitan counties.

For the 10th consecutive year, the estimated number of aggravated assaults in the United States declined. Based on law enforcement reports for 2003, the UCR estimated 857,921 aggravated assaults, a 3.8 percent decrease compared to the 2002 figure. By volume, aggravated assaults comprised 62.1 percent of the estimated total number of violent crimes. By rate, the UCR estimated that there were 295 aggravated assault offenses per 100,000 inhabitants in the United States, a 4.7 percent decline from the 2002 estimate. Aggravated assault offenders used personal weapons (hands, fists, feet, etc.) in 26.9 percent of offenses, firearms in 19.1 percent of offenses, and knives or cutting instruments in 18.2 percent of offenses. Other types of weapons were used in 35.9 percent of aggravated assaults.

3.2 THE RESPONSE TO VIOLENCE BY THE JOINT COMMISSION ON ACCREDITATION OF HEALTHCARE ORGANIZATIONS

Although the U.S. crime rate will always fluctuate, there is little doubt that violence will continue to be a part of everyday life. As such, and recognizing that the health care system will be called on to care for the victims and perpetrators of violence, one important oversight entity has led the way in developing standards aimed at addressing this complex issue.

Since 1992, the Joint Commission on Accreditation of Healthcare Organizations (JCAHO) has published standards to ensure that all staff at its accredited hospitals hospital are trained in the identification of victims of violence and protocol necessary to treat and care for these individuals. These standards include criteria to identify potential victims of physical assault, rape, or sexual molestation, as well as provide guidance for patient evaluation procedures, including patient consent, examination components, and treatment. Lynch (1995) writes:

> A mandate that unequivocally provides for the role of the forensic clinician is set forth in the hospital's responsibility in collection, retention, and safeguarding of specimens, photography, and other trace and physical evidence. Medical record documentation, including examinations, treatment referrals to other care providers and community-based family violence agencies, and required notification of authorities, are among the responsibilities of the care provider.

JCAHO also monitors its accredited health care institutions' response to adverse (sentinel) events.

JCAHO is a not-for-profit entity that provides accreditation to acute-care facilities; it evaluates and accredits more than 16,000 health care organizations and programs in the United States and is the nation's predominant standards-setting and accrediting body in health care. The JCAHO standard relevant to forensic nursing is PC.3.10.1. According to Mark Forstneger, media relations specialist for JCAHO, there are no current plans to revise these standards, which were updated for 2004 as part of the "Shared Visions, New Pathways" standards review project. Sullivan (in press) says that these standards "open the door for an important role to include the clinical forensic nurse specialist or investigator."

PC.3.10.1 mandates that victims of sexual molestation, domestic abuse, elder neglect or abuse, and child neglect or abuse are identified using criteria developed or adopted by the hospital. This standard acknowledges that these medico-legal cases have subtle clinical presentations that might not be obvious to untrained personnel; therefore, every health care institution must have in place methodology to assist medical personnel in the identification and assessment of these patients, no matter to which hospital department they first present. Following assessment, the health care provider must determine an appropriate course of treatment or referral, bearing in mind that JCAHO requires what it deems to be observable evidence as opposed to allegations.

Sullivan (in press) writes, "With the influence of forensic science on nursing assessments made by the clinical forensic nurse provider, it is more likely that a patient who is a victim of domestic abuse or neglect will be discovered. With this discovery, the appropriate assessments, documentation, and referrals will be made in a timely manner."

Because JCAHO mandates that health care providers conduct their evidentiary examinations and assessments within a medico-legal context, Sullivan believes that the clinical forensic nurse examiner "is the ideal person to collect and preserve all evidentiary material in these clinical situations. This nurse is particularly knowledgeable about the safeguarding of evidence and chain-of-custody requirements that are paramount in all cases that involve legal action. Further, this nurse should be involved in writing all policies and procedures that define these activities within the hospital setting."

Specifically, JCAHO Standard PC.3.10.1 states that victims of abuse, neglect, or exploitation might come to an organization in a variety of ways. The patient might be unable or reluctant to speak of the abuse, and it might not be obvious to the casual observer. Staff must be able to identify abuse, neglect, and exploitation as well as the extent and circumstances of the abuse, neglect, or exploitation, to give the patient appropriate care. Criteria for identifying and assessing victims of abuse, neglect, or exploitation should be used throughout the organization. The assessment of the patient must be conducted within the context of the requirements of the law to preserve evidentiary materials and support future legal actions.

Elements of performance for PC.3.10.1 include the following:

1. The organization develops or adopts criteria for identifying victims in each of the following situations:
    - Physical assault
    - Rape
    - Sexual molestation
    - Domestic abuse
    - Elder neglect or abuse
    - Child neglect or abuse
    - Exploitation
2. Staff is educated about abuse, neglect, or exploitation and how to refer as appropriate.
3. A list of private and public community agencies that provide or arrange for assessment and care of abuse victims is maintained to facilitate appropriate referrals.
4. Victims of abuse, neglect, or exploitation are identified using the criteria developed or adopted by the organization at entry into the system and on an ongoing basis.
5. The organization's staff refers appropriately or conducts the assessment of victims of abuse, neglect, or exploitation.
6. All cases of possible abuse, neglect, or exploitation are reported to appropriate agencies according to organization policy and law and regulation. State laws differ for child abuse, intimate partner violence, and elder abuse. Some states have requirements to report current victimization to law enforcement or social services. Providers should:
    - Learn applicable state statutes. View state codes specific to domestic violence.
    - If you practice in a state with a mandated reporting law, inform patients about any limits of confidentiality prior to conducting screening.
7. All cases of possible abuse, neglect, or exploitation are immediately reported in the organization.

"I believe that the Joint Commission's standards addressing victims of abuse and violence are beginning to be viewed by all health care providers as something they must keep in the forefront of their minds," says Janet Barber, MSN, RN:

> The Joint Commission has the authority to say to health care professionals, "You have a role in this, you must assess patients for abuse and neglect, you must intervene, you must refer, you must care for them, and you must manage evidence according to your community's standards." I think the fact that the Joint Commission basically has said to hospitals, "This is no longer optional; whether you want to or not, you will be involved in this process," demonstrates what good citizenry in the health care field is all about. On other health care fronts, other practitioners in nursing subspecialties have been picking up various bits of forensic protocol and practice; psychiatric nurses, pediatric nurses, OB-GYN nurses, and nurse gerontologists are beginning to see clearly how they fit into this whole realm. I think that this trend is encouraging, and it helps to further support and legitimize forensic nursing.

Because it is considered to be the gold standard for accreditation, a stamp of approval from the JCAHO carries weight in the health care community. It also appeals to third-party payers, insurance companies, and the consumer seeking exemplary health care. The managed care era has slashed reimbursement rates and created enormous competition among health care systems, so many institutions are looking for ways to differentiate themselves in the marketplace. Accreditation by the JCAHO and a progressive response to patients, especially those sustaining trauma or abuse, helps to meet that goal of providing distinguished services.

"Even hospitals who do not seek Joint Commission accreditation primarily because of cost restrictions pay attention to what JCAHO says because it's the gold standard," Barber says. "They read the manuals and they are familiar with JCAHO's mandates even though they do not seek accreditation. So when you consider the number of hospitals who are following JCAHO's mandates, there are an incredible number of hospitals who are poised to take it a step farther and employ forensic nurses to help them meet these standards."

Barber says she observes an increasing number of developments in health care that can be linked to forensic practice, including mandatory reporting of certain kinds of deaths, as well as long-standing requirements to report abuse:

> For example, the Centers for Disease Control and Prevention (CDC) has introduced a data form to record information gained during the investigation of SIDS deaths, and so I think an increasing number of agencies such as the CDC are beginning to realize the importance of quantifying data and statistics related to such medico-legal cases. Because information about these kinds of deaths is statistically vital to the government, health care institutions can no longer be apathetic about how they investigate and classify these deaths. Health care personnel can no longer say casually, "That was a natural death" or "That was an accidental death," or "That was a death stemming from intentional abuse and neglect," without the data and the evidence to back it up. This means institutions will have to pay far more attention to these issues, and that's a good thing for forensic nursing practice. Mandatory reporting and new assessments and new ways of collecting data may not directly support forensic nursing practice, but I think an increasing number of people see more clearly that in a health care institution, the nurse is the constant in the medico-legal equation. Social workers come and go, doctors are there for brief periods of time, and all other practitioners who interface with patients are fairly transient. But the nurse is the ever-present person who can put a lot of details together and who has that around-the-clock vigilance. Nurses are the keepers of the keys, so to speak, and this will heighten their visibility as various agencies continue to address issues related to violence and death.

In addition to recognizing victims of violence, hospitals must address sentinel events, defined by the JCAHO (2004) as an unexpected occurrence involving death or serious physical or psychological injury, or the risk thereof. Sullivan (in press) writes:

> Each hospital is to establish mechanisms to identify, report, analyze, and prevent these events and are expected to identify and respond appropriately to all sentinel events. Response includes conducting a timely, thorough, and credible root cause analysis; implementing improvements to reduce risks; and monitoring the effectiveness of those improvements. Utilizing the expertise of a clinical forensic nurse will assist hospitals with fulfilling these standards.

3.3 THE RESPONSE TO VIOLENCE BY THE PUBLIC HEALTH COMMUNITY

In "Strengthening the Collaboration Between Public Health and Criminal Justice to Prevent Violence," published in the *Journal of Law, Medicine & Ethics*, Prothrow-Stith (2004) reports that public health has made several contributions to the understanding and prevention of violence, including new and expanded knowledge in surveillance, delineation of risk factors, and program design, including implementation and evaluation strategies. She writes, "While public health activities generally complement those of criminal justice, confrontations, challenges, and turf issues within this cross-disciplinary enterprise remain inevitable. Continued progress is dependent upon expanded efforts and greater collaboration within both disciplines."

Prothrow-Stith explains the four reasons why interpersonal violence (IPV) became an important concern for public health professionals in the United States:

1. The contact health professionals have with victims and perpetrators of violence
2. The magnitude of the problem
3. The characteristics of violence
4. The application of public health strategies to both understanding and preventing violence, which has yielded significant positive findings and offers further promise

According to Prothrow-Stith, 30 years ago, emergency room personnel had a "stitch them up and send them out" mentality as the standard of care. She writes, "Nevertheless, the predictable and regular contact physicians and nurses have had with victims and perpetrators of violence, particularly in emergency departments, has caused many to begin to address this problem. To this day, emergency room recidivism and the high mortality rates associated with violent injury continue to compel medical personnel toward violence prevention efforts."

Since the late 1980s, Prothrow-Stith reports that the ACEP has included violence prevention on the agenda of its annual meetings, and that the American Medical Association (AMA) has published protocols and manuals for health care providers on domestic violence, youth violence, child abuse, and sexual assault. With a greater awareness has come new strategies, materials, and protocols for clinical intervention and prevention, thus "reflecting the responsiveness of health care providers to the repeated contact they have with the tragedy of violence," she adds.

In the past 20 years, public health professionals have applied traditional public health strategies to violence prevention. Prothrow-Stith writes, "They have brought a different perspective and orientation to bear on the problem by applying public-health techniques and strategies which complement and strengthen the criminal justice approach. Public health brings an analytic approach that identifies risk factors and important causes that could become the focus of preventive interventions."

A definition of violence within the public health profession was offered by the National Center for Injury Prevention and Control at the CDC. The CDC classifies both unintentional injuries (accidents) and intentional injuries (violence) as public health problems. Intentional injuries are divided into self-directed violence (suicides and suicide attempts) and IPV (assaults and homicides).

Violence is defined by the CDC, as "the threatened or actual use of physical force or power against another person, against oneself, or against a group or community that either results or is likely to result in injury, death, or deprivation."

Prothrow-Stith writes that in the last 20 years, "Violence has been increasingly accepted within mainstream public health as a problem for its consideration. The major contribution resulting from designating violence as a public health problem is the acknowledgment that violence is preventable, not inevitable." In 1983, the CDC established its Violence Epidemiology Branch for the explicit study of homicide and suicide. Prothrow-Stith calls this application of basic epidemiology and reporting techniques "part of the impetus for public health professionals across the country to confront the issue." Two years later, then-Surgeon General C. Everett Koop convened the Surgeon General's Workshop on Violence and Public Health, which looked at assault, homicide, child abuse, rape and sexual assault, domestic violence, elder abuse, and suicide. In 1994, the CDC created the National Center for Injury Prevention and Control and every surgeon general to follow Koop has encouraged the public health community to better understand and prevent violence.

Prothrow-Stith asserts that public health's venture into violence prevention "has not always been well received," adding that numerous issues divide public health and criminal justice, including proactive versus reactive strategies, and prevention efforts versus a punitive response to violence. She says that the public health and criminal justice systems have been historically separate in their conceptualization of approaches to violence and the development of activities to reduce or prevent violence. She writes, "The public health field has approached the issue through efforts to identify the risk factors related to violent behavior. The criminal justice system has approached the issue through efforts to identify and assign blame for criminal behavior, maintain public safety, and remove violent offenders from the community."

She states that the criminal justice system's response to violence is rooted in the assumptions that violence is an individual's criminal choice; punishment or the threat of punishment is a deterrent to violent acts; and violence is an inevitable aspect of the behaviors of some people. She adds that prevention of violence is resolved through the "passage of laws and the deterrence resulting from enforcement."

Prothrow-Stith is concerned that the criminal justice system does not adequately address violence among intimates. She explains, "Police and many of the laws they enforce are geared toward predatory violence that occurs among strangers on the street. As a result, the many episodes of violence among family, friend and acquaintance that emerge from insults, frustrations, festering disputes, and that take place in intimate settings are less well addressed." She advocates for a more collaborative and comprehensive set of prevention activities to address acquaintance violence. She writes, "More effective collaboration beyond the existing silos of activity and competitive strategies would greatly improve society's capacity to save children from the devastating impact of interpersonal violence. Currently, both disciplines are defensive; criminal justice for its failure to meet societal expectations to control youth violence and public health for the slowness with which it has recognized and taken on the problem." She adds that tension between the two disciplines is inevitable, fueled further by divergent perspectives and inadequate resources directed to addressing violence, which "fosters competition rather than collaboration."

Prothrow-Stith advocates for three stages of prevention of violence: primary prevention, secondary prevention (or early intervention), and tertiary prevention (or treatment and rehabilitation). Primary prevention would be directed toward dealing with the public's attitudes toward violence, whereas secondary prevention could focus on individuals who are considered to be at high risk of engaging in or being victimized by violence, and educating them in nonviolent methods of resolving disputes or displaying competence and power. Tertiary prevention would concentrate on reducing the negative consequences of a particular event after it has occurred, or on trying to find ways to use the event to reduce the likelihood of similar incidents occurring in the future. She explains. "Thus, one might think of improved trauma care, on the one hand, and increased efforts to rehabilitate or incapacitate violent offenders, on the other hand, as tertiary prevention instruments in the control of or the response to violence."

These models of violence prevention, Prothrow-Stith states, "can be very useful when applied specifically to the issue of interpersonal violence." She adds, "Traditionally, public health responded by treating the violence-related injury in the emergency setting. Today a new generation of committed health practitioners, community violence-prevention practitioners, social workers, and community activists have devised numerous intervention programs to serve medium- to high-risk (individuals)." She concludes, "The contributions made by public health professionals toward efforts to prevent violence have been tremendous. The continued application of public health strategies to the understanding and prevention of violence is essential to further progress. Also, the interface between public health and criminal justice must be continually explored to ensure complementary strategies and activities." Despite decreasing crime rates recently, she adds, "Even with our lower national rates there is far too much preventable injury daily. The emphasis of the public health system will always be on prevention and the criminal justice system must place priority on aggressive responses to violence, but much possibility lies in enhancing the collaborative effort between both disciplines."

3.4 IS THERE A FORENSIC NURSE IN THE HOUSE?

As private sector oversight entities and governmental agencies wrestle with the issue of identifying and caring for victims of violence, health care institutions scramble to do more—including meeting numerous patient-safety and quality-improvement mandates—with less, including fewer health care workers and smaller operational budgets. Many facilities cannot hire designated forensic personnel, and therefore depend on regular staff to compensate for this void.

Physicians are dedicated, well-meaning individuals who are spread as thin as other health care professionals. Some are more aware of issues of IPV than others, but they are still in the minority. Many forensic nurses say that is precisely why they can provide essential forensic services when other health care providers can't or won't. On occasion, victims have verbalized their desire that physicians pay attention to issues such as IPV.

Zink et al. (2004) undertook a study to understand how women who are victims of intimate-partner violence want physicians to manage these abusive relationships in the health care setting. Thirty-two mothers in IPV shelters or support groups in southwestern Ohio were interviewed to explore their abuse experiences and health care encounters retrospectively. The researchers discovered that participants believed physicians should screen women for IPV both on a routine basis and when symptoms indicating possible abuse are present, even if the victim does not disclose the abuse. They add that screening is an important tool to capture those women early in the process of victimization. When a victim does not recognize her relationship as abusive, participants recommended that physicians raise the issue by asking, but they also warned that doing more might alienate the victim. Participants also encouraged physicians to explore clues that victims might give about the abuse.

The researchers discovered that in later contemplation, victims are willing to disclose the abuse and are open to exploring options. Physicians were encouraged to affirm the abuse, know local resources for IPV victims, make appropriate referrals, educate victims about how the abuse affects their health, and document the abuse. Participants identified a variety of internal and external factors that had affected their processes. In hindsight, IPV victims recommended desired actions from physicians that could help them during early stages of coming to terms with their abusive relationships. According to the researchers, in the primary care environment, 11 percent to 22 percent of women are currently experiencing physical abuse. They also said that a number of studies have demonstrated that IPV affects the physical and mental health of victims and of children who witness it.

Rhodes and Levinson (2003) and Lapidus et al. (2002) as well as the Institute of Medicine report, *Confronting Chronic Neglect: The Education and Training of Health Professionals on Family Violence* (National Academies Press, 2002), state that physicians will continue to see both genders who are abused and that the early recognition of abuse might influence the outcomes of care. The literature points to the fact that physicians are not screening for IPV as they should; according to Hamberger et al. (1992), the reported barriers to screening include time constraints, discomfort with the subject, fear of offending the patient, frustration with patient's denial, lack of skills and resources to manage IPV, and the fear of opening "Pandora's box."

Because physicians generally cannot tell which patients are in abusive relationships unless there are warning signs or diagnoses (illnesses frequently found in patients with IPV) or an abusive interaction between the patient and his or her partner is observed, guidelines recommend routine screening for IPV. The researchers said that some participants did not understand why they were asked about abuse, and others who were screened by physicians appreciated being asked. Many who had not been screened wished that they had been. Once participants began to acknowledge the abuse, they also began to have expectations about how physicians should react to what they learned, the researchers discovered. They identified four relevant patient expectations of health care providers: affirm that the abuse is real, know and inform victims about local IPV resources, educate victims about the effects of the abuse on themselves and their children, and document injuries in the medical record. The researchers also discovered that patients wanted physicians to affirm or validate that their relationships were abusive, and that no one, no matter what they did, deserved to be abused; that most women wanted their physicians to address the abuse and to know about IPV resources; and that they wanted to know health care providers were documenting information in their medical records for legal purposes.

REFERENCES

Bell, K., & Benak, L D. Forensic nursing: The fastest growing discipline of nursing for the 21st century. Available online at: www.iafn.org. 2000.

Hamberger, L., Saunders, D., & Hovey, M. Prevalence of domestic violence in community practice and rate of physician inquiry. *Arch Fam Med. 24*, 283–287, 1992.

Joint Commission on Accreditation of Health care Organizations (JCAHO). *Joint Commission 2000 Hospital Accreditation Standards*. Oakbrook Terrace, IL. 2004.

Lapidus, G., Cooke, M. B., Gelven, E., Sherman, K., Duncan, M., & Banco, L. A statewide survey of domestic violence screening behaviors among pediatricians and family physicians. *Arch Pediatr Adolesc Med. 156*, 332–336, 2002.

Lynch, V. A. Clinical forensic nursing: A new perspective in the management of crime victims from trauma to trial. *Critical Care Nursing Clinics of North America. 7*, 3, 489–507, 1995.

Lynch, V. A. *Clinical Forensic Nursing: A New Perspective in Trauma*. Collins: Bearhawk Consulting Group. 1997.

Prothrow-Stith, D. Strengthening the collaboration between public health and criminal justice to prevent violence. *J Law, Med Ethics. 1*, 32, 82, 2004.

Rhodes, K. V., & Levinson, W. Interventions for intimate partner violence against women: Clinical applications. *JAMA. 289*, 601–605, 2003.

Sullivan, M. K. Opportunities and challenges in forensic nursing. In V. A. Lynch, Ed., *Forensic Nursing in the Hospital Setting*. New York: Elsevier. In press.

Zink, T., Elder, N., Jacobson, J., & Klostermann, B. Medical management of intimate partner violence considering the stages of change: Precontemplation and contemplation. *Ann Fam Med. 2*, 231–239, 2004.

RECOMMENDED READINGS

American Medical Association (AMA). American Medical Association Diagnostic and Treatment Guidelines for Domestic Violence. *Arch Fam Med. 1*, 39–47, 1992.

Campbell, J. C. Health consequences of intimate partner violence. *The Lancet. 359*, 1331–1336, 2002.

Campbell, J. C., Jones, A. S., & Dienemann, J., et. al. Intimate partner violence and physical health consequences. *Arch Intern Med. 162*, 1157–1163, 2002.

Coker, A. L., Smith, P. H., Bethea, L., King, M. R., & McKeown, R. E. Physical health consequences of physical and psychological intimate partner violence. *Arch Fam Med. 9*, 451–457, 2000.

Dienemann, J., Boyle, E., Baker, D., Resnick, W., Wiederhoen, N., & Campbell, J. C. Intimate partner abuse among women diagnosed with depression. *Iss Mental Health Nurs. 21*, 499–513, 2000.

Drossman, D. A., Lesserman, J., Rachman, G., Zhiming, L., Gluck, H., & Toomey, T. C. Sexual and physical abuse in women with functional or organic gastrointestinal disorders. *Ann Intern Med. 113*, 828, 1990.

Edleson, J. L. Children's witnessing of adult domestic violence. *J Interpers Violence. 14*, 839–870, 1999.

Elliot, B., & Johnson, M. Domestic violence in a primary care setting: Patterns and prevalence. *Arch Fam Med. 4*, 113–119, 1995.

Gin, N. E., Rucker, L., Frayne, S., Cygan, R., & Habbell, F. A. Prevalence of intimate partner violence among patients in three ambulatory care internal medicine clinics. *J Gen Intern Med. 6*, 317–322, 1991.

Kernic, M. A., Holt, V. L., Wolf, M. E., McKnight, B., Huebner, C. E., & Rivara, F. P. Academic and school health issues among children exposed to maternal intimate partner abuse. *Arch Ped Adolesc Med. 156*, 549–555, 2002.

Kolbo, J. R., Blakely, E. H., & Engleman, D. Children who witness domestic violence: A review of empirical literature. *J Interpers Violence. 11*, 281–293, 1996.

Koss, M. P., & Heslet, L. Somatic consequences of violence against women. *Arch Fam Med. 1*, 53–59, 1992.

McFarlane, J., Parker, B., & Soeken, K. Physical abuse, smoking, and substance use during pregnancy: Prevalence, interrelationships and effect on birth weight. *JOGNN. 25*, 313–320, 1996.

McNeal, C., & Amato, P. Parent's marital violence: Long-term consequences for children. *J Fam Issues. 19*, 123–139, 1998.

Plichta, S. B., & Falik, M. Prevalence of violence and its implications for women's health. *Women's Health Issues. 11*, 244–258, 2001.

Rodriquez, M., Bauer, H., McLoughlin, E., & Grumbach, K. Screening and intervention for intimate partner abuse: Practice and attitudes of primary care physicians. *JAMA. 282*, 468–474, 1999.

Sugg, N., & Inui, T. Primary care physicians response to domestic violence. *JAMA. 267*, 3157–3160, 1992.

Sugg, N., Thompson, R., Thompson, D., Maiuro, R., & Rivara, F. Domestic violence and primary care. *Arch Fam Med. 8*, 301–306, 1999.

Walker, E. A., Koss, M. P., & Katon, W. J. Medical sequelae of sexual and physical victimization of women: A pilot study. *Women's Health Issues. 5*, 77–78, 1995.

Wolak, J., & Finkelhor, D. Children exposed to partner violence. In J. Jasinski, & L. Williams, Eds., *Partner Violence: A Comprehensive Review of 20 Years of Research* (pp. 73–112). Thousand Oaks, CA: Sage. 1998.

Zuckerman, B., Augustyn, M., Groves, B., & Parker, S. Silent victims revisited: The special case of domestic violence. *Pediatrics. 96*, 511–513, 1995.

4 Forensic Issues in the Clinical Setting

CONTENTS

4.1 THE EMERGENCY DEPARTMENT AS THE FORENSIC PORTAL OF HEALTH CARE

The frontline of forensic nursing is considered by many to be the emergency department (ED), the portal through which many forensic cases first enter a health care facility. Whether individuals are brought in by first responders such as paramedics and escorted by law enforcement officers, or whether individuals present themselves to the ER of their own accord, one thing is certain: The actions of this department's personnel are the first stop on the medico-legal continuum.

4.1.1 UNDERSTANDING THE ED PHYSICIAN'S VIEWPOINT OF THE MEDICO-LEGAL CONTINUUM

One of the most common forensic cases presenting to the ED is the sexual assault victim. Michael L. Weaver, MD, FACEP, in his discussion of "Optimizing Physician/Nurse Role in the Criminal Justice System," at the September 1999 National Non-Stranger Sexual Assault Symposium, further established the health care provider's role as that of a "forensic clinician." Weaver says, "This role is not only part of the criminal justice system, but is part of a communitywide multidisciplinary response to the issue of sexual assault and abuse. That role can therefore only be optimized if the entire community is working together."

A coordinated community response, according to Weaver, integrates the sexual assault response team (SART) with representatives from the community, forensic nurses, crime labs, law enforcement, prosecutors, hospitals, and social services, and together, protocols and outcomes can be developed. This model is particularly essential, Weaver says, knowing that not every hospital employs health care providers with specific forensic knowledge.

Weaver says, "When and where patients are to be examined, chain-of-custody procedures, time limits for the evidentiary exam, who should take photographs, what type of camera, and the use of partial kits, are additional issues that impact the quality and consistency of the patient's case." He touches on a number of issues related to forensic cases, pointing to the varying levels of service that victims will encounter at health care institutions. He says:

> The importance of advocates in the criminal justice system meeting with forensic clinicians is exemplified by differences between various community hospitals. Standard protocol dictates that sexual assault victims are offered the "morning after pill." However, in Catholic hospitals physicians are not allowed to prescribe this treatment. Hence, a community plan with alternatives for patients at those hospitals should be identified. Variation between forensic clinicians will also have a dramatic effect on the overall quality of the sexual assault case and may lead to patient re-victimization. Some communities are fortunate to have strong physician and nurse sexual assault advocates. Protocols that mandate examinations be performed by board-certified emergency physicians, sexual assault nurse examiners (SANEs), or other forensic examiners have already been developed. Unfortunately in some university teaching hospitals, the examination of the sexual assault patient may be relegated to a physician with minimal clinical experience (e.g., the intern that has just graduated from medical school). The OB-GYN, family medicine, or emergency medicine intern typically has little orientation and is not well supervised in this complicated medico-legal arena. The intern's patients are usually forced to wait extended periods of time, evidence collection is frequently inadequate and the desire to compassionately care for these patients is highly variable. This may result in the degradation of crucial data, inadmissible evidence, or a patient that is emotionally re-traumatized. These concerns make it essential that a community standard be developed. A leading community organization with forensic clinician members has the additional benefit of allowing important public political pressures to be utilized for building consensus in the management of sexual assault cases.

Prior to a medico-legal case going to trial, Weaver says:

> It is important for advocates of the criminal justice system to understand that forensic clinicians may have apprehensions toward participating in sexual assault cases. Negative feelings many physicians and nurses have surrounding care for sexual assault patients are largely due to concerns about future interactions with the criminal justice system. Perceived abuses of power, disrespect, and fear of the courtroom have significant impact on their cooperation.

Weaver enumerates many forensic clinicians' concerns when he says:

> A major clinical issue is that months or years may have passed since the sexual assault evaluation. Thus, the clinician's memory of important details, such as the patient's demeanor, may have faded. Additionally a clinician may be uncomfortable because their hospital practice sees less than 50 sexually assaulted patients per year. Since sexual assault examination responsibilities are frequently rotated, forensic clinicians may ultimately examine one or two patients yearly. Typically less than 20 percent of cases actually go to trial. Therefore, it is unlikely to find a clinician that is not apprehensive about testifying in a sexual assault case. Clinical forensic examinations are usually not taught in medical or nursing school and there are few didactic postgraduate opportunities to learn. In essence, the sexual assault prosecutor who works in this area routinely must understand that in many instances, they may be more familiar with clinical issues than the average clinician.

Weaver explains that many clinicians feel inconvenienced by the criminal justice process. He says:

> Many prosecutors have their first contact with the forensic clinician indirectly through the subpoena. Health care workers usually perceive subpoenas as initial notification of a malpractice suit. Therefore their first response is full of negative emotions. After realizing that they are not personally being sued, the next emotion is frustration toward last-minute notification to appear in court. This initial encounter between the forensic clinician and the prosecutor damages a potential collegial relationship. Frequently, the forensic clinician views the subpoena as one professional being empowered over another, and the spirit of cooperation is quickly diminished. Additionally, most hospital physicians and nurses have fixed schedules, four to eight weeks in advance, and the ability to find replacements is very difficult. Last-minute notification may force them to work back-to-back shifts, or worse, work a night shift just prior to trial. In many instances the result is a hostile witness, who hasn't properly reviewed the record, is not aware of the pivotal points of the case, and isn't able to quote relevant literature that would be helpful to the prosecution.

In an attempt to resolve these and other related clinical and professional issues, Weaver suggests that a basic pretrial checklist should be developed. Citing work by Keen-Payne (1998), Weaver offers a list of things that can help prosecutors and forensic clinicians collaborate in a more efficient manner. Regarding initial forensic clinician contact, Weaver suggests it should be arranged at least one month prior to the trial date, and that subpoenas should be avoided if possible. For the formal case review, the meeting should be scheduled at least two weeks prior to trial, avoiding an on-duty or an end-of-shift time frame. The case review should include a review of the health care institution's rape kit, use of toluidine blue dye or colposcopy, chain of evidence, and routine laboratory process, and a review of the specifics of the case. Weaver suggests prosecutors evaluate the forensic clinician's qualifications to serve as a fact or expert witness, reviewing the individual's previous trial experience, professional training, certifications, and publications, and discussing the limits of the professional's clinical expertise. Weaver also suggests that the prosecutor provide written guidelines for effective testimony including courtroom etiquette, direct and cross-examination procedures, and legal implications of terminology such as probable versus possible, as well as relevant literature for review.

In the trial phase, Weaver says, "Trials are naturally unpredictable; therefore, every effort should be made to minimize variables that may diminish a successful outcome." Following the trial, Weaver adds, "The posttrial phase is most important in influencing future care and community outcomes. Clinicians and nonclinicians need to be educated as to what is occurring in their community and share lessons learned... In a typical continuous quality improvement process, benchmarks should be established and data tracked to gain necessary feedback, maintain quality, and improve outcomes."

4.1.2 Busy Doctors Make Way for Capable Nurses in the ED

Chapter 1 discussed the concepts of clinical forensic medicine and its role in the emergency department. Smock (1994) states that a patient's emergency medical evaluation must be detailed and the documentation comprehensive. He writes, "Comprehensive documentation ideally contains all three components: narrative, diagrammatic, and photographic. The failure to document a number of clinical findings comprehensively may have far-ranging consequences for a patient, an accused suspect, and, potentially, the treating physician." Carmona and Prince (1989) reviewed 100 charts of patients who presented to the ED of a level-one trauma center in California; they found poor, improper, or inadequate documentation in 70 percent of cases, and in 38 percent of cases, potential evidence was improperly secured or documented, or inadvertently discarded. Smock comments, "The forensically untrained emergency physician may easily overlook and inadvertently destroy evidence, both gross and trace, in the course of providing patient care. He may misinterpret physical injuries and evidence, and form an inaccurate opinion as to their cause."

Massachusetts CFN specialist Georgia Pasqualone, MSN, MSFS, RN, CEN, DABFN, who says she has collaborated with Smock on a number of projects, understands the pressures placed on ED physicians and identifies with Smock's call to forensic action:

> He's one of my heroes. I firmly believe that every single physician who has any plans of going into emergency medicine needs to be familiar with the concepts of clinical forensic medicine as so ably outlined by Bill Smock. For example, many ED personnel don't know enough about clinical forensic medicine as they should, and run the risk of misnaming entrance and exit wounds, for example. Worse yet is to have them not recognize that something was evidence when it truly is, and they don't collect it. I think it points to a need for clinical forensic personnel in every health care institution.

One of the assumptions of forensic nursing is that it not only provides medico-legal expertise, but also frees up physicians who are more interested in life-saving interventions than they are in following forensic protocol and going to court. "As nurses, we're the first ones to handle the clothes, the first ones the patient talks to, we're a nonthreatening entity, people will share with us a lot more than they are going to share with the busy doctor," asserts Canadian forensic nurse Linda McCracken, RN. She explains that physicians can't do it all or know it all, nor should they, especially when a capable, specially trained nurse is on the scene. "Physicians are going to burn out and they are not going to be able to do it all," she says. However, from a clinical accuracy point of view, McCracken says physicians should learn from nurses who immerse themselves in forensic protocol:

> Physicians still document gunshot wounds as "entrance" and "exit" and I tell them, "You shouldn't be saying that." Most want to know why, and that's a good sign. The trauma services director at our facility asked me to present my living forensics lecture to trauma rounds, to the heads of all the departments of trauma services. I was able to share with them that they shouldn't be writing "entrance/exit" unless they are certified forensic pathologists. Instead, they should be writing "wound No. 1," "wound No. 2." I tell them, "Don't make assumptions, and watch what you are charting."

McCracken says she tries to keep up with the tenets of clinical forensic medicine to share with physicians and nurses:

> If you have what appears to be a sharp-trauma injury, maybe some type of knife wound, a doctor might chart, "Patient has a 2-cm laceration to the right side of the chest." In actuality, that's not a laceration, that's a stab wound. A laceration is from blunt trauma. Health care personnel must change their language, but often they don't. They continue to use the word "laceration" whether the wound is a cut, an incised wound, or a defense wound. Just write "cut." How easy is that? I don't think, from the medical standpoint, physicians have had any real training in forensic principles, let alone extended forensic practice.

Lynch (1995) writes:

> These cases are generally reported from the hospital emergency department. One reason that trauma care is of concern is that for all the reported crimes of human violence, there may be three times as many unreported crimes. Failure by health care providers to recognize the subtle signs and symptoms of abuse and neglect in the early warning stages, and failure to report to an investigating agency, can contribute to further injury or death... Trauma nurses perform an important role in the investigation of crime and the legal process in terms of victims of violence, both living and deceased. For example, questions related to trauma that may be of later relevance in a court of law may remain unanswered because of an emergency department nurse's ignorance of forensic issues. Frequently, cases are won or lost based on the handling of evidence. If health care professionals fail to incorporate forensic guidelines, misinterpretation or omission of evidence may result in a miscarriage of justice. Clinical forensic nursing is designed to provide a solution to medico-legal-related problems in trauma departments. In addition to medico-legal issues, sensitivity to victims and families has historically been an exclusive concern of victim advocates from the perspective of basic human rights. As a patient advocate, it is a concern for the clinical forensic nurse.

Because the majority of victims of violence and trauma are seen in the ED, nursing personnel must be trained in the proper recognition, collection, documentation, and preservation of forensic evidence. From a bloodied shirt to hands bearing gunshot residue, ED personnel should be well versed in identifying and protecting evidence that is vulnerable to the care-giving process and could be otherwise lost forever. The difference in the way forensic evidence is recognized and handled, or tossed aside, forensic nurses emphasize, could be a miscarriage of justice.

Even as nurses continue to observe proper forensic protocol, there is still some hesitance on the part of nurses regarding where clinical intervention ends and forensic protocol begins. The answer, experts say, is that they overlap whenever and wherever possible, although medical intervention always takes precedence.

McCracken says that although this topic is starting to get more exposure in the nursing and medical literature, it might not be an automatic response. "Awareness of forensic protocol has certainly been helped by shows like *CSI: Crime Scene Investigation,* as more medical personnel are hopping onto the bandwagon," McCracken says:

> Forensic science as it relates to nursing and health care is a hot topic right now. People hear all the time that they should try not to cut through bullet holes in clothing, etc., but people still do it. Those guilty of this most often are the paramedics, who also are the ones who throw things away. They get angry when I say to them, "This spine board is staying under the patient and you're not getting it back until it has been interpreted as evidence." After all, the patient on the spine board was a naked woman found under a bush, obviously assaulted and injured. She was intubated and going into the ICU. I tell them, "We're wrapping that spine board in a sheet and it's going to the police." Other times, medical personnel will recognize a wound as a potential gunshot wound or stab wound; they're thinking about not cutting through a hole in the shirt, but then they get careless and throw it in the garbage. I ask them, "Where's the shirt?" and they say, "It's in the garbage." And I immediately tell them, "Well, let's go get it." A law enforcement officer accompanies them and they retrieve the shirt out of the garbage. So not only must nurses and other ED personnel know the right protocol, pre-hospital personnel should know it, too. We can educate people by word of mouth, by modeling behavior, by in-services—the key is to keep spreading the word about the importance of proper evidence collection and preservation within the context of life-saving intervention.

4.1.3 Nurses Under Fire in the ED

From a medico-legal perspective, it is essential that health care facilities have clear policies and procedures pertaining to health care providers' interaction with patients, particularly those who might be victims or perpetrators of violence. Lynch (1997) observes, "In the interests of maintaining the patient's rights and safeguarding the public's rights, ethical issues have been raised concerning the nurse's treatment of victims in the clinical setting." She adds, "Protecting the patient, whether victim or offender, is the primary concern of both the health care provider and the police officer in the advocacy and ministration of victims of violent crime."

A lack of medico-legal protocol for health care providers and members of law enforcement when they are within the health care environment might create contentious situations that ultimately are detrimental to all parties. For example, some courts have upheld hospitals' rights to refuse to have patients photographed by the police even though it is in the patient's best interest to have their injuries photo-documented. In another instance, a state supreme court ruled that an ER nurse should not have turned over clothing worn by a patient (and potential perpetrator) to police because the patient was not under arrest at the time. The police officer who had brought the suspect to the hospital took the clothes from the nurse and used them to obtain a warrant of arrest. The patient filed suit against the nurse and won.

Lynch (1997) cautions nurses to understand important legal precedents. She writes, "When the patient is a criminal, ethical issues have been raised concerning the nurse's treatment of the patient in the emergency department. Protecting the patient—whether offender or victim—is the primary concern of health care professionals and law enforcement. Crimes against human beings force the nurse to decide which obligations are due the patient and which to law enforcement officers." She adds, "Every hospital . . . eventually must address problems of conflict with law enforcement agencies regarding patients in legal custody. Contributing to the facilitation of interaction between police officers and the emergency department staff are policies that increase mutual understanding, define roles, and promote cooperation."

4.1.4 The Investigation of Trauma in the ED

Lynch (1995) writes:

> Nurses have a unique opportunity to contribute to forensic science as they manage problems commonly encountered in trauma care. Law enforcement officers struggle to safeguard evidence during medical interventions, and resultant conflicts of priority may ensue. Medical-legal interface is critical among multidisciplinary teams investigating traumatic injuries, whether accidental, criminal, self-inflicted, or from unknown causes. Interface can be damaged, with serious consequences, when no forensic protocols exist. This occurs when police officers and hospital staff are not familiar with procedures that each is supposed to follow. The appointment of a designated hospital liaison to network with police and the coroner and/or medical examiner can provide a systematic approach to communication and coordination. This liaison should be knowledgeable of forensic concepts, legal responsibilities, and victims' issues. The forensic clinical nurse specialist is prepared to fill this role ideally.

"A lot of forensic cases come in to the ER, so you are afforded many opportunities to learn what is forensic and what is not forensic," says Bobbi Jo O'Neal, RN, BSN, F-ABMDI, deputy coroner in Charleston, South Carolina, who was an ER nurse early in her career. "You also have to interact with law enforcement officers because they are coming into the ER to see victims and suspects. The ER is the only place in the medical community where you will see these kinds of cases, and a wide variety of them."

O'Neal says she specifically came to the ER to get exposure to forensic cases and practices. "My interest in forensic cases was piqued early. I was an oncology nurse first, and began doing some part-time work with a hospice agency in Tennessee. I would have to call the coroner, after a patient died, to get permission to call the funeral home. I started asking questions of every person I encountered along the way. I realized that nurses could become involved and valuable in many types of forensic cases."

Although O'Neal might have had an early bent toward forensic practice, the ER in which she worked was lacking in proper forensic protocol. "When I was working in the ER, the sexual assault kits were still being done by the ER physicians, so the resident on call would do them. The nurse was really just a handmaiden during that process—I don't think anyone thought of it as forensic nursing, even as late as 1996 or 1997. I don't think there was an awareness of forensic cases, even sexual assault cases, like there should have been."

As O'Neal was gaining a firmer grasp on the concepts of clinical forensic nursing, she would share them with her colleagues, but with mixed results:

> I think forensic protocols went over fairly well, but not for the reasons you might think. It went over well because they knew I was interested in doing (forensic cases), so if I was working that day, I would take care of those patients. If a sexual assault victim came in, they would say, "Give them to Bobbi Jo!" I think that my colleagues' awareness started to come about slowly; if they had questions, they now had someone who could perhaps answer them.

Even in the face of demonstrated success, acceptance was slow by her coworkers:

> The ER really wasn't interested in a more structured protocol. The hospital I was a part of eventually had an OB-GYN physician who was very interested in sexual assault, and she started to develop a team concept but it really didn't involve nurses much; it had more to do with the OB-GYN residents. They wanted a number of nurses to volunteer to help with their program. I initially sat down with her and said, "I think the way we are going about this is probably not good," because basically they were saying, "Nurse, just open the kit, this is all you need to do," and there really wasn't any training for the nurses on what they should do. Even in that effort, I felt there wasn't a lot of support for the nurses.

O'Neal explains that funding for the sexual assault program came through the facility's psychology division, which secured monies to examine how victims responded from a psychological standpoint:

> Since the funding came through them, the psych department headed up the program. The problem came when the research assistants would show up at the hospital to meet the victim; one of their goals was to make sure the victim filed a police report and went through the program to ensure that they became a part of the research project. There were times when the victims were pressured to press charges, because that's how they got into the research project. Often, I would get there and the victim would not be cooperative, so sometimes I would have to say, "Everyone out of the room" so I could sit down with them one on one and say, "You don't have to do anything; you can leave, but first, let me tell you the benefits of this program and why I am here." Ninety-nine percent of the time, the victim went through the exam, we were able to get them prophylaxis if they needed it, and attend to their needs.

The program was fraught with politics, however, O'Neal says:

> Not too long after that, all of the nurses who were part of the team resigned. They said, "By being a part of this program and how it was run, we felt we were re-victimizing them, which is not what we want to do, and we felt we had lost sight of the purpose of doing the forensic exam. Yes, we wanted to get them to counseling and all that stuff, but first and foremost, we are trying to do a forensic exam to gather the evidence that was needed so that prosecution could take place, and we hoped to do it in an atmosphere in which we wouldn't add to their harm or distress. The nurses felt that wasn't happening."

4.1.5 Recognition of Forensic Cases in the ED

Pasqualone (2003) writes, "Recognition of forensic issues that accompany patients into the emergency department is nearly as important as the priorities in rendering life-saving treatment." Pasqualone's research reveals the presence of at least 24 forensic categories among patients seen at a community hospital ED. She asserts that by identifying these categories and the numbers of patients within them, the resulting data will mandate the presence of a CNS in forensic nursing in the ED as well as on call to other departments of the hospital.

"A CNS in forensic nursing should be established as an integral component of the ED health care staff," Pasqualone adds:

> The establishment of forensic categories will further clarify the educational needs of the ED nursing staff. Nurses must be educated with regard to the forensic issues surrounding the victims of trauma and violent crime. If staffing is inadequate, the priorities of treatment may well outweigh the importance of recognizing, documenting and collecting evidence. If important evidence is destroyed and/or overlooked, a serious injustice could be rendered to the patient, suspect, or hospital.

Pasqualone says:

> A general lack of knowledge about forensic issues identifies a need for the categorization of this unique patient base. A systematic approach to the clarification and delineation of forensic categories is compulsory, should the need arise to provide evidence in a litigious situation. Concise, chronological identification and documentation of these evidentiary groupings is essential as a prerequisite of current and future ED nurses' inevitable direct involvement in judicial proceedings. ED nurses' attitudes and familiarities with the majority of forensic issues are, more often than not, limited to their initial dialogue with law enforcement personnel concerning the medical condition of a patient. ED nursing personnel must be aware at all times of the necessity to integrate the appropriate collection of any significant evidence, both demonstrative and testimonial, while providing care. This most assuredly can be accomplished in a proficient manner.

Pasqualone acquiesces that although life-saving interventions come first:

> The trail of evidence and the chain of custody are being destroyed far too many times during the flurry of saving a life. It later appears in court that justice is not being served, that the guilty are escaping punishment, and that victims are being victimized once again. Mistakes in forensic cases exist, made and then compounded by ignorance, incompetence, or indifference. By initiating a conscientious system of recognizing, assessing, collecting, documenting, photo documenting, and reporting, ED nurses can assist their patients, their local police departments, and the entire legal community by maintaining chain of custody, being aware of important issues, and detailing all evidence in the medical record.

To facilitate development of the forensic categories, Pasqualone (1998, 2003) examined the records of patients admitted through the ED of a small community hospital located just outside of a major metropolitan city in eastern Massachusetts. The ED sees approximately 22,500 patients annually. The categorization system was developed from a retrospective study of ED medical records. The population studied consisted of every person (N = 3,436) admitted to the ED during a 60-day period. Approximately 914 patients (27 percent) qualified as forensic cases. The top categories were occupation-related injuries, 289 (8.41 percent); transportation injuries, 193 (5.62 percent); substance abuse, 160 (4.66 percent); personal injury, 125 (3.64 percent); and forensic psych, 49 (1.43 percent).

In addition, Pasqualone discovered that child abuse and neglect cases numbered 464 per year (2.06 percent), abuse of the disabled numbered 130 cases per year (0.58 percent), human and animal bites numbered 90 per year (.40 percent), elder abuse and neglect numbered 56 cases per year (.25 percent), assault and battery numbered 22 per year (.64 percent), domestic violence numbered 6 cases (.17 percent), sharp force injuries numbered 7 cases per year (.03 percent), clients in police custody and sexual assault each numbered 2 cases per year (.06 percent), and firearm injuries consisted of 7 cases in three years (.01 percent). The categories of child, elder, and disabled abuse and neglect; human and animal bites; sharp force injuries; organ and tissue donation; burns; and firearm injuries were extrapolated from ED admissions and statistics of mandated reports taken over a one-year period. Although food and drug tampering, gang violence, and malpractice and negligence were not categories identified among the ED population during the study, Pasqualone reports that they are categories having the potential of occurrence at any time in any ED.

Goll-McGee et al. (2003) emphasize that:

> Clinical forensic nursing has come of age as a means of coping with the resultant increased complexity of nursing

> practice, society and the law. A living forensic population, "survivors of criminal or liability-related injuries that result in an investigation by a legal agency," is being recognized by health care professionals in varied clinical practice environments, especially in the ED. In fact, personnel frequently interface with forensic cases and therefore have the greatest potential for evaluating the associated forensic elements.

Goll-McGee et al. add, "As nurses on the front line begin to ponder the presence of a forensic patient population they will look to address their needs. As our knowledge base expands, professionals themselves develop and nursing paradigms shift." Smock (1994) says that continued attention to these types of cases and the use of this forensic nursing process could make an important contribution to safeguarding the legal rights of patients and the community and nurture clinical forensic nursing, a developing nursing specialty, within practice environments.

Once a forensic patient is identified, the nurse engages in clinical practice encompassing evidence collection, documentation, and intervention. According to Mund (1996), physical evidence is anything that has been "used, left, removed, altered or contaminated during the commission of a crime by either the suspect or victim." Forensic nurses working in the ED can look to the position statement from the Emergency Nurses Association (ENA) for guidance on the specifics of forensic evidence collection. According to the ENA:

> Victims of sexual assault, child maltreatment, elder abuse and other violent incidents are often brought to the emergency department (ED) for care, treatment, and evidence collection. Evidence can, during the course of the ED evaluation, become lost by being cut through, brushed away, or overlooked. The performance of forensic procedures is a component of emergency nursing practice. The emergency nurse identifies the need for forensic evidence collection, and for collecting and preserving the evidence. These procedures are a part of the scientific investigation, evidence collection and preservation, analysis, prevention and treatment of trauma and/or death-related medical-legal issues. The emergency nurse caring for a victim of crime also is responsible for accurate documentation and the ability to perform the duties of a witness during court proceedings. The nurse also may be requested to function as an expert witness in medical-legal investigations, including depositions and courtroom testimony.

The ENA's position statement on evidence collection says:

> ENA believes that it is the emergency nurse's role not only to provide physical and emotional care to patients, but also to help preserve the evidence collected in the emergency department. ENA supports collaboration with emergency physicians, social service, and law enforcement personnel to develop guidelines for forensic evidence collection and documentation in the emergency care setting. ENA encourages emergency nurses to become familiar with the concepts and skills of evidence collection, photographic and written documentation, as well as testifying in legal proceedings.

The ENA emphasizes, "An emergency nurse is often the first person a patient encounters after an incident of violence. Emergency nurses should have the skills needed for evidence collection and preservation. Emergency nurses are skilled in providing comprehensive care and treatment of the patient as well as in maintaining the chain of custody and appropriate documentation."

Numerous experts have addressed the importance of proper identification of forensic patients, as well as appropriate assessment and documentation. Goll-McGee et al. (2003) write, "The development of protocols for collecting available evidence may assist in assuring that collection is performed appropriately." Goll-McGee et al. add, "Proper collection of evidence is imperative to avoid the compromise of its integrity." Hoyt (1999) states, "Preservation of evidence in the clinical setting requires planning, attention to detail, and the guidance of agency policies and procedures." George et al. (1997) write, "In the duty to document . . . it is almost as important to keep extraneous material out of the medical record as it is to be sure to include pertinent information." Goll-McGee et al. (2003) add, "In many situations, important information . . . which may not be required for patient care is nonetheless vital to later investigation and requires the patient's consent to ensure that collection of the evidence will not amount to an illegal search (or perhaps malpractice)." Smock et al. (1994) state, "Thorough, objective documentation of ED evaluation and treatment of patients who present with complaints suggesting potential litigation and/or criminal activity is critical. Meticulous documentation provides evidence that something is done or not done, exists or doesn't exist, it provides evidence for the client, protection for the nurse and testimony for the court."

Perhaps most important, experts point to the need for a high index of suspicion in the ED. Winfrey and Smith (1999) state, "Intuition . . . gives the forensically educated nurse permission to trust and to act upon his or her suspicions." Goll-McGee (1999) writes, "Non-physical evidence collection suggests the use of an index of suspicion to uncover the how and why of their mechanisms of injury. This effort involves an assessment of psychosocial history, separating the injuries from the story and asking hard questions. It looks for inconsistencies in clinical presentations."

4.1.6 Evidence Documentation in the ED

One of the most important forensic steps a nurse in the ED can take is the performance of thorough photo-documentation of a patient's injuries; however, many nurses wrestle with patient privacy restrictions. McCracken says she struggles with Canada's privacy laws, the same way many nurses grapple with federal Health Insurance Portability and Accountability Act (HIPAA) compliance and state privacy laws in the United States. "The big issue related to evidence collection and recognition of injury and assessment in the ED is photo documentation," she says:

> Here, it is considered to be infringement of an individual's privacy, and the big question is, are you getting patient consent. But nurses say, "How will I get consent if the patient is unconscious?" At our facility, the photography consent form doesn't refer to documentation of suspicious injuries. I have told the people in legal services who drafted the consent form that it needs to be changed. I have gotten the support of our trauma services who say they love the pictures I take—not only does it help them from a medical-legal standpoint, but later on, if a case goes to court, those bruises are healed—but hey, I have Polaroid photos taped to the nurses' notes so medical records won't throw them away—they are good for 99 years. I encountered a lot of resistance from my managers when I said, "We need a Polaroid camera." I told them a camera is better than marking an X on a body map. Over and over again, it's proved that photographs save the day. There was a case where a patient died from her injuries, and when the chart was pulled, my photos were still in there. Hospital hierarchy is afraid of taking pictures of people.

Many ED nurses are unaware of forensic protocol and struggle with its implementation. Lynch says, "Emergency nurses become involved when a patient is admitted for trauma care as a result of suspicious injuries that may be crime-related or self-inflicted. These patients require nurses to be aware of the manner in which the assessment of injury, forensic evidence, and critical data are documented with law enforcement and crime scene officers." She adds:

> The problem of gathering evidence in the emergency department is compounded by failure to develop and implement forensic guidelines for nurses. A classic problem is the lack of an acceptable method for preserving evidence from crimes that are discovered long after the patient has been admitted or has died. This situation is further complicated when the forensic pathologist becomes involved after the destruction of the evidence, or the condition of the body has been altered by surgical intervention. Hospital emergency departments are regularly in contact with essential evidence in criminal cases.

The evidence collection process is addressed throughout this text, but a quick primer for ED nurses is appropriate. The types of evidence most commonly encountered by ED nurses include clothing, bullets, blood stains, hairs, fibers, and small pieces of material such as fragments of metal, glass, paint, and wood. Trace and physical evidence are used to establish the facts of a crime. Lynch says:

> If, however, proper precautions are not taken to ensure an unaltered condition when collecting specimens, the forensic examination is compromised. When crime victims are treated by emergency department staff, forensic evidence is often lost because medical personnel are not aware of its presence or potential value. Problems in gathering evidence in the emergency department, surgical suite, or any department in the hospital are not restricted to the failure to recognize or collect forensic evidence; often, there is failure to properly preserve fragile or perishable evidence. Documentation must reflect the accurate identification, description, and security of medico-legal evidence.

Lynch (1995) acknowledges the dual responsibility of providing medical care and following medico-legal protocol in the ED. She writes, "The dilemma of gathering evidence in the emergency department is a serious cause of concern in traumatic injury patients." She adds that ED staff should recognize the importance of recovering possible items of evidence in a legally acceptable manner in medico-legal cases, defined as a treatment situation with legal implications, such as suspicious deaths or crime-related injuries, and accidents that might trigger some form of civil or criminal litigation.

Lynch states that it is imperative for ED staff to recognize and preserve vital fragments of trace evidence through careful handling of the patient's clothing and personal property. She writes, "This is one of the most important actions nurses provide to aid the investigation process. Clothing worn at the time of the incident may contain trace evidence useful in linking the victim with the assailant or crime scene." She adds, "Careful examination of defects in clothes can be compared to wounds of the victim, and often clothes provide insight as to the type of weapon or wounding instrument used. Clothing should be checked for blood, semen, gunshot residue, or trace materials such as hair or fibers." The clothing and the trace evidence should be properly photo-documented, diagrammed, collected, and preserved.

Lynch (1995, 1997) writes, "Documentation of the condition of the patient's clothing should be carefully noted. Color, type, unusual markings, and tears or other damages should be recorded. Occasionally, fibers or foreign debris from the crime scene on the victim's clothing may be transferred to the vehicle or assailant. Clothing is often the first circumstantial evidence that may help to identify a missing person or collaborate an eyewitness statement." Clothing should be carefully removed to protect any foreign fragments adhering to them, and they should not be shaken.

"Clothing is frequently cut away during resuscitation attempts and is subject to loss of both the article itself and/or evidentiary materials," Lynch explains:

> The cutting of clothing is unavoidable in many life-threatening situations and is necessary to provide immediate access to treatment sites. When this occurs, try to avoid cutting through tears, rips, and holes that may have resulted from the weapon or the assault. Clothing should never be discarded or thrown on the floor, as this can result in cross-contamination of trace evidence with debris from the treatment environment.

She adds that due to time constraints during life-saving intervention, a clean, white sheet can be placed on an empty trauma table, Mayo stand, or on the floor in the corner of the room for clothing to be placed until time permits for effective packaging. If a victim is able to remove his or her clothes, this should be done standing on a clean sheet or a large sheet of paper to collect any microscopic evidence that might become dislodged during removal. The sheet should be packaged in a separate paper bag for transfer to the crime laboratory.

Regarding the preservation of evidence collected in the ED, moist clothing should be hung to dry in a secure location. Clean white paper should be placed over stains to avoid cross-contamination, and each item of clothing should be stored in separate paper bags, not plastic bags. Plastic bags are inappropriate because there is a tendency for condensation to accumulate, resulting in a degradation of the integrity of the evidence. Each bag should be sealed and clearly marked with the date, time, and signature or initials of the individual doing the sealing.

Health care professionals in the ED must maintain secure custody of the clothing and trace evidence until it is handed over to law enforcement. A chain of custody commences with the individual collecting the evidence; this person maintains custody of evidentiary material. The chain of custody should be defined in the health care institution's forensic protocol and generally requires a form of written documentation. Rules of evidence require a chain of custody for each item recovered from the patient, including trace and physical evidence, laboratory specimens of blood and body fluids, clothing, and personal articles. Lynch writes, "The integrity of every specimen or piece of evidence seized must be ensured to protect the admissibility in a court of law. Failure to maintain the chain of custody renders potentially important evidence worthless if lost, damaged, or unaccountable from the hands of the nurse to the police officer."

4.2 PRESENTATION OF SPECIFIC FORENSIC CASES IN THE ED

Issues of sexual assault, child abuse, and elder abuse are discussed thoroughly later in this text; however, it is appropriate to set the stage by discussing the treatment of these victims in the ED as further proof of the need for properly trained forensic health care personnel.

4.2.1 ED Care of the Sexual Assault Victim

Carr (2001) asserts that victims of sexual assault deserve competent, compassionate medical evaluation, but that many ED physicians believe they are not adequately trained or prepared to perform the time-consuming, intricate evidentiary examinations required. She writes:

> A loud, busy emergency department is a hostile type of environment for victims. Doctors and nurses pulled in many directions may be perceived as being gruff and uncaring to the victim. These patients may leave before they receive medical care, and because of this poor introduction to the system may drop out. They fail to obtain needed emotional counseling and justice is not pursued. A badly performed medical exam that is not well documented is of little value. Chain of custody for forensic evidence must be maintained or it will be worthless from a legal standpoint. Concerns regarding pregnancy, sexually transmitted infections, safety and follow up care need to be addressed before the patient is discharged.

Carr points to the burgeoning number of SANEs and SARTs, but is cautious about these programs, no surprise to forensic nurses who are well aware of physicians' skeptical—and to a large degree inaccurate—perspectives of their performance.

Carr writes:

> Several areas around the country have formed nurse examiner programs to perform the sexual assault exam. These programs are staffed by nurses specifically trained in performing the sexual assault exam. They are closely associated with EDs so that if the patient has significant injuries or medical issues, a physician is nearby. These programs seem to be the answer to all the problems that arise in the ED when a victim of sexual assault presents. There are however some problems with the programs. A review of the SANE programs found an almost ten-fold difference in the amount of education received by nurses prior to performing this service. One of the greatest problems is that only a few programs keep track of statistics. All aspects of the sexual assault exam need to be looked at critically in order to achieve a format that is both useful for prosecution and not too unpleasant for the victim. SANE programs began in the later 1970s and have doubled in numbers in the last five years. Hopefully the programs will soon become more standardized and data analyzed in order to make valid decisions about the utility of many aspects of this exam.

Carr asserts that there is a paucity of evidence-based medicine to support the current management of the sexual assault victim and as a result, numerous controversies rage. Carr writes:

> Recently I heard a former president of ACEP tell a group at a conference that the history of a sexual assault victim should be kept to a minimum in order to avoid discrepancies between the victim's story to the medical field and that to the police. Most programs feel that a well-documented medical history is needed for the evaluator to know the mindset of the victim during the assault that caused her to act as she did. The potential physical injuries are also gleaned from a good history. One of medicine's main objectives in these exams is to determine if the physical findings are consistent with the history given by the victim.

Carr recommends that ED personnel not involve themselves in what she describes as a "he said, she said" telling of the traumatic event, but to document direct quotes from the victim, or "excited utterances" that indicate the patient's state of mind during the assault. Carr writes, "Such statements can be used as testimony and are exempt from the hearsay rule because they are statements given for the purpose of medical diagnosis. Contradictions in victim statements are issues for attorneys. It is not wise for a physician with little legal training to try to decide what will be legal issues and consequences."

Carr acknowledges undiscerning health care professionals' tendency to overlook minute forensic considerations as small as the trace evidence that might be residing in the nooks and crannies of a patient's skin and clothing. Carr writes, "The physical exam needs to be carefully performed with attention to all findings including those that are typically of little medical concern. After ruling out significant injury we want to look for evidence that assists in identifying the assailant, provides proof of force or coercion, proves recent sexual contact and corroborates the victim's story." Bruises, redness, swelling, scratches, bites, or ligature marks must be documented in the medical record through a complete description, by drawing on an anatomic diagram, or by photographing the injured area.

Carr says that perineal, anal, and pelvic exams can be performed with the aid of a colposcope, with or without an attached camera. Carr writes, "Programs providing service to sexually abused children find that photographing this area is very important. Many normal variants exist in children that may otherwise be interpreted as injuries. In adults the value of the colposcope in seeing injuries not well seen by general exam is well documented. But the interpretation of findings is only as good as the medical provider." She says that the finding of micro-abrasions, redness, swelling, and bruising is of value when they corroborate the victim's statements, and must be differentiated from those caused by consensual sex, tampon placement, or constipated stool. She writes, "So far, there is only one study evaluating genital changes after consensual sex. In this small study it was determined that microtrauma can occur and it was seen with a colposcope. This microtrauma consisted of tiny broken blood vessels and micro-abrasions." She continues, "There is also a study showing no evidence of trauma in two patients with semen present who also reported a sexual assault, suggesting that physical findings do not have to be present after a sexual assault."

Carr admits physicians' discomfort in conducting examinations. "Properly obtaining forensic evidence can be distressing to the physician," she acknowledges:

> We are not used to the role of investigator. In this instance, the crime scene is the body, with evidence inside and outside. It is important to keep in mind that the evidence we want to obtain is that of the assailant. This evidence will be washed away, wear away or degrade in a short time. Most feel after 48 hours there is little likelihood of obtaining evidence. Others feel 72 hours is a better time frame. It is not unreasonable to assume that as forensic testing becomes more sensitive we will be able to obtain evidence beyond 72 hours.

Carr explains that most programs obtain evidence from only those areas of the body the patient says were involved, whereas other programs believe it is necessary to obtain evidence from all orifices because the victim might be too traumatized to know what happened to him or her. Carr adds that specimens must be sealed and a record kept of the rape kit at all locations along the path; the kit can never be left unattended if it has not been sealed. Carr concludes, "The sexual assault exam continues to be a bane of emergency physicians. Many more studies need to be done in order to determine the areas of the exam that are beneficial to the patient from a medical standpoint and the areas that are useful in the legal process."

4.2.2 ED Care of the Child Abuse Victim

Reece (2001) says that the most common injury seen in the ER is bruising. He explains that the keys to diagnosing these bruises as having been inflicted are location and patterns. Reece writes, "If they are on the posterior aspects of the body, on the sides of the face, the buttocks, the genitalia, the ears or the neck, or on the abdominal wall, they are more likely to be of abusive origin than accidental. The other key is pattern. Certain instruments are used in harsh discipline, and these leave characteristic marks."

Although clinicians are still debating the stages of bruise healing as markers for determining when an injury was sustained, clinicians agree that the presence of bruises in various stages of healing is also indicative of repetitive injuries. Reece writes:

One word of caution about judging the ages of bruises by their color: the older literature contains misinformation about judging the ages of bruises on the basis of color. For example, older textbooks display a chart indicating that certain colors suggest certain ages. When this was studied recently, the conclusions of the authors were that there are too many variables to make definitive determination of the age of the bruise based on color. Rough estimates may be made, but it must be recognized that there is a range of error of two to four days. One of the more recent articles that is helpful in judging the origin of bruising was subtitled: "Those who don't cruise rarely bruise." In this study of bruising in various age groups it was found that bruises seen in nonambulatory children were more likely to have been inflicted than in children old enough to walk, a seemingly self-evident finding but one that is often forgotten when confronted with unexplained bruises.

Head injury in children is another common presentation to the ER. According to Reece:

Head injury is the most common cause of mortality from child abuse and it is also the reason for most long term morbidity in survivors. Head injury can be the result of direct blows to the head by fists, feet, or objects, or by striking the child's head against an object. In infants, shaking or shaking with impact are the most frequent mechanisms for producing signs and symptoms referable to the central nervous system. Injuries to the head cover a wide spectrum and so the resultant signs and symptoms are also quite variable. Smaller biomechanical forces lead to smaller injuries and milder symptoms.

According to Reece, head injuries can present the following symptoms: extreme fussiness, inconsolable crying, irritability, lethargy, hypotonia, disinclination to feed, vomiting, tachypnea, bradycardia, hypothermia, seizures, gaze preferences, unequal or unreactive pupils, stupor, coma, and death.

Reece says that another common presentation in children that might be a sign of abuse is fractures. Distinguishing accidental from inflicted cases can be challenging. Reece writes:

As in all abuse, the younger the age of the child with traumatic injuries, the more likely the etiology is abusive. Fractures in children under the age of 12 months are, in the majority of cases, abusive. Fractures in certain bones are highly correlated with abuse: posterior rib fractures, metaphyseal fractures, bilateral or multiple fractures, multiple fractures in various stages of healing, digital fractures, scapular fractures and complex skull fractures. The type of fracture, however, helps little in determining the etiology.

Older literature suggested that spiral fractures were more often associated with abuse, but more recent studies have shown that this type of fracture only tells us about the mechanical forces involved in the production of the fracture, but not whether or not it was abusive. Certain fractures, such as a toddler's fracture, clavicular fractures, simple skull fractures, and long bone fractures in older children are much more likely to be of accidental origin. When evaluating for the possibility of abuse, other medical conditions that can produce fractures, such as osteogenesis imperfecta or fractures through pathologic bones, must be considered and ruled out if appropriate.

4.2.3 ED Care of the Elder Abuse Victim

In 1997, the American College of Emergency Physicians (ACEP) released a new practice guideline to address the presentation of elders to the ED. In a seven-year study of ED use by older victims of family violence, 182 physical elder abuse victims were identified, and 114 (62.6 percent) had been seen in an ED at least once during a five-year period surrounding initial identification of abuse. These 114 individuals accounted for 628 visits, 30.6 percent of which resulted in hospital admission. The patients in the study were primarily female (76.3 percent) and White (85.3 percent), with a mean age of 73.1 years. Adult sons were the abusers in 28.9 percent of cases, spouses in 26.8 percent of cases, and adult daughters in 21.6 percent of cases. Other abusers included grandchildren, other relatives, and friends. The most common weapon used was the body (punching, kicking, slapping), but knives, canes, furniture, and pipes also were described. Injury, including fractures, lacerations, and contusions, was the chief complaint. The study concluded that elder abuse victims have substantial interactions with EDs that frequently result in hospital admissions and that strategies to identify elder abuse in less acute settings would improve quality of life and likely result in substantial savings in health care expenditures.

Another survey, "Elder Mistreatment: National Survey of Emergency Physicians," was the first one to survey emergency physicians to determine the perceived magnitude of elder mistreatment, levels of physician awareness, and willingness to report suspected cases. It also sought to determine the barriers to reporting suspected cases of elder mistreatment and physician awareness of state elder abuse laws. Fifty-two percent of the more than 700 surveys completed by members of the ACEP described elder mistreatment as prevalent but less so than spouse or child abuse. Ninety-two percent of the physicians indicated their states did not have sufficient resources to meet the needs of elderly victims. Only 31 percent reported having a written protocol for reporting elder mistreatment. Physicians also were generally not familiar with applicable state laws and did not feel confident about identifying or reporting elderly victims of abuse or neglect. Until recently, research on domestic violence has been focused mainly on spouse and child abuse, and little attention has been paid to the mistreatment of older people. The results of the survey highlight the need for greater training and continuing medical education focused related on elder abuse in the field of geriatric emergency medicine.

Jones (1991) states that as many as half of the elderly patients who present in an ER will be admitted to hospitals, transported to skilled nursing homes, or placed in a protected environment for further diagnosis and treatment of their urgent care conditions. The other half will be released, and a significant number of them, because they live alone and have few family members or friends to assist them, are at risk of returning to the ER. Jones writes:

> A shortage of primary-care physicians, especially ones trained in geriatrics, in rural and low-income urban areas, seems to be one of the reasons why more elderly are going to ERs. Overloaded with patients, doctors often can't find the time to advise the elderly on preventive measures, monitor their chronic conditions, or prescribe new medications before a crisis develops. And when one does, the doctor may not be reachable. In a recent Philadelphia study, nearly two-thirds of the seniors surveyed found their doctors to be inaccessible during a crisis because of irregular office hours or lack of a 24-hour answering service.

> Research shows that most older persons have good reason to go to emergency rooms when they do, because they have proportionately as many or more emergency and urgent care needs as other age groups. Unfortunately, most ER doctors and nurses receive little training in geriatrics. The needs of some elderly ER patients are different from those of younger ones and may not be met in the middle of ER crisis and confusion . . . Time pressures may limit the ER staff's ability to take down comprehensive medical histories of an older person, (and) fully evaluate symptoms.

4.3 THE FORENSIC NURSING RESPONSE

Pasqualone says:

> There is a need to place advanced practice forensic nurse clinical specialists into our hospitals, nursing homes, schools, criminal justice system and anywhere else in our communities where nurses can act as the liaisons between medicine and the law. Nurses will be prepared to enter into this new career field as medico-legal consultants for attorneys, insurance companies, law enforcement agencies, medical examiner and coroner systems, school departments, nursing home administrations and hospital EDs. Although the contemporary media has portrayed the forensic scientist as a death-investigating Quincy, able to solve a murder in less than an hour, one can now appreciate the comprehensive involvement of forensic nursing and its far-reaching influence with this science of the 21st century. The need for a greater consciousness on the part of all health care providers with regard to delivery of more cost-efficient medical care cannot be emphasized enough. The forensic needs of the client, though, must not be jeopardized. Efficiency can be improved through a well-coordinated intelligent process that improves performance without compromising quality. More efficient utilization of resources means more resources can be available for those in need.

Pasqualone advocates for a mobile system that facilities quick, efficient response to forensic cases. She explains:

> When interfacing with a forensic patient, the ED nurse must strive to utilize a logical approach and have an algorithmic method in place for the forensic nursing process. The nurse can then recognize, assess, collect, document, photo document, preserve and report, depending on the patient category. An ED forensic cart is one way of taking the initial guesswork out of "What do I do now?" The cart can be similar to those utilized by the ED for code situations. On it should be various sizes of clean paper bags for clothing; plastic containers for leaves, fibers, buttons, paint chips and the like; clean white paper for making bundles for the smallest hairs and fibers; sterile swabs; sterile water; evidence tape; felt-tip pens; labels; clean sheets; and file folders containing all mandated reporting forms. The state's sexual assault evidence collection kit should also be included on the cart. A 35-mm camera or an instant camera system plus film should be available at all times to the ED personnel for photo documentation of injuries. If a hospital policy for chain of custody for film processing is in place, the 35-mm system can be utilized with peace of mind. Otherwise, instant photographs can be placed in the medical record immediately. There is both practicality and economy when utilizing the cart when caring for forensic patients.

> In-service education must be an ongoing process. Laws change and ED nurses must be kept informed of legislative ramifications of their care. Policies and procedures should be written and overhauled in order to manage the forensic populations properly. In fact, the study of forensic nursing should be integrated into the most basic of nursing educational processes. Evidence may present itself to paraprofessionals as easily as it is to the professional health care provider. If evidence is destroyed unknowingly, cases can be lost in the process.

Pasqualone says that hospitals should initiate a tracking mechanism for all forensic categories of patients. She explains that a facility that is unaware of the incidences of forensic situations "inhibits the gathering of valuable statistics, as well as deterring the process of addressing educational needs for all staff." She adds:

> Registration personnel could potentially track forensic categories as they register into the ED; however, nursing staff should be making note of the categories as the

> patients are seen. By identifying forensic categories and the numbers of patients within these categories, the high percentage of forensic patients (27 percent) identifies a need for a forensic clinical nurse specialist in the ED setting. A CNS in forensic nursing should be established as an integral component of the staffing patterns in the ED.

Pasqualone believes that nurses and all ED staff should be educated about the forensic issues surrounding the victims of trauma and violent crime. "Categorization will lead to recognition; recognition will lead to adequate staffing; and adequate staffing will lead to a more complete preparedness and treatment for this unique population of patients," she says. "If staffing and education are inadequate, the priorities of treatment may well outweigh the importance of recognizing, documenting, and collecting evidence. If important evidence is destroyed and/or overlooked, a serious injustice could be rendered to the patient, suspect, or hospital." She continues:

> Our rapidly evolving health care environment necessitates a change in the way we practice nursing. Nurses aware of mandated reporting cases protect patients' rights as well as maintaining patient safety. Forms should be completed correctly and expeditiously. Statistics should be recorded and this information could be utilized for greatly needed research on the cycle of violence and classification of patients. Nurses aware of the benefits of photo documentation can save their clients time and money within the judicial system due to the accuracy and supplemental recording of injuries. In addition, forensic nurse consultants can save hospitals time and litigation fees with their testimonial expertise. Knowledgeable nurses can truly decrease the number of lawsuits that are actually introduced into the court system. Nailing the evidence could potentially eliminate the need to go to trial. The application of forensic techniques is essential. The structure of the entire forensic nursing process is predicated on maintaining a certain state of mind—an investigative, interpretive, dogmatic search for the facts and the truth. The forensic nursing process, as an extension of the general nursing process, is being cultivated in an increasing number of EDs of health care facilities across the country.

4.3.1 Across the Border: Forensic Nursing in Canadian EDs Still Coming of Age

Linda McCracken, RN, describes forensic nursing in Canada as still being in its infancy, but there are signs of growth. One issue with which many nurses must contend is working with patients they might not even realize are forensic cases. McCracken says:

> I think of forensic nursing as something you are doing everyday, but there are some nurses who don't understand this. I think of it as being in the right place at the right time to be involved in forensic cases, while others may think they are in the wrong place at the wrong time. Working in emergency nursing for so many years, get involved in cases you didn't even know were forensic... until the day you get subpoenaed to go to court. I have gone to court as a factual witness many times. It's because I usually was the one who took the samples from the doctor when he did the sexual assault exam and handed them to the police officer. Because of this action, I am subpoenaed to go to court to say "Yes, I was working that day," "Yes, that patient was there," and "Yes, I took the samples and handed them over to the police."

McCracken recalls a time when she was involved in the case of a local socialite who was stopped by the police and a scuffle ensued:

> The police were charging her with assault. She came to the ER with some bruises and small scratches, nothing too significant; however, in my experience, no matter how small the presentation of injury, it is wise to document carefully, because I assume it could go to court. I'm very astute in my documentation, and I try to tell other ER nurses how important that is. Your documentation is your testimony; you may go to court years later and you won't remember the details of the case, so you'll be glad you wrote them down. So, in the socialite's case, I must have had three pages of charting for no real injuries, and sure enough, it was a year later that I was subpoenaed not for the prosecution like we usually are, but for the defense, and there was my chart, laminated as Exhibit A. It included things I had documented, and I thought, "This is something important added on to my role in the ED—being a witness to the evidence."

McCracken points to a former medical examiner in Calgary, John Butts, MD (who in 1994 had investigated the Swiss Air crash in Nova Scotia), for being one of the earliest proponents of forensic nursing. "He was and continues to be pro-nursing," she says. "As early as 1976, he recognized that emergency nurses were the ones who had important assessment skills, and began training them to work with forensic cases." McCracken explains that Butts and forensic nursing pioneer Virginia Lynch were conducting a Canadian-wide lecture tour and speaking about forensic science in the clinical environment. "They hit Calgary in 1994, and myself and a girlfriend who is now the sexual assault coordinator for a hospital here in Calgary, bought into the whole idea of forensic nursing," McCracken recalls:

> The person who set it up this lecture tour was a forensic psychiatric nurse at a hospital here who taught forensic nursing as an option in the nursing degree program. I connected with her, and in 1996, when I was president of the Canadian emergency nurses group, we brought Virginia back to Alberta. During a two-day workshop at our group's annual conference, we got Virginia connected with the people at Mount Royal College, and through

discussions, they agreed to develop a forensic studies program. And now it's booming.

McCracken believes this is a step in the right direction, but grouses over the lack of master's programs in forensic nursing, as well as the lack of nurse representation in forensic services in clinical settings to begin with:

There are just a handful of sexual assault nurse examiner programs; they had one in Edmonton and one in Ontario, but that's still spotty because here in Alberta, our physicians won't let nurses do these kinds of exams. They believe that we're not qualified as experts in sexual exams and that too many cases would be lost. Go figure. So, forensic nursing is just getting started in Canada, and we're way behind the United States, but it's catching on, though.

McCracken says that in the past, her province has not had as many crimes related to weapons due to a smaller overall ownership of weapons; however, she says she does see a significant amount of interpersonal violence and an increase in violent crime. "I have been in nursing for 31 years, with 26 of those years in emergency nursing in a tertiary trauma center, and the knife-and-gun club is thriving. We need forensic nursing in the health care system to make sure health care providers document appropriately so that the victims will get their just rewards in the end. By the time things go to court, if it's not charted, it never existed."

McCracken says that documentation is challenged by Canada's privacy act:

What we struggle with here is a privacy act that is almost turning hospitals into havens for criminals. There is no federal or provincial law that states if someone comes in as a victim of a gunshot wound, or even if they were the person who did the shooting, that says I have to report it to the authorities. It's almost like the lawyer–patient confidentiality assurance; in health care they want it to be so people will come to the hospitals for their health's sake without being afraid that we will report everything to the authorities. If many people with injuries thought we'd report everything, they believe patients would feel that they were in trouble, and would not tell us important things related to their injuries or to their overall health and long-term survival. They want hospitals to be that safe haven where people can freely say what has happened to them. Now certainly we have laws that if someone has TB or some other communicable disease, we must report it, or if you suspect child abuse, you have to report it. Physicians have to report if someone has had a seizure, but otherwise, there is nothing else required.

McCracken adds, "It's different when there has been a shooting and paramedics are responding to the scene; they have called the police, so they are already involved. It's the cases that are being tossed at our door or patients walking in off the street that provide the biggest challenges." McCracken notes that a draft of a document for the sharing of verbal information between authorities and health care workers is underway:

Officers will call and say there was a breaking-and-entering and there's a lot of blood at the scene; they ask us to alert them if someone shows up with lacerations. I have to say, "Sorry officer, I can't tell you anything." Our lawyers tell us that if a patient with those kinds of injuries walks into the hospital, what we can do is phone the police and say, "Why don't you come over for coffee?" That's just stupid. They have seen that health care workers are in conflict after all, the nurses are in the trenches, while legal advisors aren't there after hours for us to talk to. So they have developed a form so that health care workers and the police can share verbal information. The police officer would bring in the form when he is investigating a case; he has to meet certain criteria whereby he has given the nurse enough information so that the nurse can determine if a person is indeed in our department. But it's all verbal.

McCracken says the present situation is not ideal, but she hopes that future progressive thinking will address the cracks in the system, including how law enforcement interacts with nurses and other health care providers. McCracken says:

It shouldn't be about protecting one's turf or watching one's back; I have struggled to convince everybody there must be a multidisciplinary approach. I help officers when they come into the ER; after all, they are out of their turf, and they don't know what to do. But some nurses and doctors don't want them in the ER, thinking they have no business there. I did a lecture a few years ago on what forensic nursing is all about in emergency care and told attendees to "Go where there is no path and leave a trail." My mother had shared that quote with me and I thought how appropriate that was. That's exactly what forensic nurses are doing. We must be cautious because we are still working for the health care system, and you don't want to infringe on that, and we're not working for the police—we are simply trying to link everybody together for the benefit of our patients.

4.3.2 Other Realms of Forensic Practice

Although the ER is still a common portal through which forensic patients present, the operating room (OR) is another department in a health care institution in which medical personnel should be familiar with proper protocol—especially when a forensic case might pass through the ER directly to the OR.

Evans and Stagner (2003) write, "Whether or not a perioperative nurse has formal training in forensic nursing, he or she must ensure proper collection and disposition of evidence. The perpetrator of a crime should not go free because forensic evidence was mishandled; however, protocols for collecting evidence and maintaining the chain of custody often are not clearly established." For example, they ask, what happens to a bullet once it is turned over to the pathology department? Is it guarded continuously or locked in a controlled area? Can a nurse confidently state that the chain of custody remained unbroken and evidence has not been tampered with if called on to testify in a court of law? Evans and Stagner explain, "Commonly, forensic evidence collected surgically is sent to the pathology department as a biological specimen. Bullets, in particular, are pieces of evidence that can be altered by pathology procedures, and many times, the proper chain of custody is not maintained during the process. These forensic specimens should be collected as such initially and transferred to the appropriate authority as soon as possible."

According to Evans and Stagner, perioperative nurses are responsible for identifying, collecting, and preserving evidence and for securing evidence in a designated area of the OR to establish and maintain the chain of custody. Evidence collection in the OR follows similar steps of evidence collection to those elsewhere in the hospital.

The first step is to identify potential forensic evidence, including clothing, and debris caught in the patient's hair or lodged in the skin. According to Evans and Stagner,:

> The most common types of physical evidence identified in the OR are bullets; pieces of glass, wood, or paint; and bloodstained clothing. A forensic nurse examiner may be required to collect additional evidence, by hair combing, swabbing, and fingernail scraping or by performing an examination for sexual assault. If a physician requests a comprehensive medical forensic examination, the forensic nurse examiner on call should be notified to conduct the examination. A full medical forensic examination includes taking a patient history and conducting a head-to-toe assessment for trauma, including a detailed genital examination, to evaluate forensic evidence.

In the OR, evidence should be handled with equal care, with perioperative nurses wearing gloves at all times. Evidence must be collected in a manner that does not contaminate the specimens so that a medico-legal investigation of suspicious injury or death is not compromised. Clothing should be removed from the patient without cutting through tears or holes that contain important trace evidence, and because articles of clothing could contain forensic evidence such as hairs, fibers, or the assailant's blood, they should not be shaken. When removed from the patient in the OR, clothing should be placed on a clean white sheet on the floor in a corner until time permits for proper packaging. Evans and Stagner say each piece of clothing should be placed in a separate paper bag with a clean white sheet of paper placed over stains to avoid cross-contamination.

To maintain the chain of custody, Evans and Stagner say the bags should be sealed with evidence tape and labeled with the patient's name, the date, the time, and the signature of the person responsible for collecting and securing the evidence. These bags should be placed in a secured area of the OR where there is no chance of contamination by fluids. Best practice includes placing the evidence and appropriate chain of custody forms in a locked drop box that contains a refrigerator and is located in an area that has limited public access and key access for designated personnel only. Evidence must be kept in the drop box until the forensic nurse examiner or law enforcement officer takes the evidence into his or her possession.

Clothing never should be placed in plastic bags because this can result in cross-contamination and degradation of the evidence. If clothes are wet or damp, they should be allowed to air dry. If moisture still is present and there is a chance of leakage, the sealed clothing bags should be placed inside a larger paper bag with the top of the second bag left open. A label should be attached to the outside of the bag to alert crime laboratory personnel that wet evidence is present. Law enforcement officers should be notified immediately to pick up wet evidence. Wet evidence never should be stored in the drop box. Dry clothing can be stored in the drop box until it is turned over to law enforcement officers or a forensic nurse examiner. This is important to ensure the chain of custody is maintained.

Perhaps one of the most important pieces of forensic evidence might still be lodged in the patient's body. Evans and Stagner write:

> Projectiles or penetrating devices should be safeguarded against mutilation or damage. Bullets should be removed with rubber-shod forceps to avoid causing artifact to the bullet, wrapped in cotton, and placed in a peel pack. Bullets should be handled as little as possible and never should come into contact with a metal surface. The peel pack should be sealed with evidence tape, labeled, and placed in the drop box or given to the forensic nurse examiner or law enforcement officer, if one is available. Large penetrating devices, such as knives, should be placed in a double peel pack with the outside pack left open and then placed in an open paper bag with appropriate labeling. The evidence then is secured in the locked drop box.

Perioperative nurses might encounter patients coming into the OR with bagged hands to protect trace evidence or gunpowder residue. Evans and Stagner advise, "Should it become necessary to remove the bags, the gunpowder residue must be collected. Prefabricated kits are available to assist in the collection of residues from shooting suspects or victims. Either cotton swabs or adhesive applicators are used to recover gunpowder particles that later can be analyzed to determine the type of ammunition from which the gunpowder came."

Evans and Stagner emphasize:

> Perioperative nurses have a professional responsibility to ensure that their educational needs regarding evidence collection and preservation are met, whether through formal education in forensic nursing programs or reviewing the policies and procedures at their facilities. If necessary, they should seek information to help establish protocols for collecting and handling evidence and maintaining the chain of custody at their facilities. Competent handling of forensic evidence may be the deciding factor in whether a violent offender is found guilty or not guilty. It is a nurse's responsibility... to ensure that patients' rights are upheld.

4.4 SUDDEN, SUSPICIOUS, OR UNEXPECTED DEATH IN THE HEALTH CARE ENVIRONMENT

The presence of severe illness and death in the health care environment is a given; however, it is precisely this setting that invites suspicious activity of perpetrators intent on causing harm to the vulnerable patient populations who entrust their very health and welfare to hospitals who are treating them. Health care professionals must be aware of the various opportunities for assaults, injuries, and deaths triggered by outside agents and assailants, as well as their clinical colleagues.

Forensic nurses are well appointed and positioned to recognize and respond to sudden, suspicious, or unexpected death in the clinical setting. Lynch (1997) writes, "Life-saving priority is obvious to nurses in catastrophic, near-death treatment. Yet the importance of properly identifying, securing, and preserving items that can later be considered as evidence may be forgotten when the patient dies." The hospital environment can very quickly become the scene of a crime, and forensic nurses must know how to operate within these parameters. Lynch adds, "If death occurs in the trauma room, for example, the trauma room suddenly becomes a scene of legal inquiry and is listed as the place of death on the death certificate regardless of where the initial incident occurred. The death scene must be protected until the body and the evidence have been removed at the completion of the medico-legal investigation."

It is then incumbent on the forensic nurse to provide accurate documentation, detailed description of wounds, collection and preservation of physical evidence, and the gathering of medical records and reports. Georgia Pasqualone explains that forensic principles remain the same, regardless of the setting in which the death occurs:

> The principles of forensic science are the same, and the principles of the nursing process are the same, no matter the environment. Today, nursing is not bound by the four walls of the hospital; nurses are out at crime scenes in the community, too. Death is usually associated with events outside of a hospital, but no matter where a crime scene occurs, the nursing process is the same. Nurses are still in charge of essential components such as assessment, diagnosis, intervention, evaluation... the way a nurse thinks, the way a nurse puts it all together, it's the same no matter what the environment of the situation is. Nurses must recognize evidence for what it is, they must collect it, preserve it, document it, photo-document it—nurses must be especially careful to adhere to forensic science and medico-legal principles or a case is going to fall apart.

Lynch (1995) states, "Sudden and violent deaths most frequently represent the initial interface between the hospital staff and police in the emergency department. Considering the number of sudden and unexpected deaths that occur in the clinical setting, nurses have a critical role to play in providing answers in questionable death situations." She explains that deaths occur frequently in the hospital environment, and might include patients who are dead on arrival, those who die during trauma treatment, patients who die on the operating table or in the delivery room, and patients who die in the ICU. "Deaths which occur as a result of trauma or unknown causes require investigation," Lynch writes. "Generally, any death that occurs during the first 24 hours after admission is reportable to the medical examiner/coroner system regardless of the history."

Lynch (1997) explains that if a patient death occurs in the trauma room, that room instantly becomes "a scene of legal inquiry and is listed as the place of death on the death certificate regardless of where the initial incident occurred." It is essential that health care personnel protect this death scene until the body and the physical and trace evidence have been removed at the completion of the medico-legal investigation. Lynch adds, "Patients who die as a result of abuse or an accident must be reported; there must be investigation; and evidence must be retained." She emphasizes the role of the forensic nurse in these situations: "Who is responsible for preserving the scene, interviewing the witnesses, collecting evidence, and managing forensic issues until the investigation is turned over to the proper authority? The presence of a nurse skilled in forensic technique and appropriate medico-legal procedures may be essential in each of these situations."

In Chapter 1, the nurse's index of suspicion is addressed. Lynch states that "maintaining an index of suspicion is essential when considering criminal activity as a cause of sudden and unexpected death." She adds that "preservation of evidence, careful documentation of the circumstances surrounding the death, and the decedent's social and medical history may form the basis for deducing the cause of death when it is not obvious." A forensic nurse plays a pivotal role in identifying pieces of evidence that can speak volumes about the details of the case and the specific events leading up to the suspicious or sudden-death event. Lynch explains:

> Often overlooked is the proper handling of items that might subsequently be considered evidence. Full documentation of the appearance of the victim on arrival at the hospital is also often neglected. Nurses are among the first to come in contact with the patient, interview family members, and handle the patient's property and laboratory specimens. They serve as a vital link between the victim, police, and medical examiner or coroner. Generally, the nurse elicits information that may clarify important points related to the cause or manner of death, and the nurse is often the first person to have access to evidence of a criminal nature in the medico-legal sense.

The first step in any sudden, suspicious, or unexpected death is to determine "whether the initiating cause is natural or unnatural," Sullivan (in press) writes:

> It is not uncommon for physicians to incorrectly identify the cause of death because of failure to differentiate between cause, manner, and mechanism of death. Increasingly, states are passing nurse pronouncement laws, and nurses are pronouncing death. With the extent of greater involvement in death pronouncement, a clear understanding of these terms must become an essential component of nursing education. Although the nurse may not be filling out the death certificate, the data recorded in the chart is often copied by less knowledgeable people; therefore, it is vital that the entry be appropriate.

In Chapter 6, the cause, manner, and mechanism of death are explored in greater detail. In the clinical setting, nurses must remember that the cause of death is the injury or disease (or combination of the two) that is "responsible for initiating the sequence of disturbances that produce the fatal termination," according to Sullivan. Manner of death is the circumstance in which the cause of death arose, and is categorized as natural, accident, homicide, suicide, or undetermined. According to Sullivan, mechanism of death is the "physiologic derangement or biochemical disturbance incompatible with life initiated by the cause of death."

Many deaths are anticipated or can be explained by age or disease processes, and these are traditionally considered to be natural deaths. They are not subjected to investigation and are normally handled by the attending physician, who will attest to the death due to natural causes. Conversely, sudden death is any death that was not expected, and might involve the patient's respiratory system, cardiovascular system, or central nervous system. According to Sullivan, the term *sudden death* usually is attributed to deaths "occurring in less than five minutes, frequently with instantaneous immobility." She explains, "In the absence of suspicion, unexpected deaths should fall within the jurisdiction of the medical examiner/coroner if no recent medical attention for a natural disease is documented. In contrast, unexpected deaths that are unnatural may include trauma, either intentional or unintentional; suicide, self-inflicted injury with the intention of taking one's own life; and homicide (injury inflicted by another with intention to kill); these require reporting to a legal agency."

4.5 HEALTH CARE SERIAL KILLERS

Nurses serving in a forensic capacity often are the first responders to victims sustaining suspicious injuries; however, what if the nurse is the perpetrator of these injuries or even death? Health care providers who kill their patients tread on and exploit the inherent trust built into the health care profession; what better place to experiment with murder than among the ill, the injured, and the dying in a hospital environment? Interventions designed to kill can be more easily camouflaged by the interventions intended to heal; it is the subtleties that can reveal the health care professional's intentions, and no one is better trained than the forensic nurse to note these minute details and collect evidence that documents them.

Health care serial killers are nothing new, but lately they have been making headlines far more frequently. *The Philadelphia Inquirer* reports that in the last three decades, there have been at least three dozen such cases in civilized societies, with many more suspected but as yet unproved cases. "This is a more common problem than is known, and it's getting worse as the population ages," observes forensic pathologist Michael Baden, MD, chief medical examiner for the New York State Police.

According to Court TV's *Crime Library,* "Some enter the profession as 'angels of death,' while others transform into killers on the job." Since the mid-1970s, there have been 36 cases of serial murder among nurses and other health care workers in the United States. A survey shows that the incidences appear to be increasing, with 14 during the 1990s and already six since 2000. Many experts speculate that health care has contributed more serial killers than all other professions combined and that the field attracts a disproportionately high number of people with a pathological interest in life and death. They prey on vulnerable populations such as the very young, the very old, the disabled, the very ill, and anyone else who might not be able to fight back and report suspicious activity on the part of a health care provider.

Former New Jersey nurse Charles Cullen, who said he killed as many as 40 of his patients, was convicted of 16 murders; he pleaded guilty on May 19, 2004 to three counts of first-degree murder, according to Warren County Prosecutor Thomas Ferguson. The charges involved the 1983 deaths of Helen Dean, 91; Lucy Mugavero, 90; and Mary Natoli, 85. All three were patients at Warren Hospital in Phillipsburg, New Jersey, where Cullen worked. Cullen had worked as a nurse for almost 20 years at hospitals in Pennsylvania and New Jersey. He faces several consecutive life terms in prison.

Cullen, who earned his RN degree in 1987, was initially charged with murder in the death of a patient at Somerset Medical Center in New Jersey who was found to have lethal levels of the drug digoxin in his system. An original attempted-murder charge stemmed from a female patient who recovered from an overdose of the same drug. According to investigators and media reports, Cullen was fired after an investigation of six patients with abnormal lab results showed him as the only common denominator.

According to Court TV's *Crime Library,* a toxicologist at the New Jersey Poison Information and Education System had informed the medical center in July 2003 that he had identified a cluster of at least four poisoning cases. The facility's administrators ignored the warning, according to reports in the *Newark Star Ledger.* Just one year earlier, nurses at St. Luke's Hospital in Bethlehem, Pennsylvania, had cautioned the state nursing board, law enforcement officials, and the county coroner that Cullen could be a murderer, after identifying a noticeable increase in the number of code blue incidents, according to reports in the *The Morning Call.* Additionally, nurses at two other facilities demanded that Cullen be dismissed and investigated, but administrators declined.

Even with outright warnings of potentially criminal behavior on his part, Cullen's employers continued to hire and retain him; many point to the severe nursing shortage as sufficient reason to hire a nurse—any nurse—on the spot. According to *USA Today,* Somerset Medical Center representatives stated they did not know that Cullen was under investigation elsewhere, and that when his credentials were checked, there was no reason not to hire him. However, there are reports that dates of employment were the only pieces of information that were verified.

Observers might be astounded by the fact that health care serial killers go years without being detected, or when they are, can continue to work in the health care system without their criminal behavior being recognized and stopped, and eventually investigated and prosecuted. Court TV's *Crime Library* states, "While arguments have flown back and forth over the Cullen case in terms of ultimate responsibility, it's clear that patients must depend on hospitals and clinics to spot the red flags and do something about them. Too often, these killers have been allowed to drift from one hospital to another, fired under a cloud of suspicion but rarely brought to justice until after incriminating evidence has reached shocking levels."

Health care institutions state that they could be sued if they act on their suspicions in a way that prevents an individual from being hired. According to reports by *The Morning Call,* hospitals can also be sued for not doing so, and their insurance carriers will not cover them. Intentional acts of murder are not considered part of professional practice, insurers claim. Court TV states, "If families move ahead on their threats to sue those facilities that did not voice suspicions when asked or did not warn other potential employers of Cullen, this case might become a real wake-up call."

One of the more chilling cases was that of Kristen Gilbert, a 30-year-old nurse indicted in 1998 for murdering four of her patients and attempting to kill three others by injecting them with epinephrine. Gilbert worked at a Veterans Administration (VA) medical center in Northampton, Massachusetts, and although her patients often were elderly, the majority was not in acute distress or immediate danger of death, and investigators maintained they were not mercy killings. Prosecutors charged that Gilbert enjoyed injecting epinephrine into her patients and then calling codes so she could meet up with a security guard with whom she was having an affair. Defense attorneys argued that the government could not prove foul play; considerable amounts of circumstantial evidence as well as Gilbert's inculpatory statements were met with a lack of eyewitness testimony. Judge Michael Ponsor said, "The trial presented . . . a classic battle of experts" in a *Boston Globe* article, adding that the extensive prosecution and defense teams of experts cost more than $1.6 million of taxpayers' money.

More than 250 motions and hundreds of hours of hearings later, the jury began its deliberations. On March 14, 2001, after 12 days of deliberation, the jury delivered its verdict of guilty on three counts of first-degree murder as well as several lesser charges. The complexity of the Gilbert case might explain why the jury, in the penalty phase of this capital case, pronounced themselves deadlocked, and imposed the default sentence of mandatory life imprisonment without possibility of release. Three jurors said that although the evidence was strong enough to prove guilt beyond a reasonable doubt, it was too weak to justify the death penalty. There is no state death penalty in Massachusetts, but Gilbert was eligible for it under federal law because her crimes took place on federal property at the VA hospital.

On March 27, 2001, Ponsor sentenced Gilbert to four consecutive life terms without the possibility of parole for killing four patients, and also sentenced her to two 20-year terms for trying to kill two other patients. Assistant U.S. Attorney William Welch had called Gilbert "a shell of a human being" who deserved to die for the calculating way she murdered her victims. On July 25, 2003, Gilbert dropped her federal appeal. If she had won a new trial on appeal, a recent U.S. Supreme Court ruling would have allowed prosecutors to seek the death penalty.

The Gilbert killings are some of at least 35 other serial murders committed by health care personnel (mainly nurses, but also including a respiratory therapist and several physicians) since the mid-1970s, says Beatrice Crofts

Yorker, RD, JD, FAAN, an expert in psychiatric mental health nursing and nursing jurisprudence. Four occurred in the 1970s, 12 in the 1980s, 14 in the 1990s, and at least five in the 2000s, including the more recent cases of Richard Williams in Missouri in 1992, Orville Lynn Majors in Indiana in 1995, and Vicki Dawn Jackson in Texas in 2000. According to Yorker's analysis, at least 26 murders occurred in hospitals, nine of which took place in the ICU. The nurses used injection of noncontrolled medication such as insulin, digoxin, lidocaine, epinephrine, and other respiratory paralysis agents. Males are disproportionately represented, Yorker says, accounting for 38 percent of the perpetrators.

"Serial killers in health care appear to come in basically one of five guises: those who kill out of mercy, those who want to feel like God, those who kill for an erotic thrill, those who are mentally ill, and those who just feel overburdened," says Katherine Ramsland, PhD, who teaches forensic psychology at DeSales University in Pennsylvania. "All of these types have been around because all of these motives arise out of human nature."

Netherlands researcher Paula Lampe reports that since 1970 in her country, there have been four male and five female health care killers who are nurses, whereas globally, that number amounts to 81 cases. She says of these, 31 are male. Male nurses are disproportionately represented among caretakers who harm patients. Although there are many more cases, quantitatively, of women who indulge in this behavior, Yorker, director of the School of Nursing at San Francisco State University, reports that the approximately 146,000 male RNs represent 5 percent to 7 percent of all nurses, yet are responsible for more than one third of individuals who have killed patients in the United States since 1975.

When Donald Harvey worked at Marymount Hospital in London, Kentucky, in 1970, he would smother his patients with a pillow to ease them out of their suffering. Following an arrest for burglary, a stint in the Air Force, and a commitment to a mental health facility, Harvey got work as a nursing assistant at several health care facilities in the Lexington, Kentucky area, moving on to the Cincinnati VA Medical center in Ohio, where for nearly a decade he worked in various capacities as a nursing assistant, housekeeper, and autopsy assistant. In 1985 he was forced to resign on the basis of possession of a firearm at the facility. He immediately began working as a nursing assistant at Drake Memorial Hospital, where it was reported he killed more than 20 patients by injecting them with lethal substances such as arsenic, cyanide, and petroleum-based cleansers before his arrest in April 1987. According to the Court TV *Crime Library,* the death of patient John Powell "finally brought Harvey down." During Powell's autopsy, the forensic pathologist detected significantly elevated levels of cyanide, and the death was ruled a homicide. Harvey was arrested, but he pleaded not guilty by reason of insanity; it was then that he confessed to killing 33 people, then 52, then more than 80. He said that most of the murders were mercy killings. He was declared sane and competent for trial by a psychiatrist who examined him. In a Cincinnati courtroom on August 18, 1987, Harvey pled guilty to 24 counts of murder and four counts of attempted murder. Then he added another murder plea, which earned him four consecutive life sentences. In Kentucky, Harvey admitted to 12 more murders but entered a guilty plea on only nine of them; in that state, he received eight life terms, plus 20 years. In Cincinnati again, he confessed to three more killings and three more attempts at murder, amounting to a total of 37 official murder victims. Harvey is said to hold the U.S. record for the most confirmed number of victims of any health care serial killer.

"Since 1974, at least 12 nurses have been charged with murder following mysterious epidemics of adverse patient incidents," Yorker (1994) wrote in the *Journal of Nursing Law.* "In some cases, the CDC confirmed an epidemic of cardiopulmonary arrests and attributed them to the presence of a particular nurse ... Until recently, social scientists dismissed the idea that female serial killers existed. Since the 1970s, however, research shows that female serial killers do exist and are convicted." She points to research by Holmes, who discusses five types of female serial killers: women who kill in response to voices or visions, women who kill for money, hedonistic killers who obtain pleasure from killing, disciples who kill under the influence of charismatic leaders, and power seekers who deliberately put their patients at risk so they can rush in and save them to appear heroic.

Ramsland says that even though they are easier to spot these days, they are driven by centuries-old motivations. "They have had access to poisons since the earliest of times. It's more difficult for them now, because victim counts stand out, professionals are more alert to killers among them, there are better surveillance methods, and we have methods of accountability that did not exist decades ago. We know more about them now because we have better documentation, but they have been around for centuries."

"Males tend to be more involved in playing God, feeling power over human life, and finding an erotic thrill in that, although we've certainly had cases of nurses who found killing so exciting that they immediately had to have sex," Ramsland explains. "More health care workers claim they killed patients out of a sense of mercy, yet further analysis tends to dispel this motivation. Often they're seeking attention, they're acting from some delusion, or they're trying to prove something. I think it's a myth that most health care workers who kill do so because they want to do a kindness."

Richard Angelo claimed that he was motivated to save people rather than kill them, and experts believed that as a charge nurse at Good Samaritan Hospital on Long Island in New York, Angelo could capitalize on situations that made him look like a hero—similar to the Gilbert case. Injecting a foreign substance into the IV tube of a patient, John Fisher, Angelo triggered an adverse reaction in the patient, who died before Angelo could save him. This failure to rescue did not deter Angelo, however. According to Court TV, in a taped confession Angelo commented, "I wanted to create a situation where I would cause the patient to have some respiratory distress or some problem, and through my intervention or suggested intervention or whatever, come out looking like I knew what I was doing. I had no confidence in myself. I felt very inadequate."

A patient named Gerolamo Kucich was Angelo's downfall. Kucich saw a bearded man inject something into his IV, and was able to press his call button; the patient survived, and described the perpetrator to nurses who made the connection to Angelo. Kucich's urine test was positive for Pavulon and Anectine, paralysis-inducing drugs that had not been prescribed for him. When Angelo's apartment was searched, investigators located and seized vials of the drugs, and arrested Angelo. Following a confession of killing at least 10 patients, the bodies were exhumed; tests revealed traces of the drugs in those patients' systems as well. Charged with multiple counts of second-degree murder, at his 1989 trial Angelo pleaded to temporary insanity at the time of each killing. Despite being diagnosed by psychologists as having dissociative identity disorder, Angelo was convicted of two counts of second-degree murder, one count of second-degree manslaughter, one count of criminally negligent homicide, and six counts of assault; he was sentenced to 61 years to life.

Another high-profile case was that of licensed practical nurse Orville Lynn Majors. Shortly after he came to work at the 56-bed Vermillion County Hospital in Clinton, Indiana, in 1993, there was an increase in number of deaths occurring in the ICU. That year, there were 26 deaths in the ICU; in 1994, there were 101 deaths, with 67 of them occurring in the last half of the year and 63 of them during Majors's work shifts. In Majors's 22 months of employment, 147 patients died, and most of them were under Majors's care at the time. A perceptive nursing supervisor became suspicious, and when Majors's license was suspended in 1995, the hospital's death rate returned to its normal baseline. It was later determined by an independent statistical report on all of the deaths that patients were 43 percent more likely to die at the hospital if Majors was working a shift.

According to Court TV, an investigation of 160 deaths between May 1993 and February 1995 revealed that Majors sometimes provided unauthorized "treatment" to his patients. Fifteen bodies were exhumed to test the patients' tissue, and investigators found that at least six deaths were consistent with the administration of epinephrine and potassium chloride. A search of Majors's house revealed syringes, needles, and vials of the two drugs, as well as vials of potassium chloride in Majors's vehicle.

Majors was suspected of having caused as many as 130 deaths, and in December 1997, he was arrested and charged with six counts of murder. On October 17, 1999, Majors was convicted of six counts of murder, for which he received a sentence of life in prison.

There are several other notable cases of health care serial killers in the vaults of Court TV's *Crime Library*. In the United Kingdom, nurse Kevin Cobb was convicted in May 2000 of one count of manslaughter, two counts of rape, and four counts of drugging women with intent to rape. He received seven life sentences. Atlanta nurse Joseph Dewy Akin was suspected of being responsible for more than 100 deaths in a span of 10 years when working for more than 20 health care institutions; he was sentenced to 15 years in prison after pleading guilty to manslaughter. Swiss health care provider Roger Andermatt was arrested for the murder of 24 patients, and also charged with the attempted murder of three patients. Another three deaths were classified as assisted suicide. He confessed to all of the murders, which occurred between September 1995 and June 2001 in nursing homes in and around Lucerne, Switzerland. The victims, some as young as 66 and others as old as 95, either had Alzheimer's disease or were in need of high levels of care. Nine patients were killed with lethal doses of medication, eight patients were smothered with a plastic bag or a cloth, and 10 patients were killed using a combination of drugs and smothering. Trial was pending at the time of writing. In 2001, Japanese nurse Daisuke Mori was arrested and charged with the murder of an 89-year-old patient. Mori was also charged with four counts of attempted murder of a 1-year-old girl, an 11-year-old girl, a 4-year-old boy, and a 45-year-old man, also patients at the Hokuryo Clinic in Izumi Ward, Sendai. Prosecutors claimed that Mori administered a muscle relaxant to his victims through an intravenous drip, implying that he replaced a bag that was prepared by other nurses with one that contained the lethal doses. The alleged attacks occurred between February and November 2000, but there were no witnesses to the alleged acts. Mori originally confessed to the crimes, but then recanted and pleaded not guilty to the charges. At the time of writing, the case was pending.

In the Los Angeles County suburb of Glendale, California, hospital therapist Efren Saldivar was implicated in the 1996 respiratory failure of a 75-year-old woman who was found dead in her bed, even as she had been expected to recover and return to her home. In March 1998, Salvidar confessed to murdering 50 patients for "humanitarian reasons." Investigators exhumed 20 bodies and tissue samples were tested for the presence of Pavulon. Of six patients exhumed, five had not received Pavulon as part of their legitimate medical treatment prior to their deaths. Salvidar was arrested in 2001, and admitted to killing at least 60 patients; he pleaded guilty to six murders and is serving a life sentence in prison.

According to various reports by the Associated Press, Columbia, Missouri nurse Richard Williams was indicted in 2002 for killing 10 patients a decade earlier. A former VA hospital employee, Williams was charged with administering succinlycholine, a derivative of curare, to nine men and one woman in his care. Their ages ranged from 58 to 85. Helping to secure these charges was new technology able to detect this pharmaceutical in human tissue in a way that was previously impossible, as well as the statements of more than 100 witnesses. The charges were later dismissed when issues with the test developed, and Williams maintained his innocence throughout, despite being accused of as many as 24 deaths.

Although profiling has played a significant role in catching killers, Ramsland says:

> There's no way to provide a general psychological type, because each killer that I've studied is quite unique in his or her own framework. One man killed to ease his workload, another to experiment. Two women killed to prove their love to each other. Another liked watching her boyfriend come running in an emergency. A male nurse talked about supernatural issues. Another was suffering from Munchausen by Proxy Syndrome. As with most other types of crime, each case is unique to the person.

Ramsland says the most susceptible patients are children, especially babies, and the elderly, because their deaths can be easily explained by natural causes. Even using epidemiological data to connect an unusually high number of these deaths from seemingly "natural causes" has not been foolproof in building and trying a case. In one case in Maryland where an epidemiologist testified that patients of a particular nurse were 47.5 times more likely to have a cardiac arrest (100 times more likely on the night shift), the judge ruled the evidence in the case was only circumstantial and could not be used as evidence of intentional acts, Yorker says, because the state-of-mind element of proof was missing. Although not effective in a criminal case, this kind of statistical evidence can be very persuasive evidence in a wrongful death lawsuit, Yorker says, due to differences in burden of proof between criminal and civil suits. In the Maryland case, although the nurse was acquitted of murder, she faced eight civil suits that settled for $8.5 million.

Regardless of the outcome, the real challenge might be in warranting the arrest and bringing the case to trial in the first place. For six months, Gilbert went on a killing spree before several of her nursing colleagues could no longer ignore the number of sudden deaths occurring on her watch.

Says Ramsland:

> It is common that people get away with murder in a hospital or community health setting for quite a while, partly because of denial. Many people cannot believe that someone in a helping profession would actually kill his or her patients. Many people also cannot believe that women would commit serial murder (though we have many, many cases). Sometimes people are protected by a hospital trying to avoid bad publicity, so they're sent away but not stopped, as in the case of Dr. Michael Swango. I believe that Dr. Harold Shipman, who may be the worst serial killer among them with a victim count over 200, often made house calls and had such a kindly air that no one suspected. For the most part, it does seem that the medical community has a code of protection and people are loathe to turn someone in, especially if circumstances are ambiguous. We've seen cases where whistleblowers get fired or bullied, while the killer continues to work. It's often a delicate situation, and good psychopaths know how to manipulate it to their advantage.

Investigators have pinpointed the red flags that signal suspicious activity. Bruce Sackman, special agent in charge of the Northeast field office for the Office of the Inspector General, was one of the investigators on the team that played a key role in bringing Gilbert to justice. He offers the following list:

- Statistically, a patient's risk of harm is significantly greater when treated by the subject.
- The subject is uncommonly accurate in predicting patients' demise.
- Patient deaths were unexpected by staff or family, and the family was not at the patient's bedside.
- Death certificate cites the patient's last illness as the cause of death, or a catch-all is noted, such as cardiac arrest.
- Initial review usually finds insufficient evidence to pursue the case, with buy-in from management.
- The subject often continues patient care during investigation, and is removed only after allegations become public knowledge.
- Fellow employees often report allegations to investigators, not management.
- There are no eyewitnesses to the crime.
- Witnesses say they saw the subject with the patient shortly before the patient died.
- The weapon of choice is usually a sudden death chemical readily available on the ward and often considered nondetectable or not checked at autopsy.
- Syringes, IV lines, and feeding tubes are the most likely portals of entry if poison is used.
- If a code is called, EKG strips should be in the chart; their absence should raise suspicions.

- Subjects are often charming and friendly, yet have difficulty with personal relationships.
- The subject receives good written reviews from supervisors, although prior employment records show questionable incidents.
- The subject is given nicknames by the staff while still employed.
- Drugs, poisons, and related books are found in the subject's home.
- Killing is nonconfrontational.
- The subject insists patients died of natural causes.
- The subject never shows remorse for his or her victims.
- Other patients complain about the subject but their comments often are ignored.
- The subject craves notoriety.
- Evidence exists that the subject killed or attempted to kill off duty as well as on duty.
- A subject likes to arrive early or stay late on a shift.
- An individual enjoys talking about death with colleagues or shows odd behaviors related to the death, such as excitement, ownership, or undue curiosity.
- An individual keeps to himself or herself, preferring shifts where fewer colleagues are present.
- The subject makes colleagues anxious or suspicious, or attempts to prevent others from checking on patients.
- The subject lingers during the immediate death investigation.

Experts emphasize that no one specific red flag is sufficient to point to a potential health care killer, but a cluster of them occurring together should be taken seriously by health care providers and hospital administrators. Experts like Sackman and Ramsland agree that forensic nurses are in an excellent position to detect suspicious activity in their health care facilities. "If they get trained in criminal behavior, forensic nurses would have a better eye for this behavior, but not all programs offer that," Ramsland says:

> A high victim count on someone's shift is generally the first red flag. A regular incidence of patients going downhill after a particular doctor or nurse has been in their room. A health care worker who appears to have antisocial tendencies, who likes to talk about violence, who shows a high degree of excitement in emergencies, who is secretive, and whose emotional response to incidents seems shallow or superficial is someone to watch. If medicines that may cause coma or death are missing, that's a red flag. A person who pays a lot of attention to the fatalities for entertainment value rather than to learn could be showing signs of a problem. But again, there's no general psychological type. No matter what might be offered in terms of a set of red flags, psychology is a field full of novelties. There's no way to predict what new behavior might arise that we haven't seen before. But we can study the details of past cases and learn from them in order to see potential red flags sooner.

Evidence goes to the heart of any criminal investigation, and Ramsland says forensic nurses should do everything they can to identify, collect, and preserve it. "Everything is potential evidence," Ramsland emphasizes:

> One never knows what small item will make all the difference in a guilty or not guilty verdict. Even nonphysical items, such as a man discussing his fantasy of seeing children die, can have evidentiary value (and has). Forensic nurses are trained to understand the importance of handling evidence, chain of custody, ensuring that specimens are protected from degrading, etcetera. They may be trained in character disorders common to criminal behavior in ways that other nurses are not, and they can spot some of the signals more quickly. They can also use their education in criminality to put pressure on medical boards and administrators to be alert to the cases. Above all, they can keep educating themselves in these cases, because the more one knows about what has happened in the past, the more one is able to recognize an ongoing linked series of incidents and to believe that a serial killer might indeed be in their midst. Education is the best way to erode denial and naivete, perhaps the serial killer's most lethal allies in the medical system.

With several cases pending and the news of serial killers in the newspapers, one would think the medical boards and institutions are responding to this seeming epidemic of health care serial killers, but Ramsland says health care is guarded about the situation:

> My impression is that the medical community in general views serial killing as an anomaly and deals with each case after the fact. I think there's a general atmosphere of institutional self-protection and no one wants to have to make specific policies, other than to ensure better supervision. To do so would be to publicly admit that medical facilities are vulnerable to delusional workers or serial killers. That's not good for business.

M. William Phelps, author of the book *Perfect Poison,* which documents the Kristen Gilbert case, says:

> Forensics is a tool to uncover what has happened—or at least a good perception of the truth as it pertains to science. [Forensic nurses] understand that it is nothing like the TV show *CSI.* It is more meticulous, more research-oriented, and certainly more time-consuming and unromantic than the show would suggest. For example, if, after a code, you have three spent ampoules of 1:1000 strength

epinephrine in a waste basket, another used 1:10,000 bristo-jet package of epinephrine sitting empty on a crash cart, along with EKG readings with spikes that look like a silhouette of the Rocky Mountains, a forensic nurse might be able to put it all together in real time and, at the least, say, "Wait a minute, something seems suspicious here." And, perhaps the most important observation: "Let's look into it further." Granted, forensic nurses generally deal in sexual assault cases. Yet any type of nurse in any health care situation who is observing patient care by other nurses has an obligation to report suspicious activity of any kind, regardless of what it looks like, their personal feelings, or the thought that it might be "nothing." If there is any question or any doubt, it must be looked into further. I'm tired of that age-old mentality of one professional turning a blind eye to the other simply because they are colleagues. Health care professionals are in the business of saving lives, not making friends and scoring social points.

Chicago forensic nurse Catherine A. O'Brien, RN, MS, CNA, CLNC, D-ABMDI, a registered medico-legal death investigator, says that "several unconventional encounters with death" in her early years as a staff nurse in the hospital setting might have influenced her career choice. She says that she was not in the forensic mindset at the time of these medico-legal moments, but they got her thinking about sudden, unexpected death in the health care environment and how better to respond to the next unanticipated event.

She recalls the attempted murder of a known gangster under her care by someone dressed like a respiratory therapist:

As I turned the corner and approached the room with the sounding call light, I observed a male figure, dressed in white pants and lab coat, come out of the room and walk down the hall in the opposite direction. Although one of my patients in that room was on oxygen therapy, I recall thinking it odd and too early in the night for respiratory therapy to be making routine rounds. My patient told me he heard muffled, moaning sounds that awoke him. Simultaneously, coughing sounds could be heard from the other side of the curtain. When able to speak, the roommate told me of a suffocation attempt on his life that was interrupted by the ringing call light.

O'Brien says she was devastated at the thought that any patient under her care was victimized:

I regretted not having had the foresight to anticipate this possibility due to the patient's personal history, but after all, hospitals were supposed to be safe environments. I regretted not following my gut instinct about the untimely presence of someone unfamiliar in the environment. Had I been more observant of this male figure, I might have been able to provide law enforcement a more detailed physical description. Perhaps had I verbalized an inquisitive remark to this individual, it may have provided an opportunity to get a glimpse of his face, hear a verbal response, or generate a reaction to share with the police in order to make a valuable contribution to the subsequent investigation.

O'Brien characterizes her experiences as a pediatric intensive care nurse as "tragic." She reflects:

Traumatic deaths due to gunshot injuries, blunt-trauma injuries, patterned injuries, burns, neglect and battering, accidents were common denominators in the demise of many of my vulnerable patients. It was during this decade of my career that collaboration on numerous cases with law enforcement, child protective services, organ procurement teams, hospital general counsel, and the legal process came to the forefront. The intersection between medicine and law in each instance broadened my perspectives, taught numerous lessons, and strengthened my advocacy for victim's legal, civil, and human rights. The value of meticulous initial and ongoing assessments, detailed and factual documentation as well as testimony presentation cannot be understated.

This was particularly evident in one case that involved a toddler in isolation who was under the care of a registered nurse each shift. Periodically, there was a need to leave the room to obtain refrigerated medications, which sometime occurred while the parents were present. On several occasions, my colleagues and I observed that after the parents' departure, the child's behavior often would become agitated with increased vital signs and other unusual findings for no apparent reason. We verbalized our suspicions to the attending physician. A chemical assault was confirmed by toxicology reports finding the presence of phencyclidine (PCP) that was injected into the intravenous line by the child's father.

"Death, under any circumstance in the pediatric ICU, was always a somber experience," O'Brien notes:

There were those heart-wrenching encounters with devastated parents regarding consent for autopsy, who questioned exactly what the procedure would entail. I found myself inept in formulating a response that was truthful and informative, yet compassionate and sensitive since I had never witnessed the procedure. A day in pathology observing autopsies guided me in subsequent parental encounters. It was also during this period, as a critical care nurse, I experienced cognitive dissonance relative to my scope of practice and death. Critical care nursing is dedicated to the prevention of and intervention in life-threatening situations. Caring for a patient with a diagnosis of brain death was in direct conflict with this mission. Curious about the feelings of other colleagues, this became my graduate thesis subject matter. Death was a frequent by-product of the active level-one trauma center and knowing the forensic value of a dying declaration and demonstrating competence in standards of evidence collection and preservation was unmistakable in certain settings.

4.5.1 Forensic Nurses' Role in Identifying Health Care Serial Killers

Special agent Bruce Sackman (2002), one of the key investigators in the Kristen Gilbert case, points to the opening words of then-assistant U.S. Attorney William Welch in his opening remarks at Gilbert's trial in November 2001:

> It was a cold chilly day. On Ward C of the U.S. Department of Veterans Affairs Medical Center there was a different kind of chill that penetrated the floor. It was a deep eerie feeling; patients were dying unexpectedly from sudden cardiac arrest. Three nurses came together and voiced their suspicions. It was every hospital's nightmare. There was a killer among them, one who coldly and callously killed four men and attempted to kill three others by injecting them with the heart stimulant epinephrine.

Sackman (2002) writes, "Almost identical words could have been utilized in other recent health care murder cases." He points to a steady stream of newspaper headlines recounting the actions of these killers. Sackman adds, "Few criminal investigators have experience working suspicious death cases at medical centers because very few of them are ever reported to the police." He adds, "Highly trained medical professionals who have taken an oath to help heal the sick have a difficult time accepting the premise that a fellow medical professional would intentionally kill a patient." Sackman says that patients rarely question the drugs administered by health care professionals, and family members are loathe to even consider that the person who is entrusted to heal their relative is endangering their loved one's life. Sackman writes, "So high is the confidence level in hospital staff that family members refuse to believe the cordial nurse or doctor who frequently visited their mom or dad at the hospital may have intentionally caused their death."

Several factors contribute to a lack of timely response to a potential health care serial killer. Sackman says that fear of damage to a hospital's reputation has a chilling effect on administrators' willingness to inquire into allegations about their employees possibly committing murder. He adds that, "Rather than conduct a forensic inquiry, hospital administrators rely on peer reviews to determine that the cause of death was probably related to some underlying medical problem in the patient's history. Autopsies conducted by the hospital are not forensic autopsies, but are conducted to confirm the patient could have died from an underlying medical problem." Another factor is the lack of medical expertise on the part of many members of law enforcement, hampering a determination of the cause of death and further investigation. Sackman writes, "If a team of physicians has already determined through peer review that the patient's death could have resulted from existing medical conditions, why pursue the matter further?"

Sackman says that a health care institution is a perfect place for a homicide due to the level of activity of personnel, the amount of chaos present in places such as the ED, the degree of illness in places such as the ICU, and the overall ability for health care serial killers to blend in, have access to potent narcotics, and be able to cover their tracks when they are finished administering their own, potentially lethal version of clinical intervention. "Given these facts, if I were inclined to commit a series of murders, I would be well advised to choose a health care facility," Sackman writes. "And what better profession to choose than that of a health care professional, one that virtually gives me the legal power of life and death over a person?" He adds, "Working alone on a night shift, I am virtually guaranteed that there will be no witnesses to my crime. My choice of weapons is formidable. There are a number of 'sudden-death' chemicals readily available on the ward, including many that are considered undetectable or generally not tested for at autopsy." Sackman notes that during the course of an investigation, it was determined 40 sudden-death injectibles existed on just one ward.

One of the solutions to identifying suspect individuals, according to Sackman, is the presence of a forensic nurse in the health care institution. He explains that these nurses' medical skills, coupled with their increasing medico-legal skills, are formidable allies in the effort to collect critical evidence and document suspicious or questionable activity as part of their routine nursing observation and assessment. The scene of a suspicious death in a health care environment is most always the patient room, and the portal of entry of a lethal substance is usually an IV line or a feeding tube. Sackman writes, "In the case of sudden unexpected death, what happens to these crucial pieces of evidence? Are they discarded as a matter of routine? The first assignment of a forensic nurse should be to ensure all physical evidence is retained for possible future forensic examination. The forensic nurse should ensure all pertinent medical records are secured in a safe location."

Sackman explains further that in cases of sudden, suspicious deaths, extended periods of time might pass before investigations are conducted or law enforcement authorities are contacted. He states, "If suspicion only arises as a result of a pattern of untimely deaths, then it can be years before law enforcement is contacted. A review of the case early on by a forensic nurse will help ensure that a timely and correct decision regarding outside referral will be made." Sackman says that a forensic nurse's familiarity with the medical record is key to any investigation. "It is important the forensic nurse begins a review of the patient's treatment records. This nurse must have access to all medical records, including those of the pharmacy service, any correspondence between the patient, patient's family and the medical center and its personnel." He says that the forensic nurse, in acting as a liaison between the health care institution and law enforcement, might be asked to review the medical records of other patients that were treated in the same ward or by the same health care professional under question.

A nurse's familiarity with the medical record can assist criminal investigators who have little or no experience in reading a chart, and are unaware of its contents and significance, especially if a critical component of the medical record is missing or incomplete. Sackman writes, "The investigator faces a considerable learning curve when first confronted with a medical suspicious death... Cops and prosecutors need a competent guide and interpreter to assist them in their journey through this maze of science and protocol. There is simply no one better suited for this task than the forensic nurse." Sackman explains that forensic nurses are able to guide investigators through the maze of hospital regulations, numerous quality-of-care issues, and daunting medical procedures and medical terminology:

> The forensic nurse also has the important skill of evaluating the quality of care given a patient from a nursing perspective. This service cannot be understated. Nurses often reflect upon patient care from a different perspective than physicians or technicians, noting improprieties and spotting errors that other medical professionals miss. Forensic nurses are knowledgeable about drug interactions and the evaluation of prescriptions. All these skills are essential to the investigative team.

Sackman emphasizes that in many cases, the activities of health care serial killers were discovered by fellow nurses who "suspected wrongdoing on the part of a co-worker and alerted management," Sackman writes, although, "unfortunately, management's initial medical review, absent training in forensics, usually found insufficient evidence to pursue the case." Sackman is adamant about the many important contributions forensic nurses make to the medico-legal process. He observes, "Forensic nursing is still a relatively new and underutilized discipline. Health care facilities should waste no time in establishing this practice. It is simply what is most needed today to forge the link between medicine and investigation."

Sullivan (in press) explains that there are several causes of what she describes as "caregiver malfeasance." She writes, "The reality is that most medical facilities across the country are in a crisis mode when it comes to who provides hands-on patient care and how well it is accomplished." Sullivan points to hospital wards that are overflowing with critically ill patients:

> A high patient census with equally high acuity levels combined with fewer licensed registered nurses to share the workload makes for a dangerous situation... Additionally, some new applicants are not always completely honest with background histories, and screening efforts do not always catch the discrepancies. Further, there is an overall failure to discipline or terminate marginal employees, and because of short staffing it is often felt that a "warm body" is better than nobody showing up for work.

Sullivan says these factors set the stage for the entrance of an individual who does not have the best interests of patients at heart. "History has certainly shown that individuals such as former doctor Michael Swango, former nurse Gilbert, and many other former licensed health care professionals who have been successfully prosecuted for criminal acts against patients have taken advantage of these dynamics. These are additional reasons to increase the number of health care providers who are indoctrinated in forensic science in hospitals and clinics."

Pasqualone cautions that there is no blanket approach to identifying perpetrators of killing sprees or a lone incident, in the clinical setting. "All of these kinds of scenarios must be examined on a case-by-case basis," she says:

> In the case of serial murders, mercy killings, health care workers who kill, many of them aren't recognized for what they are when they are happening. Unfortunately, you sometimes recognize suspicious events only after a number of them occur because you see a pattern emerge. Then you start observing your suspect more closely. The trick is to try to get the authorities involved without letting your suspect know that you are suspicious; then, depending on how this person is killing his or her patients, you must collect whatever you think the weapon might be—the syringe or the drugs, or whatever it may be. In the Kristen Gilbert case, nurses actually retrieved the empty drug vials from the trash, but they didn't get the authorities involved soon enough. They collected the evidence but they failed to establish proper chain of custody; so although it could have been considered hard evidence, it could only be viewed as circumstantial evidence. At least they could reconstruct various events when they collected this evidence, and that's what created the index of suspicion. But if you suspect that on the spot that one of your colleagues is doing something wrong, you must treat the evidence as exigent; you have to grab it immediately, whatever it is. If something gets thrown into the sharps box, you grab the whole sharps box as evidence; you allow the criminal investigators to sort through it—you don't retrieve it out of the box yourself.

4.5.2 The VA's Response to Health Care Serial Killers

VA hospitals have been the setting of a number of high-profile cases, such as the Kristen Gilbert murders explored earlier, and the killing spree of physician Michael Swango, who might have been one of the most prolific of all known or suspected health care serial killers. A former doctor who might have killed as many as 35 or more people in a 15-year poisoning binge, Swango left a trail of suspicious deaths on two continents as he hopped from job to job. "Instead of using his medical license to become a healer, Swango embarked on a career as a killer," U.S. Attorney Loretta Lynch was quoted as saying in the *New York Daily News* on July 12, 2000, a day after he was indicted for three deaths at a Long Island hospital. "He used his skills to search for victims and take their lives," she added.

Swango had been accused of injecting lethal doses of drugs into three critically ill patients at the Northport Veterans Affairs Medical Center in 1993. He had been indicted for these killings just days after being released from federal prison after serving two years for lying about his criminal record. At the time, criminal investigators and prosecutors were scrambling to build a case against him in connection to 32 other murders. Despite a 1985 conviction for poisoning six coworkers when he worked as a paramedic in Illinois, Swango managed to secure positions at several hospitals in South Dakota and New York, all because employers failed to check his background. Called a "charming, pathological liar," Swango talked his way into a medical residency program, neglecting to mention that his medical license had been suspended due to a former conviction of a bar brawl. He was fired, hired, and roamed several continents as he continued to care for and kill patients over the course of a number of years. Following a lengthy legal course of investigations, indictments, and sentences, Swango was finally convicted on three deaths at the VA facility and was sentenced to life in prison. For a complete look at the Swango case and other health care serial killers, go to www.crimelibrary.com.

With so many cases unfolding within VA hospitals, the government began to crack down on certain loopholes that facilitated these kinds of crimes. In August 2001, a number of representatives from the Office of the Medical Inspector (OMI) and directors of various VA facilities gathered in Phoenix for a conference, coordinated by Mary Sullivan and her colleague Barbara Spence-O'Donnell. The conference was titled, "Death Investigation, Adverse Patient Events, and Evidence Collection in the Hospital Setting." During a panel presentation, "A VA Management Initiative and an Emerging Role for Forensic Nursing: Improving Patient Safety by Responding to Suspicious Adverse Events," four representatives from the Veterans Health Administration discussed how to respond to an increasing number of suspicious events in the health care environment. The panelists were Richard Sorenson, special assistant to the medical inspector; Gary Campbell, then-director of the Harry S. Truman Memorial VAMC in Columbia, Missouri; Mary Dowling, former director of the Northport VAMC; and William Boutelle, MD, then-chief of staff of the Northampton VMAC.

The VA serves close to 4 million veteran patients and more than 350,000 nonveteran patients in a mammoth health care system that has an average daily census of almost 57,000 patients. To respond to an increasing number of suspicious adverse events in VA facilities, in August 2000, the OMI created a working group to focus on the essential elements of investigating suspicious deaths, including identification of cases, protecting evidence at the scene, and developing policies and procedures to address these kinds of medico-legal cases.

The common thread of the OMI's focus was that patient care is paramount and that the safety and security of both patients and staff members was vital to all aspects of VA facility operation. Sorenson explained to the Phoenix conference attendees that the working group had identified several key measures in the identification of suspicious deaths, including establishing definitions of reportable deaths and suspicious events related to existing policies, as well as steps personnel could take to preserve the physical integrity of the death scene, to prevent further disturbance of the crime scene, and ways to maintain the integrity of all medical devices, biologicals, instruments, tubing, supplies, and other medical paraphernalia associated with the clinical setting. He added that personnel need to be alert to the possibility of suspicious, adverse patient events, and that first responders to the scene should provide care if appropriate, notify the authorities, observe the patient and the surroundings, report any alteration to the scene, and notify the medical supervisor on shift. In the same manner, the OMI identified ways that VA police and facility administrators could further protect the scene and facilitate investigation. Sorenson added that forensic nursing was emerging as a way to supplement and contribute to the investigation of any adverse patient event.

During the 2001 panel, Gary Campbell reported that there had been an increase in the number of cardiopulmonary codes identified by his facility's CPR committee, as well as an increase in the number of patient deaths on one inpatient medical and surgical ward in the summer of 1992, the same time period when an allegation of patient abuse had been filed against a registered nurse. Campbell said that a board of investigation was appointed in September 1992. The board members conducted an internal review of codes and deaths at the facility, as well as a statistical analysis that suggested that the deaths were not occurring by chance. Employees who had learned of this internal audit had alerted the media, and Campbell reported that a media crisis had developed rapidly. A joint investigation by the VA Office of the Inspector General (OIG), the FBI, and the U.S. Department of Justice ensued, followed by the exhumation of the bodies of 13 patients. The VA Inspector General for Health Care Inspections reviewed statistical information, and allegations of obstruction of justice and a cover-up were bounced around. A special inquiry by the OIG was launched, followed by congressional oversight subcommittee hearings and a wrongful death civil lawsuit filed against the U.S. government. A dispute resolution specialist undertook a program review and a site visit regarding certain staff members who had identified themselves as whistleblowers, and a review by the Government Accounting Office (GAO) was conducted.

During this lengthy process, Campbell said, a number of internal processes were in place, including ongoing quality assurance reviews by various committees, occurrence screening by registered nurses use 100 percent of the time in all deaths, mortality data tracking and trending, and all unexpected deaths forwarded for peer review. According to Campbell, corrective actions included revising an autopsy policy to request autopsy on all deaths, tracking mortality and code data by unit every month, establishment of a hospital peer review board, and an overall sense of heightened awareness created among staff members. The facility established care teams to follow every VA patient through his or her continuum of care, and implemented a patient safety reporting system. Campbell added that the investigation of adverse events should be "timely and as broad as possible." He acknowledged that there is a tendency for disciplines to "protect their own," leading to communication breakdowns and delayed decision making. He also stated that facilities must establish "a culture of patient safety" and create "a sense of openness regarding the reporting of unusual or suspicious events."

Also at the 2001 conference panel, Mary Dowling reviewed events surrounding the Michael Swango case and suggested areas of system evaluation and change when responding to adverse patient events. She advocated for a stronger system of employee background checks, a system for addressing gaps in the review process, better training for all department personnel who might come into contact with adverse-event cases, and stronger quality assurance measures. In his panel presentation, Boutelle explained that a delicate balance exists between patient safety and the rights of individuals, and that all adverse patient events must be taken seriously, documented, and investigated in a timely and efficacious manner. He added that leaving a paper trail is better than relying on memory, and the need to communicate effectively among all disciplines of a facility is paramount.

Even as the U.S. government was wrestling with a seemingly alarming outbreak of adverse patient events and suspicious deaths in its government-operated health care facilities, a movement of a different kind was slowly taking shape. One nurse at the Carl T. Hayden VA Medical Center in Phoenix, Arizona, began to see how clinical forensic nursing could play an important role in the identification and investigation of adverse patient events. Mary K. Sullivan, MSN, RNC, CARN, was advocating the role of the clinical forensic nurse for the VHA health care system.

Sullivan (in press) writes, "In some instances, this nurse will work as a member of a multidisciplinary team consisting of administrative, law enforcement, or legal personnel to provide essential subject matter expertise in cases involving suspicious, unexpected patient death or other sentinel events that have occurred in a health care facility."

Sullivan points to research conducted by Dr. George Wesley of the VA OIG, who demonstrated the link between clinical QM activities and forensic medicine and nursing. In a review conducted by the Office of Health Care Inspections of more than 1,000 cases spanning slightly more than a decade, numerous forensic issues emerged, including patient abuse and neglect, assault, suicide, homicide, medication or delivery system tampering, improper medication administration or error, and medical equipment or device tampering.

As a clinical forensic nurse coordinator for the U.S. Department of Veterans Affairs, Sullivan continues to advocate for forensic nursing in general and specifically, for the presence of clinical forensic nursing services in VA health care institutions. Not only can they protect patients, they can also protect the health care system, a win–win situation as she sees it.

Sullivan, a graduate of Creighton University, draws from extensive experience as a psychiatric nurse. Up until her clinical rotation in psychiatry, she says she struggled to find her place in nursing school; it was as if psych nursing had been created especially for her. "I found that psych nursing was immediately to my liking, and I knew instantly that I belonged there," Sullivan enthuses. "Psych unlocked the nursing process for me... I felt a natural affinity to these patients. From the very start, I was always able to get them to take their meds and do things other nurses couldn't. It all came very naturally to me, and right out of school, I went into psych nursing."

Sullivan says she attributes to her early success in the discipline to her communication and listening skills:

> I really listened to my patients, not just heard them, and that's what made me successful. I like to think that my interpersonal skills and the ability to read between the lines and connect the dots helps me be a more effective nurse. I'm also organized to a fault and I tend to be very good in a crisis situation... that's a good thing because you have the crisis *du jour* on psych units—there's always something going on. I like the challenging environment and managing that patient population.

She says psych nursing is not for shrinking violets, nor is it an appropriate setting for someone who is unable to make quick and effective decisions:

> I learned to think on my feet, to make quick, accurate assessments. I was amazed by how fast I could actually think—you don't really know what you can do until you actually have to do it. One time you might feel like you're simply lucky, but when you succeed consistently, you become confident in your skills. You don't stress about stuff before it happens because you've already demonstrated that you can function well. You must have quick thought processes and be able to reach conclusions swiftly and succinctly. These are skills that you have to develop, as you can't really learn them from a book. After all, there is no way that you can capture mentally ill people in a textbook; you have to experience it for yourself. It's a whole other world in a psych unit.

Sullivan acknowledges the challenges of caring for mentally ill patients, but she says nurses take them in stride. "It goes with the territory. Everyone prefers a quiet shift, but if something is going down, it's always better to not only be confident in your abilities to manage the situation, but to be backed up by a really good team of co-workers. In a crisis on the unit, you don't need a lot of talking to get something done—you simply look at each other and you know what needs to be done. It's instinct, it's silent communication among competent team members."

In an environment that treats the mentally ill and incapacitated, as well as in a setting that can foster malfeasance, Sullivan says a nurse must constantly be on his or her toes, ready to respond in an appropriate manner consistent with good nursing practice. "Yes, your patients may try to play and manipulate you, but an appropriate response comes with experience. You make good eye contact with your patients, and you are always thinking about your safety and the safety of your patient. Patients want to feel worthy, to feel understood," she says. "When you are on the same unit every night behind locked doors with the same patients, you start feeling like a family, actually, boundaries and all."

She adds that psych nursing has contributed to her sense of personal well-being. "I have realized how fortunate I am to have a life that is fairly under control, but I have also realized that as humans, we're all extremely frail—how easily one day you can be squared away and the next day, you're not."

Despite years on the job at VA facilities in Kansas City, Missouri and in Phoenix, Sullivan says she was oblivious not only to the inner workings of the government, but to how forensic principles could be applied to patient care. In just a short time, Sullivan would find herself in the midst of an opportunity to learn both from the inside out. She recalls:

> I can tell you exactly when all the forensic stuff hit me. I was married to a detective working with homicides and sex crimes. He often brought his work home, and I often said, you know, a nurse could do that for you, or a nurse can get in there and find that out. That was in 1990 or 1991. Every time he would have a problem with a case, I wondered, "How would I handle that?" In 1994, the *Journal of Psychosocial Nursing* produced a forensic issue and after reading it, I thought, "This is for me." I thought that nursing fit so well with forensic thinking and processes, and, complementing the work of law enforcement; my husband agreed with me, but he never thought it would go anywhere. In the early 1990s, things started gelling for me forensically, but before then, I never heard the word forensic, and never thought about it until I related it to law enforcement and began listening more closely to my husband. I was working things out for myself, and it was so exciting to discover that there was a whole slew of nurses who know this stuff.

Sullivan continued to work as an inpatient psych nurse and charge nurse on the evening shift at the Phoenix VA, and in 1994, she discovered the IAFN:

> I joined immediately, did my homework, and became familiar with every possible facet of forensic nursing. Then one of the people in the organization said, "Why don't you look into the sexual assault examiner training program? Do you think the VA would be interested in that?" I didn't know, but I certainly was, so off I went to San Diego to be trained by Diana Faugno. It was an awesome training session, six straight days, with classes often going until 10 p.m., but we loved it.
>
> We had several groups in the classroom; the nurses, a few physicians, the police officers, and some who I considered social workers who turned out later to be victim advocates. We all spoke different languages; we all were absorbing the information differently. On Monday morning, no one really talked to each other, by Friday we were all speaking the same language and I thought this process was fabulous. But on Monday morning, when I was sitting there in the first row, listening to the speakers and being totally in awe of them, I knew right away that a sexual assault agenda alone was never going to fly in the VA. It was not going to work as a program because it wasn't broad enough to meet the mission statement of the VHA.
>
> But as we were taught about the head-to-toe physical assessment, the interviewing process, the evidence collection process, things started to click in my brain. As nurses, we do all of this anyway, so forensics have to be applicable to all nurses and to all patients. I mean, all nurses conduct physical assessments and listen to patients and hear the stories right from the get-go. So I thought, "I'm going to get forensic nursing into the VA, but it can't be as a sexual assault nurse; it has to be as a generalist so that we can apply these principles across the board."

In 1996, Sullivan gave her director a proposal:

> I had five meetings with him, and finally, during the fifth meeting he said suddenly, "OK, let's do this." In fact, he not only gave me permission to put my own team together and train them, he gave me the budget to pull in trainers so that I could replicate the full training experience I had in San Diego. He also gave me two rooms in the ER to outfit as forensic exam rooms, as well as funds with which to buy forensic-related equipment. He gave me a lot of freedom to develop this forensic nursing program. To this day, I don't know what exactly convinced him to give me the go-ahead.

However, Sullivan says, problems popped up:

> We wanted to offer sexual assault exams to the community for free, as the federal government cannot make money off of the community. But, we are not supposed to lose money, either. So somehow, in taking care of the veterans, we were going to do this as a community service 24/7 with our 11 sexual assault nurses and brand-new equipment. But due to county politics, it wasn't going to work. Our county attorney's sexual assault bureau had other ideas about making money and went with a private-sector provider instead.

Feeling a bit wiser after the experience, Sullivan says she continued to approach sexual assault from new perspectives in an effort to serve the broadest range of patients possible. "We had all this talent in the VA—11 nurses, and we needed to make the most of their special training."

4.5.3 The VA Considers the Adoption of Forensic Nursing

Sullivan takes a deep breath before plunging into the story of how forensic nursing was embraced tentatively by one of the country's largest health care systems. She had been asked by longtime forensic nursing proponent Janet Barber, MSN, RN, to ponder a forensic nursing wish list if there were no obstacles to this emerging nursing specialty. "She asked me to write up a strategic plan for implementing forensic nursing into the VA, so I did, and sent it to her," Sullivan recalls:

> Unbeknownst to me, Janet ended up taking it to Washington, DC, and it landed in the hands of the Inspector General (IG). In the meantime, I had made a poster presentation at the Association of Military Surgeons of the United States in Irvine, California. I was checking out another guy's poster and he turns to me, looks at my name tag and says, "Oh, you're Mary Sullivan... I know of you." So we start chatting, and it turns out he is the medical advisor to the IG, Dr. George Wesley. He says, "I have your strategic plan on my desk." Here we are, at 9 p.m. at night after a full day at the conference, and we're both tired, and we say hey, let's talk about this proposal. He then said, "You really should be involved in the suspicious death medical evidence task force that is being organized in Washington." That's when he explained it was being formed to address suspicious adverse events and the management of medical evidence in the VA system. My attention had suddenly become diverted from the sexual assault project; and I now realized I had a vehicle with which to apply forensic nursing across the board, for all nurses and to all patients. I knew there was now a reason to step out of the sexual assault role and apply our forensic training to a much broader universe.

Sullivan says soon after, she and a colleague coordinated the aforementioned August 2001 clinical forensic nursing conference in Phoenix. "The event was attended by many high-profile people from Washington, and we were able to demonstrate our knowledge about suspicious deaths and adverse patient events, and the application of forensic nursing to these incidents," she explains. "Three of the original 11 team members were selected to serve on the OMI's medical evidence task force, so essentially, we were going back and forth to VA headquarters in Washington, DC for two years. We used every opportunity to educate anyone who would listen in VA headquarters about forensic nursing."

Although it was a slow process, Sullivan says it paid off in significant dividends eventually. "They demonstrated curiosity and fear; initially, they didn't want anything to do with us," Sullivan recalls, chuckling with laughter:

> They thought to themselves, "Who are these people?" After all, we were field personnel, staff nurses, total peons, and they were all the top leadership in the VA. Some of them embraced the concept of forensic nursing, seeing it as a gift to the VA system, while the other half said, "These people are out of their minds. It was an honor and a thrill to be on the task force, because, and I can't stress this enough, we were little people at the very big table. Most of these folks had no clue about forensic principles such as chain of custody or evidence collection. We wanted to continue to reinforce that forensic nursing bridges the gap between medicine and law enforcement. We're trained in evidence collection, we understand chain of custody, we know how to freeze a crime or death scene and we know how to preserve it until the right people arrive; we know how to take statements, and we know how to document. The people on the task force weren't sure what we were talking about half the time because we were talking medicine and nursing, and the other half was talking law enforcement—and the administrative people were in the middle. There is also a huge application of forensic nursing processes to events that are not criminal in nature. Anything that has even a remote chance of having legal implications should require a clinical forensic nursing presence.

Sullivan reports a slow, gradual understanding and acceptance of certain medico-legal concepts by the VA since the original task force meetings in 2000 and 2001:

It's 2005 and we're still in the process of convincing them. The directive that came out of that early task force did not pass, as every department in the VA signed off except one. But our work was done; that task force was a direct response to recommendations made by the IG from the health care serial-killer investigations. So in the meantime, we held the Phoenix forensic nursing conference, and we kept educating people at every turn. We know that we don't need a directive to deliver good patient care or to improve nursing practice.

Sullivan says she is encouraged by the open reception she received from the VA's chief nurse executive, Cathy Rick. "She is very supportive and has always given me her ear. She kept giving me opportunities to talk about forensic nursing, and I took her up on every one of them." In 2003, Sullivan again presented a revised strategic plan for forensic nursing, and it was reviewed by the National Nurse Executive Council, the power-base through which all nursing business is evaluated and approved in VHA.

"We're working on the first phase of education and training, what clinical forensic nurses are, and what they do. The first goal is increasing awareness among all clinicians about what constitutes medico-legal significance in the health care setting."

Sullivan believes that because of the size of the VA's size nursing force, the location of its facilities in nearly every kind of community, and its sizable patient population served, it is the perfect health care entity in which to implement forensic nursing services. In time, the VHA could set an example for private-sector health care systems to follow. "The VA is all over the country, in all settings, whether rural or urban, with different personalities, politics, and patient needs, so if forensic nursing can work there, it can work anywhere," Sullivan emphasizes.

She says she has been explaining to the VA that forensic nurses embody many different roles, as death investigators, as SANEs, as legal nurse consultants, and as forensic psychiatric nurses, to name a few, and that they practice both in the clinical setting and in the community:

I have suggested that VA nurses are practicing forensic nursing outside of the VA, and that we need to bring this expertise in-house for the benefit of our veterans. I have been approved by the NNEC to bring together qualified nurses with a forensic background in a work group to identify the aspects of forensic nursing that can be applied immediately, as well as identify long-term goals, and education and training needs of other nurses who want to be forensic nurses in the VA system. At the time of writing, we are in the process of our work, and it is moving forward.

Clinical forensic nursing is applying forensic nursing to the existing patient care process. There are two groups of nurses who need forensic awareness. First, the frontline personnel working directly with patients. In this frontline group, there are the nurses who do not have the time, money, inclination, or energy to go back to school specifically for forensic training, but they still need information about forensic principles. The other group of frontline nurses is those who do not want to pursue further training and education and eventually put this expertise into patient care delivery. Those nurses who already have a forensic background, I would hope, would be eager to serve as preceptors. Together, these nurses will open others' minds so they can see that forensic nurses have so many skills to offer health care institutions and communities, from sexual assault nurse examination, to death investigation and nursing jurisprudence and so much more.

Sullivan says that it is equally critical to reach QM personnel in health care facilities. "These nurses are like the cold case investigators," Sullivan explains. "There are situations in the hospital where the evidence is gone, nobody wants to talk to you, and you have a hard time coming up with a recommendation for change because you don't have the evidence, facts, or data."

4.5.4 The Role of the Clinical Forensic Nurse Examiner

Sullivan believes passionately in the role of the CFNE in any health care setting, as a trained individual well versed in handling tricky, potentially medico-legal events such as codes and unexpected deaths.

Sullivan (in press) writes:

The clinical forensic nurse provider would respond to all codes called whether the patient survives or not. This nurse does not participate in providing treatment during the code, but instead monitors events and accounts for all treatments provided. The nurse ensures that EKG strips are preserved along with the sequential records of medications, airway management, and other interventions such as defibrillation. In addition, all circumstances that immediately preceded the code are documented, including the names of family and staff members present before and during the code. A standard set of laboratory specimens are typically collected, especially if the patient does not survive the resuscitation attempt. This information is archived and if a suspicious trend is later identified, more complete information is available for root cause analysis or other investigation processes.

Kathleen Brown, RN, PhD (2003) writes:

Documentation of any injury created by a treatment process is also helpful to law enforcement. If the victim does not survive, leaving tubes, catheters, and any other devices used for treatment in place assists law enforcement in differentiating injuries created by medical personnel from injuries created prior to treatment. Collection and preservation of forensic evidence in a health care setting assists law enforcement and, therefore, assists the victims of the crime who are seeking justice.

Sullivan adds that forensic nurses might also be able to respond to bomb threats, fire alarms, infant abductions, environmental security breaches, or hostage scenarios. Another critical domain of the CFNE is clinical deaths. As envisioned by Sullivan, the CFNE would respond to every patient death, whether expected or unexpected. She says that ideally, the CFNE would document the circumstances of each death, collect laboratory specimens, note the last physician order changes, medication and treatments received in last 24 hours, any visitors, and other pertinent data. Sullivan writes, "If a suspicious trend is later identified, more complete information is available for root cause analysis or investigation."

She adds that if the death is suspicious or unexpected, the CFNE can "freeze the scene until further consultation with the supervisor or law enforcement. Fortunately, these events happen rarely, but it is important to have someone who realizes what may be vital evidence and is instrumental in maintaining the integrity of this potential crime scene."

A third critical purview of the CFNE is the change of shift at a health care facility. Barber has stated that the time frame between the change of shifts provides an ideal "window of opportunity" for criminal activity ranging from stealing narcotics, to tampering with life-support equipment or IVs, to in some way attempting to harm a vulnerable patient. There are numerous dynamics at work during a change of shift, including health care personnel who are going off shift disengaging from their responsibilities too soon, and personnel who are coming on to their shift engaging in work only after the preceding shift has departed. Additionally, Barber says that health care providers might use the shift change as an opportunity to engage in social interaction rather than professional communication. Barber adds that personnel who are just starting their day might be preoccupied with "nesting" activities, including getting coffee, or arranging one's work tools and supplies. She also says that at the change of shift, priorities can become "fuzzy," with documentation and oral reports taking precedence over continuing care activities. Finally, there is a tendency for health care providers to make erroneous assumptions about what their colleagues will do or have done, increasing a margin of error for the completion of critical clinical tasks.

Sullivan (in press) writes:

> Patients as well as visitors are often aware of the confusion and chaos that may occur at change of shift, and some may take advantage of these opportunities to engage in behavior not conducive to the health and welfare of other patients on the unit. Those caregivers who have ideas other than providing health care on their minds will also realize that the change of shift provides an optimum time for inappropriate, illegal, or otherwise dangerous behavior. The clinical forensic nurse provider may encourage and reinforce the heightened awareness of all staff at these particular times.

O'Brien recalls a change-of-shift incident that has stuck with her:

> The day my ventilator-dependent patient was disconnected from respiratory support while I participated in change-of-shift report was suspicious and could not have been accidental. During report, I focused on a distant but constant alarm, which I immediately recognized. I rushed to a private room, finding the door only slightly cracked open and the curtain pulled around the bed. The machine was connected to the endotracheal tube but not ventilating, and appeared to be malfunctioning. The visitor chair, occupied 15 minutes earlier by the patient's daughter, was now empty and she was nowhere in sight. The patient was in acute distress and as resuscitative efforts ensued, I frantically tried to determine what had gone so terribly wrong. Just prior to report, a physical assessment had been performed with stable findings and ventilator settings double-checked. The patient had been resting comfortably in the company of his daughter. I instructed her to call if anything was needed and said I would be in report. As other team members responded to the code, it was soon determined the ventilator was unplugged from the wall outlet behind the headboard.
>
> The prospect that his daughter was involved or responsible for his expiration left me stunned, saddened and feeling professionally violated. While I empathized with the family's plight, should I have been more suspect of a family distraught and divided over a loved one's ventilator-dependent state? Or did someone unauthorized enter the room, a person who was familiar with unit routines, and aware that staff would be clustered in report and not in close proximity to the room? Could the plug of this older model machine just happen to fall out of the outlet causing it to lose power? For weeks thereafter, I searched for clues I might have missed and struggled with feelings of guilt in failing my responsibility to keep my patient safe from harm, even if that included members of his own family, which was an inconceivable thought to me at that point in my career.

Barber says that due to the high number of incidents occurring during the time of the health care "changing of the guard," the role of the forensic investigator is to conduct a root cause analysis (RCA) through which the nurse reconstructs the event in the context of the health care facility's schedule of activities, and using tools that pinpoint the personnel present and various related timelines. Key documents to obtain early in the discovery of a suspicious event include medical records, personnel schedules, pharmacy orders, sign-out sheets for equipment and supplies, supervisor's report, housekeeping log, telephone and/or e-mail log, names and conditions of patients on the unit at the time of the event, records of charges to patients and other invoices, a list of equipment and supplies in the patient's room, monitoring records from bedside recording devices, and any appropriate photo-documentation.

According to Barber, risk-reduction strategies for the change of shift include radio-frequency tracking technology, which records personnel's activities in the patient's room and their interfaces with medical equipment; point-of-care data entry systems that allow personnel to spend more time on meaningful clinical activities in the patient's room; technology-enhanced aids such as bed-exit alarms and restraint-monitoring devices; and personnel performing walking rounds, where outgoing and incoming health care providers can meet to exchange their reports at the bedside to "clarify, rectify and validate care components," Barber says.

Regarding RCAs, Sullivan (in press) writes:

> I see the CFNE as an essential part of the hospital team with the responsibility to evaluate and perform the root cause analyses of adverse patient events. Adverse patient events range from those causing minimal concern to extremely serious action, but the vast majority are not criminal in nature. However, precise identification, collection, and management of facts, data, and medical evidence are critical, criminal or not. I am referring to ensuring a higher level of quality patient care and accurate delivery of our services. It is our duty as health care providers to be accountable for our actions and to ensure a safe environment for our patients.

Sullivan asserts that the costs associated with hiring a CFNE would be quickly recouped in terms of litigation, settlements to families and insurance reimbursements. The positive outcomes in increased accuracy of in the delivery of patient care services and more cost-effective investigation processes realized from utilizing a CFNE could be easily tracked and quantified. Research utilization information would further indicate additional areas that could be positively impacted by the CFNE. Still, the bottom line remains: There is no price that can be placed on the increased feeling of safety and satisfaction of patients who count on us for competent delivery of care or for lives we may save.

Sullivan says:

> Code events are situations where a forensic nurse would be essential. For example, have a forensic nurse arrive at every code and assess the situation from a forensic nursing point of view. This would include looking at events before, during and after the code, retrieving data, investigating what happened, determining who visited the patient, did they just eat or drink something, etc. After the code, the forensic nurse would look everywhere, including in the trash for anything unusual, and would also account for any medications administered. All data would be placed in a separate report, turned into the quality management department, and then archived. Data can be trended to see which staff members attended the code, which shifts and units are getting the codes, and other vital information. The same with every patient death... page the forensic nurse, who can reconstruct what happened in the 24 hours prior to the adverse event. And if it's a suspicious event, the forensic nurse may opt to "freeze" the scene, which would be a rare event. It doesn't necessarily have to be a suspicious or criminal event to warrant data collection. I remind people that being forensic-minded is really being medico-legal minded, which is also a risk-management strategy.

The concept of living forensics, one of the most unsung components of risk management ever, was a challenging one for the VA to grasp initially, Sullivan says. She acknowledges the significance of the VA's initial steps toward the implementation of forensic nursing in its facilities, and says she is proud that her health care system is leading the private sector in this regard:

> We will lead and we will benchmark. The private-sector health care system has to worry about bad publicity caused by adverse events, or the facility closing, or taking a major financial hit. If the hospital is in a small community, it could lose business, health care providers don't get paid, and patients don't receive care; or there are insurance issues with which to contend. There are many reasons why private-sector hospitals don't want their business aired on the evening news. At the VA, we're an open book, and we are in a very good position to be proactive about this. There is no other health care entity that has taken this bull by the horns. It's simply a more accurate, more precise delivery of care, and if we catch any funny business in the meantime, then good for us. The VA answers to the taxpayers and to Congress, and we have oversight by the Inspector General. We have every reason to be proactive. If I were in the private sector, I would never have this opportunity, which is another reason why I love being a VA nurse.

What might be most significant is the vast number of nurses who are potentially impacted by the VA's interest in forensic nursing. The VA currently employs approximately 60,000 nurses, according to Sullivan, and if half that number of nurses is interested in forensic nursing principles, that is 30,000 forensic nurses who will one day be looking after the welfare of patients and victims of violence everywhere.

4.6 QUALITY IMPROVEMENT AND RISK MANAGEMENT

In many ways, forensic nursing serves as a key quality improvement and risk management tool because it helps hospitals identify patient populations and clinical situations that pose medico-legal questions to answer and issues to resolve. Janet Barber says she sees the private health care sector fashioning itself after the government health care sector in the future as a way to cultivate greater transparency of wrong-doing and to foster increased accountability:

> With more people on Medicare and Medicaid, and with an increasing number of people on national health care plans through the military, I think the general public will eventually have the same kind of scrutiny of its hospitals as government facilities. The same goes for making a case for quality improvement in health care. If a health care institution can reduce its risks, that certainly demonstrates to the public that it is a safe place to be, and that your health care processes are of the highest quality. Within the concepts of quality assurance or quality improvement, a health care facility looks for its weak spots and fixes them. And that is precisely what forensic nursing is doing . . . it is looking for the weak spots, identifying them, handling them, and then putting into place solid solutions that become ongoing and a part of everyday practice at the facility.

Sullivan (in press) writes, "The forensic nurse specialist is adept in performing forensic medical record reviews and is the appropriate liaison to hospital risk management and legal personnel. The forensic nurse specialist is an ideal adjunct to quality management with regard to analyzing trends and performing root cause analyses to adverse patient and sentinel events." Barber (2001) adds that a clinical forensic nurse specialist assisting the quality improvement or risk management staff or other authorities in an investigation can reconstruct the event within the context of the hospital's schedule of activities. She notes, "Tools that assist in pinpointing personnel presence and timelines of activities include the following: medical and pharmacy records, equipment sign-out sheets, housekeeping log, e-mail files and computerized medical record entries, records of charges billed to patients, monitoring records from bedside recording devices, and the supervisor's report. Others include the personnel schedule or time clock records and telephone paging logs."

4.7 VIOLENCE IN THE HEALTH CARE ENVIRONMENT

Violence in almost any occupational setting is of concern, but few workplaces are as susceptible to disturbances as health care settings, the scene of trauma, chaos, and anger. The tables sometimes turn, with patients inflicting harm and injury on their health care providers. A study published in the February 2005 issue of *Annals of Emergency Medicine* found that verbal threats, physical assault, and even stalking, are not uncommon workplace problems for emergency physicians and other personnel. Of the 171 respondents surveyed, 131 (76 percent) reported experiencing at least one violent act during the previous 12 months. Three quarters (74.9 percent) of respondents said they had encountered verbal threats; nearly one third (28.1 percent) indicated they were victims of physical assaults; 11 percent indicated they were confronted outside the emergency department, and 3.5 percent reported experiencing stalking events.

"Emergency departments, by their very nature, are high-stress places for both the patient and staff," said lead author Terry Kowalenko, MD, of the University of Michigan Medical Center in Ann Arbor, Michigan. "Add to that mix patients who are intoxicated, in a state of drug withdrawal, suffering from delirium, or have psychiatric problems that may make them more prone to violence and you have a potentially volatile atmosphere."

Despite the large majority of emergency personnel experiencing a violent act, 80 percent said they are only occasionally fearful of workplace violence, and a little more than 9 percent said they were frequently fearful. In response to their fear of violence, 42 percent of emergency physicians report that they did obtain some sort of protection, including obtaining a gun (18 percent), a knife (20 percent), or a concealed weapon (13 percent) or carrying mace (7 percent) or a club (4 percent). However, most (31 percent) used a security escort as their method of choice for personal protection.

The survey also found it is not just patients who are violent. Of the emergency physicians who reported experiencing physical assaults, 89 percent came from patients, 9 percent from family members, and 2 percent from friends of patients. Drugs and alcohol appear to be the major factor in the most violent acts. Emergency physicians reported that 45 percent of physical assaults occurred with patients who were believed to be intoxicated.

Despite the potential for violence in EDs, less than one third (27 percent) of emergency physicians and other personnel report their hospital has permanent security officers assigned to the ED, and 24 percent reported having general hospital security staff that included the ED in their rounds of the hospital. However, the study authors said further research is needed to determine if increasing the presence of security personnel would decrease the violence.

Stultz (1996) documented that overall crime in hospitals participating in the 10th annual International Association for Health care Security & Safety (IAHSS) survey increased by 7 percent in 1995 versus 1994. On a per-hospital basis, five crime categories showed increases:

murder, suicide, physical assault, sexual assault, and theft. Six categories showed decreases: robbery, arson, burglary, auto thefts, bomb threats, and vandalism. Whereas crime in urban and suburban hospitals in 1995 leveled off after a sharp increase reported for 1994 over 1993, rural hospitals showed a 9 percent increase in crime in 1995 over the previous year. The 1995 crime rate was 11 percent higher than the preceding eight-year average, with physical assault 36 percent higher than the eight-year average, and sexual assault 88 percent higher on a per-hospital basis.

In "Preventing Violence in the Health care Setting," Kathleen Brewer-Smyth, RN, PhD, CRRN (2003), a postdoctoral fellow at the School of Nursing of the University of Pennsylvania, describes the hypothetical case of a young critical-care nurse who had been kicked in the face by a disoriented patient while she was attempting to preserve his arterial and central IV lines. Although the patient was unharmed and the nurse was uninjured, her confidence had been shaken, and she wondered what she had done to possibly provoke the violent incident. Brewer-Smyth says that although health care providers cannot avoid potential harm, they can be better prepared to deal with outbursts and threats of physical harm from patients or even coworkers. She writes, "Nurses heighten their awareness and expertise in dealing with violence in their professional settings by learning to identify risk factors and warning signs, and by applying interventions that could shield their patients and themselves from harm."

The hospital, like other occupational settings, can be a turbulent environment. In 1993, a survey of the general public estimated that 2.2 million Americans were attacked at work during the preceding 12 months and that another 6.3 million were threatened. In a 1994 study, one out of 12 human resources managers disclosed that at least one violent workplace death had occurred in their organization within the past four years. Brewer-Smyth says that accurate statistics from health care settings are difficult to obtain due to underreporting. In violent attacks in acute-care facilities, 36 percent to 43 percent of victims filed a report through risk-management tracking systems. "Extra paperwork, time spent explaining the incident, and fear of being blamed are a few of the reasons some have avoided alerting anyone of an incident. Combative, threatening behavior that deescalates and does not result in actual assault may not be reported at all, making the problem seem less significant than it is," Brewer-Smyth writes.

Regardless, a high prevalence of violence has been reported in the health care environment. The National Institute of Occupational Safety and Health (NIOSH, 2002) reports that violence often takes place during times of high activity and interaction with patients such as meal times, and during visiting hours and patient transportation. Additionally, assaults might occur when service is denied, a patient is involuntarily admitted, or a health care worker attempts to set limits. Violence occurred most frequently in psychiatric and ED waiting rooms, and in geriatric units.

Thackrey and Bobbitt (1990) reported that of 122 clinical and nonclinical employees surveyed on medical, surgical, and psychiatric units of a 475-bed teaching hospital, 48 percent reported at least one attack. Carmel and Hunter (1989) reported that an investigation of a state psychiatric hospital disclosed an injury rate of 16 per 100 nursing staff per year and that rate only encompassed injuries that resulted in death, medical treatment, or transfer of the staff member to another unit. Pane et al. (1991) reported that a 493-bed urban university-affiliated hospital experienced 686 incidents of violence in one year, with most situations requiring police intervention.

May and Grubbs (2002) described a survey of nurses working in the ED, ICU, and on the general floor in a 770-bed acute care medical center in which 88 percent reported being verbally assaulted and 74 percent reported being physically assaulted by patients and family members or visitors. The assaults were perpetrated most often by patients with cognitive dysfunction (79.1 percent), patients with substance abuse (60.5 percent), and persons who were angry because of the patient's condition (55.8 percent). Weapons also play a part in some violent incidents in health care facilities. Lavoie et al. (1988) reported that almost half of the respondents in a study of teaching hospitals in the United States reported that they confiscated weapons from patients and visitors at least once a month. One ED used metal detectors to seize more than 300 weapons a month.

Lanza et al. (1991) discussed various risk factors for health care providers and patients, but did not discover a significant association between violence and personnel's gender, age, length of employment, history of working with the mentally ill, organizational position, or amount of time spent in certain patient care activities. However, the researchers found that staff who had been assaulted were more likely to be unmarried, and spent more time administering medications, setting limits, and observing and talking with patients.

Brewer-Smyth reports that the likelihood of violence in health care settings has also been linked to certain patient diagnoses, work situations, and geographical areas, but cautions that "all nurses need to anticipate trouble by accurately assessing risk factors and changes in patients' behaviors" that could be triggered by underlying physiological causes such as metabolic abnormalities, drug toxicity, and acute pulmonary or neurological impairment. Brewer-Smyth warns, "Violence may still be difficult to predict when precipitated by situational factors. A patient's visitor, such as a bereaved loved one or a member of an opposing street gang, may become unexpectedly assaultive in a health care facility. Nurses need to be vigilant for clues that indicate that friction may lie ahead."

Although no single strategy for the prevention of violence in the workplace exists, Brewer-Smyth states:

> Employers need to assess the environment's risks, develop relevant policies and procedures that address prevention and intervention, and monitor the effectiveness of these standards. Employers also need to create an environment of open communication between staff and management that emphasizes the importance of reporting an incident and the actions that were taken. Additionally, employers must recognize that a rested staff which has adequate time away from the work environment is more likely to have the energy and patience to manage difficult patients, family, and visitors.

She adds that a number of studies have demonstrated that better training in violence issues is one step toward taking preventive measures. Health care providers are advised to do the following:

- Assess the environment for ways to make the health care facility's physical surroundings more conducive to a pleasant experience. High-risk areas such as ED waiting areas should be spacious and well lit, with adequate seating and access to refreshments, restrooms, and telephones. Security guards, surveillance cameras, panic buttons with silent alarms, metal detectors, and bulletproof glass might be necessary precautions. Objects that can be used as weapons, such as pictures and tables, should be affixed to the wall or floor. High-risk units should have enclosed nurses' stations, staff-only restrooms, and emergency exits.
- Assess the patient population on a unit to identify potentially violent patients and their triggers. Typical triggers include crowding, noise, irritating patients and staff, boredom, unstructured activity, and tasks that a patient might not want to perform, such as physical therapy. Whenever possible, redirect patients' attention to focus on things that do not agitate them, or take them to a quieter place. Staffing patterns should also be designed to prevent personnel from working alone and to minimize patient waiting times. Rosenthal et al. (1992) reported that when one hospital installed an electronic system that flagged records and alerted personnel to patients with histories of disruptive behavior, and used it with other interventions, violent incidents decreased 91.6 percent.
- Convey an impression of interest and caring by being cognizant of body language and facial expressions, as well as communicate in an honest and respectful manner with patients, their families, and other visitors. They should also control their own behavior and reactions to hostile actions or comments from patients or visitors.
- Acknowledge a patient or visitor's frustration at their perceived loss of control over their situation; keep patients and their families informed and involved in decisions regarding their care whenever possible, and respect their right to privacy. Brewer-Smyth writes, "Rigid, unfair, or overly strict rules and regulations, especially regarding visitors, can trigger anger and need to be avoided whenever possible. Maintaining and updating policies and procedures ensures consistency and takes the burden off the staff member for individual decisions."
- Ensure staff members' safety by coming to consensus on what constitutes unacceptable patient or visitor behavior, and being able to recognize it when it occurs, and being able to obtain immediate assistance when necessary. Brewer-Smyth writes, "Never attempt to deal with a physically aggressive patient alone. If necessary, remove yourself from danger . . . never turn your back on an angry person, corner an individual, or allow a person to get between you and the door or an escape route."

The Occupational Safety and Health Act's general duty clause requires that employers provide safe and secure workplaces for their employees, but recent fiscal constraints might tempt institutions to try to do more with less, often resulting in fewer security personnel available or other means of protection. As a result, an increasing number of health care providers are contending with violence on the job that can in turn trigger fear and anger, depression, sleeping difficulties, headaches, or a desire to leave an otherwise rewarding career. Brewer-Smyth writes, "Although many nurses who have been assaulted have not lost time from work, others have required (time) . . . to fully recover from the physiological, emotional, and social effects of the experience." Health care providers must report all incidents of violence to their risk management departments, and should consider taking advantage of their employer's various counseling programs.

"Violence may be difficult to predict and prevent," Brewer-Smyth writes:

> Sometimes there is nothing health care providers can do to avoid its occurrence, which is why additional research is needed to identify more strategies that can effectively prevent and reduce violence in the work setting. Nurses can anticipate violence and use tested interventions to prevent it or at the least, reduce its ill effects by learning to recognize risk factors and warning signs.

REFERENCES

Brewer-Smyth, K. Preventing violence in the health care setting. *Nursing Spectrum*. 2003.

Carmel, H., & Hunter, M. Staff injuries from inpatient violence. *Hosp Comm Psych. 40,* 1, 41–46, 1989.

Carmona, R., & Prince, K. Trauma and forensic medicine. *J Trauma. 29,* 1222, 1989.

Carr, M. E. Care of the victim of sexual assault. Available online at: http://www.EMedHome.com. 2001.

Evans, M. M, & Stagner, P. A. Maintaining the chain of custody: Evidence handling in forensic cases. *AORN J. Vol. 78,* October, 2003.

George, J. E., Quattrone, M. S., & Goldstone. M. The duty to document: What are the limits? *J Emerg Nurs. 23,* 5, 467, 1997.

Goll-McGee, B. The role of the clinical forensic nurse in critical care. *Crit Care Nurs Q. 22,* 1, 8–17, 1999.

Goll-McGee, B., Couto, S., Ferrandi, J., Jankowski, K., Lawlor, J., Luciani-McGillvray, I., & Robertson, M. Forensic nursing process: An evaluation of forensic patients in the clinical environment. *Forensic Nurse*. July, 2003.

Hoyt, C. A. Evidence recognition and collection in the clinical setting. *Crit Care Nurs Q. 22,* 1, 19–23, 1999.

Jones, P. Reaching the elderly through hospital emergency rooms. *Aging*. Winter, 1991.

Keen-Payne, R. Serving as an expert witness in rape cases. *Nurse Pract. 13,* 7, 59–62, 1998.

Lanza, M. L., Kayne, H. L., Hicks, C., & Milner, J. Nursing staff characteristics related to patient assault. *Issues Ment Health Nurs. 12,* 3, 253–265, 1991.

Lavoie, F. W., Carter, G. L., Danzl, D. F., & Berg, R. L. Emergency department violence in US teaching hospitals. *Ann Emerg Med. 17,* 11, 1227–1233, 1988.

Lynch, V. A. Clinical forensic nursing: A new perspective in the management of crime victims from trauma to trial. *Crit Care Nurs Clin North Am. 7,* 2, 489–507, 1995.

Lynch, V. A. *Clinical Forensic Nursing: A New Perspective in Trauma.* Collins: Bearhawk Consulting Group. 1997.

May, D. D., & Grubbs, L. M. The extent, nature, and precipitating factors of nurse assault among three groups of registered nurses in a regional medical center. *J Emerg Nurs. 28,* 1, 11–17, 2002.

Mund, S. More on evidence collection. *J Emerg Nurs. 22,* 1, 12–13, 1996.

National Institute of Occupational Safety and Health (NIOSH). Violence: Occupational hazards in hospitals. Centers for Disease Control and Prevention (CDC), Washington, DC: Department of Health and Human Services. Publication No. 2002-101. 2002.

Pane, G. A., Winiarski, A. M., & Salness, K. A. Aggression directed toward emergency department staff at a university teaching hospital. *Ann Emerg Med. 20,* 3, 283–286, 1991.

Pasqualone, G. What's behind door 24?: An examination of forensic categories among patients seen at a community hospital emergency department. Unpublished manuscript, Fitchburg State College, Fitchburg, MA. 1998.

Pasqualone, G. Forensic categories among patients in the ED. *Forensic Nurse*. July, 2003.

Reece, R. M. Identifying the abused child in the emergency department. 2001. Available online at: http://www.emedhome.com.

Rosenthal, T. L., Edwards, N. B., Rosenthal, R. H., & Ackerman, B. J. Hospital violence: Site, severity, and nurses' preventive training. *Issues Ment Health Nurs. 31,* 4, 349–356, 1992.

Sackman, B. Profile of a VA serial killer: Red flags for health care inspectors. Paper presented at Forensic Nursing Clinical Update 2001: Death Investigation, Adverse Patient Events, and Evidence Collection in the Hospital Setting, Phoenix, AZ. 2001.

Smock, W. S. Development of a clinical forensic medicine curriculum for emergency physicians in the USA. *J Clin Forensic Med. 1,* 1, 27, 1994.

Smock, W. S., Ross, C. S., & Hamilton, F. N. Clinical forensic medicine: How ED physicians can help with the sleuthing. *Emerg Legal Brief. 5,* 1, 1–8, 1994.

Stultz, M. S. Crime in Hospitals 1995: The Latest IAHSS Survey. *J Healthc Prot Manag, 13,* 1, 1–45, 1996.

Sullivan, M. K. Opportunities and challenges in forensic nursing. In V. A. Lynch, Ed., *Forensic Nursing in the Hospital Setting*. New York: Elsevier. In press.

Thackrey, M., & Bobbitt, R. G. Patient aggression against clinical and nonclinical staff in a VA medical center. *Hosp Community Psychiatry. 41,* 2, 195–197, 1990.

Winfrey, M. E., & Smith, A. R. The suspiciousness factor: Critical care nursing and forensics. *Crit Care Nurs Q. 22,* 1, 1–7, 1999.

Yorker, B. An analysis of murder charges against nurses. *J Nurs Law. 1,* 3, 35–46, 1994.

RECOMMENDED READINGS

American College of Emergency Physicians (ACEP). Evaluation and management of the sexually assaulted or sexually abused patient. Dallas, TX: ACEP. 1999.

American College of Obstetricians and Gynecologists (ACOG). Adolescent acquaintance rape. *Int J Gynecol and Obstet. 42,* 209–211, 1993.

Ball, G. G. Modifying the behavior of the violent patient. *Psychiatr Q. 64,* 4, 359–369, 1993.

Benak, L. D. Forensics and the critical role of the ER nurse. On *The Edge. 7,* 1, 20–22, 2001.

Blair, D. T. Assaultive behavior: Does provocation begin in the front office? *J Psychosoc Nurs Ment Health Serv. 29,* 5, 21–26, 1991.

Blank, C., & Mascitti-Mazur, J. E. Violence in Philadelphia emergency departments reflects national trends. *J Emerg Nurs. 17,* 5, 318–321, 1991.

Brenneman, K. Forensic nursing teaches nurses to preserve evidence. *Boston Bus J. 17,* 40, 12, 1997.

Burgess, A. W., Burgess, A. G., & Douglas, J. E. Examining violence in the workplace. *J Psychosoc Nurs Ment Health Serv. 32,* 7, 11–18, 1994.

Burgess, A. W., Douglas, J. E., Burgess, A. G., Baker, T., Sauve, H., & Gariti, K. Hospital communication threats and intervention. *J Psychosoc Nurs Ment Health Serv. 35,* 8, 9–16, 1997.

Carroll, V., & Goldsmith, J. One third of nurses are abused in the workplace. *Reflections. 25,* 3, 24–27, 1999.

Centers for Disease Control and Prevention (CDC). Violence: Occupational hazards in hospitals. Available online at: http://www.cdc.gov/niosh/2002-101.html.

Ciancone, A. C., Wilson, C., Collette, R., & Gerson, L. Sexual assault nurse examiner programs in the United States. *Ann Emerg Med. 35,* 4, 353–357, 2000.

Drummond, D. J., Sparr, L. F., & Gordon, G. H. Hospital violence reduction among high-risk patients. *JAMA. 261,* 17, 2531–2534, 1989.

Eckert, W. G., Bell, J. S., Stein, R. J., et al. Clinical forensic medicine. *Am J Forensic Med Pathol. 7,* 3, 182, 1986.

Erickson, L., & Williams-Evans, S. A. Attitudes of emergency nurses regarding patient assaults. *J Emerg Nurs. 26,* 3, 210–215, 2000.

Ernst, A., Green, E., Ferguson, M. T., Weiss, S. J., & Green, W. M. The utility of anoscopy and colposcopy in the evaluation of male sexual assault victims. *Ann Emerg Med. 36,* 5, 432–437, 2000.

Felton, J. S. Violence prevention at the health care site. *Occup Med. 12,* 4, 701–715, 1997.

Garbacz-Bader, D. M. Forensic science program: A community effort. *Am J Forensic Med Path. 19,* 3, 242–245, 1997.

Girardin, B. W., Faugno, D. K., Senski, P. C., Slaughter, L., & Whelan, M. Guidelines for giving effective testimony. In B. Girardin, D. K. Faugno, P. C. Senski, L. Slaughter, & M. Whelan (Eds.). *Color Atlas of Sexual Assault.* St. Louis, MO: Mosby. 1997.

Groth, A., & Burgess, A. W. Sexual dysfunction during rape. *New Engl J Med. 297,* 14, 764–766, 1977.

Hancock, P. Forensic nurse specialist: Forensic nursing. 2002. Available online at: www.ufcw141nurses.org/forensic %20ns.htm.

Hanson, K. A., & Gidyez, C. A. Evaluation of a sexual assault prevention program. *J Consul Clin Psycho. 61,* 6, 1046–1052, 1993.

Haywood, Y. C., & Scott, J. L. Domestic violence in the emergency department. *Emergency Medicine Clinics of North America. 17,* 3, 603–615, 1999.

Hochmeister, M. N., Whelan, M., Gehrig, C., Binda, S., Berzlanovich, A., Rauch, E., & Dirnhofer, R. Effects of toluidine blue and destaining reagents used in sexual assault examinations on the ability to obtain DNA profiles from post-coital vaginal swabs. *J Forensic Sci. 42,* 2, 316–319, 1997.

International Association of Forensic Nurses. *Scope and Standards of Forensic Nursing Practice.* Washington, DC: American Nurses Association Publishing. 1997.

Irwin, K., Edlin, B., Wong, L., Faruque, S., McCoy, H., Word, C., Schilling, R., McCoy, C., Evans, P., & Holmberg, S. Urban rape survivors: Characteristics of human immunodeficiency virus and other sexually transmitted infections. *Obstet and Gynecol. 85,* 3, 330–336, 1995.

Jenny, C., Hooton, T., Bowers, A., Copass, M., Krieger, J., Hillier, S., Kiviat, N., Corey, L., Stamm, W., & Holmes, K. Sexually transmitted diseases in victims of rape. *New Engl J Med. 322,* 11, 713–716, 1990.

Koss, M., Gidyez, C., & Wisniewski, N. The scope of rape: Incidence and prevalence of sexual aggression and victimization in a national sample of higher education students. *J Consult Clin Psycho. 55,* 162–170, 1987.

Lanza, M. L., & Carifio, J. Blaming the victim. *J Emerg Nurs. 17,* 5, 299–309, 1991.

Lanza, M. L. Environmental characteristics related to patient assault. *Issues Ment Health Nurs. 15,* 3, 319–335, 1994.

Lauber, A. A., & Souma, M. L. Use of toluidine blue for documentation of traumatic intercourse. *Obstet Gynecol. 60,* 5, 644–648, 1982.

LeBeau, M., Andollo, W., Hearn, W. L., Baselt, R., Cone, E., Finkle, B., Fraser, D., Jenkins, A., Mayer, J., Negrusz, A., Poklis, A., Walls, C., Lionel, R., Robertson, M., & Saady, J. Recommendations for toxicological investigations of drug-facilitated sexual assaults. *J Forensic Sci. 44,* 1, 227–230, 1999.

Ledray, L. Evidence collection and care of the sexual assault survivor: The SANE-SART response, violence against women. 2001. Available online at: http://www.vaw.umn.edu /FinalDocuments/CommisionedDocs/ForensicEvidence .asp.

Ledray, L. E., & Barry, L. Sexual assault: Clinical issues, SANE expert and factual testimony. *J Emerg Nurs. 24,* 3, 284–287, 1998.

Ledray, L., & Summelink, K. Sexual assault: Clinical issues: Efficacy of SANE evidence collection, a Minnesota study. *J Emerg Nurs. 23,* 1, 75–77, 1997.

Lenahan, L., Ernst, A., & Johnson, B. Colposcopy in evaluation of the adult sexual assault victim. *Am J Emerg Med. 16,* 2, 183–184, 1998.

Levin, P. F., Hewitt, J. B., & Misner, S. T. Insights of nurses about assault in hospital-based emergency departments. *Image J Nurs Sch. 30,* 3, 249–254, 1998.

Lion, J. R., Dubin, W. R., & Futrell, D. E. *Creating a Secure Workplace: Effective Policies and Practices in Health Care.* Chicago: American Hospital Publishing. 1996.

Lipscomb, J. Violence in the workplace: A growing crisis among health care workers. In G. Fragala & W. Charney, Eds. *The Epidemic of Health Care Worker Injury* (pp. 163–165). Boca Raton, FL: CRC Press. 1999.

Lurie, P., Miller, S., Hecht, F., Chesney, M., & Lo, B. Postexposure prophylaxis after nonoccupational HIV exposure. *J Am Med Assoc. 280,* 20, 1769–1773, 1998.

Mahoney, B. S. The extent, nature, and response to victimization of emergency nurses in Pennsylvania. *J Emerg Nurs. 29,* 5, 21–26, 1991.

McCauley, J., Gorman, R. L., & Guzinski, G. Toluidine blue in the detection of perineal lacerations in pediatric and adolescent sexual abuse victims. *Pediatrics. 78,* 6, 1039–1043, 1986.

McCauley, J., Guzinski, G., Welch, R., Gorman, R., & Osmers, F. Toluidine blue in corroboration of rape in the adult victim. *Am J Emerg Med. 5,* 2, 105–108, 1987.

McCracken, L. Forensic health care. 2002. Available online at: http://www.4n6links.com/forensichealthcare.htm.

McCracken, L. The forensic nurse's ABC's of trauma care. 2002. Available online at: http://www.4n6links.com/abcs.htm.

McCracken, L. Living forensics: A natural evolution of care. 2002. Available online at: http://www.4n6links.com/livingforensics.htm.

McInerney, C. In a time of crisis proper crisis intervention saves lives. *On Call. 11,* 16–19, 1998.

Merchant, R. Non-occupational HIV post-exposure prophylaxis: A new role for the emergency department. *Ann Emerg Med. 36,* 4, 2000.

Mills, C. S., & Granoff, B. J. Date and acquaintance rape among a sample of college. *Social Work. 37,* 6, 504–509, 1992.

Mittleman, R. E., Goldberg, H. S., & Waksman, D. M. Preserving evidence in the emergency department. *Am J Nurs. 83,* 1652, 1983.

Murray, M. G., and Snyder, J. C. When staff are assaulted: A nursing consultation support service. *J Psychosoc Nurs Ment Health Serv. 29,* 7, 24–29, 1991.

Nabb, D. Visitors' violence: The serious effects of aggression on nurses and others. *Nursing Standard. 14,* 23, 36–38, 2000.

Norvell, M. K., Benrubin, G. I., & Thompson, R. J. Investigation of micro-trauma after sexual intercourse. *J Repro Med. 29,* 269–271, 1984.

Occupational Health and Safety Administration (OSHA). Guidelines for preventing workplace violence for health care and social service workers. Available online at: www.osha.gov/SLTC/workplaceviolence/guideline.html.

Overman, S. Workplace violence: Threat from within. *Occup Health and Safety. 54,* 7, 24–27, 1995.

Reilly, J. L. Curriculum proposal: Masters of science in forensic nursing. 2000. Available online at: http://www.newfoundations.com/CurrProjects/ForeN.html.

Rhynard, J., Drebs, M., & Glover, J. Sexual assault in a dating relationship. *J School Health. 67,* 3, 89–93, 1997.

Rickert, V. I., & Wiemann, C. M. Date rape among adolescents and young adults. *J Pediatr Adoles Gynecol. 11,* 167–175, 1998.

Riggs, N., Houry, D., Long, G., Markovchick, V., & Feldhaus, K. Analysis of 1,076 cases of sexual assault. *Annals of Emergency Medicine. 35,* 4, 358–362, 2000.

Ritchie, E. C. Reactions to rape: A military forensics psychiatrist's perspective. *Mil Med. 163,* 505–509, 1998.

Roper, J. M., & Anderson, N. L. The interactional dynamics of violence. *Arch Psychiatr Nurs. 5,* 4, 209–215, 1991.

Rose, V. L. CDC releases the 1998 guidelines for the treatment of sexually transmitted diseases. *Am Fam Physician. 57,* 8, 2003–2008, 1998.

Sackman, B. The role of the forensic nurse as an integral part of the criminal investigative team. *Forensic Nurse. 2,* 5, 2002.

Schewe, P. A., & O'Donohue, W. Rape prevention with high-risk males: Short-term outcome of two interventions. *Arch Sex Behav. 25,* 5, 455–471, 1996.

Simmons, M. M., & Cupp, M. J. Use and abuse of flunitrazepam. *Ann Pharmacother. 32,* 117–119, 1998.

Simonowitz, J. A. Health care workers and workplace violence. *Occup Med. 11,* 2, 277–291, 1996.

Sirotnak, S. P., & Sorotnak, A. P. Child abuse and forensic pediatric medicine fellowship curriculum statement. *Child Maltreat. 5,* 1, 58–63, 2000.

Slaughter, L., & Brown, C. Colposcopy to establish physical findings in rape victims. *Am J of Obstet Gyn. 166,* 1, 83–86, 1992.

Slaughter, L., Brown, C., Crowley, S., & Peck, R. The pattern of genital injury in female sexual assault victims. *Am J Obstet Gyn. 176,* 609–669, 1997.

Smialek, J. E. Forensic medicine in the emergency department. *Emerg Med Clin North Am. 1,* 3, 1685, 1983.

Smock, W. S., Ross, C. S., & Hamilton, F. N. Clinical forensic medicine: How ED physicians can help with the sleuthing. *Emerg Legal Brief. 5,* 1, 1–8, 1994.

Sommargren, C. E. Violence as an occupational hazard in the acute care setting. *AACN Clin Iss Crit Care Nurs. 5,* 4, 516–522, 1994.

Sullivan, M. K. Clinical forensic nursing: A higher standard of care. *Forensic Nurse. 1,* 1, 2002.

Tintinalli, J., & Hoelzer, M. Clinical findings and legal resolution in sexual assault. *Ann Emerg Med. 14,* 5, 447–453, 1985.

Yehuda, R. Managing anger and aggression in patients with posttraumatic stress disorder. *J Clin Psychiatry. 60* (Suppl 15), 33–37, 1999.

Yody, B. B., Schaub, C., Conway, J., Peters, S., Strauss, D., & Helsinger, S. Applied behavior management and acquired brain injury: Approaches and assessment. *J Head Trauma Rehabil. 15,* 4, 1041–1060, 2000.

5 Forensic Nurses' Medico-Legal Skill Sets: Observation, Documentation, Photography, and Evidence Collection

CONTENTS

5.1 THE IMPORTANCE OF MEDICO-LEGAL SKILL SETS

There are a number of specific skill sets that enable forensic nurses to perform their duties effectively according to proper forensic science protocol and appropriate nursing practice. Forensic nurses must be able to document their clinical findings in a cogent manner, whether it is through the use of photo-documentation of a patient's injuries, or clear, descriptive narrations in the patient's medical record following comprehensive interview and assessment processes. It is the integration of these skills with a nurse's index of suspicion that creates a dynamic toolkit filled with clinical, psychosocial, and forensic interventions.

Clinical nurse consultant Janet Barber, MSN, RN, says that in forensic nursing, the skills inherent to nursing practice are coupled with medico-legal principles that are built on these fundamentals:

> Characteristics and abilities of nurses, such as vigilance, nurturing, caring, and concern for a patient's welfare, are everyday nursing behaviors that are engrained in individuals who become nurses; otherwise, they probably would not have become nurses in the first place. So, as a nurse, you have this commitment to taking care of human beings and you go about it through standard nursing practice and through the application of standards that protect and defend a patient. I think that is where forensic nursing comes in; it is an application of an even higher set of standards and medico-legal processes that not only protect patients, but provide a defense for them in the event that they can't speak or act for themselves.

The power of observation, which facilitates solid clinical assessment and documentation, is a key skill in a forensic nurse's toolkit. Operating one's forensic antenna and being swift on the uptake of information is critical, Barber notes, adding that it is the springboard for all other nursing practice. Barber says, historically, nurses have been dissuaded from reading too much into a patient's situation, but forensic nurses have a special license to question and to investigate more fully.

"Still there are some people who don't think it's a nurse's business to investigate and to call certain scenarios into question," Barber says:

> They think it's the exclusive domain of the police officer, or it is someone else's domain of practice. I believe most

> nurses are beginning to feel fairly sure-footed about their forensic or medico-legal responsibilities, and they are not going to allow themselves to be intimidated. I think that in general, all health care providers are realizing that they can be held legally accountable on obstruction of justice if they don't pay more attention to injuries and ensure precise documentation of them. They are beginning to understand that this kind of attention to detail is no longer optional. I think that very recently, when nurses and physicians have been made responsible for reporting abuse and suspicious injuries and if they fail to report it is an obstruction of justice . . . that's a pretty powerful motivator to observe injuries or signs of abuse, and to document, collect, and preserve medico-legal evidence.

Barber says that forensic nurses must use their keen skills of observation to corroborate the patient's story and any injuries they might or might not be seeing during the patient interview and physical evidentiary examination. "Nurses must take in a lot of information at once, then begin to sort through the details," Barber adds:

> Nurses must consider the patient's behavior and their story; is what they are telling you believable? Does it make sense? Does it correspond to or contradict the patient's injuries? Are they under the influence of drugs or alcohol? Once you can determine your patient's behavior as normal or suspicious, you can begin to put into context your observations and begin to gather concrete physical information that concurs with what the patient is saying. Sometimes, the patient's story doesn't make sense; nurses have had patients tell them really bizarre things. For example, nurses in New Mexico have had people coming into the emergency department claiming they have been abducted and injured by aliens. Well, it sounds bizarre, of course, but yet when there are enough of these stories from otherwise "normal" people, they merit attention. The same goes for forensic cases. You record what you hear and what you see, and then you try to dissect it. I can't emphasize enough the need to take down absolutely all of the information pertaining to a case, whether it makes sense at the time or not. Nurses must be absolutely obsessive-compulsive about detail when it comes to their documentation. Some of the smallest details that patients will tell you may not seem to be important at the time, but later on, you might ask yourself, "Did they tell me they were in the living room or in the kitchen when the incident happened? Who was there? Were there four people or one other person?" Forensic nurses pay attention to those details, they take it in, and they write it all down. These details may or may not ever be needed, or may never be important, but forensic nurses still document every single little detail. Sometimes your colleagues will say, "Wow, you sure wrote a lot about this case." Well, it's better to write a lot of detail and then find out you only need a little bit of that information, than wishing later on that you had remembered more of what the patient told you. If you don't write it down, how can you possibly remember everything, and what if you missed something? Forensic nursing is all about the business of being very detail-oriented.

5.2 DOCUMENTATION IN THE MEDICAL RECORD

The patient interview is one of the most important steps in the documentation process says Kathleen Brown, RN, PhD, (2003) in "Evidence Collection and Preservation in a Health Care Setting." She writes, "Whenever possible, health care personnel interview the victim, with or without a law enforcement person present. The interview guides the forensic examination by revealing what aspects of the body require the most attention. This process is similar to ED triage in which a member of the ED team asks questions to help focus the visit."

Health care personnel should record what the victim recalls in his or her own words as often as possible, Brown advises. "An ideal victim interview is a series of quotes, in quotation marks, of what the victim recalls about the crime committed. Statements made by the victim can be used in court. The role of the health care provider is not to analyze or place judgment on the words of the victim, but simply to record them . . . The victim's description should not be sanitized or interpreted, just recorded with as many exact quotes as possible." Brown adds that nurses might encounter patients who are unable to be interviewed. She states:

> Because health care concerns are always a priority, the interview may be delayed until the victim is medically stable; examination, evaluation, and treatment may proceed without interview. The interview may also be delayed if the victim is unconscious or semiconscious, and/or under the influence of alcohol or drugs. Evaluation, treatment, and testing should proceed in these situations without an interview, which can be conducted at a later time. When the victim cannot speak, careful documentation of all observations of the victim by health care personnel becomes crucial.

Mary Muscari, RN, NP, confirms, "Proper documentation is critical in forensic cases. Record direct quotes as often as possible, using quotation marks to indicate direct statements. Patients may use slang or vulgar terminology to describe what an assailant has done to them or to sanitize their own violent acts. Avoid paraphrasing the patient's descriptions, using medical terminology, or correcting the patient's grammar, since these detract from the credibility of the patient's history." She cautions nurses to avoid using potentially pejorative documentation. She writes, "The term 'alleged' may be used out of concern for making a wrongful accusation against someone. Conversely, writing the term 'alleged' in the record may imply reservations about the truthfulness of the patient's statements. Accurate, objective, and detailed documentation is required in forensic cases."

Forensic examiner Sharon Crowley, MN, RN, says forensic nurses must be "bullet-proof" when they are testifying in a court of law, and that means conscientious, complete documentation at all times:

> Documentation requires thoroughness, completeness, and objectivity. Bearing in mind that what you write in the medical record is subject to scrutiny by nursing and medical peers, and by juries in court can really change your whole perspective of documentation. As you document a patient's injuries, collect and package the evidence, and take photographs, if you imagine the most severe scrutiny possible, it changes your whole approach and you dot every "i" and cross every "t" and you don't leave anything to the imagination. Another compelling reason for careful and thorough documentation is knowing that if a case goes to court years later, you may forget the details if you don't write them down. It's like balancing a checkbook—you might let it go for a month or two but if you knew you were going to be audited tomorrow, you would make sure you made entries and balanced it every day. After a bad court experience or after testifying for the first time, it's amazing how diligent you become in your documentation. All nurses may one day have to answer for their documentation in a court of law, and besides, good documentation is the right thing to do for the sake of the patient.

Clinical forensic nurse specialist Georgia Pasqualone, MSN, MSFS, RN, CEN, says she is troubled by the state of nursing documentation today. "There's a problem with nursing documentation, and it's poor nationally," she says. "ED nurses in particular, often feel that they are too busy to document in a timely, consistent fashion, and that's wrong but they do it anyway. When it comes to saving a hemorrhaging patient or writing in the medical record, the hemorrhaging patient wins out every time, and that's the way it should be. But we need a better balance between the two."

Pasqualone believes a simple form of technology could facilitate busy nurses' charting abilities:

> The ideal documentation process would involve nurses wearing a headset attached to a recording device, so that we were continually speaking into this little microphone. While we're examining the patient, we can verbalize our findings, and it goes right into the tape recorder. Perhaps that would eliminate the fact we have to sit down and write something in the medical record. In reality, nurses are too busy to write, or sometimes you can't find the chart. Or the chart is at the nurses' station but you are in the patient's room and standing between you and it is a very long walk down the hallway. Or you take the chart into the patient's room but there's no room to write, or you have dirty gloves on and don't want to chart with them on, or whatever the scenario may be, there are many reasons why nurses don't chart immediately after providing patient care.
>
> Like a lot of ED nurses, I am guilty of sometimes leaving all of my charting until the end of the shift... after a long, busy day, who remembers the small details of patient care? It's a huge challenge and a significant problem that we must amend. We say that documentation should be complete, and we say that we should document after every assessment, every intervention, and every evaluation, but we don't have time for that. That's why I think that a great solution would be the headset and tape recorder. The tapes can be transcribed and placed in the medical record, and that way, nurses don't miss anything at the time it is happening.

Another challenge to accurate documentation, Pasqualone notes, is the terminology that nurses use to document their observations in the medical record:

> I don't teach people to name things, I teach them to describe what they see. You may not know what to call something forensically, but you certainly know how to describe it. So I tell nurses to record the dimensions of the injury, including measuring the width and length of the wound, describing its color and disposition. Nurses should never write that they think it's a bruise that is two, three, or four days old, because it may not be a bruise, and we now know it's tricky to tell how old a possible contusion might be. For example, one of my famous cases is of the elderly lady who was beaten up. Within an hour of presentation to the hospital, her bruises were deep purple and round; she had been on anti-coagulants, so her bruises looked a few days old when in fact they were only an hour or so old because her blood was so thin it turned colors rapidly. So you can never presume to know something definitively; you should only document what you see, what you smell, as well as the textures of things; use all five senses when you are documenting injuries, and don't presume what these signs mean. Just write down what you observe.

Nancy Cabelus, MSN, RN, DABFN, concurs:

> We are trying to teach nurses not to write in the medical record "This is an entrance wound" or "This is an exit wound." Instead, nurses should write that they observe two holes. Nurses must not box themselves in by what they write in a patient's chart. They should be descriptive, but be careful not to call something by the wrong name. Cuts, lacerations, and blunt trauma often get confused and interchanged, so I tell other nurses to simply write down what you see; you don't have to nail it down and say it's definitely a bite mark. Support your descriptions with photographs whenever possible. In court, if it is established that a nurse used the wrong terminology, their credibility can be destroyed instantly. When I first came to law enforcement, I was told, "The more you write, the more trouble you get into. Keep it brief and to the point."

> Well, you know what, when your murder case goes to court four years down the road, what are you going to remember? Probably very little. So you must write quite a bit, and do everything with an eye toward court. It may not seem to be forensically related at the time, but it certainly is.

"Details, details, details," emphasizes Melissa Becker, RN, D-ABMDI, when asked about documentation in the medical record. "Start broad and narrow down your narrative," she advises. "Your documentation should be thorough and detailed, providing a clear line from one end of the case to the other, which is easily followed and then easily understood whether it's read tomorrow or two years from now."

Health care providers know that if they don't document it, "it never happened." Much has been done to better educate the health care community about the importance of documentation, especially when it comes to domestic violence. In a September 2001 research brief, *Documenting Domestic Violence: How Health Care Providers Can Help Victims,* published by the U.S. Department of Justice Office of Justice Programs, National Institute of Justice authors Nancy E. Isaac, ScD, senior research scientist with the Harvard Injury Control Research Center at the Harvard School of Public Health, and V. Pualani Enos, JD, assistant clinical professor at Northeastern University School of Law, Domestic Violence Institute, write:

> Many health care protocols and training programs now note the importance of such documentation. But only if medical documentation is accurate and comprehensive can it serve as objective, third-party evidence useful in legal proceedings. For a number of reasons, documentation is not as strong as it could be in providing evidence, so medical records are not used in legal proceedings to the extent they could be. In addition to being difficult to obtain, the records are often incomplete or inaccurate and the handwriting may be illegible. These flaws can make medical records more harmful than helpful. (Isaac & Enos, 1997)

There are still many health care providers who do not consider the consequences of incomplete or careless medico-legal documentation, particularly in abuse cases. A significant number of health care professionals have received scant information about how medical records can help domestic violence victims take legal action against their abusers. Isaac and Enos write, "They often are not aware that admissibility is affected by subtle differences in the way they record the injuries. By making some fairly simple changes in documentation, physicians and other health care professionals can dramatically increase the usefulness of the information they record and thereby help their patients obtain the legal remedies they seek."

The victim's attorney, or the victim acting on her own behalf as a pro se litigant, can submit medical documentation as evidence for obtaining a range of protective relief, such as a restraining order. Victims can also use medical documentation in less formal legal contexts to support their assertions of abuse. Persuasive, factual information might qualify them for special status or exemptions in obtaining public housing, welfare, health and life insurance, victim compensation, and immigration relief related to domestic violence and in resolving landlord–tenant disputes. For formal legal proceedings, the documentation needs to be strong enough to be admissible in a court of law. Typically, the only third-party evidence available to victims of domestic violence is police reports, but these can vary in quality and completeness. Medical documentation can corroborate police data. It constitutes unbiased, factual information recorded shortly after the abuse occurs, when recall is easier. Medical records can contain a variety of information useful in legal proceedings. Photographs taken in the course of the examination record images of injuries that might fade by the time legal proceedings begin, and they capture the moment in a way that no verbal description can. Body maps can document the extent and location of injuries. The records might also hold information about the emotional impact of the abuse. However, the way the information is recorded can affect its admissibility. For instance, a statement about the injury in which the patient is clearly identified as the source of information is more likely to be accepted as evidence in legal proceedings. Even poor handwriting on written records can affect their admissibility.

There are several reasons medical recordkeeping is not generally adequate. Health care providers are concerned about confidentiality and liability. They are concerned about recording information that might inadvertently harm the victim. Many are confused about whether, how, and why to record information about domestic violence, so in an effort to be "neutral," some use language that could subvert the patient's legal case and even support the abuser's case.

Some health care providers are afraid to testify in court. They might see the risks to the patient and themselves as possibly outweighing the benefits of documenting abuse. Even health care providers who are reluctant to testify can still submit medical evidence. Although the hearsay rule prohibits out-of-court statements, an exception permits testimony about diagnosis and treatment. In addition, some states also allow the diagnosis and treatment elements of a certified medical record to be entered into the evidentiary record without the testimony of a health care provider. Thus, in some instances, physicians and other health care providers can be spared the burden of appearing in court.

The patient's "excited utterances" or "spontaneous exclamations" about the incident are another exception to the prohibition of hearsay. These are statements made by someone during or soon after an event, while in an agitated state of mind. They have exceptional credibility because of their proximity in time to the event and because they are not likely to be premeditated. Excited utterances are valuable because they allow the prosecution to proceed even if the victim is unwilling to testify. These statements need to be carefully documented. A patient's report might be admissible if the record demonstrates that the patient made the statement while responding to the event stimulating the utterance (the act or acts of abuse). Noting the time between the event and the time the statements were made or describing the patient's demeanor as she made the statement can help show she was responding to the stimulating event. Such a showing is necessary to establish that a statement is an excited utterance or spontaneous exclamation, and thus an exception to the hearsay rule.

It appears that at present, many medical records are not sufficiently well documented to provide adequate legal evidence of domestic violence. A study of 184 visits for medical care in which an injury or other evidence of abuse was noted revealed these major shortcomings in the records:

- For the 93 instances of an injury, the records contained only one photograph. There was no mention in any records of photographs filed elsewhere (e.g., with the police).
- A body map documenting the injury was included in only three of the 93 instances. Drawings of the injuries appeared in eight of the 93 instances.
- Doctors' and nurses' handwriting was illegible in key portions of the records in one third of the patients' visits in which abuse or injury was noted.
- All three criteria for considering a patient's words an excited utterance were met in only 28 of the more than 800 statements evaluated (3.4 percent). Most frequently missing was a description of the patient's demeanor, and often the patient was not clearly identified as the source of the information.

On the bright side, although photographs and body maps documenting injuries were rare, injuries were otherwise described in detail. In less than 1 percent of the visits were negative comments made about the patient's appearance, manner, or motive for stating that abuse had occurred.

5.3 HOW HEALTH CARE PROVIDERS CAN IMPROVE THEIR DOCUMENTATION SKILLS

Medical records could be much more useful to domestic violence victims in legal proceedings if some minor changes were made in documentation.

Clinicians can do the following:

- Take photographs of injuries known or suspected to have resulted from domestic violence.
- Write legibly. Computerized medical records can also help overcome the common problem of illegible handwriting.
- Set off the patient's own words in quotation marks or use such phrases as "patient states" or "patient reports" to indicate that the information recorded reflects the patient's words. To write "patient was kicked in abdomen" obscures the identity of the speaker.
- Avoid such phrases as "patient claims" or "patient alleges," which imply doubt about the patient's reliability. If the clinician's observations conflict with the patient's statements, the clinician should record the reason for the difference.
- Describe the person who hurt the patient by using quotation marks to set off the statement. The clinician would write, for example: The patient stated, "My boyfriend kicked and punched me."
- Avoid summarizing a patient's report of abuse in conclusive terms. If such language as "patient is a battered woman," "assault and battery," or "rape" lacks sufficient accompanying factual information, it is inadmissible.
- Do not place the term "domestic violence" or abbreviations such as "DV" in the diagnosis section of the medical record. Such terms do not convey factual information and are not medical terminology. The court determines whether domestic violence has occurred.
- Describe the patient's demeanor, indicating, for example, whether she is crying or shaking or seems angry, agitated, upset, calm, or happy. Even if the patient's demeanor belies the evidence of abuse, the clinician's observations of that demeanor should be recorded.
- Record the time of day the patient is examined and, if possible, indicate how much time has elapsed since the abuse occurred. For example, the clinician might write, "Patient states that early this morning her boyfriend hit her."

5.4 FORENSIC PHOTOGRAPHY

As hand washing is to the prevention of disease transmission, so is forensic photography essential to the documentation of injuries in medico-legal cases. Both nursing interventions are critical to a patient's welfare, and without them, health care providers run the risk of rejecting proper protocol. Photo documentation is one of the cornerstones of forensic nursing because it establishes a patient's injuries and preserves a visual record of those injuries for permanent documentation. Should a civil or criminal lawsuit be filed in the future, this documentation can be used as key evidence to prove or disprove a plaintiff's or a defendant's claims. Experts say that proper photodocumentation is essential in those cases in which a victim of violence might present to the health care facility repeatedly, as the result of escalating abuse, even though the individual might attempt to minimize their injuries or fabricate stories to explain away their injuries. Photo documentation makes it more challenging for individuals to downplay or deny their abusive circumstances. Photography also provides a record of injuries that might have healed fully by the time a case goes to trial. In many cases, forensic photography can be a deciding factor in the minds of jurors.

Brown (2003) writes, "Detection of injury is important to the investigation of a crime. Any injuries the victim sustained during the commission of a crime, regardless of whether they require medical intervention, must be noted and recorded. Injuries are photographed and described in the medical record, both in a narrative and drawn on a traumagram or body map." Health care professionals should look for evidence of the various classifications of violence-related injuries, including blunt-force trauma, sharp-force injury, bite marks, abrasions, and lacerations.

Although descriptions and drawings of injuries help investigations, it is photography that preserves the appearance of the victim in the immediate aftermath of the crime. Brown writes, "One photograph is worth a thousand words of narrative. And photographs of injury have a powerful effect on the law enforcement community." Brown explains that because photographs preserve critical evidence, victims can use them in matters of restraint orders, divorce, and custody arrangements. Photography can also be used to assist rape and sexual assault victims in the investigative and judicial process. It also can be used to protect children who are victims of physical or sexual abuse.

Photographs of the victim should be taken with cameras customarily used for forensic work, such as Polaroid instant, digital, or 35-mm cameras, before collection of trace evidence, Brown advises. These photographs document the appearance of the victim on arrival at the health care facility, and they must be taken before the victim is cleaned up or any part of his or her body is washed or dressed. The victim's entire body should be carefully inspected for signs of injury, which then should be photographed. "Fresh injury can be difficult to detect, which is why the interview may be important to guide the search," Brown writes. "If possible, take an initial overall picture of the victim as identification as well as documentation of the overall appearance before any medical intervention."

Brown adds that when injuries are fresh, light purple, and difficult to see in initial photographs, they can be rephotographed at a time deemed appropriate by law enforcement and health care personnel. She emphasizes, "But, if at all possible, photograph the injury before treatment ensues. Investigators want documentation of the appearance of injuries that appeared before medical intervention. If this is not possible, photograph immediately after intervention."

It is essential that all photographs be taken with a scale in place to indicate the dimensions of the injury. This scale, or forensic ruler, should not overlay any portion of the injury, but should be included in the photo and should identify the victim with a case or medical record number. A picture should be taken with and without the scale if possible, and all photographs should be taken at a 90-degree angle reduce the probability of distortion. "Photographs will be accepted in court if the distance from the injury allows for accurate evaluation, the photograph is clear and in focus, and the scale is placed to allow for good visualization and measurement of the injury," Brown adds.

The forensic nurse should take an adequate number of photographs, being mindful that in a case of trauma or other medical emergency, taking perfectly composed photos might not be possible. Brown advises, "Quickly photograph what the victim looks like upon arrival and photograph any injuries as they are detected. Do not compromise the health care of the victim, but get those pictures!"

If 35-mm film is used, it should be developed by law enforcement, Brown says, and if an instant camera is used, every photograph must be labeled with the victim's name, the examiner's name, the date, and the time the photo was taken. If digital photography is used, the disk should be given to law enforcement.

Ledray (2001) writes, "Physical injuries are probably the best proof of force and need to be photographed, described on drawings, and documented in writing on the exam report. Ledray (1992a, 1992b) and Pasqualone (1996) say that photographs are not meant to take the place of thorough charting. They advise that health care providers take at least two sets of photographs; one set should be kept in the medical record, and the second set should be given to the police with other physical or trace evidence collected.

Ledray and Pasqualone instruct that when photographs are taken, health care providers should follow a systematic order, starting with the patient's face, and working through the rest of the body from head to toe, and from front to back. They recommend that photo-documentation of injuries should be conducted using a 35-mm camera with a standard 50-mm lens and 100 or 200 speed (ASA) color film. They explain that a disadvantage of 35-mm pictures is that they must be sent out for developing and often are not available to the police when they investigate, or to the prosecutor deciding to charge the case. Polaroid pictures have the advantage of being available to the police during their initial investigation, but they have the disadvantage of poorer quality, especially for close-ups. Some experts recommend taking both Polaroid pictures for use in the initial investigation and the charging decision-making process and 35-mm pictures that can be developed and used if the case goes to court.

Although some examiners are hesitant to photograph a victim's breasts and genitals, not properly documenting injuries with pictures could result in liability for failure to document, according to Pasqualone (1996). Health care providers can preserve a patient's dignity by taking close-up pictures of the injury and by properly draping exposed areas.

Although many nurses understand the importance of photographing the patient's injuries, they are hesitant about breaking their particular state's patient privacy laws. Pasqualone says:

> Recent conversations with emergency department colleagues have revealed that some health care providers are under the misconception that photo-documentation of patient injuries will breach confidentiality. On the contrary, photographs are considered as much a part of the medical record as is the written documentation. Neither gets separated from the record, and the information enclosed within does not get revealed outside the clinical setting until subpoenaed by the legal system.

Pasqualone recalls the case of an elderly woman who was brought into the ED from a nursing home with fever of unknown origin. When the patient was prepared for catheterization, the nurse observed massive swelling, contusions, and bruises in the patient's perineal area. There were no other injuries on the woman's body:

> Was this a result of anticoagulation therapy, or was this a situation of elder abuse? The nurse wanted to photo-document the injuries and report her observations to elder services, but was discouraged from doing either by the resident on call. The resident was under the impression that photographing the woman's injuries, because they were on her genitalia, would not only be an invasive process, but would also breach her confidentiality.

Pasqualone adds, "The truth of the matter is that by not photographing the woman's injuries, health care personnel are committing an injustice to this patient. Photo-documentation preserves the injuries that will heal with time. If photo documentation does not become part of the written record, the patient will lose the impact for adjudication of this potentially abusive situation." Pasqualone continues:

> As with all narrative notes, documentation of physical findings, clinical procedures, and diagrams of patient's injuries, photographs are included in the medical record. If a patient is unable to give consent for photography, there is an implied consent, as treatable injuries are considered exigent evidence. In other words, evidence that will eventually vanish or be changed in appearance through healing or treatment is considered exigent and must be captured through photo documentation in order to complete the record.

Pasqualone advocates for all hospitals to have on hand a comprehensive photo-documentation protocol prior to the arrival of any forensic category of patient:

> Ideally, photo-documentation should be included in the blanket permission to treat. As with any treatment generated in the ED, the patient always has the option of refusing or declining. If a patient does not want photographs taken of their injuries, they still have that right to refuse. There will come a day when hospitals and health care providers will be sued for not photographing the injuries due to trauma and/or violent crime. This will be an act of neglect on the part of the clinicians. The police have been photo-documenting for many years. Their photographs lend only to the investigative process, though. Health care providers, especially those in the ED, are in the ideal situation for visualizing injuries, recognizing them as evidence, and preserving them for any future litigation. In effect, they are advocating for their patients. The knowledgeable public is becoming more and more aware of the fact that photographs provide a tremendous impact in the courtroom. It is the proactive hospital and the educated health care provider with a vision toward the future that not only treats the patient, but also protects his or her civil rights.

Cabelus raises an issue on the minds of many new forensic nurses. "It's unclear for many nurses whether or not they have the authority to take pictures," she says. "They ask, 'What if the patient says no?' 'Do I need to get consent?'" Mary Sullivan chimes in, "Nurses have a lot of trouble in their minds sorting out what's confidential and what's not, according to HIPAA regulations. Nurses just want to take care of their patients, so they just want to bypass all of those issues. I think we definitely need rules and regulations that allow us to get those pictures when we need to."

Cabelus says many nurses also raise the question of chain-of-custody issues with the film:

> Nurses ask constantly, "Where does the film go if you don't have a lab in your hospital?" I gave a lecture last year and addressed some of these issues. I told attendees to keep a camera and a stock of 35-mm film in their medication room in the ED, and that when it is ready to be processed, someone is going to have to hand carry that film to a photo-processing place and stand by for the one hour while it is being developed. So they wrote down all of this. About six months later I taught the same class and I asked who had a photography policy. This nurse raises her hand and says her hospital has a new photography policy as well as a separate consent form for photos, that they keep a camera and film handy, and that a nurse takes the film to the local Piggly Wiggly and she stands by and waits for it to be developed. I said, "That's wonderful. When did you start doing this?" And she replied, "One of our nurses took your class six months ago and that's the information she came back with." I was delighted to see somebody had been listening and then they utilized the plan. If we can get this to spread like a rash, it would be great!

Photography can have a significant impact on cases relating to interpersonal violence, and the importance of photo documentation in a forensic case cannot be understated, prosecutors emphasize. "From the moment an arrest is made, the clock is ticking," says San Diego Assistant City Attorney Gael Strack of the San Diego County Domestic Violence Unit. "In our profession, speed is essential because each suspect must be arraigned within 72 hours of the time of arrest. Evidence in the form of photographs must be collected right away." Instant photo documentation has helped San Diego achieve a 90 percent conviction rate and Los Angeles a 95 percent conviction rate when dealing with domestic violence cases.

Strack says one of the reasons for San Diego's successful prosecution track record and a 75 percent drop in domestic violence homicides since 1985 is the philosophy that cases must be prosecuted with or without the victim's participation. "If we have enough evidence to go forward, we do. This means we need to document the injuries and the statements. We rely heavily on the Polaroid instant photographs taken by police officers at the scene for our cases." She says the San Diego Police Department (SDPD) documents about 12,000 domestic violence cases annually, with more than 4,000 victims displaying visible injuries. The SDPD uses Polaroid Macro 5 and Spectra cameras equipped with the law enforcement close-up kit. "The benefit of having instant photos is that pictures don't recant, pictures don't minimize, pictures don't change their story," Strack says. "Pictures do paint a very painful picture. And that's what juries need to see to be convinced that a crime has occurred."

Strack says that proper photo documentation of injuries is essential because it is crucial in establishing the chain of evidence required to prosecute; photo documentation helps prosecutors secure early guilty pleas from offenders, reducing court costs and caseloads; and cases can be successfully prosecuted without the victim's testimony when proper documentation is provided. An instant photo imaging system is beneficial because instant photos are tamper resistant, unlike conventional 35-mm and digital images. Instant camera users can see immediately that the right image was captured, minimizing the number of photos taken per case. Instant photos provide evidence before an officer leaves the scene, unlike 35-mm photos or digital images (which can be improperly exposed or misplaced). Instant photos also become part of the case file immediately, particularly important for fast arraignments.

Injuries should be thoroughly documented in the following steps:

- When possible, take photographs before medical treatment is given.
- Photograph from different angles, full-body and close-up.
- Include the patient's face in at least one photograph.
- Hold up a coin, ruler, or other object to illustrate the size of an injury.
- Take at least two pictures of every major trauma area.
- One-on-one or close-up photos of the victim's injuries, including fresh bruising, abrasions and lacerations, should be taken.
- A second close-up or midrange set of photos that includes the victim's face for identification purposes, should be taken.
- Check for indications of past abuse, including scars, or cluster or faded bruising, which could be evidence of abuse over an extended period.
- Check for defensive injuries, especially on the forearms.
- The scene of the violence also should be thoroughly documented, including taking photos of overturned or broken furniture, smashed pictures, mirrors, glasses or dishware, or phones ripped out of the wall. These kinds of photos show the severity of the violence.
- Document any evidence of drug or alcohol abuse or any evidence of violence against children, including images showing them crying, scared, upset, or injured.
- Photograph the batterer, if present at the scene, or obtain a copy of his or her photo if he or she has fled.

- Label each photograph with patient's name, birth date, date and time photo was taken, and the signature of the person taking the photograph.
- Place in a sealed envelope and mark as confidential. Place on the left side of chart in the section marked "Do not release."
- Document in notes that photographs were taken.

"Whatever will effectively document what happened at the scene, we want recorded," Strack says. "Police will photograph the victim's injuries. If there are children present we ask the officers to take a picture of the children. If anything has been damaged, for instance, if he has put his fist through the wall, we want a picture of that. If a weapon has been used, they take a picture of that. Officers also photograph the perpetrator to capture any injuries he's sustained."

Because domestic violence includes the dynamics of love and fear, some victims recant their statements within several days after the incident. The use of detailed police reports, statements, and clear photographic evidence allow prosecutors to proceed with the case without pressuring the victim to cooperate. "The more photographs, the better," Strack says. "When we go back into court six months later to try to prove that a crime occurred, the pictures tell the story of what happened long after the physical wounds have healed."

Pictures truly can be worth a thousand words. Pasqualone (1996) writes, "There is absolutely no way that a nurse can accurately document the extent of 53 stab wounds on a victim's body with the written word. There is no way to accurately document the bridging of a laceration, blood-flow patterns showing directionality or the extent of an abrasion ring around a gunshot wound." She emphasizes that photography cannot and should not replace documentation in the medical record, but "it certainly should be the No. 1 form of supplemental documentation . . . photographic documentation in the search for the truth continues to exist after the wounds are healed, and will persist for the attorneys and judges to utilize in their pursuit of guilt or innocence."

Nurses must understand, Pasqualone says, that they can be held responsible for not documenting trauma, injuries, and signs of abuse, exposing their health care institution to potential legal liability. "By failing to properly photograph evidence related to injuries, health care providers who help restore a crime victim's physical wellbeing may ruin that patient's changes of redress through the courts, or more importantly, jeopardize that victim's future safety," she adds. Photographs of evidence on clothing, such as bullet holes, debris, stains, and tears, can corroborate the story told by the victim or the perpetrator, and Pasqualone says, "Each of these elements tells a story that could be destroyed if rolled up in a ball and thrown into the garbage or washed down a sink."

Many hospitals are including a separate patient photography release form as part of the facility's paperwork on admission, with instructions to explain to patients the purpose of photography and the reasons why these photographs might be important to the patient if legal action is taken.

5.5 EVIDENCE COLLECTION

In 1987, the first individual was convicted of sexual assault with the assistance of deoxyribonucleic acid (DNA) evidence, and in 1991, the Minnesota Bureau of Criminal Apprehension (BCA) Laboratory became the first state crime lab to identify a suspect on the basis of DNA alone. Ledray and Netzel (1997) reported that as a result of this valuable investigative resource, an otherwise unidentified rapist was found and convicted. The acknowledgment of DNA as a valuable investigative tool, as well as the fact that numerous rapists are repeat offenders, led to the development of the FBI's Combined DNA Index System (CODIS). DNA issues are described in greater detail in chapter 14.

Ledray and Netzel (1997) say that DNA evidence should be obtained by collecting any available blood evidence that could be from the assailant on the skin or clothing of the victim. If the survivor reports she scratched the assailant, fingernail scrapings should be collected in hopes of collecting the assailant's blood. DNA can also be obtained by swabbing the involved orifices with a standard-size cotton-tip swab for sperm and seminal fluid. Additionally, when the forensic examiner completes the evidentiary exam, blood evidence should be collected from the survivor for DNA analysis to distinguish her DNA from that of the assailant.

Regarding seminal fluid evidence, Tucker, Ledray, and Stehle-Werner (1990) caution that the absence of positive sperm or seminal fluid findings does not prove there was no recent sexual intercourse. Studies have indicated that 34 percent or more of rapists are sexually dysfunctional (Groth & Burgess, 1977), and as many as 40 percent wear condoms (Larkin & Paolinetti, 1998). Seminal fluid evidence is usually analyzed for sperm, motile or nonmotile, and for prostatic specific acid phosphatase. The enzyme acid phosphatase is present in large quantities in seminal fluid and minimal concentrations in vaginal fluids, so if a high level of acid phosphatase is collected in a sexual assault victim, this would ndicate that recent sexual contact occurred.

When Tucker et al. (1990) examined the results of 1,007 rape survivors, sperm was found in 1 percent of the 369 cases involving oral rape. All of the positive oral specimens were collected within three hours of the rape. Of the 210 cases with rectal involvement, only 2 percent were positive for sperm. These exams were all completed within four hours of the rape. In the 111 skin specimens collected, 19 percent were positive. All but two of the positive specimens were collected within four hours of the rape. Of the 919 vaginal specimens, 37 percent were positive. Of these, 263 were examined within five hours and 317 were examined within 12 hours of the rape. Only seven of the positive specimens were collected more than 20 hours after the rape. In the same study, the acid phosphatase results were better by approximately a factor of 10. Of the oral specimens, 11 percent were positive; 12 percent of the rectal specimens were positive; 43 percent of the skin specimens were positive; and positive responses were obtained in 62 percent of the cases involving vaginal assault.

Roach and Vladutiu (1993) compared prostatic acid phosphatase (PAP) to prostatic specific antigen (PSA) and found, in a sample of 212 women who had consensual sex within four days, that more positive results were obtained with PAP analysis. Although both were positive 59 percent of the time, PAP was positive 84 percent of the time and PSA was positive 60 percent of the time. PAP was negative only 2 percent of the time when PSA was positive, and PSA was negative 25 percent of the time when PAP was positive.

Forensic nurses must be well versed in the correct procedures and techniques for the identification, documentation, collection, and preservation of trace evidence from both the individual presenting in the clinical environment, and from the crime scene, whether it is within or separate from the health care institution. An understanding of trace evidence collection is predicated on Locard's Exchange Principle, which states that whenever two objects come into contact, a transfer of material occurs (Locard, 1930). Trace evidence that is transferred can be used to associate objects, individuals, or locations.

Kathleen Brown, RN, PhD, explains that the goal of any forensic examination within a health care setting is to identify and collect evidence that has transferred from the offender to the victim. Brown (2003) writes, "When a crime involves close contact between the victim and the offender, in such crimes as assault, sexual assault, and physical abuse, evidence transfers to the crime scene and the victim. While law enforcement personnel preserve and collect evidence from the crime scene, health care personnel can preserve and collect it from victims." She explains that evidence must be collected systematically and comprehensively "without inducing psychological or physical harm to the victim," and adds, "The system for evidence collection and preservation involves a careful search of the entire body, requiring careful identification and retention of all evidence from the victim."

Brown continues, "Health care personnel can play an important role in assisting in the investigation of crime, while providing health care to the victim. However, the forensic work of collecting and preserving evidence should never compromise the safety of a patient, the first priority. And members of the health care community should be able to handle forensic evidence without compromising health care."

The integrity and significance of trace material as associative evidence relies on proper detection, collection, and preservation, and an understanding of the transfer and persistence of trace evidence will assist the examiner in interpreting the significance of the analytical results. The U.S. Department of Justice and the FBI, through its *Trace Evidence Recovery Guidelines*, presents cogent instructions for health care providers when it comes to the collection of pertinent forensic evidence.

5.5.1 Documentation of Evidence

When a case is initiated, a specific file for that case must be created to contain the case documentation for the length of time required by the prevailing laws and nonconflicting agency policy. Documentation of questioned and known trace evidence collection must include permanent notes about the following:

- The date (and time, when appropriate) of the collection
- The name of the person collecting the evidence
- A descriptive listing of items collected
- A unique identifier for each item collected, such as an item number and case number
- The location of each item (documented by notes, sketches, measurements, photographs, or a combination of these)

The chain of custody for each item must be initiated at collection and maintained until final disposition. Recommended procedures for documenting and labeling physical evidence are outlined in ASTM Standard E 1459-92, Standard Guide for Physical Evidence Labeling and Related Documentation (9.2), and Standard E 1492-92, Standard Practice for Receiving, Documenting, Storing, and Retrieving Evidence in a Forensic Science Laboratory.

Ledray (1999) says that many experts caution against the forensic examiner collecting detailed investigative information, and suggest that the SANE should ask only for information necessary to collect the proper medical evidence, deal with the immediate physical and psychological needs of the survivor, and collect and interpret the physical and laboratory findings. The SANE should remember that he or she is conducting a medical forensic interview that centers on the survivor and not other assault details or investigative information, such as the height or weight of the assailant. The defense attorney might use details reported by the nurse, which differ from the police report, to show discrepancies in the survivor's story. The only necessary documentation is that needed to guide the exam and treat the survivor (Ledray, 1999; Slaughter, 1992).

Basic documentation should include the following:

- Site and time of assault
- Nature of physical contacts
- Race and number of assailants
- Relationship to assailants
- Weapons and restraints used
- Actual and attempted penetration of which orifice by penis, objects, or fingers
- Ejaculation, if known, and where
- Use of condom
- Activities of the victim that might have destroyed evidence, such as bathing, douching, or bowel movement
- Consensual sex within the last 72 hours and with whom
- Use of tampon
- Change of clothes
- Contraceptive use
- Current pregnancy
- Allergies
- Victim's general appearance and response during exam
- Physical injuries

Ledray adds that it is important to remember that in addition to the assault exam report, the entire chart is a part of the legal record and can be submitted as evidence if the case goes to court. All statements, procedures, and actions must be accurately, completely, and legibly recorded (Blair & Warner, 1992). It is important to accurately and completely document the emotional state of the survivor and quote important statements made by the survivor, such as threats made by the assailant (Ledray, 1999; Sheridan, 1993). When appropriate, qualifying statements such as, "patient states..." or "patient reports..." should be used. If the exam findings match the history given by the survivor, the examiner should also document "there is congruence between the victim's story and her injuries" (Sheridan, 1993). Sheridan also states that the term "alleged sexual assault" should never be used in documentation of a sexual assault, as the term has negative connotations and might be interpreted by judges and juries as indicating the victim exaggerated or lied.

5.5.2 Contamination and Loss

When collecting or examining items, care must be taken to prevent contamination and loss of trace materials. Unless circumstances dictate otherwise, the trace evidence should be collected and preserved prior to other examinations. General principles and practices to avoid evidence contamination and loss include the following:

- Contact between items and personnel before the appropriate trace evidence has been secured should be restricted.
- Appropriate protective apparel, such as laboratory coats and disposable gloves, must be worn to prevent contamination from the examiner's clothing. The apparel must be changed as necessary to avoid contamination or transfer between evidentiary items, locations, and personnel.
- Items being collected for trace evidence examination must be handled as little as possible to minimize loss of the trace evidence and to limit exposure of the items to contaminants.
- Collect, package, and seal items individually in appropriate packaging. Keep items in a secure, sealed package until the item is processed in a controlled environment.
- Equipment and work surfaces used during collection and examination must be cleaned in an appropriate manner before processing begins and as often as necessary during processing to prevent contamination.
- Adhesive-lift materials (used for collection, storage, or both) must be maintained in a manner to avoid contamination. Caution should be used to prevent tape edges from contacting any unclean surfaces.
- Evidence examination areas should have adequate lighting, easily cleaned surfaces, and a physical environment designed to restrict excessive air currents, static electricity, and general foot traffic.
- The examination of questioned and known items for trace evidence must be conducted separately in different locations, at different times, or both, to prevent contamination. It is recommended that questioned items with the most probative value be examined first.
- Any contact, condition, or situation that could cause contamination or otherwise compromise the trace evidence examination must be documented and communicated between the laboratory analyst or analysts and the submitter.

Ledray (1999) says that although it is suggested that specimens be refrigerated for long-term storage to prevent deterioration, it is essential that the evidence be kept in an area at less than 75 degrees Fahrenheit and the blood evidence not be frozen, meaning that storage in an air-conditioned room is sufficient for the short term.

5.5.3 Detection, Collection, and Preservation Techniques

When selecting detection, collection, and preservation methods and the processing sequence, consider the circumstances of the case, ambient conditions, the discriminatory power of the different techniques, and the need to preserve or collect other types of evidence. Record the techniques used for detection, collection, and preservation of the evidentiary items and the location from which they are removed. Methods used for detecting trace evidence include but are not limited to general visual searches; visual searches assisted by different types of illumination, such as oblique lighting and alternate light sources (ultraviolet, laser, high intensity); and visual searches assisted by magnification.

Trace evidence recovery or collection techniques used should be the most direct and least intrusive techniques practical. Collection techniques include picking, lifting, scraping, vacuum sweeping, combing, and clipping:

- *Picking:* Trace evidence can be separated from an item by using clean forceps or other implements. The collected samples should be immediately protected against loss or contamination.
- *Lifting:* An adhesive-bearing substrate such as tape is repeatedly and firmly patted or rolled over the item, causing loosely adhering trace evidence to stick to the tape. Do not overload the tape. The collected lifts are typically placed on a transparent backing (e.g., clear plastic sheeting, glass slides, and clear plastic or glass petri dishes). This protects against contamination and permits samples to be easily viewed and removed for further comparison.
- *Scraping:* A clean spatula or similar tool is used to dislodge trace evidence from an item onto a collection surface such as clean paper. The collected debris is immediately packaged in a manner to avoid sample loss. This technique is most often conducted within the laboratory in a controlled environment that reduces the risk of contamination or loss of the trace evidence.
- *Vacuum sweeping:* A vacuum cleaner equipped with a filter trap is used to recover trace evidence from an item or area. The filter and its contents should be immediately packaged to avoid sample loss. The appropriate vacuum parts, filter, and trap must be changed and rigorously cleaned between each vacuuming to avoid contamination. Consider using this method subsequent to other collection techniques as it is indiscriminate and might result in the collection of a large amount of extraneous material.
- *Combing:* A clean comb or brush is used to recover trace evidence from the hair of an individual. The combing device and collected debris from the hair should be packaged together.
- *Clipping:* Trace evidence can be recovered from fingernails by nail clipping, scraping, or both. Fingernails can be clipped with clean scissors or clippers and packaged in clean paper. Fingernails can be scraped with a clean implement to collect debris from underneath them. Package the collected debris and the scraping device as one unit, typically in clean paper. Commonly, fingernails from the right and left hands are packaged separately. This does not preclude the collection of each or any nail separately from all others, such as a nail with obvious damage.

Appropriate preservation and packaging of trace evidence and items to be examined for trace evidence will vary. Appropriate packaging must prevent loss or contamination of the trace evidence. All evidence packages must be properly sealed to prevent tampering and eliminate loss or contamination of the trace evidence through open edges. Small or loose trace evidence must be secured in clean, unused primary containers such as paper packets or petri dishes. The primary container should then be appropriately secured in an envelope or paper bag. Large items, such as whole garments, should be sealed individually in clean, unused packaging.

Clothing and other items that are wet must be air dried as soon as possible, without exposure to heat or sunlight, in a secured area in a manner that will prevent loss or contamination of trace evidence. An arrangement to collect any trace evidence that might fall from the item during drying should be used. Small or manageable items at a crime scene that bear visible, firmly attached trace evidence should be documented, packaged intact, and transported to the laboratory for examination. Items at a crime scene that bear visible but easily lost trace evidence, or items that are impractical to transport should be documented and the trace evidence collected by an appropriate technique.

5.5.4 Site and Special Collection Considerations

Individuals responsible for the detection and collection of trace evidence should be aware of the applicable laws governing search warrants, searches, and seizures within their jurisdiction. They should be aware that various types of evidence will be present during the processing of a crime scene or the examination of items submitted to the laboratory. Some types of evidence other than trace evidence might be more significant to a particular case and therefore should be given higher priority. Representative known samples of an item, sufficient to represent all variations that could be present within that item, should be collected for comparison with the questioned trace evidence. The areas from which these samples are collected must be documented.

Patterned marks or impressions might be encountered and might require additional documentation and collection procedures such as 1:1 scale photography. Enhancement techniques such as oblique lighting or powder dusting and preservation techniques such as adhesive lifting or casting should be considered. The possibility of physically matching a fractured, broken, torn, or cut portion of an object to its source should always be considered. The entire questioned item and possible source item should be collected, protecting the edges from further deformation. When the possibility of a physical match exists, one should not overlook the necessity of maintaining all items separately to prevent contamination.

5.5.5 Evidence Security

Trace evidence must remain in secure, controlled-access areas, protected from loss, damage, or contamination. It must have a documented and continuous chain of custody from the time of collection until the time the evidence is admitted into court or the case has been disposed and the evidence is no longer needed. The security and integrity of evidence is the responsibility of all persons who might identify, collect, package, store, transport, or examine evidentiary items.

Ledray (1993) says that maintaining a proper chain of evidence is as important as collecting the proper evidence. She writes, "Without this complete documentation, with signatures, of chain-of-custody from the individual who collected the evidence to the courtroom, the evidence will be inadmissible." Ledray adds that it is not necessary, nor is it appropriate, for the police officer to be in the exam room when the evidence is collected to maintain a proper chain of evidence. The police officer can leave the area and the forensic nurse can call him or her when the exam is completed to return and pick up the evidence. Both signatures on the chain-of-evidence document are all that is necessary.

When the police cannot immediately return, the SANE can place the evidence in a locked storage area, preferably a refrigerator with limited access, and when the police do return, any available nurse can sign.

5.5.6 Training Requirements for Trace Evidence Collection Personnel

The responsibility of trace evidence collection can be assigned to personnel of varying occupations and levels of expertise, such as crime scene technicians, law enforcement personnel, and medical personnel. These personnel must be trained in trace evidence detection, collection, and preservation techniques. Training should include but not be limited to the recordkeeping protocol of the agency; crime scene search techniques; rules of evidence handling; safety concerns of evidence handling and detection techniques; legal aspects of search warrants, seizures, and evidence recovery; chain-of-custody requirements; storage of physical evidence; the detection, collection, and preservation methods used for trace evidence; contamination prevention; and the significance of trace evidence analysis results.

5.5.7 Special Considerations in the Health Care Setting

Kathleen Brown advocates strict adherence to best practices for evidence collection and preservation in the health care setting. One of the more frequently encountered pieces of physical evidence in the ER or the OR is a bullet, and great care should be taken to handle it as little as possible. She explains that metal forceps can damage the exterior of a bullet, making it more difficult for ballistics experts to match the bullet to a particular firearm. She says that the teeth of the forceps should be covered with a plastic shield if they are used to recover a bullet; once removed, the bullet should be wrapped in gauze and placed in an envelope. Documentation of the removal of a bullet should include what it is, the patient from whom it was removed, and who removed it, as well as date and time. The bullet should be turned over to the police.

Brown (2003) adds that health care providers should bear the following in mind when observing and documenting violence-related wounds:

- Health care personnel should not take it on themselves to determine whether a wound is an entrance or an exit gunshot wound, unless the victim is able to describe entry versus exit. Brown writes, "If health care personnel determine entrance versus exit incorrectly, a discrepancy will appear when the expert is consulted. Conflicting reports can mislead investigators."
- Health care personnel should observe wounds for gunshot powder residue, which will be deposited on the patient's skin and clothing if the victim was shot at a close range (less than three feet). Photographs of the wound with surrounding gunpowder should be taken before removal of the gunpowder. Following photodocumentation, the powder residue should be removed by scraping some of it onto a piece of paper and placing the paper into an envelope. Brown writes, "In cases of suicide, gunshot powder will be found on the victim's hands. If

suicide is suspected, the victim's hands should be covered in paper bags until an expert examines them."

- Health care providers should never use stab wounds for treatment access, such as for the insertion of tubes or catheters; new insertion sites should be chosen. The victim's stab wounds should be photographed before medical intervention whenever possible.
- Clothing worn by a victim during the commission of a crime can hold important clues, including bullet holes, stab holes, rips, and tears, and should be collected by a gloved examiner and placed into clean paper bags. Each item of clothing should be placed in a separate paper bag to prevent transfer of evidence. Each bag should be sealed with evidence tape, labeled with the item of clothing, the victim's name, the collector's name, and the time and date of collection. If clothing worn during the crime must be cut for removal, cutting should avoid altering any evidence, such as rips, tears, cuts, and holes that resulted from the assault. Brown writes:

> If clothing worn during the crime has been removed before the patient arrived at the health care setting, it should be retrieved and placed in paper bags by law enforcement personnel, who will deliver it to the police crime laboratory for analysis. In medical emergencies the clothing is often forgotten and discarded. Investigators of crime would appreciate health care personnel tossing the clothing aside, at the very least, rather than losing it to the trash in the ED.

Brown explains that there are three kinds of forensic evidence that can be collected in the health care setting: evidence identifying the perpetrator, evidence indicating if force was involved, and evidence placing the victim at the crime scene.

Brown writes, "Evidence should be collected whenever possible before it is disturbed by medical intervention or cleaning. 'Cleaning up' the victim removes valuable evidence and should occur after evidence collection, if at all possible." Brown adds, "For forensic examiners, the skin is the most important organ of the body." She advocates meticulous examination of the victim's skin for any transfer of evidence from the perpetrator, including saliva, semen, or other body fluids. Forensic examiners should collect any random hair, fibers, or debris, and place it into a druggist's paper and then into a clean envelope. Each envelope must be labeled with the victim's name, the examiner's name, and the date and time of collection, as well as its contents and from where on the victim's body the evidence came. Brown says health care providers should maintain custody of the evidence at all times until it is turned over to law enforcement.

5.5.8 The Importance of Evidence Collection

Ledray, Faugno, and Speck (2001) write, "It has been only in recent years that our health care facilities have begun to recognize their responsibility to have trained staff available to provide this specialized service for victims of sexual assault. Treating injuries alone is not sufficient."

A New York hospital learned the importance of chain of custody issues the hard way. According to Ledray et al.:

> In 2000, Coney Island Hospital was fined $46,000 by state regulators after a rape victim came to the medical facility and a sexual assault evidentiary examination was not accurately performed. She was made to wait three hours before being examined and then potentially significant evidence, including her underwear and vaginal swabs, was lost. The Department of Health investigation also found that the hospital did not provide her with medication to prevent pregnancy and they failed to provide complete care. The authorities believed that had correct evidence collection and chain-of-custody occurred, the evidence may have been useful to secure a conviction against the serial sex offender charged with her rape. As a result New York passed the Sexual Assault Reform Act requiring New York State medical facilities to develop specialized sexual assault examiner evidence collection programs in 2001.

In 2000, *New York Times* writer C. J. Chivers described it as a "game of chance" that exists in most U.S. hospitals when facilities don't have the proper forensic protocols or specially trained medical staff to respond to sexual assault cases. Chivers compared two sex crime cases to illustrate the differences competency can make in the judicial process. In one case, a woman's attackers were convicted of aggravated sexual abuse and are serving long prison sentences. In another case, the one described by Ledray et al., the assailant, a serial sex offender, secured a lenient plea bargain for attempted assault and was eligible for a parole hearing.

Chivers wrote, "The drastically different outcomes of these similar cases were the result of what prosecutors, physicians and victims' advocates describe as a game of chance inside emergency rooms at New York City Hospitals. The first woman received a thorough examination that documented evidence of the attack. The second woman did not." Chivers pointed out that years after health care facilities were afforded a forensic protocol, the level of competence in administering evidentiary exams varied widely. "This uneven quality of care, experts say, can mean an uneven quality of evidence with which to prosecute some of society's most malevolent criminals."

In the first sexual assault case, the victim was met by a physician sexual assault examiner, who performed the evidentiary exam, including use of a Wood's Lamp to identify minute amounts of DNA that can be collected, and to document vaginal injury through use of a colposcope. Using the colposcope, the examiner was able to locate and photograph genital abrasions that were consistent with sexual assault and that could support a prosecutor's charge. Chivers reported that a according to a law enforcement authority, one of the defendants—who had denied all charges—was presented with the contents of the medical file; when confronted with the evidence of injury, he pleaded guilty to the maximum charge and accepted a 15-year prison sentence. Ledray et al. report that one study conducted in the Midwest showed that prosecutors introduced 48 percent more evidence in cases in which victims were treated in examiner-based programs.

REFERENCES

American Society for Testing and Materials (ASTM). ASTM E 1492-92: Standard Practice for Receiving, Documenting, Storing, and Retrieving Evidence in a Forensic Science Laboratory. West Conshohocken, PA: ASTM.

Blair, T., & Warner, C. Sexual assault. *Top Emerg Med. 14,* 4, 58–77, 1992.

Brown, K. Evidence collection and preservation in a health care setting. Available at: www.nursingspectrum.com. 2003.

Chivers, C. J. In sex crimes, evidence depends on game of chance in hospitals. *New York Times.* August 6, 2000.

Groth, A., & Burgess, A. W. Sexual dysfunction during rape. *New Engl J Med. 297,* 764–766, 1977.

Isaac, N. E., & Enos, P. Medical records as legal evidence of domestic violence (pp. 1–76). Washington, DC: U.S. Department of Justice. 1997.

Larkin, H., & Paolinetti, L. Pattern of anal/rectal injury in sexual assault victims who complain of rectal penetration. IAFN Sixth Annual Scientific Assembly. Pittsburgh, PA. October 1 5, 1998.

Ledray, L. E. The sexual assault examination: Overview and lessons learned in one program. *J Emerg Nurs. 18,* 3, 223–232, 1992a.

Ledray, L. E. The sexual assault nurse clinician: Minneapolis' 15 years experience. *J Emerg Nurs. 18,* 3, 217–221, 1992b.

Ledray, L. E. Sexual assault nurse clinician: An emerging area of nursing expertise. In L. C. Andrist, Ed., *Clinical Issues in Perinatal and Women's Health Nursing.* Philadelphia: J.B. Lippincott. 1993.

Ledray, L. E. Sexual assault: Clinical issues: Date rape drug alert. *J Emerg Nurs. 17,* 1, 1–2, 1999.

Ledray, L. E. Evidence collection and care of the sexual assault survivor: The SANE-SART response. Violence Against Women Online Resources. August 2001.

Ledray, L. E., Faugno, D., & Speck, P. Sexual assault: Clinical issues. SANE: Advocate, forensic technician, nurse? *J Emerg Nurs. 27,* 1, 91–93, 2001.

Ledray, L. E., & Netzel, L. Forensic nursing: DNA evidence collection. *J Emerg Nurs. 23,* 2, 182–186, 1997.

Locard, E. The analysis of dust traces. Part I. *Am J Police Science. 1,* 276–298, 1930.

Pasqualone, G. A. Forensic RNs as photographers: Documentation in the ED. *J Psychoso Nurs. 34,* 10, 1996.

Roach, B. A., & Vladutiu, A. O. Letter to the editor: Prostatic specific antigen and prostatic acid phosphatase measured by radioimmunoassay in vaginal washings from cases of suspected sexual assault. *Clinica Chimica Acta. 216,* 199–201, 1993.

Sheridan, D. J. The role of the battered woman specialist. *J Psychoso Nurs. 31,* 11, 1993.

Slaughter, L., & Brown, C. R. Colposcopy to establish physical findings in rape victims. *Am J Obstet Gynecol.* Jan;166, 83–86 1992.

Tucker, S., Ledray, L. E., & Stehle-Werner, J. Sexual assault evidence collection. *Wisconsin Med J. 89,* 407–411, 1990.

U.S. Department of Justice, Federal Bureau of Investigations. Trace Evidence Recovery Guidelines. *Forensic Science Communications. 1,* 3, 1999.

RECOMMENDED READINGS

De Forest, P. R., Gaensslen, R. E., & Lee, H. C. *Forensic Science: An Introduction to Criminalistics.* New York: McGraw-Hill. 1983.

Federal Bureau of Investigation. *Handbook of Forensic Science.* Washington, DC: Government Printing Office. 1994.

Fisher, B. A. J., Svensson, A., & Wendel, O. *Techniques of Crime Scene Investigation* (Fourth Edition). New York: Elsevier. 1987.

Moreau, D. M. *Physical Evidence in Sexual Assault Cases.* New York: Elsevier. 1987.

Moreau, D. M., & Allen, S. P. *Forensic Techniques Used to Search Persons for Physical Evidence in Crimes of Violence.* Washington, DC: Federal Bureau of Investigation, Forensic Science Training Unit. 1989.

Nelson, D. F., & Revell, B. C. Backward fragmentation from breaking glass. *J Forensic Sci Soc. 7,* 58–61, 1967.

Olshaker, J., Jackson, M., & Smock, W. *Forensic Emergency Medicine.* Philadelphia: Lippincott Williams & Wilkins. 2001.

Pasqualone, G. A. Capturing more than the moment. *Forensic Nurse.* 2002.

Pasqualone, G.A. The role of photography in the emergency room. Polaroid Advocate Instant Evidence e-Newsletter. 2003.

Pearson, E. F., May, R. W., & Dabbs, M. D. G. Glass and paint fragments found in men's outer clothing: Report of a survey. *J Forensic Sci. 16,* 283–300, 1971.

Pounds, C. A. The recovery of fibres from the surface of clothing for forensic examinations. *J Forensic Sci Soc. 17,* 132–140, 1972.

Pounds, C. A., & Smalldon, K. W. The transfer of fibres between clothing materials during simulated contacts and their persistence during wear. Part I: Fibre transference. *J Forensic Sci Soc. 15,* 17–27, 1975.

Pounds, C. A., & Smalldon, K. W. The transfer of fibres between clothing materials during simulated contacts and their persistence during wear. Part II: Fibre persistence. *J Forensic Sci Soc. 15,* 29–37, 1975.

Pounds, C. A., & Smalldon, K. W. The transfer of fibres between clothing materials during simulated contacts and their persistence during wear. Part III: A preliminary investigation of the mechanisms involved. *J Forensic Sci Soc. 15,* 197–207, 1975.

Pounds, C. A., & Smalldon, K. W. The distribution of glass fragments in front of a broken window and the transfer of fragments to individuals standing nearby. *J Forensic Sci Soc. 18,* 197–303, 1978.

Quill, J. L. The transfer theory of hairs applied to the normal work day. In Proceedings of the International Symposium on Forensic Hair Comparisons (pp. 141–142). Washington, DC: Federal Bureau of Investigation. 1985.

Robertson, J., Ed. The forensic examination of fibres—Protocols and approaches: An overview. In *Forensic Examination of Fibres.* New York: Ellis Horwood. 41–98, 1992.

Robertson, J., Kidd, C. B. M., & Parkinson, H. M. P. The persistence of textile fibres transferred during simulated contacts. *J Forensic Sci Soc. 22,* 353–360, 1982.

Robertson, J., & Lloyd, A. K. Observations on redistribution of textile fibres. *J Forensic Sci Soc. 24,* 3–7, 1984.

Saferstein, R., Ed. *Forensic Science Handbook* (Vol. I & II). Englewood Cliffs, NJ: Prentice Hall. 1988.

Saferstein, R. *Criminalistics: An Introduction to Forensic Science* (Seventh Edition). Englewood Cliffs, NJ: Prentice Hall. 2001.

Scott, H. G. The persistence of fibres transferred during contact of automobile carpets and clothing fabrics. *Canadian Soc Forensic Sci J. 18,* 185–199, 1985.

Simon, A. Hair evidence on laundered items. *Crime Laboratory Digest. 13,* 3, 78–81, 1986.

Spitz, W. U. *Spitz and Fisher's Medicolegal Investigation of Death* (Third Edition). Springfield, IL: Charles C Thomas. 1993.

6 Sexual Assault

CONTENTS

Sexual assault is an expansive clinical specialty that overlaps into many other aspects of forensic nursing practice. For the purposes of introduction, this chapter discusses broad principles of sexual violence, and subsequent sections take a closer look at abuse of and violence toward vulnerable populations such as children, the elderly, and the disabled.

6.1 SEXUAL VIOLENCE IS A GLOBAL PROBLEM

Sexual violence is ubiquitous; it occurs in every culture, at all levels of society, and in every country of the world. Data indicate that, in some parts of the world at least, one woman in every five has suffered an attempted or completed rape by an intimate partner during her lifetime (World Health Organization, 2003). Additionally, as many as one third of women worldwide describe their first sexual experience as being forced, not consensual. Although the vast majority of victims are women, men and children of both sexes also experience sexual violence. Sexual violence is a global problem that must be reckoned with by health care providers and members of law enforcement and the legal community.

The World Health Organization (WHO) maintains that at least one woman in five has been physically or sexually abused by a man at some time in her life. Women are more at risk from those they know—husbands, fathers, neighbors, or colleagues—than they are from strangers (WHO, 2003). Globally, gender violence includes sexual harassment, sexual coercion, assault, and rape as well as battering, trafficking, forced prostitution, dowry-related violence, female genital mutilation, sex-selective abortion, and female infanticide. The Declaration on the Elimination of Violence Against Women, adopted by the United Nations General Assembly in 1993, defines violence against women as any act of gender-based violence that results or is likely to result in physical, sexual, or psychological harm or suffering to women, including threats of such acts, coercion, or arbitrary deprivation of liberty, whether occurring in public or private life.

WHO defines sexual violence as "Any sexual act, attempt to obtain a sexual act, unwanted sexual comments, or advances, or acts to traffic a person's sexuality, using coercion, threats of harm or physical force, by any person regardless of their relationship to the victim, in any setting, including but not limited to home and work."

In a 2003 multicountry study undertaken by WHO, women who were able to give information anonymously were almost twice as likely to report having experienced sexual abuse before the age of 15 as women who were interviewed face to face. When women have more than one opportunity to do so, they are more likely to disclose violence. Violence is nearly always underreported by women because they believe it is "normal," they fear that making it public will cause them harm or shame; or they are not ready to talk about it, so levels of violence reported are often minimum levels of actual violence. Often violence does not come to light until it is specifically looked for.

In 48 surveys on intimate partner violence around the world that asked direct questions such as, "Has a current or former partner ever hit you with his fist or with something else that could hurt you?" 10 percent to 69 percent of women reported being hit or physically assaulted by a current or former husband or boyfriend and 3 percent to 52 percent reported such violence in the year preceding the study. Coercive sex in intimate partnerships is more common if women are also physically assaulted. Studies in Mexico and the United States estimate that 40 percent to 52 percent of women experiencing physical violence from an intimate partner have also been sexually abused by that partner. Intimate partner violence can also affect men, but there is a significant gender gap between women and men in terms of quantity of violence and severity of injury, with women much more heavily affected. The dynamics of violence between men and women also differ with studies reporting men seeking to exert dominance, power, or control over women or circumscribe them to particular gender roles, whereas many women who physically abuse husbands have often been abused themselves. Studies of child sexual abuse from 20 countries, including 10 national representative surveys, showed rates of childhood sexual abuse of 7 percent to 36 percent for girls and 3 percent to 29 percent for boys, with most studies reporting rates 1.5 to 3 times higher against girls (WHO, 2003).

Sexual violence has a significant negative impact on the health of the population. The potential reproductive and sexual health consequences are numerous, including unwanted pregnancy, sexually transmitted infections (STIs), human immunodeficiency virus/acquired immunodeficiency syndrome (HIV/AIDS), and increased risk for adoption of risky sexual or health behaviors. The mental health consequences of sexual violence can be just as serious and enduring. Victims of child sexual abuse, for example, are more likely to experience depression, substance abuse, posttraumatic stress disorder (PTSD), and suicide in later life than their nonabused counterparts. Worldwide child sexual abuse is a major cause of PTSD, accounting for an estimated 33 percent of cases in females and 21 percent of cases in males (WHO, 2003).

Even if they fail to disclose the event itself, persons who have experienced sexual violence often seek medical assistance. Leserman (1998) and Campbell (2002) studied the relationships between intimate partner violence, health status, and female use of health care, and found that abused women consume more medical care than nonabused women. Survivors who choose to report the assault to the police are often taken to a health care facility for examination and treatment, particularly if the assailant was a stranger. Irrespective of the circumstances, health care providers who come into contact with victims of sexual violence are pivotal to the recognition of, and response to, individual cases of sexual assault.

Victims of sexual assault require comprehensive, gender-sensitive health services to cope with the physical and mental health consequences of their experience and to aid their recovery from an extremely distressing and traumatic event. The types of services that are needed include emergency contraception, STI testing or prophylaxis, treatment of injuries, and psychosocial counseling. In addition to providing immediate health care, the health care and medical communities can act as an important referral point for other services that the victim might need, such as social welfare and legal aid. Swart (2000) says that health care providers are also prepared to collect and document the evidence necessary for corroborating the circumstances of the assault, and for identifying the perpetrator and the health consequences of the event. Such evidence is often crucial to the prosecution of cases of sexual violence.

In most countries, however, there is a gap between the health care and medico-legal needs of victims of sexual violence and the existing level of services provided in such cases (Acosta, 2002; Chaudhry, 1995; Cohen, de Vos, & Newberger, 1997). For instance, in many countries, victims of sexual violence are not examined by a specially trained medico-legal examiner or health care provider. In some cases, victims are subjected to multiple examinations in surroundings that do not meet minimum health standards. Furthermore, until now, published protocols or guidelines for health care professionals on the medical management of persons who have experienced sexual violence have not been widely available.

6.2 SEXUAL ASSAULT HITS CLOSER TO HOME: THE DOMESTIC PROBLEM

Sexual assault, including rape and attempted rape, is an equally distressing problem in the United States. Estimates of the prevalence of rape and other forms of sexual assault vary from study to study, but even the most narrowly focused estimates provide a sense of the breadth of the problem. In 2000, almost 147,000 persons over age 12, male and female, were victims of rape or attempted rape (U.S. Department of Justice, 2001). In 2002, there were 247,730 victims of rape, attempted rape, or sexual assault. Of these approximately 248,000 victims, about 87,000 were victims of completed rape, 70,000 were victims of attempted rape, and 91,000 were victims of sexual assault (U.S. Department of Justice, 2002). Because of the methodology of the NCVS of the U.S. Department of Justice Bureau of Justice Statistics, these figures do not include victims 12 or younger. Although there are no reliable annual surveys of sexual assaults on children, the Justice Department has estimated that one of six victims are under age 12.

According to the Rape, Abuse & Incest National Network (RAINN), every two minutes, somewhere in America, someone is sexually assaulted; this calculation is based on the 2002 NCVS of the Bureau of Justice Statistics of the U.S. Department of Justice.

One out of every six American women have been the victims of an attempted or completed rape in their lifetime (14.8 percent completed rape, 2.8 percent attempted rape). A total of 17.7 million women have been victims of these crimes, according to the Prevalence, Incidence, and Consequences of Violence Against Women Survey by the National Institute of Justice and Centers for Disease Control and Prevention in 1998. In 2002, seven out of every eight rape victims were female (NCVS, 2002). About 3 percent of American men—a total of 2.78 million men—have experienced an attempted or completed rape in their lifetime. In 2002, one in every eight rape victims were male (NCVS, 2002). About 44 percent of rape victims are under age 18. Three out of every 20 victims (15 percent) are under the age of 12 (U.S. Department of Justice, 1997). Seven percent of girls in grades five to eight and 12 percent of girls in grades nine through 12 said they had been sexually abused. Three percent of boys in grades five through eight and 5 percent of boys in grades nine through 12 said they had been sexually abused. Ninety-three percent of juvenile sexual assault victims knew their attacker; 34.2 percent were family members and 58.7 percent were acquaintances. Only 7 percent of the perpetrators were strangers to the victim (U.S. Department of Justice, 2000).

One of the most startling aspects of sex crimes is how many go unreported. The most common reasons given by victims for not reporting these crimes are the belief that it is a private or personal matter and that they fear reprisal from the assailant. In 2001, only 39 percent of rapes and sexual assaults were reported to law enforcement officials, or about one in every three (NCVS, 2002). Of sexually abused children in grades five through 12, 48 percent of boys and 29 percent of girls had told no one about the abuse, according to the Commonwealth Fund Survey of the Health of Adolescent Girls (1998).

Most rapists aren't masked men in the night, according to statistics. Approximately 66 percent of rape victims know their assailants (NCVS, 2000). Approximately 48 percent of victims are raped by a friend or acquaintance; 30 percent by a stranger; 16 percent by an intimate; 2 percent by another relative; and in 4 percent of cases the relationship is unknown (NCVS, 2000). Sixty-one percent of sexual assaults are not reported to the police. Those rapists, of course, never serve a day in prison (NCVS, 1999). If the rape is reported to police, there is a 50.8 percent chance that an arrest will be made. If an arrest is made, there is an 80 percent chance of prosecution. If there is a prosecution, there is a 58 percent chance of a felony conviction. If there is a felony conviction, there is a 69 percent chance the convict will spend time in jail. So, even in the 39 percent of attacks that are reported to police, there is only a 16.3 percent chance the rapist will end up in prison. Factoring in unreported rapes, about 6 percent of rapists, or one out of 16, will ever spend a day in jail; 15 out of 16 will walk free.

6.2.1 The Challenge of Underreporting

The WHO (2003) states that there is significant underreporting of sexual violence; therefore, published statistics are therefore unlikely to provide an accurate picture of the true scale of the problem. This also creates difficulties when attempting to compare studies. The reasons for nonreporting are complex and multifaceted but typically include fear of retribution or ridicule, and a lack of confidence in investigators, police, and health care professionals. Men are even less likely than women to report being a victim of sexual violence and for this reason information about the extent of sexual violence against males is especially limited. It is also very difficult to establish true incidence rates, and even prevalence estimates, of child sexual abuse, again largely because of underreporting. Child sexual abuse is rarely reported when the abuse occurs, and in many cases is never reported. Most prevalence data come from asking adults about their past experiences. Moreover, many countries lack a reliable reporting system for child sexual abuse.

The situation is compounded by the fact that definitions of child sexual abuse vary among countries, making comparisons difficult. What data are available from studies conducted in different parts of the world suggest that between 7 percent and 36 percent of girls, and between 3 percent and 29 percent of boys have suffered from child sexual abuse. The majority of studies concluded that sexual violence against girls is anywhere from 1.5 to 3 times more widespread than that against boys. Of the reported cases of child sexual abuse, only 10 percent to 15 percent involve boys, a finding that highlights the discrepancy between reporting and occurrence of sexual violence in boys. The trafficking of women and children for prostitution is becoming one of the fastest growing areas of international criminal activity. According to official estimates, somewhere between 1 million and 2 million women and children are trafficked each year worldwide for forced labor, domestic servitude, or sexual exploitation. Generally speaking, women of lower economic status are more susceptible to sexual slavery, trafficking, and sexual harassment (WHO, 2003).

6.3 SEXUAL VIOLENCE: DEFINITIONS, PREVALENCE, AND CHARACTERISTICS

6.3.1 Definitions of Sexual Assault

A challenge for the health care, law enforcement, and legal communities has been to get on the same page when it comes to how certain terms are defined. The terms *rape, sexual assault, sexual abuse,* and *sexual violence* are generally considered synonymous and are often used interchangeably. However, these terms might have very different meanings (and implications) in varying situations and locations. More significantly, legal definitions of specific types of sexual violence might differ from the medical and social definitions, and furthermore, can vary among countries and even within countries. It is important, therefore, that health care professionals are aware of the legal definitions of sexual violence within their own jurisdiction (WHO, 2003).

The word *rape* has been used to define forced or attempted sexual intercourse with a male or female, by an offender that can be of the same sex or a different sex from the victim. *Sexual assault* is usually defined to encompass rape, attempted rape, forced oral and anal sex, penetration with objects, touching of intimate parts, and other types of threats or coercion in which unwanted sexual contact is attempted or occurs between the victim and offender. Studies have attempted to group rape and attempted rape as one of several types of sexual assault. However, the NCVS defines sexual assault as a "wide range of victimizations separate from rape or attempted rape." For legal purposes, rape and sexual assault are defined by each state, and they differ in terms of what specific acts are included or excluded, what the age of consent for sexual intercourse is, and other details that affect the medico-legal process of prosecution, penalties, and sentences.

According to a 2003 report, *Guidelines for Medico-Legal Care for Victims of Sexual Violence*, commissioned by the WHO, sexual violence is defined as, "Any sexual act, attempt to obtain a sexual act, unwanted sexual comments or advances, or acts to traffic women's sexuality, using coercion, threats of harm or physical force, by any person regardless of relationship to the victim, in any setting, including but not limited to home and work" According to this definition, a wide range of behaviors, from rape at gunpoint to sexual coercion under a threat of dismissal (i.e., with false agreement), would be classified as an act of sexual violence. False agreement to sexual activity can be obtained in a variety of ways; for instance, through threats of physical violence, threats of withholding benefits, psychological pressure, or blackmail. Agreement in such circumstances does not amount to freely given consent. The same is true in cases of sexual acts involving individuals who are unable to give consent; that is to say, individuals who are not capable of understanding the significance of the act or of indicating their consent or refusal (e.g., those who are incapacitated due to the effects of alcohol or drugs, or those with a mental disability). Such acts would also be described as nonconsensual (Saltzman, 1999).

6.3.2 Types and Characteristics of Sexual Violence

Sexual violence can take many forms and take place under very different circumstances. A person can be sexually violated by one individual or several people (gang rapes), or the incident might be a planned or a surprise attack. Although sexual violence occurs most commonly in the victim's or perpetrator's home, it also takes place in many other settings.

The perpetrator of a sexual assault might be a date, an acquaintance, a friend, a family member, an intimate partner or former intimate partner, or a complete stranger; more often than not, however, it is someone known to the victim. There is no stereotypical perpetrator; sexually violent men come from all backgrounds: rich and poor, academic and uneducated, religious and nonreligious. Perpetrators could be persons in positions of authority who are respected and trusted, and thus less likely to be suspected of sexual violence.

6.3.3 Typology of Rape

There are many good texts that discuss the typology of rape; for purposes of this work, the various types of sexual offenders are summarized briefly. In "Rape Violence," authors A. Nicholas Groth, Ann Wolbert Burgess, Carol R. Hartman, and Lynda Lytle Holstrom observe that, "The most basic observation one can make regarding rapists is that not all such offenders are alike. They do not do the very same thing in the very same way or for the very same reason." In all cases of rape, however, the researchers found three ever-present components: anger, power, and sexuality. They explain, "The hierarchy and interrelationships among these three factors, together with the relative intensity with which each is experienced and the variety of ways in which each is expressed, may vary from one offense to another." They add that there is sufficient clustering so that distinguishable patterns of rape become evident: the anger rape, in which sexuality becomes a hostile act; the power rape, in which sexuality becomes an expression of conquest; and the sadistic rape, in which anger and control become eroticized.

Groth et al. write, "In every act of rape, then, both aggression and sexuality are involved; but it is clear, however, that sexuality becomes the means of expressing other, nonsexual needs and feelings which operate in the offender and motivate his assault. Rather than being primarily an expression of sexual desire, rape is, in fact, the use of sexuality to express issues of power and anger." They say that rape is a sexual act having more to do with status, aggression, control, and dominance than with sexual pleasure and satisfaction. "It is sexual behavior in the service of nonsexual needs and, in this sense, rape is clearly a distortion of human sexuality."

In cases of anger rape, the researchers explain, "sexuality becomes a means of expressing and discharging feelings of intense anger, rage, contempt, hatred, and frustration; the assault is characterized by excessive brutality." They say that the assault is one of "explosive physical violence to all parts of the victim's body. This type of offender approaches his victim by striking and beating her. He tears her clothes, knocks her to the ground, uses abusive and profane language, rapes her, and frequently makes her perform or submit to additional degrading acts." The offender in this kind of rape appears to be more impulsive than premeditated, and a precipitating stressor—such as a significant woman in the offender's life—might set him off. "The conflict he experiences in this relationship reaches a crisis level and then becomes activated by some upsetting altercation or frustrating interaction with this individual. The resulting fury is released and discharged in a sexual assault against a victim who may be, but more frequently is not, the actual person towards whom the offender harbors such feelings." The researchers add, "Sex becomes a weapon, and rape is the means by which he can use this weapon to hurt and degrade his victim. His intent is to hurt his victim, and his assault is brutal and violent. His motive is revenge and punishment. In extreme cases, this may result in homicide."

In cases of power rape, Groth et al. say, the offender typically uses only whatever force is necessary to overpower his victim. The evidence of such power and control is that the victim submits to sexual demands on the part of the offender. "The offender controls his victim through verbal threats, intimidation with a weapon, or physical force, and this provides the offender with a reassuring sense of power, security, strength, mastery, and control. In this fashion, he compensates for underlying feelings of inadequacy, vulnerability, and helplessness." This kind of offender "shows little skill in negotiating interpersonal relationships and feels inadequate in both sexual and nonsexual areas of his life." The researchers add, "Having few other avenues of personal expression, sexuality becomes the core of his self-image and self-esteem. Rape becomes the means by which he reassures himself of his sexual adequacy and identity, of his strength and potency." For this class of assailant, the offenses become repetitive and compulsive, with a possible escalation in the amount of aggressive force used in the assault. Groth et al. explain, "The power rape may be precipitated by some perceived challenge from a female or threat from a male which activates the offender's feelings of inadequacy and insecurity." To this end, sexual assault is the vehicle through which the offender can express his identity, and demonstrate his potency, mastery, strength, and dominance—all the while denying any feelings of inadequacy, rejection, and vulnerability.

In cases of sadistic rape, the researchers say, aggression is eroticized, and the assailant derives immense satisfaction in the sexual abuse of his victim:

> Sexuality and aggression become intertwined into a single psychological experience: sadism. The assault itself appears ritualistic and usually involves bondage and torture... The rape experience for this type of offender is one of intense and mounting excitement. He finds pleasure in the victim's torment, anguish, distress, and suffering. His assault is deliberate, calculated, and premeditated. The victim is stalked, captured, abused, and in extreme cases, murdered.

Groth et al. assert that all types of rape are motivated by power: controlling the victim (the power rape); hurting the victim (the anger rape); and degrading and destroying the victim (the sadistic rape). "Anger, power, and sexuality are evident in all rapes, but the role each of these components plays and the pattern in which they interface may vary from one offender to another," they write. "Rape is a complex, multidetermined act which, in addition to expressing anger and asserting control, also serves to compensate for feelings of helplessness, to reassure the offender about his sexual adequacy, to assert his identity, to retain status among peers, to defend against sexual anxieties, to achieve sexual gratification, and to discharge frustration."

The researchers point out that the by-products of rape—the victim's etiology—including the life-threatening nature of the assault, the victim's helplessness and loss of control, and being the target of her assailant's rage, might constitute the offender's pathology. They write, "The clinical typology offers one approach to differentiating offenders with regard to identification, disposition, treatment planning, and prognosis."

6.3.4 Deconstructing a Rape Case

It is essential for forensic nurses and examiners to understand the dynamics of a sexual assault case. A sweeping study conducted by Riggs et al. (2000) analyzed 1,076 cases of sexual assault to determine whether rates of sexual assault are increasing, and if demographics and characteristics are changing. The researchers endeavored to describe victim, assailant, assault, and treatment characteristics for sexual assault victims and to provide descriptive data on the evidentiary examination.

The researchers collected data on all sexual assault victims presenting to an urban Level 1 trauma center from January 1992 to December 1995 for treatment and evidentiary examination. Data from crime laboratory records were retrospectively reviewed. Presenting after a sexual assault were 1,112 patients; a total of 1,076 (97 percent) patients consented to the medical and evidentiary examination and were enrolled in the study. Age of the patients ranged from 1 to 85 years, with 96 percent (1,036) female and 4 percent (41) male victims.

In 80.1 percent of cases, the assailant acted alone; however, 10.3 percent of cases involved two assailants, and as many as 12 assailants were documented in one case. The number of assailants was greater than 1 in 20 percent (208) of cases, and the assailant was a stranger only 39 percent (409) of the time. Men were significantly (31.5 percent) more likely than women (18.6 percent) to face multiple assailants.

The assault occurred in the victim's home in 20.9 percent of cases, in the assailant's home in 20.8 percent of cases, and in automobiles in 14.6 percent of cases. The assailant was someone the victim knew or had an established relationship with in 37.8 percent of cases. The assailant was a first-time acquaintance in 23.6 percent of cases, and a stranger in 38.7 percent of cases.

Physical force was used in 80 percent (817) of reported assaults, and in 27 percent (275) of cases a weapon was present. Vaginal intercourse was involved in 83 percent (851) of female victims. Oral assault was involved in 25 percent (271) of all cases, and anal penetration was involved in 17 percent (178) of all cases. Overall, general body trauma was seen 67 percent (621) of the time, and genital trauma occurred in 53 percent (388) of cases. Twenty percent (147) of patients had no trauma noted on examination. Sperm were noted on the ED wet mount in 13 percent (93) of the victims, and of the 612 cases with both ED sperm data and crime laboratory semen data available, evidence of sperm and semen were found 48 percent (296) of the time by either. Sixty percent of all women received treatment to prevent pregnancy, and 88 percent of all victims agreed to take prophylaxis for sexually transmitted disease (STDs). Of the 12 percent who opted not to receive prophylaxis, most were likely to have been assaulted by a known assailant.

The researchers concluded, therefore, that health care professionals should be aware that general body trauma is common, that the assailant is often someone known to the victim, and that evidence of semen is commonly found by the crime laboratory even when it is not found in the ED analysis of a wet mount. (A more detailed discussion of patterns of genital injury in sexual assault victims can be found later in this chapter.)

A number of other characteristics of rape cases have been documented in the medical literature. Grossin et al. (2003) endeavored to describe the victim, the assailant, assault characteristics for sexual assault victims according to the time between the last sexual assault and the examination, and to provide descriptive data on medico-legal findings. Their study was based on 418 examined victims of sexual assault during the year 1998. Victims were referred from investigating police authorities. All examinations were performed with the use of colposcopy by physicians with special training in forensic medicine. Two groups of victims were defined: a first group of victims examined in the ED within 72 hours after the last sexual assault, and a second group of victims examined after 72 hours. About 86 percent of the cases were female victims. The average age of the cases of the first group was 22.4 years. Conversely, 76 percent of the victims examined after 72 hours were under the age of 15 years. Vulnerability was present in 31 percent of the cases examined in the ED, including disabled and pregnant victims. Sexual assault happened once in 87 percent of the cases of the first group and in 64 percent of the cases of the second group. The victim's home was the most frequent place of sexual assault (35 percent of the cases of the first group and 56 percent of the cases of the second group). The assailant was a stranger in 51 percent of the cases of the first group. In the second group of the victims, the assailant was a family member in 58 percent of the cases (the father in 30 percent of the cases). There was a single assailant in the majority of the cases for the two groups. Threats were used by the assailant on 66 percent of the victims examined in emergency and 33 percent of the cases of the second group.

Grossin et al. (2003) reported that the type of sexual assault was penetration in the majority of the cases for both groups. Vaginal, oral, and anal penetration were involved in 55 percent, 23 percent, and 13 percent, respectively, of the cases of the first group. General body trauma was found in 39.1 percent of the cases examined in the ED and in 6.3 percent of the cases of the second group. Genital trauma occurred in 35.7 percent of the cases in the first group and in 19.5 percent of the cases in the second group. Hymenal, vulvo-vaginal, and anal lesions were found in 11 percent, 20 percent, and 7 percent of the cases, respectively, examined in the ED. Toxicological analysis was performed in 14.3 percent of the cases examined in the ED. In 47 percent of the tested cases, a drug was detected. Cytology was performed in 61.5 percent of the cases examined in the ED. Detection of spermatozoa occurred in 30.3 percent of these cases.

Feldhaus, Houry, and Kaminsky (2000) acknowledged various studies suggesting significant rates of female sexual assault; the majority of them remain unreported, and few victims receive medical care. Feldhaus et al. undertook a study to determine lifetime prevalence rates of sexual assault in an ED population and to assess reporting patterns to police, physicians, and social service agencies. A verbally administered survey was given to all female patients during four-hour randomized periods in an urban Level 1 trauma center. Four hundred forty-two women were eligible; 360 (81 percent) of them agreed to participate. The lifetime prevalence rate of sexual assault was 39 percent. Ninety-seven women (70 percent) were older than 15 years at the time of the assault. Of these, 97 assaults occurred in adulthood; 49 (52 percent) reported assault by an acquaintance, family member, or friend; 28 (30 percent) by a stranger; and 17 (18 percent) by a partner. Forty-five (46 percent) women reported the crime to the police, 42 (43 percent) sought medical care, and 23 (25 percent) contacted a social service agency. Reporting patterns for victims assaulted by a stranger versus those assaulted by a partner were: reported to police, 79 percent versus 18 percent; received medical care, 70 percent versus 29 percent; and contacted a social service agency, 30 percent versus 24 percent. The researchers concluded that lifetime female sexual assault rates in ED populations are significant. Fewer than half of victims report the assault to the police or seek medical care. Women assaulted by a partner are significantly less likely to report the sexual assault to police or seek medical care.

Walch and Broadhead (1992) assert that state and federal statistics have described a lower incidence of rape and child abuse than is suggested by community prevalence rates. Victims of sexual assault can experience numerous short-term and long-term effects on psychosocial and physical health. They add that these victims tend to use medical services more than nonvictims and are also more likely to seek medical care than mental health services. Their study sought to determine the prevalence of sexual victimization in a family practice setting. Of 416 women, 405 agreed to participate. Of 147 family-practice patients, 47.6 percent reported some type of contact sexual victimization during their lifetimes; 25.2 percent reported rape or attempted rape. Of 258 student health service patients, 57 percent had experienced contact sexual victimization, and 28.7 percent reported rape or attempted rape. Of those who reported unwanted sexual contact, 30 percent of the family practice patients felt they would not be comfortable discussing the experience with medical personnel, and 44.9 percent of the student health service patients would not feel comfortable doing so. The researchers concluded that women with a history of unwanted sexual contact might be common in family practice and student health settings. Although treatment can be beneficial, many of these patients are not comfortable discussing their experiences with medical personnel. The authors say that their findings suggest that there is potential benefit in obtaining a sexual victimization history as part of routine care, but further research is necessary to assess the clinical benefit of such an approach.

6.4 HEALTH-RELATED CONSEQUENCES OF SEXUAL VIOLENCE

Regardless of the type or prevalence of sexual violence, health care providers should be aware of the numerous health-related consequences. The medical literature has thoroughly documented the myriad health consequences of sexual violence, including short- and long-term physical and psychological effects. Resnick (1997) characterizes the following sequelae of sexual violence:

1. Physical injuries can lead to chronic sequelae, such as heart attack, stroke, syncope, fractures from falling, dislocated joints, torn muscle tissue, or a loss of dexterity. Acute health problems, such as STDs, can also develop into chronic infection, dysfunction, or systemic disorders.
2. Assault-related generalized stress can impair functioning of the immune, endocrine, or autonomic systems, increasing the likelihood of the victim's contracting infectious diseases.
3. Either assault-related stress or assault-related emotional problems might increase the risk of engagement in unhealthy behaviors, such as smoking, excessive alcohol or drug use, poor diet, lack of sleep, or insufficient physical exercise. These behaviors could contribute to future health problems or immune system disorders and might lead to chronic mental health problems.
4. Assault-related inappropriate health care utilization places victims at higher risk of needing additional restorative treatment.

6.4.1 Physical Impacts

Individuals who have experienced sexual assault can suffer a range of nongenital and genital injuries. Nongenital injuries can include bruises and contusions; lacerations; ligature marks on ankles, wrists, and neck; anal or rectal trauma; and pattern injuries such as handprints, finger marks, belt marks, and bite marks. Genital injuries are most commonly seen in the posterior fourchette, the labia minora, the hymen, and the fossa navicularis. The most common types of genital injuries include tears, abrasions, bruising, redness, and swelling. Additionally, victims of sexual assault are at increased risk of unwanted pregnancy, STIs, pelvic pain, pelvic inflammatory disease, and urinary tract infections.

Goodman, Koss, and Russo (1993) and Koss and Heslet (1992) studied acute physical injuries following completed rape, including nongenital physical injury as well as vaginal tearing. Geist (1988) found that more than half of the rape victims seen in EDs have vaginal and perineal trauma, and 15 percent have significant vaginal tearing. Goodman et al. (1993) found that approximately 5 percent of reported rapes of women in childbearing years result in pregnancy. Victims are also at risk for any of 15 STDs that reportedly occur in 3 percent to 30 percent of victims of sexual violence. Kilpatrick, Edmonds, and Seymour (1992) found that most victims of sexual violence report that they did not receive standard medical care after their assault. Young, Bracken, and Goddard (1992) found that only half of all sexual assault victims who receive emergency treatment return for a follow-up examination.

6.4.2 Psychological Impacts

Although manifestations of psychological effects vary from individual to individual, the medical literature recognizes these symptoms as being common in sexual assault victims: rape trauma syndrome; PTSD; depression; social phobias; anxiety; increased substance use or abuse; suicidal behavior; and other physical distresses such as chronic headaches, fatigue, sleep disturbances, recurrent nausea, eating disorders, menstrual pain, and sexual difficulties.

6.4.2.1 Rape Trauma Syndrome

Many victims of sexual violence experience rape trauma syndrome (RTS), which is defined as "the stress response pattern of... a person who has experienced sexual violence" (WHO, 2003). RTS can be manifested in somatic, cognitive, psychological and behavioral symptoms, and usually consists of two phases: the acute phase and the long-term phase. The acute phase is a period of disorganization beginning immediately after the rape and persisting for several weeks. During the acute phase, a person usually experiences strong emotional reactions and might present with physical symptoms.

Emotional responses tend to be either expressed or controlled; they can be expressed as anger, fear, or anxiety on one end of the spectrum, or as shock and numbness on the other. The acute reaction is rooted in a fear of physical injury, mutilation, or death, and once the victim comes to terms with the violent event, he or she might experience mood swings, as well as intense feelings of shame, humiliation, degradation, guilt, embarrassment, self-blame, hopelessness, anger, and fear of another attack. The long-term phase is one of reorganization, beginning several weeks after the event, where the victim reorganizes his or her life in an adaptive or maladaptive way. Factors influencing how well a victim recovers include the age of the survivor, specific personality traits, his or her life situation, the circumstances surrounding the sexual assault, and the degree of support he or she receives from loved ones (WHO, 2003).

6.4.2.2 PTSD

Victims of sexual violence frequently experience symptoms of PTSD, which appears to be more common in persons who were threatened with a weapon or extreme physical force, those assaulted by strangers, and in cases where physical injuries were inflicted.

Symptoms of PTSD include the following:

- Reliving the experience through nightmares, flashbacks, and recurrent, intrusive thoughts of the attack
- Self-imposed isolation from family, friends, and peers
- Increased drug or alcohol use
- Engaging in high-risk behaviors
- Avoiding places, activities, or people that remind victims of the assault
- Disassociation from the attack
- Hypervigilance about one's personal safety and security

Studies indicate that the psychopathological sequelae of rape are prevalent and long term. Rothbaum and associates (1992) found that fully 90 percent of rape victims met symptom criteria for PTSD within two weeks of the rape, and about 50 percent continued to meet PTSD criteria three months later. Individuals who evinced relatively severe initial distress were more likely to meet PTSD diagnostic criteria at the three-month point. Kilpatrick et al. (1987) found that PTSD was present 17 years after assault in 16.5 percent of cases.

Resnick et al. (1993) noted that 11 percent of women who were victims of rape at any point in their lives actively met diagnostic criteria for PTSD at the time of assessment, and rape victims were 6.2 times more likely to develop PTSD than were women who had not been raped. Rates of PTSD in women following nonsexual assault are similar to those following rape. Kessler et al. (1995) found that post-sexual-assault rates of PTSD were 48 percent, and that post-physical-assault rates of PTSD were 39 percent. Resnick et al. (1993) found the rates of postrape PTSD to be 32 percent, compared with 38.5 percent following physical assault.

Koss and Heslet (1992) suggest that persistent physiological arousal, as seen in PTSD cases, might lead to actual physical impairments. McFarlane et al. (1994) discovered high rates of cardiovascular, respiratory, musculoskeletal, and neurological symptoms in men with PTSD. Litz, Keane, and Fisher (1992) established an association between persistent arousal and illness in a study of Vietnam veterans. Pitman (1993) also suggested that cue-specific physiological arousal, such as heart rate, is elevated in association with PTSD in response to trauma-related visual images. Resnick (1997) says that long-term follow-up studies with postassault samples of men and women are needed to explore other potential health effects of persistent physiological arousal.

"Post-traumatic stress disorder is very real," asserts Candice DeLong, a former psychiatric nurse and a 20-year veteran agent with the FBI:

> It has been studied extensively by Ann Wolbert Burgess, RN, PhD. She literally wrote the book on it, and is one of the finest researchers in the country. But I wouldn't have had to read her book to know that PTSD exists. Someone breaks into the victim's home and he or she never gets over it. When it comes to PTSD, similar symptoms are manifested whether the individual is a soldier on the battlefield or someone who is at home having dinner with the family and someone comes in and ties everyone up, threatens them, and steals the Picasso painting right off of the wall. The same common denominator among all types of violent crimes is the victim's fear of loss of life as well as a loss of control. You are not in control of your life when someone is threatening you. Then factor in the humiliation of sexual assault or other violent physical contact... people suffer from PTSD who go through a lot less trauma than a rape victim does. There is absolutely no doubt in my mind that it exists and that health care providers must recognize and deal with it.

In one study, Resnick (1997) found that more than half of 29 sexual assault victims who were assessed within hours after the rape reported that they experienced physical reactions of nausea or abdominal distress, rapid heart rate, shortness of breath, shaking, sweating, and choking sensations during the rape. Resnick, Kilpatrick, Dansky, and Freedy (1992) determined that physiological indicators of panic, such as dizziness, chest pain, and shortness of breath, were a major predictor of immediate trauma reactions reported by men and women who had experienced violence. Initial reactions, such as abdominal distress or pain, might become learned conditioned responses to environmental fear triggers, leading to longer term health problems that might include chronic pain syndrome or irritable bowel syndrome (IBS). Leserman (1998) assessed the prevalence of physical and sexual assault histories among 239 female gastroenterology patients and found that 67 percent had a positive history of assault. Irwin et al. (1996) studied 50 patients seeking treatment for IBS who had high rates of PTSD and other psychiatric diagnoses. Falsetti, Lydiard, Gibbs, and Resnick (1997) studied data from 3,911 men and women who were assessed for symptoms of IBS, violence histories, mental health diagnoses, and patterns of using medical services. They discovered that IBS prevalence was 2.8 percent. These findings support the reported presence of gastrointestinal symptoms during acute trauma and as a component of the physiological alarm response.

In addition to IBS, other medical complaints in connection with victimization history have been studied. Walker and Stenchever (1993) reviewed studies of chronic pelvic pain and other physical complaints in association with physical and sexual assault. They concluded that the data supported a stronger association between sexual assault and chronic pelvic pain than between pain and other types of assault. A history of physical assault or a compound history of both sexual and physical assault, however, might be associated with general chronic pain syndromes. Physical pain at the time of sexual or physical assault tends to be associated with the specific locations of later chronic pain.

6.4.3 Harmful Behaviors Triggered by Sexual Assault

Following a violent assault, victims might increase their use of substances to reduce symptoms of fear, anxiety, and depression. Kilpatrick et al. (1987) say that extreme levels of painful affect produced by assault can cause individuals to engage in behaviors that effectively diminish negative emotions, such as escaping by abusing alcohol or drugs.

In addition to its direct causal role in mortality, alcohol appears to play a facilitative role in many more deaths and injuries from accidents or violence. Jurkovich et al. (1992) and Rivara, Jurkovich, and Gurney (1993) reported that almost half of trauma victims presenting to the ED had been using alcohol. Alcohol has been detected in 63 percent of homicide victims, 49 percent of nonintentional injury fatalities, 35 percent of suicides, and 14.4 percent of natural deaths, according to Rutledge and Messick (1992).

Yates, Hadfield, and Peters (1987) reported that 60 percent of victims of violence who presented to an ED had been using alcohol. In a study of 1,770 adult ED patients, Cherpitel (1993) found that individuals with violence-related injuries were more likely to be under the influence of alcohol, to report episodes of heavy drinking, to have experienced significant negative consequences of drinking, and to have received treatment for an alcohol-related problem. Buss, Abdu, and Walker (1995) determined, on the basis of self-report and toxicology screens, that 70 percent of seriously assaulted individuals seeking hospital treatment were under the influence of either drugs or alcohol at the time they were attacked, and 60 percent reported that their assailants were drinking or using drugs.

Breslau et al. (1991) noted that the likelihood of victimization in individuals with alcohol problems was 1.47 times that of individuals without substance use problems; the likelihood of trauma and victimization was 1.79 times as likely for individuals with drug problems. Kessler et al. (1995) found that alcohol and drug abusers were about 1.5 times as likely to experience traumatic events as nonusers. Long-term effects of child abuse have been found to influence increased alcohol and drug use. Miller et al. (1987) discovered that 67 percent of alcoholic women reported having experienced sexual assault during their childhoods, in contrast to 20 percent of nonalcoholic women. Polusny and Follette (1997) found that 27 percent to 37 percent of victimized women reported lifetime alcohol-related problems, compared with only 4 percent to 20 percent of nonabused women. Burnam, Stein, and Olding (1988) observed that twice the proportion of assaulted adults developed alcohol abuse relative to nonvictimized adults.

Victimization also affects rates of drug use. Polusny and Follette (1997) noted that 14 percent to 31 percent of women who were sexually abused as children exhibited drug-related problems later in their lifetimes, compared with 3 percent to 12 percent of controls. In a study of male and female victims, Burnam et al. (1988) observed that 18 percent of assault victims but only 2 percent of matched controls reported drug abuse. Kilpatrick et al. (1997) found that the likelihood of continued drug use two years after an assault nearly doubled in newly assaulted or previously assaulted women, even after controlling for age, race, education, and first-time drug use.

An increased number of eating disorders has been found among both women and men with histories of sexual assault (Laws & Golding, 1996). Dansky (1997) found that the incidence of rape and physical assault was higher in respondents with bulimia nervosa (26.6 percent evinced a history of rape, and 26.8 percent evinced a history of physical assault) compared with respondents without bulimia (13.3 percent with past rape, and 8.5 percent with past assault). In a study of both genders, Laws and Golding (1996) reported that sexual assault victims were about twice as likely as nonassaulted individuals to weigh less than 85 percent of their normal body weight, to have one or more symptoms of anorexia nervosa, and to experience a sudden weight change. Because this was a cross-sectional study, we do not know the sequence of events. The researchers add, however, that repeated sexual victimization and assault by a parent were associated with an increased likelihood of having one or more symptoms of anorexia.

Increased promiscuity and having unprotected sex have been observed among victims of sexual violence. McGinnis and Foege (1993) studied a group of rape victims in a one-year follow-up and discovered that a history of assault and exposure to rape were associated with increased HIV risk behaviors and rates of STDs. In 430 sexually active college women, Harlow et al. (1993) found that victimization by sexual or physical assault was a significant predictor both of the partner's risk characteristics and of unprotected vaginal intercourse. Conversely, Resnick (1997) writes, "Sexual activity often becomes aversive as a result of its association with high autonomic arousal during a rape, and rape victims frequently use drugs or alcohol to cope with conditioned anxiety during sexual activity. This maladaptive coping style may impair an individual's ability to take appropriate precautions to avoid the risk of HIV and may also reduce the likelihood of avoiding truly dangerous situations." Resnick indicated that use of drugs or alcohol during sex was associated with increased rates of unprotected sex.

Elliott, Mock, and Briere (2004) examined the prevalence and impact of adult sexual assault (ASA) in a stratified random sample of the general population. Among 941 participants, ASA was reported by 22 percent of women and 3.8 percent of men. Multivariate risk factors for ASA included a younger age, being female, having been divorced, sexual abuse in childhood, and physical assault in adulthood. Childhood sexual abuse was especially common among sexually assaulted men and women (61 percent and 59 percent, respectively). ASA victims were more symptomatic than their nonassaulted cohorts on all scales of the Trauma Symptom Inventory, despite an average of 14 years having passed since the assault. Assaulted men reported greater symptomatology than assaulted women, whereas nonassaulted men reported less symptomatology than nonassaulted women.

6.5 VICTIMS' UTILIZATION OF MEDICAL SERVICES

Inappropriate or inadequate use of services by victims is an area of concern to some researchers. Resnick (1997) writes, "Misinterpretation of a variety of post-trauma signs of physiological arousal or actual post-trauma physical impairment may also play a significant role."

Golding et al. (1988) assessed the use of mental and physical health services in a community population, looking at the actions of 2,560 individuals who had been screened for a lifetime history of sexual assault. Seventeen percent of women and 9 percent of men reported being victims of sexual violence. The use of mental and medical health services in the preceding six months was significantly greater among the women with a history of sexual assault: 17.8 percent reported using mental health services, and 59.7 percent reported using medical services. The corresponding rates of mental and medical health service use among women in the sample who were not sexually assaulted were 9 percent for mental health services and 44.1 percent for medical services. Conversely, among women in the study who used medical services recently, the rate of histories of sexual assault was 20.8 percent, compared with 12 percent among medical service nonusers. The researchers found that individuals without private insurance increased their use of the services more than those who were insured, so not having medical insurance did not prevent increased usage among those with sexual assault histories. These data indicate that health perceptions and functional impairment lead to higher medical use among victims, regardless of who pays for the services.

Koss, Woodruff, and Koss (1990) and Koss, Koss, and Woodruff (1991) studied 2,291 women in a health maintenance organization (HMO) who completed a mail survey to assess stressful events, physical and sexual assault victimization, and health perceptions; 241 of the female victims also participated in in-person interviews. The researchers discovered that demographic variables, stressful life events, and crime victimization were significant predictors of how one perceived one's health status. Data from clinic records of 68 of the interviewed women with histories of assault, rape, or other crimes that occurred while they were covered by the health plan indicated that 93 percent made at least one physician visit in the year after the reported crime. All made physician visits again in the year following the assault.

Koss and Woodruff (1991) described results of interviews with 390 women who belonged to an HMO. Of the 390, 316 had experienced some type of crime. The women reported nonvictimization, 19 percent; noncontact crime, 13 percent; single incident crimes without rape, 23 percent; completed rape, 24 percent; and multiple assaults, 21 percent. The women with histories of sexual or physical assault reported poorer health overall and poorer health habits. The greatest distress was reported on gynecological symptoms, including sexual dysfunction. Multiply victimized women made 6.9 visits to a physician per year, whereas nonvictimized women averaged 3.5 visits annually.

Kimerling and Calhoun (1994) studied the medical use and health perceptions associated with violence in a study of 115 rape victims and a comparison group of 87 women for a 1-year postrape period. Rape victims reported physical symptoms, including rapid heart rate, tension headaches, stomachaches, skin problems, menstrual symptoms, weight changes, and allergies that decreased over the course of the year. In addition, rape victims displayed significantly elevated psychological distress throughout the year. Despite this diminished symptomatology, the rape victims' use of medical services was significantly greater than that of nonvictims at four months and one year following the assault.

Interestingly, Kiecolt-Glaser and Glaser (1992) discovered that the utilization of mental health services was not different for the victims and nonvictims. Kimerling and Calhoun (1994) theorized that the low rates of use of these services could be the result of misidentifying psychological distress as physical illness. Many of the reported physical symptoms were also symptoms of anxiety and depression.

Victims might also engage in health-related behaviors that could cause them long-term harm. Resnick (1997) states, "Although several studies indicate that assault tends to increase use of health care services, additional data indicate that women with histories of sexual abuse or assault may be less likely to engage in positive health care behaviors, such as obtaining regular Pap smears." Young et al. (1992) found that that almost 40 percent of urban women raped in the past year had at least one STD, compared with 19 percent of women of similar socioeconomic demographics. "This finding," Resnick (1997) says, "is consistent with a relative lack of adaptive medical care available to these women. Thus, lack of resources or avoidance of distress or anxiety may lead to failure to obtain needed preventive medical care." Poor health behaviors in general have been associated with victimization or post-trauma psychological distress, including fatalism, becoming careless about health care, drinking more alcohol, smoking, drug use, and careless eating habits.

6.6 THE HEALTH CARE RESPONSE TO SEXUAL VIOLENCE

6.6.1 Experiences in the ER

Violence has a significant impact on the physical and psychosocial health of millions of Americans every year. Because women are so often the victims of violence, it is essential that women who present to EDs for even minor trauma be thoroughly evaluated. ED staff must be aware of the types of injuries most likely resulting from violence, and the victim must be asked about the cause of the trauma to determine if it is the result of violence and further evaluation is required (Sheridan, 1993). When violence such as rape is identified, trained staff need to be available to provide services. Only in 1992 did the guidelines of the JCAHO first require emergency and ambulatory care facilities to have protocols on rape, sexual molestation, and domestic abuse (Bobak, 1992).

In chapter 1 we examined the concept that the ER is the portal for the majority of cases, both forensic and not. This portal often determines if a forensic case will be handled properly or not. In December 2003, the Texas Association Against Sexual Assault (TAASA) assembled *A Report on the Level of Care for Sexual Assault Patients in Texas Hospital Emergency Rooms*. It paints an engrossing picture of how these victims are dealt with in a state that sees its share of sexual assault and abuse cases annually. Authored by Mimi Garcia, BA, and Torie Hilton, MEd, the TAASA study was conducted to assess the level of care for sexual assault patients in Texas hospital ERs, specifically pertaining to the patient's care in the hospital before, during, and after a forensic medical examination. All hospitals with emergency rooms, including children's hospitals and members of the Catholic Health Association, were asked to participate in a survey that included measures of geographic data; routines for treating sexual assault patients before, during, and after medical examinations; hospital policies and protocols; and training of health care providers. Four hundred twelve surveys were distributed and 107 were returned (a 26 percent response rate). The average number of beds in participant hospitals was 147. Fourteen percent of these hospitals described themselves as public, 26 percent as for-profit, and 60 percent as nonprofit. Additionally, 62 percent of hospitals indicated they were in rural locations and 39 percent in urban locations. Finally, the hospitals see an average of 4.6 sexual assault patients per month.

The TAASA report presented the following results:

Before the Exam. Privacy is extremely important to sexual assault patients, as details of the assault are often embarrassing to discuss. Because of this concern TAASA recommends that a private area be provided for sexual assault patients to discuss the assault with law enforcement and medical professionals. Eighty-two percent of hospitals in this survey indicated a private area was provided, 19 percent only when possible. Because the evidence collected through the exam might be used in a trial, it is important to maintain a proper chain of custody. This is easier when the exam occurs in a dedicated exam room. Seventy-three percent of hospitals indicate these were provided, 21 percent did not provide them, and 6 percent provided them when possible. Texas state law allows a support person, including a rape crisis center advocate, in the exam room for support and comfort if the patient desires. Seventy-six percent of hospitals indicated that they gave the patient the option for contacting a rape crisis center advocate, 7 percent said no, and 16 percent indicated there was no rape crisis center in their area.

Treatment of Sexual Assault Patients. Some communities have developed a system in which one hospital in their area treats sexual assault patients. In this survey, 60 percent of hospitals treat the sexual assault patients and 40 percent stabilize and transfer. STIs, including HIV, are a common concern of rape survivors. It is standard care to provide information about STIs, including HIV, to sexual assault patients. Treatment is dependent on the circumstances of the patient. The study found that 89 percent of hospitals provided information and treatment for STIs, and 70 percent provided this care for HIV. Pregnancy is another common concern. Eighty-four percent of hospitals indicated they provide information on the risks of pregnancy. Emergency contraception can prevent pregnancy if taken within 72 hours after the assault. It is the standard of care to inform and offer female sexual assault patients emergency contraception, yet only 23 percent of Texas ERs met this standard of care. Seventy percent of ERs provide, at a minimum, information, but 13 percent do not inform sexual assault patients of emergency contraception unless the patient asks.

Hospital Policies Regarding the Treatment of Sexual Assault Patients. There should be a minimum level of care for sexual assault patients in Texas ERs. This minimum level can be indicated by the presence of hospital policy or the presence of policies and protocols published by outside entities. Seventy-eight percent of hospitals reported having a specific policy for the treatment of sexual assault patients. Sixty-five percent reported having a copy of the *Texas Evidence Collection Protocol* on file. Thirty-one percent reported having a copy of the ACEP *Guidelines for the Care of Sexual Assault Patients.* Free, confidential services are provided to all rape survivors through the local rape crisis center. Services include hospital accompaniment, individual and group counseling, criminal justice accompaniment, and advocacy. Survivors should be assisted in contacting their local rape crisis center. Seventy-seven percent of hospitals reported referring patients for rape crisis center care, 8 percent did not refer patients, and 15 percent indicated that a rape crisis center is not available.

Training Hospital Staff for the Treatment of Sexual Assault Patients. SANEs are nurses who are specially trained to conduct sexual assault exams sensitively, accurately, and as objectively as possible. The sexual assault exam usually lasts two to three hours and consists of a detailed set of steps in the evidence collection process. Training is highly recommended, as the evidence collected will be scrutinized in a court of law. Thirty-four percent of hospitals reported having a SANE program and 66 percent reported not having the program. Although a SANE program is ideal, many hospitals do not have the program and depend on their regular ER staff to perform the sexual assault exams. Typically speaking, only one fourth of ER physicians and nurses have specific training in the treatment of sexual assault patients, with less than 5 percent of respondents indicating that it is a requirement for employment. Findings also indicate that physician assistants and nurse practitioners seldom receive training on sexual assault examinations.

6.6.2 Physicians as Part of the Equation

Before the advent of the specially trained SANE—a concept that is addressed later in this chapter—physicians in the ER were expected to provide the sexual assault evidentiary examination. Lacking proper training in medico-legal protocols, the examinations these physicians provided were not always up to the standards expected today by and from SANEs. A number of studies point to the varying degrees of success physicians have had in providing medico-legal services to victims.

ED records are an important source of injury surveillance data. However, documentation regarding intentional assault has not been studied and could be suboptimal. Houry, Feldhaus, and Nyquist (1999) analyzed physician documentation of assailant, site, and object used in intentional assault. The researchers reviewed retrospectively the ED log of an urban Level 1 trauma center to identify eligible patients presenting consecutively in November 1996. From the ED log, 1,483 patients were identified as possible study subjects; 1,457 (98 percent) charts were located and reviewed and 971 (67 percent) met inclusion criteria. Of these, 288 (30 percent) cases resulted from intentional assault. In 67 percent of patients, there was no documentation of the identity of the assailant. For 13 percent of cases, there was no documentation regarding the object or force used in the assault. In 79 percent of cases there was no documentation regarding the site of assault. For 24 cases (8 percent), the assailant was documented as an intimate partner or former partner. Police involvement in these cases was documented 54 percent of the time, despite the fact that this state mandates police reports for cases of acute partner violence. Social service involvement and shelter referrals were documented in less than one fourth of domestic violence cases. The researchers concluded that although the ED commonly treats patients who have been assaulted, basic surveillance data are often omitted from the chart. Structured charting might provide more complete data collection.

Du Mont and Parnis (2004) reported on findings from a population-based study of sexual assault physicians who are responsible for both the health care of sexually assaulted persons and for conducting forensic medical examinations on them for the purpose of collecting corroborative evidence to aid in legal proceedings. Self-administered questionnaires were distributed to the 100 physicians attached to sexual assault care and treatment centers across the province of Ontario, Canada. The questionnaires were focussed on exploring their relative commitment to two assessment priorities: the collection of forensic evidence for the courts and the provision of medical care. Although most of the 31 physicians replying expressed satisfaction with their participation in the legal arena, a substantial proportion indicated that although they believed medical care to be the most important part of their work, evidence collection and court appearances were the most time-consuming. In addition, more than four fifths admitted to having deviated from the standard protocol used for evidence collection, based on the belief that a particular procedure or information item might either emotionally or legally harm the victim or her or his case. The researchers write, "We suggest that the implications of these findings point to a possible ambivalence toward the evidentiary dimension of the dual role of the sexual assault physician."

6.6.3 Emergency Physicians Address the Issue of Sexual Violence

In 1999, the ACEP published the 134-page handbook, *Evaluation and Management of the Sexually Assaulted or Sexually Abused Patient.* A quick look at the guidelines' content is prudent, as the handbook appears to embrace the contributions of forensic nurses, or at the very least, the work of SANEs. The handbook addresses clinical considerations including the following:

1. Identification of sexual assault or sexual abuse. Recent sexual assault is usually defined as within 72 hours; however, this interval can be extended, as technology such as DNA analysis advances. Because some drugs can be found in the serum up to 1 week after ingestion, for the patient with drug-facilitated rape, the collection of evidence can be performed up to 96 hours later. If the patient is in the out-of-hospital setting and the sexual assault is recent, the patient should be encouraged to go immediately to the ED, local rape crisis center, or other designated facility suitable for an evidentiary examination to collect physical evidence. The patient should be instructed to not engage in activities that might destroy important evidence that can be used to identify the perpetrator, such as urinating, defecating, vomiting, douching, removing or inserting a tampon, wiping or cleaning the genital area, bathing, showering, gargling, brushing teeth, smoking, eating, drinking, chewing gum, changing clothes, or taking medications. Nonevidentiary examinations might or might not be emergent. Nonemergent cases can be referred to appropriate local resources for collection of appropriate evidence or for follow-up care once the patient's immediate needs are met.
2. Clinical evaluation. The handbook says:

> Policies and procedures for the evaluation and management of the patient with the complaint of sexual assault should be established by all sexual assault evaluation facilities. SANE programs are an excellent option for acute and chronic sexual assault evaluations, because they standardize the sexual assault evaluation and collection of evidence. Special attention and supervision must be provided if resident physicians are involved in sexual assault evaluations to best ensure timely, efficient, and standardized treatment.

The handbook emphasizes that life-threatening injuries must be treated first. Once stabilized, the patient should be placed into a private room as soon as possible. A specially trained individual who can provide crisis intervention, such as a rape crisis advocate, mental health professional, social worker, or pastoral caregiver, should be available for emotional support. If desired by the patient, a friend or relative can be present. Throughout the encounter, privacy, safety, and confidentiality must be ensured.

Ideally, the information in the medical record should be available to outside authorities only with the consent of the patient. However, disclosure of the medical record might be mandated by law in some jurisdictions. In most states, the sexually assaulted patient is not required to report the assault to law enforcement authorities. In contrast, in many states, medical personnel are required by law to report all cases of sexual assault. Most states mandate the reporting of sexual abuse of children to police or to the child protection agency. However, in many jurisdictions, police coordinate and oversee the collection of evidence. Thus, if they determine that sexual assault has not occurred or if the patient is uncertain about pressing charges, no evidence is collected. Informed consent or refusal should be obtained for each of the following components of the sexual assault evaluation:

- Medical evaluation and treatment
- Reporting the crime
- Performing a physical examination
- Photo-documentation
- Evidence collection
- Transfer of evidence to law enforcement personnel

In many jurisdictions, hospitals are not required by law to perform examinations on suspected perpetrators without a court order or alternative means of legally mandating such an examination. Persons placed under arrest do not have the right to refuse an examination for the collection of evidence if the officer has a court order. Because states vary in requirements, check your local statutes.

In the evidentiary examination, the examiner should prevent cross-contamination of evidence by changing gloves whenever it could occur. Clearly document all findings.

1. Before the patient undresses, place a clean hospital sheet on the floor to be a barrier for the collection paper.
2. Allow the patient to remove and place each piece of clothing being collected in a separate paper bag. Handle all clothing with gloved hands to prevent contamination of evidence.
3. Simultaneously identify the presence of any physical injury, biological evidence, or foreign debris, but do not disturb.
4. Recover any trace evidence, including sand, soil, leaves, grass, and biological secretions. Note the body location of the collection; identify moist secretions.
5. Note all injuries by documenting the location, size, and complete description of any trauma, including bite marks, strangulation, or areas of

point tenderness, especially those occurring around the mouth, breasts, thighs, wrists, upper arms, legs, back, and anogenital region.

6. Perform appropriate photo-documentation of collection sites before collection, as well as documentation of other suspect areas.
7. Recover moist secretions with a dry swab. Look for areas of debris and dried secretions on the skin; flake them off onto folded paper. Recover any remaining material on these areas with a swab moistened with one drop of water (tap water is acceptable).
8. Document the Tanner Stage of the patient and describe the level of physical maturity.
9. Follow these sexual assault evidence collection instructions:
   - Toluidine blue dye can be used to identify minor external genital and anal injuries, but it might cause discomfort in prepubertal children.
   - When the vaginal examination is performed, the speculum should be lubricated with tap water because other lubricants might affect test results and decrease sperm motility. A vaginal speculum is never used in prepubertal children without general anesthesia.
   - When drug- or alcohol-facilitated sexual assault is suspected, blood and urine should be collected. If alcohol was ingested, use the law enforcement blood alcohol collection kit or collect three fluoride tubes. Check with local law enforcement for the kit. If a drug was ingested within 36 hours of examination, collect three full fluoride tubes of blood and 100 ml of nonprepped, first-void urine. If a drug was ingested more than 36 hours before the examination, collect 100 ml of nonprepped, first-void urine. Package each item separately, label and seal, and initial each package.
   - A colposcope can be used as an adjunctive examination tool. Ano-genital examination findings are enhanced through illumination, magnification, and photo documentation.
   - The collection of known samples from the patient might be indicated (buccal smear, blood, or hair). Depending on laboratory preferences, these samples can be collected later.

Regarding chain of custody, the examiner should document all historical and physical findings. Properly seal and initial all specimens and label with the following information:

- Hospital name, patient name, and patient identification number
- Date and time of collection of evidence
- Description and location of the body part of origin of the evidence
- Name and signature of the person collecting the evidence

All transfers of custody of evidence must be accountable by keeping a written record of the name and signature of the person receiving the evidence, and the date and time of the transfer.

The handbook says examiners should consider offering the following interventions depending on the circumstances:

1. Antibiotic prophylaxis for STDs
2. Hepatitis B immunization if the patient has not been previously immunized
3. HIV prophylaxis based on risk assessment of exposure
4. Pregnancy prevention

Finally, the ACEP guidelines say that the patient should be given referrals to local resources for follow-up counseling and advocate services. The patient should be referred for follow-up examinations in two weeks, three months, and six months for evaluation of pregnancy and STDs.

Despite the ACEP's acknowledgment of the issue and its handbook of protocol, many nurses have observed physicians' reluctance to work with sexual assault victims. This might be why the SANE program has increasing relevance and importance. According to Ledray (1999), "The primary mission of a SANE program is to meet the needs of the sexual assault victim by providing immediate, compassionate, culturally sensitive, and comprehensive forensic evaluation and treatment by trained, professional nurse experts within the parameters of the individual's state nurse practice act, the SANE standards of the International Association of Forensic Nurses (IAFN), and the individual agency policies." Ledray adds that SANE programs should adopt specific goals, such as the following:

- To assess, document, and treat injuries
- To provide timely, thorough, and professional forensic evidence collection, documentation, and preservation of evidence
- To evaluate and treat prophylactically for STDs
- To evaluate pregnancy risk and offer prevention
- To provide crisis intervention
- To appropriately refer victims for immediate and follow-up medical care and counseling

- To enhance the ability of law enforcement agencies to obtain evidence and successfully prosecute sexual assault cases

6.6.4 Nurses as Part of the Equation

In chapter 3, we examined the fact that in 1992, JCAHO first required health care institutions to have protocols on rape, sexual molestation, and domestic abuse (Bobak, 1992). Five years later, JCAHO required these health care institutions to train their staff members to use criteria to identify possible victims of physical assault, rape, or other sexual molestation, domestic abuse, and abuse or neglect of older adults and children. (JCAHO, 1997). Although the JCAHO does not specifically stipulate that a forensic nurse perform these duties, it is clear that the accreditation agency expects a well-trained individual to provide appropriate and complete services to victims.

The stage has been set for the work of forensic nurses, and in the arena of sexual assault cases specifically, these nurses are known as SANEs. Efforts of the SANE are magnified when the nurse works within a SART model, which encompasses the SANE (or other health care provider), an advocate, a law enforcement officer, and a prosecutor. Other members might include domestic violence victim advocates, state crime laboratory personnel, clergy, and social services staff.

Several studies confirm the idea that these nurse examiners are well suited to work with victims of violence. Du Mont and Parnis (2003) compared nurses who had participated in a SANE program to nurses who had not participated in the program on their opinions and practices in relation to the collection of forensic evidence. Self-administered surveys were distributed to all SANEs and non-SANEs employed in sexual assault care centers in Ontario, Canada. The researchers found that SANEs were more likely to indicate that certain samples, items, or questions should not be taken or asked as a regular part of the forensic examination. They were less likely to perceive the presence of physical injuries and semen or sperm as being "extremely important" to a positive legal outcome. Finally, more SANEs reported experiencing dilemmas with respect to their dual roles as caregivers and evidence collectors.

Amey and Bishai (2002) examined two aspects of ED treatment received by women who experienced sexual assault: administration of emergency contraception to prevent pregnancy and screening and treatment for STDs. The researchers analyzed seven years of data from the National Hospital Ambulatory Medical Care Survey (NHAMCS). They found that the number of rapes per year reported in the NHAMCS data is highly consistent with the number of forcible rapes reported by the FBI. Results showed statistically significant differences in patients who received screening on the basis of age and also suggested that the same difference exists for STD medications received. They added that accounting for differences in screening and medications by age does not completely explain why a large portion of the patients are neither screened nor receive STD medications.

6.6.5 A Nurse's Issue: Emergency Contraception

Although Linda Ledray, RN, PhD, LP, FAAN, believes forensic nurses have made great strides, there are major pockets of controversy and complacency that should be rooted out. One such pocket is a refusal to administer emergency prophylaxis to rape victims, an issue that she says wasn't handled appropriately in the recently released *National Protocol for Sexual Assault Medical Forensic Examinations Adults/Adolescents*, published by the U.S. Department of Justice Office on Violence Against Women in September 2004 (and discussed later in this chapter). "I worked on that protocol, but there were administrative and political limitations," she says.

> We were told as clear as can be that if we suggested, recommended, or even brought up the subject of emergency contraception, it wouldn't get published. Family-planning issues are as close as we could get. It should say that every rape victim has to be offered emergency contraception and that she can make the decision if she wants it. I also think the Centers for Disease Control and Prevention (CDC) has limited us; there is absolutely no reason they should be testing for STDs in the ER, and the CDC is very naive if they think the rape shield laws are going to keep positive results out of the courtroom. I feel like we all sold out to the current administration but it would have happened anyway. We fought over the wording in it. There were versions that were much worse than the final version; I'm not sure some people are happy with it.

Ledray is understandably concerned about emergency contraception issues. Health care providers are hit-and-miss about informing victims about the availability of contraception. Ledray (2001) writes:

> In the past, forensic examiners tested for STIs in the ED and then again at follow-up. The rationale was that if a victim was negative initially, and positive on follow-up, the assailant, if apprehended, could be tested as well. If he was positive for the same STI this could then link him to the crime. Because there are so many variables that could account for a positive STI test, this has not been useful forensic evidence and is no longer recommended practice for adult and adolescent examinations. It is still recommended for ongoing child sexual abuse.

STIs are, however, a concern for victims from a clinical perspective and must be addressed as a part of the initial examination, Ledray adds. Ledray (1999) found that although 36 percent of rape victims presenting to the ED stated their primary reason for coming was concern about having contracted an STI, the actual risk is low. The CDC estimates the risk of rape victims getting gonorrhea is 6 percent to 12 percent, chlamydia risk is 4 percent to 17 percent, syphilis risk is 0.5 percent to 3 percent, and the risk of HIV is less than 1 percent. STI testing is very expensive and time-consuming for the survivor, who must return two or three times for each test; according to Blair and Warner (1992), most victims do not return. According to Ledray (1999), 25 percent of the survivors seen in the ED returned for the initial STI follow-up visit. Tintinali and Hoelzer (1985) found that only 15 percent returned. The researchers were able to contact 47 percent of those who had not returned for follow-up and they found an additional 11 percent of these went elsewhere for medical follow-up; however, only 14 percent told the physician they saw for follow-up about the rape. Most clinicians recommend prophylactic treatment for STIs. According to Blair and Warner (1992), except in child sexual abuse cases, cultures taken need not be handled as evidence because they are not used in court.

Yuzpe, Smith, Percival, and Rademaker (1982) stated that the risk of pregnancy from a rape is approximately 2 percent to 4 percent. Although this is a low risk, some might argue, pregnancy is a victims' concern that should be addressed at the time of the initial examination, even if the treating medical personnel or the medical facility does not support termination of an existing pregnancy. The National Conference of Catholic Bishops agreed that, "A female who has been raped should be able to defend herself against a potential conception from the sexual assault. If, after appropriate testing, there is no evidence that conception has occurred already, she may be treated with medication that would prevent ovulation, or fertilization."

A look at the medical literature is in order. Holmes (1999) writes, "Sexual assault is a common occurrence that carries significant physical and mental health morbidity. Some of the most common concerns expressed by sexual assault victims can be allayed by addressing the risks of rape-related sexually transmitted infections. Although exact risks cannot be accurately quantified, it is important that health care professionals provide counseling as well as prophylaxis and/or treatment as indicated."

Holmes, Resnick, Kilpatrick, and Best (1996) attempted to determine the national rape-related pregnancy rate and provide descriptive characteristics of pregnancies that result from rape. A national probability sample of 4,008 adult American women participated in a three-year longitudinal survey that assessed the prevalence and incidence of rape and related physical and mental health outcomes. The national rape-related pregnancy rate was calculated to be 5 percent per rape among victims of reproductive age (12–45); among adult women, an estimated 32,101 pregnancies result from rape each year. Among 34 cases of rape-related pregnancy, the majority occurred among adolescents and resulted from assault by a known, often related perpetrator. Only 11.7 percent of these victims received immediate medical attention after the assault, and 47.1 percent received no medical attention related to the rape. A total of 32.4 percent of these victims did not discover they were pregnant until they had already entered the second trimester; 32.2 percent opted to keep the infant, whereas 50 percent underwent abortion and 5.9 percent placed the infant for adoption; an additional 11.8 percent had spontaneous abortion. The researchers concluded that rape-related pregnancy occurs with significant frequency, is a cause of many unwanted pregnancies, and is closely linked with family and domestic violence. They write, "As we address the epidemic of unintended pregnancies in the United States, greater attention and effort should be aimed at preventing and identifying unwanted pregnancies that result from sexual victimization."

Merchant, Keshavarz, and Low (2004) examined the extent of HIV postexposure prophylaxis (PEP) provision in a New York City pediatric ED after the release of emergency prophylaxis guidelines. Using logs of the sexual assault and violence intervention advocacy program, the researchers identified patients who had been evaluated for sexual assault in the hospital's pediatric ED from January 1999 to December 2000. These patients' medical records were reviewed retrospectively for details of their sexual assault and the medical treatment they received in the ED. Of 25 patients identified from the hospital's affiliated sexual assault and violence intervention advocacy program logs, 14 female adolescents had received HIV PEP. Each patient had sustained forced vaginal intercourse; 64 percent of the victims knew their assailant, but none knew his HIV status. No patients received HIV PEP within the optimal one-hour prescription time, but none presented within the one-hour window. Eighty-six percent presented more than 12 hours after the event and 42 percent presented more than 24 hours after the assault. HIV PEP was ordered an average of 218 minutes after the patient presented to the ED, and patients received drugs an average of 58 minutes after they were ordered. All but one patient received a three-drug regimen. The researchers encourage efforts to expedite HIV PEP provision in the ED, such as educating ED practitioners on its proper use, and making HIV PEP drugs available for direct dispense from the ED.

Keshavarz, Merchant, and McGreal (2002) undertook a study to determine ED practitioner willingness to offer emergency contraception following sexual assault and consensual sex, and to compare responses of practitioners from states whose laws permit the refusal, discussion, counseling, and referral of patients for abortions with those of practitioners from states without these laws. Using a structured questionnaire, a convenience sample of ED practitioners attending a national emergency medicine meeting was surveyed. The 600 respondents were 71 percent male, 29 percent female; 34 percent academic, 26 percent community, 33 percent resident physicians; and 7 percent nurse practitioners and physician assistants. Many respondents (88 percent) were inclined to offer emergency contraception to those sexually assaulted by unknown assailants. More practitioners said they were willing to offer emergency contraception if the assailant was known to be HIV-infected rather than if the assailant had low HIV risk factors (90 percent vs. 79 percent). More respondents would prescribe emergency contraception after sexual assault than consensual sex (88 percent vs. 73 percent). The rates of willingness to offer emergency contraception were the same for practitioners in states with abortion-related conscience clauses and those from other states.

Wiebe, Comay, McGregor, and Ducceschi (2000) reports that the the sexual assault service operated by the Children's and Women's Health Centre of British Columbia, in partnership with the Vancouver General Hospital Emergency Department, started offering HIV prophylaxis in November 1996 to patients presenting to the ED after a sexual assault. In the first 16 months of the program, a total of 258 people were seen by the service, of whom 71 accepted the offer of HIV prophylaxis. Only 29 continued with the drug treatment after receiving the initial five-day starter pack, and only eight completed the full four-week treatment regimen and returned for their final follow-up visit. Patients at highest risk for HIV infection, including those who had penetration by an assailant known to be HIV-positive, were more likely to accept prophylaxis and more likely to complete the treatment than those at lower risk. Compliance and follow-up were the main problems with implementing this service. Service providers found it difficult to give the information about HIV prophylaxis to traumatized patients. The researchers reported that following this program evaluation, the service changed its policy to offer HIV prophylaxis only to people at high risk of HIV infection. They said that this targeting of services is expected to make the service providers' jobs easier and to make the program more cost-effective while still protecting sexual assault victims against HIV infection.

Unintended pregnancy is a major medical, social, and public health problem. Emergency contraceptive pills can prevent 75 percent to 85 percent of unintended pregnancies if administered within 72 hours of intercourse. Abbott, Feldhaus, Houry, and Lowenstein (2004) performed a study to measure knowledge, attitudes, practices, and perceived needs about emergency contraception in a sample of women seeking care at an ED. The sample consisted of women presenting to an inner-city ED during an eight-week study period. Women who were aged 18 to 45 years, English speaking, and not critically ill and who presented during 56 randomly generated four-hour time blocks were eligible. Trained research assistants administered a 20-question survey that included questions on current sexual and contraceptive practices and knowledge, acceptance, and preferences about postcoital contraception. Two hundred thirty-two women met eligibility criteria; 158 (68 percent) women agreed to participate. The participants' mean age was 30 years. Twenty-five percent were married, 49 percent had never married, and 25 percent were separated or divorced. Fifty-two percent reported at least one previous unintended pregnancy; 28 percent had one or more previous elective abortions. Of women who had been sexually active in the past month, half reported unprotected intercourse during that time. Among all respondents, 122 had heard of emergency contraception as a way of preventing pregnancy after unprotected intercourse. Of these respondents, one fourth to one half did not have enough knowledge to use emergency contraceptive pills effectively. Fifty-seven percent of women were willing to use emergency contraceptive pills in the future, and 16 women said they would consider a change in regular contraception to emergency contraceptive pills if widely available. The researchers concluded that sexually active women seeking ED care have high rates of unintended pregnancy and abortion. There is broad acceptance of emergency contraceptive pills to prevent pregnancy, but knowledge of availability, timing, and proper use is limited. Emergency contraceptive pills are a safe, effective, and low-cost primary preventive and emergency care intervention, and information about their use should be made available to ED patients. Patients should be advised, however, not to abandon their use of barrier or other traditional contraceptives.

Myles et al. (2000) conducted a retrospective review of charts of sexual assault survivors who were offered PEP between April 1998 and November 1999 at San Francisco General Hospital. The total cost of PEP medications was also computed. Overall, the researchers noted that one third of the 367 sexual assault survivors chose to initiate PEP. Men who were anally raped are at the highest risk for HIV transmission and were most likely to initiate PEP. Among women, on the other hand, those who were non-White and homeless were less likely to accept PEP. In the context of cost, the total per-person cost of medication dispensed during the study period ($65 per person offered PEP) is comparable to other medications offered routinely following sexual assault, such as azithromycin for chlamydia prophylaxis ($43 per treatment). However, the researchers said there was no definitive evidence that PEP is effective in preventing HIV seroconversion after sexual assault. They suggested that in developing rational policy recommendation for offering HIV PEP after sexual assault, further studies are needed to better delineate the rates of HIV seroprevalence among sexual assailants, the efficacy of PEP after sexual exposure, and the psychological benefits or harm incurred by the sexually assaulted patients.

Gibb, McManus, and Forster (2003) assessed whether antibiotic prophylaxis should be offered to women after sexual assault by considering acceptability of prophylaxis, follow-up attendance rates, and the prevalence of STIs in these women. A retrospective case review of female survivors of sexual assault attending the Rose Clinic at Ambrose King Centre in the Royal London Hospital between January 1, 1997 and May 31, 1999 was carried out. All women were screened for STIs using standard investigation methods; antibiotic prophylaxis was offered within two weeks of the assault, and the antibiotic regimens were followed as recommended. The women were invited to attend for results at two weeks and offered a further screening at three months postassault. Bacterial vaginosis was present in 32 percent of the women screened, chlamydia trachomatis was identified in 8 percent, and none tested positive for Neisseria gonorrhoeae. Of the 25 women who were offered antibiotic prophylaxis, 88 percent accepted. Follow-up attendances were 57 percent at two weeks and 30 percent at three months. Antibiotic prophylaxis was acceptable to women. Among recent rape victims, follow-up rates are low, as confirmed by this study. These factors support the use of antibiotic prophylaxis after sexual assault. The researchers found a high prevalence of STIs among women in this study, and added that more research is required with respect to this aspect of the work and to consider the cost–benefit analysis of antibiotic prophylaxis.

According to the National Conference of State Legislatures, there are seven states that currently have statutes related to emergency contraception:

- California: Code 2704.13–2704.16 (2003–2004) authorizes a pharmacist to initiate emergency contraception drug therapy in accordance with standardized protocols developed by the pharmacist and an authorized prescriber acting within his or her scope of practice.
- Hawaii: Rev. Stat. 461-1 allows pharmacists working in collaboration with a physician and with the appropriate training to initiate emergency contraception oral drug therapy.
- Illinois: Rev. Stat. ch. 110, 1-106 (2002) finds that FDA-approved emergency contraception can significantly reduce the risk of pregnancy of taken within 72 hours after the sexual assault,. The law also finds that providing emergency contraception to rape victims in a timely manner can significantly reduce the trauma of rape. The law requires hospitals providing services to alleged sexual assault survivors to develop a protocol that ensures that each survivor of sexual assault will receive medically and factually accurate and written and oral information about emergency contraception, the risks associated with the use of emergency contraception, and a description of how victims can be provided emergency contraception. The law requires hospitals to submit a plan to provide hospital emergency services to alleged sexual assault survivors.
- Iowa: Code 144.29A (2003) requires that a pregnancy termination report include information on the method used for the induced termination of a pregnancy, including the use of mifepristone.
- Maine: Rev. Stat. Ann. Tit. 32, 13821-13825 (2003) allows a pharmacist to initiate emergency contraception drug therapy in collaboration with an authorized prescriber, provided that the pharmacist completes an emergency contraception training program. The pharmacist is also required to provide the recipient of the drug therapy with a standardized fact sheet.
- New Mexico: Stat. Ann. 16.19.26.9 authorizes a pharmacist to administer emergency contraception drug therapy in accordance with protocols established by the board of pharmacy. The statute also requires that the pharmacist complete a course in emergency contraception drug therapy.
- Washington: Rev. Code Amm. 70.41 (2002) relates to emergency care for victims of sexual assault. The law declares that it is essential that all hospital ERs provide emergency contraception as a treatment option to any woman who seeks treatment as a result of a sexual assault. The law requires hospitals providing emergency care to victims of sexual assault to provide medically and factually accurate information and emergency contraception at the hospital, orally inform victims of their option to be provided emergency contraception at the hospital, and provide emergency contraception immediately to each victim who requests it. The law mandates the development of informational materials relating to emergency contraception for the prevention of pregnancy in rape victims for distribution in all ERs.

In January 2005, the CDC announced new federal guidelines for the use of antiretroviral drugs to prevent HIV infection after exposure to HIV through sexual intercourse, sexual assault, injection drug use, or accidents. "Using antiretroviral drugs after exposure is an important safety net to prevent HIV infection in certain cases," says Ronald O. Valdiserri, MD, MPH, deputy director of the CDC's National Center for HIV, STD and TB Prevention. "But the drugs are not a substitute for abstinence, mutual monogamy, or consistent and correct condom use, and should not be viewed as a quick fix" (CDC, 2005).

The new guidelines recommend use of the approach, called nonoccupational postexposure prophylaxis (NPEP), only for patients who seek treatment no more than 72 hours after a high-risk exposure with a person known to be infected with HIV. Treatment should be initiated as soon as possible after exposure and continued for 28 days. The new guidelines update Department of Health and Human Services (HHS) guidance issued in 1998, at which time data were not sufficient to recommend for or against the NPEP approach. Since then, new data from human and animal studies, case reports, and documentation of the approach's use in several countries, including the United States, have provided evidence to support its use.

The guidance includes specific recommendations for clinicians when making decisions about use of the approach. When potentially exposed persons seek care within 72 hours of exposure but don't know the HIV status of the person who was the possible source, the guidance encourages clinicians to evaluate the risks and benefits on a case-by-case basis. When a person seeks care more than 72 hours after exposure or when HIV exposure risk is low, NPEP is not recommended. Use of the drugs is also not recommended for people whose behaviors result in frequent, recurrent exposures to HIV.

The potential benefits of using antiretroviral drugs for NPEP also must be weighed against the patient's individual circumstances and the potential risks of the medication, including the possibility of serious side effects and ability to follow a daily regimen of taking several drugs. People who are frequently at risk of exposure to HIV, such as those who have HIV-infected sex partners and rarely use condoms, or injection drug users who often share equipment, would benefit more from intensive risk-reduction interventions than from NPEP.

PEP has been recommended for health care workers exposed to HIV since 1996 and in observational studies has been associated with an 80 percent reduction in the risk of infection. Any three-drug combination of antiretroviral medications recommended by HHS can be used as NPEP, except those containing nevirapine. When used under conditions similar to the NPEP approach, nevirapine has been associated with severe reactions and liver damage.

The CDC cites a study of sexual assault survivors in Sao Paolo, Brazil. Women who sought care within 72 hours after exposure were treated for 28 days with either zidovudine and lamivudine (for those without mucosal trauma) or zidovudine, lamivudine, and indinavir (for those with mucosal trauma or those subjected to unprotected anal sex) for 28 days. Women were not treated if they sought care later than 72 hours after assault, if the assailant was HIV-negative, or if a condom was used and no mucosal trauma was seen. Of 180 women treated, none seroconverted; of 145 women not treated, four (2.7 percent) seroconverted. Although these studies demonstrate that NPEP might reduce the risk for infection after sexual HIV exposures, participants were not randomly assigned, and sample sizes were too small for statistically significant conclusions. In a study of rape survivors in South Africa, of 480 initially seronegative survivors begun on zidovudine and lamivudine and followed up for at least six weeks, one woman seroconverted. She had started taking medications 96 hours after the assault. An additional woman, who sought treatment 12 days after assault, was seronegative at that time but not offered NPEP. At retesting six weeks after the assault, she had seroconverted and had a positive polymerase chain reaction result.

According to the CDC (2005), surveys of clinicians and facilities indicate a need for more widespread implementation of guidelines and protocols for NPEP use. In a survey of Massachusetts ED directors, 52 percent of facilities had received NPEP requests during the preceding year, but only 15 percent had written NPEP protocols. Similarly, in a survey of Massachusetts clinicians, approximately 20 percent had a written NPEP protocol. Among pediatric emergency medicine specialists surveyed throughout the United States and Canada, approximately 20 percent had a written policy about NPEP use, but 33 percent had prescribed it for children and adolescents; different prescribing practices were reported. In a survey of 27 European Union countries, 23 had guidelines for occupational PEP use, but only six had guidelines for NPEP use.

Although the estimated per-act transmission risk from unprotected exposure to a partner known to be infected with HIV is relatively low for different types of exposure, different nonoccupational exposures are associated with different levels of risk. The highest levels of estimated per-act risk for HIV transmission are associated with blood transfusion, needle sharing by injection drug users, receptive anal intercourse, and percutaneous needlestick injuries. Insertive anal intercourse, penile–vaginal exposures, and oral sex represent substantially less per-act risk.

According to the CDC, a history should be taken of the specific sexual, injection drug use, or other behaviors that might have led to, or modified, a risk for acquiring HIV infection. Eliciting a complete description of the exposure and information about the HIV status of the partners can substantially lower (e.g., if the patient was the insertive partner or a condom was used) or increase (e.g., if the partner is known to be HIV-positive) the estimate of risk for HIV transmission resulting from a specific exposure. In addition to sexual and injection drug use exposures, percutaneous injuries from needles discarded in public settings result in requests for NPEP with a certain frequency. Although no HIV infections from such injuries have been documented, concern exists that syringes discarded by injection drug users (e.g., for whom the HIV infection rate is higher than that for diabetics) might pose a substantial risk. However, these injuries typically involve small-bore needles that contain only limited amounts of blood, and the viability of any virus present is limited. In a study of syringes used to administer medications to HIV-infected persons, only 3.8 percent had detectable HIV RNA. In a study of the viability of virus in needles, viable virus was recovered from 8 percent at 21 days when the needles had been stored at room temperature; less than 1 percent had viable virus after one week of storage at higher temperatures.

Another category of transmission has special significance for the SANE. Bite injuries represent another potential means of transmitting HIV; however, HIV transmission by this route has been reported rarely, according to the CDC (2005). Transmission might theoretically occur either through biting or receiving a bite from an HIV-infected person. Biting an HIV-infected person, resulting in a break in the skin, exposes the oral mucous membranes to infected blood; being bitten by an HIV-infected person exposes nonintact skin to saliva. Saliva that is contaminated with infected blood poses a substantial exposure risk. Saliva that is not contaminated with blood contains HIV in much lower titers and constitutes a negligible exposure risk.

Because of the emotional, social, and potential financial consequences of possible HIV infection, clinicians should handle NPEP evaluations with the highest level of confidentiality. Confidential reporting of STIs and newly diagnosed HIV infections to health departments should take place as dictated by local law and regulations. For cases of sexual assault, the CDC says that clinicians should document their findings and assist patients with notifying local authorities. HIV test results should be recorded separately from the findings of the sexual assault examination to protect patients' confidentiality in the event that medical records are later released for legal proceedings. Certain states and localities have special programs to provide reimbursement for medical therapy, including antiretroviral medication after sexual assault, and these areas might have specific reporting requirements. When the sexual abuse of a child is suspected or documented, the clinician should report it in compliance with state and local law and regulations.

Potential HIV exposures in children occur most often by accident (e.g., needlesticks in the community, fights, or playground incidents resulting in bleeding by an HIV-infected child) or by sexual abuse or assaults. In a review of charts from one year in the pediatric ED of one hospital, 10 children considered for NPEP were identified (six because of sexual assault and four because of needlestick injury). Eight began taking NPEP, but only two completed the four-week course, according to the CDC (2005). An analysis of 9,136 reported AIDS cases in children identified 26 who were sexually abused with confirmed or suspected exposure to HIV infection.

The American Academy of Pediatrics has issued NPEP guidelines for pediatric patients. In addition, HHS pediatric antiretroviral treatment guidelines provide information about the use of antiretroviral agents in children. For young children who cannot swallow capsules or tablets and to ensure appropriate dosing for drugs that do not have capsule or tablet formulations that allow pediatric dosing, drugs for which pediatric formulations are available might need to be prescribed. Adherence to the prescribed medications will depend on the involvement of, and support provided to, parents or guardians.

Use of NPEP for sexual assault survivors has been widely encouraged both in the United States and elsewhere, according to the CDC (2005). Sexual assault is relatively common among women; 13 percent of a national sample of adult women reported having ever been raped (60 percent before age 18), and 5 percent reported having been raped more than once. Sexual assault is not uncommon among men. In one series from an emergency department, 5 percent of reported rapes involved men sexually assaulted by men. Males accounted for 11.6 percent of rapes reported among persons aged older than 12 years who responded to the NCVS in 1999. However, only three documented cases of HIV infection resulting from sexual assault have been published, according to the CDC. In observational studies, HIV infections have been temporally associated with sexual assault. Studies have examined HIV infection rates for sexual assailants; the largest of these, an evaluation of men incarcerated in Rhode Island, determined that 1 percent of those convicted of sexual assault were infected with HIV when they entered prison, compared with 3 percent of all prisoners and 0.3 percent of the general male population, according to the CDC (2005).

Sexual assault typically has multiple characteristics that increase the risk for HIV transmission if the assailant is infected. In one prospective study of 1,076 sexual assault cases, 20 percent were attacked by multiple assailants, 39 percent were assaulted by strangers, 83 percent of females were vaginally penetrated, and 17 percent overall were sodomized. Genital trauma was documented in 53 percent of those assaulted, and sperm or semen was detected in 48 percent. In another study, in which toluidine blue dye was used as an adjunct to naked-eye examination, 40 percent of assaulted women (70 percent of nulliparas) had detectable vaginal lacerations, compared with 5 percent of women examined after consensual sex (CDC, 2005).

Despite these risks and the establishment of multidisciplinary support services, sexual assault survivors often decline NPEP, and many who do take it do not complete the 28-day course. This pattern has been reported in several countries and several programs in North America. In Vancouver, 71 of 258 assault survivors accepted the five-day starter pack of NPEP, 29 returned for additional doses, and eight completed four weeks of therapy. Those with the highest risk for HIV exposure (i.e., source known to be HIV infected, a homosexual or bisexual man, or an injection drug user) were more likely to begin and complete NPEP. Patients who have been sexually assaulted will benefit from supportive services to improve adherence to NPEP if it is prescribed, and from psychological and other support provided by sexual assault crisis centers. All sexually assaulted patients should be tested and administered prophylaxis for sexually transmitted infections, and women who might become pregnant should be offered emergency contraception (CDC, 2005).

Certain illegal behaviors that result in imprisonment (e.g., prostitution and injection drug use) also might be associated with a higher prevalence of HIV infection among prison inmates than among the general population. However, studies indicate that the risk for becoming infected in prison is probably less than the risk outside prison. However, when exposure does occur, because sexual contact and injection drug use are prohibited in jails and prisons, prisoners who have experienced such exposures might be unable or unwilling to report the behaviors to health care providers. According to the CDC (2005), administrators and health care providers working in correctional settings should develop and implement systems to make HIV education and risk-reduction counseling, NPEP, voluntary HIV testing, and HIV care confidentially available to inmates. Such programs will allow inmates to benefit from NPEP when indicated, facilitate treatment services for those with drug addiction, and assist in the identification and treatment of sexual assault survivors.

6.6.6 Development of the SANE/SART Program

It has been demonstrated that every nurse is essentially a forensic nurse, but the discipline of sexual assault examination has perhaps the deepest roots of all forensic nursing specialties. The first concerted effort to address the needs of this patient population came in the 1970s, spearheaded in clinical practice by a nurse in Minneapolis, as well as by a nurse in Boston. Ann Wolbert Burgess is considered to be one of the earliest researchers to systematically examine the needs of sexual assault victims. She developed a pattern of psychological response she called RTS, and has spent an academic career championing a scientific study of rape and sexual violence.

During the time Burgess was formulating her theories, Linda Ledray was contemplating how to better serve the victims of rape she saw in her community. Ledray is considered by many to be one of the earliest pioneers of SANE nursing, when in 1976 she created the Sexual Assault Resource Service (SARS) at Hennepin County Medical Center in Minneapolis. Her goal was to develop a nursing-focused health care delivery model that addressed the unmet needs of assault and abuse victims.

Although Ledray might have felt that she was working in a vacuum at the time, she discovered that nurses in other parts of the country, notably Texas and Tennessee, were working to implement more responsive care for sexual assault victims. Realizing that by combining their best practices and innovative approaches they could accomplish more, this small group of nurses met, brainstormed, and eventually created a national organization that came to be known as the IAFN, which championed the fledgling SANE and SART programs in the 1980s.

SANE and SART programs weren't on many people's radars until the early 1990s. In 1994, the SANE program in Tulsa, Oklahoma was awarded the Innovations in State and Local Government Award from the Ford Foundation and John F. Kennedy School of Government at Harvard University. This honor brought to light the accomplishments of the SANEs and piqued the interest of health care professionals interested in starting programs to address needs in their own communities. The first roll call of SANE programs had taken place three years earlier, when in 1991, the Emergency Nurses Association published the first list of SANE programs in its *Journal of Emergency Nursing*. It was a short list, numbering just 20, but five years later, the number had climbed to 86. The list was the impetus behind a survey conducted by Ledray to obtain more details about SANE program structure and practice. Of the 59 programs surveyed, three were established from 1976 to 1979, 10 from 1980 to 1989, and 46 from 1990 to 1996. At the time the *SANE Development and Operation Guide* was being written in 1999 by the U.S. Department of Justice Office for Victims of Crime (OVC), there were approximately 117 SANE programs in the United States. Today, Ledray estimates there are more than 400.

Prior to the creation of the modern structured sexual assault response program, such exams were a hit-or-miss proposition. Victims of sexual abuse—or any kind of violent trauma or abuse, for that matter—were lumped in with the general ED population, made to wait for seemingly endless stretches of time with their cohorts. When their turn finally came, they were treated with indifference by physicians pressed for time. Cursory examinations were conducted, and crucial steps in the evidentiary exam process weren't "invented" yet.

The impetus to develop SANE programs began with nurses, other medical professionals, counselors, and advocates working with rape victims across the country. It was obvious to these individuals that the services to victims were inadequate, and not at the same high standard of care provided to other patients presenting in the ED (Holloway & Swan, 1993; O'Brien, 1996). A number of researchers (Holloway & Swan, 1993; Sandrick, 1996; Speck & Aiken, 1995) documented sexual assault victims' long waits for care in the ED because medical personnel viewed their injuries as being less severe than those of other patients.

During their wait, which ranged from four to as long as 12 hours, victims were prohibited from eating, drinking, or urinating, for fear of losing evidence, just to meet with health care providers who were insufficiently trained to perform medicao-legal exams. Lenehan (1991), Yorker (1996), and Tobias (1990) found that among staff that had been adequately trained, it was common for health care providers not to complete a sufficient number of exams to maintain their level of proficiency. In most cases, Lenehan (1991) found the only physician available to do the vaginal exam was male, and although roughly half the victims were unconcerned about the gender of the examiner, for the other half, this was extremely problematic. Ledray (1999) stated, "Even male victims often prefer to be examined by a woman, as they too are most often raped by a man and experience the same generalized fear and anger toward men that female victims experience."

"When I got into this, there was no such thing as forensic nursing or the SANE program," Ledray says:

> Essentially, victims were coming into the ER, waiting eight or 12 hours to be seen, and no one wanted to see them, no one wanted anything to do with them. As well, no one had a clue about forensic aspects, nor did they know much about evidence collection either, although they were trying to do something akin to it. The most that ED personnel were doing back then—fighting the battle of who was going to take care of the victim—was collecting swabs to look for sperm. And, of course, treating injuries, but the documentation was just the clinical documentation, there was no forensic component because people didn't know about the importance of forensics yet. Back then, physicians didn't know about emergency contraception and actually some still don't. It amazes me how many think plan B is the abortion pill. In fact, I was doing a training recently that was attended by an OB/GYN doctor who had graduated in 2000, and she had nothing in her training about emergency contraception. Regarding the attitude of the ED physicians, it wasn't that forensic issues weren't important, it's that they didn't know what to do and they were afraid if they saw the victim they'd have to testify in court; they clearly didn't want to do that, partially because of the time and partially because they'd be asked about things they probably expected were errors because they didn't know how to do the procedure. It still amazes me that when ED staff members are doing a rape kit, they are still reading the directions to the procedure while they are doing it. I don't think there is any other patient for which we would allow that.

Ledray says she has seen the evolution of sexual assault services in the time since she started in the field. It all began when Ledray, a former member of the U.S. military, moved from Germany and came to the Hennepin County Medical Center in Minnesota.

> I got started in sexual assault issues because I agreed to do an in-service. I was the nurse manager for the psych mental health program for Hennepin County, and a nurse in the OB/GYN clinic asked me to do an in-service to help them provide better services to rape victims; at that time, the only referral made after the ED was to the OB/GYN clinic—no mental health referral, no other referrals, and they knew at best, one in four victims was making it there, the others were not making their appointments. That's when I started looking into how these victims were treated. That was in 1975, and so many years later, I am still trying to figure it out.

"There were grants available to look at rape impact and treatment projects, so I wrote a grant and started the program," she adds:

> In order to get the money to start a program, which is what I really wanted, I was forced to do research, and forced to look at what we were doing at our facility and how we were doing it systematically. Much to my surprise, I found out that even the psychological treatment the rape centers were doing—and it was only recently that they began providing services—really wasn't the best because they weren't doing research; they were providing services. What everyone thought was the best way to do it clearly wasn't. That first grant was a six-month pilot study, four-year grant. I started step by step looking at what we were doing, what was effective, and what wasn't. We had eight different treatment models that we were comparing and over the years, have taken the best, compared it to other things, and kept what we thought was best. If we found something better, we changed over to it. Obviously it was trial and error as much as anything else. And, most importantly, we didn't listen to people who said it couldn't be done. Back in the early days, nurses couldn't testify, do the exam, do research or secure grants. It really was the dark ages, of a sort.

Ledray recalls an early test of her mettle as she pushed for nurses' rights to participate in the medico-legal process:

> There was a well-known medical examiner who has since retired, who looked at the results of the evidence of sperm motility phosphotase levels and testified in court about what the levels meant. However, in a meeting at the county attorney's office, he threatened not to do so if nurses were in court, not physicians. Fortunately, at that point I was finishing up my doctorate degree, so I figured, if he didn't want to testify, I would. So the prosecutor went ahead with the case.

Ledray says she owes her earliest successes to a unique combination of clinical and scientific research skills:

> I was a researcher and a clinician and that's what made it work. I earned my PhD in clinical psychology and personality research from the University of Minnesota. I was doing the research and implementing it, and then I could test it. My staff would see the client, come up with questions, we'd develop a study, test it, and could implement

> the results and take the next step based on that. It was a relatively rare opportunity; usually researchers aren't clinicians, so they might not ask the right clinical questions, and maybe their results are never implemented, which is unfortunate.

As a part of the grant for the first five years of the SANE program development, Ledray worked as an employee of a separate organization from the Hennepin County Medical Center, the Minneapolis Medical Research Foundation. "The program started seeing patients in 1975, but it was probably in the early 1980s, when the grant was long over and I started publishing the results of the research . . . that's when I started getting calls from people who needed help with starting a program of their own. The calls were from nurses . . . nurses who were willing to start a SANE program against all odds."

Ledray's model got a boost, interestingly enough, from physicians who were spreading word of the early SANE model in the 1980s:

> Hennepin is a teaching institute, so we had physicians who were doing their ER rotation. They would graduate and go to other hospitals, including others in Hennepin County. When a rape victim would come into their ER, they would immediately say, "Call the SANE!" It was because they knew how good of a program it was. Then, I started getting calls from nurse managers, or sometimes a few physicians at other hospitals, wanting more information about the program. It didn't surprise me, because physicians don't want to do sexual assault cases. There is no money in it. I have always been somewhat afraid that if or when funding becomes better, the physicians would try to take it back.

Diana Faugno, RN, BSN, CPN, SANE, director of the SART of San Diego North County, says that the need for a SART was evident the day in 1990 when a woman in San Diego was raped and spent nine hours going from hospital to hospital, unable to find a facility that could collect forensic evidence and provide the appropriate level of care. She recalls the early days of her facility's SANE program and its quest for validation:

> Our program launched in 1990, but in 1986 we started our child abuse program, which was similar to the SART model; it had a multidisciplinary approach and members included law enforcement, a social worker, and an examiner. Several years later, the police wanted a similar model for adult victims, so the adult response team was started by Patty Seneski, who came over from Phoenix and got trained on the colposcope in the child abuse room. They asked me to join that team in 1991.

Faugno acknowledges how SANE-related issues have evolved over the years:

> Regarding examinations back then, probably the biggest issue was getting DNA from biological samples—something that hadn't fully arrived yet. We would collect a lot of evidence, but there was a lot that could not be done with it; back then, kits were only kept seven years and then they were tossed—can you imagine that? The evidentiary examination is still basically the same, with forensic nurses looking for evidence, documenting the evidence, and maintaining that chain of evidence.

Faugno remembers the day when examiners only used the colposcope for child-abuse-related cases. "Child abuse investigation has long had a colposcope as part of the investigation and documentation process; its use on adults came later, but its purpose in these cases is as important as ever." Faugno recalls that some of the earliest findings that were documented by nurse examiners using a colposcope were questioned:

> I think they might have been suspect because the injury was there, but we would go back and recheck a lot of exams to make sure that what we were seeing truly was the specific trauma we were looking at and not a congenital malformation. What was challenged was the way that the findings were stated in the literature at that time. We certainly know more today than we did back then. I think we categorized injuries; we would list them out: one, two, three, four, five, six, and we didn't break them down into specific and nonspecific. We have a little more definition, if you will, of that terminology; redness by itself, or swelling by itself are nonspecific and can be caused by many other things.

Genital injuries, a topic of great controversy and misperception, are discussed in greater detail later in the chapter.

Faugno says the early sexual assault work was challenging. Sometimes, interaction with physicians and other health care colleagues often was a walk on the tightrope. "Looking back, it was pretty cutting-edge stuff. At the time, ignorance was bliss. I have no recollection that ED physicians didn't want the nurses to do a focused sexual assault program; I believe they were very happy to get these victims out of the ED and not have to deal with them so they don't have to go to court."

6.6.6.1 Demonstrating the Need for the SANE Program

In the aforementioned *SANE Development and Operation Guide* (Ledray, 1999), Kathryn M. Turman, then-acting director of the OVC writes:

> We know that victims of sexual assault suffer psychological trauma and, all too frequently, long-term health consequences as a result of their victimization. Therefore, providing sensitive health care to victims is critically important

> in the aftermath of a sexual assault. Unfortunately, the traditional model for sexual assault medical evidentiary exams frequently compounds the traumatization of victims. Medical personnel in the emergency room setting often regard the needs of most sexual assault victims as less urgent than other patients in the emergency room. As a result, rape victims may endure long hours of waiting in the public areas of busy emergency rooms. They are not allowed to eat, drink, or even urinate while they wait for a physician to conduct the medical evidentiary exam. Frequently, the physicians or nurses who perform the exams have not been trained in medical evidence collection procedures or do not perform these procedures frequently enough to maintain their proficiency. Some physicians are reluctant even to perform the medical evidentiary exam, knowing that they might be called away to spend a day or more in court testifying or that their qualifications to testify might be questioned due to their lack of training and experience.

The *SANE Guide* explains that typically, the rape victim faced a time-consuming, cumbersome succession of examiners for one exam, some with only a few hours of orientation and little experience. ED services were inconsistent and problematic. Often the only physician available to do the vaginal exam after the rape was male (Lenehan, 1991).

There are also many anecdotal and published reports of physicians being reluctant to do the sexual assault exam for many reasons, including their lack of experience and training in forensic evidence collection (Bell, 1998; Lynch, 1993; Speck & Aiken, 1995), the time-consuming nature of the evidentiary exam in a busy ED with many other medically urgent patients (DiNitto, Martin, Norton, & Maxwell, 1986; Frank, 1996), and the potential that if they completed the exam they were then vulnerable to being subpoenaed and taken away from their work in the ED to testify in court and be questioned by a sometimes hostile defense attorney (DiNitto et al., 1986; Frank, 1996; Speck & Aiken, 1995; Thomas & Zachritz, 1993). This often resulted in documentation of evidence that was rushed, inadequate, or incomplete (Frank, 1996). Many physicians even refused to do the exam (DiNitto et al., 1986). In one case, it was reported that a rape victim was sent home from a hospital without having an evidentiary exam completed because no physician could be found to do the exam.

As research became more readily available on the complex needs and appropriate follow-up for rape victims, nurses and other professionals realized the importance of providing the best ED care possible (Lenehan, 1991). For 75 percent of these victims, the initial ED contact was the only known contact they had with medical or professional support staff (Ledray, 1999). Ledray writes, "Nurses also were very aware that while they were credited with 'only assisting the physician with the exam,' in reality they were already doing everything except the pelvic exam" (DiNitto et al., 1986; Ledray, 1992a). It was clear to these nurses that it was time to reevaluate the system and consider a new approach that would better meet the needs of sexual assault victims. Turman adds, "The services of trained, experienced SANE practitioners help to preserve the victim's dignity, enhance medical evidence collection for better prosecution, and promote community involvement and concern with crime victims and their families."

Seng and Sanubol (2004) say there are increasing opportunities for nurses to become SANEs, but in rural areas far from established SANE programs, nurses considering becoming SANEs have few opportunities to talk with or observe experienced SANEs to explore the role and determine if they are well suited to forensic work. The researchers sought to learn what the first year in practice was like for members of a new semirural SANE team in terms of role transition and role-specific stress. They conducted interviews with six members of a SANE team three times during their first year in that role. The researchers discovered that the expertise these nurses brought from their backgrounds as emergency nurses, women's health nurses, and intensive care nurses transferred well and eased their adaptation to the SANE role in a process more akin to role expansion than role transition. They identified comfort working with clients in crisis, acting on their clinical judgment, implementing complex protocols, and adding new skills to their regular nursing role as helpful in their transition to the SANE role. Themes about the first year included the contribution of prior experiences observing or assisting with examinations, concerns that diminished over time, getting used to being on call, using their usual coping skills, getting past the first examination, and finding satisfaction.

6.6.6.2 A Model SANE Program

As described by Ledray (1999), a SANE is usually available on call, off premises, 24 hours a day, seven days a week. The on-call SANE is paged immediately whenever a victim of sexual violence enters the health care facility. If the facility's protocol indicates that an advocate should be called, the staff or SANE also will page the individual who is on call. There are several models of SANE programs. In the hospital-based SANE program model, a victim can enter the health care system by calling local law enforcement who will transport him or her to the hospital ED or SANE exam clinic; by going directly to the hospital ED; or calling a designated crisis line for assistance. During the time it takes for the SANE to respond, which ideally should be less than an hour, the ED or clinic staff will evaluate and treat any urgent or life-threatening injuries. If treatment is medically necessary, the ED staff should treat the patient, always considering and documenting thoroughly the forensic ramifications of the lifesaving and stabilizing medical procedures. If clothes or objects are removed from the victim by the ED staff, care should be taken utilizing forensic principles for handling and storage of the physical evidence. If medical necessity dictates treatment prior to the arrival of the SANE, ED staff take photographs following established forensic procedures. However, it is preferable that the SANE take all forensic photographs. When the ED staff determines that the victim does not require immediate medical care, the victim should be taken to a private room adjacent to the ED, which enhances the victim's sense of safety and security and provides comfort and quiet. If the victim has not yet filed a police report and indicates that he or she wants to do so, a health care provider should contact law enforcement to take the initial report at the hospital. If the victim is upset, and a social worker is available on site, with the victim's permission, the social worker is called to wait with the victim until the SANE arrives.

In the community-based SANE program model, a victim can enter the health care system by calling local law enforcement. They are first triaged for injuries and, if only minor injuries or no injuries are present, they are transported to the community-based SANE facility. If going to the ED of a local hospital on their own, a victim is triaged for injuries, and if there are only minor injuries or no injury present, they are transported to the community-based SANE program. Victims can also get access by going directly to the community-based SANE program during business hours or by calling the designated crisis line for assistance and receiving a referral to the community-based SANE program.

No matter where the program is based, once the SANE arrives, he or she is responsible for completing the entire evidentiary examination, including crisis intervention, STD prevention, pregnancy-risk evaluation and interception, collection of forensic evidence, and referrals for additional support and care. In states with mandatory reporting laws, the SANE is required to follow established protocol for reporting felony crimes, after explaining the process to the victim. Ledray (1999) advises that if the victim has not yet decided if he or she wants to report the incident, the SANE discusses the victim's concerns and provides information necessary to make an informed decision. If the victim does not want to report at this time, but is unsure if he or she will report at a future date, the SANE should ensure that the victim is aware of his or her options and the limitations of reporting at a later date. The SANE should offer to complete an evidentiary exam kit that can be held in a locked refrigerator for a specified time (usually one month or an appropriate period of time as mandated by state law) in case the victim chooses to report the incident later. If the victim decides not to report and an evidentiary exam is not completed, the SANE still offers prophylaxis to prevent STDs, evaluate the victim's risk of pregnancy, and offer pregnancy prevention for up to 72 hours postrape. The SANE also should make referrals for follow-up medical care and counseling. When a report is made, a complete evidentiary exam is conducted following the SANE program's protocol. In most programs, the complete exam is conducted within 36 hours of the sexual assault, and an abbreviated exam is completed between 36 and 72 hours postrape—up to 96 hours in some states. (Ledray, 1999) After obtaining a signed consent form, the SANE should conduct a complete examination, including the collection of evidence in a rape kit, further assessment and documentation of injuries, prophylactic care for STDs, evaluation of pregnancy risk and preventive care, crisis intervention, and referral for follow-up medical and psychological care. When the victim is ready to be discharged, the SANE should inquire if the victim would like accompaniment by a family member or friend. Ledray (1999) writes, "Every effort will be made to find a place for her to go where she will feel safe and will not be alone."

6.6.6.3 A Model SART Program

Ledray (1999) writes, "No SANE program can operate in isolation. To be optimally effective and provide the best service possible to victims of sexual assault, the SANE must function as a part of a team of individuals from community organizations." The answer is the formation of a SART. Ideally, the SART will include representatives from the community who can best help the victims. Members of a SART often include the SANE, law enforcement officer or detective, prosecutor, victim advocate, and ED personnel.

The original SART model, developed in California, involves a coordinated response. According to Ledray (1999), "The concept is based on the belief that a team response helps prevent the victim from reporting the account of the assault repeatedly. It also helps prevent confusion among professionals trying to meet the needs of the rape victim as she progresses through the health care and criminal justice systems."

When members of law enforcement go to the scene of a violent sexual incident, they protect the victim from further harm, protect the crime scene evidence, and take a limited statement from the victim to determine if a sex crime was committed. They then call the hospital ED triage, who pages the SANE and the rape advocate on call. When the police and victim arrive at the hospital, the SANE decides if the victim should be directed to the ED for medical evaluation by a physician, or directed immediately to the SANE area for forensic examination. The SANE stays with the victim during any necessary medical evaluation and until he or she is cleared medically and transferred to the SANE examination area. With the advocate present to provide support, the SANE and the police officer or detective conduct an in-depth interview of the victim after briefly conferring to coordinate questioning. Once the interview is completed, the police officer or detective waits outside the exam room while the SANE collects the evidence, which is then turned over to law enforcement or locked in a secured area for law enforcement to pick up at a later time. With the victim's permission, the advocate remains in the exam room to provide support during the exam as well. When the exam is completed, the SANE makes any necessary arrangements for follow-up medical care, and the advocate makes arrangements to contact the victim for follow-up supportive counseling and legal advocacy.

Ledray (1999) acknowledges limitations of the SART program, particularly in the area of victim reporting:

> If the victim is uncertain about reporting, she may feel pressured to report when protocol requires law enforcement personnel to interview the victim before the SANE becomes involved. The advocate will support the victim in whatever decision she makes, even if the decision is not to prosecute. If the victim decides not to report, this also may result in a victim who cannot access health care for STD and pregnancy risk evaluation and prevention. If the victim decides not to report, the hospital care is then typically not paid by the crime victims compensation fund. When the police authorize reimbursement, they are more likely to require that a police report be made. In areas where payment is authorized through another agency, reporting is not necessarily a requirement for payment.

Reimbursement for the evidentiary exam and collection of rape kit contents are discussed elsewhere in this text.

6.6.6.4 Obstacles to the SANE/SART Program

Although SANE/SART programs have distinct advantages, Ledray (1999) has assembled from the medical literature a list of the following obstacles these programs face:

- The fear of physicians that the SANE would miss injuries in the initial exam (O'Brien, 1996)
- The concern of physicians that they will still be called to testify in court even though they did not complete the exam (Ledray & Simmelink, 1997)
- The belief of prosecutors that a physician must conduct the exam for the physical evidence to stand up in the courtroom (DiNitto et al., 1986)
- The belief of prosecutors that the SANE will not be as credible a witness in court as the physician (Antognoli-Toland, 1985; Ledray, 1992)
- Inadequate funding (O'Brien, 1996)
- Narrow interpretation of old laws requiring a physician to collect the evidence for it to be used in court and for the cost of the exam to be reimbursable (Speck & Aiken, 1995)

In the *SANE Guide* (1999), Ledray addresses these concerns in a systematic fashion:

1. Concerns about cost. Although starting and operating a SANE program requires a financial investment, having a SANE on call might actually be more cost-effective for the facility because it frees both the ED physician and nurse, saving an estimated 20 minutes of physician time and 3.5 hours of ED nursing time, according to Rambow, Adkinson, and Frost (1992). DiNitto et al. (1986) found that SANE-related costs are more modest than the costs in facilities with physicians completing even a portion of the exam; however, actual costs for the physician fee, use of the ED, laboratory fees, and medication costs often exceed the amounts reimbursed by the state. In many cases, if there are no legal restrictions on billing the victim, or no special arrangements are made with the hospital, victims might be charged these additional expenses.
2. Fear of interference. Through the course of their responsibilities, SANEs assist law enforcement and prosecutors in numerous ways. Yorker (1996) has found that as a rule, police officers prefer to work with a few forensically trained nurses, as opposed to dozens of different nurses and physicians in a busy ED, because SANEs know what evidence to collect and how to maintain the proper chain of custody.
3. Concern that the SANE will not perform the exam as well as a physician. Ledray says the reliability of the evidence collected from a rape victim has been of significant concern to other medical and law enforcement personnel. She cites the approach used in the United Kingdom: Until recently, only police surgeons (usually male) were allowed to collect evidence from victims. When a group of female general practice physicians decided they wanted to make their services available, their ability to develop the necessary forensic skills to collect evidence was challenged by the police surgeons. Wright, Wright, and Farnan (1999) report that their persistence has paid off, and they are becoming increasingly accepted for their contributions. Holloway and Swan (1993) say that this was a necessary first step before the police were willing to train nurses for this role in England.

Ledray says:

> The real issue is one of training and experience, not professional background. Just as with any other specialized clinical skill, competency in the collection of forensic evidence and the completion of a sexual assault evidentiary exam entails

> training and experience. It does not necessarily require an advanced medical degree. Unfortunately, most medical and nursing schools do not teach forensic principles. Few physicians or nurses have the opportunity to complete a sufficient number of rape exams to develop or maintain proficiency, even if they have completed the training. A primary advantage of the SANE program is that a dedicated, limited number of nurses complete all of the evidentiary exams in a given hospital or clinic, which enables them to complete an adequate number of exams to develop and maintain proficiency.
>
> When Ledray and Simmelink (1997) compared 24 sexual assault evidence kits collected by SANEs to 73 collected by non-SANEs, the SANE kits provided more complete documentation, and the SANEs always maintained proper chain of custody, whereas the others did not. Thirteen (18 percent) of the kits completed by non-SANEs either had no indication of who had collected the evidence or the records were illegible, thus making the available evidence useless. Overall, 48 percent of the non-SANE kits had some break in the chain of custody compared to none of the rape kits collected by SANEs.

4. Concern that the SANE will not be a credible witness in court. "Concerns about SANE credibility are unfounded," Ledray (1999) writes. "In fact, there are several reports of prosecutors, who were initially concerned, later finding that the SANE is an extremely credible witness in court as a result of her extensive experience and expertise in conducting the sexual assault exam." Yorker (1996) found that prosecuting attorneys who have worked with SANEs know they can rely on the competence of the SANE as a witness if the case goes to trial, and that the testimony of the SANE is backed up by solid credentials and impressive numbers of victims seen (Lenehan, 1991).

6.6.6.5 The Challenge to Nurse Examiners

Some physicians are questioning the quality of the medical record generated by the SANE in his or her documentation of the evaluation and treatment of sexual assault victims who present in the ER, based on the paucity of information that would otherwise validate SANEs' work. Minshall and Patel (2001) compared medical record documentation practices of SANEs and their medical center to the standards set forth in the medical literature, as reviews by these nurses had resulted in individual institutional protocol revisions and policy changes in an effort to continually improve the quality of care provided (Ledray, 1992a, 1992b). The researchers knew that a 1995 policy issued by the ACEP states, "As part of ongoing quality management activities, the hospital should establish patient-care criteria for the management of the sexually assaulted patient and monitor staff performance. Emergency department staff should have ongoing training and education in the management of the sexually assaulted patient." They questioned whether completion of a state-mandated medico-legal recording tool by the SANE is sufficient to meet the medical needs of patients who present to the ED with the complaint of sexual assault.

Minshall and Patel drew up a list of various items considered to be essential for comprehensive medical record documentation, drawing from OB/GYN, emergency medicine, and other relevant literature. They retrospectively reviewed the charts of survivors of sexual assault who presented to their 180-bed medical center between January 1996 and November 1998. The facility's ED, which treats about 55,000 patients annually, treated approximately 200 sexual assault victims annually. Inclusion criteria included being a survivor of recent sexual assault (presenting for evaluation with 72 hours of the assault), managed by a SANE, and being 16 years old or greater. The audit of the medical record included not only review of the state-mandated OCJP 923 form, but also all pertinent material related to that visit, including the face sheet, nursing notes, dictated summaries, laboratory slips, and so on. Elements considered to be essential based on the literature review were not noted within the OCJP 923 paperwork, including historical elements (general medical history, medication allergies, and current medications), physical examination elements (examination of the oral cavity and bimanual examination), and laboratory and disposition elements (obtaining cultures and prophylactic treatment for STDs, testing and prophylaxis for pregnancy, and referral for counseling or other social support measures).

Minshall and Patel found that there were 162 cases of sexual assault over the 36-month review period; 127 (78 percent) charts were available for review, 79 (49 percent) of which met inclusion criteria. The most common reasons for exclusion were patient age less than 16 years or survivors were not managed by a SANE. All but one patient were female, and only one male survivor met inclusion criteria. OB/GYN history and pregnancy testing statistics therefore utilize only 78 cases. In addition to the single male survivor, there was one female patient who reported only rectal penetration and refused examination of the vagina and cervix, as well as the bimanual examination. Therefore, these elements were analyzed for only 77 cases.

The researchers acknowledge the development of SANE and SART programs that utilize specially trained nurses for the management of survivors of sexual assault, and who perform evidentiary examinations; provide counseling on pregnancy and STD prophylaxis; act as liaison between the survivor and law enforcement, social service personnel, and psychological support systems; as well as provide testimony in a court of law. At their medical center's ER in Bakersfield, California, a SANE has provided evidentiary examinations of victims of sexual assault since 1995. They write, "These nurses are a valuable resource to ED physicians and nurses, law enforcement, the county prosecutor's office, and most importantly to the survivor herself. It has been asserted that the SANE has improved the quality of service that EDs are able to provide for survivors of sexual assault, and that they are, in many cases, better expert witnesses than are physicians" (Ledray, 1992a; Ledray & Simmelink, 1997). The researchers explain that in California, SANE training places significant emphasis on the completion of the mandated medicolegal form, and in their study, SANEs demonstrated high compliance levels in the completion of this form; particularly those elements with check boxes or diagrams provided; specifically OB/GYN history, history of the assault, postassault actions, general physical condition, external genitalia examination, cervix and vagina examination, and examination of the anus and rectum had high compliance frequencies. They say that this competence is the result of SANEs training in completion of OCJP 923.

However, Minshall and Patel found that several essential elements were poorly documented, despite OCJP 923 written instructions. In particular, section E7 of OCJP 923 states, "Examine the oral cavity for injury and the area around the mouth for seminal fluid. Note frenulum trauma." The researchers say there is no specific check box or diagram on which the examiner is to record results, and documentation of an examination of the oral cavity was found in only 16.5 percent of cases. The researchers write, "It is unclear whether this lack of documentation is a reflection of this element going unperformed or whether examinations were merely undocumented (perhaps those with no abnormal physical findings), as there is no specific area for documentation. Also, examinations may not have been performed in cases where the survivor did not report any assaultive actions involving the oral cavity." In addition, documentation of SANEs' use of the Wood's Lamp examination was lacking in 35 percent of the cases. Written instructions in OCJP 923 state: "Scan the entire body with a Wood's Lamp. Label Wood's lamp findings 'WL.'" The researchers say poor documentation might simply be due to not having a specific check box or diagram on which to document results, and it is likely that negative findings were not specifically charted.

Documentation by SANEs of their performance of the bimanual examination was found in 13 percent of cases, but the researchers note that there is no specific instruction, check box, or diagram provided by OCJP 923 for this element. They add, however, that this element is repeatedly found throughout the medical literature as an essential element in the comprehensive examination of the sexual assault survivor. They state, "The medical literature supports the bimanual examination as an excellent opportunity to identify injuries which otherwise might have gone undetected, such as vaginal epithelium lacerations and broad ligament injuries." Notably, a bimanual examination was not part of the routine SANE protocol at the researchers' facility at the time of their study.

Minshall and Patel reported that although the medical literature supports several standard postexamination actions, California's standard documentation form, OCJP 923, does not provide any instruction or recording area for this information. The researchers noted that SANEs completed these actions "with exceptional frequency." Specifically, the actions are cultures for STDs, pregnancy testing, STD prophylaxis, and follow-up and referral, which were documented in 98 percent to 100 percent of the medical records the researchers examined. The researchers found, however, that documentation of pregnancy prophylaxis was made in 60 percent of cases, and they acknowledge several influencing factors: three patients were known to be pregnant at the time of the assault, two patients reported no vaginal penetration, and one patient was posthysterectomy.

Minshall and Patel say that their state's mandatory form provides "only minimal consideration for the medical needs of the survivor of sexual assault. Limited space and the omission of medically prudent historical, physical examination, laboratory, and dispositional elements require that an additional recording tool be utilized for comprehensive medical documentation." They say that documentation beyond OCJP 923 allows the examiner to provide greater detail of the events and circumstances of the assault and would allow the examiner to state direct quotes from the survivor without the constraints of space limited boxes. They conclude:

> The ED care of its survivors serves multiple purposes and SANEs perform an invaluable service in patient management. The medical literature supports certain documentation standards that may not be equivalent to legal objectives. Medical-legal forms such as this state's OCJP 923 are convenient but inadequate for comprehensive medical documentation. Additional documentation is required and SANEs must be specifically trained to perform this.

6.6.6.6 In Defense of SANE and SART Programs

A number of studies have been conducted that support the efficacy of a SANE program, including a study published in the December 2003 issue of the *Journal of Emergency Nursing* showing that evidence kits collected by specially trained SANEs provide more effective evidence collection compared with non-SANE-trained nurses and physicians. Crime analysts with the Colorado Bureau of Investigation completed audits on sexual assault evidence kits submitted to the bureau from October 1999 to April 2002. Commercially prepared evidence kits contain swabs, envelopes, slides and slide holders, and other tools used to collect and preserve evidence for analysis at a crime lab. Of the kits audited, those completed by SANE nurses were more accurate and complete when compared with those prepared by non-SANE nurses and physicians. Researchers found that evidence kits prepared by SANEs were more likely to have a completed chain of custody (92 percent) compared with non-SANE-collected kits (81 percent). SANEs were also more likely to have properly sealed individual specimen envelopes (91 percent vs. 75 percent), to have labeled the individual specimen envelopes (95 percent vs. 88 percent), and to have included the appropriate number of blood tubes (95 percent vs. 80 percent).

Study coauthor Sherry Murphy, a criminal investigator with the Colorado Bureau of Investigation, points to a situation that demonstrated the quality of the work performed by SANEs:

> DNA analysis of the oral swabs in one specific case resulted in limited interpretation. The anal swabs gave no profile. However, the SANE had also collected swabs from the victim's chin. That sample was the only one that provided a complete, nonmixture profile of the suspect. The suspect pled guilty upon admission of the test results. This meant that there was not only a conviction, but the victim did not have to testify in court. The defendant in this case was sentenced to 48 years in the Department of Corrections. We have come to expect top quality collection of samples from the SANEs in Colorado and are rarely, if ever, disappointed. (Sievers, Murphy, & Miller, 2003)

Study coauthor Valerie Sievers, MSN, RN, CNS, CEN, SANE-A, a clinical forensic nurse specialist, points out that additional research is needed to document the expertise and value of SANE programs: "Despite the growth of SANE programs in Colorado and across the country, more needs to be done to evaluate the impact of forensic nursing in the areas of health care and criminal justice. It isn't enough to say that SANE programs make a difference—we need to illustrate that fact in order to secure funding, promote forensic education and ensure a comprehensive health care response to victims of crime and interpersonal violence" (Sievers et al., 2003).

"I knew Linda Ledray had conducted a similar study in Minneapolis a number of years before, so I looked at that and kept it in the back of my mind," Sievers says. But unlike Ledray's pioneering program, the relatively new SANE program in Colorado had only been in existence for 10 years:

> In comparison to other programs like Pat Speck's and Jamie Ferrel's, it was new so I felt it was important to talk to everyone I could—hospitals, crime labs. I knew it would be helpful if we looked at some sort of baseline, then conduct research to see if we could identify some kind of validation about a different approach to forensic nursing—or if not in those terms, show someone having expertise and providing the response to sexual assault patients.

Sievers says the study and the results were welcomed. "For the most part, people in Colorado were very positive about it; they were very excited that we were able to document the efforts of forensic nursing. I think they intrinsically knew what kinds of contributions that nurses were making. And the nurses were happy to know there was additional research to help support what they knew to be true all along.

Sievers, whose interest in nursing goes back to when she was a young girl, is among those who have embraced nursing as a rewarding, challenging career. When her mother became ill during her first year of nursing school, Sievers discovered critical-care nursing:

> Mom spent 10 days in the ICU. I was amazed at the skill and care provided by the ICU nurses. I've always been a fan of "the adrenaline rush" that I first felt while working in critical-care areas. After graduating, I worked in intermediate cardiac care and then a surgical-neurological intensive care unit (SNICU). It was a great learning experience. One night while working in the SNICU, an entire family came by ambulance to the emergency department with carbon monoxide poisoning. The night supervisor requested help from the ICU staff to assist with the five code blues. After several hours of working with the trauma team, I knew my next move would be to emergency nursing.

After working several years in the ED and recognizing that victims of violence were not afforded the same response provided to trauma or cardiac patients, Sievers became interested in forensic nursing:

> On a busy Saturday night, a young mother brought her 7-year-old daughter to the ED because she "couldn't sleep." When I assessed the child, despite normal vital signs, the hair on the back of my neck stood up. This girl, without any history of illness, was pale, with dark circles under her eyes and tufts of hair missing from her scalp. Over the next few hours, while snacking on graham crackers and being entertained by police officers guarding patients waiting for disposition to the county jail, this little girl told me that her parents were divorced. On the weekends, she stayed with her dad who sometimes worked at night. When her dad was at work, his male roommate would come into her room and "hurt her girl parts." She said she was having nightmares, was afraid to sleep, and pulled her own hair out. Dad's roommate had told her she had pretty blonde hair, so she thought if her hair wasn't pretty, the roommate would leave her alone.

Following a police interview and a less-than-adequate exam by the ED physician, Sievers was convinced that adult and child survivors of sexual assault deserved a better response from health care providers. "The next day I contacted the Emergency Nurses Association (ENA) for information on SANE programs. After several years of submitting proposals to the hospital and gaining the support of law enforcement, victim advocacy, and district attorneys, our hospital administrators decided to fund the education and equipment needed to initiate a SANE program."

Sievers is a clinical forensic nurse specialist and statewide SANE coordinator for the Colorado Coalition Against Sexual Assault. Her responsibility is to educate nurses and physicians on appropriate care for victims of sexual assault or abuse and standardized collection of forensic evidence. Tapping into her 16 years of emergency nursing practice, Sievers is part of the SANE team that she developed in 1995 with emergency nursing colleagues. She staffs the local Children's Advocacy Center several times a month to provide medical-forensic exams for children who require nonacute evaluation and collection of evidence.

Sievers's workdays are filled with variety:

> On a typical day I may be responding to the hospital to provide care and evidence collection, writing grant reports, reviewing current forensic literature, teaching a class, giving a presentation on forensic nursing and SANE services, working with nurses in other communities to develop a SANE program, or testifying in court. I also provide collaborative strategies for communities interested in SANE programs, present the Colorado-based SANE curriculum to nurses and physicians, and deliver ongoing technical support and education for existing SANE programs. I help inform the public about the SANE program: where to go, what to expect for the patient who has been sexually assaulted, and information on the range of forensic nursing services available to law enforcement, criminal justice, and victim advocacy groups.

"The greatest satisfaction I derive from my work is in knowing that victims of sexual violence are afforded a compassionate and comprehensive response," Sievers says. "I can stay neutral in this emotionally charged work by realizing that my care of the patient and accurate collection of evidence impacts my responsibility to provide essential courtroom testimony. The understanding of my role as a patient advocate, not a victim advocate, is pivotal in this process."

Sievers says forensic nurses are establishing a new hybrid of heath care delivery:

> Physicians are medically driven, but they must realize that the practice of the sexual assault nurse examiner is holistic; we are there not to necessarily address all of the patient's medical needs, but to address the combination of their medico-legal needs with an emphasis on forensic science. There are always those whom I think are uncomfortable or intimidated or realize they don't have the education to necessarily approach these patients and do the kind of job they might otherwise want to do. What we do is so easy to pick apart though; physicians have to realize our documentation is focused on the medical forensic exam.

Sievers says she is fortunate in that the physicians she works with in the ED have understood the role of the SANE:

> They have always been very supportive but we have a history between us. Long before we started the SANE program officially at Memorial Hospital, I had done probably five years of work with them, providing propaganda, so to speak, on SANE-related issues. I think that even before I started working with the ER doctors, I started working with the prosecutors, the victim advocates, and law enforcement because they were truly the first responders and I felt if I can get them to embrace the idea of having forensic nurses, convincing the physicians would be easier. I mean, I barely got the SANE concepts out of my mouth and law enforcement was all over it. They thought the concept sounded wonderful. Their support really helped to garner support from the ER physicians. Our physician advisor at the hospital has been the director of the ER for 20 years and what she says goes, and she very much embraces the program and is very much a nurse advocate. The ER physicians at Memorial actually use the SANE program as a recruiting tool for new ED doctors. They tell them, "We see a lot of trauma, and one of the things you have to look forward to at our facility is that we have a very diverse nursing staff and a SANE program, so you don't ever have to worry about testifying in court or providing evidence collection."

As a young program, Sievers says, Colorado probably avoided a lot of pitfalls encountered by older, more established SANE programs. "I think our program followed the progress of other programs and this was a factor in its early success." Sievers also credits the program's success to a number of individuals who helped shape and grow the program:

> We had the dynamic Jamie Ferrell, who came from Texas to do our education in Colorado Springs, and not only did the nurses love her but hospital administrators did, too. It was helpful being able to say to them, "Here is someone who has done the research and made things happen elsewhere, so we can, too." Texas had their programs in place for probably 15 years by then; their laws are very close to what we have in Colorado, so that was an easy way to say we can share, shadow, and model what they have done in Texas. We also benefited from the wonderful Dr. Mary Dudley, who is now chief medical examiner for Sedgwick County, Kansas; she's awesome. When I was starting graduate school at Beth El College of Nursing at the University of Colorado at Colorado Springs, Mary was still teaching there as a clinical nursing instructor. She

> was finishing medical school and ready to go for her residency. She was, and still is, such a great nurse advocate. She was a fabulous support system, and was the person who brought the concept of forensic nursing and a forensic nursing curriculum to Beth El. And Virginia Lynch was one of the inaugural founders of the IAFN. She has authored numerous papers that have defined forensic nursing and roles for forensic nurses, and continues to educate and mentor others. Our program really benefited from the leadership of people who believed in forensic nursing.

Sievers has strong feelings about the need for ongoing education and training opportunities for forensic nurses. She has provided the SANE curriculum in Colorado for the last eight years, and just recently, has had her victim advocacy organization coordinator duties transferred to Beth El:

> They feel that will be a more supportive and appropriate setting for advanced nursing education. I am excited that there are many available opportunities for nurses, but one of the things I get concerned about is—and I preface this by saying I haven't had the opportunity to evaluate all the education and all of these models in terms of their credibility and their foundation in nursing practice—is the credibility and quality of SANE training for nurses. I'd like to see some sort of professional organization or nursing education structure be able to accredit those programs. Things are pretty different—even in SANE training—in every state. Their rape kits are different, nurse practice acts are different . . . I get worried about those who get their SANE education on a weekend and think, "I'm really smart, I've never done this, but I can develop a curriculum and take it back to my community and use it as a moneymaker." As opposed to saying, "I am experienced, I am investing in this process, and I am going to take some of my experiential education and pass that on to nurses who need to learn how to approach victims of violence, because I have expertise in forensic nursing." There are some out there who are diluting the education or are not able to back up what they are saying with credible, professional experience.

Sievers sees changes ahead in emergency nursing:

> Without some form of universal health care, I think EDs will continue to be overcrowded and utilized by many citizens as a source of primary health care. If this trend continues, more urgent care centers will be developed; emergency departments will be federally regulated and may possibly be designated for the exclusive use of the acutely ill or injured person. ED nurses might also become more specialized; they might focus their area of practice, for instance, on pediatric emergency nursing or geriatric emergency nursing.

She also believes forensic nursing has made great strides:

> In 2004 we had our 10th annual IAFN meeting, so we've just kind of professionally jelled the concept of forensic nursing over the past decade or so, and I think we have come a long way. There are many great people doing fabulous things. The field has grown and people are realizing that forensic nurses aren't just nurses who respond to the "knife and gun club" in the ED. Growth will continue but we need to focus on not waiting until nurses have spent 12 years in the ED to realize they are forensic nurses, but incorporating that education at the baccalaureate level and cultivating continued forensic education at the graduate and doctorate levels. We need more nursing professionals who recognize the need to provide expert care to victims of violence. Basic forensic nursing should be included in the curriculum of nursing degree programs. Clinical experience, persistence, and patience go a long way in developing avenues for forensic nursing. Educating our colleagues, hospital administrators, law enforcement, and the public about forensic health care and the impact of forensic nursing can facilitate more career paths.

Other studies point to the characteritics and overall efficacy of SANE and SART programs. Ciancone, Wilson, and Collette (2000) sought to provide a descriptive study of SANE programs and their characteristics in the United States. They mailed a confidential survey addressing patient and staff demographics, administration attributes, examination procedures, and medical and legal issues to SANE programs, and received responses from 61 (66 percent) of 92 programs. They found that 55 percent of the programs had been in operation for less than five years. Thirty (52 percent) of 58 programs performed the initial sexual assault examination in hospital EDs. Written consent (57 of 59, or 97 percent) was obtained for the initial examination, and most (51 of 59, or 86 percent) programs used preprepared commercial sexual assault kits. The researchers found that program directors were predominantly registered nurses. All but one program mandated specific training requirements for their staff, with a median requirement of 80 hours. Procedures used for initial examinations varied; most offered pregnancy testing (56 of 58, or 97 percent), pregnancy prophylaxis (57 of 59, or 97 percent), and STD prophylaxis (53 of 59, or 90 percent). HIV testing was not offered in 32 (54 percent) of 59 programs. Almost all programs used Wood's lamp (51 of 59, or 86 percent), colposcopes (42 of 59, or 71 percent), and photographs (46 of 59, or 78 percent) for documentation. Median time required per patient for initial examination and evidence collection was three hours (with a range of one to eight hours). Follow-up is consistently offered to the survivor. Most programs (45 of 61, or 74 percent) could report the number of survivors treated, but few could provide information on survivor medical follow-up or the number of prosecutions by survivors and their outcomes.

Hatmaker, Pinholster, and Saye (2002) report that the community-based Athens-Clarke County SANE (ACC-SANE) program was developed to respond to the needs of sexual assault victims. The researchers say that although this type of SANE model allows for a strong nurse-managed program, there are frustrations and pitfalls that differ from most hospital-based programs. At this time, they say, the majority (71 percent) of SANE programs are based in hospitals, and few (15 percent) function in outpatient or community facilities. In the ACC-SANE program, many community agencies interact to provide a seamless approach to postassault health care, counseling, and criminal prosecution. They add that SANEs are well equipped to provide forensic examinations in a caring, out-of-hospital environment.

Derhammer, Lucente, Reed, and Young (2000) describe the impetus to the start-up of the SANE interdisciplinary approach to care of sexual assault victims at Lehigh Valley Hospital in Allentown, Pennsylvania in May 1998: "Although many aspects of rape management were in place, a busy ED with varying levels of physician response and exposure to the process of rape management contributed to a lack of standardized, objective, timely, and compassionate medical management of sexual assault victims." The researchers report that comparing a baseline group of 130 sexual assault victims with 39 patients who were evaluated after the SANE approach was implemented indicated increased clinical interaction and significant improvements in quality indicators, such as completeness of evaluation and information gathered relevant to medicolegal issues. Law enforcement staff developed a more collaborative relationship with SANE examiners through the interdisciplinary team approach. Collaborative relationships were initiated with several other hospitals in the hospital's integrated delivery system to help offset some of the program's training, continuing education, and on-call costs and to allow for joint outcomes collection. The SANE program became a core ED service in July 1999.

Smith, Homeseth, and Macgregor (1998) report that after several years of planning, the SART at Immanuel St. Joseph's/Mayo Health Systems in Minnesota became a reality in August 1997. The nurses who were trained for this program were already providing 24-hour coverage in the ED for psychiatric emergencies and patients with chemical dependency; the SANE responsibilities were added to their on-call duties. Five nurses participated in a 40-hour training program led by experts in the local community. Smith et al. write:

> As expected, nurses were apprehensive as they conducted their first examinations; however, all has gone well. Over time, the providers' and clients' satisfaction with the program has improved. The examination is completed in less time, and the person assaulted does not have to wait as long for the SANE to arrive. Members of law enforcement and the prosecutor's office are especially pleased with the quality of evidence collected and the procedures followed to maintain chain of evidence so the evidence obtained can be used in prosecution.

Smith et al. report that the program has resulted in kind and compassionate care for persons who have been sexually assaulted. The providers are continuing to meet monthly as an interdisciplinary, interagency team and are addressing concerns as they arise, and members of the SART are developing a good working relationship. "Everyone involved agrees that developing this program has been a worthwhile effort and that the hospital is providing a valued service for the community."

Ericksen et al. (2002) say that specialized services have been developed to meet the unique needs of survivors of sexual assault, and yet little research has been conducted to investigate clients' experiences with these services. The researchers conducted an interpretive study to understand the experience of women who were sexually assaulted and then cared for in an emergency setting by professionals associated with a specialized sexual assault service; to discover themes in the experiences of these women; and to discern implications of this experience for delivery of care to women who have been sexually assaulted. They found nine themes emerging from latent content analysis of the interviews, and stated that holistic woman-centered care; the importance of having one caregiver focus on the client's emotional needs; the importance of touch; and the need for an effective, sensitive, and coordinated response by police and community services were essential components of a health care service provider.

Stermac and Stirpe (2002) conducted a study of a SANE program at a hospital-based sexual assault care center in Ontario, Canada, and assess its efficacy in comparison with physician examiners. The researchers obtained data from the hospital records of 515 women who came to a Toronto sexual assault care center. A number of variables relevant to this assessment of services were examined, including client demographics and presenting history, aspects of the sexual assault, and characteristics of the treatment. They found that average assessment times were shorter for victims seen by SANEs than for victims seen by physicians (approximately three hours vs. four hours). Physicians had more interruptions (25.1 percent) than did SANEs (20.0 percent).

Greenwood (2003) shared testimonies from community members as to the effectiveness of a SANE program. "The emotional support required by these victims is best rendered by a SANE. This frees the ED nurse to care for other patients, while sexual assault victims receive a high level of care," says Nancy Donel, RN manager at St. Thomas Hospital ED. "The DOVE program benefits not only the emergency physician, but the EMS system as well," comments Michael Mackan, MD, of the Summa Health System. "It gives us a resource and a specifically identified program with well-trained, qualified providers. Through their training and knowledge, SANEs not only help victims, but also increase the number of legal convictions that take assailants off the streets. This improves the health and safety of the communities in which we live and serve."

Lewis et al. (2003) evaluated the use and effectiveness of a protocol developed for emergency nurses and other medical personnel to use with survivors of sexual assault. The Ohio Department of Health (ODH) Protocol for the Treatment of Adult Sexual Assault Survivors was developed by a multidisciplinary team in 1991–1992 as a written guide to provide comprehensive, standardized, nonjudgmental, and equitable treatment for survivors. In 1993, this 118-page manual was sent to all Ohio hospitals. In 1994, a follow-up video and training guide were also delivered. In 1997, Victims Rights Advocacy, a nonprofit agency in Ohio, and the Center for Social Work Research at The University of Texas at Austin collaboratively conducted an evaluation of the utilization and effectiveness of this protocol at Ohio hospitals. EDs at Ohio hospitals were asked to complete a mailed survey regarding their policies and procedures for treating sexual assault patients. Telephone calls were made to the hospitals that did not return a survey, and site visits were conducted at 20 hospitals in diverse areas of Ohio. Overall, Lewis et al. found that respondents concurred that hospitals can benefit from using a standardized protocol, such as the ODH Protocol, for treating victims of sexual assault. Survey participants also indicated that training is needed on several topics, especially testifying in court, cultural awareness, and the needs of special populations, such as male, gay, lesbian, and bisexual survivors. In addition, findings indicate that survivors need more follow-up services, and written information about these services should be provided to them.

6.6.7 The Evidentiary Examination

In a sexual assault case, the victim's body is the most important source of physical evidence. The victim is, in essence a walking and talking crime scene. A medical evidentiary examination is an examination done by a health professional that includes attention to the medical needs of the victim as well as to the gathering of evidence for law enforcement purposes. It typically includes medical evaluation and crisis intervention, forensic evidence collection, evaluation of emotional needs, and referral for follow-up care. A medical evidentiary examination can be a key element in the successful prosecution of sexual assault and other violent crimes. When examining a victim, providers must systematically gather evidence that will document injuries and assist in identifying the assailant, yet must also avoid or reduce further psychological distress and retraumatization of the patient. Discussions with the patient about the assault, gathering and storing of specimens that might eventually link the assailant to the crime, and documentation of injuries must be done in a painstaking, yet respectful way. Evidence must be preserved and stored without contamination or risk of tampering. As a scientist serving law enforcement, the provider might be asked to testify in court about any statements made by the victim and his or her demeanor at the time of the examination, and about the evidence collected. To do an examination correctly and to ensure that the process meets the test of reliability required by a court, a health care provider needs training and experience in what procedures are needed and how they should be done. Many health care providers are not routinely trained or familiarized with the management of victims of sexual assault and other abuse or in the performance of evidentiary examinations.

A medical evidentiary examination is given to victims of sexual assault and other forms of abuse and is performed to collect physical evidence and document findings that can be used to identify, prosecute, and convict an assailant. Although an evidentiary examination includes an array of medical components, including assessment of injuries and crisis intervention, its main purpose is to meet the needs of the legal system. It can also be called a medico-legal examination or a sexual assault forensic examination. Basic components of the examination usually include the following:

- Medical evaluation and crisis intervention: Recognition and treatment of physical injuries, risk evaluation and counseling for STDs and pregnancy.
- Forensic evidence collection: Evaluation, collection, and preservation of evidence; interpretation of findings; and the documentation of examination results for law enforcement purposes.
- Evaluation of emotional needs: Assessment of psychological functioning, response to the immediate emotional needs of the victim, and referral for appropriate follow-up mental health evaluation and treatment.
- Referral for follow-up care: Assessment of the need for follow-up treatment and services, with written instructions for the patient on recommendations for further treatment of injuries, laboratory testing, and mental health services, and the names and phone numbers of referral organizations.

The examination should be based on an integrated clinical approach that considers and responds to cultural issues for victims of diverse racial, ethnic, and economic backgrounds. Culturally congruent care includes sensitivity to victims who might be intimidated by police, such as an immigrant or homeless person; to victims who need translation services; or to women who cannot admit being violated without being ostracized from family and community. The way the examination is conducted is affected by factors such as the clinical protocols used in a particular health care institution, the type and contents of the rape kit used by the hospital, the length of time elapsed since the attack (which affects the viability of some types of evidence), whether police believe that drugs might have been used in the attack, the nature of the attack, and whether the victim has bathed or changed clothes. Examination of vulnerable populations such as the disabled, the elderly, or young children, presents special challenges to the examination process that the forensic nurses must be equipped to handle.

6.6.8 Training of Health Care Providers

To perform an evidentiary examination correctly and to ensure that the process meets the test of reliability that a court will one day demand, a health care provider needs training and experience in what procedures are needed and how they should be done. Voelker (1996) and Stobo, Salmon, and Cohn (2002) assert that most health care providers are not routinely trained or familiarized with the management of sexual assault victims and the performance of evidentiary examinations. The training model that is growing rapidly and bringing substantial change to the field, of course, is the aforementioned SANE/SART programs; however, other models exist. Other organizations that offer continuing education (CE) programs to develop the skills needed to perform medical evidentiary examinations include a handful of state-funded programs, such as the California Medical Training Center at the University of California-Davis that provides specialized multidisciplinary training and distance learning facilities, and the Texas Office of the Attorney General, which provides financial support and technical assistance for development of SANE/SART training programs throughout Texas, and has a full-time unit to encourage these programs. Several professional organizations have developed materials, policies, and course offerings related to sexual assault, including the American College of Obstetricians and Gynecologists (ACOG). The ACEP has developed a detailed examination protocol, as well as other materials and training.

Distinct from educational programs that are offered at a particular time and place and are part of a formal training process, guidelines, professional standards, and clinical practice protocols are developed by professional organizations or quality improvement bodies to help guide practicing providers toward improved health outcomes. In recent years, the development of guidelines and protocols has grown, as evidence-based medicine has become a dominant force in the way medicine is practiced. A number of specialty-specific professional organizations and accrediting bodies have developed clinical protocols, training materials, professional standards, and policy statements to assist their members in practice. These organizations include the JCAHO; the American Academy of Pediatrics (AAP), ACEP, ACOG, the AMA, the American Professional Society on the Abuse of Children (APSAC), the American Academy of Child and Adolescent Psychiatry (AACAP), the American Society for Testing and Materials (ASTM), and the CDC. Training is discussed in greater detail in chapter 15.

6.7 THE COST OF SEXUAL ASSAULT

Essential to any study of forensic nursing programs is the cost of abuse and assault to society. The most recent study to assess both immediate and long-term costs of sexual assault was published by the National Institute of Justice (NIJ) at the Department of Justice in 1996. The report indicated that costs associated with nonfatal rape and sexual assault averaged $87,000 per incident for adults, and $99,000 per incident for children. The estimates consider both immediate use of medical care and mental health services, lost productivity, and permanent disability, as well as the cost of less tangible impacts such as pain, suffering, fear, and lost quality of life. The researchers estimated that between 10 and 20 percent of mental health care expenditures in the United States might be attributable to crime victims who seek treatment as a result of their victimization. The total costs per incident of nonfatal rape and sexual assault are estimated at $87,000, including $2,200 in productivity losses, $500 for medical care expenses, $2,200 for mental health care, and $81,400 associated with reduced quality of life. The average total cost per incident of child abuse is $60,000, including $2,200 in lost productivity, $430 in medical care costs, $2,500 for mental health care, and $52,371 in reduced quality of life. The greatest losses are associated with sexual abuse ($99,000 per incident), followed by physical abuse ($67,000) and emotional abuse ($27,000). These figures were derived from the analysis of 1,106 jury awards and settlements to assault, rape, and burn survivors to compensate for pain, suffering, and lost quality of life (excluding punitive damages).

The total annual losses in the United States associated with child abuse (including sexual, physical, and emotional abuse) are estimated at $56 billion, including $23 billion specifically for rape and sexual assault. Total annual losses associated with rape and sexual assault of adults are estimated at $127 billion, including $4 billion in medical costs, $3.5 billion in other tangible costs, and $119 billion in quality of life. Total annual losses associated specifically with adult domestic violence (including fatalities, rape, other assaults and robbery) are estimated at $67 billion, including $1.8 billion for medical care, $7 billion for other tangible costs, and $58 billion for quality of life.

Injuries of sexual assault victims ranged from minor to moderate, according to results of the 1995–96 National Violence Against Women Survey (NVAWS), a telephone sample survey that collected information on medical services provided to adult victims of rape. The survey established that:

- About one third (31 percent) of female rape victims reported physical injuries. Almost three quarters of the injuries (73 percent) were minor (e.g., scratches, bruises, or welts).
- About one third (36 percent) of those injured received some type of medical care. The majority of injured female victims who received care were treated in a hospital (82 percent). Although most of those treated in a hospital were seen in the ER or an outpatient department, about 13 percent stayed for at least one night, with an average stay of 3.6 nights for those admitted on an inpatient basis.
- About half (55 percent) of all women who received medical care were treated by a physician outside of a hospital and averaged 4.8 office visits related to the injury. Somewhat less than one fifth received dental care (16.9 percent). A similar proportion visited a physical therapist (16.7 percent).

6.8 QUALITY-OF-CARE ISSUES

A number of quality-of-care issues relating to variations in SANE/SART practice have been raised by the nurses who provide this care, as well as the agencies and institutions that depend on their services. These issues include lack of standardized protocols, procedures, and rape testing kits in use; lack of trained providers and expert consultants; uneven quality of examination facilities and technologies available; and poor quality and limited capability to test for drugs and DNA. What little data exists suggests wide variations in access to and quality of services received by victims of sexual assault, including length of waiting times; provision of information or testing for STDs; the availability of nurse examiners or other providers with specialized expertise in evidentiary examinations; the presence of extraneous personnel during the examination; the availability or referral to other community resources such as advocacy organizations or social service agencies; and the availability of private waiting areas, examination rooms, showers, or the provision of clothing.

Access to medical evidentiary examinations is not uniform across the United States and access can be compromised by payment issues. Although numerous federal and state laws have been enacted to ensure that victims of sexual assault do not have to pay for medical evidentiary examinations, some states limit payment to victims who indicate a willingness to report the assault, a decision the victim might not want or be able to make immediately. Even when the victim is willing to commit to formally filing a report and cooperating with prosecution, the law enforcement agency or prosecutor still might not be willing to approve payment for an examination if they feel the case is weak, a decision that is made in the early stages of an investigation. In addition, it is the opinion of many experts working in the field that despite legal prohibitions, billing of the patient victim continues to be widespread.

6.8.1 Mandatory Reporting

At the state level, mandatory reporting seems to be one of the most important contributions that government is making toward addressing sexual assault and abuse issues. Almost all states have mandatory reporting requirements for child abuse and elder abuse, and three fifths have or are developing practice protocols on sexual assault; 45 states have or are developing standardized evidence collection kits. A few states have established mandatory educational requirements for health professionals, and about half of the states have SART/SANE programs. Mandatory reporting laws require physicians, and often nurses, other health professionals, and clergy, to report actual or suspected sexual assault and other types of abuse and neglect. In 48 states, health care professionals are required to report known or suspected instances of actual or suspected child abuse, and most states also require physicians to report if they believe that elder abuse has occurred. According to Stobo et al. (2002), four states (California, Colorado, Rhode Island, and Kentucky) specifically require physicians to report intimate partner abuse, even if the victim's wishes are otherwise. Houry, Sachs, Feldhaus, and Linden (2002) say that 42 states require health care providers to report injuries resulting from firearms, knives, and other weapons.

Opposition to mandatory reporting laws has occurred, and reasons include the following:

- Mandatory reporting might expose a victim to retaliation, as many know their assailant.
- A lack of informed consent around the reporting issue compromises the patient–provider relationship.
- It takes away the autonomy of sexual assault victims for whom a sense of regained control

over their life can be an important step to recovery. There might also be a discrepancy between the legal requirements and the health care provider's personal threshold of what they feel constitutes abuse.

6.8.2 Addressing the Issues of Quality of Care

The Institute of Medicine (IOM) report, *Confronting Chronic Neglect* (National Academy Press, 2002) identified a number of practice variations with which forensic nurses across the country are grappling.

1. Lack of standardized protocols, procedures, and rape kits. A number of protocols and procedures have been developed, but there is considerable overlap. More important, there are significant differences among the protocols in use and none have been compared or rigorously assessed, at least until now. The national sexual assault protocol, issued in September 2004 by the U.S. Department of Justice, is examined at the end of this chapter.
2. Lack of trained providers and expert consultants. Voelker (1996) asserts that although there are curricula for instructing how to perform a medical evidentiary examination, these programs have reached only a few, self-selected providers. There have been notable efforts to extend and support forensic training programs to health professionals already in practice, but the sheer number and types of providers who might see a sexual assault victim is daunting. The IOM report makes the point that all providers need basic competencies.
3. Uneven quality of examination facilities and technologies available. Most victims who seek medical care, although not all, are examined in a hospital setting. Many hospitals have developed special areas and separate facilities for examining patients, to provide a place where the lengthy examination will not impede care for other types of patients coming into an ER, to make available the special equipment and storage facilities used in such examinations, and to provide the victim a sanctuary that protects her or him from further traumatic experiences. Quiet, age-appropriate environments are thought to be especially important when examining children, who are particularly vulnerable to retraumatization and who also need examiners who are trained to meet the specialized needs of child victims. Specialized and separate sexual assault units within or near a hospital are viewed by many as ideal from a patient's perspective, but such facilities are not available in all hospitals. Reasons include lack of space; too few patients to make it an effective use of reserved space; an unwillingness or inability to spend the resources needed to establish and maintain a dedicated sexual assault unit; and a lack of understanding by administrators or the community about the importance of specialized care. Equipment and space are expensive resources, and smaller, rural hospitals might have particular difficulty creating a viable program, facility, and trained staff.
4. Limited capability to test for drugs and DNA. Most hospitals do not routinely test for the full range of drugs (including substances used in drug-facilitated rape). Even fewer have the skills and technology to handle DNA testing, which has assumed additional importance with the advent of state DNA banks. DNA evidence can easily be compromised by untrained providers who are involved in the collection and preservation process. The sample can be contaminated if someone sneezes or coughs over the evidence, or even if the examiner touches his or her own hair or body and then touches the area to be tested. According to Turman (2001), it is also affected by heat and humidity, and is easily degraded. Forensic DNA testing is a lengthy and expensive process, but one which is often paid for by law enforcement or the prosecutor's office. However, even police labs often lack adequate forensic testing capabilities.

   In partial response to these issues, a federal law, the Paul Coverdell National Forensic Sciences Improvement Act, was enacted in 2000, authorizing approximately $500 million in federal funds over a five-year period to be used by states to improve procedures for testing DNA samples, hire and train personnel, modernize laboratory equipment, and improve the quality and timeliness of forensic science services. The Justice for All Act of 2004 is another example of a federal attempt to increase capacity and resources to handle biological evidence; this piece of legislation is examined in chapter 14.
5. Challenged access to services. Reports endeavoring to characterize the type and quality of victims' services indicate sweeping variations. One survey found that 55 percent of rape victims had not been given information on HIV testing and that one third were not given information about other STD testing. The practice of immediate testing for STDs is controversial because any infection found would reflect prior exposure, and not all assaults will expose a

patient to STD risks. However, others favor it as baseline information, and virtually all experts agree that the provider should stress the need for follow-up STD evaluation and treatment for patients at risk, according to the CDC (2002). Maxwell and Soubielle (1996) surveyed 130 Florida hospitals; of the 64 facilities that responded (49 percent):

- 88 percent saw rape victims through the ER.
- Six hospitals reported that law enforcement personnel assist in the exam, a violation of the state's evidence collection protocol. (Most experts in the field agree that, except in rare cases, there is no medical or legal reason for law enforcement representatives, male or female, to be present during the exam. Maintaining the chain of custody during the examination is a function and responsibility of the attending medical personnel and one that should not require outside assistance.)
- Although the JCAHO calls for ongoing in-service training, only about one fourth of hospitals reported that they provided such training for the personnel conducting examinations.
- Most hospitals only involve local rape crisis center personnel if requested to do so by the victims, many of whom do not know that such services exist.
- Fewer than half of the hospitals reported that they provide written material on common rape reactions and community resources as a usual practice; 15 percent said they do not provide the victim with any information on resources.
- Just over half of the hospitals set aside separate rooms for rape victims and some provide showers for the rape victims after the exam, maintain a clothing closet, or provide underwear or paper jumpsuits to patients whose clothing was collected.
- Most hospitals (82 percent) discussed HIV screening with patients and dispensed prophylactic drugs for STDs (88 percent).

6. Access issues involving payment for evidentiary exams. When a sexual assault victim presents to a hospital or clinic, medical staff will typically assess and respond to serious or life-threatening injuries. However, the decision to do a formal evidentiary examination is dependent on the patient, who must give written consent, and is affected both by state laws and the judgment of local law enforcement officials or prosecutors as to whether an examination will be useful and can be justified.

Numerous federal and state laws have been enacted to ensure that victims of sexual assault do not have to pay for medical evidentiary examinations. However, some states limit payment only to victims who are willing to report the assault to police and to cooperate in any prosecution. If the assault is not reported, or the case is not prosecuted, the victim might be unable to obtain a full examination, or might have to pay for the costs of an examination. A number of states place responsibility for payment on the county where the sexual offense occurred, or on the entity that requests the examination, most often the investigating law enforcement agency or the prosecuting attorney. If the county official, police officer, or prosecutor is told that the victim does not plan to formally report the assault (a decision that the victim might not want or be able to make immediately, and a decision that sometimes changes), they might not approve payment for an examination. Similarly, if they believe that the victim's account is weak or that successful prosecution is unlikely, they might act to preserve limited resources and not provide approval for payment. Even when state laws mandate that victims not be charged for the expense of evidentiary exams, there are cases in which claims might be submitted to third-party insurance companies, compromising the victim's privacy, as insurance companies might not only be informed of the sexual assault but could also learn about exposure to HIV or other aspects of treatment that could affect insurance coverage in the future. Victims might also be forced to disclose the assault to the primary person on the insurance, such as a family member or even an employer. Victims of crime are not generally required to cover the costs of evidence collection incurred in the investigation of their cases. Despite the fact that most states have laws that designate payment sources to cover the costs of forensic exams for sexual assault victims, and some even specifically prohibit billing of victims, billing of sexual assault victims continues to be widespread, according to 2003 data from the National Center for Victims of Crisis.

6.8.3 Evidence of SANE/SART Efficacy

Ledray (2001) says that little research data is available on the efficacy of the SANE/SART model, with the bulk of the information contained in anecdotal case studies. For the nurse working as a SANE, much validity comes through a job well done; benchmarking and best practices will have to catch up with real-world performance. Until then, it has been documented by Frank (1996) that without a SANE in the ED, victims encounter rushed, overworked health care providers who might appear aloof and insensitive. The SANE is able to provide not only the evidentiary exam, but also additional resources and support that facilitate follow- through in the judicial process. (Frank, 1996;

Ledray, 1992a, 1992b) Arndt (1988) found that this assistance can trigger an increase in reporting by victims.

Ledray (1999) discovered that in one program, 38 percent of 337 rape survivors were uncertain about reporting when they first came to the hospital ED. After meeting with a SANE, an additional 12 percent opted to report, and the police were called to the ED. An additional 23 percent agreed to have an evidentiary exam completed because they thought they would report. Only 3 percent of the 337 survivors in this study did not report. Speck (1995) asserts that a SANE program satisfies a victim's physical and emotional needs because it dramatically reduces a victim's waiting time in the ED. Speck reports that in a client satisfaction questionnaire mailed to 201 survivors two weeks after they were seen by a SANE for an exam, 93 percent of those returning the questionnaire were satisfied with the care they received. SANEs also perform more efficient and accurate forensic evidence collection, the result of thorough training and competent experience on the job. Ledray (2001) notes, "A primary advantage of the SANE program is that with a limited number of dedicated nurses completing all of the evidentiary exams in a given hospital or regional area, they are able to complete an adequate number of exams to develop and maintain this proficiency." Additionally, SANEs have worked with prosecutors and law enforcement personnel to develop a better understanding of the medical competencies required to obtain forensic evidence that helps obtain convictions.

Researchers have found that SANEs also provide more thorough documentation.

Ledray and Simmelink (1997) compared 24 sexual assault evidence kits collected by SANEs to 73 evidence kits collected by non-SANEs; the SANE kits were overall better documented, more complete, and always maintained proper chain of evidence, whereas the others did not. Thirteen kits completed by non-SANEs either had no indication of who had collected the evidence or it was illegible, making the evidence useless. All of the SANE kits were properly labeled. In addition, the work of SANEs has been found to improve prosecutorial outcomes. Although there are reports of attorneys who were initially concerned about the testimony of SANEs, Ledray (2001) says they later admitted that SANEs were extremely credible witnesses in court due to their extensive experience and expertise in conducting the evidentiary exam. Yorker (1996) states that prosecutors trust the competence of the SANE as a witness if the case goes to trial, and Lenehan (1991) reports that SANEs have the credential needed to validate their work.

It is essential that health care providers, in the course of performing their duties, are objective and as free as possible from any prejudice or bias. It is possible to provide an objective service without sacrificing sensitivity or compassion. The need for impartiality is especially important when providing evidence—in the form of a written report or court testimony—in cases that proceed to criminal prosecution. Investigators, consciously or unconsciously, can bring considerable pressure to bear on health care practitioners to provide an interpretation that would resolve an issue. These forces could be direct and forceful, or subtle and insidious, and are likely to be particularly strong in situations where the practitioner has a formal relationship with an investigating authority, where a close personal relationship has developed between the investigator and the practitioner, or when the individual roles of the investigator and the practitioner become blurred. Fairness might also be compromised when the practitioner develops an unconscious or misplaced desire to help investigators.

In *The Effectiveness of Sexual Assault Nurse Examiner (SANE) Programs*, author Rebecca Campbell, PhD (2004), associate professor of community psychology and program evaluation at Michigan State University, affirms what forensic nurses have always known: They provide high-quality, effective, medico-legally sound service to victims in forensic cases. She writes, "The role of SANE nurses is complex, as they must attend to the medical, forensic, and psychological needs of their patients" (Antognoli-Toland, 1985; Littel, 2001; Taylor, 2002), adding that they minimize the victim's physical and psychological trauma and maximize the probability of collection and preservation of evidence for potential use in the legal system (Young et al., 1992). Campbell adds, "Although it is often the forensic aspects of SANE nurses' work that receive the most attention by the legal and medical communities, Ledray, Faugno, and Speck (2001) emphasize this psychological care dimension when they noted that a SANE nurse is a compassionate and supportive nurse who is also a skilled forensic technician."

Campbell points to a few studies that have systematically evaluated the psychological impact of SANE programs. In a study of the Memphis SANE program, Solola, Scott, Severs, and Howell (1983) found that 50 percent of victims in their study sample were able to return to their usual vocation within one month, and in three to six months, 85 percent felt secure alone in public areas. At the end of a year, more than 90 percent of the survivors were entirely free of their initial assault-related anxieties and emotional discomposure. Other research, Campbell says, suggests that at the very least, rape survivors perceive SANE nurses as helpful and supportive. Malloy (1991) surveyed 70 patients in crisis, and found that 85 percent of the survivors identified the nurses' listening skills as a mechanism that helped them the most during their crisis period. Ericksen et al. (2002) conducted semistructured qualitative interviews with eight survivors who were treated in a Canadian specialized sexual assault service that included specially trained physicians and SANEs. The researchers identified several common threads in the participants' narratives: Victims felt as though they were respected as a whole person, their needs were met and they were treated with dignity and respect, they felt the presence of the nursing staff provided information about what to expect, they felt safe among female caregivers who were sensitive, they felt in control because they were given options and were not pushed toward certain choices, they felt reassured and believed by the staff, they felt they were cared for by people with expertise, and they felt cared for beyond the hospital setting because they received follow-up care or the option for follow-up care.

Campbell reports that "empirical studies that directly compare the evidence collected by SANE nurses and physicians on objective criteria would better inform the debate over whether nurses are competent medical forensic examiners." She points to two such studies conducted in the United States. Ledray and Simmelink (1997) reported the findings from an audit study of rape kits sent to the Minnesota Bureau of Criminal Apprehension. Twenty-seven kits conducted by SANE nurses were compared to 73 kits collected by physicians or non-SANE nurses with respect to completeness of specimens collected, documentation, and maintenance of chain of custody. Overall, the SANE-collected kits were more thorough and had fewer errors than the non-SANE kits. For example, with respect to completeness of evidence, 96 percent of the SANE kits versus 85 percent of non-SANE kits collected the swabs to match the recorded orifice of penetration, 92 percent of the SANE kits versus 15 percent of non-SANE kits contained an extra tube of blood for alcohol and drug analysis, and in 100 percent of the SANE kits versus 81 percent of non-SANE kits, a blood stain card was properly prepared. In addition, the chain of evidence was broken in non-SANE kits but was always maintained in SANE kits. "Although these descriptive data suggest that the SANE nurses' evidence collection was more thorough and accurate, inferential statistics were not reported so it is not known whether these differences were statistically significant," Campbell says.

A larger scale, Colorado-based study by Sievers et al. (2003) explicitly tested differences between SANE and non-SANE kits, and also found support for better evidence collection by SANE nurses. Specifically, this study compared 279 kits collected by SANE nurses and 236 by doctors or non-SANE nurses on 10 quality control criteria, and found that in nine of these 10 categories, the SANE-collected kits were significantly better. The kits collected by SANE nurses were significantly more likely than kits collected by physicians to include the proper sealing and labeling of specimen envelopes, the correct number of swabs and other evidence (pubic hairs and head hairs), the correct kind of blood tubes, a vaginal motility slide, and a completed crime lab form. Sievers et al. (2003) provide the strongest evidence to date that SANE nurses are qualified to conduct forensic exams, and in fact, they perform them better than physicians. However, it is important to note that training and experience, not job title or professional degree, are the likely reasons behind these findings. Further underscoring the link between experience and evidence quality, DiNitto et al. (1986) reported that prosecutors in Florida were "satisfied with evidence collected by nurse examiners, crediting the training of the nurse examiners... Prosecutors tended to be more pleased with the quality of a physician's evidence when the examiner had conducted many exams and thus had perfected the techniques." Because SANE nurses have made it a professional priority to obtain extensive forensic training and practice, it is not surprising that both case study and empirical data suggest they are better medical forensic examiners than physicians and nurses who have not completed such training.

SANEs provide law enforcement personnel and prosecutors with detailed forensic evidence documenting crimes of sexual assault, which raises the question of whether SANE programs have an impact on prosecution rates in their communities. The literature suggests that SANE programs increase prosecution, according to Aiken and Speck (1995), Cornell (1998), Hutson (2002), Littel (2001), and Seneski (1992). For example, there are reports that SANE programs specifically increase the rate of plea bargains because when confronted with the detailed forensic evidence collected by the SANE nurses, assailants decide to plead guilty (often to a lesser charge) rather than face trial, according to research by Aiken and Speck (1995), Ledray (1992a, 1992b), Littel (2001), and Seneski (1992). Other research indicates that when cases do go to trial, the expert witness testimony provided by SANE nurses is instrumental in obtaining convictions, according to O'Brien (1996), Smith (1996), and Ledray (1999).

Yet there have been few studies that have empirically tested the hypothesis that SANE programs increase prosecution. Studies that report the prosecution rates for SANE programs rarely include a comparison group (e.g., rates before and after the SANE program was implemented, or comparisons to another community without a SANE program). However, there is already an extensive literature on what are considered to be typical rates of prosecution in communities without SANE programs. For example, arrest rates in rape cases have been found to vary between 25 percent (Frazier & Haney, 1996) and 49 percent (Spohn & Horney, 1992). Prosecution rates are substantially lower, with only 14 percent (LaFree, 1980) to 35 percent of reported cases successfully prosecuted. Only 7 percent (Galvin & Polk, 1982) to 17 percent of cases end with a guilty verdict or guilty plea bargain.

Solola et al. (1983) examined the legal outcomes for 621 victims who were treated in the Memphis SANE program in 1980. Police reports were filed in 573 of these cases (92 percent), and 124 resulted in an arrest and successful prosecution (22 percent of reported cases). However, 135 cases were still pending at the time this study was conducted, and if the rates of arrest and prosecution are examined only in closed cases, the prosecution rate was 28 percent. In either analysis, the prosecution rate of 22 percent or 28 percent is still low, but higher rates that have been found for non-SANE cases. In a study of the Santa Cruz County SANE program, Arndt (1988) noted that 42 percent of sexual assaults involving victims 14 years and older resulted in arrests of the perpetrators, and 58 percent of child molestation cases resulted in arrest. Ledray (1992a, 1992b) reported that of 417 rape cases in Minneapolis in 1990, police presented 193 cases to the county attorney (46 percent); of those 193 cases, 60 were not charged by the prosecutor (31 percent), 65 defendants pleaded guilty (34 percent), and 14 went to trial (7 percent). Six perpetrators were found guilty and eight were found not guilty (the outcomes in the remaining 54 cases were not reported). The rates of guilty plea-bargaining reported in this study are higher than those found in studies of non-SANE jurisdictions, researchers conclude.

Ledray notes that a stronger methodological design would include a direct comparison of legal outcomes for SANE cases versus non-SANE cases, and points to work by Crandall and Helitzer (2003). They compared the legal outcomes for sexual assault cases seen at the University of New Mexico's Health Sciences Center for the two years prior to the inception of a SANE program (1994–1996, $n = 242$) and four years afterward (1996–1999, $n = 715$). A significantly higher percentage of victims treated in the SANE program reported the assault to the police than did before the SANE program was launched in this community (72 percent vs. 50 percent) and significantly more survivors had evidence collected using approved kits (88 percent vs. 30 percent). Police filed more charges of sexual assault post-SANE as compared to pre-SANE (7 charges per perpetrator versus 5.4). The conviction rate for charged SANE cases was also higher (69 percent vs. 57 percent), resulting in longer average sentences (5.1 vs. 1.2 years). These data provide the strongest evidence yet that SANE programs can have a beneficial impact on the prosecution of sexual assault cases, according to Ledray.

6.8.4 Health Care Provision for Victims of Sexual Violence

According to the WHO (2003), there are a number of givens regarding the delivery of health care to victims of sexual violence:

- The health and welfare of the patient is the foremost priority.
- Ideally, the health care and medico-legal services should be provided at the same time and in the same place by the same person.
- Health care professionals should receive special training in providing services for victims of sexual violence and should also have a good understanding of local protocols, rules, and laws applicable to the field of sexual violence.
- There should be a constructive and professional relationship with the other individuals and groups treating and assisting the victim or investigating the crime, as networking with other service providers can help ensure comprehensive care.
- Health care professionals should be free of bias or prejudices and maintain high ethical standards in the provision of services.
- Resource constraints might preclude the possibility of service provision in an ideal facility, but it is possible to improve the quality of existing facilities by ensuring they are accessible, secure, clean, and private.

Kilpatrick (1992) says that even though many sexual assault survivors do not sustain serious physical injury as a result of the assault, they still access the medical system for STD treatment, HIV/AIDS testing, emergency contraception, forensic evidence collection, and medical care. Sexual assault also has health effects that extend beyond immediate medical and forensic needs. Kimerling and Calhoun (1994) found that rape victims seeking care at a rape crisis center had more self-reported physician visits than nonvictims up to one year after the sexual assault. There have been many long-lasting symptoms and illnesses that have been associated with sexual victimization including gastrointestinal disorders and a variety of chronic pain disorders including pelvic, back, and facial pain and headaches. Given the fact that health care facilities are a common point of entry for sexual assault survivors, the medical system is in a unique position to identify survivors of sexual assault and to refer them to counseling and advocacy services.

Research has shown that the response by health care professionals can either increase or diminish survivors' psychological consequences of sexual assault (Cohen, Donohue, & Kovener, 1996). As initial responders in many sexual assault cases, the medical system plays an important role in survivors' recovery. The important role that health care providers play in the lives of sexual assault victims was underscored in *The Response to Sexual Assault: Removing Barriers to Services and Justice,* a report of the Michigan Sexual Assault Systems Response Task Force (2001). This workgroup's goal was to provide health care professionals with guidelines and best practices for responding to the medical needs of victims of sexual assault. The task force identified the following issues and made the following recommendations:

Issue 1: Coordination of Supporting Disciplines. Burgess, Fawcett, Hazelwood, and Grant (1995) assert that dealing with sexual victimization requires the collaborative and cooperative efforts of a network of services, but many individuals are not informed of services available to them.

Recommendations: Where a sexual assault program advocate is available, the ED and sexual assault program should work together to enhance the provision of immediate care and support for survivors. Law enforcement is also a resource for survivors of sexual assault. Hospital staff, physicians, health department nurses, alcohol and drug treatment counselors, dentists, health educators, prenatal health care providers, HIV/AIDS counselors, psychologists, social workers, family planning specialists, and mental health providers should be aware of the services available for sexual assault survivors in their community and make appropriate referrals. The medical system should participate in or initiate the community development of a victim-centered coordinated community plan to respond to sexual assault to better serve the immediate and long-term needs of sexual assault survivors. Further, "Well-planned multidisciplinary community response plans have been demonstrated to be cost effective while diminishing further harm to the (sexual assault) patient and providing comprehensive care" (ACEP, 1999). The medical system should be included in SARTs. Regardless of where the survivor enters the system—a police station, an ED, or , phone call to a sexual assault program's crisis line—the SART can be activated. A SART has the potential to provide a greater continuum of care for sexual assault survivors, increased quality of care for survivors, and a reduction of the secondary trauma that survivors often experience as they move through the medical, judicial, and law enforcement systems. SART programs can also increase the investment in providing a better response to survivors of sexual assault by all team members and keep the focus of the response on the survivor. If survivors of sexual assault experience a more compassionate and collaborative response, they might be likely to make a police report and participate in prosecution. The ED directors should promote within the department a cooperative and professional working relationship with, and understanding and respect for, the role and responsibilities of the local sexual assault service programs, the prosecuting attorneys, and law enforcement.

Issue 2: Mandatory Reporting of Sexual Assaults by Medical Personnel. Many health care providers are confused by their state's mandatory reporting law.

Recommendations: Facilities should discuss and provide guidance on the implications of mandatory reporting due to the complexity of issues involved. The discussion should include careful consideration of the patient's right to privacy. Input should be sought from individuals representing law enforcement, prosecutors, sexual assault programs, and health care professionals.

Issue 3: Training. There is minimal training in medical and nursing schools on meeting the medical and emotional needs of sexual assault survivors as well as on conducting forensic evidence collection. Cohen et al. (1996) found that 56 percent of physicians and 63 percent of nurses indicated that they received no forensic training. Health care providers reported that the first time they became familiar with the forensic evidence collection kit was when they were forced to complete one. Lack of training often results in inconsistency of care, incorrect or incomplete forensic examinations, and inappropriate documentation. All medical professionals who currently conduct sexual assault evidence collection need specialized training. All trauma responders should possess the same level of competence in responding to sexual assault that they have in responding to other types of trauma. The goal is to improve the health care response to sexual assault survivors through ensuring that all health care professionals have a basic understanding of the dynamics of sexual assault and how to appropriately respond to survivors.

Recommendations: All health care facilities that provide treatment to sexual assault survivors should follow the recommendations outlined in *Evaluation and Management of the Sexually Assaulted or Sexually Abused Patient* (ACEP, 1999). Health care professionals who provide medical care and collect forensic evidence should demonstrate competence in the following areas: multidisciplinary team concept; dynamics of sexual assault; sexual assault forensic examination; proper handling of evidence (maintaining chain-of-evidence); anatomy and physiology as it relates to sexual assault; psychological aspects of sexual assault; the role of the forensic examiner in the criminal justice system; medical management of STIs, HIV, and pregnancy; and services available to survivors. Health care facilities should provide training on these topics. Trainers can include the local sexual assault program, the prosecutor's office, law enforcement agencies, forensic nurses, the local health department, and other local and national experts in the care of sexual assault survivors. Training should be provided to health care professionals on effective, culturally competent communication with victims including the use of interpreter services and assistive technology. Training for health care professionals should also address how to appropriately document cases of sexual assault. Documentation should be based in fact, use quotes whenever possible, and make no judgmental statements. This training should include prosecuting attorneys. Health care facilities should comply with the JCAHO guidelines requiring emergency and ambulatory care facilities to have protocols on rape, sexual molestation, and domestic violence. To meet these guidelines, health care providers must develop services that identify and document cases of sexual assault and refer victims to agencies that can provide further support and advocacy. According to the JCAHO guidelines, appropriate management of the patient requires a standardized clinical evaluation as well as effective interface with law enforcement for the handling of forensic evidence and coordination of the continuum of care with a community plan. It also requires health care providers to address the medical and emotional needs of the patient while addressing the forensic requirements of the criminal justice system. Medical issues include acute injuries and evaluation of potential STDs and pregnancy. Emotional needs include acute and nonacute crisis intervention and referral for appropriate follow-up counseling, support, and advocacy. Forensic tasks include thorough documentation of pertinent historical and physical findings, proper specimen collection and handling of evidence, and presentation of findings and conclusions in court. Health care professionals should also receive training on evidence collection techniques with suspects. It is useful in police investigations to collect forensic evidence from the suspect as well as the survivor.

Issue 4: FNE Program Development. Current treatment of sexual assault survivors in traditional ED settings often revictimizes survivors seeking care. Because the vast majority of sexual assault survivors do not sustain serious physical injuries, they can often be forced to wait, sometimes up to 12 hours, while not being allowed to urinate, drink, shower, or change clothes to preserve physical evidence (Thomas & Zachritz, 1993). In seeking ways to treat and collect evidence from sexual assault survivors with more sensitivity and effectiveness, and to ensure empowerment rather than revictimization, some communities have established FNE programs (Lang, 1999). Although most FNE programs started by conducting forensic and medical exams with sexual assault survivors, these programs have increasingly been used to conduct forensic exams (document, collect evidence, and treat injury and trauma) with domestic violence survivors. Because of the common application in sexual assault cases, many nurse examiner programs refer to themselves as SANE programs. An FNE program includes the use of a clinician (usually a registered nurse or a nurse practitioner) who conducts the forensic examination of the sexual assault victim (Lang, 1999). Forensic nursing is the application of nursing science to public or legal proceedings that involve the investigation or treatment of trauma or death of victims and perpetrators of criminal violence. The clinician is specially trained in forensic evidence collection, sexual assault trauma response, forensic techniques using specialized equipment, expert witness testimony, assessment of injuries, STD treatment, and pregnancy evaluation and treatment (Cohen et al., 1996; Ledray & Berry, 1998).

Recommendations: The medical system should promote the development of FNE programs by collaborating with other systems in the formation of the program. Utilization of medical facilities for the location of the FNE program can be an important resource that the medical community can offer. Many FNE programs are located within medical facilities such as EDs, women's health centers, and community health departments. FNE programs should be developed by a multidisciplinary task force including, but not limited to, sexual assault survivors; sexual assault program staff; hospital administrators; ED personnel including medical directors, physicians, and nurses; local law enforcement agencies; probation officers; court judges; county and city prosecuting attorneys; prosecutor's office victim advocates; and state police crime lab personnel. In addition, the task force should reflect the diversity of the community and include representatives from various cultural and other special populations in the community. All FNE programs should establish protocols and procedures to ensure the separation of team roles. Additional safeguards should be in place to maintain the actual and perceived neutrality and objectivity of the program, the credibility of the FNE, and the integrity of the forensic evidence collected. This is especially important for community-based FNE programs. FNE programs should include an on-site response by a sexual assault advocate. Although FNEs are trained in understanding sexual assault trauma response and are concerned for the emotional well-being of the patient, an advocate is able to provide support, advocacy, and validation so that the FNE can maintain his or her objectivity to preserve the forensic value of the physical exam. These roles should be clearly defined. When an FNE program is not located in a hospital, an agreement should be negotiated with the local hospital so that the FNE has access to the hospital facilities to conduct the forensic exam if the victim needs to remain in the hospital for injuries or does not wish to transfer to another location. FNE programs should be developed and operate with the holistic care of the patient being the primary focus. The forensic examination is performed for the purpose of treatment and diagnosis of a medical condition (sexual assault), and as such, the FNE can often testify to statements (made by the patient) as a medical exception to hearsay. In FNE programs it is important to base practice on sound nursing principles.

6.8.5 General Considerations for Health Care Delivery

When caring for victims of sexual violence, the overriding priority must always be the health and welfare of the patient. The provision of medico-legal services assumes secondary importance to that of general health care services, such as the treatment of injuries, assessment and management of pregnancy, and STIs. Performing a forensic examination without addressing the primary health care needs of patients is negligent. Concern for the welfare of the patient extends to ensuring that patients are able to maintain their dignity. Medical and forensic services should be offered in such a way to minimize the number of invasive physical examinations and interviews the patient is required to undergo.

6.8.5.1 Ethical Issues

It is a fundamental duty of all health care providers to use their professional skills in an ethical manner and observe the laws of the community. When providing services to victims of sexual violence, the following principles are generally considered to be fundamental:

- Autonomy: The right of patients to make decisions on their own behalf. All steps taken in providing services are based on the informed consent of the patient.
- Beneficence: The duty or obligation to act in the best interests of the patient.
- Nonmalfeasance: The duty or obligation to avoid harm to the patient.
- Fairness: Doing and giving what is rightfully due.

Health care professionals, in following the oath of "First, do no harm," must also be aware of the needs and wishes of the patient, must display sensitivity and compassion, and must maintain objectivity.

6.8.5.2 Timing of Health Care Delivery

The timing of the physical examination is largely dictated by what is best for the patient (particularly when injury intervention is required), but for a number of reasons, is best performed as soon as possible after the patient presents. Delay in accessing services could result in lost therapeutic opportunities, such as provision of emergency contraception; changes to the physical evidence, including healing of injuries; and loss of forensic material, the evidence of contact with the assailant.

6.8.5.3 The Setting of the Examination

Appropriate, high-quality care should be available to sexual assault victims. Consultations and examinations should take place at a site where there is optimal access to the full range of services and facilities that might be required by the patient, for example. Victims should be able to access services 24 hours a day; if it is not possible to keep facilities open all the time (e.g., due to financial constraints), outside normal working hours, access could be provided on an on-call basis. Regardless of the setting and location, experts say care should be ethical, compassionate, objective, and above all, patient centered. Safety, security, and privacy are also important aspects of service provision. In many regions and states, the health and medico-legal components of the service are provided at different times, in different places, and by different people, a process that is considered to be inefficient, unnecessary, and most important, places an unwarranted burden on the victim. Ideally, medico-legal and health services are provided in the same location and preferably by the same health care practitioner. Policymakers and health care professionals are encouraged to develop this model of service provision. For a look at one such model, the Family Justice Center located in San Diego, see chapter 7.

Because sexual assault victims present at any point along the health care continuum, all health care facilities should be able to recognize sexual abuse and provide services to victims of sexual violence, irrespective of whether a forensic examination is required. If not already in place, health care facilities must develop specific policies and procedures for dealing with victims of sexual violence. Given appropriate knowledge and training, any health care provider should be able to provide first-level service to victims of sexual violence. Expertise in the field will develop with further training, professional support, and adequate resources. Ideally, all health care providers who come into contact with victims of sexual violence should receive appropriate training; this applies particularly to nurses and physicians who conduct physical examinations of victims of sexual violence and to those who provide services to children and to the courts. In addition to initial training, health care practitioners should also be given the opportunity to further their education and training and to participate in quality control and peer review processes. In many settings, the sex of the health care provider might be a critical issue. Directors or managers of health care facilities should ensure that female nurses or physicians are available whenever possible. If necessary, efforts to recruit female examiners should be a priority.

6.9 THE MEDICO-LEGAL EXAMINATION ENVIRONMENT

6.9.1 Facilities for Sexual Assault Victims

The ideal location for a health care facility for sexual violence victims is either within a hospital or a medical clinic, or somewhere where there is immediate access to medical expertise. Although most SANE programs are hospital based and located in the ED, there is a growing trend toward locating SANE programs outside of a health care institution. Because the credibility of the SANE has been established and is becoming increasingly accepted, and because research shows many victims sustain injuries requiring ED care, close medical supervision of the SANE's practice is required. Wherever the practice is based, ideally, there should be at least two rooms: a waiting room and reception area plus a separate consulting and examination room (preferably with access to a toilet and waiting facilities). If the facility is providing services to children, the physical surroundings should be child-friendly and special equipment for interviewing the child, such as two-way mirrors or video-recording facilities, might be necessary.

When it comes to equipping the examination room, financial resources are likely to be the main factor in determining the quality and quantity of equipment that can be provided and maintained by any given facility. The type of equipment and volume of supplies needed will depend on the types of services offered, the location of the health care facility, and the level of access to other medical services. When considering equipment needs, service providers should consider carefully the relevance of rape kits and laboratory services to their own situation. The fundamental requirements for facilities that treat sexual assault victims include:

- Accessibility: Services should be accessible 24/7 if possible, or with health care providers on-call around the clock.
- Security: There should be adequate infrastructure in place to protect patients, staff, health records, and the facility itself.
- Cleanliness: A high standard of hygiene is required in the provision of any medical service.
- Privacy: Unauthorized people should not be able to view or hear any aspects of the consultation, so the examination rooms should have walls and a door, not merely curtains. Assailants must be kept separate from their victims.

Most important, victims need a private, discreet suite with ready access to an ED, comprising:

1. An examination room, equipped with an examination table. This space should:
   - Be of a comfortable temperature for the victim.
   - Have auditory and visual privacy.
   - Have clean table paper and a gown for each patient.
   - Have lighting sufficient to perform a genito-anal examination.
   - Have handwashing facilities.
   - Have well-organized and fully stocked forensic supplies.
   - Have a table or desk for documenting and for labeling specimens.
   - Have a lockable door to prevent entry during the examination.
   - Have access to a telephone.
2. A separate room containing a table and chairs where a support person could talk with the patient, and facilities for offering patients refreshments and a change of clothing.
3. A shower and toilet for the patient.
4. A room for the police.
5. A reception area that could also be used as a room for waiting family and friends (WHO, 2003).

6.9.2 Equipment and Supplies

The well-stocked examination suite should have the following items readily accessible:

6.9.2.1 General Medical Supplies

- Syringes, needles, and sharps container
- Sterile swabs
- Blood-collection tubes
- Speculums in various sizes
- Sterilizing equipment for sterilizing specula
- Proctoscope/anoscope
- Examination gloves
- Pregnancy testing kits
- STI testing/collection kits
- Lubricant, sterile water, or normal saline solution

6.9.2.2 Forensic Supplies

- Swabs for collection of foreign material on victim such as semen, blood, or saliva
- Containers for transporting
- Microscope slides for the plating of swabs
- Blood-collection tubes for DNA or toxicological analysis
- Urine specimen containers for pregnancy and toxicological testing
- Sheets of paper or a clean white sheet for the patient to stand on while undressing for collection of loose, fine trace-evidence materials
- Paper bags for collection of clothing
- Drying cabinet to dry wet items of clothing
- Tweezers, scissors, and a comb for collecting foreign debris on skin and hair
- Ruler for measuring the size of wounds, and a scale for forensic photography

6.9.2.3 Treatment Supplies

- Analgesics
- Emergency contraception
- Suture materials
- Tetanus and hepatitis prophylaxis and vaccination
- STI prophylaxis

6.9.2.4 Linen Supplies

- Sheets or paper for the or examination table
- Towels

- Clothing to replace any damaged or retained items of the victim's clothing
- Patient gowns to allow the patient to fully undress for examination
- Sanitary items such as pads and tampons

6.9.2.5 Sundry Supplies

- Camera and film for photo–documentation of injuries
- Colposcope or magnifying lens for obtaining a magnified view of a wound
- Microscope to check for the presence of sperm, particularly if no laboratory facility is accessible

6.9.2.6 Documentation Supplies

- Examination record for recording findings
- Labels for attaching to specimens
- Consent form
- Pathology and radiology referral forms
- Information brochure to provide the patient with information about referral and follow-up services

6.9.3 Special Considerations

6.9.3.1 Sexual Assault Kits

Rape kits are prepackaged kits that contain all the items typically required when collecting evidentiary material from victims. A rape kit readily provides busy clinicians with all of the materials required for the collection of evidence, making thenm readily accessible when needed. In addition, the contents can act as a prompt for inexperienced practitioners to take certain specimens. It also ensures that specimens are collected and packaged in such a way that is acceptable to the forensic laboratory. A disadvantage of prepackaged kits is their cost; typically, the monetary value of the individual parts is relatively small, but costs involved in the preparation and packaging of the kit add considerably to the overall price. In some cases, only a small number of the items in the kit are used, and the rest are wasted. An alternative to using prepackaged rape kits is to gather the various required items, such as swabs and slides, to create a customized rape kit from a stock of individual items. Custom-made rape kits also have the advantage of flexibility and can evolve as the facility becomes better resourced.

According to Ledray (1999) in the *Sexual Assault Nurse Examiner Development and Operation Guide,* before samples for a sexual assault kit are collected, "a dialogue among the health care, forensic, and legal entities involved should occur." Samples and collection techniques vary according to jurisdiction and will evolve as technology advances. According to the *Guide,* basic evidence collection must include oral, vaginal, and anal samples, as appropriate.

Step 1: Clothing

- Place a clean hospital sheet on the floor as a barrier, then place collection paper on the barrier sheet. The examiner must be careful to prevent evidence transfer and should change his or her gloves whenever cross-contamination could occur. Document all findings. Have the patient first remove the shoes and then undress over the collection paper to catch any debris that is dislodged.
- Collect only clothing pertinent to the assault. Place each piece of clothing and collection paper in a separate paper bag, label, seal, and initial the seal. Collect shoes, if pertinent. If additional bags are needed, use grocery-style paper bags only. Tape or seal bags closed; label, seal, and initial the seal.
- Collect obvious debris from the patient's body, including any plant material, fibers, hair, soil, and so on, on the sheet of paper provided, then bundle, label, seal, and initial the seal.
- If fingernail scrapings are collected, place the fingernail scrapings and the tool used to obtain the sample in a paper, bundle, label, seal, and initial the seal. If fingernails are broken, cut the remaining jagged edge for later comparison. Collect decorated fake nail as a known sample if one fake nail is missing.
- Place the patient in an examination gown.

Step 2: Dried Secretions

- Inspect the body carefully for dried secretions, bruises, bite marks, and burns.
- Place flake-dried secretions into a paper bundle or swab dried secretions with a swab moistened with one drop of water; or smear swabs onto two microscope slides.
- Air dry all specimens, then label, place in an envelope, seal, and initial the seal.
- Photograph all bite marks and swab them for trace evidence using the double-swab technique.
- Swab the bite marks as well as all areas the perpetrator might have kissed, licked, or sucked.

Step 3: Oral Sample

- Place two swabs together to collect a specimen from the oral cavity between gums and cheeks and under tongue; remove dentures and swab with same swabs.
- Air dry slides and swabs.

- Place slides in holder and swabs in carton; place in envelope.
- Label and seal the envelope, then initial the seal.

Step 4: Head Hair Combing

- Remove paper and comb provided in envelope; patient can do the combing.
- Unfold and place paper under the patient's head. Using comb provided, comb head hair toward the paper. If hair is matted because of stains, cut the matted hair and place on the collection paper.
- Place the comb in the center of the paper and fold into bundle with comb inside.
- Label, place in envelope, seal, and initial the seal.

Step 5: Optional Pulled Head Hair (Can Be Delayed at the Discretion of Law Enforcement and the Patient); Patient Can Collect Hairs

- Remove paper bundle and unfold.
- Use fingers; do not use forceps or tweezers.
- Pull, do not cut, a minimum of eight full-length head hairs from top, front, back, left side, and right side.
- Collect unusually colored or dyed hairs; collect hairs from wigs and hairpieces; place in separate bundle, label, and place in collection paper.
- Place hairs in bundle and refold.
- Label and seal envelope; initial the seal.

Step 6: Pubic Hair Combing

- Place collection paper under patient's buttocks and comb hair toward the paper.
- Collect secretions dried on the pubic hair by cutting the matted hair and placing on the collection paper.
- Fold comb with debris and matted hair into paper; place folded paper in envelope.
- Place in envelope, label, seal, and initial the seal.

Step 7: Pulled Pubic Hair (Can Delay Collection Until and if Requested by the Forensic Laboratory)

- Remove paper bundle and unfold.
- Pull the hair (do not cut).
- Use fingers only, as tweezers or forceps crimp the hair.
- Pull a minimum of 25 hairs from all areas of the pubis.
- If debris or semen is matted in the hair, cut it out and add to the pubic hair sample bundle.
- Place hairs in the bundle and refold.
- Place in envelope, label, seal, and initial seal.

Step 8: External Genital Sample

- Swab the external genital area with two swabs, rolling swabs together as you collect.
- Smear the swabs on the two microscope slides.
- Air dry swabs and slides for 60 minutes. If drying or desiccant agents are used, swabs must be packaged inmediately. Package swabs and two desiccant packs in an airtight container or glassine envelope folded over to be airtight.
- Place slides in holder and swabs in cartons.
- Place in envelope, label, seal, and initial the seal.

Step 9: Toluidine Blue

Toluidine blue dye (1 percent aqueous solution) is used in sexual assault examinations to aid in the identification and documentation of lacerations. Toluidine blue does not stain the surface layer of skin but will dye nucleated squamous cells in deeper layers of the epidermis exposed by even superficial lacerations. It has increased detection of trauma in children, adolescents, and adults, and it can be applied in cases suspicious for both genital and anal trauma. If used as part of the female genital exaimnation, it should be applied by cotton swab before any internal digital or speculum examination to ensure that any injuries noted are not induced by the examiner. The examiner should be careful not to allow the dye to enter the vaginal vault. The vaginal application of the dye should occur after the anal application has been completed (if indicated) to avoid any cross-contamination. Excess dye can be blotted away with 1 percent acetic acid solution (1 percent vinegar/water) or lubricating jelly. Specific injuries identified at the posterior fourchette are most consistent with trauma from recent sexual intercourse. Use of toluidine might be unnecessary if a colposcope is available or if obvious trauma is visible. Toluidine cannot separate consensual from nonconsensual lesions. Nontraumatic inflammatory or infectious lesions will be positive. Toluidine might be useful in illuminating injuries for nonmedical persons, including jurors in a courtroom setting. The steps are as follows:

1. Collect all external genital specimens as indicated by examination protocol before toluidine blue dye application.
2. Photo-document the area.
3. Apply toluidine blue dye by using a sterile cotton swab to the genital area in question. Dye application can be used on the labia majora, labia minora, posterior fourchette, penneal body, and penanal area.
4. Gently blot away excess dye with 1 percent acetic acid or lubrication jelly.
5. Photo-document area after dye application.
6. Speculum examination and other procedures can be commenced.

Step 10: Anal Sample

The examiner must consider local policy, potential issues of patient needs and wants, and the need for collection of evidence from appropriate parts of the body. There are times, however, when a patient will deny anal touching or penetration because of embarrassment, and valuable evidence would be lost. It is suggested that a routine anal swab be requested of each sexual assault patient, at the same time making it clear that, as with any other part of the examination, it can be declined after the patient is informed. The examiner must also consider the likelihood of a positive test, potential trauma to the patient, and the need to collect immediate evidence.

- Use an alternative light source on anal area and flake off or swab areas of dried secretions, place on slide (optional), air dry, and place in envelope labeled "perianal."
- Use two swabs together to collect a sample from the anal cavity (avoid contact with external skin surfaces).
- Air dry, place in holders, and place in envelope.
- Label and seal envelope, and initial the seal.

Step 11: Vaginal/Penile Sample

- Use two swabs together to collect specimen from vaginal pool.
- Optional: Smear one swab on slide for wet mount; slide is prepared by placing one drop of normal saline onto slide. Roll swab into drop and cover with a coverslip. View for presence of motile sperm under 400x (within 10 minutes). Package this swab and slide separately and label as "wet mount."
- Optional: Smear other swabs onto slides.
- Air dry all swabs and slides, place in appropriate holders (wet mount slide goes into single slide holder), and place in envelope.
- Label and seal envelope, and initial the seal.

Step 12: Optional Vaginal Washings

- Use 3 mL of sterile saline or water for vaginal lavage (use plastic catheter and 3 mL syringe).
- Aspirate and place in tube provided. Tightly secure cap.
- Label, place in envelope, and seal envelope; initial the seal.

Step 13: Toxicology

- Collect a urine sample if drug or alcohol ingestion is suspected.
- If possible, perform the vaginal examination (if applicable) before collecting the urine sample.
- Collect urine in a specimen cup.
- Label, seal, and initial the seal.
- Do not place the urine sample in the kit; package it separately according to local protocol.
- To collect a blood sample (if drug ingestion up to 12 hours), collect three Vacutainer tubes (30 mL total).

Step 14: Optional Known Reference Sample

- A buccal swab can be used instead of blood sample, depending on the jurisdiction.
- Remove sterile swab from envelope.
- Have the patient rinse his or her mouth with tap water, and then expose buccal (inner) area of cheek.
- Swab with gentle pressure.
- Place in envelope, label, seal, and initial the seal.

Bite Mark Guidelines

According to guidelines from the American Board of Forensic Odontology, forensic examiners should include a clear and complete description of the bite mark. The following demographic information should be collected: patient's name; case number; date of the assault; date of the examination; and the age, race, and sex of the patient. The examiner's name should be included. The following should be noted when documenting a bite mark:

- Location of bite mark
- Description of the anatomic location
- Describe surface contour: flat, curved, irregular
- Description of tissue characteristics
- Description of the underlying structure: boric, cartilage, muscle, fat
- Description of the skin, whether relatively fixed or mobile
- Description of the shape: round, ovoid, crescent, irregular, double
- Description of the color: red, purple, and so on
- Description of the size, including vertical and horizontal dimensions of the bite mark; the distance between canines; the circular arc should be documented with a metric scale such as the ABFO #2 scale; the presence or absence of suction applied to the bite area should be documented when possible
- Description of the type of injury: petechial hemorrhage, contusion, abrasion, laceration, incision, avulsion, or artifact

The gathering of bite mark evidence should be done with authorization from the patient. Note whether the bite mark has been affected by washing, contamination, lividity, change of position, and other factors. Bite marks should be documented through proper photography. Orientation and close-up photographs with and without a metric scale marker should be taken, with identifying information such as the case number, date, initials of the examiner, and so on included in the photographs. Photographic resolution should be of high quality (a macro lens with ring and point flash). If color film is used, accuracy of color balance should be ensured. In using the scale (including a circular and linear scale), ensure that it is on the same plane and adjacent to the bite mark. The ABFO #2 scale incorporates both of these elements. Ultraviolet light can be used to photograph bite wounds months after they occur, even when the overlying skin appears normal. This method should be used when historically indicated. The most critical photographs should be taken in a manner that will eliminate distortion. Some high-end 35mm cameras have interchangeable focusing screens. Use of an architectural grid screen in conjunction with the ABFO #2 scale will help reduce distortion. It is also beneficial to obtain serial photographs of the bite mark over a period of time.

Whenever possible, salivary trace evidence should be collected as guided by the patient history and the use of an alternative light source. Examiners should use the double-swab technique to collect the saliva, taking the following actions:

- Immerse the tip of the first swab in water.
- Roll the tip of the swab over the skin, using moderate pressure and circular motions.
- Air dry the swab for 60 minutes.
- Do not moisten the second swab, but use it dry.
- Roll the tip of the swab over the skin, using moderate pressure and circular motions.
- Air dry the swab for 60 minutes.
- Package both swabs together in a paper envelope, label, and seal.
- Do not lick the evidence envelope because it will contaminate the sample.

Taking the Assault History

1. Document the patient's description of the encounter in direct quotes if at all possible, including the following details:
   - Date of assault(s)
   - Time of assault(s)
   - Physical surrounding of assault(s)
   - Lapse of consciousness
   - Nongenital injury, pain, and/or bleeding
   - Anogenital injury, pain, and/or bleeding
   - Verbal coercion
   - Force or coercion used (including weapons threatened or used; physical assault; grabbing, holding, or pinching; physical restraints; drugs used to facilitate sexual assault; choking; burns; ingestion of a foreign substance)
   - Injuries inflicted on assailant(s) during assault
   - Acts described by patient
   - If more than one assailant, identify by number
2. Document the following acts and whether a penis, finger, or other object was used:
   - Penetration of labia majora (vulva or deeper structures)
   - Penetration of anus or deeper structures
   - Oral copulation of genitals
   - Oral copulation of anus
   - Nongenital acts
   - Biting of patient or by patient on perpetrator
   - Licking
   - Kissing
   - Other acts
   - Did ejaculation occur? If yes, note location: vulva or deeper structures; anus or deeper structures; body surface; mouth; bedding; clothing
   - Contraceptives or lubricant products used
   - Recent consensual intercourse

Performing the General Physicial Examination and Documenting Findings

- Vital signs
- Date and time of examination
- General physical appearance
- General demeanor, behavior, and orientation
- Description of clothing on arrival
- Conduct physical examination and document, draw, number injuries and findings, including size and appearance, on a diagram and use a legend for abbreviations or numbers (be specific)
- Alternate light source examination
- Collect dry and moist secretions, stains, and foreign materials from the body and from the nose, mouth, and genitals
- Collect fingernail scrapings or cuttings
- Examine the oral cavity for injury
- Swab the areas the suspect kissed, licked, or sucked

Laboratory Services

Specimens collected from victims can be broadly divided into two categories: those used for diagnostic health purposes and those used for criminal investigation. In most settings, the type of specimens collected for the purpose of forensic investigation will be dictated by the quality and sophistication of available services at medico-legal or forensic laboratories. For instance, if a laboratory is not able to perform DNA testing (or access such testing from another laboratory), there is little point in collecting specimens for DNA analysis. By the same token, there is little use for expensive rape kits if immediate access to high-quality analytical services is not available. Health care providers are advised to consult laboratory staff as to which specimens they are able to process, how samples should be collected and handled, and how long the samples will take to process.

Examination Records

There are a number of different ways of recording the details of a consultation with a victim; however, use of a standard form is generally considered to be the most convenient and reliable method. Consideration must also be given to matters of confidentiality; completed records must be stored securely and accessed only by authorized staff.

The Colposcope

The colposcope is a binocular, low-powered microscope with an integral light source. Most colposcopes have an attachable camera that allows findings to be photographed or videotaped. In recent years, the colposcope and its capacity for photo-documentation have greatly assisted the recording of genito-anal findings in abused and nonabused children. However, colposcopes are expensive and some skill is required in the interpretation of recorded findings. Genito-anal examinations conducted by an experienced person using a fixed light and a hand-held lens are generally considered to be adequate and are still the norm in many areas.

Exam Equipment

The hospital ED or clinic where the exams are being completed is often willing to donate exam supplies. In many states, the rape exam kits are provided by law enforcement at no charge. Standardized kits can also be purchased when they are not available free from law enforcement. Consult with the local state crime laboratory that will be analyzing the evidence collected before purchasing the kits. Because the price and contents of standardized kits vary greatly from manufacturer to manufacturer, ask to have a sample sent for review before making a decision to purchase a particular kit. The crime laboratory might know where to purchase standardized kits, as they are available from a number of sources. Law enforcement agencies often pay for this cost because use of standardized kits benefits law enforcement by promoting better evidence collection. Emphasize this benefit to the law enforcement agency when negotiating with them to provide these kits. Further discussion of this issue follows later in this chapter.

A Polaroid, digital, or 35mm camera will also be needed. Before making the purchase, check to see if the ED or clinic where the exams will be completed already has one available that the SANE could access. Small 35mm cameras with automatic focus that are easy to operate and will take adequate pictures of injuries are available for as little as $100. A camera with a macro lens attachment will produce higher quality, close-up photos. Later, when the budget allows, the camera equipment can be upgraded. Do not be tempted to get camera equipment that is so sophisticated that the staff will have trouble using it effectively. Also, ensure that the cost of film and film development is covered in the budget if these costs, which can be considerable, are not reimbursed by law enforcement or the prosecutor's office. If the budget allows, consider purchasing a digital camera that can transmit photo evidence directly to the police department, if it is utilizing this technology. The police department might even be willing to provide the SANE program this equipment, recognizing the value to the investigative efforts of its department. Another consideration is photographic equipment that captures ultraviolet images. Although more sophisticated, it is very effective in identifying and highlighting bruising, especially in women of color. Although this technology was once controversial and its accuracy was challenged in the courtroom, its scientific value is now widely accepted. The use of a digital camera, however, must be discussed with the local prosecuting attorney's office because digital imagery can be altered easily and, consequently, it might not be accepted by that office. Forensic photo-documentation is discussed further in chapter 5.

An alternate light source will also be needed. Much like the camera, these light sources are typically available in the ED or clinic for eye exams. If the budget is tight, arrange to have access to the equipment rather than to purchase it. If the SANE program is located in a separate clinic, a pelvic examination table also must be acquired. A microscope might be necessary to observe wet mounts for motile sperm. Additional equipment that will soon become a standard, but is still not available to many SANE programs because of the cost, are the colposcope ($10,000–$15,000 for the colposcope alone); light-staining microscope ($1,000 to $1,500); digital camera systems with direct computer links; and video equipment with print capabilities. Because of the excessive cost of the colposcope, some programs, especially those working with children, have chosen instead to purchase MedScope ($3,500; $11,500 including camera, internal lens, camera holder, monitor, printer, foot switch, VCR, and cart).

6.9.4 The Initial Assessment

6.9.4.1 Conduct of Health Care Providers

How health care professionals conduct themselves is of vital importance in the treatment of sexual assault victims. A victim is often in a heightened state of awareness and very emotional after an assault. Many survivors of sexual assault have described the kindness of the treating personnel as being beneficial to their recovery. Health care providers must choose their words with great care when dealing with sexual assault patients and take care not to contribute in any way to revictimization of the patient. Use of insensitive language can not only contribute to patient distress during the examination but also hinder long-term recovery. Health providers are advised to choose words that are gentle and soothing; there is no place for judgmental or critical comments. It is imperative that all victims of sexual violence are treated with respect and dignity throughout the entire examination irrespective of their social status, race, religion, culture, sexual orientation, lifestyle, sex or occupation. Many victims cite a fear of not being believed as a reason for not reporting sexual assault and, indeed, recovery can be hindered when others disbelieve or blame the patient for the assault. Validation of the patient's feelings is thus critical to recovery. Body language, gestures, and facial expressions all contribute to conveying an atmosphere of believing the patient's account. However, this does not relieve the health worker from his or her duty to consider carefully what he or she is being told. There is a big difference between skepticism and naivete, and it is in between these polarities that the health care provider can best satisfy the differing needs of patient, law enforcement, criminal justice system, and the wider society. To be seen to be impartial is vital for effective court testimony. Health care providers should also be aware of the impact on themselves of repeatedly hearing, seeing, and dealing with cases of IPV.

6.9.4.2 Demeanor of the Health Care Provider

The following strategies and techniques might be helpful when dealing with victims of sexual violence:

- Greet the patient by name.
- Introduce yourself to the patient and explain your role.
- Aim for an attitude of respectful, quiet professionalism.
- Have a calm demeanor, as a victim who has been frightened and has experienced fear should be in the company of people who are not frightened.
- Be unhurried and make the victim the focus of your attention.
- Maintain eye contact as much as is appropriate.
- Be empathetic and nonjudgmental as your patient recounts his or her experiences.

6.9.4.3 Obtaining Consent

Before a full medical examination of the patient can be conducted, it is essential that informed consent be obtained. In practice, obtaining informed consent means explaining all aspects of the consultation to the patient. Particular emphasis should be placed on the matter of the release of information to other parties, including the police. This is especially important in settings where there is a legal obligation to report an episode of violence (and hence details of the consultation) to the relevant authorities. Thus, having determined the medical status of the patient, the next step in the assessment process is to inform the patient of his or her options. It is crucial that patients understand the options open to them and are given sufficient information to enable them to make informed decisions about their care. It is important that the correct environment is provided (i.e., one in which the patient feels secure and does not feel pressured or intimidated in any way). This is a fundamental right of all patients but has particular relevance in this setting where patients might have been subjected to a personal and intrusive event against their will. It is also important to ensure that patients have a sense of control returned to them when in medical care. Above all, the wishes of the patient must be respected. Informed consent is a central issue in medico-legal matters. Examining a person without his or her consent could result in the examiner being charged with offenses of assault, battery, or trespass. In some jurisdictions, the results of an examination conducted without consent cannot be used in legal proceedings.

6.9.4.4 Taking a History

Once you, as the examiner, are satisfied that the patient has sufficient information to provide informed consent, ask him or her to sign or mark the consent form (if a consent form is required in your jurisdiction). Explain to the patient that should he or she decide to pursue legal action against the perpetrator, any information he or she discloses to you in the course of the examination might become part of the public record. If mandatory reporting is required in your jurisdiction, make sure the patient understands this. It is worth spending time obtaining consent as this could help to develop the patient's trust in you. It will benefit everyone if you can make your patient feel safe and secure in the environment in which you are working, as well as with yourself, as his or her examiner.

6.9.4.5 Obtaining a General Medical History

The primary purpose of taking a medical history is to obtain information that might assist in the medical management of the patient or might help to explain subsequent findings, such as easy bruising, loss of consciousness, or memory loss. Health professionals are advised to refer to national guidelines or standards for conducting clinical examinations to ensure that they are in compliance. At a minimum, the medical history should cover any known health problems, immunization status, and medications. If possible, a standard examination record should be used for recording details of the patient's medical history; use of a standard form acts as a guide for the examiner by prompting relevant questions and prevents the omission of important details. Observing an experienced practitioner taking a history is also an invaluable aid in this area.

6.9.4.6 Obtaining an Account of the Assault

The main objectives of obtaining an account of the assault are to do the following:

- Detect and assess injuries.
- Assess the risk of adverse consequences, such as pregnancy and STIs.
- Facilitate relevant evidence collection.
- Facilitate documentation.
- Guide forensic examination.

When interviewing the patient about the assault, ask him or her to tell you in his .or her own words what happened. Document the account without unnecessary interruption; if you need to clarify any details, ask questions after your patient has completed his or her account. Avoid questions commencing with the word, "Why?" as this tends to imply blame; instead use open-ended, non-leading questions. Be thorough, bearing in mind that some patients might intentionally avoid particularly embarrassing details of the assault (e.g., patients might omit details of oral sexual contact or anal penetration); others might find it difficult to talk about the assault. Explain to the patient that you are interested in different aspects of the event to the police; as his or her health care provider, you are particularly concerned about any physical contacts between the patient and his or her assailants.

The following details about the alleged assault must be documented:

- Date, time, and location of the assault, including a description of the type of surface on which the assault occurred
- Name and identity (if nonstranger) and number of assailants
- Nature of the physical contacts and detailed account of violence inflicted
- Use of weapons and restraints
- Use of medications, drugs, alcohol, or inhaled substances
- How clothing was removed

Details of actual or attempted sexual activity should also be carefully recorded, in particular whether or not the following occurred:

- Vaginal penetration of victim by offender's penis, fingers, or objects
- Rectal penetration of victim by offender's penis, fingers, or objects
- Oral penetration of victim by offender's penis or other object
- Oral contact of offender's mouth with victim's face, body, or genito-anal area
- Forced oral contact of victim's mouth with offender's face, body, or genito-anal area
- Ejaculation in victim's vagina or elsewhere on the victim's body or at the scene

The use of condoms and lubricant should be noted. Any subsequent activities by the patient that might alter evidence (example.g., bathing, douching, wiping, the use of tampons, and changes of clothing) should also be documented. Finally, details of any symptoms that have developed since the assault must be recorded, including genital bleeding, discharge, itching, sores or pain; urinary symptoms; anal pain or bleeding; and abdominal pain.

6.9.4.7 The Physical Examination

When conducting a physical examination of a victim of sexual violence, examiners are advised to proceed as follows:

1. Note the patient's general appearance, demeanor, and mental functioning. If the patient's mental functioning appears impaired, attempt to assess whether the impairment is recent or symptomatic of a longer term illness or disability.
2. Note the patient's vital signs: blood pressure, temperature, pulse, and respiration rate.
3. Examine the patient from head to toe, concluding with the genito-anal area.
4. Note and describe in detail any physical injuries, even if forensic evidence is not being collected. Use body maps to indicate location and size of injury.
5. Photograph any injuries.
6. Order diagnostic tests (e.g., x-rays, CT scan, ultrasound) to aid in diagnosing fractures, head and neck injuries, brain or spinal cord injuries, or abdominal trauma.
7. Draw blood samples for testing for HIV (informed consent must be obtained for HIV testing), hepatitis B, syphilis, and other STIs.

It is important to observe the following general principles and procedures throughout the examination:

- Before starting the physical examination, take time to explain all of the procedures to your patient and why they are necessary. Give your patient a chance to ask questions.

- Allow the patient to have a family member or friend present throughout the examination.
- A chaperone for the patient should always be present, especially if the examiner is male. The primary role of the chaperone, preferably a trained health worker, is to provide comfort and support to the patient. The chaperone also protects the health care provider in the event of a patient alleging that the examining health care provider behaved in an unprofessional manner.
- Throughout the physical examination inform the patient what you plan to do next and ask permission. Always let the patient know when and where touching will occur. Show and explain instruments and collection materials. Patients can refuse all or parts of the physical examination and you must respect the patient's decision. Allowing the patient a degree of control over the physical examination is important to his or her recovery.
- The examination should be performed in a setting that is light, warm, clean, and private.
- If the clothing removed was that worn during the assault and forensic evidence is to be collected, the patient needs to undress over a white sheet or large piece of light paper. Try to provide as much privacy as possible while the patient is undressing. Use a cover gown. If the patient has consented to the collection of his or her clothing, each item of clothing must be placed by the examiner's gloved hand into a paper bag. If clothing is to be held for forensic examination, replacement clothing needs to be provided.
- Both medical and forensic specimens should be collected during the course of the examination. Providing medical and legal services simultaneously reduces the number of examinations the patient has to undergo and can ensure the needs of the patient are addressed more comprehensively.
- The following standard precautions should be observed at all times during the examination to prevent transmission of infectious agents:
    1. Wear gloves whenever in contact with blood or other body fluids.
    2. Change gloves between patients; it might sometimes be necessary to change gloves during the examination to prevent contamination.
    3. Wash hands with soap and water after any exposure to body fluids or blood, between clients, and after removing gloves.
    4. Wear protective eyewear, masks, or face shields if there is a possibility of splashing blood or body fluids into your eyes, face, or mouth.
    5. Do not recap used needles, do not bend or break needles after use, and dispose of used needles in special impermeable sharps containers immediately after use.
- The health care provider should document all findings as the physical examination proceeds. The patient can thus expect periods of silence during the course of the examination. Make sure that the patient understands that he or she can stop the procedure at any stage if it is uncomfortable for him or her and give him or her ample opportunity to stop the examination, if necessary.
- Always address patient questions and concerns in a nonjudgmental, emphatic manner, and use a calm tone of voice.

6.9.4.8 The "Top-to-Toe" Physical Examination

According to the WHO's (2003) guidelines for the medico-legal examination, a systematic, "top-to-toe" physical examination of the patient should be conducted in the following manner:

1. First note the patient's general appearance and demeanor. Take the patient's vital signs. Start with the patient's hands, inspecting both sides of both hands for injuries. Observe the wrists for signs of ligature marks. Trace evidence might need to be collected, including fingernail scrapings.
2. Inspect the forearms for defensive injuries, which occur when the victim raises a limb to ward off force to vulnerable areas of the body. Defensive injuries include bruising, abrasions, lacerations, or incised wounds. In dark-skinned individuals, bruising can be difficult to see, and thus tenderness and swelling is of great significance. Any intravenous puncture sites should be noted.
3. The inner surfaces of the upper arms and the armpit or axilla need to be carefully observed for signs of bruising. Victims who have been restrained by hands often display fingertip bruising on the upper arms. Similarly, when clothing has been pulled, red linear petechial bruising can sometimes be seen.
4. Inspect the face. Black eyes can be subtle. Look in the nose for signs of bleeding. Gentle palpation of jaw margins and orbital margins might reveal tenderness indicating bruising. The

mouth should be inspected carefully, checking for bruising, abrasions, and lacerations of buccal mucosa. Petechiae on the hard or soft palate might indicate penetration. Check for a torn frenulum and broken teeth. Collect an oral swab, if indicated.

5. Inspect the ears, not forgetting the area behind the ears, for evidence of shadow bruising, which develops when the ear has been struck onto the scalp. Use an otoscope to inspect the eardrum.
6. Gentle palpation of the scalp might reveal tenderness and swelling, suggestive of hematomas. Hair loss due to hair pulling during the assault could cause large amounts of loose hair to be collected in the gloved hands of the examiner; alternatively, a gentle combing might recover any loose hair. Electrostatic forces can, however, cause large amounts of loose hair to be retained in the head until the patient next takes a shower or bath.
7. The neck area is of great forensic interest. Bruising on the neck can indicate a life-threatening assault. Imprint bruising might be seen from necklaces and other items of jewelry on the ears and on the neck. Suction-type bruising from bites should be noted and swabbed for saliva before being touched.
8. The breasts and trunk should be examined with as much dignity and privacy as can be afforded. It is generally most convenient to start with the back. It is possible to expose only that area that is being examined; for example, the gown can be taken aside on the right side of the back and then the left side of the back. The shoulders should be separately viewed. Subtle bruising and more obvious bruising might be seen in a variety of places on the back. If the patient is able to sit up on the examination table, the gown can be taken down to the upper breast level just exposing the upper chest on the right and left and then each breast can be examined in turn. Breasts are frequently a target of assault and are often bitten and so might reveal evidence of suction bruises or blunt trauma. If the breasts are not examined, the reasons for not doing so should be documented.
9. The patient can then be reclined for an abdominal inspection for bruising, abrasions, lacerations, and trace evidence. Abdominal palpation should be performed to exclude any internal trauma or to detect pregnancy.
10. With the patient still in a reclined position, the legs can be examined in turn, commencing with the front of the legs. Inner thighs are often the target of fingertip bruising or blunt trauma caused by the assailant's knees. The pattern of bruising on the inner thighs is often symmetrical. There might be abrasions to the knee as a consequence of the patient being forced to the ground; similarly, the feet might show evidence of abrasions or lacerations. It is important to inspect the ankles (and wrists) very closely for signs of restraint with ligatures. The soles of the feet should also be examined.
11. It is advisable, if possible, to ask the patient to stand for the inspection of the back of the legs. An inspection of the buttocks is also best achieved with the patient standing. Alternatively, the patient can be examined in a supine position and asked to lift each leg in turn and then rolled slightly to inspect each buttock. The latter method might be the only option if the patient is unsteady on his or her feet for any reason, but does not afford such a good view of the area. Any biological evidence should be collected with moistened swabs (for semen, saliva, or blood) or tweezers (for hair, fibers, grass, or soil). As a general rule, the presence of any tattoos should be documented in the examination record, together with a brief description of their size and shape, as these might become a means of assessing the accuracy of the observations of the examining practitioner in court. Similarly, obvious physical deformities should be noted. If tattoos and obvious deformities are not recorded, the examiner should be prepared to justify his or her decision for not doing so. The examiner should weigh the evidential value of observations of this nature against the prejudicial value they might have when discussed in front of a jury on a case-by-case basis. The WHO guidelines state that the use of a Wood's lamp to detect semen on areas of skin where this is suspected is no longer a recommended clinical practice, stating, "Wood's lamps do not fluoresce semen as well as previously thought, and more reliable methods of detecting semen (e.g. swabs) should therefore be used."

6.9.4.9 The Genito-Anal Examination

Before embarking on a detailed examination of the genito-anal area, according to the WHO guidelines, it is important to make the patient feel as comfortable and as relaxed as possible. It will greatly assist many patients if each step of the examination is explained to them; for example, say, "I'm going to have a careful look. I'm going to touch you here to look a bit more carefully. Please tell me if anything feels tender." Initially, the patient should be placed lying on his or her back with his or her knees drawn up, heels together, and legs gently flopped apart (in the lithotomy position). The patient's breasts, abdomen, pelvic area, and legs can be covered by a sheet until the examination actually takes place, at which point the sheet can be drawn up. Lighting should be directed onto the patient's vulval area. Injuries to the genital or anal regions can cause considerable pain when touched. In some instances, only a limited examination might be necessary; alternatively, analgesia might be required.

The following procedures form the basis of a routine genito-anal examination:

1. The external areas of the genital region and anus should be examined, as well as any markings on the thighs and buttocks. Inspect the mons pubis. The vaginal vestibule should be examined, paying special attention to the labia majora, labia minora, clitoris, hymen or hymenal remnants, posterior fourchette, and perineum. A swab of the external genitalia should be taken before any digital exploration or speculum examination is attempted. A gentle stretch at the posterior fourchette area might reveal abrasions that are otherwise difficult to see, particularly if they are hidden within slight swelling or within the folds of the mucosal tissue. Gently pulling the labia (toward the examiner) will improve visualization of the hymen. Asking the patient to bear down might assist the visualizing of the introitus.
2. If any bright blood is present, it should be gently swabbed to establish its origin—whether it is vulval or from higher in the vagina.
3. A speculum examination allows the examiner to inspect the vaginal walls for signs of injury, including abrasions, lacerations, and bruising. (Use of a transparent plastic speculum is especially helpful for visualizing the vaginal walls.) Trace evidence, such as foreign bodies and hairs, might be found and, if so, collected. The endocervical canal can also be visualized. This part of the examination might be particularly difficult for the patient, as it might remind her of the assault. It should therefore be introduced gently and its importance explained carefully. Warming of the speculum prior to use is advisable and can be achieved by immersing the instrument in warm water in a sink. Traditionally, the recommended technique for speculum examinations involved inserting the speculum along the longitudinal plane of the vulval tissues and then rotating it into its final position once the initial muscle resistance had relaxed. More recently, however, an alternative technique, one that is generally more comfortable for the patient, has gained widespread acceptance. The duckbill speculum is rested in its broader dimension on the posterior fourchette, allowing the dimension of the object to be anticipated by the vaginal tissues. This also allows some relaxation of the introital tissues prior to insertion, in much the same way as the perianal sphincters do when the examining digit is rested at the opening prior to insertion. With the duckbill speculum resting as described, and the patient in the lithotomy position, the speculum can be smoothly introduced, with no twisting, in a downward direction, opening the duckbills gently as it progresses. This avoids any contact with the urethra, which is painful, and allows the cervix to be visualized with ease. In most cases, a speculum examination should be performed as a matter of course. It is particularly relevant if there is significant vaginal or uterine pain postassault, vaginal bleeding, or suspicion of a foreign body in the vagina. Furthermore, in assaults that occurred more than 24 hours but less than 96 hours prior to the physical examination, a speculum examination should be performed to collect an endocervical canal swab (for semen). If a speculum examination is not conducted because of patient refusal, it might still be possible to collect a blind vaginal swab.
4. Although an anal examination can be performed while the patient is still in the lithotomy position, it is usually easier to do this with the patient in the left lateral position. Thus on completion of the genital examination, ask the patient to roll over on to her side and face the wall with her legs drawn up. Respectful covering of the thighs and vulva with a gown or sheet during this procedure can help prevent a feeling of exposure. The uppermost buttock needs to be lifted to view the anus. This should be explained. The patient can hold the buttock up herself, if she is comfortable and able to do so. Gentle pressure at the anal verge might reveal bruises, lacerations, and abrasions.
5. Digital rectal examinations are recommended if there is a reason to suspect that a foreign object has been inserted in the anal canal, and should be performed prior to a proctoscopy or anoscopy. In a digital rectal examination, the examining finger should be placed on the perianal tissues to allow relaxation of the natural contraction response of the sphincter. Once relaxation is sensed, insertion can take place.
6. Proctoscopy need only be used in cases of anal bleeding or severe anal pain postassault, or if

the presence of a foreign body in the rectum is suspected.

6.9.4.10 Recording and Classifying Injuries

Clinicians and pathologists are frequently required to respond to questions about injuries from investigators, lawyers, or the courts. The sorts of things that investigating teams want to know about are the following:

- The age of an injury
- The mechanism by which the injury was produced
- The amount of force required to produce the injury
- The circumstances in which the injury was sustained
- The consequences of the injury

Injury interpretation is a complex process requiring a broad comprehension of anatomical, physiological, and pathological principles. Individuals performing this role should have proven expertise in the field; this expertise should be reinforced by exposure to peer review, continuing education, and quality assurance programs. Without accurate documentation and expert interpretation of injuries, any conclusions drawn about how injuries occurred might be seriously flawed. This will have profound consequences for both the victim and the accused.

6.9.4.11 Injury Description

Injury interpretation is entirely dependent on the accuracy and completeness of the recorded observations of wounds. Adoption of a systematic approach to describing and recording the physical characteristics of wounds will ensure that none of the critical elements is omitted. Ideally, such observations should be recorded contemporaneously in the notes of the medical consultation.

6.9.4.12 Classification of Wounds

There are a number of advantages of using standard, universally accepted descriptive terms for classifying wounds. Use of a standard terminology not only assists in identifying the mechanism by which the injury was sustained but also contributes to a better understanding of the circumstances in which the injuries could have been sustained. When used correctly, a standardized system of wound classification and description might allow deductions about the weapon or object that caused the injury. Furthermore, an examination of the pattern of injuries could assist in answering questions about whether the injuries were sustained in an accidental, assaultive, or self-inflicted manner. Wounds are generally classified as either abrasions, bruises, lacerations, incisions, stab wounds, or gunshot wounds.

Describing features of physical injuries requires documentation of the following:

- Site: Record the anatomical position of the wounds.
- Size: The dimensions of the wounds should be measured.
- Shape: Describe the shape of the wounds, such as linear, curved, or irregular.
- Surrounds: Note the condition of the surrounding or the nearby tissues.
- Color: Observation of color is particularly relevant when describing bruises.
- Course: Comment on the apparent direction of the force applied.
- Contents: Note the presence of any foreign material in the wound, such as dirt, and so on.
- Age: Comment on any evidence of healing.
- Borders: The characteristics of the edges of the wounds might provide a clue as to the weapon used.
- Classification: Use accepted terminology wherever possible.
- Depth: Give an indication of the depth of the wounds; this might have to be an estimate.

6.9.4.13 Wound Categories

1. Abrasions are defined as superficial injuries to the skin caused by the application of blunt force and are produced by a combination of contact pressure and movement applied simultaneously to the skin. Careful examination of an abrasion might allow identification of the causative implement and the direction of the force applied. There are a number of different types of abrasions:
   - Scratches, such as those produced by fingernails, thorns, and so on
   - Imprint, whereby the pattern of the weapon migh leave a characteristic abrasion on the skin
   - Friction, such as grazes from contact with carpet or concrete
2. Bruises are defined as an area of hemorrhage beneath the skin. Bruises are also known as hematomas or contusions. Bruising follows blunt trauma; the discoloration is caused by blood leaking from ruptured blood vessels. Bruises might also occur within a body cavity or within an organ. When commenting on bruises, exercise caution for the following reasons:

- The current consensus view is that the age of a bruise cannot be determined with any degree of accuracy; however, this was previously thought possible and is widely taught in older textbooks.
- The apparent color of the bruise can be affected by skin pigmentation and by different types of lighting. Additionally, describing color inevitably involves a subjective element.
- The site of bruising is not necessarily the site of trauma.
- The shape of the bruise does not necessarily reflect the shape of the weapon used.
- The size of the bruise is not necessarily proportional to the amount of force delivered.

Some bruises bear features that might well assist in their interpretation:

- Bite marks are oval or circular bruises with a pale central area; there might also be some abrasion. In some instances, there might be a discernable dentition pattern.
- Fingertip bruises are caused by the forceful application of fingertips. These usually appear as 1- to 2-cm oval or round clusters of three to four bruises. There might also be a linear or curved abrasion from contact with the fingernail.
- Patterned (imprint) bruises occur when a bruise takes on the specific characteristics of the weapon used. A clothing imprint can also occur when the force is delivered through the clothing and onto the skin.
- Petechial bruises are pinpoint areas of hemorrhage and are caused by the rupture of very small blood vessels. This type of bruising is usually seen in the face, scalp, or eyes after neck compression.
- Trainline bruises are parallel linear bruises with a pale central area produced by forceful contact with a linear object.

3. Lacerations are defined as ragged or irregular tears or splits in the skin, subcutaneous tissues, or organs resulting from blunt trauma. The main characteristics of a lacerated wound are as follows:
   - Ragged, irregular, or bruised margins, which might be inverted
   - Intact nerves, tendons, and bands of tissue within the wound
   - The presence of foreign materials or hair in the wound
   - The shape of the laceration might reflect the shape of the causative implement.
   - Incised wounds are defined as injuries produced by sharp edged objects whose length is greater than their depth. Incised wounds can be produced by a knife, razor blade, scalpel, sword, or glass fragment. It is important to distinguish between lacerations and incised wounds (also referred to as incisions or cuts), as this might assist in identifying the type of causative weapon.
4. Stab wounds are defined as incised wounds whose depth is greater than their length on the skin surface. The depth of such wounds and, in particular, the degree of trauma to deeper structures, determine the seriousness of the injury. Important points to note with respect to stab wounds include the following:
   - The dimensions of the wound might not be the dimensions of the blade.
   - The depth of stab wounds is affected by a number of factors, such as the amount of force delivered, the robustness of protective clothing, the sharpness of the tip of the blade, and tissue resistance and any movement of the victim.
   - The dynamics of a stabbing (unless the victim is otherwise immobilized) demand great caution when interpreting the relative positions and movements of assailant and victim.
   - There might be no relationship between the external dimensions of the wound and the resulting trauma to internal structures.
5. Health care providers should have a reasonable working knowledge of ballistics and gunshot wounds; however, it is quite likely that treatment of gunshot wounds will become the responsibility of a surgeon and their interpretation might require the assistance of a forensic pathologist. Unless such wounds are a regular part of your practice, you should be prepared to refer cases to more experienced practitioners for analysis.

6.9.4.14 Genito-Anal Injuries Related to Penetration

Trauma to the female genitalia and anus can be caused by forceful penetration. Penetration can be by an erect or semierect male penis, by other parts of the body including the fingers and tongue, or by objects of various dimensions and characteristics. The act of penetration causes the soft tissues around the orifice to stretch. The likelihood and extent of any resultant injuries will depend on the following factors:

- The state of the tissues (i.e., size, lubrication, and durability)
- The size and characteristics of the penetrating object
- The amount of force used
- The degree of relaxation in the pelvic and perineal musculature
- The position of the perpetrator and angle of penetration

The posterior fourchette, the labia minora and majora, the hymen and the perianal folds are the most likely sites for injury, and abrasions, bruises, and lacerations are the most common forms of injury. The distinction between genital injury caused by consensual penetration and that caused by nonconsensual penetration is an important one. Genital injuries might occur during consensual intercourse, but visible signs of injuries (to the naked eye) are rare, and usually confined to minor abrasions to the posterior fourchette and introitus. Injury to the hymen, sufficient to cause bleeding, might occur in some females previously unaccustomed to sexual intercourse. Anal and rectal injuries are seldom seen after consensual penetration. On the other hand, not all women who allege sexual assault will have genital injury that is visible on examination performed without magnification. Indeed, in many cases, none would be expected. If a mature, sexually active woman does not resist, through fear of force or harm, and penile penetration of her vagina occurs, then it is likely that no injury will be sustained. This finding does not disprove her claim, however. Most studies indicate that less than 30 percent of premenopausal women will have genital injuries visible to the naked eye after nonconsensual penetration. This figure increases to less than 50 percent in postmenopausal women (WHO, 2003). An understanding of this issue is of fundamental importance in sexual assault medicine.

6.9.4.15 Injury Patterns and Their Interpretation

The classification of wounds according to their main characteristics allows certain conclusions to be drawn about their causes; however, this is an area that should be approached with caution. The interpretation of injury patterns for medico-legal purposes should only be performed by practitioners with considerable experience in the field. Assaults produce a significant range of different types of injury; indeed, injuries are as varied as the assaultive actions that caused them. This diversity complicates the task of injury interpretation and, more often than not, precludes definitive conclusions. Nevertheless, some inferences about the nature and circumstances of an assault can be made from the pattern of injury in many cases.

The following points should be kept in mind when assessing injury patterns in cases involving sexual violence:

- The pattern of injuries sustained during a sexual assault can show considerable variation. This might range from a complete absence of injuries (most frequently) to fatal injuries (very rare).
- There are few situations in which it will be possible to state that a specific injury has been sustained in a particular way or with a particular object. In many cases it can only be concluded that the injury was caused by blunt trauma or sharp trauma.
- Falls during an assault or when fleeing from an assailant can produce a number of injuries. These will usually be abrasions or bruises (and occasionally lacerations) to the bony prominences of the body, with the severity of the injuries being proportional to the distance fallen.
- In some situations, individuals might deliberately inflict injuries on themselves. Reasons for this include an underlying psychiatric illness or secondary gain. These cases require very careful consideration before the diagnosis of self-inflicted injury is made. Information about injuries and patterns of injury is often vital in cases of sexual assault. In the event of a case proceeding to criminal prosecution, health care providers might be required to answer questions about injury patterns and to draw inferences from injury patterns about the circumstances surrounding the alleged assault, either in court or in the form of a written report. A comprehensive assessment of injuries sustained might allow comments to be made about the following:
- Whether the injuries were due to blunt or sharp trauma (or both)
- How many applications of force were required to produce the injuries, and the amount of force required to produce such injuries
- Whether the injuries were sustained at or about the same time
- The likelihood of the injuries being sustained in the manner alleged or whether there might be some alternative explanation that could also explain the injuries
- The possible immediate or long-term consequences of the injuries

6.9.5 Follow-Up on Health Care Services Among Victims

Sexual assault has a negative impact on physical and mental health, health-related behaviors, and health service utilization. To study timely medical care's role in preventive services, Resnick et al. (2000) obtained cross-sectional data from a larger two-year longitudinal study, the National Women's Study (NWS). A total of 3,006 adult women participated in the final data collection wave of the NWS. During a structured telephone interview, women who reported a most-recent or only-rape incident during adulthood were asked about rape characteristics, reporting to authorities, medical care, and rape-related concerns. The main outcome measures were receipt and timing of medical care received after an adult rape, and factors influencing whether or not medical care was received. Of the sample, 214 (7.1 percent) had experienced a most-recent or only rape as an adult, and 56 (26.2 percent) received rape-related medical care following that incident. The final model multivariable logistic regression indicated that reporting the crime to police or other authorities and fear of STDs were significant predictors of receipt of postrape medical care. The researchers found that one in five victims reported an adult rape to police or other authorities; these women were nine times more likely to receive medical care than those who did not.

Putz, Thomas, and Cowles (1996) sought to determine whether patients who receive emergency care at a sexual assault treatment center (SATC) follow suggested guidelines for prevention and treatment of associated STDs. The research consisted of a descriptive study of 26 adult victims of sexual assault who had been treated initially at an SATC. A nine-item questionnaire was designed to query participants by telephone six to eight weeks after their initial care for sexual assault. Participants were questioned about their compliance with the suggested medication regimen and follow-up medical attention. In addition, health insurance coverage information was retrieved from participants' records to ascertain possible patterns of compliance by availability of health insurance. Participant perceptions of the nursing care received in the SATC also were elicited. Data were analyzed with frequencies and percentages, as well as qualitative categorization procedures. Twenty-six women, aged 19 to 43 years, participated in the study. Seventy-three percent reported taking all of the prophylactic medication prescribed or given to them at the SATC, whereas 50 percent had made and kept a recommended follow-up appointment with a physician. No association could be determined between compliance with the suggested follow-up protocol and the availability of health insurance. Reasons for not following suggested protocols varied greatly. Of particular importance for those who were noncompliant were the implied misunderstandings related to the need to take medications after a sexual assault. The researchers state that although concern has been expressed in the literature regarding sexual assault victims' compliance with follow-up regimens for the prevention and treatment of STDs, the findings from this study indicate that compliance, particularly with medication protocols, might be higher than expected. However, continuing work is needed to ensure that all victims receive all recommended information regarding follow-up care during the first encounter with the nurse and that the rationale for follow-up care is fully understood by the patient. The researchers added that nurses who interact with victims of sexual assault are in the best position to enhance compliance with follow-up regimens by identifying victims who might be at risk of noncompliance.

Holmes, Resnick, and Frampton (1998) attempted to describe medical findings and health-related concerns of sexual assault victims who returned for follow-up and to assess demographic and assault characteristics of victims who used follow-up services compared to those who did not. This study was a retrospective cohort analysis involving records from the acute sexual assault evidentiary examination and the sexual assault follow-up evaluation clinic visit. Data were extracted from the records of 389 adolescent and adult victims who reported an acute sexual assault and underwent a complete evidentiary examination between January 1, 1995, and June 30, 1997. Descriptive statistics were generated on demographic and historical information, assault characteristics, and medical and laboratory findings. There were no differences in age, race, or perpetrator factors between patients who used follow-up services and patients who did not return to the clinic. Similarly, there were no other assault characteristics, relationships, or physical examination findings that were associated with follow-up patterns. A total of 31 percent (n = 122) of all sexual assault victims returned for a follow-up visit. Physical complaints were reported by 42.6 percent, but 98 percent had normal findings at a general examination, and 94.8 percent had a normal result from a gynecologic examination. Pregnancy and STDs were identified through the follow-up clinic. Since the assault, 49.2 percent had been sexually active, 10 percent with multiple partners and 73.3 percent without consistent condom use. Disturbances in sleep, sexual function, and appetite were commonly reported among victims at follow-up, as were numerous assault-related fears.

6.10 GENITAL INJURIES IN SEXUAL ASSAULT VICTIMS

Various studies have shown that significant physical injury from a sexual assault is rare and occurs in only 3 percent to 5 percent of rape survivors, and less than 1 percent of rape victims have been found to need hospitalization. Even minor injury is usually documented in only about one third of the reported rapes. Injuries, when they do occur, are more common in stranger rapes and rapes by someone the victim knows intimately, such as a domestic partner, rather than in date rape or acquaintance rape situations, according to studies conducted by Kilpatrick et al. (1992), Ledray (1999), Bownes, Gorman, and Saters (1991), Marchbanks, Lui, and Mercy (1990), and Tucker, Ledray, and Stehle-Werner (1990).

According to Petrak and Clayton (1995), in th of 351 rape victims, the rate of physical injury rape victims (40 percent) was found to be higher female victims (26 percent). Although 25 percen men and 38 percent of the women in the study medical care after the rape for their physical inju percent of them told the treating physician they ha raped. The women expressed a strong preference fo ical treatment and counseling by a woman. The ma tims were, however, less likely to express a gende erence. A more recent study of 1,076 sexual a victims found nongenital trauma more often than pre studies, 67 percent of the time (Riggs et al., 2000). also important to note that the absence of injuries prove the lack of force or coercion and does not p consent, according to Tucker et al. (1990).

It is important that the forensic examiner is awar the likely pattern of injuries from violence to know appropriate questions to ask and where to look for inju on the basis of the history given. Intentional injuries te to be more central, and accidental injuries more tow the extremities. Especially if domestic violence is involved, injuries are most often inflicted where the victim can easily hide them. The most common injuries are broken ear drums from slapping, neck bruising from choking, punch bruising to the upper arm, and defensive posturing injuries to the outer midulnar areas of the arms. Also common are whip or cord-like injuries to the back; punch or bite injuries to the breasts and nipples; punch injuries to the abdomen, especially in pregnant women; punch and kick injuries to the lateral thighs; and facial bruising, abrasions, and lacerations (Sheridan, 1993).

The literature cautions the forensic examiner against trying to date the age of a bruise by its color. Although clinicians know that in people with light skin, recent bruising is red or dark blue in color, and older bruising might be green-blue or yellow-blue, and older still bruising might be barely visible, people vary greatly in their rates of healing. Medications could affect bleeding and healing response as well. Experts suggest that the size and color should be documented (e.g., 2 cm by 3 cm, deep blue-purple bruising) without further interpretation (Ledray, 1999). It is also important to remember that it can be very difficult to even identify bruising in individuals with dark skin if alternative light sources are not available. Unfortunately, because these light sources are very expensive, most medical facilities do not have them available.

6.10.1 Genital Trauma

The literature suggests that colposcopic genital examination is extremely useful to visualize and document genital abrasions, bruises, and tears, as they are often so minute they cannot be seen with the naked eye, according to Frank (1996), Ledray (2001), and Slaughter and Brown (1992).

ic examination
sed to magnify
readily visible
hed. It is not
ocumented in
s an accepted
and children
purpose is
ccording to
ly important
rom, 1994).
lways doc-
amination,
994).

ts that the
ut the use
to that of
0 percent
ly, 1999).
n 52 percent
reviewed; the researchers did not indicate if a colposcope was used during the examination. With colposcopic examination, genital trauma has been identified in up to 87 percent of sexual assault cases (Slaughter & Brown, 1992). Just as with nongenital trauma, the absence of genital trauma does not indicate consent. Rape victims often fear vaginal trauma, and are concerned that their genital area has been permanently damaged. Because this is rarely true, it is helpful and reassuring to a traumatized victim to have the extent of the trauma explained to them after the forensic examination is completed (Ledray, 1999). When a video colposcope is available, it can be helpful to turn the screen so that the survivor can also view the genital area during the examination.

In a study by Tintinali et al. (1985), vaginal injuries represented only 19 percent of the total injuries, and they were always accompanied by complaints of vaginal pain, discomfort, or bleeding. Geist (1988) found only 1 percent of rape victims have genital injuries so severe they require surgical repair; 75 percent of these are upper vaginal lacerations, which usually present with profuse bleeding and pain. Because the posterior fourchette is the point of greatest stress when forceful stretching occurs, and it is the point of first contact of the penis with the vagina, the resulting injury is characterized as an acute mounting injury (Slaughter & Brown, 1992). In a study that compared 311 sexual assault survivors to a group of 75 women who had consenting sexual contact, researchers identified genital trauma in 68 percent of the rape survivors, whereas only 11 percent of the women had injuries from consensual sex (Slaughter, Brown, Crowley, & Peck, 1997).

Both the colposcope and anoscope have been shown to improve the identification of rectal trauma, but the colposcope might be less helpful than the anoscope. In a study (Ernst, Houry, Weiss, & Green, 2000) of 67 male rape victims, all examined by experienced forensic examiners, 53 percent had genital trauma identified with the naked eye alone. This number increased only slightly, 8 percent, when the colposcope was used. However, the positive findings increased a significant 32 percent when an anoscope was utilized. The combination of naked eye, colposcope, and anoscope resulted in a total positive findings in 72 percent of the cases.

6.10.2 Patterns of Genital Injuries in Sexual Assault Victims and Issues of Consent

It has been demonstrated that bodily trauma is found in many victims of sexual assault, but there are a number of medico-legal issues relating to consent defenses in these types of cases, which are discussed in chapter 13. The medical literature has generally supported the view that sexual assaults by strangers are more serious and more violent than assaults by people known to the victims. However, there are a number of forensic professionals who debate this assumption. In this section we examine the many issues related to the evidentiary examination of sexual assault victims, expectations of DNA evidence, and documentation of injuries. A look at the medical literature is in order, followed by discussion.

Bowyer and Dalton (1997) report that many jurors still rely on medical evidence, in particular evidence of genital injury, to "prove" rape. They sought to ascertain the incidence of genital injury in victims of alleged rape. Conducting a retrospective review of case records of women who reported they had had been raped, the researchers found that 22 of 83 women had genital injuries; 68 of 83 women had some form of physical injury, although most of these were minor. The researchers conclude that although the study demonstrates that only a minority of women examined by specifically trained police doctors show evidence of genital injury, the absence of genital injury does not exclude rape.

Jones et al. (2004) conducted a retrospective study to compare characteristics of sexual assaults by strangers and those by people known to the victims in a community-based population of women. Study patients were consecutive female patients, 13 years or older, presenting to a sexual assault clinic during a 40-month study period. The clinic is associated with a university-affiliated emergency medicine residency program and is staffed by forensic nurses trained to perform medico-legal examinations using colposcopy with nuclear staining. Case files of 849 patients were reviewed; the age range was 13 to 82 years (mean = 22.5 years). Sexual assault by a person known to the victim accounted for 646 (76 percent) cases. The majority of these assailants (68 percent) were described as acquaintances, 139 (21 percent) were current or previous boyfriends or spouses and 33 (5 percent) involved other family members. Sexual assault by a stranger was more likely to occur in the home of the victim (43 percent vs. 28 percent), involve weapons or physical coercion (58 percent vs. 31 percent), and was associated with more nongenital injuries (61 percent vs. 40 percent). However, the overall frequency of ano-genital trauma (77 percent vs. 71 percent), the mean number of ano-genital injuries (2.0 vs. 2.3), and the types of genital trauma were similar in both groups of women. The researchers conclude the results demonstrated that 71 percent of the victims of acquaintance rape sustain ano-genital trauma and that these injuries can be as extensive as those caused by unknown assailants.

Several studies confirm what is found most often in the literature, that sexual acts and injuries frequently—but not always—vary according to the identity of the perpetrator. Stermac, Du Mont, and Kalemba (1995) examined the characteristics of sexual assaults by strangers and those by people known to the victims in an urban community-based population of women. All 677 women who presented to the health care center between June 1, 1991, and September 30, 1993, and for whom the victim–assailant relationship was known, were eligible for the study. The researchers found that sexual assault by a person known to the victim accounted for 456 (67.4 percent) of the assaults reported. In 344 cases the person was known more than 24 hours; 99 (28.8 percent) were current or previous boyfriends or spouses. Assailants who were strangers were more likely to assault the victim more than once, force the victim to perform fellatio, use weapons, and use physical coercion, whereas assailants who were known to the victims were more likely to assault a woman who was sleeping or drugged. Sexual assault by a known assailant was more likely to occur in the home of the victim or the assailant, whereas sexual assault by a stranger was more likely to occur outdoors or in a vehicle. Overall, the mean number of trauma sites was greater among victims assaulted by strangers than among those assaulted by people they knew.

Eckert, Sugar, and Fine (2004) sought to determine whether physician gender or level of experience is associated with the prevalence of trauma documented in victims after sexual assault. All female patients 15 years or older reporting to an urban hospital with a complaint of sexual assault between January 1997 and September 1999 underwent a standardized history and physical examination by a second- or third-year resident in obstetrics and gynecology. The researchers report that the overall prevalence of genital trauma was 21 percent in the 662 patients available for analysis. The prevalence of genital trauma documented was 50 of 191 patients (26.2 percent) and 90 of 471 patients (19.1 percent), respectively, despite similar assault characteristics between the two groups. The prevalence of genital trauma documented by male examiners (105 of 499, or 21 percent) and female examiners (35 of 160, or 21.9 percent) did not differ. All examiners documented a similar prevalence of body trauma (52 percent). The researchers say that their study supports the hypothesis that the examiner's experience level might influence the prevalence of genital trauma documented after a sexual assault.

Adams (2001) attempted to document the frequency and types of genital injuries in adolescent women examined acutely following a sexual assault and determine any historical correlates of injury. The study consisted of retrospective chart review in an urban community hospital served by a SART. All female patients aged 14 to 19 who were referred by law enforcement for an acute sexual assault examination and were examined between May 1994 and May 1999 were included in the study. Charts of 214 female subjects (average age 16.3) were reviewed. The most common findings were posterior fourchette tear (36 percent); erythema of the labia minora, hymen, cervix, or posterior fourchette (18 percent–32 percent); and swelling of the hymen (19 percent). The researchers report that the incidence of hymenal tears in self-described virgins was higher than in nonvirgins (19 percent vs. 3 percent); however, the total number or severity of other injuries was not significantly higher in virgins. Victims reporting anal penetration had a higher frequency of anal injuries than those who denied such contact (14 of 31, or 61 percent vs. 2 of 150, or 1 percent). The researchers conclude that tears of the posterior fourchette or fossa were the most common findings (40 percent). They report that hymenal tears were uncommon, even in self-described virginal girls, and that timely examination of adolescent victims is important to document injuries. However, they state, many victims will still not have signs of bruising, abrasions, or tears.

Slaughter (1997) emphasizes that conventional rape examination protocols have been poor in yielding genital findings (10 percent–30 percent typically). In their study, the researchers looked at a revised protocol employing colposcopy to perform genital examinations of victims and to document findings. Physical examinations were performed on rape victims seen by San Luis Obispo County's Suspected Abuse Response Team between 1985 and 1990. Of 131 patients seen within 48 hours who experienced penile penetration, 114 (87 percent) had positive findings. Colposcopic magnification allowed examiners to characterize these findings as acute mounting injuries, typically seen at 3, 6, and 9 o'clock on the posterior fourchette and consisting chiefly of lacerations, ecchymosis, and swelling. The researchers conclude that an examination protocol that includes colposcopy might be the most reliable means to document and characterize genital findings in rape victims and to evaluate whether findings can be linked to a reported sexual assault.

Reznic, Nachman, and Hiss (2004) state that in most cases of sexual assault, even following long-term abuse, genital and extragenital injuries might be very scarce or literally not found. Although the forensic experts customarily illustrate to the court that the absence of physical trauma does not rule out that the assault took place, more substantial medical evidence can be helpful in pursuing a conviction. Reznic and colleagues examined three cases at the National Center of Forensic Medicine in Tel-Aviv in which information obtained during questioning of the victims concerning genital pathology of the assailant was later verified through examination of the suspects. The researchers say that such data could provide key evidence to get an indictment when the assault is perpetrated by a stranger or a person who should not have an intimate relationship with the victim. Therefore, the researchers say, acquiring information from the victim concerning any pathology of the assailant's genitalia should be part of the routine questionnaire form for victims of suspected sexual assault or abuse, as findings of this sort might become paramount in conviction of perpetrators.

Biggs, Stermac, and Divinisky (1998) say that the literature on sexual assault has not directly addressed the question of genital injuries in women without prior sexual intercourse experience. Given the paucity of research and the current importance of physical evidence in the criminal justice system, the researchers say their study was designed to document the type and site of genital injuries from sexual assault in women without and with prior sexual intercourse experience. The charts of 132 women who had been sexually assaulted and had sought medical treatment at the Sexual Assault Care Centre at the Women's College Hospital in Toronto within 10 days after the assault were reviewed. Half (66) of the women reported that, at the time of the assault, they had no prior sexual intercourse experience. The rape kit in each patient's file was reviewed to ascertain the type and location of genital injuries. Types of injuries were classified into three categories (nonperforating soft-tissue injuries, lacerations, or current bleeding) and locations into six categories (labia majora and minora, posterior fourchette and introitus, hymen, vagina, cervix, and anus). The researchers say that significantly more women without than with prior sexual intercourse experience had visible genital injuries (65.2 percent vs. 25.8 percent). However, of the women without prior experience, only 9.1 percent had hymenal perforation. Analyses of the data for only women with genital injuries indicated no difference between those without and those with prior sexual intercourse experience in the overall mean number of injured sites (1.65 and 1.47, respectively) or in the mean number of sites with nonperforating soft-tissue injuries (0.349 and 0.706), lacerations (0.953 and 0.471), and bleeding (0.279 and 0.294). The researchers say the results suggest that genital injuries are more common in women without prior sexual intercourse experience but that substantial proportions of all women, regardless of their prior sexual experience at the time of assault, will not have visible genital injuries. They add that ED staff and members of the criminal justice system should be aware of the variable presentation of genital trauma related to sexual assault in women with and without prior sexual intercourse experience.

Jones et al. (2004) set out to determine the incidence of toluidine-blue positive findings after speculum examination of sexual assault victims. The researchers performed a prospective before and after study of 27 female patients presenting after sexual assault to a free-standing nurse examiner clinic. Before the insertion of a speculum, a 1 percent aqueous solution of toluidine blue was applied to the posterior fourchette and photographs were taken using colposcopy with digital imaging (16x magnification). After the forensic examination was completed, dye was reapplied. Photographs taken before and after speculum examination were reviewed by three emergency medicine physicians for superficial lacerations or abrasions. Before speculum examination, genital injuries from sexual assault were documented in 67 percent of the patients (mean number of genital injuries = 1.4). After speculum examination, one patient (3.7 percent) demonstrated a new genital injury, an abrasion to the labia. The researchers say that until further studies are performed, use of a speculum should be delayed until after toluidine dye application.

Rossman et al. (2004) assert that clinicians might not perform a medico-legal examination in cases in which a sexual assault was attempted but no penile–vaginal contact occurred. The researchers conducted a retrospective study to document the frequency and type of genital injuries in women in whom forced digital penetration was the only reported type of assault. Study patients were consecutive female patients presenting to an urban sexual assault clinic during a three-year study period. The clinic is associated with a university-affiliated urban hospital and is staffed by registered nurses trained to perform forensic examinations using colposcopy with nuclear staining. Case files of 941 patients were reviewed; 6 percent (53) reported only digital–vaginal contact. Genital injuries were documented in 81 percent of the patients (mean number of genital injuries = 2.4). Fifty-six percent of the injuries occurred at four sites: fossa navicularis, labia minora, cervix, and posterior fourchette. The most common type of injury was erythema (34 percent) followed by superficial tears (29 percent) and abrasions (21 percent). The researchers say that colposcopy with nuclear staining was useful in detecting these injuries and can provide valuable legal information in sexual assault victims reporting only digital–vaginal penetration.

Jones and Dunnuck et al. (2003) conducted a study to determine the usefulness of the Foley catheter balloon technique for visualizing injuries of the estrogenized hymen in adolescent sexual assault victims compared with supine labial traction. A prospective clinical trial of 20 adolescent (age 13–16) victims of sexual assault was held at a free-standing nurse examiner clinic and was conducted over a four-month study period. The clinic, affiliated with an emergency medicine residency program, was staffed by registered nurses who have been specially trained to perform medico-legal examinations using colposcopy with digital imaging. The Foley catheter technique uses an inflated balloon in the distal vaginal vault to expand the estrogenized hymen to its full capacity so that the edge can be readily visualized for signs of trauma. The Foley technique was compared with gross inspection, using supine labial traction, to photo-document hymenal abnormalities. Photographs of the hymen were obtained using the labial traction technique and then the Foley technique. Three emergency physicians independently examined each pair of photographs with high interrater agreement for the presence of injury. Twenty adolescent sexual assault victims volunteered for the study; the average age was 14.8 years. Gross inspection of the hymen using supine labial traction identified hymenal injuries in three patients (15 percent). Use of the Foley catheter balloon technique allowed identification of hymenal abnormalities in nine additional cases (60 percent). The common injuries to the hymen included lacerations (30 percent), followed by ecchymosis and abrasions. One patient (5 percent) voiced discomfort (mild pressure sensation) during inflation of the balloon. The researchers concluded that the Foley catheter balloon technique is a simple method allowing improved photo-documentation of hymenal trauma in adolescent sexual assault victims compared with supine labial traction.

Jones and Rossman et al. (2003) sought to compare the characteristics of sexual assault in pubertal girls younger than 18 and adults in a community-based population of women presenting to an urban sexual assault clinic. The researchers evaluated consecutive female patients presenting to a sexual assault clinic during a three-year study period. The clinic was associated with a university-affiliated emergency medicine residency program and is staffed by forensic nurses trained to perform medico-legal examinations using colposcopy with nuclear staining. A total of 766 cases were identified: 43 percent of the victims were 13 to 17 years old (mean = 15 years old), and 57 percent were older than 17 years old (mean = 30.8 years old). Adolescents were more likely to be assaulted by an acquaintance or relative (84 percent vs. 50 percent) and to delay medical evaluation (17 hours vs. 12 hours) than were older women. Adolescent sexual assault was less likely to involve weapons or physical coercion (29 percent vs. 57 percent) and was associated with fewer nongenital injuries (33 percent vs. 55 percent). Adolescents had a greater frequency of ano-genital injuries (83 percent vs. 64 percent), however, compared with older women. Common sites of injury in adolescents were posterior, including the fossa navicularis, hymen, fourchette, and labia minora. The injuries showed consistent topologic features, varying with the site and nature of tissue. Adult victims of sexual assault had a less consistent pattern of ano-genital injuries with fewer hymenal injuries, greater injury to the perianal area, and widespread erythema. The researchers concluded that the epidemiology of sexual trauma and the pattern of ano-genital trauma in this age group are unique and might pose special challenges to emergency health care providers.

Sugar, Fine, and Eckert (2004) sought to determine characteristics associated with physical injury in female sexual assault victims. All females who were 15 years or older presenting after sexual assault to an urban ED during a 34-month period underwent standardized evaluation. Of 819 women, 52 percent had general body and 20 percent had genital-anal trauma; 41 percent were without injury. General body trauma was independently associated with being hit or kicked, attempted strangulation, oral or anal penetration, and stranger assault. Genital-anal injury was more frequent in victims younger than 20 and older than 49 years, in virgins, and in those examined within 24 hours and after anal assault.

Jones, Dunnick, and Rossman (2003) compared the types and locations of ano-genital injuries occurring in adolescent females (13–17 years old) after consensual and nonconsensual sexual intercourse. The researchers conducted a retrospective, matched case-control study to assess ano-genital injuries in female adolescents presenting to a free-standing nurse examiner clinic during a four-year study period. Adolescents were selected for inclusion in the study if they reported consensual sexual intercourse and agreed to a medico-legal examination. Control subjects were victims of alleged sexual assault or nonconsensual sexual intercourse matched to cases by age and prior sexual intercourse experience. Genital trauma was documented using colposcopy with nuclear staining and digital photography. Fifty-one cases of consensual sexual intercourse were identified; the age range was 13 to 17 years (mean = 15.1 years). Overall, 49 percent (25 of 51) of consensual sexual intercourse subjects reported no prior sexual intercourse experience. Consensual and nonconsensual sexual intercourse were comparable in terms of race, time to physical examination, alcohol use, and frequency of genital injuries (73 percent vs. 85 percent). The mean number of documented ano-genital injuries in consensual sexual intercourse subjects was 1.9 (+/– 1.5). These injuries commonly involved the hymen, fossa navicularis, and posterior fourchette. Consensual sexual intercourse subjects had a greater number of ano-genital injuries (2.6 +/– 2.0), typically involving the fossa navicularis, labia minora, and hymen. The most common type of injury in both groups was lacerations (39 percent vs. 41 percent); however, nonconsensual sexual intercourse subjects had a greater incidence of ano-genital abrasions, ecchymosis, and edema.

Mancino et al. (2003) assert that victims of sexual assault require appropriate care, follow-up, and information regarding their legal rights. Clinicians are faced with the challenging responsibility of identifying victims and providing effective intervention and preventive counseling. They add that the most pressing medical task is to confirm the assault and to undertake correct documentation and exhibition of biological traces. They explain that performing colposcopy and vulvovaginoscopy does not allow clinicians to diagnose a sexual assault trauma, but it can help them to identify those microscopic lesions (due to the enhanced visualization and the higher resolution under which the genital areas are examined) that might not be seen during a normal clinical examination. The colposcopic and vulvovaginoscopic examination starts from the vulvar region looking for superficial lacerations and ecchymosis; the labia majora and minora are examined scrupulously, then the posterior forchette, the perineum, and the hymen, where it is possible to report micro-ulcerations, contusions, and even possible scars due to a precedent defloration. Recent advances in clinical forensic medicine show that trained examiners using colposcopy obtain evidence of genital trauma in 87 percent to 92 percent of rape victims. The researchers emphasize that colposcopy and vulvovaginoscopy must be performed within 48 hours of the sexual assault, because most of the lesions heal rapidly. Colposcopy and vulvovaginoscopy might be seen as a stressful invasion of a woman who is already vulnerable and at risk of RTS. Prior information about colposcopy might reduce the level of anxiety experienced by many women undergoing this procedure. The researchers say that incorporating colposcopy and vulvovaginoscopy into the routine assessment of sexual assault victims could be a valid way of identifying genital injuries, and the medical report will be more detailed and precise.

Sachs and Chu (2002) say that legal decisions in sexual assault cases often hinge on the presence or absence of genitor-rectal injury but add that the forensic literature does not explain why some victims sustain genitor-rectal injury and others do not. Their study attempted to explore possible predictors of genitor-rectal injury in adult female sexual assault victims. They conducted a retrospective study of cases, extracting data describing consecutive female sexual assault victims who met inclusion criteria between July 1995 and July 1998. Exclusion criteria included male sex, lack of estrogen in females, consensual intercourse within the previous 72 hours, and lack of penetration during the assault. The researchers explored associations between genitor-rectal injury and seven demographic variables, nine assault characteristics, and the time between assault and exam or postcoital interval (PCI). Five hundred forty-eight sexual assault victims were seen during the study time period; 209 of these met the inclusion criteria. Logistic regression controlling for important covariates showed an increased risk of genitor-rectal injury with a PCI of less than 24 hours, physical and verbal resistance, rectal penetration, and greater than a high school education.

Adams, Girardin, and Faugno (2000) report that adolescent females are the most frequent victims of sexual assault, but studies to document the presence of genital findings in patients examined within 72 hours, using magnification and dye, have not been published. Their study was designed to document the frequency and types of genital injuries in adolescent women following acute sexual assault, using chart and photograph review. The most common findings recorded by the nurse examiner were posterior fourchette tear (36 percent); erythema of the labia minora, hymen, cervix, or posterior fourchette (18 percent–32 percent); and swelling of the hymen (19 percent). Uptake of toluidine dye was noted in 66 percent of patients in whom it was applied. Overall, 21 percent of patients were found to have no findings, and 40 percent had tears of the posterior fourchette or fossa. Time to examination was highly correlated with the degree of injury noted. The incidence of hymenal tears in self-described virgins was higher than in nonvirgins (19 percent vs. 3 percent), however the total number or severity of other injuries was not significantly higher in virgins. Reported anal penetration was associated with a high frequency of anal bruising, abrasions, or tears (14 of 23, or 61 percent), and only two of 150 victims who denied anal penetration had tears (1 percent). Victims who reported multiple physical symptoms such as pain, nausea, or vomiting were significantly more likely to be older and to have an increased number of nongenital injuries such as bruising, abrasions, and bite marks. A higher number of nongenital injuries was also correlated with a higher number of total genital injuries.

Finally, Lincoln (2001) surveyed the available literature on genital injury to facilitate an understanding of its significance in relation to sexual offense trials, and reported that wide variation exists in research objectives, study populations, and methodology, hindering interpretation considerably. Lincoln says that the most valuable research in this field identifies the range of normal genital findings and those associated with consensual sexual intercourse, to enable interpretation of genital findings in sexual assault victims, but few studies of this nature exist. Lincoln acknowledges that difficulties arise when examining doctors are not experienced in the genital examination of those other than sexual assault victims, limiting their ability to draw conclusions about genital injury if it is detected. If the methods of genital examination employed are not the same as those used to examine a wide range of nonsexual assault victims, comparison and thus valuable interpretation is further limited. Lincoln's review of the literature finds that the most appropriate genital examinations and the most legally valuable as far as interpretation is concerned are done macroscopically by doctors with considerable experience in the examination of normal, diseased, and traumatized genitalia, and a sound knowledge of the principles of injury interpretation. Lincoln says that a deficiency exists in the literature in relation to macroscopic genital examination findings in consensually sexually active women who have been examined by forensically trained doctors. This deficiency must be addressed before the medico-legal significance of genital injury relating to sexual assault can be accurately interpreted, and before any decision is made to incorporate colposcopy or staining techniques into the routine assessment of sexual assault victims.

One of the more definitive studies of genital injury in sexual assault victims was conducted by Slaughter et al. (1997), who emphasize that the most important objective of the medico-legal examination of sexual assault vitims is "to provide competent evidence collection to assist in the investigation of the incident." The researchers say that recent advances in clinical forensic medicine have allowed forensic examiners using colposcopy to identify and obtain evidence of genital trauma in 87 percent to 92 percent of rape victims within 48 hours. They add that this is a significant improvement over protocols that have traditionally relied on gross visualization or toluidine blue dye enhancement. Because there has been little material published about the location, extent, and types of injury seen in sexual assault victims, Slaughter et al. emphasized the importance of discussing and comparing the findings of rape victims with the genital findings in women having consensual intercourse. The researchers observe, "Previous studies using nuclear staining have shown that the prevalence of genital injury in women who complain of rape is greater than that seen in women without this history," but add that the use of colposcopic magnification might provide additional findings.

The researchers studied the locations and types of genital injury seen in female assault victims compared with women engaging in consensual sex. They performed sexual assault examinations (using colposcopy to evaluate ano-genital trauma) on 311 rape victims seen by San Luis Obispo County (California)'s Suspected Abuse Response Team between 1985 and 1993 and contemporaneously on 75 women after consensual sexual intercourse.

The researchers assessed how six factors—time from complaint to examination, relationship of victim and assailant, age of victim, type of sex act reported, presence of nongenital trauma, and history of nonsensual sexual intercourse—related to physical findings in the victims. The researchers found that among the 311 assault victims, 213 (68 percent) had ano-genital trauma; among the 178 (57 percent) patients with nongenital trauma, 132 (74 percent) also had genital injury. Two patients had required hospitalization, one for head trauma, and the other for vaginal laceration. The researchers reported that penile penetration was the most common reported type of assault associated with genital injury, and the absence of penile penetration of the vagina accounted for the largest proportion of victims with normal findings. It was discovered that 41 percent of women described their assailant as an intimate partner; within this group, 49 percent had ano-genital trauma and 56 percent had nongenital injury. The researchers observe, "The proportion with ano-genital trauma was significantly higher for those women without a relationship to the offender than for those with such a relationship." One-hundred sixty-two (76 percent) of the women had an average of 3.1 sites of injury; comparatively, eight (11 percent) consenting women had just single-site trauma. Two hundred (94 percent) victims had trauma at one or more of four locations, as follows: posterior fourchette, labia minora, hymen, and fossa navicularis. The researchers report that trauma types varied by site; tears appeared most often on the posterior fourchette and fossa, abrasions appeared on the labia, and ecchymosis was seen on the hymen. Fifty-five patients reported anal contact, with six victims reporting it as the only sexual act of the assault. Hymenal or vaginal laceration was found in five victims, and vaginal laceration alone was found in nine cases. The researchers found that hymenal, vaginal, and combined tears were all associated with penile penetration with the exception of one case of penetration with a foreign object, and all patients reported vaginal bleeding. The researchers focused specifically on cases of penile penetration, as it is the most common type of assault associated with vaginal injury. Approximately 82 patients (38 percent) returned for follow-up examination within an average of 25 days after the assault. The researchers reported that all injury had resolved in 71 cases (87 percent). The researchers reported that hymenal tears and tears of the area of the fossa navicularis did not reunite, and no scarring was observed. They added that five women exhibited localized areas of hypervascularity or pigmentation that were initially viewed as trauma, necessitating an addendum to amend the first evaluation. In the consensual intercourse group, 75 women were seen within 24 hours after intercourse; trauma was noted in eight consenting women (11 percent) and was limited to one site. The injury had resolved by the time of a follow-up examination. In follow-up visits within 48 hours, six women had hypervascularity as a persistent finding. The researchers write, "Our findings show that genital trauma is common in victims of sexual assault, occurring in 68 percent of all patients, and is more commonly observed than injury associated with complaints of sodomy (56 percent). Moreover, our data confirm prior information showing that the prevalence of genital injury in rape is greater than in those women engaging in consensual intercourse." They add that the severity and extent of trauma in rape victims appear to differ from changes after consensual intercourse. The researchers also conclude that injuries showing consistent topologic features provide evidence that the most significant cause of genital trauma in rape victims occurs as entry injury, with insertion or attempts at insertion by a penis or other foreign object into the vagina. They add that the hymen was not the most common site of injury in either adults or adolescents, confirming the vulnerability of the posterior fourchette in sexual assult. Significantly, the researchers note, the average number of injury sites did not correspond to the time interval between the assault and the examination, suggesting that time could enhance the visibility of some lesions and injuries, or that the severity of the injury might cause victims to delay reporting. The researchers emphasize, "Prompt forensic assessment of all victims of sex crimes is important. Delayed reporting continues to occur with a substantial frequency . . . Nearly 50 percent of victims seen for examination at or after 72 hours had positive genital findings. Therefore, law enforcement should consider obtaining a forensic evaluation, even though trace evidence may have dissipated." They add, "Evidence of trauma has already been shown to be significantly associated with successful prosecution."

Slaughter et al. (1997) explain that ultimately, forensic examiners must be able to analyze and explain genital findings to the court. They conclude, "Now that we have more descriptive information about genital trauma in rape victims and comparative data from women engaging in consensual sex, we can better understand the mechanism of injury seen in rape victims and begin to develop taxonomy of genital trauma that is based on degree and type of injury, establishing a more reliable basis for forensic analysis." They alluded to injury to the cervix, predominantly ecchymosis, which was "difficult to see without careful inspection and magnification," and which might have been overlooked previously. Slaughter and Brown (1991) sought to provide corroborative physical data from rape victims to refute previous studies showing positive physical findings in only 10 percent to 30 percent of rape cases. They write, "This dismal result has prompted some authors to suggest that the performance of a genital examination be reserved for those who complain of pain or have a history of undergoing instrumentation." Slaughter and Brown reported on two cases of cervical findings through the use of colposcopy magnification; in one case, a 17-year-old woman was digitally penetrated, and in the other, a 30-year-old woman had been assaulted by what the victim described as something that felt like a knife in her vagina. An examination of the 17-year-old was conducted five days later; punctuated areas of hemorrhage were seen on the hymen at the 5- and 7-o'clock locations while the patient was in a supine position. Cervical examination revealed fine linear abrasions just below the cervical os. The 30-year-old was examined two hours after the assault. Genital examination revealed blood at the introitus, and a linear laceration was noted on the right in the vaginal barrel. The cervix showed several punctuate and linear lacerations. The researchers noted that armed with advanced technology afforded by the colposcope, they were able to detect and photograph trauma to the victim's cervix, a type of injury that had not been previously reported. They write, "These two cases illustrate how trauma can be reliably documented via colposcopic magnification; in both, the pattern of injury is consistent with blunt-force or penile penetration." They add that documentation of the healing process—which was observed to be within days or a few weeks in both victims—is an important part of forensic assessment. They explain, "First, it links the traumatic event to the injuries observed, establishing a reliable time frame associated with injury. Second, documentation of the victim's normal anatomy in the follow-up examination effectively establishes her as her own control against which the court can evaluate the nature, extent and cause of the injury." The researchers emphasize that this is critical when the body parts that are injured are not ones that can be seen; these injuries are easy to dismiss as trivial from a purely medical standpoint, but from a medico-legal standpoint, the researchers say, the information gathered from the colposcopic examination is significant. The information supports vaginal penetration, which is fundamental to a charge of rape, and it can also substantiate penetration with a foreign object, which is a separate crime.

By the early 1990s, Slaughter and Brown (1992) had used colposcopy to establish some of the first physical findings in rape victims. They write, "The difficulty of establishing physical findings in rape victims has been an accepted limitation in the medical and legal process that addresses sexual assault." They add that while a physical examination is a crucial part of patient management and that the findings can corroborate rape, conventional protocols have yielded an unacceptably low rate of positive findings. They also say that somewhat better results had been found when using toluidine blue dye to evaluate patients who had experienced penile penetration who are seen within 48 hours of the assault. In their study, Slaughter and Brown performed physical examinations on rape victims seen by the San Louis Obispo County's SART between 1985 and 1990. Of 131 patients examined within 48 hours and who experienced penile penetration, 114 (87 percent) had positive findings. Using colposcopic examination, the researchers were able to characrterize these findings as acute mounting injuries, typically seen at 3, 6, and 9 o'clock on the posterior fourchette and consisting mainly of lacerations, swelling, and ecchymosis.

Although toluidine blue dye has been helpful in visualization of gential injuries, forensic examiners have noted some limitations. As a nuclear stain, toluidine blue has been used to bind with and to detect lacerations that expose the deeper dermis. Various researchers, according to Slaughter and Brown, have been able to demonstrate an increase in detection of vaginal lacerations from 1 in 24 rape victims to 14 in 24 following the application of toluidine blue. Slaughter and Brown point out, however, that the dye will not be taken up in injuries that are superficial or are beginning to re-epithelialize. They note, "In our series toluidine blue did not define trauma not already seen with the colposcope. However, anticipating the need for a clear pictorial presentation of the findings in court, toluidine blue is useful to highlight injuries that a lay audience would find difficult to appreciate."

6.10.3 Postmortem Genital Examinations

The investigation of sexual homicide has traditionally not been within the nurse's purview; however, several FNEs have not only been practicing in the field, but have published what little nursing-driven research exists in this field. Skilled in the nuances of sexual assault and in come cases, in tandem with medico-legal death investigation, the FNE is uniquely qualified to assist forensic pathologists, law enforcement agencies, and prosecutors in these complex cases. Having established their expertise in the examination of living forensic patients, FNEs are extremely capable of providing postmortem examinations in suspected cases of sexual homicide through the use of advanced colposcopic technology and progressive evidentiary examination protocol. FNEs are adept at recognizing and interpreting postmortem changes in the body, which facilitates the identification of normal versus abnormal postmortem changes that point to potential criminal acts.

One examiner who has made significant strides in postmortem genital examination research is Sharon Crowley, MN, RN, a forensic clinical nurse specialist in Santa Cruz, California, who has consistently presented her research to the AAFS and has been published in the prestigious *Journal of Forensic Science*. Initiated in 1995, Crowley's work has focused on the colposcopic magnification of genital injuries in decedent victims of sexual assault. She acknowledges work by Slaughter and others, as well as her own findings that have established the common genital findings of living sexual assault victims, facilitated by the use of colposcopic magnification. However, Crowley was interested in the genital findings of decedents, and knew there was a paucity of information on this subject in the medical literature.

Crowley, author of *Sexual Assault: The Medical-Legal Examination* (1999), developed a "Sequential Methodology for the Examination of Sexual Homicide Victims" as a response to the need for a systematic examination method of decedents. Her research included a study of 18 decedents whose deaths were determined to be accidental, natural, and suicide. Using a mobile system of colposcopy that she invented, Crowley evaluated the ano-genital regions of the victims in collaboration with a forensic pathologist. The decedents ranged in age from 6 to 72, with an average age of almost 49 years. The postmortem interval ranged from less than 24 hours to more than a few days, and all bodies were in a state of active decay. Crowley examined 11 anatomical sites: labia majora, labia minora, periutereal area, posterior fourchette, fossa navicularis, hymen, vagina, cervix, perineum, anus, and rectum.

This kind of work, as well as Crowley's mobile colposcopy system, was the subject of an article in the November 2004 issue of the *Journal of Forensic Science*, "A Mobile System for Postmortem Genital Examination With Colposcopy: SART-to-Go." Crowley devised her mobile system after identifying the need to bring examiner services to the decedent in a jurisdiction that lacked a centrally located morgue. During Crowley's initial rape-homicide examinations, only gross visualization methods were available, and she knew there had to be a better way to scrutinize the ano-genital tissues at various postmortem intervals.

Crowley says this kind of examination is crucial in sexual homicide cases, where the offender's sexual motivation for homicide is based on the accurate assessment of information regarding the victim, the crime scene, forensic reports, and the nature of the behavioral exchange between the victim and the offender. She says sexually motivated offenders can be classified as organized, disorganized, mixed, and sadistic, with each characterization affecting the manner in which the sexual homicide was committed. This classification system helps examiners, investigators, and criminal profilers determine a course of forensic investigation and examination.

In her "Sequential Methodology for the Examination of Sexual Homicide Victims," Crowley (2005) outlines an approach that "incorporates all facets of the examination process" and "helps to ensure that the myriad aspects of the entire evaluation will be completed." She explains that a standardized, methodical approach minimizes omissions and avoids errors, which is particularly important in jurisdictions with varying protocols. Prior to the start of the autopsy, Crowley recommends that individual roles and responsibilities of each forensic team member should be clarified in terms of evidence collection, photography, and documentation of nongenital trauma. Crowley also advises, "If possible, conduct the genital examination and collect ano-genital specimens prior to the general autopsy. This may be done after the forensic pathologist has done a preliminary overview of the body and noted gross features such as clothing. This allows prompt collection of biological specimens and avoids obscuring the genital area by leakage of body fluids through the vaginal opening." The next step is setting up a work area with all the necessary equipment, including a still-sealed rape evidence kit to facilitate evidence collection during the postmortem examination. All pertinent case data should be documented next, including demographic data, disposition of the body at the crime scene, victim's medical history, and results of the general physical examination of the decedent. Evidence is then collected from the body, observing proper forensic protocol. Postmortem genital examination, as described by Crowley, involves a number of body sites and collection techniques, including the following:

- Oral swabs
- Vaginal swabs
- Vaginal lavage
- Cervix swabs
- Penile swabs
- External genital swabs
- Anal swabs
- Swabs of dried secretions
- Collection of debris
- Fingernail scrapings
- Collection of encrusted stains
- Collection of condoms

Crowley emphasizes that the examination creates the framework of all medico-legal reports, and the examiner must ensure its completeness and accuracy. She writes, "In the summary of findings for the postmortem anogenital evaluation, describe the nature and pattern/location of any injuries. Distinguish multiple vs. single sites of injury. Describe the overall appearance and integrity of the ano-genital tissues. This may include concomitant postmortem tissue changes, e.g., lividity, dilatation, skin slippage, or mucosal shedding."

6.10.4 Up Close and Clinical With Sharon Crowley

Crowley says her postmortem genital examination research had humble beginnings in her professional dealings with law enforcement while she was working as a nurse in San Luis Obispo. In fact, she says, laughing, "I blame the cops for getting me into this; I was quite fine in the world of the living." She explains that one day, "A detective called me and explained that he had a female homicide victim whom he wanted me to examine to determine if she had also been sexually assaulted," Crowley recalls:

> There was a tradition of doing this kind of examination where I worked, so it wasn't the first time. But when I started to do the examination, something just clicked and I thought to myself, "This is a different world altogether." I realized that it isn't the same as with a living forensic patient, and I also realized, as I began to study the subject more, that as little research as we had on living victims, there was nothing on dead victims. The more I dug, the more I realized this and by the time I did my second and third cases, I realized, "OK, this is going to be a habit. I need to get some kind of a system going." Because every time I did a post-mortem examination, it felt like it was for the first time; I needed a standardized system.

Before she developed her methodology, Crowley quips, "I flew by the seat of my pants." Now, to know Crowley is to understand that she takes nothing related to her job lightly, but she recognized the utter absence of guidance in the medical literature for these kinds of cases:

> I did what I thought worked, and as I really started studying it, I pulled from the research conducted by the FBI and the world of criminal profiling. When I got involved with homicides, I developed a burning curiosity. I wondered if all of this stuff about different kinds of rapists tied in any way to what we, as nurses and pathologists, see when we examine decedents. I started researching all the different aspects of sexual homicide cases, from the profiling of various kinds of sexual murders, and scrutinizing methods of examining living sexual assault victims in order to better perform evidence collection and documentation. After all, you are now dealing with a victim who can't give a history, at least not verbally—the body will have to tell the tale. But you have huge sections of information for which we rely on living victims that are now blank. There is no one to give you instant answers to your questions. Once I understood the parameters of working with decedents, I started assembling the equipment I needed to do post-mortem cases.

Because Crowley tended to a lot of cases in jurisdictions that lacked a central morgue, Crowley then developed her mobile system, which she calls SART-to-Go. She explains:

> I did a lot of fast talking and got a company to loan me equipment. It took at least a year or more of trial and error in setting up the equipment in the back of my truck, to see what worked and what didn't. I put together the methodology based on what worked and what I thought would work in a variety of different areas and examination settings. When I started in San Luis Obispo there was no central morgue; examinations were done at different mortuaries, which was a huge challenge logistically. Yet that's the way it is done in many rural areas, or else you go to a fancy, highly scientific morgue, which is real convenient. So I challenged myself to come up with a system that would work no matter where the examination was done.

Crowley knew that the next step, once she had perfected her methodology, was to get this system in front of her forensic peers and colleagues:

> As I wrote each protocol, because it was such a new field, I wanted to get scientific peer review. So I presented my ideas every year; I would write another abstract or a case study, and present it wherever I could, at AAFS meeting or some other professional conference. At AAFS I presented my first rape homicide, which happened in 1994. I wrote it up and collaborated with a criminal investigator/profiler on that case because we'd also examined the suspect. That's when I was first thinking along the lines of, what fits into what I see anatomically, and the kind of perpetrator who would do this crime. In 2000, I wondered if they'd let a nurse chair and conduct a workshop on post-mortem genital examination, so I asked, and ended up doing a four-hour workshop which I also chaired.

At that time, Crowley connected with an epidemiologist who helped her create a database to collect data derived from each case, including the case identification number assigned to it, and the victim's age, ethnicity, race; the date of the examination; the postmortem interval; the cause of death; medical history; gross nongenital trauma; and examination protocol performed. Crowley knew it was important to establish a framework to support the systematic collection and analysis of evidence and data, and to further classify the postmortem genital findings. "I had envisioned a database that would one day allow me to pull up whatever data I needed about a particular victim," Crowley explains:

> Say you have a Caucasian woman with such-and-such injuries sustained in a rape-homicide at four days post-mortem, and I wanted to be able to compare this victim with other victims in other age ranges, races, and genital injuries. I wanted a database that could refute the old argument based in comparing findings of living patients and decedents in court. I wanted to have something to compare apples to apples instead of apples to oranges. So the epidemiologist helped me create the mechanics of a database; I told him what variables I wanted in it and he helped me with the framework. Then I got Brian Peterson, MD, who was the pathologist that I had been working with, on board with this project. I was also interested in the work by the forensic odontologist, Bob Barsley, at Louisiana State University. He was totally supportive of my work. This kind of collaboration illustrates the fact that if I am going to publish my research findings, I need to consult professionals who can tell me if I'm on track or not. Having forensic colleagues' buy-in strengthens the project, and it tells them, "Hey, nurses can do this."

Crowley says that at every step of the way in her quest to publish her research, she involved her peers and colleagues in the forensic community, and kept her work in the full scrutiny of the AAFS membership:

> I knew it was a hot topic in a new field, and I wanted to give these scientists every reason to look over my work and comment on it. And when you start gaining acceptance, then you introduce the concept of nurses conducting this kind of research. It's a lengthy process of gaining credibility and earning their stamp of approval. I think that's the battle we have to fight as nurses. But once you get the support you need, it's awesome. Unless you screw it up, you've got them.

In February 2003, Crowley, a fellow of the AAFS, was honored by the Academy with its prestigious General Section Achievement Award. So how did this public health nurse and STD coordinator for the Santa Cruz, California Department of Health, pediatric SART examiner, and FCNS for Santa Clara Valley Medical Center's Center for Child Protection in San Jose, California, end up where she is now? She says it's been a long, glorious road full of twists and turns. As a young nurse with a freshly minted bachelor's degree, Crowley worked in med-surg, coronary care, and the ICU for a year before deciding to pursue a master's degree. She comments:

> At the time, being a clinical nurse specialist was a very new thing, but so was the nurse practitioner program. It was very new to try to have a master's of education degree in nursing and yet not be a researcher, an educator, or an administrator. I wanted to be clinically focused. So I went the CNS route, and at the time, my love and great passion in life was cardiovascular care. While I was in grad school I worked in open heart surgery. After graduating I got a job at USC Medical Center, but they didn't know what to do with me; they didn't have a position for someone with a master's degree, but they were desperate for nurses to work in their special-care units. They resembled mini ICUs; new nursing grads were placed into these units alone with five patients for 12-hour shifts. They needed someone to show these new nurses how to provide nursing care in a hands-on training environment. I devised my own role, and that's the way it's been for the last 30 years... basically creating my job as I go.

Crowley explains that when she left grad school, "I couldn't find the job I really wanted, but I found it 30 years later. Jobs tend to follow me rather than be available at the time I really want them," she says, laughing. "So I'll be 80 when I find the job I really want now!" she kids. Crowley's résumé encompasses nursing experience in nearly every setting and community, but when she was ready to take a breather, she moved to northern California to get married, have kids, and settle down. "I even explored the possibility of becoming a chiropractor, because I was getting burned out on nursing," she recalls. "Things started evolving in nursing, and in the late 1980s I got into forensic nursing. And everything changed."

Crowley says she was asked to join a child abuse prevention council in Santa Cruz, which she did. "I did that for about a year; all along, the nurse examiner program had been in operation since 1986, the first nurse examiner program in California. I joined it in 1988 and went through the SART training." She explains:

> I've never been one to sit down and put all the pieces together before I did anything. I've sort of leaped in and went for it when it felt right to do so. The pieces of the puzzle always seemed to fall into place afterward. I recognized the need for forensic nursing, and it seemed exciting; the time was certainly right for finding a way to serve victims of violence in an improved manner. I knew this was a way I could work as a nurse and be very involved in the field of rape and child abuse, which was both meaningful, exciting, and rewarding.

Crowley says that at the time, sexual assault was somewhat unchartered waters, even as child abuse was well understood and studied. However, certain medico-legal processes were still lacking:

> In 1986, it was very unusual for a young child to go to court and testify; there had to be a lot more evidence, and so much of the work forensic nurses do now in the area of child abuse—other than rote evidence collection—working with victims and doing a history—has helped a lot more of those cases get to trial. The field of child abuse has always had more of a body of literature and research than adult sexual assault. At the time, the battles we fought were, can nurses do this exam? Are we going to be adequate to testify in court? Do we have the support of the local prosecutors? Do the police want us to do their cases? Will the crime lab think we can do the rape kit correctly? Can we learn all this? And then, will the medical field accept us as colleagues?

The answer, of course, is yes, but Crowley says that at the time, nurses had to prove themselves:

> The 1980s were very much a proving ground for nurses and what they could do. The timing was right, however, so I think that had a lot to do with nurses' eventual success. Physicians didn't like the hassle of going to court on sexual assault cases, and they were overloaded in the ER, so there was a void, work that needed to be done. And the nurses filled that role beautifully. There was a definite medico-legal need because the existing system really wasn't able or willing—not unwilling, just that they were overextended. Many medical personnel didn't have the forensic training necessary. I used to affectionately be told by ER staff, "We love you and we're so glad of the work you do, but we hate to see you coming, because we know what that means." Trauma, like a motor vehicle accident, was one thing, but when a sexual assault victim came in, it was much more difficult for the staff without forensic nurses.

Whether it is sexual assault or medico-legal death investigation, Crowley says forensics is a natural fit for nurses. "The stage was already set," she says:

> Even a lay observer could tell tht forensic nursing was well within the scope of practice for a nurse. It was really no different, I don't think, than being in the ER or the ICU, when you look at the kinds of care provided and the medico-legal approach. The only thing different was, could nurses develop the technical forensic skills that typically belonged to the realm of the physician or the law enforcement officer, or even the nurse practitioner. Those were bigger issues than forensic concepts; some

people really focused on the nursing process and how forensics fit into it. For a lot of us, it was really more about learning the specific medico-legal skills because we knew we already had the expertise of documentation and working with patients down cold. It was natural to extend forensic work to the care of patients; it really became more a matter of plugging in the forensic pieces in other clinical responsibilities. I have always seen all of us—doctors, nurses, law enforcement, prosecutors—as a team. I've always been able to work well with physicians and all other allied health professionals, and now in the forensic community, collegiality extends to the criminalists and to the police. It may be different players, but it's no different in terms of the team concept. Different people bring different talents to the forensic arena. The forensic nurse is a vital member of that team.

6.10.5 Genital Injury: An Issue in the Courtroom

In the more than two decades since formal SANE/SART programs were developed, experts are still pondering the likelihood of genital injury following sexual assault. This type of injury is frequently an issue in the courts, with the expectation that injuries will be discovered and documented in "genuine" cases. In some jurisdictions, rates of conviction are higher when the complainant has genital injuries.

Palmer, McNulty, D'Este, and Donovan (2004) consulted assault records and forensic examination findings of 153 women who attended a sexual assault service in Newcastle, Australia between 1997 and 1999. All of the women were examined within 72 hours of their assault. One hundred eleven (73 percent) of the women were under the age of 30, and 4 percent were over the age of 50. Eighty-six percent of the cases were penile–vaginal penetration. Nongenital injuries were found in 46 percent of the women examined, and genital injury was found in 22 percent. Palmer et al. (2004) write, "Genital injury following sexual assault carries undue influence in obtaining convictions." Bowyer and Dalton (1997) concluded that the courts in the United Kingdom rely on medical evidence, especially genital injury, to prove sexual assault even though many studies report that a minority of women suffer such injury. Estimates of genital injury following sexual assault have ranged from 7 percent to 87 percent of women, depending on the method of detection used (Girardin, Faugno, Seneski, & Slaughter, 1997; Slaughter & Brown, 1992). Examinations using tissue staining and colposcopy have higher rates of genital injury noted than unaided examination. Some findings such as redness and swelling could have been physiological responses or due to unrelated conditions. Nevertheless, most injuries related to sexual assault are minor. Severe genital trauma was reported in less than 5 percent of women and fewer than 2 percent of genital injuries required hospital admission and medical treatment.

Palmer and colleagues reported in their study that 61 percent of the women interviewed knew their assailant, and 51 percent of the women were assaulted in either their own home or the home of the assailant. Two hundred fifty-three separate sexual acts allegedly were perpetrated on the victims, most commonly penile–vaginal penetration, either attempted or completed. A weapon was present in 11 percent of the assaults, and threats of violence were reported by 18 percent of the women. Nongenital injuries were detected in 70 women; 66 percent of injuries were deemed minor, 24 percent moderate, and 10 percent severe. Injuries consisted of bruises (54 percent), abrasions (40 percent), and lacerations (4 percent). Three women were hospitalized due to the extent of their injuries. The physical sites of the injuries were the limbs (50 percent); back and buttocks (25 percent); head, face, and neck (15 percent); and abdomen and chest (10 percent). Genital injuries were detected in 33 women; 61 percent of injuries were deemed minor, 33 percent moderate, and 9 percent severe. Injuries were chiefly abrasions (59 percent), bruises (22 percent), and lacerations (16 percent). One woman was hospitalized due to the severity of her injuries. The most common site of injury was the vulva (49 percent), upper inner thighs (22 percent), and the perianal area (20 percent); vaginal injuries represented 8 percent of cases. Half of the women had neither nongenital nor genital injuries. The researchers discovered that less than one third of the women studied had genital injuries documented, and most were minor. Their research confirms many U.S. and British studies that found a majority of women who reported sexual assault had clinical evidence of genital injuries. The researchers drew several conclusions:

- There are limitations to the measurement of injury after alleged sexual assault, as bruising can take days to appear, and some injuries might not have been present at the time of the examination. Conversely, preexisting lesions could have been assessed as being caused by the assault.
- Interobserver error could be introduced into a case, as different physicians were involved in the medical examinations of the women.
- As many sexual assaults go unreported, women with injuries might not seek care, and so it might not be appropriate to generalize findings of the study to a larger group of women who do not seek medical treatment.
- Reporting bias could be present, as the majority of the women were assaulted by known assailants.
- The likelihood and extent of genital injury following penetration is dependent on the following factors: the state of the genital tissues; their

lubrication, durability, and integrity; the dimensions of the penetrating object; and the degree of force involved.

- It is usually impossible to differentiate the effects of digital from penile penetration, regardless of the victim's age and hormonal status. Therefore, genital injuries can be due to individual factors or the combined result of penile, digital, or foreign-body penetration of the anus and the vagina.

The researchers discovered several significant factors associated with injury following sexual assault:

- The presence of nongenital injury had an odds ratio of 19 for the presence of genital injury, which reflects the findings of other studies.
- Threats of violence were independently associated with genital and nongenital injuries.
- Assault by a known assailant had lower odds of nongenital and genital injuries than assault by a stranger. The researchers conclude, "Debate persists as to the likelihood and frequency of genital injury following consensual intercourse as opposed to sexual assault. Studies comparing genital findings on unaided examination of women following consensual intercourse and of women who have been sexually assaulted are needed. Nevertheless, this study should redress the misperception that genital injury is a necessary finding following sexual assault."

6.10.6 Use of Colposcopy in Sexual Assault Examinations

In the past 15 years, a standard in the use of the colposcope for photo documentation of child and adult sexual assault cases has been established, with an increasing appreciation for the use of video colposcopy in this patient population. Although a comprehensive history and interview are crucial components of the examination process, forensic nurses must have a thorough understanding of the significant medical-clinical evidence involved in sexual assault cases. Two types of medical evidence exist: laboratory (forensic evidence and STDs) and clinical, or the documentation of traumatic and psychological injuries. It is obvious to health care providers that laboratory evidence can be definitive when there is evidence of ejaculation; however, it has become increasingly important to provide clinical documentation of trauma associated with assault, as many cases are presented without forensic evidence or with legal strategies claiming that the sexual act was consensual. In recent years there has been an increased understanding of the significance of medical (clinical) findings in sexual assault. Researchers have reached a consensus on those clinical findings of trauma and variants of normal and nonspecific changes. Colposcopy, with the addition of video and computer technology, has changed with the times and has become more sophisticated, directly addressing the medical community's increasing dependence on photo documentation in assault cases. The primary benefit of colposcopy is the single examination, which can be reviewed with experts and provided to the legal system, avoiding the need for numerous examinations and examiners.

Astrid H. Heger, MD, executive director of the Violence Intervention Program at the Los Angeles County and University of Southern California Medical Center, where she is also an associate professor of clinical pediatrics, reports that video colposcopy adds an additional dimension, as the examination can be virtually re-created via videotape—an important factor when evaluating the adolescent or adult patient. In these patients, the estrogenized hymen tends to be more dynamic and moves during the examination, so video documentation allows the examiner to evaluate all of the folds and clefts that might be missed during still photography. Additionally, video colposcopy gives teaching programs the ability to instruct through closed-circuit video, rather than having numerous evaluators in the room during the examination. Heger states:

> With the increased reliance on nurse specialists or forensic nurses, the video documentation allows for the physician back-up to review and participate in both diagnosis and treatment, and the legal processes. This collaboration improves the quality of the evaluation for the patient and the system, while giving the patient access to a medical setting staffed by caring professionals. The primary use of photographic documentation by the legal system has been in the substitution of photographs for re-examination. Defense and court-appointed experts can review prior evaluations easily without additional trauma to the patient. This use of colposcopy in the diagnosis of sexual abuse of children and adult victims of sexual assault has been upheld by the appellate court of California and its use is described as being nonexperimental... Video colposcopy will not replace the meticulous, sensitive, well-trained professional, but it can bring the best of documentation and accountability to a diagnosis which must be made accurately and scientifically for the protection of both the victim and the system. This is truly a case where a picture is worth a thousand words.

6.10.7 Sexual Assault Examination, Reporting, and the Legal Outcome of Cases

Although not completely nonexistent, there is a paucity of information on the relationship between medico-legal evidence and the laying of charges in sexual assault cases. Here is a look at several recent studies. One Canadian study outright questions the "uncritical" collection of medical forensic evidence as it relates to the laying of charges. Du Mont and Parnis (2000) say that because very little is known about the role of medical evidence in the legal resolution of sexual assault cases, they conducted a retrospective review of hospital and police records to determine whether medico-legal evidence was related to the police laying of charges. Data were obtained from 187 female sexual assault victims who presented to a large urban hospital-based sexual assault treatment center and the police in Ontario, Canada between January 1 and December 31, 1994. Using stepwise logistic regression, medico-legal variables were tested while controlling for nonmedical factors. Neither the collection of sperm, semen, and saliva, nor the documentation of clinically observed injuries, was significant in predicting an arrest and charge. In contrast, nonmedical variables such as the victim's age, use of alcohol, resistance and relationship to the assailant, and the corroborating evidence of a witness were related to charge-laying.

Wiley, Sugar, Fine, and Eckert (2003) wanted to better describe the assault characteristics and examination findings in sexual assault victims who pursue legal action. They performed a case-control study of consecutive women older than 15 years who came to an urban hospital after sexual assault over a 32-month period. All of the women underwent a standardized history and physical examination by a resident in obstetrics and gynecology. Of the 888 women undergoing evaluation in the ED, 132 (15 percent) had charges filed by the prosecutor. Characteristics positively associated with a legal outcome included being examined within 24 hours after assault, partner or spouse as an assailant, oral assault, and anogenital trauma. Amnesia at the time of assault and friend or acquaintance as assailant were negatively associated with a legal outcome.

Sexual assault and abuse crimes often go unpunished because many cases go unreported; however, even when victims do come forward, it can be a difficult crime to prosecute. A recent study by Rennison (2002) that looked at survey figures for the years 1992 to 2000 found that only about 36 percent of forcible rapes experienced by females age 12 and older were reported to law enforcement officials. Langan and Farrington (1998) say that of reported assaults, only about one fifth actually result in arrest, prosecution, and successful conviction.

A sexual assault is a personal crime that can be emotionally and physically traumatizing, and reporting it might be daunting when the assailant is someone the victim knows. Greenfeld (1997) found that in about three out of four assaults, the victim and offender are acquainted, intimate partners, or from the same family. In another study of police-recorded data on children under age 12, some 90 percent of the children raped knew the offender (DOJ, Bureau of Justice Statistics, 1993). The medical evidentiary examination then becomes an even more important component in the medico-legal process. The examination must be performed competently and comprehensively if the evidence gathered is to stand up in a court proceeding that might occur weeks, months, and sometimes years after an assault.

McGregor, Le, Marion, and Wiebe (1999) state that few studies have examined if there is a correlation between medical findings and legal outcomes in sexual assault cases. Rambow et al. (1992) found that evidence of genital or nongenital trauma was significantly associated with conviction in cases in which there was an identified suspect and the victim was willing to testify. Penttilla and Karhumen (1990) determined that little correlation existed between the severity of a victim's injuries and the outcome of the case. Schei (1995) discovered that conviction was related to the occurrence of severe violence, documentation of genital injuries, and presence of sperm at the time of the evidentiary examination. In their retrospective cohort study, McGregor et al. (1999) reviewed the charts and medico-legal reports for all cases of sexual assault handled by the BC Women's Sexual Assault Service in 1992 for which a police report had been filed. Ninety-five cases were identified; in 10 cases, no injuries were documented at the time of the examination. The degree of injury was rated as mild in 26 cases (27 percent), moderate in 56 cases (59 percent), and severe in 3 cases (3 percent). In 31 cases, there was documented genital injury. After adjustment for income level and the patient's knowledge of the assailant, the odds ratio for charge-laying in a sexual assault case with documented moderate to severe injury was 33.3. Socioeconomic status above the group median and knowledge of the assailant were also associated with charge-laying. Presence of genital injury per se, age of the patient, and the detection of sperm by microscopy at the time of the examination were not associated with the laying of charges. The researchers concluded that the extent of documented injury is associated with the laying of charges in cases of sexual assault; however, questions remain as to the effectiveness of the medical component of evidence collection. The researchers approached the study with the questions of, "Is there an association between the extent of documented physical injury and legal outcome in cases of sexual assault?" and "What other factors are associated with legal outcome in these cases?" McGregor et al. write:

> Answers to these questions should provide insight into how a health care provider should apportion his or her time between the forensic component of the exam, educating the patient about treatment after the assault, and assisting the patient to debrief after the experience. If particular aspects of the physical exam, such as detection of sperm or documentation of genital injury, are strongly associated with a positive legal outcome, sexual assault services could direct greater resources to training in the collection of forensic evidence in these areas.

In 31 cases (33 percent), charges were laid, and in 11 of these cases there was a conviction. Of the 11 convictions, 10 were for sexual assault and one was for common assault, or an assault that does not involve a weapon and does not result in serious bodily harm. For the perpetrators who were charged, there was a stay of proceedings in another 11 cases. Under Canadian law, a stay of proceedings is often entered if a victim or witness is unable or unwilling to testify, and there is insufficient evidence to proceed. McGregor et al. report that the most common outcome for the cases in which charges were not made was that the case became inactive due to lack of information (28 cases); the second most common outcome (13 cases) was a designation that the victim did not want to proceed. Among the perpetrators who were convicted, sentences ranged from 21 days to five years, and in once case of a multiple offender, a life sentence was handed down. Charges were laid in 1 of the 10 cases with no injury, 6 of the 26 cases with mild injury, 22 of the 56 cases with moderate injury, and 2 of the 3 cases with severe injury. McGregor and colleagues report that during the year of the study, too few convictions provided sufficient means for analysis; however, they say:

> The laying of charges was a reasonable positive legal outcome for the analysis, for without a charge, there can be no conviction. The proportion of cases in which there was evidence of genital injury, excluding tenderness, was similar to that reported in previous studies, which have found that visible genital trauma is relatively uncommon in sexual assault. The lack of an association between charge-laying and genital findings suggests that increasing the time devoted to documenting microtrauma of the genital region by means of colposcopy may not be appropriate.

McGregor and colleagues sum up their study by reiterating that their study results support the theory that there is an association between the laying of charges and the presence of documented moderate or severe injury. "It is important to have good evidence that the time spent on the forensic part of the examination does indeed influence the legal outcome of the case."

McGregor and colleagues readdressed the issue of evidence related to successful prosecution. This time they conducted a retrospective chart review of all police-reported cases seen from January 1993 to December 1997 at a sexual assault center. They reported that charges were filed in 151 (32.7 percent) and a conviction secured in 51 (11 percent) of 462 cases examined. Genital injury was observed in 193 cases (41.8 percent) and semen-positive forensic results were obtained in 100 cases (38.2 percent). In 197 cases (42.6 percent) the assailant was known to the victim before the attack, and 21 cases (4.5 percent) involved multiple assailants. Slightly more than three fourths of victims reported vaginal, anal, or foreign-object penetration. Genital injury was noted in 193 cases (41.8 percent), and police files documented receipt of forensic samples from the forensic examiner in 327 cases (70.8 percent). Of the 262 cases in which forensic samples were analyzed, 100 samples (38.2 percent) tested positive for the presence of sperm. DNA testing was performed in eight cases (1.7 percent). The most common documented extragenital injury was bruising, seen in 301 cases (65.2 percent), with lacerations being relatively uncommon (18.6 percent). In the McGregor (1999) study, a suspect was identified in 280 cases (60.6 percent), and a conviction was secured in 51 cases (11 percent). At the time the study was conducted, one case remained before the courts. The researchers discovered that perpetrators were found guilty as charged in 33 cases (7.1 percent) and guilty of a lesser charge in 18 cases (3.9 percent). In 40 cases (8.7 percent), a custodial sentence was rendered. The period of incarceration varied from seven days to more than 14 years. McGregor et al. write, "Previous authors have cited provision costs and time, victims' experience of the evidence collection process as invasive and traumatic, and victims' expectation that the examination would prove an assault took place as reasons for evaluating medical-legal findings in sexual assault." The researchers added that the proportion of cases with observed genital injury was somewhat higher in their study than in previous studies, which might be explained by the use of colposcopic examination. The researchers say the low rate of findings of sperm can be explained by time delays in presenting for examination, douching after an assault, variations in the vaginal environment, sexual dysfunction of the assailant, and the use of condoms. The researchers caution, "When testifying in court, examiners need to educate the judge and jury regarding how these tests should be interpreted. Failure to do so might leave the court with the false impression that negative results negate the possibility that a sexual assault has occurred." The researchers add that positive associations of documented injury with charge filing and conviction is "an important step in confirming the value of injury documentation in the forensic examination of sexual assault victims." They add that positively associating injury with conviction is consistent with other studies and that it is not surprising, "given that more than half of cases proceeding through the criminal justice system involve an assailant known previously to the victim, which is likely to make corroboration of consent through injury documentation a common issue at trial." One of the most important points the researchers tried to make was the causation between the presence of forensic evidence collected by an examiner and the increased incident of charges being filed. They write, "The greater than threefold increased likelihood of charges being filed in the presence of forensic samples collected by the examiner, irrespective of the test results, suggests that a victim's willingness to submit to a forensic examination might play a role in assessing the strength of a case." They add, "The examiner's collection of biologic samples for submission to police appears to provide some perceived scientific validation of a victim's allegations."

What this study might do for the encouragement of reporting and laying of charges is contrasted with the damage it might do to the use of colposcopic examination. McGregor and colleagues report that the lack of genital injury alone with either charge filing or convictions suggests that efforts to focus on visualizing microtrauma of the genital region in sexual assault forensic examinations "might be misguided." They say further, "This is particularly relevant considering the costs of colposcopy, the need for technical expertise and familiarity with colposcopic examination of normal patients, and care providers' need to apportion time between evidence collection, medical care, and counseling." They also add, "As described by Patel (1993), the procedure is a potentially 'stressful invasion of a woman who is already vulnerable and at risk of the rape trauma syndrome.' Future evaluation of colposcopic technology with respect to its effect on victim–provider interactions, the victim's experience of care provision, and its relationship to securing greater numbers of convictions is important."

Gray-Eurom, Seaburg, and Wears (2002) at the University of Florida Health Science Center also set out to determine the association between historical and physical evidence with the judicial outcome of sexual assault cases. They conducted a population-based, retrospective review of forensic evidence for all sexual assault cases reported in Duval County in Florida during a two-year period. The variables examined included age, race of victim, evidence of trauma—whether body, genital, or both—presence of spermatozoa at the time of the forensic examination, weapon use, and whether the victim knew the assailant. In cases in which an arrest was made, logistic regression was used to estimate the strength of association with the outcome of conviction in sexual assault cases. During the study period, 821 sexual assaults were reported, and 801 forensic examinations were performed. Seven hundred seventy-six (97 percent) of the victims were female. A suspect was identified in 355 (44 percent) of the 801 cases for which a sexual assault forensic examination was conducted. No suspect was identified in 446 (56 percent) of these cases. Two hundred seventy-one arrests were made, and police did not have enough evidence to arrest a suspect after detention in 84 cases. For those cases in which a suspect was arrested, 153 had charges dropped, 89 were found guilty, 2 were found not guilty, and 27 cases were still pending or the files were sealed and unavailable for review. There was evidence of trauma in 202 (57 percent) of the examinations, and sperm were found at the time of the forensic examination in 110 (31 percent) of the cases in which a suspect was identified. By using logistic regression, the researchers found that victims aged younger than 18 years, the presence of trauma, and the use of a weapon by the assailant were significantly associated with successful prosecution. There also was a trend toward conviction if the victim was White. The researchers concluded, "Emergency physicians have an obligation to provide care for victims of sexual assault cases. This care includes a possible legal defense. To that end, emergency physicians should be vigilant in the documentation of the history of the event and in the documentation of traumatic injuries because these factors can assist in a successful prosecution."

One of the more definitive cases involving pattern injury and court testimony in a sexual assault is a 1997 case that represented the first successful prosecution of an acquaintance rape case in a county. Hohenhaus (1998) described the case of a 40-year-old woman who presented to the ED of a tertiary-care teaching hospital in September 1997. She reported being sexually assaulted by an acquaintance earlier in the evening. When the SANE performed routine evidence collection, the nurse examined the patient's genital area with a colposcope before and after application of toluidine blue dye. On first examination, the patient had a 2-cm tear at the 6 o'clock area of the posterior fourchette, as well as redness extending from the 6 o'clock to the 7 o'clock position. The visible tear had a positive uptake of toluidine blue dye, and the speculum examination revealed petechias of the cervix, with some minimal bleeding noted from the cervical os. The SANE photographed the injuries per standard protocol, and recorded the opinion that the injuries were consistent with nonconsensual intercourse. The defendant was charged with second-degree rape, and the case went to trial on May 13, 1998. Hohenhaus reported that at the pretrial conference, the defense attorney provided the assistant district attorney and the SANE with several photographs of the defendant's penis with a metal ring through the base of the glans. The defense stated that the injuries found in the patient's genital area were the result of the defendant wearing this ring during consensual intercourse, although the patient denied during testimony that she had observed this ring. During the SANE's testimony, the defense inquired as to whether the injuries observed during the patient's examination could have been caused by the ring. Although this was possible, Hohenhaus writes, "further study of the photographs of both the patient and the defendant revealed an interesting note, based on the defense's opinion of how the injuries occurred." The defense claimed that the clasp on the ring caused the victim's genital tear, rather than injuries sustained during nonconsensual intercourse. The SANE acknowledged that this was possible, but that the tear was more consistent with blunt-force trauma as opposed to sharp-force trauma. The SANE asked the defense if the ring was inserted from the same direction each time it was used; when the defense replied that it was always placed from his right to his left, the SANE explained that it was highly unlikely that the injury noted would have been caused by the clasp on the ring because the injury then more likely would have been noted at the 7 o'clock position of the posterior fourchette. Hohenhaus reported that during the three-day trial, the SANE testified for four hours and was called back by the jury for clarification of some of the issues regarding "left and right" as presented in the medical evidence. After deliberating for two hours, and after requesting only the photographs and the medical record, the jury returned with a verdict of guilty. Hohenhaus writes, "Understanding mechanism of injury plays an important role in the examination of victims of sexual assault. In this case, the SANE's expertise in patterned injury interpretation was a major factor in the conviction of a rapist."

6.11 DRUG-FACILITATED SEXUAL ASSAULT

Although alcohol has long been used to facilitate sexual assaults, today newer, memory-erasing drugs such as rohypnol, ketamine, gamma hydroxybutyrate (GHB), gamma butyrolactone (GBL) and many others are being used in drug-facilitated sexual assault. Symptoms include a history of having only a couple of alcoholic beverages but quickly becoming extremely intoxicated. The victim can often remember very little of the incident other than flashes, sometimes referred to as cameo appearances, until she awakens. She might then find herself undressed, or partially dressed, with vaginal or rectal soreness making her believe she has been raped (Ledray, 1999). Whenever a victim of a potential drug-facilitated sexual assault (DFSA) is seen within 72 hours of the likely assault, a urine specimen should be collected for a drug screen analysis, according to the ACEP (1999). Although 72 hours is the recommended time limit because most substances cannot be detected beyond that time, newer techniques of drug analysis are being developed and the time frames might change. Although the technique is still under study, a new process of analysis can now detect a 2-mg dose of flunitrazepam for up to 28 days after ingestion. Once developed, these processes will allow for the identification of substances as long as 28 days postingestion of a single 2-mg dose of flunitrazepam (Negrusz et al., 2000).

Even though there is little memory and perhaps no certainty of a sexual assault, whenever the victim's story is consistent with a DFSA, or suspicious, the forensic examiner should collect a urine specimen for DFSA analysis as a part of the sexual assault evidentiary examination. If the victim calls prior to coming to the hospital or clinic, she should be told to not void unless necessary, and if she must void to collect her first voided urine in a clean container and bring it with her (Anglin, Spears, & Hutson, 1997).

Some assailants use drugs to facilitate sexual assault. A woman who has been plied with drugs is easier to control, to the extent that physical force is not necessary, as the drugs will render her submissive and incapacitated and, in some cases, unconscious. In this respect, the increased use of so-called "date rape" drugs in recent years has received much attention (WHO, 2003). In some cases of sexual assault, defense attorneys might tap into societal prejudices against the use of alcohol or drugs by women to cast further doubt and disdain on the victim. Forensic nurses should be aware of the facts and issues associated with DFSA.

Kintz, Villain, and Ludes (2004) explain that the use of a drug to modify a person's behavior for criminal gain is not a recent phenomenon; however, the recent increase in reports of drug-facilitated crimes such as sexual assault has caused alarm in the general public. Drugs involved in DFSA can include pharmaceuticals such as benzodiazepines (flunitrazepam or lorazepam), hypnotics (zopiclone or zolpidem), sedatives (neuroleptics, some histamine H, antagonists), or anesthetics (GHB or ketamine); drugs of abuse such as cannabis, ecstasy, or lysergide; or more often ethanol. Drugs used to facilitate sexual assaults can be difficult to detect (active products at low dosages, chemical instability), possess amnesic properties, and can be rapidly cleared from the body (short half-life). The researchers say that in these situations, blood or even urine can be of little help, and this is the reason why this laboratory developed an original approach based on hair testing. Hair was suggested as a valuable specimen in situations where, as a result of a delay in reporting the crime, natural processes have eliminated the drug from typical biologic specimens. Although there are many papers focused on the identification of drugs in hair following chronic drug use, those dealing with a single dose are very scarce, Kintz et al. state. They add that hair analysis might be a useful adjunct to conventional drug testing in sexual assault; it should not be considered an alternative to blood and urine analyses but as a complement. Testa, Vanzile-Tamsen, and Livingston (2004) examined the impact of perpetrator and victim substance use on the sexual assault outcomes of penetration and victim injury. More than 1,000 women ages 18 to 30 were recruited from households using random digit dialing. Women who reported sexual assault since age 14 (359) were interviewed face-to-face regarding their most recent sexual assault incident. As hypothesized, the researchers report that high levels of perpetrator intoxication decreased the likelihood of penetration occurring. When the victim was highly intoxicated however, penetration was more likely. Victim injury was more likely in assaults involving penetration. Higher levels of perpetrator intoxication in assaults involving a sober victim were also associated with greater odds of victim injury.

In another study, Testa, Livingston, and Collins (2000) examined the impact of alcohol consumption on women's risk perceptions and intended behaviors in a hypothetical situation in which the potential for establishing a relationship with an attractive man was coupled with the potential for sexual aggression. Fifty-nine single women, ages 21 to 29, were randomly assigned to one of three beverage conditions: (a) alcohol (dose sufficient to raise blood alcohol level to .08); (b) placebo, in which they were led to believe that they had consumed alcohol but had not; or (c) no alcohol, in which they neither expected nor received alcohol. Compared with women in the no-alcohol condition, women in the alcohol condition rated the male character in the vignette more positively, anticipated less risk and more benefit resulting from a series of behaviors likely to facilitate the relationship while increasing sexual vulnerability (e.g., engaging in consensual sexual activities), and anticipated greater involvement in those behaviors. The placebo appeared to exert similar but weaker effects.

McGregor et al. (2003) conducted a retrospective review of sexual assault cases seen in an ED from 1993 to 1999, as well as examined rates and characteristics of suspected DFSA. Overall, 12 percent of cases were identified as suspected DFSAs. The researchers reported that the rate of suspected DFSA in 1999 was more than double that in the preceding six years, and as compared to other sexual assaults, suspected DFSA cases had a longer time delay in presenting to the hospital, were less likely to involve the police, and had a lower occurrence of both genital and extragenital injury.

Ledray (2001) explains that at her facility's Sexual Assault Resource Service in Minneapolis, not every individual who might have been drugged and sexually assaulted is administered a drug screen; rather, examiners look for a presenting clinical symptom pattern consistent with DFSA and a history of drug ingestion within 72 hours. Ledray writes, "It has been our experience that what many of these men and women really want is a clear assessment of the likelihood of their having been drugged and raped. A detailed interview and examination for injuries or trauma can often be less costly and more helpful than a drug screen." Ledray adds that examiners look for the following:

- A history of being out drinking, having just one or two drinks that would not account for the extreme level of intoxication, suddenly feeling disoriented, or suddenly appearing drunk or drowsy with impaired motor skills, judgment, or amnesia.
- Reports that the victim looked or acted intoxicated within about 15 minutes after drinking a beverage that he or she accepted from someone, or drinking a beverage that was left unattended.
- The victim remembers very little of the incident after accepting the beverage until awakening.
- The victim awakens hours later and finds himself or herself undressed or partially dressed, possibly in bed with a person he or she might or might not know, or the victim awakes with vaginal or rectal soreness, indicating sexual contact might have occurred without consent.
- Possible nausea and vomiting on awakening.
- History of being at a party or a rave where drugs such as Ecstasy or "Special K" might have been available.

Ledray reports that the recommendation of the June 2000 national forum is that when the forensic examiner determines that an assault history is suspicious of DFSA, a blood and urine specimen should be collected as soon as possible, and that a chain of custody is maintained. It has been recommended that blood and urine specimens be collected for up to 72 hours after ingestion; Ledray writes:

> It is unlikely that positive results of a blood test will be obtained beyond 24 hours and that test results will be positive beyond four to six hours with substances such as GHB... urine is a better specimen than blood for detection of metabolites of most of the many drugs used to facilitate a sexual assault. With use of current technology, substances such as flunitrazepam (Rohypnol) are rarely detected beyond 24 hours after ingestion, and GHB is only detectable in the urine for six to 12 hours after ingestion, resulting in many false-negative results.

Ledray recommends to examiners that when dealing with victims who suspect that they have been drugged and raped, these victims should be instructed that if they must urinate before coming in for a forensic examination, they should save their first voided urine and bring it with them. Ledray says the examiner should take possession of the urine and begin the chain of custody from that point. "In an attempt to strengthen the chain of custody, the SANE should also document when the urine was collected by the victim, where it was kept between the time it was collected and when the SANE took possession of it, and who else had access to the urine," she writes:

> Both this urine and the first urine voided in the emergency department should be sent for toxicologic analysis. Although it is uncertain whether the results of this urine test will be admissible in the courtroom as evidence because of chain-of-custody issues that will likely be challenged, it should still be collected. It will be the most accurate specimen, and even if it has no forensic value, the information may be helpful to the survivor in putting the pieces together for recovery.

Forensic scientists say that head hair is also a source for identification of some drugs, however, false-negative results often are found, Ledray asserts. She adds:

> When hair is to be used for drug screening, it should not be collected as a part of the initial SANE evidentiary examination. The hairs do not need to be pulled, but they should be cut close to the skin. With special equipment and procedures... drugs may be detected in hair samples as early as 24 hours after ingestion; however, toxicologists prefer hair specimens collected 14 days later to allow for absorption of the drug into the hair with growth of the hair.

Ledray states that SANEs should identify those laboratories that can conduct a sensitive drug toxicology screen when a blood, urine, or hair specimen is obtained for DFSA testing, because numerous crime laboratories can identify benzodiazepines but not flunitrazepam, for example. "State crime laboratories will only do the specific test when it is requested by law enforcement agencies. It is not routine for them to do a broad drug screen, and they may have a limited capacity to do so," Ledray writes. In the same vein, SANEs should work closely with their local law enforcement agencies to ensure that all substances in question are accounted for during testing. Ledray explains:

> Current standards suggest that if a complete drug screen is going to be conducted, it is essential that the SANE inform the victim what drugs will be included in the screen. It is also important that the SANE explain that if the victim has recently used drugs recreationally or by prescription, they may be detected in the screen. If the victim has recently used drugs, it is important that the SANE know this ahead of time in order for it to have the least negative impact on the victim's credibility. In most communities, if voluntary use of illegal drugs is not disclosed until after positive results of a drug screen have been obtained, it can do irreparable damage to the victim's credibility. An otherwise good case may not go forward as a result. However, if the drug use is disclosed, it is more likely that the prosecutor will decide he or she can either exclude the information from court or deal with it in court.

Ledray adds that victims should be informed as to whether or not they might be charged criminally if they admit to illegal drug use, as well as how police and prosecutors might view a positive screen for an illegal substance and the potential impact on the investigation and charging of their case.

Drug testing is not an inexpensive proposition, and Ledray states that a comprehensive drug-toxicity screen could cost more than the total amount available to most SANE programs as reimbursement for the complete sexual assault evidentiary examination. She states:

> It is unreasonable to expect the SANE program or the medical facility to assume this cost without adequate reimbursement. The solution of many other SANE programs across the United States has been to turn over the biological specimens collected to the appropriate law enforcement department with the rape kit. The law enforcement department will then be responsible to pay for a drug screen if one is requested by their department. If a report is not made but the victim or his or her family wants a drug screen, the victim should be informed that he or she or his or her insurer will be responsible for paying for a drug screen if one is sent to a private laboratory. The victim should also be informed what the cost will be. When a drug screen is completed for other than medical purposes, many insurers will not assume the cost.

Suzanne R. White, MD, FACEP, FACMT, medical director of the Children's Hospital of Michigan Regional Poison Control Center, writes, "While it is estimated that 1 in 4 women in the United States will be raped in their lifetimes (with 75 percent of those rapes acquaintance or date rapes), this form of assault is likely underreported secondary to complex feelings of guilt or the common belief that the woman was responsible for the assault. While increasingly reported, the true incidence of chemically-mediated date rape is therefore unknown." Alcohol has long been used to facilitate nonconsensual sex and remains the most popular "drug" of choice. In recent years, however, the use of "date rape" drugs has been implicated in an increasing number of cases of sexual violence. The most commonly used drugs are flunitrazepam (Rohypnol) and other benzodiazepines, GHB, ketamine, cocaine, methamphetamine, and marijuana. Victims might be unaware that they have been drugged and that they have been sexually violated. A double standard often exists between men and women in terms of drinking alcohol or using drugs. If a woman has been drinking or using drugs she is often blamed for her victimization. Conversely, the perpetrator's behavior is excused or justified because he was "under the influence" and thus not expected to control his behavior.

Health care providers must be aware of the signs that are suggestive of drug-facilitated sexual violence. If patients present with any of the following symptoms, the use of drugs or alcohol should be suspected:

- Impaired conscious state, memory loss, disorientation, or confusion
- Impairment of speech or coordination
- Unexplained signs of trauma, particularly genital trauma
- Apparent intoxication not corresponding to stated alcohol consumption
- Unexplained loss or rearrangement of clothing
- Talking about having an "out-of-body experience"

- If drugs or alcohol are suspected, it is important to be aware of the following:
  - Any alteration in conscious state requires immediate access to full resuscitation facilities, such as those available in EDs.
  - The sooner specimens are taken (e.g., blood, urine) the greater the likelihood of successfully detecting any substances not knowingly taken.

Forty-six percent of women report that they have experienced attempted or completed forced sex by an intimate partner or ex-partner at some time in their lives. Rape and domestic violence account for an estimated 5 percent to more than 15 percent of healthy years of life lost to women of reproductive age (WHO, 2003).

The following is a closer look at common date rape drugs.

Flunitrazepam (Rohypnol) is a benzodiazepine developed by Hoffmann-La Roche in 1960 to be used for the short-term treatment of insomnia. It is 10 times more potent than diazepam, possessing both hypnotic and amnestic properties that predominate over its other sedative, anxiolytic, muscle-relaxing, and anticonvulsant effects. Sexual activities involving the use of Rohypnol have been reported by both male and females to be consensual in most instances. Authorities in numerous states and on college campuses report that the drug is increasingly being given to females without their consent. Flunitrazepam is typically combined with alcohol or other drugs as an "extender" while the user gets a high. It is odorless, colorless, and tasteless. Recent changes by the manufacturer include a reformulation of the tablet to include a dye pellet that both renders a blue discoloration to and leaves a particulate residue in dissolved liquids. Abrupt onset of action is noted within 15 to 30 minutes of ingestion. Peak levels occur within one to two hours. Active metabolites are present and the total duration of action is about eight hours. Most commonly, early effects include drowsiness, dizziness, incoordination, and impaired judgment and reaction time. Disinhibition or aggression have been associated with behavioral toxicity leading to dangerous behavior on the part of the user. Memory loss is characteristic, with blackouts lasting for eight to 24 hours. Other less common effects include gastrointestinal upset, hiccoughs, blurred vision, dry mouth, and a "hangover" sensation. Life-threatening symptoms such as coma, respiratory depression, or apnea are most commonly seen following combination with other sedatives, but death from flunitrazepam alone is also described. Early specimens are most useful as peak blood levels occur within one to two hours of ingestion. Detection of a 1-mg dose in the blood for up to 12 hours and urine for 60 to 72 hours (as the metabolite 7-aminoflunitrazepam) is possible.

Ketamine is an anesthetic agent that is diverted from legitimate human or veterinary use. It is commonly abused in the rave party setting and has been implicated in cases of date rape. It is available as a clear liquid that is usually dried and then sold in small bags, paper folds, foils, vials, or capsules. The powder is then snorted, put into drinks, injected, or smoked. The liquid form has also been abused as a nasal spray. Ketamine is a short-acting dissociative anesthetic that is structurally similar to phencyclidine (PCP). Its sites of action within the central nervous system include the N-methyl-D-asparate (NMDA) receptor complex and muscarinic receptors. With subanesthetic doses of either parenteral or oral ketamine (70 mg on average), the onset of action is one to 10 minutes, with peak levels occurring within 30 minutes. There are active metabolites, norketamine and dehydronorketamine, both psychoactive. The half-life is two to three hours. Neurologic effects predominate and include nystagmus, catalepsy, hypertonicity, nonpurposeful movements, dystonic reactions, and bizarre vocalizations. Early cardiovascular effects include a transient increase in blood pressure and heart rate. Dose-dependent respiratory depression is seen, along with increased oral secretions. Whereas at anesthetic doses, intact corneal, light, pharyngeal, and laryngeal reflexes are seen, airway crises can occur when higher doses are taken.

GHB was initially developed as an anesthetic agent, but enthusiasm for its medical application waned due to lack of any significant analgesic effect and an association with seizure-like clonic activity on emergence. In the United States, GHB entered the health food market in 1990 and was promoted illicitly as a growth hormone releaser, diet aid, sleep aid, and sexual enhancer. Fifty-nine reports of serious toxicity and death from GHB use were made to poison centers in the western and southeast United States within a few months of initial marketing. This prompted the Food and Drug Administration (FDA) and the U.S. Department of Justice to take action against its importation, manufacture, distribution, and promotion. To date, more than 5,700 overdoses in 45 states and 65 deaths have been documented by the U.S. Drug Enforcement Agency (DEA). Date rape facilitated by GHB has been reported since 1994, and to date, more than 50 cases have been documented. GHB is metabolized via the Kreb's cycle to carbon dioxide, which is then expired. The half-life is a short 27 minutes, and the duration of action is two to five hours. Predicting dose response is difficult based on the variability of drug found in one "scoop" (2.8–7.9 gm) of powder or one capful of liquid. Admixture with other substances such as ethanol, known to have a synergistic effect, or use of impure home preparations also contribute to the variable responses seen following a given dose. Nonetheless, the usual illicit dose is 1 to 2.5 gm or one to two capfuls (1 gm/5 ccs). This corresponds to an average dose of 35 mg/kg. Most patients present with a triad of gastrointestinal, respiratory, and neurologic symptoms.

Early symptoms include somnolence within 15 minutes of an oral dose, dizziness, lightheadedness, and a "high" feeling. Higher doses might be associated with nausea, vomiting, impaired judgment, hallucinations, confusion, ataxia, loss of peripheral vision, and abrupt unconsciousness, generally with doses greater than 60 mg/kg. Intermittent respiratory depression and apnea vacillate with periods of combativeness and aggression. Interestingly, increased aggression in response to direct gaze has been observed. Random clonic movements of the face and extremities might occur. Other findings may include hypothermia, bradycardia, and excessive salivation, relating to the corrosive effects of some home preparations.

Regarding management of the date rape victim, White says this type of patient requires "a meticulous physical examination." She advises the health care provider to gain an accurate time frame of ingestion through interviewing friends or bystanders, and to make early contact with law enforcement. She also suggests the retrieval of containers could be very useful for later analysis. She adds that consent should be obtained for evidence collection, examination, and involvement of authorities:

> Given the rapid clearance of these drugs, the immediate procurement of samples prior to the use of confounding medications for sedation is important. Above all, chain-of-custody must be maintained in the handling of specimens. As with the management of all sexual assault victims, counseling by an experienced professional prior to discharge is advised. Patients who are still lethargic at six hours post-ingestion should be admitted.

White adds that the prosecution of offenders might be difficult because there could be a delay in victim presentation. Furthermore, failure to detect the intoxicant does not prove that it was not used, given the rapid clearance of these agents. Health care providers should be cognizant of the narrow window of opportunity for successfully detecting the date rape drugs.

Despite the technology available, Ledray (2001) cautions that "positive results of a blood, urine, or hair specimen are rarely obtained." She says that law enforcement and prosecutors must rely on the physical evidence as well as the patient history collected by the forensic examiner. Ledray writes, "Because the SANE is conducting a medical examination and can testify in court about what the victim reported during the examination as an exception to the hearsay rule, this testimony can be important corroborating evidence and very useful in court." To this end, the forensic examiner must carefully and precisely document what the victim says, using the victim's own words whnever possible. "The victim's ability to recall past events should also be documented in detail, because the credibility of the victim will often be challenged when the case goes to trial," Ledray adds. "It is helpful for the SANE to note if the victim's speech is clear, if his or her gait is steady, and if there are any other viable physical signs of intoxication or impairment at the time of the examination."

In many DFSA cases, it is unclear whether a sexual assault took place, and if the victim cannot give an account of the assault, the forensic examiner must conduct a thorough head-to-toe visual examination, looking for areas of redness, swelling, abrasions, bruising, scratches, or cuts, as well as palpate for areas of soreness. The victim's oral, rectal, and vaginal orifices should be examined for trauma, and specimens should be collected to help determine if recent sexual contact occurred. "It's important to note that whereas positive specimens will prove that recent sexual contact did occur, negative results without trauma and without sperm or acid phosphatase do not prove that recent sexual contact did not occur," Ledray writes.

Ledray says that the role of the SANE with suspected DFSA includes much more than biologic evidence collection. "The SANE must also ensure that ED staff and other sexual assault resource team members are familiar with the clinical symptom picture that may indicate a possible DFSA so that proper referrals are made for evidence collection and testing," she says:

> The SANE must be aware of the unique victim impact issues for DFSA victims and work closely with the rape crisis advocate to ensure that the victim's counseling needs are met. Self-blame is often an even more pressing issue because the victim cannot assist with the investigation because of his or her missing memory, perhaps even because of a drug he or she took willingly, without knowing that he or she was in danger of being assaulted. The victim's fear may be more pronounced because the victim does not know who assaulted him or her or even if he or she was assaulted. Furthermore, the assault probably occurred in a place or with people whom he or she considered safe. The victim's anger at his or her own inability to remember or his or her inability to help the prosecution of the case can be devastating. Unfortunately, memory is usually not recovered in these cases.

6.12 A NATIONAL PROTOCOL FOR HANDLING SEXUAL ASSAULT CASES

In September 2004, the U.S. Department of Justice Office on Violence Against Women published *A National Protocol for Sexual Assault Medical Forensic Examinations Adults/Adolescents*, researched and written by consultant Kristin Littel. The 141-page document is an attempt to address a number of issues affecting the care of victims of violence, and to create a framework in which forensic nurses and all health care providers can work to provide exemplary service. The protocol encompasses what it calls "overarching issues" as well as operational issues, and makes practical recommendations based on the pooling of expert knowledge and experience. It is by no means a final work, but should be seen as a work in progress, as forensic nurses undoubtedly will continue to challenge its contents, particularly as current thought in health care and medicine evolves, and as new research is produced to substantiate or negate accepted protocol. The following is a summary of the protocol's overarching and operational issues, with references to sections that provide readers with additional information.

6.12.1 Overarching Issues

6.12.1.1 Coordinated Approach

A coordinated, multidisciplinary approach to conducting the exam provides victims with access to comprehensive immediate care, helps minimize trauma they might experience, and encourages their use of community resources. Such a response can also enhance public safety by facilitating investigation and prosecution, which increases the likelihood that offenders will be held accountable for their actions. Raising public awareness about the existence and benefits of a coordinated response to sexual assault could lead more victims to disclose the assault and seek help.

The following are recommendations for jurisdictions to facilitate a coordinated approach to the exam process:

- Understand the dual purposes of the exam process to address patients' needs and justice system needs. Addressing patients' needs might include evaluating and treating injuries; conducting prompt exams; providing support, crisis intervention, and advocacy; providing prophylaxis against STIs and referrals; assessing reproductive health issues; and providing follow-up contact and care. Addressing justice system needs might include obtaining a history of the assault; documenting exam findings; properly collecting, handling, and preserving evidence; and (postexam) interpreting and analyzing findings, presenting findings, and providing factual and expert opinions.
- Identify key responders and their roles.
- Develop quality assurance measures to ensure effective immediate response.

6.12.1.2 Victim-Centered Care

Victim-centered care is paramount to the success of the exam process. Response to victims should be timely, appropriate, sensitive, and respectful. Sexual assault patients are also referred to as victims, depending on which responders are primarily being discussed. The term *patients* is generally used by health care professionals. The term *victim* is not used in a strictly criminal justice context. The use of victim simply acknowledges that persons who disclose that they have been sexually assaulted should have access to certain services.

Recommendations for Health Care Providers and Other Responders to Facilitate Victim-centered Care

- Give sexual assault patients priority as emergency cases and respond in a timely manner. Provide them with as much privacy as possible, while ensuring that they are supported.
- Recognize that the medical forensic exam is an interactive process that must be adapted to the needs and circumstances of each patient.
- Be aware of issues commonly faced by victims from specific populations. For example, certain characteristics (e.g., culture, religion, language skills or mode of communication, disabilities, gender, and age) can influence a victim's behavior in the aftermath of an assault, including the exam process.
- Understand the importance of victim services within the exam process. Victim service providers and advocates typically offer victims support, crisis intervention, information and referrals, and advocacy to ensure that victims' interests are represented, their wishes respected, and their rights upheld. Providers and advocates also might offer support for family members and friends who are present. In addition, they can promote sensitive, appropriate, and coordinated interventions.
- Involve victim service providers and advocates in the exam process as soon after a victim discloses an assault as possible. Victims have the right to accept or decline victim services.
- Accommodate patients' requests to have relatives, friends, or other support persons (e.g., a religious or spiritual counselor) present during the exam, unless the presence of that person could be considered harmful.
- Accommodate victims' request for responders of a specific gender as much as possible.
- Prior to starting the exam and before each procedure, describe what is entailed and its purpose to patients. Be sure that communication and language needs are met and information is conveyed in a manner that patients will understand. After providing this information, seek patients' permission to proceed and respect their right to decline any part of the exam. However, follow exam facility and jurisdictional policy regarding minors and adults who are incompetent to give consent.
- Assess and respect patients' priorities.

- Integrate exam procedures where possible (e.g., blood samples needed for medical and evidentiary purposes should be drawn at the same time).
- Address patients' safety concerns during the exam. Sexual assault patients have legitimate reasons to fear further assaults from their attackers. Local law enforcement might be able to assist facilities in addressing patients' safety needs.
- Provide information that is easy for patients to understand and that can be reviewed at their convenience.
- After the exam is finished, provide patients with the opportunity to wash, change clothes (providing clean replacement clothing if necessary), get food or drinks, and make needed phone calls.

6.12.1.3 Informed Consent

Patients should understand the full nature of their consent to each exam procedure. When presented with relevant information, they are in a position to make an informed decision about whether to accept or decline a procedure. However, they should be aware of the impact of declining a particular procedure, as it could negatively affect the quality of care, the usefulness of evidence collection, and, ultimately, any criminal investigation or prosecution. They should understand that declining a particular procedure might also be used to discredit them in court. If a procedure is declined, reasons why should be documented if the patient provides such information.

Recommendations for Health Care Providers and Other Responders to Request Patients' Consent During the Exam Process

- Seek informed consent as appropriate throughout the exam process for medical evaluation and treatment, the forensic exam, and evidence collection. Coordinate efforts to obtain consent among responders.
- Be aware of statutes and policies governing consent in cases of minor patients, vulnerable adult patients, and patients who are unconscious, intoxicated, or under the influence of drugs. In all cases, however, the exam should never be done against the will of the patient.

6.12.1.4 Confidentiality

Involved responders must be aware of the scope and limitations of confidentiality related to information gathered during the exam process. Confidentiality is intricately linked to the scope of patients' consent. Members of a SART or other collaborating responders should inform victims of the scope of confidentiality with each responder and be cautious not to exceed the limits of victim consent to share information in each case.

Recommendations That Jurisdictions Might Take to Maintain Confidentiality of Patients

- Make sure that jurisdictional policies address confidentiality related to the medical forensic exam (e.g., of forensic documentation, photographs, and colposcopic video images).
- Increase responders' and patients' understanding of confidentiality issues (e.g., scope of confidentiality advocates can provide; scope of confidentiality of information shared with examiners, law enforcement, prosecutors, and other responders with whom patient has contact; and what happens to information once it enters the criminal justice system).
- Consider the impact of federal privacy laws regarding health information on victims of sexual assault.
- Strive to resolve intrajurisdictional conflicts.

6.12.1.5 Reporting to Law Enforcement

Reporting provides the criminal justice system with the opportunity to offer immediate protection to victims, collect evidence from all crime scenes, investigate cases, prosecute if there is sufficient evidence, and hold offenders accountable for crimes committed. Given the danger that sex offenders pose to the community, reporting can serve as a first step in efforts to stop them from reoffending. Equally important, reporting gives the justice system the chance to help victims address their needs, identify patterns of sexual violence in the jurisdiction, and educate the public about such patterns. It is recommended that service providers encourage victims to report due in part to the recognition that delayed reporting is detrimental to the prosecution and to holding offenders accountable. Victims need to know that even if they are not ready to report at the time of the exam, the best way to preserve their option to report later is to have the exam performed. Reporting requirements in sexual assault cases vary from one jurisdiction to another. Every effort should be made to facilitate treatment and evidence collection (if the patient agrees), regardless of whether the decision to report has been made at the time of the exam. Victims who are undecided about reporting who receive respectful and appropriate care and advocacy at the time of their exam are more likely to assist law enforcement and prosecution.

Recommendations for Jurisdictions and Responders to Facilitate Victim-centered Reporting Practices

- Where permitted by law, patients, not health care workers, should make the decision to report a sexual assault to law enforcement. Patients

should be provided with information about possible benefits and consequences of reporting so that they can make an informed decision.
- It is not recommended to require reporting as a condition of performing or paying for the exam. Even if patients are undecided about reporting, they should be encouraged to provide a medical forensic history, undergo the forensic exam, and have evidence collected and stored.
- Jurisdictions might want to consider alternatives to standard reporting procedures. For example, an anonymous or blind reporting system might be useful in cases in which victims do not want to report immediately or are undecided about reporting.
- Jurisdictions should consider a variety of approaches that promote a victim-centered reporting process.

6.12.1.6 Payment for the Examination Under the VAWA

Under the Violence Against Women Act (VAWA), a state, territory, or the District of Columbia is entitled to funds under the STOP Violence Against Women Formula Grant Program only if it, or another governmental entity, incurs the full out-of-pocket cost of medical forensic exams for victims of sexual assault. The VAWA provisions indicate the exam should minimally include "an examination of physical trauma; determination of penetration/force; a victim interview; and collection and evaluation of evidence." Full out-of-pocket costs means any expense that can be charged to a victim in connection with the exam for the purpose of gathering evidence of a sexual assault.

Recommendations for Jurisdictions to Facilitate Payment for the Sexual Assault Medical Forensic Exam

- Understand the scope of the VAWA provisions related to exam payment.
- Ensure that victims are notified of exam facility and jurisdictional policies regarding payment for medical care and the medical forensic exam, as well as if and how reporting decisions will impact payment. Relevant government entities are strongly encouraged to pay for medical forensic exams regardless of whether victims pursue prosecution.

6.12.2 Operational Issues

6.12.2.1 Sexual Assault Forensic Examiners

These are the health care professionals who conduct the examination. It is critical that all examiners, regardless of their discipline, are committed to providing compassionate and quality care for patients disclosing sexual assault, collecting evidence competently, and testifying in court as needed.

Recommendations for Jurisdictions to Build the Capacity of Examiners Performing These Exams

- Encourage the development of specific examiner knowledge, skills, and attitudes.
- Encourage advanced education and supervised clinical practice of examiners, as well as certification for nurses who are examiners.

6.12.2.2 Facilities

Health care facilities have an obligation to provide services to sexual assault patients. Designated exam facilities or sites served by specially educated and clinically prepared examiners increase the likelihood of a state-of-the-art exam, enhance coordination, encourage quality control, and increase quality of care for patients.

Recommendations for Jurisdictions to Build Capacity of Health Care Facilities to Respond to Sexual Assault Cases

- Recognize the obligation of health care facilities to serve sexual assault patients.
- Ensure that exams are conducted at sites served by specially educated and clinically prepared examiners. A designated facility can employ or have ready access to examiners to conduct the exam. Some jurisdictions have examiner programs that serve one or multiple exam sites within a specific area.
- Explore what is best for the community regarding locations for exam sites. It is critical to consider how accessible facilities are to patients disclosing sexual assault, as well as the facility's capacity to properly conduct these exams and treat related injuries.
- Recognize that exam facilities and examiners could benefit from networking with examiners in other facilities or areas for support with peer review of medical forensic reports, quality assurance, and information sharing (e.g., on training opportunities, practices, and referrals for patients).
- Consider developing basic jurisdictional requirements for exam sites. The analysis of evidence gathered during the examination, along with examiner documentation of findings, could help in determining whether penetration occurred or force was used. However, examiners are not responsible for drawing conclusions

about how injuries were caused or whether the assault occurred or not (although they can note consistency between patients' statements and injuries they identify).
- Promote public awareness about where exams are conducted. Use specially educated and clinically prepared forensic examiners to conduct the exam, ensuring dissemination of relevant information to appropriate agencies and community members. Encourage first responders to work together to assist victims in using these sites.
- If a transfer from one health care facility to a designated site is necessary, use an established protocol that minimizes time delays and loss of evidence while addressing a patient's needs. However, avoid transferring these patients whenever possible.

6.12.2.3 Equipment and Supplies

Certain equipment and supplies are essential to the exam process (although they might not be used in every case). These include a copy of the most current exam protocol used by the jurisdiction, standard exam room equipment and supplies, comfort supplies for patients, sexual assault evidence collection kits, an evidence drying device or method, a camera, testing and treatment supplies, an alternate light source, an anoscope, and written materials for patients. A microscope and toluidine blue dye might be required, depending on jurisdictional policy. A colposcope or other magnifying instrument is strongly suggested. Some jurisdictions are also beginning to use advanced technology (telemedicine), which allows examiners to conduct offsite consultation with medical experts using computers, software programs, and the Internet.

Recommendations for Jurisdictions and Responders to Ensure that Proper Equipment and Supplies Are Available for Examinations

- Consider what equipment and supplies are essential.
- Address cost barriers to obtaining equipment and supplies.

6.12.2.4 Sexual Assault Evidence Collection Kit

Most jurisdictions have developed their own sexual assault evidence collection kits or purchased premade kits through commercial vendors. Kits often vary from one jurisdiction to another. Despite variations, however, it is critical that every kit meets or exceeds minimum guidelines for contents: broadly including a kit container, instruction sheet or checklist, forms, and materials for collecting and preserving all evidence required by the applicable crime laboratory. Evidence that might be collected includes but is not limited to clothing, foreign materials on the body, hair (including head and pubic hair samples and combings), oral and ano-genital swabs and smears, body swabs, and a blood or saliva sample for DNA analysis and comparison. The instruction sheet or checklist should guide examiners on maintaining the chain of custody for evidence collected.

Recommendations for Jurisdictions and Responders When Developing or Customizing Kits

- Use standardized kits (across a local jurisdiction, region, state, territory, or tribal land) that meet or exceed minimum guidelines for contents, as described previously.
- Make kits readily available at any facility that conducts sexual assault medical forensic exams.
- Periodically review the kit's efficiency and usefulness and make changes as needed.

6.12.2.5 Timing Considerations for Collecting Evidence

Although many jurisdictions currently use 72 hours after the assault as the standard cutoff time for collecting evidence, evidence collection beyond that point is conceivable. Because of this, some jurisdictions have extended the standard cutoff time (e.g., to five days or one week). Advancing DNA technologies continue to extend time limits because of the stability of DNA and sensitivity of testing. These technologies are even enabling forensic scientists to analyze evidence that was previously unusable when it was collected years ago. Thus, it is critical that in every case in which patients are willing, examiners obtain the medical forensic history, examine patients, and document findings. Not only can the information gained from the history and exam help health care providers address patients' medical needs, but it can guide examiners in determining whether there is evidence to collect and, if so, what to collect.

Recommendations for Health Care Providers and Other Responders to Maximize Evidence Collection

- Whether or not evidence is collected, examiners should obtain the medical forensic history as appropriate, examine patients, and document findings (with patients' consent). Patients' demeanor and statements related to the assault should also be documented.
- Promptly examine patients to minimize loss of evidence and to identify medical needs and concerns.
- Decide whether to collect evidence and what to collect on a case-by-case basis, remembering

that outside time limits for obtaining evidence vary.

- In any case, where the need for evidence collection is in question, encourage dialogue about the potential benefits or limitations of collection. Avoid basing decisions about whether to collect evidence on a patient's characteristics or circumstances (e.g., the patient has used illegal drugs).
- Responders should seek education and resources that aid them in making well-informed decisions about evidence collection.

6.12.2.6 Evidence Integrity

Properly collecting, preserving, and maintaining the chain of custody of evidence is critical to its subsequent use in criminal justice proceedings.

Recommendations for Health Care Providers and Other Responders to Maintain Evidence Integrity

- Follow jurisdictional policies for drying, packaging, labeling, and sealing the evidence.
- Follow jurisdictional policies for documenting exam findings, the medical forensic history, and the patient's demeanor and statements, and packaging, labeling, and sealing such documentation.
- Follow jurisdictional policies for consistent evidence management and distribution. A duly authorized agent should transfer evidence from the exam site to the appropriate crime lab or other designated storage site (e.g., a law enforcement property facility).
- Make sure storage procedures maximize evidence preservation. Ensure that storage areas are kept secure and at the proper temperature for the evidence. Also, make sure jurisdictional policies are in place to address the secure storage of evidence in cases in which patients are undecided about reporting.
- Maintain the chain of custody of evidence. All those involved in handling, documenting, transferring, and storing evidence should be educated regarding the specifics of their roles in properly preserving evidence and maintaining the chain of custody.

6.12.2.7 The Examination Process

Some sexual assault patients might initially present at a designated exam facility, but most who receive immediate medical care initially contact a law enforcement or advocacy agency for help. If 911 is called, law enforcement or emergency medical services might be the first to provide assistance to victims. Communities need to have procedures in place to promptly respond to disclosures and reports of sexual assault in a standardized and victim-centered manner.

Recommendations for Jurisdictions and Responders to Facilitate Initial Contact with Victims

- Build consensus among involved agencies regarding procedures for a coordinated initial response when a recent sexual assault is disclosed or reported, and educate responders on procedures. Encourage victims to interact with advocates as soon after disclosure as possible.
- Recognize essential elements of initial response. In particular, encourage victims to seek medical care and have evidence collected. In the case of life-threatening or serious injuries, obtain emergency medical assistance according to jurisdictional policy. Any life-threatening wounds should be treated and victims' immediate safety needs should be addressed before evidence is collected.
- If victims decide to seek medical care, have evidence collected, or both, follow jurisdictional policies for preserving evidence, collecting a urine sample if needed, and transporting victims to the exam site.

6.12.2.8 Triage and Intake

Once patients arrive at the exam site, health care personnel must evaluate, stabilize, and treat them for life-threatening and serious injuries according to facility policy. Standardized procedures for response in these cases should be followed, while respecting patients and maximizing evidence preservation.

Recommendations for Health Care Providers to Facilitate Triage and Intake that Addresses Patients' Needs

- Consider sexual assault patients a priority. Use private locations in the exam facility for the primary patient consultation and initial law enforcement interviews, offer a waiting area for family members and friends, and provide child care if possible.
- Respond to acute injury, trauma care, and safety needs of patients before collecting evidence. Patients should not wash, change clothes, urinate, defecate, smoke, drink, or eat until initially evaluated by examiners, unless necessary for treating acute medical needs.
- Alert examiners to the need for their services at the exam site.

- Contact victim advocates so they can offer services to the patient, if not already done.
- Assess and respond to safety concerns, such as threats to the patient or staff, on arrival of patients at the exam site.
- Assess patients' needs for immediate medical or mental health intervention. Seek informed consent from patients before providing treatment, according to facility policy.

6.12.2.9 Documentation by Health Care Personnel

Examiners document exam findings, the medical forensic history, and evidence collected in the medical forensic report. Examiners and other involved clinicians separately document medical care in the patient's medical record.

Recommendations for Health Care Providers to Complete Needed Documentation

- Ensure completion of all appropriate documentation. The forensic details of the exam are documented in the medical forensic report, according to jurisdictional policy. The only medical issues documented in this report are acute findings that potentially relate to the assault or preexisting medical factors that could influence interpretation of findings. Separate medical documentation by examiners and other involved clinicians follows a standard approach—address acute complaints, gather pertinent historical data, describe findings, and document treatment and follow-up care.
- Ensure the accuracy and objectivity of medical forensic reports by seeking education on proper report writing.

6.12.2.10 The Medical Forensic History

Examiners ask the patient questions to obtain this history. This information guides them in examining the patient and collecting evidence.

Recommendations for Health Care Providers to Facilitate Gathering Information from Patients

- Examiners should coordinate with other responders, primarily law enforcement representatives, to facilitate information gathering that is respectful to patients and minimizes repetition of questions.
- Keep in mind that advocates can support and advocate for patients when the medical forensic history is taken (if desired by patients), but they cannot actively participate in the process. Patients should be informed that the presence of family members, friends, and others offering personal support during this time might influence or be perceived as influencing their statements. If patients choose to have others present despite this knowledge, these individuals should not actively participate in the process.
- Consider and address patients' needs prior to information gathering, including identifying the level of their communication skill and modalities and then tailoring information gathering accordingly.
- Obtain the medical forensic history in a private, quiet setting.
- Gather information for the history according to jurisdictional policy. Include the date and time of the assault, pertinent patient medical history (e.g., menstruation history), recent consensual sexual activity of the patient, the patient's activities since the assault (e.g., took a shower), the patient's assault-related history (e.g., loss of consciousness), suspect information if known (e.g., number and gender of assailants), nature of the physical assault, and description of the sexual assault.

6.12.2.11 Photography

Photographic evidence of injury on the patient's body can supplement the medical forensic history and document physical findings.

Recommendations for Health Care Providers and Other Responders to Photograph Evidence

- Come to a consensus about the extent of forensic photography necessary. Some jurisdictions routinely take photographs of both detected injuries on patients and normal (apparently uninjured) anatomy, whereas others limit photography to detected injuries.
- Consider who will take photographs and what equipment will be used. Photographers should be familiar with equipment operation and educated in forensic photography and in ways to maintain the patient's privacy and dignity while taking photographs. Consult with jurisdictional criminal justice agencies and examiners regarding the type of equipment that should be used.
- Obtain informed consent from patients before taking photographs. Patients should understand the purpose of the photographs, what will be photographed and any related procedures, the potential uses of photographs during investigation and prosecution, and the possible need for follow-up photographs.

- Consider the patient's comfort and need for modesty.
- Identify who will be present when photographs are taken.
- Take initial and follow-up photographs as appropriate, according to jurisdictional policy.

6.12.2.12 Exam and Evidence Collection Procedures

Examiners examine patients and collect evidence according to jurisdictional policy. Findings from the exam and collected evidence often help reconstruct the events in question in a scientific and objective manner.

Recommendations for Health Care Providers to Conduct the Exam and Facilitate Evidence Collection

- Strive to collect as much evidence from patients as possible, considering the scope of informed consent, the medical forensic history, the examination, and evidence collection kit instructions.
- Be aware of evidence that might be pertinent to the issue of whether the patient consented to sexual contact with the suspect. Understand how biological evidence is tested.
- Prevent exposure (of both patients and staff) to infectious materials and contamination of evidence.
- Understand the implication of the presence or lack of semen (in cases involving male suspects).
- Seek informed consent from patients for each portion of the exam and evidence collection.
- Modify the exam and evidence collection to address the specific needs and concerns of patients.
- Conduct the general physical and ano-genital examination, guided by the scope of informed consent and the medical forensic history. Document findings on body diagram forms. With the patient's consent, use an alternate light source, colposcope, and anoscope, as appropriate and if available, to increase the likelihood of detecting evidence.
- Collect evidence to submit to the crime lab for analysis, according to jurisdictional policy.
- Collect blood and urine for toxicology screening, if applicable.
- Keep medical specimens separate from forensic specimens collected during the exam.

6.12.2.13 Drug-Facilitated Sexual Assault

Responders must consider the possibility that drugs might have been used to facilitate an assault. They must know how to screen for suspected drug-facilitated sexual assault, obtain informed consent of patients for testing, and collect toxicology samples when needed.

Recommendations for Jurisdictions and Responders to Facilitate Response in Suspected Drug-facilitated Sexual Assault

- Educate examiners, 911 dispatchers, law enforcement representatives, prosecutors, judges, and advocates on related issues. Develop jurisdictional policies to clarify first responders' roles in cases involving suspected drug-facilitated assault.
- Be clear about the circumstances in which toxicology testing might be indicated (for optimal care or when there is a suspicion of drug-facilitated sexual assault). Routine toxicology testing in all sexual assault cases is not recommended.
- Informed consent of patients should be sought to collect toxicology samples. Patients should be aware of the purposes and scope of testing that will be done, potential benefits and consequences of testing, any follow-up treatment necessary, how they can obtain results, who will pay for the testing, and if they have any opportunity to revoke consent to testing.
- With patients' permission, immediately collect a urine specimen if it is suspected that ingestion of drugs used to facilitate sexual assault occurred within 96 hours prior to the exam. The first available urine should be collected; law enforcement and emergency medical services should be trained and prepared to collect a urine sample if patients must urinate prior to arrival at the health care facility for the exam. Advocates and other professionals who might have contact with patients prior to their arrival at the exam site should also be educated to provide those who suspect drug-facilitated assault with information on how to collect a sample if the patient cannot wait to urinate until getting to the site.
- Collect a blood sample if it is suspected that the ingestion of drugs used to facilitate sexual assault occurred within 24 hours of the exam. If a blood alcohol determination is needed, collect blood within 24 hours of ingestion of alcohol, according to jurisdictional policy.
- Jurisdictional policies should be in place and followed for packaging, storing, and transferring samples.

6.12.2.14 STI Evaluation and Care

Because contracting an STI from an assailant is of significant concern to patients, it should be addressed during the exam.

Recommendations for Health Care Providers to Facilitate STI Evaluation and Care

- Offer patients information about the risks of STIs (including HIV), the symptoms and what to do if symptoms occur, testing and treatment options, follow-up care, and referrals. Referrals should include free and low-cost testing, counseling, and treatment available in various sections of the community. For HIV testing, confidential and anonymous testing is recommended.
- Consider testing patients for STIs during the initial exam on a case-by-case basis. If testing is done, follow the guidelines of the CDC.
- Encourage patients to accept prophylaxis against STIs during the initial exam. (Note, however, that treatment might not be appropriate for some individuals—for example, if they have a condition that could be adversely affected by taking prophylaxis.) The CDC suggests a regimen to protect against chlamydia, gonorrhea, trichomonas, and bacterial vaginosis, as well as the hepatitis B virus. If accepted, provide care that meets or exceeds CDC guidelines. If declined, it is medically prudent to obtain cultures and arrange for a follow-up exam and testing. Seek informed consent from patients for treatment, according to facility policy.
- Encourage and facilitate follow-up STI examinations, testing, immunizations, and treatment as directed.
- Offer postexposure prophylaxis for HIV to patients at high risk for exposure, particularly when it is known that suspects have HIV/AIDS. Meet or exceed CDC recommendations. Discuss risks and benefits of the prophylaxis with patients prior to their decisions to accept or decline treatment. Careful monitoring and follow-up by a health care provider or agency experienced in HIV issues is required.

6.12.2.15 Pregnancy Risk Evaluation and Care

Female patients might fear becoming pregnant as a result of an assault. Health care providers must address this issue according to facility and jurisdictional policy.

Recommendations for Health Care Providers to Facilitate Pregnancy Evaluation and Care

- Discuss the probability of pregnancy with patients.
- Administer a baseline pregnancy test for all patients with reproductive capability.
- Discuss treatment options with patients, including reproductive health services.

6.12.2.16 Discharge and Follow-Up

Health care personnel have specific tasks to accomplish before discharging patients, as do advocates and law enforcement representatives (if involved). Responders should coordinate discharge and follow-up activities as much as possible to reduce repetition and avoid overwhelming patients.

Recommendations to Facilitate Discharge and Follow-up

- It is important to ensure that patients are fully informed about postexam care. Information might include referrals to other professionals to make sure that patients' medical and mental health needs related to the assault have been addressed, discharge instructions, follow-up appointments with the examiner or other health care providers, and contact procedures for medical follow-up. In addition to medical follow-up, follow-up might be indicated to document developing or healing injuries and complete resolution of healing.
- Advocates and law enforcement representatives, if involved, should coordinate with examiners to discuss other issues with patients, including planning for their safety and well-being, physical comfort needs, information needs, the investigative process, advocacy and counseling options, and law enforcement and advocacy follow-up contact procedures.

6.12.2.17 Examiner Court Appearances

Health care providers conducting the exam should expect to be called on to testify in court as fact or expert witnesses.

Recommendations for Jurisdictions to Maximize the Usefulness of Examiner Testimony in Court

- Encourage broad education for examiners on testifying in court.
- Promote prompt notification of examiners if there is a need for them to testify in court.
- Encourage pretrial preparation of examiners.
- Encourage examiners to seek feedback on testimony to improve effectiveness of future court appearances.

REFERENCES

Abbott, J., Feldhaus, K. M., Houry, D., & Lowenstein, S. R. Emergency contraception: What do our patients know? *Ann Emerg Med. 43*, 3, 376–381, 2004.

Acosta, M. L. Collecting evidence for domestic and sexual assault: Highlighting violence against women in health care system intervention. *International J Gynaecology and Obstetrics. 78*(Suppl. 1), S99–S104, 2002.

Adams, J. A. Evolution of a classification scale: Medical evaluation of suspected child sexual abuse. *Child Maltreatment. 6,* 31–36, 2001.

Adams, J. A., Girardin, B., & Faugno, D. Signs of genital trauma in adolescent rape victims examined acutely. *J Pediatr Adolesc Gynecol. 13,* 2, 88, 2000.

American College of Emergency Physicians (ACEP). *Evaluation and management of the sexually assaulted or sexually abused patient.* Washington, DC: U.S. Department of Health and Human Services, Health Resources and Services Administration, Maternal and Child Health Bureau. 1999.

Amey, A. L., & Bishai, D. Measuring the quality of medical care for women who experience sexual assault with data from the National Hospital Ambulatory Medical Care Survey. *Annals of Emergency Medicine. 39,* 631–663, 2002.

Anglin, D., Spears, K. L., Hutson, H. R. Flunitrazepam and its involvement in date or acquaintance rape. *Acad Emerg Med. 4,* 323–326, 1997.

Antognoli-Toland, P. Comprehensive program of examination of sexual assault victims: A hospital-based project in Texas. *J Emerg Nurs. 11,* 3, 132–135, 1985.

Arndt, S. Nurses help Santa Cruz sexual assault survivors. *California Nurse. 84,* 8, 4–5, 1988.

Bell, K. How are emergency departments using sexual assault nurse examiners (SANEs) within the ED routine? *J Emerg Nurs. 24,* 6, 440, 1998.

Biggs, M., Stermac, L. E., & Divinsky, M. Genital injuries following sexual assault of women with and without prior sexual experience. *Canadian Medical Association Journal. 159,* 33–37, 1998.

Blair, T., & Warner, C. Sexual assault. *Topics in Emergency Medicine, 14,* 4, 58–77, 1992.

Bobak, I. M. Violence against women. In *Maternity & Gynecologic Care* St. Louis: Mosby. 1992.

Bownes, I., Gorman, E., & Saters, A. A rape comparison of stranger and acquaintance assaults. *Medical Science Law. 31,* 2, 102–109, 1991.

Bowyer, L., & Dalton, M. Female victims of rape and their genital injuries. *Br J Obstet Gynaecol. May, 104,* 5, 617–620, 1997.

Breslau, N., Davis, G. C., Andreski, P., & Petersen, E. Traumatic events and posttraumatic stress disorder in an urban population of young adults. *Arch Gen Psychiatry. 48,* 216–222, 1991.

Burgess, A. W., Fawcett, J., Hazelwood, R. R., & Grant, C. A. Victim care services and the comprehensive sexual assault assessment tool. In R. R. Hazelwood & A. W. Burgess, Eds., *Rape Investigation* (pp. 263–281). New York: CRC Press. 1995.

Burnam, M. A, Stein, J. A., & Golding, J. M. Sexual assault and mental disorders in a community population. *J Consult Clin Psychol. 56,* 843–850, 1988.

Buss, T. F., Abdu, R., & Walker, J. R. Alcohol, drugs, and urban violence in a small city trauma center. *J Substance Abuse Treatment. 12,* 2, 75–83, 1995.

Campbell, J. C. Health consequences of intimate partner violence. *The Lancet. 359,* 1331–1336, 2002.

Campbell, R. The effectiveness of sexual assault nurse examiner programs. Violence Against Women Online Resources. www.vawnet.org. November 2004.

CDC. CDC issues updated guidelines on use of antiretroviral drugs to prevent HIV infection after sexual, drug use, and accidental exposure. Centers for Disease Control and Prevention National Center for HIV, STD, and TB Prevention. www.cdc.gov. Jan. 20, 2005.

Centers for Disease Control and Prevention. Sexual assault and STDs: Sexually transmitted diseases treatment guidelines. *MMWR Recomm Rep.* May 10, 51(RR-6), 69–74, 2002.

Chaudhry, S. Retrospective study of alleged sexual assault at the Aga Khan Hospital, Nairobi. *East African Medical Journal. 72,* 200–202, 1995.

Cherpitel, C. J. Alcohol and violence-related injuries: An emergency room study. *Addiction. 88,* 1, 79–88, 1993.

Ciancone, A. C., Wilson, C., & Collette, R. Sexual assault nurse examiner programs in the United States. *Ann Emerg Med.* April, 35, 4, 353–357, 2000.

Cohen, L., Donohue, J., & Kovener, M. A SANE approach to treating sexual assault survivors in Colorado: Utilizing sexual assault nurse examiners. Denver: Colorado Coalition Against Sexual Assault. 1996.

Cohen, S., de Vos, E., & Newberger, E. Barriers to physician identification and treatment of family violence: Lessons from five communities. *Academic Medicine. 72* (Suppl. 1), S19–S25, 1997.

Cornell, D. Helping victims of rape: A program called SANE. *New Jersey Medicine. 2,* 45–46, 1998.

Crandall, C., & Helitzer, D. *Impact Evaluation of a Sexual Assault Nurse Examiner (SANE) Program* (NCJ 203276). Washington, DC: National Institute of Justice. 2003.

Crowley, S. R. *Sexual assault: The medical legal examination.* New York: McGraw-Hill. 1999.

Crowley, S. R. Sequential methodology for the examination of sexual homicide victims. *J Forensic Sciences, 50,* 1, 2005.

Dansky, B. S., Brewerton, T. D., Kilpatrick, D. G., & O'Neil, P. M. The National Women's Study: Relationship of crime victimization and PTSD to bulimia nervosa. *Int J Eat Disord. 21,* 213–228, 1997.

Derhammer, F., Lucente, V., Reed, J. F., & Young M. J. Using a SANE interdisciplinary approach to care of sexual assault victims. *Jt Comm J Qual Improv. August, 26,* 8, 488–496, 2000.

DiNitto, D., Martin, P. Y., Norton, D. B., & Maxwell, M. S. After rape: Who should examine rape survivors? *American J Nursing. 86,* 5, 538–540, 1986.

Du Mont, J., & Parnis, D. Sexual assault and legal resolution: Querying the medical collection of forensic evidence. *Med Law. 19,* 4, 779–792, 2000.

Du Mont, J., & Parnis, D. Forensic nursing in the context of sexual assault: Comparing the opinions and practices of nurse examiners and nurses. *Appl Nurs Res. August, 16,* 3, 173–183, 2003.

Du Mont, J., & Parnis, D. The doctor's dilemma: Caregiving and medicolegal evidence collection. *Med Law. 23,* 3, 515–529, 2004.

Eckert, L. O., Sugar, N., & Fine, D. Factors impacting injury documentation after sexual assault: Role of examiner experience and gender. *Am J Obstet Gynecol. 190,* 6, 1739–1746, 2004.

Elliott, D. M., Mok, D. S., & Briere, J. Adult sexual assault: Prevalence, symptomatology, and sex differences in the general population. *J Trauma Stress. 17,* 3, 203–211, 2004.

Ericksen, J., Dudley, C., McIntosh, G., Ritch, L., Shumay, S., & Simpson, M. Clients' experiences with a specialized sexual assault service. *J Emerg Nurs. 28,* 1, 86–90, 2002.

Falsetti, S. A., Lydiard, R. B., Gibbs, N., & Resnick, H. S. Irritable bowel syndrome: Associations with psychiatric disorders, victimization, and health care seeking behavior. Paper presented at the Anxiety Disorders Association of America (ADAA), New Orleans, LA. 1997.

Feldhaus, K. M., Houry, D., & Kaminsky, R. Lifetime sexual assault prevalence rates and reporting practices in an emergency department population. *Ann Emerg Med. 36,* 1, 23–27, 2000.

Frank, C. The new way to catch rapists. *Redbook,* December, 61–65, 1996.

Frazier, P. A., & Haney, B. Sexual assault cases in the legal system: Police, prosecutor, and victim perspectives. *Law and Human Behavior. 20,* 607–628, 1996.

Galvin, J., & Polk, K. Attrition in case processing: Is rape unique? *J Research in Crime and Delinquency. 20,* 106–154, 1982.

Geist, R. F. Sexually related trauma. *Emerg Med Clin North Am. 6,* 3, 439–466, Aug. 1988.

Gibb, A. M., McManus, T., & Forster, G. E. Should we offer antibiotic prophylaxis post sexual assault? *Int J STD AIDS. 14,* 2, 99–102, 2003.

Girardin, B., Faugno, D., Seneski, P., & Slaughter, L. Findings in sexual assault and consensual intercourse. In M. Whelan, Ed., *Color Atlas of Sexual Assault* (pp. 19–65). St. Louis, MO: CV Mosby. 1997.

Golding, J. M., Stein, J. A., Siegel, J. M., Burnam, M. A., & Sorenson, S. B. Sexual assault history and use of health and mental health services. *Am J Community Psychol. 6,* 625–644, 1988.

Goodman, L. A., Koss, M. P., & Russo, N. F. Violence against women: Physical and mental health effects. Part I: Research findings. *Applied and Preventive Psychol. 2,* 79–89, 1993.

Gray-Eurom, K., Seaberg, D. C., & Wears, R. L. The prosecution of sexual assault cases: Correlation with forensic evidence. *Ann Emerg Med. 39,* 1, 39–46, 2002.

Greenfeld, L. *Sex Offenses and Offenders.* Washington, DC: U.S. Department of Justice, Bureau of Justice Statistics, Office of Justice Programs. NCJ 163392. 1997.

Greenwood, M. D. Community cooperatives combat sexual assault and domestic violence. *Emerg Med Serv. 32,* 2, 60–61, 2003.

Grossin, C., Sibille, I., Lorin de la Grandmaison, G., Banasr, A., Brion, F., & Durigon, M. Analysis of 418 cases of sexual assault. *Forensic Sci Int. 131,* 2–3, 125–130, 2003.

Groth, A. N., & Burgess, A. W., Hartman, C. R., & Holstrom, L. L. Rape violence. Available at: www.NursingSpectrum.com

Harlow, L. L., Quina, K., Morokoff, P. J., Rose, J. S., & Grimley, D. M. HIV risk in women: A multifaceted model. *J Appl Behav Res. 1,* 3–38, 1993.

Hatmaker, D. D., Pinholster, L., & Saye, J. J. A community-based approach to sexual assault. *Public Health Nurs. 19,* 2, 124–127, 2002.

Hohenhaus, S. SANE legislation and lessons learned: Sexual assault nurse examiner. *J Emerg Nurs. 24,* 5, 463–464, 1998.

Holloway, M., & Swan, A. A & E management of sexual assault. *Nursing Standard. 7,* 45, 31–35, 1993.

Holmes, M. Sexually transmitted infections in female rape victims. *AIDS Patient Care STDS. 13,* 12, 703–708, 1999.

Holmes, M. M., Resnick, H. S., & Frampton, D. Follow-up of sexual assault victims. *Am J Obstet Gynecol. 179,* 2, 336–342, 1998.

Holmes, M. M., Resnick, H. S., Kilpatrick, D. G., & Best, C. L. Rape-related pregnancy: Estimates and descriptive characteristics from a national sample of women. *Am J Obstet Gynecol. 175,* 320–325, 1996.

Houry, D., Feldhaus, K. M., & Nyquist, S. R. Emergency department documentation in cases of intentional assault. *Ann Emerg Med. 34,* 6, 715–719, 1999.

Houry, D., Sachs, C. J., Feldhaus, K. M., & Linden, J. Violence-inflicted injuries: Reporting laws in the 50 states. *Ann Emerg Med. 39,* 1, 56–60, 2002.

Hutson, L. A. Development of sexual assault nurse examiner programs. *Emergency Nursing. 37,* 79–88, 2002.

International Association of Forensic Nurses. *Sexual Assault Nurse Examiner Standards of Practice.* Thorofare, NJ: Slack, Inc. 1996.

Irwin, C., Falsetti, S. A., Lydiard, R. B., Ballenger, J. C., Brock, C. D., & Brener, W. Co-morbidity of posttraumatic stress disorder and irritable bowel syndrome. *J Clin Psychiatry. 57,* 12, 576–578, 1996.

Joint Commission on Accreditation of Health Organizations. *Comprehensive Accreditation Manual for Hospitals: The Official Handbook.* Oakbrook Terrace, IL: Joint Commission on Accreditation of Health Care Organization. 1997.

Jones, J. S., Dunnuck, C., Rossman, L., Wyn, B. N., & Nelson-Horan, C. Significance of toluidine blue positive findings after speculum examination for sexual assault. *Am J Emerg Med. 22,* 3, 201–203, 2004.

Jurkovich, G. J., Rivara, F. P., Gurney, J. G., Seguin, D., Fligner, C. L., & Copass, M. Effects of alcohol intoxication on the initial assessment of trauma patients. *Ann Emerg Med. 21,* 6, 704–708, 1992.

Keshavarz, R., Merchant, R. C., & McGreal, J. Emergency contraception provision: A survey of emergency department practitioners. *Acad Emerg Med. 9,* 1, 69–74, 2002.

Kessler, R. C., Sonnega, A., Bromet, E., Hughes, M., & Nelson, C. B. Posttraumatic stress disorder in the National Comorbidity Survey. *Arch Gen Psychiatry. 52,* 1048–1060, 1995.

Kiecolt-Glaser, J., & Glaser, R. Psychoneuroimmunology: Can psychological interventions modulate immunity? *J Consult Clin Psychol. 604,* 4, 569–575, 1992.

Kilpatrick, D., Edmunds, C., & Seymour, A. *Rape in America: A Report to the Nation*. Arlington, VA: National Victim Center. 1992.

Kilpatrick, D. G., Saunders, B. E., Veronen, L. J., Best, C. L., & Von, J. M. Criminal victimization: Lifetime prevalence, reporting to police, and psychological impact. *Crime and Delinquency. 334,* 479–489, 1987.

Kimerling, R., & Calhoun, K. S. Somatic symptoms, social support, and treatment seeking among sexual assault victims. *J Consult Clin Psychol. 62,* 333–340, 1994.

Kintz, P., Villain, M., & Ludes, B. Testing for the undetectable in drug-facilitated sexual assault using hair analyzed by tandem mass spectrometry as evidence. *Ther Drug Monit. 26,* 2, 211–214, 2004.

Koss, M. P., & Heslet, L. Somatic consequences of violence against women. *Arch Family Med. 1,* 53–59, 1992.

Koss, M. P., Koss, P. G., & Woodruff, W. J. Deleterious effects of criminal victimization on women's health and medical utilization. *Arch Intern Med. 151,* 342–347, 1991.

Koss, M. P., Woodruff, W. J., & Koss, P. G. Relation of criminal victimization to health perceptions among women medical patients. *J Consult Clin Psychol. 58,* 147–152, 1990.

LaFree, G. Variables affecting guilty pleas and convictions in rape cases: Toward a social theory of rape processing. *Social Forces. 58,* 833–850, 1980.

Lang, K. S. *Sexual assault nurse examiner resource guide for Michigan communities.* Okemos, MI: Michigan coalition against domestic and sexual violence. 1999.

Langan, P. A., & Farrington, D. P. Crime and justice in the United States and in England and Wales, 1981–96. Washington, DC: U.S. Department of Justice, Bureau of Justice Statistics. NCJ 169284. 1998.

Laws, A., & Golding J. M. Sexual assault history and eating disorder symptoms among White, Hispanic, and African-American women and men. *Am J Public Health. 86,* 579–581, 1996.

Ledray, L. E. The sexual assault examination: Overview and lessons learned in one program. *J Emer Nurs. 18,* 3, 223–230, 1992a.

Ledray, L. E. The sexual assault nurse clinician: A 15-year experience in Minneapolis. *J Emer Nurs. 18,* 3, 217–222, 1992b.

Ledray, L. E. *Sexual Assault Nurse Examiner (SANE) Development & Operation Guide.* Minneapolis, MN: U.S. Department of Justice, Office of Justice Programs, Office for Victims of Crime. NCJ 170609. 1999.

Ledray, L. E. *Forensic Evidence Collection and Care of the Sexual Assault Survivor: The SANE Response.* Washington, DC: U.S. Department of Justice, Office of Justice Programs. Violence Against Women Online Resources. 2001.

Ledray, L. E., & Barry, L. SANE expert and factual testimony. *J Emerg Nurs. 24,* 3, 284–287, 1998.

Ledray, L. E., Faugno, D., & Speck, P. Sexual assault: Clinical issues. SANE: Advocate, forensic technician, nurse? *J Emerg Nurs. 27,* 1, 91–93, 2001.

Ledray, L. E., & Simmelink, K. Efficacy of SANE evidence collection: A Minnesota study. *J Emerg Nurs. 23,* 1, 75–77, 1997.

Lenehan, G. P. A SANE way to care for rape victims. *J Emerg Nurs. 17,* 1, 1–2, 1991.

Leserman, J. Selected symptoms associated with sexual and physical abuse history among female patients with gastrointestinal disorders: The impact on subsequent health care visits. *Psychological Medicine. 28,* 417–425, 1998.

Lewis, C. M., DiNitto, D., Nelson, T. S., Just, M. M., & Campbell-Ruggaard, J. Evaluation of a rape protocol: A five-year follow-up with nurse managers. *J Am Acad Nurse Pract. 15,* 1, 34–39, 2003.

Lincoln, C. Genital injury: Is it significant? A review of the literature. *Med Sci Law. 41,* 3, 206–216, 2001.

Littel, *K. SANE Programs: Improving the Community Response to Sexual Assault Victims. OVC Bulletin.* Washington, DC: U.S. Department of Justice, Office of Justice Programs, Office for Victims of Crime. 2001.

Litz, B. T., Keane, T. M., & Fisher, L. Physical health complaints in combat-related post-traumatic-stress disorder: A preliminary report. *J Traumatic Stress. 5,* 1, 131–141, 1992.

Lynch, V. A. Forensic nursing: Diversity in education and practice. *J Psychosocial Nursing. 132,* 3, 7–14, 1993.

Malloy, M. Relationship of nurse identified therapeutic techniques to client satisfaction reports in a crisis program. Unpublished master's thesis, University of Minnesota, Minneapolis, MN. 1991.

Mancino, P., Parlavecchio, E., Melluso, J., Monti, M., & Russo, P. Introducing colposcopy and vulvovaginoscopy as routine examinations for victims of sexual assault. *Clin Exp Obstet Gynecol. 30,* 1, 40–42, 2003.

Marchbanks, P., Lui, K. J., & Mercy, J. Risk of injury from resisting rape. *American J Epidemiology. 132,* 3, 501–505, 1990.

Maxwell, M. S., & Soubielle, K. Hospital sexual assault needs, issues and recommendations: Sexual assault needs assessment. *Florida.* 57–68, 1996.

McFarlane, A. C., Atchison, M., Rafalowicz, E., & Papay, P. Physical symptoms in post-traumatic stress disorder. *J Psychosom Res. 38,* 715–726, 1994.

McGinnis, M., & Foege, W. H. Actual causes of death in the United States. *JAMA. 270,* 2207–2212, 1993.

McGregor, M. J., Le, G., Marion, S. A., & Wiebe, E. Examination for sexual assault: Is the documentation of physical injury associated with the laying of charges? A retrospective cohort study. *Canadian Medical Association Journal. 160,* 11, 1565–1569, 1999.

McGregor, M. J., Lipowska, M., Shah, S., Du Mont, J., & De Siato, C. An exploratory analysis of suspected drug-facilitated sexual assault seen in a hospital emergency department. *Women Health. 37,* 3, 71–80, 2003.

Merchant, R. C., Keshavarz, R., & Low, C. HIV post-exposure prophylaxis provided at an urban paediatric emergency department to female adolescents after sexual assault. *Emerg Med J. 21,* 4, 449–451, 2004.

Michigan Coalition Against Domestic and Sexual Violence. The response to sexual assault: Removing barriers to services and justice. 2004. www.mcadsv.org

Miller, B. A., Downs, W. R., Gondoli, D. M., & Keil, A. The role of childhood sexual abuse in the development of alcoholism in women. *Violence and Victims. 2,* 157–172, 1987.

Minshall, L., & Patel, M. Evaluation of documentation practices of sexual assault nurse examiners. *California J Emergency Medicine. 2,* 3, 28, 2001.

Myles, J. E., Hirozawa, A., Katz, M. H., Kimmerling, R., & Bamberger, J. D. Postexposure prophylaxis for HIV after sexual assault. *JAMA. 284,* 12, 1516–1518, 2000.

NCVS. Criminal victimization. U.S. Department of Justice, Office of Justice Programs. 1999–2000.

NCVS. Criminal victimization, 2002. U.S. Department of Justice, Office of Justice Programs. August 2003.

Negrusz, A., Moore, A., Stockham, C., Poiser, T., Kern, K., Palaparthy, J., Ngoc L. T., Janicak, P., & Levy, N. Elimination of 7-aminoflunitrazepam and flunitrazepam in urine after a single dose of Rohypnol. *J Forensic Sciences. 45,* 5, 1013–1022, 2000.

O'Brien, C. Sexual assault nurse examiner (SANE) program coordinator. *J Emerg Nurs. 23,* 5, 532–533, 1996.

Palmer, C. M., McNulty, A. M., D'Este, C., & Donovan, B. Genital injuries in women reporting sexual assault. *Sexual Health. 1,* 55–59, 2004.

Pitman, R. K. Biological findings in posttraumnatic stress disorder: Implications for DSM-IV classification. In J. R. T. Davidson & E. B. Foa, Eds., *Posttraumatic Stress Disorder: DSM-IV and Beyond* (pp. 173–189). Washington, DC: American Psychiatric Association Press. 1993.

Polusny, M. A., & Follette, V. M. Long-term correlates of child sexual abuse: Theory and review of the empirical literature. *Appl Prey Psychol. 4,* 3, 143–166, 1997.

Putz, M., Thomas, B. K., & Cowles, K. V. Sexual assault victims' compliance with follow-up care at one sexual assault treatment center. *J Emerg Nurs. 22,* 6, 560–565, 1996.

Rambow, B., Adkinson, C., & Frost, T. H. Female sexual assault: Medical and legal implications. *Ann Emerg Med. 21,* 6, 727–731, 1992.

Rennison, C. *Rape and Sexual Assault: Reporting to Police and Medical Attention, 1992–2000.* Washington, DC: U.S. Department of Justice, Office of Justice Programs, Bureau of Justice Statistics. NCJ 194530. 2002.

Resnick, H. S. Health impact of interpersonal violence.*Behav Med. 23,* 2, 53–64, 1997.

Resnick, H. S., Holmes, M. M., Kilpatrick, D. G., Clum, G., Acierno, R., Best, C. L., & Saunders, B. E. Predictors of post-rape medical care in a national sample of women. *Am J Prev Med., 19,* 4, 214–219, 2000.

Resnick, H. S., Kilpatrick, D. G., Dansky, B. S., & Freedy, J. R. Emotional and physiological responses during a variety of traumatic events. Paper presented at the annual meeting of the Association for the Advancement of Behavior Therapy, Boston, 1992.

Resnick, H. S., Kilpatrick, D. G., Dansky, B. S., Saunders, B. E., & Best, C. L. Prevalence of civilian trauma and PTSD in a representative national sample of women. *J Consult Clin Psychol. 61,* 984–991, 1993.

Reznic, M. F., Nachman, R., & Hiss, J. Penile lesions: Reinforcing the case against suspects of sexual assault. *J Clin Forensic Med. 11,* 2, 78–81, 2004.

Riggs, N., Houry, D., Long, G., Markovchick, V., & Feldhaus, K. Analysis of 1,076 cases of sexual assault. *Annals of Emergency Medicine. 35,* 4, 358–362, 2000.

Rivara, R. P., Jurkovich, G. J., & Gurney, J. G. The magnitude of acute and chronic alcohol abuse in trauma patients. *Arch Surg. 128,* 8, 907–912, 1993.

Rossman, L., Jones, J. S., Dunnuck, C., Wynn, B. N., & Bermingham, M. Genital trauma associated with forced digital penetration. *Am J Emerg Med. 22,* 2, 101–104, 2004.

Rothbaum, B. O., Foa, E. B., Riggs, D. S., Murdock, T., & Walsh, W. A prospective examination of post-traumatic stress disorder in rape victims. *J Traumatic Stress. 5,* 455–475, 1992.

Rutledge, R., & Messick, W. J. The association of trauma death and alcohol use in a rural state. *J Trauma. 31,* 5, 737–742, 1992.

Sachs, C. J., & Chu, L. D. Predictors of genitorectal injury in female victims of suspected sexual assault. *Acad Emerg Med. 9,* 2, 146–151, 2002.

Saltzman, L. E. *Intimate Partner Violence: Uniform Definitions and Recommended Data Elements, Version 1.0.* Atlanta, GA, National Center for Injury Prevention and Control, Centers for Disease Control and Prevention. 1999.

Sandrick, K. M. Medicine & law: Tightening the chain of evidence. *Hosp Health Netw., 70,* 11, 64, 66, 1996.

Schei, B., Muus, K. M., and Moen, M. H. Medical and legal aspects of rape. Referrals to a team for care of rape victims at the regional hospital in Trondheim during the period 1989–1992. *Tidsskr Nor Laegeforen. 115,* 1, 30–33, 1995.

Seneski, P. Multi-disciplinary program helps sexual assault victims. The American College of Physician Executives. 417–418, 1992.

Seng, J. S., & Sanubol, M. Johnson County (Iowa) SANE team: The first year as sexual assault nurse examiner: Role transition and role-related stress within a new SANE team. *J Emerg Nurs. 30,* 2, 126–133, 2004.

Sheridan, D. J. The role of the battered woman specialist. *J Psychosocial Nursing. 31,* 11, 1993.

Sievers, V., Murphy, S., & Miller, J. Sexual assault evidence collection more accurate when completed by sexual assault nurse examiners: Colorado's experience. *J Emerg Nurs. 29,* 511–514, 2003.

Slaughter, L., & Brown, C. R. Cervical findings in rape victims. *Am J Obstet Gynecol. 164,* 528–529, 1991.

Slaughter, L., & Brown, C. Colposcopy to establish physical findings in rape victims. *Am J Obstet Gynecol. 16,* 1, 83–86, 1992.

Slaughter, L., Brown, C. R., Crowley, S., & Peck, R. Patterns of genital injury in female sexual assault victims. *Am J Obstet Gynecol. 176,* 609–616, 1997.

Smith, H. G. SART: Special team helps net convictions. *Long Beach Press-Telegram.* June 5, 1996.

Smith, K., Holmseth, J., & Macgregor, M. Sexual assault response team: Overcoming obstacles to program development. *J Emerg Nurs. 24,* 4, 365–367, 1998.

Soderstrom, R. M. Colposcopic documentation: An objective approach to assessing sexual abuse of girls. *J Reproductive Medicine. 39,* 1, 6–8, 1994.

Solola, A., Scott, C., Severs, H., & Howell, J. Rape: Management in a non-institutional setting. *Obstetrics & Gynecology. 61,* 373–378, 1983.

Speck, P. *Patient Satisfaction Survey and Memorandum to Nurses*. Memphis, TN: Memphis Sexual Assault Resource Center. 1995.

Speck, P., & Aiken, M. 20 years of community nursing service. *Tennessee Nurse. 58,* 2, 5–18, 1995.

Stermac, L. E., Du Mont, J. A., & Kalemba, V. Comparison of sexual assaults by strangers and known assailants in an urban population of women. *CMAJ. 153,* 8, 1089–1094, 1995.

Stermac, L. E., & Stirpe, T. S. Efficacy of a two-year-old sexual assault nurse examiner program in a Canadian hospital. *J Emerg Nurs. 28,* 1, 18–23, 2002.

Stobo, J. D., Salmon, M. E., & Cohn, F., Eds. *Confronting Chronic Neglect: The Education and Training of Health Professionals on Family Violence*. Washington, DC: National Academy Press. 2002.

Sugar, N. F., Fine, D. N., & Eckert, L. O. Physical injury after sexual assault: Findings of a large case series. *Am J Obstet Gynecol. 190,* 1, 71–76, 2004.

Swart, L. A. Rape surveillance through district surgeon offices in Johannesburg, 1996–1998: Findings, evaluation and prevention implications. *South African J Psychology. 30,* 2–10, 2000.

Taylor, W. K. Collecting evidence for sexual assault: The role of the sexual assault nurse examiner (SANE). *International J Gynecology and Obstetrics. 78,* S91–S94, 2002.

Testa, M., Livingston, J. A., & Collins, R. L. The role of women's alcohol consumption in evaluation of vulnerability to sexual aggression. *Exp Clin Psychopharmacol. 8,* 2, 185–191, 2000.

Testa, M., Vanzile-Tamsen, C., & Livingston, J. A. The role of victim and perpetrator intoxication on sexual assault outcomes. *J Stud Alcohol. 65,* 3, 320–329, 2004.

Thomas, M., & Zachritz, H. Tulsa sexual assault nurse examiners (SANE) program. *J Oklahoma State Medical Association. 86,* 6, 284–286, 1993.

Tobias, G. Rape examinations by GPs. *The Practitioner. 234,* 1990.

Tucker, S., Ledray, L. E., & Stehle-Werner, J. Sexual assault evidence collection. *Wisconsin Med J. 89,* 407–411, 1990.

Turman, D. M. *Understanding DNA Evidence: A Guide for Victim Service Providers.* Office for Victims of Crime Bulletin. Washington, DC: U.S. Department of Justice, Office of Justice Programs. NCJ 185690. 2001.

Voelker, R. Experts hope team approach will improve the quality of rape exams. *JAMA. 275,* 13, 973–974, 1996.

Walch, A. G., & Broadhead, W. E. Prevalence of lifetime sexual victimization among female patients. *J Fam Pract. 35,* 5, 511–516, 1992.

Walker, E. A., & Stenchever, M. A. Sexual victimization and chronic pelvic pain. *Obstet Gynecol Clin North Am. 20,* 795–807, 1993.

Wiebe, E. R., Comay, S. E., McGregor, M., & Ducceschi, S. Offering HIV prophylaxis to people who have been sexually assaulted: 16 months' experience in a sexual assault service. *CMAJ. 162,* 5, 641–645, 2000.

Wiley, J., Sugar, N., Fine, D., & Eckert, L. O. Legal outcomes of sexual assault. *Am J Obstet Gynecol. 188,* 6, 1638–1641, 2003.

World Health Organization. *Guidelines for Medico-Legal Care for Victims of Sexual Violence*. New York: Author. 2003.

Wright, R. J., Wright, R. O., & Farnan, L. Response to child abuse in the pediatric emergency: Need for continued education. *Pediatr Emerg Care. 15,* 6, 376–382, 1999.

Yates, D. W., Hadfield, J. M., & Peters, K. Alcohol consumption of patients attending two accident and emergency departments in north-west England. *J Roy Soc Med. 80,* 8, 486–489, 1987.

Yorker, B. Crofts nurses in Georgia care for survivors of sexual assault. *Georgia Nursing. 147,* 335–341, 1996.

Young, W. W., Bracken, A. C., & Goddard, M. A. Sexual assault: Review of a national model protocol for forensic and medical evaluation. *Obstet Gynecol. 80,* 5, 878–883, 1992.

Yuzpe, A., Smith, A., Percival, R., & Rademaker, A. W. A multicenter clinical investigation employing ethinyl estradiol combined with dl-norgestrel as a post-coital contraceptive agent. *Fertility and Sterility. 37,* 4, 508–513, 1982.

RECOMMENDED READINGS

Abbey, A. Lessons learned and unanswered questions about sexual assault perpetration. *J Interpers Violence. 20,* 1, 39–42, 2005.

Abbey, A., & McAuslan, P. A longitudinal examination of male college students' perpetration of sexual assault. *J Consult Clin Psychol. 72,* 5, 747–756, 2004.

Ackerman, P. T., Newton, J. E. O., & McPherson, W. B. Prevalence of posttraumatic stress disorder and other psychiatric diagnoses in three groups of abused children (sexual, physical, and both). *Child Abuse Negl. 22,* 8, 759–774, 1998.

ACOG Issues Report on Sexual Assault. *Amer Family Phys. 57,* 5, 1144–1145, 1998.

Adams, J. A. Medical evaluation of suspected child sexual abuse: It's time for standardized training, referral centers, and routine peer review. *Arch Pediatr Adolesc Med. 153,* 11, 1121–1122, 1999.

Adams, J. A., Harper, K., & Knudson, S. Examination findings in legally confirmed child sexual abuse: It's normal to be normal. *Pediatrics. 94,* 3, 310–317, 1994.

Adams, J. A., & Wells, R. Normal vs. abnormal genital findings in children: How well do examiners agree? *Child Abuse Negl. 17,* 5, 663–675, 1993.

American College of Emergency Physicians (ACEP). Policy statements: Management of the patient with the complaint of sexual assault. *Ann Emerg Med. 25,* 728–729, 1995.

American College of Obstetricians and Gynecologists (ACOG). *Sexual Assault* (ACOG Educational Bulletin No 242). Washington DC: American College of Obstetricians and Gynecologists. 1997.

American Medical Association. *Strategies for the treatment and prevention of sexual assault.* Chicago: American Medical Association. 1995.

Ahrens, C. E., Campbell, R., Wasco, S. M., Aponte, G., Grubstein, L., & Davidson, W. S. Sexual assault nurse examiner (SANE) programs: Alternative systems for service delivery for sexual assault victims. *J Interpersonal Violence. 15,* 9, 921–943, 2000.

Aiken, M. M., & Speck, P. M. Sexual assault and multiple trauma: A sexual assault nurse examiner (SANE) challenge. *J Emerg Nurs. 2,* 466–468, 1995.

Ales, B. Community collaboration: The nursing administrator's role in implementing a child abuse prevention program. *J Nurs Admin. 28,* 6, 43–48, 1998.

Alexander, R. C., & Smith, W. L. Shaken baby syndrome. *Infants Young Child. 10,* 3, 1–9, 1998.

Allen, E. After the examination: Tracking sexual assault cases through the legal system. *J Emerg Nurs. 25,* 6, 569–571, 1999.

American Medical Association, Council on Scientific Affairs. Violence against women: Relevance for medical practitioners. *JAMA. 267,* 3184–3189, 1992.

Anderson, C. Childhood sexually transmitted diseases: One consequence of sexual abuse. *Public Health Nurs. 12,* 1, 41–46, 1995.

ASTM International. *Standard guide for sexual assault investigation, examination, and evidence.* American Society for Testing and Materials Committee (E-30) on Forensic Sciences. Available at http://www.astm.org.

Atabaki, S., & Paradise, J. E. The medical evaluation of the sexually abused child: Lessons from a decade of research. *Pediatrics. 104,* 1, 178–186, 1999.

Bauer, H. M., Mooney, D., & Larkin, H. California's mandatory reporting of domestic violence injuries: Does the law go too far or not far enough? *West J Med. 171,* 2, 118–124, 1999.

Bays, J., & Chadwick, D. Medical diagnosis of the sexually abused child. *Child Abuse Negl. 17,* 1, 91–110, 1993.

Bays, J., Chewnig, M., & Keltner, L. Changes in hymenal anatomy during examination of prepubertal girls for possible sexual abuse. *Adolesc Pedriatr Gynecol. 3,* 34–46, 1990.

Bays, J., & Lewman, L. Toluidine blue in the detection at autopsy or perineal and anal laceration in victims of sexual abuse. *Arch Pathol Lab Med. 116,* 620–621, 1992.

Beebe, D. K. Emergency management of the adult female rape victim. *Amer Family Phys. 43,* 6, 2041–2046, 1991a.

Beebe, D. K. Initial assessment of the rape victim. *J MSMA. 32,* 11, 403–406, 1991b.

Berenson, A. B. The prepubertal genital exam: What is normal and abnormal. *Curr Opin Obstet Gynecol. 6,* 6, 526–530, 1994.

Berenson, A. B., Chacko, M. R., & Wiemann, C. M. A case-control study of anatomic changes resulting from sexual abuse. *Am J Obstet Gynecol. 182,* 4, 820–31, 2000.

Berkowitz, C. D. Medical consequences of sexual abuse. *Child Abuse Negl. 22,* 6, 541–550, 1998.

Berliner, L., & Saunders, B. E. Treating fear and anxiety in sexually abused children: Results of a controlled two-year follow-up study. *Child Maltreat. 1,* 294–309, 1996.

Bernet, W. Practice parameters for the forensic evaluation of children and adolescents who may have been physically or sexually abused. *J Am Acad Child Adolesc Psychiatry. 36,* 10(Suppl), 37S–56S, 1997.

Betchel, K., & Podrazik, M. Evaluation of the adolescent rape victim. *Pediatr Clin North Am. 46,* 4, 809–823, 1999.

Black, C. T. Ano-rectal trauma in children. *J Ped Surg. 17,* 501–504, 1982.

Block, R. What doctors who perform child abuse medical evaluations want the rest of the team to know. *J Okla State Med Assoc. 91,* 8, 457, 1998.

Boney-McCoy, S., & Finkelhor, D. Prior victimization: A risk factor for child sexual abuse and for PTSD-related symptomatology among sexually abused youth. *Child Abuse Negl. 19,* 12, 1401–1421, 1995.

Botash, A. S. Examination for sexual abuse in prepubertal children: An update. *Pediatr Ann. 26,* 5, 312–320, 1997.

Briere, J., & Jordan, C. E. Violence against women: Outcome complexity and implications for assessment and treatment. *J Interpers Violence. 19,* 11, 1252–1276, 2004.

Britton, H., & Hansen, K. Sexual abuse. *Clin Obstet Gynecol. 40,* 1, 226–240, 1997.

Brown, K. Rape and sexual assault: Understanding the offense and the offender. *Adv Nurse Pract. 12,* 8, 69–70, 2004.

Burgess, A. W., & Fawcett, J. The comprehensive sexual assault assessment tool. *Nurse Pract. 21,* 4, 66, 71–76, 78, 1996.

Burgess, A. W., & Holstrum, L. The rape trauma syndrome. *Am J Psychiatry. 131,* 981–986, 1974.

California Medical Protocol for Examination of Sexual Assault and Child Sexual Abuse Victims. Sacramento, CA: Office of Criminal Justice Planning. July 1987.

Campbell, R. Mental health services for rape survivors: Issues in therapeutic practice. Violence Against Women Online Resources. 1–9, 2001.

Campbell, R., Dorey, H., Naegeli, M., Grubstein, L. K., Bennett, K. K., Bonter, F., Smith, P. K., Grzywacz, J., Baker, P. K., & Davidson, S. An empowerment evaluation model for sexual assault programs: Empirical evidence of effectiveness. *Am J Community Psychol. 34,* 3–4, 251–262, 2004.

Cardello, D. Forms, forms, and more forms: Emergency department sexual assault assessment. *J Emerg Nurs. 19,* 5, 450–451, 1993.

Centers for Disease Control and Prevention. Sexual assault and STDs: Sexually transmitted diseases treatment guidelines. *MMWR Recomm Rep 2002. 51,* RR-6, 69–74, 2002.

Child abuse and forensic pediatric medicine fellowship curriculum statement. American Academy of Pediatrics, Section on Child Abuse and Neglect, and the Forensic Pediatrics Physician Leadership Group, Committee on Fellowship Curriculum. *Child Maltreat. 5,* 1, 58–62, 2000.

Christian, C. W., Lavelle, J. M., & De Jong, A. R. Forensic evidence findings in prepubertal victims of sexual assault. *Pediatrics. 106,* 1, 100–104, 2000.

Cohen, J. A., & Mannarino, A. P. A treatment model for sexually abused preschoolers. *J Interpersonal Violence. 8,* 115–131, 1993.

Cohen, J. A., & Mannarino, A. P. A treatment outcome study for sexually abused preschool children: Initial findings. *J Am Acad Child Adolesc Psychiatry. 3,* 1, 42–50, 1996.

Coury, D. L. Recognition of child abuse: Notes from the field. *Arch Pediatr Adolesc Med. 154,* 1, 9–10, 2000.

Davidson, D. A. Physical abuse of preschoolers: Identification and intervention through occupational therapy. *Am J Occup Ther. 49,* 3, 235–243, 1995.

Davies, D., Cole, J., & Albertella, G. A model for conducting forensic interviews with child victims of abuse. *Child Maltreat. 1,* 3, 189–199, 1996.

Deblinger, E., Lippmann, U., & Steer, R. A. Sexually abused children suffering posttraumatic stress symptoms: Initial treatment outcome findings. *Child Maltreat. 1,* 310–321, 1996.

Deblinger, E., Steer, R. A., & Lippmann, J. Maternal factors associated with sexually abused children's psychosocial adjustment. *Child Maltreat. 4,* 1, 13–20, 1999a.

Deblinger, E., Steer, R. A., & Lippmann, J. Two-year follow-up study of cognitive behavioral therapy for sexually abused children suffering post-traumatic stress symptoms. *Child Abuse Negl. 23,* 12, 1371–1378, 1999b.

De Jong, A. R. Impact of child sexual abuse medical examinations on dependency and criminal systems. *Child Abuse Negl. 22,* 6, 645–652, 1998.

Deming, J., Mittelman, R., & Wetli, C. Forensic science aspects of fatal sexual assaults on women. *J Foren Sci. 28,* 3, 572–576, 1983.

Dietz, P. E., Hazelwood, R., & Warren, J. The sexually sadistic criminal and his offenses. *Bull Am Acad Psych Law. 18,* 2, 163–178, 1990.

Douglas, J., Burgess, A. W., Burgess, A. G., & Ressler, R. *Crime Classification Manual.* New York: Lexington Books. 1992.

Dubowitz, H. Children's responses to the evaluation for sexual abuse. *Child Abuse Negl. 22,* 6, 581–584, 1998.

Dubowitz, H., Giardino, A., & Gustavson, E. Child neglect: Guidance for pediatricians. *Pediatr in Rev. 21,* 4, 111–116, 2000.

Dupre, A. R., Hampton, H. L., & Morrison, H. Sexual assault. *Obstetrical and Gynecological Survey. 48,* 9, 640–648, 1993.

Dwyer, B. J. Rape: Psychological medical, and forensic aspects of emergency management. *Emergency Medicine Reports. 16,* 12, 105–116, 1995.

Echeburua, E., de Corral, P., & Sarasua, B. Treatment of acute posttraumatic stress disorder in rape victims: An experimental study. *J Anxiety Disord. 10,* 185–199, 1996.

Emergency Nurses Association (ENA). Position statement. *J Emerg Nurs. 24,* 5, 38A, 1998.

English, D. J. The extent and consequences of child maltreatment. *Future Child. 8,* 1, 39–53, 1998.

Ernst, A. A., Green, E., Ferguson, M. T., Weiss, S. J., & Green, W. M. The utility of anoscopy and colposcopy in the evaluation of male sexual assault victims. *Ann Emerg Med. 36,* 5, 432–437, 2000.

Ernst, A. A., Houry, D., Weiss, S. J., & Green, W. Domestic violence awareness in a medical school class: Two-year follow-up. *South Med J. 93,* 8, 772–776, 2000.

Ferrell, J. Foley catheter balloon technique for visualizing the hymen in female adolescent sexual abuse victims. *J Emerg Nurs. 21,* 6, 585–586, 1995.

Finkel, M. Technical conduct of the child sexual abuse medical examination. *Child Abuse Negl. 22,* 6, 555–566, 1998.

Flaherty, E. G., Sege, R., & Binns, H. J. Health care providers' experience reporting child abuse in the primary care setting. *Arch Pediatr Adolesc Med. 154,* 489–493, 2000.

Foa, E. B., Rothbaum, B. O., & Riggs, D. S. Treatment of posttraumatic stress disorder in rape victims: A comparison between cognitive-behavioral procedures and counseling. *J Consult Clin Psychol. 59,* 5, 715–723, 1991.

Friedrich, W. N., Gramsch, P., & Damon, L. Child Sexual Behavior Inventory: Normative and clinical comparisons. *Psychol Assess. 4,* 303–344, 2002.

Fulginiti, T. P., Seibert, E., Firth, V., Quattrone, J., Harner, L., Webb, J., & Vida, P. A SANE experience in a community hospital: Doylestown's first six months. *J Emergency Nursing. 22,* 422–425, 1996.

Gaffney, D. A., & Ledray, L. Sexual assault examiners and rape crisis advocates: Rising to the challenge together. *Sex Assault Rep. 3,* 2, 17–32, 1999.

Giardino, A. P., Brayden, R. M., & Sugarman, J. M. Residency training in child sexual abuse evaluation. *Child Abuse Negl. 22,* 4, 331–336, 1998.

Giardino, A. P., Christian, C. W., & Giardino, E. R. *A Practical Guide to the Evaluation of Child Physical Abuse and Neglect.* Thousand Oaks, CA: Sage. 1997.

Gostin, L. O., Lazzarini, Z., Alexander, D., Brandt, A. M., Mayer, K. H., & Silverman, D. C. HIV testing, counseling, and prophylaxis after sexual assault. *JAMA. 271,* 18, 1436–1444, 1994.

Green, S. M., Clark, R., Hostetler, M. A., Cohen, M., Carlson, D., Rothrock, S. G. Inadvertent ketamine overdose in children: Clinical manifestations and outcome. *Ann Emerg Med. 34,* 492–497, 1999.

Groth, A. N., & Burgess, A. W. Sexual dysfunction during rape. *New England J Medicine, 297,* 14, 764–766, 1977.

Gully, K. J., Britton, H., & Hansen, K. A new measure for distress during child sexual abuse examinations: The genital examination distress scale. *Child Abuse Negl. 23,* 1, 61–70, 1999.

Hadlich, S. F., & Kohl, P. K. Sexually transmitted diseases in children. *Dermatol Clin. 16,* 4, 859–861, 1998.

Hammerschlag, M. R. Sexually transmitted diseases in sexually abused children: Medical and legal implications. *Sex Transm Infect. 74,* 3, 167–174, 1998a.

Hammerschlag, M. R. The transmissibility of sexually transmitted diseases in sexually abused children. *Child Abuse Negl. 22,* 6, 623–635, 1998b.

Hampton, H. L. Care of the woman who has been raped. *N Engl J Med. 332,* 4, 234–237, 1995.

Hanson, R. F., Resnick, H. S., & Saunders, B. E. Factors related to the reporting of childhood sexual assault. *Child Abuse Negl. 23,* 6, 559–569, 1999.

Hazelwood, R., & Burgess, A., Eds. *Practical Aspects of Rape Investigation: A Multidisciplinary Approach.* New York: Elsevier. 1987.

Heger, A. H. Evaluation of sexual assault in the emergency department. *Top Emerg Med. 21,* 2, 46–57, 1999,

Heger, A. H., & Emans, S. J. *Evaluation of the Sexually Abused Child: Textbook and Atlas.* New York: Oxford University Press. 1992.

Hochmeister, M. N., Whelan, M., & Borer, U. V. Effects of toluidine blue and destaining reagents used in sexual assault examinations on the ability to obtain DNA profiles from postcoital vaginal swabs. *J Forensic Sci. 42,* 2, 316–319, 1997.

Holmes, W. S. Sexual abuse of boys: Definition, prevalence, correlates, sequelae and management. *JAMA. 280,* 21, 1855–1862, 1998.

International Association of Forensic Nurses. *Scope and Standards of Forensic Nursing Practice.* Pitman, NJ: International Association of Forensic Nurses. Available at: http://www.forensicnurse.org.

International Association of Forensic Nurses. *Sexual Assault Nurse Examiner Education Guidelines.* Pitman, NJ: International Association of Forensic Nurses. 1997. Available at: http://www.forensicnurse.org.

International Association of Forensic Nurses. Forensic nursing on trial: Virginia judge's decision in sexual assault case places forensic nursing in the forefront of law and medicine [Press release]. Pitman, NJ: International Association of Forensic Nurses. April 25, 2001. Available at: http://www.forensicnurse.org.

Jackman, T. When rape is in question, so are nurses' answers. *Washington Post.* April 2, 2001, B1, B4.

Jaeger, B. Sexual assault nurse examiners. *J Emerg Nurs. 24,* 5, 440–441, 1998.

Jansen, K. Using ketamine to induce the near-death experience: Mechanism of action and therapeutic potential. *Yearbook for Ethnomedicine and the Study of Consciousness.* 55–81, 1996.

Jaudes, P. K., & Martone, M. Interdisciplinary evaluations of alleged sexual abuse cases. *Pediatrics. 89,* 6, 1164–1168, 1992.

Jenny, C. Pediatrics and child sexual abuse: Where we've been and where we're going. *Pediatr Ann. 26,* 5, 284–286, 1997.

Jezierski, M. Sexual assault nurse examiner: A role with lifetime impact. *J Emerg Nurs. 18,* 2, 177–179, 1992.

Jones, J. S., Dunnuck, C., Rossman, L., Wynn, B. N., & Genco, M. Adolescent foley catheter technique for visualizing hymenal injuries in adolescent sexual assault. *Acad Emerg Med. 10,* 9, 1001–1004, 2003.

Jones, J. S., Rossman, L., Wynn, B. N., Dunnuck, C., & Schwartz, N. Comparative analysis of adult vs. adolescent sexual assault: Epidemiology and patterns of anogenital injury. *Acad Emerg Med. 10,* 8, 872–877, 2003.

Kaplan, D. W., Feinstein, R. A., & Fisher, M. Care of the adolescent sexual assault victim. *Pediatrics. 107,* b, 1476–1479, 2001.

Kaplan, S. J., Pelcovitz, D., & Labruna, V. Child and adolescent abuse and neglect research: A review of the past 10 years. *J Am Acad Child Adolesc Psychiatr. 38,* 10, 1214–1222, 1999.

Karch, S. B. Ketamine: The hot new drug of abuse. *Forensic Drug Abuse Advisor. 9,* 6, 1–2, 1997.

Kelley, S. J., & Yorker, B. C. The role of non-physician health care providers in the physical assessment and diagnosis of suspected child maltreatment: Results of a national survey. *Child Maltreat. 2,* 4, 331–340, 1997.

Kellogg, N. D. The pediatrician's role in child abuse: Position statement of the Texas pediatrician society, a chapter of the American Academy of Pediatrics, Committee on Child Abuse. *Tex Med. 95,* 2, 69–71, 1999.

Kenney, M. J. A sexual assault record. *J Emerg Nurs. 20,* 6, 560–561, 1994.

Kerns, D. L. Establishing a medical research agenda for child sexual abuse: Historical perspective and executive summary. *Child Abuse Negl. 22,* 6, 453–465, 1998a.

Kerns, D. L. Triage and referrals for child sexual abuse medical examinations: Which children are likely to have positive medical findings? *Child Abuse Negl. 22,* 6, 515–518, 1998.

Kiffe, B. *Perceptions: Responsibility Attributions of Rape Victims* [Thesis]. Augsburg College, Minneapolis, MN. 1996.

King, N. J., Tonge, B. J, & Mullen, P. Treating sexually abused children with post-traumatic stress symptoms: A randomized clinical trial. *J Am Acad Child Adolesc Psychiatry. 39,* 11, 1347–1355, 2000.

Kivlahan, C., Kruse R., & Furnell, D. Sexual assault examinations in children: The role of a statewide network of health care providers. *American J Diseases in Childhood. 146,* 11, 1365–1370, 1992.

Koss, M. P., Koss, P. G., Woodruff, W. J. Deleterious effects of criminal victimization on women's health and medical utilization. *Arch Intern Med. 151,* 2, 342–347, 1991.

Krugman, R. D. Child abuse and neglect: A worldwide problem. *Child Abuse Negl. 19*(3) 1995.

Lamb, M. E., Sternberg, K. J., & Esplin, P. W. Conducting investigative interviews of alleged sexual abuse victims. *Child Abuse Negl. 22,* 8, 813–823, 1998.

Lancon, J. A., Haines, D. E., & Parent, A. D. Anatomy of the shaken baby syndrome. *Anat Rec. 253,* 1, 13–18, 1998.

Lang, K. *Sexual Assault Nurse Examiner Resource Guide for Michigan Communities.* Okemos, MI: Michigan Coalition against Domestic and Sexual Violence. 1999.

Lauber, A., & Souma, M. Use of toluidine blue for documentation of traumatic intercourse. *Obstet & Gynecol. 60,* 5, 644–648, 1982.

LeBeau, M., Andollo, W., & Hearn, W. L. Recommendations for toxicological investigations of drug-facilitated sexual assaults. *J Forensic Sci. 44,* 1, 227–230, 1999.

Ledray, L. E. Counseling rape victims: The nursing challenge. *Perspectives in Psychiatric Care. 26,* 2, 21–27, 1990.

Ledray, L. E. The sexual assault examination: Overview and lessons learned in one program. *J Emer Nurs. 18,* 3, 223–230, 1992.

Ledray, L. E. Sexual assault nurse clinician: An emerging area of nursing expertise. *AWHONN's Clinical Issues in Perinatal and Women's Health Nursing. 4,* 2, 180–190, 1993.

Ledray, L. E. Sexual assault: Clinical issues: Sexual assault evidentiary exam and treatment protocol. *J Emerg Nurs. 21,* 21, 355–359, 1995.

Ledray, L. E., & Arndt, S. Examining the sexual assault victim: A new model for nursing care. *J Psychosocial Nursing Mental Health Services. 32,* 7–12, 1994.

Levitt, C. Further technical considerations regarding conducting and documenting the child sexual abuse medical examination. *Child Abuse Negl. 22,* 6, 567–568, 1998.

Lynch, L., & Faust, J. Reduction of distress in children undergoing sexual abuse medical examination. *J Pediatr. 132,* 2, 296–299, 1998.

McCann, J. Use of the colposcope in childhood sexual abuse examinations. *Pediatr Clin North Am. 37,* 4, 863–880, 1990.

McCann, J. The appearance of acute, healing, and healed anogenital trauma. *Child Abuse Negl. 22,* 6, 605–615, 1998.

McCauley, J., Guzinski, G., Welch, R., Gorman, R., & Osmers, F. Toluidine blue in the corroboration of rape in the adult victim. *Am J Emerg Med. 5,* 2, 105–108, 1987.

Merritt, D. F. Evaluation of vaginal bleeding in the preadolescent child. *Semin Pediatr Surg. 7,* 1, 35–42, 1998.

Miller, T. R., Cohen, M. A., & Wiersema, B. *Victim Costs and Consequences: A New Look.* Washington, DC: National Institute of Justice. 1996.

Mok, J. Y. When is HIV an issue after child sexual abuse? *Arch Dis Child. 75,* 1, 85–87, 1996.

Monk, M. Interviewing suspected victims of child maltreatment in the emergency department. *J Emerg Nurs. 24,* 1, 31–34, 1998.

Muram, D. Child sexual abuse: Genital tract findings in prepubertal girls: Comparison of colposcopic and unaided examinations. *Am J Obstet Gynecol. 160,* 333–335, 1989.

Muram, D. A., Aiken, M. M., & Strong, C. Children's refusal of gynecologic examinations for suspected sexual abuse. *J Clin Ethics. 8,* 2, 158–164, 1997.

Muram, D., Arheart, K. L., & Jennings, S. G. Diagnostic accuracy of colposcopic photographs in child sexual abuse evaluations. *J Pediatr Adolesc Gynecol. 12,* 2, 588–561, 1999.

Muram, D., & Laufer, M. R. Limitations of the medical evaluation for child sexual abuse. *J Reprod Med. 44,* 12, 993–999, 1999.

National Center for Injury Protection and Control Fact Sheet. Atlanta, GA: Centers for Disease Control and Prevention. 1999.

National Center for Victims of Crime and Crime Victims Research and Treatment Center. *Rape in America: A Report to the Nation.* Arlington, VA: National Center for Victims of Crime. 1992.

National Center for Victims of Crime. *Issues: Payment for Forensic Exams.* Prepared for the 2001 Sexual Assault Response Team (SART) Conference. 2001. Available at: http://www.ncvc.org/policy/issues/forensicexams/.

National Center for Victims of Crime. Payment of sexual assault forensic exams. *Victim Policy Pipeline.* 7, 1, 2001.

National Institute of Justice. *The Extent and Costs of Crime Victimization: A New Look.* Washington, DC: U.S. Department of Justice, Office of Justice Programs. 1996.

Nieves-Khouw, F. C. Recognizing victims of physical and sexual abuse. *Crit Care Nurs Clin North Am. 9,* 2, 141–148, 1997.

Norvell, M. K., Benrubi, G. I., & Thompson, R. J. Investigation of microtrauma after sexual intercourse. *J Reprod Med. 29,* 269–271, 1984.

Osatlin, A., & Short, L. M. *Intimate partner violence and sexual assault: A guide to training materials and programs for health care providers.* Atlanta, GA: Centers for Disease Control and Prevention, National Center for Injury Prevention and Control. 1998.

Osborn, M., & Bryan, S. Patient care guidelines: Evidentiary examination in sexual assault. *J Emerg Nurs. 15,* 3, 284–290, 1989.

Paolucci, E. O., Genuis, M. L., & Violato, C. A meta-analysis of the published research on the effects of child sexual abuse. *J Psychol. 135,* 1, 17–36, 2001.

Paradise, J. E., Finkel, M. A., & Beiser, A. S. Assessment of girls' genital findings and the likelihood of sexual abuse. *Arch Pediatr Adolesc Med. 151,* 9, 883–891, 1997.

Pasqualone, G. A. Forensic RNs as photographers: Documentation in the ED. *J Psychoso Nurs. 34,* 10, 47–53, 1996.

Patterson, J. J. Honing our clinical awareness of sexual abuse. *J Am Osteopath Assoc. 89,* 5, 617, 1989.

Persaud, D. I., Squires, J. E., & Rubin-Remer, D. Use of foley catheter to examine estrogenized hymens for evidence of sexual abuse. *J Pediatr Adolesc Gynecol. 10,* 2, 83–85, 1997.

Petrak, J. A., Skinner, C. J., Claydon, E.J. The prevalence of sexual assault in a genitourinary medicine clinic: Service implications. *Genitourin Med. 71,* 2, 98–102. 1995.

Pharris, M. D., & Ledray, L. E. Consent and confidentiality in the care of the sexually assaulted adolescent. *J Emerg Nurs. 23,* 3, 279–281, 1997.

Poliak, L., & Chang, E. Nancy Cabelus: Bringing forth justice: Sexual assault nurse examiners. *Am J Nurs. 104,* 9, 94–95, 2004.

Pressel, D. M. Evaluation of physical abuse in children. *Am Fam Physician. 61,* 10, 3057–3064, 2000.

Rand M. *Changes 1996–7 with Trends.* Washington, DC: U.S. Department of Justice, Office of Justice Programs, Bureau of Justice Statistics, National Crime Victimization Survey, Criminal Victimization 1997. Publication No. NCJ 173385. 1998.

Resnick, H., Acierno, R., & Holmes, M. Prevention of post-rape psychopathology: Preliminary findings of a controlled acute rape treatment study. *J Anxiety Disord. 13,* 4, 359–370, 1999.

Ricci, L. Medical forensic photography of the sexually abused child. *Child Abuse Neglect. 12,* 305–310, 1998.

Robinson, A. J., Watkeys, J., & Ridgway, G. L. Sexually transmitted organisms in sexually abused children. *Arch Dis Child. 79,* 4, 356–358, 1998.

Rodgers, G. D. Sequelae of sexual assault. *Primary Care Update for Ob/Gyns. 4,* 4, 143–146, 1997.

Rogers D. Physical aspects of alleged sexual assaults. *Med Sci Law. 36,* 2, 117–122, 1996.

Rothbaum, B. O. A controlled study of eye movement desensitization and reprocessing in the treatment of posttraumatic stress disordered sexual assault victims. *Bull Menninger Clin. 61,* 3, 317–334, 1997.

Roye, C. F., & Coonan, P. R. Emergency! Adolescent rape. *Am J Nurs. 97,* 4, 45, 1997.

Santucci, K. A., Nelson, D. G., & McQuillen, K. K. Wood's lamp utility in the identification of semen. *Pediatrics. 104,* 6, 1342–1344, 1999.

Satin, A. J., Hemsell, D. L., Stone, I. C. Jr, Theriot, S. & Wendel G.D. Jr. Sexual assault in pregnancy. *Obstetrics and Gynecology. 77,* 710–714, 1991.

Saunders, B. E., Kilpatrick, D. G., & Hanson, R. F. Prevalence, case characteristics, and long-term psychological correlates of child rape among women: A national survey. *Child Maltreat. 4,* 3, 187–200, 1999.

Savino, J. O., & Turvey, B. E., Eds. *Rape Investigation Handbook*. New York: Elsevier. 2005.

Schiff, A. F. Examination and treatment of the male rape victim. *Southern Medical J. 73,* 1498–1502, 1980.

Schwartz, R. H., & Weaver, A. B. Rohypnol the date rate drug. *Clin Ped. 36,* 321, 1998.

Scott, D. L., Schelbe, D. T., & White, L. J. An important question in the evaluation of sexual assault victims. *Acad Emerg Med. 4,* 4, 329–330, 1997.

Shapiro, R. How to interpret results of a child sexual abuse examination: What conditions may be mistaken for sexual abuse? In D. A. DePanifilis, Ed., *Handbook for Child Protection Practice*. Thousand Oaks, CA: Sage. 2000a.

Shapiro, R. The medical evaluation for possible child sexual abuse: When it is needed, who should provide it, what will be done and how to prepare the child? In D. A. DePanfilis, Ed., *Handbook for Child Protective Practice*. Thousand Oaks, CA: Sage. 2000b.

Siegel, R. M., Schubert, C. J., & Myers, P. A. The prevalence of sexually transmitted diseases in children and adolescents evaluated for sexual abuse in Cincinnati: Rationale for limited STD testing in prepubertal girls. *Pediatrics. 96,* 6, 1090–1094, 1995.

Simmons, M., & Cupp, M. J. Use and abuse of flunitrazepam. *Ann Pharmacotherapy. 32,* 117–119, 1998.

Skinner, C. J., & Forster, G. The coexistence of physical and sexual assault. *Am J Obstet Gynecol. May, 172,* 5, 1644, 1995.

Sloan, L. Sexual assault nurse examiners: The new challenges. *Sex Assault Report. 2,* 6, 81–96, 1999.

Smith, K., Holmseth, J., Macgregor, M., & Letourneau, M. Sexual assault response team: Overcoming obstacles to program development. *J Emerg Nurs. 24,* 4, 365–367, 1998.

Smock, W. S., Nichols, G. R., & Fuller, P. M. Development and implementation of the first clinical forensic medicine training program. *J Forensic Sci. 38,* 4, 835–839, 1993.

Socolar, R. R. Physician knowledge of child sexual abuse. *Child Abuse Negl. 20,* 8, 783–790, 1996.

Socolar, R. R., Raines, B., & Chen-Mok, M. Intervention to improve physician documentation and knowledge of child sexual abuse: A randomized, controlled trial. *Pediatrics. 101,* 5, 817–824, 1998.

Spohn, C., & Horney, J. *Rape law reform: A grassroots revolution and its impact*. New York: Plenum. 1992.

Springs, F. E., & Friedrich, W. N. Health risk behaviors and medical sequelae of childhood sexual abuse. *Mayo Clin Proc. 67,* 527–532, 1992.

Starling, S. P., Sirotnak, A. P., & Jenny, C. Child abuse and forensic pediatric medicine fellowship curriculum statement. *Child Maltreat. 5,* 1, 58–62, 2000.

Stephenson, T. & Bialas, Y. Estimation of the age of bruising. *Arch Dis Child. 74,* 1, 53–55, 1996.

Teixeira, R. G. Hymenal colposcopic examination in sexual offenses. *Am J Forensic Med Pathol. 2,* 209–214, 1981.

Tintinalli, J. E., & Hoelzer, M. Clinical findings and legal resolution in sexual assault. *Annals of Emerg Med. 14,* 5, 447–453, 1985.

Tjaden, P., & Thoennes, N. *Full Report of the Prevalence, Incidence, and Consequences of Violence Against Women*. Washington, DC: U.S. Department of Justice, Office of Justice Programs. NCJ 183781. 2000.

Tucker, S., Ledray, L. E., & Werner, J. S. Sexual assault evidence collection. *Wis Med J. 89,* 7, 407–411, 1990.

Ullman, S. Do social reactions to sexual assault victims vary by support provider? *Violence and Victims. 11,* 143–156, 1996.

Underhill, R. A., & Dewhurst, J. The doctor cannot always tell: Medical examination of the "intact" hymen. *The Lancet. 1,* 375–376, 1978.

U.S. Department of Health and Human Services, Administration on Children, Youth, and Families, Children's Bureau. *Child Maltreatment 2000: Reports from the States to the National Child Abuse and Neglect Data System (NCANDS)*. Washington, DC: U.S. Department of Health and Human Services. 2002.

U.S. Department of Health and Human Services, Administration on Children, Youth, and Families, Children's Bureau. *Child Abuse and Neglect State Statutes Series Compendium of Laws: Reporting Laws*. Washington, DC: National Clearinghouse on Child Abuse and Neglect Information. 2002.

U.S. Department of Health and Human Services, Administration on Children, Youth, and Families, Children's Bureau. *Statutes at a Glance 2002: Mandatory Reporters of Child Abuse and Neglect*. Child Abuse and Neglect State Statutes Series. Washington, DC: National Clearinghouse on Child Abuse and Neglect Information. 2002.

U.S. Department of Justice. *Criminal victimization 2000: Changes 1999–2000, with Trends 1993–2000, Bulletin*. Washington, DC: U.S. Department of Justice, Office of Justice Programs. NCJ 187007. 2001.

U.S. Department of Justice. *Sexual Assault Nurse Examiner (SANE) Programs: Improving the Community Response to Sexual Assault Victims*. Washington, DC: U.S. Department of Justice, Office of Justice Programs. NCJ 186366. 2001.

U.S. Department of Justice. *Sourcebook of Criminal Justice Statistics, 2000*. Washington, DC: U.S. Department of Justice, Bureau of Justice Statistics. NCJ 190251. 2001.

U.S. Department of Justice. *Criminal victimization, 1996: Changes 1995–96 with trends 1993–96*. Washington, DC: Bureau of Justice Statistics. 1997.

U.S. Department of Justice, Office on Violence Against Women. *A national protocol for sexual assault medical forensic examinations: Adults/adolescents*. Washington, DC: Office of Violence Against Women, 2004.

Uttley, L., & Petraitis, C. Rape survivors and emergency contraception: Substandard care at hospital emergency rooms. *Prochoice Ideas*. 3–4, 2000.

Veronen, L. J., & Kilpatrick, D. G. Self-reported fears of rape victims: A preliminary investigation. *Behav Modif. 4,* 383–396, 1980.

Voelker, R. Experts hope team approach will improve the quality of rape exams. *JAMA. 275,* 973–974, 1996.

Waibel-Duncan, M. K., & Sanger, M. Understanding and reacting to the anogenital exam: Implications for patient preparation. *Child Abuse Negl. 23,* 3, 281–286, 1999.

Walter, H. Genital pathology: Its impact on the interpretation of signs of genital trauma. *J Clin Forensic Med. 5,* 2, 85–89, 1998.

Woodling, B. A., & Heger A. The use of the colposcope in the diagnosis of sexual abuse in the pediatric age group. *Child Abuse Neglect. 10,* 111–114, 1986.

Woodtli, M. A., & Breslin, E. Violence-related content in the nursing curriculum: A national study. *J Nurs Ed. 35,* 8, 367–377, 1996.

Xenarios, S., Reichert, K., & Giordano, L. Implementing a multidisciplinary sexual assault forensic examiner program in an urban teaching hospital setting. Paper presented at the National Sexual Violence Prevention Conference: Coming Together to End Sexual Assault, Dallas, TX, 2000.

Young, W. W., Bracken, A. C., & Goddard, M. A. Sexual assault: Review of a national model protocol for forensic and medical evaluation. *Obstet Gynecol. 80,* 5, 878–883, 1992.

Zorza, J. Effects of childhood sexual abuse on male survivors. *Sexual Assault Report. 3,* 1, 1–13, 1999a.

Zorza, J. Male rape: Men raping men. *Sexual Assault Report. 2,* 4, 1–2, 1999b.

7 Interpersonal Violence

CONTENTS

7.1 THE SCOPE OF THE PROBLEM

Violence that hits home has many names: domestic violence, spousal abuse, interpersonal violence (IPV), and family violence. No matter the nomenclature, IPV is a serious problem with sweeping implications for men, women, and children throughout the human life span. Although statistics are disputed frequently, the CDC (2000) estimates that up to one quarter of the U.S. population is affected by some type of IPV. The determination of incidence and prevalence is made more difficult by the fact that IPV can be acute or chronic, subtle or extreme. According to *Confronting Chronic Neglect: The Education and Training of Health Professionals on Family Violence,* published by The National Academies of Sciences (2000), violence is generally divided into four categories:

1. Physical violence
2. Sexual violence
3. The threat of physical or sexual violence
4. Psychological or emotional abuse

Victims of IPV include both women and men, in heterosexual and same-sex relationships, but women abused by current or former intimate male partners are the most frequently abused and sustain the highest rates of injury. Lifetime incidence rates vary widely, depending on the type of violence assessed, but they tend to be in the 15 percent to 30 percent range. In contrast, intimate partner violence accounts for 3 percent of violence against men, and rates of violence by women against men are generally lower.

In the mid-1980s, U.S. surgeon generals began drawing attention to domestic violence and the act of victimization by an intimate partner. Men are the perpetrators in 90 percent of all reported domestic assaults, and women are 10 times as likely as men to be injured in episodes of domestic abuse. Among female murder victims in this country, about one third are slain by their husbands or boyfriends each year, whereas only 4 percent of all male victims are killed by their wives or girlfriends (Bachman, 1994; Zawitz, 1994).

In 2004, advocates and activists celebrated the 10th anniversary of the landmark Violence Against Women Act (VAWA), the ground-breaking legislation and policy that addressed violence, abuse, and assault against women. A report by Congressional Research Service (CRS) on the VAWA and its impacts stated that the law helped define the problem and enabled the health care, law enforcement, and legal communities to start putting their collective arms around this growing problem. It also stated that for the first time, IPV was being viewed as a serious crime, rather than a private family issue or personal problem. However, the report indicates that many victims, even with the passage of a decade, fail to report abuse because they still believe it is a private matter, or for fear of retaliation from the abuser. The CRS found the following:

- From 1998 to 2000, states passed more than 650 laws to combat violence, sexual assault, and stalking.
- From 1993 to 2001, the NCVS found that violence against women was cut in half from 1.1 million nonfatal violent crimes in 1993 to 588,490 female victims in 2001.
- The percentage of women who experienced violence from an intimate partner and reported it increased from 48 percent in 1993 to 59 percent in 1998. The report attributes this to stronger arrest policies (Family Violence Prevention Fund, 2004).

McFarlane et al. (2005) sought to describe the characteristics and consequences of sexual assault within intimate relationships specific to racial or ethnic group, compare the findings to a similar group of physically assaulted women, and measure the risk of reassault after victim contact with justice and health services. The researchers conducted a personal interview survey of 148 African American, Hispanic, and White English- and Spanish-speaking abused women seeking a protection order. Extent of sexual assault, prevalence of rape-related STDs and pregnancy, symptoms of PTSD and depression, and risk of reassault after treatment were measured. Sixty-eight percent of the physically abused women reported sexual assault; 15 percent of the women attributed one or more STDs to sexual assault, and 20 percent of the women experienced a rape-related pregnancy. Sexually assaulted women reported significantly more PTSD symptoms compared with nonsexually assaulted women. One significant difference occurred between ethnic groups and PTSD scores. Regardless of sexual assault or no assault, Hispanic women reported significantly higher mean PTSD scores compared with African American women and White women. The risk of sexual reassault was decreased by 59 percent and 70 percent for women who contacted the police or applied for a protection order, respectively, after the first sexual assault. Receiving medical care decreased the woman's risk of further sexual assault by 32 percent.

Stark, Flitcraft, and Frazier (1997) and McLeer and Anwar (1989) report that the first prevalence studies of domestic violence in the medical setting, which were conducted in hospital EDs, demonstrated that domestic violence accounted for 22 percent to 35 percent of women seen in the ED. Studies of patients in internal medicine, obstetrics, and family practice clinics have been conducted to estimate the prevalence of domestic violence seen in the primary-care setting. According to these studies, 12 percent to 28 percent of outpatients in these settings have reported current involvement in violent relationships. In the studies of lifetime experience with violence, between 28 percent and 54 percent of patients reported having lived with a violent partner at some previous time (Elliott & Johnson, 1995; Hamberger, Saunders, & Hovey, 1992; Gin et al., 1991; Rath, Jarratt, & Leonardson, 1989). These rates are much higher than those of the national incidence and prevalence studies (Elliott & Johnson, 1995; Koss, Koss, & Woodruff, 1991; Saunders, Hamberger, & Hovey, 1993), which documented that battered women are more frequent users of health care services than women who are not battered.

7.2 DOMESTIC VIOLENCE IN URBAN VERSUS RURAL SETTINGS

To date, most of what is known about the prevalence of domestic violence in rural settings comes from federal incidence and prevalence statistics that are based on the definition of rural as a nonmetropolitan area comprising sparsely populated areas that include cities with populations of less than 50,000. According to these statistics, women have the same risk of experiencing domestic violence regardless of where they live, although women living in central cities are more vulnerable to all types of violent crime perpetrated by strangers. Marilou Johnson, MD, and Barbara A. Elliott, PhD, compared the domestic violence experiences of female patients in rural outpatient clinics with what the authors learned from their earlier research about the prevalence and characteristics of domestic violence among women patients in the larger community setting. The study's sample was comprised of women seen in one family practice clinic (FPC) in a city of 85,000 people, as well as in two FPCs in rural communities of less than 10,000. Of the 219 women seen in all three clinics, 200 were eligible by study parameters, and 127 participated. The women seen in the rural clinics were significantly older than those served by the clinic in the largest community, and they had significantly more and older children. The rural women were also less likely to be employed and were more likely to have either dropped out of high school or not to have pursued education beyond high school.

Elliott and Johnson (1995) found that 46 percent of the 127 women interviewed reported some experience with violence; 21 percent reported ongoing abuse by their current partner, and 28 percent reported violence in past relationships. Twenty-two women (17 percent) reported violence only in their current relationship, 31 (24 percent) only in past relationships, and 4 (3 percent) reported violence in both past and ongoing relationships. There was only one difference between women battered in the larger community compared with those battered in rural settings: Involvement in an ongoing abusive relationship was significantly more common among rural women than among women in the city (25 percent vs. 12 percent). The researchers found that the women reported various abusive experiences. Some form of physical abuse was reported by 37 women (29 percent); sexual abuse was reported by 19 women (15 percent), and threats involving weapons by 118 women (4 percent). Every woman who reported physical violence also reported emotional and social abuse. Twenty-three percent of the women with a history of abuse—10 percent of the entire sample—reported experiencing physical abuse and threats with weapons, in addition to emotional and social abuse. Twenty-one percent of those with any history of abuse had experienced emotional and social abuse only. For the group with a past history of abuse, 11 percent reported emotional and social abuse only, whereas 31 percent of those currently in an abusive relationship reported emotional and social abuse only. When asked to detail the frequency of abusive episodes, 13 currently abused women commented. Six of these women reported that abusive events tended to occur at least once a week, and for eight of the women, physical violence occurred at least every three months. Five women reported a single episode of physical violence. The researchers say that correlations among the types of abuse indicate that women commonly experience more than one type of domestic violence; moderate battery and severe battery often occur together. Threatened or actual use of weapons does not often occur with severe battery or sexual violence, although it usually accompanies emotional and social abuse. Sexual abuse also accompanies moderate battery. Of the women reporting moderate battery and sexual violence, 62 percent also reported severe battery. Interestingly, sexual abuse was not correlated with social abuse.

Elliott and Johnson looked at the purpose of their participants' medical visits on the day of the interview. Of those who had never been battered, 38 percent were in the clinic for preventive care, including physical and prenatal examinations. Only half as many of the women currently being abused were being seen for preventive visits; 81 percent of them had come in for episodic care with specific complaints, including neck stiffness, twisted ankles, refills of antidepressant medication, migraine headaches, injured arms, sinus infection, hip pain, and depression. The primary reasons for the clinic visit given by women who had been abused in the past included depression, leg injury, sinus infection, amenorrhea, and pelvic pain, although more of them came for preventive care than currently abused women did.

In their interviews of study participants, Elliott and Johnson heard vivid stories about the severity and frequency of physical violence, and the women's fears that they were going to be killed. They reported that several women said they had been beaten during pregnancy, and one reported that she lost a pregnancy as a result of a beating. Another woman reported an episode in which she was forcibly held in a door frame for 30 minutes. Still another woman described having her head banged on the sidewalk, and another told of being shoved down the steps and dragged through the hallway by her hair. Many women reported acts of physical violence that occurred at least once a week, and fear of an upcoming violent episode was a constant theme. One woman reported that if more than a week went by between abusive episodes, she "huddled around the corner waiting for what would come next." At least two of the women reported being beaten or choked as they slept. Expressions of violence also included weapons. The husband of one woman cleaned his guns during arguments. Other men reportedly threw kitchen knives at their partners or actually held a knife blade to their throats.

Some women reported that their partners threatened to kill them and then take their own lives. One man wrote suicide letters to his children during an initial separation from his wife, and another held a loaded gun to his head in front of his daughter and her friend. Despite being divorced from her husband for four years, another woman stated that her biggest fear was that "I'll be walking around one day and he will simply kill me." When asked how she coped with such a frightening threat to her life, still another woman explained that she never really thought of the danger of it, but that she had to "keep a sort of even tone" to her thoughts so that she would not lose her mind. Equally striking was the woman whose husband held a loaded gun to her head every day. She denied being abused, saying, "My face isn't covered with bruises like those women in the posters."

The women also reported sexual abuse that intensified the sexual humiliation and degradation they experienced. When asked if she had been forced to have sex, one woman explained that she had not been physically forced but had been asked to do "terrible things which I went along with because I didn't know any better." For some women, sexual humiliation became public. Over the course of their marriage, one man frequently made sexually explicit and degrading remarks about his wife in public, usually in front of their friends. Several women reported being forced to have intercourse when their partners were drunk, and another reported that if she wanted something, she had to earn it by having sex with her husband; toward the end of this pair's relationship, however, he would simply throw her on the floor and rape her.

Elliott and Johnson say, "An insidious form of abuse that accompanies physical violence is the gradual social and psychological isolation created by the batterer." Regardless of location, most of the women participating in this study reported being isolated from their friends and family. Rural women live with an additional dimension of separation: By living in a rural area, the batterer ensures geographic isolation. One woman who lived 13 miles out of town reported that no car was available to her because either she did not have her partner's permission to use it or he intentionally disabled the car. Several rural women also reported that they had been regularly left to care for their small children without access to vehicles until medical emergencies convinced their partners to leave a car at home "for the sake of the kids."

Elliott and Johnson say their study underscores the need for health care providers to have a high index of suspicion regarding potential cases of domestic violence. They write, "Women in battering relationships present to family practice clinics primarily for episodic care. Therefore, if physicians ask about violence only during extended visits, such as those for preventive care, these women will be missed." They add, "The prevalence rates and the characteristics of violence experienced by women documented in our study indicate that physicians should routinely screen their patients for battery, educate all patients about domestic violence, assess the level of danger, review safety plans with their patients, and refer those who are living with its consequences. This screening process will help identify women in abusive relationships."

7.3 THE HEALTH CARE SYSTEM'S RESPONSE TO INTERPERSONAL VIOLENCE

In Improving the Health and Mental Health Care Systems' Responses to Violence Against Women, Toolkit to End Violence Against Women (2001), the Violence Against Women Office of the U.S. Justice Department outlines what health care and mental health care systems can do to make a difference in the lives of victims of violence. The white paper states:

> Millions of women are victims of sexual assault, dating or domestic violence, or stalking at some point in their lives, and the traumatic effects of this violence have a tremendous impact on survivors' physical and mental health. Too many victims never discuss incidents of violence with anyone or approach the health and mental health care, criminal justice, or other system for assistance. However, most women come to health care settings for regular exams, for treatment of specific problems both caused by and independent of the abuse, and for the care of their children and other family members. Health care providers may be the first and only professionals who see a battered woman or sexual assault victim. This makes the health and mental health care systems crucial points for early intervention and prevention for women who have survived or are experiencing violence.

The health effects of violence against women are extensive. In addition to possible acute injuries sustained during sexual assault or domestic violence, physical, sexual, and psychological abuse are linked to numerous adverse chronic health conditions, including arthritis, chronic neck or back pain, frequent migraines or other types of headaches, visual problems, STIs, chronic pelvic pain, increased gynecological symptoms, peptic ulcers, and functional or irritable bowel disease (Coker et al., 1997). Violence against women is also directly related to adverse mental health effects. Sexual assault trauma and domestic violence are often life-altering experiences resulting in numerous emotional and behavioral responses.

Kilpatrick, Edmunds, and Seymour (1992) found that sexual assault victims are more likely than other crime victims to attempt suicide, while Housekamp and Foy (1991) discovered that more than one third of sexual assault victims and battered women experience symptoms of depression. Kilpatrick et al. reported that 46 percent of domestic violence victims have symptoms of anxiety disorder, and victims of both sexual assault and domestic violence experience symptoms consistent with PTSD. Persistent sexual victimization occurring early in childhood can lead to a range of disorders that can arise anytime after the traumatic event and last indefinitely until appropriate treatment is received (Golding, 1999; Housekamp & Foy, 1991; Kilpatrick et al., 1985) Resulting behaviors, such as drug abuse or prostitution, might be deemed criminal and could result in the person being punished. Numerous studies nationwide consistently show prevalence rates of sexual abuse histories at 22 percent to 54 percent among women receiving case management mental health services and 50 percent to 70 percent among women in inpatient psychiatric facilities (Briere et al., 1997; Craine, Henson, Collier, & MacLean, 1998; Nibert, Cooper, & Crossmaker, 1989).

Many health care and mental health care providers still do not view sexual assault, dating and domestic violence, and stalking as public health issues and lack the knowledge, skills, and incentives to intervene appropriately. For example, only 9 percent to 11 percent of the primary care physicians in California routinely screen patients for domestic violence during new patient visits, periodic checkups, and prenatal care (Rodriguez, Bauer, McLaughlin, & Grumbach, 1999). Friedman et al. (1992) found that patients and physicians at both a private and a public hospital favored the practice of doctors inquiring about physical and sexual abuse, yet 89 percent of the physicians never made such inquiries. Health problems of the magnitude described earlier require a broad public health approach with comprehensive prevention strategies and commitment to ongoing evaluation. When such strategies are effective, they can prevent health problems (primary prevention) or identify a problem in its earliest stages (secondary prevention). In this way, harm to individuals is reduced, and the long-term adverse impact on a patient's health (including mental health) is minimized. For example, early detection programs for breast, cervical, and prostate cancer can identify and treat these problems before the disease reaches advanced stages. When primary or secondary prevention strategies are not implemented or are ineffective, tertiary prevention—a strategy that limits the impact of an injury or disability once it has become serious—is needed.

Until recently, the health care system has addressed sexual assault and domestic violence predominantly through tertiary prevention strategies. Sexual assault programs handle crisis calls from victims and survivors, and shelters provide temporary housing for women and children seeking refuge from abuse. The criminal justice system reacts to violent incidents with sanctions for perpetrators. Similarly, health and mental health care professionals treat the presenting problem (suturing lacerations, setting broken bones, and prescribing antidepressants) usually without exploring the underlying problem. In one study of 476 consecutive women seen by an FPC in the midwest, 394 (82.7 percent) agreed to be surveyed. Of these patients, 22.7 percent had been physically assaulted by their partners within the last year, and 38.8 percent of them endured lifetime physical abuse. However, only six women said they had ever been asked about the occurrence of domestic violence by their physician (Hamberger et al., 1992).

If violence against women is to be stopped, screening and intervention in the health care setting must be supplemented with broad-based public education efforts that inform and address deep-seated attitudes and give people tools for action in the communities in which they live. Despite some gains, far too many Americans continue to hold attitudes that can be construed as excusing the sexual abuser or batterer for his behavior or blaming victims for precipitating the violence. These attitudes contribute to pervasive social norms that tolerate and permit abuse.

Almost every clinical health and mental health care provider treats victims of sexual assault and domestic violence, although most are unaware that their patients have formerly or recently been abused. Historically, health care providers have viewed violence against women as a social or legal issue or even as a private family problem, outside their purview and inappropriate to address in a clinical setting. Only recently has the situation begun to change. At the clinical care level, health care and mental health care institutions and systems are encouraged to implement changes designed to create comprehensive standards of care for victims of violence against women. The standards should include the following:

- Access to health and mental health care. Basic, quality, affordable services should be available to all women regardless of age, geographic or language barriers, sexual orientation, or ability to pay.
- Routine screening by trained health care providers. All adult and teenage women should be screened routinely for intimate partner violence following a screening protocol that ensures patient privacy, safety, and confidentiality. Resources must be invested to develop and test sexual assault screening instruments and to train providers across all health specialties on the use of these tools and appropriate referrals. Screening for violence based on observed injuries alone does not account for the toll of psychological abuse or unseen injuries and eliminates many opportunities for early intervention and prevention. By asking simple and direct questions regarding abuse and sexual assault, trained health care providers engage in vital prevention and early intervention by sending a message to women that violence against

them is a health issue, that they are not alone, and that health care providers know and care about sexual assault and domestic violence.

- Documenting violence against women. Acute incidents of sexual assault and domestic violence should be documented accurately, nonjudgmentally, and in detail in the medical record. Documentation of sexual and domestic violence improves both continuity and quality of care by allowing the provider to understand the impact of violence on current and future health problems or injuries. Proper documentation also facilitates reimbursement and referral to additional services, but confidentiality must be maintained throughout the process. Detailed documentation in the medical record also serves as compelling evidence when a victim seeks legal recourse. On a system level, a large number of documented abuse and sexual assault incidents justifies the allocation of additional dedicated services for victims in the medical and mental health care setting. However, more study is needed to determine the best approach to documenting an adult patient's history of child sexual abuse and adult nonacute sexual assault, given how prejudicial such information can be if used improperly.
- Intervention and referral. Once abuse is identified and documented, an appropriate response should ensue. This response can vary depending on the internal and community-based resources of the health care facility and the desires of each survivor. Multidisciplinary protocols that incorporate the roles and responsibilities of all staff who interact with victims of violence against women can ensure that victims receive the support and services they need. Although some health care facilities have in-house advocates to provide victims with resources and support, such as safety assessment and planning or counseling, others might need to partner with local sexual assault and domestic violence victim advocates and refer appropriately. Regardless of the setting, health care providers must develop culturally competent, creative, and effective strategies to assist victims. Development of a coordinated and collaborative system of referral, follow-up care, and onsite services is critical in improving the safety, recovery process, and health status of victims. Clinical interventions should be tailored to respond to the range of racial, ethnic, and socioeconomic characteristics of patients, as well as address the particular needs of women with disabilities and women of all ages and sexual orientations. Literacy levels should also be considered when developing screening questions and patient information.

The clear lesson of the past two decades of efforts to improve health care's response to violence against women is that the system must be engaged at every level to ensure that meaningful public health efforts and effective sustainable clinical interventions occur. Early efforts focused on creating protocols to guide the care of victims of domestic violence. Although the JCAHO mandated that health care settings develop protocols on identifying and responding to sexual assault and domestic violence, protocols unaccompanied by other strategies did not improve screening and intervention. Efforts shifted to supplementing protocols with training for individual providers on the dynamics of and responses to sexual assault and dating and domestic violence. Training, along with increasingly strengthened JCAHO requirements, successfully raised individual provider awareness of and sensitivity to the issue. Single providers, however, have often lacked the organizational support necessary to continue to respond to victims.

Those striving to improve the health care system's response to domestic violence began by training multidisciplinary teams consisting of nurses, physicians, advocates, social workers, and administrators. By organizing and training a range of stakeholders in an institution, awareness and response was more widespread, consistent, and long-lasting. These teams met with more success in screening and assisting victims through their policy change efforts, creating a multidisciplinary response, and instituting new clinical tools, but the demands of the increasingly complicated health care system, as well as staff turnover, still make routine screening and response difficult.

To address the particular needs of sexual assault victims who sought medical assistance soon after an assault, a multidisciplinary response was developed, coordinating crisis intervention services and professional forensic evidence collection when the victim wanted to report the assault to law enforcement. For these victims, a new area of medical specialization has evolved, the SANE or SAFE. SANEs are trained medical professionals who have advanced education and clinical preparation in the forensic examination of sexual assault victims and who partner with local victim advocates to provide support during the forensic exam and coordinate follow-up services. When a victim wants to report an assault to law enforcement, existing relationships between the SANE, victim advocate, and police department facilitate a victim-centered response. Some communities have established SARTs to coordinate these efforts. Protocols and individual and team training are all crucial, but they must be joined by broader reforms of institutions and policies that affect health care delivery and inform public health strategies, according to the Violence Against Women Office of the U.S. Justice Department. This agency suggests the following steps:

- Confidentiality of health records. An essential corollary to documentation of abuse in medical records is the confidentiality of these medical records. Women who have been sexually assaulted, abused, or stalked share with many other health care consumers concerns about inappropriate access to and use of medical record information by insurance companies, employers, and law enforcement agencies. In addition, victims of domestic violence have the added concern of potential perpetrator access. Few laws exist to prevent spousal access to medical records.
- Removing barriers to forensic sexual assault exams and related treatment. One problem is the practice of conditioning medical or forensic services to requirements that the victim report to law enforcement agencies or participate in court proceedings. Such practices compromise sexual assault survivors' access to the emergency health care services they might need and could place them at further risk.
- Mandatory reporting to law enforcement by health care providers. With increased recognition that violence against women is a public health issue, some jurisdictions have instituted policies that require a health care provider to report domestic violence, and sometimes sexual assault, to law enforcement authorities. Growing evidence suggests that mandatory reporting might not improve a patient's health and safety and might discourage some victims from seeking medical care. More research is needed on the unintended consequences of these policies and how they affect victims' safety and health before they are established in any more institutions.
- Creating reimbursement mechanisms, coding, and other incentives to provide care for victims of violence against women. Currently, no specific current procedural terminology (CPT) codes for domestic violence screening or intervention exist. However, diagnostic codes capture additional information such as the nature of the abuse and perpetrators. Although clinicians can use the general preventive medicine codes to bill for domestic violence screening performed in the context of a comprehensive preventive medicine assessment and preventive medicine counseling codes for domestic violence safety assessment and referral processes, there are many compelling reasons to develop codes specific to domestic violence screening and intervention. First, a specific billing code would provide a direct financial incentive to reward clinicians for the time spent screening and intervening in cases of domestic violence. Second, specific codes would facilitate the process of evaluating how frequently screening is being performed. Third, specific codes for screening and intervention would make it easier for population-based delivery systems to provide feedback to medical groups and individual clinicians on how well they are performing compared with national standards and peers. For example, a review of specific coding might reveal how many women per 1,000 were screened in cases of domestic violence or what percentage of screened women received an intervention. Measured performance can be tied to both financial and nonfinancial incentives to drive more rapid improvement. Finally, specific codes for domestic violence screening and intervention would indicate to the health care community that these services are as valuable as other services for which specific codes already exist. Appropriate use of existing diagnostic codes can be an important source of data about domestic violence and can be used by health plans and other population-based delivery systems to track incidence, associated costs, utilization patterns, and effectiveness of interventions. This type of administrative data can also be used by researchers to answer many important questions about how to design programs that will improve the health care system's response to victims of domestic violence. As documentation and coding for domestic abuse and dating violence is improved, issues concerning confidentiality of the information must be rigorously addressed.
- Financial and nonfinancial incentives that promote evaluation and intervention services for victims of domestic violence at all levels of the health care system must be developed and implemented. Purchasers, health plans, and other insurers might be motivated to "buy" or implement comprehensive domestic violence programs if they are presented with the business case for such programs. In addition to being paid for delivering domestic violence services, clinicians should be encouraged to improve performance. Institutions must prioritize the creation of comprehensive packaged services for victims of domestic violence. Models that require multifaceted responses including medical care, counseling, assessment, case management, and

mental health counseling and referrals should be used to create systems that encourage response to dating and domestic violence.

- Creating appropriate measures of health outcomes. Much of contemporary health care delivery is shaped by health-outcome measures. Many health issues have obvious means to measure successful treatment or intervention. Effective outcome measures must be established to guide care delivery to victims of violence against women.

7.3.1 Ways to Increase Understanding of Violence Against Women as a Critical Public Health Problem

1. Conduct public health campaigns about violence against women at the same level as other large-scale public education campaigns.
   - Communicate the serious consequences that violence against women has on all aspects of health and mental health so that the public no longer minimizes the problems or views them as solely private or criminal justice issues.
   - Encourage public health leaders, including the Secretary of Health and Human Services, the Surgeon General, and state and local public health figures, to continue to identify sexual assault, dating and domestic violence, and stalking as serious public health issues and call for comprehensive responses.
   - Emulate campaign strategies that addressed other health issues that were considered largely private or social in nature. Consider those that resulted in greater willingness of individual providers to screen and intervene and in patient willingness to turn to health care providers for assistance.
   - Integrate messages about violence against women into other health education campaigns. Look for opportunities to include information about sexual assault, dating and domestic violence, and stalking into education that targets behavior often associated with the aftereffects of sexual assault, including but not limited to teen pregnancy, unsafe sex, STDs, and alcohol and other drug use.
   - Target funds to develop campaigns that respond to a wide range of factors, such as race, ethnicity, socioeconomic level, age, disability, and literacy level. Research shows that linguistically and culturally appropriate campaigns are significantly more effective.
2. Educate all health care providers and public health professionals on violence against women.
   - Because violence affects so many aspects of physical and mental health and women enter the health care system through various types of providers, institutions, government health programs, and managed care systems, engage every type of provider, institution, and system in education efforts.
3. Develop professional school curricula that address violence against women.
   - Fully integrate information on violence against women into standard curriculums at all health care and public health professional schools.
   - Include information on the dynamics, epidemiology, and direct and indirect effects of sexual assault, dating and domestic violence, and stalking, as well as clinical skills such as screening, documentation, and response.
   - Although specialized sections on specific issues are necessary, integrate information about violence against women throughout course work whenever appropriate.
   - Offer specific modules on improving the cultural and linguistic competence of practices for all levels of providers. Integrate examples of culturally and linguistically competent practices and cases that deal with various patient populations in training that addresses violence against women.
4. As part of continuing education for providers, offer specific modules on violence against women, and recognize achievements in the field.
   - Ensure that training related to violence against women is a component providers receive to become or remain licensed to practice.
   - Involve sexual assault and domestic violence advocates and survivors in the development and implementation of continuing education on violence against women.
   - Include questions related to both the dynamics and effects of violence against women and appropriate clinical responses on licensure and certification examinations.
   - Provide training and promote effective clinical guidelines and standards of care that reflect routine screening, documentation, appropriate assessment, intervention, and referral.
   - Create association-wide member awareness campaigns around sexual assault, dating and domestic violence, and stalking.

- Target primary care, reproductive health, emergency, mental health, pediatric, and other specialty organizations that see women regularly.
- Integrate violence against women into association member recognition programs.
- Increase the availability of technical assistance and training for health care providers who want to become SANEs and professionals who want to improve multidisciplinary responses to sexual assault.
- Follow recommendations of the IAFN, which requires the completion of 40 contact hours approved through a recognized continuing education body or offered through a college or university.
- Participate in continuing education and ongoing training to maintain proficiency with new technologies and research findings.

5. Engage all types of providers and institutions.
    - Primary-care settings offer opportunities for early intervention, and even primary prevention, by identifying sexual or domestic abuse as a health issue in its early stages or before it begins.
    - Mental health professionals are key points of contact who see victims for problems of anxiety, depression, PTSD, suicide attempts, and other psychological problems highly associated with violence against women.
    - Obstetricians, gynecologists, women's health nurse practitioners, and nurse midwives are important players because sexual assault survivors often experience anxiety about pelvic examinations and because data suggest that the onset of abuse is often associated with pregnancy.
    - Pediatricians and pediatric nurse practitioners can identify victims of domestic violence and offer the resources and support necessary to stop the abuse before it takes its toll on the mothers and children they are treating.
    - SANEs see victims of sexual assault as well as victims of domestic violence.
    - Dentists and oral surgeons might see women for treatment of oral injuries, such as fractured jaws, and for regular check-ups, during which abuse can be identified by routine screening even in the absence of acute injuries. They might also have patients who have specific fears or reactions concerning their dental care because of a history of sexual assault.
    - Substance abuse counselors see many women who are victims of sexual assault and domestic violence and who use alcohol or other drugs as a way of coping with the trauma. Research has shown victimization to be a risk factor for substance abuse.
    - Specialists such as orthopedic and plastic surgeons, radiologists, and home health care nurses and attendants each have an important stake in identifying and responding to abuse among their patients. Pain management centers could see many women who suffer from chronic pain due to abuse.
    - Inpatient health care settings, such as psychiatric facilities and nursing homes, are urged to work with community sexual assault and domestic violence programs to provide training and develop policies and services that respond to the needs of patients who enter with a history of assault or who are assaulted while in the institution.
    - All types of health care organizations must be engaged, including community health centers; home health and visiting nurses agencies; managed care organizations; private hospitals and practices; alternative healing centers; Indian Health Services; military health entities; Women, Infants, and Children (WIC) and Medicaid programs; and state and federal public health departments and agencies.
    - Businesses and other health care purchasers can create the institutional support and incentives that promote training and an improved response by their providers and insurers.
6. Expand SANE programs to all communities throughout the country.
    - Increase the capacity of existing SANEs to address the complex health and forensic needs of victims, including the domestic violence victims experiencing forced sex by their partners.
    - Provide increased funding and technical assistance to support program development in underserved areas, in collaboration with local and state sexual assault programs and coalitions.
7. Design mental health services to respond to the needs of victims and survivors of sexual assault, dating and domestic violence, and stalking.
    - Designate funds to provide quality mental health services for treating the traumatic sequelae of abuse for victims of sexual assault, dating and domestic violence, and

stalking, including adult survivors of child sexual abuse living in rural areas.
- Develop collaborative models for addressing the social and advocacy needs and the psychological needs of survivors of sexual assault, dating and domestic violence, and stalking.
- Designate program and training resources to improve quality of care in public mental health systems to address trauma and its sequelae across the life span.
- Provide training for community mental health centers to address sexual assault and domestic violence for women diagnosed with serious mental illness and for women who are experiencing other mental health sequelae of sexual assault, dating and domestic violence, and stalking.
- Provide resources for sexual assault and domestic violence victim advocacy programs to provide onsite services and develop contractual arrangements with mental health providers and agencies to address the mental health sequelae of violence against women. Foster greater collaboration between mental health professionals, sexual assault victim advocates, alcohol and other drug abuse treatment providers, and criminal justice personnel.
- Develop curriculums and training materials for mental health providers (e.g., psychiatrists, psychologists, social workers, and marital and family therapists) to address issues faced by women who are being or have been sexually, emotionally, or physically abused.

8. Develop and support the widespread use of provider and institution clinical tools that respond to sexual assault and domestic violence.
   - Develop patient charts, new-patient intake forms, and other clinical tools that support appropriate screening, documentation, and response to victims of sexual assault, dating and domestic violence, and stalking.
   - Include prompts for providing sexual assault victims with information on available forensic medical examinations in sexual assault protocols, and ensure access to appropriate equipment and staff training on its proper use.
   - Post local, state, and national hotline telephone numbers for victims of sexual assault and domestic violence in all examination rooms and patient bathrooms.
   - Develop practitioner reference cards that address sexual assault, dating and domestic violence, and stalking. Include sexual assault and domestic violence information on Web sites designed for health care provider and patient reference.
   - Equip examination rooms with body maps available for documenting injuries. Equip EDs, acute care centers, and other sites that see injuries caused by domestic violence with instant cameras.
   - Scrutinize all standard tools to ensure they include information about violence against women.
9. Use funding, licensing, and credentialing mechanisms to ensure that health care institutions have relevant response protocols for violence against women.
   - Require grantees to have policies, protocols, training requirements, incentives, and other relevant responses to violence against women.
   - Create and strengthen guidelines regarding sexual assault, dating and domestic violence, and stalking, including guidelines for screening.
10. Fully protect the confidentiality of victims' health records.
    - Implement safeguards, under federal, tribal, and state laws, to ensure that health records of victims of sexual assault, dating and domestic violence, and stalking are not accessed inappropriately by insurance companies, employers, or spouses and partners. Protect privileged medical and mental health information from discovery and other legal actions during the course of a criminal proceeding.
    - Build into current policy necessary protections for patients who might be endangered under routine directory information, next of kin, and other practices in health care institutions. Allow victims to restrict access to their patient information.
    - Allow victims to request that bills and explanations of benefits be sent to alternate addresses.
    - Remove information regarding abuse from the records of victims and their children before releasing them to spouses or partners. Notify victims before any required release of abuse-related information to facilitate their safety planning.
    - Allow minors who lawfully receive care on their own to restrict access to records regarding abuse.

11. Reduce or eliminate cost and reporting requirements for victims needing forensic medical exams or related treatment after a sexual assault.
    - Earmark state funds to cover costs of forensic medical exams for victims of sexual assault without seeking reimbursement from the victim or from any public or private health insurance under which the victim might otherwise be covered.
    - Adopt current federal guidelines governing victim compensation agencies, which permit reimbursement of examination costs to hospitals and other medical facilities regardless of whether the assault is reported to law enforcement authorities.
    - Include care for acute symptoms and prophylaxis for pregnancy, STD transmission, and treatment for the hepatitis B virus when appropriate as part of emergency medical care associated with an assault.
12. Amend mandatory reporting laws regarding adult victims of violence to ensure that the laws increase victim safety and health status and do not deter women from seeking care.
    - Require patient consent—except in cases of gunshot wounds or life-threatening injuries—before health care providers report violent incidents to law enforcement agencies.
    - Increase awareness of the problems that arise from mandatory reporting for women who are undocumented and the subsequent immigration problems.
13. Create reimbursement mechanisms, coding, and other incentives to provide quality care to victims of violence against women.
    - Educate clinicians and medical coders on the importance of including the existing International Classification of Diseases, Ninth Revision (ICD-9) codes for adult abuse and e-codes, particularly those that describe the relationship of the perpetrator to the patient, either as primary or secondary diagnostic codes. Failure to add an adult abuse code to the medical record means that information about the root cause of an injury or illness is not captured and therefore might not be appropriately addressed in follow-up encounters.
    - Promote the use of existing ICD-9 codes, including the use of e-codes to define the relationship of the perpetrator to the patient, through medical coder professional organizations, national health care provider organizations, state medical boards, and the use of federal and state government advisories.
    - Develop and implement at least two CPT codes specific to domestic violence screening and intervention.
    - Develop the business case for domestic violence services in the health care setting.
    - Develop model incentive programs that reward purchasers, plans, other insurers, and clinicians for domestic violence screening and intervention.
14. Provide incentives for individual health care providers to address the violence against women issues of their patients.
    - Provide feedback on performance compared to peers and national standards.
    - Tie monetary rewards to attaining defined performance goals with respect to screening and intervention.
    - Provide public recognition for high performers (e.g., newspaper articles, plaques presented at medical society meetings).
    - Design and implement formal mechanisms to give providers feedback from patients who value these services.
    - Support the clinician's role in responding to sexual assault and domestic violence by developing in-house services for victims of sexual assault and domestic violence or by contracting with community organizations to provide onsite or on-call access to their specialized services.
15. Prioritize the creation of comprehensive packaged services for victims of sexual assault, dating and domestic violence, and stalking.
    - Develop models for delivering multifaceted responses, including medical care, counseling, assessment, case management, and mental health counseling and referrals.
    - Examine Medicaid program models that could reimburse health plans for the provision of patient education and case management, safety assessment, and referrals in violence against women cases in low-income communities.
16. Establish appropriate health outcome measures related to improved health care response to violence against women.
    - Convene a task force of leading advocates, survivors, health care providers, researchers, and federal representatives to create health plan employer data and information set measures for sexual assault and domestic violence.
    - Explore the full range of possible outcome measures, including decreased health care use, fewer secondary health effects related

to violence, and victim perception of improved physical and mental health status and safety.
- Develop and provide funds to implement a research agenda that establishes the medical evidence for effective intervention and improved health outcomes and increased safety.

17. Increase funding to improve the health and mental health care systems' response to violence against women.
    - Explore the creation of new funding streams that can be dedicated to improving the health and mental health care systems' responses to violence against women.
    - Earmark specific funding within state and local health department budgets for improving health care responses to sexual assault and domestic violence.
    - Provide funds for health care provider training, institutional reform, patient education, and public health campaigns to reflect the prevalence of violence and its impact on health costs.

7.4 HEALTH CARE PROVIDERS' ROLE IN IPV CASES

7.4.1 Attitudes of Health Care Providers Toward IPV

Moore, Zaccaro, and Parsons (1998) compared the education, attitudes, and practices related to domestic violence of nurses from three types of practice sites: public health, hospital, and physician's offices. The sample consisted of 275 nurses. The researchers found some differences in beliefs among the nurses, but even greater differences were identified in their behaviors. Only 54 percent of the nurses reported receiving education about domestic violence in formal or continuing education programs. Public health nurses were the most likely to have such education. In the total sample, 31 percent of nurses reported personal accounts of abuse or abuse toward family members. The researchers concluded that many nurses in this study lacked education about domestic violence, and that the provision of education about abuse and domestic violence is an important first step toward a change in nursing practice.

High rates of family violence and low rates of detection, reporting, and therapeutic intervention by health professionals are well documented. Tilden et al. (1994) attempted to determine what factors influence clinicians' decision making about identifying abuse and intervening with victims. Survey data about clinicians' experiences with and attitudes toward family violence were gathered through mailed questionnaires to a random sample of practicing clinicians in six disciplines. Data showed similarities within and wide differences among three groups of participants: dentists and dental hygienists, nurses and physicians, and psychologists and social workers. Overall, a third of the study participants reported having received no educational content on child, spouse, or elder abuse in their professional training programs. Those with education on the topic more commonly suspected abuse in their patients than those without; among all participants, spouse abuse was suspected more often than child abuse, whereas elder abuse was suspected infrequently. Significant numbers of participants did not view themselves as responsible for dealing with problems of family violence. Respondents indicated low confidence in and low compliance with mandatory reporting laws. The researchers concluded that there is a need for educators to expand curricula on family violence, and for legislators to reexamine mandatory reporting laws.

7.4.2 Training of Health Care Providers in IPV Issues

In 1998, the American Academy of Pediatrics (AAP) issued guidelines for pediatricians to screen for domestic violence and for residency programs to include domestic violence education. Bair-Merritt et al. (2004) attempted to assess chief residents' attitudes and training regarding domestic violence screening. A 53-question survey was mailed to the chief residents of 194 nonmilitary U.S. pediatric residency programs, and 68 percent of surveys were returned. Although 93 percent of chief residents felt that pediatricians should screen for domestic violence, only 21 percent screen every patient. Just 24 percent agreed or strongly agreed that they felt experienced in handling domestic violence cases. Although 60 percent of respondents said that they received 11 or more hours of residency training in how to handle child abuse, the majority (80 percent) received four hours or less of training. Seventy-one percent agreed or strongly agreed that pediatricians do not screen secondary to lack of training. The researchers conclude that although many pediatric chief residents believe that domestic violence is a significant pediatric health problem, screening practices are variable. They add, "Most chief residents feel that their training was not sufficient to make them comfortable screening for DV. Chief residents demonstrated openness to incorporating DV training into their programs, indicating a positive environment for DV curricula."

Several studies have demonstrated that textbooks for physicians and nurses are lacking in content addressing IPV issues. Parsons and Moore (1997) evaluated major texts in obstetrics and gynecology, primary care, and nursing for their content in the area of family violence. The study included 48 medical texts and 19 nursing texts published between 1990 and 1996. Key words and phrases were identified and indexes were searched; the minimum requirements for content on domestic violence included 12 issues identified as important. If the text contained any information on an issue, it received one point. A domestic violence content score was calculated, and a maximum score of 12 was possible. Textbooks were evaluated for content related to domestic violence as well as rape, child sexual abuse, abuse in pregnancy, and elder abuse. Thirty-seven percent of physician texts and 63 percent of nursing texts included some content on domestic violence. On the researchers' domestic violence content scale, 16 percent of medicine texts and 10 percent of nursing texts scored 9 to 12. The researchers concluded, "The availability of information on family violence is limited in both medical and nursing texts."

Appropriate educational preparation about violence prevention, assessment, and treatment provides critical knowledge and skills that enable nurses to provide competent care to violence survivors. Woodtli and Breslin (2002) conducted a national survey that examined changes in the extent, placement, and faculty responsible for violence-related content in baccalaureate nursing curricula since their original 1995 survey was conducted. This national study used a 31-item mailed questionnaire that requested demographic information; data related to course content, clinical experiences, curriculum and faculty development; curriculum evaluation; and recommendations. Usable questionnaires were returned from 395 (61 percent) of 648 programs surveyed. Findings indicated that content related to women, children, and suicide and self-destructive behavior was taught primarily in two to four hours; 46 percent of schools presented sexual and elder abuse content in one hour or in readings only; and related clinical experiences were primarily coincidental. The majority of schools (63 percent) reported no violence-related faculty development activities during the past four years despite previous indication of need. More than two thirds of programs (68 percent) did not systematically evaluate violence content, and three quarters had not developed violence-focused student competencies. Although small gains were found in hours of presentation in some content, the researchers discovered that little has changed in the nursing curriculum overall. The authors of the study call into question the relevance of nursing education to preparing students and faculty to address the social and health problems of increasing violence and abuse.

In *Intimate Partner Violence: A Death Sentence for Women*, Joellen W. Hawkins (2002), RNC, PhD, FAAN, says that nurse practitioners can play a valuable role in assisting victims of violence. "Making screening for violence an integral part of every patient visit will ensure that women know that our practice sites are safe places to talk about their concerns when they are ready and able to do so," she writes. "We should explore conflict in relationships, how women handle crises in their lives, and relate health concerns to abuse. We need to raise the index of suspicion when women present with recurrent health problems or injuries and children exhibit signs of witnessing violence." She points to Campbell, Sharps, Campbell, and Lopez (2002), who said, "Each entry point into a health care setting has the potential for initiating an intervention or referral to prevent or reduce further violence against women."

7.5 THE MENTAL AND PHYSICAL IMPACTS OF IPV

Numerous studies have documented IPV's impact on the health and well-being of adults and children. The effects of child abuse and neglect range from the negligible to severe injury and even death. Physical abuse can consist of single or multiple bruises, burns, fractures, abdominal injuries, and head injuries. The consequences of sexual abuse of a child depend on the age of the child, the duration of the abuse, the relationship of the child to the abuser, and the amount of coercion used to sustain the abusive relationship. Emotional neglect can lead to significant developmental, emotional, and behavioral problems later in life. In addition to the immediate effects of the mistreatment of children, there are well-documented, long-term consequences that can occur in adulthood, including increased risk for somatic, psychosomatic, and psychiatric problems. The effects of witnessing IPV in the home are not yet fully understood, but there is some evidence to suggest that there are emotional and developmental effects. As with other forms of IPV, the most severe medical consequence is death, and intimate partners constitute the largest single category of perpetrators in the homicide of women, according to the CDC (2000). Nonfatal intimate partner violence is also associated with a variety of physical, psychological, and psychosomatic complaints, including headache, chronic pain, gastrointestinal and gynecological symptoms, STDs, unintended pregnancies, urinary tract infections, depression and anxiety, suicide, substance abuse, and PTSD.

Tjaden and Thoennes (2000) found that of the 4.8 million cases of intimate partner physical and sexual abuse of women estimated annually, approximately 2 million resulted in injury to the victim, and of these, 552,192 resulted in medical treatment. Wisner (1999) states that intimate partner violence appears to be a significant predictor of hospitalizations, general clinic use, mental health service use, and out-of-plan referrals. Kimerling and Calhoun (1994) found that 72 percent of sexual assault victims in the study sample sought medical attention, and 19 percent sought psychiatric treatment.

The full economic cost of IPV has not been determined, but what is known suggests that it is quite high. Rudman

(2002) suggests that a hospitalized patient who has been identified as a victim of IPV will cost a median of $873 more than a patient with the same condition who has not been identified as a victim. Direct medical costs of care for victims of IPV are estimated at $1.8 billion annually (Miller et al., 1993). Between 850,000 and 1.5 million women are assaulted by their partners each year. The 2001 crime statistics showed that physical abuse (including sexual assaults) occurred in 172 women every 60 minutes. These same statistics showed that an episode of rape occurred every two minutes, and that a woman was abused by her male partner every nine seconds. In 1998, estimates of violence against women included 876,340 rapes, sexual assaults, robberies, aggravated assaults, and simple assaults. The 1998 statistics also showed 160,000 violent crimes against men. However, domestic violence occurred most frequently against women, and 95 percent of all victims of intimate partner abuse were female. Researchers suggested that violence results in more injuries than rape, motor vehicle crashes, and muggings combined. In 1999, 1,218 women were murdered by intimate partners. In a study from 1993 to 1999, 45 percent of female murder victims between the ages of 20 and 24 were killed by intimate partners. Another study showed that 50 percent of all female murder victims were killed by male partners. An estimated 4,084 cases of same-sex domestic violence were reported in 2000 with an almost 50 percent division between women and men. The National Domestic Violence Hotline reported that from February 1996 to December 2001, 700,000 calls were placed for assistance. Reports also indicated that an estimated 324,000 pregnant women are victims of intimate partner violence each year. Of 10,000 women visiting EDs each year, at least 40 percent had some form of domestic violence in her past or present history.

In 2000, approximately 1,200 children died of maltreatment, a rate of 1.71 per 100,000 children. Child protective services agencies reported that 3 million referrals concerning 5 million children were made to their offices in the year 2000. Of these referrals, approximately 879,000 children (32 percent) were cases of maltreatment of children from birth to 3 years of age. This age group had the highest rate of 13.9 per 1,000 children and included neglect, physical abuse, sexual abuse, and psychological maltreatment.

A comparison of abuse and neglect of children over time showed a decline in cases since 1993, but a possible increase in 2000. In 1993, 15.3 children per 1,000 were victims. In 1999, the number dropped to 11.8 victims per 1,000, but increased to 12.2 per 1,000 in 2000. Authorities believe that the recent increase is due, at least in part, to "more timely completion of investigations, a cleared backlog of investigations awaiting dispositions or a reduced rate in 1999 ... due to census population estimates." There also has been an increased awareness and ease of reporting. Neglect, a subset of violence, is much harder to define or detect. It has not been spotlighted for the public's information as much as physical violence. It has been defined as the failure of a caretaker to provide the goods or services that are necessary to avoid physical harm, mental anguish, or mental illness. Patients, often children and the elderly, who are dehydrated, malnourished, have poor hygiene, are inappropriately dressed, or have received medications improperly should be further assessed for neglect.

7.5.1 Women's Childhood Abuse Linked to Later Poor Health

Women who were physically abused as children are more likely to report having poor health than those who did not experience such abuse, according to a 2003 study in the *American Journal of Preventive Medicine*. The study, based on survey results from 3,527 women in the state of Washington, also suggests that that women who were physically abused or who witnessed violence between their parents are also more likely to experience intimate partner violence and emotional abuse as adults. Women who were sexually abused but did not suffer other physical abuse or witness parental violence, on the other hand, did not appear to be at a higher risk for intimate partner violence or poor health, according to Lillian Bensley, PhD, and colleagues at the Washington State Department of Health (2003). The association between childhood abuse and poor health persisted even among women who had not recently experienced partner violence, say the researchers. They suggest the link between abuse and poor health could be due to many factors, including the lingering physical and mental effects of childhood abuse or possibly risky health behaviors. Although the findings suggest a link between childhood experience and adult risks, the researchers say the association might not necessarily lead to health problems in all abused women. "The role of childhood experiences in adult mental health may depend on the life course that follows; other experiences, such as a positive therapeutic experience or a supportive spouse, may be able to counteract these long-term associations," Bensley and colleagues say. The researchers also found that women younger than 36 had more than 10 times the risk of intimate partner violence and twice the risk of emotional abuse compared to women 46 years and older, regardless of their childhood experiences.

7.6 DOMESTIC VIOLENCE CASES: THE ED PORTAL

Approximately 7 percent of victims of nonfatal intimate partner violence sought care in EDs, which represents about 15 percent of those who experience an injury. Less than 1 percent of victims were hospitalized, according to *Confronting Chronic Neglect: The Education and Training of Health Professionals on Family Violence*, published in 2000 by the National Academies of Sciences.

Bell, Jenkins, Kpo, and Rhodes (1994) explored whether EDs in a metropolitan county had standard procedures or offered services that address the needs of victims of IPV. Fifty EDs (75 percent of the facilities eligible to participate in the survey) responded to a 55-item questionnaire about their handling of victims of IPV. The researchers discovered that EDs generally rely on patient self-reports to determine whether a patient is a victim of violence. Standard operating procedures for reporting cases to state agencies and referrals for additional services were most likely to exist for areas in which hospitals' response is mandated by law, such as sexual assault and child abuse. In addition, three fourths of the hospitals had procedures for dealing with elder abuse, an area in which reporting is strongly encouraged. Most direct services received by victims were not specifically targeted to them but were services offered to the general ED population. The most frequent referrals were to rape advocacy groups and battered women's groups.

McGrath et al. (1997) attempted to determine provider behavior in screening for domestic violence and sexual assault, provider training in domestic violence and sexual assault, provider knowledge of available protocols for domestic violence and sexual assault, and provider perception of barriers to intervention. The researchers distributed anonymous surveys to physicians, nurses, and social workers at an adult ED trauma center, an affiliated pediatric ED, and a women's urgent care center between July and September 1995. Of 207 staff members (59 percent) responding, 54 percent and 68 percent indicated that they never or rarely screen for domestic violence or sexual assault, respectively. Thirty-five percent had received no domestic violence training and 27 percent had received no sexual assault training. Thirty-one percent of the staff had knowledge of existing protocols for domestic violence and 63 percent had knowledge of existing protocols for sexual assault. Providers trained in domestic violence were more likely to screen for domestic violence and sexual assault, and providers trained in sexual assault were more likely to screen for sexual assault and domestic violence. Barriers that the majority of staff experienced in the care of domestic violence or sexual assault victims included frustration that the victim would return to an abusive partner, concerns about misdiagnosis, lack of time, personal discomfort, reluctance to intrude into familial privacy, and lack of 24-hour social service support. Researchers concluded, "Providers surveyed had received little training in and rarely screen for violence, and there are a range of personal and institutional barriers impeding intervention with victims of SA and DV. Institutional changes to enhance training and support providers working in the front line of this epidemic may improve services for victims of violence."

Sachs, Baraff, and Peek (1998) desired to quantify the proportion of men and women seen in a university ED for treatment of injuries resulting from intimate partner violence that require reports to law enforcement. A total of 1,516 adult ED patients were asked to complete a written survey instrument, and 1,003 patients (66.2 percent) completed the survey. Two percent of patients reported they presented to the ED for treatment of injuries resulting from IPV. Three percent reported IPV within the last year, and 10 percent reported that they had ever been physically abused by a partner. Six percent of respondents reported that they had ever been threatened with a gun or knife by a partner, 2 percent within the past year. Only the lifetime prevalence of IPV was significantly greater among female patients (15 percent vs. 6 percent). The researchers determined that approximately 2 percent of the sample ED patients required law enforcement intervention for IPV.

Stuart (2004) sought to identify risk factors for physical or sexual assault as a result of domestic violence in patients presenting to the ED. The backward prevalence study of two urban teaching hospital EDs measured the one-year period prevalence, acute incidence of ED presentation, and risk factors of domestic physical assault. Of the 1,326 patients (62 percent female) completing the study, 115 reported assault by a partner or ex-partner within the preceding 12 months, and 31 reported domestic physical assault as the cause of their presentation. Risk factors for recent domestic physical assault included female gender, age of less than 25 years, past presentation to an ED for assault, and a past history of child abuse. Stuart found no association between health care utilization or mental illness and the reporting of recent domestic physical assault.

Sethi et al. (2004) report that one in three women seeking emergency medical care in inner-city hospitals has suffered domestic violence at some point in her life. The authors base their findings on questionnaire responses from 198 women seeking emergency medical treatment at one inner-city hospital during the course of 22 nursing shifts covering all times of the day and week. None of the women was drunk, confused, or critically ill. The responses indicated that physical assault by a sexual partner was the reason for seeking emergency medical care for 1 percent of the women surveyed. An additional 6 percent said that they had been physically assaulted during the preceding 12 months. One in three of the women (almost 35 percent) confessed that they had been the victims of domestic violence at some point during their life. One in 10 said that the abuse had been life threatening. Three out of four of the women said they did not mind being asked questions about domestic violence while in the ED, and well over half (60.5 percent) felt that they should be routinely asked about these issues. The authors acknowledge the practical difficulties of surveying women in a busy emergency care facility, with the need to protect women's safety and confidentiality. Nevertheless, it might be easier for women to talk about it when directly asked by emergency medical staff, they say. Health professionals need to be more proactive in detecting it, they add: "Few health professionals directly ask about domestic violence and most do not consider it as part of their differential diagnosis. Despite recommendations from professional bodies, little routine health information has been collected or research conducted on the extent to which abused women present to health care services."

7.6.1 The Health Care Provider's Response to Domestic Violence Presenting in the ER

In 1994, the ENA published a position statement on domestic violence, maltreatment, and neglect. It acknowledges the following:

- Domestic violence consists of all forms of child abuse, violence against intimate partners, and violence against the elderly.
- Priorities for the domestic violence patient are safety and confidentiality.
- The victim of domestic violence has a right to be treated in a physical and social environment conducive to compassionate and unbiased care.
- The emergency nurse is an advocate for the victim of domestic violence.
- Emergency nurses have the duty to identify and report suspected domestic violence, maltreatment, and neglect.

Therefore, the ENA urges the following:

- Emergency nurses take an active role in the development, implementation, and ongoing maintenance of hospital and community protective service teams to ensure consistent and accurate assessments and protection of all individuals and families at risk for domestic violence, maltreatment, and neglect.
- The early mobilization of social services in suspected or confirmed cases of domestic violence, maltreatment, and neglect.

The ENA supports the following goals related to violence and abuse prevention:

- Reduce homicides
- Reduce maltreatment and maltreatment fatalities of children.
- Reduce the rate of physical assault by current or former intimate partners.
- Reduce the annual rate of rape or attempted rape.
- Reduce sexual assault other than rape.
- Reduce physical assaults.
- The development and use of routine protocols and procedures for assessment, identification, and referral for survivors of domestic violence, maltreatment, and neglect.
- Active promotion of a national format for reporting domestic violence, maltreatment, and neglect.
- Mandatory professional training, curriculum development, and continuing education including the importance of proper documentation and reporting for all health professionals on domestic violence, maltreatment, and neglect.
- Continued dissemination of information to emergency nurses regarding domestic violence, maltreatment, and neglect, in the form of journal articles, legislative updates, and research activities.
- The development of outreach programs and appropriate funding for education and prevention programs that help decrease the morbidity and mortality associated with domestic violence, maltreatment, and neglect.
- Increased public education for the prevention, detection, treatment, reporting, and follow-up of domestic violence, maltreatment, and neglect.
- Efforts to increase the public's awareness of neglect as a form of domestic violence.
- Research efforts in the early identification and treatment of victims of domestic violence, maltreatment, and neglect.
- Funding for additional personnel and resources, such as advocates and shelters to provide for the protection and treatment of victims of domestic violence.
- Allocation of funding and resources for the continuation of educational, legislative, and preventive measures regarding domestic violence, maltreatment, and neglect.

The ENA states:

> By increasing knowledge and understanding through education, the emergency nurse will become more cognizant of the problems of domestic violence, and incorporate the skills of identification and intervention into practice. Nurses are in key positions to assess and detect actual and potential cases of abuse. The emergency nurse must act as the advocate for the victims of domestic violence. Universal screening and identification of victims of domestic violence is the first step to patient advocacy.

7.6.2 Screening for IPV by Health Care Providers

In the early 2000s, the U.S. Preventive Services Task Force (USPSTF) published a recommendation statement on screening for family and intimate partner violence, based on its examination of evidence. It updates the 1996 recommendations contained in the *Guide to Clinical Preventive Services.* In 1996, the USPSTF found insufficient evidence to recommend for or against the use of specific instruments to detect domestic violence. The task force now uses an explicit process in which the balance of benefits and harms is determined exclusively by the quality and magnitude of the evidence. As a result, current letter grades are based on different criteria than those in 1996. (The complete information on which this statement is based, including evidence tables and references, is available through the USPSTF Web site at *http://www. preventiveservices.ahrq.gov* and through the National Guideline Clearinghouse at *http:// www.guideline.gov.*). The USPSTF found insufficient evidence to recommend for or against routine screening of parents or guardians for the physical abuse or neglect of children, of women for intimate partner violence, or of older adults or their caregivers for elder abuse. The USPSTF found no direct evidence that screening for family and intimate partner violence leads to decreased disability or premature death, and found no existing studies that determine the accuracy of screening tools for identifying family and intimate partner violence among children, women, or older adults in the general population. The USPSTF found fair to good evidence that interventions reduce harm to children when child abuse or neglect has been assessed. The USPSTF also found limited evidence as to whether interventions reduce harm to women, and no studies that examined the effectiveness of interventions in older adults. No studies have directly addressed the harms of screening and interventions for family and intimate partner violence. As a result, the USPSTF could not determine the balance between the benefits and harms of screening for family and intimate partner violence among children, women, or older adults.

The USPSTF did not review the evidence for the effectiveness of case-finding tools; however, all clinicians examining children and adults should be alert to physical and behavioral signs and symptoms associated with abuse or neglect. Patients in whom abuse is suspected should receive proper documentation of the incident and physical findings; treatment for physical injuries; arrangements for skilled counseling by a mental health professional; and the telephone numbers of local crisis centers, shelters, and protective service agencies. Several instruments to screen patients for child abuse have been studied, but their ability to predict child abuse or neglect is limited. Instruments to screen for intimate partner violence also have been developed, and although some have demonstrated good internal consistency (e.g., the HITS instrument: Hurt, Insulted, Threatened, Screamed at; the Partner Abuse Interview; and the Women's Experience with Battering Scale), none have been validated against measurable outcomes. Only a few screening instruments have been developed to identify potential older victims of abuse or their abusive caretakers. Both of these tools correlated well with previously validated instruments when administered in the community but have not been tested in the primary care clinical setting, the USPSTF stated.

The USPSTF reviewed the evidence for the effectiveness of screening procedures and interventions in the primary care setting in reducing harmful outcomes of domestic violence against children, women, and older adults. Because no studies were found that directly addressed the impact of screening on reducing harmful outcomes, the USPSTF examined the accuracy of clinical screening instruments in identifying risk for current or future abuse and the efficacy of clinic-based interventions in reducing harmful outcomes. USPSTF found few screening instruments for the detection of older adults who are the potential victims of abuse or their caretakers. None of the instruments available has been widely validated. No studies have directly addressed the harms of screening and intervention for family and intimate partner violence. False-positive test results, most common in low-risk populations, could compromise the clinician–patient relationship. Additional possible harms of screening could include loss of contact with established support systems, psychological distress, and an escalation of abuse; however, none of these potential harms have been studied.

The AAP and the AMA recommend that physicians and other health care providers remain alert for the signs and symptoms of child physical abuse and child sexual abuse in the routine examination. The AMA encourages physicians to inquire routinely about their patients' domestic violence histories and refer those patients with violence-related problems for medical or community-based services. The American Academy of Family Physicians notes that family physicians can provide early intervention in family violence through routine screening and the identification of abuse, and recommends that physicians be alert for the presence of family violence in virtually every patient encounter.

Taking issue with the USPSTF's statement that there is insufficient evidence to screen patients for IPV are a number of medical experts and health care providers that assert that less screening and intervention will endanger victims of abuse. Medical leaders insist that the task force used the wrong criteria to assess screening. "We agree that there should be more research exploring the best ways to screen for abuse and help victims," says Esta Soler, president of the Family Violence Prevention Fund (FVPF):

> But the task force is wrong, and, worse, potentially very harmful. The task force assessed screening for abuse as a medical screen rather than a behavioral assessment tool, which was a mistake. Furthermore, they ignored hundred of studies on this topic, simply because researchers did not use control groups. But highly respected researchers around the world have expressed concern about using control groups because they raise ethical questions about withholding help from patients in danger. The task force should have recognized that and examined existing research more fully.

"We stand by our existing policy of routine inquiry about abuse," says John Nelson, president of the AMA. "Our experience confirms what common sense tells us: when doctors and other health care providers talk to patients about domestic violence and offer referrals and help to those who are victims, battered patients are more likely to take steps to protect themselves and their children. It would be a tragedy if any provider stopped inquiring about family violence as a result of this recommendation."

"There is strong, clear evidence that health care providers can improve women's safety by intervening to help those who are battered," says Debbie Lee, managing director of the FVPF. "Health care providers across this nation, some of who were once reluctant to ask about abuse, can speak to the life-saving benefits of intervention to help victims of domestic violence."

Medical experts criticized the task force for relying on an evidence report that used an overly narrow approach by examining screening for domestic violence as a medical screen rather than a behavioral assessment tool; excluded from their analysis all studies that looked at patients presenting with trauma; discounted a significant body of research; and misapplied a study that examined mandatory reporting for domestic violence to reach conclusions about screening for domestic violence. "Evidence-based medicine is not yet mature regarding behavioral health issues," says Carden Johnston, MD, FAAP, President of the AAP. "Practitioners have to rely on experiences that work and can be replicated. We know that early screening has real positive effects even though some aspects of emotional and psychological stress of child abuse won't show up in evidence-based studies. We should never minimize the positive things that we can do to help." The FVPF's full response to the task force recommendations can be found at http://www.endabuse.org.

7.6.3 Mandatory Reporting of IPV by Health Care Providers

A study conducted in 2000 of 290 women found no difference in the percentage of women reporting domestic violence, whether or not the women were told of a law mandating that physicians report such incidents to a state agency. This study, conducted at the Northern Kentucky Children's Advocacy Center at St. Luke Hospital, compared the frequency of domestic violence reported by women who were informed of a state-mandated reporting law to the frequency among women who were not informed of the mandated reporting. In an effort to aid battered women, many states, including Kentucky, have required physicians to report incidents of domestic violence to a state agency. Many physicians are concerned that informing women of the requirement of reporting domestic violence to the state will make these women less likely to reveal the information. The women were screened using a six-question tool in a pediatric office setting. After the screening, the incidence of domestic violence was compared between the two groups. Of the 154 women screened who were not told about the mandatory reporting, 31 percent revealed a domestic violence episode, 17 percent within the last 24 months. Of the 136 women screened who were told about the mandatory reporting to the state, 21 percent revealed a domestic violence episode, only 6 percent within the last 24 months. Overall, the difference is not significant. The incidence of abuse within the past 24 months was significantly lower. "States should consider this study, and others like it, when re-evaluating their policies for the mandatory reporting of domestic violence," says Robert Siegel, MD, medical director of the Northern Kentucky Children's Advocacy Center.

Sachs et al. (1998) endeavored to assess the effect of California's 1994 mandatory domestic violence reporting law on Los Angeles Sheriff's Department dispatches to medical facilities for domestic violence incidents. Researchers analyzed data from the 26,051 dispatches for domestic violence offenses from January 1, 1993, to December 31, 1995. The outcome measures were changes in biweekly department dispatches for domestic violence offenses resulting from the implementation of the mandatory domestic violence reporting law adjusted for seasonal variation and the Nicole Simpson and Ron Goldman murders. The researchers discovered that the percentage of biweekly dispatches to medical facilities for domestic violence offenses did not increase in response to the law. Total domestic violence dispatches increased significantly after the Simpson and Goldman murders but not after passage of the law.

Physicians and other health care providers have an important role in the diagnosis, treatment, and documentation of violence-inflicted injuries. These health care professionals can also be legally mandated to report these assault-related injuries to law enforcement. Previous studies have shown that physicians might not be aware of the reporting laws in their state. Houry, Sachs, Feldhaus, and Linden (2002) reviewed the reporting laws for violence-inflicted injuries in adults in the 50 states and the District of Columbia, with particular emphasis on domestic violence. Members of a domestic violence research interest group contacted individual state legislatures regarding mandated reporting by health providers of violence-inflicted injuries in adults. This information was then verified by each state's domestic violence coalition. Statutes regarding child abuse or sexual assault and statutes concerning injuries in incapacitated adults were not included in the study. The researchers found that five states—Alabama, New Mexico, South Carolina, Washington, and Wyoming—have no specific reporting requirements for health care providers treating patients with assault-related injuries. Forty-two states have reporting requirements for injuries resulting from firearms, knives, or other weapons. Twenty-three states have reporting requirements for injuries resulting from crimes. Seven states have statutes that specifically require health providers to report injuries resulting from domestic violence.

State laws mandating health care personnel to contact police when treating patients injured as a result of domestic violence are controversial. Attitudes toward these laws have been studied in select groups, but never in a large population-based sample. Sachs et al. (2002) measured support for mandatory reporting among 845 women in 11 cities who participated in a telephone survey assessing risk factors for intimate partner violence. Abused women were oversampled to create equal groups (427 abused and 418 nonabused), and results were presented stratified by abuse status or weighted based on prevalence of abuse among women who were screened. Researchers found that the estimated prevalence of physical violence or threat of physical violence from an intimate partner during the past two years was 11.7 percent. Seventy-two percent of women supported mandatory reporting. Abused women were significantly less likely to support mandatory reporting compared to nonabused women (59 percent vs. 73 percent). Reasons that endorsed support included the belief that victims would find it easier to get help (81 percent) and would like health care personnel to call the police (68 percent). Reasons that endorsed opposition included the belief that victims would be less likely to disclose abuse (77 percent), would resent someone else having control (61 percent), and reporting would increase the risk of perpetrator retaliation (44 percent).

7.6.4 The Physician's Role in IPV Cases

According to *Confronting Chronic Neglect: The Education and Training of Health Professionals on Family Violence* (National Academies of Sciences, 2000), a majority of medical schools report the existence of educational content on at least one form of family violence. Most often, this education concentrates on reporting requirements, patient interviewing skills, screening tools, health conditions associated with violence, and services to which victims can be referred. The amount of training varies, from very brief to more extensive. About 95 percent of medical schools report curricular inclusion of material related to child abuse and neglect, and teaching is both didactic and interactive. When it comes to IPV, schools are trying harder; most instruction is on sexual assault, and the least amount of instruction seems to be on elder abuse. Additionally, family violence training during residency appears to be most common among programs with residents who are considered most likely to encounter victims: pediatrics, obstetrics-gynecology, internal medicine, geriatrics, psychiatry, and emergency medicine.

In the August 6, 1996 issue of the *Morbidity and Mortality Weekly Report* issued by the U.S. Department of Health and Human Services and the CDC, a study looked at family violence education in medical-school-based residency programs in Virginia in 1995. In the United States, family violence (e.g., intimate partner violence, child abuse, and elder abuse) is a well-documented social and public health problem that physicians are uniquely positioned to address. However, few schools of medicine or residency training programs provide substantial attention to family violence in their curricula. To assess the status of graduate medical education regarding family violence at Virginia's three medical schools, Eastern Virginia Medical School, Medical College of Virginia, and the University of Virginia, the Task Force on Violence Education and Awareness for Physicians, established by the Virginia Commission on Family Violence, conducted a survey of these medical schools in 1995. The task force distributed questionnaires to directors of the 69 fully accredited medical-school-based residency programs in the three schools, asking them to indicate the presence in the curriculum of instruction on specific types of family abuse and sexual assault, to indicate whether such teaching was required or elective, and to describe materials and methods used in the curriculum. In addition, the directors were asked to identify faculty at their institution who were experts in the area of family violence and to list the area of their expertise. To increase the likelihood of response to the survey, respondents were informed that only aggregate results would be reported. Therefore, program-specific findings were not included in the report. Of the 69 residency programs surveyed, 48 (70 percent) responded. Of the 48, a total of 26 (54 percent) indicated they included content related to family violence in their curricula. A total of 20 (42 percent) covered child abuse (the content area most frequently covered), 13 (27 percent) covered battered women, and nine (19 percent) covered elder abuse. Whether instruction courses were required or elective varied substantially among the programs. Sixteen of the 20 programs that provided some instruction on child abuse had required courses, as did 10 of the 13 programs that covered battered women and seven of the nine programs that covered elder abuse. In addition, the instructional methods for the existing curricula varied; they included regularly scheduled grand rounds on family violence topics, occasional discussion of these topics as part of noontime conferences, informal instruction from attending physicians during rounds, and "brown bag" series discussions and presentations. Of the 27 experts on family violence identified, 16 had expertise in identifying and treating family-violence-related injuries. Other areas in which experts were identified included child abuse, elder abuse, violence against women during pregnancy, PTSD in children, and community response to violence. No experts were identified in the areas of mental health sequelae of family violence, transgenerational transmission of violence, and violence prevention. The results of the survey described in this report are subject to at least three limitations. First, no attempt was made to contact nonresponding residency programs; survey responses from those programs could have differed from those that did respond. Second, the survey did not have precise criteria for defining presence of family violence instruction in program curricula (e.g., the amount of time spent teaching specific areas of family violence), which could have resulted in overestimating the amount of family violence curricula in place. Finally, no assessment of the quality of curricula was made. The task force used results of this survey to develop five recommendations regarding medical education about family violence in Virginia: 1) formally integrate family violence curricula into medical school and internship/residency programs; 2) use model curricula developed nationally as a base for training programs; 3) develop an in-school assessment tool to track each school's efforts; 4) have the medical schools, the commission, and the state medical society jointly sponsor a statewide medical-education conference for faculty and other interested persons; and 5) develop statewide mechanisms to coordinate family violence prevention services available through medical, legal, judicial, social services, political, and business agencies and services. These recommendations were adopted by the commission and presented in a report of the commission to the governor and the 1996 General Assembly of Virginia; the General Assembly accepted the recommendations and agreed to continue support for the commission's activities. In addition, the deans of the three medical schools agreed to collaborate on efforts to more thoroughly and systematically integrate violence education into their residency programs and to develop longitudinal, multidisciplinary instruction at the predoctoral level.

In U.S. medical schools and residency programs, family violence education in the curriculum often is brief and not reinforced in residency programs. Most hospitals do not have programs or policies to train and support physicians for work with abuse victims. The study in Virginia illustrates the need for a nationwide assessment of curricula and faculty development in medical school and residency programs and creation of an ongoing reinforcement protocol throughout the health care system, with evaluation instituted at all levels within each program. The CDC developed an annotative bibliography of training programs to assist medical training programs, health care organizations, and advocacy groups in identifying curricula and protocols, as well as a framework for evaluating these programs.

7.6.5 Domestic Violence Recognized, Not Always Investigated by Medical Students

In a study in October 2004, most medical students were able to identify domestic violence in a simulated ED encounter. However, say the Temple University researchers who conducted the study, some students didn't take the next step, inquiring about dangers that might remain once the patient returned home, a step that could help stop the cycle of domestic violence. The study, *Medical Interviewing Skills of Fourth Year Medical Students Encountering a Simulated Case of Intimate Partner Violence*, was presented at the ACEP annual meeting by Sachin J. Shah, MD, assistant professor of emergency medicine at Temple University School of Medicine. Shah explained, "Students and physicians working in an emergency room may be in a unique position to identify victims of intimate partner violence, a significant public health problem affecting millions of women in the United States. The objective of our study was to determine the ability of fourth-year medical students to identify a victim of intimate partner violence using a simulated emergency department encounter."

Simulated patient encounters are an increasingly common teaching tool for medical students. The exercises help prepare students for what they'll see when they are physicians and allow them to learn in a controlled teaching environment without consequences. "Our study was designed to measure both how we as teachers are doing and how well the students are learning. What do we need to teach better or emphasize more?" says David Wald, DO, assistant professor of emergency medicine at Temple. In the study, all 196 fourth-year medical students at Temple University School of Medicine completed an exercise with an actor trained to portray a 46-year-old female coming to the ER with lower back pain caused by intimate partner violence. At the end of each 20-minute encounter, the patient documented how the student performed, noting the questions asked, as well as the student's manner, tone, and professionalism. "In most cases, medical students identified that the actor was portraying a victim of intimate partner violence," says Shah. "It is unclear whether this occurred by way of routine screening or as a result of deductive reasoning. Even after identification of intimate partner violence, however, few students inquired into the social history of the spouse, whether the patient had ever been sexually abused, whether she wanted to make a report to the police, or whether a firearm was present in the home." "Some students didn't go on to ask other pertinent questions, ensuring the safety of the patient at home,"

Wald says. "These findings will help us shape and improve our curriculum." As a result of these findings, a discussion regarding domestic violence screening has been incorporated into the emergency medicine clerkship orientation. Hill (2005) asserts that medical schools around the country have initiated ad hoc teaching around family violence issues, especially child abuse and intimate partner violence; however, these activities typically are not integrated with other aspects of the curriculum, or with each other. Consequently, students do not have the opportunity to learn the broader issues related to family violence prevention and intervention. Hill describes how students at the Southern Illinois University School of Medicine participated in an elective to develop a model family violence curriculum encompassing child abuse, IPV, sexual assault, and elder abuse. The activities use standardized patients and resource people, including hotline and shelter staff, legal professionals, and law enforcement. Hill says that family violence teaching in medical schools is merely a first step, and that continuing medical education in violence-related issues must also be available for all clinicians.

7.6.6 Physicians Less Likely to Screen, But More Likely to Intervene in Domestic Violence

Despite the fact that only a small percentage of physicians screen new patients for domestic violence compared to other health problems, their interventions are more intensive, according to findings in 2002. "Only 19 percent of physicians surveyed reported screening new patients for domestic violence compared with 98 percent for tobacco use, 90 percent for alcohol abuse, and 47 percent for HIV and sexually transmitted disease risks," says lead investigator Barbara Gerbert, PhD, from the University of California San Francisco. However, once the problem of domestic violence was identified, the "respondents reported intervening at comparable or greater frequencies—compared with tobacco, alcohol, or HIV/STD risks," Gerbert reports. Her team's findings also indicate that physicians spent longer time periods counseling identified domestic violence victims than patients identified as having any of the other three health risks. The study appeared the *American Journal of Preventive Medicine.* Previous research has shown that between 1.5 million and 3.9 million women are physically abused each year by their intimate partners, with domestic violence affecting an estimated 8 to 14 percent of primary care patients. "In addition to death and immediate trauma, domestic violence results in a number of chronic health problems," Gerbert explains. These problems include depression, anxiety, and substance abuse. Despite these observations—as well as repeated findings that appropriate screening can be both effective and beneficial and recommendations for routine screening from medical organizations and domestic violence experts—Gerbert notes that investigators have repeatedly shown that only a small minority of physicians ask about domestic violence. Previous research shows that physicians' attitudes and responses regarding domestic violence might affect screening rates, Gerbert and her colleagues note, so they compared physicians' beliefs and practices on domestic violence and other stigmatized health behaviors for which screening is recommended. The researchers mailed questionnaires to a random, national sample of 1,200 physicians specializing in internal medicine or family practice. Questions on the 32-item survey centered on four health behaviors: domestic violence, tobacco use, alcohol abuse, and HIV/STD risks. The 610 physicians who replied echoed previous reports of particularly low screening rates for domestic violence. At the same time, they reported knowing "less about how to screen for or intervene with domestic violence than the other health risks—and, compared with alcohol abuse and STDs, believe they lack appropriate referral resources," according to Gerbert and her co-authors. The answers also indicated that although the majority of physicians (86 percent) believe that intervening with domestic violence is an essential or nearly essential part of their role, even more (at least 95 percent) feel that way about the other three problems. Yet physicians' self-described interventions to domestic violence, once identified, were most intense. Gerbert notes that physicians were far more likely to "provide counseling, arrange for follow-up visits or calls, and refer patients to additional resources for domestic violence victims than–for patients identified with the other three health risks."

7.6.7 Women's Shame Stalls Abuse Disclosure to Health Care Providers

Shame, denial, and fear of others' reactions keep many abused women from confiding in their physicians, a 1998 Johns Hopkins study of women in Baltimore discovered. Although most of the women queried had sought medical attention for a variety of problems during the past year, only one in three discussed their abuse with doctors. Although half of the women reported positive experiences with their physicians, some noted that the clinicians didn't listen or seemed uncaring, uncomfortable with the topic of abuse, too busy, or only interested in money. The study, published in the *Journal of General Internal Medicine,* used questionnaires and focus groups to survey 21 Baltimore-area victims of domestic violence who already were participating in group therapy. Most of the women were single, separated, or divorced, from a mix of income levels. The feelings of fear, shame, and distrust crossed all class lines. "Other studies indicate that as many as 44 percent of women who seek medical attention have been abused at some point in their lives, yet most physicians do not routinely screen their patients for abuse," says Jeanne McCauley, MD, MPH, lead author of the study and a physician advisor for the Johns Hopkins Medical Services Corp. "Our study suggests that many of the barriers to discussing abuse could be overcome by a physician's understanding of the emotions surrounding abuse and the unique treatment concerns of abused women." Eighteen of the women (88 percent) sought medical attention during the previous year. Their symptoms, which either began or worsened with abuse, included asthma, hypertension, headaches, eye pain, chest pain, stomach pains, back problems, vaginal bleeding, weight changes, insomnia, depression, and anxiety. Although most women did not recognize an association between abuse and these symptoms, one in three noticed improvement when she left the relationship or discussed it with a health professional. The study also found that:

- The doctor's gender was less of a barrier to discussing abuse than whether he or she appeared caring, easy to talk to, and supportive.
- Domestic violence posters displayed in the medical office helped prompt some victims to speak up. Questionnaires, when administered in private, also helped.
- Although nearly all of the women who received prescription medications for depression, anxiety, or sleep disturbances benefited from them, many feared addiction or decreased alertness in the presence of an abusive partner.

The fact that all of the women were in group therapy, however, might have introduced bias in the study, McCauley says. "More studies need to be performed to confirm the findings of this study," she says.

7.6.8 Health Care Providers Need More Training to Spot and Intervene in Cases of Domestic Violence

Research has shown that the prevalence of people, particularly women, being beaten by their partners is high and that such victims are frequent users of medical services. For example, recent studies have shown that the incidence of women seeking care for a domestic violence injury in primary care medical settings ranges between 17 and 25 percent and between 22 and 35 percent in hospital ERs. However, additional research suggests that these women are often not identified as partner abuse victims and are not provided appropriate services based on their unique needs. A study presented in 2000 at the 108th Annual Convention of the American Psychological Association (APA) found that although medical delivery settings provide ample opportunity for domestic violence victims to be identified and assisted, medical personnel often fail to screen for domestic violence or make appropriate referrals because doctors and nurses aren't confident in their ability to intervene or provide appropriate help to victims. Other barriers to screening identified by the study were often specific to the individual hospital facilities; lack of private rooms in the ED, for example. Psychologists L. Kevin Hamberger, PhD, of the Medical College of Wisconsin, Deb Pape, PhD, and Debbie Minsky, MSW, of All Saints Health Care Systems, Inc., Racine, Wisconsin, and their co-authors Clare Guse, Jennifer Boerger, and Christine Folsom (2000), measured the amount of training in domestic violence intervention provided to 752 health care professionals in two hospitals in a midsize midwestern city. Through the use of a survey, the Healthcare Provider Survey on Intimate Partner Violence, the health care providers (including doctors, nurses, certified medical assistants, radiology technicians, laboratory technicians, and social workers) were asked about the amount of training they had received, whether they routinely asked patients about violence in their relationships, and what their sense of efficacy was in screening for domestic violence. Forty-eight percent of the study participants reported some prior type of domestic violence intervention training, and 25 percent reported having identified a victim of partner violence in the past year. However, this and other studies have also identified serious barriers to intervention that health providers feel when confronted with a situation involving battering. Based on their study and earlier research, which shows that medical personnel who have received training in how to screen for domestic violence and how to provide help to its victims are much more likely to ask patients about violence in their relationships, the authors recommend that all health care providers receive partner violence education designed to increase their sense of efficacy to identify and help victims of partner violence: "Providing trainees (medical personnel) with didactic information about domestic violence and the health care provider's role in intervention and prevention, together with role modeling and skill rehearsal, should result in increases in perceived judgments of self-efficacy to screen and help battered victims," conclude the authors. However, they also emphasized that "one-size training will not fit all." Their survey shows that different medical personnel are going to need different training, most often dependent on their previous training and experience with domestic violence victims.

7.6.9 Nurses Can Help Violence Victims Find a Solution

In a study of 298 schools of nursing, 100 percent had at least some kind of family-violence-related content in their curricula, but only 53 percent of the schools felt it was adequately addressed (Woodtli & Breslin, 1996). In spite of reports like this, a random sample survey of 1,571 practicing clinicians in six disciplines, including nursing, demonstrated that more than one third of these clinicians reported no educational content in family violence. On the plus side, attention to the issue is increasing rapidly in the nursing literature. Curriculum content on intimate partner violence has increased with official nursing organization attention to the issue, such as that coming from the ANA and the American Association of Colleges of Nursing (AACN). Studies estimate that as many as 3 million incidents of domestic violence occur worldwide every year. An estimated half of all domestic violence victims report their injuries, so nurses are in a unique position to offer victims of domestic violence real ways to find safety, according to June Sheehan Berlinger, RN, BSN, a survivor of domestic violence, a nurse, and an expert on domestic abuse. She shared her thoughts in an article in *Nursing2001*. Berlinger, who was the coordinator of clinical programs for the Florida State University Center for Prevention and Early Intervention, says that knowing the tactics used by nurses to identify and assist victims can be helpful to victims or those who suspect a friend might be a victim. Berlinger provides inside details on why people stay in abusive relationships and why abusers feel entitled to control their partners, along with a list of conditions and behaviors that people who are abused often display. "A nurse's job isn't to cure a patient or solve her problems," said Berlinger. "But, she will offer tools and options that will help the patient make her own decisions." A nurse will also take other appropriate actions to keep the victim safe, such as asking questions about domestic violence only when she and the victim have total privacy. She will make sure that the victim's chart isn't left where unauthorized people, such as the abuser, could read it. The nurse will listen without judging, provide emotional support, and help the woman get in touch with a victim advocate. She will also document the woman's condition carefully and completely. The victim's patient records can help her successfully prosecute the abuser, resolve child custody issues, or obtain court protection. "A nurse may be the first nonfamily member that a victim turns to for help," says Berlinger. However, friends or family members can use the same professional approach that nurses take to help a victim of abuse.

7.7 THE SCOPE OF PARTNER VIOLENCE

A study of violence between intimate partners by two University of Wisconsin–Madison psychologists reveals a problem of disturbing scope, with as many as one third of respondents reporting being either victims or perpetrators of physical abuse. Surprisingly, the researchers found that results by gender were not as lopsided as one would presume: Women reported being perpetrators of physical violence toward their partners slightly more than men. The study, released by the National Institute of Justice, chronicles the responses of 861 21-year-olds on their experiences with violence within their relationships over the past year. Relationships included current or former intimate partners—spouses, boyfriends, or girlfriends. The participants are part of a longitudinal study carried out in New Zealand by University of Wisconsin–Madison psychologists Terrie Moffitt and Avshalom Caspi (1999). "This field is full of surprises," says Moffitt. "Almost everything we thought we knew isn't true when we use sound scientific methods to examine it correctly." The researchers conducted interviews with the participants and used a standardized measure of physical abuse, which includes more than a dozen violent acts from shoving, slapping, or punching to using a knife or gun. "One of the first lessons learned from this study is there are no tidy and distinct groups of victims or perpetrators," Moffitt said, adding that "mutual violence" between both men and women was a strong trend. However, the consequences of violence against women are more consequential, as women are more likely to be injured by men, she said. Unlike the women, physically abusive men also tend to have other extremely deviant patterns such as drug abuse, chronic unemployment, and dropping out of school. Some of the major findings of the study were as follows:

- About 27 percent of women and 34 percent of men in the study reported physical abuse by their partner. The abuse was most prevalent among couples living together.
- Young adults most likely to be involved in violent relationships are also most likely to be parents. Women who had children by age 21 were twice as likely to be victims of domestic violence, and men who were fathers by age 21 were three times as likely to be physical abusers.
- The strongest risk factor for both male and female perpetrators was a history of physical aggression before age 15. Male perpetrators were more likely to have backgrounds of poverty and low academic achievement, whereas disturbed family relationships and harsh discipline were common backgrounds for female perpetrators.

Moffitt suggests that future interventions include the teaching of nonviolent problem solving to teenagers and young parents, and better coordination among police, the judiciary, and psychiatric professionals. The methodology of the study was solid, Moffitt says. The New Zealand study group includes all the males and females born in the city of Dunedin in 1972, so it represents a snapshot of the full population. Researchers also interviewed 360 of the partners independently, and there was 80 percent agreement about the violence reports. Moffitt noted that the results are quite similar to two other national studies of domestic violence that were used for comparison. The Dunedin study participants have been surveyed over a variety of ages during childhood, adolescence, and young adulthood. Although the primary focus of the study was on teen behavioral problems and delinquency, the partner violence question became a natural extension of that earlier work, Moffitt says.

7.7.1 The Three Faces of Domestic Violence

Psychologists at the University of Arkansas's Center for Research on Aggression and Violence (CRAV) who are currently investigating domestic violence have discovered that men who beat women fall into three main categories of offenders. Such insight could eventually lead to improved treatment methodologies and the possibility of early intervention. Jeffrey Lohr began researching this topic in the mid-1990s in response to the idea that men who batter women might not represent a single homogenous group, but instead might be of several distinct personality types. Along with former graduate student Kevin Hamberger of the Department of Community and Family Medicine at the Medical College of Wisconsin, Lohr investigated the personality characteristics of a group of 800 male court-referred domestic violence offenders in the state of Wisconsin. These men completed several questionnaires, including the Millon Clinical Multiaxial Inventory, designed to detect various character disorders, as well as anger and depression. Statistical analysis of the data revealed three main types of offenders.

The first of these groups is composed of psychopathic men. Psychopathy is a personality trait marked by a lack of empathy and poor impulse control. Almost everyone has the trait to some extent, but it appears to be concentrated in some individuals more than in others, Lohr states. These men have frequent run-ins with the law for both violent and nonviolent offenses. Men in this category tend to use drugs and alcohol. They are also more likely to have been abused themselves as children compared to men in the other two groups.

The second type of abusers has noncharacterizable personality disorders but appear to be "chronically angry, unhappy, have problems with drugs and alcohol use, but are not psychopathic," explains Lohr. These men tend to have the most extensive police records for both family-oriented and nonfamily-oriented violence, as well as a myriad of other criminal offenses. "These men tend to be generally violent individuals, and their wives just happen to be there," Lohr adds.

The third distinct type of domestic violence perpetrator comprises individuals with no identifiable character disorders but, unlike the other two groups, the men seem to limit their violence to their families. "They tend to be depressed and unhappy, but do not show obvious or severe personality problems," says Lohr, referring to the fact that these men appear to function normally in all other aspects of their lives. "This is the group that we are interested in discovering the psychological variables that lead these otherwise normal men to beat their wives." These men, like those in the first group, might also display a heightened degree of psychopathy compared to the average population, explains Lohr. Lohr and his colleagues want to investigate exactly how far down the developmental sequence psychopathy extends to investigate its relationship with other personality characteristics and attitudes commonly associated with domestic violence. The main focus of this research remains on the possibility for improved treatment and intervention. As a first step in testing whether these perpetrator categories could be a useful tool for clinicians, 12 individual profiles typifying each category have been sent to trained clinical psychologists to see if they can sort them into the appropriate groups. This is done because those in the position to provide treatment must first find these categories identifiable to be useful. Such categories might ultimately facilitate the treatment of domestic violence offenders by maximizing the match between therapy and client characteristics. "If there are three distinct types of perpetrators, then a 'one size fits all' therapy approach might not be the most effective approach," emphasizes Lohr. "There has really been very little research done in this area, so it will be awhile before any new therapy techniques are actually realized."

7.7.2 Intimate Partner Violence and Homicide

A woman who leaves her abusive partner is at a higher risk of being killed by her partner than a woman who stays with her abuser is, according to a recent report. The risk of homicide increases nine-fold in cases in which a couple separates after living together and when the abuser has a highly controlling personality, says Jacquelyn C. Campbell, PhD, RN, of Johns Hopkins University, and colleagues in the *American Journal of Public Health.* Abused women are also more likely to be killed by their intimate partner if the partner is unemployed or has access to a gun, or if stepchildren live in the home with the couple. Campbell and colleagues say that physicians should be alert to such factors among their abused female patients. "Under these conditions of extreme danger, it is incumbent on health care professionals to be extremely assertive with abused women about their risk of homicide and their need for shelter," Campbell says. For instance, "if a woman confides that she is planning to leave her abuser, it is critical to warn her not to confront him personally with her decision," she says.

Homicide is the leading cause of death among African American women ages 15 to 45 and the seventh-leading cause of premature death among women overall. These women are most often killed by an intimate partner and the majority of these homicides involve abuse, say the researchers. To identify risk factors related to these deaths, Campbell and colleagues collected data on abusive intimate partner relationships and partner homicides in 11 cities, combing through police records and asking close friends or family members of the victim about her relationship with the abusive partner. The data came from Baltimore; Tampa/St. Petersburg, Florida; New York; Kansas City, Kansas; Kansas City, Missouri; Los Angeles; Chicago; Houston; Wichita, Kansas; Portland, Oregon; and Seattle. Women who never lived with their abusive partners had a significantly lower risk of being killed. The risk was also lower in cases in which the abusive partner had been arrested previously for domestic violence, possibly because arrest can trigger a set of court-ordered protections, Campbell says.

7.7.3 The Disturbing Trend of "Femicide"

Health care providers should know about the increase of an alarming trend called *femicide,* which was documented in a 2004 report, *Femicide in New York City: 1995–2002* (New York City Department of Health, 2004). In 1999, homicide was the second leading cause of death among women aged 15 to 19 and 20 to 24 in the United States, with rates of 3.6 and 5.2 per 100,000, respectively. Although men comprised the majority of homicide victims—75 percent between 1976 and 1996—homicide of women, or femicide, represents a significant source of premature mortality among young women in New York City today. However, because male victims constitute the bulk of overall homicide counts, trends unique to homicides of women are often overlooked. When women are killed, they are most often killed by people they know: friends, family members, and intimate partners. For example, in the 20 years between 1976 and 1996, approximately a third of all women who were homicide victims in the United States were killed by current or former intimate partners. The proportion was similar in New York City. In contrast, just 6 percent of male homicide victims were killed by intimate partners. Further, women make up the great majority of all intimate partner homicide victims; in 1998, they constituted 72 percent of all victims. The New York City Department of Health's Bureau of Injury Epidemiology has collected data on all femicides in New York City since 1990. The goal of this research is to identify risk factors for femicide in New York City to bolster prevention efforts. A 1997 report presented data on femicides that occurred between 1990 and 1994; the most recent report updates the data through 2002. Data was collected on all femicides with victims aged 12 and older from the records of the Office of the Chief Medical Examiner (OCME) of New York City. Records included autopsy, crime scene, and police reports, as well as demographic characteristics of the victim and perpetrator. Data was collected annually, at least six months after the end of the previous calendar year, to ensure that the OCME records were complete. The data collectors were public health epidemiologists and student interns who were trained on data collection methods, standardized coding techniques, and confidentiality issues.

Using both the motive recorded on the police report and information on the victim–perpetrator relationship from the OCME records, cases were categorized as intimate partner femicides and nonintimate-partner femicides. Intimate partner femicides included all homicides characterized as intimate partner femicides, probable intimate partner femicides, secondary intimate partner femicides, and intimate partner accidents. Intimate partner femicides were those in which the alleged perpetrator was either a current or former husband, or an opposite-sex or same-sex partner (includes boyfriends, girlfriends, common-law marriages, lovers, etc.). Probable intimate partner femicides were those for which the research team concluded that the perpetrator was an intimate partner, based on relative or informant reporting, regardless of whether the police identified the perpetrator as the intimate partner. Secondary intimate partner femicides were homicides in which the victim was killed during a dispute between two intimate partners; for example, a woman was killed by her stepfather while attempting to interrupt a fight between him and her mother. Intimate partner "accidents" were homicides in which an intimate partner and perpetrator alleged that the homicide was an accident; for example, it was reported that the boyfriend was "playing" with a gun, holding it to the victim's head, when it went off. Nonintimate-partner femicides include family (nonintimate partner) homicides, family violence "accidents," homicides committed in association with other crimes (i.e., robbery, drugs, sex crimes), random homicides (such as those caused by stray bullets), justifiable homicides (such as police-perpetrated homicides during an attempted arrest), and other types of homicides. Perpetrators were considered family if they were biological, adopted, step or foster parents, children, siblings, grandparents, cousins, nieces, nephews, or other relatives.

In the remaining femicides, the motive was unknown and thus the cases were classified as "unknown." It is possible that some of these cases were, in fact, intimate partner femicides. The victim–perpetrator relationship was used to categorize intimate partner femicides and family violence femicides, whereas all other motive types (sex crime, narcotics, etc.) were categorized based on the circumstantial information of the crime. This number reflects the possibility that the police misclassify a number of intimate partner femicides each year. It is also possible that the police classify some proportion of these probable intimate partner femicides as such, but after the end of the official data collection period; thus, the OCME records did not reflect this classification at the time of data collection.

One thousand thirty deaths of women were classified as homicides by the OCME between 1995 and 2002. Of these, 339 were intimate partner homicides, 369 were nonintimate-partner homicides, and 322 were classified as having an unknown motive. On average, intimate partner femicide victims were younger than nonintimate-partner femicide victims (34.2 vs. 41.5). A little more than one third of all intimate partner femicide victims were between the ages of 20 and 29 (34 percent), whereas 29 percent of nonintimate-partner femicide victims were 50 years of age and older. Both findings were statistically significant. Most of the nonintimate-partner femicide victims over 50 years of age were victims of robbery (40 percent) or family violence (31 percent). Women ages 30 to 39 made up the largest age group of all femicide victims, including those with an unknown motive. Twenty-nine percent of all intimate partner femicides were 30 to 39, as were 25 percent of all nonintimate-partner femicides. Almost half (49 percent) of all femicide victims were Black women. Blacks made up the largest percentage of intimate partner femicides (46 percent) and this was true for nonintimate-partner femicide victims as well (50 percent). Among Black women, there is no statistically significant difference between those killed by an intimate partner and those killed by someone else. Among Hispanic and White victims, that difference was statistically significant. A third of all intimate partner femicides were Hispanic women, and 23 percent of nonintimate-partner femicide victims were Hispanic. Among White femicide victims with a known motive, 37 percent were victims of intimate partner femicide and 63 percent were victims of nonintimate-partner femicide. Foreign-born women were significantly more likely to be killed by their intimate partners than U.S.-born women. Fifty-seven percent of foreign-born women were victims of intimate partner femicide. Foreign-born women comprised 35 percent of nonintimate-partner femicide victims and 51 percent of intimate partner victims. Victims of intimate partner femicide were 87 percent more likely than victims of nonintimate-partner femicide to be foreign-born.

Lower, middle, and upper median income groups were evenly distributed across intimate versus nonintimate-partner femicides. Each median income group comprised approximately one third of all femicides (including unknowns). Although all three groups were evenly distributed by motive, the lower and middle groups consist of relatively poor women (with an income of less than $34,900), indicating that a disproportionate number of poor women were victims of femicide. Women who tested positive for drugs were less likely to be killed by their intimate partners (40 percent) than victims of other crimes (60 percent). Victims of intimate partner femicide were 45 percent less likely to test positive for drugs (including alcohol) than nonintimate-partner femicides. Most femicide victims for whom a motive was known were killed in their own home (59 percent); however, victims of intimate partner femicide were 2.9 times more likely than victims of nonintimate-partner femicide to be found in their own residence. Of those femicide victims found outside, 76 percent were victims of crimes other than intimate partner violence. A firearm was used in one third of all femicides. Femicides committed with a firearm made up the largest percentage of method used for intimate partner femicides (40 percent) as well as nonintimate-partner femicides (32.2 percent). One third of all intimate partner femicide victims were stabbed by their assailant compared to 17.4 percent of all nonintimate-partner femicide victims. Women who were stabbed to death were 2.1 times more likely to have been killed by an intimate partner than someone who was not an intimate partner.

Victims of intimate partner femicide were less likely than nonintimate-partner femicides to be victims of rape or sexual assault. Of those women who were sexually assaulted, 86 percent were victims of nonintimate-partner femicide. The majority of all perpetrators whose gender is known are male (94.3 percent). Only 4 percent of the femicides in which the gender of the perpetrator was known were committed by women, and only three of the intimate partner homicides were committed by women. There was a correlation between intimate partner femicides and perpetrators who committed suicide. Of those perpetrators who committed suicide, 87 percent were intimate partners and 13 percent had some other relationship to the victim. Perpetrators who committed suicide were 8.4 times more likely to have killed an intimate partner than to have killed someone else.

Finally, the rate of intimate partner femicide remained fairly stable from 1995 through 2002, with a slight increase in 2002 indicating that intimate partner femicide remains a major public health issue in New York City. Interventions that have contributed to an overall decrease in femicides do not appear to have contributed to a decrease in femicides perpetrated by intimate partners. This study demonstrates that young, foreign-born, and minority women are overrepresented among intimate partner femicide victims. To reduce deaths among these population subgroups, public health officials must fund research-driven programs, founded on identifying risk factors for serious and lethal intimate partner violence.

7.8 A NATIONAL CONSENSUS ON DOMESTIC VIOLENCE

In the last 15 to 20 years, an increasing number of health care providers have been given the tools they need to identify and address the needs of victims of domestic violence, also known as intimate partner violence. At some point in their lives, most Americans see a health care provider; therefore the health care setting offers a critical opportunity for early identification and even primary prevention of abuse. Studies have demonstrated that assessing for intimate partner violence in medical settings has been effective in identifying women who are victims and that patients are not offended when asked about current or past incidents of intimate partner violence. Numerous professional health care associations have issued position statements to their members describing the impact of IPV on patients and suggesting strategies for assessment and identification of abuse. These statements represent important steps in raising awareness about intimate partner violence in health care settings. Generally, however, they offer neither specific guidelines for intervening and responding, nor criteria that promote the utilization and evaluation of recommended practice. To help fill this void, the FVPF assembled a significant body of thought titled *National Consensus Guidelines on Identifying and Responding to Domestic Violence Victimization in Healthcare Settings.* For more than two decades, the FVPF has worked to end violence against women and children around the world. Instrumental in developing the landmark VAWA passed by Congress in 1994, the FVPF has continued to break new ground by reaching new audiences, promoting leadership within communities to ensure that violence prevention efforts become self-sustaining, and transforming the way that health care providers, police, judges, employers, and others address violence. The FVPF is a national nonprofit organization committed to mobilizing concerned individuals, allied professionals, women's rights groups, civil rights groups, other social justice organizations, and children's groups through public education and prevention campaigns, public policy reform, model training, advocacy programs, and organizing. This important consensus document gathers recommendations from some of the leading experts in the field, and should be required reading for any forensic nurse wishing to expand his or her knowledge base of IPV. The guidelines offer specific recommendations for assessing for and responding to IPV that can be applied to multiple health settings. The next section examines the consensus document to glean important suggestions for the health care provider.

Intimate partner violence is a pattern of assaultive and coercive behaviors that can include inflicted physical injury, psychological abuse, sexual assault, progressive social isolation, stalking, deprivation, intimidation, and threats. These behaviors are perpetrated by someone who is, was, or wishes to be involved in an intimate or dating relationship with an adult or adolescent, and are aimed at establishing control by one partner over the other.

Intimate partner violence is a health problem of enormous proportions. It is estimated that between 20 percent and 30 percent of women and 7.5 percent of men in the United States have been physically or sexually abused by an intimate partner at some point in their adult lives. Heterosexual women are five to eight times more likely than heterosexual men to be victimized by an intimate partner. From 1993 to 1998, victimization by an intimate accounted for 22 percent of the violent crime experienced by females and 3 percent of the violent crime sustained by males. Women aged 16 to 24 experience the highest per-capita rate of intimate partner violence. For adolescents, the rates of experiencing some form of dating violence vary from 25 percent to 60 percent. Although studies indicate that boys and girls might accept physical and sexual aggression as normative in dating and intimate partner relationships, adolescent females are more likely to receive significant physical injuries than boys and are more likely to be sexually victimized by their partners.

No one is immune from the risk of abuse. The National Center on Elder Abuse estimates that 818,000 elderly Americans were victims of domestic abuse in 1994. There are far fewer data on lesbian, gay, transgender, and bisexual (LGTB) victimization. However, the available literature suggests similarly high rates for LGTB adolescent and adult populations with higher rates in male same-sex relationships than female. Intimate partner violence occurs in every urban, suburban, rural, and remote community; in all social classes; and in all ethnic and religious groups including immigrant and refugee populations.

Consequently, all health care settings and professionals providing care to patients are treating patients affected by intimate partner violence and are in a position to identify and intervene on behalf of victims. The estimates of children exposed to intimate partner violence vary from 3.3 million to 10 million per year, depending on the specific definition of witnessing violence, the source of interview, and the age of child included in the survey. In the Adverse Childhood Experiences Study, conducted on a large sample of members (30,000 adults) of the Kaiser Health Plan in California, 12.5 percent of respondents indicated childhood exposure to intimate partner violence and 10.8 percent indicated a personal history of child abuse including physical, sexual, and emotional abuse. This research and other studies indicate that children who witness intimate partner violence are seen with both frequency and regularity in the health care system as children and as adults.

7.8.1 Health Effects of Intimate Partner Violence

In addition to injuries sustained by women during violent episodes, physical and psychological abuse are linked to a number of adverse medical health effects, including arthritis, chronic neck or back pain, migraine or other types of headache, STIs (including HIV/AIDS), chronic pelvic pain, peptic ulcers, chronic irritable bowel syndrome, and frequent indigestion, diarrhea, or constipation.

Six percent of all pregnant women are battered and pregnancy complications, including low weight gain, anemia, infections, and first and second trimester bleeding, are significantly higher for abused women, as are maternal rates of depression, suicide attempts, and substance abuse. Optimal management of other chronic illnesses such as asthma, HIV/AIDS, seizures, diabetes, gastrointestinal disorders, and hypertension can be problematic in women who are being abused or have been abused in the past. Often the perpetrator controls the victim's access to and compliance with health protocols. Emerging research shows that women who are abused are less likely to engage in important preventive health care behaviors such as regular mammograms, and they are more likely to participate in injurious health behaviors including smoking, alcohol abuse, and substance abuse. In many controlled studies, intimate partner violence significantly increases the risk for serious mental health consequences for victims, including depression, traumatic and posttraumatic stress disorder, anxiety, and suicidal ideation. The health consequences of abuse can continue for years after the abuse has ended. Intimate partner violence can also result in homicide; in 1996, 1,800 murders were attributed to intimates.

More than 100 studies have explored the short- and long-term effects of intimate partner violence on children. In 30 percent to 60 percent of families affected by intimate partner violence, children are also directly abused. Children exposed to intimate partner violence, particularly chronic abuse, often show symptoms associated with PTSD. One study found that a child's exposure to intimate partner violence (without being directly assaulted) was sufficiently traumatic to precipitate moderate to severe symptoms of PTSD in 85 percent of the children surveyed. Although physical health problems have seldom been measured in children exposed to intimate partner violence, one study found that they are more likely to exhibit physical health problems including chronic somatic complaints, and behavioral problems such as depression, anxiety, and violence toward peers. Another study found that exposed children were also more likely to attempt suicide, abuse drugs and alcohol, run away from home, engage in teenage prostitution, and commit sexual assault crimes. There is a growing body of research regarding the impact of violence on early brain development that could have implications for children growing up in violent homes.

There is an urgent need to address family violence over the life span because the health effects of victimization often persist for years after the abuse has ended. Adults who were abused as children, witnessed intimate partner violence, had a parent with a mental illness, or witnessed parental substance abuse are at significantly high risk for obesity, heart disease, hepatitis, diabetes, depression, and suicide. These adverse childhood experiences frequently cluster in households and have a cumulative effect: The more adverse exposures in a household, the higher the likelihood of long-term health problems as an adult.

7.8.2 Identifying and Responding to Abuse Can Make a Difference

The National Consensus says that the health care system plays an important role in identifying and preventing public health problems. Models developed to identify other chronic health problems can effectively be applied to intimate partner violence. Routine inquiry, with a focus on early identification of all victims of intimate partner violence whether or not symptoms are immediately apparent, is a primary starting point for this improved approach to medical practice for intimate partner violence. Regular, face-to-face screening of women by skilled health care providers significantly increases the identification of victims of intimate partner violence, as well as those who are at risk for verbal, physical, and sexual abuse. Routine inquiry of all patients, as opposed to indicator-based assessment, increases opportunities for both identification and effective interventions, validates intimate partner violence as a central and legitimate health care issue, and enables providers to assist both victims and their children. When victims or children exposed to intimate partner violence are identified early, providers might be able to break the isolation and coordinate with domestic violence victim advocates to help patients understand their options, live more safely within the relationship, or safely leave the relationship. Expert opinion suggests that such interventions in adult health settings could lead to reduced morbidity and mortality. Talking with patients about intimate partner violence provides a valuable opportunity for providers to learn about their experiences with abuse. Battered women report that one of the most important aspects of their interactions with a physician was being listened to about the abuse. Even if a patient chooses not to disclose being abused, the provider's inquiry can often communicate support and increase the likelihood of future discussion of the issue.

The National Consensus says that all health care settings, including acute-care hospitals, clinics, and primary care environments, are prime settings for the identification of domestic violence and intimate partner violence cases. It says that inquiry and initial response should be conducted by a health care provider who:

- Has been educated about the dynamics of intimate partner violence, the safety and autonomy of abused patients, and elements of culturally competent care.
- Has been trained how to ask about abuse, to provide information about intimate partner

violence and local community resources, and to intervene with identified victims.

- Is authorized to record in the patient's medical record.
- Has established a relationship or some trust with the patient in a primary care setting.
- Has a clearly defined role in a specialty, urgent care, or emergency setting.

7.8.3 Conducting the Intimate Partner Violence Inquiry

According to the National Consensus, health care providers should ask patients about current and lifetime exposure to intimate partner violence victimization, including direct questions about physical, emotional, and sexual abuse. Recipients of this inquiry should be all adolescent and adult patients regardless of cultural background, as well as parents or caregivers of children in pediatric care. The intimate partner violence assessment should be:

- Conducted routinely, regardless of the presence or absence of indicators of abuse.
- Conducted orally as part of a face-to-face health care encounter.
- Included in written or computer-based health questionnaires.
- Direct and nonjudgmental, using language that is culturally and linguistically appropriate.
- Conducted in private: no friends, relatives (except for children under the age of 3), or caregivers should be present.
- Confidential: prior to inquiry, patients should be informed of any reporting requirements or other limits to provider–patient confidentiality.
- Assisted, if needed, by interpreters who have been trained to ask about abuse and who do not know the patient or the patient's partner, caregiver, friends, or family socially.

The inquiry for past and present intimate partner violence victimization should take place:

- As part of the routine health history (e.g., social history and review of systems).
- As part of the standard health assessment (or at every encounter in urgent care).
- During every new patient encounter.
- During periodic comprehensive health visits (assess for current intimate partner violence victimization only).
- During a visit for a new chief complaint (assess for current intimate partner violence victimization only).
- At every new intimate relationship (assess for current intimate partner violence victimization only).
- When signs and symptoms raise concerns or at other times at the provider's discretion.

The inquiry should not be made if:

- The health care provider cannot secure a private space in which to conduct inquiry.
- There are concerns that assessing the patient is unsafe for either patient or provider.
- The provider is unable to secure an appropriate interpreter.

If the inquiry does not occur, the health care provider should note in the medical record that the inquiry was not completed, and schedule a follow-up appointment (or if in an urgent-care setting, refer the patient to a primary care provider). Also, the health care provider should have on hand posters, safety cards, and patient education materials about intimate partner violence available in exam or waiting rooms, bathrooms, or on discharge instructions.

7.8.3.1 Conducting the Health and Safety Assessment

The goals of the assessment are to create a supportive environment in which the patient can discuss the abuse, enable the health care provider to gather information about health problems associated with the abuse, and assess the immediate and long-term health and safety needs for the patient to develop and implement a response. Assessment should take place immediately after disclosure, and repeat or expanded assessments should occur during follow-up appointments with health care providers and domestic violence victim advocates. According to the National Consensus, for the patient who discloses current abuse, assessment should include, at a minimum, the following questions:

- Are you in immediate danger?
- Is your partner at the health facility now?
- Do you want to (or have to) go home with your partner?
- Do you have somewhere safe to go?
- Have there been threats or direct abuse of the children (if he or she has children)?
- Are you afraid your life might be in danger?
- Has the violence gotten worse or is it getting scarier? Is it happening more often?
- Has your partner used weapons, alcohol, or drugs?
- Has your partner ever held you or your children against your will?

- Does your partner ever watch you closely, follow you, or stalk you?
- Has your partner ever threatened to kill you, himself or herself, or your children?

If the patient states that there has been an escalation in the frequency or severity of violence, that weapons have been used, or that there has been hostage taking, stalking, homicide or suicide threats, health care providers are advised to conduct an assessment for homicide or suicide.

To assess the pattern and the history of current abuse, the following questions should be asked:

- How long has the violence been going on?
- Have you ever been hospitalized because of the abuse?
- Can you tell me about your most serious event?
- Has your partner forced you to have sex, hurt you sexually, or forced you into sexual acts that made you uncomfortable?
- Have other family members, children, or pets been hurt by your partner?
- Does your partner control your activities, money, or children?

If a patient says there have been no episodes of intimate partner violence, the health care provider should respect the patient's response, letting him or her know that help is available should the situation ever change. Assessment should be made again at previously recommended intervals. If the health care provider believes the patient might be at risk, discuss the specific risk factors and offer information and resources in exam and waiting rooms.

Providing intervention services and advocacy might be done by the health care provider or by the advocate. Interventions will vary based on the severity of the abuse, the patient's decisions about what he or she wants for assistance at that time, and if the abuse is happening currently. For all patients who disclose current abuse, providers should provide validation by listening nonjudgmentally, provide information, respond to the patient's safety issues, and make referrals to local resources.

7.8.3.2 Reporting Cases of Intimate Partner Violence

Some states have requirements to report current victimization to law enforcement or to social services. Health care providers should learn applicable statutes in their state, and if they practice in a state with a mandated reporting law, they should inform patients about any limits of confidentiality prior to conducting an assessment. Regarding confidentiality, the National Consensus emphasizes that inappropriate disclosure of health information could violate patient–provider confidentiality and threaten patient safety. Perpetrators who discover that a victim has sought care might retaliate with further violence. Employers, insurers, law enforcement agencies, and community members who discover abuse might discriminate against a victim or alert the perpetrator. It is imperative that policy, protocol, and practice surrounding the use and disclosure of health information regarding victims of intimate partner violence should respect patient confidentiality and autonomy and serve to improve the safety and health status of victims. The federal medical records privacy regulations issued in August 2002 (which went into effect on April 14, 2003) have specific implications for victims of violence.

7.8.3.3 Documentation

The National Consensus states that documentation should be conducted by a health care provider who is authorized to record in the patient's medical record. Providers should document the patient's statements and avoid pejorative or judgmental documentation (e.g., write "patient declines services" rather than "patient refuses services," and "patient states" rather than "patient alleges"). Health care providers should document relevant history, including the following:

- Chief complaint or history of present illness.
- Details of the abuse and its relationship to the presenting problem.
- Any concurrent medical problems that might be related to the abuse.
- For current intimate partner violence victims, a summary of past and current abuse including social history, relationship to abuser, and abuser's name, if possible.
- Patient's statement about what happened, not what led up to the abuse (e.g., "boyfriend John Smith hit me in the face" not "patient arguing over money").
- Date, time, and location of incidents where possible.
- Patient's appearance and demeanor (e.g., "tearful, shirt ripped" not "distraught").
- Any objects or weapons used in an assault (e.g., knife, iron, closed or open fist).
- Patient's accounts of any threats made or other psychological abuse.
- Names or descriptions of any witnesses to the abuse.

Health care providers should document the results of physical examination, including the following:

- Findings related to intimate partner violence, neurological, gynecological, and mental status exam if indicated.

- If there are injuries (present or past), describe type, color, texture, size, and location.
- A body map or photographs to supplement written description.
- A consent form prior to photographing patient. Include a label and date.

Health care providers should document laboratory and other diagnostic procedures, including recording the results of any lab tests, X-rays, or other diagnostic procedures and their relationship to the current or past abuse. Health care providers should document the results of assessment, intervention, and referral:

- Record information pertaining to the patient's health and safety assessment including your assessment of potential for serious harm, suicide, and health impact of intimate partner violence.
- Document referrals made and options discussed.
- Document follow-up arrangements.

If the patient does not disclose intimate partner violence victimization, the health care provider should document that assessment was conducted and that the patient did not disclose abuse. If you suspect abuse, document your reasons for concern (i.e., "physical findings are not congruent with history or description," or "patient presents with indications of abuse").

7.8.3.4 Continuity of Care for the Patient

At least one follow-up appointment (or referral) with a health care provider, social worker, or domestic violence victim advocate should be offered after disclosure of current or past abuse. At every follow-up visit with patients currently in abusive relationships, the health care provider should review the medical record and ask about current and past episodes of intimate partner violence, as well as communicate concern and assess both safety and coping or survival strategies. For current and previous victims, the health care provider should ensure that the patient has a connection to a primary care provider, and coordinate and monitor an integrated care plan with community-based experts as needed.

7.8.3.5 Challenges for the Health Care Provider When Screening Patients for Intimate Partner Violence

The National Consensus acknowledges that regularly assessing all patients for intimate partner violence victimization raises additional policy and practice issues for providers and there is debate in the field about appropriate responses. Those opposed to these policies assert that the risks of alerting perpetrators to the practice of assessing for intimate partner violence outweigh the benefits. There are concerns that perpetrators might limit their partners' access to health care, might threaten victims who disclose, or might learn about safety planning materials, which could ultimately undermine victim safety. Proponents of policies to assess men and women assert that because men in same-sex relationships experience intimate partner violence at equal rates as women in heterosexual relationships, and some men in heterosexual couples experience abuse, it is critical to identify and assist as many victims as possible. Proponents also argue that determined perpetrators can already access safety planning materials and that assessing all patients offers unparalleled opportunities for abuse prevention. Still others maintain that because the majority of victims are women, providers should begin by assessing all female patients and integrate assessing men as a second step, after gaining more experience in assessment for victimization and developing policies to address some of the difficult practical concerns that are raised when assessing all patients.

Frequently, it might be difficult to assess who the victim is, as the accounts of one or both parties could lead to confusion about the incident. Male perpetrators often claim victimization to avoid consequences or as a tactic to further control victims. Because the majority of intimate partner violence perpetrators are male, assessing men increases the likelihood of assessing perpetrators who might claim they are victims. There is not sufficient experience with female perpetrators of violence to know if this is also true of them. Victims might take the blame for the abuse because their partners have told them repeatedly that the problems in the relationship are their fault or because they used violence or other tactics in self-defense. Both parties might use physical force in an incident. Whether the patient is viewed as a victim or perpetrator will influence the health care provider's response and could lead to inappropriate treatment:

- A victim who takes the blame for the abuse might prevent providers from offering support and information about intimate partner violence.
- Perpetrators who falsely claim they are victims might lead providers to share safety planning strategies with them, inadvertently colluding and undermining victims' safety planning efforts.
- What is recorded in the medical record by the health care provider can have legal ramifications for the victim, particularly in divorce, custody, or other legal cases.

Although it is not the role of the health care provider to determine if the patient is telling the truth, the provider should take care in evaluating the patient's information and in identifying whether or not the patients is a victim of intimate partner violence, just as they take care in evaluating other patients' reports of health concerns. Understanding the definition of intimate partner violence and being skilled in behavioral inquiry assists providers in making accurate identification of victimization. Prior to implementing a protocol to assess all patients for abuse, providers should be trained on the dynamics of intimate partner violence and perpetrator issues, including the context and intent of abuse and how the abuse affects both the perpetrator and the victim. Training should include but not be limited to what is known about perpetrator and victim dynamics.

The following behaviors are characteristic of perpetrators:

- They often control access to money, property, and other shared commodities.
- They are often notably jealous of friends, family, co-workers, and others.
- They are often scornful of their partner's perspective.
- They can use various forms of status to claim authority, knowledge, or power.
- They often minimize or explain their behavior, make excuses, or become defensive.
- They are often vague about violent incidents.
- The might have a documented prior use of violence.
- They often have offensive wounds (i.e., scratches or bite marks when injuries are present).
- They use physical force against people or property.

Victims often display these characteristics:

- They are often fearful of their partners.
- They are often not allowed access to family, friends, or other support networks.
- They often experience reduced autonomy, and when they exercise autonomy, there are negative or abusive consequences.
- They often feel guilty or wonder if they are to blame for their partner's violence.
- They might experience problems sleeping, chronic pain, gastrointestinal disorders, nervousness, depression, or signs of PTSD.
- They are more likely to have more serious injuries (injuries to the head, neck, and torso).
- They can often articulate what precipitated specific incidents or the progression of violence.
- They have been told by others (family, friends, etc.) about the concern for the patient's safety.

7.9 THE FAMILY JUSTICE CENTER CONCEPT

Other chapters have described the average plight of the victim of IPV or sexual assault; the person who is bounced back and forth (often across town) among health care providers, advocates, and law enforcement; and often made to wait for long periods of time while the reporting and documentation process unfolds. There had to be a better way to serve victims of abuse, thought then San Diego City Attorney Casey Gwinn, who, on October 10, 2002, with then San Diego Police Chief Dave Bejarano, launched the San Diego Family Justice Center (SDFJC). The concept of the one-stop center received full support from elected officials from the city and county of San Diego, corporate and community leaders, nonprofit agencies, state and federal governmental agencies, foundations, and individuals from the community.

The SDFJC was a new community initiative designed to help domestic violence victims and their children by bringing together 120 professionals from 24 agencies under one roof. For the first time in San Diego history, victims had easy access to advocates, police officers, prosecutors, probation officers, civil attorneys, counselors, doctors, and other professionals in one location in downtown San Diego. The center's goals were simple: to provide more services from one location, reduce child abuse and domestic violence incidents, hold batterers accountable, and ultimately be the first large-city jurisdiction in the United States to see domestic violence homicides eliminated.

Organizers of the SDFJC knew that, despite increased efforts over the last decade, domestic violence continued to be a significant problem throughout San Diego. Each year, law enforcement agencies document approximately 25,000 domestic violence incidents within the city and county of San Diego. This figure is even more alarming when one considers that experts estimate that only 25 percent of domestic violence cases are actually reported. Prior to the SDFJC, the criminal justice system made it difficult for victims to seek help and unintentionally wore them down, its supporters say. Victims were often required to travel from location to location to seek services that were scattered through the city and county. Victims had to tell their story repeatedly to law enforcement, courts, legal aid, medical professionals, transportation officials, housing, social services, mental health, rehabilitation, financial assistance, and many more entities. Prior to the launch of a one-stop concept, the criminal justice system made it easier for victims to become frustrated and ultimately give up on seeking the assistance they needed. The old system, many believed, allowed sophisticated or seasoned offenders to slip through the cracks and avoid accountability due to the high volume of cases, lack of resources, and a lack of communication among the various professionals involved in these cases. It became evident that sweeping changes were necessary to bring perpetrators to justice and to resolve the fractured nature of the provision of services to victims. A coordinated community response was needed.

Diana Faugno, RN, BSN, CPN, FAAFS, SANE-A, district director of forensic health services at Palomar-Pomerado Hospital in North County, San Diego, recalls early discussion of a one-stop shop concept for her county:

> I remember talking to Assistant City Attorney Gael Strack years ago and saying, "Gael, here's the vision: picture an umbrella; hang all those hooks under it when you are looking at forensic services, whether it is domestic violence, sexual assault, child abuse or elder abuse—they all need to be under one umbrella and we have to get out of those individual silos." I know we like to stay in them because we have our comfort zones, but the interpersonal violence won't stop; it crosses everything that we do here, and that's part of the problem.

The center provides a combination of services and interventions from one location to help victims and offenders break the cycle of violence and develop healthy relationships. A collaborative effort also provides more support to victims and children involved in domestic violence through improved case management and a more fluid exchange of information and resources. Bridging existing gaps improves victims' accessibility to services and resources, and makes the entire process of reporting a domestic violence incident much less overwhelming for the victims and children involved. Not only does the center assist victims, it dramatically improves the quality of police investigations and ultimately increases the number of convictions of domestic violence perpetrators. By increasing the conviction rates, there is also an increase in the number of perpetrators who complete the mandatory 52-week domestic violence rehabilitation program.

Supporters of the SDFJC say that the combination of this extensive counseling for perpetrators, in conjunction with the empowerment and education of victims and children, works in a synergistic fashion to reduce the rates of child abuse and domestic violence recidivism in San Diego.

The scope of the SDFJC is far reaching; phasing plans include offering comprehensive medical and legal services; counseling to victims and children; links to juvenile, family, and criminal courts; as well as access to on-site professionals such as child protective service workers, probation, parole, and border patrol officers, advocates, and the Kids in Court program. Intervention initiatives include case management and risk assessments for every case, providing increased supervision of repeat offenders, assisting high-risk victims, providing meaningful probation for misdemeanor offenders, providing a systemwide audit, apprehending fugitives, and improving investigation techniques. Prevention initiatives include assisting pregnant victims exposed to domestic violence, outreach efforts to young adults and underserved victims, and increased community training.

The San Diego medical, legal, and law enforcement communities had been planning and preparing for the establishment of the SDFJC since 1989, when the concept first became the subject of a wide variety of community forums, focus groups, and strategic planning meetings. Organizers visited other sites to see what worked and what didn't, and a feasibility study was conducted by the San Diego Police Department. As a result of these efforts, a model that was right for the demographics of San Diego was developed. This model includes best practices, local partners, proven strategies, innovative programs, and an ideal site. San Diego knew it had the expertise, skills, and partnerships to ensure the success of this important project. During the last 15 years, San Diego has developed a comprehensive community response to domestic violence. This response included the creation in 1989 of the countywide San Diego Domestic Violence Council, comprised of more than 200 agencies, which functions through a network of 14 working committees. As part of its vision and mission, the council developed many protocols, including the San Diego Domestic Violence Law Enforcement Protocol, a medical facilities protocol, treatment standards, and much more. San Diego also established specialized domestic violence units in the City and District Attorney's offices, city and county law enforcement, probation, and the Superior Court. This collaborative regional effort resulted in strong community partnerships and significant reductions in reported incidents of domestic violence and homicides. In 1986, there were fewer than 5,000 cases and 30 domestic violence homicides. In 1991, the city faced 11,739 cases and 22 homicides. In 2001, it had 10,666 cases and 10 homicides, including the deaths of two children and one unborn child.

The SDFJC has some restrictions and jurisdictional limitations, however. The San Diego Police Department has jurisdiction over only criminal (felony and misdemeanor) cases that occur within the city of San Diego; the City Attorney's office has jurisdiction to prosecute misdemeanor cases that occur only within the incorporated cities of San Diego and Poway.

At its inception, the SDFJC was housed in a 27,000-square-foot space spread out over three floors. Floor plans were specifically developed to handle the volume, put victims and children at ease, and provide accessible services. The center has special waiting rooms for victims and children, medical facilities, and state-of-the-art interview rooms. There are multiple large and small conference rooms to allow for community meetings and training. The center received substantial funding from government, public, and private entities in its first year, and sustainability is important for the SDFJC to continue to provide these crucial services. The center's staff and board continue to take aggressive steps to ensure the longevity of the project, including cultivating funding from the city and the county. They also are seeking grants at the local, state, and federal level. Protracted financial security arrived in 2003 when Attorney General John Ashcroft announced that $30 million had been earmarked for 15 communities pursuing the family justice center concept. These communities were selected for funding under President George W. Bush's Family Justice Center Initiative, which was designed to prevent and respond to violence against women. The initiative, unveiled by President Bush in October 2003, was an unprecedented pilot program charged with making a victim's search for help and justice more efficient and effective by bringing professionals who provide an array of necessary services together under one roof. The Justice Department's Office on Violence Against Women (OVW) has taken the lead in this pilot program to develop comprehensive domestic violence victim service and support centers in these 15 communities across the country. "The Family Justice Center Initiative Awards will make a tremendous difference for women in these communities who are victimized by domestic violence, allowing those who desperately need help to find it in one place," said Ashcroft. "The cause of justice is served not only when we prosecute criminals, but also when we reach out to the victims of crime. The Family Justice Centers will ease their burden and demonstrate that the most compassionate way of helping victims can also be the best and most effective way."

"Offering centralized, comprehensive services to domestic violence victims is the coordinated community response at its best," said Office on Violence Against Women Director Diane M. Stuart. "Whether it's obtaining a protection order, talking to an advocate, or meeting with a prosecutor, these centers will enable victims to get the assistance they need to put their lives and their children's lives back on track."

Often, the services designed to help these victims are uncoordinated and scattered throughout communities. The Family Justice Center Initiative sites are designed to bring together advocates from nonprofit, nongovernmental domestic violence victim services organizations, law enforcement officers, prosecutors, probation officers, governmental victim assistants, forensic medical professionals, civil legal attorneys, chaplains, and representatives from community-based organizations into one centralized location. The 15 newest family justice centers were encouraged to look to those centers pioneered in San Diego, Indianapolis, and Hennepin County, Minnesota, for the comprehensive development and creation of their own facilities. U.S. Justice Department efforts will be further supported by its partners from the Department of Health and Human Services, Department of Agriculture, Department of Defense, Department of Education, Department of Housing and Urban Development, and Department of Labor. "The problem with these big justice centers is that it takes tremendous resources to maintain them," Diana Faugno adds, tapping into one of the main reasons so many fledgling centers are seeking local, state, and federal assistance. "Expenses are everywhere—running the program, paying the staff... those huge expenses are what kills everyone."

At the announcement of the $20 million funding in October 2003, President Bush acknowledged the numerous difficulties victims encounter in the reporting process, and how family justice centers can alleviate or eliminate completely any unnecessary waiting times, paperwork, and redundant examinations and questionings. "Too often, the services designed to help victims are uncoordinated and scattered throughout communities," Bush stated. "Imagine what it would be like if you were an abused person trying to find help and you went from one place to another. With laws and police and all the rules and regulations of a free society, it must be confusing and disheartening. The victim has been so traumatized, and then she has to tell her story over and over again, which repeats the trauma. There's a better way to do this. There's a better way to help people who need help in our society." He also acknowledged the hard work and vision of family justice center organizers:

> San Diego figured it out. They've got a city attorney named Casey Gwinn who recognized that there's a more compassionate way to help people who have been abused. And so he did something about it. He created what's called the San Diego Family Justice Center. It's a full-service center for domestic violence victims, where police officers and prosecutors and probation officers and civil attorneys and counselors and doctors and victims' advocates and chaplains all come together to help somebody. The run-around is over in San Diego. There's a central location where somebody who desperately needs help can find compassion and help. Victims can pick up food vouchers; they can get help with transportation; they can file for a temporary restraining order against their abusers; they can sign up for supervised visitation programs to keep their children safe; they can get their cell phone there. They can find help.

Bush continued:

> The San Diego Family Justice Center opened a year ago. It has already served thousands of victims. They tell me the story of Caitlin Effgen, who is a brave woman who lives in San Diego. It's probably, unfortunately, a typical story I'm about to tell you. What's atypical is that she found help in a brand new way of helping victims of domestic violence. Her boyfriend started hitting her. She tried to break up with him and he began to stalk her. She went to the authorities and got a restraining order, which, as the experts will tell you, sometimes works and some-

> times it doesn't; in her case, the boyfriend continued to harass her. You can imagine the fear she felt. He pleaded guilty to charges, but he still stalked her. And then she discovered the center. They helped her get counseling. They got another restraining order. A victim's advocate joined her and her dad in court. She got all the help she needed. I can imagine the relief that she must have felt when somebody who heard the call to love a neighbor did just that. The guy ended up behind bars, which is the right thing to (have happened). I congratulate the San Diego law enforcement officers. But more important, she got to remember what life was like without her misery. Those are her words, not mine. She found compassion. The funding I've set aside will help begin a national movement toward more of these centers. Fifteen will be funded through this initiative. When they work, there's another 12 or 15 to fund, maybe even more. Maybe we can escalate the request. But the point is, we have found what can work.

Casey Gwinn, one of the SDFJC's visionaries and most ardent supporters of the family justice center concept, worked tirelessly to lead a group of dedicated individuals to success that October day in 2002 when the center opened its doors. What many outside of San Diego County don't realize is that Gwinn had testified relentlessly to city government to remove the barriers in the center's path toward fruition. In a written testimony on March 12, 1992, Gwinn, who at the time was chairman of the San Diego Domestic Violence Council, related some of his experiences as a city attorney fighting on behalf of victims of violence. He recalled:

> In 1985, "Karen" walked into a hospital emergency room in San Diego and collapsed in the reception area. Nurses rushed out and determined she had been beaten by her husband. She had broken ribs, a collapsed lung, and internal bleeding. As they rushed her into surgery she was asked one question, "Do you want to press charges against your husband?" Predictably, she answered, "No." The police were never called. Social workers had minimal involvement with her and four days later her husband drove her home from the hospital to three more years of abuse before she left the relationship for good. In 1991, "Margaret" called 911 and said she had fallen in her kitchen and injured her head and needed paramedics. Paramedics arrived within 10 minutes. These paramedics, however, were trained in domestic violence issues. They quickly suspected nonaccidental injury based on the victim's description of the incident and the scene. They transported her to a hospital emergency room where domestic violence-trained nurses spent time talking to her about how the injury occurred. Within 20 minutes, Margaret admitted that she had not tripped but her husband had swung her by the arm into the door frame during an argument. Consistent with the hospital's new domestic violence protocol, the police were called and came directly to the emergency room where they interviewed Margaret. Police officers located her husband and arrested him. Margaret's case came to the City Attorney's Domestic Violence Unit for prosecution. We filed misdemeanor spousal abuse charges against Margaret's husband. Within days, Margaret became uncooperative. She refused to testify against her husband. We proceeded with the prosecution, based on the 911 tape, statements to the paramedics, statements to the nurses, medical records, photographs, and a partial admission from the defendant. He was ultimately convicted of spousal abuse and put in a one-year, 30-session treatment program for batterers. He has now been in counseling for six months and the violence in the relationship has stopped.

Gwinn continued:

> What happened in San Diego between 1986 and 1991 to cause the dramatic differences in these two real-life cases? The changes resulted from a coordinated effort of the San Diego City Attorney and the San Diego County Task Force on Domestic Violence. The task force has now concluded its work and a copy of the Final Report has been submitted to this panel. We still have many issues to address in San Diego but the changes, through multiagency cooperation, have been dramatic. We have implemented a comprehensive law enforcement protocol including an aggressive mandatory arrest policy on all probable cause felonies and a pro-arrest policy on all misdemeanors. We adopted a countywide medical service provider protocol for urgent care clinics and hospital emergency rooms. We coordinated a new protocol with our military community for the arrest of batterers within off-base military housing rather than releasing them to shore patrol. Finally, we adopted a comprehensive set of treatment standards for all counseling programs in San Diego County who receive court-ordered batterers. The task force has now resulted in the creation of the San Diego Domestic Violence Council. The permanent council includes the district attorney, city attorney, Superior Court, Municipal Court, Public Defender, San Diego Police Department, San Diego Sheriff's Department, Probation Department, Department of Social Services, military, San Diego Hospital Council, shelter community, and treatment providers. The council also has a committee system which includes representatives from over 40 agencies in San Diego County.

In his lobbying, Gwinn delivered a set of recommendations, some of which would eventually serve as a basis for the SDFJC, and some of which still presented solid ideas for future implementation. They include the following:

- Creating a pilot project for postplea diversion on domestic violence cases or eliminating domestic violence diversion.
- Allowing municipal and superior court judges to sit for criminal, civil, and juvenile purposes when criminal prosecution is pending.

- Creating batterers' work furlough facilities where batterers are in custody, obtaining treatment, and working to pay for it.
- Creating standardized reporting forms for hospitals.
- Creating standardized consent forms for hospitals regarding release of information to law enforcement.
- Giving incentives to medical insurance carriers to pay for batterers' treatment or for support groups or counseling for victims of domestic violence, including services for particular ethnic groups.
- Creating a hotline within the Attorney General's office for the handling and investigation of complaints on the handling of domestic violence incidents.
- Maintaining funding for domestic violence information sheets circulated by local law enforcement agencies.
- Expanding the hiring of bicultural, bilingual employees by city and county governments to provide more assistance to monolingual victims and clients served by the public workforce.
- Targeting corporate wellness programs statewide for expansion into services and awareness raising for domestic violence victims and perpetrators.
- Coordinate services for domestic violence and child abuse with substance abuse programs throughout the state.
- Allocating substance abuse treatment and prevention funds for treatment and intervention in domestic violence cases.
- Prohibiting "book and release" or "detention only" in domestic violence cases where probable cause exists for arrest.
- Mandating domestic violence training for all licensed clinical social workers, marriage and family counselors, and other psychotherapists.
- Restoring child abuse prevention program funding by the state of California and including domestic violence prevention in all new programming.
- Prohibiting juvenile court referrals for psychotherapy for victims of domestic violence unless the court finds that the victim is not amenable to a support group for battered women and that psychotherapy is appropriate.
- Increasing marriage license fees to fund shelter, prosecution, and advocacy programs.
- Expanding the mandated hours for law enforcement training on domestic violence issues.
- Providing legislation to clarify the role of school authorities in transporting children to court for testimony in domestic violence cases.
- Mandating juvenile court procedures and restraining order forms that provide that restraining orders issued by juvenile court judges be immediately entered into systems for recording of orders to enable domestic violence victims to have enforceable orders.
- Creating a statewide system for the compiling of restraining orders and access by law enforcement, prosecutors, and court personnel.
- Mandating domestic violence materials to be provided by all ministers or judicial officers to every couple obtaining a marriage license.
- Creating a pilot project for a domestic violence crisis response team to respond in cooperation with law enforcement to domestic violence scenes to provide support for victims and children and to refer for appropriate social service assistance.
- Mandating the creation of protocols for coordination between family court personnel and law enforcement when domestic violence situations are identified during restraining order proceedings.
- Creating a Standing Committee on Domestic Violence within the California District Attorneys Association.
- Mandating training on domestic violence for all child abuse professionals.
- Creating funding for treatment services to children of abused women.
- Calling for the development of intensive advocacy programs for abused mothers who face juvenile court, criminal court, and family court issues as well as issues of job training, employment, and child care.
- Calling for consequences throughout the criminal justice system for batterers who fail to complete counseling programs.
- Developing a strategy for extensive public education on domestic violence issues throughout society similar to child abuse awareness programs of years past.
- Requiring registration of domestic violence offenders.
- Calling on law enforcement agencies to allocate resources based on how officers spend their time, thereby allowing adequate resources for domestic violence enforcement and investigation activities.
- Mandating domestic violence reporting by professionals who deal with domestic violence

similar to current reporting requirements for child abuse.

- Allocating a portion of lottery proceeds to address domestic violence education within the school system.
- Calling for parent awareness sessions within the public school system to raise the consciousness of parents to the consequences of domestic violence in the home.
- Allocating a percentage of alcohol taxes for community-based domestic violence treatment programs for indigent abusers and for shelter and support services for victims.
- Creating a working group within the California Criminal Justice Council to identify domestic violence issues and coordinate strategies for effective intervention.
- Calling for local sales tax initiatives to fund advocacy and intervention efforts for battered women and their children.
- Creating batterers' treatment programs within the Department of Corrections to provide long-term batterers with treatment while felony abusers are incarcerated.
- Calling for the Department of Corrections to utilize private batterers' programs for domestic violence offenders and parolees after release from state prison.
- Allocating funding for regional shelters for battered women to ensure availability throughout each county in California.

Gwinn recalls the day he got the phone call he'd anxiously been waiting for:

> It was September, 1989. After a phone call from City Attorney John Witt, the district attorney had agreed to listen to my proposal for a "one-stop shop" domestic violence service center in San Diego. I had written a 10-page proposal to be distributed to all the supervisors in the DA's Office. The premise was simple: Victims would have an easier time receiving needed services if they only had to go one place to get all the necessary help. I arrived in the DA's office on the 14th floor of the Wells Fargo Building downtown and was ushered into the main conference room. The heads of each branch were present, along with the assistant district attorney and the chief deputy. My proposal was passed out and I was given the floor for 20 minutes. After the conclusion of my presentation, there were a few questions and I was ushered out. I never got a formal response to my proposal; not a week later, not a month later. It was fair to say that a one-stop shop for domestic violence victims was an idea whose time had not come. Even after that discouraging day, though, Assistant City Attorney Gael Strack and I remained determined to move forward with the concept. By the early 1990s, we had the YWCA and CCS on site with full-time staff. We expanded our own advocacy program with grants and city eneral fund revenue. Soon thereafter, we had staff from the district attorney's Victim Witness Program in our unit, and our attorneys were cross-deputized to handle felonies as well as misdemeanors. As part of our determination to move forward with a limited one-stop shop, we began rotating prosecutors over to the police department on a weekly basis and had detectives coming over to our office on a weekly basis. We successfully pursued grants for partnerships with Children's Hospital and Child Protective Services. Within a year of that humble beginning to a multidisciplinary service center it was abundantly clear that the idea was the right one. Victims could get a restraining order and see a prosecutor. They could talk to a detective and meet with an advocate from Children's Hospital.

A turning point came in 1998, Gwinn says:

> Finally, David Bejarano became the police chief of San Diego. It was an answer to prayer. Within six months, he and I sat down and talked about two initiatives: creation of a Neighborhood Prosecution Unit, and creation of a one-stop shop for victims of domestic violence. The rest, as they say, is now history. With a cast of hundreds and the passion of a small core, we did it! We took our small, limited idea of co-located services and exploded it into a national model now becoming known as the San Diego Family Justice Center. And we are not done. Even as the rest of the country begins to follow our lead, we will keep moving forward to the next level. We will not stop. We will not rest on our laurels. We will not bruise each other with pats on the back. We will refuse to settle. We will continue to aspire until one day women, men, and children do not die in domestic violence homicides in San Diego. We will continue to strive until services are coordinated countywide and hurting families get the help they need in every corner of San Diego County. Nothing will be good enough until every child from a domestic violence home has the opportunity to break free from violence and discover their God-given gifts and abilities. We will build the best camping facilities in America for domestic violence victims and their children. And we will push for prevention initiatives as never before. The goal is not too ambitious. The vision is not too lofty. The San Diego Family Justice Center is, without question, an idea whose time has now come.

One of the most significant components of the SDFJC is the Forensic Medical Unit (FMU), which was the first freestanding forensic medical unit in the country at the time of its inception in 2002. The FMU is a private suite with two medical exam rooms and staff offices. It provides a safe, comfortable area for victims so that they will not be forced to wait in nonsecure public areas or busy hospital-based ED for care. The unit is staffed by a full-time forensic nurse practitioner and two half-time emergency medicine physicians who are national experts in the field of domestic violence injuries, George McClane, MD and Ellen Taliaferro, MD. Additional staff will be added as the unit continues to grow. "What makes the Forensic Medical Unit truly unique is that it is part of a collaborative effort involving law enforcement, forensic medicine and the City Attorney's Office," says McClane, who serves as the FMU's medical director. "It is a place where victims of domestic violence, whether they are young or old, can go to be treated and where injuries can be forensically evaluated." McClane adds that forensic medicine is a crucial element in prosecuting perpetrators of domestic violence. "The forensically-based evidence plays a major role in solving the crime," McClane says.

The FMU at the SDFJC began its operations on April 1, 2003, and saw its first patient on May 1, 2003. To date, it has provided medical care to more than 100 victims of domestic violence, including both men and women. The types of injuries handled at the FMU include contusions, abrasions, minor lacerations or sprains, as well as injuries to the head, neck, chest, breasts, abdomen, arms, and legs. Life-threatening injuries are referred to local hospital ERs. Victims have sought medical care at the FMU or have been referred by the San Diego Police Department. "In many domestic violence cases, it is essential to document the victim's injuries as quickly as possible," said San Diego Police Chief William Lansdowne. "The Family Justice Center's Forensic Medical Unit provides one more opportunity to collect detailed evidence and share it with prosecutors housed at the Family Justice Center. When abusers are prosecuted and held accountable for their crimes, it is much more difficult for them to reoffend." The FMU's care includes documentation of external and internal injuries and follow-up documentation; preservation of physical evidence for prosecution of abusers; detection of internal injuries caused by strangulation or blunt force trauma; detection of mental health and psychiatric symptoms; intervention in cases involving pregnant women; patient and victim education and safety; continuity of care and long-term support for victims; communication and collaboration among all intervention professionals; statistical record keeping and research; and education, awareness, and outreach to hospitals and clinics about the FMU and the SDFJC. The unit also provides referrals for well-child checkups and women's care. According to McClane, who is also a Sharp Grossmont Hospital ED physician, other similar forensic units across the country might work only with specific populations such as child abuse victims, or are located within a hospital and do not provide the comprehensive services and access to the continuum of care. "Most importantly, after they receive their medical exam, all the social services and law enforcement services they need are right there in the building," says Assistant City Attorney Gael Strack, the on-site coordinator of the SDFLC.

Although some professionals might be skeptical of the one-stop shop concept, there's no denying the positive impact that these types of centers can have on the community. In its very first year of operation, the SDFJC:

- Assisted 5,700 victims, including 750 children.
- Facilitated 4,962 meetings between professionals assisting domestic violence victims.
- Fielded 31,578 phone calls.
- Had 20,665 hits on its Web site.
- Saw the filing of 11,368 SDPD police reports.
- Facilitated 4,393 cases with the City Attorney.
- Saw 712 trials set.
- Saw 70 trials conducted.
- Saw 3,942 cases reviewed by probation in DV Court.
- Cared for 131 clients in the FMU.
- Benefited from 5,204 volunteer hours.

Since it opened in 2002, the SDFJC has had visitors from more than 35 states and 18 countries. The number of walk-in victims of domestic violence has gone from 87 in its first month of operation to 636 walk-in victims in September 2003. City officials report that the center has been an integral part of their efforts to prevent domestic violence and assist victims. "Most importantly," Gwinn says, "we are seeing domestic violence murders continue to decline. We have gone from 30 domestic violence homicides in the city in 1985 to nine in 2002, to four in 2003."

The SDFJC engaged in participatory strategic planning from the very beginning. This process was viewed as essential to successfully forge the multiple partnerships and complex service systems that are housed under a single roof in the SDFJC model. By working together in a strategically planned synergistic fashion, this collaborative effort has and will continue to provide victims and children involved in domestic violence with more support, improved accessibility to services and resources, and make the entire process of reporting a domestic violence incident much less overwhelming for the victims and children involved.

Organizers say it will take two phases to bring the SDFJC to life fully. Phase I was implemented in October 2002 when the SDFJC became the first in the country to house an entire police department's Domestic Violence Unit and a city's Prosecutorial Domestic Violence Unit. During Phase I, victim injuries were evaluated, documented, and treated. Phase II is the ultimate dream, a permanent home. On October 19, 2002, the SDFJC gala kicked off a $10 million capital campaign to make this part of the dream a reality. Phase II envisions the purchase and renovation of a specialized facility that will allow the inclusion of professionals handling child abuse, elder abuse, and sexual assault cases. Phase II implementation is projected to take approximately three to five years.

Through January 2004, the SDFJC saw an additional 1,067 victims (including 216 children), fielded 5,821 more phone calls, received 5,335 more hits on its Web site, saw 88 more trials set, treated 54 more people in the FMU, and benefited from 1,509 additional volunteer hours. By 2007, the center plans to offer comprehensive medical and legal services, counseling to victims and children; links to juvenile, family, and criminal court; as well as access to on-site professionals such as child protective service workers, probation, parole and border patrol officers, and others.

The SDFJC is unique in many of its configurations and operations, as it should be, experts say. A cookie-cutter approach will not be sufficient to address numerous socioeconomic factors that affect jurisdictions and communities across the country. "There are going to be many different models that come out of the one-stop shop concept," Diana Faugno says:

> It will be up to each community to determine which one is best for them. For example, the SDFJC isn't able to help us here in North County San Diego, and I can't use any of their services because of distance and cost. Whether the family justice center and the community are connected by the dotted lines on paper or is actually connected to the community, whatever is going to work in that specific community will be the best model or the best practice. What you are looking for is volume of victims and where is it located in the region; from there, it's just a matter of finding the pole upon which you're going to hang your hat.

7.10 THE FUTURE

Carlson (2005) says that in the past 20 years, important insights have been gained regarding violence and trauma, how complications occur, their causes, and their effects on victims. Carlson adds that violence and abuse toward women—physical, sexual, and emotional—are not rare events and are most often perpetrated by partners or acquaintances rather than strangers. These events occur in nonmarital as well as marital relationships, including same-sex relationships. Carlson emphasizes that future research should address increased understanding of variation in individual responses to violence and trauma, matching of treatment to different types of male offenders, better understanding of how culture affects violence perpetration and victimization, and evaluation of domestic violence interventions.

REFERENCES

American Psychological Association. *Medical Providers Need More Training to Spot and Intervene in Cases of Domestic Violence, According to New Study.* [Press release, August, 2000]. Available at www.apa.org/releases/domviolence.html

Bachman, R., Ed. *Violence Against Women: A National Crime Victimization Survey Report.* Washington, DC: U.S. Department of Justice. 1994.

Bair-Merritt, M. H., Giardino, A. P, Turner, M., Ganetsky, M., & Christian, C. W. Pediatric residency training on domestic violence: A national survey. *Ambul Pediatr. 4,* 1, 24–27, 2004.

Bell, C. C., Jenkins, E. J., Kpo, W., & Rhodes, H. Response of emergency rooms to victims of interpersonal violence. *Hosp Community Psychiatry. 45,* 2, 142–146, 1994.

Briere, J., Woo, R., McRae, B., Foltz, J., & Sitzman, R. Lifetime victimization history, demographics, and clinical status in female psychiatric emergency room patients. *J Nerv Men Dis. 185,* 95–101, 1997.

Campbell, D. W., Sharps, P. W., Campbell, J. C., & Lopez, L. M. Intimate partner violence in African American women. *Online J Issues in Nursing. 7,* 1, 5, 2002.

Campbell, J. C. *Risk Factors for Femicide in Abusive Relationships: Results from a Multi-site Case Control Study.* [Press release] Johns Hopkins University. 2003.

Carlson, B. E. The most important things learned about violence and trauma in the past 20 years. *J Interpers Violence. 20,* 1, 119–126, 2005.

Centers for Disease Control and Prevention, National Center for Injury Prevention and Control. Intimate partner violence fact sheet. 2000. Available at: www.cdc.gov/ncipc/dvp/dvam.htm.

Coker, A., Smith, P., Bethea, L., King, M., & McKeown, R. Physical health consequences of physical and psychological intimate partner violence. *Arch Fam Med. 9,* 5, 451–457, 1997.

Craine, L., Henson, C., Colliver, J., & MacLean, D. Prevalence of a history of sexual abuse among female psychiatric patients in a state hospital system. *Hosp Community Psych. 39,* 3, 300–304, 1988.

Elliott, B. A., & Johnson, M. M. Domestic violence in a primary care setting: Patterns and prevalence. *Arch Fam Med. 4,* 113–119, 1995.

Family Violence Prevention Fund. Catalog of training and education materials on domestic violence. Available at: http://www.fvpf.org.

Family Violence Prevention Fund. *Identifying and Responding to Domestic Violence: Consensus Recommendations for Child Adolescent Health.* Washington, DC: U.S. Department of Justice, Office for Victims of Crime. 2002.

Family Violence Prevention Fund. Improving health care response to domestic violence: A resource manual for health care providers. Available at: http://www.fvpf.org.

Family Violence Prevention Fund. Improving health care response to domestic violence: A training manual for health care providers. Available at: http://www.fvpf.org.

Family Violence Prevention Fund. Preventing domestic violence: Clinical guidelines on routine screening. 1999. Available at: http://www.fvpf.org.

Family Violence Prevention Fund. State-by-state report card on health care laws and domestic violence. 2000.

Family Violence Prevention Fund. National consensus guidelines on identifying and responding to domestic violence victimization in health care settings. Available at: http://endabuse.org/programs/healthcare/files/consensus.pdf

Freidman, L. S., Samet, J. H., Roberts, M. S., Hudlin, M., & Hans, P. Inquiry about victimization experiences: A survey of patient preferences and physician practices. *Arch Intern Med. 152,* 6, 1186–1190, 1992.

Gin, N. E., Rucker, L., Frayne S., Cygan R., & Hubbell, F.A. Prevalence of domestic violence among patients in three ambulatory care internal medicine clinics. *J Gen Internal Med. 6,* 317–222, 1991.

Golding, J. Sexual assault history and long-term physical health problems: Evidence from clinical and population epidemiology. *Current Directions in Psycho Sci. 8,* 191–194, 1999.

Hamberger, L. K., Saunders, D. G., & Hovey, M. Prevalence of domestic violence in community practice and rate of physician inquiry. *Fam Med. 24,* 283–287, 1992.

Houry, D., Sachs, C. J., Feldhaus, K. M., & Linden, J. Violence-inflicted injuries: Reporting laws in the 50 states. *Ann Emerg Med. 39,* 1, 56–60, 2002.

Housekamp, B. M., & Foy, D. The assessment of posttraumatic stress disorder in battered women. *J Interpers Violence. 6,* 3, 367–375, 1991.

Kilpatrick, D., Best, C. L., Veronen, L. J., Amick, A. E., Villeponteaux, L.A., & Ruff, G. A. Mental health correlates of criminal victimization: A random community survey. *J Consult Clin Psycho. 53,* 6, 866–873, 1985.

Kilpatrick, D., Edmunds, C., & Seymour, A. *Rape in America: A Report to the Nation.* Charleston, SC: National Victim Center and the Crime Victims Research and Treatment Center, Medical University of South Carolina. 1992.

Kimerling, R., & Calhoun, K. S. Somatic symptoms, social support, and treatment seeking among sexual assault victims. *J Consult Clin Psychol. 62,* 333–340, 1994.

Koss, M. P., Koss, P. G., & Woodruff, W. J. Deleterious effects of criminal victimization on women's health and medical utilization. *Arch Intern Med. 151,* 342–347, 1991.

McFarlane, J., Malecha, A., Watson, K., Gist, J., Batten, E., Hall, I., & Smith, S. Intimate partner sexual assault against women: Frequency, health consequences, and treatment outcomes. *Obstet Gynecol. 105,* 1, 99–108, 2005.

McGrath, M. E., Bettacchi, A., Duffy, S. J., Peipert, J. F., Becker, B. M., & Angelo, L. Violence against women: Provider barriers to intervention in emergency departments. *Acad Emerg Med. 4,* 4, 297–300, 1997.

McLeer, S. V., & Anwar, R. A study of battered women presenting in an emergency department. *Am J Public Health. 79,* 65–66, 1989.

Miller, T. R., Cohen, M. A., Rossman, S. B. Victim costs of violent crime and resulting injuries. *Health Aff. 12,* 4, 186–197, 1993.

Moffitt, T., & A. Caspi. *New Study Examines Scope of Partner Violence* [Press release, July 14, 1999]. University of Wisconsin–Madison. Available at www.news.wisc.edu/353.html

Moore, M. L., Zaccaro, D., & Parsons, L. H. Attitudes and practices of registered nurses toward women who have experienced abuse/domestic violence. *J Obstet Gynecol Neonatal Nurs. 27,* 2, 175–182, 1998.

National Academies of Sciences. *Confronting Chronic Neglect: The Education and Training of Health Professionals on Family Violence.* Washington, DC. 2000.

New York City Department of Health, Bureau of Injury Epidemiology. *Femicide in New York City: 1995–2002.* www.health.state.ny.us. 2004.

Nibert, D., Cooper, S., & Crossmaker, M. Assaults against residents of a psychiatric institution: Residents' history of abuse. *J Interpers Violence. 4,* 3, 342–349, 1989.

Parsons, L. H., & Moore, M. L. Family violence issues in obstetrics and gynecology, primary care, and nursing texts. *Obstet Gynecol. 90,* 4 (Pt 1), 596, 1997.

Rath, G. D., Jarratt, L. G., & Leonardson, G. Rates of domestic violence against adult women by men partners. *J Am Board Fam Pract. 2,* 227–233, 1989.

Rodriguez, M., Bauer, H., McLoughlin, E., & Grumbach, K. Screening and intervention for intimate partner abuse. *JAMA. 282,* 5, 468–474, 1999.

Sachs, C. J., Baraff, L. J., & Peek, C. Need for law enforcement in cases of intimate partner violence in a university ED. *Am J Emerg Med. 16,* 1, 60–63, 1998.

Sachs, C. J., Koziol-McLain, J., Glass, N., Webster, D., & Campbell, J. A population-based survey assessing support for mandatory domestic violence reporting by health care personnel. *Women Health. 35,* 2–3, 121–133, 2002.

Sachs, C. J., Peek, C., Baraff, L. J., & Hasselblad, V. Failure of the mandatory domestic violence reporting law to increase medical facility referral to police. *Ann Emerg Med. 31,* 4, 488–494, 1998.

Saunders, D. G., Hamberger, L. K., & Hovey, M. Indicators of woman abuse based on a chart review at a family practice center. *Arch Fam Med. 2,* 537–543, 1993.

Sethi, D., Watts, S., Zwi, A., Watson, J., McCarthy, C. Experience of domestic violence by women attending an inner city accident and emergency department. *Emerg Med J. 21,* 2, 180–184. 2004.

Stark, E., Flitcraft, A., & Frazier, W. Medicine and patriarchal violence: The social construction of a private event. *Int J Health Serv. 9,* 461–493, 1997.

Stuart, P. Risk factors for recent domestic physical assault in patients presenting to the emergency department. *Emerg Med Australas. 16,* 3, 216–224, 2004.

Surgeon General's Workshop on Violence and Public Health: Report. Washington, DC: U.S. Department of Health and Human Services, Public Health Service. 1986.

Tilden, V. P., Schmidt, T. A., Limandri, B. J., Chiodo, G. T., Garland, M. J., & Loveless, P. A. Factors that influence clinicians' assessment and management of family violence. *Am J Public Health. 84,* 4, 628–633, 1994.

Tjaden, P., & Thoennes, N. *Prevalence, Incidence, and Consequences of Violence Against Women: Findings from the National Violence Against Women Survey.* Washington, DC: National Institute of Justice, Centers for Disease Control, Bureau of Justice Statistics. 2000.

U.S. Department of Justice. *Improving the Health and Mental Health Care Systems' Responses to Violence Against Women, Toolkit to End Violence Against Women.* Washington, DC. 2001.

Washington State Department of Health. *Women's Childhood Abuse Liked to Later Poor Health.* [Press release, June 26, 2003]. Available at www.hbns.org.

Woodtli, M. B., & Breslin, E. Violence-related content in the nursing curriculum: A national study. *J Nurs Educ. 35,* 8, 367–374, 1996.

Woodtli, M., & Breslin, E. Violence-related content in the nursing curriculum: A follow-up national survey. *J Nurs Educ. 41,* 8, 340–348, 2002.

Zawitz, M. W., Ed. *Violence Between Intimates.* Washington, DC: U.S. Department of Justice, Bureau of Justice Statistics. 1994.

RECOMMENDED READINGS

Abbott, J., Johnson, R., Koziol-McLain, J., Lowenstein, S. R. Domestic violence against women incidence and prevalence in an emergency department population. *JAMA. 273,* 1763–1767, 1995.

Adams, D. Guidelines for doctors on identifying and helping in their patients who batter. *J M Women's Association. 51,* 123–126, 1996.

Alpert, E. T., Seeherman, A., & Holtz, H. Family violence curricula in U.S. medical schools. *Am J Prevent Med. 14,* 4, 273–282, 1998.

American Academy of Pediatrics. The role of the pediatrician in recognizing and intervening on behalf of abused women. *Am Acad Pediatr. Jun, 101,* 6, 1–5, 1998.

American Academy of Pediatrics Task Force on Adolescent Assault Victim Needs. Adolescent assault victim needs: A review of issues and model protocol. *Pediatrics. 98,* 5, 991–1001, 1996.

American Association of Colleges of Nursing. *Violence as a Public Health Problem.* Washington, DC: American Association of Colleges of Nursing. 1999.

American Association of Health Plans/Commonwealth Fund. *Best Practices in Women's Health: Identifying Exemplary Care: Domestic Violence.* Washington, DC: American Association of Health Plans. 1999.

American Association of Health Plans/Commonwealth Fund. *Advancing Women's Health: Health Plan Innovative Programs in Domestic Violence.* Washington, DC: American Association of Health Plans. 1998.

American College of Emergency Physicians. List of key elements of family violence protocols. Emergency Medicine Practice Committee Subcommittee on Key Elements of Domestic Violence Protocols. Available at: http://www.acep.org.

American College of Obstetricians and Gynecologists. Domestic violence: The role of the physician in identification, intervention, and prevention: A slide lecture presentation. Washington, DC: American College of Obstetricians and Gynecologists. 1995.

American College of Obstetricians and Gynecologists. *Intimate Partner Violence During Pregnancy: A Guide for Clinicians.* Washington, DC: American College of Obstetricians and Gynecologists. 2000.

American College of Physicians/American Society of Internal Medicine. *Medical Knowledge Self-Assessment Program: MKSAP 12—Ambulatory Medicine.* Chicago: American College of Physicians/American Society of Internal Medicine. 2001.

American Medical Association. *Diagnostic and Treatment Guidelines on Domestic Violence.* Chicago: American Medical Association. 1992.

American Medical Association. Prevention of Violence and Abuse Resolution (419). 2000. Available at: http://www.ama-assn.org.

American Osteopathic Association. Domestic, family and school violence education. Adopted by the House of Delegates of the American Osteopathic Association (originally in 1991; revised 1996, 2001).

American Osteopathic Association. Violence—Development of programs to reduce. Adopted by the House of Delegates of the American Osteopathic Association (originally in 1991; revised 1996, 2001).

American Physical Therapy Association. Excerpts from American Physical Therapy Association's guidelines for recognizing and providing care for victims of domestic abuse. *Phys Ther. 6,* 10, 81–82, 84, 1998.

Anderson, D., Harris, M., & McCosker, H. Violence against women: An education program for rural community health workers. *Aust J Rural Health. 5,* 1, 17–21, 1997.

Bergman, B., & Brismar, B. A five-year follow-up study of 117 battered women. *Am J Public Health. 81,* 11, 1486–1489, 1991.

Brannen, S. J., Bradshaw, R. D., Hamlin, E. R., Fogarty, J. P., Colligan, T. W. Spouse abuse: Physician guidelines to identification, diagnosis, and management in the uniformed services. *Mil Med. 164,* 1, 30–36, 1999.

Bullock, K. Domestic violence training at an inner-city hospital found helpful. *J Emerg Nurs. 23,* 4, 299–300, 1997.

Bureau of Justice Statistics. *Special Report: Intimate Partner Violence and Age of Victim, 1993–99.* Washington, DC: U.S. Department of Justice. 2001.

California Medical Training Center. Advanced training in domestic violence for health care providers. Training Course and Manual. Available at: http://web.ucdmc.ucdavis.edu/medtrng/training/events.html.

California Medical Training Center. Forensic examination for victims of domestic violence. Available at: http://web.ucdmc.ucdavis.edu/medtrng/training/events.html.

California Medical Training Center. Improving the health care response to violence. 1999. Available at: http://web.ucdmc.ucdavis.edu/medtrng/training/events.html.

Callaghan, J. Elder abuse and one community's response. *Int J Health Care Quality Assurance Inc Leadersh Health Serv. 11,* 2–3, vi–xi, 1998.

Capezuti, E., & Siegler, E. L. Educating health and social service professionals in the detection and management of mistreated nursing home residents. *J Elder Abuse Negl. 8,* 3, 73–86, 1996.

Caralis, P., & Musialowski, R. Women's experiences with domestic violence and their attitudes and expectations regarding medical care of abuse victims. *South Med J. 90,* 1075–1080, 1997.

Chamberlain, L. P., & Perham-Hester, K. A. Physicians' screening practices for female partner abuse during prenatal visits. *Matern Child Health J. 4,* 2, 141–148, 2000.

Chez, R. H., & Horan, D. L. Response of obstetrics and gynecology program directors to a domestic violence lecture module. *Am J Obstetr Gynecol. 180,* 2 (Pt 1), 496–498, 1999.

Clark, C., Becker, M., Giard, J., Mazelis, R., Savage, A., & Vogel, W. The role of coercion in the treatment of women with co-occurring disorders and histories of abuse. *J Behav Health Serv Res. 32,* 2, 167–181, 2005.

Clarke, M. E., & Pierson, W. Management of elder abuse in the emergency department. *Emerg Med Clin North Am. 17,* 3, 631–644, 1999.

Cohall, A., Cohall, R., Bannister, H., & Northridge, M. Love shouldn't hurt: Strategies for health care providers to address adolescent dating violence. *J Am Med Women's Association. 54,* 3, 144–148, 1999.

Coker, A., Smith, P., Bethea, L., King, M., & McKeown, R. Physical health consequences of physical and psychological intimate partner violence. *Arch Fam Med. 9,* 5, 451–457, 2000.

Cole, T. B. Is domestic violence screening helpful? *JAMA. 284,* 5, 551–553, 2000.

Coonrod, D. V., Bay, R. C., Rowley, B. D., Del Mar, N. B., Gabriele, L., Tessman, T. D., & Chambliss, L. R. A randomized controlled study of brief interventions to teach residents about domestic violence. *Acad Med. 75,* 1, 55–57, 2000.

Cowley, S., Rush, J., Lenton, L., & Lukasik-Foss, L. Care of the abused woman: A hospital's educational program assesses values and beliefs. *Health Progress. 77,* 2, 26–29, 1996.

Culross, P. L. Healthcare system responses to children exposed to domestic violence. *Future Child. 9,* 3, 111–121, 1999.

Currier, G. W., Barthaeur, L. M., Begier, E., & Bruce, M. L. Training and experience of psychiatric residents in identifying domestic violence. *Psychiatr Serv. 47,* 5, 529–530, 1996.

Davenport, S. Domestic violence policy and procedure: Carondelet Health Network. Tucson, AZ: St. Mary's Hospital. 1996.

Dearwater, S. R., Coben, J. H., Campbell, J. C., Nah, G., Glass, N., McLoughlin, E., & Bekemeier, B. Prevalence of intimate partner abuse in women treated at community hospital emergency departments. *JAMA. 280,* 433–438, 1998.

DeLahunta, E. T. Resistance to adding curricula about domestic violence. *Acad Med. 73,* 7, 726–727, 1998.

Dienemann, J., Trautman, D., Shahan, J., Pinnella, K., Krishnan, P., Whyne, D., Bekemeier, B., & Campbell, J. Developing a domestic violence program in an inner city academic health center emergency department: The first three years. *J Emerg Nurs. 25,* 2, 110–115, 1999.

Edleson, J. L. Children's witnessing of adult domestic violence. *J Interpers Violence. 14,* 8, 839–870, 1999.

Edleson, J. L. The overlap between child maltreatment and woman battering. *Violence Against Women. 5,* 2, 134–154, 1999.

Eisenstat, S. A., & Bancroft, L. Domestic violence. *N Engl J Med. 341,* 12, 886–892, 1999.

Emergency Nurses Association. Domestic violence & child maltreatment: Position Statement. Available at: http://www.ena.org/services/posistate/data/tresex.htm.

Family Violence Prevention Fund. *Preventing Domestic Violence: Clinical Guidelines on Routine Screening.* San Francisco: Family Violence Prevention Fund. 1999.

Fanslow, J. L., Norton, R. N., & Robinson, E. M. One-year follow-up of an emergency department protocol for abused women. *Aust N Z J Public Health. 23,* 4, 418–421, 1999.

Fanslow, J. L., Norton, R., Robinson, E. M., & Spinola, C. G. Outcome evaluation of an emergency department protocol of care on partner abuse. *Aust N Z J Public Health. 22,* 5, 598–603, 1998.

Felitti, V. J., Anda, R. F., Nordenberg, D., Williamson, D. F., Spitz, A. M., Edwards, V., Kiss, M. P., & Marks, J. Relationship of childhood abuse and household dysfunction to many of the leading causes of death in adults. *Am J Prevent Med. 14,* 4, 245–258, 1998.

Flitcraft, A. Project SAFE: Domestic violence education for practicing physicians. *Women's Health Issues. 5,* 4, 183–188, 1995.

Freeman, J. Old law, new bite mandatory abuse training. *J Iowa Med Soc. 90,* 15, 15, 2000.

Friedman, L., Samet, J., Roberts, M., Hudlin, M., & Hans, P. Inquiry about victimization experiences: A survey of patient preferences and physician practices. *Arch Internal Med. 152,* 1186–1190, 1992.

Frieze, I. R. Investigating the causes and consequences of marital rape. *J Women Culture Soc. 8,* 532–553, 1983.

Gantt, L., & Bickford, A. Screening for domestic violence: How one hospital network started asking about abuse. *AWHONN Lifelines. 3,* 2, 36–42, 1999.

Gelles, R. J., & Harrop, J. W. Violence, battering, and psychological distress among women. *J Interpers Violence. 4,* 1, 400–420, 1989.

Gerbert, B. M., Caspers, N., Bronstone, A., Moe, J., & Abercrombie, P. A qualitative analysis of how physicians with expertise in domestic violence approach the identification of victims. *Ann Intern Med. 131,* 8, 578–584, 1999.

Gerbert, B. M., Moe, J., Caspers, N., Salber, P., Feldman, M., Herzig, K., & Bronstone, A. Simplifying physicians' response to domestic violence. *West J Med. 172,* 329–331, 2000.

Glass, N., & Campbell, J. C. Mandatory reporting of intimate partner violence by health care professionals: A policy review. *Nurs Outlook. 46,* 6, 279–283, 1998.

Haack, D. Suggested Protocols for Victims of Spousal and Elder Abuse: *A Task Force Reference Document for Colorado Hospitals.* Denver: Colorado Department of Health. 1996.

Haase, C. S., Short, P. D., Chapman, D. M., & Dersch, S.A. Domestic violence education in medical school: Does it make a difference? *Acad Emerg Med. 6,* 8, 855–857, 1999.

Hadley, S. M. Documentation in the medical record of potential cases of domestic violence. In *WomanKind Policies and Procedures* (pp. 1–7). Minneapolis, MN: Fairview Health Services. 1995.

Hadley, S. S., Lezin, N., & Zook, E. An innovative model of health care response to domestic abuse. *Women's Health Issues. 5,* 4, 189–198, 1995.

Hamberger, L. K., Ambuel, B., Marbella, A., & Donze, J. Physician interaction with battered women: The women's perspective. *Arch Fam Med. 7,* 575–582, 1998.

Harwell, T. S., Casten, R. J., Armstrong, K. A., Dempsey, S., Coons, H. L., & Davis, M. Results of a domestic violence training program offered to the staff of urban community health centers. *Am J Prevent Med. 15,* 3, 235–242, 1998.

Hawkins, J. W. Intimate partner violence: A death sentance for women. *Clinical Excellence for Nurse Practitioners, 6,* 3, 2002.

Hill, J. R. Teaching about family violence: A proposed model curriculum. *Teach Learn Med. 17,* 2, 169–178, 2005.

Horan, D. L., Chapin, J., Klein, L., Schmidt, L.A., & Schulkin, J. Domestic violence screening practices of obstetricians and gynecologists. *Obstet Gynecol. 92,* 5, 785–789, 1998.

Hotch, D., Grunfeld, A., Mackay, K., et al. Improving your health care facility's response to domestic violence: Objectives and expectations. In *Domestic Violence Intervention by Emergency Department Staff* (pp. 1–4). Vancouver, BC: Vancouver Hospital and Health Sciences Centre. 1995.

Hotch, D., Grunfeld, A., Mackay, K., & Ritch L. Policy and procedures for domestic violence patients in Canadian emergency departments: A national survey. *J Emerg Nurs. 22,* 4, 278–282, 1996.

Hoyt, C. A. Evidence recognition and collection in the clinical setting. *Crit Care Nurs Q. 22,* 1, 19–26, 1999.

Jonassen, J. A., Pugnaire, M. P., Mazor, K., Regan, M. B., Jacobson, E. W., Gammon, W., Doepel, D. G., & Cohen, A. J. The effect of a domestic violence interclerkship on the knowledge, attitudes, and skills of third-year medical students. *Acad Med. 74,* 7, 821–828, 1999.

Kilpatrick, D. G. What is violence against women: Defining and measuring the problem. *J Interpers Violence. 19,* 11, 1209–1234, 2004.

Kilpatrick, D. G., Edmunds, C. N., & Seymour, A. K. *Rape in America: A report to the nation.* Arlington, VA: National Victim Center and Medical University of South Carolina. 1992.

Kilpatrick, K. I., Litt, M., & Williams, L. Post-traumatic stress disorder in child witnesses to domestic violence. *Am J Orthopsychiatry. 67,* 4, 639–644, 1997.

Kingston, P., Penhale, B., & Bennett, G. Is elder abuse on the curriculum? The relative contribution of child abuse, domestic violence and elder abuse in social work, nursing and medicine qualifying curricula. *Health Soc Care Community. 3,* 6, 353–362, 1995.

Knight, R. A., & Remington, P. L. Training internal medicine residents to screen for domestic violence. *J Womens Health Gend Based Med. 9,* 2, 167–174, 2000.

Konchak, P. S. Domestic violence: A primer for the primary care physician. *J Am Osteopath Assoc. 98,* 12, S11–S14, 1998.

Koss, M. P., Dinero, T. E., Seibel, C. A., & Cox, S. L. Stranger and acquaintance rape: Are there differences in the victim's experience. *Psychol Women Q. 12,* 1–24, 1988.

Koss, M. P., & Heslet, L. Somatic consequences of violence against women. *Arch Fam Med. 1,* 53–59, 1992.

Koziol-McLain, J., Coates, C., & Lowenstein, S. Predictive validity of a screen for partner violence against women. *Am J Prevent Med. 21,* 2, 93–100, 2001.

Kripke, E., Steele, G., O'Brien, M. K., & Novack, D. H. Domestic violence training program for residents. *J Genl Intern Med. 13,* 12, 839–841, 1998.

Krueger, P. M., & Schafer, S. Physician awareness of domestic violence: Does continuing medical education have an impact? *J Am Osteopath Assoc. 100,* 3, 145–148, 2000.

Lanzilotti, S. S., Jones, P., Dai, J., & Bentzien, V. EMS and the domestic violence patient: A report card of existing policy, protocol & training. *J Emerg Med Serv. 24,* 6, 58–66, 1999.

Larkin, G. L., Rolniak, S., Hyman, K. B., MacLeod, B. A., & Savage, R. Effect of an administrative intervention on rates of screening for domestic violence in an urban emergency department. *Am J Public Health. 90,* 9, 1444–1448, 2000.

Lawrence, L. L., & Brannen, S. J. The impact of physician training on child maltreatment reporting: A multi-specialty study. *Mil Med. 165,* 8, 607–611, 2000.

Limandri, B. J., & Tilden, V. P. Nurses' reasoning in the assessment of family violence. *Image J Nurs Sch. 28,* 3, 247–252, 1996.

Limbos, M. P., & Berkowitz, C. D. Documentation of child physical abuse: How far have we come? *Pediatrics. 102,* 1, 53–58, 1998.

Lo Vecchio, F., Bhatia, A., & Sciallo, D. Screening for domestic violence in the emergency department. *Eur J Emerg Med. 5,* 4, 441–444, 1998.

Lucas D'Olivera, A. F., Diniz, S. G., & Schraiber, L. B. Violence against women in health care institutions: An emerging problem. *Lancet. 359,* 1681, 2002.

MacMillan, H. L., MacMillan, J., & Offord, D. R. *Primary Prevention of Child Maltreatment.* Canadian Task Force on Preventive Health Care. Ottawa, Ontario, Canada: Canadian Medical Association. 1993.

Markin, D. A. Fighting the silent epidemic: Hospital launches comprehensive program against domestic violence. *Health Prog. 77,* 2, 30–33, 1996.

Martin, S., Rodriguez, M., Lee, D., & Heilig, S. *San Francisco Domestic Violence Healthcare Protocol.* San Francisco: San Francisco Family Violence Council's Health Care Committee. 1997.

McCauley, J., Kern, D. E., Kolodner, K., Dill, L., Schroeder, A. F., DeChant, H. K., Ryden, J., Bass, E. B., & Derogatis, L. R. The battering syndrome: Prevalence and clinical characteristics of domestic violence in primary care internal medicine practices. *Ann Internal Med. 123,* 737–746, 1995.

McCauley, J., Yurk, R., Jenckes, M., & Ford, D. Inside Pandora's box: Abused women's experiences with clinicians and health services. *Arch Internal Med. 13,* 549–555, 1998.

McFarlane, J., Christoffel, K., Bateman, L., Miller, V., & Bullock, L. Assessing for abuse: Self-report vs. nurse interview. *Public Health Nurs. 8,* 242–250, 1991.

McFarlane, J., Greenberg, L., Weltge, A., & Watson, M. Identification of abuse in emergency departments: Effectiveness of a two-question screening tool. *J Emerg Nurs. 21,* 391–394, 1995.

McGrath, M. E., Hogan, J. W., & Peipert, J. F. A prevalence survey of abuse and screening for abuse in urgent care patients. *Obstet Gynecol. 91,* 4, 511–514, 1998.

Moore, M. L., Zaccaro, D., & Parsons, L. H. Attitudes and practices of registered nurses toward women who have experienced abuse/domestic violence. *J Obstet Gynecol Neonatal Nurs. 27,* 2, 175–182, 1998.

Morrison, L. J., Allan, R., & Grunfeld, A. Improving the emergency department detection rate of domestic violence using direct questioning. *J Emerg Med. 19,* 2, 117–124, 2000.

Mouden, L. D. The role for dental professionals in preventing child abuse and neglect. *J Calif Dent Assoc. 26,* 10, 737–739, 741–743, 1998.

Muelleman, R. A., Lenaghan, P. A., & Pakieser, R. A. Battered women: Injury locations and types. *Ann Emerg Med. 28,* 486–492, 1996.

Myers, J. L. Workshop effectiveness: Nurses as witnesses in court cases involving physical child abuse. *J Nurs Law. 3,* 2, 35–44, 1996.

National Institute of Justice and Centers for Disease Control and Prevention. *Prevalence, Incidence, and Consequences of Violence Against Women: Findings from the National Violence Against Women Survey.* Washington, DC: National Institute of Justice and Centers for Disease Control and Prevention. 1998.

Olson, L., Anctil, C., Fullerton, L., Brillman, J., Arbuckle, J., & Sklar, D. Increasing emergency physician recognition of domestic violence. *Ann Emerg. 27,* 6, 741–746, 1996.

Oriel, K. A., & Fleming, M. F. Screening men for partner violence in a primary care setting. *J Fam Pract. 46,* 6, 493–498, 1998.

Osatlin, A., & Short, L. M. *Intimate Partner Violence and Sexual Assault: A Guide to Training Materials and Programs for Healthcare Providers.* Atlanta, GA: Centers for Disease Control and Prevention, National Center for Injury Protection and Control. 1998.

Payne, M. R. Self-study modules help health care professionals recognize and prevent abuse. *NLN Update. 2,* 4, 7, 1996.

Plichta, S. B. Intimate partner violence and physical health consequences: Policy and practice implications. *J Interpers Violence. 19,* 11, 1296–1323, 2004.

Rennison, M. *Intimate Partner Violence and Age of Victim, 1993–1999: Bureau of Justice Statistics Special Report.* Washington, DC: U.S. Department of Justice. Publication NCJ 187635. 2001.

Rhatigan, D. L., Moore, T. M., & Street, A. E. Reflections on partner violence: 20 years of research and beyond. *J Interpers Violence. 20,* 1, 82–88, 2005.

Roberts, G. L., Raphael, B., Lawrence, J. M., O'Toole, B., & O'Brien, D. Impact of an education program about domestic violence on nurses and doctors in an Australian emergency department. *J Emerg Nurs. 23,* 3, 220–227, 1997.

Rodriguez, M. A., Bauer, H. M., McLoughlin, E., & Grumbach, K. Screening and intervention for intimate partner abuse: Practices and attitudes of primary care physicians. *JAMA. 282,* 5, 468–474, 1999.

Rodriguez, M. A., Craig, A. M., Mooney, D., & Bauer, H. M. Patient attitudes about mandatory reporting of domestic violence: Implications for health care professionals. *West J Med. 169,* 6, 337–341, 1998.

Rodriguez, M., Quiroga, S. S., & Bauer, H. Breaking the silence: Battered women's perspectives on medical care. *Arch Fam Med. 5,* 153–158, 1996.

Ross, M. M., Hoff, L. A., & Coutu-Wakulczyk, G. Nursing curricula and violence issues. *J Nurs Educ. 37,* 2, 53–60, 1998.

Rovi, S., & Mouton, C. P. Domestic violence education in family practice residencies. *Fam Med. 31,* 6, 398–403, 1999.

Rupp, R. P. Conditions to be considered in the differential diagnosis of child abuse and neglect. *Gen Dent. 46,* 1, 96–100, 1998.

Sadler, D. W. The value of a thorough protocol in the investigation of sudden infant deaths. *J Clin Pathol. 51,* 9, 689–694, 1998.

Salber, P. R., & Taliaferro, E. *The Physician's Guide to Domestic Violence: How to Ask the Right Questions and Recognize Abuse . . . Another Way to Save a Life.* Volcano, CA: Volcano Press. 1995.

Saltzman, L. E., Salmi, L. R., Branche, C. M., & Bolen, J. C. Public health screening for intimate violence. *Violence Against Women. 3,* 319–331, 1997.

Saywitz, K., & Camparo, L. Interviewing child witnesses: A developmental perspective. *Child Abuse Negl. 22,* 8, 825–843, 1998.

Schroeder, M., & Weber, J. R. Promoting domestic violence education for nurses. *Nurs Forum. 33,* 4, 13–21, 1998.

Schwartz, I. L. Sexual violence against women: Prevalence, consequences, societal factors, and prevention. *Am J Prev Med. 7,* 363–371, 1991.

Schwartz, M. D. The past and the future of violence against women. *J Interpers Violence. 20,* 1, 7–11, 2005.

Sheridan, D. Forensic documentation of battered pregnant women. *J Nurse Midwifery. 41,* 6, 467–472, 1996.

Sherin, K. M., Sinacore, J. M., & Li, X. O. A short domestic violence screening tool for use in a family practice setting. *Fam Med. 30,* 7, 508–512, 1998.

Shields, G., Baer, J., Leininger, K., Marlow, J., & DeKeyser, P. Interdisciplinary health care and female victims of domestic violence. *Soc Work Health Care. 27,* 2, 27–48, 1998.

Short, L. M., Johnson, D., & Osattin, A. Recommended components of health care provider training programs on intimate partner violence. *Am J Prevent Med. 14,* 4, 283–288, 1998.

Sinai, S. H., & Stewart, C. D. Physical abuse of children: A review for orthopedic surgeons. *J South Orthop Assoc. 7,* 4, 264–276, 1998.

Smock, W. S., Nicholas, G. R., & Fuller, P. M. Development and implementation of the first clinical forensic medicine training program. *J Forensic Sci. 38,* 4, 835–839, 1993.

Spinola, C., Stewart, L., Fanslow, J., & Norton, R. Developing and implementing an intervention: Evaluation of an emergency department pilot on partner abuse. *Eval Health Prof. 21,* 1, 91–119, 1998.

Spivak, H. The role of the pediatrician in youth violence prevention in clinical practice and at the community level. *Pediatrics. 103,* 5 (Pt. 1), 1080–1081, 1999.

Stobo, J. D., Salmon, M. E., & Cohn, F, Eds. *Confronting Chronic Neglect: The Education and Training of Health Professionals on Family Violence.* Washington, DC: National Academy Press. 2002.

Taylor, W., Sheridan, D., Campbell, J. C., et al. *Battered Women: Identification, Treatment, and Referral of Nursing Network on Violence Against Women International.* 1994.

Thompson, R. S., Meyer, B. A., & Smith-DiJulio, K., Caplow, M. P., Maiuro, R. D., Thompson, D. C., Sugg, N. K., & Rivara, F. P. A training program to improve domestic violence identification and management in primary care: Preliminary results. *Violence Vict. 13,* 4, 395–410, 1998.

Thurston, W. E., & McLeod, L. Teaching second-year medical students about wife battering. *Womens Health Issues. 7,* 2, 92–98, 1997.

Tjaden, P. T. *Full Report of the Prevalence, Incidence, and Consequences of Violence Against Women: Findings From the National Violence Against Women Survey.* Washington, DC: U.S. Department of Justice, Office of Justice Programs, National Institute of Justice. 2000.

Trezona, P., Zink, T., Schlossberg, L., et al. *Healthcare guideline: Domestic violence.* Bloomington, IN: ICSI. 1996.

U.S. Department of Health and Human Services. *Child Maltreatment 1999: Reports from the States to the National Child Abuse and Neglect Data System (NCANDS).* Washington, DC: U.S. Government Printing Office. 2001.

U.S. Department of Justice. *Violence by Intimates: Analysis of Data on Crimes by Current or Former Spouses, Boyfriends, and Girlfriends.* Washington, DC: U.S. Department of Justice, Bureau of Justice Statistics. 1998.

U.S. Department of Justice. *Intimate Partner Violence.* Washington, DC: U.S. Department of Justice, Bureau of Justice Statistics. 2000.

Varvaro, F. F. Violence against women: The role of orthopedic nurses in the identification, assessment, treatment, and care for the abused women. *Orthop Nurs. 17,* 2, 33–40, 1998.

Varvaro, F. F., & Gesmond, S. ED physician house staff response to training on domestic violence. *J Emerg Nurs. 23,* 1, 17–22, 1997.

Vivio, D. Comments to the committee on training needs of health professionals to respond to family violence. Silver Spring, MD: American College of Nurse Midwives. 1–3, 2000.

Waller, A. E., Hohenhaus, S. M., Shah, P. J., & Stern, E. A. Development and validation of an emergency department screening and referral protocol for victims of domestic violence. *Ann Emerg Med. 27,* 6, 754–760, 1996.

Warshaw, C. Minimal elements of a domestic violence protocol. Harrisburg, PA: Family Violence Prevention Fund. 1995.

Warshaw, C. Intimate partner abuse: Developing a framework for change in medical education. *Acad Med. 72,* 1, S26–S37, 1997.

Weiss, S. J., Ernst, A. A., Blanton, D., Sewell, D., & Nick, T. G. EMT domestic violence knowledge and the results of an educational intervention. *Am J Emerg Med. 18,* 2, 168–171, 2000.

Weiss, S., Garza, A., Casaletto, J., Stratton, M., Ernst, A., Blanton, D., & Nick, T. G. The out-of-hospital use of a domestic violence screen for assessing patient risk. *Prehosp Emerg Care. 4,* 1, 24–27, 2000.

Welbury, R. R., & Murphy, J. M. The dental practitioner's role in protecting children from abuse: Reporting and subsequent management of abuse. *Br Dent J. 184,* 3, 115–119, 1998.

Whittaker, D. K., Aitken, M., Burfitt, E., & Sibert, J. R. Assessing bite marks in children: Working with a forensic dentist. *Ambul Child Health. 3,* 3, 225–229, 1997.

Wiist, W. H., & McFarlane, J. The effectiveness of an abuse assessment protocol in public health prenatal clinics. *Am J Public Health. 89,* 8, 1217–1221, 1999.

Wingfield, D. A., & Blocker, S. L. Development of a certificate training curriculum for domestic violence counseling. *J Addiction Offender Counsel. 18,* 2, 86–94, 1998.

Wisehart, B. Pilot project offers help to victims of domestic violence. *California Hospitals. 9,* 4, 24–25, 1995.

Woodtli, M. A. Domestic violence and the nursing curriculum: Tuning in and tuning up. *J Nurs Educ. 39,* 4, 173–82, 2000.

Yexley, M., Borowsky, I., & Ireland, M. Correlation between different experiences of intrafamilial physical violence and violent adolescent behavior. *J Interpers Violence. 17,* 7, 707–720, 2002.

8 Vulnerable Populations

CONTENTS

According to the WHO (2003), although any person can be victimized, there are some individuals or groups of individuals who might be more vulnerable, and so appear to be overrepresented as victims of interpersonal violence, and of sexual violence in particular. These include the following groups:

- Single women and lone female heads of household.
- Children and young adults.
- Children in foster care.
- Physically and mentally disabled men and women.
- Individuals in prison or held in detention.
- Individuals with drug or alcohol problems.
- Individuals with a past history of rape or sexual abuse.
- Individuals involved in prostitution.
- Individuals in an abusive intimate or dependent relationship.
- Victims of war or armed-conflict situations.
- The homeless or impoverished.

Just as there is no typical victim, perpetrators also come from all walks of life. Many times, perpetrators are the very individuals entrusted with the health, safety, and supervision of these vulnerable populations, including teachers, health care workers, day care workers, priests, community leaders, and other authority figures. Forensic nurses must be familiar with the types of violence perpetrated against members of vulnerable populations, as well as the specific makeup of each group of patients who might present to the health care facility as victims of violence, abuse, or neglect.

Barbara Moynihan, RN, APRN, PhD, assistant professor of nursing at Quinnipiac University in Connecticut, says that there are numerous opportunities for forensic nurses to work among vulnerable populations:

> Counted among these populations are individuals from other countries who flee oppression, and people who have been terrorized, abused, assaulted, and held hostage. Cultural sensitivity is so important, whether a forensic nurse is dealing with someone from a different race or culture. Everyone does not think, feel, or act the same way, even though they may look the same. Migrant populations, illegal immigrants, and others who are in minority populations have health care needs that are largely ignored by the system. Look at the returning military personnel who have been traumatized and suffer from posttraumatic stress disorder. They are dealing with horrendous injuries and mental trauma as they attempt to integrate back into society. So there are many challenges and opportunities within these kinds of underserved populations with which forensic nurses may become involved.

Moynihan says that medico-legal issues such as elder abuse are starting to gain increasing awareness. "There is much more information about elder abuse today than ever before; it's coming out of the closet; and the unspeakable is being spoken. We're broadening our scope of assessment to identify these kinds of forensic clients."

8.1 VIOLENCE AGAINST DISABLED INDIVIDUALS

8.1.1 A Portrait of Individuals With Disabilities

The most widely accepted estimate of the number of people with disabilities is 49 million noninstitutionalized Americans (McNeil, 1993). As such, people with disabilities constitute the single largest minority group identified in the United States, surpassing the elderly (about 33.2 million) and African Americans (about 32.7 million), according to the U.S. Bureau of the Census in 1995. An October 1997 update to this report indicates 54 million Americans report having some level of disability, with 26 million of those having a severe disability. The percentage of people with a disability increases with age. Whereas 5 percent of the population younger than age 18 has a disability, 84.2 percent of those age 85 and over have a disability. Of those between 18 and 44, 13.6 percent have a disability, and of those between 45 and 64, 29.2 percent have a disability. Males had a disability rate of 18.7 percent and a severe disability rate of 8.1 percent. For females, the corresponding rates were 20.2 percent and

11 percent. These Americans live with a wide array of physical, cognitive, and emotional disabilities. Some disabilities are more easily discernable than others. People who use wheelchairs, service animals, or walkers are easy to identify. Less obvious are those with intellectual or mental disabilities (such as people who have learning disabilities or schizophrenia) and those with chronic illnesses (such as chronic fatigue syndrome, seizure disorders, arthritis, alcoholism, drug addiction, and HIV disease). As with any crime victims, people with disabilities can be victims of domestic violence, child abuse, sexual assault, homicide, fraud, and other types of crimes. They are victimized by family members, acquaintances, strangers, institutional personnel, and caregivers. Many are victimized multiple times.

In addition to people who have been disabled since birth, some people are disabled as a result of violent assaults. Catastrophic physical injuries can result in loss of abilities to see, hear, touch, taste, feel, move, and think in the usual ways. Although statistics on crime-related physical injuries are imperfect, it has been estimated that at least 6 million serious injuries occur each year due to crime, resulting in either temporary or permanent disability. The National Rehabilitation Information Center (NARIC) has estimated that a large percentage—perhaps as many as 50 percent—of patients who are long-term residents of hospitals and specialized rehabilitation centers are there due to crime-related injuries. Those patients seldom receive outreach from a crime victim assistance or compensation program (National Organization for Victim Assistance [NOVA], 1998).

Baladerian (2001) reports that individuals with disabilities number approximately 43 million, representing about12 percent of the population. "Those with disabilities do not have anywhere near the presence in the political scene. They are seen . . . or mostly unseen . . . only when there is a protest, or a White House event. This is still one of the most invisible minorities in the United States." The Crime Victims With Disabilities Awareness Act of 1998 defines developmental disabilities as:

> A severe, chronic disability of an individual 5 years of age or older that is attributable to a mental or physical impairment or combination of mental and physical impairments; is manifested before the individual attains age 22; is likely to continue indefinitely; results in substantial functional limitations in three or more of the following areas of major life activity: self-care; receptive and expressive language; learning mobility; self-direction; capacity for independent living; and economic self-sufficiency; and reflects the individual's need for a combination and sequence of special, interdisciplinary or generic services, support or other services that is of lifelong or extended duration.

Baladerian says there are several misperceptions associated with persons with disabilities that can "hamper their due process of the law, and perpetuate stereotypes which often results in discrimination against people with disabilities." The first myth is the perception that people with disabilities are "suffering." She says that rather than extending legal rights and protections, as with other oppressed groups, a societal response prior to passage of the Americans with Disabilities Act (ADA) typically was to extend "charity." Baladerian states, "Being kind to a person with a disability is not an acceptable substitute for the provision of civil rights protections."

The second myth is that people with disabilities lack the ability to make choices or determine for themselves what is best for them in all areas of life, including physical, mental, emotional, spiritual, political, sexual, and financial aspects. "Although individuals with severe cognitive impairments may need greater support and advocacy services, this does not impede their ability or preclude their right to participate actively in decisions affecting their lives," Baladerian states. The third myth, according to crime victim advocates, is that many people in society fear contact with crime victims generally, as though their distresses are contagious. An even stronger stigma has been attached to those with disabilities. According to NOVA (1998):

> Society is not socialized to integrate differences in abilities as a part of people's perception of "normality." The cultural norms for functioning include good hearing and vision, physical independence and mobility, mental alertness, the ability to communicate primarily through the written and spoken word, and physical attractiveness. Deviations from those norms tend to frighten those in the "able-bodied majority" who define the concept of normal abilities.

Many individuals with disabling conditions are especially vulnerable to victimization because of their real or perceived inability to fight or flee, or to notify others and testify about the victimization. Frequently, because a person with a disability might be more physically frail, the victimization could exacerbate existing health or mental health problems. For those who hope that their disability might "protect" them from criminal victimization, it is shocking to learn that many criminals do not act on a perceived "desirability" of the intended victim, according to Baladerian, who adds that some perpetrators might be unaware that their victims have a disability. "Here, the victim is truly random, in the wrong place at the wrong time, although that victim's ability to frustrate the criminal's intent may be less than a person's without a disability," Baladerian (1997) writes. Another reality is that many offenders are motivated by a desire to obtain control over the victim and measure their potential prey for vulnerabilities. Many people with disabilities, because they are perceived as unable to physically defend themselves, identify the attacker, or call for help, are perfect targets for such offenders. People with disabilities are also vulnerable to abuse by the very professionals and other caregivers who provide them with services. Just as many pedophiles gravitate to youth-serving occupations, so do many other predators seek work as caregivers to people with disabilities. According to NOVA (1998), virtually half of the perpetrators of sexual abuse against people with disabilities gained access to their victims through disability services.

8.1.2 Victimization of Disabled Individuals

Oktay and Tompkins (2004) describe a survey of 84 adults with disabilities who received personal assistance with activities of daily living from family members, informal providers, or agency personnel. Results showed that 30 percent reported mistreatment from their primary provider, and 61 percent reported mistreatment by another provider. Verbal abuse, physical abuse, and theft or extortion were the most common forms of mistreatment by primary providers. Verbal abuse, neglect, poor care, and theft were the most common forms of mistreatment by other providers. Adults with lower incomes were the most likely to experience mistreatment. Male providers were more likely to mistreat, as were inexperienced providers, and those who provided more than 50 hours of care per week.

Studies have shown that 68 percent to 83 percent of women with developmental disabilities will be sexually assaulted in their lifetime, which represents a 50 percent higher rate than the rest of the population (NOVA, 1998). According to Pease and Frantz (1994) those with developmental disabilities are more likely to be revictimized by the same person and more than half never seek assistance from legal or treatment services. It is not just individuals with developmental disabilities who suffer very high rates of victimization. A study of psychiatric inpatients found that 81 percent had been physically or sexually assaulted. The 1998 NOVA study described several eye-opening case studies. In California, a woman was stabbed in the back during a robbery attempt. As a result of the assault, she became paraplegic. Unfortunately, neither the police nor hospital staff told her about victim assistance or independent living services. Because the assailant was never apprehended, the prosecutor-based victim assistance program did not provide her with services. In her anger and depression, she became suicidal. She survived a suicide attempt only because an alert nurse resuscitated her in time. In another case, an elderly woman who was unable to walk was cared for at home by family members. Her grandson, a drug user, frequently stole money from her, especially after the third of each month, when her Social Security disability income check arrived. The woman would tuck her money under her to hide it from her grandson. Once, in a state of anger when he could not find her money, he flipped her over and she fell out of the bed onto the floor. She sustained several bruises but was not seen by a physician. She did not report the abuse or the theft to the police out of fear that her family would no longer want to care for her.

These case studies illustrate the fact that persons with disabilities face unique obstacles, including the following:

- Isolation. Today's society often segregates persons with disabilities through physical and social isolation, with institutionalization representing the extreme. As a result of pervasive isolation, people with disabilities might not learn about available services and resources, nor are they routinely informed of rights they have by law. This is particularly true for people with more severe disabling conditions, older people with disabilities, and younger people with developmental disabilities. Indeed, many individuals who are chronically victimized do not even know that society condemns such predatory conduct and has tools to end and redress that wrong.
- Limited access. In many instances, crime victims with disabilities do not have physical access to services. Architectural barriers in buildings and public transportation systems mean that many crime victims with disabilities cannot visit criminal justice agencies or victim assistance programs. The ADA addresses key issues of accessibility, but there is an extensive lack of understanding of how Titles II and III of the ADA pertain to the criminal justice and victim assistance fields. Moreover, this lack of understanding is frequently coupled with a fear that making services accessible to crime victims with disabilities will require expensive, disruptive adaptations.

Attitudes toward the person with a disability are as important or more so than physical accessibility. In addition to accessible physical environments, program staff must be welcoming toward people with disabilities and show in their demeanor and in the quality of their programs that they sincerely want to work collaboratively to serve the community.

In 1999, a workshop was held to bring together policymakers from the Department if Justice, the Department of Health and Human Services, the Department of Education, and the California Department of Developmental Services. The discourse was eventually assembled into a report, *Crime Victims With Developmental Disabilities: Report of a Workshop*, a product of the Committee on Law and Justice of the Commission on Behavioral and Social

Sciences and Education (CBSSCE) National Research Council (2001). The report draws on eight white papers presented at the event, and assembles a critical mass of current thought on the topic of violence toward persons with disabilities. At the forum, a presentation by the California Department of Developmental Services included a study that found during the past decade, while the state of California's population increased by 20 percent, the number of persons with developmental disabilities doubled. Many of these individuals reside in communities where they receive little health care, have access to few social services, and are easy targets for violent crime.

Disabilities come in many forms, and definitions of disability relate to physical, cognitive, or behavioral characteristics, as well as to the individual's ability to perform specific functions. The report estimated that 2 percent of the U.S. population has mental retardation or a developmental disability, but it is only an estimate because the data do not reflect individuals in institutions, the correctional system, or the military. Violent crimes committed against people with disabilities include conventional violent crimes such as homicide, assault, theft, and robbery; abuse and neglect; family violence; and specialized crimes such as abduction; and noncriminal violent acts such as assaults by other children or sibling bullying. However, persons with disabilities are especially vulnerable to certain types of crimes. Anecdotal evidence suggests that they face unusually high risks of physical abuse and sexual assault. Studies from the United States, United Kingdom, Canada, and Australia confirm high rates of violence and abuse of disabled persons at the hands of caregivers. The report also estimated that 83 percent of women with developmental disabilities in their sample had been sexually assaulted, and of those, nearly 50 percent had been sexually assaulted 10 or more times. Wilson and Brewer (1992) found that 40 percent of crime against people with mild mental retardation went unreported, whereas 71 percent of crime against people with severe mental retardation went unreported. Crosse, Kaye, and Ratnofsky (1993) found that children with developmental disabilities were at twice the risk of physical and sexual abuse than children without such disabilities.

Young et al. (1997) found that women with disabilities were significantly more at risk for suffering abuse by nonintimate caretakers, and that women with disabilities stay in abusive relationships for many of the same reasons women without disabilities do, including fear of further violence or retaliation, belief that the batterer will change, love of the abuser, having no economic support if they leave, and religious beliefs, among other concerns. However, women with disabilities have limitations on their ability to leave an abusive relationship in a caregiving situation, being hampered by not physically being able to leave, fear of losing caregiver service if the abuse is reported, and lack of resources to live independently.

Baladerian (1999) writes, "While representing a significant percentage within the population, attention to issues affecting individuals with disabilities is almost none. This is particularly true regarding criminal victimization either as children or as adults. Reporting of crimes, investigations, prosecutions and even sentencing issues are major problems. Research of the victimization and data collection remains nearly nonexistent."

In 1991, the National Center on Child Abuse and Neglect, a branch of the Department of Health and Human Services, reported to Congress on the breadth and depth of the problem of abuse of the disabled. The study was conducted using a retrospective review of substantiated cases of child abuse in 36 departments of Child Protective Services (CPS) across the country. Their research found that children with disabilities are abused at approximately twice the rate of children who do not have disabilities. Baladerian says that CPS departments did not did not consistently identify or document the child's disability, and adds, "It can be interpreted that the data are far from realistic due to these problems, and the well-known problem of under reporting and inadequate investigations." She points to other studies that have demonstrated the incidence of abuse of children with disabilities to be anywhere from four to 10 times the rate among children. Researchers have documented the trend toward victims knowing their assailants. For both children and adults with disabilities, the perpetrator is well known to and trusted by the victim and/or the victim's family. Perpetrators can include family members, friends of the family, service providers (transportation, personal assistants, teachers, teacher aides, workshop staff, supervisors, and counselors), one-on-one care providers, and professionals such as physicians and social workers, among others. Those with both frequent direct care responsibilities (daily staff) and those with more distant relationships (administrators) have been identified as perpetrators of abuse (Baladerian, 1999). Sexual abuse tends to be the most publicized form of abuse; however, other types of abuse, such as murder, physical assaults, and financial exploitation have received much less attention. Baladerian (1999) classifies perpetrators of abuse against individuals with developmental disabilities as being in the "nonstranger" category in 99 percent of the cases. In the general population, the rate is closer to 70 percent, depending on the type of crime. Authorities place emphasis on avoiding so-called "stranger danger," although closer to home, a perpetrator might be the victim's father, mother, personal care assistant, foster parent, residential program staff, or work supervisor.

8.1.3 A Meeting of the Minds

A great amount of data on victimization of persons with disabilities came out of the Symposium on Working with Crime Victims With Disabilities, funded by the OVC and coordinated by NOVA. Held in January 1998 in Arlington, Virginia, the symposium brought together experts from the disability advocacy and victim assistance and research fields, who raised as many questions as they answered, thus opening the way for the victim assistance field to look more closely at a large and underserved crime victim population. As a result of their discussions, they developed recommendations for OVC and the victim assistance field on improving the response in serving crime victims with disabilities, which are discussed here for the benefit of health care providers struggling to understand this underserved and often "invisible" population. At this symposium, experts agreed on the following:

- Crime victims with disabilities have a higher risk of victimization than crime victims without disabilities, and face a greater risk of being revictimized, often at the hands of a caregiver or family member. Consequently, victims might not be in a position to report the crime without fear of retaliation from the care provider.
- A crime victim with a disability or a person who becomes disabled due to crime might not have the resources or the physical stamina to cope with the many delays and hurdles that typically occur in the criminal justice system. For example, if a victim is paralyzed as a result of a crime, the victim will be adjusting to this recent disability at the same time that he or she is interacting with the criminal justice system. The combination could be overwhelming.
- Child custody issues are typically complex in cases of domestic violence. When the victim has a disability, the issues can be further complicated. According to disability advocates, some courts have awarded custody to the batterer, based on an assumption that children might be better off with an able-bodied offender than with a victim who has a disability.

At the end of the two-day symposium, experts agreed on the following recommendations:

- Physical accessibility
    1. Criminal justice agencies and victim assistance programs should receive training on the requirements of the ADA and should support its vigorous enforcement. Agencies and programs should take advantage of technical assistance provided by the federal government to help ensure enforcement of the ADA. Programs that are not required to abide by the letter of the law should commit to adhering to the spirit of the law. This will help to ensure equal access to the justice system, as called for by federal law and state constitutional amendments and statutes.
    2. When full physical accessibility is not immediately achievable, criminal justice agencies and victim assistance programs should initiate transition planning that focuses on obtaining accessibility by a designated date. Public and nonprofit agencies should understand that development of compliance plans are typically mandated under Titles II and III of the ADA, and with some exceptions, compliance plans are required, not optional. These compliance plans serve as a roadmap for taking incremental steps to improve accessibility, even if complete implementation of the plan must be delayed. The victim assistance sector should join with disability advocates and representatives of the various populations within the community to conduct a community needs assessment survey to ensure that the compliance plan is appropriate and effective.
- Networking and cross-training
    1. Criminal justice and victim assistance personnel should receive training on disabilities, including developing an understanding of disability cultures. Special efforts should be made to identify qualified victim advocates with disabilities as trainers. In addition, criminal justice agencies and victim assistance programs should enlist qualified people with a wide range of different disabilities to lead in all stages of policy development, decision making, program development, and service delivery for crime victims with disabilities from the time of the crime through case disposition and beyond. People with disabilities should be proactively recruited and trained to become volunteers and paid staff members in criminal justice-oriented programs, especially in system-based or private victim assistance programs.
    2. Criminal justice agencies and victim assistance programs should reach out proactively to local disability service organizations. They should provide them with information about victim rights and services. The service organizations, in turn, can inform their constituents on how better to access the criminal justice system, particularly the victim assistance programs.

3. Criminal justice agencies and victim assistance programs must develop coalitions, cross-training, and joint training opportunities with disability advocacy and services programs to build better working relationships and to better understand the services each offer when working with people with disabilities. In some communities, this coalition could be formalized as an interagency team or coordinating council, including involvement of local or state governmental task forces on disabilities. Communities might wish to emulate the models developed within the domestic violence victim advocacy community.
4. Collaborative partnerships must also be fostered with other community-based entities, such as schools, social service agencies, citizen groups, and churches or synagogues. Utilizing the resources of the entire community will help to ensure that service delivery is seamless, more inclusive, and does not duplicate or waste limited resources.
5. Leaders in the victim assistance and disability advocacy fields should work together to develop and utilize innovative ways to communicate, such as e-mail listservs. These links would allow the timely sharing of information and ideas between disability groups and individuals with expertise in disability rights and services with similar experts in victim rights and services. Regional and state Web sites devoted to the needs of crime victims offer another way of fostering this exchange.

- Direct services
  1. Agencies should implement or extend streamlined interviewing and intake procedures so that crime victims with disabilities, particularly those with cognitive or communications disabilities, do not have to bear repeated interviewing in different locations. A multidisciplinary approach involving a law enforcement officer, a prosecutor, a victim assistance specialist, and others, as needed, in victim-friendly environments would be more effective and cost-efficient.
  2. Agencies should develop and implement specific protocols on disclosures, confidentiality, and safety for crime victims with disabilities, particularly where there is potential for retaliation by a caregiver or a disability services agency. For example, when a crime victim reports to a law enforcement officer (or, when it does not get reported to a police agency, to a victim advocate) that he or she is being victimized by a caregiver and has reason to fear for his or her safety, that victim should be provided with assistance to relocate if necessary and have emergency replacement caregiver services provided.
  3. Criminal justice agencies and victim assistance programs should be proactive in acquiring assistive technology that would help crime victims with disabilities to be informed, present, heard, and understood more effectively when they communicate with law enforcement officers, prosecutors, judges, and victim advocates. For example, victim assistance service providers should know what accommodations will be needed so that a person with a communication disability can make a victim impact statement at the time of sentencing. Assistive technology and accommodations costs (i.e., for computer software, sign language interpreters, paratransit, etc.) should be considered part of the cost of "doing business." Victim assistance agencies should be aware that under federal victim of crimes act (VOCA) guidelines, VOCA funds can be used to make services accessible to victims with disabilities. Specific allowable costs include the purchase of items such as Braille equipment or TTY/TTD machines, or for minor building improvements that make services more accessible to victims with disabilities.
  4. Once the agency is accessible and staff is trained, criminal justice agencies and victim assistance programs should publicize their ability to work with crime victims with disabilities by putting the universal symbol of access (the line drawing of a wheelchair) and a TTY/TTD number on all literature, promotional materials, business cards, and so on, used by the agency.
  5. Victim assistance and criminal justice agencies should incorporate into existing policies, procedures, and protocols the specific inclusion of persons with disabilities who are victims or witnesses of domestic violence, sexual violence, child abuse, impaired driving crashes, survivors of homicide victims, or other violent personal crimes. Parallel policies should be written

to cover economic crimes committed against people with disabilities.

6. Statistical information about crime victims with disabilities should be systematically collected by criminal justice agencies and victim assistance programs, using the ADA to define disability status.
7. Prosecutors should invoke hate crimes statutes, if indicated, when prosecuting crimes against people with disabilities. Judges should apply equal sentencing or sentencing enhancements, when allowed, for offenders who victimize people with disabilities.
8. When a violent personal crime occurs against a person with a disability who is institutionalized, the investigation of the crime should not be handled administratively or informally by the institution's own investigators. Several studies suggest that 80 percent to 85 percent of criminal abuse of residents of institutions (an estimated 2.3 million people) never is brought to the attention of law enforcement authorities. Criminal prosecution should be pursued in cases of violent crime.

8.1.4 Underreporting Among Disabled Victims and Interface With the Criminal Justice System

Experts say that historically, all victims of crime have been denied full participation in the criminal justice process. Crime victims with disabilities and their families are even less likely to reap the benefits of the criminal justice system. Disability advocates report that crimes against people with disabilities are often not reported to police. Of those that lead to an investigation and an arrest, very few are prosecuted. When proceeding through the criminal justice process, few victims with disabilities come into contact with a crime victim advocate. Often when victim services are provided, they might be inappropriate due to inadequate training of victim service providers. As with most types of crime and crime victims, underreporting of crimes perpetrated against people with disabilities is a major problem. Currently there is no authoritative research that details how many individuals with a disability become crime victims or how many people become disabled by criminal attacks. Nor has the victim assistance field adequately identified the best practices for serving victims with unique needs or how to train criminal justice system personnel—including victim specialists—and health care providers to make services truly accessible to all crime victims.

Underreporting of crime is a pervasive problem that victim assistance advocates are addressing on many fronts. For example, RAINN estimates that 1,000 rapes occur every day in the United States, but only about 300 will ever be reported to the police. A crime might go unreported for many reasons: mobility or communication barriers, the social or physical isolation of the victim, a victim's normal feelings of shame and self-blame, ignorance of the justice system, or the perpetrator is a family member or primary caregiver. In crimes involving a victim with a disability, one or more of these factors might prevent the crime from ever being reported. When the crime is reported, the reporting agency often fails to note that the victim had a disability, especially if the crime is reported by someone other than the victim. Later, assumptions and prejudice about the reliability of the testimony of victims with disabilities can deny them access to justice in the courts. Despite progress by disability rights activists, advocacy on their own behalf is still limited. Again, just as with many crime victims, a person who wants to access criminal justice decision-making processes is unable to do so without the adequate tools to enable full participation (NOVA, 1998).

Limited information exists regarding the criminal victimization of people with disabilities, but the little that is available is horrifying in nature and scope. During the 1998 NOVA symposium, Joan Petersilia, a researcher and professor of criminology at the University of California, Irvine, stated that persons with developmental disabilities have a four- to ten-fold higher risk of becoming crime victims than persons without a disability, in her Report to the California Senate Public Safety Committee hearings on "Persons With Developmental Disabilities in the Criminal Justice System." In addition, she says, "Children with any kind of disability are more than twice as likely as nondisabled children to be physically abused and almost twice as likely to be sexually abused." Others in the field recount anecdotal experiences from their work that illustrate that crimes against people with disabilities are often extremely violent and calculatedly intended to injure, control, and humiliate the victim.

There are many reasons why crimes against persons with disabilities go unreported. A significant obstacle to reporting is the victim's fear of not being believed or taken seriously. Hickman (1998, as cited in NOVA, 1998), Roeher (1994, as cited in NOVA, 1998), and Sanders (1997, as cited in NOVA, 1998) report that women with disabilities often have negative experiences with members of law enforcement, which makes it unlikely they would pursue future contact with them. The researchers also say police share many of the myths that the public holds about these individuals. Police might believe these victims lack credibility, and in turn, police departments often have to protocols with which to respond to these biases. Hickman (1998) suggests that police might dismiss a woman who has a speech impairment as drunk if she calls and asks for help.

Underreporting is a significant problem, experts say, as children and adults with developmental disabilities, as well as mental illness, communications disorders, and learning disabilities, are not taught about what constitutes abuse or how to report it. Many individuals with developmental disabilities are not allowed access to the telephone, thus obstructing legitimate autonomous reporting (Baladerian, 1999). If a report is made, it is not likely to be reported by the perpetrator, but by someone who knows the victim and whom the victim has told about the abuse or who notices the victims' behavior or physical well-being is compromised in some way. Either scenario is unlikely, according to Baladerian, and more likely is that the abuse is not noticed, reported, or known to anyone but the victim for many years, unless and until someone makes a direct inquiry. A related challenge is the fact that not all disability advocates support mandatory reporting of crimes against people with disabilities. An individual struggling to maintain independence might perceive mandatory reporting as excessive "protectionism," whereas others believe that the legal requirement to report crimes against "vulnerable adults" is integral to ensuring their safety (NOVA, 1998).

There is much improvement to be made in the way individuals with disabilities are interviewed when a report of abuse is filed. The first contact is usually with a member of law enforcement, and among child abuse experts, a police officer's uniform is considered to be threatening or intimidating. Their presence can sometimes undermine the interview process. Baladerian (1999) discusses a case in Los Angeles County that illustrates the need for follow-up interviews to illicit much-needed details. Following an unsuccessful interview by police, the deputy district attorney interviewed the victim; this interview resulted in the filing of charges against the alleged perpetrator. In many cases, follow-up interviews are not conducted and the case is closed with an "unable to interview" or "interview inconclusive" remark. Baladerian writes:

> In the case cited here, it was only due to the insistence of the mother of the adult victim that further interviewing occurred. As it turns out, her adult child's complaint was one of five, three of which had been made prior to the assaults this person experienced, and nothing had been done. The perseverance of this mother will in all likelihood be the one factor that most contributes to the conviction of this predator. In this case, the perpetrator is well known to the victim, being a work supervisor.

Baladerian points out that some interviewers have not been adequately trained in working with individuals with mental retardation, mental illness, communication and speech impairments, or other psychiatric or physical disabilities. Some victims have been dismissed as unable to be interviewed, and in some cases, everyone but the victim has been interviewed, leaving a wide margin for a miscarriage of justice:

> This problem arises from preconceived notions of the abilities of individuals identified and/or perceived as having a disability or inabilities to effectively participate in an information-gathering interview. Thus, feeble attempts are made, or the specific interviewing strategies that could be effective have not been used by the interviewer. And, the investigator or detective does not seek consultation or supervision assistance to assure that an effective interview is conducted—consultation with a specialist in forensic interviewing of individuals with disabilities, or with a specialist in the particular disability of the victim, or even someone who knows the victim and could provide information and strategies to use for the interview.

When a productive, effective interview takes place, Balderian (1999) says two things should happen simultaneously: A case is filed with the district attorney's office for prosecution, and the victim is referred for a psychotherapy evaluation. "Since most trauma victims could benefit from at least a few sessions with a mental health provider who specializes in the treatment of trauma, the recommendation for a referral for evaluation for the appropriateness or need for treatment is indicated. Yet, it is the rare victim with a disability who is referred directly from the law enforcement agency to the victim's assistance program, either for therapy or advocacy."

Very little research exists that documents the interaction of people with disabilities within the criminal justice system. Individuals can be involved in the court system in three different ways. They can be defendants in criminal cases, they can be witnesses to crimes allegedly committed by defendants against others, and they can be victims of crimes themselves. Capacity, which is considered to be a person's inherent ability to make a rational decision or give meaningful consent, figures into the ability of a person with disabilities to participate in a court proceeding. When there is question as to a person's competence as a participant, a competency hearing might be held. Determining if a witness or a victim is competent to testify does not mean that the testimony will necessarily be believed. It is for the trier of fact to determine if the witness's testimony is credible.

Capacity is particularly relevant to people with developmental disabilities who are victims of sexual assault and abuse. Every state's rape law criminalizes sexual intercourse with a woman who lacks capacity or is unable to give consent; typically, state statutes define sexual offenses aggravated by the victim's incapacity as those based on her ability to understand the nature of the sexual conduct or to appraise its consequences. A number of prosecutors are taking it on themselves to become better educated about and better prepared for handling cases involving disabled individuals. They have learned that to achieve a successful prosecution, individuals with disabilities should be viewed as any other person, highlighting the victim's particular vulnerability to maltreatment. There are several erroneous approaches used by some prosecutors in the courtroom, including the following:

- Making the adolescent or adult with disabilities look like an infant, or identifying the person as having a "chronological" age of 30 but a "mental" age of 6. By assuming that the adult has never had grown-up experiences, the individual is erased and a story replaces the victim's actual life and functioning skills. The use of mental age in psychological testing is designed for clinical application to address intellectual skills, not to be used to globally identify the individual's adaptive skills, language abilities, hopes, dreams, and life abilities. When the victim has a developmental or communication disability, the prosecutor must remark on the distinction between having a communication disorder and having an intellectual impairment, as many individuals have communication difficulties and have no deficits intellectually (Baladerian, 1999).
- Use of the concept referred to as *spread,* the belief that if an individual has one disability he or she probably has others. These assumptions are based in societal prejudices that are ingrained and difficult to undo. In many cases, judge and jury have been lost due to this false belief on the part of the trier of fact; the victim could not be believed, even when clear evidence had been presented (Baladerian, 1999).

8.1.5 Women With Disabilities and Sexual Violence

Spies (1999) writes, "Society is uncomfortable with crime, victimization and disability. When these two factors are combined, an increased level of discomfort usually results. Therefore, when people with disabilities are victims of crime, they often do not receive adequate attention." When it comes to violence, three assumptions are made about women with disabilities:

- People with disabilities are abused at a far greater rate than the general population.
- Family members, caregivers, and acquaintances, not strangers, are perpetrating a large percentage of the abuse.
- Often no one is told of the abuse. If a victim does tell someone, very often she is blamed and not believed.

Sobsey (1994) reported that 90 percent of the perpetrators are men known to female victims of violence. In 1990, the California State Department of Developmental Disability Studies found sexual abuse to occur at a rate of 50 percent to 90 percent for this population. Tyiska (1998) reported that catastrophic injuries as the result of violent assaults can trigger the loss of abilities to see, hear, touch, taste, feel, move, and think in the usual ways. A 1998 report by the National Clearinghouse on Family Violence in Canada states that women have cited violence by their husbands or intimate partner as causing a loss of vision or mobility. Kemp (1995) found that 81 percent of battered women suffered from some degree of PTSD.

8.1.6 Children With Disabilities and Violence

Schilling and Schinke (1984) argue that children with mental retardation are at greater risk for abuse by parents and caregivers than other children because ordinary standards of care are insufficient for them, and Neutra (1977) said they are less protected from incest than other children. Also, some children with development disabilities exhibit behavior such as tantrums and noncompliance that negatively impact caregivers and increase the risk of abuse (Solomons, 1979). Some settings or specific caretaking roles set the stage for potential abuse. Finkelhor (1988) suggests that the majority of day care abuse occurs around toileting activity, while a study of deaf children found that sexual abuse tended to occur as a result of caretaker access to residents in private settings such as bathrooms and bedrooms at residential facilities (Sullivan, 1987). Disabilities can also result from an act of violence or some other form of child maltreatment. It is estimated that approximately 33 percent of all spinal cord injuries are the result of intentional violence, although it was not known if there were other preexisting disabilities among those who suffered injury (Waters, 1996). Additionally, approximately 50,000 adolescents sustain permanent disability as the result of brain injury (Stylianos, 1998). Institutional abuse is another challenge, as approximately 2 percent of 4.5 million children with disabilities in the United States live in institutions. Brookhouser (1987) and Sullivan (1987) suggest that residential placement is a risk factor for experiencing physical or sexual abuse.

For persons with disabilities to receive adequate services and support, Spies (1999) says the following issues must be addressed:

- Active enforcement of existing discrimination laws (i.e., federally funded shelters for battered women need to be responsible for providing adequate services to women and children with disabilities).
- Grievance procedures need to be responsive to complaints about discrimination based on disability.
- When protocols are developed outlining the process that will be used when a person with a disability is victimized, they must be taken seriously. Persons with disabilities must determine what those protocols will be and must be in charge of their development.
- The disability community must apply pressure to home health agencies, rehabilitation facilities, independent living centers, hospitals, nursing homes, social services, and medical personnel to acknowledge the existence of physical, sexual, and psychological abuse against people with disabilities.
- More attention must be given by policymakers to the needs of the disability community and studies need to be funded to research the true extent of the problem.
- There must be increased funding for victim service programs to make them more accessible. Line items for accessibility provisions need to be included in budgets.
- Programs must seek in-service training on disability issues to reduce fear and ignorance.
- Medical providers who treat crime victims must be educated to ensure that people with severe disabilities receive appropriate medical treatment, safely and with dignity.
- There must be recognition by all parties that women with disabilities face double discrimination.
- There must be recognition that individuals with disabilities are being excluded from meetings, conferences, and events because of inaccessibility.
- The persons-with-disabilities culture must be recognized and honored, as disability is not a medical issue, but a civil rights issue.
- Service providers and policymaking bodies must have people with disabilities on their boards of directors and we must be involved in all levels of operation.

8.2 VIOLENCE AGAINST MEN

About 3 percent of American men, or a total of 2.78 million men, have experienced an attempted or completed rape in their lifetime, according to the *Prevalence, Incidence and Consequences of Violence Against Women* report (Tjaden & Thoennes, 1998); in 2002, one in every eight rape victims were male, according to the U.S. Department of Justice NCVS (2002). Although males are not seen by many as a vulnerable population, the act of male sexual abuse is still considered a taboo subject in numerous communities. It is a crime with a justice process that is hampered by the fear of stigmas and underreporting to law enforcement and health care providers. It is crucial for FNEs to recognize that male victims of sexual violence do exist, and to be watchful for signs and symptoms of injury when these victims present to the clinical setting. Men most commonly experience sexual violence in the form of:

- Receptive anal intercourse
- Forced masturbation of the perpetrator
- Receptive oral sex
- Forced masturbation of the victim

Sexual violence against males is underreported, far more than in the case of women, largely because of the reluctance of men to report acts of sexual violence to the police. This in turn is likely to be due to extreme embarrassment experienced by most males at being a victim of sexual violence. There are, however, certain settings in which acts of sexual violence against males might be more prevalent; for example, in prisons and the armed forces. Generally speaking, men have the same physical and psychological responses to sexual violence as women, including the following:

- Fear
- Depression
- Suicidal ideation
- Anger
- Sexual and relationship problems

Men also experience RTS in much the same way as women. However, men are likely to be particularly concerned about:

- Their masculinity
- Their sexuality
- Opinions of other people (i.e., afraid that others will think they are homosexual)
- The fact that they were unable to prevent the rape

These concerns about masculinity and sexuality might stem from the misconceptions that only homosexual men are raped and that heterosexual men would never rape another heterosexual man. Julia M. Whealin, PhD, asserts that at least 10 percent of men in the United States have suffered from trauma as a result of sexual assault. "Like women, men who experience sexual assault may suffer from depression, PTSD, and other emotional problems as a result. However, because men and women have different life experiences due to their different gender roles, emotional symptoms following trauma can look different in men than they do in women."

Perpetrators of male sexual assault differ in a number of ways from those who assault only females. Boys are more likely than girls to be sexually abused by strangers or by authority figures in organizations such as schools, churches, or athletics programs.

Those who sexually assault males usually choose young men and male adolescents (the average age is 17 years old) as their victims and are more likely to assault many victims, compared to those who sexually assault females. Perpetrators often assault young males in isolated areas where help is not readily available. For instance, a perpetrator who assaults males might pick up a teenage hitchhiker on a remote road or find some other way to isolate his intended victim. As is true about those who assault and sexually abuse women and girls, most perpetrators of males are men. Specifically, men are perpetrators in about 86 percent of male victimization cases, Whealin says. Despite the popular belief that only gay men would sexually assault men or boys, most male perpetrators identify themselves as heterosexuals and often have consensual sexual relationships with women. Particularly when the assailant is a woman, the impact of sexual assault on men might be downplayed by professionals and the public. However, men who have early sexual experiences with adults report problems in various areas at a much higher rate than those who do not. Men and boys who have been sexually assaulted are more likely to suffer from PTSD, other anxiety disorders, and depression than those who have never been abused sexually. Men who have been sexually assaulted have a high incidence of alcohol and drug use. For example, the probability for alcohol problems in adulthood is about 80 percent for men who have experienced sexual abuse, as compared to 11 percent for men who have never been sexually abused, Whealin says. One study revealed that a percentage of boys who suffer from bowel incontinence had been sexually abused.

Exposure to sexual trauma can lead to risk-taking behavior during adolescence, such as running away and other delinquent behaviors. Having been sexually assaulted also makes boys more likely to engage in behaviors that put them at risk for contracting HIV (such as having sex without using condoms).

Gender socialization has been found to affect the recognition of male sexual assault. Men who have not dealt with the symptoms of their sexual assault might experience confusion about their sexuality and role as men (their gender role). This confusion occurs for many reasons. The traditional gender role for men in the American cultures dictates that they be strong, self-reliant, and in control. Our culture traditionally does not recognize that men and boys can also be victims. Boys and men might be taught that being victimized implies that they are weak and, thus, not men. Furthermore, when the perpetrator of a sexual assault is a man, feelings of shame, stigmatization, and negative reactions from others might also result from the social taboos. When the perpetrator of a sexual assault is a woman, some people do not take the assault seriously, and men might feel as though they are unheard and unrecognized as victims. Parents often know very little about male sexual assault and might harm their male children who are sexually abused by downplaying or denying the experience. Whealin says that because of their experience of sexual assault, some men attempt to prove their masculinity by becoming hypermasculine. For example, some men deal with their experience of sexual assault by having multiple female sexual partners or engaging in dangerous "macho" behaviors to prove their masculinity. Parents of boys who have been sexually abused might inadvertently encourage this process. Men who acknowledge their assault might have to struggle with feeling ignored and invalidated by others who do not recognize that men can also be victimized.

Because of ignorance and myths about sexual abuse, men sometimes fear that the sexual assault by another man will cause them to become gay. This belief is false. Sexual assault does not cause someone to have a particular sexual orientation. Because of these various gender-related issues, men are more likely than women to feel ashamed of the assault, to not talk about it, and to not seek help from professionals. Another myth that male victims of sexual assault face is the assumption that they will become abusers themselves. For instance, they might have heard that survivors of sexual abuse tend to repeat the cycle of abuse by abusing children themselves. Some research has shown that men who were sexually abused by men during their childhood have a greater number of sexual thoughts and fantasies about sexual contact with male children and adolescents. However, it is important to know that most male victims of child sexual abuse do not become sex offenders. Furthermore, many male perpetrators do not have a history of child sexual abuse. Rather, sexual offenders more often grew up in families in which they suffered from several other forms of abuse, such as physical and emotional. Men who assault others also have difficulty with empathy, and thus put their own needs above the needs of their victims. Health care providers should realize that men who have been assaulted often feel stigmatized, which can be the most damaging aspect of the assault. It is important for men to discuss the assault with a caring and unbiased support person, whether that person is a friend, clergyman, or clinician. However, it is vital that this person be knowledgeable about sexual assault and men. A local rape crisis center might be able to refer men to mental health practitioners who are well-informed about the needs of male sexual assault victims.

8.2.1 Male Victims of Sexual Assault: A Review of the Literature

McLean, Balding, and White (2004) report that male-on-male rapes and sexual assaults comprise fewer than 10 percent of such assaults reported to the police, so many physicians seldom encounter them. The researchers sought to explore the nature of sexual assault encountered by males, ensuing injuries, and comparisons with male-on-female assault cases. Their retrospective epidemiological study was conducted on two cohorts seen at St. Mary's Sexual Assault Referral Centre in Manchester, England, between October 1986 and mid-May 2003: 376 male eases (370 individual clients) and 7,789 female cases (7,403 individual clients). The main outcome measure was the presence of injury (abrasion, laceration, or bruise) to defined body areas. The researchers found that 66 percent of male cases (when assault type was known) had been raped, significantly fewer than in female cases (95 percent). Eighteen percent of male cases that had a forensic medical examination presented with an anal injury; there were significantly more in females. Significantly fewer males than females sustained injuries to other body areas. Their conclusion was that males were significantly more likely (six times) than females to receive at least one injury to the anal area. Even so, males are five times more likely to have no anal injury, they reported.

Stermac, Del Bove, and Addison (2004) examined victim and assault characteristics and the nature and extent of coercion, violence, and physical injuries among adult male victims of sexual assaults. Client records of three groups presenting to a sexual assault care center were included: males assaulted by a stranger (64), males assaulted by an acquaintance (81), and females assaulted by an acquaintance (106). The researchers found that male victims of sexual assault tended to be young, single men who reported high rates of vulnerabilities such as homelessness and physical, psychiatric, and cognitive disabilities. They also found that male stranger assailant victims were more likely to experience assaults involving weapons and physical violence, and that injuries sustained by victims and services delivered at the sexual assault care center were similar for both male and female clients.

Lipscomb, Muram, Speck, and Mercer (1992) compared the demographics, physical findings, and assault characteristics of incarcerated, sexually assaulted men with those of nonincarcerated, sexually assaulted men. A case series of 99 adult male victims of sexual assault was evaluated over a three-year period at the Memphis Sexual Assault Resource Center, a nonhospital-based clinic that serves as the primary resource for sexually assaulted victims in the Memphis and Shelby County, Tennessee area. All adult male victims of sexual assault evaluated during the study period were included in the study; 99 victims were studied, including 80 incarcerated men and 19 men from the community. The researchers discovered that victims of sexual assault in the community group were older than the victims in the incarcerated group. Apart from the age difference and weapon use, there were no statistically significant differences between the incarcerated and nonincarcerated victims. The researchers concluded that the similarities between the two groups suggest that sexual assault of men might not be unique to prisons, and all men are potential victims. They added that further studies are required to better understand these crimes and to develop education and prevention programs.

King and Woollett (1997) investigated the nature of sexual assault on men and their help seeking following the assault. The study encompassed all men who were seen at least once for face-to-face counseling at Survivors, a counseling service for male victims. Data on 115 men were analyzed; 69 were assaulted while under age 16.The average time from assault to contact with Survivors was 16.4 years. Fifty-one men (44 percent) were assaulted more than once. The assailant was known to the victim in all but 16 cases. One hundred men (87 percent) were assaulted by at least one man, seven (6 percent) by a man and a woman, and eight (7 percent) by women. Forced anal penetration took place in 88 cases. Twenty-seven men (23 percent) said they feared for their lives during the assault; 88 men (79 percent) sought no help and only 17 men (15 percent) reported the assault to police. For victims assaulted under the age of 16, the assault was more likely to be their first sexual experience and they were more likely to delay contact with Survivors for more than 17 years. They were also less likely to report to police. Victims assaulted by more than one person were more likely to have been assaulted by strangers, by women, and to have suffered physical harm; they were less likely to have experienced the assault as their first sexual experience, the researchers reported.

Coxell and King (1996) reviewed sexual assault prevalence data from 1,480 males and found that these victims suffer from PTSD, sexual problems, difficulties forming close relationships, mistrust of adult men, suicide attempts, confusion about sexual orientation, and various mood disorders. Darves-Bornoz, Choquet, Ledoux, and Manfredi (1998) reported on a nationwide survey of school-age adolescents in France. In all, 121 boys and 344 girls reported having been sexually assaulted (mean age = 15.4 years). Results indicated that girls exhibited more somatic symptoms and mood disorders, whereas boys more frequently demonstrated behavioral symptoms such as running away, suicide attempts, violent outbursts, and substance use.

Hodge and Canter (1998) report on two different accounts of male sexual assault in the literature. The first view is that rapes are perpetrated by homosexual offenders. The other view is that rape is predominantly an example of heterosexual violence. This paper reports on the results of a study constructed to explore both possibilities. Data from 83 male sexual assault victims and 36 investigated police reports was reviewed. Results indicated that homosexual offenders knew their victims for some time and targeted males under the age of 25 years. Heterosexual offenders were more likely to attack strangers of all ages and tended to operate in gangs. Consistent with the literature on the rape of females, the data indicated that acquaintance rape was less likely to be reported to the police. Isely, Busse, and Isely (1998) report that adolescent males, 16 years of age and older, are at risk of sexual assault. The sexual assault of adolescent males, however, has not been thoroughly explored. Much like sexually abused children, these survivors display significant emotional difficulties as a consequence of the sexual assault. An awareness of this type of abuse might assist in the early identification and treatment of this unacknowledged population. Isely and Gehrenbeck-Shim (1997) report on an attempt to determine the extent of male sexual assault. Agencies that work with sexual assault victims reported contact with 3,635 men who had sought treatment for sexual assault. Most assaults occurred between the ages of 16 and 30 years and a majority of these men experienced symptoms of PTSD.

King and Woollett (1997) collected data on 115 male sexual assault victims who were seen at least once for face-to-face counseling. Analysis revealed that 69 men were assaulted prior to age 16. The average time from assault to obtaining counseling services was 16.4 years. Fifty-one men were assaulted more than once. The victim knew the perpetrator in the majority of cases. One-hundred respondents were assaulted by one or more men. Of the sample, 88 men did not seek help at the time and only 17 men reported the assault to the police. Victims under the age of 16 who were assaulted were more likely to report that this was their first sexual experience. Victims under the age of 16 were also more likely to delay contact with counseling and less likely to report to police. Victims assaulted by more than one person were less likely to have experienced the incident as their first sexual experience, and more likely to have been assaulted by strangers and to have suffered physical injuries.

Stermac, Sheridan, Davidson, and Dunn (1996) studied the incidence and characteristics of sexual assault against 29 males (aged 18–65 years) who were seen in a crisis unit. The men's personal history, demographic, and assault information were reviewed. Results showed that 86 percent of the sexual assaults involved male perpetrators, one involved a female perpetrator, and two involved both. Within this sample, 50 percent of the male–male assaults and both of the female–male assaults involved friends or acquaintances. Most victims were young gay men, many of whom had cognitive or physical disabilities that made them vulnerable; however, only a few of the stranger assaults appeared to be related to antigay violence.

Vearnals and Campbell (2001) discussed the surprising fact that recently in the United Kingdom, males were incorporated into the legal definition of rape. Prior to that, it was legally impossible for a male to be a victim of sexual assault. Not only in the United Kingdom, but worldwide, the issue of male sexual assault is underaddressed. The authors discuss the health consequences of sexual assault and the lack of research in this area, and they stress the need for appropriate treatment interventions for victims. Further research is urged in this area, especially in the epidemiology of sexual assault; the emotional, physical, and psychological consequences; and the most effective psychological interventions.

8.3 VIOLENCE AGAINST LGTB INDIVIDUALS

Health care providers must also be aware of sexual victimization within the LGTB communities. In 2003, 12 member organizations of the National Coalition of Anti-Violence Programs (NCAVP) documented a record 6,523 LGTB domestic violence incidents reported in 11 cities and regions across the United States and in Toronto, Canada. This figure represents a 13 percent increase over the 5,718 cases reported by the same agencies in 2002, and includes six reported domestic-violence-related deaths. A significant large majority (4,964 or 76 percent) of incidents were reported in Los Angeles, a region that accounts for almost 93 percent of the net growth in LGTB domestic violence cases reported nationally in 2003. A disproportionate number of cases can be attributed to the presence of a large number of NCAVP member organizations, the availability of equal legal standing and remedies for LGTB domestic violence victims, and unparalleled support for data collection and reporting by a network of affiliated domestic violence law enforcement and service providers, including police and county sheriff's departments. Boston reported 290 cases, New York City reported 501 cases, and San Francisco reported 388 cases, all of which represented significant increases in the number of cases documented. In smaller regions, 2003 case numbers declined or barely changed at all. Examples include Chicago (65 cases and a decrease of 12.2 percent), Colorado (139 cases and a decrease of 2.8 percent), Pennsylvania (19 cases, and a decrease of 42.4 percent), and Burlington, Vermont (21 cases and a decrease of 24 percent). NCAVP's newest domestic violence report contributor, Toronto, recorded 26 cases, one more than the 25 it reported internally to NCAVP last year.

A number of trends have been identified by the NCAVP. Increased public attention to the LGTB community, especially in connection with the debate over same-gender marriage that heated up in 2004, appears to have spurred increases in the amount of bias and hate-motivated violence targeting LGTB individuals. Most of the agencies represented in the 2003 report assist victims of bias violence and hate crimes, so that nearly all have found it necessary to accommodate growth in services for these individuals. A second trend is new investments of funding and resources in domestic-violence services, especially outreach and public education campaigns needed to encourage victims to seek help. Experts say that the debate over gay marriage, and especially the threat of a constitutional amendment banning any civil recognition for LGTB unions, has prevented some LGTB individuals from reporting their experience of domestic violence. In the future, an increasing number of LGTB domestic violence victims might decide to endure a partner's abuse for the sake of a marriage proposal, or even an actual marriage. Others might be more hesitant to come forward because they feel that being the victim of domestic violence will somehow harm their community's struggle for advancement. Experts add that there is no evidence that LGTB domestic violence occurs with any more frequency, or has any worse outcomes, than domestic violence between heterosexuals.

8.3.1 Murders and Domestic-Violence-Related Deaths in LGTB Communities

NCAVP documented six murders or other deaths of individuals in the context of actual or suspected LGTB domestic violence in 2003, an increase of two deaths over 2002. Two cities and regions reported murders in 2003: Arizona, with one (none in 2002), and New York City with five (compared with just two in 2002). The following recaps of homicides and attempted homicides illustrate the violence within LGTB communities. In a community in rural Arizona, there was an attempted murder of one woman by her roommate, who was then shot and killed by police as she fled the scene. The victim sustained multiple gunshot wounds before managing to call 911 before lapsing into a coma. Her assailant escaped and was pursued by sheriff's deputies. When the woman was stopped, she raised her weapon and was shot by a deputy. The perpetrator had previously spoken about the victim as her girlfriend and told acquaintances that they were in a relationship. When the victim regained consciousness, she denied there had been any romantic involvement between them.

In Kansas City, Missouri, a 28-year-old man was charged with second-degree murder and armed criminal action in the death of a 22-year-old man. The assailant had threatened to kill the victim if the victim ended the relationship. The victim had rejected the assailant's marriage proposal, and the next day, the assailant was seen moving out of the apartment both men shared. A few days later, the victim was reported missing by his family. An unidentified witness reported seeing the victim's car early in the morning, and when police arrived at the vehicle's location, they found his body in the car's trunk. Police searched the apartment and found blood evidence in the main room and a blood trail leading out of the apartment to the parking lot. Blood was also found on the assailant's shoes when police arrested him shortly thereafter.

In New York City, a 38-year-old man was convicted of second-degree manslaughter and sentenced to 22 years to life in jail for fatally beating and stabbing his lover, a 32-year-old man, during an argument in their home. The assailant claimed that the victim was killed accidentally; however, medical examiners testified that the victim died from multiple skull fractures from a baseball bat and 17 stab wounds to the chest. Also in New York state, an 88-year-old African American male was slashed across his neck while he was eating dinner. A neighbor found him dead in his home. The victim's wallet was missing, but detectives found no evidence of a break-in. They did find photographs of nude men the victim had paid to pose for him. One of the men, age 29, who was the last individual photographed, admitted to having an ongoing intimate relationship with the victim. The young man confessed to killing the elderly man and pleaded guilty to second-degree murder. Robbery, not domestic violence, was officially cited as the motivation for the murder. In a third New York case, a 53-year-old man died of a heart attack in a hospital four days after his roommate, a 51-year-old man, gouged out his eyes with his fingernails during a physical argument in the home that they shared. The men were reportedly arguing over a broken television antenna. Police arrived and arrested the assailant for assault. It is unclear whether the medical examiners linked the victim's death to the assault, and the two men were referred to only as "longtime roommates" in media accounts.

In Pittsburgh, a 15-year-old boy beat his 18-year-old brother on the head with a claw hammer approximately 18 times in the family's home and dumped the body into a bathtub. The assailant then phoned a friend, who came to the home and found the body. The assailant and another friend, who was present during the assault, left the home while the victim was being rushed to the hospital. The victim died from severe head injuries.

The perpetrator had reportedly met friends at a local mall and bragged about attacking his brother, referring to him as a "faggot." The perpetrator also reportedly told friends that he wanted to kill his brother because he was gay and that he also wanted to kill his family. The assailant was convicted of both murder and conspiracy to commit murder; the friend who witnessed the assault was also convicted of first-degree murder.

8.3.1.1 Gender of LGTB Victims

Of the total 6,523 domestic violence incidents reported by NCAVP's member organizations in 2003, the victims in 3,344 cases (44 percent) were identified as men, whereas those in 2,357 cases (36 percent) were identified as women. The next largest group (623 cases, or 9 percent) represents incidents in which information about the victim's gender was not recorded. There was a smaller group of incidents (161 cases, or 2 percent) in which the victims were identified as transgender: either male to female (M–F), or female to male (F–M). A considerably larger number of victims were transgender M–F individuals (161) than F–M (31). Relative to the comparable figures for 2002, the numbers in nearly all of these categories show growth, some of it attributable to a compensating reduction (minus 27.3 percent) in the number of 2003 victims whose gender was reported unknown, especially in Los Angeles. Los Angeles also accounted for the bulk of growth reported nationally in the number of incidents involving victims who were male (an increase of 26 percent overall) and transgender (an increase of 33 percent overall). Within the transgender category, however, considerably higher growth was seen both in Los Angeles and nationally in the number of cases involving those who identified themselves as female (an increase of 44 percent) versus those who identified as male (an increase of 16 percent).

However, this unequal growth alone cannot account for all of the continuing difference in size between the transgender M–F and F–M victim populations. Accordingly, although women made up a smaller overall proportion of domestic violence victims documented by NCAVP in 2003 than in 2002, little should be drawn from that fact. Among the other NCAVP agencies reporting increases in the number of domestic violence incidents in 2003, the tendency for most was to serve relatively higher proportions of women (and especially transgender M–F individuals) than in 2002. A significant exception was San Francisco, which reported a modest reduction in incidents involving women as victims (from 165 to 154) and significant growth among those involving men (from 168 to 196, or an increase of 16.7 percent). However, San Francisco also reported a 50 percent increase (from 18 to 27) in the number of transgender M–F victims between the two years. By contrast, at almost all of the NCAVP agencies reporting a decrease in the number of incidents, reductions involving women as victims were steeper than those involving men. This fact suggests that women might be more sensitive to limitations or constraints in LGTB domestic violence services, at least at these agencies. Another reason could be that some lesbian and bisexual women victimized by domestic violence find ways to obtain services from mainstream domestic violence organizations. The question, like most others relating to LGTB domestic violence, begs further research.

8.3.1.2 Sexual Orientation of LGTB Victims

As in past years, the great majority (5,374 cases, or 82 percent) of domestic violence incidents reported to NCAVP in 2003 involved victims who identified themselves as lesbian or gay. The next largest category (575 cases, or 9 percent) included cases in which a victim declined to specify a sexual orientation, or it wasn't recorded. In 263 other instances (4 percent), the victims identified themselves as bisexual, and in an additional 44 cases (0.6 percent), they said they questioned their sexual orientation or weren't sure. Self-identified heterosexuals (a category that can include transgender individuals) were the victims in 263 cases (4 percent), coincidentally the same number as were reported bisexual. Experts say these numbers encompass some curious changes with respect to the ones reported by NCAVP in 2002, but the significance of these changes is questionable. First, the proportion of incidents involving victims who identified themselves as lesbian or gay appeared to grow last year by six percentage points relative to 2002. Further, this trend was one of the few encountered by an actual majority of NCAVP members contributing to this report. Although some of the increase appears attributable to a decline in incidents involving victims whose sexual orientation was unknown, it cannot be fully accounted for in this way. The range of possible explanations for this shift, however, is large. Some of these explanations might appear positive: growing awareness of the problem of domestic violence among lesbians and gay men, for example, or an increased willingness to self-identify as such. However, it is also possible that the explanation is negative. Perhaps the higher concentration of self-identified LGTB clients encountered by NCAVP member agencies in 2003 means they are doing less well serving people and groups who might be at higher risk to experience domestic violence. These could include those who hide their sexual orientation, question it, or otherwise do not identify themselves in this way. Again, research is needed to shed light on all these possible explanations.

8.3.1.3 Ages of LGTB Victims

In 2002, most NCAVP member agencies used an instrument in which victims' ages were reported in several discrete categories: under 18, 18 to 22, 23 to 29, 30 to 44, 45 to 64, and 65 and over. In 2003, several (but not all) of NCAVP's members switched to a new instrument with a different set of age categories: under 14, 15 to 18, 19 to 29, 30 to 39, 40 to 49, 50 to 59, 60 to 69, 70 to 79, and 80 and over. This makes it challenging to describe any but the most general trends in the age distribution of victims in 2003. In fact, the only valid way to compare age information using both sets of categories is to divide all the reported victims into just two age groups: those under 30, and those who are older. However, within these two categories, there appears to have been an unusually large change in 2003: The number of victims whose ages were under 30 grew to 1,472 from 954 in 2002 (an increase of 54 percent), whereas the number of those 30 and older increased by just one fifth of that rate (and less than the rate of growth in new cases overall), from 1,845 to 2,040. Further, this trend was general, experienced by all but four of the agencies reporting data this year (and in all but one of those agencies, the 2003 decline in younger victims was very modest). It should be noted that there remain a very large number of cases, nearly half of those reported in both years, in which the ages of victims were not recorded. However, because most of these cases are from a single city, Los Angeles, and because their number did not change significantly in 2003 (and actually declined as a percentage of the whole) it appears that a majority of NCAVP members are providing more domestic violence interventions for LGTB and questioning youth and young adults. In fact, many of NCAVP's member organizations and affiliated programs have endeavored to develop services more appropriate for younger people over the past several years, and the figures in this report are the best indication yet of their success.

8.3.1.4 Race and Ethnicity of LGTB Victims

NCAVP member agencies also attempt to record the race and ethnicity of victims of domestic violence incidents. They do this partly to measure how well their programs are providing accessible, sensitive services for all members of the LGTB community, but also because, in some instances, a victim's racial or ethnic identity could become a weapon in the hands of abusers. However, as with other demographic questions, not all victims answer queries regarding their race or ethnicity, nor are these questions always appropriate to ask. NCAVP agencies reported the race and ethnicity of domestic violence victims in just 42 percent of all the incidents recorded in 2003. Of the victims for whom this information was known, 1,211 (44 percent) were White, 684 (25 percent) were Latino, 413 (15 percent) were people of African descent, 153 (5 percent) were Asian/Pacific Islander, and 125 (4 percent) were reported as multiracial. The number of known Asian/Pacific Islander victims grew by 104 percent over 2002, but virtually all of this increase occurred in Los Angeles. The number of known White victims declined by 11 percent, and the number of Latinos by 10 percent, but in these instances, too, most of the change was restricted to Los Angeles, and the experience of many of NCAVP's members was the reverse. For example, in San Francisco, Chicago, Boston, New York and Toronto, the number of victims who were White increased slightly (albeit not necessarily as fast as increases in cases overall), and San Francisco, Colorado, Chicago, and New York reported increases in the number of Latino clients as well. Of note in the 2003 statistics collected by NCAVP is the number of domestic violence incidents recorded by its member agencies. This data suggests that such incidents continued to peak at three points throughout the course of the year: during May and June, when many are preparing to participate in annual LGTB pride celebrations around the country and LGTB organizational and program outreach reaches a peak; again in October during the observance of Domestic Violence Awareness Month; and once more with the new year.

8.3.2 The Health Care Provider's Response to LGTB Victims

The FVPF's (2004) *National Consensus Guidelines on Identifying and Responding to Domestic Violence Victimization in Healthcare Settings* acknowledges that IPV occurs at similar rates in LGTB adolescent and adult populations as in heterosexual populations, with higher rates in male same-sex relationships than female. However, it is important to realize that the statistics might be low because those in same-sex relationships might not be comfortable stating their sexual preference. A policy to assess all patients should include specific recommendations for responding to LGTB and heterosexual victims. Specialized services might be limited in your area, so when unavailable, refer patients to national organizations or the national domestic violence hotline. Prior to implementing a program to assess all patients, it is important that health care providers do the following:

- Be aware of their own biases about who is a victim and homophobia.
- Call the local IPV program and determine what resources are available for LGTB clients.
- Call any local programs for LGTB communities and determine what resources they offer for victims of IPV.
- In addition (or if no programs exist in your area) provide LGTB victims with the national domestic violence hotline number for more information or materials
- Have educational and safety materials available that are appropriate for LGTB victims. (For clinic materials go to the FVPF Web site at http://www.endabuse.org.).
- Refer gay male victims of IPV to Anti-Violence Project (AVP), Community United Against Violence (CUAV), Gay Men's Domestic Violence

Project, or other like organizations for information and support.

- Refer lesbian victims to CUAV, the Network for Battered Lesbians and Bisexual Women, AVP, or other local organizations for information and support.

8.4 VIOLENCE AGAINST ELDERS

One of the most significant areas of opportunity for the contributions of forensic nurses is elder abuse. Griffin and Williams (1992) suggest that the effects of the baby boom and increased life expectancy have both contributed to the immediate and projected increase in the number of elderly Americans. Additionally, medical advances and the implementation of protective legislation have greatly increased the length of life for many Americans. However, generational changes in the family structure mean that fewer members of the elderly population are cared for by family members or friends; instead, this important task falls to strangers tasked with caring for an increasing number of individuals. According to the U.S. Bureau of the Census (2000), nearly 77 million people, more than a quarter of the total U.S. population, are 50 or older. By 2030, as baby boomers become the retiree majority, one third of American voters will be over 55, somewhere between a fifth and a quarter of them over 65. Issues of elder abuse are of significant interest to baby boomers who have aging parents, as well as those who themselves face issues of aging and victimization. Between now and 2030, the number of adults over 65 will double to more than 70 million, from 12 percent of the population to more than 21 percent. The health care system, crippled by an intense shortage of nurses, might not be prepared to bear this skyrocketing number of admissions into acute care, subacute care, and long-term care facilities.

Koenig and Deguerre (2005) state that older Americans constitute the fastest growing segment of the U.S. population and might account for 20 percent of the U.S. population by 2050. They assert that the federal government has taken minimal action to identify and solve elders' problems. Due to the federal government's inaction, states have become the primary engine for combating abuse. They say this is most often seen through adult protective services (APS), which primarily consist of mandatory reporting laws, involuntary interventions, and educational programs. Koenig and Deguerre add that funding is the primary roadblock to the successful execution of state laws targeting domestic elder abuse. They say that the proposed federal Elder Justice Act of 2003, if passed, might fill in the gaps of current federal legislation by implementing a uniform method of response to domestic elder abuse and providing funding to the states to rectify instances of abuse. (This piece of legislation is discussed later in this chapter.)

"Elder abuse is where we were with child abuse about 20 years ago," asserts Diana Faugno, RN, BSN, CPN, SANE:

> I think there is a lot more that needs to be done for this special population. When you think about it, we are all getting older. We need nurses who are specialists in gerontology, who can spot the many types of elder abuse and neglect, from verbal and physical abuse to fiduciary abuse, and help victims feel comfortable with reporting the abuse. Victims are scared to death to tell. They are intimidated, so they back off, and the cycle of abuse continues. We need nurses who have that basic forensic knowledge, and see the red flags of elder abuse.

8.4.1 Importance of Ending Ageism Increases as Life Expectancy Lengthens

The U.S. Bureau of the Census also estimates that by the year 2050, approximately 25 percent of Americans will be over the age of 65, yet the U.S. culture has done little to eliminate the one accepted prejudice that could relegate one quarter of the population to second-class citizenship: ageism. As the U.S. population continues to age, the need to halt ageism and ageist practices becomes more urgent, according to the recently published issue brief by the International Longevity Center USA, an independent affiliate of Mount Sinai School of Medicine, titled, "The Future of Ageism." Ageism, like racism and sexism, is prejudice and discrimination against members of a group—in this case, older individuals. It is a universal prejudice, because increased longevity means that all individuals can eventually become its victims. Unlike racism and sexism, it is rarely discussed through public discourse. It is a relatively new concept first noted in 1969 by Robert N. Butler, MD, president and CEO of the ILC-USA.

8.4.2 Painting a Picture of Violence Against Elders

Look in 10 different places for statistics on elder abuse, and you will undoubtedly find 10 different sets of figures. The NCVS of the Bureau of Justice Statistics (2001) reported that the rate of violent crime victimization of persons ages 65 or older was about four per 1,000. Persons ages 65 or older numbered 34.5 million in 1999, about 13 percent of the U.S. population, according to the Administration on Aging (2000). The 1998 National Elder Abuse Incident Study (NEAIS) reports that an estimated total of 551,011 elderly persons aged 60 and over experienced abuse, neglect, or self-neglect in domestic settings in 1996. The most frequent forms of elder abuse reported to APS agencies included neglect (48.7 percent), emotional or psychological abuse (35.4 percent), financial or material exploitation (30.2 percent), physical abuse (25.6 percent), and abandonment (3.5 percent), according to the National Center on Elder Abuse (NCEA). The agency also reports that adult children are the largest perpetrators of elder abuse (47.3 percent), followed by spouses (19.3 percent), other relatives (8.8 percent), and grandchildren (8.6 percent).

The definitions and statistics regarding elder abuse vary. They range from estimates that one out of 10 persons living with a family member is subject to abuse—approximately 2.5 million a year (Griffin & Williams, 1992)—to 1 in 25 elderly persons being victimized annually (Heisler, 1991). Other studies suggest that 3.6 percent of elderly citizens are victims of abuse each year (Commonwealth of Pennsylvania, 1988). According to the NCEA, the major types of elder abuse are categorized as follows:

- Physical abuse is defined as the use of physical force that can result in bodily injury, physical pain, or impairment. Physical abuse can include but is not limited to such acts of violence as striking (with or without an object), hitting, beating, pushing, shoving, shaking, slapping, kicking, pinching, and burning. In addition, inappropriate use of drugs and physical restraints, force-feeding, and physical punishment of any kind also are examples of physical abuse. Signs and symptoms of physical abuse include but are not limited to:
  - Bruises, black eyes, welts, lacerations, and rope marks
  - Bone fractures, broken bones, and skull fractures
  - Open wounds, cuts, punctures, and untreated injuries in various stages of healing
  - Sprains, dislocations, and internal injuries or bleeding
  - Broken eyeglasses or frames, physical signs of being subjected to punishment, and signs of being restrained
  - Laboratory findings of medication overdose or underutilization of prescribed drugs
  - An elder's report of being hit, slapped, kicked, or mistreated
  - An elder's sudden change in behavior
  - The caregiver's refusal to allow visitors to see an elder alone
- Sexual abuse is defined as nonconsensual sexual contact of any kind with an elderly person. Sexual contact with any person incapable of giving consent is also considered sexual abuse. It includes, but is not limited to, unwanted touching, all types of sexual assault or battery, such as rape, sodomy, coerced nudity, and sexually explicit photographing. Signs and symptoms of sexual abuse include but are not limited to the following:
  - Bruises around the breasts or genital area
  - Unexplained venereal disease or genital infections
  - Unexplained vaginal or anal bleeding
  - Torn, stained, or bloody underclothing
  - An elder's report of being sexually assaulted or raped
- Emotional or psychological abuse is defined as the infliction of anguish, pain, or distress through verbal or nonverbal acts. Emotional or psychological abuse includes but is not limited to verbal assaults, insults, threats, intimidation, humiliation, and harassment. In addition, treating an older person like an infant; isolating an elderly person from his or her family, friends, or regular activities; giving an older person the silent treatment; and enforced social isolation are examples of emotional and psychological abuse. Signs and symptoms of emotional and psychological abuse include but are not limited to the following:
  - Being emotionally upset or agitated
  - Being extremely withdrawn and noncommunicative or nonresponsive
  - Unusual behavior usually attributed to dementia (e.g., sucking, biting, rocking)
  - An elder's report of being verbally or emotionally mistreated
- Neglect is defined as the refusal or failure to fulfill any part of a person's obligations or duties to an elder. Neglect can also include failure of a person who has fiduciary responsibilities to provide care for an elder (e.g., pay for necessary home care services) or the failure on the part of an in-home service provider to provide necessary care. Neglect typically means the refusal or failure to provide an elderly person with such life necessities as food, water, clothing, shelter, personal hygiene, medicine, comfort, personal safety, and other essentials included in an implied or agreed-on responsibility to an elder. Signs and symptoms of neglect include but are not limited to the following:
  - Dehydration, malnutrition, untreated bed sores, and poor personal hygiene
  - Unattended or untreated health problems
  - Hazardous or unsafe living condition or arrangements (e.g., improper wiring, no heat, or no running water)
  - Unsanitary and unclean living conditions (e.g., dirt, fleas, lice on person, soiled bedding, fecal or urine smell, inadequate clothing)
  - An elder's report of being mistreated

- Abandonment is defined as the desertion of an elderly person by an individual who has assumed responsibility for providing care for an elder or physical custody of an elder. Signs and symptoms of abandonment include but are not limited to the following:
  - The desertion of an elder at a hospital, a nursing facility, or other similar institution
  - The desertion of an elder at a shopping center or other public location
  - An elder's own report of being abandoned
- Financial or material exploitation is defined as the illegal or improper use of an elder's funds, property, or assets. Examples include, but are not limited to, cashing an elderly person's checks without authorization or permission; forging an older person's signature; misusing or stealing an older person's money or possessions; coercing or deceiving an older person into signing any document (e.g., contracts or will); and the improper use of conservatorship, guardianship, or power of attorney. Signs and symptoms of financial or material exploitation include but are not limited to the following:
  - Sudden changes in bank accounts or banking practice, including an unexplained withdrawal of large sums of money by a person accompanying the elder
  - The inclusion of additional names on an elder's bank signature card
  - Unauthorized withdrawal of the elder's funds using his or her ATM card
  - Abrupt changes in a will or other financial documents
  - Unexplained disappearance of funds or valuable possessions
  - Substandard care being provided or bills unpaid despite the availability of adequate financial resources
  - Discovery of an elder's signature being forged for financial transactions or for the titles of his or her possessions
  - Sudden appearance of previously uninvolved relatives claiming their rights to an elder's affairs and possessions
  - Unexplained sudden transfer of assets to a family member or someone outside the family
  - The provision of unnecessary services
  - An elder's report of financial exploitation
- Self-neglect is characterized as the behavior of an elderly person that threatens his or her own health or safety. Self-neglect generally manifests itself in an older person as a refusal or failure to provide himself or herself with adequate food, water, clothing, shelter, personal hygiene, medication (when indicated), and safety precautions. The definition of self-neglect excludes a situation in which a mentally competent older person, who understands the consequences of his or her decisions, makes a conscious and voluntary decision to engage in acts that threaten his or her health or safety as a matter of personal choice. Signs and symptoms of self-neglect include but are not limited to the following:
  - Dehydration, malnutrition, untreated or improperly attended medical conditions, and poor personal hygiene
  - Hazardous or unsafe living conditions or arrangements (e.g., improper wiring, no indoor plumbing, no heat, no running water)
  - Unsanitary or unclean living quarters (e.g., animal or insect infestation, no functioning toilet, fecal or urine smell)
  - Inappropriate or inadequate clothing, lack of the necessary medical aids (e.g., eyeglasses, hearing aids, dentures)
  - Grossly inadequate housing or homelessness

8.4.2.1 Prevalence and Incidence of Elder Abuse

The NCEA, in its April 2005 *Fact Sheet on Elder Abuse Prevalence and Incidence*, states, "No one knows precisely how many older Americans are being abused, neglected, or exploited. While evidence accumulated to date suggests that many thousands have been harmed, there are no official national statistics." The agency points to several reasons, including:

- Definitions of elder abuse vary. It is difficult to pinpoint exactly what actions or inactions constitute abuse, and the problem remains greatly hidden.
- State statistics vary widely, as there is no uniform reporting system.
- Comprehensive national data are not collected.

In the absence of a large-scale, nationwide tracking system, studies of prevalence and incidence conducted in the past few years by investigators have been crucial in helping health care providers understand the magnitude of the problem. Regarding the prevalence of elder abuse, between 1 and 2 million Americans age 65 or older have been injured, exploited, or otherwise mistreated by someone on whom they depended for care or protection, according to the 2002 report, *Elder Mistreatment: Abuse, Neglect and Exploitation in an Aging America*, produced by the National Research Council Panel to Review Risk and Prevalence of Elder Abuse and Neglect (Bonnie & Wallace, 2002). Lachs and Pillemer (2004) estimated the frequency of elder abuse from 2 percent to 10 percent, based on various sampling, survey methods, and case definitions. Pillemer and Finkelhor (1988) suggest that regarding elder abuse in domestic settings, 1 in 14 incidents, excluding incidents of self-neglect, come to the attention of authorities. In addition, the ground-breaking 1998 NEAIS conducted by the NCEA estimated that for every case of elder abuse, neglect, exploitation, or self-neglect reported to authorities, about five more cases go unreported. In 2000, a survey of state APS, conducted by the NCEA, determined the number of elder and adult reports received in the most recent year for which data were available. Based on figures from 54 states, the total number of reports was 472,813. In 2003, state long-term care ombudsman programs nationally investigated 20,673 complaints of abuse, gross neglect, and exploitation on behalf of nursing home and board-and-care residents. Among seven types of abuse categories, physical abuse was the most common type reported.

8.4.2.2 Elders: Protected by the Law?

According to the NCEA, federal laws on child abuse and domestic violence fund services and shelters for victims, but there is no comparable federal law on elder abuse. The federal Older Americans Act (42 U.S.C. 3001 et seq., as amended) does provide definitions of elder abuse and authorizes the use of federal funds for the NCEA and for certain elder abuse awareness, training, and coordination activities in states and local communities, but does not fund APS or shelters for abused older persons. On February 10, 2003, Senator John Breaux, then-ranking member of the Senate Special Committee on Aging, and Senator Orrin Hatch, then-chairman of the Senate Judiciary Committee, introduced the Elder Justice Act (SB 333) in the Senate. If passed, the new law would, among other things, establish dual Offices of Elder Justice in the U.S. Department of Health and Human Services/Administration on Aging and the U.S. Department of Justice to coordinate elder abuse prevention efforts nationally. It also would require an FBI criminal background check for long-term care nursing assistants and better training for workers in the detection of elder abuse. It would also establish an Office of Adult Protective Services within the U.S. Department of Health and Human Services, Administration for Children and Families. Finally, it would enhance law enforcement response to elder abuse. The bill was referred to the Senate Committee on Finance and no further action has been taken so far at the time of this writing.

According to the NCEA, all 50 states and the District of Columbia have enacted legislation authorizing the provision of APS in cases of elder abuse. Generally, these APS laws establish a system for the reporting and investigation of elder abuse and for the provision of social services to help the victim and ameliorate the abuse. In most jurisdictions, these laws pertain to abused adults who have a disability, vulnerability, or impairment as defined by state law, not just to older persons. These statutes vary widely in the age at or circumstances under which a victim is eligible to receive protective services; the definition of abuse; types of abuse, neglect, and exploitation that are covered; classification of the abuse as criminal or civil; reporting (mandatory or voluntary); investigation responsibility and procedures; and remedies for abuse. Some state APS laws only relate to individuals who reside in the community, whereas other APS laws also include individuals who reside in long-term care facilities. In some states where the APS law only covers individuals who reside in the community, a separate law addresses institutional abuse. Like the APS laws, institutional abuse statutes create a mechanism for reporting, investigating, and addressing incidents of elder abuse that occur in long-term care facilities or other facilities covered under the law. Additionally, all states and the District of Columbia have laws authorizing the Long Term Care Ombudsman Program (LTCOP), which is responsible for advocating on behalf of long-term care facility residents who experience abuse, violations of their rights, or other problems. LTCOPs are mandated in each state as a condition of receiving federal funds under the Older Americans Act. LTCOPs are an integral part of the systemic response to institutional elder abuse. LTCOPs might discover an abusive situation when responding to complaints within a facility and then, if appropriate, make a referral to an APS program, a law enforcement agency, or the agency responsible for licensing and certifying such facilities. Moreover, in some states, the LTCOP actually fulfills the role of APS and has the legal authority to investigate and respond to abuse occurring within long-term care facilities.

An increasing number of states are passing laws that provide explicit criminal penalties for various forms of elder abuse. Legislatures are also signaling their intent that elder abuse should be treated as a crime in other ways. For example, some APS laws include a provision stating that elder abuse can be prosecuted criminally, and others define certain acts (e.g., sexual abuse) in the same words or by reference to definitions that are used in the criminal laws. Even if there is not a specific statute or provision authorizing criminal prosecution for elder abuse, a jurisdiction's basic criminal laws (e.g., battery, assault, theft, fraud, rape, manslaughter, or murder) can be used to prosecute someone who has committed an act of abuse against an older person. Some legislatures have enacted enhanced penalties for certain crimes against older persons. Other state laws might be pertinent in cases involving elder abuse, even though they are not cited in this document. Such laws include those addressing guardianship or conservatorship, durable powers of attorney, and domestic violence or family violence prevention.

8.4.3 Elder Abuse: A Review of the Literature

Several years ago, researchers Bonnie Brandl, MSW, senior project specialist for the National Clearinghouse on Abuse in Later Life, and Loree Cook-Daniels, a consultant for the NCEA, set out to document the incidence of domestic violence later in life. They discovered that battered middle-aged women were essentially falling through the cracks when it came to epidemiological data, studies, and services that focused on this underserved vulnerable population. Because they are neither young (domestic violence programs predominantly serve women between the ages of 18 and 45 abused by intimate partners) nor old (most APS address elderly and incompetent victims), mature battered women have no particular support system to which they can turn for assistance. Likewise, although both domestic violence and elder abuse research are presumed to address domestic abuse in later life, researchers often define their target populations in ways that exclude these victims (Brandl & Cook-Daniels, 2002). The researchers define domestic abuse in later life as male and female victims, age 50 and older, abused by someone in a trusted, ongoing relationship such as a spouse or partner, family member, or some caregivers.

Brandl and Cook-Daniels reviewed 54 articles published in the literature from 1988 to 2002 pertaining to domestic abuse, excluding studies that focused on younger and older populations of victims. Ten articles studied prevalence and incidence rates of elder abuse in general and domestic violence specifically. Mouton and Espino (1999) found that 4.3 percent of their sample of older women responding to a health survey were currently in an abusive relationship. Harris (1996) found that 5.8 percent of the older couples responding to the survey had experienced domestic violence in the past year. Lachs et al. (1997a, 1997b) examined APS records and found that 1.6 percent of elders had been abused, neglected, or exploited over a nine-year period. Hudson and Carlson (1999) discovered that 6.2 percent of the older adults in their sample admitted to hurting an elder; in another study, the figure was 2 percent (Hudson & Carlson, 1999).

Five studies examined abuse occurring at any point in an individual's lifetime. Hudson and Carlson (1999) found 19.1 percent of women in six counties experienced domestic violence at some point in their lives. Mouton and Espino (1999) and Pittaway and Westhues (1993) discovered that 31.9 percent of men and women had experienced some form of domestic violence. Pillemer and Finklehor (1988) estimated 701,000 to 1,093,560 older Americans were victims of abuse each year. More recently, the U.S. NEAIS estimated that approximately 450,000 older people were being abused in 1996.

In their review of the literature, Brandl and Cook-Daniels (2002) discovered that most of the 28 studies in which a type of abuse in later life was identified involved more than one type of abuse. For example, 19 percent of victims were abused or neglected in more than one way in Podnieks's (1992) study and 20 percent in Greenberg, McKibben, and Raymond's (1990) study. Anetzberger (1997) found that psychological abuse accompanied other types of abuse in 89.7 percent of the sample. Fourteen of the 28 articles Brandl and Cook-Daniels reviewed compared the frequency of different types of abuse in later life. Four studies found neglect was the most prevalent type of abuse: Brown (1989), Lachs et al. (1997a, 1997b), NCEA (1998), and Otiniano, Herrera, and Teasdale (1998). Greenberg et al. (1990), Pillemer and Finkelhor (1988), and Wolf and Pillemer (1997) found that physical abuse was the most prevalent type of abuse. Brandl and Cook-Daniels also reviewed data suggesting that older women can be victims of sexual assault whether they are healthy and married or frail and living in an institution. Nearly all the sexual abuse victims studied were women, and all but one identified perpetrator were male. Mouton and Espino (1999) found that 7 percent of older battered women had been forced to have sexual intercourse with their husbands. In three studies, victims were overwhelmingly impaired: 80 percent of the sample in Burgess, Dowdell, and Prentky (2000) used a wheelchair or were bedridden, and 60 percent had dementia.

Teaster, Roberto, Duke, and Myenonghwan (2000) found that 80.9 percent of the sample lived in a nursing home and fewer than one quarter could walk without assistance. Seventy-one percent of the sample in Ramsey-Klawsnik (1991) were classified as "totally dependent" or functioning "poorly" to "very poorly." Many of the sexual abuse cases had witnesses: 76.2 percent of the Teaster et al. (2000) sample, and nearly one third of both the Ramsey-Klawsnik (1991) and Burgess et al. (2000) samples. Spouses or intimate partners were the abusers in 29 percent of the Ramsey-Klawsnik (1991) sample. Other sexual abusers were residents of the nursing home (Teaster et al., 2000), sons (Ramsey-Klawsnik, 1991), paid caregivers (Teaster et al., 2000), and brothers (Ramsey-Klawsnik, 1991).

Brandl and Cook-Daniels discovered through their 2002 review of the literature that differences might exist among racial and ethnic groups' definitions of what behaviors constitute elder abuse, according to Anetzberger (1997), Hudson and Carlson (1999), and Moon and Williams (1993). Many individuals are reluctant to report abuse due to ingrained cultural beliefs (Le, 1997; Moon & Benton, 2000; Moon & Williams, 1993; Otiniano, 1998; Sanchez, 1999; Tomita, 1999). Reasons cited for not reporting abuse included shame, embarrassment, not wanting to create conflict in the family, and protecting the community. Moon and Williams (1993) and Sanchez (1999) discovered that some victims preferred to talk to relatives rather than to health care, mental health, or law enforcement professionals. Family members are often the abusers in numerous cases of abuse in later life, Brandl and Cook-Daniels discovered (Brownell, Berman, & Salamone, 1999; Godkin, Wolf, & Pillemer, 1989; Lithwick, Beaulieu, Gravel, & Straka, 1999; Otiniano, Herrera, & Teasdale, 1998; Pillemer & Finkelhor, 1988; Podnieks, 1992a, 1992b; Ramsey-Klawsnik, 1991; Vinton, 1992; Vladescu, 1999). The abuser can be an adult child (Brownell et al., 1999; Lachs et al., 1997a, 1997b; Otiniano et al., 1998; Vladescu, 1999; Wolf & Pillemer, 1997), or a spouse (Pillemer & Finkelhor, 1988; Podnieks, 1992a, 1992b). Seaver (1996) and Vinton (1992) found that 58 percent to 95 percent of older women were abused by spouses. Teaster et al. (2000) suggest that other facility residents perpetrated the majority of sexual assaults in institutions. Sometimes, the spouses are beating up on each other; Crichton, Bond, Harvey, and Ristock (1999) found more husbands abusing wives, whereas Pillemer and Finkelhor (1988) found wives reported having used physical aggression against their husbands more than vice versa. Pillemer and Finkelhor also found that 6 percent of men abused by wives were injured versus 57 percent of women abused by husbands. Crichton et al. (1999), Greenberg et al. (1990), Pillemer and Finkelhor (1988), Wolf and Pillemer (1997), and Vinton (1992) suggested that grown sons were more abusive than grown daughters. Ramsey-Klawsnik (1991) found that some adult sons also sexually abused their mothers.

Brandl and Cook-Daniels, in undertaking this review of the literature, looked for causation and found several emerging themes. Several studies pointed to power struggles as influencing risk for abuse (Harris, 1996; Pillemer & Finkelhor, 1988). Contrary to what is presumed, a few studies indicated that aggravated caregivers do not work out their frustrations on their vulnerable charges (Phillips, Torres de Ardon, & Briones, 2000; Pillemer & Finkelhor, 1988; Reis & Nahmiash, 1998). However, the literature does support that the abuser is dependent on the victim in some way (Godkin et al., 1989; Pillemer & Finkelhor, 1988; Seaver, 1996; Wolf & Pillemer, 1997). Brandl and Cook-Daniels (2002) write, "Current thinking about intergenerational cycles of abuse suggests that child abuse victims may retaliate against their aging parents when they become adults. Currently, not enough research exists to support or rule out this idea." They cite two studies that indicate intergenerational transmission of violence is not an inevitable process but might be a factor in some cases: Korbin, Anetzberger, and Austin (1995) and Podnieks (1992a, 1992b). Many abusers suffer from some sort of impairment, including substance abuse, mental illness, depression, or cognitive impairments (Brownell et al., 1999; Cohen, Llorente, & Eisdorfer, 1998; Godkin et al., 1989; Greenberg et al., 1990; Pillemer & Finkelhor, 1988; Reis & Nahmiash, 1997, 1998; Seaver, 1996).

Regarding incidence rates of intervention, it is clear from the literature that many older domestic abuse victims do not seek assistance from health care providers or law enforcement (Brownell et al., 1999; Phillips et al., 2000), and many might not reveal the abuse at all (Podnieks, 1992a, 1992b). Many victims do not see themselves as being victimized, suggests Phillips et al. (2000). Elder mistreatment is a widespread societal issue that often flies under the radar of health care providers and law enforcement professionals; however, in recent years, a greater awareness of this growing problem has triggered mandated reporting by all health care professionals in most states. Swagerty et al. (1999) defines the word *mistreatment* as including physical abuse and neglect, psychological abuse, financial exploitation, and violation of rights. Poor health, physical or cognitive impairment, alcohol abuse, and a history of domestic violence are some of the risk factors for elder mistreatment. Diagnosis of elder mistreatment depends on acquiring a detailed history from the patient and the caregiver. It also involves performing a comprehensive physical examination. Only through awareness, a healthy suspicion, and the performance of certain procedures are physicians able to detect elder mistreatment. Once it is suspected, elder mistreatment should be reported to APS. It is estimated that more than 2 million older adults are mistreated each year in the United States. Elder abuse first gained attention about 20 years ago, when the term *granny battering* first appeared in a British medical journal (Burston, 1975). Since then, elder abuse has become a significant global issue. Although this newfound heightened awareness has followed a growing awareness of child and spousal abuse, because of differing definitions, poor detection, and underreporting, the extent of elder mistreatment is unknown. Published studies estimate that the prevalence of elder mistreatment ranges from 1 percent to 5 percent (Kurrle, Sadler, Lockwood, & Cameron, 1997). Although estimates of the prevalence of elder abuse in the United States have ranged from about 4 to 10 percent of the population 65 years and older, Wolf (1996) says there has been only one community-based study. A study of 2,020 elderly persons in Boston established an overall prevalence of 3.2 percent, which subdivided into 2.2 percent physical abuse, 1.1 percent verbal abuse, and 0.4 percent neglect (Pillemer & Finkelhor, 1988). Spouse abuse (58 percent) was more prevalent than abuse by adult children (24 percent), the proportion of victims was roughly equally divided between males and females, and economic status and age were not related to the risk of abuse. This survey, to which the category of financial abuse was added, was repeated in Canada. Four percent of Canadian elders able to respond on the telephone were found to have recently experienced one or more forms of mistreatment. Again, the rates for men and women were about equal, but financial abuse was more prevalent than physical abuse, verbal aggression, or neglect. As a means for general comparison, a British study, which combined the aforementioned Boston and

Canadian survey forms, and added several questions, found prevalence of physical abuse of 2 percent, verbal abuse of 5 percent, and financial abuse of 2 percent (Ogg & Bennett, 1992).

Although studies of elder abuse in the medical literature appear to be numerous, in a white paper published in the medical journal *The Lancet* Mark S. Lachs, co-chief of the Division of Geriatrics and Gerontology at the Weill Cornell Medical College in New York City, and Karl Pillemer, professor of human development in the College of Human Ecology at Cornell University, examined the lack of quality research concerning the physical and mental abuse of elderly persons (Lachs & Pillemer, 2004). Restricting their review of what data exists to domestic abuse, they highlight two startling statistics: The rate of elder abuse is probably between 2 percent and 10 percent, and people who have been mistreated are more than three times more likely to die within three years compared with those not abused, even when corrected for comorbidities and other confounding factors. "This vastly unrecognized and under-treated problem compromises the quality of life for millions of older people worldwide," Pillemer says. "A busy physician, who might see 20 to 40 elderly patients a day, might encounter a case of possible elder abuse every day, but because of a lack of time, resources, and a general lack of recognition of the problem, many cases go undetected and untreated, putting our elderly at heightened risk of physical and mental harm, and even death."

The researchers also discussed possible approaches for screening programs to identify elder abuse, but stated that clinicians' awareness of the phenomenon is more of a priority to enhance the detection of abuse. They also highlighted the difficulties of accurate diagnosis given the high risk of false positive and false negative judgments. They placed emphasis on the importance of a multidisciplinary approach, with a definite role for health care professionals, including physicians, nurses, social workers, advocates, and members of law enforcement. Lachs comments:

> Although there are gaps in knowledge with respect to the clinical manifestations and treatment of elder abuse, they should not prevent clinicians from taking an active role in identification and management. Family violence directly affects quality of life, and removal of a patient from an abusive situation is one of the most gratifying experiences for physicians and other health care professionals. Despite the need for more data on interventions, a reasonable approach is a multidisciplinary one, specifically tailored to the situation, ideally involving multiple team members with varied expertise (the model used in other geriatric syndromes). Future research should focus on the creation of clinically useful screening techniques and evidence-based assessments of replicable interventions.

Lachs and Pillemer assert that elder abuse directly affects quality of life, and helping patients resolve an abusive situation is one of the most gratifying experiences for physicians and other health care professionals.

Shields, Hunsaker, and Hunsaker (2004) conducted a 10-year (1992–2001) retrospective case review of morbidity and mortality among individuals age 60 years and older at a state medical examiner's office serving a major metropolitan region in Kentucky and Indiana. The researchers examined medico-legal autopsies and examinations of living subjects pursuant to a clinical forensic medicine program. They examined 74 postmortem cases in which 52 deaths were attributed to a homicidal act, with 22 deaths that were suspicious for neglect. Of the 22 living victims of elder abuse and neglect, 19 cases constituted physical or sexual assault, and three individuals suffered from neglect.

Jones, Veenstra, Seamon, and Kohmer (1997) sought to determine the perceived magnitude of elder mistreatment, physician awareness of applicable state laws, and the barriers to reporting suspected cases. They surveyed a random sample of 3,000 members of the ACEP; survey questions included practice characteristics, number and type of suspected cases of elder mistreatment seen in the ED, the number of cases actually reported, and reasons for not reporting abuse. Physicians were also asked about the availability of elder-mistreatment protocols and their familiarity with local laws and reporting requirements. The researchers received 705 completed surveys, for a response rate of 24 percent. Most physicians (52 percent) described elder mistreatment as prevalent but less so than spouse or child abuse. The respondents had evaluated an average of 93 suspected cases of elder mistreatment in the preceding 12 months; approximately 50 percent were reported. Only 31 percent of emergency physicians reported having a written protocol for the reporting of elder mistreatment, and physicians were generally not familiar with applicable state laws. Twenty-five percent were able to recall educational content pertaining to elder mistreatment during their emergency medicine residencies. Most physicians were not certain or did not believe that clear-cut medical definitions of elder abuse or neglect exist (74 percent); that emergency physicians can accurately identify cases of mistreatment (58 percent); or that their states had sufficient resources to meet the needs of victims (92 percent). The researchers concluded that practicing emergency physicians are not confident in identifying or reporting geriatric victims of abuse or neglect. This lack of confidence might reflect inadequacies of training, research, and continuing education with regard to mistreatment of older people.

Comijs et al. (1998) endeavored to assess the prevalence and the consequences of chronic verbal aggression, physical aggression, financial mistreatment, and neglect in a community-based sample, as well as to investigate the circumstances that led to the abuse and the ways in which the victims handled the problem. Prevalence was assessed in a population-based sample of 1,797 older people living independently in Amsterdam. In a follow-up study one year later, the victims were questioned again about the background and consequences of the abuse. The one-year prevalence of elder abuse was 5.6 percent, and the prevalence of the various types of elder abuse was as follows: verbal aggression, 3.2 percent; physical aggression, 1.2 percent; financial mistreatment, 1.4 percent; and neglect, 0.2 percent. Most victims reported emotional reactions immediately after the abuse. Seven of 36 victims experienced physical or financial damage as a consequence of the abuse, and more than 70 percent of the victims were able to stop the abuse, either by themselves or with the help of others. The researchers concluded that elder abuse is more widely spread if not only close relatives or people with whom the older person lives are considered as possible perpetrators, but other familiar and trusted people are considered as well. Intervention should be focused on the roughly 40 percent of victims who were not able to stop the abuse, they stated.

With constant improvements in socioeconomic conditions, the people of most industrialized nations are living longer. Most elderly individuals lead productive lives within the community. Unfortunately, when elderly individuals suffer from a debilitating disease or injury, society seems ill equipped to care for them. The frailty and social isolation that comes with illness or advanced age renders the elderly more vulnerable to crime. Falzon and Davis (1998) examined the circumstances that surrounded the homicides of individuals 65 years of age or older that occurred in Jefferson County, Alabama over a 15-year span. The researchers conducted a retrospective study of all decedents brought to the Jefferson County Coroner and Medical Examiner Office during the period from 1981 to 1995. Their computer search identified 150 homicide victims who were 65 years or older. In these 150 cases, the causes of death were as follows: gunshot wound, 50 percent; blunt force injuries, 19 percent; knife wounds, 14 percent; and asphyxiation, 10 percent. Younger homicide victims were much less likely to be killed as the result of a direct physical assault; blunt force injuries and asphyxiation combined caused death in only 7 percent of the younger population. Robbery was the most common motive for death in the elderly population, accounting for 37 percent of cases. The most common location for homicides in the elderly population was in their own residence, which accounted for 71 percent of cases. Four elderly homicide victims were shot by the police, and three elderly decedents died as a result of abuse.

Kleinschmidt (1997) comments that elder abuse receives less attention than other forms of domestic violence, and fewer than 10 percent of cases are reported. Although all states have legislation addressing elder abuse, financial support for evaluation and protective services is lacking. Most states have mandatory reporting; however, it might infringe on the autonomy of competent geriatric individuals. Physicians infrequently report elder abuse because they are not familiar with reporting laws, fear offending patients, are concerned with time limitations, and believe they do not have appropriate evaluation skills. Victims often have low self-esteem, blame themselves for the abuse, and do not want to admit their vulnerabilities or betray their families. Kleinschmidt puts forth the caregiver stress hypothesis, which suggests abuse stems from caregiver stress and resentment resulting from chronic care of dependent geriatric patients, as a misconception. Abuse is actually better correlated with the emotional and financial dependence of the caregivers on the geriatric victims. Older patients are most commonly abused by the people with whom they live. Older men and women have similar per-capita abuse rates. Assessment and management should be supportive without assigning blame and should focus on both the patient and the caregiver. Patients in immediate danger should be hospitalized or placed in emergency shelters. Suspected abuse should be reported directly to the appropriate state agency, which can provide a thorough long-term assessment.

Although elder mistreatment is suspected to be life threatening in some instances, little is known about the survival of elderly persons who have been mistreated. Lachs et al. (1998) endeavored to estimate the independent contribution of reported elder abuse and neglect to all-cause mortality in an observational cohort of community-dwelling older adults. The sample included 2,812 community-dwelling adults who were older than 65 years in 1982, a subset of whom were referred to protective services for the elderly. The researchers reported that in the first nine years after cohort inception, 176 cohort members were seen by elderly protective services for verified allegations; 10 (5.7 percent) of these were for abuse, 30 (17 percent) for neglect, 8 (4.5 percent) for exploitation, and 128 (72.7 percent) for self-neglect. At the end of a 13-year follow-up period from cohort inception, cohort members seen for elder mistreatment at any time during the follow-up had poorer survival (9 percent) than either those seen for self-neglect (17 percent) or other noninvestigated cohort members (40 percent). In a pooled logistic regression that adjusted for demographic characteristics, chronic diseases, functional status, social networks, cognitive status, and depressive symptomatology, the researchers found that risk of death remained elevated for cohort members experiencing either elder mistreatment or self-neglect, when compared with other members of the cohort.

Lachs et al. (1997a, 1997b) wanted to determine longitudinal risk factors for elder abuse and neglect. The researchers linked an established cohort of 2,812 community-dwelling older adults with elderly protective service records over a nine-year follow-up period. Protective services saw 184 (6.5 percent) individuals in the cohort for any indication, and 47 cohort members were seen for corroborated elder abuse or neglect, for a sampling-adjusted nine-year prevalence of 1.6 percent. In pooled logistic regression, age, race, poverty, functional disability, and cognitive impairment were identified as risk factors for reported elder mistreatment. Additionally, the onset of new cognitive impairment was also associated with elder abuse and neglect. Because the mechanism of elder mistreatment case finding in this study was a social welfare system (protective services), the influence of race and poverty as risk factors is likely to be overestimated due to reporting bias.

Lachs et al. (1997a, 1997b) sought to determine the nature and frequency of ED use by victims of physical elder abuse. Community-dwelling victims of abuse were identified through a state elderly protective service program independent of the health care system in a geographic area served by two EDs. The researchers reviewed ED records and abstracted to determine if and how victims used emergency services. During a seven-year period, 182 elderly victims of physical abuse were identified in the catchment area of the study, and 114 (62.6 percent) had been seen in one or both EDs at least once during a five-year window surrounding the initial identification of abuse. These 114 individuals accounted for 628 visits (an average of three); 30.6 percent of these visits resulted in a hospital admission. An ordinal system was used that assigned a probability of any single ED visit being referable to abuse; 37.8 percent of subjects had at least one visit categorized as being of high probability, and 66 percent of subjects had at least one visit that resulted in an injury-related chief symptom or ICD-9 discharge diagnosis.

Little is known about the epidemiology of APS agency utilization, the state entities charged with assessment and advocacy for disenfranchised older adults. Lachs et al. (2002) sought to determine the prevalence of utilization by older adults and risk factors for APS. The researchers studied a cohort of 2,812 community-dwelling adults who were older than 65 years in 1982. The main outcome measure was referral to the state ombudsman on aging for protective services. Over the 11-year follow-up period, 209 cohort members (7.4 percent) were referred to the ombudsman 302 times as protective service cases, for a community prevalence of 6.4 percent after adjusting for the sampling strategy of the cohort. Self-neglect was the most common indication for referral (73 percent of the cases). Whereas in bivariate analyses a variety of baseline sociodemographic features, functional impairments, medical conditions, and social network factors were associated with APS use, in multivariable analysis only sociodemographic variables remained independent risk factors, including low income, non-White race, and age older than 75 years at cohort inception.

Lachs, Berkman, and Fulmer (1994) studied a sample of 2,812 community-living men and women in Connecticut who were over age 65 in 1982, and whose cases had been investigated by Connecticut's State Ombudsman on Aging in 1985 or 1986. The researchers found that 68 (2.4 percent) members of the cohort received investigation. Features at cohort entry significantly associated with investigation in multiple logistic regression included requiring assistance with feeding, being a minority elder, being over age 75 at cohort inception, and having a poor social network as defined by a social network index. The researchers concluded that functional disability, minority status, older age, and poor social networks were associated with investigation for elder mistreatment in this prospective, community-based population of men and women over the age of 65.

Lachs and Fulmer (1993) state that the signs and symptoms of elder abuse and neglect can mimic those of many common chronic medical conditions in elderly persons. They say that a complete assessment for elder abuse and neglect is time-consuming and is best performed as a regimented evaluation that includes separate histories from the patient and suspected party and a clinical assessment that emphasizes function, cognition, and specific aspects of the physical examination. The management of elder abuse and neglect should be multidisciplinary with several key personnel participating. An elderly person in immediate danger should be removed from his or her environment. For less acute cases, a variety of interventions aimed at decreasing the stress of caregiving or ameliorating other family stressors might be appropriate. Most states require that clinicians who suspect elder abuse and neglect report their concerns to a designated authority. There are many gaps in our knowledge about elder abuse and neglect. It is hoped that with the future application of rigorous epidemiologic methodology as has been employed in the study of child abuse, this social ill can be better understood and prevented. Until then, clinicians must integrate their clinical experience and social skills to recognize the problem and provide thoughtful and compassionate intervention.

Rosenblatt, Cho, and Durance (1996) sought to characterize elder mistreatment reporting patterns over time and by reporting source with specific focus on physician reporting, and to determine whether demographic or socioeconomic factors influenced the reporting of elder abuse in Michigan between 1989 and 1993 and whether these factors affected physician reporting rates. A total of 27,371 cases of possible abuse were reported, with 17,238 in persons older than age 65. Physicians reported only 2 percent of cases, and physician reporting rates did not increase over the five-year period. Physician reporting rates were highest in small counties with low physician-to-population ratios. There was a high percentage of primary care physicians in these counties. Forty-seven percent of all reported cases were substantiated. There was no difference in substantiation rate for physician-reported cases compared with other professional reporting sources. The researchers concluded that increasing physician awareness of the problem of elder mistreatment and providing physicians with the tools to screen for mistreatment should increase the number of cases that are reported to the agencies responsible for assisting mistreated older people.

Akaza et al. (2003) examined the elder abuse cases that occurred in Gifu Prefecture, Japan between 1990 and 2000. The researchers conducted a retrospective study of all the cases in which the victim was 65 years or older and autopsied in the Department of Legal Medicine at Gifu University School of Medicine. Fifteen victims were classified as elder abuse victims: five men and 10 women. The victims ranged in age from 66 to 87 years (average age = 74.5 years). The types of abuse were as follows: physical abuse, 13 cases; emotional abuse, five cases; neglect, four cases; and financial abuse, three cases. In eight cases, the victims were subjected to two or more types of abuse. The cause of death of the victims varied with the type of abuse. In the physical abuse cases, subdural hemorrhage was the most common cause, followed by other violence-related deaths and hypothermia. In the neglect cases, the victims died of either starvation or suffocation after the aspiration of food into the airway. In the domestic abuse cases, one of the victim's sons was the most common perpetrator, and little or no income was considered to be a risk factor for perpetrators. In the neglect cases, dementia and difficulty in performing activities of daily living were considered to be risk factors for victims, in addition to living in social isolation.

Kahan and Paris (2003) state that elderly men and women of all socioeconomic and ethnic backgrounds are vulnerable to mistreatment, and most often it goes undetected. For many elderly victims of abuse, the hospital is the only potential site for outside contact and support. An elder abuse program has been created at Mount Sinai Hospital in New York City, and funding was granted to assist victims with compensation claims, provide counsel and advocacy for victims, and provide support via ongoing telephone contact and referrals to community agencies. Simultaneously, hospital-wide educational seminars and rounds have provided the staff and students with information concerning detection of abuse and neglect. Over a two-year period, 182 cases were identified and assessed. More than 50 percent of these cases involved patients with a diagnosis of memory impairment. Five percent of the cases involved a long history of domestic violence. In most cases a family member was identified as the abuser, and in a majority of instances the victim either denied the suspected abuse or tried to rationalize the abuser's behavior. Patients were afraid of reporting abuse or changing their situation, despite being informed of possible resources. To combat this escalating problem in our growing elderly population, interdisciplinary collaboration between physicians and social workers is often crucial. Communication via the medical record can be key to monitoring patients in the community. There also needs to be ongoing education of all hospital staff in an effort to continually promote awareness of this problem.

Mosqueda, Burnight, Liao, and Kemp (2004) described the development and operation of a new model for integration of medical and social services. The Vulnerable Adult Specialist Team (VAST) provides APS and criminal justice agencies with access to medical experts who examine medical and psychological injuries of elder abuse victims. They conducted a retrospective, descriptive analysis that included community-dwelling elders and adults with disabilities who were reported for mistreatment and referred to VAST. The researchers found that most cases came from APS for mental status and physical examination for evidence of abuse. Cases referred to a medical response team (269) were significantly different from cases that were not referred (9,505). Ninety-seven percent of those who referred cases to VAST indicated that the team was helpful in confirming abuse, documenting impaired capacity, reviewing medications and medical conditions, facilitating the conservatorship process, persuading the client or family to take action, and supporting the need for law enforcement involvement. As a result, VAST has become institutionalized in that county. Amenable to replication, medical response teams for elder abuse might be useful in other counties across the nation.

8.4.4 Aging: A Women's Issue

"Aging is a women's issue," declared the International Longevity Center's current annual report. Among older women, 40 percent live alone and 20 percent live below the poverty line. Older women suffer the most elder abuse and make up more than 80 percent of the nursing home population (Jones, 2004). In a 1992 forum sponsored by the American Association of Retired Persons (AARP), a study was presented on abused elders and older battered women. It reported that although there is evidence that spouse or partner abuse might constitute a large portion of all elder abuse, older women abused by their husbands or partners might be falling through the cracks in both the elder abuse and domestic violence communities. The forum assembled a body of representatives of these communities to exchange information, begin a dialogue, and identify initial recommendations about how to better meet the needs of older battered women. Researchers, advocates, service providers, and medical and legal professionals from the fields of elder abuse and domestic violence participated. Prior to the forum, AARP asked battered women to write about their experiences with abuse and with seeking help. Within a month of the request, more than 500 letters arrived from women who wanted to tell their stories in the hope their experiences could help others. Some women were in their 80s and had suffered verbal, physical, and mental abuse for 35, 40, or 50 years. Common threads emerging from these letters included the following:

- The women described years of silent suffering, as many said this was the first time they had ever told anyone of the abuse.
- Many women were isolated from family and friends as a result of the abuse or of trying to keep the abuse secret.
- Many women described examples of extreme physical violence, such as being pushed, hit, and even shoved down flights of stairs, suffering fractures, dislocated joints, and deep muscle bruises that took weeks to heal.
- Almost all of the women wrote about emotional abuse, describing name calling, degrading accusations, and constant verbal battering.
- Alcohol abuse was a very frequent companion to violent behavior.
- Many described seeking help from professionals, clergy, and the police, only to be told they must have done something wrong to provoke their husbands. Some had received the help they needed from local services; however, many more had not.

The AARP forum attendees agreed that a paucity of information about the over-50 age group makes improved research among the first among steps to link the elder abuse and battered women's communities. Experts said some questions to be addressed include these:

- What are the specific risk factors for battering in later years?
- What roles are played by physical dependency, substance abuse, and other observed phenomena?
- How often is abuse triggered by age-related events such as retirement or illness?
- What are the barriers in service systems that prevent older women from seeking and receiving help?
- What roles do ethnicity, race, and culture play in the way people perceive the problem, seek services, and make decisions?

The experts who convened at the AARP forum concurred that improving the legal response to a complaint of abuse is another important component in stopping abuse and preventing further incidents, including these actions:

- Strengthening abuse laws to cover all abusing partners
- Educating judges, police, and other legal personnel about the problem
- Increasing access to affordable legal services through specially trained nonlawyers and developing more user-friendly information about the court system
- Creating a national registry of abusers

To enhance protective services, forum participants recommended that communities do the following:

- Ensure that appropriate, accessible, and safe shelters are available that take into account the needs of older women, with special attention to rural communities. Programs should be designed and operated to be multicultural and multilingual.
- Provide cross-training, coordination, and coalition-building between the elder abuse and domestic violence communities.
- Sensitize all medical and legal professionals, counselors, and religious leaders about sexism, racism, and ageism.
- Build coalitions to respond to diversity and help empower battered women.
- Reach out to older women by disseminating information about domestic violence through senior centers and home services, health clinics and physicians, civic associations, and public benefits offices. Conduct outreach to women whose partners are substance abusers or mentally ill.
- Provide victim advocates and create sister-to-sister "buddy" programs between recently battered and formerly battered women.

A gathering of experts at a symposium sponsored by the U.S. Department of Justice in 2000 discussed approaches to addressing domestic violence and sexual assault against older individuals. Bonnie Brandl, program director of the National Clearinghouse on Abuse in Later Life at the Wisconsin Coalition Against Domestic Violence, noted several factors that are important for effectively identifying and responding to the needs of older victims of abuse or assault:

- Documenting the number of older people experiencing abuse or assault and documenting the types of services needed is important when developing services or building a case for funding. Brandl suggests collecting information from a variety of sources, including APS, aging programs, and domestic violence programs.

- A multidisciplinary approach to problem exploration, service design and delivery, and fundraising is more effective than organizing a single entity to do it all. This collaborative approach, although difficult in the beginning, is more likely to sustain the effort over the long term because it allows each organization to contribute based on its recognized strengths.
- Participants in a collaboration should take time to develop a common language and clear definitions of terms so that all participants understand the values, principles, governance,
- and operating structures that direct the provision of services.
- The collaborative environment should allow for honest, up-front discussions about inevitable issues of turf, ego, and control. To get through this difficult time in collaboration building, it is critical that relationships of trust and respect be established early in the process. One way to develop these relationships, Brandl says, is by sharing quality information with each other, both in terms of organizational limitations and strengths.

Using the development of her organization as an example, Brandl noted there were several struggles among various entities in the early stages. These struggles often resulted from the fact that most organizations that were being asked to collaborate were already overwhelmed by the demand for services and yet were underfunded. Brandl recalled the initial response from many providers to a call to focus on older victims was, "We don't do that work . . . we see our population as 18 to 40 years of age and we're having a hard time even keeping up with that population. We can't begin to think about how we'd start working with older victims."

8.4.5 The 1998 Report on Elder Abuse That Shocked a Nation

Although not completely definitive by its own admission, the NEAIS of 1998 is one of the most comprehensive studies of elder abuse and neglect, and the source of a shocking finding that 450,000 elderly persons in domestic settings were abused or neglected in 1996. The NEAIS was conducted by the NCEA at the American Public Human Services Association. It gathered data on domestic elder abuse, neglect, and self-neglect through a nationally representative sample of 20 counties, collecting data from two sources: reports from the local APS agency responsible for receiving and investigating reports in each county, and reports from approximately 1,100 "sentinels," or specially trained individuals in a variety of community agencies having frequent contact with the elderly. Many sentinels were mandatory or voluntary reporters of elder abuse, as defined by state laws. The study established the following definitions:

- Physical abuse was defined as the use of physical force that could result in bodily injury, physical pain, or impairment. Physical punishments of any kind were examples of physical abuse.
- Sexual abuse was defined as nonconsensual sexual contact of any kind with an elderly person.
- Emotional or psychological abuse was defined as the infliction of anguish, pain, or distress.
- Financial or material exploitation was defined as the illegal or improper use of an elder's funds, property, or assets.
- Abandonment was defined as the desertion of an elderly person by an individual who had physical custody or otherwise had assumed responsibility for providing care for an elder or physical custody of an elder.
- Neglect was defined as the refusal or failure to fulfill any part of a person's obligations or duties to an elder.
- Self-neglect was characterized as the behaviors of an elderly person that threaten his or her own health or safety. The definition of self-neglect excludes a situation in which a mentally competent older person (who understands the consequences of his or her decisions) makes a conscious and voluntary decision to engage in acts that threaten his or her health or safety.

The NEAIS estimated that a total of 449,924 elderly persons aged 60 and older experienced abuse or neglect in domestic settings in 1996. Of this total, 70,942 (16 percent) were reported to and substantiated by APS agencies, but the remaining 378,982 (84 percent) were not reported to APS. From these figures, one can conclude that more than five times as many new incidents of abuse and neglect were unreported than those that were reported to and substantiated by APS agencies in 1996. Of 236,479 reports of abuse, neglect, and self-neglect to APS in 1996, 48.7 percent, or 115,110 reports, were substantiated after investigation, 39.3 percent were unsubstantiated, and 8.2 percent were still under investigation at the end of 1996. The remaining 3.8 percent of reports had other outcomes (e.g., suspected victim died, could not be located, or had moved away). Of the 115,110 substantiated reports in 1996 for which information was available, 61.6 percent (70,942) were reports of incidents in which other people maltreated elders, and the remaining 38.4 percent (44,168) were incidents of self-neglecting elders. Of the 70,942 unduplicated substantiated reports of elder abuse attributable to perpetrators (which excludes self-neglect), the most common types were: neglect (34,525), emotional or psychological abuse (25,142), financial exploitation (21,427), and physical abuse (18,144). Whereas the substantiation rate for all types of investigations of elder abuse combined was 48.7 percent, the substantiation rates for different types of maltreatment varied as follows: physical abuse, 61.9 percent; abandonment, 56 percent; emotional or psychological abuse, 54.1 percent; financial abuse, 44.5 percent; and neglect, 41 percent.

A wide variety of reporters of domestic elder abuse were found in the 70,942 substantiated reports of abuse and neglect. The most frequent reporters were family members, who were responsible for 20 percent of all reports, followed by hospitals (17.3 percent), and law enforcement (11.3 percent). In-home service providers, friends or neighbors, and health care providers each made between 8 percent and 10 percent of total reports. Out-of-home service providers, banks, public health departments, and other reporters were responsible for the remaining reports. Hospitals (19.8 percent) and friends or neighbors (19.1 percent) were the most frequent reporters of substantiated reports of self-neglect in 1996. Law enforcement, in-home service providers, and health care providers each made 12 percent of total reports. Out-of-home providers, family members, banks, the victims themselves, and others made the remaining reports.

The report examined the age of victims of different types of abuse reported to APS. The oldest elders (those over 80 years of age), who made up about 19 percent of the U.S. elderly population in 1996, were far more likely to be the victims of all categories of abuse, with the exception of abandonment. They accounted for over half the reports of neglect (51.8 percent), and 48 percent of financial or material abuse reports, 43.7 percent of physical abuse reports, and 41.3 percent of emotional or psychological abuse reports. In all types of abuse and neglect, elderly victims in the 60 to 64 and 65 to 69 age groups accounted for the smallest percentages. Female elders were more likely to be the victims of all categories of abuse, except for abandonment. Although making up about 58 percent of the total national elderly population in 1996, women were the victims in 76.3 percent of emotional or psychological abuse, 71.4 percent of physical abuse, 63 percent of financial exploitation, and 60 percent of neglect, which was the most frequent type of maltreatment. A majority of the victims of abandonment were men (62.2 percent). The study found that elders who are unable to care for themselves were more likely to suffer from abuse. Approximately one half (47.9 percent) of the substantiated incidents of elder abuse involved elderly persons who were not able to care for themselves, 28.7 percent were somewhat able to do so, and 22.9 percent were able to care for themselves. For the national elderly population as a whole, the federal government estimates that 14 percent have difficulties with one or more activities of daily living. Approximately six out of 10 substantiated elder abuse victims experienced some degree of confusion (31.6 percent were very confused or disoriented, and 27.9 percent were sometimes confused). This represents a high degree of potential mental impairment among this group of abused elders, particularly when compared with the estimated 10 percent of the total national elderly population suffering with some form of dementia.

Overall, men were the perpetrators of abuse and neglect 52.5 percent of the time. Of the substantiated cases of abuse and neglect, men were the most frequent perpetrators for abandonment (83.4 percent), physical abuse (62.6 percent), emotional abuse (60.1 percent), and financial exploitation (59 percent). Only in cases of neglect were women slightly more frequent (52.4 percent) perpetrators than men. The age category with the most perpetrators was the 41 to 59 age group (38.4 percent), followed by those in the 40 years or less group, who were perpetrators in more than one quarter of reports (27.4 percent). About one third of perpetrators (34.3 percent) were elderly persons themselves (60 and older). Perpetrators of financial or material exploitation were particularly younger compared to other types of abuse, with 45.1 percent being 40 or younger and another 39.5 percent being 41 to 59 years old. Eighty-five percent of the perpetrators of financial exploitation were under age 60. Data show that family members were the perpetrators in 89.7 percent of substantiated incidents of domestic elder abuse and neglect. Adult children of elder abuse victims were the most likely perpetrators of substantiated maltreatment (47.3 percent). Spouses represented the second largest group of perpetrators (19.3 percent). Other relatives and grandchildren, at 8.8 percent and 8.6 percent, respectively, were the next largest groups of perpetrators. Nonfamily perpetrators included friends or neighbors (6.2 percent), in-home service providers (2.8 percent), and out-of home service providers (1.4 percent). The report provides details about the relationship of perpetrators to the victims for the different types of maltreatment.

Self-neglect was included in the NEAIS and a common definition and signs and symptoms were adopted for it, as with all the specific types of abuse and neglect. Self-neglect is defined as the behaviors of an elderly person that threaten his or her own health or safety. Self-neglect generally manifests itself in an older person's refusal or failure to provide himself or herself with adequate food, water, clothing, shelter, safety, personal hygiene, and medication. Approximately 65.3 percent of substantiated self-neglecting elders were female, even through women make up 58 percent of the overall elderly population. About 65.1 percent of self-neglecting elders were 75 years or older. The largest proportion of self-neglecting elders were in the oldest age category of 80 and older (44.7 percent), and the proportion decreased in each declining age group, with only 6.3 percent of self-neglecting elders being in the 60 to 64 year age group (compared to being 23 percent of the total elderly population). Most (93.3 percent) self-neglecting elders have difficulty caring for themselves. Of these elders, 34.3 percent are not capable of caring for themselves, and 59 percent are somewhat able to care for themselves. Three out of 10 self-neglecting elders (29.9 percent) are very confused or disoriented, and 45.4 percent are sometimes confused. Approximately 75 percent of substantiated self-neglecting elders suffer from some degree of confusion.

The following conclusions can be drawn from the NEAIS:

- Domestic elder abuse and neglect is a significant problem. NEAIS research shows that about 450,000 unduplicated elders experienced abuse and neglect in domestic settings in 1996. More than five times as many of these incidents of abuse and neglect were unreported than were reported to and substantiated by APS agencies.
- When elders who experienced only self-neglect are included with those who were abused and neglected, the number increases to 551,000 unduplicated elder persons in 1996. Almost four times as many of these incidents were unreported than were reported to and substantiated by APS agencies.
- The NEAIS measured a large and previously unidentified and unreported portion of elder abuse and neglect, and also has learned much about the characteristics of the victims and perpetrators of abuse and neglect. At the same time, it was not possible to identify and report on all previously hidden domestic elder abuse and neglect, including the most isolated elders who do not leave their homes or who rarely come in contact with others in the community.
- Several of the characteristics of abused and neglected elderly persons are particularly worrisome and challenge health care providers, law enforcement, and social services agencies to intervene:
  1. The oldest elders (80 and older) are abused and neglected at two to three times their proportion of the elderly population.
  2. Female elders are abused at a higher rate than males.
  3. Almost half of substantiated abused and neglected elderly were not physically able to care for themselves.
  4. In almost nine out of 10 incidents of domestic elder abuse and neglect, the perpetrator is a family member. Adult children are responsible for almost half of elder abuse and neglect.
  5. Elderly self-neglect also is a problem, as evidenced by about 139,000 unduplicated reports (some of the self-neglecting elderly might also be counted as being abused or neglected). Most victims of self-neglect are unable to care for themselves and are confused.
  6. Using precisely developed standard errors, the NEAIS estimates that as many as 688,948 or as few as 210,900 elder persons might have been abused or neglected in domestic settings in 1996. When self-neglecting elders are added, the estimate range is that as many as 787,027 or as few as 314,995 elder persons might have been abused, neglected, or self-neglecting in domestic settings in 1996.
  7. Still more of the unidentified and unreported area of the iceberg remains to be revealed, especially instances of abuse and neglect among seriously isolated elderly persons and those with little contact with community organizations.

Most important, the NEAIS documented the existence of a previously unidentified and unreported stratum of elder abuse and neglect, thus advancing the understanding of the "iceberg" theory of elder abuse. The NEAIS estimated that for every abused or neglected elder reported to and substantiated by APS, there are more than five abused or neglected elders that are not reported. The study also documented similar patterns of underreporting of self-neglecting elders. The collective challenge for policymakers, service providers, advocates, researchers, and society as a whole is to utilize this data to help educate those whose purpose it is to assist the elderly.

8.4.6 Detection and Management of Elder Abuse in the Clinical Setting

In 2000, Sidney Stahl, chief of health care organizations and social institutions at the National Institute on Aging, chaired a workshop sponsored by the U.S. Department of Justice in which experts were seeking answers to the problem of elder abuse. He said that medical issues, not just social issues, can play a key role in the genesis of elder abuse and neglect at home:

> Although the connections might not be obvious at first glance, underlying ailments that may contribute to these problems include dementia, depression, psychosis, alcoholism, and early cognitive loss. This relatively new understanding highlights the need for medical professionals to work with Adult Protective Services, law enforcement, and other parties to help diagnose and treat elder abuse and neglect. Yet physicians generally have

> done a poor job in this regard. Among other reasons, doctors are unaware of the need, have not been trained to recognize abuse and neglect cases, or fear that such cases will drag them into court or obligate them to provide free services. Lessons can be learned from experts in child abuse, criminal justice, social services, and victim advocacy, in addition to the medical community, that can help overcome these problems.

Health care providers are well positioned to detect and manage elder mistreatment, because they might be the only individuals who regularly see the older adult. They also order the testing, hospital admissions, and support services that are sometimes needed to correct elder mistreatment. Vernon (1995) writes:

> The geriatrician is well accustomed to compiling a differential diagnosis from nonspecific and puzzling presentations. Delay in seeking medical help, inconsistent or implausible history, examination and laboratory findings, absence of a designated care-giver at presentation and chronic disease disequilibrium in the presence of an adequate care plan all raise the possibility of abuse or neglect. Armed with a greater awareness of abuse and in the familiar setting of a multidisciplinary team, the geriatrician can therefore proceed to evaluate a given presentation for its abusive or neglectful content. Furthermore the alert clinician can readily screen for such issues by routinely asking elderly patients about their perception of personal safety and experience of physical, verbal or psychological abuse or neglect. Such questions logically form part of an expanded social history. Routine clinical practice calls for full physical, neurological and cognitive assessment of a patient.

Gray-Vickery (2004) writes, "In some cases, you may need assessment radar to detect elder abuse. Keep in mind that normal effects of aging, disease pathology, and functional limitations can mask the signs and symptoms. For example, thin aging skin is susceptible to tearing and bruising, but don't fall into the trap of assuming that skin tears and bruises in an older person are always predictable signs of aging." Gray-Vickery says that health care providers can learn a lot about a patient's relationship with his or her caregiver by observing their behavior when together. Is the caregiver's demeanor calm and reassuring, or threatening? Do they converse or sit in silence? Writes Gray-Vickery, "A subtle tip-off to physical abuse is when a caregiver underreacts or overreacts to findings from the older person's physical examination. For example, he may refuse to have the patient hospitalized for serious injuries; at the other extreme, he may be extremely anxious to have her admitted." If abuse or neglect is suspected, Gray-Vickery advises providing an interview environment where the patient can feel safe to talk about his or her situation. "Although you may at some point interview him/her and his/her caregiver together to assess their interactions, conduct your initial discussions one-on-one." To protect the patient against possible retaliation by the caregiver, Gray-Vickery suggests conducting the interview in a private location. "Remember that a victim may not want to report abuse or her abuser because she feels shame and fears abandonment or retaliation. She may be reluctant to undress because she doesn't want to reveal her injuries." Gray-Vickery suggests approaching the patient with a warm, empathetic manner, and after exchanging pleasantries, the clinician should make a statement that lets the patient know he/she can speak up. "For example, if you note bilateral bruising or other signs of physical abuse, you might say, 'Injuries like this usually don't happen by accident. Perhaps someone else was involved.' Ask her directly about the possibility of abuse. Assure her that you'll take her seriously and that she'll be protected from retaliation." The caregiver should also be interviewed. Once the patient and the caregiver have been questioned, Gray-Vickery suggests considering whether or not the nature of the patient's injuries is consistent with the patient's and the caregiver's stories. "For example, a patient may say that she's come to the hospital because of flu-like symptoms, but you note untreated bruises and burns over her torso. Or the caregiver may blame suspicious injuries on the older person, saying that 'She's clumsy.'" If a patient has dementia or some other cognitive impairment, or when a patient denies suspected abuse, Gray-Vickery advises, "Base your determination of potential abuse on the patient's physical assessment, your interview with her caregiver, and your assessment of their interactions."

Regarding the documentation of suspected abuse, Gray-Vickery emphasizes that health care providers should document the results of assessment and all the data collected. "Include what she and her caregiver said about her injuries. Identify each speaker and use exact words within quotation marks. 'Patient states, 'He kicked me in my head and back' carries more weight than 'Patient was allegedly kicked by son.' Direct quotes help eliminate liability issues because your opinions aren't included, and they may be invaluable evidence if the case ever goes to court." Health care providers should document any discrepancy in the patient's and caregiver's stories. If the patient says she tripped and fell down a flight of stair and the caregiver says the patient fell out of bed, include both accounts. Use a body map to document the location of all injuries, and identify the type of injuries on a checklist or in a narrative description. Include photographs of the injuries in the medical record, ensuring first that the patient gives informed consent. Most states require nurses to report suspected abuse. Health care providers should follow their facility's reporting policy if they encounter an older adult in any of the following situations:

- Detection of evidence of an injury or neglect without a reasonable clinical explanation.
- The patient complains of abuse.
- The health care provider believes, based on observation and experience, that the risk of abuse and neglect is high.

Gray-Vickery says:

> Many facilities have multidisciplinary teams that specialize in handling abuse cases, and all states have statutes on reporting them. Laws differ from state to state, but most states require professionals to report all suspected incidents of elder abuse to officially designated agents. If an older patient has been abused or you suspect imminent risk, initiate a safety plan for her. She and her caregiver may benefit from referrals to social services, counseling services, and legal assistance. She may need court protection, hospital admission, or placement in elder abuse transitional housing known as a "safe house."

Gray-Vickery adds, "With careful assessment, documentation, and reporting, you can make a critical difference to the welfare of an older person who's a victim of abuse. And by teaching older people how to avoid abuse, you can target the problem before it becomes a reality."

8.4.6.1 Red Flags for Abuse

Indicators of physical abuse include the following:

- Multiple fractures or injuries in various stages of healing.
- Bruises clustered together and in regular patterns, especially in unusual locations such as the neck or groin. Lashes from a belt can cause injuries extending over several planes, such as the front, side, and back of the legs.
- Bilateral bruises or parallel injuries, "control marks," a sign of forceful restraining. Frequent shaking causes parallel injuries on the upper arms.
- Injuries to the trunk, abdomen, genitalia, buttocks, and upper thighs, which might signal sexual abuse. Forced sexual activity can cause visible injuries, pain, or itching in the genital region; evidence of STD; fractured teeth; and ecchymosis of the uvula.
- Injuries around the face, ears, and neck, including tooth fractures and whiplash injuries. (Accidental bruises usually affect the forehead, knees, shins, and elbows; senile purpura marks typically appear on the forearms and backs of the hands.)
- Burns to the soles, palms, or buttocks or circular cigarette or cigar burns. Being tied up or restrained can cause rope burns on the extremities, neck, or torso.
- Patterned injuries that can give clues to the size and the shape of the object that caused them, such as belt buckles or hands.
- Sprains or dislocations caused by pulling or pushing.
- Patchy hair loss, redness, and swelling over the scalp or areas of hemorrhaging just below the scalp line, which can occur with violent hair pulling.
- A history of frequent visits to the ED or a delay between the time of injury and going to the ED. Repeated falls, fractures, or bruises in various stages of healing, and a verbal report of physical abuse are high-risk indicators of abuse.
- Withdrawn behavior or flinching when approached.
- Indicators of neglect include the following:
- Deterioration of health
- Dehydration, malnutrition, or cachexia
- Pressure ulcers or contractures
- Dirt and odor on the body or clothing
- Assistive devices missing or in poor repair, such as broken glasses
- Inappropriate dress
- Fleas or lice
- Urine burns
- Listlessness and fatigue
- Any indication that the older person was left in an unsafe situation or alone for long periods
- Poor personal hygiene

Indicators of emotional abuse include the following:

- Confusion and disorientation
- Paranoia, depression, or anger
- Fear of strangers
- Exhibiting fear in one's own environment
- Ambivalence toward caregiver
- Being quiet when caregiver is present
- Low self-esteem
- Hunger for attention and socialization

8.4.6.2 Clinical and Medical Forensics of Elder Abuse

Dyer, Connolly and McFeeley (2002) assert, "The medical forensics aspects of elder abuse and neglect are largely unexplored and undocumented. Those who work in the field of elder abuse and neglect believe that the state of medical knowledge and forensic science regarding elder abuse and neglect is approximately equivalent to that of child abuse and neglect three decades ago and domestic violence 10 to 15 years ago." They explain that there is a set of what they call "forensic markers" of elder abuse and neglect, including abrasions, lacerations, bruising, fractures, decubiti, weight loss, dehydration, medication use, burns, cognitive and mental health problems, poor hygiene, and sexual abuse. They add, "Expanding our medical forensic knowledge base is vital to all the myriad ways in which the law is expected to address elder abuse and neglect."

Elder abuse often goes undetected and unreported, which precludes intervention, investigation, and prosecution. It falls within the health care provider's purview to identify clinical cases of suspected abuse and neglect, document and collect evidence, and in doing so, assist law enforcement and prosecutors in the criminal justice process.

The AMA defines physical abuse as an act of violence that can result in pain, injury, impairment, or disease. Neglect is the failure to provide the goods and services necessary for functioning and avoiding harm. Dyer et al. (2002) underscore the health care provider's role by pointing out that actual abuse is rarely directly observed by medical, legal, or protective-services personnel, so in the absence of eyewitness testimony, the law enforcement and criminal justice communities must depend on evidence to prove the existence of suspected abuse. Although a bruise might resolve and a bone can heal in time, health care providers are in an excellent position to add meaning to such injuries using their medico-legal-related knowledge and skills of observation and documentation. The most extreme cases of abuse—the gunshot wounds or the knife wounds—are obvious, and bite marks or starvation can indicate extreme neglect. However, it is in the cases with subtle presentations, where abuse and neglect are not clear-cut, that health care providers can excel. Dyer et al. (2002) say that because there is no gold standard when it comes to the detection and substantiation of abuse cases, health care workers must rely on these forensic markers. However, Dyer et al. point out, "The difficulty with this approach is that there is often a great overlap among the markers of disease and neglect (and sometimes abuse). Although abuse often is considered to require an overt act, whereas neglect is considered to require an omission, it is sometimes difficult to distinguish between the two." A more thorough discussion of forensic markers that can help health care providers recognize abuse follows.

- Crane (2002) defines abrasions as superficial injuries involving the outer layer of skin, whereas lacerations are characterized by full-thickness splitting of the skin. Abrasions are caused by movement of the skin over a rough surface; lacerations are the result of blunt force. Malone, Rozario, Gavinski, and Goodwin (1991) say that skin tears are a common type of laceration seen in the elderly; they are defined as a splitting of the epidermis from the underlying connective tissue, resulting in a skin flap. Health care providers should be aware of age-related changes in the skin, including the reduction of tensile strength and the increased susceptibility to shearing-force trauma. Knight (1997) suggests that because abrasions retain the pattern of the causative agent better than any other kind of injury, health care providers should document these kinds of injuries very carefully and completely. Skin tears in areas other than the arms and legs, or multiple tears or abrasions could raise suspicion. Abrasions and lacerations are most commonly seen in cases involving physical abuse, or sometimes in cases of caregiver neglect.
- Bruises are caused by blunt force trauma with concomitant rupture of small blood vessels under the skin. They are most often seen in abuse cases, but can also be the result of caregiver neglect. Bruises occur more frequently and resolve more slowly in the elderly, and can be the source of patterns suggesting the weapon. Bruises can retain the shape of knuckles or fingers, they can present in the form of tramline bruising (parallel marks) indicating injury from a stick, or they can reflect the imprint of cords. The most common locations for nonaccidental bruising are the face and neck, chest wall, abdomen, and buttocks.
- Fractures are broken bones and include a severing of the bone or a compression of intact bone. Age-related changes in the bones of elderly persons include thinning from osteoporosis or some other disease. Fractures of the wrist, hip, and vertebra are particularly prevalent among the elderly. The resolution of fractures in children has been much more widely studied than the resolution of fractures in the elderly, Dyer et al. (2002) assert. Because 50 percent of nursing home residents fall, injuries from falls alone cannot necessarily increase a health care provider's index of suspicion. Dentists frequently see physically abused patients with fractured, subluxed, or avulsed teeth or fractures of the mandible and maxilla (Fenton, Bouquot, & Unkel, 2000). A spiral fracture of a large bone with no history of gross injury is diagnostic of abuse, as are fractures with a rotational component (Dyer et al., 2002).
- A decubitus is the breakdown of skin integrity, resulting in an ulcer. Decubiti are the result of circulatory failure due to pressure; shearing forces cause thrombosis of the microcirculation, resulting in tissue necrosis (Barton & Barton, 1981). Decubiti, divided into four stages,

can be deep or superficial, and they are usually found over the sacrum, the hip, and the heels. They most often occur in medically ill or cognitively impaired individuals, and nutritional status and incontinence place the elderly at risk for these ulcers. Schor, Selby, and Bertone (1995) say that there is divided thought on whether decubiti are due to illness, neglect, or even abuse. The failure to adhere to the standard of care could be due to institutional, medical, or caregiver neglect.

- *Malnutrition and dehydration*. Gerontologists know that with age comes a decrease in the ability to smell and to taste, requisites for a healthy appetite. Poor dentition, dementia, and depression can also contribute to malnutrition. Malnutrition is a common marker of caregiver neglect in institutional settings; Knight (1997) says that more than 40 percent loss of body weight can lead to death. Improper feeding techniques, such as forceful assistance that can lead to choking and aspiration of food or liquids into the lungs, can lead to serious injury or death. Similarly, dehydration is a common marker of caretaker neglect in the elderly. Lowenstein, Crescenzi, Kern, and Steel (1986) found that dehydration is a common reason for visits to the ER by elderly persons.
- A burn results from tissue injury following exposure to heat above 50 degrees Celsius, according to Knight (1997). Burns are categorized according to the depth of tissue destruction and the percentage of body surface affected. The National Fire Protection Association says that persons over the age of 65 have twice the national average death rate due to burns. Although the association between burns and child abuse has been well documented, the same cannot be said for burns in the elderly. Bowden, Grant, Vogel, and Prasad (1988) found that 70 percent of burn cases presenting at a university-associated burn center were attributed to neglect and abuse. Bird et al. (1998) found that 40 percent of burn cases occurring in individuals 60 and older were due to abuse or neglect. In a paper about forensic nurses, White (2000) recommends that burns be considered a marker for elder neglect.
- *Cognitive and mental health problems*. Dyer et al. (2002) write, "Cognitive and mental health disorders are some of the most pervasive and clinically challenging problems of old age." Dyer and Goins (2000) report that the Texas Elder Abuse and Mistreatment Institute has treated more than 300 abused or neglected elders; the most common mental and cognitive disorders noted are depression, dementia, psychosis, and alcohol abuse. Dementia, in particular, is a prevalent condition in today's elders. This progressive impairment of memory and other areas of cognition results in an eventually reduced ability to care of oneself. It is often a triggering factor for self-neglect, which in turn makes the individual more vulnerable to mistreatment by others who would prey on them.
- *Hygiene*. Dyer et al. (2002) say that although there are no changes in one's hygiene that occur strictly with age, poor eyesight or other cognitive impairments might make it harder to keep oneself clean. Aravanis et al. (1993), Lachs and Pillemer (1995), and Butler (1999) have suggested that a marked decline in hygiene could be a marker of neglect. Age-related physiological changes in the genital areas have been documented. There is some research to suggest that changes in hygiene habits could indicate sexual abuse. Mickish (1993) categorized sexual abuse as the least perceived, acknowledged, detected, and reported type of elder abuse.

8.4.6.3 Screening for Elder Abuse in the Clinical Setting

In 1987, the AMA provided physicians with a tool to help identify elder abuse. It published a position paper on elder mistreatment that proposed a standard definition: "'Abuse' shall mean an act or omission which results in harm or threatened harm to the health or welfare of an elderly person. Abuse includes intentional infliction of physical or mental injury; sexual abuse; or withholding of necessary food, clothing, and medical care to meet the physical and mental needs of an elderly person by one having the care, custody or responsibility of an elderly person." In 1993, the AMA published *Diagnostic and Treatment Guidelines on Elder Abuse and Neglect*, which listed the following questions that health care providers can ask elderly patients:

- Has anyone at home ever hurt you?
- Has anyone ever touched you without your consent?
- Has anyone ever made you do things you didn't want to do?
- Has anyone taken anything that was yours without asking?
- Has anyone ever scolded or threatened you?

- Have you ever signed any document that you didn't understand?
- Are you afraid of anyone at home?
- Are you alone a lot?
- Has anyone ever failed to help you take care of yourself when you needed help?

"We've talked a lot about elder abuse (by caregivers, such as nursing home aides), but we have not been willing to admit the prevalence of elder abuse by family members," commented then-AMA board member Palmer E. Formica at the time of the guidelines' issuance. In 2000, the U.S. Department of Health and Human Services vowed, as one of its health goals, to ensure that at least 90 percent of the nation's hospital ERs use written protocols for identifying, treating, and referring victims of domestic abuse.

The 1987 AMA position paper explains that elder abuse takes many forms, including physical abuse and neglect, psychological abuse, financial exploitation, and violation of rights. A major obstacle to prevention of and intervention for elder mistreatment is a lack of awareness on the part of health care professionals. Lachs (1994, as cited in AMA, 1987) says that cognitive impairment and the need for assistance with activities of daily living are important risk factors for elder mistreatment. Lachs (1996, as cited in AMA, 1987) adds that caregiver burnout also can lead to elder abuse. Hwalek, Neale, Goodrich, and Quinn (1996) discovered that substance abuse by the caregiver or the patient significantly increases the risk of physical violence and neglect, and that psychological and character pathology in the caregiver and patient are also major risk factors.

8.4.6.4 The Patient History and Physical Examination

It is essential that health care providers obtain a comprehensive patient history; however, this is a challenging task due to the presence of cognitive impairment in the older adult, or the elder's fear of retribution at the hands of the abuser. Elders who have been abused frequently present with somatic complaints. Because mistreatment can sometimes be subtle or confused with other behavior, health care providers should inquire about instances of rough handling, confinement, and verbal or emotional abuse. These confusing incidents might be discovered during the older adult's routine visits to a health care facility (Swagerty, Takahashi, & Evans, 1999). Essential components of the patient history include the following:

- Medical problems and diagnoses
- Detailed description of home
- Accurate description of events related to injury or trauma
- History of prior violence
- Description of prior injuries and events surrounding them
- Description of berating, threats, or emotional abuse
- Improper care of medical problems, untreated injuries, poor hygiene, prolonged periods before presenting for medical attention
- Depression or other mental illness
- Extent of confusion or dementia
- Drug or alcohol abuse
- Quality and nature of relationships with caregivers (Swagerty, et al., 1999)

If an elder is being cared for by a caretaker, it is generally advisable that the patient be interviewed without the caregiver present. The health care provider should endeavor to piece together an accurate idea of the patient's daily life, including meals, medication, and social interaction. It is also crucial to ask the patient about the nature and quality of the relationship with the caregiver. If issues of mistreatment are raised, the caregiver should be interviewed as well. The physician must be careful not to overinterpret or to make suggestive comments, especially when the patient is cognitively impaired (Swagerty, et al., 1999).

Essential components of the patient physical examination include thorough inspection of the patient's body for possible signs of mistreatment:

- Head: Traumatic alopecia or other evidence of direct physical violence; poor oral hygiene
- Skin: Bruises, welts, bite marks, burns, or decubitus ulcers
- Musculoskeletal: Fractures or signs of previous fractures
- Neurologic: Cognitive impairment that is a risk factor for mistreatment and influences management decisions regarding competency
- Genito-rectal: Poor hygiene, inguinal rash, impaction of feces
- General: Weight loss, dehydration, poor hygiene, unkempt appearance (Swagerty, et al., 1999)

The physical examination is often used as legal evidence of mistreatment, and often dictates the need to perform additional clinical or imaging interventions to confirm any suspicious findings. The presence of dehydration and malnutrition can be established with simple laboratory tests such as a complete blood count and measurement of blood urea nitrogen, creatinine, total protein, and albumin levels. Radiographic studies provide evidence of old and new fractures, although proving that a fracture was caused by abuse can be difficult (Swagerty, et al., 1999). Documentation of all findings by health care providers is critical, because it can be entered as evidence in criminal trials or in guardianship hearings. Chain of evidence must be followed, including the collection of physical evidence in cases of suspected sexual or physical abuse.

8.4.6.5 Screening Tools for Elder Abuse

There is consensus that elder abuse and neglect are significantly underreported and underidentified, making screening tools vitally important. Dyer et al. (2002) write, "It is essential to screen for elder mistreatment, particularly in older persons who are either unable, due to cognitive impairment, or unwilling, due to fear, to report it." Jones, Daougherty, Schelbic, and Cunningham (1988) found that 72 percent of elder abuse victims did not complain of the abuse at the time they presented to the ER. In a 1997 survey of ER physicians by Jones and colleagues, 31 percent worked in a department that had elder abuse screening protocols, 33 percent worked in departments without these protocols, and 36 percent were unsure. Fulmer and Birkenhauer (1992) and Mouton and Espino (1999) recommend that screening for elder abuse be a part of the routine health assessment for all older individuals. A number of screening tools for elder abuse exist. The Comprehensive Geriatric Assessment (CGA) is an ideal tool for evaluation of abused or neglected persons, according to Aravanis et al. (1993), Lachs and Pillemer (1995), and Dyer and Goins (2000). The CGA requires obtaining a comprehensive history and physical examination, and the use of validated instruments to quantify measures of psychosocial health and function. Alessi, Struck, and Aronow (1997) found that the CGA has been shown to be effective in at least eight randomized trials. The Elder Assessment Instrument (EAI) was developed in 1981 and includes a checklist for assessing five domains, a summary, a disposition, and a narrative if the examiner chooses to use one. It is used by ED nurses and physicians, and Fulmer and Paveza (2000) demonstrated that the sensitivity and specificity were 71 percent and 93 percent, respectively, when compared with a panel of experts. These are just a few of the screening tools that currently exist. Dyer et al. (2002) report that several regions in the United States have formed multidisciplinary forensics teams that review and respond to suspected cases of elder abuse or neglect. Not only do the teams provide better coordinated intervention and response, but they are developing experience and expertise in providing a more sophisticated forensic analysis than was previously available from nonaffiliated professionals working outside of a team structure. Dyer et al. write, "Because there are so few such teams and because the data are so scarce, multidisciplinary efforts dedicated to addressing elder abuse and neglect should be studied, encouraged, and supported."

8.4.6.6 Special Considerations for Postmortem Analysis

Dyer et al. (2002) assert, "Many of the same potential markers for elder abuse and neglect in the context of living persons also apply in a post-mortem evaluation but are limited by inability to interview the patient and evaluate such things as mental status and capacity."

Dyer et al. say that the external examination by a forensic pathologist should include evaluation of the person's state of nutrition and documentation of cleanliness. He writes, "A body with crusted fecal material and secretions of dirt in skin creases, which is clad in very clean or new-appearing clothing should suggest an attempt to disguise poor hygiene and living conditions." Decubiti should be documented, as should bruising, skin lacerations, and fractures. The examiner should provide a detailed description of the size, color, extent, and location of these injuries in the medico-legal record. Patterned bruising or abrasions might indicate the object(s) causing the injury; for example, a line of circular bruises could represent finger marks. Injuries suggestive of defensive maneuvering could also prompt suspicions (Brogdon, 1998). Internal examination could provide additional evidence of markers of abuse or neglect. Organ examination can provide the state of nutrition and hydration, as well as the presence of natural disease. Inspection of the external and internal genitalia should be done to evaluate for sexual assault. "Post-mortem examination in many cases provides less information than would a complete physical examination in a living person," assert Dyer et al. (2002). "On the other hand, some post-mortem examination procedures yield more information than physical examination and laboratory testing of a living patient."

8.4.7 Elder Abuse in the Home Setting

In a 2000 OVC of the U.S. Department of Justice symposium, experts gathered to discuss the problem of elder abuse in the home. According to a report coming out of this event:

> Despite the fact that elder abuse and neglect in the home is an increasing phenomenon, only about one in five incidents gets reported and efforts to identify and address situations of abuse are often ill informed, disjointed, lacking in resources, and ineffective. This is partly due to the complexity of the issue; elder abuse in the home is often carried out by family members, which not only inverts societal expectations of familial care but also makes it difficult for investigators to detect and determine the extent of the abuse. Long-term patterns of domestic abuse make it less likely that an older person will seek help, the isolation of the victim is more easily enforced by the abuser when the older person lives at home, and consideration of civil liberties makes the job of the investigator who suspects elder abuse in the home an extremely difficult one.

Until recently there has been minimal funding directed toward educating professionals and the public on the issue of elder abuse in the home, and laws concerning the rights of the abused and prosecution of the abuser vary considerably from state to state. Numerous agencies and individuals who work with older persons are attempting to rectify this situation, and panelists presented different ways of understanding, responding to, and addressing the problem.

Speaking at the symposium, California resident Joyce Speakman related a personal experience that highlighted the importance of the issue and the suffering that can be caused by elder abuse by family members. Speakman said that her mother, Hazel Speakman, who died in August 1998 at the age of 78, endured years of physical and emotional abuse and neglect in her own home at the hands of a relative. Five years before her mother's death, Speakman knew nothing about elder abuse and thought her suspicions were disloyal to the family, but she eventually contacted the county's APS agency. She found the agency representatives to be committed, compassionate, and eager to get at the truth, but each labored under the same limitations: Her sister prohibited APS workers from interviewing her mother and thus they concluded that no determination of elder abuse could be made. In her quest to discover the extent of her mother's abuse, Speakman involved numerous other agencies and individuals, including a nonprofit case worker who was sympathetic but inexperienced, a church pastor who was conciliatory but ineffectual, and the local mental health system, which attempted to address, although only temporarily, her sister's mental health disorders. No one suggested involving the police, and when Speakman contacted them after her mother's death, they reported they would not investigate the prior circumstances of a dead victim. Medical records obtained after her death revealed that, among other things, Hazel Speakman had suffered 12 serious falls and numerous broken ribs. Although Speakman realizes that her relative's efforts to isolate her mother made the APS agency's original investigation difficult, she was disillusioned by their conclusions and believes a more in-depth understanding of the dynamics of elder abuse and risk factors for potential abusers would have been helpful.

The National Association of Adult Protective Service Administrators (NAAPSA) provides the system that receives reports of elder and adult abuse, investigates complaints, and attempts to ameliorate abuse. It operates under a mandate to protect safety, health, and civil liberties, and the social services it provides can include linkage with law enforcement, and legal, medical, transportation, housing, and psychiatric services. APS caseworkers must make critical, life-changing decisions in complex situations, which can include matters of financial concern, legal issues, mental health concerns, issues regarding physical and sexual assault, and a wide variety of family situations. Consequently, agency administrators attempt to develop multidisciplinary teams that bring together representatives from the mental health system, law enforcement, victim services, domestic violence, and others. In 1999, NAAPSA conducted a survey of state APS programs. Analysis of the survey data indicated that APS agencies in 48 jurisdictions, including the District of Columbia and Guam, had received 443,000 complaints of abuse, neglect, and exploitation, and that a majority of these incidents had occurred in the victim's home. As research indicates that one of every five cases of elder abuse is reported, there might be millions of older people who are abused, neglected, or exploited. Despite this overwhelming need, APS is resource-poor, funded primarily by state and local dollars. The only federal funding available for elder abuse services continues to be directed solely at prevention, and has remained stable at $4 million to $5 million per year. In comparison, NAAPSA has determined that domestic violence services receive approximately $200 million in federal funding, and those addressing problems of child abuse receive about $4 billion. APS systems differ significantly from state to state, but there is no federal elder abuse statute.

At the symposium, Bonnie Brandl, program director of the National Clearinghouse on Abuse in Later Life, Wisconsin Coalition Against Domestic Violence, discussed elder abuse in the context of domestic violence. Although many people find the actions of those who abuse older persons to be incomprehensible, it is important to understand that both abusers and those who seek to intervene on the behalf of the abused operate within particular belief systems. Brandl said that to understand what type of tactics abusers use and how victims are affected by abuse, belief systems on both sides of the problem must be examined. She noted that family members who abuse other family members believe they are entitled to use whatever tactic they want to dominate or punish their victims, including physical abuse, sexual abuse, financial exploitation, isolation from other family members, the withholding of medication, the abuse of beloved pets, the ridiculing of spiritual beliefs, and a range of other behaviors and threats. Some of the belief systems subscribed to by abuse prevention and treatment professionals are more complex. They include the following theories about elder abuse:

- It is a problem of caregiver stress, and should involve social services rather than law enforcement.
- What happens within the family is a private matter, and law enforcement should make every attempt to fix the situation without making arrests.
- Some abusive situations are not particularly dangerous, and law enforcement officers should

be discouraged from bringing abusers who might be older or disabled into a system that has no place for them.
- Most elder abuse victims will not access services anyway, so money and effort spent supplying them is wasted.

These belief systems do not consider the victim's safety to be of paramount importance. As a result, victims are caught between their abuser and a community that does not want to think of this as an issue of power and control, or is not looking to make an arrest, or is not developing services for the abused. It is necessary to understand what barriers the victims face when the system fails them, said Brandl, and to use victim input to inform what types of programs are developed. "A lot of us measure success by whether we close cases or get funding or start a new program," she said, "but I would encourage you to measure success based on whether victims are safer as a result of the intervention options you create in your state."

Also at the symposium, Dr. Holly Ramsey-Klawsnik, a social worker and family therapist, noted that one form of elder abuse often overlooked or ignored is sexual abuse, as there is a prevailing myth that elders and sex do not go together. She warned, however, "We've unfortunately had to get used to the idea that sometimes parents molest their children, and we also have to get used to the idea that sometimes adult children molest their elders. It is a difficult but necessary piece of information to swallow." Elder sexual abuse occurs when a senior is forced, manipulated, or coerced into unwanted sexual activity, or when a senior lacks the capacity to grant informed consent to sexual activity. Ramsey-Klawsnik discussed a number of substantiated cases of sexual assault of elderly victims perpetrated by paid or volunteer caregivers, family members, or spouses. Her cases illustrated that although the majority of identified victims are female, disabled men also are vulnerable. Most identified perpetrators are male; however, some cases have involved female perpetrators. Several factors are correlated with the impact of sexual abuse on victims. These include the victim's preabuse level of function, and the type of abuse sustained ("hands-off" offense such as sexual harassment, "hands-on" offense such as rape or molestation, or harmful genital practices such as a caregiver unnecessarily performing invasive cleansing procedures). Victim impact also is related to the extent of abuse suffered (one-time vs. recurrent episodes), and whether or not appropriate interventions are offered to assist the victim. Professional and community response to elder sexual abuse often is denial or minimization. It is an abhorrent issue to contemplate and discuss, and therefore it is easy to dismiss indicators and deny the existence of this type of victimization. Those involved with older persons need to realize that if signs and symptoms exist in an older person that would suggest sexual assault in an 8-, 20-, or 40-year-old, the matter should be investigated.

8.4.8 Institutional Abuse and Neglect

In March 2002, the U.S. GAO delivered a report to the Senate Special Committee on Aging on the results of 18 months of interviews with relatives of residents in nursing homes around the country and with officials in Georgia, Illinois, and Pennsylvania. The GAO documented instances of alleged physical and sexual abuse that were frequently not reported or prosecuted. At risk for further abuse were the 1.5 million residents of 17,000 nursing homes in the United States. According to the GAO report, most of the local police departments in those three states reported that they were seldom summoned to a nursing home following an alleged instance of abuse; instead, state survey agencies were typically notified of allegations of abuse, but these notifications were frequently delayed. Allegations of abuse might not be reported immediately for a variety of reasons, including reluctance to report abuse on the part of residents, family members, nursing home employees, and administrators, according to GAO investigators. Victims of crimes ordinarily call the police to report instances of physical and sexual abuse, but when the victim is a nursing home resident, the police appear to be notified infrequently, according to the report. Residents and family members are not required to notify local police of abusive incidents.

Several police officials told the GAO that when they do learn of an allegation of abuse involving a nursing home resident, it is sometimes after another entity, such as the state survey agency, has begun to investigate, thus hampering law enforcement's evidence collection and limiting their investigations. Most of the police departments also indicated that they did not track reports of abuse allegations involving nursing home residents and thus did not have data on the number of such reports. When residents and family members do report allegations of abuse, they might complain directly to the nursing home administrator rather than contacting police. According to one long-term care ombudsman, residents and family members do not always view the abuse as a criminal matter. Nursing homes are usually not compelled to notify local law enforcement when they learn of such reports. There is no federal requirement that they contact police, although some states have instituted such a requirement. GAO investigators' discussions with officials from 19 local law enforcement agencies indicated that police are rarely called to investigate allegations of the abuse of nursing home residents.

The GAO's review of 158 case files from 1999 and 2000 indicated state survey agencies were often not promptly notified of abuse allegations, with reports made sometimes days and weeks after the abuse occurred. Although individuals filing complaints are not compelled to report allegations within a prescribed time frame, nursing homes in the states the GAO visited are required to notify the state survey agency of abuse allegations the day they learn of the allegation or the following day. Experts say that allegations of abuse of nursing home residents might not be reported promptly for a variety of reasons. For example, a recent study by Burgess and Dowdell (2000) found that nursing home staff might be skeptical that abuse occurred. Residents might also be afraid to report abuse because of fear of retribution. According to one law enforcement official interviewed by GAO investigators, family members are sometimes fearful that the resident will be asked to leave the home and are troubled by the prospect of finding a new place for the resident to live. Additionally, nursing home staff and management do not always report abuse promptly, despite requirements to do so. According to law enforcement and state survey agency officials, staff fear losing their jobs or facing recrimination from coworkers and nursing home management. Similarly, they also said that nursing home management is sometimes reluctant to risk adverse publicity or sanctions from the state. GAO investigators encountered a number of examples of delayed reporting by health care providers.

A nursing home resident reported to a nurse that she had been raped. Although the nurse recorded this information in the resident's medical record, she did not notify the facility's management. She also allegedly discouraged the resident from telling anyone else. Two months later, the resident was admitted to a hospital for unrelated reasons and told hospital officials that she had been raped. It was not until hospital officials notified police of the resident's complaint that an investigation was conducted. Investigators then discovered that the resident had also informed her daughter of the incident, but the daughter had dismissed it. The resident later told police that she did not report the incident to other nursing home staff because she did not want to cause trouble. The case was closed because the resident could not describe the alleged perpetrator. However, the nurse was counseled about the need to immediately report such incidents.

In another instance, a nursing assistant angered by a resident who soiled his bed threw a pitcher of cold water on the patient and refused to clean him; another aide witnessed the incident. Instead of informing management, the witness confided in a third employee, who reported the incident to the nursing home administrator five days after the abuse took place. The abusive aide was fired, and a finding of abuse was recorded in her nurse aide registry file. In another case, one nursing home employee witnessed an aide slap a resident; two other employees heard the incident. The aide denied the allegation, yet the resident developed redness, swelling, and bruising around her eye. The witnesses reported the matter to nursing home management, which investigated the situation and suspended the aide the next day; the aide was subsequently fired. However, the state survey agency was not notified of the incident by the home until 11 days after the abuse took place.

The GAO report identified the fact that relatively few prosecutions result from allegations of physical and sexual abuse of nursing home residents. Investigators identified two impediments to the successful prosecution of employees who abuse nursing home residents: Allegations of abuse were not always referred to local law enforcement, and a lack of witnesses to instances of abuse made prosecutions difficult and convictions unlikely. The lack of compelling evidence often precludes prosecution of those who have abused nursing home residents, the GAO report discovered, adding that according to law enforcement officials, nursing home residents are often unwilling or unable to provide testimony. GAO file reviews confirmed that residents were reluctant or unable to provide evidence against an accused abuser in 32 of the 158 cases the agency reviewed, thus making it difficult to pursue a criminal investigation. GAO investigators noted several instances in which residents sustained unexplained black eyes, lacerations, and fractures; however, despite the existence of serious injuries, investigators could neither rule out accidental injuries nor identify a perpetrator.

Prosecutions of individuals accused of abusing nursing home residents are often weakened by the time lapse between the incident and the trial. Law enforcement officials and prosecutors told the GAO that the amount of time that elapses between an incident and a trial could ruin an otherwise successful case because witnesses do not always remember important details about the incident. The GAO's review demonstrated that nursing home residents might become incapable of testifying months after they were abused. For example, in one case, a victim's roommate witnessed the abuse and positively identified the abuser during the investigation. However, by the time of the trial, nearly five months later, she could no longer identify the suspect in the courtroom, prompting the judge to dismiss the charges. Moreover, given the age and medical condition of many nursing home residents, many might not survive long enough to participate in a trial. Burgess and Dowdell's (2000) study of 20 sexually abused nursing home residents revealed that 11 died within one year of the abuse. The GAO report stated that law enforcement officials believe that without testimony from either a victim or a witness, conviction is unlikely. One of the safeguards against elder abuse should be the screening of health care providers. Requirements by the Centers for Medicare and Medicaid (CMS) preclude facilities from employing an individual convicted of abusing nursing home residents but permit the hiring of those convicted of other abusive acts, such as child abuse. Although some states have established more stringent requirements, criminal background checks typically do not identify individuals who have committed a crime in another state, according to the GAO report.

Nursing homes can be cited for deficiencies if they fail to adequately protect residents from abuse, but these deficiencies rarely result in the imposition of sanctions, such as civil monetary penalties, by state survey agencies. State survey agencies, which also oversee the operation of state nurse aide registries, do not adequately ensure that residents will be protected from aides who previously abused residents. Finally, states are unable to take professional disciplinary actions against other employees, such as security guards or housekeeping staff, who might have abused residents but who are neither licensed nor certified to care for residents. Although CMS requires nursing homes to establish policies that prevent the hiring of individuals who have been convicted of abusing nursing home residents, this requirement does not include offenses committed against individuals outside the nursing home setting, nor does it specify that states conduct background checks on all prospective employees. CMS's requirement does not preclude individuals with similar convictions, such as assault, battery, and child abuse, from obtaining nursing home employment. Nationwide background checks on prospective nursing home employees can be performed by the FBI if nursing homes request them. These checks could identify offenses committed elsewhere, but not all states take advantage of this option. According to the GAO report, 21 states have requirements that subject some health care employees to these checks, but state requirements vary and do not always apply to prospective nursing home employees.

The GAO report revealed that many states do not levy sanctions against nursing homes for deficiencies associated with their handling of instances of abuse. According to the report, severe deficiencies, including those resulting in actual harm or immediate jeopardy to resident health or safety, could result in an immediate sanction such as a civil monetary penalty. Deficiencies not resulting in actual harm or immediate jeopardy usually resulted in nursing homes being required to submit a plan of corrective action. In the GAO's review of 158 cases, 26 nursing homes were cited for abuse-related deficiencies such as failing to report allegations of abuse in a timely manner or failing to properly investigate them, as well as inadequately screening employees for criminal backgrounds. Bertsch (2003) suggests that nursing homes can fight against incidences of elder abuse by doing the following:

- Hire licensed nurses who have geriatric experience.
- Ensure that allegations of abuse are reported immediately to the administrator responsible for reporting to officials in accordance with state law.
- Implement written policies and procedures that prohibit mistreatment, neglect, and abuse of residents and misappropriation of resident property; include expected consequences for abusers and those who do not report abuse.
- Conduct criminal background checks on all nursing employees by referring to state boards of nursing, nurse aides' registries, and police records.
- Before hiring applicants, check references from former employers and instructors even if they are permitted to supply dates of employment only; for certified nursing assistants, check state registries for current certification and status, and for licensed nurses, verify current licenses, and check with state licensing boards to ensure no penalties are pending.
- Provide regular educational programs on how to understand residents' behavior and provide care, including simulation of residents' physical impairments.
- Require written accident reports for all resident accidents; evaluate them quarterly, and track for ongoing trends.
- Initiate an open-door policy to encourage staff to freely discuss suspicions of abuse and share suggestions.
- Emphasize residents' rights when hiring new nursing staff.

Bertsch (2003) also suggests that nurses who work in long-term care facilities do the following:

- Learn how to identify abuse and potential elder abuse.
- Monitor trends of potential and actual abuse.
- Physically assess all residents while making rounds.
- Observe staff members who provide direct patient care.
- Become familiar with your state's advocacy system, including ombudsman, state licensing agency, and consumer advocacy groups.
- Facilitate staff participation in educational programs on abuse that emphasize the recognition of signs of elder abuse, its causes, and reporting protocols.

"Even in the most proactive nursing homes, daily demands on staff continue to put residents at risk for abuse," Bertsch writes. "Residents' inability to protect themselves accentuates the need for protective measures in both nursing homes and agencies that oversee them. But even efforts to screen employees and prompt reporting can fall short of creating a tight enough net to protect residents from potential offenders."

Several recent initiatives have emerged to address abuse. CMS has created the Internet-based program Nursing Home Compare at www.medicare.gov/Nhcompare/home.asp. All nursing homes participating in Medicare and Medicaid are subject to review on nine quality measures, such as how often a facility uses physical restraints to manage residents, the percentage of residents with pressure sores and weight loss, and a list of deficiencies found by state licensing surveyors that details the scope and severity of each deficiency.

The GAO report made the following recommendations to CMS:

- Ensure that state survey agencies immediately notify local law enforcement agencies or the Medicaid Fraud Control Unit (MFCU) when nursing homes report allegations of physical or sexual abuse of residents or when the survey agency has confirmed complaints of alleged abuse.
- Accelerate the agency's educational campaign on reporting nursing home abuse by distributing its new poster with clearly displayed complaint telephone numbers and requiring state survey agencies to ensure that the numbers are prominently listed in local telephone directories.
- Systematically assess state policy and practices for complying with the federal requirement to prohibit employment of people convicted of abusing nursing home residents and, if necessary, develop more specific guidance to ensure compliance.
- Clarify the definition of abuse and otherwise ensure that states apply that definition consistently and appropriately.
- Shorten the state survey agencies' time frame for determining whether to include findings of abuse in nurse aide registry files.

"Nurses who are aware of nursing home abuse can educate others about ways to prevent it," Bertsch writes. "In particular, RNs who work in nursing homes know the importance of immediate notification of resident abuse to state survey agencies. Likewise, nurses in hospitals should be on the alert for signs of abuse when residents are admitted from nursing homes and must know how to notify authorities when necessary. Community health nurses should also be on the alert for signs of abuse when their patients are discharged from nursing homes to prior or new living arrangements." Bertsch points to the current nursing shortage as an aggravating factor of elder abuse. "A serious shortage situation confronts the nursing profession, including an RN vacancy rate of 18 percent in nursing homes." To address this challenge, Bertsch advocates incorporation of long-term care experience in nursing school curricula, increased promotion of the ANA credentialing program in gerontology, and support for nurses who wish to study gerontology in graduate programs. "One day federal regulations may mandate nursing homes to staff with RNs skilled in geriatric nursing," Bertsch writes. "As professional nurses move into geriatric settings as role models, their presence could have an impact on employee attitudes, work habits, and relationships with residents leading to the decline and perhaps eradication of nursing home abuse."

8.4.8.1 The New Nursing Home Challenge: Resident-on-Resident Violence

Gray-Vickery (2004) reports that between 1999 and 2001, 30 percent of nursing homes in the United States were cited for abuse. Abuse in institutions is often triggered by stressful working conditions, staff burnout, patient aggression, or negative attitudes toward the elderly. Abuse and neglect of elders at the hands of caretakers in nursing homes and other institutions has been well documented in the lay press, in the medical literature, and in countless books, but a new problem is developing that some experts say could be addressed by forensically trained health care providers.

In 2004, an 88-year-old patient in a Stamford, Connecticut nursing home was bludgeoned to death by his 82-year-old roommate, who used the footboard of a bed as the weapon. This case of an assailant who suffered from dementia is casting new light on the emerging problem of violence among facility residents. Even as policymakers, investigators, and advocates have focused on complaints of staff abuse, resident-on-resident violence is triggering an increasing number of complaints, studies, and conferences, according to an October 6, 2004 Associated Press story. The article reported, "Nationwide, more than 3,700 complaints about such abuse were lodged with state ombudsmen programs in 2002, up from about 2,500 in 1997." Pennsylvania, New York, and Florida have reported cases in recent years of patients killed by fellow residents suffering from dementia. "There's so many situations occurring now where there is resident-on-resident abuse, including cases where people are killed occasionally," said Janet Wells, director of public policy for the National Citizens Coalition for Nursing Home Reform, who was quoted in the AP story. Patient advocates say more staff and better training, as well as improved screening of patients for mental illness or criminal backgrounds is needed to address the problem. In the AP story, Wells said that nursing homes are eager to fill beds and might not inquire as to a patient's background. In Oklahoma, a group called A Perfect Cause warned that violent offenders were being warehoused in nursing homes. In 1999, an 83-year-old woman died after she was thrown against a wall by another resident who had an extensive criminal record. In

2003, 16 residents were killed in a Hartford, Connecticut nursing home when the facility caught fire. The blaze was set by a 24-year-old resident who was known to be mentally ill. In another case, a 23-year-old mentally ill man slashed an elderly resident's throat because he was upset that the man had taken a cookie from him.

In the summer of 2004, Minnesota Attorney General Mike Hatch filed a lawsuit against a nursing home, alleging that it jeopardized the health and safety of vulnerable adults patients by accepting multiple convicted sex offenders to its facility, and by condoning the presence of other deplorable conditions. The lawsuit alleged that the 94-bed nursing home accepted referrals of convicted sex offenders from Minnesota prisons in 2002, 2003, and 2004. One of the sex offenders, a 44-year-old man, had been charged with first- and second-degree criminal sexual conduct against a vulnerable adult. Within days of arriving at the facility named in the lawsuit, the offender had developed a friendship with a female resident. After the patient learned of the man's criminal history, she attempted to end the friendship. The man began to follow the female resident and one night was found in her room, hovering over her while she was in bed. He was discharged back to the Minnesota Correctional Facility a month after arriving at the nursing home. The facility had also admitted a 26-year-old male sex offender, JA, who had a history of pedophilia. Around the same time, a 43-year-old female, NM, with diagnoses including mental retardation, borderline intelligence, and schizophrenia, had been admitted. Less than 10 days after NM's admission to the facility, JA was found in NM's room, fondling her "private parts." A few days later, NM was taken to the ER for abdominal bleeding. JA admitted penetrating NM's vagina. Witnesses also observed JA grabbing NM's buttocks. A picture of NM naked from the waist down, lying on her back with her legs spread apart, was found in JA's wallet. The facility had instructed an employee of the facility to destroy this piece of evidence, but he refused to do so. Allegedly, the facility management thought that the relationship between JA and NM was "cute" and talked about buying a ring for JA to present to NM. Hatch's lawsuit alleges that the facility failed to inform its staff, residents, their families and others that convicted sex offenders were residing there, among other charges of unsafe, inappropriate, and deplorable conditions.

Noted forensic pathologist Vincent DiMaio, MD, says forensic nurses are needed in nursing homes to help identify and document forensic cases, both obvious and subtle. "While I see forensic nurses excelling in working as investigators for medical examiners, I see them in an equally important role," DiMaio says:

> One of the major problems we are having in society now is care of the elderly. The nursing homes are horror stories in many areas, and in my office we get 2,000 deaths a year reported to us in nursing homes... we can't investigate them all. How can I send my investigator, a certified, commissioned peace officer to review the medical records of someone in a nursing home? They don't understand what they are reading. You can tell them what happened, but they won't be able to pick up on the medical and clinical nuances like forensic nurses can. The U.S. population is getting older and attention is being drawn to the problem of abuse and neglect in nursing homes. There is some talk of making a law that says the family of a victim is entitled to an autopsy of anyone who dies in a nursing home so that the circumstances can be investigated... the problem is, some medical examiners are fighting it. I would like it, but it's hard for me to handle all of these nursing home cases already. That's why we need nurse investigators. I testified in a case in Honolulu which centered on a nursing home in which one of the residents died of decubitus ulcers. The facility operator was charged with murder, was convicted, and got 20 years. In that case, it was all done retrospectively; think about how easy it would be for me to investigate these cases if I had nurse investigators who are familiar with natural disease as well as suspicious injury and death.

8.4.8.2 Underreporting of Elder Abuse

Although all states have laws and services in place to detect elder abuse, a 1996 study indicated that only about one in five cases of elder abuse is reported and substantiated. This low level of intervention, despite laws and services, prompted University of Iowa Health Care researchers to pursue their own study. The findings, which appeared in the December 2004 issue of the *American Journal of Public Health*, indicate that how domestic elder abuse cases are detected and handled differs significantly across states because the relevant state laws and regulations vary greatly. In particular, the study found that states that require mandatory reporting and tracking of domestic elder abuse reports have much higher investigation rates than states without these mandatory requirements. The study is believed to be the first to comprehensively relate domestic elder abuse rates to laws and regulations in all 50 states and the District of Columbia. The University of Iowa study suggests that particular professions need not be singled out in statutes as mandatory reporters, and that types of abuse need to be better defined within many state regulations.

In addition, the findings indicate that it might be more effective to have caseworkers handle only adult abuse cases rather than both child and adult cases. "Laws do have an impact on public health, and this study demonstrates that different aspects of laws related to domestic elder abuse impact the amount of abuse reported, investigated and found to be actual abuse," says Gerald Jogerst, MD, associate professor and interim head of family medicine in the University of Iowa Roy J. and Lucille A. Carver College of Medicine and lead investigator of the study. "Our findings suggest that improvements and standardization are needed nationwide in how information on elder abuse is collected and how state laws are created."

The University of Iowa study was based on data for 1999 that included all available domestic elder abuse reports, investigations, and substantiations. Specifically, there were 190,005 reports from 17 states (not all states keep track of reports); 242,530 investigations from 46 states and the District of Columbia; and 102,879 substantiations from 35 states. A total of four states were not included in the investigation totals because they either reported no data (Georgia, North Dakota, Ohio) or were not sure of its accuracy (Colorado). In addition, not all states were able to provide substantiation of investigation data. A report is an allegation or suspicion of abuse received by a state's APS; an investigation involves actually going to a potential victim's home to see whether abuse is taking place; and substantiation is the finding of abuse as defined by that state's law. The University of Iowa team analyzed each state's statute and regulation regarding APS. The team of researchers found that domestic elder abuse reports ranged from 4.5 per 1,000 elders in New Hampshire to 14.6 in California. "The range of reporting rates is very high, and is one of the indicators that there is high variability in how states document elder abuse," Jogerst says. Elder abuse investigations rates ranged from .5 per 1,000 elders in Wyoming to 12.1 in Texas. Substantiations ranged from .1 per 1,000 elders in Wyoming to 8.6 in Minnesota. Forty-five percent of cases investigated were substantiated as actual abuse according to state laws. The terminology used to describe elder abuse varies greatly. As a result, the University of Iowa team first had to review and recodify terms used so that appropriate comparisons could be made across states, says Jeanette Daly, PhD, a University of Iowa geriatric nurse researcher in family medicine and the study's coprincipal investigator. "The team members drew on the disciplines of nursing, medicine, law, biostatistics and social work. We worked together to code more than 80 aspects of the different statutes and come to consensus about categorizing these definitions," Daly adds. In addition, variations are widespread in how states document cases. For example, some states, including Iowa, used the term *report* in summaries when referring to what, by standard definition, is considered an investigation. "The National Association of Adult Protective Services has a model reporting system for states to mimic. However, some states are hindered in implementing the model because their adult and child protection services share a computerized system," Daly says. The team found that mandatory reporting, which was part of the law in 44 states during the year studied, is linked to higher investigation rates. Although mandatory reporting apparently affects how many elder abuse cases are investigated, the researchers found that it is not necessary for states to spend time and resources defining who should be a mandatory reporter. "Some states list 'any person' as a mandatory reporter and other states list professionals such as physicians, nurses and bankers," Jogerst says. "However, when you compare these two groups of states, there is no overall difference in the number of reports, investigations or substantiations. The law simply should say 'any person.'" States that tracked reports had more investigations and nearly three times as many substantiated cases as did states that did not track reports. This was true even when considering how much funding a state has to track such cases. "We think an aspect of this requirement to track reports puts administrators and workers on alert that they are being monitored in their performance," Jogerst says. "It also sends a message that the state government feels that tracking reports is important."

The team also found that states where investigators handle only elder abuse cases had a nearly 50 percent substantiation ratio compared to a 34 percent substantiation ratio in states where investigators handle both child and elder abuse cases. The substantiation ratio was determined by dividing the number of substantiations by the number of investigations. "This substantiation difference may exist because investigators devoted to one type of abuse probably acquire more expertise by doing more elder abuse investigations," Jogerst says. Iowa is one of 11 states that currently have protective services caseworkers handling both elder and child abuse cases.

The team also determined that it is "worth the time to spell out abuse definitions within regulations." Abuse definitions are broken down into eight categories: abandonment, emotional or psychological, exploitation (usually financial), sexual, self-neglect, neglect (by another person), physical, and abuse not otherwise specified. Self-neglect is the failure, either by the adult's action or inaction, to provide the proper or necessary support or medical or any other care necessary for his or her own well-being. "We saw that state regulations that included most or all of the abuse definitions have increased substantiation rates and ratios," Jogerst says. "This suggests investigators can do a better job of documenting abuse when they have more to go on and the definitions are clear and precise."

8.4.9 The Public Health Response to Elder Abuse ... or Lack Thereof

With elder abuse coming to light in the United States in the 1970s through congressional hearings, scientific research, and exposure in the media, came enactment of state adult protective service and elder abuse reporting laws to identify and treat elder abuse. The majority of the laws were passed during the early 1980s, and today all states have some kind of law for victims of elder abuse, although they differ widely in content. In the early 1990s, Ehrlich (1991) reported that state laws include mandatory reporting, a provision regarded by some as important for case finding. Ehrlich writes, "The usefulness of mandatory reporting rests in the ability of those identified as reporters to recognize elder abuse and make effective referrals for service. Elder abuse protocols help facilitate this."

Health care providers are major referral sources for elder abuse, and also are most commonly identified as mandatory reporters in elder abuse reporting laws (Fulmer & O'Malley, 1987). Ehrlich (1991) says, "Conventional wisdom suggests that public-health officials are the most informed health care providers about laws affecting the safety and welfare of vulnerable populations. It is reasonable to think, therefore, that they are knowledgeable about state elder abuse reporting laws and procedures for their appropriate implementation." To test this assumption, a survey (consisting of a two-page questionnaire) was conducted of the 50 state health department officials between April 1989 and October 1989. A cover letter accompanying the survey also identified these staff members as "front-line workers who can make a significant contribution to the early identification of abuse situations." Abuse was defined to include physical abuse, neglect, exploitation, and abandonment. Two follow-up mailings to nonrespondents plus five telephone interviews resulted in a response rate of 100 percent.

The Survey of State Health Departments on Elder Abuse Reporting Procedures uncovered the following:

- Thirty-eight departments reported that they had no protocol specifically prepared for staff members or related community professionals. More than half (18) of them indicated that it was not the responsibility of their department. One respondent wrote, "Protocols are not necessary, the law is clear."
- Ten health departments reported that they had protocols. A review of the materials submitted suggests, however, that these were either for use in reporting abuse in long-term care facilities or consisted of brochures and manuals prepared by the responsible investigating agency for general use. Four departments used the general-use brochures and manuals in mailings, in one case to 2,100 community physicians and 165 ER physicians.
- Fourteen departments indicated that they conducted training or awareness campaigns, or both, for physicians and nurses at the time their state law was implemented. Six departments maintain ongoing in-service, particularly to clarify legal requirements.
- Less than one third of the departments knew of difficulties encountered by health care practitioners in reporting abuse. This group of respondents identified a number of general reporting issues applicable to the total reporting system as well as to the health professional. These were lack of clarity with the law, including limited familiarity with the requirements, procedures, investigative agencies, and differences between reporting community-based and long-term care facility abuse; different definitions of abuse used by health department staff members and abuse investigators; lack of adequate number of investigators and timely investigations; lack of public awareness; uneasiness about reporting, including professional denial of abuse occurrence or the unwillingness of families to cooperate, or both; and lack of confidentiality for the person reporting abuse.

Ehrlich (1991) writes, "The findings suggest that state departments of health are aware of elder abuse reporting laws, but it appears that little has been done to further their implementation." Specifically, none of the 50 departments surveyed developed an actual protocol around abuse identification and referral; 64 percent lacked related in-service training of health care providers, and almost 75 percent offered no awareness campaign regarding the law. Ehrlich acknowledges that "the responsibility for developing abuse protocols and initiating awareness campaigns probably cannot rest at the national level because variability among state elder abuse reporting laws precludes a uniform design that can be implemented," and that local action is necessary. She adds, "State departments of health familiar with the law and concerned about the welfare of vulnerable populations are critically situated to ensure that health providers are aware of elder abuse as a problem, know its signs, and can effectively carry out reporting obligations."

8.5 VIOLENCE AGAINST CHILDREN

This section is in no way a comprehensive reference to all child abuse issues, as other works have addressed the full range of clinical and psychological considerations. Instead, it touches on items of interest to health care providers and other members of the professional community who wish to understand the overall framework of child abuse as it relates to clinical forensic medicine and medico-legal cases.

8.5.1 The Scope of the Problem

Child abuse is probably one of the most studied and researched forms of family violence, representing a critical mass of information and statistics quantifying and qualifying this subset of human mistreatment. It is little wonder, as the statistics can be staggering. In 1995, local CPS agencies identified 126,000 children who were victims of either substantiated or indicated sexual abuse; of these, 75 percent were girls. Nearly 30 percent of child victims were between the ages of 4 and 7 according to the U.S. Department of Health and Human Services Administration for Children and Families. And according to the U.S. Bureau of Justice Statistics, in 1997, approximately 44 percent of rape victims were under age 18. Ninety-three percent of juvenile sexual assault victims knew their attacker; 34.2 percent were family members and 58.7 percent were acquaintances. Only 7 percent of the perpetrators were strangers to the victim, according to *Sexual Assault of Young Children as Reported to Law Enforcement*, issued by the Bureau of Justice Statistics (U.S. Department of Justice, 2000).

As an introduction to the clinical presentation of child abuse, it is appropriate to examine the work of Keshavarz, Kawashima, and Low (2002), who described the epidemiology of reported abuse (physical, sexual, and neglect) in a teaching, metropolitan pediatric ED with approximately 30,000 annual visits. A retrospective chart review was conducted of all cases from the pediatric ED that were referred to the Department of Social Work and reported to the Administration for Children's Services (ACS), the New York children's protective services, from May 1996 through December 1998. Demographic information about the victims as well as past medical history, number of previous pediatric ED visits, information about the perpetrator, and the nature of the injuries were obtained. The researchers identified 106 cases over this period of time that were reported for child abuse or neglect from the pediatric ED. Fifty-five percent of cases were reported for suspected physical abuse, 15 percent for sexual abuse, and 30 percent for neglect. The suspected perpetrator was the mother in 41 percent of cases and the father in 21 percent of cases. Bruises were the most frequent injury reported, seen in 25 percent of cases. The average age of the patients was 6.4 years old, and they averaged 4.6 previous pediatric ED visits. The majority of patients lived near the hospital. Sixty-nine percent of the patients presented for care between the hours of 5 p.m. and 9 a.m. Most of the patients claimed their primary physician was located in a clinic near their home (44 percent); only 12.7 percent were unsure of their primary physician. Significantly more victims (89 percent) had Medicaid or no insurance compared with other pediatric ED patients (71 percent). Victims did not live in zip codes with lower incomes compared with other pediatric ED patients. After complete investigation by ACS, 49 cases (46 percent) were deemed "indicated," 21 cases (20 percent) were "unfounded," and for the remaining 36 cases (34 percent), follow-up information could not be determined. The researchers concluded that the majority of reported cases (especially those of sexual abuse) did not have any physical findings at the time of presentation, stressing the need for a careful search for both abuse and neglect.

8.5.2 What Is Child Abuse and Neglect?

The National Clearinghouse on Child Abuse and Neglect Information says that federal legislation provides a foundation for states by identifying a minimum set of acts or behaviors that define child abuse and neglect. The Federal Child Abuse Prevention and Treatment Act (CAPTA), as amended by the Keeping Children and Families Safe Act of 2003, defines child abuse and neglect as, at minimum:

- Any recent act or failure to act on the part of a parent or caretaker that results in death, serious physical or emotional harm, sexual abuse or exploitation.
- An act or failure to act that presents an imminent risk of serious harm.

Within the minimum standards set by CAPTA, each state is responsible for providing its own definitions of child abuse and neglect. Most states recognize four major types of maltreatment: neglect, physical abuse, sexual abuse, and emotional abuse. Although any of the forms of child maltreatment can be found separately, they often occur in combination.

Neglect is failure to provide for a child's basic needs. Neglect can be:

- Physical (e.g., failure to provide necessary food or shelter, or lack of appropriate supervision)
- Medical (e.g., failure to provide necessary medical or mental health treatment)
- Educational (e.g., failure to educate a child or attend to special education needs)
- Emotional (e.g., inattention to a child's emotional needs, failure to provide psychological care, or permitting the child to use alcohol or other drugs)

These situations do not always mean a child is neglected. Sometimes cultural values, the standards of care in the community, and poverty can be contributing factors, indicating the family is in need of information or assistance. When a family fails to use information and resources, and the child's health or safety is at risk, then child welfare intervention might be required.

Physical abuse is physical injury (ranging from minor bruises to severe fractures or death) as a result of punching, beating, kicking, biting, shaking, throwing, stabbing, choking, hitting (with a hand, stick, strap, or other object), burning, or otherwise harming a child. Such injury is considered abuse regardless of whether the caretaker intended to hurt the child.

Sexual abuse includes activities by a parent or caretaker such as fondling a child's genitals, penetration, incest, rape, sodomy, indecent exposure, and exploitation through prostitution or the production of pornographic materials.

Emotional abuse is a pattern of behavior that impairs a child's emotional development or sense of self-worth. This can include constant criticism, threats, or rejection, as well as withholding love, support, or guidance. Emotional abuse is often difficult to prove and, therefore, CPS might not be able to intervene without evidence of harm to the child. Emotional abuse is almost always present when other forms are identified.

8.5.3 Signs and Symptoms of Child Abuse and Neglect

According to the National Clearinghouse on Child Abuse and Neglect Information, the first step in helping abused or neglected children is learning to recognize the signs of child abuse and neglect. The presence of a single sign does not prove child abuse is occurring in a family; however, when these signs appear repeatedly or in combination you should take a closer look at the situation and consider the possibility of child abuse. If you, as a health care provider, do suspect a child is being harmed, reporting your suspicions could protect the child and get help for the family. The following checklist for use in suspected cases of physical child abuse was adapted from the U.S. Department of Justice (1996).

- Have you asked about the child's family history, substance abuse or other environmental factors in the home, and the parents' marital status, employment history, or unrealistic expectations of the child?
- How could the child's behavior or the caretaker's stress have contributed to the crisis?
- Could the child do what the caretakers told you he or she did?
- Is the child a "target" child (a child perceived by the caretaker(s) as having negative characteristics), or are there target children present?
- Was there any delay in treatment or was hospital "shopping" involved?
- What are the locations, configurations, and distributions of the bruises, welts, lacerations, abrasions, or burns?
- Do the injuries appear to have been caused by the hands or an instrument? Can you determine what instrument might have been used?
- Are multiple injuries (in various stages of healing) present?
- Are the injuries in areas commonly targeted in abuse (the back, from the neck to the back of the knees including the shoulders and arms)?
- Can you determine the positions of the offender and the child during the attack?
- Is there any evidence of attempts to hold the child in a certain position or at a certain angle during the attack? Are there control marks on the wrists, forearms, or biceps?
- Was a careful check made for injuries on the head, mouth, ears, and nose?

8.5.3.1 Recognizing Child Abuse

The following signs might signal the presence of child abuse or neglect.

The child:

- Shows sudden changes in behavior or school performance.
- Has not received help for physical or medical problems brought to the parents' attention.
- Has learning problems (or difficulty concentrating) that cannot be attributed to specific physical or psychological causes.
- Is always watchful, as though preparing for something bad to happen.
- Lacks adult supervision.
- Is overly compliant, passive, or withdrawn.

The parent:

- Shows little concern for the child.
- Denies the existence of—or blames the child for—the child's problems in school or at home.
- Asks caretakers to use harsh physical discipline if the child misbehaves.
- Sees the child as entirely bad, worthless, or burdensome.
- Demands a level of physical or academic performance the child cannot achieve.
- Looks primarily to the child for care, attention, and satisfaction of emotional needs.

The parent and child:

- Rarely touch or look at each other.
- Consider their relationship entirely negative.
- State that they do not like each other.

8.5.3.2 Types of Abuse

The following are some signs often associated with particular types of child abuse and neglect: physical abuse, neglect, sexual abuse, and emotional abuse. It is important to note, however, these types of abuse are more typically found in combination rather than alone. A physically abused child, for example, is often emotionally abused as well, and a sexually abused child also might be neglected.

8.5.3.2.1 Signs of Physical Abuse

Consider the possibility of physical abuse when the child:

- Has unexplained burns, bites, bruises, broken bones, or black eyes.
- Has fading bruises or other marks noticeable after an absence from school.
- Seems frightened of the parents and protests or cries when it is time to go home.
- Shrinks at the approach of adults.
- Reports injury by a parent or another adult caregiver.

Consider the possibility of physical abuse when the parent or other adult caregiver:

- Offers conflicting, unconvincing, or no explanation for the child's injury.
- Describes the child in some negative way.
- Uses harsh physical discipline with the child.
- Has a history of abuse as a child.

Signs of Neglect

Consider the possibility of neglect when the child:

- Is frequently absent from school.
- Begs or steals food or money.
- Lacks needed medical or dental care, immunizations, or glasses.
- Is consistently dirty and has severe body odor.
- Lacks sufficient clothing for the weather.
- Abuses alcohol or other drugs.
- States that there is no one at home to provide care.

Consider the possibility of neglect when the parent or other adult caregiver:

- Appears to be indifferent to the child.
- Seems apathetic or depressed.
- Behaves irrationally or in a bizarre manner.
- Is abusing alcohol or other drugs.

Signs of Sexual Abuse

Consider the possibility of sexual abuse when the child:

- Has difficulty walking or sitting.
- Suddenly refuses to change for gym or participate in physical activities.
- Reports nightmares or bedwetting.
- Experiences a sudden change in appetite.
- Demonstrates bizarre, sophisticated, or unusual sexual knowledge or behavior.
- Becomes pregnant or contracts a venereal disease, particularly if under age 14.
- Reports sexual abuse by a parent or another adult caregiver.

Consider the possibility of sexual abuse when the parent or other adult caregiver:

- Is unduly protective of the child or severely limits the child's contact with other children, especially of the opposite sex.
- Is secretive and isolated.
- Is jealous or controlling with family members.

Signs of Emotional Maltreatment

Consider the possibility of emotional maltreatment when the child:

- Shows extremes in behavior, such as overly compliant or demanding behavior, extreme passivity, or aggression.
- Is either inappropriately adult (e.g., parenting other children) or inappropriately infantile (e.g., frequently rocking or head-banging).
- Is delayed in physical or emotional development.
- Has attempted suicide.
- Reports a lack of attachment to the parent.

Consider the possibility of emotional maltreatment when the parent or other adult caregiver:

- Constantly blames, belittles, or berates the child.
- Is unconcerned about the child and refuses to consider offers of help for the child's problems.
- Overtly rejects the child.

There are a number of more specific physical and behavioral signs and symptoms that are common indicators of child abuse and neglect. It is critical for health care providers to be able to distinguish abuse and neglect from nonintentional injury, as many of the indicators to follow can result from nonabusive incidents. The following was adapted from the Massachusetts Department of Social Services Investigation Training manual, *Evidence and Indicators of Maltreatment*.

Signs of Possible Inflicted Injury

- Unsuspected fractures "accidentally" discovered in the course of an examination
- Injuries inconsistent with, or out of proportion to the history provided or with the child's age or developmental stage

- Multiple fractures, often symmetrical, or fractures at different stages of healing; any fractures in nonambulatory children are suspicious
- Skeletal trauma combined with other types of injuries, such as burns
- Subdural hematoma
- Failure to thrive—the child may appear malnourished, chronically underweight, or be losing weight.

Bruises and Welts

- Caused by pinching or hitting the child with a hand or an object.
- Bruises of identical age and cause on the same person might not appear the same color and might not change at the same rate.
- Bruise sites: Neither the ears or buttocks are injured frequently in accidents; bruises on knees, shins, foreheads, and elbows can be either intentional or unintentional.
- Pinch bruises: Often symmetrical pattern (e.g., on each earlobe).
- Loop or belt marks: Caused by whipping the child with a looped cord (e.g., an electrical cord) or belt; no disease or accident looks like a loop or belt mark.
- Ligature bruises: Can be caused by ropes tied around the child's ankles or neck, resulting in a bruise or a burn.
- Slap marks: Fingers might leave bruises on the face. Loose tissue with little bony structure underneath (i.e., eyelids, genitals) bruise most easily and retain bruises longest.
- Genital bruises: Be suspicious if a caretaker delays seeking treatment for a child with a genital injury. Bruises in the inner thigh or genital area could indicate sexual abuse.
- Note that Mongolian spots (birthmarks) might be mistaken for abuse; these are usually grayish-blue, clearly defined spots on the buttocks, back, or extremities, and are most common in African American and American Indian babies.

Lacerations

- Occur on soft tissue areas such as abdomen, throat, buttocks, and thighs.
- Injuries to buttocks, lower back, or thighs can be caused by whipping.
- Some areas of the body are normally protected by being inside or covered by other body parts (i.e., medial aspects of extremities); it would be difficult to fall and injure these areas.
- Lacerations of the ear, nose, or throat do not tend to occur accidentally and should arouse suspicion.
- A torn frenulum of the upper lip, especially in an infant, is very concerning for abuse in the absence of a plausible history.

Bites

- Determine if bite marks are human or animal: Torn flesh is usually a dog bite, whereas compressed flesh is usually a human bite.
- If the wound is fresh, swab for possible recovery of the offender's saliva for DNA evidence.
- Human bites appear as distinctive oval to horseshoe-shaped marks in which tooth impressions appear as bruises facing each other.
- If the distance between the canines is greater than 3 cm, the bite is most likely from a human adult. Victim's teeth should be examined and measured to exclude the possibility of a self-inflicted bite.
- A forensic odontologist or pathologist should evaluate the size, contour, and color(s) of the bite marks, as well as make molds of a suspected abuser's teeth and possibly of the bite itself because each individual has a characteristic bite pattern.

Burns and Scalds

- Burns from hot water are the most common whether abusive or nonintentional.
- Accidental burns tend to be asymmetrical in distribution.
- A burn covering more than 20 percent of the body is severe regardless of the child's age; a burn covering more than 65 percent of the body can be fatal, even if it is a first-degree burn.
- Medical conditions mistaken for burns include scalded skin syndrome, impetigo, and severe diaper rash.
- Immersion burns have a "water line" or sharp demarcation border; document the absence of splash marks; symmetric burns with sharp edges are very suspicious.
- Doughnut hole burns are caused when a child is forced into a bathtub; parts of the body, usually the buttocks, rest on the bottom of the tub and thus will not burn, creating a patch of unburned skin in the center of the burn (like a doughnut hole).
- Dunking burns are caused by dunking the child into scalding water (often as punishment for wetting the bed); hands and feet are not burned

because the child is held and dunked; sharp demarcations—often called parallel lines—because the child is held but not forced to the bottom of a tub or pot on the stove (so no doughnut burn); document the absence of splash marks.

- Stocking or glove burns are caused by immersing the child's hands or feet in hot water or holding the hands or feet under very hot running water; usually shows sharp demarcation.
- Splash burns are caused by the offender throwing hot liquid at the child. Unintentional splash burns are usually on the head or top of the chest and run downward (might be caused by a child reaching upward to grab a pot handle). Liquids thrown at a child hit at a horizontal angle, so the burns will be concentrated on the child's face or chest, and will run toward the back of the body. Splash burns on the back or buttocks are highly suspicious.
- Cigarette burns usually appear on the trunk, external genitalia, or extremities, often the palms of the hands or soles of the feet; usually symmetrical in shape (impetigo blisters are irregular and can be ruled out by testing for signs of strep); often multiple burns in various stages of healing.
- Chemical burns are caused by household products. Some parents or caretakers force children to drink lye derivatives (toilet bowl cleaner, detergents, or oils), causing chemical burns of the mouth and throat, vomiting, and esophageal damage.

Fractures and Dislocations

- Fractures are usually inflicted in nonambulatory children; 90 percent of all abusive fractures in children 2 years or younger include the ribs.
- Metaphyseal fractures: A chip of the metaphysis is pulled off by a ligament; can only occur from a jerking force applied to the extremities (e.g., by shaking or swinging a child by the arms or legs).
- Spiral fracture: Diagonal fracture usually caused by the twisting of an extremity; common in children due to more pliant bones; it can occur very easily in small children by twisting their own leg or ankle in an accidental injury. Thus, spiral fractures are not necessarily indicative of abuse.
- Pelvic fractures: Double vertical fractures through superior and inferior pubic rami and sacroiliac joint dislocation on the contralateral side; do not normally result from accidental injuries.
- Periosteal elevation: Injury to this highly vascular tissue occurs when an infant's extremities are twisted or shaken, causing the periosteum to be separated from the bone and blood to collect in the new space; if symmetric, it might be a normal variant.
- Rib fractures: Can be caused by a caretaker squeezing the baby forcefully; victims might present with signs of respiratory distress, although they are usually asymptomatic.

Internal Injuries

- Injuries to internal organs are caused by blows to the abdomen or squeezing; significant violent force is required to cause a life-threatening abdominal injury.
- Only a small percentage of children receive internal injuries from abuse; for those who do, the mortality rate is 40 percent to 50 percent.
- Signs and symptoms include abdominal, chest, flank, or back pain; visible bruising of the chest or abdomen; distended, swollen abdomen; tense abdominal muscles; labored breathing or dyspnea; pleuritic pain; and nausea or vomiting. However, many children exhibit minimal symptoms after abdominal trauma.

Neurological Damage: Skull Fracture, Brain or Spinal Cord Damage, and Intracranial Hemorrhage

- Serious life-threatening cranial injuries, with the exception of epidural hematomas, do not result from a child falling from a short height such as a bed or crib.
- Skull fractures: More likely in young children—any pressure from cerebritis or hemorrhage can separate fontanelles; brain injury is more likely due to increased subdural space in young children.
- Subdural hematoma: Ruptured vessels in subdural space.
- Subgaleal hematoma: The scalp separates from the skull; often a sign of skull fracture and reason to image the skull; can be caused by jerking or twisting a child's hair—especially in girls with pigtails—and might be evident by a bald spot. (Alopecia can be caused by neglect if the child lies on his or her back for long periods of time.)

Shaken Baby Syndrome

- A child has been held around the upper thorax, under the arms, and shaken back and forth with

great force or held upside down by the feet and shaken up and down.
- Many infants die, especially if there is a delay in getting treatment; those who survive often have permanent brain damage and can be paralyzed, developmentally delayed, or develop cerebral palsy.
- There is often an absence of externally visible injuries, but retinal hemorrhage is pathognomonic; subdural hematoma and metaphyseal lesions are common.

Other Physical Injury

- Asphyxiation, suffocation, and drowning might be due to abuse.
- Blinding and eye injuries: Blows to the eyes can result in a dislocated lens and, later, to cataracts; blows to the front or back of the head can result in bilateral black eyes and massive swelling of the eyelids. Subconjunctival hemorrhage is caused by direct trauma (i.e., a blow to the face), but can be caused by birthing trauma; unrelated to retinal hemorrhage.
- Injuries to teeth, jaws, mouth, and lips: A strong blow is required to completely dislodge a tooth from its socket; injuries to the maxilla are rarely seen in accidents. Forced feeding of infants could cause bruised lips or a torn frenulum, which is pathognomonic of abuse.
- Damage to ears and hearing: Blows to the ears or pinching and twisting of the ears can result in bruised pinna.
- Hair pulling: Might see irregular patches of missing hair with broken hair visible, but no completely bald areas; be sure to distinguish from alopecia.

Poisoning

- 17 percent mortality rate, but more are nonintentional.
- Salt poisoning: Forcing a child to swallow salt (often as a punishment for bedwetting); causes hypernatremia, which can lead to dehydration, vomiting, and seizures.
- Water poisoning: Forcing a child to ingest water (often as a punishment for involuntary urination); causes hyponatremia, which can lead to convulsions, confusion, lethargy, and coma.
- Laxatives: Cause diarrhea, which can lead to severe dehydration, fever, and bloody stools.
- Sedatives: Symptoms include lethargy and coma.
- Pepper: Ingesting black pepper can damage the mucous membranes of the oropharynx and stomach and might clog the throat and lungs, which can lead to apnea.

Physical Abuse: Behavioral and Emotional Indicators

The following factors could influence the intensity and type of reaction a child has to the experience of maltreatment (although some important issues related to any one child's experience might not be included in this list):

- Parental support (willingness to entertain the possibility that sexual abuse might have occured)
- Identity of perpetrator and perpetrator's relationship with child (closer relationships are associated with longer delays in disclosure and more severe aftereffects)
- Child's age
- Child's developmental status, including whether or not the child has any developmental disabilities
- History of prior, or concurrent maltreatment, trauma, or stress
- Duration (time span) of the abuse
- Circumstances or context of the abuse (e.g., has the child been afraid, embarrassed, etc?)
- Type and intensity of abuse or neglect
- Family, social, and community support
- Child's coping strategies, and generality personal characteristics (i.e., temperament)
- A child's reactions might involve behaviors that can be observed by other people, or might simply involve the child's innermost thoughts or subjective emotional feelings. Some of the reactions to maltreatment can be similar across age groups, whereas other reactions might be more common in younger or in older children. In general, it can be difficult to differentiate children who have been abused or neglected from children who have experienced other kinds of stressful experiences. It is important to remember that research in the area of child abuse suggests that many abused children do not exhibit any obvious reactions to maltreatment. Therefore, if a child is not exhibiting concerning behaviors, but you have reason to suspect child abuse, it is strongly recommended that you consult a professional with expertise in the area of child maltreatment for guidance.

The following list includes general signs and symptoms that might sometimes be observed in maltreated children. When reviewing this list, it is very important to remember that fears and behavioral difficulties are commonly associated with normal child development. Many of the following are concerning only when behavioral changes are extreme or occur suddenly. If you have concerns, it is often helpful to consult a professional with expertise in this area.

Behavioral Indicators

- Running away from home frequently
- Staying at school beyond class time
- Threatening self-harm or suicide
- Assaulting others
- Trying to deny or hide signs of abuse
- Verbalizing a poor self-image
- Thumb sucking or nail biting
- Poor relationships with other children
- Verbal abuse of other children
- Irrational fears
- Overly compliant behavior
- Being inattentive or absent from school frequently
- Indiscriminant friendliness with strangers
- Fearfulness when other children cry and are approached by an adult
- Hypervigilance
- Rocking or uncontrollable crying
- Excessive daydreaming
- Unawareness of others
- Perfectionism
- Eating problems
- Compulsive behavior
- Never looking to caretaker(s) for comfort
- Passivity, maintaining a "low profile"
- Regression or delayed development
- Constant overactivity
- Sleep disturbances
- Doesn't expect needs to be met
- Aggressiveness
- Unusual interpretations and perceptions of others; maltreated children, especially children exposed to physical violence, might interpret innocuous or neutral interactions or situations as hostile and respond with unwarranted aggression

Emotional Indicators

- Extremely low self-esteem
- Feeling unwanted and deserving of abuse
- Irrational fears
- Blaming, placing responsibility on others
- Constant anger or temper tantrums
- Fear of family members
- Out-of-control feelings
- Constant worrying and tenseness
- Fear of leaving school
- Attribution of own feelings to others
- Depression

8.5.3.3 Munchausen Syndrome by Proxy

Dowdell and Foster (2003) say that Munchausen syndrome by proxy (MSBP), an unusual and potentially lethal form of child abuse, warrants more attention from nurses. They report that approximately 10 percent of cases are fatal and more than 25 percent involve more than one child. The syndrome is characterized by a parent, usually the mother, who induces or reports physical symptoms in a child and fabricates a corresponding history that results in unnecessary medical evaluation and treatment. Dowdell and Foster explain that parents might "commit many deceptions," such as adding their own blood, paint, or dye to a child's urine or feces so that it appears bloody, or feeding a child large amounts of salts or sugars to create an electrolyte imbalance. Parents have scraped a child's skin with a sharp object or applied irritating chemicals to cause rashes that can last for days, weeks, or even months. Parents have also administered sedatives and tranquilizers to their child to induce neurological symptoms. Dowdell and Foster write, "Only the imaginations of these parents limit the variety of believable signs and symptoms. The children not only suffer from the parents' actions, but also are subjected to an extensive array of invasive radiological, medical, and surgical procedures that are unnecessary and painful." Because unfamiliarity with MSBP might allow the abuse to continue, Dowdell and Foster say it is imperative for clinicians to recognize its victims. They write, "Because nurses can play a vital role in profiling and aiding in the diagnosis of MSBP, they must be able to identify symptoms, warning signs, and the typical characteristics of a perpetrator, as well as the psychosocial dynamics. Nurses must understand that their careful documentation of forensic evidence may be a prime factor in ultimately keeping the children safe from further harm."

The term *Munchausen syndrome* was first described by London physician Richard Asher, MD, in the 1950s to describe patients who continually fabricated false stories about themselves to receive needless medical investigations, operations, and treatments. Asher named the syndrome for a German soldier, Baron Von Munchausen, who was known for entertaining guests with his tales of unbelievable travels and brave military exploits. Munchausen syndrome by proxy was first used in 1977 to describe a condition in which parents falsified illnesses or fabricated symptoms for their children. According to the 1996 U.S. Department of Justice guide, *Child Neglect and Munchausen Syndrome by Proxy Diagnostic Criteria*, MSBP occurs when there is:

- Illness in a child that is simulated or produced by a parent or other caretaker, or both.
- Presentation of the child for medical assessment and care, usually persistently, often resulting in multiple medical procedures.
- Denial of knowledge by the parent or caretaker as to the cause of the child's illness.
- Subsiding of acute symptoms and signs when the child is separated from the parent or caretaker.

Typically, but not always, the mother spends a good deal of time at the hospital with the child and exhibits a remarkable familiarity with medical terminology. She might be "confidentially friendly" with the hospital staff and other patients, although she might show frustration with her child's chronic illness and anger at the medical staff's inadequate vigor in pursuing her child's problems. She might insist that she is the "only one" for whom the child will eat, drink, or swallow medications. If more than one child in a family dies of sudden infant death syndrome (SIDS) or of any other ill-defined disease, MSBP (i.e., homicide) along with some genetic, metabolic, environmental, and toxicological causes of death, must be considered as more likely explanations. Common presentation of MSBP and the usual methods of deception (presentation and mechanism) include the following:

- Apnea: Suffocation, drugs, poisoning, lying
- Seizures: Lying, drugs, poisons, asphyxiation
- Bleeding: Adding blood to urine, vomit, and so on; opening IV line
- Fevers, sepsis: Injecting feces, saliva, or contaminated water into child
- Vomiting: Poisoning with drugs that cause vomiting; lying
- Diarrhea: Poisoning with laxatives, salt, mineral oil

Dowdell and Foster (2003) write, "Reported cases of MSBP vary in complexity from simply fabricating symptoms, tampering with laboratory specimens, or altering health records, to using direct methods to induce symptoms. Abuse occurs when the parent seeks medical attention that subjects the child to unnecessary extensive testing and medical interventions. The spectrum of illnesses reflected in cases of MSBP is startling." According to Dowdell and Foster, there could be apnea, seizures, hematuria, bleeding from the upper respiratory tract, vomiting, diarrhea, skin infections or lesions, pyogenic arthritis, vaginal and rectal bleeding, cardio-respiratory arrests, induced seizures, and nonaccidental poisoning. One high-profile case of MSBP involved a young girl who experienced more than 200 hospitalizations and 40 surgeries, including the removal of her gall bladder, appendix, and part of her intestines, which might have been triggered by MSBP on the part of her mother.

Experts have assembled a profile of the MSBP perpetrator that reflects all socioeconomic classes, intact but highly dysfunctional families, and a higher proportion of mothers as opposed to fathers as the assailant. They believe that these mothers have experienced an emotionally deprived childhood with a high probability of a history of physical abuse, and use MSBP as a mechanism for expressing anger and fear and seeking emotional support, love, and nurturing in the context of disease and illness. Dowdell and Foster state that the health care environment

> May allow the mother to escape some of the responsibilities of parenthood and the reality of unpleasant events in her life or provide her with the attention she seeks. When confronted with a sick, young child, the health care team will turn to the mother for a history, and in an effort to provide holistic care, she will be included in decisions and treatments. This inclusion and consultation regarding her child reinforces the mother's need for attention and support. So every time the child is ill or brought in for treatment, unsuspecting nursing and medical personnel are meeting her dysfunctional psychological needs.

Experts also believe that mothers exhibiting MSBP tendencies often have medical knowledge stemming from past experience as a health care provider. Frequently, Dowdell and Foster say, MSBP perpetrators have a history of Munchausen syndrome themselves, a history of attempted suicide, or ongoing marital problems. They write, "The identification of the perpetrator's pattern of behavior is critical because, without treatment, some mothers will continue and perhaps intensify their deceptions." In many cases, perpetrators will inflict harm on a child's siblings, explaining that the illness "runs in the family." Dowdell and Foster write, "Thus, if the syndrome goes undetected in one child, the abuse is committed against the siblings as well. Between 25 percent to 33 percent of MSBP cases suggest the involvement of more than one child. This may still underrepresent cases that go undiagnosed."

MSBP presents a unique challenge to health care workers because the syndrome can take months or years to be diagnosed, experts say. Dowdell and Foster explain that MSBP cases begin at infancy or by the age of 2, and the average length of time to the diagnosis of MSBP generally exceeds six months. They write, "The victims are generally children less than six years of age, because older children are out of the home attending school and are more likely to reveal the truth about their so-called symptoms. If MSBP continues as the child ages, the victim may accommodate to the parent's deceptions." Recognizing MSBP is the responsibility of all health care providers. Dowdell and Foster state, "Nurses play a vital role in the observation and confirmation of the profile of MSBP."

Clinicians should first educate themselves about the signs and symptoms of the syndrome, as well as create a multidisciplinary team that meets regularly to conduct ongoing case reviews. Dowdell and Foster note, "These meetings should focus on fact-finding, gathering data, and building a case to establish the diagnosis. If team members feel that they are getting close to confirming a case of child abuse and/or MSBP, they may want to notify the hospital attorney, risk manager, or administrator. Law enforcement personnel may be included at this stage."

Dowdell and Foster make the following suggestions for nurses who want to ferret out possible cases of MSBP:

- Solicit a comprehensive history to determine if the history matches physical findings. "When taking a history, the nurse should ask questions to determine if the suspected perpetrator was present each time symptoms occurred, and to gather a detailed health history of the mother and family, as well as the child," Dowdell and Foster suggest.
- Scrutinize the frequency of hospitalizations, testing, and treatments.
- Observe the child carefully, looking for verbal and nonverbal clues.
- Separate the mother from the child to determine whether the symptoms continue or abate in her absence.
- Document the child's symptoms in relation to the mother's participation. For example, a nurse can collect the urine specimen from the child, eliminating the mother's opportunity to contaminate the specimen.

Dowdell and Foster write, "Steps in obtaining a thorough history and physical assessment lay the groundwork for determining the extent of the deception and the length of time involved." Following the history, nurses should launch a fact-finding mission that might include indisputable evidence, such as catching the perpetrator in the act, and video camera surveillance. "While covert video surveillance eliminates some of the problems of close observation, legal, ethical, and financial problems complicate this method," Dowdell and Foster comment. "Detailed documentation of assessments and observations is necessary for use in courts and aids in removing the child from the abusive situation, but use of video surveillance must be handled properly. Involvement of law enforcement personnel is recommended. The video becomes part of the child's medical record and may be able to be viewed in court."

"It has been more than two decades since Munchausen Syndrome by Proxy has been identified," writes Beatrice Crofts Yorker, RN, JD (1995). "MSBP continues to be one of the most bizarre and baffling forms of child abuse to all who encounter it." Yorker explains that most victims of MSBP are under the age of 6 and usually unable to verbalize their abuse. She describes the obstacles to intervention: "First, health professionals lack the awareness that an illness may be intentionally produced. Second, the mother who falsifies her child's illness usually is portrayed as a model parent. Third, securing evidence of a patient who is secretively producing symptoms is most difficult to obtain. Finally, the courts are reluctant to believe this type of abuse is occurring." Some hospitals have debated the merits of installing video cameras to capture covert, potential MSBP activity by perpetrators. Yorker says she has personally observed a videotape of a hospitalized child that showed a mother rinsing a thermometer under running water then calling the nurse to read an elevated temperature. However, this act of surveillance can run counter to the provisions of the Fourth Amendment to the U.S. Constitution, which states, "The right of the people to be secure in their persons, houses, papers, and effects, against unreasonable searches and seizures, shall not be violated and no warrants shall issue, but upon probable cause, supported by oath or affirmation, and particularly describing the place to be searched and the person or things to be seized." Yorker explains, "Evidence seized in violation of the Fourth Amendment is not admissible in court under the 'exclusionary rule' of the Fourth Amendment. Is video camera surveillance in a child's hospital room, which is intended to view the mother's action with the child, an unreasonable search and seizure?" Yorker says that the most critical factors when determining the legality of a hidden camera in a hospital room are the reasonable expectation of privacy and state action. Yorker explains that the U.S. Supreme Court recognizes exceptions to the exclusionary rule for a search warrant in exigent circumstances, such as when a suspect will destroy the evidence or there is an immediate threat to human life. She says that court cases support warrantless searches if danger to human life is imminent. "Therefore, child health care providers would argue that a mother who is suspected of smothering her child certainly poses an immediate danger to the child. Of course, arguments can be made that obtaining a warrant takes only a short time and allows for an objective legal review on the exigent circumstances."

The 1967 case of *Katz v. United States* first established the reasonable expectation of privacy, providing that where a person could reasonably expect that his or her conversation or actions would not be overheard or observed, a search warrant was necessary to listen or look in. Yorker says that the Fourth Amendment (as applied to the states and to the federal government) requires state action, meaning that actions are taken for some state purpose. For example, Yorker explains, if the police request that a health care institution videotape a particular patient room so that law enforcement can gather evidence of a crime, this would be considered as state action and would require a warrant for it to be lawful.

Yorker cautions that state and federal statutes on wiretapping vary. In general, wiretapping covers audio surveillance, with or without video; videotape without audio generally does not violate the statutes. Yorker writes, "By its very nature, a hospital is a place where patients are assessed, observed, and monitored. This can be accomplished only if patients are viewed by nurses, doctors, and other health care personnel. The mother is aware of this monitoring. This, of course, is part of the attention she craves. It should follow that the mother would have only a limited expectation of privacy in a hospital room." Yorker points to *United States v. White*, in which the Supreme Court clarified the expectation of privacy by the use of evidence of electronic surveillance in courts of law with the consent of only one party. Yorker explains that the nurse or the physician, therefore, can be considered as the consulting party. "For example, in *Avery v. State*, 292 A.2d 728 743 (MD. Ct Spec. App. 1972), a woman who was sexually assaulted by her physician was allowed to introduce evidence obtained by a hidden camera in her room," Yorker writes. Yorker continues, "Of course, a warrant by the police to video/audiotape may be applied for through the court system of the applicable state. This warrant application must specifically name the child (victim), the mother, the hospital, and all items to be seized as evidence." Yorker says such items can include body fluids, diapers, clothing, vomitus, blood, other secretions from the victim, and devices and instruments that might have inflicted bodily injury on the mother herself or others for the purpose of using these results of false injury to the victim as evidence, such as fake blood or animal blood that might represent falsely illness or injury to the child. Yorker writes, "Many other questions need to be answered when a hospital make a decision to use covert video surveillance. There are potential legal liabilities to the hospital as well as child-safety, allowable child abuse, intervention/lack of intervention, and the consequences of not initiating video surveillance." Experts have suggested that hospitals can obtain consent by adding the word *videotaping* to its consent form that parents must sign on admission to the hospital to permit medical treatment for their child, with the idea that limiting the surveillance to videotape, and not audio, is less invasive should legal questions arise. Yorker comments, "This, of course, brings up the issue of the alleged perpetrator having access to the child. If such a step is taken, investigators should be available for immediate intervention when viewing suspicious acts by the mother."

Yorker emphasizes the important role health care providers can play in identifying MSBP, but cautions that right-to-privacy issues could exist among health professionals themselves. "Child abuse is one of so many ways in which nurses are involved in forensics. The nursing staff caring for these children will also be observed (most likely unknowingly). This might be another arena of legal debate concerning employees' rights to privacy, if any." Yorker adds that nurses should be exposed to these kinds of legal issues early in the nursing curricula. "Further, to understand forensic nursing interventions, as is the case in child abuse, the nurse must have a working understanding of the applicable criminal law, its procedures, and evidence. Such education allays anxiety while fostering interdisciplinary collaboration so necessary in MSBP cases."

Dowdell and Foster (2003) write, "Every nurse needs to be aware of the forensic issues involved in MSBP. RNs are legally mandated to report any child who may be the victim or suspected victim of abuse to their city/state department of child protective services. As in any case of child abuse, the goal of treatment for MSBP is to stop the abuse and protect the child. Identifying abusive situations as early as possible is critical." The first step, they say, is ensuring the safety of the child; if he or she is in immediate danger, nurses might need to summon child advocates who can initiate the process of protective custody. Dowdell and Foster advise, "The team treating the child should be together when confronting the mother, and child protection services may also need to be present... The mother usually denies the abuse, even after being presented with the evidence. She may try to take the child out of the hospital." Dowdell and Foster acknowledge the controversial and emotional nature of MSBP and that health care providers might have difficulty believing that the individuals on whom they rely for accurate histories and proper care of children actually cause their illness. They add:

> Nurses play a vital role in the observation and confirmation of the profile of an MSBP case... Careful documentation is an important forensic aspect of these cases, as nurses will be called to testify in court regarding their observations. Nurses in many areas are in the position to break the cycle by assessment and facilitation of profiling and early identification. These interventions may be the critical link in the survival of these children.

8.5.3.4 Child Abuse Versus SIDS

According to the U.S. Department of Justice (1996) guide, *Recognizing When a Child's Injury Is Caused by Abuse*, SIDS is the "sudden death of an infant under one year which remains unexplained after a thorough case investigation, including performance of a complete autopsy, examination of the death scene, including performance of a complete autopsy, and review of the clinical history." SIDS is unexpected, usually occurring in apparently healthy infants ages 1 month to 1 year. Most deaths from SIDS occur by the end of the sixth month, with the greatest number taking place between the ages of 2 and 4 months. These are some other identifying characteristics of SIDS:

- SIDS currently cannot be predicted or prevented.
- SIDS deaths appear to cause no pain or suffering; death occurs very rapidly, usually during sleep.
- SIDS is not child abuse.
- SIDS is not caused by external suffocation.
- SIDS is not caused by vomiting and choking or by minor illnesses such as colds or infections.
- SIDS is not caused by the DPT vaccine or other immunizations.
- SIDS is not contagious.
- SIDS is not the cause of every unexplained infant death.

8.5.3.5 Shaken Baby Syndrome

Reece (2001), explains that shaken baby syndrome (also called shaken impact syndrome) is usually seen in infants under 1 year of age, but can be seen in older children as well. He reports that clinicians have seen isolated cases of shaken adult syndrome under extraordinary conditions, such as in the case of a prisoner under interrogation, or the act of violence against a woman, but the usual victim is an infant. Reece says it occurs when a person of much larger size (usually four times the weight of the victim) grasps the infant, either by the thorax, the upper arms, or the neck, and violently shakes the infant, causing the head to rotate wildly about the axis of the cervical spine. The shaking can last from three to 20 seconds, but seldom longer. The number of shakes per second varies, as do the number of oscillations of the head, depending both on the time of shaking and the rapidity. Reese says, "If the number and violence of the shakes are small, then the resultant injury to the brain and consequent symptomatology will be mild. If there are many shakes, the resultant pathology and signs and symptoms will be much more dramatic."

Reece says signs and symptoms could be so mild as to lead the diagnosing physician to look elsewhere for the cause. In a study from Denver, 173 cases of acute subdural hematoma were analyzed and it was found that in these shaken infants, there was evidence on the CT scan of both old and new subdural hematomas, indicating that there had been previous shaking episodes. When the investigators reviewed the old medical records, they found that many of these infants had been seen by physicians with mild symptoms, such as vomiting or irritability, and diagnoses of gastroenteritis, otitis media, and seizure disorder had been made. Reece says that the classic triad of subdural or subarachnoid bleeding, cerebral edema, and retinal hemorrhages is seen in the majority of cases. However, some cases might not show one of these signs, particularly retinal hemorrhages. Associated injuries, such as bruises on the upper arms or thorax where the child was held during shaking, or rib fractures, might be present but are often absent, making the presence of external evidence of trauma an unreliable sign. Injuries to the neck muscles or cervical spine are extremely rare in shaken baby syndrome, probably because of the underdevelopment of these structures in this age group. Reece advises that the use of head CT to diagnose intracranial bleeding or cerebral injury is the best approach in the ED; MR might be a good complementary study afterward. Experts say that skeletal surveys should be obtained on all children under the age of 2 years in which there is suspicion of physical abuse, and at some point in the workup of the suspected shaken baby case, but it can wait until the child is stable. Inflicted abusive visceral injuries commonly involve the hollow viscera more than solid organs. Intramural hematomas of the duodenum and jejunum are commonly the result of blunt injury to the upper abdomen and result from a blow from a fist, foot, or blunt instrument such as a stick. Hollow viscera and the pancreas are seldom injured from falls onto flat surfaces, but are commonly the result of blunt trauma to the abdomen. Injuries to the hypopharynx are rarer, but are usually easily diagnosed because of subcutaneous air in the neck and mediastinum, and because of gagging, coughing and, hemoptysis. Fever might be present because of mediastinitis. Injuries to the heart, particularly the left atrium, can be caused by a sharp blow to the chest, and Reece says an occasional child has died because of commotio cordis, where a blow to the sternum has produced cardiac standstill because of an interruption in the cardiac electrical cycle.

8.5.4 Other Clinical Considerations Related to Child Abuse and Neglect: A Brief Review of the Literature

There are a number of other clinical issues related to child abuse and neglect of which health care providers should be aware.

8.5.4.1 Intentional Burns and Scalds

Daria et al. (2004) explain that experience with several previously unreported, intentional face-first immersion burns led them to evaluate the distribution of inflicted and unintentional immersion scald burns in a hospital series. The researchers examined cases presenting to the burn center at a regional level-one trauma hospital. Their subjects were consecutive hospitalized scald burn victims younger than 5 years old, seen from January 1996 to March 2000. The researchers conducted a retrospective records review and described six cases of inflicted head and neck immersion injury. Four were caused by tap water and two were caused by food or drink scalds. Twenty-two of 195 hospitalized victims had sustained immersion burns, 13 from tap water and nine from other fluids. Six (46 percent) tap water immersions and no (0 percent) other immersions had inflicted injuries. Two of the tap water immersions and one other source immersion included burning of the head and neck; of these, one tap water immersion, but no other immersion, was inflicted. In no patients were head and neck injuries the sole or predominant site of scalding, according to the researchers. In all, nine children sustained inflicted scalds. Bilateral lower extremity tap water immersion scalds occurred in 100 percent (six cases) of abusive injuries and 29 percent (two) of unintentional injuries. Buttock and perineal injuries occurred in 67 percent inflicted versus 29 percent unintentional tap water immersion scalds. Other fluids caused bilateral lower extremity immersion burns in 33 percent of unintentionally injured patients, but no abused children. The researchers concluded that craniofacial immersion injury, although seen in legal cases, is infrequent; it was present incidentally in one inflicted tap water burn in the consecutive hospital series. The researchers say this series affirms the predominance of bilateral lower extremity burns in inflicted tap water immersions. Buttock and perineal immersions were more common with abuse than with unintentional injury.

8.5.4.2 Bruises

Sugar, Taylor, and Feldman (1999) sought to determine the frequency and location of bruises in normal infants and toddlers, and to determine the relationship of age and developmental stage to bruising. They conducted a cross-sectional survey in community primary care pediatric offices of children younger than 36 months attending well-child visits. The researchers found bruises in 203 (20.9 percent) of 973 children who had no known medical cause for bruising and in whom abuse was not suspected. Two (0.6 percent) of 366 children who were younger than 6 months, and eight (1.7 percent) of 473 children younger than 9 months had any bruises. Bruises were noted in 11 (2.2 percent) of 511 children who were not yet walking with support (cruising). However, 17.8 percent of cruisers and 51.9 percent of walkers had bruises. The average bruise frequency ranged from 1.3 bruises per injured child among precruisers (range of 1–2 bruises) to 2.4 per injured child among walkers (range of 1–11 bruises). The most frequent site of bruises was over the anterior tibia and knee. Bruises on the forehead and upper leg were common among walkers, but bruises on the face and trunk were rare, and bruises on the hands and buttocks were not observed at any age. The researchers concluded that bruises are rare in normal infants and precruisers, and become common among cruisers and walkers. Bruises in infants younger than 9 months who are not yet beginning to ambulate should lead to consideration of abuse or illness as the cause. Bruises in toddlers that are located in atypical areas, such as the trunk, hands, or buttocks, should prompt similar concerns.

8.5.4.3 Head Injury

Head injury is the leading cause of death in abused children under 2 years of age, and some experts assert that evidence for establishing guidelines regarding screening for occult head injury in a neurologically asymptomatic child with other evidence of abuse is lacking. This is particularly important, they say, given that many children with acute inflicted head injury have evidence of old injury when they are diagnosed.

Rubin et al. (2003) endeavored to estimate the prevalence of occult head injury in a high-risk sample of abused children with normal neurological examinations. The study's sample consisted of children under 2 years of age admitted to an urban children's hospital between January 1998 and December 2001 with injuries suspicious for child abuse. Subjects were selected if they met one high-risk criteria of rib fractures, multiple fractures, facial injury, or age less than 6 months. Subjects were excluded if they had a history of neurological dysfunction, seizures, respiratory arrest, or if their initial physical examination revealed scalp injury. Of the 65 patients who met these criteria, the researchers found that 51 (78.5 percent) had a head CT or MRI in addition to skeletal survey. Of these 51 patients, 19 (37.3 percent) had an occult head injury. Injuries included scalp swelling (74 percent), skull fracture (74 percent), and intracranial injury (53 percent). All except three of the head-injured patients had at least a skull fracture or intracranial injury. Skeletal survey alone missed 26 percent of the cases. Head-injured children were younger than nonhead-injured children (average age 2.5 vs. 5.1 months); all but one head-injured child was less than 1 year of age. Among the head-injured children, 72 percent came from single-parent households, 37 percent had mothers whose age was younger than 21 years, and 26 percent had a history of prior child welfare involvement in their families. Ophthalmologic examination was performed in 14 of the 19 cases; no retinal hemorrhages were noted. The researchers said that their results support a recommendation for universal screening in neurologically asymptomatic abused children with any of the high-risk criteria used in their study, particularly if that child is under 1 year of age. They added that ophthalmologic examination is a poor screening method for occult head injury, and that CT or MRI is a preferred screening tool. Given the high prevalence of occult head injury detected in their study, they believe that further study is warranted to estimate the prevalence of occult head injury in lower risk populations of abused children.

Abused children might have hidden head injuries that go undetected by routine examination and screening, according to research from The Children's Hospital of Philadelphia. The researchers recommend that health care personnel perform brain scans to screen for occult head injuries in children with suspected abuse injuries who are less than six months of age or who present with high-risk injuries, including rib fractures, multiple skeletal fractures, or facial injuries. The research team found that children with suspected high-risk child abuse injuries had a high incidence of occult head injuries, even when their neurological examinations were otherwise normal. Those head injuries, such as scalp swelling, skull fractures, and more serious intracranial injuries, were often missed by routine physical, neurological, and ophthalmologic exams and skeletal surveys, but were detected by brain scans, which are not universally used for screening in this high-risk population. The study was the first to estimate the prevalence of occult head injury in a high-risk cohort of abused children.

"Head injury is the leading cause of death among abused children under age two years," says David M. Rubin, MD, MSCE, a physician at Safe Place: The Center for Child Protection and Health at The Children's Hospital of Philadelphia, and lead author of the study. "Because asymptomatic head injury can be difficult to diagnose, especially in young children, it is necessary to use additional measures to determine which children have sustained these injuries so we can intervene early to prevent death, long-term neurological damage or future abuse." Children's Hospital researchers studied hospital records for 51 children under age two who presented to The Children's Hospital of Philadelphia with suspected abuse injuries between 1998 and 2001. Patients were included if they had one of the following "high-risk" characteristics or injuries: age less than six months for any abusive injury, rib fractures, more than one fracture of any type, or facial injury. The children underwent routine screening measures and a brain scan using CT or MRI technology. Also, patients included in the study had normal neurological examination on admission and showed no overt signs of head injuries. Of the 51 patient records with complete data, 19 (37 percent) showed signs of occult head injuries, with more than half suffering from intracranial injuries. Skeletal survey alone missed five of the 19 children with an occult head injury. An ophthalmologic examination was performed on 14 patients to determine the presence of retinal hemorrhages, a sign of head trauma. No evidence of hemorrhage was present in any of the children, suggesting ophthalmologic exam is not an accurate screening measure for occult head injury in asymptomatic children. Children with head injury were also found to be younger than children without head injury, with all but one of the head-injured children less than one year of age. The study results support a recommendation for universal CT or MRI screening in all children under six months of age with any signs of abuse and children under one year of age with high-risk injuries, including rib fractures, multiple fractures, and facial injuries. "Additional research is also needed to help determine the presence of occult head injury in the broader population of children who are abused, and whether universal or targeted screening would be most appropriate," adds Cindy W. Christian, MD, medical director of Safe Place and coauthor of the study. "Thanks to past research, there has for a long time been an effective universal recommendation that children under age two years who have acute head injury should be screened for hidden fractures, but no comparable guidelines have existed for head injury screening," said Rubin. "We are hopeful that this study sets the stage for new guidelines to better diagnose, treat, and protect these children."

8.5.4.4 Fractures

A recent Children's Hospital Medical Center of Cincinnati study is helping child abuse experts evaluate alleged cases of child physical abuse. The study found that follow-up X-rays of alleged victims taken two or more weeks after the original evaluation yielded additional information—in some cases previously undetected broken bones—in 48 percent of cases studied. Because of the study, Cincinnati Children's now takes follow-up X-rays of virtually all alleged victims of child physical abuse who are evaluated at the medical center. "Many injuries are hard to pick up on initial examination," says Stephanie Zimmerman, MD, an emergency medicine physician at Cincinnati Children's Hospital. "But if there has been an injury to bone, new bone builds up around the injured area. Two weeks later, you can see those that have healed, enabling us to pick up the injury a second time." The researchers studied 27 children under the age of four who were suspected victims of physical child abuse. Two weeks after their initial examination, identical X-rays were taken again, except for X-rays of the skull, which were omitted. These follow-up X-rays yielded new information in 13 of the 27 cases. Fourteen previously undetected fractures were seen on the follow-up studies of seven patients. In addition, the initial X-rays of nine children revealed 11 possible extremity fractures and five possible rib fractures. Follow-up examinations, however, confirmed only three extremity fractures. In four cases, the impression of child abuse was reversed based on the findings of the follow-up X-rays, according to Zimmerman. "Repeat skeletal surveys are a valuable addition in the evaluation of alleged child physical abuse," Zimmerman adds. "Because these radiographs may reveal new fractures and/or clarify questionable fractures, physicians will be able to more accurately diagnose or exclude child physical abuse."

8.5.4.5 Criterion for Diagnosing Child Abuse Based on Faulty Evidence

At least one of the "definitive" criteria used to diagnose child abuse might be wrong, report researchers from Wake Forest University Baptist Medical Center in the March 2004 issue of the *British Medical Journal*. "If you read the medical literature, certain eye findings have been considered diagnostic for shaken baby syndrome," says Patrick E. Lantz, MD, a forensic pathologist at Wake Forest University Baptist Medical Center. "This isn't supported by objective scientific evidence and could result in innocent caregivers going to jail." Lantz and colleagues researched published reports about perimacular retinal folds, which is a buckling of the retina, the light-sensitive membrane that lines the back of the eye. The injury has been reported in shaken baby syndrome, caused by vigorous shaking of an infant or young child. The shaking can cause bleeding around the brain and in the eyes, resulting in blindness, and can also result in brain damage leading to death. "Statements in the medical literature indicate that perimacular retinal folds result from the movement of the gel within the eye when an infant or young child is shaken, and that they have no other cause in young children with head injuries," said Lantz. "But our literature review showed that this conclusion is not based on scientifically valid comparative or experimental studies." Lantz and colleagues researched the issue after being involved in the case of a 14-month-old-child who died with perimacular retinal folds and other injuries. The child's father reported that a television set had toppled over, landing on the child's head. However, because of the diagnosis of perimacular retinal folds and hemorrhages, CPS suspected child abuse and removed a sibling from the home. "Our investigation found no indication of child abuse other than the eye findings," said Lantz.

A review of the current medical literature showed that the condition has been reported in cases of shaken baby syndrome. However, no studies have compared whether the condition is also present in similar accidental head injuries in young children. "Some physicians observed perimacular retinal folds in diagnosed cases of shaken baby syndrome and jumped to conclusions," said Lantz. In the case of the 14-month-old child, an investigation by police, a child abuse specialist, and a medical examiner corroborated the father's report and the sibling was returned to the home. "We found that the eye findings in this case were caused by an accident," said Lantz:

> But when you read the current medical literature, the presence of perimacular retinal folds and hemorrhages in a young child with a serious head injury are considered diagnostic for shaken baby syndrome and cannot be from anything else. When physicians read that, they may stop investigating other potential causes, which could have serious consequences. Until good scientific evidence is available, we urge caution in interpreting eye finds out of context.

Lantz said the 14-month-old child also had other eye injuries that some professionals consider diagnostic for child abuse. He said the evidence base for these assumptions has problems similar to the evidence surrounding perimacular retinal folds and could also lead to false allegations.

8.5.5 Risk and Protective Factors for Child Abuse and Neglect

The U.S. Department of Health and Human Services Administration for Children and Families (2003) white paper, *Emerging Practices in the Prevention of Child Abuse and Neglect,* provides health care providers with a solid overview of risk and protective factors for child abuse and neglect. Most experts attribute the cause of child maltreatment to four sources: the child, the family, the community, and society. Although children are not responsible for the abuse inflicted on them, certain child characteristics have been found to increase the risk or potential for maltreatment. Children with disabilities or mental retardation, for example, are significantly more likely to be abused, according to Crosse et al. (1993) and Schilling and Schinke (1984). Evidence also suggests that age and gender are predictive of maltreatment risk. Younger children are more likely to be neglected, whereas the risk for sexual abuse increases with age, suggest Mraovick and Wilson (1999). Female children and adolescents are significantly more likely than males to suffer sexual abuse. Important characteristics of the family are linked with child maltreatment.

Families in which there is substance abuse are more likely to experience abuse or are at a higher risk of abuse (Ammerman et al., 1999; Besinger, Garland, Litrownik, & Landsverk, 1999). However, identifying families in which substance abuse is present can be difficult. The Child Welfare League of America (2001) recently found that substance abuse is present in 40 percent to 80 percent of families in which children are abuse victims.

Recent studies also have established a link between having a history of childhood abuse and becoming a victimizer later in life, including Clarke et al. (1999), confirming some of the earliest work in the field. DiLillo, Tremblay, and Peterson (2000) found that childhood sexual abuse increased the risk of perpetrating physical abuse on children as adults. Domestic violence and lack of parenting or communication skills also increase the risks of maltreatment to children.

Factors related to the community and the larger society also are linked with child maltreatment. Poverty, for example, has been linked with maltreatment, particularly neglect, in each of the national incidence studies (Sedlak & Broadhurst, 1996), has been associated with child neglect by Black (2000), and has been found to be a strong predictor of substantiated child maltreatment by Lee and Goerge (1999). Bishop and Leadbeater (1999) found that abusive mothers reported fewer friends in their social support networks, less contact with friends, and lower ratings of quality support received from friends. Violence and unemployment are other community-level variables that have been found to be associated with child maltreatment. Perhaps the least understood and studied level of child maltreatment is that of societal factors. Ecological theories postulate that factors such as the narrow legal definitions of child maltreatment, the social acceptance of violence (as evidenced by video games, television and films, and music lyrics), and political or religious views that value noninterference in families above all may be associated with child maltreatment (Tzeng, Jackson, & Karlson, 1991).

8.5.5.1 Protective Factors

Researchers, practitioners, and policymakers are now increasingly thinking about protective factors within children and families that can reduce risks, build family capacity, and foster resilience. In 1987, case studies of three victims of child maltreatment began to shed light on the dynamics of survival in high-risk settings. Resilience in maltreated children was found to be related to personal characteristics including a child's ability to recognize danger and adapt, distance oneself from intense feelings, create relationships that are crucial for support, and project oneself into a time and place in the future in which the perpetrator is no longer present (Mrazek & Mrazek, 1987). Since then, researchers have continued to explore why certain children with risk factors become victims and other children with the same factors do not.

What are the factors that appear to protect children from the risks of maltreatment? In a recent overview by the Family Support Network, factors that might protect children from maltreatment include child factors, parent and family factors, and social and environmental factors. Child factors that might protect children include good health, above-average intelligence, hobbies or interests, good peer relationships, an easy temperament, a positive disposition, an active coping style, positive self-esteem, good social skills, an internal locus of control, and a balance between seeking help and autonomy. Parent and family protective factors that might protect children include secure attachment with children, parental reconciliation with their own childhood history of abuse, supportive family environment, household rules and monitoring of the child, extended family support, stable relationship with parents, family expectations of prosocial behavior, and high levels of parental education. Social and environmental risk factors that might protect children include middle to high socioeconomic status, access to health care and social services, consistent parental employment, adequate housing, family participation in a religious faith, good schools, and supportive adults outside the family who serve as role models or mentors (Family Support Network, 2002). Some recent studies have found that families with two married parents encounter more stable home environments, fewer years in poverty, and diminished material hardship (Lerman, 2002). The following sections include a summary of common risk and protective factors for child abuse and neglect.

8.5.5.2 Child Risk Factors

- Premature birth, birth anomalies, low birth weight, exposure to toxins in utero
- Temperament: Difficult or slow to warm up
- Physical, cognitive, or emotional disability; chronic or serious illness
- Childhood trauma
- Antisocial peer group
- Age
- Child aggression, behavior problems, attention deficits

8.5.5.3 Parental and Family Risk Factors

- Personality factors
- External locus of control
- Poor impulse control
- Depression or anxiety
- Low tolerance for frustration
- Feelings of insecurity
- Lack of trust
- Insecure attachment with own parents
- Childhood history of abuse
- High parental conflict, domestic violence
- Family structure: Single parent with lack of support, high number of children in household
- Social isolation, lack of support
- Parental psychopathology
- Substance abuse
- Separation or divorce, especially high-conflict divorce
- Age
- High general stress level
- Poor parent–child interaction, negative attitudes and attributions about child's behavior
- Inaccurate knowledge and expectations about child development

8.5.5.4 Social and Environmental Risk Factors

- Low socioeconomic status
- Stressful life events
- Lack of access to medical care, health insurance, adequate child care, and social services
- Parental unemployment; homelessness
- Social isolation and lack of social support
- Exposure to racism and discrimination
- Poor schools
- Exposure to environmental toxins

- Dangerous or violent neighborhood
- Community violence

8.5.5.5 Child Protective Factors

- Good health, history of adequate development
- Above-average intelligence
- Hobbies and interests
- Good peer relationships
- Personality factors
- Easy temperament
- Positive disposition
- Active coping style
- Positive self-esteem
- Good social skills
- Internal locus of control
- Balance between help seeking and autonomy

8.5.5.6 Parental and Family Protective Factors

- Secure attachment; positive and warm parent–child relationship
- Supportive family environment
- Household rules and structure; parental monitoring of child
- Extended family support and involvement, including caregiving help
- Stable relationship with parents
- Parents have a model of competence and good coping skills
- Family expectations of prosocial behavior
- High parental education

8.5.5.7 Social and Environmental Protective Factors

- Mid- to high socioeconomic status
- Access to health care and social services
- Consistent parental employment
- Adequate housing
- Family religious faith participation
- Good schools
- Supportive adults outside of family who serve as role models and mentors to child

8.5.6 Mandatory Reporting of Child Abuse

All 50 states have passed some form of mandatory child abuse and neglect reporting legislation to qualify for funding under CAPTA. This key piece of federal legislation addressing child abuse and neglect was originally enacted in 1974. This act was amended several times and was most recently amended and reauthorized on June 25, 2003, by the Keeping Children and Families Safe Act of 2003. CAPTA provides federal funding to states in support of prevention, assessment, investigation, prosecution, and treatment activities. It also provides grants to public agencies and nonprofit organizations for demonstration programs and projects. Additionally, CAPTA identifies the federal role in supporting research, evaluation, technical assistance, and data collection activities; establishes the Office on Child Abuse and Neglect; and mandates the National Clearinghouse on Child Abuse and Neglect Information. CAPTA also sets forth a minimum definition of child abuse and neglect. The complete text of the law (U.S. Code title 42, chapter 67) can be downloaded from the Cornell University Legal Information Institute Web site at www.4.law.cornell.edu/ uscode/42/ch67.html.

All states require certain professionals and institutions to report suspected child abuse, including health care providers and facilities of all types, mental health care providers of all types, teachers and other school personnel, social workers, day care providers, and law enforcement personnel. Many states require commercial film developers to report photographs depicting or containing incidences of abuse. Failure to report suspected child abuse can result in criminal liability, although the liability is typically a misdemeanor punishable by a fine. Failure to report also can result in civil liability. CAPTA requires states to enact legislation that provides for immunity from prosecution arising out of the reporting of abuse or neglect. In most states, a person who reports suspected child abuse in good faith is absolutely immune from criminal and civil liability. For that reason, "most health care attorneys will advise a client that it is much better, in theory, to be faced with defending a civil action for reporting suspected abuse rather than the bleak alternative of defending a civil action if a child is injured or killed as a result of failing to make a report of suspected child abuse," according to attorneys Jennifer L. Cox and Jennifer A. Osowiecki in *Mandatory Reporting: Hidden Dangers*.

False reporting also is addressed. The 1993 CAPTA amendments require states to enact legislation providing for prosecution in false-reporting cases, or reports made without a reasonable belief that the report is true. The false-reporting laws must be read together with the immunity statutes and case law; however, persons who report in good faith are immune from civil and criminal liability. As a matter of public policy, prosecutors should be extremely selective in initiating false reporting prosecutions so that reporting is not discouraged.

In recent years, increased attention has been focused on children who might be impacted by violence in the home, either as direct victims or as witnesses to domestic violence. Although mandatory reporting laws have been the primary means for protecting abused and neglected children, many states now provide additional protection for children in their domestic violence laws. Domestic violence can be defined generally as "a pattern of assaultive and/or coercive behaviors, including physical, sexual, and emotional abuse, as well as economic coercion, that adults use against their intimate partners to gain power and control in that relationship" (Schecter & Edleson, 1999). All jurisdictions in the United States have laws that define domestic or family violence. In some states, domestic violence is defined broadly with terms such as abuse, harassment, threats of harm, or intimidation. In other states, the definition can include more specific behaviors such as burglary, criminal trespass, arson, sexual assault, or violation of a protective order.

The persons protected by domestic violence laws can include spouses or former spouses, persons who live or have lived together or have a dating relationship, or other family or household members. According to the National Clearinghouse on Child Abuse and Neglect Information (as of March 2004), 40 states, the District of Columbia, and the U.S. territories of Guam, Northern Mariana Islands, and Puerto Rico include children as a class of protected persons in some way within their definitions of domestic violence. Colorado, Iowa, Kansas, Massachusetts, New Hampshire, New Jersey, Oregon, South Carolina, Wisconsin, and Wyoming do not currently include children in their definitions of domestic violence. Most commonly, a child who is a member of the household or a child of either adult in the relationship is protected by the law. Five states (Arizona, Hawaii, Ohio, Utah, and Vermont) include child abuse in their definition of domestic violence. Four states (Arizona, North Carolina, Virginia, and Washington) specifically include grandchildren as protected persons, and three states (Georgia, Louisiana, and Texas) include foster children. A small number of states provide exceptions for certain acts in their definitions of domestic violence. The most common exception, in seven states (Delaware, Indiana, Louisiana, Michigan, North Carolina, North Dakota, and Texas provide this exception) and Guam, is for acts of self-defense. Guam also exempts defense of others, and Delaware and Louisiana exempt acts committed in defense of a child. Three states, Georgia, Illinois, and Maryland, provide an exception for reasonable acts of discipline of a child. Verbal abuse or argument is exempted by Connecticut. The National Clearinghouse on Child Abuse and Neglect Information is legislatively mandated to maintain information about mandatory reporting statutes and child abuse prevention laws in all 50 states. For more information, access http://nccanch.acf.hhs.gov/.

Emalee Flaherty, MD, head of the Protective Services Team at Children's Memorial Hospital in Illinois, recently completed a year-long study evaluating the office-based practitioner's experience identifying and reporting injuries caused by child abuse. Child abuse is a primary cause of death for young children and results in serious injury for more than 500,000 children each year. Although medical personnel are responsible for the largest percentage of reports from mandated reports to the Illinois State Central Register, only a handful of these reports come from office-based physicians. The study's objective was to evaluate primary care health providers' self-reported experiences in reporting abused children to CPS. Eighty-five providers, including 76 physicians, eight nurse practitioners, and one physician assistant completed the survey. Thirty-five (42 percent) providers reported that they had not reported any cases of suspected abuse in the preceding 12 months. The remaining providers reported having detected a total of 152 cases of child abuse. Seven (5 percent) providers who saw at least one child with suspected abuse did not report the case to CPS, meaning a total of seven children were not reported. "We were told that the number one reason why providers did not report their findings is that they were not sure the injury was caused by abuse. They also said they could intervene more effectively than CPS," Flaherty says. "Although the providers indicated that CPS workers responded promptly and professionally, they felt that 63 percent of children and 47 percent of families had not benefited from CPS intervention. Only a third of providers indicated that they were kept informed by CPS concerning the progress and disposition of the investigation. Forty-nine percent of providers stated that their experience would make them less willing to report future cases." Although previous efforts at improving child abuse reporting have focused exclusively on improved case identification, this study suggests that improving the health care provider's experience with CPS could result in more frequent reporting of suspected child abuse (Flaherty, 2000).

8.5.7 Two Important National Reports on Child Abuse and Neglect

Two studies (from 1996 and from 2002) of significant merit are presented in the following section as a means to present some of the most current data on child abuse and neglect.

8.5.7.1 The 1996 National Incidence Study

In the 1996 report *Third National Incidence Study of Child Abuse and Neglect* issued by the U.S. Department of Health and Human Services, authors Andrea J. Sedlak, PhD, and Diane D. Broadhurst, MLA, document the national incidence of child abuse and neglect through the congressionally mandated Third National Incidence Study of Child Abuse and Neglect (NIS-3). The National Incidence Study (NIS) is a congressionally mandated, periodic effort of the National Center on Child Abuse and Neglect. The first NIS (NIS-1) was conducted in 1979 and 1980 and published in 1981. The second NIS (NIS-2) was conducted in 1986 and 1987 and published in 1988. The NIS-3 data were collected in 1993 and 1994, analyses conducted in 1995 and 1996, and results published in 1996.

A key objective of the NIS-3 was to provide updated estimates of the incidence of child abuse and neglect in the United States and measure changes in incidence from the earlier studies. The NIS-3 findings are based on a nationally representative sample of more than 5,600 professionals in 842 agencies serving 42 counties. The NIS-3 used two sets of standardized definitions of abuse and neglect. Under the Harm Standard, children identified in the study were considered to be maltreated only if they had experienced harm from abuse or neglect. Under the Endangerment Standard, children who experienced abuse or neglect that put them at risk of harm were included in the set of those considered to be maltreated, together with the already-harmed children. The NIS-3 offers an important perspective on the scope of child abuse and neglect. The NIS includes children who were investigated by CPS agencies, but it also obtains data on children seen by community professionals who were not reported to CPS or who were screened out by CPS without investigation. This means that the NIS estimates provide a more comprehensive measure of the scope of child abuse and neglect known to community professionals, including abused and neglected children who are both in the official statistics and those who are not.

Like the NIS-1 and NIS-2 before it, the NIS-3 employed a sentinel survey methodology, in which community professionals serving children and families in various categories of non-CPS agencies were also recruited into the study. In each county, these sentinels were a representative sample of all professional staff who were likely to come into contact with maltreated children in police and sheriffs' departments, public schools, day care centers, hospitals, voluntary social service agencies, mental health agencies, and the county juvenile probation and public health departments. The participating sentinels in the NIS-3 were 5,612 professionals in 800 non-CPS agencies who remained on the lookout for maltreated children during the study period. The NIS-3 provides important insights about the incidence and distribution of child abuse and neglect and about changes in incidence since the previous studies. This section examines these findings that might be useful to health care providers and other professionals studying child abuse and neglect.

Incidence

There have been substantial and significant increases in the incidence of child abuse and neglect since the last national incidence study was conducted in 1986. The total number of children seriously injured and the total number endangered both quadrupled during this time.

Estimated Incidence as Defined by the Harm Standard

An estimated 1,553,800 children in the United States were abused or neglected under the Harm Standard in 1993. The NIS-3 total reflects a 67 percent increase since the NIS-2 estimate, which indicated that the total was 931,000 children in 1986, and it corresponds to a 149 percent increase since the NIS-1 estimate for 1980 of 625,100 children. Significant or close-to-significant increases were found in both abuse and neglect. The number of abused children who were countable under the Harm Standard rose by 46 percent from an estimated 507,700 in the NIS-2 to 743,200 in the NIS-3. The number of neglected children who fit the Harm Standard increased significantly from 474,800 during the NIS-2 data collection in 1986 to 879,000 at the time of the NIS-3 data period in 1993. Considering specific types of abuse and neglect as defined by the Harm Standard, significant increases since the NIS-2 were found in the incidence of sexual abuse, physical neglect, and emotional neglect, and a close-to-significant (i.e., statistically marginal) increase was observed in the incidence of physical abuse:

- The estimated number of sexually abused children under the Harm Standard rose from 119,200 in 1986 to 217,700 in 1993 (an 83 percent increase).
- The number of physically neglected children under the Harm Standard increased from an estimated 167,800 at the time of the NIS-2 to an estimated 338,900 in the NIS-3 (a 102 percent rise in incidence).
- There was a 333 percent increase in the estimated number of emotionally neglected children using the Harm Standard, from 49,200 in the NIS-2 to 212,800 in the NIS-3.
- The estimated number of physically abused children under the Harm Standard was 269,700 at the time of the NIS-2, but it had increased to 381,700 during the NIS-3 (a 42 percent increase).

When these abused and neglected children were classified according to the injury or harm they suffered from maltreatment that fit the Harm Standard, there was a substantial and significant increase in the incidence of children who were seriously harmed and a statistically marginal increase in the number for whom injury could be inferred due to the severe nature of their maltreatment. The estimated number of seriously injured children essentially quadrupled from 141,700 to 565,000 in the intervening seven years between the NIS-2 and the NIS-3 (a 299 percent increase). The number for whom injury could be inferred increased from an estimated 105,500 children in the NIS-2 to an estimated 165,300 children in the NIS-3 (a 57 percent increase).

Estimated Incidence Using the Endangerment Standard

Between 1986 and 1993, the total estimated number of abused and neglected children in the United States who fit the Endangerment Standard nearly doubled: In 1986, there were an estimated 1,424,400 abused and neglected children in the United States. The NIS-3 estimate of 2,815,600 reflects a 98 percent increase over the NIS-2 figure. Significant increases were found in both abuse and neglect. The number of abused children more than doubled from an estimated 590,800 to 1,221,800 (a 107 percent increase), and the estimated number of neglected children also more than doubled from 917,200 to 1,961,300 (a 114 percent increase). The increases were substantial and significant for all types of abuse and neglect except educational neglect:

- The estimated number of physically abused children rose from 311,500 to 614,100 (a 97 percent increase).
- The estimated number of sexually abused children increased from an estimated 133,600 children to 300,200 (a 125 percent increase).
- The more recent estimate of the number of emotionally abused children was 183 percent higher than the previous estimate (188,100 in 1986 vs. 532,200 in 1993).
- The estimated number of physically neglected children increased from 507,700 to 1,335,100 (a 163 percent increase)
- The estimated number of emotionally neglected children nearly tripled in the interval between the studies, rising from 203,000 in 1986 to 585,100 in 1993 (a 188 percent increase).

When the children whose abuse or neglect met the Endangerment Standard were classified according to the injury or harm they suffered, significant increases were evident in two categories. First, the 1993 estimate of the number of children who were endangered by their maltreatment (but not yet harmed) was more than four times the corresponding 1986 estimate. That is, the number of endangered children rose from an estimated 254,000 in 1986 to an estimated 1,032,000 in 1993 (a 306 percent increase). Second, the number of children who were seriously injured or harmed by abuse or neglect that fit the Endangerment Standard in 1993 was well over half a million, which is nearly quadruple the 1986 estimate for this category. In 1986, an estimated 143,300 children had been seriously injured by abuse or neglect; in 1993, the figure was 569,900 children (a 298 percent increase). Note that nearly all (99 percent) of the children who counted as seriously injured here were also countable under the Harm Standard, so the near-quadrupling of their numbers since 1986 essentially reiterates what was already reported in connection with the Harm Standard.

Distribution of Child Abuse and Neglect by the Child's Characteristics

- Girls were sexually abused three times more often than boys.
- Boys had a greater risk of emotional neglect and of serious injury than girls.
- Children are consistently vulnerable to sexual abuse from age three on.
- There were no significant race differences in the incidence of maltreatment or maltreatment-related injuries uncovered in either the NIS-2 or the NIS-3.

Child's Sex

Girls were sexually abused about three times more often than boys, under both the Harm Standard and the Endangerment Standard. This finding reiterates the NIS-2 result, so girls' disproportionately greater risk of sexual abuse has been stable over time. This sex difference in incidence rates of sexual abuse leads to higher rates of abuse in general among girls. Also, because the definitional guidelines permit the inference that injury or harm occurred in connection with the more extreme forms of sexual abuse, girls' greater risk of sexual abuse also accounts for their higher incidence rates for inferred injury.

At the same time, boys had higher incidence rates than girls in some arenas, and boys' maltreatment risks also demonstrated some increases since the NIS-2. Boys were at somewhat greater risk of serious injury (24 percent higher than girls' risk under both definitional standards), and boys were significantly more likely to be emotionally neglected (boys' risk was 18 percent greater than girls'). Also, boys' rates of physical neglect defined by the Harm Standard and of emotional abuse using the Endangerment Standard increased more since the NIS-2 than girls' rates did. Moreover, trends in the incidence of fatal injuries from maltreatment moved in opposite directions for girls and boys; the incidence of fatally injured girls declined slightly since the NIS-2, whereas the incidence of fatally injured boys rose.

Child's Age

A consistent feature of the age differences in incidence rates within the NIS-3 was the lower incidence of maltreatment among the younger children under both definitional standards. In most cases, the differentiation was between the 0- to 2-year-olds and older children or between the 0- to 5-year-olds and older children. It is possible that the lower rates at these younger ages reflect undercoverage of these age groups. That is, prior to attaining school age, children are less observable to community professionals. Another recurring theme in connection with age is that of disproportionate increases in the incidence of maltreatment among the younger children (under 12 years old) and especially among children in their middle-childhood years (ages 6–11). Note that as circumstances deteriorate and maltreatment becomes more prevalent and more severe, older children have greater opportunities for escape. Also, older children are more able to defend themselves and retaliate. These factors might have moderated the increases in maltreatment that were observed among the older age groups. The disproportionate increases during the younger and middle-childhood years mean that the overall profiles of age differences in maltreatment were different in the NIS-3 than they had been in the NIS-2. During the NIS-2, the risk of maltreatment generally increased with the age of the child in a close-to-linear fashion. With the lopsided increases among the younger children and among children in their middle-childhood years, the profile has changed toward a curvilinear configuration, where the middle years of childhood are associated with the maximum risk of maltreatment, and toward a somewhat flatter distribution, where age differences are somewhat attenuated overall compared to their NIS-2 patterns. One of the most striking findings is the age distribution of sexual abuse, which combined the general flattening of the age differences in incidence rates with a very low age transition in the distribution of incidence rates. The rate of sexual abuse as defined under the Endangerment Standard was very low for 0- to 2-year-olds, but then relatively constant for children ages 3 and older, indicating a very broad age range of vulnerability from preschool age on.

Child's Race

The NIS-3 found no race differences in maltreatment incidence. The NIS-3 reiterates the findings of the earlier national incidence studies in this regard. That is, the NIS-1 and the NIS-2 also found no significant race differences in the incidence of maltreatment or maltreatment-related injuries. Service providers might find these results somewhat surprising in view of the disproportionate representation of children of color in the child welfare population and in the clientele of other public agencies. However, it should be recognized that the NIS methodology identifies a much broader range of children than those who come to the attention of any one type of service agency or the even smaller subset who receive child protective and other child welfare services. The NIS findings suggest that the different races receive differential attention somewhere during the process of referral, investigation, and service allocation, and that the differential representation of minorities in the child welfare population does not derive from inherent differences in the rates at which they are abused or neglected. It is also important to recognize that although there are no overall race differences in the incidence of child abuse and neglect in the NIS-3 findings, subsequent analyses that simultaneously consider multiple characteristics might reveal race differences in maltreatment incidence among specific subsets of children (e.g., for children of certain ages, for one sex but not the other, etc.).

Distribution of Child Abuse and Neglect by Family Characteristics

The incidence of child maltreatment varied as a function of family income, family structure, family size, and the metropolitan status of the county.

- Children of single parents had a 77 percent greater risk of being harmed by physical abuse, an 87 percent greater risk of being harmed by physical neglect, and an 80 percent greater risk of suffering serious injury or harm from abuse or neglect than children living with both parents.
- Children in the largest families were physically neglected at nearly three times the rate of those who came from single-child families.
- Children from families with annual incomes below $15,000 as compared to children from families with annual incomes above $30,000 per year were more than 22 times more likely to experience some form of maltreatment that fit the Harm Standard and more than 25 times more likely to suffer some form of maltreatment as defined by the Endangerment Standard.
- Children from the lowest income families were 18 times more likely to be sexually abused, almost 56 times more likely to be educationally neglected, and more than 22 times more likely to be seriously injured from maltreatment as defined under the Harm Standard than children from the higher income families.

Family Structure. Children of single parents were at higher risk of physical abuse and of all types of neglect and were overrepresented among seriously injured, moderately injured, and endangered children. Compared with their counterparts living with both parents, children in single-parent families had:

- A 77 percent greater risk of being harmed by physical abuse (using the stringent Harm Standard) and a 63 percent greater risk of experiencing any countable physical abuse (using the Endangerment Standard).
- An 87 percent greater risk of being harmed by physical neglect and a 165 percent greater risk of experiencing any countable physical neglect.
- A 74 percent greater risk of being harmed by emotional neglect and a 64 percent greater risk

of experiencing any countable emotional neglect.

- A 220 percent (or more than three times) greater risk of being educationally neglected; an approximately 80 percent greater risk of suffering serious injury or harm from abuse or neglect.
- An approximately 90 percent greater risk of receiving moderate injury or harm as a result of child maltreatment.
- A 120 percent (or more than two times) greater risk of being endangered by some type of child abuse or neglect.

Among children in single-parent households, those living with only their fathers were almost twice as likely to be physically abused than those living with only their mothers. Although parents are not necessarily, nor even most frequently, the perpetrators of maltreatment, the relationship between parent structure and maltreatment incidence is understandable, considering the added responsibilities and stresses of single parenting together with the likelihood that surrounding social and practical support might be inadequate.

Family Size. The incidence of maltreatment was related to the number of dependent children in the family, especially in the categories of physical and educational neglect. For educational neglect, and for physical neglect according to the Harm Standard, the pattern was nonlinear: The incidence rates were highest for children in the largest families (those with four or more children), intermediate for "only" children, and lowest for children in families with two to three children. Children in the largest families were almost three times more likely to be educationally neglected, and nearly two-and-a-half times more likely to be physically neglected under the Harm Standard, compared to children in families with two or three children. Under the Endangerment Standard, the pattern was one of increasing incidence of physical neglect with greater numbers of children. Children in the largest families were physically neglected at nearly three times the rate of those who came from single-child families. Additional children in a household mean additional tasks and responsibilities, so it is understandable that incidence rates of child abuse and neglect might be higher when there are more children. Accounting for why "only" children have higher rates of educational neglect and physical neglect under the Harm Standard than children in families with two or three children requires a different explanation. One possibility is that there might be too many expectations focused on "only" children, whereas expectations (and disappointments) are diffused over multiple children in the larger families. Another possibility is that many "only" child households represent the early stages in their families' development, as a number of these families will have additional children in time. Thus, many "only" children are in families with relatively young and inexperienced parents and caretakers.

County Metropolitan Status. The incidence of children who had been moderately harmed by maltreatment was significantly lower among children in large urban counties than among children who lived in other urban counties. This was interpreted as reflecting a general undercoverage of moderately injured maltreated children in the large urban counties. It was not clear whether this was because the moderately injured children are less likely to be encountered by community professionals in the large urban centers, because community professionals in these locales are less likely to identify these children as maltreated, or because the NIS information sources in these counties are less likely to submit data about these maltreated children.

Family Income. Despite the fact that only a rather gross index of family income was available, and despite a substantial percentage of cases with missing data on this factor, family income was significantly related to incidence rates in nearly every category of maltreatment. Compared to children whose families earned $30,000 per year or more, those in families with annual incomes below $15,000 per year were:

- More than 22 times more likely to experience some form of maltreatment under the Harm Standard and more than 25 times more likely to suffer maltreatment of some type using the Endangerment Standard.
- Almost 14 times more likely to be harmed by some variety of abuse and nearly 15 times more likely to be abused using the Endangerment Standard criteria.
- More than 44 times more likely to be neglected, by either definitional standard; almost 16 times more likely to be a victim of physical abuse under the Harm Standard and nearly 12 times more likely to be a victim of physical abuse using the Endangerment Standard.
- Almost 18 times more likely to be sexually abused by either definitional standard.
- Thirteen times more likely to be emotionally abused under the Harm Standard criteria and more than 18 times more likely to be emotionally abused in a manner that fit Endangerment Standard requirements.
- Forty times more likely to experience physical neglect under the Harm Standard and more than 48 times more likely to be a victim of physical neglect using the Endangerment Standard.

- More than 29 times more likely to be emotionally neglected under the Harm Standard definitions and more than 27 times more likely to be emotionally neglected by Endangerment Standard criteria.
- Nearly 56 times more likely to be educationally neglected by either definitional standard.
- Sixty times more likely to die from maltreatment of some type under the Harm Standard and more than 22 times more likely to die from abuse or neglect using the Endangerment Standard.
- More than 22 times more likely to be seriously injured by maltreatment under the Harm Standard and almost 22 times more likely to be seriously injured by maltreatment that fits the Endangerment Standard requirements.
- About 18 times more likely to be moderately injured by abuse or neglect under the Harm Standard and nearly 20 times more likely to have a moderate injury from maltreatment as defined by the Endangerment Standard.
- Fifty-seven times more likely to be classified as having an inferred injury under the Harm Standard and 39 times more likely to meet the criteria for inferred injury as defined by the Endangerment Standard.
- More than 31 times more likely to be considered endangered, although not yet injured, by some type of abusive or neglectful treatment.

The NIS-3 findings on the correlation between family income and child maltreatment are entirely consistent with the earlier findings of the NIS-2. Moreover, they cannot be plausibly explained on the basis of the higher visibility of lower income families to community professionals. On the one hand, the NIS sentinels observed substantial numbers of children and families at the middle- and upper-income levels. The large majority of maltreated children were recognized by professionals likely to encounter children and families at all income levels, such as sentinels in hospitals, schools, day care centers, mental health agencies, and voluntary social service agencies; by professionals not represented by NIS sentinel categories; and by the general public. Sentinels in schools alone recognized the majority of the maltreated children. Although the NIS design includes only public schools, approximately 89 percent of the U.S. population of school-age children attends public schools, so children attending public schools represent a broad spectrum of family income levels. Moreover, the private schools not reflected in the NIS include religiously affiliated schools, which have sliding scales for poorer children, so children who attend private schools are not necessarily from better economic circumstances than children enrolled in public schools.

Conversely, if the income finding is interpreted as an artifact of selective observation of low-income families, it would mean that there have to be enough undetected abused and neglected children in the middle- and upper-income brackets used here to equalize the incidence rates across different income categories. That would require an astounding number of still-undetected children in the nation who experience countable maltreatment. Specifically, it would mean that an additional 2,138,700 children suffered maltreatment according to the Harm Standard yet remained hidden to the NIS. Similarly, it would mean there were an additional 4,500,700 children in 1993 who experienced maltreatment under the Endangerment Standard but escaped observation by community professionals. To add some perspective as to what this would entail, consider that almost 7 percent of the total U.S. child population would be maltreated in countable ways yet entirely escape the attention of the spectrum of community professionals who serve as NIS sentinels, and all of these additional children would have to be in families with incomes of $15,000 per year or more. Considering the implications of the alternative, it appears more plausible to assume that the income-related differences in incidence found in the NIS reflect real differences in the extent to which children in different income levels are being abused or neglected. Note that there are a number of problems associated with poverty that could contribute to child maltreatment: more transient residence, poorer education, and higher rates of substance abuse and emotional disorders. Moreover, families at lower socioeconomic levels have less adequate social support systems to assist parents in their child care responsibilities.

Distribution of Child Abuse and Neglect by Perpetrator Characteristics

Children who had been maltreated as defined by the Harm Standard were categorized according to their relationship to the most closely related perpetrator and according to this perpetrator's sex, age, and employment status. These categorizations were examined in relation to the type of maltreatment and the severity of the child's injury or harm. Perpetrators' relationships to the children also were examined in relation to the children's race. The findings represent only a preliminary exploration of perpetrator characteristics in the NIS-3 data, as they lack significance tests concerning potential relationships and substantial percentages of the children were missing information concerning certain perpetrator characteristics.

Perpetrator's Relationship to the Child

The majority of all children countable under the Harm Standard (78 percent) were maltreated by their birth parents, and this held true both for children who were abused (62 percent were maltreated by birth parents) and for those who were neglected (91 percent experienced neglect by birth parents). Birth parents were the most closely related perpetrators for 72 percent of the physically abused children and for 81 percent of the emotionally abused children. The pattern was distinctly different for sexual abuse. Nearly half of the sexually abused children were sexually abused by someone other than a parent or parent substitute, whereas just over one fourth were sexually abused by a birth parent, and one fourth were sexually abused by other than a birth parent or parent substitute. In addition, a sexually abused child was most likely to sustain a serious injury or impairment when a birth parent was the perpetrator.

Perpetrator's Sex

Children were somewhat more likely to be maltreated by female perpetrators than by males: 65 percent of the maltreated children had been maltreated by a female, whereas 54 percent had been maltreated by a male. Of children who were maltreated by their birth parents, the majority (75 percent) were maltreated by their mothers and a sizable minority (46 percent) were maltreated by their fathers (some children were maltreated by both parents). In contrast, children who were maltreated by other parents or parent substitutes, or by other persons, were more likely to have been maltreated by a male than by a female (80 percent to 85 percent were maltreated by males; 14 percent to 41 percent by females). Abused children presented a different pattern in connection with the sex of their perpetrators than did the neglected children. Children were more often neglected by female perpetrators (87 percent by females vs. 43 percent by males). This finding is congruent with the fact that mothers and mother substitutes tend to be the primary caretakers and are the primary persons held accountable for any omissions or failings in caretaking. In contrast, children were more often abused by males (67 percent were abused by males vs. 40 percent by females). The prevalence of male perpetrators was strongest in the category of sexual abuse, where 89 percent of the children were abused by a male compared to only 11 percent by a female. Among all abused children, those abused by their birth parents were about equally likely to have been abused by mothers as by fathers (50 percent and 58 percent, respectively), but those abused by other parents, parentsubstitutes, or other non parental perpetrators were much more likely to be abused by males (80 percent to 90 percent by males vs. 14 percent to 15 percent by females). This general pattern held for emotional abuse, but was slightly different in the area of physical abuse. Children who had been physically abused by their birth parents were more likely to have suffered at the hands of their mothers than their fathers (60 percent vs. 48 percent), whereas those who had been physically abused by other parents or parent substitutes were much more likely to have been abused by their fathers or father substitutes (90 percent by their fathers vs. 19 percent by their mothers). For sexual abuse, the child's relationship to the perpetrator made very little difference, because males clearly predominated as perpetrators, whatever their relationship to the child. Moreover, the severity of the injury or impairment that the child experienced as a result of maltreatment did not appear to bear any relationship to the sex of the perpetrator.

Perpetrator's Age

The perpetrator's age was entirely unknown for one third of the children who were countable under the Harm Standard. Given the prevalence of children maltreated by perpetrators of unknown age, the findings here are tentative, as they could easily be eradicated if all perpetrators' ages were known. Among all maltreated children, only a small percentage (13 percent) had been maltreated by a perpetrator in the youngest age bracket (under 26 years of age). However, younger perpetrators were slightly more predominant among children who had been sexually abused (where 22 percent had been sexually abused by a perpetrator under 26 years of age) and among children who had been maltreated in any way by someone who was not their parent or parent substitute (among whom 40 percent had been maltreated by a perpetrator in the youngest age bracket). A child's severity of injury or harm from maltreatment appeared not to be associated with the age of the perpetrator.

Perpetrator's Employment Status

Perpetrators' employment status was unknown for more than one third of the maltreated children, limiting the value of the findings on this issue. Nearly half of all maltreated children were abused by a perpetrator who was employed, and this held true for both abuse and neglect. Of the children who sustained serious injury, the majority were maltreated by an employed perpetrator. In no category were the majority of children maltreated by a perpetrator who was unemployed.

Child's Race and Relationship to the Perpetrator

Because the perpetrator's race was not known for children submitted to the study solely through non-CPS sources, the child's race was examined in connection with the relationship to the perpetrator and with the nature and severity of the maltreatment. For overall abuse, child's race reflected no notable connection to the relationship with the perpetrator. However, among sexually abused children, White children constituted a greater proportion of children who were sexually abused by their birth parents than of those sexually abused by other parents and parent substitutes, and by others. Among physically abused children, White children were more prevalent among those who were physically abused by other parents and parent substitutes than among those who were physically abused by their birth parents or those physically abused by other types of perpetrators. Although non-White children were the minority of victims in all categories, they were more prevalent among children who were physically or sexually abused by perpetrators other than parents or parent substitutes. White children are a larger majority of those who suffered serious injury, whereas non-White children's representation was strongest among those who experienced moderate injury and those for whom injury could be inferred based on the severity of their maltreatment.

Sources of Recognition for Maltreated Children

School staff predominated as a source of recognition for maltreated children. School sentinels recognized 59 percent of the children who suffered maltreatment as defined by the Harm Standard and 54 percent of the Endangerment Standard total. Other important sources of recognizing abused and neglected children were hospitals, police departments, social service agencies, and the general public. For maltreatment defined under the Endangerment Standard, day care centers also joined in the group of agency categories that encountered more than 100,000 abused and neglected children. Since the NIS-2, hospitals more than tripled the rate at which they recognized maltreated children; mental health agencies nearly quadrupled their rate of recognition of children who met the Harm Standard and increased their recognition fivefold of children who met the Endangerment Standard; schools more than doubled their rate of recognition of children who met the Endangerment Standard, which included a 70 percent increase in their recognition rate for the Harm Standard sector. Endangerment Standard recognition more than doubled in law enforcement agencies. Interestingly, there were no changes in the contributions of sources that are tapped in the NIS only through their reports to CPS (e.g., private physicians and the general public). This finding probably reflects the relatively stable level of CPS involvement with the abused and neglected children countable in the NIS over the time period, as noted next.

Official Reporting of Maltreated Children and Their Investigation by CPS

- CPS investigated only 28 percent of the recognized children who met the Harm Standard. This was a significant decrease from the 44 percent investigated in 1986. Although the percentage of children whose abuse or neglect was investigated declined, the actual number of children investigated remained constant.
- CPS investigated less than half of all Harm Standard children recognized by any source and less than half of all Endangerment Standard children recognized by any source except police and sheriffs' departments (52 percent).
- Schools recognized the largest number of children maltreated under the Harm Standard, but only 16 percent of these children were investigated by CPS.
- CPS investigated only 26 percent of the seriously injured and 26 percent of the moderately injured children.

The NIS methodology provides information that speaks only to the end result of several processes, indicating whether or not a given maltreated child was or was not among the children whose maltreatment was investigated by CPS. Children who do not receive CPS investigation of their maltreatment represent an enigma to the study, as it cannot be determined whether this was because they were not reported to CPS or because CPS screened their reports out without an investigation. Despite that limitation, the NIS-3 findings concerning the percentages of abused and neglected children whose maltreatment received CPS investigation are cause for serious concern. Only a minority of the children who were abused or neglected, by either definitional standard, received CPS attention for their maltreatment. CPS investigated the maltreatment of only 28 percent of children who were countable under the Harm Standard and only 33 percent of those whose maltreatment fit the Endangerment Standard. Moreover, the percentages of those who received CPS investigation represented less than half of the maltreated children in all categories of maltreatment except fatalities, and across nearly all recognition sources. Especially remarkable was the finding that CPS investigation extended to only slightly more than one-fourth of the children who were seriously harmed or injured by abuse or neglect.

Another important finding was that the percentages of maltreated children who receive CPS investigation have decreased significantly since the NIS-2. The percentage of children receiving investigation among those who met the Harm Standard dropped from 44 percent to 28 percent, and the percentage of CPS investigation of children who met the Endangerment Standard fell from 51 percent to 33 percent. Although the decline was significant only among children recognized in law enforcement agencies and hospitals, it nevertheless cut across every type of recognition source. The decline in rates of CPS investigation affected abuse under the Harm Standard, all categories of maltreatment under the Endangerment Standard, and all levels of outcomes except fatalities. At the same time, the actual numbers of countable children investigated by CPS remained stable (when considering Harm Standard totals) or even slightly increased (considering the Endangerment Standard totals). Thus, as the total number of maltreated children has risen, it means that a larger percentage of them have not had access to CPS investigation of their maltreatment. This picture suggests that the CPS system has reached its capacity to respond to the maltreated child population. Are the observed increases in the incidence of child abuse and neglect, especially the quadrupling of the numbers of children who were seriously injured or endangered by maltreatment, real increases in the scope of the problem, or do they instead reflect improved recognition on the part of sentinels and other reporters to CPS? The fact that the increases occurred where they did among children who were seriously injured and among children who were endangered suggests that both of these dynamics contributed to the observed increases, each affecting a different sector of the abused and neglected population.

More Children Are Now Being Abused and Neglected Than in 1986, and Their Injuries Are More Serious

The rise in the number of seriously injured children probably reflects a real increase in child abuse and neglect, because it cannot plausibly be explained on the basis of heightened sensitivity. It is unreasonable to suppose that quadruple the number of seriously injured victims of abuse and neglect existed at the time of the NIS-2 and somehow escaped notice by community professionals. The fact that the seriously injured group has quadrupled during the seven years since the NIS-2, and now comprises more than one-half million children, appears to herald a true rise in the scope and severity of child abuse and neglect in the United States. Although the NIS does not address the causes of abuse and neglect, it was striking how often illicit drug use was noted in the narrative descriptions on the NIS data forms. The increase in illicit drug use since the fall of 1986 when the NIS-2 data were collected might have contributed to the rise in incidence observed in the NIS-3. Economics is another factor that might have enlarged the problem. Family income is the strongest correlate of incidence in nearly all categories of abuse and neglect, with the lowest income families evidencing the highest rates of maltreatment. Increases in incidence since 1986 could partially derive from decreased economic resources among the poorer families and the increase in the number of children living in poverty.

Community Professionals Are Better at Recognizing Abused and Neglected Children, Especially Those Endangered but Not Yet Harmed by Maltreatment

The rise in the number of endangered children probably stems from improved recognition of more subtle cues that indicate abusive and neglectful behaviors that have not yet resulted in harm or injury. It is quite plausible to suppose that some (even sizable) portion of the endangered children escaped attention in the NIS-2, but that by the time of the NIS-3, community professionals had learned to pay better attention to information that might indicate endangering maltreatment. Note that this explanation also completes an account of consistent progression in recognition across the three national incidence studies. The NIS-2 demonstrated an increase in the number of moderately injured children. In interpreting that finding, it was considered likely to have derived from improved attentiveness to moderate-injury indicators of abuse and neglect. The NIS-3 found no statistical change in the numbers of moderately injured children, which suggests that professionals had reached close-to-maximum recognition rates for this category of children at the time of the NIS-2. The fourfold increase in the number of endangered children in the NIS-3 implies that the subsequent further improvements in recognition have now shifted toward even subtler cues associated with not-yet-injurious abusive actions and neglectful omissions.

Better Targeting Is Needed to Ensure CPS Investigation for the Children Who Most Need It

The number of NIS-countable children who are investigated by CPS has remained fairly stable, or risen slightly, since the last national incidence study in 1986. As a result, CPS investigation has not kept up with the dramatic rise in the incidence of these children, so the percentages who receive CPS investigation of their maltreatment have fallen significantly. The low rates of CPS investigation of the maltreated children, especially of those already seriously injured by maltreatment, warrant immediate attention. These findings emphasize the need for better targeting, whether by reporters in referring children to CPS, by CPS screening practices in connection with reports, or by both. One possibility is that, although reporters now demonstrate considerable perceptiveness in identifying maltreated children, they have not reliably translated this into reports to CPS, or are unclear as to how to do so. Another possibility is that CPS, which has increasingly turned to screening cases to keep its workload manageably within the range of its resources, has not been using effective screening criteria or has been unclear or inconsistent about the criteria to be applied. Note that these are not independent dynamics, because the response of CPS to a report provides feedback that has consequences for future reporting behaviors.

The main NIS-3 data can offer some guidance in targeting. Neglect warrants more attention. It affects the greatest number of maltreated children, and their injuries are often serious. Children from the poorest families are at the greatest risk of maltreatment, so these children warrant increased CPS attention as well. Children in single-parent families also experienced higher rates of maltreatment. A number of characteristics explored here are not unrelated to each other; for instance, single-parent families often have lower incomes. Further analyses of the NIS-3 data can address the independent contributions of different characteristics to better clarify risk factors that can guide CPS screening activities. Narratives on the NIS data forms can also be more systematically explored. The narratives often included spontaneous comments about illegal drug use, indicated whether the perpetrator had a history (sometimes a criminal record) of sexually or physically abusing or assaulting other children or adults, or noted that the incident described was not the first time the child had been abused or neglected. As part of improving CPS targeting of the more serious cases, efforts should also focus on achieving better consensus about what types of cases should not receive CPS investigation. Very few of the educationally neglected children currently have their maltreatment investigated by CPS, and those who do might have been maltreated in multiple ways, with the CPS investigation focusing on abuse or other types of neglect. The current role of CPS in relation to educational neglect might be the centerpiece of an emerging consensus on what specific forms of abuse or neglect should not receive CPS investigation.

8.5.7.2 National Child Maltreatment Findings From 2002

Much of the most recent information on child abuse and neglect comes from *Child Maltreatment 2002*, a 2004 report based on data submissions by the states for calendar year 2002 to the National Child Abuse and Neglect Data System (NCANDS). This system was developed by the Children's Bureau of the U.S. Department of Health and Human Services in partnership with the states to collect annual statistics on child maltreatment from state CPS agencies.

Victims

An estimated 896,000 children were determined to be victims of child abuse or neglect in 2002. The rate of victimization per 1,000 children in the national population has dropped from 13.4 children in 1990 to 12.3 children in 2002. More than 60 percent of child victims experienced neglect. Almost 20 percent were physically abused, 10 percent were sexually abused, and 7 percent were emotionally maltreated. In addition, almost 20 percent were associated with "other" types of maltreatment based on specific state laws and policies. Children from birth to three years had the highest rates of victimization at 16.0 per 1,000 children. Girls were slightly more likely to be victims than boys. American Indian or Alaska Native and African American children had the highest rates of victimization when compared to their national population. Whereas the rate of White victims of child abuse or neglect was 10.7 per 1,000 children of the same race, the rate for American Indian or Alaska Natives was 21.7 per 1,000 children and for African Americans 20.2 per 1,000 children. In 2002, an estimated total of 2.6 million referrals concerning the welfare of approximately 4.5 million children were made to CPS agencies throughout the United States. Of these, approximately two thirds (an estimated 1.8 million) were accepted for investigation or assessment; the remaining referrals were not accepted.

Reports of Child Abuse and Neglect

More than half (56.5 percent) of all reports of alleged child abuse or neglect were made by such professionals as educators, law enforcement and legal personnel, social services personnel, medical personnel, mental health personnel, child day care providers, and foster care providers. Such nonprofessionals as friends, neighbors, and relatives submitted approximately 43.6 percent of reports. Approximately 30 percent of the reports included at least one child who was found to be a victim of abuse or neglect. Sixty-one percent of the reports were found to be unsubstantiated (including intentionally false); the remaining reports were closed for additional reasons.

Fatalities

Child fatalities are the most tragic consequence of maltreatment. In 2002, an estimated 1,400 children died due to abuse or neglect. Three quarters (76 percent) of children who were killed were younger than 4 years old; 12 percent were 4 to 7 years old; 6 percent were 8 to 11 years old; and 6 percent were 12 to 17 years old. Infant boys (younger than 1 year old) had the highest rate of fatalities, with nearly 19 deaths per 100,000 boys of the same age in the national population. Infant girls (younger than 1 year old) had a rate of 12 deaths per 100,000. The overall rate of child fatalities was 2 deaths per 100,000 children. One third of child fatalities were attributed to neglect. Physical abuse and sexual abuse also were major contributors to fatalities.

Perpetrators

More than 80 percent of perpetrators were parents. Other relatives accounted for 7 percent, and unmarried partners of parents accounted for 3 percent of perpetrators. The remaining perpetrators include persons with other (camp counselor, school employee, etc.) or unknown relationships to the child victims. Female perpetrators, who were mostly mothers, were typically younger than male perpetrators, who were mostly fathers. Women also comprised a larger percentage of all perpetrators than men, 58 percent compared to 42 percent. Of all parents who were perpetrators, less than 3 percent were associated with sexual abuse. Of all perpetrators of sexual abuse, nearly 29 percent were other relatives, and nearly one quarter were in nonrelative or nonchild-care roles. Approximately 59 percent of victims and 31 percent of nonvictims received services as a result of an investigation or assessment. Additional analyses indicated that children who were prior victims of maltreatment were more than 80 percent more likely to receive services than first-time victims. Additionally, children with multiple types of maltreatment were more than 80 percent more likely to receive services than children with only one type of recorded maltreatment.

Services

Services included both in-home and foster care services. Almost one fifth of child victims were placed in foster care. About 4 percent of nonvictims also experienced a removal—usually a short-term placement during the course of the investigation.

The Link Between Women and Children in Violence Scenarios

Currently estimates are that between 2 million and 4 million women are physically battered annually in the United States by their male partners. At least 25 percent to 30 percent of all American women are at risk for domestic violence during their lifetime. Studies have demonstrated that woman battering and child abuse are intricately linked. Within a group of children that had been flagged as suspected victims of child abuse or neglect, 45 percent of their mothers had also been battered. A study in Massachusetts assessed a sample of 200 substantiated child abuse cases and found documentation of abuse of the mother in 30 percent of those cases. A medical record review done at Boston City Hospital showed that 59 percent of mothers of abused children were suspected victims of battering. In addition, child abuse occurs disproportionately in homes where domestic violence exists. Children of battered mothers are 6 to 15 times more likely to be abused. In cases of severe wife abuse, the coexistence of child abuse might be as high as 77 percent.

Moreover, children who witness family violence significantly outnumber those who are direct victims of abuse. In the United States, from 3.3 million to 10 million children are estimated to witness parental violence annually. Studies indicate that 40 percent to 60 percent of child abuse victims have witnessed abuse of their mothers on one or more occasions. The impact of domestic violence on children reaches beyond suffering direct physical abuse or neglect. Witnessing the battering of their mothers could be as traumatic to children as being a direct victim of abuse, and both result in similar psychosocial and developmental sequelae. Indeed, the witnessing of one's mother being battered has been called the most insidious form of child abuse.

8.5.8 Sexual Assault of Children

In *Sexual Assault of Young Children as Reported to Law Enforcement: Victim, Incident, and Offender Characteristics* (produced by the U.S. Department of Justice Office of Justice Programs and the Bureau of Justice Statistics, July 2000) author Howard N. Snyder, PhD (2000), of the National Center for Juvenile Justice, presented data from the National Incident-Based Reporting System (NIBRS). Snyder writes:

> To law enforcement and the public, sexual assaults, and especially the sexual assaults of young children, are a major social concern. Caretakers worry about such attacks when their children are out of sight. Law enforcement, child protective services, and legislatures work to reduce the incidence of these crimes. However, while a few highly publicized incidents are engraved in the public's consciousness, there is little empirically based information on these crimes. Until recently, law enforcement and policymakers had few hard facts on which to base their response to these crimes, their victims, and their offenders.

Snyder says that the NIBRS has the potential to yield detailed descriptions of sexual assaults because it captures a wide range of information on each incident of sexual assault reported to law enforcement. This information includes demographic information on all victims; the levels of victim injury; victims' perceptions of offenders' ages, gender, race, and Hispanic ethnicity; and the victim–offender relationships. NIBRS also collects information on all offenses involved in the incident; the types of weapons used; the locations of the incident, the dates and times of the incident; the demographics of arrestees (if any); and the methods of clearance, such as arrest or victim refusal to cooperate with the investigation. The 1991–1996 NIBRS master files contain reports from law enforcement agencies in 12 states: Alabama, Colorado, Idaho, Illinois, Iowa, Massachusetts, Michigan, North Dakota, South Carolina, Utah, Vermont, and Virginia. These reports were scanned to identify incidents of sexual assault. The FBI's offense coding structure classifies sexual assault into four separate offense categories. From most to least serious, these crimes are forcible rape, forcible sodomy, sexual assault with an object, and forcible fondling. If more than one of these offenses occurred, the most severe sexual charge was used to classify the sexual assault in the incident. Snyder reports that to study the sexual assault of young children, two research bases (differing by unit of count) were extracted from the 1991 through 1996 NIBRS master files. One base summarized the information for each of the 60,991 victims of sexual assault, the incident characteristics, and (where available) information on their offenders. The second base compiled information for each of the 57,762 victim-identified offenders in sexual assault incidents, their victims, and related incident characteristics.

8.5.8.1 Age of Sexual Assault Victims

The most serious sexual assault charge was forcible fondling in 45 percent of all sexual assaults reported to law enforcement in the 1991 through 1996 NIBRS master files. Incidents of forcible rape were nearly as common (42 percent), whereas incidents of forcible sodomy (8 percent) and sexual assault with an object (4 percent) were far less frequent. One percent of victims of these crimes were age 54 or older. Seven percent of victims were over age 34. Another 12 percent were ages 25 through 34, and 14 percent were between ages 18 and 24. More than two thirds (67 percent) of all victims of sexual assault reported to law enforcement agencies were juveniles (under the age of 18 at the time of the crime). More than half of all juvenile victims were under age 12; 33 percent of all victims of sexual assault reported to law enforcement were ages 12 through 17, and 34 percent were under age 12. One of every seven victims of sexual assault (14 percent of all victims) reported to law enforcement agencies was under age 6.

The age profile of sexual assault victims varied with the nature of the crime. Juveniles were the large majority of the victims of forcible fondling (84 percent), forcible sodomy (79 percent), and sexual assault with an object (75 percent). In contrast, juveniles were the victims in less than half (46 percent) of forcible rapes. In each sexual assault category except forcible rape, children below the age of 12 were about half of all victims. Snyder says that the detailed age distribution of the victims of sexual assault emphasizes the high proportion of juvenile victims. The single age with the greatest proportion of sexual assault victims reported to law enforcement was age 14. There were more victims in each individual age group between 3 and 17 than in any individual age group over age 17 (any adult age group), and more victims age 2 than in any age group above age 40. For victims under age 12, 4-year-olds were at greatest risk of being the victim of a sexual assault. The victim age distribution differed with the nature of the offense. The risk of being the victim of forcible rape increased dramatically from age 10 to age 14, where it peaked. By age 20, the risk had dropped to less than half the peak 14-year-old rate, and dropped to a one tenth of the 14-year-old peak by age 40. For the other types of sexual assault, the victim age curves had two peaks, one (as in forcible rape) around age 13 or 14 and the other around age 4. The risk of being the victim of forcible sodomy peaked at age 4. By age 11 the risk of forcible sodomy dropped to half the peak rate, then increased for a couple of years through age 13, before falling to a tenth of the peak rate by the early 20s. The risk of being the victim of sexual assault with an object peaked at ages 3 and 4, then fell to less than half the peak rate by age 8. After age 8 the risk of sexual assault with an object increased through age 14 to almost three fourths the 3- and 4-year-old peak, and then dropped to a tenth of the peak rate by the mid-20s. The risk of forcible fondling, the other high-volume sex assault offense along with forcible rape, first peaked at age 4, dropped marginally through the preteen years, and then increased to its absolute peak for victims age 13. After age 13, the risk of forcible fondling dropped precipitously, so that by age 24 the risk was a tenth of that of 13-year-olds.

8.5.8.2 Gender of Sexual Assault Victims

Females were more than six times as likely as males to be the victims of sexual assaults known to law enforcement agencies. More specifically, 86 percent of all victims of sexual assault were female. The relative proportion of female victims generally increased with age. Sixty-nine percent of victims under age 6 were female, compared with 73 percent of victims under age 12, and 82 percent of all juvenile (under age 18) victims. The female proportion of sexual assault victims reached 90 percent at age 13 and 95 percent at age 19. Nearly 99 percent involved a female victim. Males can be victims of a forcible rape when the perpetrator is a female. Females were the large majority of victims in incidents of sexual assault with an object (87 percent) and forcible fondling (82 percent). In contrast, the majority of victims of forcible sodomy (54%) were males. In general, across all specific offense categories, the proportion of female victims increased with the age of the victim. A greater percentage of juvenile sexual assault victims were male (18 percent) than were adult sexual assault victims (4 percent). Males were 15 percent of the juvenile victims of sexual assault with an object, 20 percent of the juvenile victims of forcible fondling, and 59 percent of the juvenile victims of forcible sodomy. For victims under age 12, the male proportions were even greater: sexual assault with an object (19 percent), forcible fondling (26 percent), and forcible sodomy (64 percent). Snyder asserts, based on the NIBRS data, that the year in a male's life when he is most likely to be the victim of a sexual assault is age 4. By age 17 his risk of victimization has been cut by a factor of five. A female's year of greatest risk is age 14. Her risk drops to half the peak level by age 17 and to a fifth of the peak level by age 27. At his peak victimization age of 4, a male's risk of sexual assault victimization is just half that of females of the same age. In the later juvenile years (ages 14–17), the female victimization rates are at least 10 times greater than the male rates for similar age groups.

8.5.8.3 Other Offenses in Sexual Assault Incidents

Snyder explains that in 92 percent of sexual assault victimizations, a single sexual assault was the only crime against the victim recorded for the offender. Crimes against adults were more likely to involve multiple charges than were crimes against juveniles. That is, law enforcement recorded that 16 percent of all adult sexual assault victims also experienced another offense in the incident, compared with 5 percent of juvenile victims. Overall, female victims of sexual assault were more likely to experience multiple offenses than were male victims (10 percent vs. 4 percent). This gender difference was far less for juvenile victims; 5 percent of female juvenile victims experienced multiple offenses compare with 3 percent of male juvenile victims. When juvenile victims experienced multiple offenses, the most serious other charge in 47 percent of the incidents was another sex offense, 21 percent involved a nonsexual assault, 17 percent a kidnapping, and 8 percent a burglary. When adult victims experienced multiple offenses, in 13 percent of the incidents the most serious other charge was another sex offense, in 20 percent a nonsexual assault, in 30 percent a kidnapping, in 10 percent a robbery, and in 21 percent a burglary.

8.5.8.4 Other Victims in Sexual Assault Incidents

When adults were sexually assaulted, the adult was the only victim in the incident in the vast majority of victimizations (96 percent). Juvenile victimizations were far more likely to include other victims. In 19 percent of juvenile sexual assault victimizations, the juvenile was victimized along with another individual. Thirteen percent of juvenile victimizations involved a second victim; the remaining 6 percent involved three or more victims (not necessarily victims of sexual assault). Younger juvenile victims were more likely than older juvenile victims to be sexually assaulted with other victims. The proportion of youth victimized with others was greater for juvenile victims under age 12 (25 percent) than for older juveniles (13 percent). However, within the younger juvenile group, this age-related pattern was reversed; that is, youth ages 6 through 11 were more likely to be victimized with others than were youth under age 6. Twenty-one percent of victims under age 6 were victimized with others compared to 28 percent of victims ages 6 through 11.

Forcible rapes were more likely to involve a single victim than any other sexual assault. In 94 percent of forcible rape victimizations, there were no other victims involved, compared with 79 percent of forcible fondling, 81 percent of forcible sodomy, and 85 percent of victimizations of sexual assault with an object. Within each type of sexual assault, juvenile victims were more likely to be victimized with others than were adults. Regardless of the nature of the sexual assault, juveniles under age 12 were more likely than older juveniles to be victimized with others. However, as in the overall pattern, within each detailed offense category, youth ages 6 through 11 were more likely to be victimized with others than were the youngest victims, under age 6. Females were more likely to be victimized alone than were males. In 96 percent of adult female sexual assault victimizations, the female was the only victim, compared with 88 percent of adult male victimizations. This discrepancy held for juvenile victims; in 83 percent of juvenile female sexual assault victimizations, the female was the only victim, compared with 71 percent of male victimizations. This discrepancy also held for victims under age 12; girls under age 12 were the lone victims in 77 percent of their sexual assaults compared with 69 percent of young males.

Similar gender differences were found in each specific sexual assault offense category. When there was more than one victim in the incident, the victims were likely to be of similar ages. This relationship was stronger for juvenile victims than adult victims. In adult victimizations involving more than one victim, 71 percent of the victimizations involved another adult and 35 percent involved a juvenile victim, with 6 percent involving both another adult and a juvenile victim. However, in juvenile victimizations with more than one victim, 96 percent of the victimizations involved another juvenile and 6 percent involved an adult victim, with 2 percent involving both another juvenile and an adult victim. For victims under age 12 who were victimized with others, 90 percent of victimizations involved another youth under age 12, 15 percent involved older juveniles, and 4 percent involved adult victims.

8.5.8.5 Location of Sexual Assault

Most (70 percent) of the sexual assaults reported to law enforcement occurred in the residence of the victim, the offender, or another individual. Less than two thirds of forcible rapes (64 percent) occur in a residence compared with three quarters of other sexual assaults: forcible sodomy (74 percent), sexual assault with an object (76 percent), and forcible fondling (74 percent). Sexual assaults against females were less likely to occur in a residence than were those against male victims (69 percent vs. 77 percent).

Young victims were generally more likely to be victimized in a residence than were older victims. The age of the victim was strongly related to where the assault occurred. Seventy-seven percent of sexual assaults with juvenile victims occurred in a residence compared with 55 percent of adult victimizations. Older juveniles were more likely than younger juveniles to be victimized in a location other than a residence. Whereas just 16 percent of the sexual assaults of youth below the age of 12 occurred in a place other than a residence, 31 percent of the victimizations of youth ages 12 through 17 occurred in such locations. The most common nonresident locations for sexual assaults of juveniles were roadways, fields or woods, schools, and hotels or motels. For adults the most likely locations after a residence included roadways, fields or woods, hotels or motels, parking lots, and commercial or office buildings. When a juvenile female was the victim of a sexual assault, the incident was almost as likely to occur in a residence as when a juvenile male was the victim. Seventy-six percent of juvenile female victims of sexual assault were victimized in their home or in another residence compared with 80 percent of juvenile male victims. The proportion of victimizations that occurred in residences was also similar for female and male victims under age 12 (85 percent vs. 83 percent) and for female and male victims ages 12 through 17 (69 percent vs. 72 percent).

8.5.8.6 Weapons Used in Sexual Assault

In 93 percent of sexual assault victimizations, Snyder says the NIBRS data provided information on the most serious weapon used in the incident. In 77 percent of sexual assaults for which weapon information was available, the only weapon involved was what the FBI labels as a personal weapon, such as hands, feet, or fists. A firearm was used or brandished in just 2 percent of sexual assault victimizations. Other nonpersonal weapons such as a knife or club were used or brandished in another 6 percent of sexual assaults. In 14 percent of victimizations the records indicate that no weapon was involved. The use of a weapon other than a personal weapon increased with the age of the victim. Rarely did the sexual assaults of youth under age 12 involve a firearm. A firearm was involved in just 1 percent of the sexual assaults of youth ages 12 through 17. Other nonpersonal weapons were more common in these crimes, being involved in 4 percent of crimes against both juveniles under age 12 and victims between ages 12 and 17. For adult victims, firearms were a slightly more common attribute of sexual assault, being used in 5 percent of victimizations. Other nonpersonal weapons were more common in adult, rather than in juvenile assaults, being used in 11 percent of the sexual assaults of persons ages 18 and over.

8.5.8.7 Time of Day of the Sexual Assault

Snyder reports that the time of day when sexual assaults occurred was related primarily to the age of the victim. For adult victims, sexual assaults were most common between midnight and 2 a.m. From morning through 7 p.m. the number of adult sexual assaults committed in each one-hour period was essentially constant. The number of adult assaults began to increase in the 8 p.m. hour and increased consistently until the peak in the 2 a.m. hour. The primary temporal pattern for child sexual assault has a peak in the 3 p.m. hour. This is also the hour other research has found to be the period when juveniles are most likely to be the victims of violent crime in general (Snyder & Sickmund, 1999). This primary temporal pattern shows a consistent increase in the frequency of sexual assaults of very young victims before 3 p.m. and a consistent decline in the hours after 3 p.m. The secondary temporal pattern for the sexual assaults of very young children shows the hours of 8 a.m., noon, and 6 p.m. (traditional meal times) to be periods when the numbers of sexual assaults of very young victims spike. The temporal patterns of sexual assault of youth ages 6 through 11 and juveniles ages 12 through 17 appear to be a combination of the patterns of the very young, and the adult victims. These temporal distributions combine the after-school and mealtime hour patterns of very young victims and the temporal patterns of sexual assault for adults.

8.5.8.8 Gender and Age of Offenders in Sexual Assault

Nearly all of the offenders in sexual assaults reported to law enforcement were male (96 percent). Female offenders were most common in assaults against victims under age 6. For these youngest victims, 12 percent of offenders were females, compared with 6 percent for victims ages 6 through 12, and 3 percent for victims ages 12 through 17. Overall, 6 percent of the offenders who sexually assaulted juveniles were female, compared with just 1 percent of the female offenders who sexually assaulted adults.

The age profile of offenders in sexual assault varied with the nature of the crime. Overall, 23 percent of sexual assault offenders were under age 18 and 77 percent were adults. Juveniles were a substantially smaller proportion of the offenders in forcible rapes (17 percent) than in sexual assaults with an object (23 percent), forcible fondlings (27 percent), and incidents of forcible sodomy (36 percent). Sixteen percent of juvenile offenders were under the age of 12. These very young offenders were seldom the offenders in forcible rapes (1 percent of all offenders and 7 percent of juvenile offenders), although they made up greater proportions of the juvenile offenders in forcible fondlings (19 percent), sexual assaults with an object (17 percent), and forcible sodomies (23 percent). Young adults (persons 18–24) were 22 percent of adult offenders in forcible fondlings; however, they were 35 percent of adult offenders in forcible rapes. Correspondingly, adults over age 34 were 28 percent of all adult offenders in forcible rapes and 47 percent of the adult offenders in forcible fondlings. In general, the detailed age profile of offenders in sexual assault crimes shows that the single age with the greatest number of offenders from the perspective of law enforcement was age 14. The age profile of offenders varied with the age of the victim.

Juvenile offenders assaulted 4 percent of adult victims, whereas adult offenders assaulted 67 percent of juvenile victims. Younger juvenile victims tended to have a greater proportion of juvenile offenders than did older juvenile victims. Thirteen percent of offenders of victims under age 6 were ages 7 through 11, and 27 percent of the offenders of these very young victims were ages 12 through 17. That is, 40 percent of the offenders of victims under age 6 were themselves juveniles. A similar proportion (39 percent) of offenders of victims ages 6 through 11 were also juveniles. For older juvenile victims, the proportion of juvenile offenders dropped to 27 percent.

8.5.8.9 Victim–Offender Relationships in Sexual Assault

About one quarter (27 percent) of all offenders were family members of their victims. The offenders of young victims were more likely than the offenders of older victims to be family members. Almost half (49 percent) of the offenders of victims under age 6 were family members, compared with 42 percent of the offenders who sexually assaulted youth ages 6 through 11, and 24 percent of offenders who sexually assaulted juveniles ages 12 through 17. Overall, just 12 percent of the offenders who sexually assaulted adults were family members of the victims, compared with 34 percent of the offenders of juvenile victims. Except for victims under age 6, most sexual assault offenders were not family members but were otherwise known to the victim. Sixty percent of all sexual assault offenders were classified by law enforcement as acquaintances of the victim. Just 14 percent of offenders were strangers to their victims. Strangers were a greater proportion of the offenders of adult victims (27 percent) than juvenile victims (7 percent). The youngest juveniles were least likely to have an offender who was a stranger. Just 3 percent of the offenders in the sexual assaults of children under age 6 were strangers, compared with 5 percent of the offenders of youth ages 6 through 12, and 10 percent of offenders of juveniles ages 12 through 17. In general, the victim–offender relationships were similar for male and female victims; however, there were differences in the offender profiles for victims under age 12. Compared with young male victims, a greater proportion of female victims under age 12 were assaulted by family members. For male victims under age 12, 40 percent of offenders were family members compared with 47 percent of the offenders of females under age 12.

8.5.8.10 Offender Profiling

Snyder says that, using NIBRS data, it is possible to develop probability statements about the characteristics of the offenders given certain characteristics of the incident. For example, knowing that a victim under age 6 was assaulted in a residence, the NIBRS data indicate that the most likely offender was a juvenile acquaintance age 12 through 17 (probability = 15.2 percent) or a family member age 25 through 34 (probability = 15 percent). When a very young victim was assaulted some place other than a residence, the probability that the offender was an adult family member declines, whereas the probability that the offender was a juvenile acquaintance under age 12 increases substantially. When the victim was a little older (ages 6–11) and assaulted in some place other than a residence, the likelihood that the offender was a juvenile acquaintance increases even more (probability = 41 percent). The offenders of adolescents (victims ages 12–17) were five times more likely to be adult family members when the crime was committed in a residence than when it was committed elsewhere. The probability that the offender was a juvenile age 12 through 17 was twice as great when the crime occurred outside of a residence. For adult victims, the offender profile was also related to the location of the crime. Offenders of adult victims were three times more likely to be adult strangers when the crime occurred outside of a residence than when it occurred inside a residence.

8.5.8.11 Probability of Arrest and Clearance

Snyder says that the NIBRS data indicate that an arrest was made in 27 percent of all sexual assault victimizations. There were only minor offense-related differences in arrest probabilities: forcible rape (25 percent), forcible sodomy (30 percent), sexual assault with an object (28 percent), and forcible fondling (27 percent). Crimes were also cleared by means other than arrest, or what the FBI has labeled clearances by exceptional means. More specifically, in 7 percent of sexual assault victimizations the victim refused to cooperate. Prosecution was declined in 6 percent of sexual assaults, implying that there was insufficient evidence to charge or convict the offender. In a small proportion of cases, the offender had died, making arrest impossible. Overall, in the NIBRS sample, 42 percent of all sexual assaults were cleared by law enforcement through arrest or by exceptional means.

In general, the assaults of juvenile victims were more likely to result in an arrest (29 percent) than were adult victimizations (22 percent). Assaults against the youngest victims were the least likely of juvenile victimizations to result in arrest. An offender was arrested in just 19 percent of the sexual assaults of children under age 6, compared to 33 percent of victims ages 6 through 11, and 32 percent of victims ages 12 through 17. In all, arrest probabilities were similar in victimizations of children under age 6 and of adults, whereas the probability of arrest was greater when the victim was between the ages of 6 and 17.

One factor in the relatively lower arrest probability for crimes against adult victims can be found in a study of clearances by other means. When considering both arrest and other exceptional means, the probability that adult victimizations were cleared (39 percent) was closer to the clearance probabilities for crimes against victims ages 6 through 11 (45 percent) and victims ages 12 through 17 (45 percent). These clearance probabilities were more similar than the arrest probabilities because a much larger proportion of adult crimes were classified as cleared by law enforcement when the victim refused to cooperate. However, even when considering all means of clearances, the youngest victims (under age 6) still had the smallest proportion of their victimizations cleared by law enforcement (34 percent). The probability that an offender would be arrested or the matter cleared by arrest or exceptional means was largely unrelated to the offender's age. The only age-related difference was for very young offenders. Although the crimes of very young offenders were far less likely to result in arrest than were those of other offenders, the proportion of their crimes cleared were similar. The reason for this pattern is that law enforcement considered many of these crimes to be cleared because the offender had been identified, but due to the young age of the offender no arrest was made.

Whereas age of the offender was differentially related to the likelihood of arrest only for the very young offender, other incident characteristics were correlated with the probability of arrest and the probability that the offense would be otherwise cleared by law enforcement. Based on the results of a logistic regression, the factors that had the largest influence on the probability of arrest (in order of their odds ratios) were as follows:

- The number of victims in the incident—with more than one victim increasing arrest probabilities
- The number of offenders in the incident—with incidents with just one offender increasing arrest probabilities
- The age of the victim—with juvenile victims increasing arrest probabilities
- The sex of the victim—with male victims decreasing arrest probabilities

Other incident characteristics that influenced the probability of arrest to a lesser degree, but still remained statistically significant were the following:

- The relationship of the victim and the offender—with offenders who were strangers decreasing arrest probabilities
- The location of the incident—with incidents occurring outside of residences decreasing arrest probabilities
- The injury to the victim—with incidents in which the victim was injured decreasing arrest probabilities

These correlates were roughly similar for predictions of clearances with one exception. Incidents with offenders who were known to the victim were substantially more likely to be cleared than those in which the offender was a stranger to the victim. This difference between the arrests and clearance correlates reflects those incidents in which the offender is known to the victim but the victim refuses to cooperate with law enforcement.

The NIBRS also defines forcible-sex offenses:

- Forcible sex offenses: Any sexual act directed against another person, forcibly or against that person's will; or not forcibly or against the person's will where the victim is incapable of giving consent because of his or her temporary or permanent mental or physical incapacity.
- Forcible rape (except statutory rape): The carnal knowledge of a person, forcibly or against that person's will; or not forcibly or against the person's will where the victim is incapable of giving consent because of his or her temporary or permanent mental or physical incapacity. If force was used or threatened, the crime should be classified as forcible rape regardless of the age of the victim. If no force was used or threatened and the victim was under the statutory age of consent, the crime should be classified as statutory rape.
- Forcible sodomy: Oral or anal sexual intercourse with another person, forcibly or against that person's will; or not forcibly or against the person's will where the victim is incapable of giving consent because of his or her youth or because of his or her temporary or permanent mental or physical incapacity.
- Sexual assault with an object: To use an object or instrument to unlawfully penetrate, however slightly, the genital or anal opening of the body of another person, forcibly or against that person's will; or not forcibly or against the person's will where the victim is incapable of giving consent because of his or her youth or because of his or her temporary or permanent mental or physical incapacity. An object or instrument is anything used by the offender other than the offender's genitalia. Examples are a finger, bottle, handgun, stick, and so on.
- Forcible fondling: The touching of the private body parts of another person for the purpose of sexual gratification, forcibly or against that person's will; or not forcibly or against the person's will where the victim is incapable of giving consent because of his or her youth or because of his or her temporary or permanent mental or physical incapacity. Forcible fondling includes indecent liberties and child molesting. Because forcible fondling is an element of forcible rape, forcible sodomy, and sexual assault with an object, it should be reported only if it is the sole forcible sex offense committed against a victim.

8.5.9 A Decline in Child Sexual Abuse Cases?

In January 2004, a report issued by the U.S. Department of Justice's Office of Justice Programs Office of Juvenile

Justice and Delinquency Prevention (OJJDP), *Explanations for the Decline in Child Sexual Abuse Cases,* investigated an apparent nationwide decrease in child sexual abuse cases. Report authors David Finkelhor and Lisa M. Jones (2004) state that the number of sexual abuse cases substantiated by CPS agencies dropped 40 percent between 1992 and 2000, down from an estimated 150,000 cases to 89,500 cases. However, professional opinion is divided as to the reasons for this startling decrease. Finkelhor and Jones write:

> It is possible that the incidence of sexual abuse has declined as a result of two decades of prevention, treatment, and aggressive criminal justice activity. It is also possible that there has been no real decline, and that the apparent decline is explained by a drop in the number of cases being identified and reported or by changes in practices of child protection agencies. Identifying the source or sources of the decline in the number of substantiated sexual abuse cases is important. The possibility that a real decline occurred is heartening and could point the way to more effective strategies for preventing all kinds of child maltreatment. On the other hand, if the decline is due solely to decreased reporting or changes in CPS procedures, it could mean that more children are failing to get the help and services they need.

Finkelhor and Jones report that detailed data provided by four state CPS agencies offered little evidence that the decline was due either to more conservative judgment by CPS about the types of sexual abuse cases they would investigate or substantiate or to increasing reluctance by CPS to become involved in cases in which the perpetrator is not a primary caregiver. There also was no strong evidence that the decline was largely due to a diminishing reservoir of older, ongoing cases available for new disclosures. There was some evidence that the sexual abuse decline in one state could be partly explained by changes in CPS procedures and data collection methods. According to national data, however, this explanation does not successfully account for the declines seen in the majority of states. There was mixed evidence that reporting of sexual abuse to CPS declined because of a greater public and professional skepticism about reports of sexual abuse. Evidence from a number of different sources, including NCVS data showing a 56 percent decline in self-reported sexual assault against juveniles, is consistent with a real decline in sexual abuse. Finally, additional studies and improved data are needed to make crucially important decisions for public policy based on the factors that are most responsible for the decline.

8.5.9.1 Evidence for the Decline

Finkelhor and Jones explain that early estimates of substantiated sexual abuse from 1992 to 2000 were calculated from CPS administrative data collected by NCANDS. The number of states that submitted data to this system each year varied from 43 to 49, making published totals difficult to compare across years. To arrive at more comparable numbers, sexual abuse totals were extrapolated to account for the population of all 50 states and the District of Columbia as estimated annually by the U.S. Census. These extrapolated totals show that the number of substantiated sexual abuse cases reached a peak of approximately 149,800 in 1992, followed by declines of 2 to 11 percent each year through 2000, the last year for which data are available. In 2000, estimated cases of sexual abuse reached a low of approximately 89,355, for a total decline of 40 percent in identified sexual abuse cases over the eight-year period. The trend is not universal, they say, but it has occurred in the majority of states. Of 49 states, 39 experienced a total decline of 30 percent or more in substantiated cases of sexual abuse from their peak year to 2000, and 19 of these states saw declines of more than 50 percent in their sexual abuse caseloads. Finkelhor and Jones write:

> The decline in sexual abuse does not appear to be just an extension of a general declining trend in overall child maltreatment or of some other demographic factor. According to estimates based on the NCANDS data, the decline in sexual abuse appears to account for a large part of the 15 percent decline in child maltreatment. Neglect cases have fluctuated during the 1990s with no overall decline while physical abuse has declined 30 percent since peak in 1995. The decline in physical abuse is significant, but it is smaller and more recent than the decline in sexual abuse. In fact, the largest proportion of the decline in physical abuse (15 percent) occurred between 1998 and 1999, whereas the more gradual 40 percent decline for sexual abuse occurred over an eight-year period.

8.5.9.2 Explanations for the Decline

The authors conducted a survey of state child protection administrators to gather hypotheses and evidence about the decline in sexual abuse (Jones, Finkelhor, & Kopiec, 2001). Although the administrators expressed many ideas about the decline, six explanations were offered frequently and backed by some anecdotal support:

- Increasing conservatism within CPS. In this view, sexual abuse cases were declining in state caseloads because CPS was adopting more conservative standards regarding "questionable" cases (e.g., allegations arising in divorces and custody disputes) or cases with weak initial evidence.
- Exclusion of cases that do not involve caretakers. In this view, CPS was increasingly excluding from its jurisdiction sexual abuse cases in

which the perpetrator was not a primary caregiver.
- Changes in CPS data collection methods or definitions. In this view, the decline was due to changes in the way CPS tabulated or counted its cases, such as changing from a three-tiered classification system (substantiated, indicated, and unsubstantiated) to a two-tiered system (substantiated and unsubstantiated).
- Less reporting to CPS due to a sexual abuse backlash. In this view, negative publicity about sexual abuse cases and the potential liability of professionals who report suspected abuse made the public and professionals more reluctant to report sexual abuse.
- A diminishing reservoir of older cases. In this view, there had been a reduction in the supply of older but previously undisclosed cases available for new disclosures but no true decline in new cases.
- A real decline in the incidence of sexual abuse. In this view, there was a reduction in the number of children actually being abused as a result of increased prevention efforts, more prosecution and incarceration of offenders, or other social or cultural changes.

8.5.9.3 A Real Decline in the Incidence of Sexual Abuse?

Finkelhor and Jones state that if the decline in child sexual abuse cannot be fully explained by various hypotheses in their 2004 report, is the decline real? They suggest that there are several predictions that would be consistent with a true reduction in the number of children and youth being sexually abused:

- Decline in the number of self-reports of sexual abuse by victims
- Decline in related social problems
- Greater decline in the most readily preventable cases
- Increase in the incarceration of offenders

Regarding a decline in the number of self-reports of sexual abuse by victims, the authors say that sexual abuse is not a crime category tracked by the nation's most reliable measure of self-reported crime victimization, the NCVS. However, NCVS does ask about rape and sexual assault for victims ages 12 and older, and these crimes include acts counted within the broader definition of child sexual abuse. The NCVS data show that sex offenses against juveniles (ages 12–17) declined 56 percent between 1993 and 2000, with virtually all the decline occurring in offenses committed by known (family and acquaintance) perpetrators (down 72 percent). Cases involving known perpetrators are the type most likely to be categorized as sexual abuse.

The timing and magnitude of this decline in self-reports are parallel to the trend in CPS data on sexual abuse. Another source of self-report information on sexual abuse comes from the Minnesota Student Survey. The survey includes two questions about experiences with sexual abuse. For sexual abuse by both family and nonfamily perpetrators, these data show a slight rise between 1989 and 1992 and a 22 percent drop from 1992 to 2001. This trend also parallels the trend in the CPS data.

Regarding a decline in related social problems, the authors say that if sexual abuse were truly declining, the decrease might be paralleled by drops in indicators of other related social problems. These problems could be considered precursors of sexual abuse, or they could be affected by similar causal factors. The period in which the decline in sexual abuse occurred also saw declines in a number of other child welfare problems, including crime and violent crime, births to teenage mothers, children running away or living in poverty, and teen suicide. In general, Finkelhor and Jones say the evidence for these other declines is more reliable than the evidence for the decline in sexual abuse.

The decline in crime and violent crime during the 1990s has been widely publicized. The evidence for that decline is based both on self-reports from NCVS and on police reports. NCVS shows a 46 percent decrease in violent crime from 1994 to 2000 (Rennison, 2001), and a 21 percent decrease in intimate partner assault from 1993 to 1998 (Rennison & Welchans, 2000). The decline in intimate partner assault is particularly noteworthy, the authors say, because of its connections to sexual abuse. Child sexual abuse is thought to be more common in families where there is intimate partner violence (Rumm et al., 2000). Like child sexual abuse, intimate partner violence has in recent years been the subject of substantial publicity, increasingly aggressive efforts at case detection, upgraded law enforcement activity, and stiffened legal sanctions.

Another social problem that has declined markedly over the same period is the number of out-of-wedlock teenage pregnancies. The rate of live births to teenage mothers dropped 28 percent from a high of 39 live births per 1,000 females ages 15 to 17 in 1991 to 28 per 1,000 in 2000 (Moore et al., 2001). Teen pregnancy has often been an outcome of sexual abuse, both in the form of conceptions resulting from abuse (Boyer & Fine, 1992) and in conceptions resulting from the sexualized behaviors that victims sometimes manifest in the wake of abuse (Butler & Burton, 1990). The number of teens who reported being currently sexually active or ever having sexual intercourse also fell during the 1990s (Terry & Manlove, 2000).

Yet another related indicator that experienced a decline is the frequency of children running away. Police reported 28 percent fewer incidents of taking children into custody for running away in 1999 than in 1995 (Federal Bureau of Investigation, 2001). A comparison of data from the Second National Incidence Studies of Missing, Abducted, Runaway, and Thrownaway Children (NISMART–2) with data from NISMART–1 also indicates a decline in the runaway problem between 1988 and 1999 (Hammer, Finkelhor, & Sedlak, 2002). Running away is frequently cited as a coping strategy used by children who are being sexually abused at home, and it is a behavior that also increases a youth's risk for sexual assault and exploitation (Famularo et al., 1990). The decline in running away is consistent with a decline in sexual abuse. Also consistent with a decline in sexual abuse is a drop in teen suicide. Vital statistics show a modest 18 percent reduction in suicide among 15- to 19-year-olds between 1990 and 1999 (Annie E. Casey Foundation, 2002).

In the same period, the percentage of children living in poverty dropped 27 percent, from 22 percent of children younger than 18 in 1992 to 16 percent of children younger than 18 in 1999 (Federal Interagency Forum on Child and Family Statistics, 2000). This decline was accompanied by a decrease in unemployment and a reduction of families on welfare. Poverty, unemployment, and welfare have generally been viewed more as risk factors for forms of child maltreatment other than sexual abuse. It is possible, however, that increased employment, particularly among potential offenders, might have reduced both opportunities to molest and some of the motivations (such as discouragement and anxiety) behind offending.

8.5.9.4 A Greater Decline in the Most Readily Preventable Cases

Finkelhor and Jones write, "Intensive public awareness about child sexual abuse, combined with aggressive efforts at case finding, prosecution, and incarceration, may have had some deterrent effect on potential offenders. They may be increasingly inhibited by fears of detection and prosecution." They add that deterrence generally has its greatest effect on those offenders with the most potential for self-control, the biggest stake in conformity, and the fewest other pressures to deviate. Based on this logic, a true decline in sexual abuse would be expected to occur differentially among biological fathers in intact families. They tend to be the least compulsive offenders with a lesser tendency to recidivate, the most responsiveness to treatment, and a considerable stake in conformity (Hanson, 2001). Finkelhor and Jones report that state data confirm a particularly large decline in sexual abuse by biological fathers in intact families. This trend could be interpreted as consistent with an argument that deterrence has played a role in a true decline.

8.5.9.5 Increase in the Incarceration of Offenders

Among explanations for the general decline in crime during the 1990s, the large increase in the incarceration of offenders has received the most extensive empirical support (Blumstein, 2000; Conklin, 2003). Although detailed data are insufficient to conduct a careful analysis of the possible impact of incarceration on sexual abuse, the overall pattern is certainly consistent with the idea that increased incarceration played a part in a true decline. Surveys of state correctional facilities suggest that between 1991 and 1997, the number of persons incarcerated for sex crimes against children increased 39 percent, from 43,500 to 60,700 (Finkelhor & Ormrod, 2001), after more than doubling from 19,900 in 1986. This does not include the many sexual abuse offenders who receive sanctions that do not involve incarceration for a year or more.

Compared with people who commit other forms of child maltreatment, people who commit sexual abuse are much more likely to lose access to their victims (as a result of court order or divorce) or to lose their liberty altogether. The incapacitation of offenders alone should be expected to have some effect on the number of new cases. Finkelhor and Jones conclude:

> No solid and convincing explanation exists for why sexual abuse cases declined in the 1990s, although it is important to try to find out why a decline occurred. The answer, if it can be determined, is not likely to be a simple one. In all likelihood, multiple factors were involved in the trend. Based on the strength of current evidence, one of those factors was probably a true decline in the occurrence of sexual abuse. Changes in the practices of professionals who report suspected abuse and of the child protective system probably also have played a part, but how large a part is difficult to ascertain.
>
> Many observers of the decline in the number of substantiated sexual abuse cases, including state officials, have seemed resistant to the possibility that the numbers represent a true decline, preferring almost any other explanation as an alternative. This attitude may stem from a concern that if people believe sexual abuse is waning, their vigilance and concern about the problem and willingness to support funding will disappear. Increasing numbers of cases were part of what mobilized people and resources during the 1980s, so declining numbers of cases might have the opposite effect.
>
> Although social problems go through a well-recognized issue/attention cycle and some changes have occurred in the media attitude toward sexual abuse, there are reasons to doubt that a true decline in incidence of the current magnitude could, if recognized, result in a massive desertion of interest or funding. For one, the public and professional interest in the issue of sexual abuse has roots that go far beyond the matter of whether it involves 50,000 or 150,000 cases per year, and relate to the now well-

established role that it plays in discussions of family problems, gender relations, sexuality, and mental health. The high-profile public and professional role this problem has achieved in recent years will not easily change.

Finkelhor and Jones add:

Researchers may not be able to fully answer the question of why this most recent decline has occurred; however, it is important to be better prepared to understand the sources of any continuing or future declines. To what extent do prevention education, increased public awareness, greater prosecution, and incarceration play roles? Answering such questions can help policymakers formulate policies that will extend and accelerate the decline in sexual abuse and, perhaps, in other forms of child maltreatment.

8.5.10 Child Sexual Assault Guidelines for Health Care Professionals

One state with child sexual abuse guidelines that have been modeled by other states is North Carolina. In its *Child Sexual Abuse Guidelines: Recommendations for Professionals*, the North Carolina Department of Justice (1997) has laid out a solid set of recommendations for health care providers to follow. The guidelines acknowledge, "The evaluation of children for concerns of sexual abuse can be compared to fitting together the pieces of a complicated jigsaw puzzle. The more pieces that fit together, the more clear the picture becomes. One important piece of the puzzle is the medical evaluation."

8.5.10.1 Medical Evaluation

The North Carolina guidelines suggest that referrals for medical evaluation of child sexual abuse should be made to a medical care provider or medical evaluation team that is well trained and experienced in performing evaluations for concerns of sexual abuse. Referrals should be made in a timely fashion, especially if the alleged incident has occurred within the last 72 hours. Often medical findings such as recent tears, abrasions, bruises, swelling, or other signs of trauma can heal very rapidly and efficiently, leaving little or no definitive physical signs of trauma. In some cases, specific diagnostic findings that were initially present might become more obscure when the child is examined weeks, months, or years after the abusive act(s) have occurred. Consequently, nonspecific or even normal physical findings do not rule out that a child might have been sexually abused.

Pediatric and Adolescent Patient Physical Findings in Child Sexual Abuse

The likelihood of finding physical evidence of abuse depends on the following factors:

- Whether force was used
- The size and age differences of the perpetrator and the patient
- Whether a foreign object was placed or forced into the mouth, vulva, or anus
- Positioning of the child and use of lubricants during the abuse
- Type of abuse and its frequency and chronicity (McCann, 1992, found that in children with genital injury from sexual assault, healing occurred rapidly and little scar formation resulted; irregular hymenal edges and narrow rims at the point of injury were the most persistent findings.)
- Whether the child resisted

Physical Examination Findings Consistent With Child Sexual Abuse

These occur in approximately 25 percent of cases. Findings consistent with abuse but not diagnostic include the following:

- Female patient (Note: The size of the hymenal opening is based on relaxation, position, technique used, and anatomic structure and thus is not useful information to be included.)
  - Vaginal discharge, urethral inflammation, lymph gland inflammation, pregnancy, recurrent atypical abdominal pain, blood stains on underwear, genital bleeding, genital pruritis, genital bruising
  - Abrasions, chafing, or bruising to medial thighs
  - Bite marks to the thighs, breasts, or other areas
  - Scarring, tears, or distortion to the hymen
  - Injury to or scarring of the fossa navicularis or posterior fourchette
  - Scars or tearing of the labia minora

(Note: Nonintentional trauma such as straddle injury or falls often results in injury to anterior structures such as the periurethral area or labia minora or majora; the hymen is rarely affected. Intentional trauma usually results in injury to posterior structures such as the hymen, posterior fourchette, fossa navicularis, and anus.)

- Male patient
  - Chafing or bruising to the genital region, anus, or back
  - Penile discharge, painful urination, penile swelling
  - Bite marks to the genital region, anus, or back

- Male and female patients
  - Bruises, scars, or anal tears
  - Other anal findings include: the loss of rugal pattern to anus, loss of sphincter tone, scars, anal dilation (without stool present), edema, venous congestion, skin tags, or contusions to natal cleft or perianal tissues
  - Tears to the labial frenulum or palatal petechiae
  - STDs, enuresis, encopresis

(Note: Sixty-six percent of patients with a history of anal penetration have normal exams according to Muram, 1989a, 1989b, and reflexive dilatation is controversial because it can be found in 49 percent of children without abuse according to McCann, 1992.)

A normal physical examination is most often what is found and can be consistent with abuse, the ACEP states.

8.5.10.2 Emergency Room Examinations

Whenever possible, the medical evaluation should be done in a calm, child-friendly environment by a physician trained to conduct medical examinations of children and knowledgeable in child abuse issues. In the past, most physical examinations of child abuse victims were conducted in ERs or physician's offices, by doctors inadequately trained to perform such specialized exams. However, as awareness of child abuse and its traumatic effects on victims has increased, advocates and medical professionals have worked to provide child victims with services that are more sensitive to their physical and emotional needs. The North Carolina guidelines state:

> The emergency room (ER) can be a frightening environment for a child. Whenever possible, the sexual abuse evaluation should be postponed a few hours or even overnight until the child can be evaluated in an appropriate clinic setting. If deferring the evaluation might result in diminished quality of care or loss of evidence, then a careful, thorough, sensitive evaluation should be completed in the ER, preferably by a medical professional trained through the SANE, CMEP or similar programs.

The different parts of the medical evaluation can be performed by a single health care provider or can be divided among a medical team with members who are specifically trained for their roles in the evaluation. Although the composition of a particular medical team might vary, typically members include physicians or physician extenders, medical social workers or mental health professionals, nursing staff, and ancillary support staff. At the completion of the medical evaluation process, the medical care provider or team will use all of the information obtained to reach a medical diagnosis (e.g., abuse confirmed, abuse suspected, abuse ruled out or abuse unknown). Health care providers should also be available to help clarify information contained in the medical report or related to the medical diagnosis, as well as to serve as witnesses of fact or expert witnesses in cases that proceed into the legal system.

Information Intake Process

The evaluation involves all of the standard methods of medical diagnosis, including the following:

- An intake process to understand why a child is being referred for evaluation.
- Obtaining available information from other professionals involved in the child's care or case.
- Obtaining a thorough social history and an account of events from the child's caretaker(s). Also document basic family information (e.g., name, address, and phone number of child, caretaker, other children at risk, etc.).
- Documenting the evaluation by written medical report, diagrams and/or slides, or photographs.
- Conducting a separate diagnostic interview with the child.
- Obtaining a thorough past medical history and recent review of systems.
- Performing a forensic physical examination of the child with special attention to the genital and anal areas.
- Performing appropriate laboratory tests or studies as indicated by the exam or history.

Obtaining the Medical and Social History

The North Carolina guidelines state that whenever possible, the child should be given choices about the evaluation process. This process can be awkward and confusing both for the child and the caretaker, and all available support should be provided to both. During the evaluation process, the child should never have to be exposed to or deal with a suspected perpetrator or a nonsupportive caretaker. If an appropriate caretaker is not available, a child advocate (nurse, social worker, or other supportive personnel) should accompany the child during the evaluation. A general medical history should be obtained, including all significant medical conditions, prior hospitalizations, significant illnesses, serious accidents, and so on. In addition, a medication history, history of recent use of antibiotics, and history of drug allergies should be obtained. It is helpful to obtain any day care or school history, including concerns or behavioral issues that might have been noted. Any prior concerns of abuse or neglect should be explored, as well as physical signs or symptoms of earlier injuries that might be associated with abuse. Current and prior medical care providers should be identified, as requests for medical records could be indicated.

Review of Physical Systems

A standard medical review of systems should be completed, including pulmonary, cardiovascular, gastrointestinal, genitourinary, and musculoskeletal systems, as well as skin, and so on. Any existing medical conditions should be identified. In particular, gastrointestinal complaints such as diarrhea, constipation, stomach discomfort, blood in stools; and genitourinary complaints such as dysuria, hematuria, vaginal discharge, genital spotting or bleeding, genital or anal pruritus or pain, and genital redness or lesions should be specifically addressed. Status of the child's toilet training should be obtained, and identification of bathing or washing techniques that involve the genital area should be noted (e.g., specific cleaning or scrubbing of the genital or anal areas, use of bubble bath or harsh soaps, complaints by the child during bathing, etc.). It is also helpful to get general information about any eating, sleeping, voiding, or stooling problems, or other behaviors of concern the child might have exhibited.

Physical Examination

In the exam room, the child should be able to move freely around the room or remain close to the caretaker if he or she prefers. Spend time building rapport with the child, letting him or her explore the room and showing him or her the different pieces of equipment that will be used. The examiner should explain that his or her job is to examine children to make sure they are healthy and not having any problems. It might be helpful to ask the child if he or she understands the reason for the exam. The exam room should have good lighting. The child should be dressed in a clinic gown or loose clothing that allows easy access during the physical exam. Older children and teens might prefer having an additional drape or cover during the abdominal and genital and anal parts of the exam. The examiner should wear standard exam gloves to avoid the risk of communicable infections.

Note the child's reaction to the general physical exam, as well as to the supine and knee–chest exams that are utilized in examining the genital and anal areas. Try to assess if the child is overly anxious or overly compliant and passive. Perform the general physical exam beginning with the parts of the exam the child is familiar with and those that are the least traumatic or invasive. This should include a thorough head–eyes–ears–nose–throat–neck exam, especially noting any oral lesions or redness. Next, the pulmonary and cardiovascular exams can be done, followed by an examination of the breasts to determine Tanner staging and the armpit to determine if any axillary hair is present. The abdominal exam with the child reclining on the examining table is usually well tolerated if done gently. This position easily leads to the examination of boys' genitalia or to assisting girls in positioning their legs in a supine "frog-leg" position for examination of the genital area. Following the supine exam, the child can be asked to roll over and curl up "like a sleeping kitten" to place him or her in the knee–chest position.

The child's extremities and skin surfaces should also be examined to assess whether there are any lesions, marks, or findings of concern. Descriptions, diagrams, slides, or photographs of any notable physical findings should be made. The genital and anal exams can be performed with the child on the examining table, or if the child prefers, on the caretaker's lap. Both the child and the caretaker need to be prepared for what will be done during the exam. Time should be spent explaining the exam and possibly demonstrating with a stuffed animal or doll in what positions the child will be examined. In some cases, the child might need to return for a follow-up visit if the exam is not tolerated on that day. The exam is greatly aided by use of a magnifying device such as an otoscope (which might be handheld) or a colposcope, which can stand independently and can be used with a camera attachment for photo documentation.

The examiner needs to have a standard method of locating and obtaining accurate measurements of genital findings and of the hymenal opening size. A metric tape attached to the end of a tongue depressor can be used after assuring the child that this device will not touch him or her. When describing lesions or findings, it is important to note which position the child is in (supine frog-leg or knee–chest) and to use the face of a clock to locate the area of a finding.

In the frog-leg position, the child is positioned lying on his or her back with feet together and hips and knees flexed and externally rotated so that the lateral surfaces of the legs are resting on the exam table. The purpose of this position is to examine the external genitalia. The North Carolina guidelines note that this is not meant to be a pelvic exam, and a speculum should never be used when examining prepubertal girls or young teens who cannot tolerate a speculum exam. If a speculum exam needs to be done to assess genital bleeding, persistent infection, or possible vaginal foreign body in a prepubertal girl, this should be done under anesthesia. For girls who are Tanner III or greater in sexual development, a speculum exam with a Pederson speculum can be carefully attempted, but this should be immediately discontinued if the child is unable to tolerate the procedure. In the supine frog-leg position, the labia majora, clitoral hood, and the perineal areas can be examined before ever touching the child. Following external inspection, the labia majora should be gently separated using lateral separation (labial separation technique). This permits a good view of the perivaginal tissues, including the posterior fourchette, the fossa navicularis, the urethral meatus, and the lateral perihymenal tissues. Next, the labia majora should be gently grasped between thumbs and forefingers with gentle outward and either upward or downward traction applied (labial traction technique). This technique allows the best view of the hymenal margin and edge, and results in an average of a 1 to 2-mm increase in hymenal opening size as compared with the labial separation technique. The hymenal opening size can be measured using either labial separation or labial traction, or preferably both. It is important to record which technique is being used when the measurement is taken. Tables showing mean hymenal opening sizes for various age groups, as well as the upper and lower ranges of these measurements, have been published. It is important to note the type of hymen (annular, crescentic, septated, cribiform, redundant, or noninterpretable). Findings to be noted during the supine frog-leg exam include the following:

- Hymenal notches or clefts (areas where part of the hymen is narrowed or absent); hymenal mounds, projections, ortags; hymenal septal remnants; markedly narrowed hymenal rims, and so on
- Exposed intravaginal mucosal ridges, perihymenal bands (anterior or posterior), and so on
- Markedly dilated urethral meatus, urethral prolapse, labial adhesions, inclusion cysts, lesions, hemangiomas, tears, scars, bruises, edema, ulcers, pustules, warts, redness, friability, discharge, and so on

For boys, the genital exam should consist of noting whether the penis is circumcised or not; whether there is any abnormality, discharge, or redness of the urethral meatus; if the scrotum and testes are normal; and if there are any lesions, warts, or other significant findings.

The Knee–Chest Position

For this position, the child is placed in a prone position with the knees and lower legs drawn up onto the table, the head and shoulders resting on the pillow, and the buttocks raised up for examination. If the knee–chest exam is simply not tolerated, the anus can be examined in either the supine or lateral decubitus positions. In the knee–chest position, the buttocks should be gently separated and the external anal sphincter observed for at least 30 to 40 seconds. This allows visualization of any redness, discharge, lesions, fissures, tears, warts, or anal gaping that might be present. Rapid, repeated, or sustained anal gaping to greater than 1.0 cm in horizontal diameter of both the internal and external anal sphincters with absence of stool in the rectal vault is significant. If stool is present in the rectal vault or if the child is tense, a repeat exam is recommended several hours after the child has voided and when the child is more relaxed.

For girls, after examination of the anus, the buttocks should be gently lifted upward to open up the area of the vaginal introitus. In the knee–chest position, the hymenal margin can be clearly viewed as it hangs down with gravity. If the tissues are adherent and poorly visualized due to redundancy or stickiness of the hymen, it might be helpful to rinse the genital tissues with water or normal saline. In some cases, it might be necessary to gently touch and spread out the hymenal edge with a moistened swab, but the child should be prepared for this and agree to the touch.

Assessment for Sexually Transmitted Diseases

Children might or might not have genital or anal signs or symptoms when STIs are present. The decision of whether to obtain cultures for STIs should rely on the physical signs (redness, discharge, lesions, etc.), symptoms (pain, dysuria, pruritis, etc.), and history or disclosure of sexual contact. Children do not have to experience penetrating sexual trauma to acquire an STD, but there must be close, intimate contact with the secretions of an infected perpetrator. Fomite transmission of STDs from such objects as toilet seats, towels, bathtubs, and so on, are generally discounted.

In general, when obtaining cultures for STDs, a cotton-tipped or Dacron swab (e.g., that provided in the routine culturette tube) should be used for all cultures. Calgi swabs and wooden-handled swabs generally should not be used, especially for chlamydia cultures. It is helpful to premoisten the swab with sterile saline so that it is softer when touched to the child's tissue. This is particularly important when culturing prepubertal girls. Vaginal cultures can be obtained in either the supine or knee–chest positions, depending on the child's preference. It is important to try to avoid touching or bumping the hymen as this is very sensitive, whereas the vaginal walls are much less sensitive in young children. Cervical swabs are not necessary in culturing prepubertal girls, as most infectious organisms in young girls readily grow in the outer vaginal and introital areas. Cervical cultures are recommended only in pubertal girls. Use of a speculum is not required for obtaining cervical cultures; in the knee–chest position the cervix can often be well visualized and a swab inserted to obtain a culture. Anal swabs are most easily obtained by having the child "bear down" as though he or she is having a bowel movement, which will help relax and open the external anal sphincter.

Sexual Assault Evidence Collection Kit

In cases where a sexual assault of a child or teen has occurred within 24 to 72 hours of the time of the medical evaluation, further information can be gathered via the sexual assault evidence collection kit (also known as the rape kit). The kit's required procedures are completed by the medical care provider, given to a law enforcement officer according to the chain of evidence method, and sent by law enforcement to the state laboratory to be processed. Motile sperm or traces of semen might only be present for 48 to 72 hours after an assault has occurred.

The steps of completing the rape kit should be clearly outlined in the instruction sheets included in the kit. A Woods lamp or fluorescent lamp can be used to shine on the mucus membranes or skin to reveal areas of green fluorescence to be sampled for possible semen. Fluorescence alone does not indicate that semen is present, as other fluids such as urine and Vaseline can also fluoresce. As with the other cultures and samples, all samples should be clearly identified with the child's name, any other identifiers, name of person collecting the samples, date, and time.

Documentation

Medical reports should be prepared in the standard method of the local medical center or practice. These medical documents, written and typed reports, as well as photographic documentation, can be required by subpoena to be presented or used in legal cases. Medical notes and reports should be legible and complete with final assessment, conclusions, and recommendations clearly stated. Medical records and other documentation should be stored per the standard methods of the local medical center or practice. When working with a medical diagnostic team, it is important to routinely review the medical reports and medical slides or photographs with team members as part of the evaluation and diagnostic process. Conclusions of these team reviews should also be documented. Diagnostic criteria for categorizing the information obtained through the interviewing process and the medical exam should be standardized and routinely used by the health care provider or medical evaluation team. Standard diagnostic categories include the following:

- Abuse confirmed
- Abuse unknown
- Abuse suspected
- Abuse ruled out

At the conclusion of the medical evaluation, a community team review will help incorporate the medical portion of the child sexual abuse jigsaw puzzle into the entire case.

Mental Health Referral

In most cases in which the evaluating medical care provider diagnoses confirmed or suspected child sexual abuse, a timely referral for mental health evaluation or therapy should be made for the child. In some cases, a referral for support or therapy for the nonoffending caretakers and siblings should also be made. In any case in which the child is exhibiting behavioral problems, even those unrelated to issues of child sexual abuse, a mental health referral should be made.

Tracking

Children should return for a follow-up visit to assess the success of treatment of medical problems, such as STDs. Follow-up for a sexual abuse case is no different than for any doctor–patient relationship. However, there is another dimension to sexual abuse cases for which all the involved professionals have at least a moral responsibility, if not a legal one. That responsibility is to track the situation to determine whether the abuse has ceased and whether the child and nonoffending caretaker are receiving the recommended support services. This type of follow-up is called *tracking*. Tracking provides the data necessary for continued efforts to serve victims of abuse. Tracking also provides the basis for ongoing evaluation of process and outcome, and opportunity for improvement in case management. When there is a committed, believing, nonoffending caretaker, tracking can be accomplished by simply being in contact with that individual. However, when there is no such person with whom to communicate periodically, data should be gathered from other professionals and agencies that have been involved, such as mental health, social services, law enforcement, and public health.

8.5.11 Child Witnesses of Domestic Violence

Although the direct physical and mental impacts of abuse on a child are significant, so are the consequences of a child witnessing violence to his or her mother. Research shows that even when children are not the direct targets of violence in the home, they can be harmed by witnessing the occurrence of such violence. The witnessing of domestic violence can be auditory, visual, or inferred, including cases in which the child witnesses the aftermath of violence, such as cuts, bruises, or broken limbs. Children who witness domestic violence can suffer severe emotional and developmental difficulties similar to children who are the direct victims of abuse (Schecter & Edleson, 1999).

The legal system is beginning to recognize the need to protect and care for these children. More than 20 states (Alaska, Arizona, Arkansas, California, Delaware, Florida, Georgia, Hawaii, Idaho, Illinois, Indiana, Minnesota, Mississippi, Montana, North Carolina, Ohio, Oklahoma, Oregon, Utah, and Washington, plus Puerto Rico) have enacted legislation that specifically includes children who witness domestic violence as a class of persons in need of legal protection. A child is a witness to domestic violence when an act that is defined as domestic violence is committed in the presence of or witnessed by the child. In some states, the definition goes no further than that. In other states (Alaska, Arizona, Arkansas, California, Florida, Georgia, Hawaii, Idaho, Illinois, Mississippi, Oklahoma, Oregon, and Utah) the definition is more specific, stating that witnessing by a child occurs when the offender commits the violence "in the physical presence of the child or knowing that the child is present and can see or hear" the act of violence. Washington uses the language "within sight or sound of victim's or offender's children." Ohio law states that witnessing occurs when the domestic violence is committed "in the vicinity of a child," meaning within 30 feet or within the same residential unit occupied by the child, regardless of whether the child is actually present or can actually see the commission of the offense. Minnesota includes chronic and severe use of alcohol or a controlled substance by a parent as part of the definition of "exposed to domestic violence." In many states, a conviction of domestic violence committed in the presence of a child can result in harsher penalties. Thus, when the presence of a child during domestic violence is considered to be "aggravating circumstances," sentencing guidelines in most states mandate that such aggravating circumstances result in a harsher criminal penalty, such as a longer jail or prison term or an increased fine. Eight states (Alaska, Arizona, California, Hawaii, Mississippi, Montana, Ohio, and Washington) include committing an act of domestic violence in the presence of a child as an aggravating circumstance. An additional seven states (Arkansas, Florida, Idaho [where penalties are doubled], North Carolina, Oklahoma, Oregon, and Utah) and Puerto Rico provide for enhanced penalties when domestic violence is committed in the presence of a child. Illinois and Nevada require perpetrators of domestic violence to pay for any counseling that a child victim might require. In Delaware, committing domestic violence in the presence of a child is considered an act of child endangerment. In Georgia, it is considered cruelty to children. Indiana requires a noncustodial parent who is convicted of domestic violence in the presence of a child to have visitation with the child supervised for at least one year and not more than two years following the act of domestic violence.

8.5.11.1 Children Who Witness Violence Are at Risk of Violence in Adulthood

Children who witness their parents using violence against each other and who regularly receive excessive punishment are at increased risk of being involved in an abusive relationship as an adult, according to a 20-year study that followed children into adult romantic relationships. In partner violence cases that result in injury, the study finds that being the victim of physical abuse and conduct disorders as a child are also important risk factors. The findings were reported in the August 2003 issue of the *Journal of Consulting and Clinical Psychology.* Research shows that violent behavior toward a romantic partner is difficult to change and that more needs to be done to develop prevention programs that identify major risk factors for partner violence before adult relationships develop. Working toward that goal, psychologist Miriam K. Ehrensaft, PhD, and other researchers from Columbia University College of Physicians and Surgeons and the New York State Psychiatric Institute studied 543 randomly selected children who were first contacted in 1975. The youths and their mothers were assessed separately in three follow-up interviews (1983, 1985–86, and 1991–93) regarding demographic, psychiatric, and other psychosocial factors. In 1999, a questionnaire on recent life changes, work history, aggressive behavior, intimate partner history, and partner violence was mailed to the participants. Results indicated that child behavior problems (conduct disorder) are important predictors of adult partner violence and that exposure to violence between parents and harsh punishment are also risk factors that seem to predict later relationship violence. "It appears that it is not necessary to develop conduct disorder in order for early family lessons of coercive, aggressive conflict resolution within intimate relationships to generalize to youth's own intimate relationships," say the researchers. "Punishment from mothers may serve as a model for physical expression of anger. This acceptance of coercive, power-based norms as ways of regulating conflict may have direct implications for young adults' means of conflict resolution with partners, independent of a disruptive behavior disorder."

The study also found that a history of physical abuse by a caretaker appears to directly increase the odds of using similar tactics of conflict resolution in adult close relationships. However, in looking at factors that might predict being on the receiving end of partner violence, the researchers say they were surprised to find that being the victim of child abuse was not a significant risk factor once exposure to violence between parents and harsh punishment were included. "Exposure to violence between parents, which probably begins when a child is young, seems to pose the greatest independent risk for being the victim of any act of partner violence," say the authors. The findings have important implications for prevention programs, according to Ehrensaft, including targeting families before children reach adolescence. "If families are targeted before children reach late childhood, patterns of excessive punishment may be prevented from becoming entrenched and later reproduced in adolescents' fledgling romantic relationships." Prevention programs should not just target boys, adds Ehrensaft, because no sex differences were found in predictors of partner violence. Both males and females who were abused as children or displayed conduct disorders as adolescents were found to be at risk for partner violence. "Preventing women's partner violence as well as men's may be necessary to prevent adverse consequences of partner violence for women." Finally, the researchers say preventing and treating child disruptive behavior disorders could be a major factor in preventing partner violence.

8.5.11.2 Children Whose Mothers Suffer from Abuse Are More Likely to Be Abused

Children whose mothers suffer domestic abuse are much more likely to be abused themselves. Wahl, Sisk, and Ball (2004) showed that active screening significantly helps physicians identify families that experience domestic abuse, and thus to protect children. The AAP notes that, "child abuse occurs in one-third to three-quarters of families that experience domestic violence." Identifying these women, and taking steps to intervene, may be one of the most effective ways to prevent child abuse. Pediatrician Richard Wahl, MD, and his colleagues asked all families who visited the University of Arizona pediatric clinic over a two-year period to fill in a child safety questionnaire. This questionnaire explicitly asked parents questions about their experiences of domestic violence, such as "Have you ever been in a relationship with someone who has hit you, kicked you, slapped you, punched you or threatened to hurt you?" A total of 7,070 questionnaires were completed, and 138 people revealed that they were currently exposed to domestic violence. This is equivalent to 2 percent of those screened. The researchers then compared the number of cases of domestic violence identified prior to the implementation of active screening with those identified when the questionnaires were in use. "Using the child safety questionnaire significantly increased the odds of detecting current domestic violence, with 73 percent of the cases identified being attributable to the use of the questionnaire," write the study's authors. "An estimated 40-plus cases per year of current domestic violence would probably have been missed in our clinic without active screening. With the implementation of active screening for domestic violence, those parents were assessed and referred to social service agencies while still in our clinic." The researchers noted that the initiation of active screening dramatically increased the need for clinical social services support. Once the staff at the clinic had begun to ask questions about domestic violence, they received requests for assistance on an almost daily basis. "The pediatric clinics may be the ideal environment in which to screen for domestic violence," said the researchers. As the AAP notes, "abused women are often reluctant to seek care for their own injuries but usually continue seeking routine care for their children."

8.5.11.3 Overlap of Violence Against Women, Child Abuse, and Youth Violence

Child abuse and youth violence remain serious social problems in the United States and, according to some research, have strong connections to domestic violence. Slightly more than half of female victims of intimate violence live in households with children under age 12 (U.S. Department of Justice, 2001). An increasing number of studies document the concurrent incidence of domestic violence and child abuse within families. Most of this research indicates that 30 to 60 percent of families experiencing child maltreatment also experience domestic violence. In a national survey of more than 6,000 families, researchers found that 50 percent of the men who frequently assaulted their wives also frequently assaulted their children. Studies also suggest the presence of domestic violence in approximately 40 percent of lethal child abuse cases. In fact, in 1995 the U.S. Advisory Board on Child Abuse and Neglect suggested that domestic violence might be the single major precursor to child abuse and neglect fatalities in this country. An estimated 34 percent of rapes occur in the victim's home where children are likely to see or hear the assault on their mothers or caregivers. When mothers are sexually assaulted or stalked, their children are also likely to be affected. However, to what degree and with what consequences to children has not been addressed by either researchers or practitioners.

Many children might not be direct victims of abuse but rather are exposed to violence in their homes. Data from a 1995 Gallup Poll of family violence suggest that 1.5 million to 3.3 million children witness or experience parental domestic violence each year. Another leading family violence researcher estimates that as many as 10 million children are exposed to parental violence each year. Domestic violence, child abuse, and youth violence often occur within the same families and have serious consequences for the safety of family members, as well as members of the larger community. First, where one form of violence exists, others are often present. Second, the impact on children who witness or experience parental domestic violence might be similar to the consequences of being abused by a parent, and both experiences can significantly contribute to youth violence. The linkages have important implications for intervention and prevention efforts.

8.5.11.4 Effects of Physical and Sexual Violence on Children and Families

Although most maltreated children do not engage in delinquent behavior, if a child is abused or neglected, his or her likelihood of arrest increases by 53 percent as a juvenile, by 38 percent as an adult, and by 38 percent for being involved in a violent crime. A significant risk factor for becoming a child abuser, domestic violence perpetrator, and violent juvenile offender is having been abused or witnessing violence at home. Close to 70 percent of girls involved in the juvenile justice system have histories of physical abuse. Also, surveys of girls in the juvenile justice system and in shelters indicate rates of sexual abuse and assault of more than 70 percent. These girls often respond by running away from home, which too frequently leads to engaging in prostitution. Girls now constitute 25 percent of juvenile arrests in the United States, an increase of 31 percent over the past decade.

Exposure to parental domestic violence, although not considered automatically a form of child abuse, might be associated with a series of childhood problems, primarily behavioral and emotional. Child witnesses of domestic violence on average exhibit more aggressive and antisocial behaviors, fearful and inhibited behaviors, anxiety, depression, trauma-related symptoms, temperament problems, and lowered social competence than children who do not witness such violence. Research also indicates that exposure to domestic violence can affect cognitive functioning. The harm that individual children experience as a result of exposure to domestic violence varies depending on many factors, including the level of violence in the family, the child's exposure to it, the child's ability to cope, and the protective factors in the child's environment. Problems associated with exposure to domestic violence vary with the age and gender of the child, the length of time since the last exposure to violence, and the child's connections to the nonabusive parent and other significant individuals and social supports in his or her life. The impact of a child's exposure to domestic violence and child abuse can continue through adolescence if safety and other interventions are not provided. Many adolescents who have grown up in violent homes are at risk for re-creating the abusive relationships they have observed. They are more likely to attempt suicide, abuse drugs and alcohol, run away from home, and commit other delinquent behavior; engage in teenage prostitution; and commit sexual assault crimes. Research has found that violent adolescents suffered serious physical abuse by a parent and witnessed the use of weapons in their homes significantly more often than nonviolent adolescents. These variables, both independently and combined, have been significantly associated with adolescents' use of violence. Witnessing violence as a child is also associated with adult reports of depression, trauma-related symptoms, and low self-esteem among women, and trauma-related symptoms among men. Research has found that men who as children witnessed their parents' domestic violence are twice as likely to abuse their own wives than sons of nonviolent parents. Domestic violence and child abuse put the next generation at greater risk of becoming abusers and violent juveniles, as well as contribute to other antisocial behavior that continues to affect our communities. Exposure to physical or sexual abuse or domestic violence as a child is not the only risk factor for juvenile violence. Living in a crime-infested community; frequent exposure to drugs, guns, and crime; having parents that use harsh or erratic discipline; and being isolated from the community, family, or school are all circumstances that put children at higher risk.

Although little is known about protective factors that mitigate the effects on children who witness domestic violence, research has identified protective factors for child abuse and youth violence. These factors include economic opportunity, mentors and role models who provide a strong sense of moral development, organized community programs for youth and families, involvement in a faith community, a school environment that promotes prevention, and nurturing adult family members who provide consistent, structured supervision. Research suggests that a successful family and youth violence prevention program targets children's shared risk factors of poverty, social isolation, and the witnessing of violence in the home or on the street. Prevention should also focus on strengthening protective factors, reaching parents with young children, providing services over several years, and conducting rigorous longitudinal evaluations of these measures.

8.5.12 Consequences of Child Abuse and Neglect

An estimated 903,000 children were victims of child abuse or neglect in 2001, according to the U.S. Department of Health and Human Services. Although physical injuries might or might not be immediately visible, abuse and neglect can have consequences for children, families, and society that last lifetimes, if not generations. The impact of child abuse and neglect is often discussed in terms of physical, psychological, behavioral, and societal consequences. In reality, however, it is impossible to separate them completely. Physical consequences (such as damage to a child's growing brain) can have psychological implications (e.g., cognitive delays or emotional difficulties). Psychological problems often manifest as high-risk behaviors. Depression and anxiety, for example, might make a person more likely to smoke, abuse alcohol or illicit drugs, or overeat. High-risk behaviors, in turn, can lead to long-term physical health problems such as STDs, cancer, and obesity. This fact sheet provides an overview of some of the most common physical, psychological, behavioral, and societal consequences of child abuse and neglect, while acknowledging that much crossover among categories exists.

8.5.12.1 Factors Affecting the Consequences of Child Abuse

Not all abused and neglected children will experience long-term consequences. Outcomes of individual cases vary widely and are affected by a combination of factors, including the following:

- The child's age and developmental status when the abuse or neglect occurred
- The type of abuse (physical abuse, neglect, sexual abuse, etc.)
- Frequency, duration, and severity of abuse
- Relationship between the victim and his or her abuser (Chalk, Gibbons, & Scarupa, 2002)

According to data from the National Clearinghouse on Child Abuse and Neglect Information, researchers also have begun to explore why, given similar conditions, some children experience long-term consequences of abuse and neglect whereas others emerge relatively unscathed. The ability to cope, and even thrive, following a negative experience is sometimes referred to as *resilience*. A number of protective factors could contribute to an abused or neglected child's resilience, including individual characteristics, such as optimism, self-esteem, intelligence, creativity, humor, and independence. Protective factors can also include the family or social environment, such as a child's access to social support, particularly a caring adult in the child's life. Community well-being, including neighborhood stability and access to health care, is also a protective factor (Thomlison, 1997).

8.5.12.2 Physical Health Consequences

The immediate physical effects of abuse or neglect can be relatively minor (bruises or cuts) or severe (broken bones, hemorrhage, or even death). In some cases the physical effects are temporary; however, the pain and suffering they cause a child should not be discounted. Meanwhile, the long-term impact of child abuse and neglect on physical health is just beginning to be explored. The following are some outcomes researchers have identified:

- Shaken baby syndrome. The immediate effects of shaking a baby (a common form of child abuse in infants) can include vomiting, concussion, respiratory distress, seizures, and death. Long-term consequences can include blindness, learning disabilities, mental retardation, cerebral palsy, or paralysis (Conway, 1998).
- Impaired brain development. Child abuse and neglect have been shown, in some cases, to cause important regions of the brain to fail to form properly, resulting in impaired physical, mental, and emotional development (Perry, 2002; Shore, 1997). In other cases, the stress of chronic abuse causes a "hyperarousal" response by certain areas of the brain, which can result in hyperactivity, sleep disturbances, and anxiety, as well as increased vulnerability to PTSD, attention deficit/hyperactivity disorder, conduct disorder, and learning and memory difficulties (Dallam, 2001; Perry, 2001).
- Poor physical health. A study of 700 children who had been in foster care for one year found more than one quarter of the children had some kind of recurring physical or mental health problem, according to the National Survey of Child and Adolescent Well-Being. A study of 9,500 HMO participants showed a relationship between various forms of household dysfunction (including childhood abuse) and long-term health problems such as STDs, heart disease, cancer, chronic lung disease, skeletal fractures, and liver disease (Felitti et al., 1998; Hillis et al., 2000).

8.5.12.3 Psychological Consequences

The immediate emotional effects of abuse and neglect—isolation, fear, and an inability to trust—can translate into lifelong consequences including low self-esteem, depression, and relationship difficulties. Researchers have identified links between child abuse and neglect and the following:

- Poor mental and emotional health. In one long-term study, as many as 80 percent of young adults who had been abused met the diagnostic criteria for at least one psychiatric disorder at age 21. These young adults exhibited many problems, including depression, anxiety, eating disorders, and suicide attempts (Silverman, Reinherz, & Giaconia, 1996). Other psychological and emotional conditions associated with abuse and neglect include panic disorder, dissociative disorders, attention deficit/hyperactivity disorder, PTSD, and reactive attachment disorder (Teicher, 2000).
- Cognitive difficulties. The National Survey of Child and Adolescent Well-Being (U.S. Department of Health and Human Services, 2003) recently found children placed in out-of-home care due to abuse or neglect tended to score lower than the general population on measures of cognitive capacity, language development, and academic achievement
- Social difficulties. Children who are abused and neglected by caretakers often do not form secure attachments to them. These early attachment difficulties can lead to later difficulties in relationships with other adults as well as with peers (Morrison, Frank, Holland, & Kates, 1999).

Not all victims of child abuse and neglect experience behavioral consequences; however, child abuse and neglect appear to make the consequences covered next more likely.

8.5.12.4 Behavioral Consequences

- Difficulties during adolescence. Studies have found abused and neglected children to be at least 25 percent more likely to experience problems such as delinquency, teen pregnancy, low academic achievement, drug use, and mental health problems (Kelley, Thornberry, & Smith, 1997).

- Juvenile delinquency and adult criminality. A National Institute of Justice study indicated being abused or neglected as a child increased the likelihood of arrest as a juvenile by 59 percent. Abuse and neglect increased the likelihood of adult criminal behavior by 28 percent and violent crime by 30 percent (Widom & Maxfield, 2001).
- Alcohol and other drug abuse. Research consistently reflects an increased likelihood that abused and neglected children will smoke cigarettes, abuse alcohol, or take illicit drugs. According to the National Institute on Drug Abuse, as many as two thirds of people in drug treatment programs reported being abused as children.
- Abusive behavior. Abusive parents often have experienced abuse during their own childhoods. It is estimated approximately one third of abused and neglected children will eventually victimize their own children.

8.5.12.5 Societal Consequences

Although child abuse and neglect almost always occur within the family, the impact does not end there. Society as a whole pays a price for child abuse and neglect, in terms of both direct and indirect costs. Max et al. (2004) provide estimates of the economic cost of intimate partner violence perpetrated against women and children in the United States, including expenditures for medical care and mental health services, and lost productivity from injury and premature death. The analysis uses national survey data, including the National Violence Against Women Survey and the Medical Expenditure Panel Survey, to estimate costs for 1995. Intimate partner violence against women cost $5.8 billion in 1995, including $320 million for rapes, $4.2 billion for physical assault, $342 million for stalking, and $893 million for murders. Updated to 2003 dollars, costs would total more than $8.3 billion.

- Direct costs. Direct costs include those associated with maintaining a child welfare system to investigate allegations of child abuse and neglect, as well as expenditures by the judicial, law enforcement, health, and mental health systems to respond to and treat abused children and their families. A 2001 report by Prevent Child Abuse America estimates these costs at $24 billion per year.
- Indirect costs. Indirect costs represent the long-term economic consequences of child abuse and neglect. These include juvenile and adult criminal activity, mental illness, substance abuse, and domestic violence. They can also include loss of productivity due to unemployment and underemployment, the cost of special education services, and increased use of the health care system. Prevent Child Abuse America in 2001 estimated these costs at more than $69 billion per year.

8.5.12.6 Risk Factors for Chronic Child Maltreatment

Results from a recent study published in the *Journal of Family Violence* indicate that certain psychosocial risk factors are associated with a mother's high potential for child abuse and neglect over time. These results can help health care practitioners identify families who are at greatest risk of chronic maltreatment and implement long-term interventions that take these risk factors into account. The study involved 56 mothers who either maltreated their children or were at high risk for maltreatment. After four years, the women who still had an open case with a child protection agency or displayed strong tendencies for abuse (chronic abuse problems) were compared with those women with inactive child protection cases and those who displayed weak tendencies for abuse (transitory abuse problems). Results show that six of the 14 risk factors studied were associated with chronic abuse problems after four years:

- High potential for abuse and neglect at intake.
- Presence of both a mother and father in the home.
- Large number of children.
- Mother had been in foster care as a child.
- Mother had been sexually abused.
- Mother had run away as an adolescent.

Additionally, mothers with more than eight risk factors were found to be much more likely to have chronic abuse problems than mothers with fewer than eight risk factors.

8.5.13 Presentation to the Emergency Room

As with other forms of physical abuse, victims usually find their way into the health care system through the ER. In the article "Response to Battered Mothers in the Pediatric Emergency Department: A Call for an Interdisciplinary Approach to Family Violence," Rosalind J. Wright, a research fellow in medicine at Brigham & Women's Hospital in Boston, confirms, "Often the first place a battered woman presents for help is in the health care system with the hospital emergency department frequently being the frontline." Consequently, much research has been conducted that examines the response to woman battering in the adult ED, often focusing on women who present with injuries. Pediatric ED physicians are in a unique position to identify and respond to battered mothers through their children, even though the mother is not the primary patient. "Indeed, some women who are battered for years may only seek help in the medical community when injury to their child occurs," Wright adds.

Wright and colleagues surveyed pediatric ED physicians in training to measure their level of preparedness to respond to battered mothers, and to determine the potential obstacles and attitudinal barriers to their effective response. The study was conducted by the Injury Control Center at the Harvard School of Public Health, which identified pediatric emergency medicine training programs. The researchers developed a 30-item, self-administered questionnaire to obtain information on the extent of training pediatric emergency medicine fellows receive on adult domestic violence and child abuse, and to quantify their level of preparedness for identifying and dealing with battered women and children who are neglected or abused. The researchers mailed out 162 questionnaires in March 1995, with a follow-up mailing to all nonresponders approximately one month later. Response was anonymous; 175 pediatric emergency medicine fellows returned the survey for a response rate of 77.2 percent. The surveyed population was 54.7 percent women, which is consistent with national estimates of the gender distribution in pediatrics. Among the respondents, 59.2 percent were women. Nearly all respondents were first- and second-year fellows. Only three were doing a third year of training, which, at the time of this survey, was not a requirement. The majority (90.4 percent) had completed residency training in pediatrics. Most fellows (63.2 percent) trained in a freestanding children's hospital without an adult ED in the same facility.

Information was obtained on the extent of training received in various aspects of adult domestic violence before current fellowship training. Less than one third of respondents had received training on woman abuse or battered women (29.6 percent) or adult sexual abuse (28.8 percent). The reported proportions receiving training on dating violence and elder abuse were even lower (25.6 percent and 15.2 percent, respectively). The mean number of hours devoted to all topics combined was 16.8 (with a range of 1–136 hours); 58.6 percent of responders reported 10 hours of training in all categories combined. Half (51.8 percent) of the responding fellows believed some formal instruction would be moderately to very helpful to add to the curriculum.

When asked what they would do if they suspected that a child's mother was being battered, almost all responded that they would refer them to a social worker who could then make appropriate referrals. This was equally true whether they were training in hospitals with an adult ED in their facility or in freestanding pediatric hospitals. No data were obtained on whether the social workers were trained to respond to and refer battered women. When given an opportunity to comment in an open-ended format, a number of survey respondents reiterated that caring for battered women was not in the scope of pediatrics. One fellow stated, "I do not treat the mother as a patient." Another fellow wrote, "Not sure how to approach this, given that the women are not our patients." Other respondents commented, "I feel it is out of my jurisdiction as a pediatrician," and "I feel it is not part of my job." A few re-emphasized their lack of training and remarked: "Not my area of comfort/expertise" and "Unsure what to do, lack formal training." Others expressed frustration over not being able to control the mother's behavior: "They protect the batterer and won't agree to seek help for themselves," and "There is resistance of mother to questioning/intervention." Clearly, there is a disconnection occurring both between the health care provider and the pediatric patient's mother, as well as a distancing of the mother from taking responsibility to act to protect the child from the abuser. Wright states, "Many lines of research stress the important link between child abuse and adult domestic violence, specifically battering of the child's mother." She points to Stark and Flitcraft (1988), who indicated that identifying battered mothers might be the single most important means of identifying child abuse. Conversely, when child abuse is suspected, the potential that the child's mother is being battered cannot be ignored. Also, the need to intervene for children who are secondary victims of domestic violence, as they witness the battering of their mothers, is emerging as a crucial factor in responding effectively to family violence:

> Given the complex relationship between battered women and their children, it can be argued that identifying battered mothers may be the best way to protect their children. Those in a position to identify child witnesses and victims of domestic violence are in an excellent position to respond to battered mothers. The pediatric emergency room is recognizably one medical care setting where this unique opportunity exists. This study, however, demonstrates that battered women are rarely identified in the PED. We also identify major obstacles to effective intervention, including lack of training and experience, and confirm internal barriers cited by the responding physicians.

The link between women and children in a violence scenario is examined in this section shortly. Wright's study underscores the need for more comprehensive training of physicians pertaining to domestic violence, and unwittingly emphasizes the need for clinical forensic nurse specialists in EDs that can help these physicians with identification of potential forensic cases, both adult and pediatric. Wright says that physicians are better educated about child abuse and neglect compared to other forms of domestic violence, due in part to the adoption of mandatory child abuse reporting laws in the 1960s. "With the implementation of such laws came an increase in reporting and a consequent rise in demand for professional and community education and programs to facilitate systematic response to victims of child abuse," she says. The lack of required training on adult domestic violence, including woman battering, in medical schools has previously been documented. In a study of all 143 accredited U.S. and Canadian medical schools surveyed in 1987 and 1988, 58 percent of the 116 responding schools did not require instruction about battering in their curriculum (CDC, 1989). Wright says that the skewed training on child abuse in her survey was also likely influenced by the fact that nearly the entire study population trained in pediatrics before fellowship, and thus had limited contact with adult patients. The most frequently confirmed obstacle to identifying battered women was lack of experience with these kinds of cases, Wright says. Many of Wright's findings on perceived obstacles to responding to battered women parallel those revealed in a study of primary care physicians' responses to domestic violence. Sugg and Inui (1992) conducted open-ended interviews with 38 physicians and found that the most frequently identified perceived barriers to the recognition of domestic violence and intervention in the primary care setting were time constraints (71 percent), powerlessness (50 percent), lack of comfort (39 percent), loss of control (42 percent), and fear of offending the patient (55 percent). In that same study, many physicians who expressed a sense of powerlessness also pointed to their lack of training on domestic violence during medical school and residency or in continuing medical education courses. Sixty-one percent revealed they had no training, whereas only 8 percent said they had good training on this issue. "We would agree that physicians' education on domestic violence may be most lacking with respect to understanding the dynamics that maintain women in abusive relationships," Wright says. "To overcome the obstacle, we must overcome the prejudices that exist toward women in battering relationships by educating all physicians about the battered woman's syndrome." Wright adds that health care professionals who receive formal training on domestic violence are less likely to hold the battered persons responsible for their situation. In general, Wright's study found that protocols on the treatment of battered women are rare in pediatric EDs. In one study of female trauma victims in the ED, the implementation of such a protocol increased the proportion of all patients identified as battered from 5.6 percent to 30 percent (McLeer & Anwar, 1989). Although protocols facilitate the response to abused women, they do not preclude the need for continued education on identifying domestic violence. McLeer, Anwar, Herman, and Maquiling (1989) found that without continued presence of staff who were knowledgeable about and interested in the issue of family violence, the level of identification of domestic violence in the ER returned to the low levels seen before implementing the protocol. A frequently cited obstacle to providing care to the battered mother of a pediatric patient was lack of time. Wright says, "The time constraints of treating a battered child, much less a battered woman, are indeed enormous and understandably daunting in the context of a busy PED. Implementation of programs and policies involving many care providers (including nurses) to facilitate response to suspected battered women and children would help take the burden off the physician and alleviate time constraints."

A program called the Advocacy for Women and Kids in Emergencies, pioneered at Children's Hospital of Boston, is an interdisciplinary team that assesses the mother of any child reported for abuse. An advocate is assigned to refer suspected battered mothers to the appropriate services. The advocate continues to advise the mother as she interacts with the different agencies and guides her through the process. The role of the physician is crucial for such a program to succeed, as the physician needs to be trained to identify these patients and make the initial referral. "As we formulate approaches to family violence in an interdisciplinary fashion we must be mindful of the unique issues existing around responding to abused children and battered women, paying particular attention to how they differ," Wright says. There areexisting programs in place to facilitate a systematic response to child victims; however, mandatory reporting for woman battering could threaten the safety of battered women. Some experts believe that patient autonomy and confidentiality are also threatened through this approach. "Strategies sensitive to these differences need to be a part of any approach taken to responding to battered mothers," Wright adds.

Wright isn't afraid to play the gender card. She explains that self-determined obstacles to responding to battered women might be different for male and female physicians. In her study, the reported frequency of obstacles was significantly different based on the physician's gender. Sugg and Inui (1992) also found gender differences in the responses given by male and female physicians when exploring attitudes about domestic violence. "It may be that we need to explore how societal determinants of gender roles affect a physician's response to domestic violence," Wright says. "Further research is necessary to explore this issue as it may be important to account for such gender differences when designing curricula to enhance appropriate response to domestic violence."

8.5.14 Child Abuse: Investigation, Prosecution, and Expert Witness Testimony Issues

8.5.14.1 The Key to Convicting Child Molesters

Despite the importance given to courtroom statements made by victims in cases of child sexual abuse, a child's testimony is not necessarily the key to convicting child molesters, say researchers at the University of Michigan and Western Michigan University. Rather, effective cooperation among police, prosecutors, and professionals in CPS can help reduce further trauma to children and increase the number of criminal convictions—largely through higher confession and plea rates.

"Decisions about sexual abuse usually come down to a child's word against an adult's," says Kathleen C. Faller, University of Michigan professor of social work:

> Often, sexually abused children are at a disadvantage because they lack adult communication skills, don't know what to do when they are sexually abused, and are under the power and control of the offender. Our research suggests attention should be focused elsewhere, on the professionals and system coordination. Adults can and should bear primary responsibility for obtaining successful outcomes in child sexual abuse cases, not child witnesses.

In a study published in the February 2000 issue of *Child Abuse & Neglect*, Faller and James Henry, Western Michigan University assistant professor of social work, found that defendants in 64 percent of cases in which they were accused of child sex offenses confessed to their crimes and in 70 percent of cases entered into a plea bargaining agreement, thanks mostly to successful intervention by law enforcement officials and CPS. Less than 5 percent of the cases studied actually went to trial, sparing a large number of children from rehashing details of the traumatic incident in open court. The researchers used data from 323 cases of alleged sex crimes against children in St. Joseph County in southwestern Michigan from 1988 to 1998. Specific information gathered—with the help of St. Joseph County Prosecutor Jeffrey Middleton—included child and suspect demographic data, involvement of police and CPS, child disclosure patterns and caretaker responses, offender confessions, offender pleas, trial and child testimony information, and sentences received by offenders.

According to the study, in nearly all (96 percent) of the confessed cases (206 out of 323), offenders either completely or partially corroborated the statements given to investigators by victims. A little more than a third of the alleged offenders took a polygraph and about 63 percent of them failed the test, Faller and Henry say. Lie detector tests were not given to the remaining majority of suspects because they admitted to at least some of what their victims had described. Overall, charges were brought against 69 percent of the defendants in child sexual abuse cases referred to the prosecutor's office by police or CPS, the study shows. About three-fourths of all suspects received some sort of punishment, with about 90 percent of those found guilty sentenced to jail or prison. The researchers say that CPS was active in 57 percent of all cases. Specifically, CPS was involved in about 87 percent of the cases in which alleged offenders lived with the child and in roughly 42 percent of cases in which they did not. Nearly three fourths of the cases included videotaped interviews of the victims, although an interview was more likely to occur if CPS was involved (85 percent of the time vs. 57 percent with law enforcement, but no CPS involvement), Faller and Henry say. Most children (81 percent) initially reported their abuse to someone they knew (parent, caretaker, other relative, etc.) before telling police or CPS, they say. The disclosures of 54 percent of the children in the entire sample were intentional, 28 percent were unintentional, and 2 percent involved both intentional and unintentional elements.

"Although children and families in the criminal justice system may not be representative of all sexual abuse cases, these cases show that children confide their sexual abuse in trusted adults, are believed and supported by their caretakers, and can prevail in the criminal justice system," Faller says. "However, in the overwhelming majority of cases, these children did not prevail by providing testimony in criminal trials. The victims' success in these cases derives almost entirely from effective intervention by professionals with offenders so that they confess and plead to their crimes."

8.5.14.2 New Strategies to Prevent Child Homicide Needed

In what may be the largest study of child homicide, two University of California, Irvine researchers have identified significant differences in child and adult homicides, as well as age-related risk factors, that could lead to more effective prevention of child abuse and child homicide. Results of the study of nearly 1,500 child homicide cases from the California Attorney General's files were reported in the May 1999 issue of *Homicide Studies*. In their review of 30,929 California homicides that occurred between 1981 and 1990, Kenneth Chew and Richard McCleary (1999), professors in University of California, Irvine's School of Social Ecology, focused on the 5 percent of victims who were younger than 15. Their findings suggest a need for age-specific approaches to prevention of child homicide.

"Adult murders are most likely to occur in a public place on a Friday or Saturday night around 1 a.m. . . . about the time that bars close. Victims typically are men between the ages of 20 and 29, and more than 60 percent are killed by firearms," Chew says. In contrast, children of both sexes typically are killed at home, in the middle of a weekday, by a parent or other caregiver. The weapon of choice, overwhelmingly, is the human hand. Homicide is the nation's second leading cause—after auto accidents—of preventable deaths of children, according to the California Department of Health Services. "It's relatively rare," Chew says, "but unlike other causes of childhood death, the child homicide rate has increased steadily since 1960. It's a serious public health issue. Still, very few parents who commit homicide set out to do murder. They're under stress; they go too far. In more than half of all infant and toddler homicides, the precipitating event is child abuse/shaken baby syndrome." Although most child homicides are the result of "child abuse gone too far," McCleary confirms, he and Chew label a significant number of them "altruistic killings." "Between 15 percent and 30 percent of homicides of children under age 10 are related to adult suicides," says McCleary. "The parent decides to commit suicide, and can't bear to leave the child behind. Sometimes the suicide-homicide is related to a custody dispute."

According to the study, child homicides show two distinct peaks: The first occurs between birth and age 4, the second between ages 10 and 14. Nearly 60 percent of the 1,498 child homicides studied were infants and toddlers younger than 4. About 27 percent were middle-school children ages 10 to 14. Less than 15 percent were primary school children between the ages of 5 and 9. "Infants and toddlers are home all the time, alone with one adult, and they're physically weak," Chew points out. In addition, although their study did not include socioeconomic data, Chew and McCleary suggest that parents or caregivers of these littlest victims often lack the education, support, and financial resources to handle the constant demands of caring for young children. "By age 14, the pattern is beginning to look like adult homicide," Chew continues. "Middle-school students start to hang out with older brothers, in gangs. They follow bad counsel, get in over their heads—now it's guns, drugs, money, 'honor.' The homicide begins with a dispute, or in commission of a felony, and a gun happens to be there." But what is happening with the middle range of kids, those between the ages of 4 and 10, for whom the risk of homicide seems to decrease? "There appears to be a developmental 'victimology' at work," Chew says. "Children in the middle are physically more robust, they're smarter, they can run away. Away all day at school, they are less likely than younger kids to be killed during the day on a weekday."

What Chew and McCleary learned about the time, place, and people—victims and killers—involved in child homicides has led them to recommend prevention approaches that take into account developmental stages. "For child homicide prevention, the approach needs to be different—they're not like adult homicides," Chew says. "Stricter gun control, for example, might have an effect on teen or adult homicide rates. But it won't save babies. Infants don't die of gunshot wounds—they die at their parents' hands." What could make a difference for infants and toddlers, the researchers say, is education. They recommend prenatal and parenting classes that cover anger management as well as child development. Parents also need respite child care, advice and support from visiting nurses, and suicide hotline counseling. "We know whom to target—young parents with limited resources. And we know when to target them—before the child is born," McCleary says. "Young parents get information in prenatal classes on sudden infant death syndrome (SIDS) and postpartum depression, but they aren't told about child abuse. Many of them don't know that infants and toddlers are built like tootsie-pops, with oversized heads that make them especially vulnerable to shaking or jerking. No one tells young parents that anger is normal, and there are ways to manage it safely." Child homicide is the tip of the iceberg of child abuse, according to Chew and McCleary. "Child homicide provides a window on child abuse," McCleary says. "There's no way to know the exact circumstances of an abuse incident, but we get a detailed picture of homicide. Our findings in the study of 1,498 child homicides suggest that an age-developmental perspective can produce a more focused prevention strategy."

8.5.14.3 Child Abuse and Neglect Fatalities

Statistics from the National Clearinghouse on Child Abuse and Neglect Information make it evident that, despite the efforts of the child protection system, child maltreatment fatalities remain a serious problem. Although the untimely deaths of children due to illness and accidents have been closely monitored, deaths that result from physical assault or severe neglect can be more difficult to track. Intervention strategies targeted at resolving this problem face complex challenges. The NCANDS reported an estimated 1,400 child fatalities in 2002. This translates to a rate of 1.98 children per 100,000 children in the general population. NCANDS defines "child fatality" as the death of a child caused by an injury resulting from abuse or neglect, or in which abuse or neglect were contributing factors. Many researchers and practitioners believe child fatalities due to abuse and neglect are underreported. States' definitions of key terms such as child homicide, abuse, and neglect vary (therefore, so do the numbers and types of child fatalities they report). In addition, some deaths officially labeled as accidents, child homicides, or SIDS might be attributed to child abuse or neglect if more comprehensive investigations were conducted or if there were consensus on the coding of abuse on death certificates. Recent studies in Colorado and North Carolina have estimated as many as 50 to 60 percent of deaths resulting from abuse or neglect are not recorded (Crume et al., 2002; Herman-Giddens et al., 1999). These studies indicate that neglect is the most underrecorded form of fatal maltreatment. The rate of child abuse and neglect fatalities reported by NCANDS has increased slightly over the last several years from 1.84 per 100,000 children in 2000 to 1.96 in 2001 and 1.98 in 2002. However, experts do not agree whether this represents an actual increase in child abuse and neglect fatalities, or whether it can be attributed to improvements in reporting procedures. For example, statistics on approximately 20 percent of fatalities were from health departments and fatality review boards for 2002, compared to 11.4 percent for 2001, an indication of greater coordination of data collection among agencies. A number of issues affecting the accuracy and consistency of child fatality data from year to year have been identified, including the following:

- Variation among reporting requirements and definitions of child abuse and neglect
- Variation in state child fatality review processes
- The amount of time (as long as a year, in some cases) it could take a fatality review team to declare abuse or neglect as the cause of death
- Miscoding of death certificates

Research indicates very young children (ages 3 and younger) are the most frequent victims of child fatalities. NCANDS data for 2002 demonstrated children younger than 1 year accounted for 41 percent of fatalities, and children younger than 4 years accounted for 76 percent of fatalities. This population of children is the most vulnerable for many reasons, including their dependency, small size, and inability to defend themselves. In 2002, more than one third (38 percent) of child maltreatment fatalities were associated with neglect alone. Physical abuse alone was cited in 30 percent of reported fatalities. Another 29 percent of fatalities were the result of multiple maltreatment types. Fatal child abuse might involve repeated abuse over a period of time (e.g., battered child syndrome), or it might involve a single, impulsive incident (e.g., drowning, suffocating, or shaking a baby). In cases of fatal neglect, the child's death results not from anything the caregiver does, but from a caregiver's failure to act. The neglect can be chronic (e.g., extended malnourishment) or acute (e.g., an infant who drowns because she is left unsupervised in the bathtub).

No matter how the fatal abuse occurs, one fact of great concern is that the perpetrators are, by definition, individuals responsible for the care and supervision of their victims. In 2002, one or both parents were involved in 79 percent of child abuse or neglect fatalities. Of the other 21 percent of fatalities, 16 percent were the result of maltreatment by nonparent caretakers, and 5 percent were unknown or missing. These percentages are consistent with findings from previous years. There is no single profile of a perpetrator of fatal child abuse, although certain characteristics reappear in many studies. Frequently the perpetrator is a young adult in his or her mid-20s without a high school diploma, living at or below the poverty level, depressed, and someone who might have difficulty coping with stressful situations. In many instances, the perpetrator has experienced violence firsthand. Most fatalities from physical abuse are caused by fathers and other male caretakers. Mothers are most often held responsible for deaths resulting from child neglect. However, in some cases this might be because women are most often responsible (or assumed to be responsible) for children's care. The response to the problem of child abuse and neglect fatalities is often hampered by inconsistencies, including the following:

- Inaccurate reporting of the number of children who die each year as a result of abuse and neglect
- Lack of national standards for child autopsies or death investigations
- The different roles CPS agencies in different jurisdictions play in the investigation process
- The use in some states of medical examiners or elected coroners who do not have specific child abuse and neglect training

To address some of these inconsistencies, multidisciplinary and multiagency child fatality review teams have emerged to provide a coordinated approach to the investigation of child deaths. These teams, which now exist at a state, local, or state and local level in every state and in the District of Columbia, are comprised of prosecutors, coroners or medical examiners, law enforcement personnel, CPS workers, public health care providers, and others. Child fatality review teams offer many benefits, including improved interagency communication, identification of gaps in community child protection systems, and the development of data information systems that can guide agency policy and practice (National Center on Child Fatality Review, 2003). The teams review cases of child deaths and facilitate appropriate follow-up. This might include ensuring that services are provided for surviving family members, providing information to assist in the prosecution of perpetrators, and developing recommendations to improve child protection and community support systems. When addressing the issue of child maltreatment, and especially child fatalities, prevention is a recurring theme. Well-designed, properly organized child fatality review teams appear to offer hope for defining the underlying nature and scope of fatalities due to child abuse and neglect. The child fatality review process helps identify risk factors that might assist prevention professionals, such as those engaged in home visiting and parenting education, to prevent future deaths.

In 2003, the Office on Child Abuse and Neglect, within the Children's Bureau, Administration for Children and Families, U.S. Department of Health and Human Services, launched a Child Abuse Prevention Initiative to raise awareness of the issue in a much more visible and comprehensive way than ever before. The Prevention Initiative is an opportunity to work together in communities across the country to keep children safe, provide the support families need to stay together, and raise children and youth to be happy, secure, and stable adults. For more information, visit the Prevention Initiative Web site at http://nccanch.acf.hhs.gov/topics/prevention/index.cfm.

Although the exact number of children affected is uncertain, child fatalities due to abuse and neglect remain a serious problem in the United States. Fatalities disproportionately affect young children and are most often caused by one or both of the child's parents. Child fatality review teams appear to be among the most promising current approaches to responding to and preventing child abuse and neglect fatalities.

8.5.14.4 Nurses' Expert Testimony in Child Abuse Cases

In *Health Professional Exams of Suspected Child Victims*, noted medico-legal expert Beatrice Yorker (2001), RN, JD, embraces the SANE model of specialized health care delivery to adult and pediatric cases of sexual assault. She says, "SANE nurses have reported generally positive experiences with the courts in being recognized as experts in conducting health care exams related to sexual assault and testifying as expert witnesses." Yorker explains that although the acceptance of nonphysician providers of forensic medical examinations varies, the rapid growth in the number of nurse practitioners and physician assistants is a by-product of the unmet consumer demand for primary health care. Yorker says, "Concerns regarding the use of nonphysicians include competition and scope of practice. Even in collaborative physician extender relationships, physicians may be vicariously liable for the practice of an employee, independently liable for poor protocols and inadequate supervision of mid-level providers in their practice, or liable for aiding and abetting the unauthorized practice of medicine if a provider exceeds his or her scope of practice." Yorker reports that many states authorize independent practice and prescriptive authority for nurse practitioners, physician assistants, and nurse midwives, who are regulated under medical practice acts. Yorker says, "The courts have clearly interpreted state legislative intent to recognize the 'existence of overlapping functions between physicians and registered nurses (RNs) and to permit additional sharing of functions within organized health systems' and are suspect of any attempt to restrict trade," she adds, citing the case of *Fein v. Permanente Medical Group* (1985). Yorker points to an increasing number of nonphysicians who are being qualified in court as able "to exercise that degree of skill practiced by the average prudent practitioner in the same or similar circumstances" (*Avret v. McCormick, 1980*; *Fein v. Permanente Medical Group, 1985*; Hirsch, 1991). She cites research by Doss (1994) showing that judges are less likely to view nonphysicians as qualified to testify in child abuse cases than are prosecutors. Yorker adds that even though the 1994 survey by Doss was limited to prosecutors, it has implications for judges who conduct child abuse cases.

Two studies provide data regarding the prevalence of nonphysicians in the examination, diagnosis, and treatment of child abuse cases, Yorker suggests. Giardino, Montoya, Richardson, and Leventhal (1999) sent 118 questionnaires to child protection programs identified by the Executive Committee on Child Abuse and Neglect of the AAP under the sponsorship of the Special Interest Group on Child Abuse of the Ambulatory Pediatric Association. Seventy-three surveys from 31 states were returned. The respondents were required to have either a physician or a nurse practitioner on staff to qualify as a medically oriented child protection team; 49 percent of the respondents had nurses on the teams. Yorker says that the inclusion of nurses in their survey, the requirement that either an MD or nurse practitioner staff a "medically oriented" child protection team, and the response that approximately half of these teams use nurses, demonstrates acceptance of nonphysician practice by the AAP.

Kelley and Yorker (1997) conducted a survey of 221 nonphysician health care providers (including nurse practitioners, physician assistants, and RNs) who provided child abuse examinations. Out of the 104 respondents, 95.2 percent performed examinations in cases of sexual abuse and 70 percent in cases of physical abuse. The practice settings of the respondents included clinics (70 percent), EDs (41.4 percent), child abuse programs (27.9 percent), and child advocacy centers (23.4 percent). The respondents had an average of six years of experience working in the field of child abuse and 76.9 percent provided colposcopic examinations. Approximately 80 percent reported being supervised by a physician. The data from this study regarding court experiences of nonphysicians who work in the field of child abuse are particularly relevant to the current study. Seventy-eight percent of the respondents had qualified as an expert witness and testified in court, only 12 percent ever had a judge refuse to qualify them as an expert, and the average number of times each had testified in court was 25.6, with a range from 0 to 360 times. Kelley and Yorker asked respondents if they perceived that their credibility was an issue with other disciplines involved in child maltreatment; they report that respondents believed they had credibility problems with defense attorneys (35.6 percent), physicians (16.7 percent), prosecutors (11.5 percent), judges (10.6 percent), police (6.8 percent), and CPS (3.9 percent).

In Yorker's search for related case law involving nurses or physician assistants who provided expert witness testimony in legal appeals, she located five published cases. The first of these was tried in Georgia (*Hyde v. State*, 1988) by a father who appealed his conviction for molesting his then 4-year-old daughter. He alleged that the testimony of a nurse practitioner was improperly admitted because her qualifications were less than those of a medical doctor. He also appealed the portion of the nurse's testimony that identified the father and perpetrator as hearsay and therefore inadmissible. Yorker reports that the court responded to the first issue by enumerating the qualifications of the expert witness. The nurse held two advanced degrees in nursing, had been trained at a reputable hospital-based rape crisis center to evaluate adult and child victims of sexual abuse, and had completed two days of intensive training in child sexual abuse issues. The court cited previous case law that recognized "an overlap of medical and nursing expertise" and overruled the objection. The court responded to the hearsay objection, concluding that the portion of the nurse practitioner's testimony that identified the father as the perpetrator fell under laws that permit, as an exception to the hearsay rule, testimony concerning statements made as part of the medical history when relevant to diagnosis or treatment. Yorker says that the published opinion referred to the nurse practice act, OCGA 43-26-1(3), which defines the practice of nursing as "the performance or compensation of any act in the observation, care, and counsel of the ill, injured, or infirm . . . which requires substantial specialized judgment and skill based on knowledge and application of the principles of physical . . . science" and concluded the nurse was "merely fulfilling her professional duty." Yorker adds, "Perhaps the most compelling conclusion of the appellate court, was its decision to allow the expert to testify regarding causation. The court upheld her clinical findings from the examination of the child's pubic and pelvic areas and her testimony that her findings 'were consistent with the history that (the child) related to me' and that vaginal scarring of the sort she found 'would occur from an object being placed in the vagina, a blunt type.'"

In a case in 1991, Yorker reports that the state of Tennessee decided two appeals that involved expert testimony nurses in prosecutions (*State of Tennessee v. Brunetti*, 1991; *State of Tennessee v. Fields, 1991*). In the *Brunetti* case, the defendant appealed a conviction for molesting his girlfriend's 10-year-old daughter, alleging error in permitting a nurse to qualify as an expert and in allowing testimony regarding the cause of injuries. Specifically, the nurse stated "lesions on the girl's vagina and a tear in the hymen" were abnormal and could be caused by trauma, infection, or penetration. The court responded that there was no abuse of discretion on the part of the trial court. They upheld the nurse's testimony and qualifications, which included a master's degree, employment at the Memphis Rape Crisis Center since 1984, and more than 1,000 examinations of victims of sexual abuse. The defendant's sentence of 18 years in prison was affirmed. The *Fields* case involved the testimony of a SANE in the rape of an adult female victim. The court upheld the qualifications of a master's degree, nine years of experience with the rape crisis program, and numerous prior occasions testifying in rape cases to allow the nurse's expert testimony regarding the nature and the cause of the genital injuries and the statements made by the victim describing her assailant.

In Ohio, the court heard two appeals of sexual assault convictions that challenged a nurse's expert testimony. In *Ohio v. Brooks* (1996), the court upheld a clinical nurse specialist and assistant professor of nursing's testimony that "evidence found in her examination was consistent with the type of abuse that was alleged by the victim." The court also allowed a presumption of force based on the age differential between the 6-year-old victim and the 40-year-old defendant, as well as the inherent power relationship between parent and child. The court also allowed testimony that explained why the victim delayed reporting the abuse for more than a year. Yorker points to the 1995 case of *Ohio v. Brant*, which involved the appeal of a conviction of date rape on a college campus. The court upheld the opinion of a nurse practitioner at the children's hospital where the 19-year-old was examined that the trauma was caused by forcible rape. The court concluded that since the defense had used this expert on cross-examination to establish a slight blood-alcohol level, her testimony regarding physical findings of trauma to the vaginal area, swelling, tearing, and discoloration consistent with forcible intercourse should also be allowed. In the 1993 case of *Daubert v. Merrell Dow Pharmaceuticals*, the U.S. Supreme Court clarified that for expert testimony to be admitted, it must be relevant and reliable. The court established four factors a judge can use in scrutinizing scientific evidence:

- Whether a theory or technique has been tested
- Whether it "has been subjected to peer review and publication"
- Whether there is a known or potential rate of error
- The degree to which it has "acceptability in the relevant scientific community"

Yorker writes:

> Very recently, this "gatekeeping" obligation of a trial court to limit scientific testimony has been extended to all expert testimony in *Kumho Tire v. Carmichael* (1999). Furthermore, the Supreme Court in *General Electric v. Joiner* (1997) upheld Daubert as a way to exclude "expertise that is false and science that is junky." The court allows appellate review of the admission of expert scientific testimony only if the trial court showed abuse of discretion. Thus, it is unlikely that the cases permitting nurses to provide expert testimony will be overturned if they continue to comply with the Daubert factors.

Chadwick and Krous (1997) described irresponsible medical testimony in three child abuse prosecutions, and outlined the following recommendations regarding the minimal credentials for any professional to testify regarding the medical findings of child abuse:

- General training or experience in child abuse and neglect
- Specific training or experience relative to the particular type of case being adjudicated
- Membership in relevant professional societies
- Child abuse and neglect conference presentations and attendance
- Relevant professional publications

8.5.15 The School Nurse: A New Opportunity for Forensic Nurses

Although the rates of violent incidents in U.S. schools fluctuate, few would argue that school-related violence is not prevalent. For the sake of perspective, in 1933, 75 percent of adolescent deaths resulted from natural causes; 50 years later, 80 percent of adolescent deaths were the result of homicide and unintentional injuries, according to Mann et al. (1998). In a 1992–93 survey of more than 2,000 school districts, student-on-student assaults, student-on-teacher assaults, and students carrying weapons were reported as common problems (Weist & Warner, 1996). The approximately 58,000 school nurses in the United States are in a particularly unique position to identify and document incidents of violence in schools, as well as to treat and advocate for youthful victims. The National Association of School Nurses (NASN, 1999) defines school nursing as "a specialized practice of professional nursing that advances the well being, academic success, and life-long achievement of students. School nurses facilitate positive student responses to normal development; promote health and safety; intervene with actual and potential health problems; provide case management services; and actively collaborate with others to build student and family capacity for adaptation, self management, self advocacy, and learning." Bell and Benak (2000) write:

> Local law enforcement agencies have been asked to provide full-time, uniformed police officers in the position of student resource officers in an effort to deter crime and serve as a "watch dog" in high schools; nurses are already employed in the health clinics of public schools. As one might imagine, the presence of law enforcement has been accepted with mixed responses but surprisingly, mostly positive ones. This is an example of combining the community policing efforts discussed by Codish and the advanced roles of nurses addressed by Lynch. Wallen describes nurses and teachers as adjuncts for detecting anti-social or aberrant behavior, injuries, and student conversations. Information communicated between law enforcement and a school nurse that understands forensic principles within a high school environment provides unique opportunities to demonstrate collaborative practice and recognize the early warning signs of a youth at risk. This example of collaborative practice may be beneficial in deterring the type of event that occurred at Columbine High School. Nurses must be encouraged to stand on their credentials and work toward the development of partnerships that promote health and safety in all their contact environments.

In its position statement (adopted in 1997 and revised in 2003), *The Role of the Advanced Practice Registered Nurse in the School Setting*, the NASN states, "The practice of school nursing is both complex and multidimensional. School nurses come from many specialty areas and function in a number of different roles and practice settings (Christeson, 2003). One of the specialty areas found in school nursing is advanced practice."

The first expanded role for nurses was developed during the 1960s at the University of Colorado with the inception of the pediatric nurse practitioner program. Pediatric nurse practitioners were educated to provide pediatric care in ambulatory community health settings (Wold, 1981). Since that time, other nurse practitioner and clinical nurse specialties have been developed, and advanced practice RNs now function as nurse practitioners or clinical nurse specialists in a variety of areas and settings. In 2000, the National Sample Survey of Registered Nurses estimated there were 102,829 nurse practitioners with 14,643 also prepared as clinical nurse specialists. The advanced practice areas most appropriate for nurses working in the school setting are pediatric, school, family, and psychiatric and mental health.

The NASN reports that the title of advanced practice registered nurse (APRN) is being increasingly used by legislative and governing bodies to describe the collection of RNs who practice in the extended role beyond the normal role of basic registered nursing. The APRN has education beyond the four-year baccalaureate degree in nursing. In addition to increased education, the APRN role requires extra responsibility, critical thinking, and judgment. There are four major groups of APRNs: nurse practitioners, clinical nurse specialists, certified nurse midwives, and certified registered nurse anesthetists. Those groups appropriate to work in schools are nurse practitioners and clinical nurse specialists. The nurse practitioner and clinical nurse specialist are differentiated by educational preparation and clinical practice (Advanced Practice Registered Nurses Council, 2003). Some states require certification from a nationally recognized body to be licensed as an APRN (American Nurses Association, 1996). Clinical nurse specialists are APRNs who are educated in the disciplines of nursing and a clinical practice specialty of primary or acute care. Clinical nurse specialists can practice in the advanced role with specialized education, national certification, and official recognition from a state licensing board (Advanced Practice Registered Nurses Council, 2003). Nurse practitioners are RNs with advanced academic and clinical experience that enables them to diagnose and manage most common and many chronic illnesses, independently or as part of a health care team. Nurse practitioners provide some care that was previously only performed by physicians. In most states, nurse practitioners have the ability to prescribe medications. Nurse practitioners focus mainly on health maintenance, disease prevention, counseling, and patient education. Nurse practitioner education programs grant either a certificate or a master's degree (American College of Nurse Practitioners, 2003b). Currently, entry-level preparation for nurse practitioner practice is a master's degree (American Academy of Nurse Practitioners, 2003). A key component to most nurse practitioner programs is an intensive preceptorship under the direct supervision of a physician or an experienced nurse practitioner. There is also instruction in nursing theory. The scope of practice for nurse practitioners varies depending on each state's nurse practice act (American College of Nurse Practitioners, 2003b). The competencies that all nurse practitioners should be able to demonstrate regardless of specialty area are available in the document "Nurse Practitioner Primary Care Competencies in Specialty Areas" from the National Organization of Nurse Practitioner Faculties.

The NASN states:

> Health services provided in school districts may include enhanced health services as an alternative to school-based or school-linked health centers. A number of school districts throughout the country offer health services beyond the basic core services. This is due in part to the fact that health care reforms have not solved the problem of students' access to health care and health problems continue to interfere with students' learning (Marx & Wooley, 1998). As good health is important to a child's ability to learn and succeed in school and life, the need for quality, affordable health programs in or near schools is unavoidable. Employment of an advanced practice registered nurse enables a school district to offer more than the core health services. An enhanced school health services team may include school nurses, advanced practice registered nurses, licensed practical nurses, unlicensed assistive personnel, clerical staff, school physicians, school counselors, school psychologists, and school social workers (American Academy of Pediatrics, 2001). On an enhanced school health services team that includes both school nurses and advanced practice nurses, school nurses are able to assist in the identification of students with health problems and provide triage services for the advanced practice registered nurse.

The position paper adds:

> It is the position of the National Association of School Nurses that advanced practice registered nurses can provide unique and valuable services for students. In those communities where students do not receive consistent, appropriate medical care, advanced practice registered nurses offer a cost effective solution to this need. School districts that include both school nurses and advanced practice nurses on their staffs will be able to offer a broader range of health services. The anticipated outcome is more health needs of students being met, resulting in a positive impact on the health and educational performance of students.

8.5.15.1 The Role of School Nurses in Youth Violence

Nurses are well equipped to deal with interpersonal violence, and an area in which they can make significant contributions is in the education system. Student-on-student violence, as demonstrated by the shootings at Columbine High School in Littleton, Colorado in 1999, is of concern to policymakers, educators, and parents. Although daily news reports of violence in the nation's primary and secondary institutions of learning would seem to indicate otherwise, a report issued in late 2004 seems to indicate that the rate of violent crimes in schools is decreasing. The rate of violent crimes in school settings against students ages 12 to 18 dropped by half between 1992 and 2002, according to a report released by the U.S. Department of Education and the U.S. Department of Justice.

Indicators of School Crime and Safety: 2004 is the seventh in a series of annual reports on school crime and safety. The report presents data on student and teacher victimization, students' perception of personal safety, gangs, student reports of bullying, students being called hate-related words and seeing hate-related graffiti, and student alcohol and drug abuse. "This report shows that over the past 10 years or so that violent incidents among teenagers have declined in our schools, as have the number of students who bring weapons to school," says Deborah Price, deputy undersecretary for the Office of Safe and Drug-Free Schools. "This annual report helps us monitor school safety. It is a necessary reminder that we need to ensure that public schools are safe places where parents feel secure in sending their children." The following are some other key findings from the report:

- Between 1992 and 2002, the total crime rate for students ages 12 to 18, as well as rates of theft, violent crimes (including serious violent crimes and simple assault), and serious violent crimes (including rape, sexual assault, robbery, and aggravated assault) declined.
- Between 1993 and 2003, the percentage of students in grades 9 through 12 who reported being in a fight on school property declined from 16 percent to 13 percent.

- In 2003, 7 percent of students ages 12 to 18 reported that they had been bullied at school. The percentage of students in this age range who had been bullied increased from 5 percent in 1999 to 8 percent in 2001, but no difference was detected between 2001 and 2003.
- Between 1993 and 2003, the percentage of students in grades 9 through 12 who reported carrying a weapon such as a gun, knife, or club on school property within the previous 30 days dropped by half, from 12 percent to 6 percent.
- In 2003, 12 percent of students ages 12 to 18 reported that someone at school had used hate-related words against them (i.e., derogatory words related to race, religion, ethnicity, disability, gender, or sexual orientation). During the same period, about 36 percent of students ages 12 to 18 saw hate-related graffiti at school.
- Twenty-one percent of students ages 12 to 18 reported that street gangs were present at their schools in 2003. Students in urban schools were the most likely to report the presence of street gangs at their school (31 percent), followed by suburban students and rural students (18 and 12 percent, respectively).
- In 2003, students in grades 9 through 12 were asked about using drugs on school property. In the 30 days prior to the survey, 5 percent of students reported having at least one drink of alcohol on school property and 6 percent reported using marijuana.
- Every year from 1998 to 2002, teachers were the victims of approximately 234,000 total nonfatal crimes at school, including 144,000 thefts and 90,000 violent crimes. On average, these figures translate into a rate of 32 thefts, 20 violent crimes, and 2 serious violent crimes per 1,000 teachers annually.

The NASN (2001b) created a position statement, *The Role of the School Nurse in Violence Prevention,* which acknowledges nurses' pivotal involvement in cases of youth-on-youth violence. The position paper was first adopted in 1994 and was revised in 1995 and 2000. According to the NASN position paper:

> Escalating incidents of threats and acts of violence in society are putting communities at risk. Exposure to violence has significant emotional, behavioral and cognitive effects on children. Children who are exposed to violence are likely to exhibit fear, behavioral, cognitive and concentration problems and resultant difficulty achieving optimal academic success. Children who are not successful in schools are more likely to be violent than those who are successful (Remboldt, 1994; Weist & Warner, 1994). Although schools are some of the safest places in America (Schiraldi, 1998), it has become necessary for school districts to be proactive in preventing and/or addressing these situations.

The NASN says that societal influences, which have contributed to the increased incidence of violence, include the following:

- Changing family structure
- Changing societal roles
- Easy access to dangerous weapons
- Media influence, which has sensationalized and desensitized individuals to the impact of violence
- Lack of acceptance of diversity
- Increasing demands on young people that negatively affect coping abilities
- Increasing incidence of all forms of domestic abuse
- Increased incidence of hopelessness and helplessness
- Perceived need for instant gratification

The NASN paper says that the dramatic escalation in incidents of violence on school campuses has created a sense of urgency in American society. It adds:

> Schools should be "safe zones" and adopt positions of no tolerance for weapons, crime and violence. Schools and communities must thoughtfully plan to proactively change behaviors in their quest to create a positive, healthy, and safe environment. School nurses have the unique ability to address problems holistically, including physical, emotional, and social perspectives. School nurses are prepared to deal with the physical and emotional results of violence, to contribute to positive youth development and academic success and to collaborate with school and community teams toward violence prevention and intervention.

The NASN states:

> It is the position of the National Association of School Nurses that school nurses have expertise to assist students to develop problem solving and conflict resolution techniques, coping and anger management skills, and a positive self-image. Furthermore, it is the position of the National Association of School Nurses that school nurses should be active members of crisis intervention teams and curriculum committees, and be involved in the development and planning of intervention and prevention programs.

8.5.15.2 School Nurses and Child Abuse

In its position paper (adopted in 1974 and revised in 1982, 1985, 1996 and 2002), *Child Abuse and Neglect*, the NASN says school nurses can play an important role in the identification and reporting of suspected child abuse cases. The NASN acknowledges the prevalence of these kinds of cases:

> Many children are at risk for, or are victims of, variable degrees of child abuse and/or neglect. Maltreatment of children may include physical, emotional, medical, religious, spiritual, educational, or social developmental abuse or neglect; sexual abuse, rape, sexual exploitation, profanity, pornography, prostitution; threat of harm; or child abandonment and infanticide (Menrick, 1996). Abuse or neglect of a child involves actions that result in significant harm to a child's well-being or inactions that result in a child not having the basic need for nurturance, support, and safety met (Hootman, 1996). The actual prevalence of child abuse and neglect is difficult to determine because numerous cases of abuse or neglect are not reported (Shaw, 2002). Each of the 50 states has enacted laws defining child abuse and maltreatment and has determined criteria for outside intervention when necessary. Data from the Administration of Children and Families in 1998 revealed that nearly 54 percent of substantiated reported cases were for child neglect, 11.5 percent were for sexual abuse, and almost 23 percent were for physical abuse. In all forms of substantiated abuse, parents were about 75 percent of the identified perpetrators (Policy News Publishing, 2001).

The NASN suggests:

> School personnel and volunteers have an opportunity to interact with children on a daily basis over an extended period of time. This regular interaction allows for observation of unusual behavior(s) and for the opportunity to develop trusting relationships that may lead to direct or indirect disclosures of child abuse and/or neglect. All employees and volunteers within the school setting must be knowledgeable of, and strictly adhere to, district policy and mandated reporting, as determined by individual state laws regarding disclosures or suspicions of child abuse and/or neglect. In many states, it is a school employee's or volunteer's legal, moral, and ethical obligation to report suspected or disclosed incidents to the local agency identified to receive such complaints. It is important to remember that a school employee's or volunteer's obligation is fulfilled by making the initial factual report; it then becomes the responsibility of the department of family services and/or law enforcement agencies to initiate and complete the investigation (Child and Family Services Division, Montana, 2000). In order to ensure the privacy and protection of children and their families, many state laws prohibit dissemination of confidential information to school employees after the initial interview of a child. Promoting an awareness of child abuse and/or neglect within communities is a vital step in identifying victims and perpetrators so that risk assessment, intervention, access to care, and prevention programs can be provided to create a safer society for our children and prevent re-victimization (Shaw, 2002). It is of utmost importance to remember that child abuse and neglect must be reported before a child can be protected and services offered to the family (Child and Family Services Division, Montana, 2000).

The NASN further advises:

> Each community needs a mechanism to protect victims, to offer support for resolving physical and psychological damage to child victims, and to clearly convey social intolerance of the abuse and/or neglect of any child. All individuals working with children must be taught to observe signs and symptoms of child abuse and/or neglect. In addition, they must work together to ensure mandated reporting is strictly adhered to. Direct instruction curriculums defining appropriate touch and empowering victims to tell about inappropriate physical or sexual touch can strengthen a child's ability to resist abusive situations (Shaw, 2002). As the primary health care provider in the educational setting, the school nurse is frequently consulted about suspicions of child abuse and/or neglect. It is the professional responsibility of school nurses to keep current on mandated reporting requirements so they can provide leadership and support to staff members, especially when making a report, to assure that the reporting procedure is properly carried out for each and every child, as mandated by law.

The position paper concludes:

> It is the position of the National Association of School Nurses that school nurses comply with applicable laws that identify them as mandated reporters and shall be actively involved in establishing safe environments for all children. School nurses are in a unique position to provide personal body safety education to students. In addition, they are available to educate and support staff on the signs and symptoms of child abuse and/or neglect and on mandated reporting laws. Further, it is the role of the school nurse to support victims of child abuse and/or neglect, reassuring them that it was not their fault. Lastly, the school nurse is an essential link to community resources that are available to assist victims and families.

In *Forensic Nursing and Violent Schoolchildren,* (2003), authors Ann Wolbert Burgess, RN, DNSc, professor of psychiatric nursing at Boston College School of Nursing, and Elizabeth B. Dowdell (2003), RN, PhD, assistant professor in the College of Nursing at Villanova University, write, "At one time, schools—a workplace for students, teachers, and nurses—were considered safe. But there is growing alarm that violence on school grounds and inside school buildings is increasing in the aftermath of several high-profile cases of shooting homicides in these settings. School, community, emergency, and psychiatric nurses can play a better role in the prevention of violence by understanding the dynamics and youth profiles behind recent homicides." Health care providers and school nurses should first understand the basics of homicide classification to try to make sense of events such as the Columbine shootings. Burgess and Dowdell explain that homicides classified by motive provide answers as to why the offender killed, and "can assist in prosecution, direct a legal defense, define a psychological intervention, and render information for violence prevention programs."

The Crime Classification Manual was created by the Behavioral Science Unit at the FBI Academy to classify violent crimes, to standardize language for the apprehension of suspects, and to encourage research among law enforcement agents and mental health professionals. Using this manual, Burgess and Dowdell examined four recent school shootings that were classified as personal-cause homicides and subtyped as nonspecific, revenge, patricide or matricide, and authority homicides. They explain, "Personal-cause homicide is an act of interpersonal aggression that results in death to people who may not know each other. This homicide is not motivated by material gain or sexual intent. It is the result of an underlying emotional conflict that propels the offender to kill."

Burgess and Dowdell explain that a nonspecific motive homicide "appears irrational and is committed for a reason known only to the offender." They say that these types of homicides are usually committed during the daytime and in public because the offender desires as many victims as possible. This kind of disorganized, open crime scene presents a high risk of capture to the offender, they say, and there is no effort made to conceal the victim. The weapon of choice for this offender is usually a firearm, they say, and it is brought to the scene. This crime often becomes a massacre caused by guns that offer optimal lethality and an abundance of ammunition. The motive for such killings remains with the offender, who might be unable to state why he or she committed the killing, Burgess and Dowdell say. As an example of a nonspecific homicide, Burgess and Dowdell point to the 1997 case of a 14-year-old in Kentucky who opened fire on a group of classmates as they were attending a prayer meeting. The assailant wounded five and killed three; additional killings were contained due to the quick capture of the shooter by a peer. Prior to the attack, the boy had warned classmates that something "big" would happen. Burgess and Dowdell say that this crime scene was disorganized, but the shooting was planned because the shooter came to the scene armed with a gun and fired at random with no plan of escape or an escape route. They write, "Of note in this case is the prior warning and bragging about the prospect of killing. The perpetrator feels an alienation from others and little regard for the value of life except his own. The shooting ... indicates knowledge of the school schedule and that students would be together as a contained target. It is unclear if there was any motive against the prayer meeting."

Burgess and Dowdell explain that revenge killing involves the murder of another person in retaliation for perceived wrongs, real or imagined, committed against the offender. The victim might not personally know the offender; however, some element in the victim's life is related directly to the offender's actions. In other words, some kind of significant event or interaction links the offender to the victim. As an example of a revenge homicide, Burgess and Dowdell recall a 1998 case involving an 11-year-old boy who first had triggered a fire alarm in an elementary school in Arkansas. The boy and a 13-year-old friend were seated on a hill 100 yards away and opened fire on students and teachers who were walking out of the classrooms. In less than four minutes, the youths had fired 22 rounds of ammunition, killing five and wounding 15. Burgess and Dowdell say that this crime scene was organized and focused, and the shootings were well calculated. The boys had stolen unsecured guns from their parents' homes and had hidden in high grass and a wooded area overlooking the school. After the shooting, their escape was planned, but not well enough. Bystanders spotted gunsmoke rising from the woods and called police, who disarmed the boys as they headed toward a getaway vehicle. One of the boys was proficient with guns and had a reputation for being "mean-spirited." He wore military fatigues and talked of hunting and shooting targets. The other boy had a long history of trouble, including charges pending of molesting a very young girl.

Burgess and Dowdell explain that patricide or matricide homicide involves a child who kills his father, mother, or both. The killings are triggered either by a recent stressful event or by a cumulative buildup of stress, and the offender is mission oriented. In a 1997 case, a 16-year-old boy was charged with the stabbing death of his mother and the shooting deaths of two classmates in Mississippi. The boy was convicted and given three life sentences. At trial, he testified that he had told his mother she did not love him and that she picked on him. He said that a breakup with a girlfriend caused him to become involved in the occult, which ultimately led to the stabbing of his mother and to his reign of terror over his classmates. He told jurors he befriended a 19-year-old boy with whom he explored the occult. The 19-year-old and several others of the cult group they formed were charged with conspiracy in the school shootings. Burgess and Dowdell say that in this case, there are two crime scenes. The stabbing indicates a close personal killing, with the triggering event unknown. The crime scene for the student shootings is disorganized in that there is no escape route and the assailant is well identified and captured at the scene. They explain that the 16-year-old's situation is a case of a youth positioning himself against the world, implying that everyone is out to get him.

Burgess and Dowdell say that an authority killing involves an individual who kills people who have an authority or symbolic relationship by which the killer perceives that he or she has been wronged. The target of the assault could be people or a building, structure, or institution that symbolizes the authority. Random victims are often wounded or killed during the assault as a result of their actual or perceived association with the authority figure or institution under attack. They add that the offender enters the crime scene with little or no intention to abort the plan and escape from the scene or from responsibility for the act. "The offender may desire to die at the scene, either by suicide or police bullets, and thereby attain martyrdom for his acts. Because of the obsession of being wronged, the offender gathers and usually brings multiple weapons to the scene of the confrontation. The assault may develop into a mass killing." In a 1998 case in Oregon, a 15-year-old opened fire at his high school, shooting 22 students, two of whom died. Earlier he had shot his parents to death at home. The boy was reported as asking the police officer who led him away to shoot him. Burgess and Dowdell write, "Killing parents is a close and personal act of focused emotion, usually rage or anger.... When a parent is killed and then classmates and/or teachers are killed, the dynamics are compounded."

Experts say there is a specific violent youth profile for which school nurses can look. "Thinking drives behavior, and troubled youths live in an inner fantasy world with constant thoughts of anger, revenge, retribution, and justifiable rage," Burgess and Dowdell write. "They think of violent solutions to perceived offenses against them. Although 'offenses' by others can be minor, such as being told to study for class or clean a room, it involves control by authority." They point to surging hormones, the underlying neurobiology that can contribute to homicidal thoughts and actions. They add that anger and frustration can set off adolescents who perceive adult authority figures as restrictive or constraining in some way, and they are driven to act with little concern for consequences either to himself or herself, or to others. Burgess and Dowdell write, "When troubled juveniles have minimal bonding to people, are not involved in school, and lack a sense of participating and getting along with others, their increased isolation reinforces reliance on their own internal psychological worlds. In the case of these violent juveniles, that internal psychological world is filled with bitterness, resentment, and rage." They add, "One cause of this developmental situation in juveniles is interpersonal failure or conflict. For example, failure in school or peer relationships or rejection by a group can precipitate acting out against peers or authority. Frustration, accompanied by the inability to handle or resolve such situations, is precipitating events. Suicidal thoughts or attempts before killing are common." Burgess and Dowdell also point to the frequency with which students are bullied, harassed, and teased by their peers. "Until recently, teasing and bullying has been viewed somewhat as a normative social experience of childhood that has to be endured... Contemporary research indicates that the social and emotional problems of being teased and bullied are well documented. Students who are victimized by bullies view school as an unsafe environment and certain peers as tormentors." They add, "Prevention and intervention programs will only be effective if we learn more about how bullying occurs where students are vying for power and status within peer groups." Armed with this kind of information, Burgess and Dowdell say that educators can "then design programs to educate students about the harmful effects of teasing and harassment and give them skills to manage, and potentially change, the pressure to hurt their classmates in order to fit in."

School nurses are particularly well equipped to help prevent violence, Burgess and Dowdell emphasize. They advise the following:

- Be educated about violent youth, especially factors leading to the violence; be knowledgeable about motives and dynamics of killings, injuries, or other violent events and discuss them with colleagues.
- If a health care worker is involved in the violence, provide careful documentation.
- Learn the early warning signs of teen violence; involve parents and teachers in working with the youth and recommend mental health referrals.

"The degree of danger is always difficult to assess," Burgess and Dowdell write. "Nursing staff in psychiatric hospitals, emergency departments, clinics, schools, and the community have struggled with this for years. General profile characteristics exist, but there are no formulas or observations that are totally accurate." They add, "School nurses have access to schoolchildren. In addition to being aware of violent youth profile characteristics that place children at risk for aggressive behavior, pay attention and listen for youths who are communicating threats." Burgess and Dowdell emphasize that nurses in a school setting should pay particular attention to documentation. "Documentation is a key to interfacing with the judicial system. Forensic nurses need to provide objective documentation and record significant data as dictated by the nature and extent of a situation or injury. As with any documentation, the record must hold up in court as a clear, concise presentation of the facts." They add that when nurses come in contact with potentially violent youths, standard information should include the nature of the visit or interaction, statements placed within quotations, and complaints and findings. They also advise that any action taken on a statement should also be in the record, as well as follow-up conversations or services that were provided for the client. "Nurses are in prime positions to assess violent youths because they have access to them, their families, and their potential victims in the workplace, community, schools, and inpatient and psychiatric settings," Burgess and Dowdell write. "Nurses can hopefully intervene in a manner that not only identifies the risks, but also protects others and the youth himself from violence."

8.5.15.3 School Nurses' Role in Bioterrorism

In addition to issues of campus violence, forensic nurses working as school nurses have opportunities to work in areas such as bioterrorism preparedness. On many fronts, policymakers and health care providers are pushing for a greater contribution from nurses in this specialized arena. On January 23, 2002 (National School Nurse Day), Representative Steve Israel (D-NY) introduced HR 298, the Protecting Our Schools Homeland Defense Act, regarding the role of the school nurse in response to bioterrorism. This bill amends the Public Health Service Act to direct the Secretary of Health and Human Services to make grants to designated eligible entities to train school nurses as first responders in the event of a biological or chemical attack on the nation. On the day before the resolution was introduced, NASN president Linda Wolfe participated in Israel's news conference to announce his intentions. The bill read, in part:

> Expressing the sense of the Congress that State and local officials should designate school nurses as "first responders" and remove any legal or regulatory barriers that would impede school nurses from responding to a biological or chemical attack. Whereas there are more than 47,000 nurses in the Nation's elementary and secondary schools; Whereas some children spend up to 10 hours in school each day; Whereas school children and teachers work in close proximity to other people, quickening the spread of airborne diseases; Whereas school nurses are the only professional health care providers in many schools; Whereas if a child becomes sick or arrives at school sick, a school nurse is often the first medical professional to see, diagnose, and treat the child; Whereas in a biological or chemical attack on the United States, school nurses would be among the first medical professionals to respond, would put themselves at risk, and would be responsible even for the children and teachers not subject to the attack; and Whereas school children, including a large number of mainstreamed children with disabilities, may be more vulnerable to biological or chemical attack, and therefore show symptoms sooner than the general population: Now, therefore, be it resolved by the House of Representatives (the Senate concurring), that it is the sense of the Congress that, in response to the terrorist attacks on the United States on September 11, 2001, State and local officials should (1) designate school nurses as "first responders," conferring upon them all rights and responsibilities such status implies in a particular State or locality; and (2) remove any legal or regulatory barriers that would impede school nurses from doing everything within medical guidelines for responding to a biological or chemical attack.

About a year later, on May 8, 2003, Wolfe also testified before the Subcommittee on Labor, Health and Human Services Education and Related Agencies regarding bioterrorism preparedness for school nurses. She stated:

> NASN believes funding for the training of school nurses is crucial, yet is not in any current allocation of funds for bioterrorism. NASN believes that $5 million would allow for this much-needed training to begin around the country. Such funding would protect our most vulnerable population, the children. School nurses are uniquely positioned to participate in our nation's preparedness to bioterrorism. We can provide surveillance and be first responders. First, let me speak to the role of surveillance. The school nurse interacts with a large segment of the populations, which reflects the community at large. We see the first signs of an epidemic because of the symptoms of staff and students. We know when a significant number of staff or children are ill or absent. As medical professionals, we can assess our findings and share this information with public health. With proper training, the school nurse can be a critical member of community surveillance. The second role of the school nurse is as a first responder. A chemical, bioterrorist or radiological attack within this country could be subtle in nature or a well-known event. Either way, it would directly affect the community, including school children. If a chemical is used in the water, food or air, children may be the first to show symptoms because of their increased sensitivity. If a radiological event occurs, children will need to immediately receive potassium iodide tablets at the school site. If a bioterrorism attack occurs, such as smallpox or anthrax, children may be the first to show symptoms. If their symptoms go unnoticed or misdiagnosed the risk of further exposing their families and larger community to serious illness is increased. Children are especially vulnerable because they breathe faster, have lower body surface area and thinner skin. This means they would receive higher doses, in terms of percentage, of a chemical, radioactive or bioterrorism agent. Additionally, children have less fluid reserve if nausea and vomiting occur and lack the cognitive ability to flee or sometimes follow directions in an emergency. Indications of a chemical or biological attack could be manifested by skin rashes, difficulty breathing, nausea and vomiting or other symptoms. Symptoms may be insidious and difficult to diagnose, treat and stop. School nurses know that we are often the first, and sometimes the only, health care provider for many children. Many working families consult with the school nurse before contacting an emergency department or primary physician. Every day, children come to our offices complaining of "not feeling well" and we must assess their symptoms. Typical health assessments identify symptoms of viruses, chronic health problems and metal health concerns. Now with the recent code orange alerts, school nurses can no longer just consider viruses and common medical conditions, we

must consider the possibility of bioterrorism. The symptoms, treatments and responses to bioterrorism are new to school nurses, but our fundamental role is the same. We assess the child and determine the appropriate intervention. In other words, should the child go back to class, be isolated, be sent home or be referred for immediate medical attention? The correct decision could determine the fate of a community. School nurses also care for a large number of children with chronic and severe health problems, including children in wheelchairs, on ventilator support or with special health procedures. Managing these children's care, either in a school evacuation or a school shutdown, requires pre-planned and special procedures. There must be cooperation between schools and emergency services for safe evacuation.

Currently the majority of America's 58,000 school nurses have not received the educational training required to adequately respond to an attack. The anthrax attacks two years ago showed that there was a lack of knowledge about germ warfare and appropriate health measures. If school nurses had the needed education on the signs and symptoms that would be used in a bioterrorist attack, they could provide necessary early treatment and cooperation with other emergency services. It would dramatically decrease the spread of illness and increase the likelihood of a favorable outcome for the child, their community and our nation. That knowledge and training is currently lacking and must be funded to occur. Because children and adults spend so many hours in the school setting, it makes good sense to prepare school nurses to be effective at surveillance, to identify early warning signs, and skilled as first responders who quickly intervene to stop the spread of disease. Currently, NASN is only aware of two states where the school nurse is being actively included in the bioterrorism preparedness for schools: Delaware and Wyoming. In Wyoming, a large number of school nurses received smallpox inoculations and are part of the public health team that would respond to an outbreak. In Delaware, the Division of Public Health and the Department of Education collaborated to assure that every school nurse received training in passive syndromic surveillance and in first response. These two examples show what can be done, but unfortunately is not occurring. School districts are creating crisis plans for responding to assaults, but are forgetting to include the school nurse. Without federal and state resources and guidance, the schools are unable to provide the necessary training to the professionals they will rely on in the event of a bioterrorist attack.

Wolfe concluded, "NASN recommends initial and ongoing training for all school nurses throughout this country. School nurses must have access to emergency communication systems already in place to respond to a terrorist attack. NASN recommends the allocation of $5 million to begin training programs for school nurses."

8.5.15.4 School Nurses: A Resource Stretched Thin

Stewart (1998) states, "The balkanization of the nation's educational system into about 15,000 school districts with wildly varying resources and student populations has stretched to the limit many school nurses' abilities to provide care." He points to recent efforts by lawmakers to strengthen the capacities of school nurses on a local, state, and national level. California Congresswoman Lois Capps, a former school nurse, has said, "In treating our schoolchildren, school nurses are treating their families and their communities. They are irreplaceable. As a member of Congress, I clearly see the need to spotlight the health of America's children at school." Capps represents San Luis Obispo County, Santa Barbara County, and Ventura County. Stewart says political representatives must address funding challenges that are hampering school nurses' abilities to perform their jobs. He quotes Marykay Haas, MPH, RN, CNS, nursing practice specialist for the Minnesota Nurses Association, as saying, "The push to cost-containment has put a lot of pressure on school districts. School nursing is a public health function, but we haven't had a basis to fund school nursing out of the public health funding stream. The resulting danger, being realized today, is that we have unqualified individuals providing health care in schools without the proper nursing background and skills."

Through conversations with school nurses across the country, Stewart reports stories of school nurses being laid off during short- and long-term fiscal constraints in school districts. He says, "When school budgets are on the chopping block, nurses may be the first to go." Stewart adds, "While some states are getting the message on the importance of school nurses—Alabama, Florida, Massachusetts, Mississippi, Missouri and Tennessee all have proposed or recently passed legislation adding school nurses and enhancing their roles—large pockets of areas nationwide still struggle with this issue." In Colorado, Stewart reports, school district populations are swelling, yet the number of school nurses has been trimmed from 50 to 55 to barely 17, with each nurse having to serve an average of five to seven schools. At issue in many districts is the hiring of unlicensed assistive personnel (UAP) to assist with this personnel crunch. Stewart quotes Kansas State Nurses Association member Susan McLoughlin, MSN, RN, CPNP, as saying, "One of the things the professional nurse has that you really can't delegate is the knowledge base that comes with education and experience. The registered nurse can do triaging and assessment. UAP tend to panic or not do a full assessment that would take into account the full scope of possibilities." Haas adds, "School nursing is a public health function, but we haven't had a basis to fund school nursing out of the public health funding stream. The resulting danger, being realized today, is that we have unqualified individuals providing health care in schools without the proper nursing background and skills." One category of UAP is school health assistants, who number approximately 500,000 nationwide, according to Stewart, who adds, "These individuals work under the dual supervision of the school nurse and the school principal, who may not always agree about these UAPs' responsibilities and their supervision."

A smaller category of UAP is the school assistants for children with health care needs in special education. These UAP take care of some of the most complex health situations faced by non-RNs in the schools. If taught well by a school nurse, these assistants might be able to perform a step-by-step protocol correctly, experts say. The school nurse also is responsible for monitoring the health assistant's performance and for ensuring compliance with the set procedures However, nursing experts caution that these assistants might not have the required nursing judgment that a school nurse, particularly a nurse with forensic instincts, might have.

Another challenge is the graying of the American nurse; at least 40 percent of the estimated 45,000 school nurses in practice will be retiring within the next 10 years, according to Stewart. In the face of demographic and fiscal challenges, experts say, school nurses will need to make a case for organizational restructuring; an increased number of differentiated models of practice; the strategic use of nurses educated at the baccalaureate, master's, and doctoral levels; and discussion of evidence-based practice networks. Connor says, "School nursing is a coveted job—it's a good place to be. I don't know of any nurse who's not satisfied with the job; they'd just like not to be stretched so thin. You should be able to do health promotion with the children and with parents."

The U.S. Department of Justice's (2001) *Toolkit to End Violence Against Women: Intervention and Prevention for Children and Youth* outlines the following ways schools can enhance their response to child abuse and youth-related violence:

- Develop policies, applicable to all employees and students, that define a school's response to violence and policies or codes of conduct prohibiting sexual harassment, assault, and dating violence.
- Ensure that policies are consistent with existing laws. Provide training for teachers, administrators, and other school personnel on policies and their implementation.
- Widely disseminate information on these policies throughout the school system, including distribution to school administrators, teachers, and other personnel; students; and parents.
- Design and implement core training for all school personnel on effective prevention strategies, the impact of violence against women and children and other forms of violence, and how to respond appropriately to disclosures of abuse.
- Provide this training throughout the school system, and include principals, school superintendents, school boards, teachers, school social workers, guidance counselors, school nurses, school resource officers, administrative and office personnel, security personnel, coaches, bus drivers, and janitorial and cafeteria staff.
- Implement intervention and prevention programs that address bullying and physical and sexual assault, and teach youth social skills that enable them to develop healthy, nonviolent relationships.
- Provide age-appropriate information on the prevalence of acquaintance rape and other forms of community and family violence, including the warning signs that might signal risks to a student's safety, situations and circumstances that foster nonconsensual sexual conduct, the kinds of behaviors that constitute stalking, and appropriate response strategies.
- Provide information to students about how to ask for help from parents (or when necessary, teachers and other adults) and how to respond appropriately to physical, emotional, or sexual violence among their peers.
- Include information on the role of bystanders, including age-appropriate strategies students can use to assist victims of physical, sexual, or emotional abuse or bullying and safely challenge perpetrator behavior, as well as how to report incidents.
- Destigmatize mental health services, and offer a wide variety of services with parental notification and consent, such as support groups, peer mediation and counseling, 12-step models, and individual counseling.
- Develop a comprehensive school safety plan that incorporates strategies to prevent violence against women and girls and includes personal safety planning for staff and students.
- Include students and parents, mental health providers, police and juvenile justice authorities, and local sexual assault and domestic violence advocacy groups in the development and implementation of the safety plan.
- Widely disseminate information on the plan to students, parents, all school personnel, and community leaders.
- Develop a school plan to address students who sexually assault or batter that responsibly balances the requirement to educate all students with the need to ensure that school is a safe place.

REFERENCES

Administration on Aging. *Profile of Older Americans: 2000.* Washington, DC: U.S. Department of Health and Human Services. 2000.

Advanced Practice Registered Nurses Council. Information on APRNs. Available at www.scnurses.org. 2003.

Akaza, K., Bunai, Y., Tsujinaka, M., Nakamura, I., Nagai, A., Tsukata, Y., & Ohya, I. Elder abuse and neglect: Social problems revealed from 15 autopsy cases. *Leg Med. (Tokyo). 5,* 1, 7–14, 2003.

Alessi, C. A., Struck, A. E., & Aronow, H. U. The process of care in preventive in-home comprehensive geriatric assessment. *J Amer Geriatrics Society. 45,* 1044–1050, 1997.

American Academy of Nurse Practitioners. Position statement on nurse practitioner curriculum. Available at: www.aanp.org. 2003.

American Academy of Pediatrics. The Role of the School Nurse in Providing School Health Services. *Pediatrics, 108,* 5, November 2001.

American College of Nurse Practitioners. Facts about nurse practitioners. Available at: www.nurse.org/acnp/facts/index.shtml. 2003a.

American College of Nurse Practitioners. What is a nurse practitioner? Available at: www.nurse.org/acnp/facts/whatis.shtml. 2003b.

American Medical Association. *Diagnostic and Treatment Guidelines on Elder Abuse and Neglect.* Chicago: American Medical Association. 1993.

American Nurses Association. Scope and standards of advanced practice registered nursing (brochure). Washington, DC. 1996.

Ammerman, R., Kolko, D., Kirisci, L., Blackson, T., & Dawes, M. Child abuse potential in parents with histories of substance abuse disorder. *Child Abuse Negl. 23,* 1225–1238, 1999.

Annie E. Casey Foundation. *Kids count 2002.* Available at: www.aecf.org/kidscount/kc2002/pdfs/summary.pdf

Anetzberger, G. J. Elderly adult survivors of family violence. Implications for clinical practice. *Violence Against Women. 3,* 5, 499–514, 1997.

Aravanis, S. C., Adelman, R. D., Breckman, R., Fulmer, T. T., Holder, E., Lachs, M., O'Brien, J. G., & Sanders, A. B. Diagnostic and treatment guidelines on elder abuse and neglect. *Arch Fam Med. 2,* 371–388, 1993.

Avret v. McCormick, 246 Ga. 401 (1980).

Baladerian, N. J. Recognizing abuse and neglect in people with severe cognative and/or communication impairments. *J Elder Abuse Negl. 9,* 2, 93–104, 1997.

Baladerian, N. J. *Criminal Justice System Response to Victimization of Adults With Disabilities. 1999 State of the Art Report.* National Non-Stranger Sexual Assault Symposium Proceedings Report. Denver Sexual Assault Interagency Council. Denver, CO. Sept. 15–17, 1999.

Baladerian, N. J.*Crime Victims with Developmental Disabilities: Report of a Workshop Commission on Behavioral and Social Sciences and Education.* Washington, DC: National Academies Press. 2001.

Barton, A., & Barton, M., Eds. *The Management and Prevention of Pressure Sores.* London: Faber & Faber. 1981.

Bell, K., & Benak, L. D. Forensic nursing: The fastest growing discipline of nursing for the 21st century. Available at: http://www.iafn.org. 2000.

Besinger, B., Garland, A., Litrownik, A., & Landsverk, J. Caregiver substance abuse among maltreated children placed in out-of-home care. *Child Welfare. 78,* 2, 221–239, 1999.

Bird, P. E., Harrington, D. T., Barillo, D. J., McSweeney, A., Shirani, K. Z., & Goodwin, C. W. Elder abuse: A call to action. *J Burn Care Rehab. 19,* 6, 522–527. 1998.

Bishop, S., & Leadbeater, B. Maternal social support patterns and child maltreatment: Comparison of maltreating and nonmaltreating mothers. *Am J Orthopsychiatry. 69,* 172–181, 1999.

Black, M. The roots of child neglect. In R. M. Reece, Ed. *Treatment of Child Abuse: Common Mental Health, Medical, and Legal Practitioners.* Baltimore, MD: Johns Hopkins University Press. 2000.

Blumstein, A. Disaggregating the violence trends. In A. Blumstein & J. Wallman, Eds. *The Crime Drop in America* (pp. 13–44). Cambridge, England: Cambridge University Press. 2000.

Bonnie, R. J., & Wallace, R. B. *Elder mistreatment: Abuse, neglect, and exploitation in an aging America.* National Academies Press. 2002.

Bowden, M. L., Grant, S. T., Vogel, B., & Prasad, J. K. The elderly, disabled and handicapped adults burned through abuse and neglect. *Burns, Including Thermal Injury. 14,* 6, 447–450. 1988.

Boyer, D., & Fine, D. Sexual abuse as a factor in adolescent pregnancy and child mistreatment. *Fam Plann Perspect. 24,* 1, 4–11, 19, 1992.

Brandl, B., & Cook-Daniels, L. *Domestic Abuse in Later Life.* National Clearinghouse on Abuse in Later Life. Violence Against Women Net. Pennsylvania Coalition Against Domestic Violence. Harrisburg, PA 2002.

Brogdon, B. G. *Forensic Radiology.* Boca Raton, FL: CRC Press. 1998.

Brookhouser, P. E. Ensuring the safety of deaf children in residential schools. *Otolaryngol Head Neck Surg. 97,* 4, 361–368, 1987.

Brown, A. A survey on elder abuse at one Native American tribe. *J Elder Abuse Negl. 1,* 2, 17–37, 1989.

Brownell, P., Berman, J., & Salamone, A. Mental health and criminal-justice issues among perpetrators of elder abuse. *J Elder Abuse Negl. 11,* 4, 81–94, 1999.

Burgess, A. W., Dowdell, E. B., & Prentky, R. A. Sexual abuse of nursing home residents. *J Psychosoc Nurs Ment Health Serv. 38,* 6, 10–18, 2000.

Burston, G. R. Granny-battering. *Br Med J. 3,* 592, 1975.

Butler, R. N. Warning signs of elder abuse: The family physician may be the patient's only protection from family violence. *Geriatrics. 54,* 3, 3–4. 1999.

Butler, J. R., & Burton, L. M. Rethinking teenage childbearing: Is sexual abuse a missing link? *Fam Relations, 39,* 73–80, 1990.

Centers for Disease Control and Prevention. Education about adult domestic violence in U.S. and Canadian medical schools, 1987–1988. *JAMA. 261,* 972, 1989.

Chadwick, D., & Krous, H. F. Irresponsible medical testimony. *Child maltreatment 2,* 4, 313–321, 1997.

Chalk, R., Gibbons, A., & Scarupa, H. J. *The Multiple Dimensions of Child Abuse and Neglect: New Insights Into an Old Problem.* Washington, DC: Child Trends. Available at: www.childtrends.org/files/ChildAbuseRB.pdf. 2002.

Chew, K. S., McCleary, R., Lew, M. A., & Wang, J. C. The epidemiology of child homocide in California, 1981 through 1990. *Homicide Stud. 3,* 2, 151–169, 1999.

Child and Family Services Division, Montana Department of Public Health & Human Services. Montana school guidelines for the identification and reporting of child abuse and neglect, 3, 4, 5. 2000.

Child Welfare League of America. *National fact sheet 2001.* Available at: www.cwla.org/advocacy. 2001.

Christeson, E. P. The health of the school nurse community: A framework. *J School Nurs. 19,* 2, 73–80, 2003.

Clarke, J., Stein, M., Sobota, M., Marisi, M., & Hanna, L. Victims as victimizers: Physical aggression by persons with a history of childhood abuse. *Arch Intern Med. 159,* 1920–1924, 1999.

Cohen, D., Llorente, M., & Eisdorfer, C. Homicide-suicide in older persons. *Am J Psych. 155,* 3, 390–396, 1998.

Comijs, H. C., Pot, A. M., Smit, J. H., Bouter, L. M., & Jonker, C. Elder abuse in the community: Prevalence and consequences. *J Am Geriatr Soc. 46,* 7, 885–888, 1998.

Committee on Law and Justice of the Commission on Behavioral and Social Sciences and Education (CBSSCE) National Research Council. *Crime Victims With Developmental Disabilities: Report of a Workshop.* 2001.

Commonwealth of Pennsylvania. *Attorney General's Family Violence Task Force: Violence Against Elders.* 1988.

Conklin, J. E. 2003. *Why Crime Rates Fell.* Boston: Allyn & Bacon.

Conway, E. E. Non-accidental head injury in infants: The shaken baby syndrome revisited. *Ped Ann. 27,* 10, 677–690, 1998.

Cox, J. L., & Osowiecki, J. A. Child abuse reporting: Hidden dangers. Available at www.smith-lawfirm.com/mandatory-hiddendangers.htm

Coxell, A. W., & King, M. B. Male victims of rape and sexual abuse. *Sexual and Marital Therapy, 11,* 3, 297–308, 1996.

Crane, J. Injury interpretation. In M. M. Star, Ed. *Forensic Science: A Physician's Guide to Clinical Forensic Medicine.* Totowa, NJ: Humana Press. 2000.

Crichton, S., Bond, J., Harvey, C., & Ristock, J. Elder abuse: Feminist and ageist perspectives. *J Elder Abuse Negl. 10,* 3–4, 115–130, 1999.

Crosse, S., Kaye, E., & Ratnofsky, A. *A Report on the Maltreatment of Children With Disabilities.* Washington, DC: National Clearinghouse on Child Abuse and Neglect Information. 1993.

Crume, T., DiGuiseppi, C., Byers, T., Sirotnak, A., & Garrett, C. Under-ascertainment of child maltreatment fatalities by death certificates, 1990–1998. *Pediatrics. 110,* 2, 2002.

Dallam, S. J. The long-term medical consequences of childhood maltreatment. In K. Franey, R. Geffner, & R. Falconer, Eds. *The Cost of Child Maltreatment: Who Pays? We All Do.* San Diego, CA: Family Violence & Sexual Assault Institute. 2001.

Daria, S., Sugar, N. F., Feldman, K. W., Boos, S. C., Benton, S. A., & Ornstein, A. Into hot water head first: Distribution of intentional and unintentional immersion burns. *Pediatr Emerg Care. 20,* 5, 302–310, 2004.

Darves-Bornoz, J. M., Choquet, M., Ledoux, S., & Manfredi, R. Gender differences in symptoms of adolescents reporting sexual assault. *Social Psychiatry & Psychiatric Epidemiology. 33,* 111–117, 1998.

Daubert v. Merrell Dow Pharmaceuticals 113 S. Ct. 2786. 1993.

DiLillo, D., Tremblay, G., & Peterson, L. Maternal anger. *Child Abuse Negl. 24,* 6, 767–779, 2000.

Doss, C. B. The use of medical personnel as expert witnesses in child abuse cases. Report from the Center for Urban Policy Research, Georgia State University. 1994.

Dowdell, E. B., & Foster, K. L. Munchausen syndrome by proxy: Recognizing a form of child abuse. *Nursing Spectrum.* 2003.

Dyer, C. B., Connolly, M. T., & McFeeley, P. The clinical and medical forensics of elder abuse and neglect. In *Elder Mistreatment: Abuse, Neglect, and Exploitation in an Aging America.* The National Academies Press. 2002.

Dyer, C. G., & Goins, A. M. The role of the interdisciplinary geriatric assessment in addressing self-neglect of the elderly. *Generations. 24,* 2, 23–27, 2000.

Ehrlich, P. Survey of state public health departments on procedures for reporting elder abuse. *Public Health Reports. March–April, 106,* 2, 151–154, 1991.

Exposure to Violence Between Parents and Harsh Punishment During Childhood Significantly Increases the Risk for Adult Partner Violene, Study Finds. [Press release, July 24, 2003]. American Psychological Association. Available at: www.apa.org/releases/partnerviolence.html.

Falzon, A. L. & Davis, G. G. A 15-year retrospective review of homicide in the elderly. *J Forensic Sci. 43,* 2, 371–374, 1998.

Family Support Network. Child abuse and neglect. 2002. Available at: http://www.familysupport.org/Abuse.cfm.

Family Violence Prevention Fund (FVPF). *National Consensus Guidelines on Identifying and Responding to Domestic Violence Victimization in Healthcare Settings.* San Francisco, 2004.

Famularo, R., Kinscherff, R., Fenton, T., & Bolduc, S. M. Child maltreatment histories among runaway and deliquent children. *Clin Ped. 29,* 12, 713–718, 1990.

Federal Bureau of Investigation. *Crime in the United States, 1999: Uniform crime reports.* Washington, DC: U.S. Department of Justice. 2001.

Federal Interagency Forum on Child and Family Statistics. *America's children: Key national indicators of well-being, 2000.* Washington, DC: Government Printing Office. 2000.

Fein v. Permanente Medical Group, 695 P 2d 665 (Cal. 1985).

Felitti, V. J., Anda, R. F., Nordenberg, D., Williamson, D. F., Spitz, A. M., Edwards, V., Koss, M. P., & Marks, J. S. Relationship of childhood abuse and household dysfunction to many of the leading causes of death in adults: The adverse childhood experiences (ACE) study. *Amer J Preventive Med. 14,* 4, 245–258, 1998.

Fenton, S. J., Bouquot, J. E., & Unkel, J. I. Orofacial considerations for pediatric, adult, and elderly victims of abuse. *Emergency Medical Clinic of North America. 18,* 3, 601–617, 2000.

Finkelhor, D., & Jones, L. M. *Explanations for the decline in child sexual abuse cases.* Juvenile Justice Bulletin. U.S. Department of Justice. January 2004.

Finkelhor, D., & Ormrod, R. K. *Offenders Incarcerated for Crimes Against Juveniles. Bulletin.* Washington, DC: U.S. Department of Justice, Office of Justice Programs, Office of Juvenile Justice and Delinquency Prevention. 2001.

Finkelhor, D., Williams, L. M., Burns, N., & Kalinowski, M. *Sexual abuse in daycare: A national study.* Durham, NH: Family Research Laboratory, University of New Hampshire. 1988.

Flaherty, E. Sege, R., & Binns, H. J. Healthcare providers' experience reporting child abuse in the primary care setting. *Arch. Ped. Add. Med. 154,* 489–493, May 2000.

Fulmer, T., & Birkenhauer, D. Elder mistreatment assessment as a part of everyday practice. *J Gerontol Nurs. 18,* 3, 42–45, 1992.

Fulmer, T., & Paveza, G. Social assessment. In J. Gallo, T. Fulmer, & G. Paveza (Eds.), *Handbook of geriatric assessment,* 159–190, Baltimore: Aspen Publishers. 2000.

Fulmer, T. T., & O'Malley, T. A. *Inadequate Care of the Elderly: A Healthcare Perspective on Abuse and Neglect.* New York: Springer. 1987.

General Electric Company v. Joiner 118 S. Ct. 512 (1997).

Giardino, A. P., Montoya, L. A., Richardson, A. C., & Leventhal, J. M. Funding realities: Child abuse diagnostic evaluations in the health care setting. *Child Abuse Negl. 23,* 6, 531–538, 1999.

Godkin, M., Wolf, R., & Pillemer, K. A case-comparison analysis of elder abuse and neglect. *International J Aging Human Develop. 28,* 3, 207–225, 1989.

Gray-Vickery, P. Combating elder abuse. *Nursing. 34,* 10, 47–51, 2004.

Greenberg, J., McKibben, M., & Raymond, J. Dependent adult children and elder abuse. *J Elder Abuse Negl. 2,* 1/2, 73–86, 1990.

Griffin, L. W., & Williams, O. J. Abuse among African-American elderly. *J Fam Violence. 7,* 1, 19–35, 1992.

Hammer, H., Finkelhor, D., & Sedlak, A. J. *Runaway/Thrownaway Children: National Estimates and Characteristics. Bulletin.* Washington, DC: U.S. Department of Justice, Office of Justice Programs, Office of Juvenile Justice and Delinquency Prevention. 2002.

Hanson, R. K. *Age and Sexual Recidivism: A Comparison of Rapists and Child Molesters.* Ottawa, Canada: Solicitor General of Canada. 2001.

Harris, S. For better or worse: Spouse abuse grown old. *J Elder Abuse Negl. 8,* 1, 1–33, 1996.

Heisler, C. J. The role of the criminal justice system in elder abuse cases. *J Elder Abuse Negl. 3,* 1, 5–33, 1991.

Herman-Giddens, M., Brown, G., Verbiest, S., Carlson, P., Hooten, E., Howell, E., & Butts, J. Under-ascertainment of child abuse mortality in the United States. *JAMA.* 282, 5, 463–467, 1999.

Hillis, S. D., Anda, R. F., Felitti, V. J., Nordenberg, D., & Marchbanks, P. A. Adverse childhood experiences and sexually transmitted diseases in men and women: A retrospective study. *Pediatrics. 106,* 1, E11, 2000.

Hirsch, H. L. Medico-legal considerations in the use of physician extenders. *Legal Medicine 1,* 127–205, 1991.

Hodge, S., & Canter, D. Victims and perpetrators of male sexual assault. *J Interpers Violence.* 13, 2, 222–239, 1998.

Hootman, J. *Quality Nursing Interventions in the School Setting: Procedures, Models and Guidelines.* Scarborough, ME: NASN. 1996.

Hudson, M., & Carlson, J. Elder abuse: Its meaning to Caucasians, African Americans, and Native Americans. In T. Tatara (Ed.), *Understanding elder abuse in minority populations,* 187–204. New York: Brunner-Routledge. 1999.

Hwalek, M. A., Neale, A. V., Goodrich, C. S., & Quinn, K. The association of elder abuse and substance abuse in the Illinois elder abuse system. *Gerontologist. 36,* 694–700, 1996.

Hyde v. State, 189 Ga. App. 27, 377 So. 2d 187 (1988).

Isely, P. J., Busse, W., & Isely, P. Sexual assault of males in late adolescence: A hidden phenomenon. *Professional School Counseling. 2,* 2, 153–160, 1998.

Isely, P. J., & Gehrenbeck-Shim, D. Sexual assault of men in the community. *J Comm Psycho. 25,* 2, 159–166, 1997.

Jones, A. U.S. faces oncoming aging boom: Political shake-up predicted as numbers of elderly set to double. *Natl Catholic Reporter.* April 30, 2004.

Jones, J., Daougherty, J. D., Schelbic, D., & Cunningham, W. Emergency department protocol for the diagnosis and evaluation of geriatric abuse. *Ann Emerg Med. 17,* 1006–1015, 1988.

Jones, J. S., Veenstra, T. R., Seamon, J. P., & Krohmer, J. Elder mistreatment: National survey of emergency physicians. *Ann Emerg Med. 30,* 4, 473–479, 1997.

Jones, L. M., Finkelhor, D., & Kopiec, K. Why is sexual abuse declining? A survey of state child-protection administrators. *Child Abuse Negl. 25,* 9, 1139–1158, 2001.

Kahan, F. S., & Paris, B. E. Why elder abuse continues to elude the health care system. *Mt Sinai J Med. 70,* 1, 62–68, 2003.

Kelley, B. T., Thornberry, T. P., & Smith, C. A. *In the Wake of Childhood Maltreatment.* Washington, DC: National Institute of Justice. 1997.

Kelley, S. J., & Yorker, B. C. The role of non-physician health care providers in the physical assessment and diagnosis of suspected maltreatment: Results of a national survey. *Child Maltreat. 2,* 331–340, 1997.

Kemp, A. Incidence and correlates of posttraumatic stress disorder in battered women. *J Interpersonal Violence, 10,* 1, 43–55, 1995.

Keshavarz, R., Kawashima, R., & Low, C. Child abuse and neglect presentations to a pediatric emergency department. *J Emerg Med. 23,* 4, 341–345, 2002.

King, M., & Woollett, E. Sexually assaulted males: 115 men consulting a counseling service. *Arch Sex Behav. 26,* 6, 579–588, 1997.

Kleinschmidt, K, C. Elder abuse: A review. *Ann Emerg Med. 30,* 4, 463–472, 1997.

Knight B, Ed. *Simpson's Forensic Medicine* (11th edition). New York: Oxford University Press. 1997.

Koenig, R. J., & Deguerre, C. R. The legal and governmental response to domestic elder abuse. *Clin Geriatr Med. 21,* 2, 383–398, 2005.

Korbin, J., Anetzberger, G., & Austin, C. The intergenerational cycle of violence in child and elder abuse. *J Elder Abuse Negl. 7,* 1, 1–15, 1995.

Kumho Tire Company v. Charmichael 119 S. Ct. 1167 (1999).

Kurrle, S. E., Sadler, P. M., Lockwood, K., & Cameron, I. D. Elder abuse: Prevalence, intervention and outcomes in patients referred to four aged care assessment teams. *Med J Aust. 166,* 119–122, 1997.

Lachs, M. S., Berkman, L., Fulmer, T., & Horwitz, R. I. A prospective community-based pilot study of risk factors for the investigation of elder mistreatment. *J Am Geriatr Soc. 42,* 2, 169–173, 1994.

Lachs, M. S., & Fulmer, T. Recognizing elder abuse and neglect. *Clin Geriatr Med. 9,* 3, 665–681, 1993.

Lachs, M. S., & Pillemer, K. Elder abuse. *The Lancet. 364,* 1192–1263, 2004.

Lachs, M. S., & Pillemer, K. Abuse and neglect of elderly persons. *New England J Medicine. 332,* 7, 437–443, 1995.

Lachs, M. S., Williams, C., O'Brien, S., Hurst, L., & Horwitz, R. Risk factors for reported elder abuse and neglect: A nine-year observational cohort study. *Gerontologist. 37,* 4, 469–474, 1997a.

Lachs, M. S., Williams, C. S., O'Brien, S., Hurst, L., Kossack, A., Siegal, A., & Tinetti, M. E. ED use by older victims of family violence. *Ann Emerg Med. 30,* 4, 448–454, 1997b.

Lachs, M. S., Williams, C., O'Brien, S., Hurst, L., & Horwitz, R. Adult protective service use and nursing home placement. *Gerontologist. 42,* 734–739, 2002.

Lachs, M. S., Williams, C. S., O'Brien, S., Pillemer, K. A., & Charlson, M. E. The mortality of elder mistreatment. *JAMA. 280,* 5, 428–432, 1998.

Le, Q. Mistreatment of Vietnamese elderly by their families in the United States. *J Elder Abuse Negl. 9,* 2, 51–62, 1997.

Lee, B., & Goerge, R. Poverty, early childbearing, and child maltreatment: A multi-nomial analysis. *Child and Youth Services Review. 21,* 9–10, 755–780, 1999.

Lerman, R. Wedding bells ring in stability and economic gains for mothers and children. 2002. Available at: http://www.urban.org/Template.cfm?NavMenuID=24&template=/TaggedContent/ViewPublication.cfm&PublicationID=7858.

Lipscomb, G. H., Muram, D., Speck, P. M., & Mercer, B. M. Male victims of sexual assault. *JAMA. 267,* 22, 3064–3066, 1992.

Lithwick, M., Beaulieu, M., Gravel, S., and Straka, S. The mistreatment of older adults: Perpetrator–Victim relationships and interventions. *J Elder Abuse Negl. 11,* 4, 95–112, 1999.

Lowenstein, S. R., Crescenzi, C. A., Kern, D. C., & Steel, K. Care of the elderly in the emergency department. *Ann Emerg Med. 15,* 528–535, 1986.

Malone, M. L., Rozario, N., Gavinski, M., and Goodwin, J. The epidemiology of skin tears in the institutionalized elderly. *J Am Geriatric Society, 39,* 591–595, 1991.

Mann Rinehart, P., Borowsky, I., Stoltz, A., Latta, E., Cart, C. U., and Brindis, C. D. *Youth violence: Lessons from the experts.* University of Minnesota and University of California. 1998.

Marx, E., & Wooley, S. F., Eds. *Health Is Academic: A Guide to Coordinated School Health Programs.* New York: Teachers College Press. 1998.

Max, W. Rice, D. P., Finkelstein, E., Bardwell, R. A., & Leadbetter, S. The economic toll of intimate partner violence against women in the United States. *Violence Vict. 19,* 3, 259–272, 2004.

McCann, J. Genital injuries resulting from sexual abuse: A longitudinal study. *Pediatrics. 89,* 307, 1992.

McLean, I. A., Balding, V., & White, C. Forensic medical aspects of male-on-male rape and sexual assault in greater Manchester. *Med Sci Law. 44,* 2, 165–169, 2004.

McLeer, S. V., & Anwar, R. A. A study of battered women presenting in an emergency department. *Am J Public Health. 79,* 65, 66, 1989.

McLeer, S. V., Anwar, R. A. H., Herman, S., & Maquiling, K. Education is not enough: A systems failure in protecting battered women. *Ann Emerg Med. 18,* 651–653, 1989.

McNeil, J. M. (1993). Americans with disabilities: 1991–92. (U.S. Bureau of the Census, Current Population Reports, p. 70–73). Washington, DC: Government Printing Office.

Mennick, D. Cameroon society for the prevention of child abuse and neglect. Available at: www.ispcan.org/resources.htm. 1996.

Mickish, J. Abuse and neglect: The adult and elder. In B. Byers & J. Hendricks, Eds. *Adult Protective Service: Reach and Practice.* Springfield, IL: Charles C Thomas. 1993.

Moon, A., & Benton, D. Tolerance of elder abuse and attitudes toward third-party intervention among African Americans, Korean American, and white elderly. *J Multicultural Social Work. 8,* 3/4, 283–303, 2000.

Moon, A., & Williams, O. J. Perceptions of elder abuse and help-seeking patterns among African-American, Caucasian American and Korean-American elderly women. *Gerontologist. 33,* 386–395, 1993.

Moore, K. A., Manlove, J., Terry-Humen, E., Williams, S., Papillo, A. R., & Scarpa, J. *CTS Facts at a Glance.* Washington, DC: Child Trends. 2001.

Morrison, J. A., Frank, S. J., Holland, C. C., & Kates, W. R. Emotional development and disorders in young children in the child welfare system. In J. A. Silver, B. J. Amster, & T. Haecker, Eds. *Young Children and Foster Care: A Guide for Professionals* (pp. 33–64). Baltimore, MD: Paul H. Brookes. 1999.

Mosqueda, L., Burnight, K., Liao, S., & Kemp, B. Advancing the field of elder mistreatment: A new model for integration of social and medical services. *Gerontologist. 44,* 5, 703–708, 2004.

Mouton, C. P., & Espino, D. V. Health screening in older women. *American Family Physician. 59,* 7, 1835–1842, 1999.

Mouton, C., Rovi, S., Furniss, K., & Lasser, N. The associations between health and domestic violence in older women: Results of a pilot study. *J of Women's Health and Gender-Based Medicine. 1,* 9, 1173–1179, 1999.

Mraovick, L., & Wilson, J. Patterns of child abuse and neglect associated with chronological age of children living in a Midwestern county. *Child Abuse Negl. 23,* 9, 899–903, 1999.

Mrazek, P., & Mrazek, D. Resilience in child maltreatment victims: A conceptual exploration. *Child Abuse Negl. 11,* 357–366, 1987.

National Association of School Nurses (NASN). Position statement: Role of the school nurse in violence prevention. Available at: www.nasn.org/positions/2000psviolence.htm. June 2000.

National Association of School Nurses (NASN). Position statement: The role of the school nurse in school based health centers. Available at: http://www.nasn.org/positions/schoolbased.htm. 2001.

National Association of School Nurses (NASN). Position statement: Child abuse and neglect. Available at: www.nasn.org/positions/2002pschild.htm. June 2002.

National Association of School Nurses (NASN). The role of the advanced practice Registered Nurse in the school setting. Available at: www.nasn.org/positions/2003psadvanced.htm. June 2003.

National Center on Child Fatality Review. *A 'how to' guide for child fatality review teams.* Available from www.ican-ncfr.org/documents/How_To.pdf. 2003.

National Center on Elder Abuse (NCEA). *The national elder abuse incidence study: Final report.* Madison, WI: Older Women's Network. 1998.

National Center on Elder Abuse. *What are the major types of elder abuse?* Available at: http://elderabusecenter.org/basic/index.html.

National Center on Elder Abuse. *Fact sheet on elder abuse prevalence and incidence.* Available at www.elderabuse-center.org. April 2005.

National Organization for Victim Assistance (NOVA). *Symposium on Working with Crime Victims With Disabilities.* Washington, DC: Office for Victims of Crime. 1998.

Neutra, R., Levy, J., & Parker, D. Cultural expectations versus reality in Navajo seizure patterns and sick roles. *Culture, Medicine, and Psychiatry, 1,* 225–275, 1977.

North Carolina Department of Justice. *Child sexual abuse guidelines: Recommendations for professionals.* Available at: www.jus.state.nc.us/NCJA/juvlaw.pdf. 1997.

Ogg, J., & Bennett, G. C. J. Elder abuse: A national survey. *Br Med J. 305,* 998–999, 1992.

Ohio v. Brant, No. 94-P-011 Ohio App. Lexis 4121 (1995).

Ohio v. Brooks, No. L-95-188 Ohio App. Lexis 4099 (1996).

Oktay, J. S., & Tompkins, C. J. Personal assistance providers' mistreatment of disabled adults. *Health Soc Work. 29,* 3, 177–188, 2004.

Otiniano, M., Herrera, C., & Teasdale, T. *Hispanic elder abuse.* Archstone Foundation Understanding and Combating Elder Abuse in Minority Communities, 194. Long Beach, CA. 1998.

Pease, T., & Frantz, B. *Your safety . . . Your rights & personal safety and abuse prevention education program to empower adults with disabilities and train service providers.* Doylestown, PA: Network of Victim Assistance. 1994.

Perry, B. D. The neurodevelopmental impact of violence in childhood. In D. Schetky & E. Benedek, Eds. *Textbook of Child and Adolescent Forensic Psychiatry.* Washington, DC: American Psychiatric Press. 2001.

Perry, B. D. Childhood experience and the expression of genetic potential: What childhood neglect tells us about nature and nurture. *Brain and Mind. 3,* 79–100, 2002.

Phillips, L., Torres de Ardon, E., & Briones, G. Abuse of female caregivers by care recipients: Another form of elder abuse. *J Elder Abuse Negl. 12,* 3–4, 123–144, 2000.

Pillemer, K. A., & Finkelhor, D. The prevalence of elder abuse: A random sample survey. *Gerontologist. 28,* 51–57, 1988.

Pittaway, E., & Westhues, A. The prevalence of elder abuse and neglect of older adults who access health and social services in London, Ontario, Canada. *J Elder Abuse Negl. 5,* 4, 77–93, 1993.

Podnieks, E. Emerging themes from a follow-up study of Canadian victims of elder abuse. *J Elder Abuse Negl. 4,* 1–2, 59–111, 1992a.

Podnieks, E. National survey on abuse of the elderly in Canada. *J Elder Abuse Negl. 4,* 1–2, 5–58, 1992b.

Policy News Publishing. *Almanac of policy issues: Child abuse.* Retrieved from http://www.policyalmanac.org/social_welfare/child_abuse.shtml. 2001.

Ramin, S. M., Satin, A., Stone, I., & Wendel, G. Sexual assault in postmenopausal women. *Obstetrics and Gynecology, 80,* 5, 860–864, 1992.

Ramsey-Klawsnik, H. Elder sexual abuse: Preliminary findings. *J Elder Abuse Negl. 3,* 3, 73–90, 1991.

Reece, R. M. Identifying the abused child in the emergency department. Available at: www.emedhome.com. January 2001.

Reis, M., & Nahmiash, D. Abuse of seniors: Personality, stress, and other indicators. *J Mental Health Aging, 3,* 3, 337–356, 1997.

Reis, M., & Nahmiash, D. Validation of the indicators of abuse (IOA) screen. *The Gerontologist, 38,* 4, 471–480, 1998.

Remboldt, C. *Solving Violence Problems in Your School: Why a Systematic Approach is Necessary: A Guide for Educators.* Minneapolis, MN: Johnson Institute. 1994

Rennison, C. M. *Criminal Victimization 2000: Changes 1999–2000 With Trends 1993–2000. Bulletin.* Washington, DC: U.S. Department of Justice, Office of Justice Programs, Bureau of Justice Statistics. 2001.

Rennison, C. M., & Welchans, S. *Intimate Partner Violence. Special Report.* Washington, DC: U.S. Department of Justice, Office of Justice Programs, Bureau of Justice Statistics. 2000.

Rosenblatt, D. E., Cho, K. H., & Durance, P. W. Reporting mistreatment of older adults: The role of physicians. *J Am Geriatr Soc. 44,* 1, 65–70, 1996.

Rubin, D. M., Christian, C. W., Bilaniuk, L. T., Zazyczny, K. A., & Durbin, D. R. Occult head injury in high-risk abused children. *Pediatrics. 111,* (Pt. 1), 1382–1386, 2003.

Rumm, P. D., Cummings, P., Kraus, M. R., Bell, M. A., & Rivara, F. P. Identified spouse abuse as a risk factor for child abuse. *Child Abuse & Neglect. 24,* 11, 1375–1381, 2000.

Sanchez, Y. Elder mistreatment in Mexican American communities: The Nevada and Michigan experiences. In T. Tatara (Ed.), *Understanding elder abuse in minority populations,* 67–77. Long Beach, CA: Archstone Foundation. 1999.

Schecter, S., & Edleson, J. *Effective Intervention in Domestic Violence and Child Maltreatment Cases: Guidelines for Policy and Practice.* Reno, NV: National Council of Juvenile and Family Court Judges. 1999.

Schilling, R., & Schinke, S. Personal coping and social support for parents of handicapped children. *Child and Youth Services Review. 6,* 195–206, 1984.

Schiraldi, V. Finally, state release the pressure on prisons. Washington Post: Justice Policy Institute. November 30, 2003.

Schor, J. D., Selby, A., & Bertone, C. A. Geriatric assessment in the diagnosis and treatment of elder abuse. *New Jersey Medicine. 92,* 2, 108–110, 1995.

Seaver, C. Muted lives: Older battered women. *J Elder Abuse Negl. 8,* 2, 3–21, 1996.

Sedlak, A., & Broadhurst, D. *Third National Incidence Study of Child Abuse and Neglect: Final Report.* Washington, DC: U.S. Government Printing Office. 1996.

Shaw, K. A summary of the literature on child sexual abuse and exploitation. Available at http://www.ispcan.org/Resources/Literature%20Search%20Project.htm. 2002.

Shields, L. B., Hunsaker, D. M., & Hunsaker, J. C. Abuse and neglect: A 10-year review of mortality and morbidity in our elders in a large metropolitan area. *J Forensic Sci. 49,* 1, 122–127, 2004.

Shore, R. *Rethinking the Brain.* New York: Families and Work Institute. 1997.

Silverman, A. B., Reinherz, H. Z., & Giaconia, R. M. The long-term sequelae of child and adolescent abuse: A longitudinal community study. *Child Abuse Negl. 20,* 8, 709–723, 1996.

Snyder, H. N. *Sexual assault of young children as reported to law enforcement: Victim, incident, and offender characteristics.* Washington, DC: U.S. Department of Justice, Bureau of Justice Statistics. July 2000.

Snyder, H., & Sickmund, M. *Juvenile Offenders and Victims: 1999 National Report.* Washington, DC: U.S. Department of Justice, Office of Juvenile Justice and Delinquency Prevention. 1999.

Sobsey, D. *Violence and abuse in the lives of people with disabilities: The end of silent acceptance?* Baltimore: Brocks Publishing. 1994.

Solomons, G. Child abuse and developmental disabilities. *Dev Med Child Neurology, 21,* 101–105, 1979.

Spies, L. Non-stranger sexual assault. National Non-Stranger Sexual Assault Symposium. Proceedings Report. Denver Sexual Assault Interagency Council. Denver. 1999.

Stark, E., & Flitcraft, A. H. Women and children at risk: A feminist perspective on child abuse. *Int J Health Serv. 18,* 97–119, 1988.

State of Tennessee v. Brunetti, 1991 WL 7818 (Tenn. Cr. App. Jan. 30, 1991).

State of Tennessee v. Fields, 1991 WL 35747 (Tenn. Cr. App. Mar. 20, 1991)

Stermac, L., Del Bove, G., & Addison, M. Stranger and acquaintance sexual assault of adult males. *J Interpers Violence. 19,* 8, 901–915, 2004.

Stermac, L., Sheridan, P. M., Davidson, A., & Dunn, S. Sexual assault of adult males. *J Interpersonal Violence. 11,* 1, 52–64, 1996.

Stewart, M. School nurses: Who is caring for our nation's children? *Am Nurse. 30,* 3, 13, 1998.

Stylianos, S. Late sequelae of major trauma in children. *Pediatr Clin North Am. 45,* 4, 853–859, 1998.

Sugar, N. F., Taylor, J. A., & Feldman, K. W. Bruises in infants and toddlers: Those who don't cruise rarely bruise: Puget Sound Pediatric Research Network. *Arch Pediatr Adolesc Med. 153,* 4, 399–403, 1999.

Sugg, N. K., & Inui, T. Primary care physician's response to domestic violence: Opening Pandora's box. *JAMA. 267,* 3157–3160, 1992.

Sullivan, P. M., Vernon, M., & Scanlan, J. M. Sexual abuse of deaf youth. *Am Ann Deaf. 132,* 4, 256–262, 1987.

Swagerty, D. L., Takahashi, P. Y., & Evans, J. M. Elder mistreatment. *American Family Physician. 59,* 10, 2804–2808, 1999.

Teaster, P., Roberto, K., Duke, J., & Myenonghwan, K. Sexual abuse of older adults: Preliminary findings of cases in Virginia. *J Elder Abuse Negl.* 12, 3–4, 1–16, 2000.

Teicher, M. D. Wounds that time won't heal: The neurobiology of child abuse. Cerebrum: *The Dana Forum on Brain Science. 2,* 4, 50–67, 2000.

Terry, E., & Manlove, J. *Trends in Sexual Activity and Contraceptive Use Among Teens. Research Brief.* Washington, DC: U.S. Department of Health and Human Services, Child Trends. 2000.

Thomlison, B. Risk and protective factors in child maltreatment. In M. W. Fraser, Ed. *Risk and Resilience in Childhood: An Ecological Perspective.* Washington, DC: NASW Press. 1997.

Tjaden, P., & Thoennes, N. *Prevalence, incidence, and consequences of violence against women: Findings from the national violence against women survey.* National Istitute of Justice Research Brief. November 1998.

Tomita, S. Exploration of elder mistreatment among the Japanese. In T. Tatara (Ed.), *Understanding elder abuse in minority populations,* 119–139. Long Beach, CA: Archstone Foundation. 1999.

Tyiska, C. G. Working with victims of crime with disabilities. *OVC Bulletin,* pp. 1–16. Washington, DC: U.S. Department of Justice, Office for Victims of Crime. 1998.

Tzeng, O., Jackson, J., & Karlson, H. *Theories of Child Abuse and Neglect: Differential Perspectives, Summaries, and Evaluations.* New York: Praeger. 1991.

U.S. Census Bureau. *Census Bureau report profiles older population* [Press release, November 1, 2000]. Available at www.census.gov.

U.S. Department of Health and Human Services. *National survey of child and adolescent well-being: Baseline report for one-year-in-foster-care sample*. Washington, DC: U.S. Department of Health and Human Services. 2003.

U.S. Department of Health and Human Services. *Emerging practices in the prevention of child abuse and neglect*. Available at: www.acfhhs.gov 2003.

U.S. Department of Health and Human Services, National Clearinghouse on Child Abuse and Neglect Information. *Child maltreatment 2002*. Washington, DC: U.S. Department of Health and Human Services. 2004.

U.S. Department of Justice. *Portable guides to investigating child abuse: Child neglect and Munchausen Syndrome by Proxy*. Washington, DC U.S. Department of Justice. September 1996.

U.S. Department of Justice, Office of Justice Programs and the Bureau of Justice Statistics. *Sexual Assault of Young Children as Reported to Law Enforcement: Victim, Incident, and Offender Characteristics*. Washington, DC: U.S. Department of Justice. 2000.

U.S. Department of Justice, Office of Justice Programs, National Criminal Justice Reference Service. Toolkit to end violence against women: Intervention and prevention for children and youth. Available at: http://toolkit.ncjrs.org. 2001.

U.S. Department of Justice, Office of Juvenile Justice and Delinquincy Prevention. *Recognizing when a child's injury or illness is caused by abuse*. Available at www.ncjrs.org. 1996.

Vearnals, S., & Campbell, T. Male victims of male sexual assault: A review of psychological consequences and treatment. *Sex Relation Therapy. 16*, 3, 279–286, 2001.

Vernon, M. Elder abuse: The case for greater involvement of geriatricians. *Age and Ageing. 24*, 3, 177–179, 1995.

Vinton, L. Battered women's shelters and older women: The Florida experience. *J Fam Violence. 7*, 1, 63–72, 1992.

Vladescu, D., Eveleigh, K., Ploeg, J., & Patterson, C. An evaluation of a client-centered case management program for elder abuse. *J Elder Abuse Negl. 11*, 4, 5–22, 1999.

Wahl, R. A., Sisk, D. J., & Ball, T. M. Clinic-based screening for domestic violence: Use of a child safety questionnaire. *Medicine. 2*, 25, 2004.

Waters, R. L., Cressy, J. & Adkins, A. H. Spinal cord injuries due to violence. *Am Rehabilitation, 22*, 3, 10–15, 1996.

Weist, M. D., Paskewitz, D. A., & Warner, B. S., et al. Treatment outcome of school-based mental health services for urban teenagers. *Community Ment Health J. 32, 2, 149–157, 1996.*

White, S. W. Elder abuse. Critical care nurse role in detection. *Crit Care Nurs Q. 23*, 2, 20–25, 2000.

Widom, C. S., & Maxfield, M. G. *An Update on the Cycle of Violence*. Washington, DC: National Institute of Justice. 2001.

Wilson, C & Brewer, N. The incidence of criminal victimization of individuals with an intellectual disability. *Australian Psychologist, 27*, 2, 114–117, 1992.

Wold, S. J. *School Nursing: A Framework for Practice*. St. Louis, MO: Mosby. 1981.

Wolf, R. S. Understanding elder abuse and neglect: Physical and emotional abuse. *Aging. 367*, 4–9, Spring, 1996.

Wolf, R., & Pillemer, K. The older battered woman: Wives and mothers compared. *J Mental Health Aging. 3*, 3, 325–336, 1997.

World Health Organization. *Guidelines for Medico-Legal Care for Victims of Sexual Violence*. New York: World Health Organization. 2003.

Yorker, B. Covert video surveillance of Munchausen Syndrome by Proxy: The exigent circumstances exception. Health Matrix: *J Law-Medicine. 5*, 2, 325–346, 1995.

Young, M. E., Nosek, M. A., Howland, C., Chanpong, G., Rintala, D. H. Prevalence of abuse of women with physical disabilities. *Arch Phys Med Rehabil. 78*, 12, Suppl. 5, S34–S38, 1997.

RECOMMENDED READINGS

Abbott, J., Johnson, R., Koziol-Mclain, J., & Lowenstein, S. R. Domestic violence against women: Incidence and prevalence in an emergency department population. *JAMA. 273*, 1763 1767, 1995.

Ahmad, M., & Lachs, M. S. Elder abuse and neglect: What physicians can and should do. *Cleve Clin J Med. 69*, 10, 801–808, 2002.

Alexander, R., Smith, W., & Stevenson, R. Serial Munchausen syndrome by proxy. *Pediatr. 86*, 581–585, 1990.

Allison, E. J., Ellis, P. C., & Wilson, S. E. Elder abuse and neglect: The emergency medicine perspective. *Eur J Emerg Med. 5*, 3, 355–363, 1998.

American Academy of Pediatrics, Committee on Child Abuse and Neglect. Guidelines for the evaluation of sexual abuse in children. *Pediatrics. 87*, 254, 1991.

American College of Emergency Physicians. Management of elder abuse and neglect. *Ann Emerg Med. 31*, 1, 149–150, 1998.

American College of Emergency Physicians. Recognition and management of elder abuse: Policy resource and education paper. Available at: http://www.acep.org. 1999.

Anetzberger, G. J., Palmisano, B. R., & Sanders, M. A model intervention for elder abuse and dementia. *Gerontologist. 40*, 4, 492–497, 2000.

Aravanis, S. C., Adelman, R. D., Breckman, R., Fulmer, T. T., Holder, E., & Lachs, M. Diagnostic and treatment guidelines on elder abuse and neglect. *Arch Fam Med. 2*, 371–388, 1993.

Artingstall, K. *Practical Aspects of Munchausen by Proxy and Munchausen Syndrome Investigation*. Boca Raton, FL: CRC Press. 1999.

Asher, R. Munchausen's syndrome. *The Lancet. 1*, 339–341, 1951.

Bachman, R., Dillaway, H., & Lachs, M. S. Violence against the elderly: A comparative analysis of robbery and assault across age and gender groups. *Research on Aging. 20*, 2, 183–198, 1998.

Baker, A. A. Granny battering. *Mod Geriatr. 8*, 20–24, 1975.

Bays, J. Changes in the hymenal anatomy during examination of prepubertal girls for possible sexual abuse. *Adolescent Pediatric Gynecology. 3,* 42, 1990.

Bear, Z. G. Crime scene responders: The imperative sequential steps. *Crit Care Nurs Q. 22,* 1, 75–89, 1999.

Benecke, M., Josephi, E., & Zweihoff, R. Neglect of the elderly: Forensic entomology cases and considerations. *Forensic Sci Int. 146,* Suppl., S195–199, 2004.

Bennett, G. C. J. Elder abuse: Shifting emphasis from abused to abuser. *Geriatr Med. 20,* 5, 45–49, 1990.

Bennett, K. Munchausen Syndrome by Proxy abuse. *J Child Health Care. 4,* 163–166, 2000.

Benton, D., & Marshall, C. Elder abuse. *Clinics in Geriatric Medicine. 7,* 4, 831–845, 1991.

Berenson, A., Heger, A., & Andrews, S. Appearance of the hymen in newborns. *Pediatrics. 87,* 458, 1991.

Bergeron, L., & Gray, B. Ethical dilemmas of reporting suspected elder abuse. *Social Work. 48,* 1, 96–105, 2003.

Black, C. A., & DeBlassie, R. R. Sexual abuse in male children and adolescents: Indicators, effects, and treatments. *Adolescence. 28,* 123–133, 1993.

Black, D. A., Heyman, R. E., & Smith Slep, A. M. Risk factors for child physical abuse. *Aggression and Violent Behavior. 6,* 121–188, 2001.

Bloom, J. S., Ansell, P., & Bloom, M. N. Detecting elder abuse: A guide for physicians. *Geriatrics. 44,* 6, 40–44, 1989.

Boersma, R. R. Forensic nursing practice with asylum seekers in the USA: Advocacy and international human rights: A pilot study. *J Psychiatr Ment Health Nurs. 10,* 5, 526–533, 2003.

Brady, M. Munchhausen Syndrome by Proxy: How should we weigh our options? *Law and Psychology Review. 18,* 361, 1994.

Brewer, R. A., & Jones, J. S. Reporting elder abuse: Limitations of statutes. *Ann Emerg Med. 18,* 1217–1221, 1989.

Brown, K., Streubert, G. E., & Burgess, A. W. Effectively detect and manage elder abuse. *Nurse Pract. 29,* 8, 22–27, 31, 2004.

Brown, M. L. Dilemmas facing nurses who care for Munchausen syndrome by proxy. *Pediatr Nurs. 23,* 416–418, 1997.

Bureau of Justice Statistics. *Criminal Victimization 2000.* Washington, DC: U.S. Department of Justice. 2001.

Burgess, A. W. *Advance Practice in Psychiatric Nursing.* Stamford, CT: Appleton & Lang. 1997.

Burgess, A. W. Elder justice: Medical forensic issues concerning abuse and neglect. Paper presented at the Department of Justice medical forensic roundtable discussion, Washington, DC, October 18, 2000.

Burgess, A. W. *Violence Through a Forensic Lens.* King of Prussia, PA: Nursing Spectrum. 2000.

Burgess, A. W., Berger, A. D., & Boersma, R. R. Forensic nursing. *Am J Nurs. 104,* 3, 58–64, 2004.

Burgess, A. W., Dowdell, E. B., & Brown, K. The elderly rape victim: Stereotypes, perpetrators, and implications for practice. *J Emerg Nurs. 26,* 5, 2000.

Burgess, A. W., Dowdell, E. B., & Prentky, R. A. Sexual abuse of nursing home residents. *J Psychosocial Nursing. 38,* 6, 2000.

Burgess, A. W., Hanrahan, N. P., & Baker, T. Forensic markers in elder female sexual abuse cases. *Clin Geriatr Med. 21,* 2, 399–412, 2005.

Burke, L. K., & Follingstad, D. R. Violence in lesbian and gay relationships: Theory, prevalence, and correlational factors. *Clin Psych Rev. 19,* 5, 487–512, 1999.

California Medical Training Center. Advanced training in elder abuse (version 1.0). Available at: http://web.ucdmc.ucdavis.edu/medtrng/training/events.html.

Campbell, J. C. Child abuse and wife abuse: The connections. *Md Med J. 43,* 349–350, 1994.

Campbell, R., & Wasco, S. M. Understanding rape and sexual assault: 20 years of progress and future directions. *J Interpers Violence. 20,* 1, 127–131, 2005.

Castledine, G. Acting manager who ignored a care assistant physically abusing a patient. *Br J Nurs. 13,* 15, 925, 2004a.

Castledine, G. Senior nurse who physically and verbally abused elderly residents. *Br J Nurs. 13,* 22, 1329, 2004b.

Chalk, R., & King, R. A. *Violence in Families: Assessing Prevention and Treatment Programs.* Washington, DC: National Academy Press. 1998.

Clements, P. T., & Averill, J. B. Patterns of knowing as a method of assessment and intervention for children exposed to family-member homicide. *Arch Psychiatr Nurs. 18,* 4, 143–150, 2004.

Clements, P. T., Speck, P. M., Crane, P. A., & Faulkner, M. J. Issues and dynamics of sexually assaulted adolescents and their families. *Int J Ment Health Nurs. 13,* 4, 267–274, 2004.

Collins, S. E., & Hamilton-Skipper, B. Forensic nursing in action: Physical assessment of child abuse. *Fla Nurse. 48,* 1, 26–27, 2000.

Cook-Daniels, L. Interpreting the National Elder Abuse Incidence Study. *Victimization of the Elderly and Disabled. 2,* 1, 1–2, 1999.

Coombes, R. Forensic nursing: Nurse to examine sex crime victims. *Nurs Times. 96,* 35, 8, 2000.

Coxell, A., King, M., Mezey, G., & Gordon, D. Lifetime prevalence, characteristics, and associated problems of nonconsensual sex in men: Cross sectional survey. *BMJ. 318,* 7187, 846–850, 1999.

Daniels, R. S., Baumhover, L. A., & Clark-Daniels, C. L. Physician's mandatory reporting of elder abuse. *Gerontologist. 29,* 321–327, 1989.

Danielson, C. K., & Holmes, M. M. Adolescent sexual assault: An update of the literature. *Curr Opin Obstet Gynecol. 16,* 5, 383–388, 2004.

Daro, D. Child sexual abuse prevention: Separating fact from fiction. *Child Abuse Neglect. 15,* 1, 1–4, 1991.

Davies, D. *Child Development: A Practitioner's Guide.* New York: Guilford. 1999.

Dick, T. Maggots: Are you a medical advocate for the elderly? *Emerg Med Serv. 33,* 9, 42, 2004.

Dong, X. Medical implications of elder abuse and neglect. *Clin Geriatr Med. 21,* 2, 293–313, 2005.

Dubowitz, H. Pediatrician's role in preventing child maltreatment. *Pediatric Clinics of North America. 37,* 989, 1990.

Dunlap, H., Brazeau, P., Stermac, L., & Addison, M. Acute forensic medical procedures used following a sexual assault among treatment-seeking women. *Women Health. 40,* 2, 53–65, 2004.

Dyer, C. B., Heisler, C. J., Hill, C. A., & Kim, L. C. Community approaches to elder abuse. *Clin Geriatr Med. 21,* 2, 429–447, 2005.

Emans, S. J. Genital findings in sexually abused, symptomatic, and asymptomatic girls. *Pediatrics. 79,* 778, 1987.

Fanslow, J., Norton, R., & Spinola, C. Indicators of assault-related injuries among women presenting to the emergency department. *Annals of Emerg Med. 32,* 341–348. 1998.

Finkel, M. A. Anogenital trauma in sexually abused children. *Pediatrics. 84,* 317, 1989.

Flannery, M. Munchausen Syndrome by Proxy: Broadening the scope of child abuse. *University of Richmond Law Review. 28,* 1175, 1994.

Flinck, A., Paavilainen, E., & Astedt-Kurki, P. Survival of intimate partner violence as experienced by women. *J Clin Nurs. 14,* 3, 383–393, 2005.

Fredriksen, H. I. Adult protective services: Changes with the introduction of mandatory reporting. *J Elder Abuse & Neglect. 1,* 59–70, 1989.

Francois, I., Moutel, G., Plu, I., Fauriel, I., & Herve, C. Domestic violence: What are the difficulties for practitioners? *Presse Med. 33,* 22, 1561–1565, 2004.

Friedrich, W. N. Normative sexual behavior in children. *Pediatrics. 88,* 456, 1991.

Fulmer, T. Mistreatment of elders: Assessment, diagnosis, and intervention. *Nursing Clinics of North America. 24,* 3, 707–716, 1989.

Fulmer, T. Elder abuse and neglect assessment. *J Gerontological Nursing. 29,* 6, 4–5, 2003.

Fulmer, T., Guadagno, L., & Bolton, M. M. Elder mistreatment in women. *J Obstet Gynecol Neonatal Nurs. 33,* 5, 657–663, 2004.

Fulmer, T., Guadagno, L., Bitondo Dyer, C., & Connolly, M. T. Progress in elder abuse screening and assessment instruments. *J Am Geriatr Soc. 52,* 2, 297–304, 2004.

Fulmer, T., & O'Malley, T. A. *Inadequate Care of the Elderly: A Healthcare Perspective on Abuse and Neglect.* New York: Springer. 1987.

Fulmer, T., Paveza, G., Abraham, L. I., & Fairchild, S. Elder neglect assessment in the emergency department. *J Emerg Nurs. 26,* 436–443, 2000.

Fulmer, T., Street, S., & Carr, K. Abuse of the elderly: Screening and detection. *J Emergency Nursing. 10,* 3, 131–140, 1984.

Fulton, D. R. Early recognition of Munchausen syndrome by proxy: Assessment problems. *Crit Care Nurs Q. 23,* 2, 35–42, 2000.

Garnefski, N., & Diekstra, R. F. W. Child sexual abuse and emotional and behavioral problems in adolescence: Gender differences. *J Amer Acad of Child and Adolescent Psychiatry. 36,* 323–329, 1997.

Glassman, P. D., Chavez, E. M., & Hawks, D. Abuse and neglect of elderly individuals: Guidelines for oral health professionals. *J Calif Dent Assoc. 32,* 4, 323–335, 2004.

Goldberg, W. G., & Tomlanovich, M. D. Domestic violence victims in the emergency department: New findings. *JAMA. 251,* 3259–3264, 1984.

Golden, G. S. Forensic odontology and elder abuse: A case study. *J Calif Dent Assoc. 32,* 4, 336–340, 2004.

Gorbien, M. J., & Eisenstein, A. R. Elder abuse and neglect: An overview. *Clin Geriatr Med. 21,* 2, 279–292, 2005.

Gordon, M. Males and females as victims of childhood sexual abuse: An examination of the gender effect. *J Fam Violence. 5,* 321–332, 1990.

Gorman, M. A. Forensic nursing: RN practice in prison populations. *Alta RN. 58,* 9, 4–5, 2002.

Gray-Vickery, P. Protecting the older adult. *Nurs Manage. 32,* 10, 36–40, 2001.

Greenbaum, A. R., Donne, J., Wilson, D., & Dunn, K. W. Intentional burn injury: An evidence-based, clinical and forensic review. *Burns. 30,* 7, 628–642, 2004.

Groves, B. M. Mental health services for children who witness domestic violence. *The Future of Children: Domestic Violence and Children, 9,* 3, 122–132, 1999.

Gutman, L. T. Human immunodeficiency virus transmission by child sexual abuse. *American J Diseases of Children. 145,* 137, 1991.

Haack, D. *Suggested Protocols for Victims of Spousal and Elder Abuse: A Task Force Reference Document for Colorado Hospitals.* Denver: Colorado Department of Health. 1996.

Hammerschlag, M. R. Sexually transmitted diseases in sexually abused children. *Advances in Pediatric Infectious Diseases. 3,* 1, 1988.

Hammerschlag, M. R. Chlamydial infections. *J Pediatrics. 114,* 727, 1989.

Hanrahan, N. P., Burgess, A. W., & Gerolamo, A. M. Core data elements tracking elder sexual abuse. *Clin Geriatr Med. 21,* 2, 413–427, 2005.

Hansberry, M. R., Chen, E., & Gorbien, M. J. Dementia and elder abuse. *Clin Geriatr Med. 21,* 2, 315–332, 2005.

Hardin, E., & Khan-Hudson, A. Elder abuse: Society's dilemma. *J Natl Med Assoc. 97,* 1, 91–94, 2005.

Harrington, C., Kovner, C., Mezey, M., Kayser-Jones, J., Burger, S., Mohler, M., Burke, R., & Zimmerman, D. Experts recommend minimum nurse staffing standards for nursing facilities in the United States. *Gerontologist. 40,* 1, 5–16, 2000.

Harrington, D., & Dubowitz, H. Preventing child maltreatment. In R. L. Hampton, Ed. *Family Violence: Prevention and Treatment* (second edition). (pp. 122–147). Thousand Oaks, CA: Sage. 1999.

Hassouneh-Phillips, D. Understanding abuse of women with physical disabilities: An overview of the abuse pathways model. *ANS Adv Nurs Sci. 28,* 1, 70–80, 2005.

Heger, A., & Emans, S. J. Introital diameter as the criteria for sexual abuse. *Pediatrics. 85,* 222, 1990.

Heger, A., & Emans, S. J. *Evaluation of the Sexually Abused Child: A Medical Textbook and Photographic Atlas.* New York: Oxford University Press. 1992.

Herman-Giddens, M. E., & Frothingham, T. E. Prepubertal female genitalia: Examination for evidence of sexual abuse. *Pediatrics. 80,* 203, 1987.

Heyman, R. E., & Smith-Slep, A. M. Risk factors for family violence: Introduction to the special series. *Aggression and Violent Behavior. 6,* 115–119, 2001.

Holden, G. W., & Ritchie, K. L. Linking extreme marital discord, child rearing, and child behavior problems: Evidence from battered women. *Child Dev. 62,* 311–327, 1991.

Hudson, M. F., Armachain, W. D., Beasley, C. M., & Carlson, J. R. Elder abuse: Two Native American views. *Gerontologist. 38,* 5, 538–548, 1998.

Hughes, H. H. Psychological and behavioral correlates of family violence in child witnesses and victims. *Am I Orthopsychiatry. 58,* 77–90, 1987.

Hughes, L. M., & Corbo-Richert, B. Munchausen syndrome by proxy: Literature review and implications for critical care nurses. *Crit Care Nurs. 19,* 3, 71–79, 1999.

Hyman, A., Schillinger, D., & Bernard, L. Laws mandating reporting of domestic violence: Do they promote patient well-being? *JAMA. 273,* 1781–1787, 1995.

Hyman, J. A. From the frontlines: Financial abuse and legal assistance. *NARCEA Exchange. 2,* 4, 1990.

Isaac, N. E., & Sanchez, R. L. Emergency department response to battered women in Massachusetts. *Ann Emerg Med. 23,* 855–858, 1994.

Iyer, P. Liability in the care of the elderly. *J Obstet Gynecol Neonatal Nurs. 33,* 1, 124–131, 2004.

Jogerst, G. J., Brady, M. J., & Dyer, C. B. Elder abuse and the law: New science, new tools. *J Law Med Ethics. 32,* 4, Suppl., 62–3, 2004.

Jones, J. S., Veenstra, T. R., Seamon, J. P., & Krohmer, J. Elder mistreatment: National survey of emergency physicians. *Ann Emerg Med. 30,* 4, 473–479, 1997.

Jones, L., & Finkelhor, D. *The Decline in Child Sexual Abuse Cases. Bulletin.* Washington, DC: U.S. Department of Justice, Office of Justice Programs, Office of Juvenile Justice and Delinquency Prevention. 2001.

Joshi, S., & Flaherty, J. H. Elder abuse and neglect in long-term care. *Clin Geriatr Med. 21,* 2, 333–354, 2005.

Klingbeil, K. S., & Boyd, V. D. Emergency room intervention: Detection, assessment, and treatment. In A. R. Roberts, Ed. *Battered Women and Their Families.* New York: Springer. 1984.

Kohm, C., McNally, M. J., & Tiivel, J. Abuse policies for health care institutions. *Leadersh Health Serv. 5,* 5, 36–39, 1996.

Kosberg, J. I. Preventing elder abuse: Identification of high risk factors prior to placement decisions. *Gerontologist. 28,* 43–50, 1988.

Krueger, P., & Patterson, C. *Detecting and Managing Elder Abuse: Challenges in Primary Care.* The Research Subcommittee of the Elder Abuse and Self-Neglect Task Force of Hamilton-Wentworth. Ottawa, Ontario, Canada: Canadian Medical Association.

Lachs, M. S., & Pillemer, K. Elder abuse. *The Lancet. 364,* 9441, 1263–1272, 2004.

Lachs, M. S., Williams, C., O'Brien, S., Hurst, L., & Horwitz, R. Older adults: An 11-year longitudinal study of adult protective service use. *Arch Intern Med. 26,* 4, 449–453, 1996.

Lau, E. E., & Kosberg, J. I. Abuse of the elderly by informal care providers. *Aging. 299–300,* 10–15, 1979.

Lessing, J. E. Primary-care provider interventions for the delayed disclosure of adolescent sexual assault. *J Pediatr Health Care. 19,* 1, 17–24, 2005.

Lisak, D. The psychological impact of sexual abuse: Content analysis of interviews with male survivors. *J Traumatic Stress. 7,* 525–548, 1994.

Lo Fo Wong, S. H., & Lagro-Janssen, A. L. Intimate partner abuse of women: Identification of victims in medical practice. *Ned Tijdschr Geneeskd. 149,* 1, 6–9, 2005.

Makar, A. F., & Squier, P. J. Munchausen syndrome by proxy: Father as a perpetrator. *Pediatr. 85,* 370–373, 1990.

Markowitz, J. R., Steer, S., & Garland, M. Hospital-based intervention for intimate partner violence victims: A forensic nursing model. *J Emerg Nurs. 31,* 2, 166–170, 2005.

Marshall, C. E., Benton, D., & Brazier, J. M. Elder Abuse: Using clinical tools to identify clues of mistreatment. *Geriatrics. 55,* 2, 42–53, 2000.

McCabe, M. P., & Wauchope, M. Behavioral characteristics of men accused of rape: Evidence for different types of rapists. *Arch Sex Behav. 34,* 2, 241–253, 2005.

McCann, J. Labial adhesions and posterior fourchette injuries in child sexual abuse. *American J Diseases of Children. 142,* 659, 1988.

McCann, J. Use of the colposcope in childhood sexual abuse examinations. *Pediatric Clinics of North America. 37,* 863, 1990.

McCann, J., Voris, J., Simon, M., & Wells R. Perianal findings in prepubertal children selected for non-abuse: A descriptive study. *Child Abuse & Neglect. 13,* 179–183, 1989.

McCann, J., Wells, R., Simon, M., & Voris, J. Genital findings in prepubertal girls selected for non-abuse: A descriptive study. *Pediatrics. 86,* 428–439, 1990.

McCreadie, C., & Tinker, A. Abuse of elderly people in the domestic setting: A UK perspective. *Age Ageing. 22,* 65–69, 1993.

McKay, M. M. The link between domestic violence and child abuse: Assessment and treatment considerations. *Child Welfare. 73,* 29–39, 1994.

McKibben, L., DeVos, E., & Newberger, E. Victimization of mothers of abused children: A controlled study. *Pediatrics. 4,* 531–535, 1989.

Meadows, R. Munchausen syndrome by proxy: The hinterland of child abuse. *The Lancet. 2,* 343–345, 1977.

Meeks-Sjostrom, D. A comparison of three measures of elder abuse. *J Nurs Scholarsh. 36,* 3, 247–250, 2004.

Morris, M. R. Elder Abuse: What the law requires. *RN. 61,* 8, 52–54, 1998.

Morrison, C. A. Cameras in hospital rooms: The Fourth Amendment to the Constitution and Munchausen Syndrome by Proxy. *Criti Care Nurs Q. 22,* 1, 65–68, 1999.

Mosqueda, L., Burnight, K., Liao, S., & Kemp, B. Advancing the field of elder mistreatment: A new model for integration of social and medical services. *Gerontologist. 44,* 5, 703–708, 2004.

Muram, D. Anal and perianal abnormalities in prepubertal victims of sexual abuse. *Am J Obstet Gynecol. 161,* 278, 1989a.

Muram, D. Child sexual abuse: Relationship between sexual acts and genital findings. *Child Abuse Negl. 13,* 211, 1989b.

Muram, D., Miller, K., & Cutler, A. Sexual assault of the elderly victim. *J Interpersonal Violence. 7,* 1, 70–76, 1992.

Myers, W. C., Scott, K., Burgess, A. W., & Burgess, A. G. Psychopathology, biopsychosocial factors, crime characteristics, and classification of 25 homicidal youths. *J Am Acad Child Adolesc Psychiatry. 34,* 11, 1483–1489, 1995.

National Association of School Nurses (NASN). Issue brief: Integrated service delivery. 2001a. Available at: http://www.nasn.org/briefs/integratedsvcdel.htm.

National Center on Elder Abuse. *National Elder Abuse Incident Study; Final Report.* Washington, DC: Administration for Children and Families, Administration on Aging, U.S. Department of Health and Human Services. 1998.

National Clearinghouse on Child Abuse and Neglect Information. *Child Fatalities Resource Listing.* Washington, DC: U.S. Department of Health and Human Services. 2003.

National Research Council. *Understanding Child Abuse and Neglect.* Washington, DC: National Academy Press. 1993.

Nelson, J. C., & Johnston, C. Screening for family and intimate partner violence. *Ann Intern Med. 141,* 1, 81, 2004.

Nolan, M. Elder abuse: A wake-up call to nurse educationalists. *Br J Nurs. 13,* 9, 510, 2004.

Nosek, M. A., Rintala, D. H., Young, M. E., Howland, C. A., Foley, C. C., Rossi, D., & Chanpong, G. Sexual functioning among women with physical disabilities. *Arch Phys Med Rehabil. 77,* 2, 107–115, 1996.

NOVA. The elderly crime victim. *Network Information Bulletin. 2,* 2, 1985.

Office for Victims of Crime. *Breaking the Cycle of Violence: Recommendations to Improve the Criminal Justice Response to Child Victims and Witnesses.* Washington, DC: U.S. Department of Justice. 1999.

Otiniano, M. E., Lorimor, R., Macdonald, E., & Du, X. L. Common fraud experienced by the elderly: Findings from a 1998 survey in Houston, Texas. *Tex Med. 98,* 10, 46–50, 2002.

Otto, J., & Quinn, K. The National Elder Abuse Incidence Study: An evaluation by the National Association of Adult Protective Service Administrators. *Victimization of the Elderly and Disabled. 2,* 1, 4, 1999.

Paradise, J. E. The medical evaluation of the sexually abused child. *Pediatric Clinics of North America. 37,* 839, 1990.

Paris, B. E., Meier, D. E., Goldstein, T., Weiss, M., & Fein, E. D. Elder abuse and neglect: How to recognize warning signs and intervene. *Geriatrics. 50,* 47–51, 1995.

Pasqualone, G. A., & Fitzgerald, S. M. Munchausen by proxy syndrome: The forensic challenge of recognition, diagnosis, and reporting. *Crit Care Nurs Q. 22,* 52–64, 1999.

Pillemer, K. A. Ten tentative truths about elder abuse. *J Health Home Rehabil Adult. 12,* 4, 465–483, 1990.

Plotkin, M. R. Improving the police response to domestic elder abuse victims. *Aging. 367,* 28–33, 1996.

Quinn, K., & Zielke, H. Elder abuse, neglect, and exploitation: Policy issues. *Clin Geriatr Med. 21,* 2, 449–457, 2005.

Reece, R. *Child Abuse: Medical Diagnosis and Management.* Philadelphia: Lea & Febiger. 1994.

Reed, K. When elders lose their cents: Financial abuse of the elderly. *Clin Geriatr Med. 21,* 2, 365–382, 2005.

Robinson, E. Munchausen Syndrome by Proxy and covert video surveillance: Exploring legal problems and solutions for hospitals. *Medical Trial Technique Q. 44,* 159–187, 1997.

Rose, K., & Saunders, D. G. Nurses' and physicians' attitudes about women abuse. *Health Care Women Int. 17,* 427–438, 1986.

Rosenberg, M., Stark, E., & Zahn, M. Interpersonal violence: Homicide and spouse abuse. In J. M. Last, Ed. *Public Health and Preventive Medicine* (12th ed.). (pp. 1399–1426). Norwalk, CT: Appleton-Century-Crofts. 1986.

Sapp, M. V., & Vandeven, A. M. Update on childhood sexual abuse. *Curr Opin Pediatr. 17,* 2, 258–264, 2005.

Schreier, H. Munchausen syndrome by proxy defined. *Pediatr. 110,* 985–988, 2002.

Schumaker, J. A., Smith-Slep, A. M., & Heyman, R. E. Risk factors for child neglect. *Aggression and Violent Behavior. 6,* 231–254, 2001.

Scott, C. J., & Matricciani, R. M. Joint Commission on Accreditation of Healthcare Organizations standards to improve care for victims of abuse. *Md Med J. 43,* 891–898, 1994.

Scott, H. S., & Beaman, R. Demographic and situational factors affecting injury, resistance, completion, and charges brought in sexual assault cases: What is best for arrest? *Violence Vict. 19,* 4, 479–494, 2004.

Siegel, S. Facility liability for patient abuse by staff. *Health Care Law Mon.* July, 3–7, 2004.

Simpson, A. R. Cultural issues and elder mistreatment. *Clin Geriatr Med. 21,* 2, 355–364, 2005.

Skeates, E., & Douglas, I. Abuse of elderly people. *Nursing. 4,* 6, 1990.

Skipper, B. H., & Collins, S. E. Forensic nursing in action: Nursing diagnosis in alleged sexual abuse of children. *Fla Nurse. 48,* 2, 33–34, 2000.

Soler, E., & Campbell, J. Screening for family and intimate partner violence. *Ann Intern Med. 141,* 1, 82, 2004.

Spies, L., & Parker, J. *Victims of violence who have disabilities: How do policies reflect societal attitudes?* 1990.

Stark, E., & Flitcraft, A. H. Violence among intimates: An epidemiological review. In V. N. Hasselt, et al., Eds. *Handbook of Family Violence.* New York; Plenum. 1987.

Steen, K., & Hunskaar, S. Violence in an urban community from the perspective of an accident and emergency department: A two-year prospective study. *Med Sci Monit. 10,* 2, CR75–79, 2004.

Steinmetz, S. K. Overlooked aspects of family violence: Battered husbands, battered siblings, and battered elderly. Testimony presented to the U.S. House Committee on Science and Technology, Washington, DC, 1978.

Stevens, S. Cracking the case: Your role in forensic nursing. *Nursing. 34,* 11, 54–56, 2004.

Straus, M. A. Children as witness to marital violence: A risk factor for lifelong problems among a nationally representative sample of American men and women. Presented at the Ross Roundtable on Children and Violence, Washington, DC, 1991.

Tanabe, M. K. Skull fracture? Not! *J Am Geriatr Soc. 52,* 8, 1402–1403, 2004.

Tatara, T. *Summaries of National Elder Abuse Data: An Exploratory Study of State Statistics*. Washington, DC: National Aging Resource Center on Elder Abuse. 1990.

Taylor, K. Perceptions of battered women. *J Pediatr Health Care. 19,* 1, 66, 2005.

Thomas, K. Munchausen syndrome by proxy: Identification and diagnosis. *J Pediatr Nurs. 18,* 174–180, 2003.

Tomlin, S. *Abuse of Elderly People: An Unnecessary and Preventable Problem*. London: British Geriatrics Society. 1988.

U.S. Department of Health and Human Services. *National Elder Abuse Incidence Study: Final Report*. Washington, DC: Administration on Aging. Administration for Children and Families. 1998. Available at: http://www.aoa.gov/abuse/report/default.htm.

U.S. Department of Health and Human Services. *Child Maltreatment 2001*. Washington, DC: Government Printing Office. 2003.

U.S. Department of Health and Human Services, Children's Bureau. *Child Maltreatment 2002*. Washington, DC: U.S. Government Printing Office. 2004.

U.S. Department of Justice. *Elder Justice: Medical Forensic Issues Concerning Abuse and Neglect: Draft Report*. Washington, DC: U.S. Department of Justice, National Institute of Justice. 2002.

U.S. House Select Committee on Aging. *Elder Abuse: An Examination of a Hidden Problem*. Washington, DC,: U.S. House of Representatives. April 3, 1981.

U.S. Preventive Services Task Force. Screening for family and intimate partner violence: Recommendation statement. *Ann Fam Med. 2*, 2, 156–160, 2004.

Voltz, A.G. Nursing interventions in Munchausen syndrome by proxy. *J Psychosoc Nurs. 33,* 9, 51–54, 1995.

Wick, J. M. Forensic nursing. *AORN J. 79,* 3, 585, 2004.

Wiese, M., Armitage, C., Delaforce, J., & Welch, J. Emergency care for complainants of sexual assault. *J R Soc Med. 98,* 2, 49–53, 2005.

Wolf, R. S. Elder abuse: Ten years later. *J Am Geriatrics Society. 36,* 758–762, 1988.

Wolf, R. The nature and scope of elder abuse. *Generations. 24,* 2, 6–12, 2000.

Women and Disability Project. *Building Community: A Manual Exploring Issues of Women and Disability.* New York: Women and Disability Project. 1984.

Woods, S. J. Intimate partner violence and post-traumatic stress disorder symptoms in women: What we know and need to know. *J Interpers Violence. 20,* 4, 394–402, 2005.

9 Sexual Violence in the Military

CONTENTS

Despite the chasm that might exist between private-sector nursing and military health care, forensic nursing has tremendous relevance for and application to military operations. Whether it is addressing sexual violence or suspicious injury or death in the field of operations, forensic nurses have a place in the military. At the time of this writing, various branches of the U.S. military are exploring ways that forensic principles can be integrated into standard military operations and its proprietary health care system.

9.1 DEPARTMENT OF JUSTICE RECOMMENDATIONS

In *The Role of the U.S. Military in Preventing and Responding to Violence Against Women: Toolkit to End Violence Against Women,* the Violence Against Women (VAW) Office of the U.S. Department of Justice (2001) outlines a number of steps that the U.S. military can take to improve the lives of those affected by violence:

- Use the Defense Task Force on Domestic Violence. Review, evaluate, support, and enhance the efforts of the U.S. Department of Defense (DOD) to end domestic violence.
- Establish a task force to address acts of sexual assault. Create a complementary body to the Defense Task Force on Domestic Violence to address acts of sexual assault that occur within the military or are committed by service personnel.
- Assess the incidence of sexual assault, dating and domestic violence, and stalking among unmarried military members and their intimate partners. Continue to identify and evaluate any policies or practices within units that directly or indirectly encourage activities that compromise women's safety.
- Improve coordination between the military and civilian communities. Implement a coordinated community response to crimes that involve sexual assault, including forced prostitution, dating and domestic violence, and stalking committed on and off the military base.
- Enhance and continue to use military intervention to address and eliminate domestic violence at its early stages. Work collaboratively with military and civilian communities to improve intervention and prevention efforts.
- Continue to teach command and service members how to prevent unauthorized use of violence throughout their active duty service. Stress that strong leadership is needed at every level to strengthen the training and management of personnel.
- Ensure that trained victim advocates are available on every installation and that women on military bases also have access to victim advocates from the local civilian community. Publicize the availability of civilian and military sexual assault and domestic violence hotlines and crisis intervention services throughout every installation.
- Continue to offer victims and offenders multidisciplinary interventions. Recommend additional resources and funding or the redirection of existing resources.
- Record all reported cases of sexual assault, dating and domestic violence, stalking, and military personnel involvement with women in forced prostitution in an appropriate DOD database.

> Review record-keeping efforts and recommend ways to improve how cases involving violence against women are tracked.

In the 2001 toolkit, the VAW Office states, "The military has undertaken significant initiatives to end violence against women." The group points to the creation of the Family Advocacy Program (FAP), which conducts an annual public awareness campaign at every installation in October during National Domestic Violence Awareness Month, plus a variety of year-round efforts to prevent domestic violence. FAP, which includes clinically licensed professionals trained in family violence, is responsible for ensuring victim safety and access to support and advocacy services as well as seeing that abusers receive appropriate intervention services.

The VAW Office asserts that DOD policymakers must address fears that military spouses and female service personnel have about reporting incidents of sexual assault, dating and domestic violence, and stalking, as well as "definitional issues." According to the VAW Office, to help reduce the economic disincentive that discourages victims from reporting abuse by a service member, Congress authorized DOD in 1993 to provide financial support and other benefits to spousal abuse victims. DOD provides transitional compensation for up to three years to family members when a service member is discharged from the military or has been court-martialed for abusing a family member. The definitional issues that must be resolved, the VAW Office says, include FAP's use of the term *spousal abuse* to refer to assault, battery, threat to injure or kill, other acts of force or violence, and emotional maltreatment committed by one spouse against another. The VAW Office asserts that FAP's definition does not refer to violence between unmarried intimate partners and therefore significantly limits the FAP's response. The VAW Office maintains that positive change can be effected through collaboration among unit commanders, military police, and local judges, prosecutors, law enforcement, and the victim advocacy community, which must create protocols for communication and cooperation. Comprehensive, multilevel training is an essential component of this process, the VAW Office says, adding, "Strong leadership also is needed at every level, from senior public officials at the Pentagon to senior nonenlisted officers and other command, to strengthen the training and management of personnel on issues of sexual assault, domestic violence, and stalking." The VAW Office acknowledges that the constitutional allocation of powers between the federal government and states, the requirements of treaties, the Uniform Code of Military Justice, federal laws, the role of the commander, and the culture of the military "all have an impact on the way the military responds to violence against women." It continues, "Each of the armed services has different structures and methods of response that reflect their different missions. These factors create both opportunities and challenges to efforts to respond to sexual assault, dating and domestic violence, and stalking."

In October 1999, the Defense Authorization Act for fiscal year 2000 was signed into law, establishing a task force on domestic violence in the military. The Defense Task Force on Domestic Violence submitted to the Secretary of Defense in February 2001 a strategic plan detailing how to address matters relating to domestic violence in the military more effectively. The plan includes an assessment of and recommendations for measures to improve the following:

- Ongoing victims' safety programs
- Offender accountability
- The climate for effective prevention of domestic violence
- Coordination and collaboration among all military organizations with responsibility or jurisdiction with respect to domestic violence
- Coordination between military and civilian communities with respect to domestic violence
- Research priorities
- Data collection
- Curricula and training for military commanders
- Prevention of and response to domestic violence at overseas military installations

9.2 SEXUAL ASSAULT AND ABUSE IN THE MILITARY

A U.S. serviceman waited outside of a latrine and hit a servicewoman on the back of the head as she exited, knocking her unconscious. He tied her hands with cord, blindfolded her, cut her clothes off with a knife, stuffed her underwear in her mouth, and then raped her. When she regained consciousness and began to resist, he threatened to rape her with the knife. He hit her in the head again, this time forcefully between the eyes, again causing her to lose consciousness. When she came to, she was transported to another facility where she was interrogated for three hours. She received no medical treatment for her head injuries. She was left in isolation for an extended period, and her requests for religious counsel were denied.

This incident is just one of more than 100 incidents of rape, sexual assault, and other forms of sexual misconduct reported in a recent 18-month span by U.S. women soldiers currently serving in Iraq and Afghanistan who have been sexually assaulted by fellow U.S. service members. According to reports and allegations, the military's response to these victims has been "grossly inadequate." Many victims have claimed that they did not receive even the most basic medical care, including emergency contraception, rape kits, testing for STIs, prophylactic treatment or testing for HIV, and rape crisis counseling. Prosecution of these crimes is delayed indefinitely, and servicewomen must often continue to serve in the same unit, and sometimes sleep in the same barracks as their assailant.

9.2.1 The Department of Defense Examines Incidence of Sexual Assault in the Services

In a DOD memorandum, U.S. Secretary of Defense Donald Rumsfeld stated that "the Department of Defense is unequivocal in its commitment to ensure that victims of sexual assault be protected, treated with dignity and respect, provided proper medical and psychological care, and that the perpetrators of such assaults be held accountable." However, around that same time, Pentagon officials admitted receiving 112 reports of sexual assault of troops deployed in the Middle East during the previous 18 months. To investigate, on February 5, 2004, Rumsfeld directed the Undersecretary of Defense for Personnel and Readiness to undertake a 90-day review of all sexual assault policies and programs among the Services and DOD, and recommend changes necessary to increase prevention, promote reporting, and enhance the quality and support provided to victims. Rumsfeld appointed a task force to investigate the problem and make recommendations. Those findings by the DOD were released in April 2004 in a 114-page document, *Task Force Report on Care for Victims of Sexual Assault.* This report acknowledges the widespread problem of sexual assault in all branches of the military, as well as lack of leadership in addressing the issue, noting everything from confusing definitions as to what constitutes sexual assault to poor data tracking to a deficiency of sound policies for preventing or responding—most notably a lack of privacy or confidentiality for victims who report. The report notes that victim advocacy and integrated services are often not available, that offenders are rarely held accountable, and that consistent, timely, sensitive responses to victim medical and psychological needs are frequently lacking. The report also reveals that the DOD does not have any mandated requirements to provide advocacy for sexual assault victims.

The task force conducted visits with 21 military locations, and had personal contact with more than 1,300 individuals. Working from scripted questions used at every site, the focus groups discussed issues such as command climate, barriers to reporting, prevention and support policies and practices, feedback mechanisms, best practices, and recommendations for improvements. Comments from focus group participants were obtained with the assurance that their individual comments would not be attributed to them or their organizations. The task force reviewed DOD, Service, and Combatant Commander policies and education and training requirements relative to sexual assault. The task force also reviewed selected 2002 and 2003 case and care reports at the sites visited in which the identified victim was a uniformed service member. The task force also consulted with other principal staff elements within the Office of the Secretary of Defense, outside experts from the Department of Justice and the Department of Veterans Affairs (VA), as well as respected experts from academia and rape crisis support organizations.

In the April 2004 report, the task force intended to provide a high-level, comprehensive assessment of the strengths, weaknesses, and gaps in current DOD and Service policies regarding care for sexual assault victims. The Task Force identified 35 key findings relevant to current sexual assault policies and programs among the Services and DOD, and proposed nine broad recommendations for immediate, near-term, and long-term corrective action. The DOD report found that data systems and records on reports of sexual assault are incomplete and not integrated. Although mechanisms such as serious incident reports, situation reports, and special interest reporting frequently report cases of sexual assault, these reporting methods do not capture all incidents, they are not standardized, they are not intended to analyze data, and the lack of record-keeping and follow-up by higher levels of command make it difficult to assess risk factors, trends, and accountability. The report stated, "What is needed is a system to help senior-level commanders understand and manage trends and characteristics of Service-level crime for the purpose of better understanding risk environments and mitigating those risks."

A lack of integration and coordination was also noted with respect to the task force's request that each installation visited provide 10 reports of investigations, with corresponding records reflecting any and all support services provided to victims in those cases. With the exception of one installation that made a conscientious attempt to provide information on mental health support provided to victims in the identified cases, the information provided could not establish the timeliness or extent of support services provided to victims. The report also discovered that there is no integrated system or strategy for reporting, tracking, or reviewing reports of sexual assault and actions taken. It stated:

> The DoD has no data-collection requirement to systematically aid commanders (mission-centric), service providers (victim-centric) and legal and law enforcement (offender-centric) officials in understanding the scope of the problem, how timely and effectively the services are provided, or how consistent and timely we are in resolving the issues for both victims and alleged offenders. Evaluating program effectiveness, assessing system accountability, and implementing data-informed process and program improvements is seriously compromised without more effective and integrated methods of data collection.

The report documented rates of reported alleged sexual assaults at 69.1 and 70 per 100,000 uniformed service members for 2002 and 2003, respectively. Across DOD, there were 901 and 1,012 alleged cases of sexual assault with uniformed service member victims reported to criminal investigations in 2002 and 2003, respectively. These figures include 24 (2002) and 94 (2003) reported cases in the CENTCOM AOR. Sexual assault, as referred to here, includes the alleged offenses of rape, forcible sodomy, assault with intent to commit rape or sodomy, indecent assault, or an attempt to commit any of these offenses. There were 2,012 identified service member victims in the 1,913 alleged cases of sexual assault. Males constituted 9 percent of identified victims in these cases. Of the 1,913 cases of alleged sexual assault across DOD for 2002 and 2003, 1,634 alleged offenders were service members at the time of the incident. Males represented 99 percent of alleged service member offenders.

Differences in definition create significant challenges for DOD in evaluating sexual assault trends and program execution, the report stated. The task force realized that there is considerable inconsistency in the terminology used and the behaviors included in related terms. To complicate matters, the same term might be used variably within and between DOD, the Services, and federal and civilian agencies. This disparity in defining terminology and behaviors makes it very difficult to compare data within DOD or with non-DOD agencies and research. For example, in an anonymous DOD survey pertaining to sexual harassment (Lipari & Lancaster, 2003), sexual assault was defined as "had sex with you without your consent or against your will." In contrast, the NCVS collects information on rape (which includes attempted rape) and sexual assault, which covers a wide range of victimizations, including completed or attempted attacks generally involving unwanted sexual contact that does not involve penetration (Hart, 2003). When discussing "military sexual trauma," the VA refers to either sexual harassment or sexual assault occurring during military service, both of which are defined further.

Perhaps the area with the greatest potential for confusion within the military system is the overlap between the terms *sexual harassment* and *sexual assault*. The DOD report explains that at the beginning of each focus group, participants were asked their understanding of the meeting purpose. Almost without exception, participants responded that they were there to discuss sexual harassment. This occurred even though all task force communication with installations identified the focus as sexual assault. Participants continued to use the terms interchangeably until redirected several times, according to the report. At the policy level, there is reason for confusion. The DOD Equal Opportunity Program directive defines sexual harassment to include unwelcome "verbal or physical contact of a sexual nature." Although contact could often form the basis for a criminal charge, commanders and service members are often confused about the proper avenue for reporting these allegations when they arise. Notably, the equal opportunity representative (the appropriate resource for reports of sexual harassment) was often identified by focus group participants as the point of contact for reporting sexual assault, the report noted.

The DOD report asserted that sexual assault risk factors in the military are not significantly different from those reported in civilian literature. Research has demonstrated that youth are at greater risk of sexual assault (e.g., Hart, 2003; Perkins, 1997; Tjaden & Thoennes, 2000), and according to the DOD report, data reported by the Services indicated the same. For those cases in which the age of the service member victim was available, ages 17 to 24 represented, on average, 87 percent of Air Force victims, 85 percent of Department of the Navy victims and 83 percent of Army victims for the two years reported. For service-member offenders, ages 17 to 24 represented, on average, 68 percent of Air Force offenders, 66 percent of Navy offenders, and 40 percent of Army offenders. Additionally, in a national survey of college women, almost all of the completed rapes occurred in campus living quarters (Fisher, Cullen, & Turner, 2000). Service data reported a consistent trend, the DDD report says; however, the task force could not ascertain the number of cases that occurred in mixed-gender living quarters on military installations. The report does say that data supplied by the Army and Navy was informative. In the Army, 52 percent of the total cases occurred in living quarters on military installations. In the Navy, 47 percent of the total cases occurred in living quarters under military control. However, when cases not occurring in areas under military control were excluded, 79 percent of Navy cases occurred in living quarters. In the Air Force, 19 percent of cases occurred in mixed-gender living quarters or military installations across the two years.

Data provided by two of the Services indicated that the use of alcohol was associated with 50 percent of alleged sexual assault cases involving service member victims during 2002 and 2003. With respect to the CENTCOM AOR, the percentage of associated alcohol use ranged from 19 percent in the Army to 48 percent in the Navy. The use of alcohol as a risk factor was a prevailing theme during discussions with leaders, junior enlisted, providers and investigators, the DOD reports found. The focus groups suggested that alcohol is involved in most reported cases of sexual assault in circumstances when the victim and alleged offender were engaged in social drinking before the alleged assault occurred. It is believed that training environments are also at risk for the occurrence of sexual assault, because arrival at training might be the first time away from home and away from parental controls. This newfound independence, coupled with peer pressure and easy access to alcohol, can lead to reckless and risky behavior. Although in most circumstances it is illegal to drink under the age of 21 and illegal to provide alcohol to someone under the age of 21, alcohol is easily accessible to service members. Alcohol is restricted within the combat theater; however, the task force observed that it is accessible in this environment. It was also noted by the DOD report that close quarters, integration of units, and limitation on privacy and personnel unfamiliar with each other could increase the risk of sexual assault.

When it comes to prevention of sexual assault, the DOD report found that existing policies and programs are inconsistent and incomplete. Several studies have been conducted to identify best practices for the prevention of sexual assault. Some promote mixed-gender training, whereas others identify the benefits of single-gender training. Regardless of the approach, education and awareness is an effective tool for the prevention of sexual assault, the DOD report said. Although there are well-defined policies and programs for the prevention of sexual harassment, there is not a clearly defined DOD-wide policy or program aimed at preventing sexual assault. Although some commands have made efforts in sexual assault prevention training, a DOD-wide set of standards for sexual assault prevention would give this subject the emphasis it merits. Whereas sexual harassment training is taught at basic officer and enlisted entry-level schools and throughout the career life cycle, sexual assault prevention and awareness training is rarely included. If addressed at all, its treatment is cursory, according to the DOD report. Junior enlisted personnel noted that installation "newcomer" and holiday safety briefings would be an excellent opportunity for commanders to address sexual assault concerns with their personnel.

Limited instruction on sexual assault awareness is conducted at formal military schools during entry-level instruction for officers and enlisted personnel. Training and education beyond the institutional setting is sporadic and varies among the Services. The Navy requires annual training on the prevention of sexual assault during general military training instruction for all Navy and Marine Corps personnel. In 1997, the Marine Corps also established the Mentors in Violence Prevention (MVP) program. MVP provides tools to assist and encourage male Marines to actively participate in efforts to prevent rape, battering, sexual harassment, and all forms of male violence against women. Because the MVP program is currently only offered during senior noncommissioned officer (NCO) and staff NCO courses, many junior enlisted personnel were not familiar with MVP, the DOD report discovered.

The report also documented that at some installations, commanders have developed local sexual assault awareness training. The task force discovered some locally developed educational materials related to sexual assault based on information from other federal, state, and local government agencies or educational tools published by various college and university experts. Often in response to a specific incident, commanders developed programs to ensure service members are better informed on the dangers of risky behavior. For example, the Dorm Awareness Program at Travis Air Force Base provides invaluable information to young airmen on improving situational awareness, how to avoid becoming a victim of sexual assault, and appropriate dating behavior. Kusan Air Force Base in Korea has created a Sexual Assault Free Environment (SAFE) program for all personnel assigned to the base. The program includes briefings by the wing commander, the military equal opportunity representative, and expert guest speakers. Enlisted personnel participating during the focus groups commented that the SAFE program enhanced their awareness of issues related to sexual assault. With the assistance of the Department of Justice, Nellis Air Force Base in Nevada has developed and implemented the Nellis Sexual Assault Prevention Program (NSAPP), focusing on prevention, education, and on- and off-post community outreach. The training is mandatory for commanders, first sergeants, and all personnel. Some installations have also adopted a local "buddy system" program requiring service members to travel in pairs. In spite of the potential of these programs as preventive measures, they have not been shared or adopted Service-wide, the DOD report said.

Despite a desire to provide sexual assault awareness training in the joint operational environment, military personnel said the operations tempo presents serious challenges. In the operational environment, commanders must maintain a high degree of readiness and their focus is mission accomplishment. Commanders expect that prior to arrival in a combat theater, units will have completed the array of mandatory training, including equal opportunity, sexual harassment, and cultural awareness training. The operational environment is also transitory, with more 200,000 troops deploying at any given time; for this reason, the DOD report says it is difficult to maintain unit integrity in living accommodations while also providing separate quarters for both genders. Although coed living presented no major sexual assault issues during field exercises with their parent unit, Army female enlisted personnel did not like having to bunk in the same area with men they did not know, according to the report. Lack of privacy for women and men was widely discussed among focus group participants, the task force reported.

The challenges for providing sexual assault awareness and prevention training in the joint environment are further complicated because of the large number of reserve component personnel (21 percent of deployed forces) in the CENTCOM theater, the DOD report asserts. Reserve component personnel who participated in focus groups identified a lack of training on the prevention of sexual assault at the home station and on arrival in theater. This insight, coupled with increased utilization of reserve component personnel, cross-leveling of service members to fill unit vacancies, and lack of predeployment awareness training, was highlighted during the task force's visits throughout the CENTCOM theater of operation. Commanders identified the need to conduct sexual assault awareness training prior to arrival in theater due to the high operations tempo. In addition, enlisted personnel also expressed a strong desire for training that was not "death by PowerPoint." Junior enlisted focus group participants that had deployed to a combat theater overwhelmingly endorsed the need for sexual assault awareness training prior to arrival in theater. They also indicated that, to be better prepared to protect themselves in a transitional wartime environment, the training might also need to be reinforced in theater, primarily because conditions and circumstances could not be anticipated in predeployment training. They noted that such training should be interactive in nature, using realistic scenarios, and come directly from their commanders. Many male focus group participants observed that current awareness training is directed primarily toward women. They noted that many all-male units tend to believe such training efforts are wasted on them, because there are no women in their units. However, in the combat environment, mixed-gender support and service support units become integrated into their command, and require service members not used to working with women to quickly assimilate appropriate sensitivity not previously required. In many focus group discussions, male participants indicated that awareness training on sexual assaults should be directed toward men, especially regarding male behaviors and risky situations that male service members should be aware of (and seek to avoid) that might lead to being accused of sexual assault or becoming victims themselves.

There was general consensus among focus group participants that in-theater training on sexual assault be given to all personnel assigned to the theater, and that such training should be standard.

When it came to sexual assault education, the DOD report found that it is limited and varies from location to location. Because the DOD has not developed or required standardized education and training materials for the prevention of sexual assault, most service members lack a basic understanding of what constitutes sexual assault, risk factors, or preventive measures, the report added. This lack of knowledge and understanding of sexual assault was prevalent across both officer and enlisted ranks. Service members at all levels often confuse the definition of sexual assault with that of sexual harassment and sexual misconduct. During focus group sessions, it was also apparent that many did not know the situations and circumstances in which most sexual assaults occur, and were unprepared to recognize and handle the risks. There is a common misperception that most cases of sexual assault involve a stranger waiting to attack an unsuspecting victim; service members were surprised to learn that men could also be victims of sexual assault. Although several commands have written zero-tolerance policies that condemn sexual assault, these policies are not widely publicized and were not reinforced through awareness or sexual assault prevention training. At the time of the focus groups, enlisted participants stated that they had not received or could not remember receiving any training specifically on sexual assault. Those who had received special training in this area through the Navy's Sexual Assault Victims Intervention (SAVI) program were the exception to this finding, but these individuals still recommended training relevant to risks, what sexual assault is and is not, and the local process for reporting and receiving support and assistance if a sexual assault occurs, the task force stated.

The DOD task force also encountered barriers to reporting incidents of sexual assault; some were consistent with those in the civilian community, and others were unique to the military setting. Data indicated that there is little delay in reporting when cases are reported to investigators. Roughly two thirds of the sexual assault cases with service member victims in 2002 and 2003 were reported within 72 hours of the alleged sexual assault, according to the DOD report; nevertheless, focus-group participants consistently articulated reasons why uniformed victims of sexual assault might choose to forgo reporting sexual assault in a timely fashion, or at all. Some of the barriers they expressed were concerns that they would not be believed, feelings of embarrassment and stigma, ambiguity about what constitutes sexual assault, concerns that the criminal justice system is largely ineffective at responding to or preventing such incidents, and fear of reprisal from the offender. Individuals were concerned that the chain of command and other unit personnel would not believe them and would ignore the complaint altogether. This was of particular concern when an alleged offender is of superior rank, has a good military record and reputation, controls the victim's professional success, or is very popular. Focus group participants also expressed concern of embarrassment and stigma because they believed that everyone in their unit would know and talk about what occurred once the investigative process began. They also expressed a lack of confidence in the chain of command's ability to effectively address a report of sexual assault. These comments were based on individuals' observations within their units and often stemmed from a lack of understanding about what had previously occurred in response to an allegation of sexual assault. Another barrier that the task force heard about was fear of repercussions from the chain of command because of the victim's own misconduct, such as underage drinking, fraternization, adultery, or sexual relations in prohibited areas. Participants also thought that reporting a sexual assault would damage their reputation, have negative career implications, or cause them to be ostracized by friends and unit personnel. For men, in particular, there was a general perception that reporting a male-against-male sexual assault might cause people to question the victim's sexual orientation. They also articulated that they were reluctant to report a sexual assault because the investigative process might disrupt the unit mission or negatively impact unit morale and cohesion. Others indicated sexual assaults went unreported because victims were concerned that if they reported it would delay their redeployment or change of assignment date.

Generally, the DOD report said, individuals are not aware of the full range of reporting options available to them. Focus group participants believed that their chain of command was the sole avenue for reporting sexual assaults. They also thought they would be more likely to report a sexual assault to a friend. When focus group participants were informed of other reporting options outside the chain of command, they perceived there would be negative consequences for failing to notify their superiors. In other words, reporting anywhere else would be viewed as "jumping the chain of command' and disloyal to the unit. Regardless of the entry point for reporting, focus group participants repeatedly stated that they believe there is a critical need for education and training on where to report and how to support a victim of sexual assault. They also felt that it was critical for all service members to receive this education because a victim is more likely to report a sexual assault to a friend or junior enlisted than to a superior in their chain of command. Service members reported to the task force that they wanted to avoid the scrutiny of their chain of command and peers. In general, individuals had no awareness of the quality of the support "outside" and lacked awareness that in some cases, the support provided would be at their own expense. They expressed a preference to use outside sources, if available near the installation, to preserve privacy. "Currently within DOD, there is not a way for victims of sexual assault to get military-sponsored medical or mental health treatment without reporting the incident and triggering the investigative and judicial processes," the DOD report stated.

A recurring theme of the desire for privacy was found throughout the DOD report. Commanders bear the primary burden of responsibility for protecting the privacy of victims under their command; however, current chain-of-command reporting mechanisms might intensify the problem, the report said. Many focus group participants indicated that, although identifiers were not shown, the facts of these offenses appear in blotter reports, on serious incident reports, and on incident reports maintained on the shared drive of a computer network, so they are seen by noncommand personnel and command personnel alike. In small ships and commands, the names don't have to be on the reports for people to intuitively derive the victim's and offender's identities. Service members said that the NCOs and officers within their command structure who have no disposition responsibility in the case should not be informed of the details of the alleged incident, and others expressed frustration that leaders and NCOs were not doing enough to positively assure the victim's privacy. Some participants suggested that individuals questioned in connection with the investigative process be required to sign nondisclosure statements with stiff penalties for violation. According to the DOD report, currently, a report to authorities of a sexual assault triggers an investigative process involving interviews with witnesses, friends, coworkers, and unit personnel. Collection of physical evidence, sometimes in the victim's or offender's room, the report stated, is equally invasive. This activity, necessary to hold the offender accountable, often serves to engage the "grapevine" and further erode the victim's privacy and reputation.

Some victims, in response to rumors and not-so-veiled innuendos about their conduct and judgment, reported that they regretted their decision to report. After seeing this happen to others, several focus group participants cited this circumstance as a key barrier to reporting. Balancing the issue of confidentiality for sexual assault victims with the commander's responsibility to ensure due process of law is complicated, but must be addressed. "The perceived lack of privacy and confidentiality within DOD is thought by many to be one of the most significant barriers to reporting by military sexual assault victims," the DOD report stated. Experts consulted by the task force suggested that sexual assault victims benefit significantly from access to a safe haven, referrals for needed medical and social services, and feeling safe and protected from physical and verbal attacks. The report said, "For military victims, this would mean providing a means to receive immediate care, legal advice, and support following the incident without, at least initially, having to advise his/her chain of command or trigger an investigation. However, there is considerable confusion at all levels with respect to issues of mandatory reporting of sexual assault, and whether confidentiality or privilege applies under our current policies and regulations."

One of the DOD report's findings is the consistent need for DOD guidelines that ensure victim safety and protection. Several focus group participants reported that steps to provide for the safety and protection of sexual assault victims are not fully understood, inadequately applied, or take too long. Commander focus group participants indicated that they did not have, or were unaware of, clear-cut guidelines for actions that could be taken to address the physical and emotional needs of the victim. The lower the rank of the command or NCO leader participants, the less was known, according to the report. Currently, Staff Judge Advocates (SJAs) are available to consult with commanders regarding what steps need to be taken to protect the victim from the alleged offender if the latter is an active-duty service member (e.g., issuing a military protective order, ordering the service member—if the victim requests it—into barracks away from victim, temporarily suspending the suspected service member's access to firearms and ammunition, temporarily reassigning the alleged offender or the victim to ensure workplace separation of both). Additionally, the SJA can advise on steps to be taken to protect the victim from the alleged offender if the latter is a civilian. At DOD installations, legal offices are also available to advise commanders on how to ensure the safety of victims of sexual assault, including information on military and civilian protection orders; the scope and applicability of the Armed Forces Domestic Security Act; a basic description of the immigration provisions of the Violence Against Women Act; and the scope and applicability of the Lautenberg Amendment to the Gun Control Act.

Unfortunately, the DOD report found that actions to segregate alleged victim and alleged offender are not always timely. Quickly segregating the victim and the offender, especially if they live in the same building or tent, is important, the DOD study stated. Several victims who spoke to the task force noted that actions to provide for their safety and protection were either not initiated, inadequate, or took too long. Commander focus group participants acknowledged that they had the ability to move or transfer victims or offenders to another location, temporarily, but said that it was based on their personal judgment of the situation rather than on any specific set of guidelines or sensitivity training about the importance of assuring safety or protection of sexual assault victims. Commanders expressed that they have had a more difficult time accommodating the need to segregate victims from their assailants in a combat theater, when limited options are available, even temporarily. One commander noted that movement of one or both trained service members out of a unit supporting a critical war-fighting mission could significantly erode it's the unit's ability to accomplish that mission, particularly if either party performed a critical skill. Another officer indicated that he would immediately send both the victim and the offender out of the theater, to different but appropriate locations, even while the investigation was ongoing. The rationale offered for sending the victim out was there were limited support services available to provide timely ongoing assistance to a traumatized victim, whose performance might be impaired by the event. The rationale for sending the alleged offender out, often with no public indication of the basis for the action, is to remove the potentially criminal behavior from an environment where judgments being made were supposed to save lives, not ruin them. Some victims reported that they felt they had been revictimized by the commander's unilateral decision to send them home. They expressed frustration that their commanders had not consulted them prior to deciding to relocate them. Commanders expressed difficulty in making decisions to move either party because of the career implications and other consequences that might potentially occur if the investigation later finds that the report was not substantiated.

The DOD report uncovered the fact that commanders have variable responses in support for victims. Several victims told the task force that the emotional and physical consequences of sexual assault might make it difficult to continue working and maintain levels of proficiency required for success. Focus group participants noted that the chain-of-command response to sexual assault victims varied. Some commands were reported to be very supportive, whereas others were noted to respond with indifference or disbelief. Some commands communicated, either directly or indirectly,that "the mission comes first," according to the report. "Over time, it became apparent from discussion in the leadership focus groups that this apparent insensitivity may be related to an absence of training that specifically addresses the needs of sexual assault victims rather than general disregard. Furthermore, it was not uncommon in these focus groups for leaders to indicate that the group discussion had enlightened them and they expressed a need for further education and information," the report stated. The DOD has not mandated requirements to provide advocacy for sexual assault victims. In the report, participants agreed that sexual assault victim advocate policy and programming is needed throughout DOD.

Although DoD policies require designated personnel to provide victim support, mostly in conjunction with the legal process, implementing regulations do not mandate appointment of liaisons to accompany and guide victims of sexual assault throughout the medical, counseling, and investigative processes. "In the end, there is no one person or office across the military departments who are mandated to principally and exclusively serve the needs of sexual assault victims," the DOD report stated. Notably, the task force found that victim and witness liaison officers in the combat theater were far more proactive in contacting sexual assault victims during the initial stages of an investigation and facilitating services on behalf of victims. These liaison officers were always Judge Advocate General Corps (JAGC) officers who took a personal interest in performing duties that would normally be performed by an advocate. They acknowledged that their effort to contact and provide support to victims early in the investigative process was beyond the mandate of DOD VWAP. Nevertheless, these liaison officers are not required, nor are they routinely trained, to provide the scope of services typically found within civilian advocacy models.

Although victim advocates within the Navy and Marine Corps provide a range of services and support more in keeping with civilian advocacy models, their programs are resourced and implemented differently, the report said. The Navy's SAVI program is resourced with service funds and the Marine Corps victim advocacy program is funded through their FAP. The success of the Navy and Marine Corps' programs at installations visited is largely dependent on individual command attention, the resources available, and the experience and training of personnel acting as victim advocates. Although trained volunteers are available within Navy units ashore and deployed on ships, the adequacy of this support is largely dependent on the experience and training of individuals selected to fill those positions. The Marine Corps trained civilian victim advocates are generally not available for deployment to the combat theater.

Another report finding was that there is a perception that some victims are not consistently informed on the status of their cases. Some victims interviewed by the task force felt that their needs were not being met with respect to obtaining information on the status or outcome of their cases during the investigatory, command decision-making, and legal processes. The continuity and relative success of programs under the VWAP tend to work better at those locations where the liaison personnel are full-time civilian employees who are proactively involved with victims, according to the report:

> Unfortunately, because of lack of funding, this function often becomes an additional or shared duty among personnel assigned to the local staff judge advocate office. Too frequently, this results in victims feeling as though nobody cares about them and is especially problematic when the victim and alleged offender are stationed in geographically dispersed locations. Strong coordination between victim advocates, where available, and VWAP personnel is critical in reducing this perceived gap.

As in civilian cases, there are multiple factors causing delays in immediate response to victims in military cases. During focus group discussions, the DOD report said it became apparent that if the victim went to a military treatment facility, care was rendered; however, timeliness of care was identified as a problem for several reasons. These included long waiting times in ERs, waiting for responders to arrive, waiting for medical evaluation of any other traumas, and delays in arranging for transportation of victims to "outside the gate" civilian facilities. Many medical commands, according to the DOD report, have partnered with civilian agencies to obtain forensic evidence, as their experienced SANEs ensure reliable evidence for trial and because a significant number of installations no longer have full military hospitals and instead provide Monday-through-Friday clinical support. The report said:

> While these agreements are practical for a number of reasons, they may have unintended consequences. Through the eyes of a victim who recently experienced the trauma of a sexual assault, it is difficult for them to be forced to wait longer than absolutely necessary before showering. It may also unnecessarily require them to relate events to more than one medical provider. The response protocol at Nellis Air Force Base was notable in that victims are transported directly to the civilian facility by investigators, bypassing the military treatment facility except on rare occasions when the victim has other additional trauma. Delays associated with investigation can also be a significant problem. Some delays noted during this review included geographic separation of the personnel involved that were caused by cases occurring during deployment or other temporary duty situations, and those reported after personnel have been redeployed or reassigned.

The report acknowledged that a system to coordinate and track victim-support services for effective case management does not exist at all military installations. With respect to Service data call information pertaining to the care provided to victims, the Army reported that for cases of alleged sexual assault involving active duty victims, 86 percent of the victims accessed military or civilian services. Of the total number of Army victims, 48 percent received military medical care, 27 percent received behavioral health care, and 12 percent received civilian purchased care. Service member victims who accessed care received a total of 1,272 clinic visits, with behavioral health visits being the greatest. With respect to the Navy, 63 percent of active-duty victims received either medical or mental health care within Navy medical facilities. Of those, only 71 percent of the victims seen had diagnostic codes that reflected the sexual assault as the reason for the visit. In the Air Force, 98 percent of uniformed victims received medical care. Of the total number of victims, 52 percent received medical care within seven days of the alleged sexual assault, and 5 percent received behavioral health care within seven days. Although multiple services are available for victims at most locations, many victims were unaware of them and were unable to identify a centralized individual or process responsible for ensuring the timely and coordinated delivery of those services, according to the report. The Navy utilizes SAVI program coordinators and a SAVI program coordinating committee on a quarterly basis to address system issues that might limit access to care for victims. "While an excellent model, focus-group participants reported inconsistency in practice," the report said. The Army has a MEDCOM regulation requiring Sexual Assault Review Boards (SARBs) at medical treatment facilities to perform quarterly reviews on how well the various providers coordinated their services to support the victim; however these boards have not been consistently implemented Service-wide, the DOD report added. The NSAPP also uses a SART concept to ensure that all team members are notified of an alleged assault. The SART concept allows for follow-up evaluation on how support services provided coordinated care for the victim, and a forum to address any gaps in care. This SART reports directly to the installation Community

Action Information Board (CAIB) to close any loops and keep the command informed. The report concluded:

> While Services have policies and procedures concerning each of the separate support services that may be used to help victims, many of these policies are outdated and are not consistently applied or not designed to insure integrated support for each victim's case. A system is needed to assess how well each sexual assault case was managed, facilitate local policy changes and address any trends or risk factors. Additionally, a mechanism to report significant installation findings to the Service level is needed to perform Service-level system review and improvement. This process would allow the Services to obtain consistent data, assess trends, and be able to adjust policies or training materials on an ongoing basis.

The report found that resourcing to deliver integrated case management support for victims in a combat theater is currently not a part of force planning. At many continental United States (CONUS) locations, the report said, military treatment facilities have entered into memoranda of understanding (MOUs) with local organizations to provide specialized, expert medical and supportive care for victims. These facilities often utilize SANEs. The report stated:

> We found these relationships to be of great benefit to sexual assault victims, providing expert forensic evidence collection, advocacy, and on going medical and psychological support. Active duty victims we spoke to who chose to receive confidential care through these agencies were generally satisfied with the care and assistance received. However, these programs differ with respect to the scope of assistance provided from location to location, they may not be affordable for all victims if not otherwise reimbursed by the Services or through health care benefits, and may require significant travel time for the victim.

One common complaint of many service members is that although the use of civilian experts has improved the military's ability to provide optimal care for victims of sexual assault, it has diluted professional training, development, and expertise. Lt. Cynthia Ferguson, CNM, MSN, in Baltimore acknowledges a series of professional meetings that were held in 2004 and 2005 among high-level representatives from the various branches of the military and from professionals in the civilian world, to discuss issues of sexual abuse in the military. She says she is uneasy about relying too much on the civilian community and contractors for providing care to military vicitms, and training military professionals. "I believe we should be cautious when contracting with civilian personnel, and that we should be sure that we are not contracting with too many individual companies. Many civilian groups are attempting to provide the military with training and instruction, when they themselves have never served in the military and do not even understand its culture," Ferguson says. "In terms of the overall issue of sexual assault I think it's wonderful to share ideas; we need to send our people to civilian courses, but I feel very strongly that the people who should be involved in doing the sexual assault exams should be our military medical personnel." Ferguson says that in training courses, civilian educators will miss the particulars of the military mindset. "When we talk about SART, not everyone's team is the same. Our military teams are very different from what someone would expect out in the civilian community," she explains:

> Yes, you have investigative services, and yes, you have law enforcement; however, it's very different—the military is its own culture. Unless you are part of it and understand it fully, you will never be able to completely relate to that audience. It's very important that civilian community sexual assault training programs that train military personnel integrate military aspects of procedure and culture into their programs and that they also receive training from our military professionals. In regard to the Department of Defense forming a permanent office for Sexual Assault Prevention and Response, Ferguson would like to see the continuous presence of one professional representative from each branch of the military; the Army, Navy, Air Force and Marines, working together to provide current updates on sexual assault information and policy. She stated she would like to see an office that incorporates at least a lead advocate representative, a forensic nurse or forensic medical specialist, and a law enforcement representative. Other professionals that typically serve on a SART team, such as a lawyer, a chaplain or a behavioral health specialist could be consulted as needed. She believes that any decision to transfer policy decision-making capabilities completely to a civilian staff would only do the military a disservice. Military resources for military professionals providing care to sexual assault victims, and other victims of violence, are essential.

Ferguson's commitment to promoting the role of forensic clinical nurse specialist has much to do with one of her earliest experiences with a sexual assault patient. Ferguson had been working as a midwife on an Indian reservation when one morning, she was called by the hospital emergency room physician:

> He said, "Hey, we have a sexual assault cases that we need you to do." I said, "I've never done one of those before" but he insisted, "We need someone to do a rape kit on a patient in the ER." When I got there, I was handed a rectangular white box, (the sexual assault evidence kit), which I had never before seen in my life. I had no idea how to perform a sexual assault exam at the time. I remember asking the physician how to perform the exam, and I was told, "It's easy. All you have to do is follow the directions." And so I did just that. I sat there in front of the 17-year-old patient, and read through step one, step two, step three and so on, until I completed the entire

> exam. I'm an expert in well-woman care, and I perform exams every day, but at that time I knew nothing about evidence collection. Even now, to this day, I feel that I did not do justice to the young girl for whom I did the exam. Afterward, I made a vow to learn all about the sexual assault examination and evidence collection procedure. I made a promise to myself, "I will learn to do this because it is ridiculous that no one here knows how to do this type of exam properly." This poor girl was passed around like a hot potato because no one wanted to, or knew how to, do her exam. It also seemed as if no one was particularly worried about collecting the evidence correctly. That was the incident that spurred me to learn all I could about caring for patients who had been victims of sexual violence.

Ferguson works as a staff midwife at the Naval Hospital in Bethesda, Maryland, but also spends a great deal of time developing the DOD's sexual assault examiner course. She hopes to eventually get the military, particularly the Navy, to acknowledge the forensic nurse specialty by developing what is called an "additional qualifier." It would essentially be a specialty code for a nursing specialty, for nursing personnel who collect evidence from victims of sexual assault and other forensic cases.

She explains:

> In the military there are several different nursing specialties, such as ER nurse specialists, pediatric nurse practitioners and certified nurse midwives. They all carry unique identifier codes. So, if someone in medical operations needed a nurse for a mission overseas, they could see from the nurse's file what their skills background is by looking at their identifier codes. Or, as another example, if the military had a specialty code for any medical personnel certified in sexual assault care (MDs, NPs, PAs, or RNs), and they were trying to assign one of them to an operational platform where they needed someone qualified in sexual assault care, assignment officers could look at the qualifiers and be able to recognize someone with that forensic skill set.

Ferguson adds,

> The Navy doesn't yet recognize the profession of the clinical forensic nurse specialist, and one of my main hopes is that by meeting with senior officers at conferences and presentations, I will be able to show them the benefits of doing this. Perhaps they will see the many possibilities of utilizing this specialty.

While on tour in Japan from January 2001 to January 2004, Ferguson had coordinated the sexual assault examiner program there, taught sexual assault examination courses and had served as one of the primary examiners on call. When asked why she decided to teach courses on sexual assault examination, she says, "Because the military doesn't officially recognize SANEs in our communities and because they haven't felt it was important to assign a separate duty for that area, many nurses have pursued SANE certification and training on their own," she says. "By providing training for them, I'm able to assist in increasing the quality of care for the victims that may come through the doors of our emergency rooms."

Ferguson went on to explain,

> The military has typically relied on the ER physicians to be able to do the sexual assault exams; the problem with that is there is usually only one ER physician on call at most military treatment facilities. If someone were to come in to the emergency room with a life-threatening injury, the ER physician would have to leave the sexual assault case in order to care for the trauma patient. Meanwhile, the sexual assault victim's evidence is in jeopardy if the chain of custody is broken in any way, and the processing of their case is interrupted and delayed. I've also found that many ER physicians—much like in the civilian world—don't want to have to worry about the possibility of spending time in court testifying about sexual assault cases. Serving as an expert witness takes time and education. You don't just show up on the day of an Article 32 ready to testify. You have to prepare, be interviewed by lawyers, review your case and provide background research that supports your findings.

Ferguson says that the handling of a forensic case can be also be extremely complex at times due to jurisdictional issues:

> If a case happens in a nearby town, the victim is usually taken to a local rape crisis center or civilian hospital. But if the crime occurs on the military base, the victim is usually taken to the military hospital if there is one available. Sometimes OB-GYN physicians are the medical specialty on call for female sexual assault exams and general surgery is supposed to be on call for male exams. Now, you tell me, logically, do you think you need a surgeon to perform a sexual assault exam? Don't you think a trained forensic nurse or sexual assault examiner might be able to recognize the presence an injury, or a need for a medical consult, and say, "Hey I need a consult because I think this person may have rectal trauma." Certainly. Utilizing a surgical specialist for something like a sexual assault exam is both ineffective in terms of manpower and in terms of cost. Sexual assault nurse examiners, forensic nurses, or other medical personnel trained in forensic care in the military should be utilized in the best possible way in order to allow for other professions, such as surgeons, to practice their own medical specialty. For the military, it's also a question of staffing. The military has several nurses who have clinic or administrative jobs during the day but could easily be on call at night to come in for a sexual assault care. Keeping up their qualifications is not very difficult if they practice using a CPR model of training, and then these nurses would be available when they were needed.

The DOD report indicated:

> With respect to forensic medical examination, we have SANEs in the active and reserve components, but have not strategically developed or implemented these assets throughout DOD. Medical and mental health professionals deployed to combat theaters are specifically trained and resourced to provide care for casualties and combat stress, but are not trained to provide specialized assistance to sexual assault victims. In addition, access to victim advocacy is minimal in the combat theatre. Where available, victim advocacy is an additional responsibility to the member's routine duties in support of the combat mission. While the Navy SAVI program purposefully utilizes military deployable victim advocates, ensuring that these assets are available in Navy units deployed to support joint forces has not occurred. There is no specific mechanism within the Navy to insure effective multifunctional case management and integration when commands are deployed away from Naval installations.

Ferguson believes forensic nurses are ideal to work closely with the advocacy components such as the SAVI program. "We need to work together as a cohesive and caring unit." Ferguson also talked about the future of forensic nursing in the military. "What I would really like to see the military do is allow for the professional training of forensic nurses and regognize the forensic nurse specialty." She says:

> I want the military to recognize that nurses can do these exams, and much more. In the long run I just don't want to limit nurses' practice to just sexual assault, though that is where the focus is right now. If nurses were able to secure these important specialty identifiers and be recognized in their field of forensic expertise, it would pave the way for them to work in areas of domestic violence evidence collection, death investigation, assisting the Office of the Armed Forces Medical Examiner with fatality cases, assisting with evidence collection from terrorist attacks or disasters, and even serving as a legal nurse consultant for the Judge Advocate General (JAG). In addition, there is so much research that could be done in the areas of interpersonal violence in the military. This research would assist with the military's prevention efforts and provide them with another avenue for recognizing whether or not the military's efforts at change are effective. There is so much that a forensic nurse specialist could be utilized for. But, with all of the reported rapes in areas such as Iraq, the focus of any type of forensic care will most likely remain on sexual assault.

The 2004 Care for Victims report revealed that at the time of its investigation, a DOD-wide uniform training of providers, and standards of care for victims of sexual assault, did not exist. The report added that numerous focus-group providers, including physicians and nurses, expressed concerns about inadequacy of specialized training in that area. As well, due to the frequent movement of both providers and victims, a focus group found that identifying continuity of mental health care was a significant issue. Another frequent comment from focus groups was the desire for routine access to "after hours" support groups on military installations. Very recently, the Department of Veterans Affairs established a continuing medical education program to assist primary care providers in identifying victims of military sexual trauma. This program is aimed at enhancing the clinician's awareness of specific conditions and sensitivities associated with a veteran who has experienced sexual trauma to ensure that these victims receive the care they deserve. This program might be useful for DOD to evaluate for potential use in training of providers.

In its examination of systems to investigate and prosecute sexual assault cases, the DOD report found a backlog of DNA evidence waiting for processing at the U.S. Army Criminal Investigation Laboratory (USACIL), and that this can significantly delay investigations and prosecutions. These lengthy delays cause hardship to sexual assault victims who must wait for the test results and any command decision with respect to the disposition of the alleged offenses. Finally, the delays contribute to perceptions that the justice system is too slow in holding offenders accountable. According to the DOD report, during focus group sessions at installations, prosecutors and investigators said it normally takes six months to get laboratory reports on DNA or similar analysis, and that USACIL will not allow cases to be expedited unless charges in a case have already been proferred. However, the results of laboratory analysis frequently are needed before deciding to bring charges against an alleged offender and, even if they are not required, referral of charges starts the 120-day speedy trial clock. Prosecutors and investigators also noted that the waiting list for expedited results could still mean delays of several months. In some cases, investigators have sought and received higher headquarters authorization to pay for and use state or local laboratories to expedite cases. The military has taken affirmative steps to address this issue, according to the report. A Process Action Team (PAT) from the Army, in coordination with the other Services, is conducting a review of current laboratory practices and any required immediate action to eliminate the current backlog and improve efficiencies. The Air Force senior leadership approved resources to provide additional manpower to USACIL, thus attempting to decrease the evidence processing time for these tests.

Another significant finding of the DOD report is that the environment in the combat theater can have a detrimental impact on the ability to timely and effectively investigate and prosecute cases. The report stated:

> In theater, agents working for AFOSI, NCIS, and USACID are often tasked to perform counter-intelligence and force protection duties in addition to their criminal investigations responsibilities. Those agents who deployed to Kuwait and Iraq during the initial months of Operation Iraqi Freedom reported that they lacked sufficient manpower and transportation resources to cover every forward operating location in a timely manner. These shortages are compounded by new missions, such as investigating mass gravesites for potential war crimes prosecutions and being required to investigate all combat deaths as possible homicides or violations of the law of war. Some investigators acknowledged that current shortages in investigative resources within the combat theater might mean they would have to rely on "reach back" capability. Furthermore, the focus of their efforts was on trying to gather intelligence and protect U.S. personnel from enemy forces.

Other than being able to preserve perishable evidence and secure an initial statement from a victim reporting a sexual assault, any case that would have arisen would have required outside, additional resources. Judge advocates deployed in theater during this period reported having to conduct large portions of criminal investigations on their own. "It is possible the unavailability and workload of investigative agents also may have been a reason why a number of sexual assaults reported in the combat theater were first investigated by the command rather than by investigative agencies with appropriate expertise," the report stated. The DOD report also found that investigations run by the command, both formal and informal, without involvement of investigative agencies might compromise cases of sexual assault. Pursuant to R.C.M. 303, commanders "shall make or cause to be made a preliminary inquiry" into suspected offenses that are triable by court martial. The discussion to that rule notes that commanders can conduct investigations personally or with members of the command, but that they should consider whether to seek the assistance of law enforcement personnel in conducting any inquiry or investigation in serious or complex cases. Generally, commanders immediately contact investigative agencies whenever serious crimes that have not been investigated come to their attention. Occasionally, commanders initiate commander-directed inquiries or investigations before contacting investigative agencies when allegations of serious criminal misconduct arise within their command. Although there might be a myriad of reasons for this, such as lack of investigative resources, or not realizing the seriousness of the allegation as reported, many focus group participants questioned this practice because cases of sexual assault are serious crimes that fall within the regulatory jurisdiction of the investigative agencies for each military department (AFOSI, USACID, and NCIS). Some focus group participants, according to the report, complained that the current emphasis on chain-of-command reporting results in commands trying to ascertain facts surrounding sexual assault reports before investigators are on scene. This can often negatively impact an investigation, including tainting potential evidence or testimony. "This informal process of trying to ascertain facts can produce multiple victim statements that may be viewed as inconsistent or, even worse, increase a victim's anxiety to the point that he or she shuts down because of being required to continually repeat what happened," the report said.

Commanders were challenged by the issue of false allegations of sexual assault, the report also found. It stated:

> The Task Force is extremely sensitive to the challenge presented when individuals make a false allegation of sexual assault. The reasons for these vary, and often the allegation is not the result of conscious deception, but rather the result of multiple other factors impacting the individual making the allegation. Nonetheless, the issue is of particular concern because of the negative effect these false allegations have on all involved. Many service members expressed concerns about the effect of false allegations, but in truth, there is little formal research to help us understand the various reasons why a victim might allege sexual assault when it has not occurred. We currently do not know the number of circumstances where the alleged victim deliberately and maliciously makes a false claim. Often there are other mechanisms at play, involving complex individual factors not well understood.

According to the report, enlisted personnel expressed the belief that there were individuals who made such allegations for secondary gain and that the alleged accused was at a disadvantage. Commanders expressed concerns in terms of the impact on unit cohesion and mission accomplishment. Investigators and legal personnel expressed the negative impact on limited resources and their ability to investigate and litigate legitimate cases. Some victims expressed their experience in encountering skeptical commanders, investigators, and peers as questioning the assault claim. The report also stated that a number of focus group participants expressed a desire to require commanders to take unambiguous action against malicious false accusers. "The challenge is, however, that rarely is there clear and unambiguous understanding of the factors that lead a person to use an unconventional and undesirable act to get needed help via a truly malicious act. This requires recognition that the individual, despite negative behavior, may need to be assessed by a professional behavioral health counselor," the report added.

A distressing finding from the DOD report is that military investigative and legal communities do not have adequate funding to provide investigators and prosecutors with specialized training in handling sexual assault cases. The report stated, "Installation law enforcement, judge advocates, and investigator resources are scarce, have heavy caseloads, and have no specific requirement to be trained in how to effectively handle sexual assault cases; in a combat theater, such resources are even more limited." For the most part, investigators and judge advocates participating in focus groups reported that they did not have formal, specialized training in handling sexual assault cases. However, because sex offense cases represent a large percentage of cases within the criminal justice system, many investigators and prosecutors had extensive experience in handling sexual assault cases. In addition, AFOSI, NCIS, and Army CID all reported having agents with specialized training (often forensic consultants) available at the regional and headquarters levels. The Federal Law Enforcement Training Center (FLETC) now has a block of instruction specifically related to investigating cases of sexual assault. AFOSI and NCIS conduct all basic investigator training at FLETC. AFOSI established an Advanced Sexual Assault Investigations Workshop, conducted at the Air Force Academy, in December 2003. They are in the process of expanding this course for investigators from each MAJCOM. Many prosecutors reported they were exposed to the issues involved with sexual assault cases as part of overall litigation training programs. Recently, the Air Force Judge Advocate General School offered its first course of instruction devoted solely to the prosecution of sexual assault cases and the course is open to judge advocates from all military departments. In addition, some judge advocates were able to attend various types of specialized training through civilian training programs offered by the Department of Justice, the National College of District Attorneys, and some state-run programs.

Whether or not there are adequate numbers of trained prosecutors, the report found that many service members believe a lack of system transparency encourages commanders to not take appropriate action and to not hold alleged offenders accountable. The report acknowledged, "There is very little transparency during the investigation of sexual assault cases and the decision-making process for individual cases. Consequently, most service members (especially more junior personnel) do not understand why cases are handled a particular way. This lack of transparency is due to, in part, the need for investigative operational security and the Privacy Act protections afforded to both the victim and alleged offender." Because of the military's inability to tell "its side of the story" in individual cases of sexual assault, due to Privacy Act restrictions and other victim or alleged offender privacy concerns, most commanders, investigators, and judge advocates expressed frustration at not being able to address the specific factors in individual cases that caused particular findings or dispositions. Because most reports of sexual assault involved fact patterns that make burdens of proof very difficult to meet, this often drives individual results. "Everyone involved with the investigation and prosecution of cases acknowledged that DOD must devise better ways to educate members within DOD and the civilian community that cases are taken seriously," the report stated.

There was universal recognition, the report added, that commanders are usually unable to advise unit and installation personnel how cases were handled or what action was taken against alleged offenders, unless the case involved a public proceeding, such as a court martial. At some installations, attempts by the command backfired when it tried to get out the word on disciplinary action taken in individual cases. Service members told the task force that they had seen military newspaper articles where reported cases involved the same or similar offense, and where the more senior offender received nonjudicial punishment and the junior offender received a stiff sentence by a court martial. Because the actual facts of each case were unknown, the DOD report pointed out, this reinforced the misperception that the system treats senior enlisted and officer offenders more favorably. The report refutes the notion that military commanders are not taking action. It stated:

> Because of the nature of the crime and the circumstances that are typically involved, obtaining the quality of evidence required to meet the criminal burden of proof is very difficult in cases involving sexual assault. Very often, there is no issue with respect to whether sexual activity occurred between the parties involved and, therefore, the issues of consent and the exact nature of the sexual conduct become central to the case. Given the prevalence of alcohol involved in these cases, the frequency of cases where the victim and alleged offender are social acquaintances or have been consensual sexual partners prior to the allegation, and the lack of corroborating witness testimony, investigators are often faced with the difficult task of trying to evaluate the credibility of two conflicting stories; the one of the victim and the other of the alleged offender. Every consistency and inconsistency in the statements given by both parties becomes critical. Add these factors to those discussed earlier in this chapter related to the barriers and problems with reporting, and commanders are often faced with extremely difficult decisions in deciding the best way to handle allegations.

The Navy statistics on cases of insufficient evidence show how difficult these cases can be for investigators, prosecutors, and commanders. The Department of the Navy (which includes both Navy and Marine Corps data) identified 235 of its cases that resulted in a determination of insufficient evidence and more than 38 percent of those determinations were because the victim refused to cooperate (59 cases) or victim fabrication was involved (31 cases). The data provided by the military departments for the DOD report revealed there were 1,634 military individuals identified and accused of sexual assault during

2002 and 2003. Of the 1,634 alleged offenders identified, 401 were from the Air Force, 670 were from the Army, 440 were from the Navy, and 123 were from the Marine Corps. Of the 401 Air Force cases, charges were initiated against 97 (just over 24 percent) of the alleged offenders and nonjudicial punishment proceedings under the uniform code of military justice (UCMJ) were initiated against another 42. Consequently, 139 cases (nearly 35 percent) resulted in some type of military justice action. The report said that none of the other military departments was able to provide information on the initial command actions taken in the cases reported. Due to the Army's self-identified problem of receiving timely and accurate commander's reports of disciplinary action for entry into its criminal databases, the Army was unable to identify final dispositions in 45 percent of its cases. The Army was only able to determine that there was court martial action in 76 cases and nonjudicial punishment proceedings in another 97 cases. Of the 563 Department of the Navy cases, there was court martial action in 154 cases and nonjudicial punishment proceedings in another 85 cases. This data showed that some type of military justice action was taken in nearly 43 percent of cases. Excluding the Army's incomplete data on command actions taken, the combined data provided by the Air Force, Navy, and Marine Corps show that court martial charges were at least initiated in 26 percent of cases, and military justice action was taken in more than 39 percent of cases.

Regarding system accountability for sexual assault, the report found no overarching policies, programs, and procedures to ensure all sectors responsible for dealing with victims of sexual assault provide an integrated response to reported cases of sexual assault. Additionally, the DOD report found that accountability for resolving sexual assault problems is diffused. Currently, Service-specific programs, policies, and organizational structures that provide care for victims of sexual assault are either addressing specific systemic needs or have augmented and reinforced program offices established for other purposes. In all cases, resources to execute these programs were accomplished through application of the discretionary funds of the Service, primarily because no DOD-wide policy or program guidance exists to reinforce the need to specifically apply resources to this issue. Each of the Services evolved its focus on this issue in response to internal management awareness that these problems needed management attention. The report said:

> The Services deserve credit for the individual initiatives across the functional spectrum to increase capability to respond to risks relating to sexual assault, improve care for victims of sexual assault, and establish command emphasis to rapidly report sexual assault incidents. However, pockets of excellence in each of the Services in establishing sexual assault-focused management initiatives are not adequate. The absence of DOD-wide policies and programs to deal with this pervasive, underreported problem has led to this situation, coupled with the fact that, except in the Navy, Service-wide command emphasis on supporting victims and preventing sexual assault is lacking.

The DOD, in its April 2004 report, made several sets of recommendations for immediate action. One recommendation is to establish a single point of accountability for all sexual assault policy matters within the DOD. This office would support the Undersecretary of Defense for Personnel and Readiness in advising the Secretary of Defense on all policy, program development and resourcing, and program oversight matters relating to sexual assault within the DOD. It would address the gaps in the current systems created by the absence of any specific sexual assault policies and programs not otherwise covered by FAP, and would address the issues of standardization of definitions, and create outcome-based accountability for the Services. It would also develop strategic program guidance and joint planning objectives to ensure that needed resources are available within the same time frame across all Services and combatant commands for sexual assault prevention, reporting, and response.

Another recommendation is to ensure broad dissemination of relevant sexual assault information through DOD-wide communication outlets. This could be accomplished by updating and leveraging existing information sources and communication structures available within the DOD and the military departments with reliable information regarding sexual assault prevention, reporting, response, protection, and accountability. Potential outlets include official Web sites, toll-free hotlines, and other print, voice, and telecommunication mediums. Each of these should ensure that it has the ability to provide updated and accurate information for reporting and obtaining services.

A third recommendation is to convene a summit of DOD leaders (military and civilian) and recognized experts on sexual assault to develop strategic courses of action on critical, unresolved issues. This would include courses of action that would develop better operational definitions and delineation of distinctions between terms like sexual harassment, sexual misconduct, and sexual assault, and how those definitions relate to crimes under the Uniform Code of Military Justice. It would also establish ways to increase transparency of the reasons for the handling and disposition of reported sexual assault cases, as well as develop and maintain an expert, full-spectrum sexual assault response capability in operational environments, such as through the use of SARTs.

It would also encourage partnerships with civilian agencies to ensure an expert response to sexual assault, as well as the provision of specially trained and experienced medical, investigative, legal, and advocacy personnel in all locations. This presents an ongoing challenge, given the mobility of the armed forces.

Another recommendation is to establish an Armed Forces Sexual Assault Advisory Council composed of key DOD officials and officials of other federal agencies with recognized expertise in dealing with issues surrounding sexual assault. The council could also seek input from other nationally recognized sexual assault experts, as needed. The council would develop policies, guidelines, and standards for sexual assault prevention, reporting, response, and accountability, and would encourage reporting through well-established, publicized, and unobstructed reporting channels. Also, the council would be tasked with developing DOD-wide medical standards of care and clinical practice guidelines for treatment and care of victims of sexual assault, including establishment of a health care integrated process team to consider how to better incorporate SANEs within the military health system in both the active and reserve component force structure. It would review and consider adopting the Department of Justice National Protocol for sexual assault forensic exams (see chapter 6), assess the need for and propose operational and combat-theater-specific adjustments to standards of medical care and clinical practice guidelines, determine standards of training required for personnel providing medical support services for victims of sexual assault, assess the need and mechanisms for periodical screening of service members for sexual assault, and assess the adequacy of the number of qualified, appropriately trained mental health professionals available to support victims of sexual assaults in the workforce. In addition, the council would develop DOD guidance to positively assure a victim's privacy, including restrictions on "need to know," what information is released in reports up the chain of command, and possibly a requirement to sign nondisclosure statements, with stiff penalties for violating it, as well as review the process and institute guidelines on how and when reports of sexual assault are forwarded up the chain of command and what information is included in those reports.

9.3 LOOKING TO THE FUTURE

From the 1991 Tailhook incidents to the 2003 incidents at the U.S. Air Force Academy in which 56 female cadets said they were raped, reports of sexual assault and abuse in the media have been pervasive in the last 15 years, yet little has been done to directly address and remediate these reported crimes. Ferguson believes improvement in the way sexual assault and other abuse has been identified and reckoned with is evident, if not a little slow in coming.

"I think the military is becoming better at identifying and addressing abuse," Ferguson says:

> The military has been going through its growing pains in regard to sexual assault prevention and response. We may have been a bit more behind the curve in our response to improving our care than the civilian community, but we are on the right track. There are a lot of rapid changes coming in the future, I believe, and in the end the military will be sure do the right thing. I have to have faith in that.

She continues,

> I think that if you compare the military life of the newly enlisted person or the young military academy student to civilian college life, there are similarities in the demographics. A lot of the people who come in to each of these scenarios are young, maybe 18 to 24, and many of them are away from home for the first time. Some of them are out partying and drinking on their off time and are just trying to have a good time. They don't have a lot of life plans at the moment. They are just there to study, to work and when they get some free time, go out and enjoy themselves. The last thing they are thinking about is that they may be a target for a social predator. They go out with friends, sometimes people they barely know, and become vulnerable due to the quantities of alcohol they may ingest. Those scenarios often lead to incidences of date or acquaintance rape because alcohol, and/or date-rape drugs are involved. They are plied to drink alcohol by the predator, and drugs are sometimes slipped into the victim's drink by the predator too. Those are the types of cases we often see. We may also see a scenario such as group of guys who may invite a female sailor or soldier out on the town, and say "Let's party." They'll make her feel special, and she won't pay for a single drink that night. Later she wakes up around 2 a.m. with two or three guys on top of her, wondering what happened. Maybe she's underage, has been engaging in underage drinking, and if she goes back to her ship and reports the sexual assault, she can get in a great deal of trouble for the underage drinking. So this girl struggles with the dilemma of going back to her command and reporting the rape, and being punished for underage drinking. Is it any wonder that she keeps it quiet? It's a very real fear to report a rape under those circumstances. The other factor that may inhibit a victim from reporting a rape is embarrassment. At one point, the military used to report the names of people who were sexually assaulted to their commands. It wasn't publicized, but the commanding officer knew who they were. Now it's confidential, but there is still a long way to go to make people feel comfortable about reporting sexual assault.

Ferguson continues:

> I have seen some senior officers support sexual assault care for victims, but there are some individuals, even female personnel, who think this is a waste time, that it's not mission essential, that it doesn't relate to the command's needs, so let's move on . . . which I find surprising.

There are also men suffering from these types of indignities that will never report because of the fear of the way they would be treated by their peers, or what people would think of them. You can imagine that male victims are frustrated that women are seen as freer to report the assault.

Ferguson says that in the end, the concern over the issue of sexual assault in the military is all about the ability the change.

It's hard to change people's views about stigmas attached to sexual assault, and the military tends to move a little slower than the rest of the world on these types of issues. I personally would like to see the military lead the way when it comes to the handling of forensic cases, including sexual assault, but also moving beyond, to becoming experts in processing mass fatalities or death investigation.

Ferguson believes that a move away from standard training techniques will afford greater learning opportunities for all military personnel, when considering general training and prevention of sexual assault across the services. "I think there is a lot more focus on the awareness of sexual assault issues now; however, I think the military tends to engage in what has been called 'death by PowerPoint,'" she says:

A lot of these young sailors and soldiers have complained about the way the military educates on topics like sexual assault or sexual violence. They have all of these people lecturing at them, telling them to pay attention, be aware, know when you are in a precarious situation, but what I think is called for is a greater presence of nurses and other medical professionals. The forensic nurse specialist can go out and be with the troops, and talk with them up close and personal about these issues, even if it means hanging out in a health care booth at the Exchange or the Commissary from time to time.

Ferguson recalls a personal approach that she used in Yokosuka Japan, to help service members become more aware about the issue of sexual assault.

I once had a bright yellow T-shirt I used to wear outside the military base gate on Friday and Saturday nights. On the front it had a big stop sign and above it said, "Put a halt" and underneath it said "to sexual assault." On the back it said, "Sexual Assault Forensic Examiner" with a picture of a large thumbprint. I would hand out educational pamphlets to people going out to the bars, and they'd see the T-shirt and stop to talk. They were curious about the shirt and would about what I was doing. It gave me a chance to teach people about the dangers of sexual assault and how to avoid putting themselves in a vulnerable position. It also gave them a chance to ask questions. Doing this provided me with an opportunity to reach out to people with my message. It is important to supply that constant stream of education to our communities, whether it's formal in a classroom or casual on the street. The military has an ever-changing population, so we are constantly striving to reach new people in our education process. Some people stay in the service for three to four years and some stay in a lifetime. Most of us never stay in one place for more than a few rotations. We are always moving around. Service members may or may not have been exposed to education about sexual assault prevention, and it takes more than just a lecture. It might be mandatory in our training, but unless our trainers are up close and personal about it, we can't be sure the message is even heard. The same can be said about the civilian world, too. In any community, people need awareness that predators are everywhere and there are ways to diminish our chances of being targets. Forensic nurses can help raise that awareness.

9.4 SEXUAL VIOLENCE IN THE U.S. MILITARY: A REVIEW OF THE LITERATURE

Violence toward women in the military has identifiable risk factors, according to a study by Iowa City Veterans Affairs Medical Center (VAMC) and University of Iowa researchers. The study, involving more than 500 female veterans, found that workplace factors, such as the behavior of superiors, were highly associated with military women's risk of sexual assault during their military service. "While violence towards working women is commonplace, surprisingly little is known about predictors of workplace sexual violence," said Anne Sadler, PhD, a researcher at the Iowa City VAMC who led the study (Sadler, Booth, Cook, & Doebbeling, 2003). "Our findings suggest that if sexual harassment is allowed in the workplace, women in those environments have a significantly increased risk of being raped." The researchers interviewed a nationwide sample of 556 female veterans who served in the Vietnam, post-Vietnam and Persian Gulf War eras. The women were selected from the U.S. Department of Veterans Affairs comprehensive women's health care registries. Participants completed an extensive structured interview to determine the characteristics of rape victims and perpetrators, as well as environmental factors associated with rape occurring during military service.

The researchers found that 79 percent of participants reported experiences of sexual harassment during their military service; 30 percent of the women reported an attempted or completed rape. Risk factors related to violence toward military women were present in both on-duty and off-duty base settings. Assailant alcohol or drug use at the time of rape was notable. Women who experienced unwanted sexual advances or sexual remarks when they were on duty or in their sleeping quarters were approximately four times more likely to be raped. In the absence of harassment, the issue of mixed-gender sleeping quarters was not a significant risk factor. "Our findings were consistent with research in civilian populations demonstrating that younger women entering male-dominated work groups at lower levels of authority are those most likely to be harassed," Sadler said. The behavior of superiors was associated with women's frequency of rape. Women working with superiors who made sexually demeaning comments or allowed such behavior were found to have a nearly fourfold risk of rape while in the military. The researchers noted that superiors' conduct could also promote a healthy work environment for women, and interventions should focus on training and supervision of leaders and greater oversight and accountability for behaviors in the day-to-day military workplace and barracks. The researchers hope the study findings will help create interventions and policies to increase the safety of women in the workplace. "Given that the rates of rape were consistent from all eras of military service among the women we interviewed, this issue remains an unresolved health concern," Sadler said.

In another study, Sadler and colleagues (2001) emphasized that little is known regarding environmental exposures for nonfatal violence toward women in the workplace. Sadler et al. sought to identify factors associated with nonfatal physical assault occurring to women during military service. A cross-sectional telephone survey of a national sample of 558 women veterans who served in Vietnam and subsequent eras of military service was conducted; 537 women were interviewed. Twenty-three percent experienced nonfatal physical assault during military service. Rates of assault were consistent across eras of service. Military environmental exposures, including sexual harassment allowed by officers and unwanted sexual advances while on duty and in sleeping quarters, were independent risk factors for assault. Environmental factors in the military workplace, including leadership behavior, appeared to promote violence toward military women. Such occupational factors can be identified and should be eliminated, the researchers asserted.

There are limited data on the extent to which spouse abuse in a family is a risk factor for child abuse. Rumm et al. (2000) attempted to estimate the subsequent relative risk of child abuse in families with a report of spouse abuse compared with other families. The cohort study analyzed a centralized U.S. Army database of married couples with children with at least one spouse on active duty in the U.S. Army during 1989 to 1995. The U.S. Army FAP's Central Database was used to identify child and spouse abuse. The exposure was an episode of identified spouse abuse and the main outcome was a substantiated episode of subsequent child abuse. During the study period of an estimated 2,019,949 person years, 14,270 incident child abuse cases were substantiated. Families with an incident case of spouse abuse identified during the study period were twice as likely to have a substantiated report of child abuse compared with other military families, rate ratio, 2.0. Young parental age had the highest rate ratio (4.9) in the subgroup analysis controlling for rank. Identified spouse abuse was associated with physical abuse of a child (rate ratio 2.4), and with sexual abuse of a child (rate ratio 1.5). Identified spouse abuse was not associated with child neglect or maltreatment. The researchers concluded that an identified episode of spouse abuse in a family appears to be associated with an increased risk of subsequent child abuse and serves as an independent risk factor; therefore, care providers should consider the potential risk to children when dealing with spouse abuse.

A few studies have examined the maltreatment of military dependents. The transitional compensation (TC) program of the U.S. Army provides financial and other benefits to the families of service members discharged for child or spouse maltreatment. McCarroll, Ursano, Fan, and Newby (2004a, 2004b) analyzed the TC records of the 347 offenders, 337 spouses (160 victims and 177 nonvictims) who were applicants for benefits, and 820 children (244 victims and 576 nonvictims). One hundred fifty-two spouses were physically abused and eight were sexually abused. One hundred eighty-two children were sexually abused, 61 were physically abused, and one was emotionally abused. The researchers examined the Army Central Registry (ACR) of child and spouse maltreatment cases to determine whether the TC offenders and victims had a history of prior maltreatment and to assess its severity. Ninety percent of the TC offenders had an ACR history as child or spouse maltreatment offenders. Seventy-four percent of the TC child abuse victims had an ACR history as victims, and 81 percent of the TC spouse abuse victims had such a history. The severity of maltreatment in the ACR of TC child and spouse victims was greater than the overall severity of maltreatment for those in the ACR database who were not in the TC database. Other children in the family who had not been identified as TC victims also had an ACR history that was more severe.

McCarroll et al. (2004a, 2004b) also compared the reports of the severity of child maltreatment for the U.S. Army and a civilian jurisdiction, Washington State, to determine important information on risk and protective factors in designing prevention programs. The researchers explained that an understanding of the differences facilitates the tailoring of interventions to better fit the characteristics of each community. The ages of the children in the Washington State cases were significantly older than the cases of the Army children. In both populations, neglect was the most prevalent form of maltreatment, followed in order by physical abuse, sexual abuse, and emotional abuse. The percentages of physical abuse, sexual abuse, and neglect were not statistically different, but the Army classified three times the number of emotional abuse cases as Washington State. The Army also classified more cases of physical abuse as severe (11 percent) compared with Washington State (5 percent). However, 16 percent of Washington State neglect cases were classified severe compared with 3 percent of Army cases.

Other researchers have examined the impact of abuse and utilization of health care by maltreated dependents. DeRoma, Root, and Smith (2003) asserted that the incidence of episodes of harassment and rape among military populations has only recently been examined. In their study of a sample of 336 female veterans in a primary care setting, the researchers found that the incidences of lifetime sexual victimization, anxiety, depression, and impact of trauma for victims of specific trauma contexts were presented. Results of the study indicated that female veterans with a history of cumulative rape experiences and civilian rape experiences are more at risk for anxiety and depression than those with only a military experience of rape. No significant differences were found for impact of event scores for different contexts of rape, however. Reporting of trauma was not associated with psychological well-being for women veterans. The researchers say that results highlight the role of the socioenvironmental context of abuse as an important variable to examine, especially in military populations.

Martin et al. (1998) conducted a study to assess the prevalence and timing of sexual assault experiences in a sample of U.S. Army soldiers. Self-administered surveys were completed by 555 male and 573 female soldiers in combat service and combat service support units. One fifth of the women reported a completed rape (22.6 percent), and 50.9 percent of women and 6.7 percent of men reported any sexual assault. The majority of sexual assaults occurred before the soldiers entered the military, and 25 percent of women and 1 percent of men reported an attempted or completed rape during childhood. Sexual assault history also varied by sociodemographic characteristics. The researchers concluded that a history of childhood sexual abuse might be more widespread among female soldiers than among civilian women, and that ascribed and achieved status characteristics might differentially expose soldiers to sexual assaults both before and after they enter the military. They recommended that health care assessments should include details of a soldier's sexual assault history.

Sadler, Booth, Mengeling, and Doebbeling (2004) conducted a study to determine whether the type or frequency of intentional violence experiences among women during military service influences health status or health care utilization. Differences in utilization and health status were also examined while controlling for life span violence exposures and important patient characteristic confounders. A cross-sectional survey of women veterans was conducted using a random sample stratified by region and era of service. Women veterans who served in the Vietnam and subsequent eras were selected from comprehensive women's health care centers' registries at Department of Veterans Affairs medical centers in Boston, Durham, Tampa, Minneapolis, Chicago, and Los Angeles. Socioeconomic information, violence exposure history, outpatient health care utilization, and assessment of health status were obtained by structured telephone interview. The type of violence women experienced was unrelated to differences in medical utilization. Women reporting repeated violence exposures during military service had significantly more outpatient visits in the year preceding the interview than singly or nontraumatized peers (16 vs. nine and eight visits, respectively). Repeatedly assaulted women also had poorer health status, and more often reported a history of childhood violence and postmilitary violence. The researchers concluded that repeated violence exposure is a relatively common experience among women in the military, and this has substantial implications for their health.

Sadler, Booth, Nielson, and Doebbeling (2000) sought to identify differences in health-related quality of life among women veterans who were raped, physically assaulted (not in the context of rape or domestic violence), both, or neither during military service. The researchers conducted a cross-sectional telephone survey of a national sample of 558 women veterans who served in Vietnam and subsequent eras of military service. A stratified survey design selected subjects according to era of service and location. The interview included socioeconomic information, lifetime violence history, the Women's Military Environment Survey to assess women's military experiences, and the Medical Outcomes Study Short Form-36 to assess health-related quality of life. Five hundred thirty-seven women completed the interview; of these, 48 percent experienced violence during military service, including rape (30 percent), physical assault (35 percent), or both (16 percent). Women who were raped or dually victimized were more likely to report chronic health problems, prescription medication use for emotional problems, failure to complete college, and annual incomes less than $25,000. Women who were physically assaulted or raped reported significantly lower health-related quality of life. Those who had both traumas reported the most severe impairment, comparable to women with chronic illnesses. The researchers say that the sequelae of violence against women are an important public health concern. More than a decade after rape or physical assault during military service, women reported severely decreased health-related quality of life, with limitations of physical and emotional health, educational and financial attainment, and severe, recurrent problems with work and social activities.

Hankin et al. (1999) studied a national sample of 3,632 women who visited VA hospitals as outpatients. The researchers determined self-reported prevalence of sexual assault experienced during military service and compared screening prevalence for current symptoms of depression and alcohol abuse between those who did and did not report this history. Data were obtained by mailed questionnaire. Military-related sexual assault was reported by 23 percent, and screening prevalence for symptoms of current depression was three times higher and for current alcohol abuse was two times higher among those who reported experiencing military-related sexual assault. Recent mental health treatment was reported by 50 percent of those who reported experiencing sexual assault during military service and screened positive for symptoms of depression, and by 40 percent of those who screened positive for symptoms of alcohol abuse.

To profile differences in current physical symptoms and medical conditions among women users of VA health services with and without a self-reported history of sexual assault sustained during military service, Frayne et al. (1999) conducted a cross-sectional analysis of a nationally representative, random sample of 3,632 women veterans using VA outpatient services. A self-administered, mailed survey asked whether women had sustained sexual assault while in the military and requested information about a spectrum of physical symptoms and medical conditions. A history of sexual assault while in the military was reported by 23 percent of women VA users and was associated with current physical symptoms and medical conditions in every domain assessed. For example, women who reported sexual assault were more likely to indicate that they had a heart attack within the past year, even after adjusting for age, hypertension, diabetes, and smoking history. Among women reporting a history of sexual assault while in the military, 26 percent endorsed more than 12 of 24 symptoms and conditions, compared with 11 percent of women with no reported sexual assault while in the military.

An increasing number of researchers have explored connections among substance abuse, PTSD, and sexual assault histories in civilian women. Despite literature suggesting the prevalence of substance abuse and sexual assault for female veterans, few studies have investigated these variables in a female veteran population. Davis and Wood (1999) suggest that a high incidence of PTSD related to sexual trauma in a substance-abusing population of female veterans and a high incidence of substance abuse among female veterans who presented requesting help for sexual trauma. Suggestions for future study include examination of comparison samples of female veterans with and without PTSD and substance abuse across a variety of dimensions, including psychiatric symptoms, substance use, treatment utilization, and impact of treatment.

Stretch, Knudson, and Durand (1998) surveyed more than 1,000 female and male active-duty soldiers to assess the effect of premilitary and military trauma on their psychological well-being. Questionnaire data were obtained on pertinent demographic information, history of trauma exposure, and symptoms of PTSD. The results indicated significant gender differences in the types of traumatic events experienced, with women reporting more sexual traumas and men reporting more nonsexual traumas. In addition, men reported experiencing more military-related traumas, whereas women reported experiencing more premilitary traumas. The prevalence of PTSD symptoms was 8.6 percent for women and 5 percent for men.

Rosen and Martin (1998b) examined the effects of three types of unwanted sexual experiences in the workplace on the psychological well-being of male and female U.S. Army soldiers, and the mediating or moderating roles of appraisal of sexual harassment, organizational climate, and the sociodemographic profile of victims. A survey was administered to 1,060 male soldiers and 305 female soldiers between May and July 1995 at three Army posts in the United States. Unwanted sexual experiences were found to be significant predictors of psychological symptoms for male and female soldiers. Certain aspects of organizational climate and appraisal of sexual harassment were also significant predictors of psychological symptoms.

Stander, Olson, and Merrill (2002) explored how specific childhood sexual experiences might be related to self-identification as a victim of sexual abuse and to gender differences in self-defined victimization. Hierarchical logistic regression was used to estimate the relationship of demographic and childhood sexual experience characteristics with self-definitions. The characteristics most strongly associated were threats, force, incest, and younger age at the time of the experience. Men were less likely than were women to acknowledge abuse and to report childhood sexual experience characteristics indicative of abuse. Women were more likely to identify themselves as victims the more childhood sexual experiences they reported involving sexual penetration. Finally, in an analysis of familial abuse, men were more likely to define themselves as victims if the perpetrator was also male.

Merrill (2001) surveyed a sample of 1,051 female U.S. Navy recruits for histories of childhood abuse and current trauma symptomatology. Victims of only childhood sexual abuse and victims of both childhood sexual abuse and childhood physical abuse had significantly higher scores on all 10 Trauma Symptom Inventory (TSI) clinical scales than did participants who did not report a history of childhood abuse. Victims of only childhood physical abuse had significantly higher scores on all TSI clinical scales, except the Sexual Concerns scale, than participants who did not report a childhood history of childhood physical abuse or childhood sexual abuse. Additionally, more victims of childhood abuse positively endorsed TSI items related to suicidal behavior and ideation than did nonvictims. Overall, the women who experienced childhood physical abuse or childhood sexual abuse reported substantially higher levels of trauma symptomatology.

Raiha and Soma (1997) wanted to contrast child maltreatment victim rates in U.S. Army and civilian populations, and to identify the demographic characteristics of Army children at increased risk for the following types of child maltreatment: major physical abuse, minor physical abuse, emotional maltreatment, sexual maltreatment, and neglect. Their study presented a descriptive analysis of child maltreatment victims in the U.S. Army during the years 1992 and 1993. Data on all substantiated child maltreatment cases in the Army Family Advocacy Central Registry were obtained from the Army Medical Department's Patient Administration System and Biostatistics Activity. Rates of abuse for demographic subsets of the population were calculated and compared. The researchers found that the overall rate of child maltreatment appears to be lower in the Army than in the general population, and rates of neglect were markedly lower in the Army population. Young children and children with lower ranking sponsors were at greatest risk for major physical abuse and neglect. Boys were neglect victims more frequently than girls. Teenage girls were the highest risk group for minor physical abuse, emotional abuse, and sexual abuse. At younger ages, boys had greater risk of minor physical abuse, and girls again had greater risk of sexual abuse.

Physical and sexual abuse are increasingly recognized as common harmful experiences for women. Coyle, Wolan, and Van Horn (1996) surveyed 828 women veterans seeking care at the Baltimore Veterans Affairs Medical Center to determine the prevalence of physical and sexual abuse experiences, both during and outside of military service. Data were collected through an anonymous, mailed questionnaire, with a response rate of 52 percent. Sixty-eight percent of respondents reported at least one form of abuse, and 27 percent reported all three. Sexual abuse was most common (55 percent), followed by physical abuse (48 percent) and rape (41 percent). Enlisted women, women younger than 50, and single, separated, or divorced women were significantly more likely to report abusive experiences. More than 40 percent of the women reporting abuse were never victimized while on active duty, and these women were less likely to receive counseling. Physical and sexual abuse experiences are disturbingly common among women veterans and demonstrate the need for additional services to assist these women.

Rosen and Martin (1998b) conducted a study to test the hypothesis that different types of gender-related personality attributes are associated with a past history of different types of childhood maltreatment. A survey was administered to 1,060 male soldiers and 305 female soldiers in the U.S. Army. The survey instrument included the Extended Personal Attributes Questionnaire, which is a self-assessment instrument of personality characteristics associated with gender, and includes measures of positive masculinity (self-assertive/instrumental traits), positive femininity (expressive/interpersonal traits), negative masculinity (hypermasculine/macho traits), and negative femininity (subordination of self to others). The survey instrument also included the Childhood Trauma Questionnaire (CTQ), which contains scales measuring sexual abuse, physical-emotional abuse, physical neglect, and emotional neglect, and four questions on childhood sexual abuse developed for a national survey of U.S. adults. The researchers found that negative masculinity was predicted by male gender, younger age, and childhood physical-emotional abuse. Negative femininity was predicted by physical-emotional abuse and sexual abuse. The relationship to sexual abuse was mainly evident for men. Positive femininity was positively correlated with sexual abuse for women and negatively correlated with sexual abuse for men. Positive masculinity was negatively correlated with emotional neglect for men but not for women. Positive femininity was negatively correlated with emotional neglect for both genders.

In a study by Rosen and Martin (1998b), 1,365 soldiers from the U.S. Army completed a 30-item version of the CTQ together with four questions on sexual abuse developed for a national survey of U.S. adults. A four-factor solution to the CTQ produced four subscales that were similar to those found in the original study, namely, emotional neglect, physical and emotional abuse, sexual abuse, and physical neglect. The researchers found that half of female soldiers reported a childhood history of sexual abuse, compared with one sixth of male soldiers. Half of both male and female soldiers reported a childhood history of physical abuse. Combined abuse histories were noted in 34 percent of female and 11 percent of male soldiers. Abused soldiers reported more psychological symptoms on the Brief Symptom Inventory than nonabused soldiers.

To examine the effects of childhood abuse on adult rape, Merrill et al. (1999) surveyed 1,887 female Navy recruits. Overall, 35 percent of recruits had been raped and 57 percent had experienced childhood physical abuse or childhood sexual abuse. Controlling for childhood physical abuse, rape was significantly (4.8 times) more likely among women who had experienced childhood sexual abuse than among women who had not. In contrast, childhood physical abuse (controlling for childhood sexual abuse) was unrelated to likelihood of adult rape. Alcohol problems and number of sex partners were examined as mediators. Although both variables predicted rape, their effects were independent of the effects of childhood sexual abuse. Finally, despite ethnic group differences in the prevalence of victimization, the predictors of rape did not differ significantly across ethnic groups.

Rosen and Martin (1998b) investigated four different types of childhood maltreatment as predictors of unwanted sexual experiences and acknowledged sexual harassment among male and female active-duty soldiers in the U.S. Army. Predictor variables included childhood sexual abuse, physical-emotional abuse, physical neglect, and emotional neglect. Three types of unwanted sexual experiences in the workplace were examined as outcome variables: gender harassment, unwanted sexual attention, and coercion. Both sexual and physical-emotional abuse during childhood were found to be predictors of unwanted sexual experiences and acknowledged sexual harassment in the workplace. Among female soldiers, the most severe type of unwanted experience—coercion—was predicted only by childhood physical-emotional abuse. Among male soldiers childhood sexual abuse was the strongest predictor of coercion. A greater variety of types of childhood maltreatment predicted sexual harassment outcomes for male soldiers. Childhood maltreatment and adult sexual harassment were predictors of psychological well-being for soldiers of both genders.

Researchers have documented that both sexual and nonsexual traumatic experiences in childhood and adulthood are associated with long-term psychological and physical health conditions, and their studies have demonstrated that the cumulative effect of traumatic experiences over time is associated with increased morbidity. According to Lee Martin of the University of Maryland School of Medicine in Baltimore, "It may be particularly important to include consideration of lifetime traumatic experiences when assessing the health and well-being of individuals who may be placed at increased risk of experiencing traumatic events because of their role, occupation, or special circumstances."

One of the more exhaustive studies of the psychological and physical effects of sexual assault among male and female members of the military was undertaken by Martin (2000), who studied the health effects of lifetime potentially traumatic events in the high-risk population of the U.S. military. Martin says:

> It remains unknown whether lifetime trauma history is distributed differently overall for military personnel compared with civilians when adjusted for differences in the demographic structures of the two populations. The current U.S. military population is predominantly male, and also comprises better educated personnel compared with age-matched civilian labor-force participants. Military service members are also more likely to be black than comparable civilians, particularly when comparing female enlisted personnel with female civilian labor force participants. Also, enlisted service members appear to come disproportionately from homes of somewhat lower socioeconomic status than comparable young men and women who do not enter the military.

Martin adds, "There is clear evidence that many military personnel enter the armed forces with histories of potentially traumatic experiences and that some are further traumatized during active duty by combat exposure or other stressful experiences that may also be common to civilians."

In a national retrospective telephone survey, 27 percent of adult women and 15 percent of adult men described a history of childhood sexual abuse (Finkelhor, Hotaling, Lewis, & Smith, 1990), whereas a survey of U.S. Army soldiers in combat support and combat service support units found that 49 percent of the female soldiers and 15 percent of the male soldiers reported a history of childhood sexual abuse using the same screening questions as those used in the national study (Rosen & Martin, 1996a). Rosen and Martin also found that 48 percent of the female soldiers and 50 percent of the male soldiers were physically abused before the age of 18 years, and that both childhood sexual and physical abuse were related to current psychological distresses.

Other studies have found that military personnel with histories of childhood sexual and physical abuse were more likely than service members without such experiences to develop PTSD symptoms after exposure to war (Bremner et al., 1993; Engel et al., 1993; Zaidi & Foy, 1994) In a reanalysis of data (Kulka et al., 1990) from the National Vietnam Veteran's Readjustment Study, King, King, Foy, and Gudanowski (1996) found that a trauma history prior to war experiences directly predicted PTSD among men and disproportionately affected high-combat-exposed male veterans. Engaging in military combat is obviously a potentially traumatic situation and might itself have contributed to a higher mortality rate of male veterans in the 15 years after fighting in World War II (Elder, Shanahan, & Clipp, 1997). By contrast, it appears that the U.S. military might promote health and well-being and regulate behavior in such a way that age-adjusted death rates of U.S. Army soldiers were half those of their civilian counterparts in 1986, with Black male soldiers' homicide rate being especially low when compared with the rate for Black civilian men (Rothberg, Bartone, Holloway, & Marlowe, 1990). Among the potentially positive influences of the military environment, social support is particularly important. Soldiers receive social support from family and friends just as their civilian counterparts do, but soldiers are also immersed in an institution that provides other sources of support and solidarity—specifically unit cohesion—that might intervene in the relationship between trauma exposure and long-term health problems.

"Unit cohesion is a sense of group integration and personal bonding among service members as a result of their regular face-to-face interactions during work, training, or war-fighting maneuvers that is ultimately directed toward meeting the goals of the unit's military mission," Martin writes:

> Such cohesion has long been recognized as a vital situational component of intimate small-group association that promotes the cooperation necessary to sustain service members when under the stress of combat or the demands of accomplishing their military mission in peacetime

> (Jones, Sparacino, Wilcox, & Rothberg, 1994; Shils, 1950). Unit cohesion is evidence of social solidarity in that it creates greater group effectiveness through a sense of *espirit de corps* and confidence in the readiness of the unit. The quality of relationships with military peers and superiors plays a major role in the well-being, social functioning, and combat readiness of individual soldiers (Bliese & Halverson, 1996; Manning & Ingraham, 1987; Vaitkus & Griffith, 1990) and it has positive effects on service members' mental and physical health.

The goals of Martin's study were to develop documentation of lifetime trauma history among active-duty personnel, to evaluate potential health consequences following qualitatively different types of events, and to determine if social support from various sources and unit cohesion would moderate the long-term harmful consequences of trauma exposure. The researchers sampled across 14 different types of potentially traumatic stressors in a checklist format so that accumulated traumas refer to exposure to multiple types of events rather than the number of instances of exposure to any single type of event. The researchers reported that sources of ascribed and achieved power and prestige were determined as important in the potentially traumatic stress–health outcome relationship because gender, race, age, education, and military rank have been associated with the type and number of exposures to potentially traumatic events over time (Martin et al., 1998; Sampson & Lauritsen, 1993; Zawitz et al., 1993).

Martin and colleagues' sample consisted of male and female soldiers on active duty in the U.S. Army who completed a survey on lifetime history of potentially traumatic experiences and current psychological and physical health symptoms. Five hundred fifty-five male soldiers and 573 female soldiers completed the survey. Service members were selected for participation in the study from six active duty Army posts in the continental United States. For three posts, the opportunity afforded by the Forces Command (FORSCOM) Umbrella Week provided available soldiers to participate in the study. Umbrella Week, scheduled once a year at FORSCOM posts, allows researchers with approved protocols to administer questionnaires or to conduct interviews with Army personnel. Martin and colleagues forwarded a request to each FORSCOM post for approximately 200 male and 200 female soldiers from combat support and combat service support units. Each post was asked to schedule small groups of 20 to 30 soldiers, divided by gender, for self-administration of the questionnaire. The posts selected the units to participate in the study, and the units selected the individuals. For the three non-FORSCOM posts, the unit commanders were briefed about the study to obtain their support. Times and dates were set up for self-administration of the questionnaire, and the units were asked to send their soldiers separately by gender to the small-group sessions (approximately 15 male and 15 female soldiers). Both at FORSCOM and non-FORSCOM posts, the sample was drawn by convenience. The selection of participants was based on availability of soldiers on a particular day, and the officials doing the selection were not informed of the purpose of the study.

The junior enlisted category of survey participants comprised 65 percent of the men and 70 percent of the women, NCOs represented 32 percent of the men and 25 percent of the women, and 3 percent of the men and 4 percent of the women were officers. Average length of time on active duty was 5.6 years for the men and 4.7 years for the women. Fifty-four percent of the men and 44 percent of the women said they were White; 27 percent of the men and 40 percent of the women were Black; 13 percent of the men and 8 percent of the women were Hispanic, 2 percent of the men and 1 percent of the women were Asian, and 3 percent of the men and 5 percent of the women were "other." Age ranged from 18 to 49 years for the men and from 18 to 46 for the women. Thirty-seven percent of the men and 34 percent of the women had a high school diploma or equivalent, 48 percent of the men and 50 percent of the women had some college or vocational or technical schooling, and 15 percent of the men and 16 percent of the women had a four-year college degree or beyond. Men were more likely to be married (59.8 percent) than women (38.5 percent), but women were more likely to be divorced or separated than men (17.4 percent vs. 7.4 percent, respectively). Thirty-two percent of men and 38.5 percent of women were single and never married.

The researchers reported that a comparison of the demographic and status characteristics of this sample with the overall U.S. Army revealed that soldiers in this study were on average about the same age, but there were relatively more enlisted personnel and fewer officers in this sample than in the entire Army. The enlisted soldiers were better educated on average than their counterparts in the active-duty force. Their racial and ethnic status was roughly similar to the overall Army, except that proportionately more Hispanic male soldiers are represented in this sample. The sample was not designed to be representative of the U.S. Army population. The researchers assessed the respondents' lifetime history of sexual assault with three yes or no questions:

- Have you ever experienced an attempted rape?
- Have you ever experienced a completed rape?
- Other than the incidents described above, have there been any other situations that did not involve actual sexual contact between you and another person, but did involve an attempt by someone to force you to have some kind of unwanted sexual contact?

Nonsexual potentially traumatic experiences were measured with the remaining 11 dichotomous items that referred to a variety of situations including close family members having been murdered or killed by a drunk driver, respondents having been violently assaulted with weapons or without weapons but with intent to kill or seriously harm them, serious accidents, natural disasters, other situations resulting in serious injury or that posed a threat to life, and witnessing events of killing or serious injury. Most of these queries about nonsexual violent events were adaptations of questions asked of a representative national sample of women. Respondents were also asked about the cohesiveness of their military units and about their regard for their leaders.

Overall, Martin and colleagues found that women reported more psychological symptoms and more physical health symptoms than did men. The experience of at least one lifetime potentially traumatic event was reported by 92 percent of the men and 91 percent of the women. The number of event types ranged from 0 to 12 among men and 0 to 13 among women. At least two types of experiences were reported by 71 percent of the men and 75 percent of the women.

The lifetime number of types of potentially traumatic experiences did not differ by gender, but men reported significantly more nonsexual events than women did, and women reported significantly more sexual events than men. Half of the women but only 6 percent of the men reported at least one type of sexual assault, and 36 percent of the female victims had experienced multiple types. Twenty-two percent of the women and 1 percent of the men reported having experienced a completed rape, 30 percent of the women and 2 percent of the men reported having experienced an attempted rape, and 29 percent of the women and 5 percent of the men reported some other attempt at unwanted and forced sexual contact. Fifty percent of the men and 29 percent of the women reported having been physically attacked by someone with or without a weapon, and 34 percent of the men and 20 percent of the women experienced some other situation in which they feared death or injury. Finally, more than a quarter of the men and women reported having a family member or close friend who was deliberately killed or murdered. Black men (48 percent) and Black women (42 percent) were significantly more likely than other groups to have experienced this type of potentially traumatic event. Information on whether the events happened before or after entering the military showed that the majority of experiences occurred prior to entering the military. This was the case for 80 percent of the women who were raped, 73 percent of the men and 74 percent of the women who were attacked with a weapon, and 71 percent of the men and 67 percent of the women who reported the deliberate murder of a significant other. Only experiencing some unspecified situation involving fear or death or another unspecified extraordinarily stressful situation was more likely to have occurred after the individual entered the military.

Unit cohesion scores were based on the summed average of three items dealing with overall unit cohesiveness, and the supportiveness of officers and NCOs. All other social support variables comprised single items measured on 5-point Likert-type scales ranging from 1 to 5 with a midpoint of 3. The lowest mean score for both women and men was for unit cohesion. Responses to the statements that the unit is highly cohesive tended, overall, toward disagreement. Social support helpfulness from unit leaders and other unit members was rated on average as neither helpful nor unhelpful. The mean scores on friend support for both women and men were substantially higher than scores for support from other unit members, suggesting divergent construct validity for differentiating these two sources of support. The only significant gender difference was for social support from friends, indicating that women had greater expressive support from friends than did men.

The researchers determined that female gender, lower education, Asian ethnicity, and junior enlisted rank predicted increased psychological symptoms. When accumulated traumas were added to the model, completed rape, attempted sexual assaults, and number of nonsexual traumas to self all predicted increased psychological symptoms. When different types of social supports were added to the model, lower unit cohesion and lower leadership support predicted increased psychological symptoms. In the final model, lower education, Asian ethnicity, all of the trauma variables, and unit cohesion showed significant main effects on psychological symptoms. A significant interaction effect was found for leadership support by number of traumas. Splitting the sample into high leadership support (scores of 4 and 5) and low support (scores of 1 to 3), the researchers found that number of traumas had a stronger correlation with psychological symptoms under conditions of low leadership support, compared with high leadership support. Regarding physical health symptoms, the researchers discovered that female gender, lower education, being divorced or separated, and junior enlisted rank predicted increased symptoms. When traumas were added to the model, completed rape, attempted sexual assault, and number of nonsexual traumas to self-predicted increased health symptoms. When types of social supports were added to the model, unit cohesion and leadership support predicted fewer symptoms.

In the final model, main effects were found for female gender, sexual and nonsexual traumas to self, and unit cohesion. A significant interaction effect was found for leadership support by number of traumas. The number of traumas had a stronger correlation with physical health symptoms among low leadership support scorers, compared with high leadership support scorers. The researchers found overall that for both men and women in their sample, exposure to a range of 14 different types of potentially traumatic experiences was widespread. The lifetime prevalence for sexual and nonsexual violent events to self were somewhat higher than those of civilian men and women as reported in studies that sampled across a variety of different types of extreme stressors (Finkelhor, 1991; Kessler & McLeod, 1984; Norris, 1992; Stein, Walker, Hazen, & Forde, 1997; Turner & Lloyd, 1995) The finding that half of all women had ever suffered a sexual assault, and that 22 percent reported a completed rape, is within the range of estimates from studies of civilian women, the researchers say (Koss et al., 1994). The higher number of Black men and women who experienced the murder of a close friend or family member is consistent with the disproportionately high representation of Blacks among homicide victims (Amick-McMullan, Kilpatrick, & Resnick, 1991; U.S. Department of Justice, 1994). Regarding levels of social support, the only significant gender difference was for social support from friends, which is consistent with literature indicating that women have greater expressive support from friends than men do (Fuhrer, Stansfield, Chemali, & Shipley, 1999; Thoits, 1995).

"This study of Army personnel demonstrates the same general relationship between long-term health problems and trauma history—including sexual assaults and exposure to sudden, shocking physical violence or environmental disruption—that has been found consistently across a wide range of civilian populations," Martin et al. (1998) write:

> The number of sexual assaults and nonsexual traumas that happened to self, including physical violence, serious accidents, and natural disasters was related to long-term health problems, even when taking into account other nonsexual traumas. Nonsexual traumas that happened to others, but to which soldiers were exposed, do not contribute much to long-term health problems when controlling for other types of potentially traumatic exposure. Overall, the physical health effect of exposure to potentially traumatic experiences found in this study is consistent with studies among civilians that have found long-term somatic complaints and poor health perceptions associated with sexual assaults (Golding, 1994), violent nonsexual criminal victimization, and potentially traumatic accidents (Malt, 1994). The consequences of accumulated sexual assaults and nonsexual traumas to self appear to be diffuse, encompassing a global sense of psychological discomfort and common physical health complaints.

Martin et al. continue:

> Although we emphasize that long-term posttraumatic responses may be manifested in a diffuse and generalized sense of lower well-being, the development of PTSD symptoms may intervene in the course of potential physical health problems and development of other psychological symptoms. Experiencing psychological and physical distress is frequently co-morbid with PTSD (Davidson & Foa, 1993; Davidson, Hughes, Blazer, & George, 1991; Stretch, 1991). The National Vietnam Veterans Readjustment Survey found that veterans with current diagnosable PTSD reported more current and chronic health problems than other veterans. Other research among veterans (Litz et al., 1992; Shalev, Bleich, & Ursano, 1990; Wolfe, Schnurr, Brown, & Furey, 1994) suggests that posttraumatic physical health responses can emerge from or be sustained by physiological hyperarousal of various bodily systems among victims who develop PTSD compared with victims who do not develop it. Similarly, military veterans' current levels of global distress have been found to be mediated by PTSD symptoms subsequent to earlier military-related or premilitary potentially traumatic experiences (Friedman, Schnurr, & McDonagh-Coyle, 1994; Wolfe, Brown, & Buscela, 1992).

With regard to the effects of social support, unit cohesion in military companies and work groups had direct beneficial effects on soldiers' mental and physical health. Furthermore, although most exposure to potentially traumatic events in our study group occurred to soldiers before they entered the military, the immediate military social environment was important in moderating the deleterious consequences of accumulated potentially traumatic experiences. Active-duty soldiers with the most extensive trauma histories manifested more symptoms under conditions of low perceived social support from their unit leaders. The significant main effect of female gender on increased health symptoms is consistent with the results of previous research showing that women report more health symptoms than men do—an issue that is the subject of ongoing debate in the literature (Sheridan, Mulhern, & Martin, 1999; Van Wijk & Kolk, 1997). However, the significantly greater reporting of general psychological distress of women, compared with men, might be a function of women's greater exposure to rape and other sexual assaults, because the effect of gender was no longer significant when traumas were included in the model. The researchers concluded that the psychological and physical health impact of sexual and nonsexual potentially traumatic experiences among this sample of servicemen and women implied a need for increased sensitivity to determining the number and types of traumas that have occurred over a lifetime among active-duty soldiers and veterans. They write, "Healthcare assessments of both groups should include questioning about pre-military potentially traumatic experiences, military-related and unrelated traumas that occurred while on active duty, and the quality of relationships within active-duty units during military service."

REFERENCES

Amick-McMullan, A., Kilpatrick, D. G., & Resnick, H. S. Homicide as a risk factor for PTSD among surviving family members. *Behav Modif. 15,* 545–559, 1991.

Bliese, P. D., & Halverson, R. R. Individual and nomothetic models of job stress: An examination of work hours, cohesion, and well-being. *J Appl Soc Psychol. 26,* 1171–1189, 1996.

Bremner, J. D., Southwick, S. M., Johnson, D. J., Yehuda, R., & Charney, D. S. Childhood physical abuse and combat-related posttraumatic stress disorder in Vietnam veterans. *Am J Psychiatry. 150,* 235–239, 1993.

Coyle, B. S., Wolan, D. L., & Van Horn, A. S. The prevalence of physical and sexual abuse in women veterans seeking care at a Veterans Affairs Medical Center. *Mil Med. 161,* 10, 588–593, 1996.

Davidson, J. T. R., & Foa, E. B. (Eds.) Introduction. In *Post-Traumatic Stress Disorder: DSM-IV and Beyond.* Washington, DC: American Psychiatric Press. 1993.

Davidson, J. T. R., Hughes, D., Blazer, D. G., & George, L. K. Post-traumatic stress disorder in the community: An epidemiological study. *Psychol Med. 21,* 713–721, 1991.

Davis, T. M., & Wood, P. S. Substance abuse and sexual trauma in a female veteran population. *J Subst Abuse Treat. 16,* 2, 123–127, 1999.

DeRoma, V. M., Root, L. P., & Smith, B. S. Socio-environmental context of sexual trauma and well-being of women veterans. *Mil Med. 168,* 5, 399–403, 2003.

Elder, G. H., Shanahan, M. J., & Clipp, E. C. Linking combat and physical health: The legacy of World War II in men's lives. *Am J Psychiatry. 154,* 330–336, 1997.

Engel, C. C., Engel, A. L., Campbell, S. J., McFall, M. R., Russo, J., & Katon, W. Post-traumatic stress disorder symptoms and precombat sexual and physical abuse in Desert Storm veterans. *J Nerv Ment Dis. 181,* 683–688, 1993.

Finkelhor, D. Child sexual abuse. In M. L. Rosenberg & M. A. Fenley, Eds. *Violence in America* (pp. 79–94). New York: Oxford University Press. 1991.

Finkelhor, D., Hotaling, G., Lewis, I. A., & Smith, C. Sexual abuse in a national survey of adult men and women: Prevalence, characteristics, and risk factors. *Child Abuse Negl. 14,* 19–29, 1990.

Fisher, B. S., Cullen, F. T., & Turner, M. G. *The Sexual Victimization of College Women.* Washington, DC: National Institute of Justice. 2000.

Frayne, S. M., Skinner, K. M., Sullivan, L. M., Tripp, T. J., Hankin, C. S., Kressin, N. R., & Miller, D. R. Medical profile of women Veterans Administration outpatients who report a history of sexual assault occurring while in the military. *Womens Health Gend Based Med. 8,* 6, 835–845, 1999.

Friedman, M. J., Schnurr, P. P., & McDonagh-Coyle, A. Post-traumatic stress disorder in the military veteran. *Psychiatr Clin North Am. 17,* 263–277, 1994.

Fuhrer, R., Stansfield, S. A., Chemali, J., & Shipley, M. J. Gender, social relations and mental health: Prospective findings from an occupational cohort. *Soc Sci Med. 48,* 77–87, 1999.

Golding, J. M. Sexual assault history and physical health in randomly selected Los Angeles women. *Health Psychol. 13,* 130–138, 1994.

Hankin, C. S., Skinner, K. M., Sullivan, L. M., Miller, D. R., Frayne, S., & Tripp, T. J. Prevalence of depressive and alcohol abuse symptoms among women VA outpatients who report experiencing sexual assault while in the military. *J Trauma Stress. 12,* 4, 601–612, 1999.

Hart, T. C. *Violent Victimization of College Students: National Crime Victimization Survey, 1995–2000. Special Report.* Washington, DC: U.S. Department of Justice, Bureau of Justice Statistics. 2003.

Jones, F. D., Sparacino, L. R., Wilcox, V. L., & Rothberg, J. M. *Military Psychiatry: Preparing in Peace for War.* Falls Church, VA: Office of the Surgeon General. 1994.

Kessler, R. C., & McLeod, J. D. Sex differences in vulnerability to undesirable life events. *Am Sociological Review. 46,* 620–631, 1984.

King, D. W., King, L. A., Foy, D., & Gudanowski, D. M. Prewar factors in combat-related posttraumatic stress disorder: Structural equation modeling with a national sample of female and male Vietnam veterans. *J Consult Clin Psychol. 64,* 520–531, 1996.

Koss, M. P., Goodman, L. A., Browne, A., Fitzgerald, L. F., Keita, G. P., & Russo, N. F. *No Safe Haven: Male Violence Against Women at Home, at Work, and in the Community.* Washington, DC: American Psychological Association. 1994.

Kulka, R. A., Schlenger, W. E., Fairbanks, J. A., Hough, R. L., Jordan, B. K., & Marmar, C. R. *Trauma and the Vietnam War Generation: Report of Findings from the National Vietnam Veterans' Readjustment Study.* New York: Brunner/Mazel. 1990.

Lipari, R. N., & Lancaster, A. R. *Armed Forces 2002 Sexual Harassment Survey.* Arlington, VA: Defense Manpower Data Center. 2003.

Litz, B. T., Keane, T. M., Fisher, L., Marx, B., & Monaco, V. Physical health complaints in combat-related post-traumatic stress disorder: A preliminary report. *J Trauma Stress. 5,* 131–141, 1992.

Malt, U. F. Traumatic effects of accidents. In R. J. Ursano, B. G. McCaughey, & C. S. Fullerton, Eds. *Individual and Community Responses to Trauma and Disaster: The Structure of Human Chaos* (pp. 103–135). New York: Cambridge University Press. 1994.

Manning, F. J., & Ingraham, L. H. An investigation into the value of unit cohesion in peacetime. In G. Belenky, Ed. *Contemporary Studies in Combat Psychiatry* (pp. 47–67). New York: Greenwood. 1987.

Martin, L. *Behavioral Medicine. Psychological and Physical Health Effects of Sexual Assaults and Nonsexual Traumas Among Male and Female United States Army Soldiers.* Washington, DC: Heldref Publications. 2000.

Martin, L., Rosen, L. N., Durand, D. B., Stretch, R. H., & Knudson, K. H. Prevalence and timing of sexual assaults in a sample of male and female U.S. Army soldiers. *Mil Med. 163,* 4, 213–216, 1998.

McCarroll J. E., Ursano, R. J., Fan, Z., & Newby, J. H. Classification of the severity of U.S. Army and civilian reports of child maltreatment. *Mil Med. 169,* 6, 461–464, 2004a.

McCarroll, J. E., Ursano, R. J., Fan, Z., & Newby, J. H. Patterns of spouse and child maltreatment by discharged U.S. Army soldiers. *J Am Acad Psychiatry Law. 32,* 1, 53–62, 2004b.

Merrill, L. L. Trauma symptomatology among female U.S. Navy recruits. *Mil Med. 166,* 7, 621–624, 2001.

Merrill, L. L., Newell, C. E., Thomsen, C. J., Gold, S. R., Milner, J. S., Koss, M. P., & Rosswork, S. G. Childhood abuse and sexual re-victimization in a female Navy recruit sample. *J Trauma Stress. 12,* 2, 211–225, 1999.

Norris, F. H. Epidemiology of trauma: Frequency and impact of different potentially traumatic events on different demographic groups. *J Consult Clin Psychol. 60,* 409–418, 1992.

Perkins, C. A. *Age Patterns of Victims of Serious Violent Crime.* Washington, DC: U.S. Department of Justice, Bureau of Justice Statistics. 1997.

Raiha, N. K., & Soma, D. J. Victims of child abuse and neglect in the U.S. Army. *Child Abuse Negl. 21,* 8, 759–768, 1997.

Rosen, L. N., & Martin, L. Impact of childhood abuse history on psychological symptoms among male and female soldiers in the U.S. Army. *Child Abuse Negl. 20,* 1149–1160, 1996a.

Rosen, L. N., & Martin, L. The measurement of childhood trauma among male and female soldiers in the U.S. Army. *Mil Med. 161,* 342–345, 1996b.

Rosen, L. N., & Martin, L. Childhood maltreatment history as a risk factor for sexual harassment among U.S. Army soldiers. *Violence Vict. 13,* 3, 269–286, 1998a.

Rosen, L. N., & Martin, L. Long-term effects of childhood maltreatment history on gender-related personality characteristics. *Child Abuse Negl. 22,* 3, 197–211, 1998b.

Rosen, L. N., & Martin, L. Psychological effects of sexual harassment, appraisal of harassment, and organizational climate among U.S. Army soldiers. *Mil Med. 163,* 2, 63–67, 1998c.

Rothberg, J. M., Bartone, P. T., Holloway, H. C., & Marlowe, D. H. Life and death in the U.S. Army. *JAMA. 264,* 2241–2244, 1990.

Rumm, P. D., Cummings, P., Kraus, M. R., Bell, M. A., & Rivara, F. P. Identified spouse abuse as a risk factor for child abuse. *Child Abuse & Neglect. 24,* 11, 1375–1381, 2000.

Sadler, A. G., Booth, B. M., Cook, B. L., & Doebbeling, B. N. Factors associated with women's risk of rape in the military environment. *Am J Ind Med. 43,* 3, 262–273, 2003.

Sadler, A. G., Booth, B. M., Cook, B. L., Torner, J. C., & Doebbeling, B. N. The military environment: Risk factors for women's non-fatal assaults. *J Occup Environ Med. 43,* 4, 325–334, 2001.

Sadler, A. G., Booth, B. M., Mengeling, M. A., & Doebbeling, B. N. Life span and repeated violence against women during military service: Effects on health status and outpatient utilization. *Women's Health. 13,* 7, 799–811, 2004.

Sadler, A. G., Booth, B. M., Nielson, D., & Doebbeling, N. Health-related consequences of physical and sexual violence: Women in the military. *Obstet Gynecol. 96,* 3, 473–480, 2000.

Sampson, R. J., & Lauritsen, J. L. Violent victimization and offending: Individual-, situational-, and community-level risk factors. In A. J. Reiss, Jr., & J. A. Roth, Eds. *Understanding and Preventing Violence: Social Influences* (pp. 1–114). Washington, DC: National Academy Press. 1993.

Shalev, A., Bleich, A., & Ursano, R. J. Posttraumatic stress disorder: Somatic co-morbidity and effort tolerance. *Psychosomatics. 31,* 197–203, 1990.

Sheridan, C. L., Mulhern, M. A., & Martin, D. The role of social desirability, negative affectivity and female reproductive system symptoms in differences in reporting symptoms by men and women. *Psychol Rep. 85,* 54–62, 1999.

Shils, E. A. Primary groups in the American army. In R. K. Merton & P. F. Lazarsfeld, Eds. *Studies in the Scope and Method of the American Soldier* (pp. 16–39). Glencoe, IL: The Free Press. 1950.

Stander, V. A., Olson, C. B., & Merrill, L. L. Self-definition as a survivor of childhood sexual abuse among navy recruits. *J Consult Clin Psychol. 70,* 2, 369–377, 2002.

Stein, M. B., Walker, J. R., Hazen, A. L., & Forde, D. R. Full and partial posttraumatic stress disorder: Findings from a community survey. *Am J Psychiatry. 154,* 1114–1119, 1997.

Stretch, R. H. Psychosocial readjustment of Canadian Vietnam veterans. *J Consult Clin Psychol. 59,* 188–189, 1991.

Stretch, R. H., Knudson, K. H., & Durand, D. Effects of premilitary and military trauma on the development of posttraumatic stress disorder symptoms in female and male active duty soldiers. *Mil Med. 163,* 7, 466–470, 1998.

Thoits, P. A. Stress, coping and social support processes: Where are we? What next? *J Health Social Support.* Spec No., 53–79, 1995

Tjaden, P., & Thoennes, N. *Full Report of the Prevalence, Incidence and Consequences of Violence Against Women: Findings from the National Violence Against Women Survey.* Washington, DC: U.S. Department of Justice, National Institute of Justice. 2000.

Turner, R. J., & Lloyd, D. A. Lifetime traumas and mental health: The significance of cumulative adversity. *J Health Soc Behav. 36,* 360–376, 1995.

U.S. Department of Defense. *Task Force Report on Care for Victims of Sexual Assault.* Washington, DC: Author. 2004.

U.S. Department of Justice. *Violent Crime: Bureau of Justice Statistics Report, NCJ- 147486.* Washington, DC: National Criminal Justice Reference Service, Office of Justice Programs. 1994.

U.S. Department of Justice. *The Role of the U.S. Military in Preventing and Responding to Violence Against Women: Toolkit To End Violence Against Women.* Washington, DC: Author. 2001.

Vaitkus, M., & Griffith, J. An evaluation of unit replacement on unit cohesion and individual morale in the U.S. Army all-volunteer force. *Mil Psychol. 2,* 221–239, 1990.

Van Wijk, C. M., & Kolk, A. M. Sex differences in physical symptoms: The contribution of symptoms perception theory. *Soc Sci Med. 45,* 231–246, 1997.

Wolfe, J., Brown, P. J., & Buscela, M. L. Symptom responses of female Vietnam veterans to Operation Desert Storm. *Am J Psych. 149,* 676–679, 1992.

Wolfe, J., Schnurr, P. P., Brown, P. J., & Furey, J. Posttraumatic stress disorder and war-zone exposure as correlates of perceived health in female Vietnam veterans. *J Consult Clin Psychol. 62,* 1235–1240, 1994.

Zaidi, L. Y., & Foy, D. W. Childhood abuse experiences and combat-related PTSD. *J Trauma Stress. 7,* 33–42, 1994.

Zawitz, M. W., Klaus, P. A., Bachman, R., et al. *Highlights From 20 Years of Surveying Crime Victims: The National Crime Victimization Survey, 1973–92. Bureau of Justice Statistics Report NCJ-144525.* Washington, DC: U.S. Department of Justice. 1993.

RECOMMENDED READINGS

Felitti, V. J., Anfa, R. F., Nordenberg, D., Williamson, D. F., Spitz, A. M., Edwards, V., Koss, M. P., & Marks, J. S. Relationship of childhood abuse and household dysfunction to many of the leading causes of death in adults. *Am J Prev Med. 14,* 245–258, 1998.

Kilpatrick, D. G., Saunders, B. E., Veronen, L. J., Best, C. L., & Von, J. M. Criminal victimization: Lifetime prevalence, reporting to police, and psychological health. *Crime and Delinquency. 33,* 479–489, 1987.

Koss, M. P., Koss, P. G., & Woodruff, W. J. Deleterious effects of criminal victimization on women's health and medical utilization. *Arch Intern Med. 151,* 342–347, 1991.

Leidig, M. W. The continuum of violence against women: Psychological and physical consequences. *J Am Coll Health. 40,* 149–155, 1992.

Link, B. G., & Phelan, J. Social conditions as fundamental causes of disease. *J Health Soc Behav.* Spec No., 80–94, 1995.

Moeller, T. P., Bachman, G. A., & Moeller, J. The combined effects of physical, sexual, and emotional abuse during childhood: Long-term consequences for women. *Child Abuse Negl. 17,* 523–640, 1993.

Resnick, H. S., Acierno, R., & Kilpatrick, D. G. Health impact of interpersonal violence 2: Medical and mental health outcomes. *Behav Med. 23,* 65–78, 1997.

Resnick, H. S., Kilpatrick, D. H., Dansky, B. S., Saunders, B. E., & Best, C. L. Prevalence of civilian trauma and posttraumatic stress disorder in a representative national sample of women. *J Consult Clin Psychol. 61,* 984–991, 1993.

Skinner, K. M., Kressin, N., Frayne, S., Tripp, T. J., Hankin, C. S., Miller, D. R, & Sullivan, L. M. The prevalence of military sexual assault among female Veteran's Administration outpatients. *J Interpers Violence. 15,* 291–310, 2000.

Teachman, J. D., Call, V. R. A., & Segal, M. W. The selectivity of military enlistment. *J Political and Military Sociology. 21,* 287–309, 1993.

Vrana, T. W., & Lauterbach, D. Prevalence of traumatic events and post-traumatic psychological symptoms in a nonclinical sample of college students. *J Trauma Stress. 7,* 289–302, 1994.

Wyatt, G. E., & Powell, G. J. *Lasting Effects of Child Sexual Abuse.* Newbury Park, CA: Sage. 1988.

10 Sexual Violence on Campus

In chapter 8, the need for forensic nurses on elementary school and high school campuses was discussed. Another opportunity for the presence of forensic nurses is on university and college campuses. These campuses traditionally have provided an intellectual safe haven, an environment in which young people can explore new ideas and learn about the world. Experts say that one of the most pivotal lessons that educational institutions can communicate to all students is that violence against women should not be tolerated, and that creating a safe and supportive campus community is an obligation to be borne by administrators, faculty and staff, other campus personnel, and students.

In its *Toolkit to End Violence Against Women: Promoting Safety and Nonviolence on College and University Campuses*, the Violence Against Women Office of the U.S Department of Justice (2001) documents that sexual assault, dating and domestic violence, and stalking are serious issues on college and university campuses, and that college-age women are at high risk for all forms of violence. For example, more than half of all stalking victims are between 18 and 29 years old (Fisher, 1998). Other findings include the fact that sexual assault is the second most common violent crime committed on college campuses; most perpetrators are students known by the victim. At least half of these sexual assaults occur in the victim's residence, and an additional one third take place in off-campus student housing such as fraternity houses (Sloan, Fisher, & Cullen, 1997). Although current national attention focuses on the use of "rape drugs" to facilitate sexual assault, alcohol continues to play an important role in campus-related assaults. Excessive use of alcohol on college campuses has also been linked to increased risk of violence against women, although alcohol use is not the cause of sexual assault, domestic violence, or stalking (Fisher, 1995).

The problem of underreporting of sexual violence is present on college campuses, and is not limited to the general population of victims of violence. Fisher, Sloan, and Cullen (1995) says that an estimated 81 percent of on-campus and 84 percent of off-campus sexual assaults are not reported to the police. Unlike their counterparts in the larger community, women students victimized by other students often face challenges specific to a "closed" campus environment. Given the unique and progressive nature of many stalking cases, student victims are often unaware or unsure when they are being stalked or they might have difficulty convincing others that there is a problem. The stalker could have seemingly legitimate reasons for remaining in contact with or in proximity to the victim in class, the dining hall, or the library. Victims of sexual assault or dating violence might continue to encounter their assailants in residence halls or at campus events. Even changing one's living arrangements or class schedule might not eliminate the threat or additional trauma caused by ongoing contact.

In response to the realities of campus violence, the 2001 Department of Justice report states that an increasing number of institutions are implementing campus-wide responses to violence against women designed to coordinate victim services, campus law enforcement, health services, campus housing, student organizations, and disciplinary boards. The report states:

> Education and prevention initiatives that shift norms, attitudes, and beliefs about violence against women are also critical components of a comprehensive strategy, as are capital improvements and risk-reduction efforts. Effective intervention and prevention programs stress perpetrator accountability for sexual and physical violence; call attention to bystander behavior; highlight the prevalence and impact of acquaintance rape, dating and domestic violence, and stalking; and clearly define the role that campus communities can play in ending violence against women.

Sexual violence on campus requires the involvement of the criminal justice system, and experts emphasize:

> Campus adjudication procedures are critical for increasing the safety and security of women on campus but cannot substitute for criminal investigation or prosecution. Effective campus adjudication procedures complement other legal system processes. Ideally both options will be available to victims of sexual assault, dating or domestic violence, or stalking. The most successful responses link campus efforts with local criminal justice agencies and

community-based sexual assault and domestic violence programs. (Violence Against Women Office, 2001)

The federal Campus Security Act provides important guidelines for collecting and reporting data on campus sexual assaults. Title IX of the Education Amendments of 1972 provisions offer guidance and mandates related to preventing, redressing, and eliminating sexual harassment by students or school employees. Campus communities can influence large-scale social change by fully complying with the Campus Security Act and Title IX, adopting comprehensive policies that treat violence against women as serious offenses, and developing interventions that prioritize victim safety, offender accountability, and prevention. Failure to address violence against women on college campuses could not only result in institutional liability, but also send the dangerous message that certain forms of violence are not serious and, therefore, are acceptable.

In September 2004, campus crime victim advocates hailed a landmark federal ruling that they hope will help improve safety on college and university campuses across the country. In a July 2004 ruling against Georgetown University, the U.S. Department of Education held that it is illegal for a college to make a campus rape victim sign a confidentiality agreement to learn the results of disciplinary action taken against his or her alleged assailant.

Under the federal Jeanne Clery Disclosure of Campus Security Policy and Campus Crime Statistics Act, sexual assault victims must unconditionally be told these results, the federal agency ruled. Institutions that violate the law face fines of up to $27,500 per violation or loss of eligibility to participate in federal student aid programs.

"This ruling significantly advances student safety and marks a major improvement in the way our nation treats campus sexual assault victims," remarked Connie Clery, CEO and cofounder of the national nonprofit victim assistance organization Security on Campus, Inc. Clery and her husband Howard championed federal campus crime reporting and victims' rights legislation after they experienced firsthand the tragedy of campus violence. "As our own family learned, after my daughter Jeanne was brutally raped and murdered on campus, colleges don't want their images sullied by public crime reports," said Clery (Security on Campus, Inc., 2004):

> This ruling ensures that rape victims won't be silenced by schools which are more concerned about their image than keeping their students safe. If they want to talk to their friends about what happened to them, they can. If they want to tell them who did it, they can. If they want to put up a poster when the school lets the guy off with hardly any punishment, they can. If they want to hold a news conference and announce to the campus just how the school handled the case, they can. If doing this will help them heal, then they should do just that, and the school can't stop them.

Colleges and universities have come under fire in recent years for operating a secret system of on-campus justice that handles everything from routine alcohol violations to crimes as serious as rape and even cases involving student deaths. Often the police are never involved in these campus court cases. Students frequently aren't warned about crimes handled there, depriving them of information about dangers to their safety.

Security on Campus, Inc. asserts that colleges abuse student privacy laws to operate these "star chamber" courts, which hand down relatively light sentences such as 500-word essays or short suspensions from school for serious crimes such as rape. Such courts often require witnesses and victims to sign confidentiality agreements, threatening disciplinary action against them if they disclose any information about the cases to which they are a party.

"Forcing a victim to sign a confidentiality agreement in order to find out the outcome of a hearing which they initiated, is not only against the law, it's inhumane," said Kate Dieringer, the Georgetown student who complained to the Department of Education about having to sign a confidentiality agreement in her campus sexual assault case. The fellow student Dieringer accused of raping her as a freshman in the fall of 2001 was initially expelled from school in the spring of 2002, but appealed the sanction down to a one-year suspension. The confidentiality agreement that she had signed barred her from making public her concerns about how the process was handled.

"The Georgetown ruling helps to break the culture of silence that campus rape thrives in," commented S. Daniel Carter, senior vice president of Security on Campus, Inc. "Now victims will better be able to heal, complain about problems with student disciplinary proceedings, and warn their fellow students if another student who is a potential threat to their safety has been allowed to remain on campus. All of these things will help combat campus sexual assault, and make our nation's campuses safer."

One of the more definitive research reports on the subject of campus sexual violence is *The Sexual Victimization of College Women*, authored by Bonnie S. Fisher, Francis T. Cullen, and Michael G. Turner (2000). Based on their findings, Fisher and her colleagues estimated that women at a college that has 10,000 female students could experience more than 350 rapes a year—a finding with serious policy implications for college administrators. Fisher et al. also discovered that many women do not characterize their sexual victimizations as a crime for a number of reasons (such as embarrassment, not clearly understanding the legal definition of rape, or not wanting to define someone they know who victimized them as a rapist) or because they blame themselves for their sexual assault. The study reinforces the importance of many organizations' efforts to improve education and knowledge about sexual assault.

Fisher et al. write:

> During the past decade, concern over the sexual victimization of female college students has escalated. In part, the interest in this problem has been spurred by increasing attention to the victimization of women in general; until the relatively recent past, female victims received very little attention. However, this is no longer true. Terms such as "date rape" and "domestic violence" have entered the public lexicon and signify the unprecedented, if still insufficient, notice given to women who have been victimized. Attention to the sexual victimization of college women, however, also has been prompted by the rising fear that college campuses are not ivory towers but, instead, have become hot spots for criminal activity.

This NIJ report notes that large concentrations of young women come into contact with young men in a variety of public and private settings at various times on college campuses. The report explains:

> Previous research suggests that these women are at greater risk for rape and other forms of sexual assault than women in the general population or in a comparable age group. College women might, therefore, be a group whose victimization warrants special attention. Recognizing these risks, the U.S. Congress passed the Student Right-to-Know and Campus Security Act of 1990. This legislation mandates that colleges and universities participating in federal student aid programs "prepare, publish, and distribute, through appropriate publications or mailings, to all current students and employees, and to any applicant for enrollment or employment upon request, an annual security report" containing campus security policies and campus crime statistics for that institution.

Congress has maintained an interest in campus crime issues, passing legislation that requires higher educational institutions to address the rights of victims of sexual victimization and to collect and publish additional crime statistics, such as murder and nonnegligent manslaughter. In 1992, Congress amended the act to include the Campus Sexual Assault Victims' Bill of Rights, which requires colleges and universities to develop and publish as part of their annual security report their policies regarding the awareness and prevention of sexual assaults, and to afford basic rights to sexual assault victims. The act was amended again in 1998 to include additional reporting obligations, extensive campus security-related provisions, and the requirement to keep a daily public crime log. Some states already required a public log (Fisher, 1995). The 1998 amendments also officially changed the name of the act to the Jeanne Clery Disclosure of Campus Security Policy and Campus Crime Statistics Act. In 1999, the U.S. Department of Justice awarded $8.1 million to 21 colleges and universities to combat sexual assault, domestic violence, and stalking.

Fisher and colleagues assert that much of what researchers know about campus violence is limited by the following:

- The failure to use a randomly selected, national sample of college women. Numerous studies have sampled students at only one college or at a limited number of institutions.
- The failure to assess the various ways in which women can be victimized. Many studies have focused on a limited number of types of sexual victimization.
- The failure to use question wording or sufficiently detailed measures that prevent biases that might cause researchers to underestimate or overestimate the extent of sexual victimization.
- The failure to collect detailed information on what occurred during the victimization incident.
- The failure to explore systematically the factors that place female students at risk for sexual victimization.
- The failure to study whether women have been stalked, a victimization that, until recently, had not been the subject of systematic research.

Fisher et al. report that the National College Women Sexual Victimization (NCWSV) study, funded by the NIJ, attempted to build on, and surmount the limitations of, existing research on the sexual victimization of college students by employing a nationally representative sample of college women; assessing a range of sexual victimizations, including stalking; acquiring detailed information on each victimization incident, including the type of penetration(s) or unwanted sexual contact experienced and the means of coercion, if any, used by the offender; and examining how the risk of being sexually victimized was affected by a variety of variables, including demographic characteristics, lifestyles, prior victimization, and the characteristics of the college or university attended.

Fisher et al. add that the research project contained a comparison component designed to assess how rape estimates that use the two-stage process of behaviorally specific questions and incident reports compared with rape estimates drawn from a sample of college women who completed a survey based on the NCVS. The comparison component was funded by the BJS. The resulting data furnished a systematic analysis of the extent and nature of the sexual victimization of college women in the past decade.

The NCWSV study results were based on a telephone survey of a randomly selected national sample of 4,446 women who were attending a two- or four-year college or university during the fall of 1996. The questions were asked between February and May 1997. The sample was limited to schools with at least 1,000 students and was stratified by the size of the total student enrollment and the school's location. Schools were randomly chosen using a probability proportional with the size of the total female enrollment.

Each sample member was sent a letter describing the study and research protocol approximately two weeks prior to when a trained female interviewer called using a computer-aided telephone interviewing system. The response rate was 85.6 percent.

Measures of 12 types of sexual victimization were constructed, and the study included measures of both completed and attempted rape as well as threats of rape. The study also measured completed, attempted, and threatened sexual coercion (penetration with the use of nonphysical forms of coercion) and unwanted sexual contact (sexual contact, but not penetration, with force or threat of force). In addition, the study measured stalking and visual and verbal forms of sexual victimization.

According to the study, 2.8 percent of the sample had experienced either a completed rape (1.7 percent) or an attempted rape incident (1.1 percent). The victimization rate was 27.7 rapes per 1,000 female students. Because some women were victimized more than once, the rate of incidents was higher than the rate of victims (35.3 per 1,000 students). Of the 123 victims, 22.8 percent (28) were multiple-rape victims.

A separate analysis found that when rates were computed for only undergraduate students, the percentage of students victimized was 1.8 percent for rape and 1.3 percent for attempted rape. The comparable figures for graduate students were, respectively, 0.8 percent and 0 percent.

Fisher et al. write:

> At first glance, one might conclude that the risk of rape victimization for college women is not high; "only" about 1 in 36 college women (2.8 percent) experience a completed rape or attempted rape in an academic year. Such a conclusion, however, misses critical, and potentially disquieting, implications. The figures measure victimization for slightly more than half a year (6.91 months). Projecting results beyond this reference period is problematic for a number of reasons, such as assuming that the risk of victimization is the same during summer months and remains stable over a person's time in college. However, if the 2.8 percent victimization figure is calculated for a one-year period, the data suggest that nearly 5 percent (4.9 percent) of college women are victimized in any given calendar year. Over the course of a college career, which now lasts an average of five years, the percentage of completed or attempted rape victimization among women in higher educational institutions might climb to between one-fifth and one-quarter.

Fisher and colleagues wondered if college-age women defined their victimization as rape. In each incident report, the researchers asked respondents, "Do you consider this incident to be a rape?" They reported that for the 86 incidents categorized as a completed rape, 46.5 percent (40) of the women answered yes, 48.8 percent (42) answered no, and 4.7 percent (four) answered that they didn't know. Among women who experienced other forms of sexual victimization (1,318), the researchers noted that 3.4 percent (42) defined their sexual victimization as a rape and 1.1 percent (14) answered that they didn't know.

Fisher et al. comment:

> Some scholars believe that the failure of women to define a victimization as a rape calls into question whether researchers have truly measured the crime of rape. Others suggest, however, that the true prevalence of rape is best measured by carefully worded questions on victimization surveys. Women may not define a victimization as a rape for many reasons (such as embarrassment, not clearly understanding the legal definition of the term, or not wanting to define someone they know who victimized them as a rapist) or because others blame them for their sexual assault. Which of these reasons is more or less correct cannot be definitively substantiated here because little systematic research has examined why women do or do not define as a rape an incident that has met the researcher's criteria for a rape.

The researchers found that threats of sexual victimization occurred less often than other forms of sexual victimization. Across 10 types of victimization, the incident rate per 1,000 female students ranged from a low of 9.5 to a high of 66.4. Slightly more than 15 percent of the college women sampled were sexually victimized during the current academic year. In the sample, 7.7 percent experienced an incident involving the use or threat of physical force, and 11.0 percent experienced a victimization that did not involve force.

The researchers also asked survey participants if they had experienced sexual victimization incidents before starting school in fall 1996. About 1 in 10 college women said they had experienced a rape, and the same proportion stated that they were victims of an attempted rape. Almost the same proportion also had sexual intercourse or contact in which they were subject to threats of nonphysical punishment or promises of reward. Unwanted or uninvited sexual contacts were widespread, with more than one third of the sample reporting these incidents. Most victims knew the person who sexually victimized them. For both completed and attempted rapes, about 9 in 10 offenders were known to the victim. Most often, a boyfriend, ex-boyfriend, classmate, friend, acquaintance, or coworker sexually victimized the women. College professors were not identified as committing any rapes or sexual coercions, but they were cited as the offender in a low percentage of cases involving unwanted sexual contact.

Variation in the type of sexual victimization that occurred on a date was evident, according to researchers. With regard to date rape, 12.8 percent of completed rapes, 35.0 percent of attempted rapes, and 22.9 percent of threatened rapes took place on a date. The vast majority of sexual victimizations occurred in the evening (after 6 p.m.). For example, 51.8 percent of completed rapes took place after midnight, 36.5 percent occurred between 6 p.m. and midnight, and only 11.8 percent took place between 6 a.m. and 6 p.m. The majority of sexual victimizations, especially rapes and physically coerced sexual contact, occurred in living quarters. Almost 60 percent of the completed rapes that occurred on campus took place in the victim's residence, 31 percent occurred in other living quarters on campus, and 10.3 percent took place in a fraternity house. Off-campus sexual victimizations, especially rapes, also occurred in residences. However, particularly for sexual contacts and threatened victimizations, incidents also took place in settings such as bars, dance clubs or nightclubs, and work settings. The researchers also found that college women are victimized both on and off campus; for nearly all types of sexual victimization, however, off-campus victimization was more common.

For nearly all forms of sexual victimization, the majority of female students reported attempting to take protective actions during the incident. For both completed rape and sexual coercion, victims of completed acts were less likely to take protective action than those who experienced attempted victimization. The most common protective action was using physical force against the assailant. Nearly 70 percent of victims of attempted rape used this response; other common physical responses included removing the offender's hand, running away, and trying to avoid the offender. Verbal responses also were common, including pleading with the offender to stop, screaming, and trying to negotiate with the offender.

According to researchers, victims in the sample generally did not state that their victimization resulted in physical or emotional injuries. In about one in five rape and attempted rape incidents, victims reported being injured, most often citing the response "bruises, black eye, cuts, scratches, swelling, or chipped teeth." The percentage injured by other types of victimization was lower, ranging from 0 percent (completed sexual contact without force) to 16.7 percent (threatened rape). The researchers also discovered that four factors increased the risk of sexual victimization: frequently drinking enough to get drunk, being unmarried, having been a victim of a sexual assault before the start of the current school year, and living on campus.

Few incidents of sexual victimization were reported to law enforcement officials: Fewer than 5 percent of completed and attempted rapes were reported to law enforcement officials. In about two thirds of the rape incidents, however, the victim did tell another person about the incidents. Most often this person was a friend, not a family member or college official. Victims gave a number of reasons for not reporting their victimizations to law enforcement officials. Some reasons indicated that they did not see the incidents as harmful or important enough to bring in the authorities. Thus, common answers included that the incident was not serious enough to report and that it was not clear that a crime was committed. Other reasons, however, suggested that there were barriers to reporting. Such answers included not wanting family or other people to know about the incident, lack of proof the incident happened, fear of reprisal by the assailant, fear of being treated with hostility by the police, and anticipation that the police would not believe the incident was serious enough or would not want to be bothered with the incident.

Fisher et al. write:

> The sexual victimization of college students has emerged as a controversial issue, pitting feminist scholars who claim that the sexual victimization of women is a serious problem against conservative commentators who claim that such victimization is rare and mostly a fictitious creation of ideologically tainted research. The research reported here undoubtedly will not settle this debate; battle lines are solidly entrenched and how the data are interpreted will, to a degree, lie in the eye of the beholder. However, the current study attempts to add a judicious voice to this conversation by attempting to furnish a methodologically sound assessment of the extent and nature of the sexual victimization of female students.

The U.S. Department of Justice outlines the following specific actions that communities can take to promote safety and nonviolence on their campuses:

1. Establish an interdisciplinary, campus-wide violence against women task force to develop policies and oversee antiviolence efforts, including the periodic evaluation of those efforts.
   - Secure representation from every sector of campus life, including administrators, health care and mental health professionals, faculty, and students, as well as experts from community-based sexual assault and domestic violence programs.
   - Provide comprehensive training about violence against women to all task force members.
   - Arrange regular task force meetings to develop short- and long-term plans for addressing violence against women on campus and oversee their implementation.
   - Periodically evaluate campus-wide antiviolence efforts and use findings to enhance intervention and prevention initiatives.
2. Develop and distribute clear, concise, and comprehensive written policies and procedures

regarding appropriate behavior by students with respect to violence against women.

- Develop and disseminate a campus code of conduct, including descriptions of expected behavior and responsibilities of the entire campus community.
- Require consistent enforcement of the campus code of conduct.
- Provide clear definitions of sexual assault, dating and domestic violence, and stalking that are consistent with state criminal statutes.
- Articulate clearly that sexual assault, dating and domestic violence, and stalking will not be tolerated.
- Describe procedures for reporting incidents (including steps that take place after a report is filed) and protecting the victim's rights throughout the process.
- Detail services available on and off campus.
- Outline options for pursuing justice and enhancing safety on campus through community-based service providers and the criminal justice system.
- Disseminate policies every academic year to all students (new and returning), faculty, staff, parents of students, campus organizations, counseling centers, health care centers, residence halls, and trustees.
- Publish campus policies in student handbooks, residence life guidelines, and through campus media such as the student newspaper. Post information on policies in appropriate public places.
- Share information with other campuses regarding policies, training programs, and effective practices for providing services to victims and holding offenders accountable.

3. Educate students, faculty, and staff about the problem of violence against women.
   - Provide information on the prevalence of acquaintance rape and other forms of violence against women on college campuses, including the situations and circumstances that foster nonconsensual sexual conduct.
   - Offer special programs that educate all students about the warning signs that might signal risks to a student's safety, behaviors that constitute stalking, and appropriate response strategies.
   - Focus on the role of bystanders, including strategies students can use to prevent violence against women, address or challenge perpetrator behavior, identify and assist a victim, and make appropriate referrals.
   - Highlight men's responsibility to prevent violence, especially in programs designed for all-male groups such as fraternities or athletic groups.
   - Reduce victim blaming and promote perpetrator accountability by challenging widely held misconceptions about sexual assault, dating and domestic violence, and stalking.
   - Provide information on the role of alcohol and other drugs, including "date-rape drugs" such as Rohypnol (flunitrazepam) and GHB, in sexual assault and dating violence in a manner that does not promote the myth that alcohol consumption causes or excuses violent or abusive behavior.
   - Share information about faculty–student dating and the potential link between and ramifications of power imbalances and sexual harassment or sexual assault.
   - Involve advocates from local sexual assault and domestic violence programs in the design and implementation of training and education programs.
4. Use a variety of outreach strategies to support educational efforts.
   - Incorporate discussion of sexual assault, dating and domestic violence, and stalking into orientation programs and materials for all incoming students with an emphasis on reaching young students, international students, and others who might be unfamiliar with campus laws, policies, and procedures.
   - Integrate prevention education into relevant core curriculum classes, classes on criminal justice and victimology, and academic discourse.
   - Disseminate prevention materials and messages through student newspapers, e-mail announcements, campus radio stations, posters, and similar mechanisms.
   - Use common space (such as the student union, campus library, and dormitories) for widely publicized all-campus events about sexual assault, dating and domestic violence, and stalking.
   - Invite college or university presidents, members of the board of trustees, prominent alumni, and other influential figures to speak out against sexual assault, dating and domestic violence, and stalking.
   - Design peer educator programs to conduct outreach to students and specific groups, including fraternities, athletic clubs, or religious groups.

- Reach out to marginalized communities that are less likely to access campus services, including students of color; LGBT students; and students with physical, cognitive, or sensory disabilities.
- Use various points of access, such as international groups, churches, and child care facilities, to reach international students, commuting students, and partners or spouses of students.
- Distribute materials on antiviolence programs to prospective students.

5. Provide adequate and appropriate risk-reduction measures on campus.
   - Establish escort services for students on campus and for those traveling to nearby off-campus locations. Conduct background checks on all escort service volunteers and supervise and monitor them carefully.
   - Provide security devices for students to activate when in danger and develop an emergency alert system on campus.
   - Install adequate lighting on all parts of campus.
   - Secure entry into residence halls, student rooms, and late-night computer labs and work areas. Patrol residence halls, parking lots, and other common areas.
   - Widely publicize emergency numbers for police and medical services and crisis hotline numbers for sexual assault, dating and domestic violence, and stalking programs.
   - Support campus security efforts to gather accurate statistics on crime rates and the outcomes of violence against women on campus.
6. Mandate training and education for all campus police and security officers on sexual assault, dating and domestic violence, and stalking as well as related policies and protocols.
   - Include data about the prevalence and unique characteristics of violence against women on college campuses.
   - Provide guidelines for responding to victims in a nonjudgmental and appropriate manner; referring victims to campus and community-based services, including medical care and forensic sexual assault examinations as appropriate and requested; facilitating incident reporting to local law enforcement; and working collaboratively with local criminal justice agencies and community sexual assault and domestic violence programs.
   - Develop investigation skills to build evidence-based cases.
   - Promote full compliance with the Campus Security Act and its reporting requirements and work to ensure that all institutions maintain accurate data.
7. Involve campus housing and residence life staff in campus efforts to address and prevent sexual assault, dating and domestic violence, and stalking.
   - Provide yearly training to campus housing and residence staff on sexual assault (including sexual harassment), dating and domestic violence, stalking, and campus policies and programs.
   - Use residence hall programming to create opportunities for discussion and support groups on issues related to violence against women.
   - Post hotline and referral information for campus and community-based sexual assault and domestic violence programs in residence hall bathrooms and on public notice boards.
8. Urge national associations of higher education professionals to prioritize violence against women as a key administrative and academic issue.
   - Encourage national associations to work collaboratively with violence against women experts to develop common principles, guidelines, policy directives, and curriculum materials to help colleges and universities develop comprehensive approaches to address and prevent violence against college women and to educate college students about sexual assault, dating and domestic violence, and stalking.
9. Facilitate students' access to both on-campus adjudication processes and off-campus criminal justice agencies.
   - Ensure that campus judicial processes and sanctions do not inhibit criminal prosecution of perpetrators of sexual assault, dating and domestic violence, and stalking.
   - Create statutes of limitation for campus adjudication that are not less than those in the state criminal and civil justice systems.
   - Provide information to all victims about options for on-campus adjudication and off-campus law enforcement involvement.
   - Enable every victim to pursue campus judicial processes, civil actions, and criminal charges concurrently, without concern that one outcome will affect the others.
   - Foster working relationships between the campus and the local community, including campus service providers, campus police,

campus adjudication officials, off-campus service providers, local law enforcement agencies, prosecutors and probation officers, and other criminal justice professionals.

10. Ensure a fair, victim-centered campus adjudication process through training and representative composition of the campus adjudication board.
    - Provide annual training for all adjudication board members.
    - When appropriate, involve violence against women experts in campus adjudication programs, including local sexual assault and domestic violence program advocates.
    - Provide adjudicators with information on appropriate and inappropriate questions for victims and alleged perpetrators and the range of victim behavior patterns, including the delayed response of some sexual assault victims (especially in cases involving drugs or alcohol) and its impact on victim reporting and testimony.
    - Ensure that the membership of the campus adjudication board reflects the composition of the campus community and, when appropriate, includes people not connected to the university who embrace a victim advocacy perspective.
11. Ensure that campus-based hearing procedures minimize victim trauma and maintain victims' rights without violating the rights of the accused.
    - Ensure victim confidentiality throughout adjudication procedures.
    - Apply the principles of rape shield laws to testimony (e.g., limiting inquiry into the victim's sexual history).
    - Employ a clearly defined standard of proof.
    - Allow the victim to have an advocate or similar figure accompany her through the judicial process, including legal counsel at her own expense.
    - Inform the victim of the time and location of all hearings and proceedings related to the case and provide the option of being present during the entire hearing if the accused has that right. Minimize inconvenience and disruption to the victim to the extent possible.
    - Allow the victim to testify at any hearings to recommend sanctions, remedial actions, or outcomes for the adjudication and, on request, to testify at a different time than the accused perpetrator.
    - Include the option of an expedited hearing to determine issues of immediate concern, such as the need to alter campus housing or class schedules. Special considerations, such as flexibility relative to class work, testing, or leaves of absence without tuition penalties, should be provided to the victim to accommodate academic circumstances affected by the victimization.
    - Inform the victim of the outcome of the case, including any conditions placed on the accused relative to the victim and her safety.
    - Ensure that a victim's rights in campus adjudication procedures mirror those built into the criminal justice system.
12. Adequately and appropriately address victim safety in campus-based sanctions and the adjudication process.
    - Establish a system of referral to law enforcement if the victim wants a protection order and is eligible for one under state law.
    - Provide the victim with updates about sanctions against a perpetrator, as necessary.
    - If feasible, allow students to obtain the administrative equivalent of a restraining or protection order against an offender, when appropriate, that accommodates the victim's academic schedule, needs, and preferences.
13. Administer sanctions in a manner that ensures offender accountability and victim and community safety.
    - Provide the adjudication board a range of formal and informal options to recommend for perpetrators of sexual assault, dating and domestic violence, and stalking, including removal or suspension from athletics, fraternal organizations, student government, and other student organizations; loss of financial aid and grants; restricted access to residence halls or removal from campus housing; termination of campus employment; loss of eligibility for academic scholarships and fellowships; mandated counseling sessions; inclusion of the conviction in the offender's permanent transcript; and expulsion or suspension from the college or university.
    - Avoid the use of mediation or counseling between the survivor and perpetrator to keep from revictimizing or endangering the victim.
    - Ensure that sanctions are not influenced by the racial, ethnic, or socioeconomic status of the perpetrator or his or her social, academic, or athletic standing within the campus community.
14. Provide free or low-cost comprehensive, accessible on-campus and community-based services to survivors.
    - Designate at least one advocate responsible for assisting victims through the on- and off-

campus systems following sexual assault, dating or domestic violence, or stalking.

- Ensure that sexually assaulted students have access to expert evidence collection through on-campus trained SANEs or off-campus health and law enforcement facilities.
- Train health clinic staff on violence against women issues and how to provide appropriate, respectful screening and services to victims.
- Consider providing transportation for victims to and from the hospital, police station, courthouse, and counseling appointments in vehicles not marked as campus security or police.
- Provide appropriate services for all victims regardless of disability, race, national origin, sexual orientation, or gender.
- Make services accessible to students who commute, have limited English skills, are older than the average student population, or have children.
- Do not require that victims report the incident to campus security or local law enforcement as a condition for receiving services, but do encourage such reporting.
- To minimize future victim–perpetrator contact when perpetrators are not removed from campus settings, help survivors who request such assistance transfer from a campus dormitory, access safe housing or a shelter, obtain an unlisted phone number, set up a new e-mail account, and take other relevant security measures.
- Establish free short- and long-term counseling services and support groups on campus administered by counselors who have been trained to address the emotional and psychological needs of victims.

15. Widely publicize the availability of services for victims of sexual assault, dating and domestic violence, and stalking.
    - Establish and publicize a point of contact on campus for survivors where all communications are confidential.
    - Distribute brochures and literature about violence against women in places frequented by students, including health and mental health service centers.

REFERENCES

Bureau of Justice Statistics. *Violence by Intimates: Analysis of Data on Crimes by Current or Former Spouses, Boyfriends, and Girlfriends.* Washington, DC: U.S. Department of Justice. 1998.

Fisher, B. S. Campus crime and fear of victimization: Judicial, legislative, and administrative responses. *Ann Am Acad Polit Soc Science. 539,* 85–101, 1995.

Fisher, B. S. Crime in the ivory tower: The level and sources of student victimization. *Criminology. 36,* 671–710, 1998.

Fisher, B. S., Cullen, F. T., & Turner, M. G. *The Sexual Victimization of College Women.* Washington, DC: National Institute of Justice. 2000.

Jeanne Clery Act Information page at Security On Campus: College and University Campus Safety Information On-Line. King of Prussia, PA: Security on Campus, Inc. Available at: www.securityoncampus.org. 2000.

Security On Campus, Inc. Security On Campus, Inc. hails landmark federal ruling that says colleges & universities can't silence campus rape victims. [Press release]. Available at: www.securityoncampus.org/reporters/releases/08042004.html. 2004.

Sloan, J. J., Fisher, B. S., & Cullen, F. T. Assessing the Student Right-to-Know and Campus Security Act of 1990: An analysis of the victim reporting practices of college and university students. *Crime and Delinquency. 43,* 248–268, 1997.

Violence Against Women Office, U.S. Department of Justice. *Toolkit to End Violence Against Women: Promoting Safety and Nonviolence on College and University Campuses.* Washington, DC: U.S. Department of Justice. 2001.

Violence Against Women Grants Office. *Stalking and Domestic Violence: The Third Annual Report to Congress Under the Violence Against Women Act.* Washington, DC: U.S. Department of Justice. 1998.

RECOMMENDED READINGS

Crowell, N. A., & Burges,s A. W., Eds. *Understanding Violence Against Women, by the Panel on Violence Against Women, National Research Council.* Washington, DC: National Academy Press. 1996.

DeKeseredy, W., & Kelly, K. The incidence and prevalence of women abuse in Canadian university and college dating relationships. *Can J Socio. 18,* 137–159, 1993.

Fisher, B. S., & Cullen, F. T. Measuring the sexual victimization of women: evolution, current controversies and future research. In D. Duffee, Ed. *Criminal Justice 2000, Volume 4: Measurement and Analysis of Crime.* Washington, DC: U.S. Department of Justice, National Institute of Justice. 2000.

Fisher, B., Sloan, J. J., & Cullen, F. T. *Final Report: Understanding Crime Victimization Among College Students: Implications for Crime Prevention.* Washington, DC: U.S. Department of Justice. 1995.

Griffaton, M. C. State-level initiatives and campus crime. In B. S. Fisher & J. J. Sloan III, Eds. *Campus Crime: Legal, Social, and Policy Perspectives.* Springfield, IL: Charles C Thomas. 1995.

Koss, M. P., Gidycz, C. A., & Wisniewski, N. The scope of rape: Incidence and prevalence of sexual aggression and victimization in a national sample of higher education students. *J Counseling Clin Psych. 55,* 162–170, 1987.

11 Forensic Psychiatric Nursing and Corrections Nursing

CONTENTS

11.1 BALANCING THE DEMANDS OF CARE AND CUSTODY IN AN "INVISIBLE" NURSING SPECIALTY

Care and custody: They are responsibilities intrinsic to one another, yet create an intriguing paradox for the forensic nurse who must balance clinical intervention with security and risk management in an environment with custodial overtones. Forensic psychiatric nursing is still a widely misunderstood specialty in which practitioners struggle with stigmas associated with their work and the mentally ill or incarcerated patient population they serve.

Colleen Carney Love, DNSc, RN, director of the Clinical Safety Project at Atascadero State Hospital and a member of the adjunct faculty of California State Long Beach School of Nursing, is adamant about raising the profile of forensic psychiatric nursing. Love and Eileen F. Morrison, PhD, RN, a nurse consultant at Central State

Hospital in Richmond, Virginia, asserted that forensic psychiatric nursing remains virtually "invisible" (Love & Morrison, 2002). They added that despite forensic psychiatric nurses having provided services in the United States for more than a century, "written material on forensic psychiatric nursing in this country is difficult to find." They reported that this subject rarely appears in nursing textbooks, nursing journals, or nursing educational programs. "Even in the International Association of Forensic Nurses (IAFN), the forensic psychiatric contingent is a tiny, far-flung minority among a vast and passionate majority of sexual assault nurse examiners (SANEs)," they wrote. "This invisibility and professional isolation of forensic psychiatric nursing practice has had crippling effects on its development as a public service nursing specialty in the United States."

Professional isolation, Love and Morrison observed, is fostered by a lack of vehicles that forensic psychiatric nurses can call their own:

> The virtual invisibility of forensic psychiatric nursing in nursing professional journals, textbooks and educational programs is curious and contrasts markedly from our neighboring disciplines.... Both psychiatry and psychology have fully developed professional publications and texts, forensic subspecialties and postgraduate, university-based forensic fellowship programs. A high-quality body of literature is produced, characterized by valuable research trajectories, lively scholarly and philosophical debates and high profile involvement in shaping public policy (which significantly impacts forensic practice) and media coverage of forensic topics.

Love and Morrison point to writings by Moritz (1982) that reflected on the lack of development of nursing's work with offenders. Love and Morrison say Bernier (1986) speculated about the slow professional development of correctional nursing, which rings true for forensic psychiatric nursing as well: "Nurses who practice in the correctional system are a silent minority. It is rare that they publish in nursing journals and unusual for nurse educators to enlist their expertise in an effort to introduce this area as a practice option when considering career choices. The majority of these nurses are further limited in their scope of practice because they are not baccalaureate prepared." "Little progress has been made in the development of forensic psychiatric nursing practice during the past 20 years," Love and Morrison asserted, pointing to the advances made across the pond. "Forensic psychiatric nurses in the United Kingdom have contributed significantly to the growth of the field in the UK countries and, despite cultural and legal differences, serve as an important resource as the specialty develops in the United States."

11.2 THE UNITED KINGDOM EXPERIENCE

The United Kingdom has enjoyed a much longer history of nurses working in secure hospitals and prisons, although it has struggled with many of the same issues that the United States has. In 1998, the United Kingdom Central Council (UKCC) commissioned the University of Central Lancashire to undertake a sweeping study of the state of nursing in secure environments, creating a comprehensive picture of the educational, occupational, and professional practice expectations placed on these nurses. The report, *Nursing in Secure Environments: Summary and Action Plan From a Scoping Study,* (UKCC, 1998) is the culmination of an exhaustive review of the British medical literature, which identified 630 references from 147 periodicals, journals, and books spanning 18 years and the work of 425 authors, as well as the input of 22 focus groups (250 practitioners from more than 80 organizations), a series of 34 interviews with experts in the field, an organizational survey (with a 39 percent response rate) of all prisons and all hospitals providing secure care, and a staff survey (yielding 715 responses) of all nurses working in prisons and of a sample of nurses working in high-, medium-, and low-security units. Researchers discovered that nursing in secure environments requires staff members with specific expertise who have considerable continuing professional development and supervision requirements. Nurses are responsible not only for providing care but also for maintaining much of the security framework and processes within which this care can be delivered. Key issues identified in the U.K. report relate to the preparation of nurses to work in secure environments, occupational and professional competence, the difficulty of developing professional practice in "closed" institutions, and the complexities of personal and professional relationships with clients. The study identified the following issues related to nursing in secure hospitals:

- Caring for those deemed dangerously mentally ill is a long-standing public policy problem.
- The number of secure beds for mentally disordered offenders has increased significantly in the last 10 years, so nursing in secure environments is likely to be a significant and enduring feature of provision for these groups.
- Problems in secure mental health care are exacerbated by a lack of access to general psychiatric services.
- Inpatients have higher levels of disadvantage, social exclusion, and homelessness, coupled with more complex needs, than in the past.
- The number of clients who have problems both with substance abuse and mental illness has risen sharply; they place great demands on the clinical

skills of nurses, who are often not trained to provide the complexity of care required.

- Professional education and research should take account of race and culture, and employers and managers should identify staff training needs and establish programs to address these issues.
- Among current admissions, the largest single group is those with a history of violence.
- The number of clients convicted or prosecuted for sexual offences has increased by 300 percent in the last 10 years.
- It is difficult for RNs to distinguish between the range of clinical problems and the treatment needs of individuals with different diagnoses and different levels of security.
- Registered mental health nurses working in general mental health services appear to be poorly equipped to deal with the rehabilitation and treatment of clients from secure settings.
- There is a need further to develop the theoretical and practical base of nursing in the psychopathologies of forensic clients.
- Nurses working in secure hospitals face significant and enduring role conflict in attempting to reconcile their responsibilities for therapeutic care with those for maintaining security.
- Clients in secure hospitals have extremely complex health, social, psychological, and forensic backgrounds, all of which continue to impose challenging demands on those who provide their nursing care.

Regarding nursing in prisons, the UKCC study identified these key issues:

- There has been a move to recognize the rights of prisoners to appropriate health care and to accept its importance from a humane and rehabilitative perspective.
- The recruitment and retention of RNs must be addressed to maintain an effective and efficient workforce.
- Differences in local management arrangements and priorities within the prison services have, on occasions, made the implementation of services-wide standards of health care extremely difficult.
- Rights and access to health care have been influenced by prisoners' legal action, rather than being based on health need.
- The health needs of prisoners are diverse and encompass severe mental illness, personality disorder, poor physical health, drug and alcohol dependency, trauma, primary care, and health promotion.
- Personnel and occupational arrangements within the prison services, especially in England, have meant that the role and contribution of nurses has been unclear and often confused with the custodial role of prison officers.

In its review of the British medical literature, the UKCC study revealed the following:

- Although there is significant literature on nursing in secure environments, it has not been used to inform the development of an evidence base that could improve standards of professional practice.
- Published research is generally derived from clinical anecdotes and concentrates on discussion rather than the presentation of empirical data.
- There is clear evidence that nurses in secure environments, both in the health and prison services, have reasonable access to sources of evidence through libraries and professional journals.
- Even though nurses working in secure environments appear to believe that the standards they are expected to implement are evidence-based, there is little evidence from the literature, survey questionnaires, and audits to support this belief.
- Closed environments in particular are motivated, at least in part, by a reliance on routines, rituals, and regimes; evidence-based practice appears to have difficulty penetrating this culture.
- Employers need to develop and maintain a culture in which nurses are enabled to review and adjust their professional practice.
- Much nursing practice is "incident and inquiry"-based and derives from a risk management perspective; the limitations of this approach mean that professional practice might become focused on containment rather than therapy.
- Political sensitivities relating to secure environments, and the media attention that they attract, result in defensive reactions to incidents rather than a considered, research-based approach to the solution of problems.

Regarding practice standards in secure environments, the UKCC study concluded that the following:

- There would be clear advantages in targeting sensitive and problematic areas for staff and working toward the setting and implementation

of standards, using external expertise and guidance where necessary.
- Standards must be systematically monitored through regular audit, training, and education, and job descriptions should reflect expectations of staff.
- There is a need to determine national minimum criteria for security issues, seclusion, leave of absence, and physical health monitoring.
- A wide range of practice standards has been developed in some aspects of secure care but there is little coordination across and between services and there is poor dissemination and application of standards.
- Neither the practice standards themselves nor their audit are supported by research evidence.
- Auditing of standards across the services is haphazard and minimal.
- Practitioners feel excluded from the development of organizational standards.
- There is confusion among nurses and their employers about what practice standards are, particularly in relation to protocols and guidelines.
- Practice standards are not made known to clients and they have little input to the development of standards.
- The development and implementation of practice standards needs to be incorporated into the overall performance indicators for an organization and subjected to regular audit and review.

11.3 FORENSIC PSYCHIATRIC NURSING: A REVIEW OF THE LITERATURE

Much of what is in the medical literature reflects the content of the UKCC study as well as the experience of forensic psychiatric nurses in the United States.

11.3.1 The Role of Forensic Psychiatric Nursing

Peternelj-Taylor (1999) states that forensic psychiatric nursing bridges the gap between the mental health care system and the criminal justice system, and is defined as the integration of mental health nursing philosophy and practice within a sociocultural context that includes the criminal justice system. Peternelj-Taylor explains that the dual responsibility toward the legal system (custody) and the individual (health care) creates a paradox that most commonly differentiates forensic psychiatric nursing from forensic nursing in general. She adds that forensic psychiatric nursing provides a multidisciplinary approach that addresses the needs of the health care and criminal justice systems. Hammer (2000) states that the hallmark for all nursing, especially for the various subspecialties of forensic nursing, is caring for victims and for offenders. This a dichotomous role in that nurses must not make conclusions regarding innocence or guilt; the nurse's need to preserve human dignity could be seen as in conflict with the objectives of the other members of the forensic team. Maeve and Vaughn (2001) acknowledge that providing high levels of quality health care for prisoners is not always popular with members of society, and that the nurse is faced with certain social and professional stigmas related to serving the incarcerated or the mentally ill. They state that because caring is fundamental to nursing, caring encompasses victims of violence as well as perpetrators, so these nurses must find ways to overcome obstacles to caring for the incarcerated population. They add that role ambiguity has been created by the word *forensic* being added to these nurses' job titles, and that it has created a new set of expectations for the outcomes of psychiatric nurses' evaluations and treatment interventions.

Martin (2001) refutes the idea that forensic psychiatric nursing has achieved the status of a distinct nursing specialty, and points toward work by Lynch (1997) and Peternelj-Taylor and Johnson (1995) that does not establish consensus regarding the development of forensic psychiatric nursing as a specialty. Martin adds that Burnard (1992) and Burrow (1993) agree that it is a specialty. Martin asserts that forensic psychiatric nursing will continue to be a subspecialty of psychiatric nursing until what is distinct and therapeutic about the practice is documented, and that nurses wishing to achieve this specialty status must consolidate their role in the containment and care of patients, return to the nurse– patient relationship as the foundation of psychiatric nursing practice, and within that relationship, expand their practice to include dealing with offense issues. Because nurses' assessment can dictate ongoing treatment and discharge, Martin says they need additional training in criminal justice and counseling skills.

Mason (2002) states that nurses are frequently doubtful about their ability to effectively treat mentally ill offenders, and that they express contentment about feeling appreciated. With regard to roles and security efforts in correctional facilities, Mason observed that in the United Kingdom, security falls to nursing staff, whereas in the United States and Canada, security personnel undertake the responsibility. Mason reports that nurses believe their patients see them as part of the prison system, thus making therapeutic treatment more difficult to conduct, and that there is indeed a very fine line between therapy and security. Sekula et al. (2001) assert that traditionally, nurses have been trained as generalists, and that nurses with extensive clinical experience in a particular area of practice are considered to be specialists. They add that by this definition, no formal education beyond the entry level is required to call oneself a specialist. The researchers cite the opinion of Whyte (1997), who argues that forensic nursing is not a legitimate specialty within nursing, as well as Lynch (1993, 1995) and Burrow (1993), who maintain that forensic nursing is a specialty of its own with unique responsibilities created by the intersection of the mentally ill person as both the patient and the criminal.

Sekula et al. acknowledge that a varying definition of the role makes it challenging to identify forensic nursing as a specialty, as well as to provide education and set standards. They argue that acceptance of this specialty could facilitate further development of a knowledge base, accelerate the development of assessment and intervention skills, encourage research in the area, and promote a sense of identity for nurses working in this marginalized domain of practice. Mason and Gerry (2002) studied the workings of a multidisciplinary team in a medium-secure forensic unit in the United Kingdom and reported that different members of the team contribute specialized knowledge and skills, and that they must have an understanding of their colleagues' roles to better function collaboratively. Mason also found that the focus of forensic mental health care is the delivery of service through a systemic structure incorporating mental health and criminal justice issues. The researchers note that a search of the literature produced other studies that confirm the need for teamwork, including Brooker and Whyte (2000), who found that professionals working in forensic settings were clear about their role in teams, and agreed about the core skills needed by all team members, despite some tensions; and Robinson and Kettles (1998), who found that forensic nurses believe that they provide a link between disciplines in a pivotal role central to communication; however, some have difficulties contributing to the team and feel they have low status within it. Mason and Gerry (2002) establish that central to forensic practice is the multidisciplinary approach that encompasses forensic nursing, but that a diffused educational platform among the team members could hamper cohesion.

11.3.2 Education of Forensic Psychiatric Nurses

Rask and Aberg (2002) point to the work of Niskala (1986), who states that forensic psychiatric nurses must possess competencies in communication, the upholding of security, the performance of the nursing process, and the maintenance of a professional role. Niskala reports that the skills nurses believe are essential to their job performance are the abilities to initiate relationships, to listen effectively, to document in a clear and concise manner, to maintain confidentiality, and to cope with institutional and environmental stressors. In addition, Rask and Aberg asked nurses working in five Swedish forensic psychiatric units to complete a questionnaire that asked them how nursing could contribute to improved care and the organizational changes needed. The researchers discovered that an interpersonal nurse–patient relationship was the essence of nursing care and a way to improve care, and that care should be influenced by nurses. The nurses also identified the need for greater improvement in treatment techniques and modalities, psychopathology and medication, more advanced training adapted to ward-specific problems, documentation and evaluation, and clinical supervision.

11.3.3 Burnout of Forensic Psychiatric Nurses

Ewers, Bradshaw, McGovern, and Ewers (2002) demonstrated that in the United Kingdom, mental health nurses working in secure environments with patients suffering from serious mental illness have been shown to be at risk of burnout, as well as demonstrating emotional and physical exhaustion and reduced job performance. The researchers stated that burnout negatively impacts staff well-being and the quality of interactions between staff and patients. The study sought to evaluate the effect of psychosocial intervention training (a strategy that helps clinicians to conceptualize their patients' problems within a more empathetic framework and trains them in the skills to intervene effectively) on the attitudes of a group of forensic mental health nurses. The researchers discovered that nurses in the experimental group showed significant improvements in their knowledge and attitudes about serious mental illness and a significant decrease in burnout rates.

11.3.4 Workplace Violence

Morrison et al. (2002) assert that little to no progress has been made toward improving health care providers' understanding of violence by the mentally ill, and that programs aimed at the prevention of such violence are uncommon. The researchers examined efforts on the part of administrative and clinical staff to reduce the incidences of workplace violence and staff injuries in a maximum-security psychiatric facility in the United States. The administrative team was found to have developed strategies for protecting staff members during outbreaks of violence, including a more lenient definition of what constituted an "emergency" for the use of seclusion or restraint, new restraint products, the implementation of a security management team, and aggression-management plans for particular high-risk patients. A nurse consultant with expertise in violence issues was hired to work with the staff in managing risks. The researchers concluded that the institution studied had significantly reduced staff injuries as well as the overall amount of aggression and violence without increased use of seclusion or restraint.

Terpstra, Terpstra, Pettee, and Hunter (2001) studied the attitudes of U.S. forensic mental health staff toward the use of restraint and their interactions with their patients. Terpstra states that nurses, who serve as frontline workers with violent offenders, can choose restraint and isolation interventions, even though physicians and therapists have viewed such interventions as punitive and violations of patients' rights. Steele (1993), who surveyed 28 employees in four inpatient psychiatric facilities, found that although 60 percent recognized the use of restraint or seclusion as therapeutic, others expressed concern about potential abuse of rights, loss of dignity, and control over persons who are at a disadvantage in the power equation.

Woods (2001) acknowledges that violence in the workplace is prevalent, particularly in forensic mental health settings, and calls for regular incident monitoring. These reporting systems should be easy to use, be based on a standard definition of incidents, allow for the timely collection of data and investigation, and be able to record detailed information about the incident. Woods, citing the literature, maintains that a number of factors relating to violence exist, including factors predisposing to violence (age, gender, ethnicity, length of stay, and previous history of violence) and environmental factors (type of ward, location of incident, patient density, time of day, day of the week, and seasonal variation). Woods adds that nurses often bear the brunt of the violence, as they provide direct patient care.

Borum (1996) states that few efforts have been made to develop clinical frameworks for risk assessments; however, risk assessment is aided by identification of factors that predispose an individual to behave in a violent manner. Risk markers can include a previous history of violence, age under 30, male gender, concurrent drug and alcohol abuse, and active psychotic symptoms. McClelland (1995) and Quintal (2002), recognizing that forensic psychiatric nurses continue to be assaulted by their patients, add that these assaults are the intersection of sociopsychological, interpersonal, situational, and sociocultural factors. Steps to avoid violence include performing thorough assessments on every patient on admission, educating health care providers about self-defense and communication strategies, and advocating for safety-promoting regulation and legislation, such as the Occupational Safety and Health Administration (OSHA)'s *Guidelines for Preventing Workplace Violence for Health Care and Social Service Workers* (1998). Harrison (2003) maintains that risk assessment is inherent in nursing as a core competency, and should be exercised as part of a multidisciplinary approach. Nurses conduct risk assessment when structuring care plans and then regularly reassessing them. Harrison says that active listening and empathy can reduce the risk of violence, and that training and continuing education and clinical supervision increase the effectiveness of clinical work and risk assessment practice.

11.3.5 Opportunities for Interventions

Austin (2001) states that forensic psychiatric nurses must connect with their patients despite their capacity to evoke strong, negative emotions, their possible histories of committing morally reprehensible acts, and those who are continually threatening. Nurses must engage in mutual respect, follow an ethical course of interaction with their patients, and relate to them through their caring despite the inherent tension between this care and custodial responsibilities.

11.4 THE CARE AND FEEDING OF FORENSIC PSYCHIATRIC NURSES

Love and Morrison (2002) point to the lack of baccalaureate- and graduate-prepared nurses working in forensic settings, which they say has severely limited its development as a specialty and left nursing at a disadvantage compared to other disciplines. "Even if graduate programs were available for advanced practice forensic nurses, few incentives exist for administrators in public sector forensic settings to create positions for advanced practice forensic nurses," they write. Love and Morrison argue that even if the clinical contributions and the cost-effectiveness of advanced practice nurses in forensic settings were proved in more numerous studies, "most public-sector environments are shaped by seriously outdated civil service systems that have no designation for advanced practice nursing roles. In situations where organizations have managed to allocate funding to hire advanced practice nurses, the salaries are often not competitive with other advanced practice nursing options, such as private practice, particularly when the hazards of forensic work are taken into consideration." They look to work by Smoyak (1991), who noted that public-sector psychiatric agencies "tend to be battlegrounds for conflicting interests." They say that when the author was establishing a forensic psychiatric nurse practitioner program in a large forensic hospital, "unforeseen obstacles became apparent. Not only were there few incentives and mixed enthusiasm for the inclusion of advanced practice nurses, turf battles and defensive guild issues emerged (and persist) from other mental health disciplines." In addition, Love and Morrison have argued that "the tendency for forensic and correctional agencies to be insular and regionally-shaped environments leads to a form of staff institutionalization." They say that unless the forensic setting is affiliated with a university or located in a major metropolitan area,

> Forensic psychiatric environments tend to be colloquial organizations with direct care staff made up of local community members trained on the job. The staff develops and perpetuates idiosyncratic cultures with neither benchmarks from other forensic settings nor feedback from the larger profession. The challenges of the work, the relatively low

salaries, and the conflicts with other disciplines are reality-based recruitment and retention problems for both the generalist and the advanced practice forensic psychiatric nurse.

11.5 ONE NURSE'S STORY

One of Colleen Carney Love's earliest vocation-related memories is memorialized by a photograph that hangs on her office bulletin board. She is 7 years old and she is posing in front of the family's Christmas tree, wearing a Nancy Nurse outfit. She is resplendent in nursing cape and cap, holding a medical bag, and grinning from ear to ear. "Nursing has always been in my bones," she says. "The specific calling to nurse the criminally insane, however, came at a much later time in my life."

When asked why she chose the field of forensic psychiatric nursing, Love says:

> As I reflect on this question, I realize that a convergence of factors contributed to my decision to devote my career to care of mentally ill offenders. Probably the most influential catalysts were two of my professors who mentored me in graduate school. In my master's program, in the mid-1980s, I worked with Dr. Kitty Buckwalter on an NIMH Geriatric Mental Health Grant. Kitty showed me how nurses could make a difference in the lives of people who were highly stigmatized and disenfranchised. In my doctoral program, Dr. Patricia Underwood from UCSF emphasized the need for advanced practice nursing in large, public-sector psychiatric facilities. In state hospitals, we are caring for the most mentally ill people on the planet. Our direct-care nursing colleagues are often practicing in professional isolation. This isolation has had crippling effects on the development of forensic psychiatric nursing. The state hospitals are serving more and more people who have both mental illness and criminal backgrounds. I guess I am naturally drawn to areas of high need.

Considering the challenging nature of the work, Love explains that she has leaned heavily on her educational background to better equip her for the rigors of her job:

> My nursing education prepared me well in the following areas: prioritizing, responding to crisis calmly and effectively, and in caring and seeking to understand my patients without judgment. The occupational health faculty I worked for in my doctoral program helped me to understand the hazards of working with and around chronically violent and abusive people relative to the occupational health needs of the staff. It raised my awareness of violence as a poorly understood occupational health hazard to nursing staff in these institutions. Also, my study of nursing history exposed me to great nursing role models who lead various challenging and effective reform movements. In my work and my consulting, I see myself in many ways "nursing the culture" of these large bureaucratic institutions. I seek to create environments that are more humane and supportive both of the recovery of our patients and in the health and professional development of our staff.

However, Love says that no amount of textbook learning or early experiences in doctoral work could have prepared her for the political maneuvering inherent in the field. "I was not prepared for the political challenges in all health care settings, particularly public sector settings," she shares.

> I did not fully appreciate that for nursing to survive in health care settings today, and to advocate for the needs of our staff and our patients, we must have thick skin, be assertive, and be strategic. Right now, the professional turf battles faced by the psychiatric nurse practitioners in my setting are creating a truly toxic environment. This situation and others, such as the midwife class-action battle in Texas, has made it clear to me that nursing must extract itself from the strangle-hold of medicine. The condoned and strategically maintained medical hegemony in health care today is doing a disservice to the consumer and to the taxpayer. Nursing must stop burying itself under the umbrella of the medical model and be able and willing to self-regulate and no longer position ourselves in positions beholden to physicians. We are an autonomous profession with a distinct practice model.

Love says that like most nurses, there is no "average" day, as "every day is really different," she says. On any given day, Love meets with one or more staff members who need debriefing or special training in therapeutic technique, or she might teach a class for orientation or required training. She might look at data on violence or seclusion and restraint use and generate policy change or training from the analysis, and talk to professionals from another state seeking resources or consultation. Her day can be filled with meetings, coaching sessions with nurse practitioners, and sessions with patients for individual or group work. She also is "always advocating for better and safer working conditions for staff." Like other nurses, Love says she maintains a strong sense of purpose about what she does and the contributions she makes daily to the field:

> When I was an ICU nurse I always received lots of positive regard in social settings for my choice of career. Now, in social settings, when I say I work with the criminally insane and sex offenders, I get a much different reaction. The stigma associated with this work is evident to me every day. Nevertheless, I have a deeply held belief that caring well for society's most deviant and outcast members is fundamentally right. I often refer to what I call the "double barrel" stigma associated with this work; that is, criminality and mental illness or caring for the mad and bad. As forensic nurses, we get very little positive regard

> from the general public for our work, yet this is a great social good that we are doing. It's a high moral calling.

In the article she co-authored with Morrison, Love had expressed that forensic psychiatric nursing has a "public relations problem." She refers to the stigma associated with the work as another reason forensic nursing has failed to develop and thrive as it should. She points to work by Goffman that defines stigma as "a spoiled identity." She says that the forensic psychiatric patient, due to the comingling of psychiatric disorder and criminality, is encumbered with this "mad–bad" stigma, which is not only part of the public's perception, as it exists within the correctional environment. "The mentally disordered offender (MDO) is stigmatized among his otherwise socially undesirable prison inmates," Love and Morrison (2002) write. They explain that even among hardened prison cultures, "a moral hierarchy of sorts exists. In most correctional settings, sex offenders, particularly child molesters, are considered inferior and deviant among their peers in prison. Sex offenders often experience sexual abuse and serious assault at the hands of inmates who view them with derision and contempt." Love and Morrison have said that a guilt by association exists, a stigma that spoils the identity of the MDO and rubs off on nurses caring for them. "Nurses working in forensic environments encounter negative reactions to their work from a public that has low tolerance for crime. The status and public appreciation enjoyed by nurses in other settings is not available to forensic psychiatric nurses," they write. "In social settings, forensic psychiatric nurses may be asked with disdain and contempt, 'How can you stand to work there?'" Love and Morrison have reported that some forensic psychiatric nurses do not disclose their place of employment in social settings.

The bad rap that forensic psychiatric nursing gets is sometimes so detrimental that administrators and policymakers in the field start believing their own bad press. "The social stigma also influences knowledge development," Love and Morrison confirm. "As much as we like to think that science is apolitical and unencumbered with subjective bias, it is not." Love says that grants for research about treatment approaches for incarcerated violent sexual predators often take a back seat to more "palatable" studies. Love and Morrison assert, "The mad–bad stigma is likely part of the reason that a limited number of research studies are published relative to the disorders encountered by forensic nurses. The phenomenon of sex offending is particularly lacking in biologically-based evidence." They charge that the best and the brightest biological scientists are not being recruited to find a cure for MDOs, and that there are few, if any, high-profile pharmaceutical companies championing treatments specific to the forensic population. "The effect of stigma on knowledge development and resource allocation becomes readily apparent when examined within the larger social context," they say.

Although many forensic nurses realize their role in the medico-legal community and thus enjoy a sense of justice about their work, Love takes a more philosophical approach:

> I understand that there are various theories of justice. There are two theories of justice I find most relevant to reflect upon in this work. The first theory, referred to as "retributive justice," is based upon the Old Testament eye-for-an-eye way of thinking. The second theory, referred to as "restorative justice," is based upon the New Testament, Buddhist and other faith systems values of forgiveness, compassion, and respect for all humans. Eye-for-an-eye punishment does little to help our patients, aside from preventing them from reoffending by keeping them locked up. The high recidivism rates are evidence that retribution does not provide our patients with the new skills they need to live productive, prosocial lives. It also provides us with little information relative to the cause of antisocial behavior and strategies to prevent it. Restorative justice calls upon us to put more resources into prevention, rather than into building more prisons. It also emphasizes that to best help our patients we need to understand them without judgment, and give them a fresh experience in relationship.

Love is quick to point out that even despite a "Hollywood-ized," forensic-science-saturated popular culture, many laypersons hold a very limited understanding of forensic science in general, and forensic psychiatric practice and treatment in particular. "We forensic mental health nurses have a serious public relations problem," Love says:

> Few people ever set foot in our institutions. The general public's impression of our work comes mainly from Hollywood. Hollywood is not our friend. The exaggerations, sensationalizing, stigmatizing and demonizing that is pervasive in Hollywood films colors the public's impression of our work. We must strive for transparency in practice and be ambassadors of our work to the public. I don't think lawyers, decision-makers, etc. need or would be able to fully understand my work. I don't fully understand theirs nor do I need to. We nurses seem to lament that people don't understand what we do. Sure, the stigma is a significant roadblock to getting funding or furthering the science, but if I am seeking to be understood so that I can be appreciated, I am being naïve. We don't need to be understood, we need to be savvy.

"It is public policy, more so than science or consumer preference, that defines our practice and the populations we serve in the public sector," Love and Morrison write. "While public relations and visibility are important in all areas of nursing, the stigma associated with forensic psychiatric work and the legislative policy that influences practice and public safety, makes assertive public relations particularly important in our field." They add, "Explaining what exactly a nurse does, and explaining what a forensic psychiatric nurse does is difficult. Communicating the effectiveness of our work among ourselves, our colleagues and to our customers (the tax-paying public) is critical." Love clarifies the specific role she plays:

> I don't use the term "medico-legal" and I am not really sure what it means. I do not work "in medicine" nor do I work "in psychiatry." I work in forensic mental health nursing, which I define as the subspecialty of nursing that assists the mental health and legal systems by caring for individuals who have come to the attention of both. Most of my work is focused on the care dimension of this work. My work is embedded in and shaped by complex and rigid social systems. I paraphrase Scott Turrow when I explain that I work in the murkiness that churns under the sharp edges of the law. Insofar as my work—direct patient care—contributes to decisions regarding the interface of my patient's mental condition and his crime, then I suppose that is the forensic cornerstone of my work. I do not, nor do I feel the need to, take a lead role in courtroom testimony regarding risk assessment for release, recommitment hearings or competency evaluations. I know other forensic mental health nurses do not agree with me on this. It is my observation that there are plenty of psychologists and psychiatrists that take on those roles. I do not see those activities as nursing.

In her writings, Love has defined a forensic psychiatric nurse as functioning "as a therapeutic agent, employing the nurse/patient therapeutic alliance and milieu interventions to assist each forensic patient to manage the symptoms of his chronic mental illness until such time as he is able to manage them for himself." She says:

> Our medical colleagues treat the underlying disease state, or biochemical pathology. Nursing, on the other hand, treats the human response to that disease state, which manifests itself in the patient's gross disturbances in thought, behavior and emotion. Forensic psychiatric nursing work is grounded in the thoughtful and purposive establishment and monitoring of the therapeutic alliance within a secure treatment milieu. All interactions with patients have the potential to be therapeutic and interactions that are built upon a solid therapeutic alliance are potentiated.

Love and Morrison say:

> Functioning effectively as a therapeutic agent and establishing and maintaining a therapeutic alliance with forensic patients is a formidable undertaking fraught with potential pitfalls, pathological manipulation and deception. In highly psychopathic patients, forming an alliance in the traditional sense may not be possible or recommended. The interpersonal work in forensic nursing requires finely honed communication skills, advanced preparation in psychodynamic theory and adequate and ongoing self-monitoring and clinical supervision. The extreme character pathology, life long patterns of exploitation and perversion of interpersonal relations, deviant violent impulses and intractable psychotic symptoms encountered in the forensic patient population calls for a constellation of personal characteristics and specialized technical competencies including physical and emotional self protection strategies. Ideally, forensic psychiatric nurses think, train and act like an elite specialty force developed to treat the big leagues of mental illness.

In working as a part of this specialty force, Love says collaborations are key:

> I always say, "the cohesion of the team has to be stronger than the pathology we treat." If my vision came to fruition, my colleagues and I would be more respectful and compassionate toward each other. This forensic care is in a sense spiritual warfare. To overshadow the dark side of human nature surrounding us, we must bring in the light... our higher angels so to speak. The antidote to that which is fundamentally wrong, is the cultivation of that which is fundamentally right.... As nurses, we need to let go of the vestiges of oppressed group behavior, and we need to be able to hold our own at the multidisciplinary table. Advanced education for nursing is critical for nursing leaders. Education is critical because nursing staff tend to be at an educational disadvantage relative to the other disciplines—knowledge is power for nursing. Respect is earned not given; we must earn respect. We also need to be able to use data effectively. Dispel the position power of the medical model that is holding authority over the other disciplines through policy changes and political challenges.

Love has said that forensic psychiatric nurses bear a heavy burden when it comes to all that is expected of them by the public, their colleagues, their employers, their patients—and themselves. "In addition to clinical competencies, forensic psychiatric nurses must have intact ego boundaries, hardiness, insight, receptivity to feedback, self-confidence and a commitment to ongoing professional development," Love and Morrison write:

> The unique and complex ethical issues that arise in practice call for ethical sophistication and the capacity for ethical reflection. Because of their treatment orientation and exposure to patients, forensic psychiatric nurses have the potential to be major forces for change, yet because of limited educational preparation and lack of adequate clinical supervision, are vastly underutilized in this regard. Until nurses can convince the public that it is cost effective and desirable for advance practice nurses to function in public sector agencies, this situation is not likely to change any time soon.

Coupled with gigantic expectations are miniscule resources. "We have a serious nursing shortage in my facility and nationwide," Love confirms:

> The private sector has responded to this problem by improving salary and working conditions. The public sector, with our drawn-out, policy-driven decision-making and economic conservatism, is lagging behind and will likely deal with the nursing shortage with too little, too late. The understaffing is serious and recruitment to the field is difficult for all the issues I have already mentioned. Additionally, not many nursing schools encourage their nurses to work with the criminally insane. Educational programs have really lagged behind and when they do offer forensic nursing programs, they are usually focused on SANE competencies and care of victims.

Love notes that barriers to excellence include poor working conditions and nonsensical regulations. For the future, Love wants to see "better working conditions for nurses, and external regulatory bodies, such as JCAHO and OSHA that are enlightened and rational relative to the unique and challenging work we do."

Love and Morrison explain, "the main unifying forces shaping forensic nursing practice come from external regulatory bodies such as the Joint Commission on Accreditation of Healthcare Organizations and state licensing which have the authority to enforce standards in forensic hospitals." They report that the requirements put forth by JCAHO in particular have forced forensic psychiatric settings to hire additional RNs (rather than relying largely on orderlies, psychiatric technicians, and aides), to use performance improvement principles, to manage seclusion and restraint use conservatively, and to document practice outcomes and staffing by acuity. They comment, "In many cases, these required standards seem unrealistic or only tangentially relevant to forensic psychiatric care while other needed standards are absent. For example, patient violence and behavior management are the top-ranked problems in forensic settings, yet JCAHO and other external regulatory agencies do not require comprehensive violence prevention or behavior management programs." Love recalls a consultation she conducted at an acute forensic psychiatric unit. A staff member had remarked, "JCAHO made us put flowerpots in the day room." She says anecdotes like these "illustrate a fairly widespread perception among direct-care forensic staff that the JCAHO standards are not responsive to the hazards and unique challenges of the forensic environment. In spite of shortcomings encountered whenever standards are enforced widely, JCAHO has been a friend to nursing in forensic settings by emphasizing the importance of nursing care relative to treatment and evaluation of the forensic patient."

The forensic psychiatric patient is one of the most challenging patient populations a nurse can encounter. Love and Morrison (2002) acknowledge:

> Patients who make their way to maximum-security forensic settings are among the most complex, dangerous and refractory to treatment. Severe and persistent mental illness combined with criminality distinguishes the forensic psychiatric patient from psychiatric patients in other involuntary, public sector institutions. The forensic psychiatric patient population presents with a variety of extremely complex clinical phenomena relative to the intermingling of severe mental illness, psychopathy, antisocial characteristics, and other forms of severe character pathology.

Several studies have documented burnout among nurses; Love says she combats professional fatigue by proactively shaping her work environment:

> I strive to diffuse the negative effects of working with and around violent mentally ill by creating a compassionate work environment that overshadows the negativity with therapeutically titrated kindness, offered with skill and sensitivity. We can and should strive to always do better in this area for both staff and patients. This work has significant occupational health hazards. Public sector environments can really grind on staff with its rigidity and emphasis on care of the patients while disregarding the needs of staff. The health of the staff is as important as the health of the patients; I often try to give my colleagues support and validation. Also, I think a personal spiritual practice is critical, as is balance in one's life. The ability to put boundaries on how much emotional energy we devote to work issues, especially after hours, at home is critical. The ability to totally shift gears and restore ourselves with deliberate self care is necessary actually, to maintain competency. This is highly emotional work we are doing and we must keep our emotions in check.

Love and Morrison point to work by Schaefer, who emphasizes the importance of attention to boundaries. "She notes that the nurse works in the patient's living space where boundaries are therefore blurred by the physical setting. Additionally, the patient's life-long patterns of exploitation, intimidation, pathological manipulation and perverted intimacy further stress boundary formation and maintenance," they write. "The structure of the nurse–patient relationship must communicate and maintain the boundaries of the relationship. While forensic settings are technically health care settings, many vestiges of the prison culture infuse the forensic milieu. Violence is a pressing reality, as are suicide, criminal activity and interpersonal boundary problems."

One challenge inherent to the work, Love says, is something she characterizes as the "double agent role," which raises complex issues, she says:

> When we serve the public (protection), the patient (treatment), and the courts (evaluation) there are many inherent dilemmas. There has been a substantive amount of debate regarding custody and care dilemmas. I do not struggle with this in my practice. I understand that prosecution for criminal activity and serving time are natural consequences for rule breaking or exploitation of others. My patients own their own behavior. I do all I can to provide opportunities for behavior change. If a patient is in denial or "precontemplation" and he is unable or unwilling to change, or he relapses, then natural consequences are part of the treatment. We tell them this and try as hard as we can to prevent reoffense and overly custodial environments. In prison, the challenge is no doubt greater relative to the tensions between custody and care.

Love has a short list of grievances that she says policymakers should address. "First, the death penalty has to go. Second, it should be a felony to assault a health care worker. Third, it should be a felony for a sexual violent predator to escape from a hospital. Fourth, nursing ratios should be scientifically based and legislated." In addition to these priorities for the field, Love adds:

> Destigmatizing mental illness would be helpful. Also, pressing for occupational health protections for our staff. Assault is not part of the job for forensic mental health nurses. We need to advocate for the direct-care staff so that their health is considered as important as the health of the patient. Also, we need to advocate for additional training for the direct care staff so they can master the competencies necessary to work effectively with our complex patients.

Despite the challenges, Love says she is buoyed by the moments when she is able to teach and "able to inspire others who are in this field with my vision and my passion... those opportunities feed me. This work has taught me what a privileged life I have had. This work has shown me the extremes of human behavior... that evil and good reside in all of us. That the only difference between myself and my patients is a matter of a few molecules and the presence or absence of love." She adds that she relishes teaching and building relationships with coworkers and with patients, and at times must bear with "bureaucracy that is slow moving, impersonal and at times, completely devoid of rationality."

With an eye toward the future, Love says there is room for growth in the field. "Forensic populations are growing and spilling over into the civil populations," she confirms. "Correctional facilities are being pressured to provide better psychiatric services, so there are lifetimes of growth here, indeed. I imagine as the biological sciences advance, our understanding of social deviance, sex offending, and mental illness will vastly improve; however, unless we become totally robotic, relationships will always be a necessary vehicle for change in our patients." She believes that succeeding generations will be able to carry on this work, but only if nurses engage in due diligence. "We are laying the path for future generations of caregivers by publishing, advancing the biological sciences, creating graduate programs for forensic mental health nursing, and destigmatizing the work as our society continues to evolve morally." Until the torch is passed, Love says she feels "privileged and well prepared both professionally and personally" to continue to advance the field.

For those expressing an interest in forensic psychiatric nursing, Love advises, "Give it a try, but remember, it is not for everyone and there is no shame in that." She adds that this specialty is "highly likely to improve slowly... very slowly." She says that a key to the specialty's success in the future is addressing ongoing myths about forensic nursing. "The misperceptions begin right in our own backyard, where our own profession is not sure what a forensic nurse is. Education and standards specific to each subspecialty of forensic nursing are greatly needed."

When asked what she considers to be the five most important principles of her work, Love makes this list: restorative justice and respect for persons, a commitment to lifelong learning and professional development, the fact that her job is principally a change agent, the fact that violence is not part of the job, and that the cohesion of the team is as important as the pathology treated. She adds that the five best practices relating to her work are these: Cognitive behavioral therapy is essential to assist patients to develop prosocial ways of thinking and behaving; milieu therapy, in which the environment is used to meet the treatment needs of each individual patient while meeting the treatment needs of the patient community; a relationship security program where staff–patient boundaries are monitored and maintained using training, clinical supervision, risk management and harm reduction; a compassionate administrative philosophy that takes the hard edges off the chain-of-command model of management; and emotional intelligence, or knowing how to interpret fear and how to assist staff who work with and around dangerous individuals using emotional intelligence.

11.6 THE HUMAN PSYCHE AND THE FORENSIC PSYCHIATRIC NURSE

As a former psychiatric nurse and 20-year veteran of the FBI, Candice DeLong is an expert in understanding and assessing the human psyche. She says that nurses, especially veteran nurses, are in an excellent position to evaluate a patient's or an offender's state of mind when the individual presents to the health care institution. "I have learned over the years that veteran nurses are so much better at performing their job than younger nurses, because by the time you have been dealing with people for 20 years, you should be able to easily identify individuals under some kind of duress," DeLong says. "Forensic nurses deal with people who are under circumstances that heighten their levels of anxiety and stress, such as those who present at hospital ERs, where there is usually a lot going on in an already chaotic environment." DeLong says the first step a forensic nurse must take is to understand the parameters of the interaction, the purpose of the patient's visit to the ER, and what the specific circumstances of the traumatic event are, when conducting the initial assessment. She adds that forensic nurses must maintain their level of suspicion throughout the process:

> Chances are, when you are dealing with a patient under stress, what you hear them saying is not necessarily what happened. In stressful circumstances, some people deliberately lie, or they minimize their involvement in anything that makes them look bad or suspicious. As a forensic nurse, you must be circumspect about that first interview. It has been my experience that people under duress, whether they are in a law enforcement setting or in a clinical setting, are worked up because they have been victimized in some way. You should not believe everything that you hear, and you should not necessarily believe your own eyes. Just be very scientific and look at the data you are getting. What is the patient really saying? Ask the patient the same question from different angles, and be prepared to accept that the first story that you get from the patient may not be accurate.

DeLong acknowledges that this type of discernment is a skill that is cultivated over years of experience, and might not be something that can be learned from a textbook in nursing school. DeLong recalls her early days at Northwestern University:

> I don't remember being taught these concepts. I was naive when I was a young nurse, but after working the psych wards of the hospital, getting my law enforcement training, and working as an agent for the FBI, I have learned to develop a sharp intuition. I can tell you from experience that it is really hard for nurses to understand that people do lie. They deliberately mislead you and I think that's hard for nurses to accept. "After all," they say, "Why would someone lie to me? I am here to help them." Well, patients and suspects do lie, of course, and not just necessarily because they may have something to hide. Nurses must be able to ferret out the truth, find the motivations behind the actions. Nurses must keep an open mind that maybe they need to verify what they are getting from their patients. If you can, you need to talk to other sources, other witnesses. You are not there as the patient's advocate if you are a forensic clinician. You are there to gather evidence and preserve and document it. I think it is important for nurses to remember, especially in a forensic setting, that the patient is going to say things to him or her that are critical to document.

DeLong emphasizes that a patient's utterances are an important form of evidence that must be documented accurately in the medical record:

> The very first things that people say after trauma—whether it's a rape, or being thrown out of a car or being shot—are very, very important to listen to and write down, including the time and exactly what they said. Don't put your own spin on it. If the patient said, "That bastard shot me," then write, "The patient said, 'that bastard shot me.'" Make sure it's in quotes so it can't be challenged later. You never know what a patient's going to say, and in law enforcement we call it the excited utterance. An excited utterance is given weight in law enforcement matters because it is generally believed that when people are excited, what they say probably has validity. We've all heard that one's first gut reaction is probably right, but it might not be. We've all been fooled before, so it's essential to keep an open mind.

When it comes to forensic documentation, DeLong says nurses shouldn't tarry:

> Don't write out your nursing notes the next day. Pick up a pen and put it to paper as soon as possible. Your first instincts are just that. It is entirely possible that what you are seeing or hearing in the clinical setting, you can take on face value; however, bear in mind that you may be seeing something else masked by inappropriate responses brought on by stress. I have interviewed rape victims who have giggled throughout the entire interview. Without the proper training, you'd think, what is this, some kind of a joke? What is so funny? The truth is, many people have nervous laughs or they demonstrate behavior that is not in keeping with the nature of the trauma. I'll say it again—it's critical to keep an open mind about what you see and what you hear.

DeLong recalls cases in which victims described seemingly implausible scenarios, but upon more thorough consideration and interpretation, investigators were able to determine a factual basis for the allegations. "I don't think nurses are trained in deception, and they should be," DeLong asserts:

> It's not just deception, either. Nurses should be familiar with the ways in which different patient populations express themselves. For example, the older patient under stress is going to be the least reliable. And in the cases of very young victims, a child doesn't have the worldly experience to explain what happened to her in adult terms. Children may say things that sound far out, so far out, in fact, that the nurse or the investigator might be tempted to say, "This kid is making this up," or that the trauma simply couldn't have happened the way the child is describing it. Further questioning is required because the child is simply explaining what happened in his or her own terms according to what their limited experience is.

Look at what some of the children in the McMartin preschool case said, a case which I believe shouldn't have been dismissed. Some of the kids were saying they were on an airplane when they were molested. When the jurors heard that, they thought it was ridiculous. Well, let's look at this a little closer. Upon further questioning, you might discover that at the preschool, the kids played a game called "airplane." They simply put their seats together like airplane seating, and pretended they were on a plane. This is a good example of never automatically dismissing something.

If an elderly woman says, "I was raped by a werewolf," you might be tempted to roll your eyes and think, "I'd better get the shrink involved in this case." The 80-year-old victim may not have been dreaming or hallucinating... maybe some really hairy guy with a beard raped her when she wasn't wearing her glasses, so the take-home lesson here is, absolutely everything requires further questioning and examination.

DeLong acknowledges that there can be friction between law enforcement and nurses when it comes to believing a patient or suspect who presents to the ER for medical care. Having been on both sides of the argument, DeLong explains that cops and nurses can learn from each other:

When it comes to the initial interview and assessment, I think it would be a good idea for cops to learn how the nurses think, and vice versa. Then there are the stereotypes. Nurses tend to think that the patrol officers and other first responders don't know anything, and that they don't have as good of an education as the nurse does. And many cops see nurses as bleeding hearts—that's why they went into nursing, after all. In my dealings with cops as a nurse, I was straightforward and direct, which has always been my style. In the back of my mind I was always thinking, "You are dealing with someone who has a different job to do and a different agenda than I do, and he's not the enemy... we need to be together on this."

DeLong says nurses have been trained to trust their patients, whereas cops have been indoctrinated in offenders' evasion and deception strategies. "Cops know things about human nature that some nurses don't," she says:

I think that some nurses tend to be naive in thinking that people—their patients especially—always tell the truth. Because of that, cops may roll their eyes as soon as nurses leave the room. Cops really do see many more instances of people lying, minimizing their own involvement to make them look good, and leaving out half of a story when they are saying, "Hey, this guy just came up to me on the street and shot me." I'm not saying that cops aren't naive too, regarding medical issues, but frankly, it's my impression that most nurses can have 10, 15, 20 years of experience, but if they are not used to dealing with people who lie, they can be fooled. I think that nurses see people who also lie by omission, such as when they purposely leave out a very important fact. For example, when a person reports that she was raped and says, "I don't know how this happened," but neglects to tell you that she was out in the yard sunbathing naked because they think that will make them look bad. To my way of thinking, it's not a lie, but you might as well lie to me to leave something important like that out of the story. Nurses just need to be aware that cops are suspicious of human behavior for a reason; they have been exposed to a lot of it. So nurses should keep an open mind when they are dealing with cops on a case. Yes, nurses know the medical stuff probably better than cops do, but cops also might know a thing or two in that area, and they may very well know people better than nurses do. It's a give-and-take thing.

When I was a psych nurse, the concept of forensic nursing didn't exist. If you were to put those two words together somebody would have said, "What is that?" But I did periodically work with police, because many times, they would bring someone into the psych unit, and I also worked ER, where you see forensic cases brought in. I never questioned my right to be there with forensic patients; I think I probably felt more of a proprietary feeling toward my patients than anyone else did; after all, I am spending eight hours a day with the patient, or I am the one with the patient on the gurney who's bleeding and I'm trying to stop the gushing. I am the one trying to assist the doctor in inserting the chest tube. But I always liked working with police. I found them to be colorful and fun, but looking back in those days, it would have been unlikely for me to listen to what a patient said with an open mind insofar as they might not be telling the whole story. That's something that comes with age... well, hopefully it still does. I can see where a nurse who doesn't interview a lot of perpetrators would have those feelings of uncertainty. You really will not be particularly effective in your job and might make very serious mistakes if you can't put those feelings in check. You might be talking to a suspect and you cannot prejudge. There are a few innocent people in prisons, yes, but I also have a tendency to assume that most suspects rarely confess, so they are probably guilty of what they are questioned about—but you have to keep an open mind with them as you do with the victim.

DeLong tackles the related issues of boundaries without apology:

It's the same reason that you don't say to your psych patient, "Hey, when you get out, let's go to dinner." There has to be a professional distance and objectivity or you will not be a good psych nurse or forensic nurse. You can't establish a personal relationship with the victim or the suspect, and you can't take sides. But I understand nurses' temptation to do so. I used to hate it when drunks would be brought into the ER; we would let them sit on a gurney and bleed, thinking to ourselves, "We have to work on the person you hit first." That's a pretty common feeling among ER personnel. Or when a shooter is brought in bleeding and his victim is bleeding, too. You always take care of the victim first. As nurses, we have to make all kinds of split-second judgments and decisions, right or wrong. And you have to make decisions about what the cops are telling you, too.

It all comes down to a nurse's control of her thoughts and opinions. Is it your goal, in interviewing a suspect during medical care, to get the true story or to get a story that you can put down on paper and give to the police? You are not going to get the true story if you prejudge and if you are standing there with a smirk on your face and your arms folded across your chest—as if to say, "This guy has nothing to say that I want to hear." Plus, if the suspect already believes he is guilty, he already believes you probably think he is, too. The goal is to get a solid interview. Even if he sits there and lies to you, that's great, you are going to be recording it all. You could end up testifying in court, and that lie that he is telling you, you will give your documentation to the cops and they may be able to prove that he was lying. Your goal is to get a good interview, and you will not get it if you are giving off signals that you don't believe a word the person says. What I just said may counter what I said previously, but it's about balancing one's suspicions.

Although treating the suspect with clinical respect, DeLong also cautions nurses about crossing the line by identifying too closely with the victim:

People enter various vocations for personal reasons, and sometimes those reasons may not be very good ones. If you are getting into the field because you were raped, forensic nursing may not be the best field for you to be in. Some people think it takes one to know one; in the field of alcohol and drug rehabilitation, half of any staff are recovering from alcohol or drug dependency themselves. They can be very effective in this role, as you can't kid a kidder, and the patients won't be able to scam them. They are not naive, as they have been there, done that. But I think recovery from alcohol and drug abuse is not the same as being traumatized at the hands of someone who has put you in fear of your life, which most rape victims are. Many victims experience rape trauma, and suffer from post-traumatic stress syndrome; to then enter a field where you are dealing with rape victims on a regular basis... I'm not so sure that is such a good idea. I guess it depends on the individual's capacity to be professional at all times. It would seem to me there would be better vocations to enter than one in which I would encounter other victims of the same trauma daily. My fear is that these forensic nurses might have a tendency to believe everything a patient is telling them, more so than a forensic nurse who has not been victimized. And objectivity is absolutely crucial in everything health care providers do.

11.7 VICTIMOLOGY AND PROFILING: IS IT IN A FORENSIC NURSE'S PURVIEW?

There is some divided thought on whether or not a forensic nurse should engage in any degree of criminal profiling or victimology when working with the patient or the suspect in a forensic case. Some nurses say it is important to be aware of the basics of profiling criminal offenders because this knowledge facilitates the nurse's interview and forensic evidence collection. An understanding of the offender's motives could frequently dictate where on the victim's body the nurse examiner might swab for biological evidence.

11.7.1 PROFILING SEX OFFENDERS

Turvey (1995) states, "To date, no universally accepted typology for violent serial offenders exists. There is no common language that both the law enforcement community and the mental health community use to describe violent criminal behavior, or to discuss motive and means." He says that even the best classification efforts, produced by such groups of motivated and respected individuals as the National Center for the Analysis of Violent Crime, have yet to be widely accepted because opinions about the criminal mind differ so widely. He adds, "The progeny of this unhappy relationship between law enforcement and mental health is a lack of mutual understanding and discarded professional respect on both sides." He observes that not enough mental health professionals have been to a crime scene, and too few investigators have studied the principles of criminal psychology and human behavior. "Each could greatly benefit from the experiences of the other. More importantly, the successful investigation of a violent serial offender often takes skills from both disciplines."

Turvey explains that, "The science and art of profiling crime scenes, and subsequently offenders, from physical and psychological evidence is key to the investigation of a violent serial sex crime for which there is no known perpetrator." Turvey points to a profiling method based on Locard's Principle of Exchange: Anyone who enters the scene both takes something of the scene with them and leaves something of themselves behind. "However, profiling goes beyond a scientific reconstruction of a crime scene. The unintended psychological ramifications of Locard's Principle are powerful, but often ignored by even the most seasoned investigator. It has been demonstrated that what can be recovered at a crime scene, utilizing basic principles of psychology applied to the physical evidence, is an impression of the man who committed the crime."

Turvey outlines some general concepts and guidelines to assist the investigator of violent serial sex crimes in profiling and in mentally navigating the inefficient coexistence between mental health and law enforcement. He says the foundation of working up the profile of a violent serial sex offender is the crime scene, what he describes as "a living document of the offender's actions, and it is the basis for much of the objective behavioral interpretation." He adds that victimology provides objective and subjective interpretation, but is not less valuable. "It is critical to preserve the crime scene and then process it, documenting the physical evidence and being attentive to the smallest detail. Any recovered physical evidence is grist for profiling."

Turvey explains that profiling tends to rely on varied offender typologies, but says these can be flawed due to perspective. "The offender is described in terms that express the investigator's understanding of the motivation behind the offender's behavior," he explains. "This can be very subjective and may be misleading to an investigative effort to understand an offender and link him to another crime. Many investigators... start from possible subjective motives, then pick and choose offender behaviors to explain their motive theories. That is backwards. Profiling does not mean coming up with a theory and then inserting an offender as best he fits." Turvey says that profiling allows the physical evidence to tell an investigator what behaviors occurred; the investigator can then consider what was intended by those behaviors. Turvey says it is essential for investigators and examiners to "think as offenders think." He adds:

> The most useful profile of a violent serial offender should include objective terms that best describe an offender's perspective and behavior towards the scene and towards the victim. Start first by thinking about what it is that they did at the scene. Describe offenders first by their behaviors. Then begin asking what desires those behaviors satisfy. Remember, violent serial sex offenders, in general, do not commit their crimes by accident. They are in possession, however elusive, of their own reasons for the behavior they act out with a victim.

Turvey alludes to the seminal work of Ann Wolbert Burgess, DNSc, RN, CS, FAAN, which discusses organized and disorganized crime scenes left by sexual killers, and demonstrates evidence of the frequency of certain offender behaviors over time. Burgess and colleagues showed evidence from their population of violent sexual offenders that several characteristic offender behaviors were frequent. Most notably consistent at a high rate of frequency were (reported in more than 80 percent of the sex offender population in the study): compulsive, chronic masturbation; constant daydreaming; social isolation; more likely to force fellatio and anal intercourse on their victims (also showing a decrease in the frequency of vaginal intercourse over time); and average to superior intelligence, with 15 percent of offenders in the very superior range. The first three behaviors were reported to be consistent from childhood to adulthood, according to Turvey.

Warren, Reboussin, Hazelwood, and Wright (1991) generated serial sex offender research supporting the theory that the increase of force and sadism at each progressive crime scene is correlated positively with offenders who have more victims over a shorter period of time. Earlier research by Hazelwood and colleagues (1989) on the same population of offenders indicated that increased offender sexual satisfaction was positively correlated with victim resistance and an increased duration of the crime. That data shows that the mean average duration of an offense increased from 36 minutes to 94 minutes when the victim resisted. Turvey writes:

> The bottom line here for the investigator of violent serial sex offenders is this: violent serial sex offenders have the most number of victims, over the shortest periods of time, and victim resistance evokes offender sexual arousal and subsequently offense duration is increased. Again, violent serial offenders commit more offenses in less time, and spend more time at the scene with the victim when the victim resists, because sexual arousal is increased. In such cases of victim resistance and increased arousal, it is noted that intercourse was delayed significantly by the offender.

11.8 PSYCHIATRIC NURSING IN THE CORRECTIONAL SETTING

A disheveled, agitated 39-year-old man, dressed in blood-soaked clothing, presents to the ED, escorted by police officers who report he allegedly murdered his wife by stabbing her repeatedly. While the suspect is treated for minor injuries sustained during a struggle, the nurse observes the man gesturing and shouting at an unseen person to "leave him alone." He is combative and insistent that for weeks, this "person" has been telling him to kill his wife. A case such as this presents with numerous forensic aspects for clinical and mental health care providers, and is typical of the kinds of cases that nurses working in correctional facilities see on a regular basis. Judith D. Johnson, RN, MN, program director of University of California Davis, Department of Psychiatry, Jail Psychiatric Services, in Sacramento, California, writes, "The nurse's ability to perform mental health assessments and make critical decisions are key factors for intervening in these challenging, complex cases" (Johnson & Laffa, 2004).

Teplin (1990) reported that a little more than 6 percent of jail detainees have a severe mental disorder, including major depression, mania, or schizophrenia, and other researchers have estimated that 5 percent to 20 percent of incarcerated individuals are mentally ill. The census of jails and prisons is increasing, as is the number of incarcerated mentally ill. Between 1993 and 1999, the population in jails in the United States increased from 459,804 to 605,943, according to the U.S. Department of Justice, Bureau of Justice Statistics (Harrison & Beck, 2003). The number of people in prisons has also increased. Approximately 1.2 million people were in custody in state and federal prisons at the end of 1997, which represents an increase of almost 434,000 since 1990. Subsequently, correctional facilities struggle with issues of overcrowding and understaffing, a limited number of medical and psychiatric resources, and physical space restrictions. In response, Johnson says, "mental health services have been expanding to meet the needs of this growing population. This expansion provides an opportunity for psychiatric nurses to move from community-based mental health to correctional mental health." These environments share similarities, but their differences create unique challenges, Johnson adds. Because correctional mental health programs focus on identification and treatment of the mentally ill, and continuity of psychiatric treatment, the psychiatric nurse can play a pivotal role in these programs. Roles can be varied; the psychiatric nurse can serve as a staff nurse in an inpatient unit, providing psychiatric nursing care to inmates, or act as an outpatient nurse, providing evaluations, counseling, or crisis intervention to inmates in the general population. The psychiatric nurse's role can vary depending on the program's size and scope of services in proportion to the incarcerated population, funding issues, court mandates, and other variables. For example, some nurses might be employed full time by a larger correctional facility, whereas smaller institutions might contract for part-time work through the local psychiatric hospital. "Differences in the scopes of services provided at each correctional facility vary according to human and financial resources, state regulations, and court mandates. Despite differences in services, the patient/inmate has certain rights under the Constitution and through state regulation or constitution," Johnson says. The most important of these rights, she asserts, is access to care. "Therefore, screening and triage of referrals, timely response, assessment, and psychiatrist availability and accessibility are critical components in any correctional psychiatric program."

When working in a correctional facility, the psychiatric nurse's duties are as varied as the institution itself. The nurse might interact daily with inmates and correctional staff when providing mental health care that is imperative to the functionality of the facility. A psychiatric nurse can provide staff in-services on topics such as identification of the mentally ill, suicide prevention, psychotropic medications, and management of the mentally ill in the correctional environment. The nurse will also engage in case management. "Continuation of any treatment and medication from jail and transition to the community-based treatment in a swift manner is critical to success," Johnson observes. She adds that nurses are vital members of the interdisciplinary team and "play significant roles in the assessment, planning, implementation, and evaluation of the case management plan to best meet the needs of patients/inmates."

A key responsibility of the psychiatric nurse is to provide assessment in a challenging environment. "When interviewing a combative or potentially dangerous person, custody staff must stand by, which often influences the amount of information the patient/inmate is willing to provide," Johnson cautions. "Nurses have to become skillful in engaging the patient/inmate and building a trusting relationship quickly." Although nurses should know the patient/inmate's arrest charges, Johnson says nurses should not ask questions specific to the nature of the charges or circumstances of the crime, especially of an unsentenced individual; disclosure of this information could then involve nurses in the legal system.

Throughout the assessment, Johnson says, the psychiatric nurse collects data through observations of verbal and nonverbal behaviors and through learned interactive and interviewing skills, based on a broad bio-psychosocial knowledge base. "The purpose of the assessment is to gather enough data to formulate a plan of care," she explains. A mental health assessment consists of the psychosocial assessment and the mental status examination. The psychosocial assessment should include demographic information, the presenting problem and nature of the referral, problem chronology, medical information, substance-abuse history, and the socioeconomic factors affecting the patient. Johnson suggests that arrest and incarceration information can give nurses a sense of the person's "criminal sophistication" and whether the inmate/patient "knows the system." She adds that the nature of the criminal charges, such as the severity of charges and notoriety of the case, may indicate the potential for violence, antisocial tendencies, or the degree of stress the person is facing, assessment for suicidal and homicidal thoughts, and the general level of functioning. During the mental status examination, Johnson says, "The nurse gathers data through observation and interview. The mental status examination consists of assessing appearance, behavior and activity, attitude, speech, mood and affect, perceptions, thoughts, sensorium and cognition, judgment, insight, and reliability." The nurse should also note the individual's appearance and hygiene, body language, movements, and facial expressions, as well as the patient's attitude and affect, and thought form and content, defined in descriptive terms.

Echoing the thoughts of Candice DeLong, Johnson writes, "Patients are not always reliable in the general community. Unreliability is even more common in the correctional setting where an accurate medical history is so important. An accurate history is essential for medical staff to know how to treat a person, what preexisting conditions exist, what to expect in terms of the patient/inmate's baseline, and how to avoid being manipulated or inadvertently making changes in a treatment plan based on erroneous information." She adds that numerous factors influence individuals' reliability. "At times, patient/inmates may be afraid that what they say may be used against them. Other times, they may possess character traits in which dishonesty is used as a coping or survival skill." Critical to assessment, Johnson adds, is the collection of information about the patient/inmates' mental health and level of functioning from various sources, including relatives, prior treatment agencies and medical staff, and law enforcement officers. Another important source of information is old medical or mental health records the correctional facility has onsite and at other agencies. "The nurse may also collect information on the patient's current behavior from officers and inmate peers," Johnson writes. "This is often helpful in determining how the patient/inmate has been functioning and may help in identifying needs not always apparent in the interview."

Psychiatric nurses in the correctional setting face additional challenges such as substance abuse, suicide, and malingering among the patient population. According to the National Institute of Justice, Arrestee Drug Abuse Monitoring Program, more than 50 percent of adult male arrestees tested positive for at least one drug, and the median rate for use of any drug among female adult arrestees was 67 percent in 1999. "Psychiatric nurses in correctional settings must have a solid foundation in substance abuse and withdrawal in order to assess patient/inmates accurately and act swiftly to obtain urgent medical intervention if withdrawal symptoms are suspected," Johnson urges. "Acute drug or alcohol withdrawal should be considered in any patient/inmate exhibiting bizarre behavior or a change in mental status during the initial two weeks of incarceration." The nurse should also be aware of the high rates of infectious diseases, such as hepatitis and AIDS, associated with intravenous drug use. Malingering, or the feigning of mental illness, is a common mental health manifestation among the incarcerated. "In the correctional setting, inmates may act 'crazy' because they are having problems with custody staff or peers and want to change their housing location," Johnson writes. "Sometimes, they simply want to talk to someone or want emotional support. A long-term secondary gain may be that inmates believe that a psychiatric diagnosis will somehow help their court process. Therefore, a thorough assessment is critical." Johnson adds, "When a nurse suspects that an inmate is malingering, a judgment may be made that the inmate is 'faking.' The nurse may feel that he or she is being used, and this arouses angers and feelings of exploitation. The nurse may lose objectivity." To maintain objectivity, Johnson advises that the nurse should discuss these kinds of cases with colleagues or supervisors and employ self-reflection strategies with which to monitor emotional responses to avoid labeling. "The nurse should refocus inmates on coping skills with the intended goal of assisting them to learn healthier, more appropriate ways of coping."

Inmate suicide is an important issue facing psychiatric nurses in the correctional setting. Hayes (1995) reported suicide rates among the incarcerated population as being 20.6 suicides per 100,000 in the prison population, and 107 suicides per 100,000 in the jail population; the suicide rate among the general public was 12.2 suicides per 100,000. "Incarcerated people often experience the correctional setting as insensitive and unresponsive to their needs," Johnson writes. "Many inmates verbalize feelings of overwhelming stress, hopelessness, and fear of the unknown. The life they knew before incarceration may be changed forever." Johnson adds that inmates with adequate coping skills before being incarcerated will adapt, but "are at risk when additional stressors during or as a result of their incarceration are experienced."

Nurses should conduct a thorough suicide assessment, including the following components: historical, environmental, and geographic factors; lethality of suicidal thinking; psychological factors such as psychiatric disorders, evaluation of risk potential, and reporting of risk by documenting the assessment in a legally defensible way; developing a treatment plan; and seeking peer consultation. More than in any other clinical setting, psychiatric nurses in the correctional environment must possess a heightened awareness of institutional safety protocol and interventions. "Facilities should have a suicide prevention plan that includes inmate screening, observation and treatment for suicidal inmates, humanistic approach, training for correctional staff, and physical plant considerations," Johnson writes, adding that suicide prevention plans are often incorporated into the overall facility safety measures to reduce contraband, provide safety-proof cells, limit dangerous objects carried by staff, and restrict objects possessed by inmates. "The nurse's goal in interacting with the suicidal patient/inmate is to provide ongoing suicide assessment and to assist that person to develop improved coping skills by teaching stress management techniques and discussing ways to adapt to the general population." Johnson adds, "Correctional psychiatric nursing is a challenging field. Psychiatric nurses in correctional settings face exciting cases that require strong assessment skills, decision-making abilities, crisis-intervention acumen, and a solid psychiatric nursing foundation. These nurses play critical roles in the treatment team and often find advocating for the mentally ill in the complex world of corrections professionally satisfying and rewarding."

11.9 NURSES AND CORRECTIONAL OFFICERS: AN INTERDISCIPLINARY APPROACH

Correctional nursing, like any other discipline of nursing, requires the nurse to work as part of an interdisciplinary team. In a correctional facility, forensic nurses must work with correctional officers. In *Correctional Officers as Members of a Psychiatric Team,* author Glen Brown, associate warden of the Regional Reception and Assessment Centre in Abbotsford, British Columbia, examines the integration of correctional officers as members of an interdisciplinary team in a secure forensic psychiatric environment in Canada.

"Forensic practice provides for the treatment of mentally disordered patients who are deemed to be dangerous, or violent, or to have criminal propensities," Brown writes. "The delivery of forensic psychiatric treatment is at the interface of the mental health and criminal justice systems. Services are delivered across a continuum of care and a continuum of risk." He adds, "Improved understanding of the integration of correctional staff into health care teams within a secure forensic psychiatric environment could contribute to the better delivery of psychiatric services, respect for the dignity of patients, and ultimately, to the reduction of risk to the public." Brown explains that correctional officers and nurses interact in both treatment and operational domains. Forensic psychiatric nurses are responsible for the 24/7 management and care of patients, whereas correctional officers interface with other treatment professionals and staff members on the treatment team. Brown writes, "The responsibilities of psychiatric nurses and correctional officers overlap and are generalist in nature in order to respond to the variety of needs that the patients present, and the variety of tasks which must be performed in the ongoing operation of the unit." Mutual responsibilities include unit supervision, meal line supervision, delivering meals, conducting rounds and counts, responding to incidents, and responding to patient requests. "Nurses obviously have exclusive responsibility for certain medical functions such as the administration of medication. Correctional officers are more exclusively responsible for searching, counting, any pre-planned use of force. However, nursing duties do overlap into the custodial domain more extensively and more readily than correctional officer duties extend into the nursing realm," Brown adds.

Although correctional officers are more likely to discipline patients/prisoners, Brown says, nurses can mandate "consequences for patients, particularly in response to persistently poor behavior and abusive conduct and language toward staff." He states that many nurses are prepared to physically intervene with patients, although all staff members are instructed to respond to an incident requiring immediate physical intervention or restraint.

"Psychiatric nurses and correctional officers overlap their efforts in the areas of patient supervision and support. This helps concentrate both the medical and supervisory effort, especially for those patients exhibiting more severe behavioral or psychiatric difficulties," Brown adds. This arrangement also facilitates greater flexibility in response to changing patient needs and workloads and also can balance the team's workload. Brown says it is his observation that nurses and correctional staff members are "comfortable interacting with and working with each other," and points to Schein (1992), who says that every group must work out its rules for peer relationships, openness, and intimacy. "The informal working relationship between correctional officers with nurses is closer than with correctional officers and other treatment staff," Brown says, adding, "This more intimate relationship is supported by shift work, proximity, increased opportunity for casual conversation, as well as working and solving problems together." Brown addresses the dichotomy between care and custody by noting that, "Even without correctional officers secure forensic psychiatric environments are inherently custodial." He refers to Baxter who interviewed a number of forensic nurses and discovered that there was a blurring of the nursing role, with nurses sometimes being mistaken for prison officers, and security issues often outweighing therapeutic ones. Brown comments, "The custodial environment is not defined only by security hardware, security systems and security staff... patient management includes the physical structure, security infrastructure, staff intervention, communication, movement control, formal discipline, assessment, observation, correctional planning and treatment planning. Physical space, routine, rules, treatment and intervention all provide for a comprehensive behavioral envelope for each patient." Brown says that the closer the working relationship of correctional officers with clinical personnel, the more likely there will be integration of treatment and correctional efforts.

In his interaction with and observation of nurses and correctional officers, he reports, "None of the staff interviewed saw security and treatment goals as necessarily being in conflict. All staff agreed that they wanted to create a safe environment which supported effective treatment." Brown says that one correctional officer noted, "Some specific nurses are 99 percent treatment driven, and have no concern for security. Conversely, there are some officers who are totally security focused. Overall, however, there is very little conflict between the mandates for care and custody."

11.10 CORRECTIONS NURSING

As the number of incarcerated individuals in the United States grows, there will be increased opportunities for forensic nurses to work in federal, state, and county correctional facilities. As violence within these institutions escalates, forensic correctional nurses are present to document and treat injury or alleged abuse.

11.10.1 The Scope of the Incarcerated Population

The Human Rights Watch report, *No Escape: Male Rape in U.S. Prisons* (Mariner, 2001), characterizes the U.S. inmate population as "enormous," in both absolute numbers, in the proportion of U.S. residents behind bars, and in comparison with global figures. With a nationwide incarcerated population of 2 million adults, or roughly one in every 140 persons, the rate of incarceration in the United States is about 727 prisoners per 100,000 residents. The report asserts, "These high figures do not represent long-standing patterns of incarceration, but instead are the consequence of radical changes in criminal justice policies over the past two decades." The report says that incarceration rates began to climb in the mid-1970s, with the growth rate accelerating in the 1980s and particularly the 1990s. In 1985, the inmate population stood at three quarters of a million; by 1990 it was more than 1.1 million. Since that time, on average, the inmate population has grown 6.5 percent annually, with the federal prison population growing at an even faster rate than that of the states. "These increases," the report says, "reflect an important overall shift in state and federal sentencing rules. In particular, they are indicative of a general trend toward longer prison terms, more stringent parole policies, mandatory minimum sentences and, most recently, three-strikes laws." Nearly $40 billion annually is spent on prisons and jails, making corrections one of the largest single items on many states' budgets, above their spending on higher education or child care. The report states, "Overcrowded and understaffed, filled with too many idle prisoners facing long terms of incarceration, many U.S. penal facilities are rife with extortion, violence, and other abuses . . . a small minority of correctional staff physically abuse inmates; many more are simply indifferent to abuses that inmates inflict on each other."

According to the report, violence is no respecter of persons; it can be perpetrated by correctional staff as well as by prisoners. There are reports of prison guards beating, raping, and shooting inmates. For example, a March 1999 federal court decision concluded that the frequency of "wholly unnecessary physical aggression" perpetrated by guards in Texas prisons reflected a "culture of sadistic and malicious violence" found there. Interprisoner violence, extortion, harassment, and other abuse is common; studies have found that as many as 70 percent of inmates are assaulted by other inmates each year. In 1998, 79 inmates were killed and many thousands more were injured so severely that they required medical attention. Abuses against inmates, whether committed by other prisoners or by guards, are rarely prosecuted or prosecuted effectively, according to Human Rights Watch. Although overall figures are lacking, the group says it is evident that criminal charges are brought only in the most egregious cases. In December 2000, the *Prison Journal* published a study based on a survey of inmates in seven men's prison facilities in four states. The results showed that 21 percent of the inmates had experienced at least one episode of pressured or forced sexual contact since being incarcerated, and at least 7 percent had been raped in their facility. A 1996 study of the Nebraska prison system produced similar findings, with 22 percent of male inmates reporting that they had been pressured or forced to have sexual contact against their will while incarcerated. Of these, over 50 percent had submitted to forced anal sex at least once. Extrapolating these findings to the national level gives a total of at least 140,000 inmates who have been raped, Human Rights Watch states.

11.10.2 Origins of Correctional Nursing

"Nursing's formal role in correctional health care emerged from a flurry of litigation, a series of prison uprisings, and a landmark U.S. Supreme Court decision in the 1970s," explains Catherine Duddy Sloan (2003), RN, MS, in "Legal Origins and Issues Behind Correctional Nursing." Sloan adds, "Before the 1970s, comprehensive nursing was nonexistent in many adult correctional facilities. Instead, matrons, corrections officers, and even inmates doled out medical care in dingy, unsanitary, and in most cases, deplorable conditions." However, subsequent legislation fueled health care reform in both prison and jail settings that eventually led to the official recognition of correctional nursing as a specialty by professional nursing organizations, such as the ANA. According to the 1995 *Scope and Standards of Nursing Practice in Correctional Facilities*, throughout most of its history, the U.S. corrections system had little or no medical care available to inmates, as the courts avoided interfering in the administration and operation of correctional facilities. The document states:

> This gave correctional administrators enormous freedom with little regulation or accountability imposed on daily operations. Public interest was minimal and government agencies saw no reason to pour tax money into the prison system. The lack of oversight generated by this philosophy allowed serious abuses to occur behind the walls of correctional institutions. The civil rights movement in the 1960s focused public attention on reform and the improvement of conditions for the less fortunate. The inevitable scrutiny of conditions and practices in correctional facilities forced the American judicial system to begin to respond to inmate claims.

In 1976, the U.S. Supreme Court established a constitutional standard for inmate health care in the Texas case of *Estelle v. Gamble*. Gamble, an inmate, claimed that prison officials inflicted undue suffering on him when they failed to provide adequate care for an injury sustained in prison. The court ruled that "deliberate indifference to serious medical needs constitutes cruel and unusual punishment, which is prohibited by the Eighth Amendment to the United States Constitution. The indifference does not have to be intended maliciously to count as deliberate." The decision led to several reforms in inmate litigation that included the following list of inmate rights related to health care:

- The right to access care
- The right to professional judgment
- The right to care that is ordered
- The right to informed consent
- The right to refuse treatment
- The right to medical confidentiality

Federal enforcement of these rights forced correctional agencies to restructure their inmate health care systems. During the years since the *Estelle v. Gamble* decision, the development of case law and national standards on correctional health care have affirmed that prisoners had a right to be free of "deliberate indifference to their serious health care needs."

11.10.3 The Population Served

According to the Sourcebook of Criminal Justice Statistics, in 2002, 6.7 million people were mandated to some form of correctional supervision in more than 7,500 adult and juvenile correctional facilities in the United States. The adult incarcerated population is about 2 million, or approximately one out of every 32 adults (or 3.1 percent of all U.S. adult residents). An estimated 106,000 juveniles are incarcerated in residential facilities. After dramatic increases in the 1980s and 1990s, the incarceration rate has leveled off at a 3.6 percent increase per year. An additional challenge to health care providers working in correctional facilities is that the current generation of inmates is generally older, sicker, and remains imprisoned longer when compared to the inmates of 20 years ago. Inmates typically come from socioeconomic groups at high risk for poor health and have not had access to regular medical care or proper treatment for medical conditions. They also have a disproportionately greater number of chronic illnesses and infectious diseases than the nonincarcerated population. Additionally, the incidence of AIDS in correctional facilities is substantially higher than in the population at large due to an overrepresentation of those with a history of high-risk behaviors. According to the CDC, in 1997, approximately 17 percent of all persons with HIV had been released from corrections facilities. As of 2001, state and federal prisoners known to be positive for HIV and confirmed AIDS cases totaled 24,147 (21,268 male and 2,265 female), according to the Sourcebook of Criminal Justice Statistics (2002). Other infectious diseases are a threat to the incarcerated population. An estimated 35 percent of all active tuberculosis cases in 1996 passed through the U.S. correctional system. In 2002, the National Commission on Correctional Health Care (NCCHC) identified the prevalence of active TB among inmates as between four and 17 times greater than among the total U.S. population. The NCCHC also estimates that hepatitis C has infected an estimated 3.9 million Americans. The most common form of transmission is through intravenous drug use, and approximately 83 percent of the nation's drug users are incarcerated at some time. Research indicates that 80 percent of inmates have a history of substance abuse. Advances in medical science, longer prison terms, mandatory sentences, and more restrictive policies are keeping inmates in prison longer with lower chances of parole, thereby resulting in a much older population. Anno, Graham, Lawrence, and Shansky (2004) found that from 1992 to 2001, the number of state and federal inmates age 50 and older increased from 41,586 to 113,358, an increase of 172.6 percent. As of 2001, inmates age 50 and older represented 7.9 percent of the prison population. Inmates suffer from age-related conditions earlier in life, and histories of poor nutrition, lack of preventive care, and high-risk behavior such as smoking and drug use are all common in the general incarcerated population. This makes a 50-year-old inmate's health status comparable to that of a free 65-year-old living in the community. Of demographic significance is the number of women in the incarcerated population. Greenfeld and Snell (1999) found that in 1998, the nearly 150,000 women behind bars represented about 11 percent of the total jail population and 6 percent of the state and federal prison population. Although more than half of these women are under the age of 35, the majority have unhealthy past lifestyles that include drug and alcohol abuse, sex work, and multiple partners, which put them at high risk for chronic and communicable diseases, according to Anno (1997). Women offenders use health services more frequently than do their male counterparts, Goldkuhle (1999) found, and they have higher rates of HIV and STDs than male offenders. Women inmates also have higher rates of serious mental illnesses, drug abuse, depression, and other emotional problems than the male population. Approximately 6 percent are pregnant on admission to jails and prisons and account for an estimated 8,820 of the 3.8 million births in the United States each year. Due to unhealthy lifestyles prior to incarceration, most of these pregnancies are classified as high risk, Greenfeld (1999) discovered.

11.10.4 The Nursing Role in the Correctional Environment

According to the ANA, correctional nursing has its roots in 1797, with the opening of the New York City Newgate Prison. Warden Thomas Eddy believed that criminals could be rehabilitated and established a school, hospital, and pharmacy for the inmates. However, nursing as a profession in the correctional setting did not appear until the 1960s, and began to gain some increased visibility toward the end of the 20th century. In 1975, Rena Murtin described entering a large correctional facility where the nurse was perceived as a "tool of the warden, a slave of the physician and an unknown to the patient." Since that time, the ANA says, "the role of the nurse has evolved from that of a pill pusher to that of an equal and respected member of the health care provider team, a case manager, a crisis intervener, a suicidologist, a counselor and more."

According to the ANA, the specialty of correctional nursing is not widely represented in statistical reporting about nurses and their work environments. The ANA points to the 2000 National Sample Survey of Registered Nurses, which projected the number of 18,033 RNs working in prisons or jails. The ANA maintains that "the American public is unaware of the complex conditions and great strains on the essential qualities of nursing that face nurses working in correctional health care settings. Even corrections nurses themselves are often unaware of how their colleagues practice behind these closed doors." The ANA adds:

> Correctional systems are under increasing pressure from the federal courts to provide adequate and humane levels of health care with limited resources and little public sympathy. Social and political conditions facing nurses in these settings are demanding and appeal to the noblest of humanitarian instincts. Nurses are often the foundation of the correctional health care system and in many cases the only providers of health care services in correctional systems. Utilizing the expertise and unique knowledge and skills of registered nurses provides correctional systems the opportunity to meet their responsibility to provide adequate and safe health care delivery to those incarcerated.

Nurses who work in correctional facilities must be prepared to practice in what the ANA calls "a very litigious environment where patients frequently file legal action against the health care providers," as much of the early reform in correctional health care was as a result of inmate-initiated lawsuits. They also must be aware of demands made on their loyalties. The ANA explains:

> Nurses are usually direct employees of the correctional facility and may be in the same organizational hierarchy as the correctional officers. Nurses can often experience a division of interest and personal and professional conflict in these practice settings. On one hand, they are employees of an institution whose mission is security and public safety. On the other hand, they are health care providers whose mission is health and wellness. The goals of security and nursing are often incompatible, and the nurses may be asked to compromise their philosophy by performing activities that are not related to nursing or health care.

There is firm support in national standards to support the restriction of participation by nursing in activities related strictly to security (NCCHC, 2002). It is imperative that nurses in correctional settings recognize their professional responsibility to role development and clarification based on a commitment to quality nursing care according to recognized standards.

11.10.5 The Cornerstone Beliefs of Corrections Nursing

The ANA (2004) stated that "nursing is the protection, promotion, and optimization of health and abilities, prevention of illness and injury, alleviation of suffering through the diagnosis and treatment of human response, and advocacy in the care of individuals, families, communities, and populations. Nursing is a science and an art, the essence of which is caring for and respecting human beings, including those in the corrections environment."

In the *Scope and Standards of Nursing Practice in Correctional Facilities,* the ANA lists the following as underpinnings for corrections nursing:

- An RN's primary duty in the corrections setting is to restore and maintain the health of patients in a spirit of compassion, concern, and professionalism.
- Each patient, regardless of circumstances, possesses intrinsic value and should be treated with dignity and respect.
- Each encounter with patients and families should portray professionalism, compassion, and concern.
- Each patient should receive quality care that is cost-effective and congruent with the latest treatment parameters and clinical guidelines.
- Patient confidentiality and privacy should be preserved.
- Nurses should collaborate with other health care team members, correctional staff, and community colleagues to meet the holistic needs of patients, which include physical, psychosocial, and spiritual aspects of care.
- Nurses should encourage each individual, through patient and family education, to take responsibility for disease prevention and health promotion.
- Monitoring and evaluating nursing practice is each nurse's responsibility and is necessary for continuous quality improvement.

- Nurses should resist assuming custodial functions that compromise the nurse's role in providing therapeutic health care.
- Nursing leadership should promote the highest quality of patient care through application of fair and equitable policies and procedures in collaboration with other health care services team members and corrections staff.
- Nursing services should be guided by responsible leaders who are sensitive to employee needs and give support, praise, and recognition to encourage professional and personal development. These nurse administrators should encourage professional growth and development through continuing education, participation in professional organizations, and generation of knowledge through research.

11.10.6 The Role of the Corrections Nurse

Correctional nursing is the practice of nursing and the delivery of patient care within the unique and distinct environment of the criminal justice system. The criminal justice system includes jails, prisons, juvenile detention centers, substance abuse treatment, and other facilities of detainment. Unlike the majority of their nursing colleagues, RNs working in corrections must demonstrate the essence of nursing in a practice environment that does not have health care as its primary mission. Matters of nursing judgment are solely the domain of the RN. The incarcerated vary from youths to aged adults, include men and women, and are individuals of all racial and ethnic backgrounds who are often disenfranchised, economically challenged, educationally limited, and largely ignored by society. These individuals enter the corrections system with communicable and chronic diseases and complications resulting from a previous lack of appropriate health care services. The work of corrections nurses contributes to limiting the health care disparities experienced by this unique and extremely diversified corrections population.

Corrections nurses are expected to deliver patient care with compassion, empathy, commitment, competency, dedication, and a positive attitude undaunted by the circumstances surrounding incarceration. Although the length of incarceration differs in the various settings, the corrections nurse plays an integral role in providing health services to this population through patient education, patient advocacy, and the delivery of patient care. Therefore, it is inappropriate for nurses to be involved in the security aspects of the facility, disciplinary decisions or committees, or participate in procedures performed solely for correctional purposes, such as body cavity searches or executions by lethal injection.

Correctional health care is one of the fastest growing specialties in health services today and offers new and unique roles for nursing in the evolving correctional health care settings. Because health care services are provided within juvenile detention centers, community corrections facilities, jails, and both juvenile and adult correctional institutions, the RN must be prepared in women's health and pediatric through geriatric and end-of-life care.

The major emphasis of nursing care in correctional settings is the provision of primary care services for the population. RNs, as the primary health care providers in correctional settings, are challenged in dealing with public health issues, providing health education and health promotion activities, evaluating the effectiveness of planned care, and encouraging preventive behavior within the prison setting as it relates to infectious diseases. In addition, the RN coordinates the linkage to community resources prior to the offender's release from incarceration, a critical function that provides the inmate the opportunity for continuity of care and facilitates a successful return to the community.

According to the ANA, nursing care within the corrections setting can be provided in collaboration with other nurses and health professionals, or independently, which is most often the case in a small or rural facility. The RN, in addition to providing direct nursing care, assesses the patient's health care status, analyzes the assessment data, develops or modifies diagnoses, develops or modifies the plan of care based on those assessments and diagnoses, and evaluates the effectiveness of the plan of care. The preferred educational preparation of the RN for entry into corrections nursing practice is at the baccalaureate level. Continuing professional development is expected, including further educational preparation leading to one or more graduate degrees.

The corrections nurse is often the only health care provider on site and must be able to demonstrate good assessment and organizational skills as well as critical decision-making and thinking skills. The RN is involved in caring for patients with multiple and complex diagnoses requiring an increased intensity of care. Nursing activities include patient assessment, decisions about medication and treatment delivery and assessment of their effects, crisis intervention, triage, education, and patient advocacy. The needs of the correctional population demand the corrections nurse have a sound background in medical-surgical, psychiatric, emergency, and in some settings, critical care nursing. Skills in negotiation, problem solving, listening, and communication are invaluable.

Working inside a correctional setting requires the corrections nurse to have knowledge of the legal aspects of nursing and litigation related to correctional health care. The corrections nurse must be acutely aware of the need for appropriate documentation of care rendered. Maintaining confidentiality of patient health information often requires special attention, especially when corrections staff must assist in monitoring the health status of patients.

The corrections nurse is expected to demonstrate integrity, highly ethical and moral practice appreciating the legally mandated obligation to deliver nursing care regardless of the individual's circumstances or offenses.

According to the ANA, corrections nursing, by nature of the practice environment, lends itself to considerations of maintaining public safety. Security issues and concerns are paramount within the correctional institution. Delegation of the authority of patient care is done in collaboration with the corrections administrators. Nurses do not work independently of security but in partnership to provide nursing and medical care to confined individuals. The focus of maintaining security makes correctional nursing practice unique and dynamic, requiring a careful balance of priorities. The maintenance of professional boundaries is essential in the corrections environment. The nurse must act in a manner that is in the best interest of the patient's medical condition while maintaining a safe and secure environment. Those actions taken by the nurse establish the difference between providing care for the patient and meeting the nurse's own personal needs. Those who cross professional boundaries place themselves, their peers, and others, including the patient, in a position of compromised security.

11.10.7 Corrections Nursing: The Scope of Practice

At the time of writing, the Scope and Standards of Nursing Practice in Correctional Facilities, published in 1995, was undergoing revision by the ANA Corrections Working Group. The proposed standards of practice include:

1. Assessment: The corrections nurse collects comprehensive data pertinent to the patient's health and condition or the situation. The corrections nurse:
   - Collects data in a systematic and ongoing process.
   - Involves the patient, family, other health care and community providers, as appropriate, in holistic data collection.
   - Prioritizes data collection activities based on the patient's immediate condition, the environment of care, or anticipated needs of the patient or situation.
   - Uses appropriate evidence-based assessment techniques and instruments in collecting pertinent data.
   - Uses analytical models and problem-solving tools.
   - Synthesizes available data, information, and knowledge relevant to the situation to identify patterns and variances.
   - Documents relevant data in a retrievable format.
2. Diagnosis: The corrections nurse analyzes the assessment data to determine the diagnoses or issues. The corrections nurse:
   - Derives the diagnoses or related issues based on assessment data.
   - Validates the diagnoses or issues with the patient, family, and other health care and community providers when possible and appropriate.
   - Documents diagnoses or issues in a manner that facilitates the determination of the expected outcomes and plan.
3. Outcomes identification: The corrections nurse identifies expected outcomes for a plan individualized to the patient or the situation. The corrections nurse:
   - Involves the patient, family, and other health care and community providers in formulating expected outcomes when possible and appropriate.
   - Derives culturally appropriate expected outcomes from the diagnoses.
   - Considers associated risks, security issues, benefits, costs, current scientific evidence, and clinical expertise when formulating expected outcomes.
   - Defines expected outcomes in terms of the patient, patient values, ethical considerations, environment or situation with such consideration as associated risks, security issues, benefits and costs, and current scientific evidence.
   - Includes a time estimate for attainment of expected outcomes.
   - Develops expected outcomes that provide direction for continuity of care.
   - Modifies expected outcomes based on changes in the status of the patient or evaluation of the situation.
   - Documents expected outcomes as measurable goals.
4. Planning: The corrections nurse develops a plan that prescribes strategies and alternatives to attain expected outcomes. The corrections nurse:
   - Develops an individualized plan considering patient characteristics or the situation.
   - Develops the plan in conjunction with the patient, family, community and public health resources, security personnel, and others, as appropriate.
   - Includes strategies within the plan that address each of the identified diagnoses or issues, which might include strategies for

promotion and restoration of health and prevention of illness, injury, and disease.
- Provides for continuity of care within the plan.
- Incorporates an implementation pathway or timeline within the plan.
- Establishes the plan priorities with the patient, family, security personnel, and others as appropriate.
- Utilizes the plan to provide direction to other members of the health care team and the security personnel.
- Defines the plan to reflect current statutes, rules and regulations, guidelines, and standards.
- Integrates current trends and research affecting care in the planning process.
- Considers the economic impact of the plan.
- Uses standardized language or recognized terminology to document the plan.

5. Implementation: The corrections nurse implements the identified plan. The corrections nurse:
   - Implements the plan in a safe and timely manner.
   - Documents implementation and any modifications, including changes or omissions, of the identified plan.
   - Utilizes evidence-based interventions and treatments specific to the diagnosis or problem.
   - Utilizes corrections facility and community resources and systems to implement the plan.
   - Collaborates with nursing colleagues, health care team members, security personnel, and others to implement the plan.
6. Evaluation: The corrections nurse evaluates progress toward attainment of outcomes. The corrections nurse:

- Conducts a systematic, ongoing, and criterion-based evaluation of the outcomes in relation to the structures and processes prescribed by the plan and the indicated timeline.
- Includes the patient and others involved in the care or situation in the evaluative process.
- Evaluates the effectiveness of the planned strategies in relation to patient responses and the attainment of the expected outcomes.
- Documents the results of the evaluation.
- Uses ongoing assessment data to revise the diagnoses, outcomes, the plan, and the implementation as needed.
- Disseminates the results to the patient and others involved in the care or situation, as appropriate, in accordance with state and federal laws and regulations.

7. Quality of practice: The corrections nurse systematically enhances the quality and effectiveness of nursing practice. The corrections nurse:
   - Demonstrates quality by documenting the application of the nursing process in a responsible, accountable, and ethical manner.
   - Uses creativity and innovation in nursing practice to improve care delivery.
   - Incorporates new knowledge to initiate changes in nursing practice if desired outcomes are not achieved.
   - Participates in quality improvement activities. Such activities might include the following:
     - Identifying aspects of practice important for quality monitoring
     - Using indicators developed to monitor quality and effectiveness of nursing practice
     - Collecting data to monitor quality and effectiveness of nursing practice
     - Analyzing quality data to identify opportunities for improving nursing practice
     - Formulating recommendations to improve nursing practice or outcomes
     - Implementing activities to enhance the quality of nursing practice
     - Developing, implementing, and evaluating policies, procedures, and guidelines to improve the quality of practice
     - Participating on interdisciplinary teams to evaluate clinical care or health services
     - Participating in efforts to minimize costs and unnecessary duplication
     - Analyzing factors related to safety, satisfaction, effectiveness, and cost–benefit options.
     - Analyzing organizational systems for barriers
     - Implementing processes to remove or decrease barriers within organizational systems
   - Uses the results of quality improvement activities to initiate changes in nursing practice, in the health care delivery, and in the correctional system.
8. Education: The corrections nurse attains knowledge and competency that reflects current nursing practice. The corrections nurse:
   - Participates in ongoing educational activities related to appropriate knowledge bases and professional issues.

- Demonstrates a commitment to lifelong learning through self-reflection and inquiry to identify learning needs.
- Seeks experiences that reflect current practice to maintain skills and competence in clinical practice or role performance.
- Acquires knowledge and skills appropriate to the specialty area, practice setting, role, or situation.
- Maintains professional records that provide evidence of competency and lifelong learning.
- Seeks experiences and formal and independent learning activities to maintain and develop clinical and professional skills and knowledge.

9. Professional practice evaluation: The corrections nurse evaluates one's own nursing practice in relation to professional practice standards and guidelines, relevant statutes, rules, and regulations. The corrections nurse's practice reflects the application of knowledge of current practice standards, guidelines, statutes, rules, and regulations. The corrections nurse:
   - Provides nursing care considering age, culture, ethnicity, and the unique aspects of the correctional environment.
   - Engages in self-evaluation of practice on a regular basis, identifying areas of strength as well as areas in which professional development would be beneficial.
   - Obtains informal feedback regarding one's own practice from patients, peers, professional colleagues, and others.
   - Participates in systematic peer review as appropriate.
   - Takes action to achieve goals identified during the evaluation process.
   - Provides rationales for practice beliefs, decisions, and actions as part of the informal and formal evaluation processes.
10. Collegiality: The corrections nurse interacts with and contributes to the professional development of peers and colleagues. The corrections nurse:
    - Shares knowledge and skills with peers and colleagues as evidenced by such activities as patient care conferences or presentations at formal or informal meetings.
    - Provides peers with feedback regarding their practice and/or role performance.
    - Interacts with peers and colleagues to enhance one's own professional nursing practice and/or role performance.
    - Maintains compassionate and caring relationships with peers and colleagues.
    - Contributes to an environment that is conducive to the education of health care professionals.
    - Contributes to a supportive and healthy work environment.
11. Collaboration: The corrections nurse collaborates with patient, family, and others in the conduct of nursing practice. The corrections nurse:
    - Communicates with patient, family, health care providers, and corrections staff regarding patient care and the nurse's role in the provision of that care.
    - Collaborates in creating a documented plan focused on outcomes and decisions related to care and delivery of services that indicates communication with patients, families, and others.
    - Partners with others to effect change and generate positive outcomes through knowledge of the patient or situation.
    - Documents referrals, including provisions for continuity of care.
12. Ethics: The corrections nurse integrates ethical provisions in all areas of practice. The corrections nurse:
    - Delivers care in a manner that preserves and protects patient autonomy, dignity and rights
    - Maintains patient confidentiality within legal and regulatory parameters considering the unique corrections environment
    - Serves as a patient advocate assisting patients in developing skills for self advocacy
    - Maintains a therapeutic and professional patient-nurse relationship with appropriate professional role boundaries
    - Demonstrates a commitment to practicing self-care, managing stress, and connecting with self and others
    - Contributes to resolving ethical issues of patients, colleagues, or systems as evidenced in such activities as participating on ethics committees
    - Reports illegal, incompetent, or impaired practices.
13. Research: The corrections nurse integrates research findings into practice. The corrections nurse:
    - Utilizes the best available evidence, including research findings, to guide practice decisions.
    - Actively participates in research activities at various levels appropriate to the nurse's level of education and position, including identifying clinical problems specific to nursing research, participating in data collection,

participating in a formal committee or program, sharing research activities and findings with peers and others, conducting research, critically analyzing and interpreting research for application to practice, using research findings in the development of policies, procedures, and standards of practice in patient care, incorporating research as a basis for learning, and recognizing the unique requirements of human subjects' protection in the corrections environment.

14. Resource utilization: The corrections nurse considers factors related to safety, effectiveness, cost, benefits, and impact on practice in the planning and delivery of nursing services. The corrections nurse:
    - Evaluates factors such as safety, security, effectiveness, availability, cost and benefits, efficiencies, and impact on practice, when choosing practice options that would result in the same expected outcome.
    - Assists the patient, family, corrections staff, and community resources in identifying and securing appropriate and available services to address health-related needs.
    - Assigns or delegates tasks, based on the needs and condition of the patient, potential for harm, stability of the patient's condition, complexity of the task, and predictability of the outcome.
    - Assists the patient and family in becoming informed consumers about the options, risks, and benefits of treatment and care.
15. Leadership: The corrections nurse provides leadership in the professional practice setting and the profession. The corrections nurse:
    - Engages in teamwork as a team player and a team builder.
    - Works to create and maintain healthy work environments in local, regional, national, or international communities.
    - Displays the ability to define a clear vision, the associated goals, and a plan to implement and measure progress.
    - Demonstrates a commitment to continuous, lifelong learning for self and others.
    - Teaches others to succeed by mentoring and other strategies.
    - Exhibits creativity and flexibility through times of change.
    - Demonstrates energy, excitement, and a passion for quality work.
    - Willingly accepts mistakes by self and others, thereby creating a culture in which risk-taking is not only safe, but expected.
    - Inspires loyalty through valuing of people as the most precious asset in an organization.
    - Directs the coordination of care across settings and among caregivers, including oversight of licensed and unlicensed personnel in any assigned or delegated tasks.
    - Serves in key roles in the work setting by participating on committees, councils, and administrative teams.
    - Promotes advancement of the profession through participation in professional organizations.

11.11 SPECIAL ISSUES: WOMEN IN PRISON

Women in prison represent a special challenge to the nurse working in a correctional facility, equal to the challenge of significant burden of medical and mental health problems—often related to poverty, violence in their lives, and a lack of social support—faced by female inmates. "Incarcerated women are a marginalized and medically underserved population with a high prevalence of physical and sexual abuse histories, high-risk sex and drug-using behaviors, and a multitude of needs that can benefit from prevention education, treatment programs, and compassionate nursing care," writes Christine Johnsen, RN, MPH, MS, NP, in the article, "Women in Prison."

Statistics from the U.S. Department of Justice reveal that 1 million women, or approximately 1 percent of all adult American women, are incarcerated. Furthermore, women comprise 16 percent of the total U.S. incarcerated population and 14 percent of all violent offenders. The majority of their offenses are related to drugs or alcohol, either directly, as in the possession or sale or illegal substances, driving while intoxicated, or commercial sex work in exchange for drugs or money for drugs; or committed while the offender was under the influence of drugs or alcohol, according to the Bureau of Justice Statistics (1999). Three out of four violent women offenders committed simple assault, and 40 percent were perceived by their victims as being under the influence of alcohol or drugs at the time of the crime. In recent years, the number of women inmates has been increasing faster than the incarceration rate for men. When it comes to demographics, women inmates can be characterized as having lower incomes, lower levels of education, and younger than the rest of the U.S. female population. One study found that 55 percent of women in jails and 73 percent of women in prisons were at least high-school graduates; 30 percent to 40 percent of the high-school graduates had at least some college. Forty percent of incarcerated women were employed full-time before arrest and 30 percent were receiving welfare assistance. About 37 percent of women had incomes less than $600 per month before their arrest. Approximately 64 percent of women in state prisons had prior convictions, and 19 percent had a juvenile history. Seventy-seven percent of women under correctional care were between 25 and 44 years of age, with 12 percent younger and 11 percent older. Nearly six in 10 women in state prisons had experienced physical or sexual abuse in the past. About two thirds of women state inmates lived with their children before imprisonment. About six in 10 women state inmates reported using drugs in the month before the offense.

The juvenile arrest rate for violent offenses in 1995 was about two and a half times the rate in 1985, but has been declining since then. The arrest rate for violent offenses in young women increased 80 percent in 1997, compared with the rate 10 years earlier, and continues to climb.

Demographics are not the only diverse characteristic of women in the correctional system; they also have special physical, mental, and emotional health needs. Johnsen writes, "Correctional facilities are reservoirs of physical and mental illness, especially infectious diseases and substance-abuse disorders. Left untreated, these problems will continue to affect the communities to which inmates return." In 1997, 34 percent of women state inmates reported a physical or mental impairment that limited their ability to work. The correctional population carries a disproportionate share of the burden of infectious diseases. The rates of HIV, hepatitis C infection, and tuberculosis are much higher in inmates. Hammett, Harmon, and Rhodes (2002) reported that 3 percent of the U.S. population spent time in a correctional facility that year, yet these inmates accounted for between 16 percent and 43 percent of these infectious diseases. The prevalence of STIs is high among women entering correctional facilities. Conklin, Lincoln, and Tuthill (2000) reported that women were twice as likely as men to report a history of chlamydia, gonorrhea, syphilis, genital warts, or trichomoniasis. The HIV infection rate in the incarcerated population is five times that in the general U.S. population. Women who pass through the correctional system have a disproportionate burden, with HIV infection rates higher in incarcerated women than men. In 2000, 2 percent of male inmates and nearly 4 percent of women inmates were known to be HIV-positive. In two jurisdictions, Washington, DC, and New York, the rates of HIV-infected women soared to 41 percent and 18 percent, respectively. New York state was the only jurisdiction to have a male infection rate greater than 5 percent, with 8 percent of men inmates in New York HIV-infected, according to the Bureau of Justice Statistics (2000).

In recent Bureau of Justice surveys, more than half of women state inmates reported that they had been abused before admission to the correctional facility; 46.5 percent reported prior physical abuse and 39 percent reported sexual abuse; and 25 percent experienced abuse before age 18. Illegal drug use and alcohol were higher among abused inmates than nonabused inmates. A study of incarcerated women in Rhode Island found PTSD to be the most common disorder among women inmates, and the rate of PTSD was twice the rate of PTSD in a community sample of women. These women were likely to have comorbid depression, borderline personality, and a history of substance abuse. Trauma, especially in childhood, has been associated with mental illness. The author concluded that women with early-abuse histories were more likely to have substance use, excessive risk-taking behaviors, and anger—factors that increase the risk of arrest—and underscores the importance of offering mental health services in the correctional setting (Zlotnick, 1997).

In an evaluation of the prevalence of psychiatric disorders in women detainees in a Chicago jail, 80 percent of the women were found to have one or more lifetime psychiatric disorders, and 70 percent were symptomatic within six months of the interview. Not surprisingly, substance-use disorders were the most common. PTSD and major depression are also significant problems in jail, where suicide is the second most common cause of death. Adverse childhood experiences, including child abuse, can have long-term consequences on adult behaviors. Women who have been previously victimized experience low self-esteem and are often unable to negotiate safer sex or protect themselves from further victimization. Psychiatric interventions that target PTSD might result in reduced recidivism in incarcerated women. The Women's Interagency HIV Study (WIHS) discovered that childhood sexual abuse is associated with an increased lifetime history of domestic violence and high-risk behaviors, including drugs; more than 10 male sexual partners; and exchanging sex for money, drugs, or shelter. Previous physical and sexual abuse might be a predisposing factor for drug abuse (Whynot, 1998). For the majority of incarcerated women for whom substance abuse is a problem, drug treatment is largely unavailable, either while they are incarcerated or when they are released. With limited access to mental health treatment in the correctional setting, women are released to the streets with the same problems that led them to substance abuse and incarceration in the first place. Recidivism is high; 65 percent of women have prior convictions (Bureau of Justice Statistics, 1999).

A unique challenge to women is being incarcerated in a facility designed to house male prisoners. "The criminal justice system has not adapted its security procedures to address the special physical needs and circumstances of women," Johnsen writes. "This can be particularly traumatic to the many women inmates who have previously been victimized by men. Women are confined to institutions designed and run by men. No prisons for women in the U.S. have all-women staff." Johnsen adds that male prison staff are present when women dress, shower, and toilet, and for strip and pat-down body searches.

11.12 SPECIAL ISSUES: SEXUAL COERCION OF WOMEN IN PRISON

The sexual coercion of women in prison can be defined as being pressured or coerced into unwanted sexual contact while incarcerated. Experts have documented the prevalence of sexual harassment, molestation during strip searches, coercive sexual fondling, and pressured and forced sexual intercourse, most likely perpetrated by prison staff. These are incidences of IPV that have been uncovered by human-rights groups, investigative agencies, and in an increasing number of court cases in which inmates have sued prisons for sexual exploitation (Bell et al., 1999; Springfield, 2000). The group Human Rights Watch (1996) documented numerous cases of sexual abuse of imprisoned women by male correctional officers in 11 state prison systems, and according to Amnesty International, documented cases of custodial sexual misconduct have been found in all 50 states.

Specifically, the Human Rights Watch (1996) released a report, *All Too Familiar: Sexual Abuse of Women in U.S. State Prisons,* which analyzed the response of the U.S. government to the issue of sexual abuse of female prisoners in California, the District of Columbia, Georgia, Illinois, Michigan, and New York. The report made recommendations for remedy in the areas of training, legislation, and policy. Due in large part to the well-publicized litigation and the Human Rights Watch report, the special rapporteur for violence against women, Radhika Coomeraswamey, issued a stinging report on the treatment of women in U.S. prisons and focused most particularly on the issues of sexual misconduct and cross-gender supervision. Amnesty International (1999) issued *Not Part of My Sentence: Violations of the Human Rights of Women in Custody,* a report that focused on a number of issues affecting women in custody, including sexual abuse. This report reached the same conclusions as the Human Rights Watch report and called for the following:

- Same-sex supervision of female inmates
- More explicit policies and laws prohibiting sexual abuse of inmates
- Stronger mechanisms for investigating and prosecuting sexual abuse of prisoners
- Appropriate supportive services and redress for sexual abuse
- Greater protection from retaliation for inmates who reported sexual misconduct.

Beck and Harrison (2001) report that the female prisoner population in the United States has more than doubled since 1990 and stood at more than 9,600 in 2000. Therefore, the number of incarcerated women at risk for sexual coercion could be substantial. A small number of studies have been conducted on coercive sex in prison, but most have focused on male victims. Struckman-Johnson et al. (1996) reports that between 1960 and 1990, a dozen studies were conducted in men's prisons, but could find only two that included female inmates: Kassebaum (1972) suggested that many women in prison were vulnerable to sexual exploitation by prison staff and other female inmates, and Bartollas and Sieverdes (1983) found that 9.1 percent of 561 adolescent offenders in six coeducational corrections facilities for juveniles had been sexually victimized.

Struckman-Johnson et al. add, "It was not until the mid-1990s that this topic was investigated in depth by social scientists." Baro (1997) discussed the chronic problems of custodial sexual abuse in a small women's prison facility in Hawaii. Baro interviewed female inmates and collected court and prison records of abusive practices, and discovered that between 1982 and 1994, Hawaii had 38 officially acknowledged cases of custodial sexual abuse. Thirty of the cases involved men and eight involved female perpetrators. Alleged abuses included forced intercourse, unwanted pregnancies, and service as prostitutes in a hotel near the prison. Baro concluded that many female inmates, vulnerable due to past histories of sexual abuse and drug addiction, were easy targets for male prison staff.

In 1996, Struckman-Johnson and colleagues surveyed a small women's facility and found that three of 42 respondents had been sexually coerced. Two victims had been sexually fondled and one had been groped by a group of inmates. The researchers identified higher coercion rates in three men's facilities that were surveyed, and theorized that the lower rate for women reflected the smaller size of the women's facility, the less violent criminal history of female inmates, or perhaps women's general disinclination to initiate sexual coercion.

Butler (1997) assessed the prevalence of sexual assault in adult female prisons in New South Wales. One-hundred female inmates were interviewed in depth; just two females reported engaging in nonconsensual sex while in prison. However, 23 women reported awareness of sexual assaults occurring in prison in the previous 12 months. Alarid (2000) published an analysis of one female inmate's observations and experiences of sexual assault during a five-year period of incarceration. Although the researcher did not provide rates of sexual coercion, evidence suggested female inmates regularly encountered sexual pressure in their daily interactions with other female inmates. Also in 2000, Greer published data from the interviews of 35 female inmates about their sexual relationships while incarcerated in a Midwestern prison. Inmates reported that most of the sexual interactions among inmates were triggered by "game playing and economic manipulation."

One of the most comprehensive studies of the sexual coercion of women was conducted by Cindy Struckman-Johnson (2002), PhD, of the Department of Psychology at the University of South Dakota, which was published in the August 2002 issue of the *Journal of Sex Research.* She writes, "Although sexual coercion of women in prison is increasingly recognized as a serious social issue, the topic has received-scant attention from social and sex scientists." Struckman-Johnson et al. (1996) assert that research into sexual coercion in prison is hampered by the difficulty in gaining access to inmate participants because prison administrations have been reluctant to allow research on coercive sexuality. Other obstacles include prison internal review boards that are wary of sex research. Struckman-Johnson explains that the impetus behind her study included reports that sexual coercion of women in prison were "rampant" (Bell et al., 1999), and "extensive" (Springfield, 2000), but there were almost no data on how many women are affected. She also asserts, "Prison records of sexual coercion rates are also rare. Many corrections agencies do not keep records or are reluctant to publish them." She points to a recent survey by the National Institute of Corrections (2000), which reported that only 36 of 54 state and federal departments of corrections (DOCs) were willing or able to provide data on substantiated incidents of sexual misconduct involving prison staff and female inmates for 1998. Of the 36 DOCs, 14 reported no incidents, 17 had between one and five incidents, and 5 reported more than five cases. Struckman-Johnson comments, "These numbers suggest that sexual coercion rates are low. However, experts caution that statistics released by prison authorities may be serious underestimates because of the difficulties female inmates have in reporting and substantiating incidents."

Struckman-Johnson had several goals in mind when conducting her study:

- Estimate what percentage of female inmates had experienced at least one incident of sexual coercion while incarcerated.
- Obtain inmates' and prison staff's perceptions of the sexual assault climate in a facility.
- Describe the characteristics of women who were the targets of sexual coercion and what happened in their worst incident.
- Assess inmates' emotional and physical reactions to incidents.
- Determine how many women reported the incident to authorities.

Struckman-Johnson sent research requests to the DOCs in 14 states; five agreed to participate. The researchers were given access to three women's facilities and seven men's facilities, all located in Midwestern states. Only the procedures and results of the women's facilities were presented in their study. Surveys were administered to the total inmate population and security-related staff of the three facilities. Facility 1 was a maximum–medium–minimum security facility with 295 female inmates and 100 prison staff. Facility 2 was a maximum–medium–minimum security facility with 113 inmates and 26 staff. Facility 3 was a maximum–medium–minimum security facility with 60 female inmates and 154 staff who were responsible for male and female inmates. The inmate survey collected demographic data and crime background, perceptions of the prison environment, and opinions about sexual coercion. Sample questions included, "Since the time you have been in prison, has anyone ever pressured or forced you to have sexual contact (touching of genitals, oral, anal, or vaginal sex) against your will?" and "In the prison you are in now, about what percentage of inmates do you think have been pressured or forced to have sexual contact against their will?" Also, inmates were asked to rate the facility protection level: "In the prison you are in now, do you think that the prison system protects inmates from pressured or forced sexual contact?"

Respondents with sexual-coercion experiences were asked about one worst case incident, either the only one that happened or the one time that was the "most serious or harmful to you." They answered questions about the number, race, and relationship of the perpetrators, the type of tactics used, and the sexual outcome. The staff survey collected demographic data and work history in corrections, perceptions of the prison environment, and opinions about sexual coercion. As in the inmate survey, staff answered questions about the perceived sexual coercion rate and facility protection level. In Facility 1, 148 inmates (50 percent) and 30 staff (30 percent) returned usable surveys. In Facility 2, 79 of the inmates (70 percent) and 13 staff (50 percent) sent back usable surveys. In Facility 3, 36 inmates (60 percent) and 57 staff (37 percent) returned usable surveys. The 30 staff respondents from Facility 1 were 12 men (40 percent) and 18 women (60 percent) who were White (73 percent) and Hispanic (20 percent). Twenty-five staff (80 percent) were correctional or security officers. In Facility 2, the 13 staff were five men (38 percent) and eight (62 percent) women who were White (100 percent). Ten (77 percent) were correctional or security officers. In Facility 3, the 57 staff respondents (all correctional officers) were 44 men (77 percent) and 13 women (23 percent) who were White (98 percent).

In Facility 1, 19 percent had experienced an incident while residing there; and 18 percent of the respondents described a worst-case incident that took occurred there. Five percent of the respondents' worst-case incidents were classified as rape, involving a force tactic and an outcome of oral, vaginal, or anal intercourse. In the 30 months before the survey, 12 percent of the respondents had experienced their worst incident, and 3 percent had been raped. Inmates guessed that 21 percent of the women in the facility had been pressured or forced into sex, and staff guessed that 10 percent of the inmates had been sexually coerced. Inmates generally disagreed and staff generally agreed that their prison system protected them from sexual coercion. In Facility 2, 9 percent of responding inmates said that they had been sexually coerced. None of the worst incidents that took place in the facility were classifiable as rape, and most of these had occurred during the 30-month period preceding the survey. The inmate guess of an 11 percent sexual coercion rate was several points higher than the reported statewide and facility rates, whereas the staff guess of 2 percent was much lower than the reported rates. Inmates generally agreed and staff strongly agreed that that the prison system protected them from sexual coercion. In Facility 3, statewide and facility sexual coercion rates were 8 percent. None of the worst incidents qualified as rape, and all happened in the 30 months preceding the survey. The inmate guess of a 13 percent sexual coercion rate was several points higher than the 8 percent report rate, and the staff guess was 4 percent. Inmates generally agreed and staff strongly agreed that the facility protected inmates from sexual coercion.

Regarding worst-case incidents, Struckman-Johnson reported that in Facility 1, 27 out of 28 women who had been coerced described a worst-case incident. Targets were predominantly heterosexual and about 25 percent were bisexual or homosexual. More than one third of the targets said that they had been assaulted by one person, whereas more than 40 percent had been attacked by a group of two to three persons. Fifty percent of the perpetrators were women and the other half were men. About half of the incidents were perpetrated by inmates, and 45 percent of the incidents involved one or more staff persons. The perpetrator(s) used only a pressure tactic in 37 percent of the cases, and the most common force tactics (used in 63 percent of the incidents) were threats of harm and intimidation by size. One third of the targets were physically restrained and 11 percent were harmed. Most of the incidents resulted in sexual touching as opposed to completed intercourse; about one fourth of the targets were raped.

Struckman-Johnson also reported that a majority of the inmate-perpetrated incidents in Facility 1 involved forceful sexual touching, such as when a perpetrator would block the door to a woman's cell and try to fondle her as the woman tried to escape. Or, a perpetrator would push a woman up against the wall and attempt to rub her body. There were more serious incidents when one or more inmates would isolate and trap a target and force her to submit to a variety of sexual acts. Staff-perpetrated incidents typically involved a male staff person who would sneak up behind female inmates at work or in their cells and attempt to fondle or kiss them. Most of the targets were able to escape the situation, but they feared that the officer would repeat the attempt. Victims of assault in Facility 1 complained of nervousness around people, distrust of people, and worry that it would happen again, and 50 percent of the victims reported experiencing flashbacks and depression. Three victims reported physical injuries. Approximately 60 percent of the victims reported the incident, but only 30 percent informed prison administration about the incident. In Facility 2, five women reported a worst-case incident, one of which involved a prison staff person. No incidents were classifiable as rape, and most of the targets encountered a single, sexually aggressive female inmate who attempted to fondle and seduce them. In the one reported staff incident, a male officer propositioned the woman. Only one victim reported the incident to a prison administrator. In Facility 3, two women reported a worst-case incident, and neither was raped. According to written descriptions, one woman was forcefully held down and touched by another female inmate; the other was forcefully restrained and sexually touched by a female staff member during a strip search. They did not report the incidents to the prison administration.

Struckman-Johnson says that her study "revealed that sexual aggression does take place in women's prisons, but that the frequency of the behavior may depend upon the characteristics of the facility and its inmate population." The researchers anticipated that the sexual coercion rates would be somewhere close to the 7 percent rate found by Struckman-Johnson et al. (1996). While the facility rates of 9 percent and 8 percent for Facilities 2 and 3, respectively, were not unexpected, the researchers reported surprise at the 27 percent statewide rate and 19 percent facility rate for women in Facility 1. The researchers report that these rates were comparable to those reported for several men's prisons in the Midwest (Struckman-Johnson & Struckman-Johnson, 2000). Struckman-Johnson writes, "Our data suggested that Facility 1 was a vastly different place than Facilities 2 and 3. Facility 1 could be described as a rough prison where nearly half of the inmates had committed serious crimes against persons." Struckman-Johnson said the study revealed that this facility had security and management problems; offered inmates an unusually low level of protection against assault; had inadequate surveillance; hired predatory, noncaring, and unresponsive staff; and upheld policies that protected rather than punished staff and inmate sexual predators. By contrast, inmates in Facilities 2 and 3 generally had a favorable view of their prison's security level and management policies. Inmates in both facilities frequently commented that their staff watched out for them. Facility 2 inmates, in particular, praised their prison administration's zero tolerance policy for sexual coercion. However, there were dissenters in both facilities who alleged that staff covered up sexual coercion incidents. The researchers discovered that most victims of self-described worst-case incidents were in their 30s, and that female targets were most likely to be heterosexual and White, but women from all racial groups reported victimization.

Struckman-Johnson writes, "One of our most important findings was that nearly one half of the incidents of sexual coercion were carried out by female inmates. Incidents ranged from casual sexual grabs to injurious gang rapes. This finding contrasts with the assertion that same-sex sexual abuse in women's prison is rare." She adds, "We conclude that prison conditions can potentially foster female sexual aggression. We speculate that many women who go to prison are more aggressive than the typical woman, as evidenced by their crime background. Their aggressive tendencies may translate into sexual aggression in the confinement of a prison setting." This observation meshes with Greer (2000), who reported that some women's prisons are becoming more like men's prisons in that many inmates meet their needs through manipulation and exploitation of other inmates.

Another important finding of Struckman-Johnson's study is that almost half of the incidents reported by female inmates were perpetrated by staff. The typical scenario was when a male staff member would corner an inmate in an isolated area and forcefully fondle her. However, Struckman-Johnson says, a number of incidents involved female staff who used similar strategies to victimize women. "We note this finding because so much of the literature presumes that male staff members are the sole perpetrators of custodial sexual abuse. According to our findings, both men and women working at the prison used their authority to bribe, blackmail, and force inmates into sexual contact," she writes. Most of the incidents involved forceful fondling of genitals and breasts, but not forced oral, anal, or vaginal intercourse, the researchers discovered. About one out of five incidents qualified as rape. The researchers also documented that the women experienced strong negative reactions to all types of incidents, and two inmates said that they attempted suicide as a result of a sexual coercion incident. Many women came to hate their assailant(s) and one in five said that they were moved to commit violence. "Our impression is that much of this trauma occurred because victims could not avoid the perpetrators," Struckman-Johnson comments. "Many women said that their assailants, whether they were staff or other inmates, found ways to track them and harass them almost daily in the confines of the prison. One woman wrote that she wanted to cut her own face in order to make people leave her alone." Most important, the study revealed women's reluctance to report these incidents; just one third of the inmates told a prison administrator about an incidence of IPV. When asked why they did not report, inmates typically responded that they feared retaliation from the perpetrators, especially staff who could make prison life very difficult for them. Also, targeted women anticipated that no one would believe them. Struckman-Johnson writes, "Our study revealed a serious problem with sexual coercion in one prison facility for women and minor to moderate problems in two other facilities. This finding does not support the sweeping conclusions appearing in much of the literature that sexual abuse is extensive in women's prisons. Our recommendation for future research is to assess sexual coercion on a facility-by-facility basis because rates may be highly variable."

11.13 SPECIAL ISSUES: VICTIMS OF PRISON RAPE

11.13.1 The Scope of the Problem

More than 2 million people are currently incarcerated in the United States, and this number continues to increase. According to congressional findings, the number of inmates sexually assaulted in the past two decades likely exceeds 1 million. Sexual assault occurs in both male and female prisons and is committed by other inmates as well as correctional staff members. For many victims, the assaults are repeated throughout their period of confinement and involve numerous assailants. Experts say that research efforts to date have had to rely on various reports of victimization, inmate interviews, and written surveys, reporting mechanisms that are of questionable value. Anonymous prisoner surveys have demonstrated to be the best available evidence of the scope of sexual assault in U.S. prisons. Estimates of the extent of inmate sexual assault produced from survey data vary widely, and there is debate among researchers about the extent of the problem. Criminal justice researchers attribute this variation to study design issues such as differing definitions of sexual assault and differing methodologies, as well as to real variation among prisons (reflecting such effects as crowding, administrative approaches to the problem, and single vs. multicell occupancy) and inmate characteristics (such as age and criminal history).

Despite the challenges associated with measurement, the current literature generally estimates sexual coercion (less serious violations involving aggressive behaviors, propositions, and touching) as more common than completed rapes. For example, in a recent study of seven Midwestern prisons, 16 percent of inmates reported experiencing sexual coercion in their current facility. By contrast, rape victims constituted 7 percent of the sample. Of note, reported offenses varied widely among the seven participating prisons: Reported sexual coercion ranged from 4 to 21 percent, and reported rape included one facility with no reported rapes, and one facility where 11 percent of the sample reported having been raped.

11.13.2 The Sequelae of Prison Sexual Assault

In addition to the trauma from the actual assault, the available research suggests that victims of prison sexual assault have a high risk of suicide, contracting HIV and other communicable sexual diseases, and experiencing lifelong psychological and emotional trauma. A significant amount of the other violence in prison might be related to sexual assault or the threat of such assault, placing all inmates and correctional staff in those institutions at risk of violent attack. Prison sexual assault also affects society at large. Anecdotal evidence suggests that many victims of sexual assault become violent aggressors both while incarcerated and after their release, with some preemptively raping in prison to avoid rape themselves. Many victims unable to adjust to mainstream society become homeless or return to prison. The congressional findings note that prison sexual assault has other impacts on society, such as increasing the costs incurred by federal, state, and local governments to administer prison systems and increasing health care expenditures to treat and stop the spread of HIV and other communicable diseases both in and out of prison. The Prison Rape Elimination Act (PREA) also cites treatment costs associated with mental health illnesses as an additional burden to society. The true impact on individuals, their families, and society is unknown because relatively few studies have been conducted on this issue. Clearly there is a need to better understand the problem of prison sexual violence. The Act represents a step toward understanding and preventing this long-ignored problem.

11.13.3 The Prison Rape Elimination Act of 2003

On September 4, 2003, President George Bush signed into law Senate Bill 1435, known as the Prison Rape Elimination Act of 2003. The bill had received overwhelming bipartisan support in the House from Representatives Frank Wolfe (R-VA) and Robert C. Scott (D-VA) and in the Senate from bill sponsor Senator Jeff Sessions (R-AL) and among cosponsors, Senator Ted Kennedy (D-MA). The bill had enjoyed swift passage in both chambers of Congress; it was introduced into the Senate on July 21, 2003, and in less than a week passed both the Senate and House by unanimous consent. The bill was presented to President Bush on September 2, 2003, and he signed it two days later. The purposes of the act are as follows:

- To establish a zero-tolerance standard for the incidence of prison rape in prisons in the United States.
- To make the prevention of prison rape a top priority in each prison system.
- To develop and implement national standards for the detection, prevention, reduction, and punishment of prison rape.
- To increase the available data and information on the incidence of prison rape, consequently improving the management and administration of correctional facilities.
- To standardize the definitions used for collecting data on the incidence of prison rape.
- To increase the accountability of prison officials who fail to detect, prevent, reduce, and punish prison rape.
- To protect the Eighth Amendment rights of federal, state, and local prisoners.
- To increase the efficiency and effectiveness of federal expenditures through grant programs such as those dealing with health care; mental health care; disease prevention; crime prevention, investigation, and prosecution; prison construction, maintenance, and operation; race relations; poverty; unemployment; and homelessness.
- To reduce the costs that prison rape imposes on interstate commerce.

Mair (2003) writes, "The speed by which Congress passed the Prison Rape Elimination Act is surprising. Since the 1970s, the tenor of U.S. criminal justice policies has become increasingly punitive." Mair attributes this trend to the growth of "supermax" facilities, the enactment of "three-strikes" laws, the banning of federal funding for some amenities in federal prisons and other "no-frills" prison initiatives, trying young teenagers as adults and housing them in the general population of adult prisons, and the imposition of juvenile death sentences. Mair adds, "Even more surprising is that Congress acted absent popular demand; the Congressional findings specifically state that: 'Members of the public and government officials are largely unaware of the epidemic character of prison rape and the day-to-day horror experienced by victimized inmates.'"

The PREA consists of five main components to accomplish its stated purposes. First, the PREA requires the Bureau of Justice Statistics to conduct an annual comprehensive statistical review and analysis of the incidence and impact of prison rape. This process must identify common characteristics of victims and perpetrators of prison rape and prisons and prison systems that have a high incidence of rape, and the analysis must be based on annual surveys of at least 10 percent of all federal, state, and county prisons. Officials and administrators of the selected prisons are required to participate in these studies and to allow access to any inmates in their custody.

To facilitate this review and analysis process, the PREA establishes a Review Panel on Prison Rape within the U.S. Department of Justice. Annually, this new entity must hold public hearings on the operation of the three prisons with the highest incidence of prison rape and the two prisons with the lowest incidence in each of three categories of prison facilities surveyed to identify the common characteristics of both victims and perpetrators of prison rape, prisons and prison systems with high incidence of rape, and prisons and prison systems that appear to have successfully deterred rape. As follow up, each year the Attorney General must submit a report to Congress and the Secretary of Health and Human Services on the Bureau's and Review Panel's PREA-directed activities. The PREA also created a national clearinghouse within the National Institute of Corrections, which must provide periodic training and education programs to these authorities and submit a yearly report to Congress and the Secretary of Health and Human Services on their activities. An additional provision of the PREA is the requirement that the Attorney General provide funding to states for personnel, training, technical assistance, data collection, and equipment to prevent and prosecute prison rape. This funding will ensure that budgetary circumstances do not undermine state efforts to protect inmates and to safeguard communities from inmates returning to the community. The PREA also establishes a National Prison Rape Reduction Commission consisting of nine members who have expertise in the issue of prison rape. This body will conduct a comprehensive legal and factual study of the physical, mental, medical, social, and economic impacts of prison rape in the United States on federal, state, and local governments, communities, and social institutions, as well as on individuals, families, and businesses within these communities.

Within two years after the commission's initial meeting, it must submit a report to the President, Congress, Attorney General, Secretary of Health and Human Services, the director of the Federal Bureau of Prisons, the chief executive of each state, and the head of the DOC of each state. The commission must also recommend national standards for enhancing the detection, prevention, reduction, and punishment of prison rape. A final component of the PREA requires the Attorney General to publish a final rule within one year after receiving the commission's report establishing national standards for detecting, preventing, reducing, and punishing prison rape.

Mair (2003) says that the PREA is a "particularly important piece of legislation because litigation has failed to serve as a tool for protecting many inmates from sexual assault." She adds that the Eighth Amendment of the United States Constitution prohibits cruel and unusual punishment, and points to the seminal Supreme Court case on this issue, *Farmer v. Brennan*, which held that a prison official's "deliberate indifference" to a substantial risk of serious harm violates the Eighth Amendment. Mair writes, "Requiring proof of a particular prison official's state of mind, rather than what an objectively reasonable official should perceive, has been widely criticized; many victims of prison rape cannot prove the requisite level of awareness." Congress appears to address this concern in the PREA, Mair says, by noting, "States that do not take basic steps to abate prison rape by adopting standards that do not generate significant additional expenditures demonstrate such indifference."

In his opinion in *Farmer v. Brennan*, Justice Harry A. Blackman describes what happens in some correctional facilities:

> The horrors experienced by many young inmates, particularly those who, like petitioner, are convicted of nonviolent offenses, border on the unimaginable. Prison rape not only threatens the lives of those who fall prey to their aggressors, but is potentially devastating to the human spirit. Shame, depression, and a shattering loss of self-esteem accompany the perpetual terror the victim thereafter must endure ... Unable to fend for himself without the protection of prison officials, the victim finds himself at the mercy of larger, stronger, and ruthless inmates. Although formally sentenced to a term of incarceration, many inmates discover that their punishment, even for nonviolent offenses like credit card fraud or tax evasion, degenerates into a reign of terror unmitigated by the protection supposedly afforded by prison officials.

The PREA is several decades too late for Stephen Donaldson, who was the victim of a two-day gang rape in a Washington, DC jail after a Quaker pray-in on the White House lawn in 1973. In an article in a 1995 issue of *USA Today,* "Can We Put an End to Inmate Rape?" Donaldson, then-president of Stop Prison Rape, Inc., wrote:

> The fight against the crime of rape is doomed to failure, and will remain an exercise in futility, as long as it ignores the vast network of training schools for rapists: jails, prisons, and reform schools. The nation long has turned a blind eye to these facilities... There, rape is an institutionalized tradition, considered by prisoners a way to prove their manhood and satisfy sexual and power needs. Most of these inmates return to the streets with such attitudes, many of them having become rapists while locked up.

Donaldson adds that once victimized, "a prisoner is marked as a continual target for sexual exploitation and repeatedly is subjected to gang rapes, or must trade sexual use by one or a few men for protection from the remainder. An estimated 60,000 prisoners are subjected to involuntary sex each day. Very few of these rapes ever are reported to administrators, much less prosecuted." Donaldson adds, "This general silence on the vast extent of sexual victimization of adult males blocks the development of programs to acknowledge and help treat survivors, and thus promotes the vicious cycle that produces further assaults on women and men. It is an irrational and self-defeating taboo."

11.14 A CAREER WITH CROSS-OVER APPEAL: CORRECTIONS NURSING AND MEDICO-LEGAL DEATH INVESTIGATION

One forensic nurse who is in the process of crossing over from corrections nursing to medico-legal death investigation is Kathy Delaney, LPN, a former corrections nurse and current inpatient psychiatric nurse living in Arizona who is transitioning to the field of medico-legal death investigation but is able to integrate all of her nursing and forensic skills into a comprehensive set of skills with far-reaching application. She believes that corrections and forensic nursing is a natural fit within the scope and practice of nursing in general:

> While I don't believe that this type of nursing is for everyone, for those whom it does fit, it fits well. For anyone who enjoys being challenged in their nursing practice, this is the type of nursing to move to. While it is less structured than a traditional nursing floor or unit, it requires much more understanding and use of your nursing skills. You really have to be confident in your skills and assessments. You have to really look at your situations and scenes. You don't have doctors and varied tests painting you a nice picture of what is happening with your patient . . . you have to figure that out and then be able to report it to a doctor or medical examiner. You have to paint the picture for them.

Delaney explains how the nursing process is used in corrections nursing as well as in the investigation of sudden death:

> You are working on a yard or in a clinic in prison. You are very isolated, and you never know who is going to walk through your door or what you will have to respond to. You have to have excellent assessment skills. You have to be able to see and know what is going on. Most of the information you receive is from your correction officers. Even though they have had training in CPR and first aid, they are very reluctant to get involved, especially with describing what is going on. They are taught, "You are not medical," so you really have to get in there, assess, triage, observe, implement care, document, and evaluate what is happening. As for death investigation, you have to use this process after the fact. You are coming into a scene or situation that most probably has already happened. You are taking your information and working almost backward to identify what has happened. You assess the scene, you observe, document, and evaluate. Instead of asking what is going on, you are asking what happened.

Delaney's interesting career path had its start in the VA system, where she worked as a nurse. One day, a coworker had discovered corrections nursing and suggested to Delaney that she consider it herself. "She told me I had to try it," Delaney recalls.

> She said, "Kathy, it's so you! You'd love it!" So with that, I had to try. I worked pool at first to see if I liked it, and within a few months, I was working full time. I never knew this kind of nursing existed. As for death investigation, I have wanted to do that for a very long time, but there was never a place for nurses. You were either a medical examiner, a lab tech, or someone who worked as an assistant. I have always been interested in being able to go back to a scene and try to figure out what happened. Sometimes, family members just want to know what happened.

Delaney sees her transition from corrections nursing to death investigation as simply transferring one set of nursing skills to another toolbox full of skills that are highly complementary. "For me, I see a natural progression," Delaney explains:

> You use the same skills in both arenas. Oftentimes in corrections, you will have an assault or attempted murder. The inmate won't talk for fear of further retaliation. You have to work with the officers and inmate and try to piece together what has happened. Often the inmate will tell you something he or she would not tell an officer. You have to maintain a great rapport with your staff and officers, just like you do in death investigation. There has to be a great deal of trust and cooperation. There is no room for egos. I think that all of my corrections nursing fits with death investigation. You never know from moment to moment what you'll encounter, where you will need to respond, and who will be there. You must remain professional at all times, but ready to spring into action at a moment's notice. You must work in chaos, noise and the elements. You have to assess quickly and be able to assess what is going on around you, and you must remember personal safety and that of your co-workers.

As is the experience of many nurses working in forensic-related practice, Delaney says nothing prepared her for the rigors of this kind of work, simply because it was a discipline that was not explored in the nursing curriculum. "Nothing prepared me for the world of correctional nursing," Delaney confirms:

> It was never discussed in nursing school. I didn't know anyone who did it until I started in this field. Training was definitely on the job, and I think I learned the most from my officers and inmates. Now, correctional nursing has helped me prepare for medico-legal death investigation. I learned that you will be out in the elements, there will be confusion, noise, and lots of other people around the crime scene. I have learned that you prepare yourself to be able to jump in and hit the ground running, just like you do in corrections nursing.

Without a specific curriculum that addressed corrections nursing, Delaney says she relied on on-the-job experience as well as gleaning information from any available source. Many times, that meant forensic-related television shows, although, she admits, the science presented doesn't often reflect real-life scenarios. "I really did learn everything on the job, and in fact, most people don't know that the disciplines of corrections nursing or nurse death investigation even exist. With all of the forensic TV shows, like the *CSI* series, people are more aware of forensics, but you only see the crime scene units. They don't feature nurses, just fancy toys and solving the case in one hour." Lacking formal education in forensic nursing, Delaney did what many nurses in her situation do, which is simply to meet the demands of the job head-on and learn the subtleties of the work as it unfolds:

> I never had a forensic curriculum, so I started working in corrections and came to forensics through "the back door," so to speak. As for corrections nursing, it is pretty much learn as you go. Nursing programs are not even mentioning forensics as a specialty practice. When I decided to become a death investigator, I had to go out on my own and find someone who taught the class. Forensics is popular with crime scene investigation, thanks to TV, but it never clearly shows nurses. There is a big difference in being a blood spatter/fingerprint expert than being a forensic nurse. For some reason, schools of nursing are still not acknowledging this nursing specialty, and there is no clinical preparation to be had. There is no formal training that begins to explain the demands of the job or the expectations of the victims. Unfortunately this type of nursing is still trial by fire. The good news is that no one works under pressure and trial by fire like a nurse.

Delaney says that no matter how much experience a nurse might have, there are some elements of corrections nursing that might hold unexpected surprises:

> I don't think there is any preparation you can make for the first time you hear that big steel door close in a prison. I also didn't know that I would be walking in the cell blocks with inmates or that I would be responding to fights or riots. I didn't know that I'd be responding to a stabbed inmate in a recreation yard, surrounded by riled-up inmates. I didn't know I'd be delivering meds in the rain or in a dust storm. I thought I'd be in a little clinic and the inmates would come to me because they had a headache or a sprained ankle. I never knew I'd be standing in the middle of rival gangs or examining a suicide attempt on someone from death row. I learned everything firsthand, and experience was my teacher. I think it would have been nice if the correctional system required even medical personnel to attend one or two days of training at the officer academy. That way, nurses would learn about basic safety and the manipulation of inmates, and boy, are they manipulative! They have nothing else to do, so everything they do has some little purpose for them. It is an extremely challenging environment in this regard.

Delaney's interest in forensic nursing was sparked by several exposures to forensic science when she was younger:

> This is going to date me, but I fell in love with the whole forensic idea from the TV show *Quincy*. To be able to figure out how someone died absolutely fascinated me. When I was 16 and in the 4-H Club, we attended meetings that often featured guest speakers. During one meeting, the county medical examiner spoke to us; five minutes after he started, I was the only one left in the room. I must have talked with him for two hours. Each picture he showed me was more fascinating than the last. I will never forget when he explained to me that he could tell if someone died in a fire or was just placed in a fire. I was amazed, to say the least. I never forgot that the absence of soot in the lungs meant a decedent did not die in a fire. Then he told me how much school was involved in becoming an ME, especially chemistry, and my hopes were dashed. It has only been in the last few years that forensic nursing has come to the forefront of practice. For me, part of its allure was working with the police and being able to figure out what had happened at a scene, as well as to know that things are seldom as they appear. I also liked the idea of being able to find out what actually happened and to give a family or a loved one some closure. Sometimes why or how something happened can be so important.

Delaney says she has a strong sense of purpose about her occupation, a necessary component to be able to do this challenging type of work in the first place. "You are trying your best to find out what happened; this can offer closure to the family," she reiterates. She also says that working in corrections nursing has helped her to cultivate a strong sense of justice. "An injury or a death may be something simple like a heart attack or it may be a result of a crime. Either way, you are working to find the truth." Finding that truth, Delaney says, assures her a spot in the medico-legal continuum. "You are working and investigating right alongside law enforcement. If your case turns out to be criminal, then you are working in the legal portion. It brings the two together. In some cases, you are lucky to find out what happened and see it go through the legal process; you get to work in both arenas." To this end, Delaney says good communication is essential. "You must have that skill to improve your working relationships. I also feel it is important to leave your ego at home, because cooperation is vital. Everyone has a job to do, no matter how small or large. Teamwork allows you to be twice as productive, and by working together, anything is possible."

Sometimes, Delaney says, the complexity of her job is compounded by the fact that many of her medical and forensic colleagues, as well as laypersons, do not comprehend how nurses contribute to the field:

> I don't feel that members of the general public understand what a death investigator is; their perception is what they see on TV. Most people would not be interested in a case of an elderly person who died in his or her home due to cardiac complications. It is not glamorous or exciting; it is rather simple and mundane. It is, however, important, especially to the individual's family. My regular nursing colleagues really do not understand what forensics is

> about. Most think that if a person is dead, then it's not really a nurse's prerogative. In my county, our medical examiner is not very open to the contributions of nurses, and I think a lot of that attitude has to do with the perception that hiring nurses costs too much money. As for lawmakers' understanding of what we do, it seems to be the same story. There is never enough money in the budget. I feel that nurses working in forensics can fulfill many tasks. We can be the liaison between law enforcement and the ME's office. We possess awesome assessment, writing, and communication skills. We are able to multitask and we learn on our feet. We also have the ability to be empathetic to family members. I think that once we can show lawmakers what we can do, we can prove to them that when it comes to saving money in the long run, nurses are the best bang for the buck!

Faced with obvious challenges to local and state budgets, Delaney agrees that there are neither enough resources for nor enough support of forensic nursing. "At this point, nurses are not really recognized or supported in the field of forensics. The only arena that is truly recognized is the sexual assault nurse examiner role. Law enforcement is wary of nurses and very protective of their crime scenes. It takes a long time to build up trust, and we are not thought of as colleagues." Delaney adds:

> The biggest barrier is the "us vs. them" mentality. Law enforcement feels that nurses are going to take over their scene somehow, and we don't. I want to talk to police departments and show how nurses would make a great addition to their departments. We come already possessing the skills that take years to develop. Essentially, we come ready made. Nurses work hard; we're not afraid to work strange hours or to work on call. We also work underpaid. Who else is better suited to work with law enforcement?

Like forensic psychiatric nursing, corrections nursing is a high-voltage environment that can trigger feelings of burnout in its nurses. Delaney says she copes in a number of ways, including maintaining an upbeat attitude:

> I deal with burnout the same way I did with traditional nursing. For me, the first antidote is humor. Let's face it, nursing and law enforcement have the same sense of humor. I also keep myself busy with other things. I love going to movies, and I enjoy music. I write poetry and I am a published poet; I cross-stitch. Having hobbies and things you like to do really helps take your mind off of work and your cases. Don't be afraid to have fun and to leave your work when you are not at work.

Burnout also can be thwarted by taking great pride and satisfaction in one's accomplishments. Many nurses can point to instances in which a particular case or a certain patient served as a reminder of why the work is worth doing in the first place. Delaney points to a case that helped to clinch her interest in forensics. "I had a patient who came to us from a nursing home," Delaney recalls:

> He was dirty, had terrible bedsores, and was in generally poor condition. It turned out that he wandered away from home seven years before. He was from Chicago and somehow had wound up in Phoenix. His daughters couldn't find him, and the police became involved. They were able to reunite him with a daughter in California who decided to sue the nursing home for his terrible care. I became involved by working with the police to photograph his wounds and assist with documentation of his care and injuries. I assisted the detectives in interpreting information found in his chart and securing the medical records. In the end, we got his life stabilized; I never did find out if the case went to court, but it was great to be part of the team. It was quite a feeling of accomplishment to put all those pieces together.

It's the kind of work that can teach a nurse something about herself, Delaney says:

> In working with law enforcement, I have learned a great deal about cooperation and communication. You are working with so many different people from different areas, that good communication is a must. Working in this area has taught me to work under pressure, and to be extremely flexible because anything can and usually does happen. As for surprises, I never expected to see the things I have seen and be able to work so well in this environment. It is definitely not for everyone, but I was surprised to find out just how well it suited me.

Nurturing her love of forensic investigation has brought Delaney to a point where she has encountered several frustrating yet surmountable obstacles. "Gender has been a factor for me," Delaney reveals:

> The county and state that I am in is very conservative and has a "good 'ol boys" mentality. Education plays a little into it, I think. Law enforcement tends to look at us and say, "Oh, she's a nurse, not a cop." They love to see us in the ER, but working with them in the field is something else. How do I handle it? Well, I am persistent. I am confident in my skills and I'm not afraid to ask questions... usually I ask a lot of them, and this shows that I'm serious. Eventually, they relax a little. Once the ice is broken and they have the chance to see what I can do, then I usually get the support I need. I just approach it like this: "Anything you can do, I can do." I think that being a consummate professional and being a little thick-skinned can help nurses cope until slowly, this bias can be eliminated. The concept of nurses in law enforcement is still relatively new and it will take a while for all of this to work itself out.

Delaney balances the ups and the downs of her journey by enjoying the process as it unfolds. "I really like not knowing what is going to happen," she enthuses:

> I enjoy being part of a team. I like it when you can get something solved or contribute a piece of the puzzle. Sometimes it can be very difficult because you will see some pretty brutal stuff during your career. Crime scene images may be hard to get out of your mind... especially in corrections where I have seen so much brutality. When you enter a crime scene, whatever happened has happened. In corrections, you have people severely injured, but still alive and needing treatment. When it is over, you know that that person is going right back into that same situation. Some days that fact is hard to deal with.

When asked to describe an average day in corrections nursing, Delaney responds:

> An average day... do we even have those? In the world of corrections, you have your clinic with your sick call. Inmates are scheduled to see the nurse or physician for a variety of complaints, such as a sore throat, sprained ankle, or sore back. Sometimes it may be a medication renewal. You also see the diabetics and give insulin, as well as any treatments. You typically see about 150 to 200 inmates in an eight-hour shift, with about seven nurses and two to three other health care providers working with you. You are busy all day, not to mention that there is a med pass per shift. While all this is going on, of course, there are the fights, the injuries, and other emergencies to which you must respond. You are on the move all during your shift. Anything can happen, and it usually does. Anything can interrupt your routine, such as a sudden busload of new arrivals that must be seen, or even the eruption of a riot. It is an environment where anything can happen at any time. You have to be sharp and safe.

Recognizing the work's rewards, challenges, and difficulties, Delaney says someone wanting to break into the field should have a realistic idea of what they are about to encounter:

> I would tell them that the work can be difficult, stressful, and often chaotic. They would need to be very organized and flexible, and possess good communication and interpersonal skills. They would need to understand that humor, even bad humor, is important for people in this line of work to relieve stress. I would recommend that they come out and shadow someone working in the field to see what it is like, because it is nothing like what is portrayed on TV. Corrections can be tough, in that you are locked up with the inmates. I have been assaulted in a riot, and a fellow officer was killed by an inmate. I can't emphasize enough that this work is tough; it is a difficult job and not everyone is suited for it. You will come face to face with people who have killed and don't think twice about it. You have to be firm, fair, and consistent. You have to be able to hold your own. You learn to look over your shoulder, or never have an inmate between you and an exit. These are people who are in prison because they can't follow the rules of society. They are not nice, but they *are* people. You have to show respect to get respect. You are not the judge and jury; you are there to help care for them. It is not your job to punish or judge them. That doesn't mean that there are not rules to be followed, as there are. There are consequences for not following the rules. It is hard not to judge them, so that is why I prefer not to know why they are there. Sometimes you can't help it, especially if they are involved in a high-profile case.

Delaney adds, "There was an inmate who had done seven years for rape and was cleared through DNA. That really sent the message that innocent people occasionally wind up in prison. He had been labeled a felon and treated with little respect. Although inmates are sentenced to do time, they are entitled to medical care and medications regardless of the crime committed. That really helped me not to be judgmental."

Delaney believes there will always be a need for good corrections nurses, and says the occupational outlook is a solid one. "Crime rates continue to rise, and more prisons and jails are being built. For this reason, corrections nursing will remain a good, steady job opportunity. For death investigation, I think it is just coming to light. I think that this will be a growing area of nursing. Once we can crack the ice and show our skills, I think that this will be a promising nursing specialty." She continues, "I definitely feel that there is room for growth. Forensic nursing is changing all the time. I think that if we get more nurses working with law enforcement, that this will open up a whole area of practice. I think that the possibilities can become endless. In forensic nursing, there is something new to learn every day.

Regarding advocacy work in support of forensic nursing, Delaney says nurses should "get out there and show law enforcement and medical examiners that we are qualified and up to the challenge." She continues:

> We know how to assess things. We are observant. We have a great attention to details. We are motivated. We are team players. We learn easily and can teach. We are excellent in working with people and would be a huge asset in working with grieving family members. We can be the go-between for the medical examiner and law enforcement. We can be an excellent source of assistance to law enforcement. Given a chance, I know that we can be a valuable member of the team.

On occasion, Delaney also has to disprove a few common misperceptions:

> Most other professionals have not heard of either corrections nursing or nurse death investigation, while others don't really think that forensic or correctional nursing is

> really a nursing subspecialty. Most other nurses think that this particular discipline is easy nursing. It is actually some of the most challenging forms of nursing. While you are not saving a life like you might in the ICU perhaps, you are working with an inmate on death row who is demanding medical attention. I would like to see these specialties addressed in nursing programs so that the myths can be debunked. And I'd like to see these nursing specialties getting more professional exposure. Forensics has gotten a boost in general due to television and shows like *CSI*; the word *forensic* has become a household word, so that's a step in the right direction.

Another assumption about the field is that corrections nursing is a bridge between the criminal justice system and the mental health system. "Mental health is fairly territorial regarding their practice. They often make statements like, 'Oh, we don't deal with that, we work with the head, the mental processes.' I always felt that we covered mental health on off times but that we work fairly independently. We deal with a lot of medical and emergency issues. I think that we work together but yet we are independent." There is also the assumption that forensic psych nursing and correctional nursing are one and the same. "While this assumption exists, I don't feel that it is damaging," Delaney comments. "This is still a fairly new nursing specialty. I think that continued education and awareness of the differences will help. Most other clinicians just seem to think, 'Oh, they work in corrections; that's an easy job.'"

Regarding misconceptions about the care of offenders Delaney notes:

> I think the most common yet difficult thing to grasp for practitioners is the general attitude toward inmates. Yes, they are people who have done some pretty horrific things. They have been judged and sentenced already, so that is not our job. We are not the jury. We shouldn't judge. Some times you can't help but find out what they did and that is a challenge to be able to treat and care for them. But, we have chosen this particular field of practice, and we must rise above that. Often a practitioner may feel that they are an inmate and they don't deserve certain treatment or medication. By law, they are required to receive medical care. You need to remember that you are there in a medical capacity, not a legal one.

Delaney would also like to see increased opportunities for forensic nurses to advance their education and capture credentials that better reflect their skill levels. "I think that forensic psych nursing and SANE/SART programs have made the most headway recently. They have worked hard to have certifications to advance their practice. Corrections nursing has come a long way and offers certification for nurses, physicians, and even CNAs and techs. It is a difficult test, but worth the effort. I would like to see more levels offered, and I'm sure that will come along one day."

As for correcting nursing's identity in the community, Delaney is quick to say, "I don't think that there *is* an identity out in the community. Most people have no concept or even interest in what goes on in prison. Once the drama of the trial is over, the accused and the convicted are forgotten. When I mention that I was in prison, people will first look amazed and ask what I did to get in there," she says, laughing. "Then they look embarrassed and ask, 'Oh, you were a guard?' They really have no idea that nurses or doctors actually work in jails and prisons. They are always amazed by it. Forensic colleagues tend to think of correctional nursing as the blue-collar, hard-labor part of the correctional environment. We are accepted, but not thought of as the elite."

Whether or not forensic nursing will ever be truly accepted remains to be seen, but Delaney comments:

> I think that one day it will be respected fully by others in the scientific community. I think that there has been an improvement in forensic scientists and physicians' acceptance of forensic nurses. They are beginning to acknowledge our skills and credentials. In law enforcement, we have a lot more respect than traditional nursing. I think that we must promote ourselves and become much more visible. We must ensure that we have educational opportunities to grow and market ourselves in the medical community.

REFERENCES

Alarid, L. F. Sexual assault and coercion among incarcerated women prisoners: Excerpts from prison letters. *Prison J. 80*, 391–406, 2000.

American Nurses Association. *Nursing: Scope and Standards of Practice*. Washington, DC: nursesbooks.org. 2004.

Amnesty International, United States of America. *Not Part of My Sentence: Violations of the Human Rights of Women in Custody*. Amnesty International. 1999.

Anno, B. J. Health behaviors in prisons and correctional facilities. In D. S. Goehman, Ed. *Handbook of Health Behaviors Research III*. New York: Plenum. 1997.

Anno, B. J., Graham, C., Lawrence, J. E., & Shansky, R. *Correctional Health Care: Addressing the Needs of Elderly, Chronically Ill, and Terminally Ill Inmates*. Washington, DC: Criminal Justice Institute, National Institute of Corrections. 2004.

Austin, W. Relational ethics in forensic psychiatric settings. *J Psycho Nurs Mental Health Serv. 39*, 9, 12–17, 2001.

Baro, A. L. Spheres of consent: An analysis of the sexual abuse and sexual exploitation of women incarcerated in the state of Hawaii. *Women Crim Justice. 8*, 61–84, 1997.

Bartollas, C., & Sieverdes, C. M. The sexual victim in a coeducational juvenile correctional institution. *Prison J. 58*, 80–90, 1983.

Beck, A. J., & Harrison, P. M. *Prisoners in 2000: Bureau of Justice Statistics Bulletin* (NCJ 188207). Washington, DC: U.S. Department of Justice. 2001.

Bell, C., Coven, M., Cronan, J. P., Garza, C. A., Guggemos, J., & Storto, L. Rape and sexual misconduct in the prison system: Analyzing America's most "open" secret. *Yale Law Policy Rev. 18,* 195–223, 1999.

Bernier, S. L. Corrections in mental health nursing. *J Psycho Nurs Mental Health Serv. 24,* 6, 20–25, 1986.

Borum, R. Improving the clinical practice of violence risk assessment. *Am Psycho. 51,* 9, 945–956, 1996.

Brooker, C., & Whyte, L. *Multidisciplinary Team Working in Secure Psychiatric Environments.* London: High Security Psychiatric Services Commissioning Board. 2000.

Brown, G. Correctional officers as members of a psychiatric team. Available at: http://www.educ.uvic.ca/epls/faculty/storey/Brown.htm.

Bureau of Justice Statistics. *Special Report: Women Offenders* (NCJ 175688). Washington, DC: Bureau of Justice Statistics. 1999.

Bureau of Justice Statistics. *Bulletin: HIV in Prisons, 2000* (NCJ 196023). Washington, DC: Bureau of Justice Statistics. 2002.

Burnard, P. The expanded role of the forensic psychiatric nurse. In P. Morrison & P. Burnard, Eds. *Aspects of Forensic Psychiatric Nursing* (pp. 139–154). Aldershot, England: Avebury. 1992.

Burrow, S. The role conflict of the forensic nurse. *Senior Nurse. 13,* 20–25, 1993.

Butler, T. Preliminary findings from the inmate health survey of the inmate population in the New South Wales Correctional System (Corrections Health Service; NSW Department of Health Report No. 365/66 09944). Sydney: NSWCHS. 1997.

Conklin, T. J., Lincoln, T., & Tuthill, R. W. Self-reported health and prior health behaviors of newly admitted correctional inmates. *Am J Public Health. 90,* 1939–1941, 2000.

Donaldson, S. Can we put an end to inmate rape? *USA Today.* May 1, 1995.

Estelle v. Gamble, 429 U.S. 97, 106, 1996.

Ewers, P., Bradshaw, T., McGovern, J. M., & Ewers, B. Does training in psychosocial interventions reduce burnout rates in forensic nurses? *J Adv Nurs. 37,* 5, 470–476, 2002.

Farmer v. Brennan, 511 U.S. 825, 838, 1994.

Goldkuhle, U. Health service utilization by women in prison: Health needs indicators and response effects. *J Correctional Healthcare. 1,* 63–83, 1999.

Greenfeld, L. A., & Snell, T. L. *Women Offenders.* Washington, DC: U.S. Department of Justice, Bureau of Justice Statistics. 1999.

Greer, K. R. The changing nature of interpersonal relationships in a women's prison. *Prison J. 80,* 442–468, 2000.

Hammer, R. Caring in forensic nursing: Expanding the holistic model. *J Psychoso Nurs Mental Health Serv. 38,* 11, 18–24, 2000.

Hammett, T., Harmon, M. P., & Rhodes, W. The burden of infectious disease among inmates of and releasees from U.S. correctional facilities. *Am J Public Health. 92,* 1789–1794, 2002.

Harrison, A. A guide to risk assessment. *Nurs Times. 99,* 9, 44, 2003.

Harrison, P. M., & Beck, A. J. Prisoners in 2002. U.S. Department of Justice, Bureau of Justice Statistics Bulletin (NCJ 198877). 2003. Available at: http:// www.ojp.usdoj.gov/bjs/pub/pdf/p02.pdf.

Hayes, L. M. *Prison Suicide: An Overview and Guide to Prevention.* Washington, DC: U.S. Justice Department, National Institute of Corrections. 1995.

Hazelwood, R., Reboussin, R., & Warren, J. Serial rape: Correlates of increased aggression and the relationship of offender pleasure to victim resistance. *J Interpersonal Violence, 4,* 1, 65–78, 1989.

Human Rights Watch. *All too familiar: Sexual abuse of women in U.S. state prisons.* New York: Human Rights Watch. Available at: www.hrw.org/summaries/s.us96d.html. 1996.

Johnsen, C. Women in prison. *Nurse Week.* Available at: www.nurseweek.com.

Johnson, J. D., & Laffa, S. Psychiatric nursing in the correctional setting. Nursing Spectrum. 2004.

Kassebaum, G. Sex in prison. *Sexual Behavior. 2,* 39–45, 1972.

Love, C. L., & Morrison, E. F. Forensic psychiatric nursing: Struggling to happen, failing to thrive. Forensic Nurse. 2002.

Lynch, V. A. Forensic aspects of health care: New roles, new responsibilities. *J Psychosoc Nurs and Ment Health Serv. 31,* 11, 5–6, 1993.

Lynch, V. A. Clinical forensic nursing: A new perspective in the management of crime victims from trauma to trial. *Critical Care Nursing Clinics of North America. 7,* 3, 489–507, 1995.

Lynch, V. A. *Clinical forensic nursing: A new perspective in trauma.* Collins: Bearhawk Consulting Group. 1997.

Maeve, M. K., & Vaughn, M. S. Nursing with prisoners: The practice of caring, forensic nursing or penal harm nursing? *Adv Nurs Sci. 24,* 2, 47–64, 2001.

Mair, J. S. New hope for victims of prison sexual assault. *J Law, Med Ethics. Winter, 31,* 4, 606–606, 2003.

Mariner, J. *No Escape: Male Rape in U.S. Prisons.* New York: Human Rights Watch. 2001. Available at: http://hrw.org/reports/2001/prison/report.html.

Martin, T. Something special: Forensic psychiatric nursing. *J Psych Mental Health Nurs. 8,* 25–32, 2001.

Mason, T. Forensic psychiatric nursing: A literature review and thematic analysis of role tensions. *J Psych Mental Health Nurs. 9,* 511–520, 2002.

Mason, T., & Gerry, C. Toward a "forensic lens" model of multidisciplinary training. *J Psych Mental Health Nurs. 9,* 541–551, 2002.

McClelland, N. Mental health. Look back at anger. *Nurs Times. 91,* 6, 59–61, 1995.

Moritz, P. Healthcare in correctional facilities: A nursing challenge. *Nurs Outlook. 30,* 253–259, 1982.

Morrison, E., Morman, G., Bonner, G., Taylor, C., Abraham, I., & Lathan, L. Reducing staff injuries and violence in a forensic psychiatric setting. *Arch Psych Nurs. 16,* 3, 108–117, 2002.

National Commission on Correctional Health Care. *The Health Status of Soon-To-Be-Released Inmates.* Washington, DC: National Commission on Correctional Health. 2002. Available at: http://www.ncchc.org/pubs/pubs_stbr.vol1.html.

National Institute of Corrections. Sexual misconduct in prisons: Law, remedies, and incidence (Special Issues in Corrections, NIC Information Center). Longmont, CO: LIS, Inc. 2000.

Niskala, H. Competencies and skills required by nurses working in forensic areas. *Western J Nurs Res. 8,* 400–413, 1986.

Occupational Safety and Health Administration. *Guidelines for Preventing Workplace Violence for Health Care and Social Service Workers.* Washington, DC: Occupational Safety and Health Administration. 1998.

Peternelj-Taylor, C. Forensic psychiatric nursing: The paradox of custody and caring. *J Psycho Nurs Mental Health Serv. 37,* 9, 9–11, 1999.

Peternelj-Taylor, C. A., & Johnson, R. L. Serving time: Psychiatric mental health nursing in corrections. *J Psycho Nurs. 33,* 12–19, 1995.

Prison Rape Elimination Act of 2003, Pub. Law. No. 108-79, 117 Stat. 972-989 (codified at 42 U.S.C.S. 15601-15609) (enacted Sept. 4, 2003).

Quintal, S. A. Violence against psychiatric nurses: An untreated epidemic? *J Psycho Nurs Mental Health Serv. 40,* 1, 46–55, 2002.

Rask, M., & Aberg, J. Swedish forensic nursing care: Nurses' professional contributions and educational needs. *J Psych Mental Health Nurs. 9,* 531–539, 2002.

Robinson, D., & Kettles, A. The emerging profession of forensic nursing: Myth or reality? *Psychiatric Care, 5,* 6, 146–152, 1998.

Schein, E. *Organizational culture and leadership.* San Francisco, CA: Jossey-Bass. 1992.

Sekula, K., Holmes, D., Zoucha, R., Desantis, J., & Olshansky, E. Forensic psychiatric nursing: Discursive practices and the emergence of a specialty. *J Psycho Nurs Mental Health Serv. 39,* 9, 51–57, 2001.

Sloan, C. D. Legal origins and issues behind correctional nursing. *Nursing Spectrum.* April 13, 2003.

Smoyak, S. A. Psychosocial nursing in public vs. private sectors: An introduction. *J Psycho Nurs. 29,* 8, 6–12, 1991.

Springfield, D. Sisters in misery: Utilizing international law to protect United States female prisoners from sexual abuse. *Indiana Intl Comp Law Rev. 10,* 457–486, 2000.

Steele, R. L. Staff attitudes toward seclusion and restraint: Anything new? *Perspect Psychiatr Care. 29,* 3, 23–28, 1993.

Struckman-Johnson, C., & Struckman-Johnson, D. Sexual coercion rates in seven midwestern prison facilities for men. *Prison J. 80,* 379–390, 2000.

Struckman-Johnson, C., & Struckman-Johnson, D. Sexual coercion reported by women in three midwestern prisons. *J Sex Res. 39,* 3, 217–227, 2002.

Struckman-Johnson, C. J., Struckman-Johnson, D. L., Rucker, L., Bumby, K., & Donaldson, S. Sexual coercion reported by men and women in prison. *J Sex Res. 33,* 67–76, 1996.

Teplin, L. A. The prevalence of severe mental disorder among male urban jail detainees: Comparison with the Epidemiologic Catchment Area Program. *Am J Public Health. 80,* 6, 663–669, 1990.

Terpstra, T. L., Terpstra, T. L., Pettee, E. J., & Hunter, M. Nursing staff's attitudes toward seclusions and restraint. *J Psycho Nurs Mental Health Serv. 39,* 5, 20–28, 2001.

Turvey, B. E. The impressions of a man: An objective forensic guideline to profiling violent serial sex offenders. San Leanaro, CA: Knowledge Solutions. 1995.

United Kingdom Central Council. *Nursing in Secure Environments: Summary and Action Plan From a Scoping Study.* Lancashire, England: University of Central Lancashire. 1998.

Warren, J., Reboussin, R., Hazelwood, R., & Wright J. Prediction of rapist type and violence from verbal, physical and sexual scales. *J Interpersonal Violence, 6,* 1, 55–67, 1991.

Whynot, E. M. Women who use injection drugs: The social context of risk. *Can Med Assoc J. 159,* 355–358, 1998.

Whyte, L. Forensic nursing: A review of concepts and definitions. *Nurs Stan. 11,* 23, 46–7, 1997.

Woods, P. Incidents: Reporting and management. In C. Dale, T. Thompson, & P. Woods, Eds. *Forensic Mental Health: Issues in Practice* (pp. 99–107). London: Bailliere Tindal in association with the Royal College of Nursing. 2001.

Zlotnick, C. Posttraumatic stress disorder, PTSD co-morbidity, and childhood abuse among incarcerated women. *J Nervous Mental Dis. 185,* 761–763, 1997.

RECOMMENDED READINGS

Akhavain, P. Collaborative practice: A nursing perspective of the psychiatric interdisciplinary treatment team. *Holistic Nurs Pract. 13,* 1–11, 1999.

Allen, B., & Bosta, D. *Games Criminals Play.* Sacramento, CA: Rae John. 1993.

Altice, F. L., Mostashari, F., & Friedland, G. H. Trust and the acceptance of and adherence to antiretroviral therapy. *J Acquir Immune Defic Synd. 28,* 1, 47–58, 2001.

Amaro, H. An expensive policy: The impact of inadequate funding for substance abuse treatment. *Am J Public Health. 89,* 657–659, 1999.

American Nurses Association. *Code of Ethics for Nurses With Interpretive Statements.* Washington, DC: American Nurses Publishing. 2001.

American Nurses Association. *Nursing's Social Policy Statement* (Second edition). Washington, DC: nursesbooks.org. 2003.

Baer, R., Goebel, G., & Flexer, R. W. An interdisciplinary team approach to rehabilitation. In R. Flexer & P. Solomon, Eds. *Psychiatric Rehabilitation in Practice* (pp. 63–78). New York: Butterworth-Heinemann. 1993.

Bureau of Justice Statistics. *Special Report: Incarcerated Parents and Their Children* (NCJ 182335). Washington, DC: Bureau of Justice Statistics. 2000.

Bureau of Justice Statistics. *Special Report: Medical Problems of Inmates, 1997* (NCJ 181644). 2001.

Cotton, D. J., & Groth, A. N. Inmate rape: Prevention and intervention. *J Prison Jail Health. 2,* 1, 47–57, 1982.

Dumond, R. W. The sexual assault of male inmates in incarcerated settings. *Intl J Socio Law.* 137–157, 1992.

Eigenberg, H. M. Correctional officers' definitions of rape in male prisons. *J Crim Justice. 28,* 435–449, 2000.

Encinares, M., & Lorbergs, K. A. Framing nursing practice within a forensic outpatient service. *J Psychosoc Nurs. 39,* 35–41, 2001.

Finn, P. No frills prisons and jails: A movement in flux. *Fed Prob. 60,* 3, 35–44, 1996.

Fogel, C. I., & Belyea, M. Psychosocial risk factors in pregnant inmates: A challenge for nursing. *Am J Mat Child Nurs. 26,* 1, 10–16, 2001.

Freudenberg, N. Adverse effects of U.S. jail and prison policies on the health and well-being of women of color. *Am J Public Health. 92,* 1895–1899, 2002.

Friel, C., & Chaloner, C. The developing role of the forensic community nurse. *Nurs Times. 92,* 29, 33–35, 1996.

Hensley, C., Struckman-Johnson, C., & Eigenberg, H. The history of prison sex research. *Prison J. 80,* 360–367, 2000.

Holmes, D. Police and pastoral power: Governmentality and correctional forensic psychiatric nursing. *Nurs Inquiry. 9,* 2, 84–92, 2002.

Hufft, A. G. The role of the forensic nurse in the USA. In D. Robinson & A. Kettles, Eds. *Forensic Nursing and Multidisciplinary Care of the Mentally Disordered Offender.* London: Jessica Kingsley Publishers. 2000.

Human Rights Watch. (1996). *All Too Familiar: Sexual Abuse of Women in U.S. State Prisons.* New York: Yale University Press.

Ibrahim, A. I. Deviant sexual behavior in men's prisons. *Crime Delin. 20,* 38–44, 1974.

Kunselman, J., Tewksbury, R., Dumond, R. W., & Dumond, D. A. Nonconsensual sexual behavior. In C. Hensley, Ed. *Prison Sex: Practice and Policy* (pp. 27–47). Boulder, CO: Rienner. 2002.

Laumann, E. O., Gagnon, J. H., Michael, R. T., & Michaels, S. *The Social Organization of Sexuality: Sexual Practices in the United States.* Chicago: University of Chicago Press. 1994.

Lepnurm, J. *Multi vs. Inter vs. Transdisciplinary Approaches: A Literature Review and Recommendation for the RPC.* Saskatoon, Canada: Correctional Service of Canada. 1999.

Lockwood, D. Issues in prison sexual violence. In M. C. Braswell, R. H. Montgomery, Jr., & L. X. Lombardo, Eds. *Prison Violence in America* (Second edition, pp. 97–102). Cincinnati, OH: Anderson Publishing. 1994.

Love, C. C., & Hunter, M. E. Types of weapons and patterns of use in a forensic state hospital. *Hosp Comm Psych. 44,* 11, 1082–1085, 1993.

Love, C. C., & Hunter, M. E. Engaging patients in violence prevention: The Atascadero State Hospital experience. *J Psychoso Nurs Mental Health Serv. 37,* 9, 32–36, 1999.

Maeve, M. K., & Vaughn, M. S. Nursing with prisoners: The practice of caring, forensic nursing or penal harm nursing? *Adv Nurs Sci. 24,* 2, 47–64, 2001.

Maier, G. J., Bernstein, M., & Musholt, E. A. Personal coping mechanisms for prison clinicians: Toward transformation. *J Prison Jail Health. 8,* 1, 29–39, 1989.

Maitland, A. S., & Sluder, R. D. Victimization and youthful inmates: An empirical analysis. *Prison J. 78,* 1, 55–73, 1998.

Martin, R. E. Would female inmates accept Papanicolaou smear screening if it was offered to them during their incarceration? *Can Med Assoc J. 162,* 657–658, 2000.

Mason, T., Williams, R., & Vivian-Byrne, S. Multi-disciplinary working in a forensic mental health setting: Ethical codes of reference. *J Psych Mental Health Nurs. 9,* 563–572, 2002.

McCorkle, R. C. Personal precautions to violence in prisons. *Crim Justice Behav. 19,* 2, 160–173, 1992.

Miller, R. K., Maier, G. J., Van Rybroek, G. J., & Weidman, J. Treating patients doing time: A forensic perspective. *Hosp Comm Psych. 40,* 960–962, 1989.

Moore, M. S. *Law and Psychiatry: Rethinking the Relationship.* London: Cambridge University Press. 1984.

Muehlenhard, C. L., Harney, P. A., & Jones, J. M. From victim precipitated rape to date rape: How far have we come? *Ann Rev Sex Res. 3,* 219–253, 1992.

Myers, W. C., Burton, P., Sanders, P. D., Donat, K., Cheney, J., Fitzpatrick, T., & Monaco, L. Project back-on track at one year: A delinquency treatment program for early-career juvenile offenders. *J Am Acad Child Adolesc Psychiatr. 39,* 1127–1134, 2000.

Neeley, C. L., Addison, L., & Moreland, D. C. Addressing the needs of elderly offenders. *Correct Today. 59,* 5, 120–124, 1997.

Ong, A. D., & Weiss, D. J. The impact of anonymity on responses to sensitive questions. *J App Soc Psych. 30,* 1691–1708, 2000.

Orr, D., & Helderstein, D. HIPAA in state correctional systems. *J Correct Health Care. 9,* 3, 345–359, 2002.

Peternelj-Taylor, C. A., & Johnson, R. L. Serving time: Psychiatric mental health nursing in corrections. *J Psycho Nurs. 33,* 8, 12–19, 1995.

Saum, C. H., Surratt, J., & Bennett, R. Sex in prison: Exploring the myths and realities. *Prison J. 75,* 4, 413–430, 1995.

Scales, C. J., Phillips, R. T., & Crysler, D. Security aspects of clinical care. *Am J Forensic Psych. 7,* 2, 49–57, 1989.

Schaefer, P. When a client develops an attraction: Successful resolution vs. boundary violation. *J Psych Mental Health Nurs. 4,* 203–211, 1997.

Selling, L. S. The pseudo family. *Am J Soc. 37,* 247–253, 1931.

Shelton, D. Health status of young offenders and their families. *J Nurs Scholarship. 32,* 2, 173–178, 2000.

Shuter, J., Bell, D., Graham, D., Holbrook, K. A., & Bellin, E. Y. Rates of and risk factors for trichomoniasis among pregnant inmates in New York City. *Sexually Transmitted Dis. 25,* 6, 303–307, 1998.

Stephson, J. Drug treatment behind bars. *JAMA. 278,* 536, 1997.

Stone, A. *Law, Psychiatry and Morality.* Washington, DC: American Psychiatric Press. 1984.

Struckman-Johnson, C., & Anderson, P. Men do and women don't: Difficulties in researching sexually aggressive women. In P. B. Anderson & C. Struckman-Johnson, Eds. *Sexually Aggressive Women: Current Perspectives and Controversies* (pp. 9–18). New York: Guilford. 1998.

Swinton, J., & Boyd, J. Autonomy and personhood: The forensic nurse as moral agent. In D. Robinson & A. Kettles, Eds. *Forensic Nursing and Multidisciplinary Care of the Mentally Disordered Offender.* London: Jessica Kingsley Publishers. 2000.

Teplin, L. A., Abram, K. M., & McClelland, G. M. Prevalence of psychiatric disorders among incarcerated women: Pretrial jail detainees. *Arch Gen Psychiatr. 53,* 505–512, 1996.

Tewksbury, R., & West, A. Research on sex in prison during the late 1980s and early 1990s. *Prison J. 80,* 368–378, 2000.

U.S. Department of Health and Human Services. *The Registered Nurse Population: Findings From the National Sample Survey of Registered Nurses, March 2000.* Washington, DC: Health Resource and Services Administration, Bureau of Health Professions, Division of Nursing. 2002.

Wilcock, K., Hammett, T. M., Widom, R., & Epstein, J. Tuberculosis in correctional facilities. *Chest. 119,* 681–683, 2001.

Woods, P., Reed, V., & Robinson, D. The behavioural status index: Therapeutic assessments of risk, insight, communication and social skills. *J Psych Mental Health Nurs. 6,* 2, 79–90, 1999.

Wortley, R. *Situational Prison Control: Crime Prevention in Correctional Institutions.* Cambridge, England: Cambridge University Press. 2002.

12 Medico-Legal Death Investigation

CONTENTS

12.1 MAKING THE TRANSITION FROM THE LIVING TO THE DEAD

It has always been the purview of the nurse to work in the land of the living, leaving forays into the world of the deceased to medical examiners, coroners, law enforcement, and members of mortuary services. However, within the last decade or so, well-qualified and specially trained nurses have fared well in medico-legal death investigation. A nurse is well versed in all aspects of anatomy and physiology, psychology, pharmacology, and chemistry, areas the nurse explored while caring for living patients and continuing to grow in living forensics expertise. Now, nurses are poised to contribute to the investigation of both natural and suspicious deaths, fully engaging skill sets that allow them to identify and document postmortem findings at a death scene. "I think it's much easier for people to grasp the concept of nurses taking care of living people," says clinical nurse specialist Janet Barber, MSN, RN:

> It is far more difficult for people to see nurses as working with decedents. Initially, they say, "Wait a minute, nurses have enough trouble taking care of people who are alive; why do they want to get involved with dead people?" However, when they are indoctrinated fully, they get it... they begin to understand that advocacy for people is a process that encompasses the entire life cycle, from birth to death, and beyond, when the body is handled after death.

A similar discernment must occur within the clinician to embrace the full spectrum of forensic duties when transitioning to medico-legal death investigation. "Nurses are very capable of transitioning from caring for the living patient to caring for the decedent," Barber adds:

> But it can be difficult for some nurses at first, if they haven't adjusted their approach and their mindset. First of all, when people are living, the responsibility is sort of from breath to breath and heartbeat to heartbeat; once people are dead, it's like the clock stops... the urgency seems less apparent. They may tend to think, "Here is this person who is already dead, and so whether we do their autopsy today or tomorrow, or whether we go back to the crime scene today or 12 hours from now"... they may be tempted to think processes are less time specific. I don't think that nurses who really get it feel there is any less importance attached to the care of the decedent.

Barber likens the defense of death investigation by nurses to the defense of a certain medical specialty related to societal prejudices. "There are some physicians who say they really have to defend themselves when they go into a specialty like cosmetic surgery," she explains:

> People will think, "We need so many people to deal with diseases and illnesses and you're going to waste your medical education on making women more beautiful? That doesn't seem right." The same thing happens in forensic nursing; everyone can see very clearly that nurses function well within the realm of sexual assault or child abuse examinations and there's little concern about appropriating personnel and budgets for that, but when you start asking nursing directors to think about allowing their nurses to get involved in clinical death investigation, it's very difficult to make the case.

Barber points to the VA's tentative support of forensic nursing being introduced into its hospitals (see chapter 5). "It's interesting to me that the VA has been able to make that leap of faith," she comments:

> I think what has driven them to do this is the fact they have had so many issues relating to sudden or suspicious death in their facilities. In government health care institutions, from my own personal experience, there is not as much opportunity to hide and suppress as there is in private health care institutions. When you have private medical staff and when you have hospital budgets that

aren't accountable to anybody but the board of directors, it's easy to hide skeletons in the closet. But when you have the U.S. government, the veterans' organization, and all of the American people saying, "Your hospital has to be safe for our loved ones who have fought in the war and Lord help you if you harm them in your facility," there is extra accountability. That degree of accountability is not present in the rest of the health care arena, mainly because the rest of the health care world operates in relative secrecy.

Barber continues:

When I worked for private hospitals, there were many things that were kept very much below the radar. People didn't talk about them, these issues weren't dealt with definitively, and things were hidden. I think the government agencies, because of their accountability to the American public and because of their very strict, ongoing review processes, are far more transparent. For example, the abuse in Iraqi prisons at the hands of American soldiers was horrible, but even though it occurred, the processes that identified it, dealt with it, and managed the aftermath, were pretty definitive. If this kind of abuse of power or human rights occurred in a private facility of some kind, I can tell you, very few people—if anyone at all—would have ever known about it.

12.2 APPLYING A NURSE'S SKILL SETS TO DEATH INVESTIGATION

Making the leap from clinical forensic nursing to medico-legal death investigation was an intuitive move for Chicago forensic nurse and registered medico-legal death investigator Catherine O'Brien, RN, MS, CNA, CLNC, D-ABMDI. O'Brien sees it as a holistic career path, being able to draw on a diverse set of clinical nursing and death investigation skills. She has taken multifaceted courses in criminal justice administration, legal nurse consulting, and numerous forensic-related courses that have helped her build an admirable foundation to further hone her medico-legal principles, processes, techniques, and skills. She emphasizes that a varied work and education background has exposed her to a number of incredible experiences. "Time spent with the Chicago Police Forensic Services Unit and the Miami-Dade Crime Scene Investigation Unit allowed for death scene investigation outside the walls of a hospital, as we responded to gang shootings, natural deaths, and suicide," she explains:

Participating with the multidisciplinary team and learning the delineation of roles was important as we secured and analyzed the scenes, photographed, conducted the physical exam, processed the evidence, and completed all associated documentation. Participating in numerous scene investigations with a child death investigator, whose style of interview, skill in body language interpretation, and seasoned knowledge of human behavior has been invaluable. This relationship exposed me to investigations for SIDS, failure to thrive, pediatric homicide, and deaths deemed suspicious which result in requests by the forensic pathologists for a scene investigation.

It was this medico-legal experience that introduced her to the art of handling firearms:

The number of deaths annually associated with firearms drove my desire to experience handling a loaded gun, understand safety mechanisms, and evaluate the ease or difficulty in pulling a trigger. A visit to the firing range with a supportive colleague allowed me such experience, firing rounds from a 9-mm semiautomatic and 38-caliber revolver. As I aimed at the target of a human figure, I will not soon forget the overwhelming feeling of empowerment which was laced with sinister feelings of control that I sense may fuel much of the domestic and gang-related shootings seen in the community.

Time with a forensic pathologist taught me a tremendous amount in the area of estimating time of death, external and internal examination, identification of traumatic injury versus artifact, ante-mortem injury, and postmortem artifact. The value of a well-documented scene report to augment clinical findings was appreciated. As I observed numerous cases, my reverence for the fragility of life and finality of death was renewed. The autopsy of an 18-month-old boy, weighing only 1.5 pounds more at death than at birth, was very disturbing. This child was the offspring of 24-year-old parents from affluent families who had "discarded" their son almost immediately after birth. The teary eyes of hardened pathologists all consulted around the cold steel table as law enforcement and I waited anxiously for the decision as to the cause and manner of death. In this very somber environment, there was a fascination in watching the medical and legal systems traverse as starvation and homicide was ruled, which promptly resulted in first-degree murder charges announced in the press that same day. Another intense experience was the autopsy of a 17-year-old female who had been brutally beaten, strangled, shot, and stabbed multiple times, her body dumped in a swampy area of the county. Finding that she was pregnant, her uterus was removed and photographed, and specimens were taken. There lay a male fetus of an estimated 16 weeks gestation. At that moment, the dichotomy between innocence and evil, safety and violence, life and death was dramatic and profound for me.

O'Brien revels in these difficult scenarios not for their gruesome indications of man's inhumanity to man, but for what they can teach forensic professionals about identifying and investigating suspicious circumstances. "These personal experiences have influenced me in my quest to become a competent forensic nurse and qualified death investigator," O'Brien says:

> As a more seasoned practitioner today, I maintain a much higher index of suspicion at all times and wear a much tougher skin. Situations exist all around us, both in the hospital setting and the community at large, with forensic implications relevant to the living and the dead. Death, all too often, is the outcome of reckless human behavior or tragic unintentional circumstances. Nurses, in all professional practice segments, must be educated and astute to acts with criminal or civil forensic implications. Surround your practice with behaviors that question and do not assume, exhibit curiosity not apathy, challenge instead of yield, assert instead of submit. From my perspective, this is of paramount value in perusing truth in life and truth in death along the continuum of care for the betterment of humanity.

Mary Sullivan, MSN, RNC, CARN, says that instead of death investigation being within the scope of forensic nursing, she prefers looking at it as nursing practice existing within the role of the death investigation. "Traditionally, nursing practice is all about caring for the patient, preventing death, understanding disease processes, and knowing how to respond to these processes," she says:

> Nurses bring to death investigation the knowledge of assessment and evaluation, but they must learn new ways of "intervention" pertinent to death investigation through appropriate coursework and training. I think nurses already possess many of the skills necessary to succeed in death investigation; they bring to the role a tremendous amount of experience. One of the first skills which nurses find second nature is assessment; in the death investigator role, a nurse would assess the decedent, looking things over and taking in the whole scene—that is something nurses are used to doing. For example, we also know the difference between clean and sterile, which would translate into not contaminating a crime scene. And we know the various side effects of medications that may manifest themselves. Nurses, especially those who are comfortable and confident in their abilities, are very good at seeing the bigger picture and knowing what is normal and abnormal. They can spot the subtle inconsisstencies that can aid them in their work as death investigators. They are extremely adept at identifying scenarios where things just don't add up. It's a skill nurses use every day, and something which makes us a natural death investigator.

The investigation of natural and unnatural deaths is a complex process requiring the highest levels of comprehension and the meticulous exercise of the scientific method. The tasks of data collection, assessment, interpretation, and correlation require a multidisciplinary approach to death investigation—a standard to which the accomplished nurse easily rises thanks to his or her clinical education and experience. Armed with critical thinking skills and forensic protocol, the forensic nurse is uniquely qualified to differentiate between the natural disease process and suspicious injury and death. Fulton (2003) writes, "Forensic nurses already possess the nursing knowledge of anatomy, physiology, pharmacology and growth and development necessary to investigate deaths. This nursing knowledge allows the investigator to sort predisposing and precipitating factors involved in a death. In addition, forensic nurses also possess advanced communication skills and knowledge of the grief process. These skills are imperative for notifying next-of-kin and interviewing witnesses."

Indeed, forensic nurses carry with them an impressive skill set that often surpasses those of other investigators, including coroners and police officers, who lack the medical background a nurse wields. John McPhail, PhD, RN, BS, an expert in the concept of living forensics, maintains that it is less difficult to teach investigative skills to nurses than it is for law enforcement professionals to grasp complex medical concepts. McPhail, who is retired from the Forensic Division of the Colorado Mental Health Institute in Pueblo, is a former police investigator, certified medico-legal death investigator, and a member of Necrosearch International. He has lectured across the country on the concept of the body as the crime scene, and believes that nurses have an uncanny ability to absorb and process advanced medico-legal concepts.

12.3 UNDERSTANDING THE CAUSE, MANNER, AND MECHANISM OF DEATH

To work as death investigators, nurses must be familiar with the cause, manner, and mechanism of death. Fulton (2003) explains that the cause of death is the injury or disease or combination of the two that is responsible for initiating the sequence of disturbances, brief or prolonged, that produce the death. Fulton writes, "Cause and mechanism of death are frequently misrepresented on death certificates due to a lack of understanding and knowledge of the differences between cause and mechanism of death." Fulton further explains that mechanism of death is the physiologic derangement or biochemical disturbance incompatible with life, which is initiated by the cause of death. "Forensic nurses are well educated in physiology and are therefore prepared to accurately distinguish between the cause and the physiologic mechanism of death," Fulton adds. Manner of death is the circumstances in which the cause of death arose (i.e., natural, accident, homicide, suicide, and undetermined). Fulton observes, "Forensic nurses possess the skills necessary to complete a psychological autopsy and interpret the subtle nuances of medications, health history and circumstances surrounding suspicious deaths." Fulton notes that inaccurate death certificates can cause misrepresentation of homicide and suicide rates that can affect, among other things, public health policy and medical research. Insurance companies can deny payment if a death certificate inaccurately reports a death as suicide when in fact it was accidental. Also, care should be taken to provide accurate information for the next of kin. The death certificate also is the next of kin's final link to the decedent.

12.3.1 Natural Versus Suspicious Deaths

The forensic investigative system in the United States consists of a network of medical examiners and coroners, depending on the specific jurisdiction. In a coroner system, the individual is elected to hold a four-year term, and is not required to be a medical doctor or health care provider. In a medical examiner system, the appointed individual is a forensic pathologist who holds an MD degree and has undergone five years of additional advanced training in forensic pathology and a one-year forensic pathology fellowship. Guidelines as to what constitutes a case for the medical examiner or coroner are based on the types of death, reporting procedures, and state statutes. Most states require the reporting of certain deaths to the medical examiner or coroner; failure to do so can result in a misdemeanor, punishable by imprisonment or a fine (Dudley, 2002). Deaths are classified as natural or unnatural (suspicious), although most forensic practitioners will say that any death should be regarded with a high level of suspicion until all the facts are known and the case has been thoroughly investigated. Nurses are supremely qualified to evaluate potential forensic cases based on the differences between natural and suspicious deaths, given their knowledge of anatomy and physiology, pharmacology, and presentation of signs and symptoms of medical conditions that would suggest whether a death is natural or unnatural. Allert and Becker (2002) write:

> Nurses are valued members of the coroner/medical examiner's office. Often, nursing/medical knowledge is key in helping to determine if deaths are due to natural or other causes. Knowledge of medications and medical paraphernalia found at scenes assists in identifying and documenting the extent of underlying medical disease(s) that may have contributed to the death. Consulting with the decedent's personal physician(s) to obtain medical history and discuss signing the death certificate is also an aspect of the investigative process that draws heavily on nursing knowledge and experience.

Allert and Becker add, "Although overt homicides, suicides and accidents are easily identifiable as reportable deaths, there are many other cases, which are less obvious. It is these cases that often present unique and complicated challenges for the medico-legal death investigator."

Reportable deaths include the following:

- Any death that might be due entirely or in part to any factor other than natural disease
- Any death that might be an accident, suicide, or homicide
- Any sudden, unexpected death in which there is no previous history of significant heart disease or any other condition associated with sudden death
- Any death that is apparently due to natural causes but in which the deceased does not have a personal physician familiar with the patient's medical history, social/environmental situation, or the circumstances of the terminal event
- Any death considered to be a result of SIDS
- Any death that occurs during, in association with, or as a consequence of a diagnostic, therapeutic, or anesthetic procedure
- Any death in which a fracture of a major bone has occurred within the past six months
- Any death in which the person was an inmate of a public institution or was in the custody of law enforcement personnel
- Any death related to accident or disease associated with the decedent's occupation
- Any death that occurs during surgery or while under anesthesia
- Any death of a prisoner while in custody

According to Dudley (2002), examples of reportable deaths are sharp-force injuries, blunt-force injuries, fatal gunshot wounds, falls, fatal electric shocks, fatal explosions, fatal motor vehicle accidents, drug overdoses, fatal burns or fires, rapid fatal illnesses, occupational deaths, clusters of undiagnosed infectious disease, and persons found dead.

Among the various manners of morbidity, death from natural causes constitutes the largest category. Leading causes of natural death include cardiovascular disease, diseases related to the respiratory system, deaths due to intracranial lesions, diseases related to the urogenital and gastrointestinal tract, and diseases related to other body systems and organs, including the pancreas, spleen, liver, and adrenal and reproductive systems.

It is important to determine if a death is natural or unnatural, and one of the most problematic deaths is suspected suicide. Suicide is defined as the deliberate termination of one's life. According to the CDC, as many as 30,000 people commit suicide annually in the United States. Two elements are required to cite suicide as a manner of death: an intent to commit suicide, and a specific act that carries out that intent. Suicide can be demonstrated by one or more of the following pieces of evidence: a suicide note in the victim's own handwriting, as determined by a forensic graphologist; the body is found in a room that has been locked from the inside; a neutral witness testifies to the event; firearm residue on hands; or evidence of prior rehearsal, to name a few. A probable suicide can be suggested by locations of wounds, contact gunshot wounds, practice or hesitation marks on the wrists or neck, and drug ingestion determined by contents of the stomach. However, more thorough investigation is needed to make a final determination.

Methods of suicide include gunshot wounds, hanging, drug overdoses or poisonings, asphyxia, cutting or stabbing, and electrocution. Death investigation of suicide begins with the victim's prior history. Interviews with the individual's relatives, friends, and colleagues can provide what Dudley (2002) describes as a "psychological autopsy." Medical records should be reviewed for physical or mental illness, and the body searched for signs of previous suicide attempts, notably hesitation marks, such as scars on the wrist, forearm, or neck. Investigators should be aware of family members' or others' attempts to conceal the suicide, which Dudley says can be motivated by financial gain, religious reasons, social stigmas, or insurance claims issues. Removing evidence or altering the scene might be attempted, so the investigator should be aware of attempts to sanitize the scene; removal of any notes, weapons, or drug paraphernalia or other incriminating items; planting evidence; and withholding key information.

There are a number of legal issues associated with death, including notification of the next of kin, death certification, worker's compensation claims, insurance claims and settlement, and, of course, criminal and civil death investigation. Essential to this process is proper identification of the decedent. If the decedent cannot be identified, for example, in situations such as decomposition or skeletal remains, fire deaths, or airplane crashes, the death investigator might call in other members of the forensic investigatory team, including highly trained forensic pathologists, forensic anthropologists (for skeletal remains), forensic odontologists (for dental identification), DNA experts, and others. Once the decedent is properly identified, the investigator should proceed with notification of the next of kin.

The medico-legal imperatives of any death investigation include determination of the manner of death, which is critical for criminal and civil investigations, as well as for insurance claims. Determination of the death as caused by accident, suicide, or intention is conducted by the medical examiner or coroner, and facilitated by the scene investigator. This determination is essential in situations of insurance policies that will not compensate the next of kin for a suicide death. The manner of death is determined by investigation of the circumstances of death at the death scene (Dudley, 2002). According to Dudley (2003), the cause of death is the injury or disease responsible for initiating the lethal sequence of events that results in death, whereas the underlying cause of death is that which, in a natural and continuous sequence unbroken by sufficient intervening cause, produces the fatality and without which the end result would not have occurred; it is the cause of death and should be recorded as such on the death certificate. The immediate cause of death is the event or sequence of events in the underlying cause that immediately precedes the death. The mechanism of death is altered physiology and biochemistry whereby the cause exerts its lethal effect. Mechanisms of death lack etiological specificity and are unacceptable as substitutes for causes of death. Manner of death explains how the cause arose, whether natural or violent. A death falls into one of five classifications with regard to manner: natural, accident, homicide, suicide, or undetermined. Any physician can sign a death certificate for a natural death; however, only the medical examiner or coroner is legally authorized to sign a death certificate if the manner of death is decided to be an accident, homicide, suicide, or undetermined. "The certainty with which an ME/coroner can determine cause of death is governed by his or her ability to identify and document the mechanisms," Dudley (2002) writes. "In fatalities due to injuries, this is usually simple; in natural deaths, this is usually impossible."

Death can be classified according to the certainty with which autopsy findings demonstrate causes. Class I refers to absolute certainty because pathological findings are inconsistent with continued life and the mechanism is obvious. Class II refers to pathological findings able to explain death but without the development of complications that promote them to Class I. Class III refers to marginal pathological findings, compelling history, and exclusion of other causes. Class IV refers to pathologically negative, positive history, and exclusion of other causes. Class V refers to cause of death undetermined. "In most ME/coroner jurisdictions, the classification of death shows the greatest number is attributed to natural deaths where people died at home (60 percent); the remaining are attributed to accidental deaths (20 percent), homicides (10 percent) and suicides (10 percent)," Dudley writes. "All agencies have cases that are undetermined and sometimes it is impossible to determine the manner of death. It is better for the ME/coroner to leave those cases open as undetermined in the event the case is reopened for investigation in the future."

12.3.2 Sudden, Natural, and Accidental Deaths

As trained clinicians, nurses are particularly well suited to understanding and identifying instances of death that are classified as sudden, natural, and accidental. Craniocerebral trauma refers to traumatic force applied to the skull and injuries to the brain. Dudley (2002) reports that homicides and accidents frequently encompass head injuries as a manner of death, although in some cases of intentional falls from significant heights, intentional motor vehicle accidents, and self-inflicted gunshot wounds might present as a suicidal manner of death. External head injuries include contusions, lacerations, and abrasions, and this blunt-force trauma is commonly associated with fatal internal craniocerebral injuries. Internal head injuries encompass subscalpular hemorrhage, skull fractures (including open, closed, complete, incomplete, linear, complex, depressed, and nondepressed), intracranial extracerebral hemorrhage, subarachnoid hemorrhage, and brain trauma, including contusions, concussions, lacerations, penetrating injuries, crushing injuries, and axonal injuries.

Injuries in motor vehicle accidents include head injuries, spinal and brain stem injuries, facial injuries, chest injuries, abdominal injuries, and injuries to the extremities. Injuries can vary according to the location of the impact; head-on collisions impact the occupants of a vehicle differently. The driver's injuries can result from impact with the windshield, steering wheel or dashboard, and airbags. The investigator should consider the pattern of blood stains on the windshield or side window, trace evidence in the vehicle, brake or accelerator pedal impression on the sole of the shoe, seatbelt abrasions (or lack thereof) on the body, and pattern and location of dicing injuries. Front and rear passengers should be examined for head, chest, and abdomen injuries, whereas rear passengers should be checked for evidence of hitting the vehicle roof, and injuries to the spine, pelvis, and thorax. Side-impact collisions can also inflict injuries to the head, chest, abdomen, and extremities. In cases of intentional motor vehicle accidents, accident reconstructionists can piece together clues yielded by the scene, including the position of the vehicle, location of the victim struck by the vehicle, and other pertinent information relating to the mechanisms of the incident, including the type of the vehicle, speed of the vehicle, and other environmental factors. Hit-and-run victims frequently sustain injuries from the undersurfaces of cars, abrasions from being dragged on cement or asphalt, tire imprints, and crushing injuries. Skin avulsions can point to the direction of the turning wheels, and lacerations can result from braking tires; abrasions occur where the body was scraped along the ground, and compression injuries occur when the victim is run over. Primary impact is when the vehicle strikes the victim; secondary impact injuries occur when the victim hits the ground or other objects after primary impact (Dudley, 2002).

Dudley (2003) also states that firearms can kill by perforating vital organs and causing hemorrhage; damaging organs that control important body functions, causing complications that result in immediate or eventual death; and causing blast injuries that can cause tissue to swell. Fatal gunshot wounds are commonly found in the brain (40 percent of the time), heart (25 percent of the time), aorta or other major vessel (25 percent of the time), and solid viscera (10 percent of the time).

Asphyxiation, which refers to the process of denying the body oxygen for any length of time, is also known as suffocation. Asphyxiation-related deaths can be caused by choking, toxic gases (including carbon monoxide), electric shock, narcotics, injuries to or compression of the chest, injury to the respiratory system, and hemorrhage and foreign bodies in the throat. The primary cause of suffocation deaths is the obstruction of arterial blood supply to the brain, which can result in unconsciousness, coma, and death. Death by asphyxia can be indicated by cyanosis and petechial hemorrhages in the face, eye sclera, pleura, and epicardium. Manners of death can include hanging, choke holds, and smothering. In cases of strangulation by ligature, as opposed to hanging, there is abrasion caused by horizontal neck pressure, and a neck mark is commonly below the level of the thyroid cartilage. A hanging mark is normally at or above the level of the thyroid cartilage.

In the case of drownings, Dudley (2002) states it is a diagnosis of exclusion, as other causes of death, including trauma, natural disease, drug overdoes, and disposal of a homicide victim, must first be ruled out. A drowning death is death by asphyxiation with subsequent hypoxemia and cerebral anoxia. No definitive diagnosis of drowning can be made based on autopsy findings, therefore, circumstances, toxicology reports, and other evidence must be used to arrive at a cause of death. Nonspecific autopsy findings in these cases can include edema fluid in the airways, lungs filled with fluid, water in the stomach, right ventricular dilation, cerebral edema, and hemorrhage in the petrous or mastoid bones.

Deaths related to exposure to the elements are seen; however, there are no diagnostic anatomic abnormalities exclusive to hypothermia. The determination of exposure as a cause of death depends on recognition of associated anatomic findings coupled with circumstantial evidence and toxicology reports. Hypothermia-related deaths can result from exposure during intoxication, the elderly exposed to extreme cold, and being a victim of natural disasters. Hyperthermia-related deaths are caused when the body becomes overheated due to illness, disease, or environmental factors. Affected pathology includes the central nervous system and the cardiovascular system, as evidenced by cerebral edema, petechiae, and gross hemorrhage. In hyperthermia-related cases, the manner of death is usually ruled as accidental; however, neglect or homicide can be considered.

Death by electrocution is an infrequent event; the causes of these kinds of deaths include contact with high-voltage current, lightning strikes, and low-voltage current. Accidental electrocution is the most common instance of electrocution death; suicide by electrocution is even less frequent, and homicide by this method is uncommon. At autopsy, nonspecific findings might sometimes mimic asphyxial deaths (Dudley, 2002).

Narcotics use can result in accidental injuries as well as trigger homicides; drug intake is usually by ingestion, inhalation, or injection. Signs of intravenous drug abuse are manifested through needle punctures over veins, visible on arms, hands, legs, feet, or the neck. Narcotics used can include opiates, stimulants, volatile substances such as spray paint or glue, sedatives and tranquilizers, and other chemicals. Forensic toxicology screening can detect the presence of these narcotics, as well as the presence of alcohol. Alcohol can be detected in the blood, urine, cerebral spinal fluid, vitreous humor, brain, and even air found in the lungs; as much as 95 percent of alcohol, however, is metabolized through the liver.

12.4 MECHANISM OF INJURIES AND WOUND IDENTIFICATION

12.4.1 Shotgun Wounds

The clinical presentation of a shotgun wound can vary, depending on the type of ammunition used. Buckshot, which are multiple small lead pellets, produce entrance wounds that vary depending on the distance between the gun and its target. Long-range wounds produce multiple smaller wounds from individual shot as it separates in the air. Intermediate-range wounds have a central defect with surrounding lead shot wounds. Close-range wounds produce a single large defect and might have a rectangular contusion from the small plastic cup that holds the shot. Buckshot injuries rarely cause exit wounds because the energy is dissipated among the numerous shot projectiles. Entrance wounds are classified as long-range, intermediate-range, close-range, and contact wounds. A contact wound is caused when the muzzle of a gun is pressed against the skin. On discharge, hot gases and soot are injected into the subcutaneous space, forcing soot into the wound. Pressure by the muzzle against the skin can produce a contusion and stellate lacerations of the skin. Close-range wounds are produced by gunshots fired approximately 6 to 12 inches from the skin and are identified by the presence of soot on the skin or on the clothing around the entrance wound. Intermediate-range wounds can be identified by the stippling effect created by shots that are fired within 1 meter; the tattooing effect is caused by partially burned gunpowder that is released when the gun is fired. Although they have no stellate lacerations, soot, muzzle marks, or identifiable stippling, long-range wounds can be identified by an abrasion collar, which consists of a contused ring of tissue surrounding the entrance wound, resulting from friction between the bullet and the skin. The wounds are produced by a gunshot of more than 1 meter of distance. Of considerable note to ER clinicians is the admonishment to never document an interpretation of a wound as "entrance" or "exit" in the medical record. Best practices in this situation include describing the wound in detail and photographing it if possible. Although these kinds of wounds have typical appearances, this determination is not always clear in the acute-care setting and misinterpretation could convolute medico-legal investigations. Typical signs of entrance wounds include tattooing, muzzle marks, and soot, whereas typical signs of exit wounds include everted, irregular edges with stellate lacerations.

12.4.2 Blunt-Force Injuries

Blunt-force injuries encompass contusions, pattern abrasions, or lacerations that mimic the striking object. Pattern abrasions are marks left by teeth or fingernails; contusions can present in the form of linear, central clearing flanked by parallel contusions; finger impressions leave circular or oval contusions that are sometimes grouped; and bite marks can present in the form of two curvilinear abrasions or contusions, or both.

12.4.3 Sharp-Force Injuries

Sharp-force injuries comprise stab wounds and incised wounds. Stab wounds are deeper than they are wide and might or might not reflect the weapon that produced the wound. These wounds can reflect a blade that is single- or double-edged, and hilted knives can sometimes leave a V-shaped or C-shaped bruise around the stab wound. Incised wounds are caused by the drawing of a sharp weapon across the skin, resulting in a broad, shallow wound with regular edges. The word *lacerations* should not be used to describe injuries that are caused by sharp weapons, as lacerations can only be caused by blunt force or by a tearing motion on the skin

12.4.4 Smothering and Strangulation

Smothering refers to asphyxiation caused by external blockage of the airway. Typical signs of smothering include abrasions and contusions of the mouth, avulsion of the teeth, and bite marks on the tongue resulting from trauma to the perioral area. More subtle signs include facial petechiae and subconjunctival hemorrhages. Strangulation refers to asphyxiation caused by external pressure applied to the neck. Hangings and significant drops can cause fracture of the upper cervical vertebrae, with medullary disruption leading to unconsciousness and cessation of respiratory effort. Lesser ligature strangulation can obstruct venous or arterial flow in the neck. Typical signs include facial plethora, petechiae, and subconjunctival hemorrhages.

12.5 POSTMORTEM CHANGES

"Changes in body temperature, stiffness of the body, or color changes at the time of the scene investigation can help establish the time a person died" (Dudley, 2002). Livor mortis refers to the pooling of blood in gravitationally dependent areas of the body, typically the sacrum in a supine or seated body. It manifests as a purplish-red discoloration in the body's tissue. Accentuated livor mortis can mimic bruising. Tardieu spots, which are red or purple patches on the body, refer to actual bleeding into area of intense livor mortis. These spots are sometimes seen in asphyxial deaths and hangings (Dudley, 2002). Cherry-red lividity is seen in situations of carbon monoxide poisoning, cold (when the body is refrigerated), and cyanide poisoning (Dudley, 2002).

Rigor mortis refers to a stiffening of the muscles of the body caused by postmortem reduction of adenosine triphosphate (ATP), which is required in muscle relaxation. Rigor mortis begins to develop shortly after death, increases to full rigidity, and then decreases as the muscle cells decompose. Maximum rigidity typically occurs by 12 hours and resolves by 24 hours; however, this timetable is dependent on a number of environmental factors such as air temperature and body habitus. Temperature affects muscle tension; if the area is warm, rigor accelerates and then begins to disappear earlier or in approximately eight hours (Dudley, 2002).

Algor mortis is the cooling of the body as heat is lost. Early core temperature taken at the scene can be helpful in establishing the time of death as the body eventually equalizes with the room or environment temperature (Dudley, 2002). The body will begin to dehydrate after death; however, the extent and rate of drying depends on the climate and the level of humidity. Some signs of postmortem drying might be misinterpreted as signs of injury; for example, mucous membranes around the lips dry to a dark red or purple color that might mimic contusions.

Putrefaction changes are triggered by the presence of bacteria on and in the body, and are influenced by the temperature. Over time, the skin might become discolored, and internal organs become soft and decompose. Purge, a brown-red decomposition fluid that might drain from the nose and mouth, could be misinterpreted as hemorrhage (Dudley, 2002). Bloating is triggered by gas produced by bacteria in the gut; it might also manifest if the body has been in water or a damp environment. Skin slippage refers to the skin sliding from its attachment, most notably on extremities. The outer layer of skin slips away and the underlying surface becomes red with the drying process, and might mimic an abrasion.

Varying stages of insect activity on or within the body can be used to estimate the approximate time of death. Forensic entomologists can read the timetable of the life cycle of flies and other insects to help determine how long the person has been dead. In the immediate postmortem time period, insects and animals might cause damage to the body that can be misinterpreted as premortem injury. Insects, in their varying stages of development, can be collected and analyzed by entomologists and toxicologists to determine levels of drugs or other chemicals in the body. Investigators should also be aware of postmortem injuries, including contusions, lacerations, abrasions, fractures, and burns that can be incurred after death and might be indistinguishable from those occurring shortly before or at the time of death.

12.6 CRIME SCENE INVESTIGATION

"Scene investigation is of paramount importance in any medico-legal inquiry of death," Dudley (2002) writes. "As in clinical medicine where a comprehensive medical history provides 50 percent to 75 percent of the information necessary for a diagnosis, scene investigation provides the forensic pathologist with the majority of information about a particular case." Information from the death or crime scene is essential to do the following:

- Estimate the time of death.
- Assess and interpret wounds.
- Determine the extent of injuries.
- Determine the cause and manner of death.
- Correlate scene findings with the circumstance of death, medical history, and autopsy.
- Provide clues to distinguish between pre-, ante-, and postmortem artifacts.
- Reconstruct events. (Dudley, 2002)

Duties of the investigator include the following:

- Verifying that death has occurred
- Collecting and documenting information and evidence regarding the circumstances of the death and background information, including medical history, of the decedent
- Assuming jurisdiction of the body, clothing, and physical evidence associated with the body
- Observing and documenting these observations regarding the crime scene with diagrams, sketches, videos, and still photographs
- Examining the body
- Preventing alteration, contamination, destruction, or concealment of evidence
- Preserving clothing, personal effects, and trace evidence
- Recognizing extraneous items at the scene that might have been used for attempts at resuscitation or treatment of the victims, as well as items that might have been planted at the scene
- Preventing postmortem injury to or contamination of the body
- Establishing and maintaining chain of custody (Dudley, 2002)

12.6.1 A National Death Investigation Protocol

In the late 1990s, the U.S. Department of Justice's Office of Justice Programs in the National Institute of Justice released a report, *Death Investigation: A Guide for the Scene Investigator* (U.S. Department of Justice, 1999), which outlines the proper steps in any medico-legal death investigation.

12.6.1.1 Arrival at the Scene

Death investigators should identify themselves on arrival at the scene and before entering the scene, and establish contact with other law enforcement agencies there. The investigator should seek out the first responder (i.e., the first agency representative at the scene) to ascertain if any artificial evidence might have been introduced to the death scene or if it has been contaminated in any way. The investigator also should determine the safety of the death scene before entering it, as the risk of environmental and physical injury must be removed prior to initiating a scene investigation. Risks include curious or hostile crowds, collapsing structures, traffic, and environmental and chemical threats. If necessary, the death investigator should contact appropriate agencies for assistance with other scene-safety issues.

On arrival at the scene, the investigator should do the following:

- Assess or establish physical boundaries.
- Identify incident command.
- Obtain clearance or authorization to enter scene from the individual responsible for scene safety.

It is key for the death investigator to remember that during the process of exercising scene safety, the integrity of the death scene and evidence contained within must be protected to the extent possible from contamination or loss by people, animals, and the elements. If external dangers and scene hazards such as collapsing structures or poisonous gases threaten the safety of scene responders, the body (or bodies) might have to be removed before scene investigation can continue.

12.6.1.2 Confirm or Pronounce Death

The most appropriate medical or civil individual, such as the medical examiner or the coroner in the local jurisdiction, must confirm and pronounce death. The death investigator must ensure that appropriate personnel have viewed the body and that death has been confirmed. On arrival at the scene, the investigator should do the following:

- Locate and view the body.
- Check for pulse, respiration, and reflexes, as appropriate.
- Identify and document the individual who made the official determination of death, including the date and time of determination.
- Ensure death is pronounced by the coroner or the medical examiner, as required by law.

12.6.1.3 Participate in Scene Briefing

Scene investigators must recognize the varying jurisdictional and statutory responsibilities that apply to individual agency representatives, such as law enforcement officers. Determining each agency's investigative responsibility at the scene is essential in planning the scope and depth of each scene investigation and the release of information to the public. Together, specific responsibilities can be identified, appropriate preliminary information can be shared, and investigative goals of each agency present at the scene can be established. When participating in the scene briefing, the death investigator should do the following:

- Locate the staging area (entry point to scene, command post, etc.).
- Document the scene location consistent with other agencies.
- Determine nature and scope of investigation by obtaining preliminary investigative details
- Ensure that initial accounts of the incident are obtained from the first witness(es).

12.6.1.4 Conduct the Scene Walk-Through

Conducting a scene walk-through provides the death investigator with an overview of the entire scene and the first opportunity to locate and view the body, identify valuable and fragile evidence, and determine initial investigative procedures providing for a systematic examination and documentation of the scene and body. On arrival at the scene, the investigator should do the following:

- Reassess scene boundaries and adjust as appropriate.
- Establish a path of entry and exit.
- Document and photograph fragile evidence immediately and collect if appropriate.
- Locate and view the decedent.

A suggested way to approach the crime scene is to work inward toward the body from the outside scene perimeter to identify all potential evidence (Dudley, 2002).

12.6.1.5 Establish Chain of Custody

Ensuring the integrity of the evidence by establishing and maintaining proper chain of custody is vital to an investigation. This process helps safeguard against allegations of tampering, theft, planting, and contamination of evidence. Prior to the removal of any evidence, the custodian(s) of evidence should be designated and should generate and maintain a chain of custody for all evidence collected. A properly maintained chain of custody and prompt transfer will reduce the likelihood of a challenge to the integrity of the evidence. Throughout the investigation, those responsible for preserving the chain of custody should do the following:

- Document location of the scene and time of arrival of the death investigator at the scene.
- Determine custodian(s) of evidence and determine which agencies are responsible for collection of specific types of evidence.
- Identify, secure, and preserve evidence with proper containers, labels, and preservatives.
- Document the collection of evidence by recording its location.
- Develop personnel lists, witness lists, and documentation of times of arrival and departure of personnel.

12.6.1.6 Follow Laws Related to the Collection of Evidence

The death investigator must follow local, state, and federal laws for the collection of evidence to ensure its admissibility, and should collaborate with local law enforcement and legal authorities to determine these laws regarding evidence collection. Following these laws will ensure a complete and proper investigation in compliance with state and local laws, admissibility in court, and adherence to office policies and protocols. Prior to or on arrival at the death scene, the investigator should work with other agencies to do the following:

- Determine the need for a search warrant.
- Identify local, state, federal, and international laws.
- Identify medical examiner or coroner statutes and office standard operating procedures.

12.6.1.7 Photograph the Scene

Photographic documentation of the scene creates a permanent historical record of the scene and provides detailed corroborating evidence that constructs a system of redundancy should questions arise concerning the report, witness statements, or position of evidence at the scene. The death investigator should take detailed photos of the scene that provide both instant (digital) and permanent (35-mm) high-quality images. On arrival at the scene, and prior to moving the body or evidence, the investigator should do the following:

- Remove all nonessential personnel from the scene.
- Obtain a wide-angle view of the scene to spatially locate the specific scene to the surrounding area.
- Photograph specific areas of the scene to provide more detailed views of specific areas within the larger scene.
- Photograph the scene from different angles to provide various perspectives that might uncover additional evidence.
- Obtain some photographs with scales.
- Obtain photographs even if the body or other evidence has been moved.

12.6.1.8 Documenting and Evaluating the Scene

1. Photograph the scene. If evidence has been moved prior to photography, it should be noted in the report, but the body or other evidence should not be reintroduced into the scene to take photographs. Photography allows for the best permanent documentation of the death scene. It is essential that accurate scene photographs are available for other investigators, agencies, and authorities to re-create the scene. Photographs are a permanent record of the terminal event and retain evidentiary value and authenticity. It is essential that the investigator obtain accurate photographs before releasing the scene.
2. Develop a descriptive. Written documentation of the scene provides a permanent record that can be used to correlate with and enhance photographic documentation, refresh recollections, and record observations. After photographic documentation of the scene and prior to removal of the body or other evidence, the investigator should do the following:
   - Diagram and describe in writing items of evidence and their relationship to the body with necessary measurements.
   - Describe and document, with necessary measurements, blood and body fluid evidence including volume, patterns, spatters, and other characteristics.
   - Describe scene environments including odors, lights, temperatures, and other fragile evidence.
3. Establish probable location of injury or illness. The location where the decedent is found might

not be the actual location where the injury or illness that contributed to the death occurred. It is imperative that the investigator attempt to determine the locations of any and all injuries or illnesses that might have contributed to the death. Physical evidence at any and all locations could be pertinent in establishing the cause, manner, and circumstances of death. The investigator should do the following:

- Document location where death was confirmed.
- Determine location from which decedent was transported and how the body was transported to the scene.
- Identify and record discrepancies in rigor mortis, livor mortis, and body temperature.
- Check body, clothing, and scene for consistency or inconsistency of trace evidence and indicate location where artifacts are found.
- Check for drag marks (on body and ground).
- Establish postinjury activity.
- Obtain dispatch (e.g., police, ambulance) records.
- Interview family members and associates as needed.

4. Collect, inventory, and safeguard property and evidence. The decedent's valuables and property must be safeguarded to ensure proper processing and eventual return to next of kin. Evidence on or near the body must be protected to ensure its availability for further evaluation. After personal property and evidence have been identified at the scene, the investigator (with a witness) should do the following:
   - Inventory, collect, and safeguard illicit drugs and paraphernalia at the scene or the office.
   - Inventory, collect, and safeguard prescription medication at the scene or the office.
   - Inventory, collect, and safeguard over-the-counter medications at the scene or the office.
   - Inventory, collect, and safeguard money at the scene and at the office.
   - Inventory, collect, and safeguard personal valuables and property at the scene and at the office.
5. Interview witnesses at the scene. The documented comments of witnesses at the scene allow the investigator to obtain primary source data regarding discovery of body, witness corroboration, and terminal history. The documented interview provides essential information for the investigative process. This documentation must exist as a permanent record to establish a chain of events. On arriving at the scene, the investigator should do the following:
   - Collect all available identifying data on witnesses (e.g., full name, address, date of birth, work and home telephone numbers, etc.).
   - Establish witness's relationship or association to the deceased.
   - Establish the basis of witness's knowledge.
   - Obtain information from each witness.
   - Note discrepancies from the scene briefing.
   - Tape statements where such equipment is available and retain them.

12.6.1.9 Documenting and Evaluating the Body

1. Photograph the body. The photographic documentation of the body at the scene creates a permanent record that preserves essential details of the body position, appearance, identity, and final movements. Photographs allow sharing of information with other agencies investigating the death. On arrival at the scene, and prior to moving the body or evidence, the investigator should do the following:
   - Photograph the body and immediate scene (including the decedent as initially found).
   - Photograph the decedent's face.
   - Take additional photographs after removal of objects that interfere with photographic documentation of the decedent.
   - Photograph the decedent with and without measurements.
   - Photograph the surface beneath the body (after the body has been removed, as appropriate).
2. Conduct external body examination (superficial). Conducting the external body examination provides the investigator with objective data regarding the single most important piece of evidence at the scene, the body. This documentation provides detailed information regarding the decedent's physical attributes, his or her relationship to the scene, and possible cause, manner, and circumstances of death. After arrival at the scene and prior to moving the decedent, the investigator should, without removing decedent's clothing, do the following:
   - Photograph the decedent with and without measurements (as appropriate), including a photograph of the decedent's face.
   - Document the decedent's position with and without measurements (as appropriate).
   - Document the decedent's physical characteristics.

- Document the presence or absence of clothing and personal effects.
- Document the presence or absence of any items that might be relevant.
- Document the presence or absence of marks, scars, and tattoos.
- Document the presence or absence of injury or trauma, petechiae, and so on.
- Based on the findings, determine the need for further evaluation or assistance of forensic specialists such pathologists or odontologists.

3. Preserve evidence (on body). The photographic and written documentation of evidence on the body allows the investigator to obtain a permanent historical record of that evidence. To maintain chain of custody, evidence must be collected, preserved, and transported properly. In addition to all of the physical evidence visible on the body, blood and other body fluids present must be photographed and documented prior to collection and transport. Fragile evidence must also be collected or preserved to maintain chain of custody and to assist in determination of cause, manner, and circumstances of death. Once evidence on the body is recognized, the investigator should do the following:
   - Photograph the evidence.
   - Document blood or body fluids on the body (froth/purge, substances from orifices), location, and pattern before transporting.
   - Place decedent's hands and feet in unused paper bags (as determined by the scene).
   - Collect trace evidence before transporting the body (e.g., blood, hair, fibers, etc.).
   - Arrange for the collection and transport of evidence at the scene.
   - Ensure the proper collection of blood and body fluids for subsequent analysis (if body will be released from scene to an outside agency without an autopsy).
4. Establish decedent identification. The establishment or confirmation of the decedent's identity is paramount to the death investigation. Proper identification allows notification of next of kin, settlement of estates, resolution of criminal and civil litigation, and the proper completion of the death certificate. To establish identity, the investigator should document use of the following methods:
   - Direct visual or photographic identification of the decedent if visually recognizable
   - Scientific methods such as fingerprints, dental, radiographic, and DNA comparisons
   - Circumstantial methods such as (but not restricted to) personal effects, circumstances, physical characteristics, tattoos, and anthropologic data
5. Document postmortem changes. The documentation of postmortem changes to the body assists the investigator in explaining body appearance in the interval following death. Inconsistencies between postmortem changes and body location can indicate movement of the body and validate or invalidate witness statements. In addition, postmortem changes to the body, when correlated with circumstantial information, can assist the investigators in estimating the approximate time of death. On arrival at the scene and prior to moving the body, the investigator should note the presence of each of the following in his or her report:
   - Livor (color, location, blanchability, Tardieu spots) consistent or inconsistent with position of the body
   - Rigor (stage and intensity, location on the body, broken, inconsistent with the scene)
   - Degree of decomposition (putrefaction, adipocere, mummification, skeletonization, as appropriate)
   - Insect and animal activity
   - Description of body temperature (e.g., warm, cold, frozen) or measurement of body temperature (document method used and time of measurement)
6. Participate in scene debriefing. The scene debriefing helps investigators from all participating agencies to establish postscene responsibilities by sharing data regarding particular scene findings. The scene debriefing provides each agency the opportunity for input regarding special requests for assistance, additional information, special examinations, and other requests requiring interagency communication, cooperation, and education. When participating in scene debriefing, the investigator should do the following:
   - Determine postscene responsibilities (identification, notification, press relations, and evidence transportation).
   - Determine and identify the need for a specialist (e.g., crime laboratory technicians, social services, entomologists, OSHA).
   - Communicate with the pathologist about responding to the scene or to the autopsy schedule (as needed).
   - Share investigative data (as required in furtherance of the investigation).
   - Communicate special requests to appropriate agencies, being mindful of the necessity for confidentiality.

7. Determine notification procedures. Every reasonable effort should be made to notify the next of kin as soon as possible. Notification of next of kin initiates closure for the family, disposition of remains, and facilitates the collection of additional information relative to the case. When determining notification procedures, the investigator should do the following:
   - Identify next of kin.
   - Locate next of kin.
   - Notify next of kin (assign person(s) to perform task) and record time of notification, or, if delegated to another agency, gain confirmation when notification is made.
   - Notify concerned agencies of status of the notification.
8. Ensure security of remains. Ensuring security of the body requires the investigator to supervise the labeling, packaging, and removal of the remains. An appropriate identification tag is placed on the body to preclude misidentification on receipt at the examining agency. This function also includes safeguarding all potential physical evidence and property and clothing that remain on the body. Prior to leaving the scene, the investigator should do the following:
   - Ensure that the body is protected from further trauma or contamination (if not, document) and unauthorized removal of therapeutic and resuscitative equipment.
   - Inventory and secure property, clothing, and personal effects that are on the body (remove in a controlled environment with witness present).
   - Identify property and clothing to be retained as evidence (in a controlled environment).
   - Recover blood and vitreous samples prior to release of remains.
   - Place identification on the body and body bag.
   - Ensure and supervise the placement of the body into the bag.
   - Ensure and supervise the removal of the body from the scene.

- Secure transportation.

12.6.1.10 Establishing and Recording Decedent Profile Information

1. Document the discovery history. Establishing a decedent profile includes documenting a discovery history and circumstances surrounding the discovery. The investigator must produce clear, concise, documented information concerning who discovered the body, the circumstances of discovery, where the discovery occurred, when the discovery was made, and how the discovery was made. The basic profile will dictate subsequent levels of investigation, jurisdiction, and authority. The focus of further investigation is dependent on this information. For an investigator to correctly document the discovery history, he or she should do the following:
   - Establish and record person(s) who discovered the body and when.
   - Document the circumstances surrounding the discovery (who, what, where, when, how).
2. Determine terminal episode history. Preterminal circumstances play a significant role in determining cause and manner of death. Documentation of medical intervention and procurement of ante-mortem specimens help to establish the decedent's condition prior to death. For the investigator to determine terminal episode history, he or she should do the following:
   - Document when, where, how, and by whom decedent was last known to be alive.
   - Document the incidents prior to the death.
   - Document complaints or symptoms prior to the death.
   - Document and review complete EMS records (including the initial electrocardiogram).
   - Obtain relevant ante-mortem specimens.
3. Document decedent medical history. The majority of deaths referred to the medical examiner or coroner are natural deaths. Establishing the decedent's medical history helps to focus the investigation. Documenting the decedent's medical signs or symptoms prior to death determines the need for subsequent examinations. The relationship between disease and injury might play a role in the cause, manner, and circumstances of death. Through interviews and review of written records, the investigator should do the following:
   - Document medical history, including medications taken, alcohol and drug use, and family medical history from family members and witnesses.
   - Document information from treating physicians and hospitals to confirm history and treatment.
   - Document physical characteristics and traits (e.g., left-/right-handedness, missing appendages, tattoos, etc.).

4. Document decedent mental health history. The decedent's mental health history can provide insight into the behavior or state of mind of the individual, which might produce clues that will aid in establishing the cause, manner, and circumstances of the death. The investigator should do the following:
   - Document the decedent's mental health history, including hospitalizations and medications.
   - Document the history of suicidal ideations, gestures, and attempts.
   - Document mental health professionals (e.g., psychiatrists, psychologists, counselors, etc.) who treated the decedent.
   - Document family mental health history.
5. Document social history. Social history includes marital, family, sexual, educational, employment, and financial information. Daily routines, habits and activities, and friends and associates of the decedent help in developing the decedent's profile. This information will aid in establishing the cause, manner, and circumstances of death. When collecting relevant social history information, the investigator should do the following:
   - Document marital and domestic history.
   - Document family history (similar deaths, significant dates).
   - Document sexual history.
   - Document employment history.
   - Document financial history.
   - Document daily routines, habits, and activities.
   - Document relationships, friends, and associates.
   - Document religious, ethnic, or other pertinent information (e.g., religious objection to autopsy).
   - Document educational background.
   - Document criminal history.

12.6.1.11 Completing the Scene Investigation

1. Maintain jurisdiction over the body. Maintaining jurisdiction over the body allows the investigator to protect the chain of custody as the body is transported from the scene for autopsy, specimen collection, or storage. When maintaining jurisdiction over the body, the investigator should do the following:
   - Arrange for, and document, secure transportation of the body to a medical or autopsy facility for further examination or storage.
   - Coordinate and document procedures to be performed when the body is received at the facility.
2. Release jurisdiction of the Body. Prior to releasing jurisdiction of the body to an authorized receiving agent or funeral director, it is necessary to determine the person responsible for certification of the death. Information to complete the death certificate includes demographic information and the date, time, and location of death. When releasing jurisdiction over the body, the investigator should do the following:
   - Determine who will sign the death certificate (name, agency, etc.).
   - Confirm the date, time, and location of death.
   - Collect, when appropriate, blood, vitreous fluid, and other evidence prior to release of the body from the scene.
   - Document and arrange with the authorized receiving agent to reconcile all death certificate information.
   - Release the body to a funeral director or other authorized receiving agent.
3. Perform exit procedures. Bringing closure to the scene investigation ensures that important evidence has been collected and the scene has been processed. In addition, a systematic review of the scene ensures that artifacts or equipment are not inadvertently left behind (e.g., used disposable gloves, paramedical debris, film wrappers, etc.), and any dangerous materials or conditions have been reported. When performing exit procedures, the investigator should do the following:
   - Identify, inventory, and remove all evidence collected at the scene.
   - Remove all personal equipment and materials from the scene.
   - Report and document any dangerous materials or conditions.
4. Assist the family. The investigator provides the family with a timetable so they can arrange for final disposition and provides information on available community and professional resources that can assist the family. When the investigator is assisting the family, it is important to do the following:
   - Inform the family if an autopsy is required.
   - Inform the family of available support services (e.g., victim assistance, police, social services, etc.).
   - Inform the family of appropriate agencies to contact with questions (medical examiner or coroner offices, law enforcement, etc.).

- Ensure family is not left alone with body (if circumstances warrant).
- Inform the family of approximate body release timetable.
- Inform the family of information release timetable (toxicology, autopsy results, etc., as required).
- Inform the family of available reports, including cost, if any.

Investigative Tools and Equipment of the Death Investigator

1. Gloves and other pieces of personal protective equipment
2. Writing implements
3. Body bags
4. Communication equipment (cell phone, pager, radio)
5. Flashlight
6. Body ID tags
7. Camera: 35-mm (with extra batteries, film, etc.) or digital camera
8. Investigative notebook (for scene notes, etc.)
9. Measurement instruments (tape measure, ruler, rolling measuring tape, etc.)
10. Official identification (for yourself)
11. Watch
12. Paper bags (for hands, feet, etc.)
13. Specimen containers (for evidence items and toxicology specimens)
14. Disinfectant (universal precautions)
15. Departmental scene forms
16. Camera: Polaroid (with extra film)
17. Blood collection tubes (syringes and needles)
18. Inventory lists (clothes, drugs, etc.)
19. Paper envelopes
20. Clean white linen sheet (stored in plastic bag)
21. Evidence tape
22. Business cards or office cards with phone numbers
23. Foul-weather gear (raincoat, umbrella, etc.)
24. Medical equipment kit (scissors, forceps, tweezers, exposure suit, scalpel handle, blades, disposable syringe, large gauge needles, cotton-tipped swabs, etc.)
25. Phone listing (important phone numbers)
26. Tape or rubber bands
27. Disposable (paper) jumpsuits, hair covers, face shield, and so on
28. Evidence seal (use with body bags and locks)
29. Pocketknife
30. Shoe covers
31. Trace evidence kit (tape, etc.)
32. Waterless hand wash
33. Thermometer
34. Crime scene tape
35. First aid kit
36. Latent print kit
37. Local maps
38. Plastic trash bags
39. Gunshot residue analysis kits
40. Photo placards (signage to ID case in photo)
41. Boots (for wet conditions, construction sites, etc.)
42. Hand lens (magnifying glass)
43. Portable electric area lighting
44. Barrier sheeting (to shield body or an area from public view)
45. Purification mask (disposable)
46. Reflective vest
47. Tape recorder
48. Basic hand tools (bolt cutter, screwdrivers, hammer, shovel, trowel, paintbrushes, etc.)
49. Body bag locks (to secure body inside bag)
50. Camera: Video (with extra battery)
51. Personal comfort supplies (insect spray, sunscreen, hat, etc.)
52. Presumptive blood test kit

12.6.2 Types of Crime Scenes

Lee (2001) says that crime scenes can be classified by the origin of the crime, the boundary of the scene, and the condition of the scene. Primary and secondary crime scenes are based on the original location where the crime occurred, and whether the body was moved from the originating scene to another scene. A crime scene can further be defined as macroscopic or microscopic. The macroscopic view of the crime scene includes the location, the victim's body, the suspect's body, and any vehicle of transport involved in the crime; essentially it is an investigation of a crime scene within a crime scene. The microscopic view of the crime scene includes any specific piece of physical evidence or object related to the crime, including trace evidence. Scenes can also be classified according to the type of crime committed, the location of the crime (indoor or outdoor), and the condition of the scene (organized or disorganized).

12.6.3 Crime Scene Search

A crime scene should be systematically and methodically processed in its entirety, with the investigator conducting an inventory of objects and structures present. "This approach ensures the critical evidence will not be damaged or overlooked. Also look for what is not present or missing from the scene. These findings often provide invaluable investigative information, and if that item is later located on the suspect's body, in a vehicle or at another location, it may provide a critical linkage between a suspect and the crime scene," Lee (2001) writes. Crime scenes can be primary or secondary, so they must be thoroughly evaluated and triaged. Any scene in which evidence is subject to loss or destruction should be processed first. A primary crime scene is the location where the principal elements or activity associated with the crime occurred; a secondary scene is a location where peripheral activity occurred, such as when a person is killed in one crime scene and the body dumped at another location. A crime scene contains both focal points and ancillary areas; focal points are defined as the areas known to have the highest probability of containing relevant physical and pattern evidence. Once the focal point has been documented, searched, and all evidence collected and preserved, any ancillary areas should be addressed. For indoor crime scene searches, Eliopulos (2003) recommends starting at the area in which the body is located and zoning off areas apart from the body, then beginning examination of these zones for evidence. Investigators should check and note the condition of scene elements such as entrances and exits like doors, windows, and staircases, as well as lighting, odors present, environmental heating or cooling conditions, contents of trash cans, contents of bathroom facilities and kitchens, and general state of order or disorder (including evidence of a struggle). For outdoor scenes, Eliopulos recommends conducting a detailed search in a methodical manner. Crime scene search patterns are varied but provide the common goal of "providing structure and organization to ensure that no physical or pattern evidence is overlooked. There is no single correct method for a specific type of crime scene. Rather, an experienced crime scene investigator will evaluate all available data and peculiarities associated with that specific scene" (Lee, 2001).

The six basic crime scene search patterns are the line, grid, spiral, ray, zone, and link methods. The link method seeks to discover associations among the scene, victim, suspect, and physical evidence. Although not based on a geometric pattern, the link method is predicated on each step being based on findings and observations, and through application of reasonable probability, the evidence will be located in a particular location. Hypotheses about the motives and the circumstances of the crime can be developed that dictate the search for correlating physical evidence. The line method can be effective in large, outdoor crime scenes that can be difficult to search due to vegetation, topography, and sizeable areas to cover. In this method, the crime scene is divided into a series of lines, blocked out in a rectangular shape. Members of the search team, separated at arm's length, proceed to walk forward in a straight line, identifying and marking any evidence in their direct path. The grid method is a modified double-line search in which investigators follow a line pattern, then realign on a perpendicular pattern in a grid format. In the zone method, a team of investigators can search a crime scene by room or by specific area, documenting and collecting all pertinent evidence in a concentrated area at a time. In the wheel or ray method, the crime scene is considered to be circular; an investigator starts from a fixed point and travels along lines extending from this critical point. The spiral method is similar to the wheel method, but the investigator travels along an inward or outward spiral. With the completion of each circuit, the diameter of the circle is progressively decreased until a central point is reached.

12.6.4 Crime Scene Documentation

12.6.4.1 Photographing the Crime Scene

One of the best methods of evidence documentation is photography, which can establish that a crime was committed, discover how a crime was committed, help prove the identity of a suspect and collectively connect a suspect to the crime. Photographs are essential to preserve evidence that might otherwise deteriorate or vanish with time, to depict a scene more thoroughly, and to lend credibility to testimony and help jurors better visualize the variables of the crime scene (Dudley, 2002). Lee (2001) states that the purpose of crime scene photography is to "provide a visual record of the scene and related areas, to record the initial appearance of the crime scene and physical evidence, to provide investigators and others with the permanent record to the courts." He adds, "As one of the primary documentation components, a systematic, organized visual record of an undisturbed crime scene must be achieved." The most systematic method of crime scene photography involves a "progressive general to specific" approach, according to Lee, which encompasses overall views, midrange views, and close-up views. This progressive method allows the photographer to capture the orientation of the crime scene in its entirety, as well as the orientation of the evidence within the crime scene, plus the documentation of specific pieces of evidence such as fingerprints or footprint impressions. Crime scene photographers are admonished to take a sufficient number of photographs, as "hindsight will not be 20/20 when a part of a crime scene or a piece of evidence appeared to have no significance and was not photographed and then subsequently becomes immensely important at a later date," Lee states.

Eliopulos (2003) recommends that crime scene photographers thoroughly capture and catalog the exterior and interior of the crime scene. Regarding the exterior, photographers should document elements such as the relationship of the building or the vehicle to other landmarks; the address or location of the building and the vehicle identification if a vehicle is involved; tire and footwear impressions; discarded items such as cigarette packs or butts, cans, drinking cups, and so on; broken branches or disturbed landscaping; drag marks; any items left behind during the crime; any weapons and other evidence related to the weapon; and blood spatter patterns. Regarding the interior, photographers should document the room or area in which the decedent was found, adjoining rooms, evidence of a struggle, objects that indicate a disruption in the decedent's activities at the time of death, areas that indicate an object might have been removed, and trace evidence. Although aerial photographs might not always be feasible, when possible, they can capture the overall crime scene. At the ground level, the areas surrounding and leading into and out of the crime scene should be photo-documented. Overall photographs of the crime scene should illustrate the victim's andsuspect's approach to the crime scene, entrance to the scene, commission of the crime, and exit from the scene. The interior of the crime scene should be approached in a systematic manner, with the photographer documenting the following: overall orientation of the scene; close-range photos that can document pattern evidence at the entrance of the scene; overlapping photos of the scene taken at four compass points of the room, as well as any pertinent adjunct areas; and individual items of evidence documented at midrange and close-range for both orientation and detail purposes. The location of items of evidence should be established through the use of numbered markers or cones to "identify" the evidence in subsequent photos or videos. Close-up photos document the details of pieces of evidence at the crime scene and can supplement forensic comparison of this evidence at the crime lab. Typical pieces of evidence warranting close-up photography include fingerprints, footwear impressions, bloodstain patterns, gunshot residue, and glass-fracture patterns. Items of evidence should be photographed in natural lighting, with additional oblique lighting, and photographed at right angles with and without a scale along two axes of the plane along which the items rest. Examination-quality photographs used for comparison purposes will exhibit a greater amount of contrast if shot with black-and-white film; color film should also be used to document the color, designs, and trace textures of the evidence.

When photographing the body specifically, Eliopulos (2003) recommends that investigators photograph the decedent in relation to the room or vehicle from all compass-point directions, photograph the body in relation to pieces of evidence, take close-up photos of the wound(s) and other areas of injury, photograph blood spatter on the decedent's clothing and other areas of bloodletting, document any signs of unusual activity around the body, photograph the decedent's hands and feet, photo-document any trace evidence found on the body, and photograph the area underneath the body once it has been removed. Crime scene photographers should use a tripod to prevent blurry photographs and to keep the subject in sharp focus. To achieve good depth of field, the camera's aperture (larger f-stop number) should be kept small, thus slowing the shutter speed and achieving greater crispness and focus. For reasonable exposures, photographers should remember the f/16 rule: Set the camera's shutter speed near the speed of the camera and set the aperture to f/16. Be sure to use a flash attachment to bring out details of the crime scene that might be overlooked otherwise. Photographers should be familiar with their equipment, keep it in reliable working condition, and always carry fresh film and backup batteries. The significant number of photos taken at the crime scene should be chronologically recorded. The photographer should also maintain a log of all photographs taken, including the following the information: date and time the photograph was taken, name of the photographer, type of equipment used, description of the angle at which the photograph was taken in relation to the subject, and any clarifying comments. A chain of custody is as essential for photographs as it is for other pieces of evidence; otherwise, the credibility and validity of the photographs might be discredited in the courtroom. Accountability must be assumed for every step of the process, including development and transportation to the authorities. A log should be kept of the number of prints made, the person submitting the film and where it was developed, the date and time of development, the person receiving the film, and a notation of every time that a photograph is released, returned, moved, or handled. Photographs cannot prejudice or mislead the jury; therefore photographs admitted as evidence must be accurate and not overdramatized or touched up in any way. The crime scene photographer is responsible for identifying the evidence portrayed in the photograph and testifying to the accuracy with which the evidence is depicted, as well as that it was not subject to tampering or altering in any way.

12.6.4.2 Sketching the Crime Scene

The spatial relationship of objects within the crime scene should be captured in a sketch or diagram of the scene. The diagram is the permanent record of the actual size and distance relationships within the scene and its physical evidence, to supplement and correlate photo-documentation of the scene and the surrounding areas. There are two types of crime scene sketches: a rough sketch, and a final sketch; perspectives include an overhead and a side view. The rough sketch is usually made before evidence collection, and illustrates the items of evidence to be collected, structures present in the crime scene, and other relevant items in or near the crime scene. A finished, or final sketch, is drawn up from the rough sketch, and it is traditionally prepared for presentation in the courtroom. Measurements of the crime scene are taken through three different methods: triangulation, in which the distance between two fixed points is measured and everything in the crime scene is then measured from these two points; polar coordinates, in which all evidence is measured for distance from a fixed point, and measured for angle or direction; and rectangular coordinates, in which a straight line is established between two fixed points and evidence is measured along this baseline and at the perpendiculars to this line.

12.6.5 Evidence Collection

Fisher (2000) states that physical evidence can do the following:

- Prove a crime has been committed or establish key elements of a crime
- Place the suspect in contact with the victim or with the crime scene
- Exonerate the innocent
- Corroborate the victim's testimony
- Force the suspect to make an admission or confess
- Provide more reliability than eyewitnesses to crimes

Fisher adds that the job of crime scene investigators is to "apply science and technology to the solution of criminal acts." As well, investigators

> shoulder an important role in the criminal justice system. It is their skill and knowledge in the criminal investigation that may result in establishing the innocence or guilt of a defendant... all forensic practitioners owe a duty to the truth. They should never be biased for or against a suspect in an investigation. The forensic practitioner's sole obligation is to serve the aims of justice. It is irrelevant whether or not a defendant is subsequently found guilty of the crime. What is important is that the forensic scientist or practitioner conducts the investigation in a thorough, competent, unbiased manner.

12.6.5.1 General Considerations

Most of the clues that lead to the solution of a crime are at the crime scene in the form of physical evidence. Investigators should not only understand the value of physical evidence and its limitations, but also the theory of evidence transfer, and the proper techniques for identification, collection, preservation, and documentation of evidence. Crime scene investigators must employ their knowledge of physical evidence as part of their overall ability to classify and define the crime scene. Lee (2001) states:

> The experienced crime investigator also knows to expect the unexpected, and that classifying and defining crime scenes is the guiding procedure for proper investigations. It is from the analysis of the crime scene that the investigator can determine what type of physical evidence will most likely be found at a particular type of crime scene, where to find the physical evidence, how to recognize, collect, preserve and process the physical evidence, and based upon the evidence examination in the laboratory combined with the scene appearance, reconstruct the crime scene.

12.6.5.2 Examining the Body

The literal definition of the Latin word *corpus delicti* is the body in a death investigation, but the term can also encompass the essential facts that can determine that a crime has occurred. These essential facts include the physical evidence, patterns of evidence at the scene, and any laboratory results stemming from the testing of the crime scene evidence. According to Eliopulos (2003), once the scene has been cleared by the medical examiner or coroner, investigators should work all evidence from the outside of the scene toward the inside of a scene, making their way carefully toward the body of the victim. "The faster the investigator can work in processing the body, the greater the chances for the death investigator to develop viable physical evidence," Eliopulos writes. "The more the victim is handled or moved, the greater the chances for physical evidence to be lost, missed, or destroyed."

Investigators should clear a path leading to and from the area where the decedent is, all the while looking for physical evidence; an alternate light source can be used to examine this pathway. Any footsteps leading to or away from the body should be identified and documented, and the investigator should collect any evidence throughout this process. The body should be examined closely for signs that it might have been moved, posed, or dressed and undressed; it should be searched for physical evidence. The investigator should consider which areas of the body might have been touched by the perpetrator, which might dictate further evidence collection and documentation. If the body looks as though it might have been dragged or carried, those areas of the body most affected by such movement should be examined closely. In some cases, investigators might be able to detect latent fingerprints on the victim's skin. Eliopulos (2003) says that the type of incident can indicate the likelihood of detecting latent prints on remains; some homicides and suicides might involve the potential of placing prints on the body on an ante-mortem, perimortem, and postmortem basis. Other elements of the crime scene that might indicate the possibility of identifying latent fingerprints on the victim's body include the posing of the decedent, removal of clothing, physical confrontation, handling of the body postmortem, and injuries made through the use of fingers. Latent prints are generally made when the perpetrator's fingers are contaminated with substances such as blood, dirt, paint, or other chemicals. Identifying latent prints depends on several factors, including contaminants that could affect the ridge detail on the gripping surface of the fingers, the area of the body touched by the perpetrator, conditions of the decedent's skin, environmental factors affecting the skin's temperature, and the amount of elapsed time between the deposition of the print and the examination by the investigator. Eliopulos (2003) writes:

> In the real world of homicide investigation, it is often considered impractical to spend an exorbitant amount of time processing bodies for latent print development... since the 1970s, the cases in which a print has been recovered have numbered only a couple dozen, and prints ultimately linked to the bad guy have been even more remote... Throughout their entire careers, most practitioners will never experience a case in which a latent print is successfully lifted from a dead body.

12.6.5.3 Examining the Scene

The physical evidence also can establish the pattern of the suspect's modus operandi (MO), or the perpetrator's characteristic way of committing a crime. Connection of cases through use of the MO and the physical evidence is important in the solving of serial cases. Physical evidence from the crime scene can establish a link from the victim to the suspect; Locard's Exchange Principle comes into play in the exchanging of trace evidence from person to person through interaction. Physical evidence can also link a victim or a suspect to a crime scene, and it can link persons, objects, and crime scenes to a particular crime. Crime scene evidence can corroborate or disprove the credibility and accuracy of the statements made by victims, suspects, and witnesses, and it can assist in the identification of a suspect by providing solid investigatory leads. It can identify unknown substances at crime scenes, such as chemicals or accelerants in the case of arson, and it also assists in the reconstruction of the crime.

In many crime scenes it is more important to determine how the evidence was created than to determine how the crime scene came to exist. This type of information is generated by examining how the evidence presents at the crime scene to reconstruct the events leading up to and during the actual crime. Lee (2001) states that in some jurisdictions, the role of the crime scene investigator has been limited to the work of a technician, who mechanically identifies, collects, preserves, and documents physical evidence at a scene. Lee advocates for a more comprehensive approach to crime scene investigation, where the process not only includes the aforementioned steps, but adds to it more dynamic approaches such as scene survey, scene analysis, development of the link between physical evidence and persons, and reconstruction of the crime scene. The forensic investigative process, Lee adds, is based on the scientific method and should be a systematic, methodical process. It begins with the initial response to the crime scene and continues through scene security, scene survey, scene documentation, recognition of physical evidence, collection, packaging and preservation of physical evidence, examination of the crime scene, crime scene analysis, and finally, reconstruction of the crime scene. Following the documentation and search of the crime scene, evidence collection and preservation can commence, starting with evidence considered to be the most fragile, transient, or easily lost.

12.6.5.4 Transfer Theory

Dr. Edmund Locard's work formed the basis for what is widely regarded as a cornerstone of the forensic sciences, Locard's Exchange Principle. Locard advocated the application of scientific methods and logic to criminal investigation and identification. As stated by Dr. John Thornton, a criminalist and a former professor of forensic science at the University of California, Berkeley, "Forensic scientists have almost universally accepted the Locard Exchange Principle." This doctrine was enunciated early in the 20th century by Locard, the director of the first crime laboratory, in Lyon, France. Locard's Exchange Principle states that with contact between two items, there will be an exchange of evidence.

Locard's belief and assertion is that when any person comes into contact with an object or another person, a cross-transfer of physical evidence occurs. By recognizing, documenting, and examining the nature and extent of this evidentiary exchange, Locard observed that criminals could be associated with particular locations, items of evidence, and victims. The detection of the exchanged materials is interpreted to mean that the two objects were in contact. This is the cause-and-effect principle reversed; the effect is observed and the cause is concluded. Forensic scientists also recognize that the nature and extent of this exchange can be used not only to associate a criminal with locations, items, and victims, but with specific actions as well. Locard's Exhange Principle dictates that a mutual exchange of matter (trace evidence) results whenever two surfaces come in contact with each other. In other words, when a suspect enters a scene, he brings material with him, and when he leaves the scene, he takes material with him. Transfers can be direct or secondary; a fingerprint or a palm print might be examples of direct transfer, whereas blood spatters deposited on a piece of clothing is an example of secondary transfer. There are two types of transfer evidence: trace transfer, such as blood, glass, fibers, or soil; and pattern transfer evidence, such as bloody shoeprints or fabric impressions.

These pieces of trace evidence can be challenging to identify, locate, and collect because of their diverse nature of biological or chemical components and the wide spectrum of detection and collection methods available. Trace evidence collection methods include collection of the entire object, tape lifts, swabbing, and vacuum sweepings of select portions of the evidence for analysis. Most physical evidence will be collected into paper folds, packets, or envelopes, as well as paper bags so that evidence is not degraded further. Outer containers are sealed with evidence tape and include documentation of the following: descriptive information about the item collected; identification of the collector; date, time, and location collected; and agency case numbers. Most items of evidence can be easily packaged and preserved in the aforementioned containers; however, volatile evidence can be secured in jars or metal paint cans, and liquid evidence can be secured in unbreakable, leakproof containers. Moist or wet biological evidence can be packaged and then transferred to a secure, controlled drying chamber where it is allowed to air dry and then repackaged into airtight containers. The original packages must be retained and packaged with the dried evidence. All pieces of evidence must be packaged separately to avoid cross-contamination, and all packages must be closed and sealed at the time of collection to avoid comingling during transport to a police evidence locker or to the crime lab for analysis.

12.6.5.5 Types of Physical Evidence

Transient evidence is evidence, which, by its very nature, is temporary and can easily be degraded or lost. Examples include temporary markings, some biological and physical phenomena, odors, and temperatures. Conditional evidence is generated by an action or an event, and can also be easily lost if not observed, documented, or collected promptly. Examples include the precise location of the body, the precise locations of pieces of evidence, and lighting conditions. Pattern evidence can take the form of markings, striations, depositions, imprints, or indentions. Examples include blood spatter or blood stains, tire or skid marks, powder or residue patterns, or furniture position patterns. Transfer (trace) evidence is generated by the physical contact of objects or persons, or between persons and objects. Associative evidence consists of items that can be used to associate a victim or a suspect with a specific scene or to each other.

Fingerprints

Because of their nearly foolproof ability to help identify the victim, fingerprints are some of the best pieces of evidence at a crime scene. Investigators should bear in mind that palm prints, bare footprints, ear prints, and lip prints also are viable forms of evidence. Fingerprints are classified into three categories. Plastic fingerprints occur when a finger touches or presses against a plastic material and produces a negative impression of the friction ridge pattern. These types of fingerprints can be found on fresh paint, substances that melt easily when touched, adhesive tape, thick layers of dust, putty or wax that has not hardened, soap, grease, tar, resin, and clay, to name a few. Prints of fingers contaminated with foreign matter result when the finger is pressed into a layer of material and then pressed against a surface. A print can be left when a finger is contaminated with pigments, ink, soot, dust, oils, and blood, to name a few substances. Latent fingerprints result when small amounts of oil, sweat, or dirt are deposited on the object touched. Latent prints can be visible or invisible to the naked eye. They can be developed by using a fingerprint powder applied with a special brush; a special adhesive is then used to lift the print and preserve it for future analysis and identification. Latent prints can also be developed by use of iodine, silver nitrate solution, ninhydrin solution, and cyanoacrylate fuming.

Investigators should look for fingerprints at locations and on objects the suspect might have touched or handled at the time of the crime. Fingerprints vary in the length of time that they are viable. Plastic prints remain for any length of time unless the object on which they are left is disturbed. Prints resulting from contamination of the fingers are quickly destroyed and should be collected and documented as soon as possible. Latent prints can remain for years if they are in a well-protected location. For comparison purposes, the investigator should take samples of known prints from every individual who might have been present at the crime scene. These elimination prints should be inked onto 10-print cards. Postmortem elimination prints of the deceased can be taken once evidence has been collected and the medical examiner has granted permission. If the decedent has been exposed to water and there is skin slippage present on the fingertips, the investigator can remove the loose epidermis, drying it with care so that the friction ridge details are not lost, then placing the skin over a mold or the investigator's own gloved fingers so that it can be inked and rolled onto a 10-print card.

Impression Evidence

Impression evidence consists of two-dimensional impressions or imprints, and three-dimensional impressions, or indentions. Imprints are frequently found in indoor scenes, on objects, and occasionally on nonporous surfaces in outdoor scenes. The most common examples are fingerprints. Indentions are frequently found at outdoor scenes, and deposited in softer receiving surfaces. The most common examples are footwear indentions in soil or other soft surfaces.

Blood

Information that can be derived from blood evidence at the scene includes blood spatter pattern to determine the parameters of the assault and resulting injury, DNA information, and blood and enzyme typing. Before collecting any blood evidence, photographs should be taken in situ to help determine the importance of this biological evidence to the investigation. Following photo-documentation, collection can commence. In general, the most easily lost blood, such as blood in high-volume traffic areas of the scene, should be collected first. Blood stains that are detected on movable surfaces or items can be protected by moving the item to a safer location until the stain or object can be collected later. Blood found at a crime scene will be observed as a dried stain or in a liquid state. Lee (2001) states, "Generally, if blood at the crime scene is liquid, then let it air dry. If the object with the blood stain is movable, then collect the entire object."

Blood and blood-stained items should be placed in the appropriate containers and packaged per proper protocol. Blood and blood-stained items should be packaged separately to prevent cross-contamination, and these pieces of evidence should not be exposed to excessive heat or humidity, or the samples will degrade. This type of evidence should be refrigerated, if possible, and transported to a forensic laboratory as soon as possible. Liquid blood samples, if small, can be collected using sterile cotton swabs and then allowing them to air dry. If the blood sample is large, it can be collected through a sterile pipette or syringe and placed in a vacutainer test tube. If the blood is on a movable object, it should be collected in an appropriate paper container and laid out for air drying. For dried blood stains, if the object is movable, it should be collected in a primary container and then placed in an outer, non-airtight container. For blood stains on bulky or immovable objects, the blood can be absorbed onto sterile cotton, it can be cut out and removed, it can be scraped using a sterile sharp instrument such as a blade into a paper receptacle, or it can be lifted using gel lifters or fingerprint tape.

Other Biological Evidence

Seminal stains found on clothing, bedding, or other surfaces should be documented, collected, packaged, and preserved in a similar way to blood stains. These stains are often detected using alternate light sources. Saliva, urine, or perspiration stains are documented, collected, packaged, and preserved in a similar manner to other biological evidence.

Clothing

Clothing should be collected in nearly every homicide, assault, fire death, firearms death, electrical death, or motor vehicle accident. Evidence from clothing can provide trace evidence, including blood, body fluids, hair and fibers, paint chips from a hit-and-run accident, and accelerants from an arson fire; evidence in the form of blood stains, burns, or tire mark impressions that help with reconstruction efforts; and the type and size of the weapon used, such as the caliber of the gun or the width of a knife blade.

Fibers and Hairs

An examination of hair can determine whether it is human or animal; the body region from which it originated; whether it fell out or was forcibly removed; whether it was burned, dried, or bleached; blood groups if the root is attached; and information provided through DNA analysis. Oblique lighting, alternate light sources, and lasers are efficient techniques for finding hairs at the crime scene or on the victim's body and clothing. Hairs can be collected through picking, vacuuming, or tape lifts. If hair is attached to another item of evidence, it should be left on the item and collected in its original condition. Lab analysis can determine the fiber type and possible origin. This type of evidence is searched, collected, and packaged like hair evidence, and collection methods include picking, vacuuming, tape lifting, and scraping. If fiber evidence is found attached to another object, such as in the case of fabric being caught on sharp edges of broken windows or ripped screens, it should be packaged intact. Other types of trace evidence can include glass, paint, and soil; this kind of evidence should be collected with similar care, and collected with suspected sources of the trace evidence.

Firearms and Tool Marks

Firearms evidence includes weapons, bullets, casings, and parts found at crime scenes involving shooting incidents. The firearm can be analyzed for fingerprints, biological fluids, and other trace evidence, and can be test-fired to determine the characteristics of the projectiles. Gunshot residue found at the crime scene or on the victim's body is fragile and should be documented and collected as soon as possible using standard techniques of disc lifting or swabbing. Gunshot residue is sometimes helpful in determining the range of fire, so any clothing displaying or suspected of displaying gunshot residue should be photographed, collected in a paper bag, and packaged carefully for further analysis. Tool marks are treated as impression evidence and should be photographed and collected, or marked and photographed if they are located on a movable surface.

Field Tests

There are numerous presumptive field-test reagents, including tests for the presence of blood (phenolphthalein, leucomalachite green, ortho-tolidine, luminal, tetra-mrthylbenzidine, and florescin); tests for the presence of body fluids including semen (acid phosphatase), saliva (amylase), urine (creatinine), fecal matter (urobilinogen), and gastric contents (gastric acid); a test for gunshot residue; and tests for controlled substances and narcotics.

12.6.5.6 Crime Scene Reconstruction

Chisum and Turvey (2000) define reconstruction as "the determination of the actions surrounding the commission of a crime." They add that, "Careful and competent examination of the physical evidence the documentation of the crime scene allows for this determination. The systematic documentation and recording of the crime scene is required for this analysis. The veracity of statements by witnesses, victims, and suspects can be established by reconstruction." Lee (2001) states:

> Crime scene reconstruction is the process of determining or eliminating the events and actions that occurred at the crime scene through analysis of the crime scene pattern, the location and position of the physical evidence, and the laboratory examination of the physical evidence. Reconstruction not only involves scientific scene analysis, interpretation of the scene pattern evidence and laboratory examination of physical evidence, but also involves systematic study of relayed information and the logical formulation of a theory.

The basic principles of crime scene reconstruction include recognition of the potential evidence and separation of this material from that material that has no evidentiary value. Analysis and comparison of physical evidence at a forensic laboratory can identify objects, substances, and materials; trace their origins; and compare them to known materials and standards. A second component of crime scene reconstruction is identification of evidence, which is a comparison process that utilizes the characteristics of a known item to match it with evidence collected at the crime scene. An item of evidence is scrutinized to determine its physical, chemical, biological, and morphological properties. A third component of crime scene reconstruction is individualization, which refers to the forensic demonstration that a piece of evidence is unique among members of its class.

According to Lee (2001), reconstruction consists of five stages: data collection, conjecture, hypothesis formulation, testing, and theory formation. Data collection involves the assembling of all information pertinent to the crime scene, including the condition of the evidence, obvious patterns and impressions, and condition of the victim. Conjecture refers to the possible explanation of events involved in a criminal act; it is by no means the only explanation for the crime, and it is usually conducted prior to extensive analysis of the evidence. A hypothesis, or educated guess about the probable course of events, is formed based on the examination of the evidence. Testing confirms or disproves a hypothesis, and a theory can be formulated from verified investigative information, evidence analysis, and interpretation.

12.6.5.7 Blood Stain Pattern Identification and Analysis

Lee (2001) says that blood stain patterns can reveal not only the "who" but the "what" with regard to the circumstance of bloodshed. Eliopulos (2003) states that blood spatter interpretation can determine the distance between the target surface and the origin of the blood at the time of the bloodshed, the point of origin of the blood, the movement and direction of the person or object, the number of blows or shots causing the dispersal of blood, the type and direction of impact that produced the blood, the position of the victim and the object during bloodshed, and movement of the victim after bloodshed. Lee confirms that investigators should study the direction of travel of the blood droplets; distance of the blood source to the target surface; the angle of the impact of the blood droplet; the type of blood droplets; identification of blood trails, direction, and relative speed of motion; the nature of the force used to create the bloodshed; the nature of the object used to cause bloodshed, the number of blows involved, and the location of the person or object relative to the bloodshed; the sequence of events leading up to the bloodshed; interpretation of contact or transfer patterns; and the estimation of elapsed time and the volume of the blood that was shed.

There are three kinds of blood stain patterns: dropping blood stain patterns, impacted blood stain spatters, and special blood stain configuration patterns. The dropping blood stain's diameter can determine the distance the blood drop fell, as drops get larger as the height from which the drop fell increases. The target surface texture for dropping blood can also affect the size and shape of the blood stain pattern. Nonporous, hard surfaces will produce circular stain patterns with smooth edges, whereas softer, more porous surfaces produce spatter stains with rough edges. The shape of the blood stain changes when the angle at which a blood drop impacts a surface is altered; the blood stain pattern becomes more elongated as the angle of impact is made smaller or more acute. The length and width of the blood stain can help investigators determine the angle of impact. Blood drops are often found in trails at the crime scene, and the pattern of the trail possesses directionality and distance characteristics. Impacted blood stains are created by more force than gravity; the energy added to a drop of blood causes it to break up into smaller drops, or spatters, relative to the amount of force employed. Internal force comes from arterial pressure, whereas external force is that which created the bleeding. The point of origin is determined by the point of convergence, which is the process of determining the two-dimensional point of origin of blood spatter. Impacted blood stain patterns are classified by the amount of force used to create the pattern. Low-velocity impact spatter produces blood stain patterns in which most of the blood drops are not broken into smaller droplets. Medium-velocity impact spatter is produced when most of the blood drops are broken into spatters of 2 mm to 4 mm. High-velocity impact spatter is characterized by drops measuring 2 mm or smaller. High-velocity impact spatter is frequently seen in cases of gunshot wounds, for example.

Other patterns include dispersion effects of forward and back spatter, found in medium- and high-velocity impact blood stain patterns. Projected blood is frequently associated with major injuries that create open wounds, such as arterial gushes, and produce patterns with sharp edges and movement. Flow pattern refers to a large quantity of blood deposited on vertical surfaces that flows downward. The repetitive dripping pattern refers to blood dripping into a pool; the edges of these blood spots are not as spineous, and show no motion. A cast-off blood stain pattern refers to an arc motion that transfers blood to an object or a body part; an example of this is a bloody object that is flung, such as a moving arm, that can produce a cast-off pattern on a wall, for example. Pooling of blood provides information about the amount of blood deposited at the scene, and contact-transfer blood stain patterns are the result of blood adhering to an object or a body through direct contact and then transferring to another location. Wiper patterns are created when an unstained object moves through a blood surface and creates a pattern.

12.6.5.8 Other Patterns

Broken glass is most frequently associated with shooting incidents, burglary, and fire scenes. Glass-fracture patterns can provide the investigator with information about the direction of the impact force applied; approximate force of the impact; approximate angle of the impact force; determination of the type of glass structure; determination of the sequence of firing, direction of firing, and the type of firearm for the projectile holes present; and estimation of the fire temperatures, direction of fire travel, and intensity of the heat. In crime scenes that occur indoors, furniture position patterns can yield information about the events that caused the patterns, and possible actions of victims and suspects. Track-trail patterns, such as those created by vehicle tires, can tell investigators how many persons or vehicles were at the scene, whether they were moving around, the direction of travel, and whether objects were dragged or carried. Footprint patterns also can help determine a suspect's shoe size, weight, stride length, and any abnormalities of gait.

12.6.5.9 Shooting Incidents

Reconstruction of the scene of shooting incidents can yield investigative information and assist in accurate conclusions. Lee (2001) states that "the components of a successful shooting investigation include crime scene processing, autopsy and medical records, laboratory examination of physical and pattern evidence, and related reconstruction experiments." Steps in the investigation of shooting incidents include collecting gunshot residue from the hands of the victim and the victim's clothing. Investigators should locate all firearms-associated evidence at the crime scene by conducting a thorough inventory of the number of bullets each firearm can store, as well as how many bullets are missing, the number of casings recovered, the number of bullet holes, the number and type of wounds, and any comments from witnesses. Following this preliminary accounting, investigators should reconcile the data to address any shots or evidence that are unaccounted for. Markings on projectiles can be examined by analysts at forensic laboratories for valuable information about the types of firearms used and the rifling characteristics that can point to the origin of manufacturing. Microscopic examination might also reveal any surfaces contacted by the projectile after firing. Muzzle-to-target distance determinations can be made by comparing the gunshot residue found on the item collected at the crime scene to laboratory-controlled gunshot residue patterns created at various distances by test fires of firearms. Routes of the projectiles can be determined through geometric, physical methods or trajectory methods of rods, strings, and probes. Optical projection methods refer to visual sightings and low-power lasers. Shell casings at the crime scene can be used for comparisons to suspect firearms to determine if they fired a particular cartridge.

12.7 DEATH INVESTIGATION: THE PROCESS

Eliopulos (2003) states that three factors solve crime: physical evidence, witness statements, and confessions. After processing the scene, death investigation proceeds to a systematic series of steps including canvassing, interviewing, and interrogation. For the purposes of examining nurses' roles in death investigation, we will look at the first two steps in greater detail, as appropriate to nurse death investigators' practice. Eliopulos defines canvassing as a questioning of people in the general vicinity of the crime scene to elicit information and possibly develop witnesses to some aspect of the case. The investigator should look for potential eyewitnesses to the event, individuals who have knowledge of the circumstance of the incident, individuals who have knowledge of the decedent, and individuals who have information related to the suspect(s). Interviewing is a three-step process encompassing preparation, questioning, and closing. Eliopulos writes, "The investigator should approach the information supplied by each witness with a critical eye to determine if it is accurate." The investigator should consider the physiological abilities of the witness (such as the accuracy of the witness's five senses), external factors involving the witness (such as weather or lighting conditions that would impair the witness's ability to see the crime in accurate detail), the emotional state of the witness, and personal screening abilities of the witness (such as any specific perceptions or knowledge that might have a bearing on the case).

12.7.1 Homicide Investigation

The U.S. Department of Justice characterized homicide victims as being predominantly male, aged 25 to 34, and African American; firearms were used in the majority of crimes (Eliopulos, 2003). The types of homicides can include anger, murder–suicide, jealousy, personal gain, triangle situations, revenge, self-defense, thrill killing, and random killing. Eliopulos states, "Traditionally, the investigation of homicides is painted with a broad brush. That is, all homicides are treated equally. No distinction is made in investigative technique with regard to the various motives." Eliopulos adds that homicides can be classified as follows:

- Altercation homicides: These comprise the largest number of homicides and frequently involve a domestic incident between known spouses, relatives, and acquaintances.
- Contract murder: This crime involves a suspect hired to kill for an individual who will benefit from the crime.
- Drug-related: This type of murder involves parties involved in the selling and purchase or use of drugs.
- Robbery homicides: These involve a death resulting from or preceding a burglary or robbery.
- Sexual homicides: This category includes any murder with an overtone of sexual violence, and can include rape and torture.
- Miscellaneous homicides: The category refers to murders that cannot be classified in the aforementioned categories and can include hate crimes, killing sprees, mass murders, and euthanasia.

12.7.2 General Considerations

Eliopulos (2003) states that altercation homicides are the most common types of murder and are the "most easily solved type of homicide because the development of a motive will usually produce a suspect." Cases are complicated by the suspect attempting to conceal the crime, including circumstances such as the body of a spouse is found in a vehicle after being reported missing; the spouse is reported to have been shot during an accidental discharge of a firearm; the victim is reported to have been killed as an act of self-defense; or the victim has been reported missing, with foul play suspected and no body recovered. In contract murders, the motive is usually developed during the course of the investigation and is commonly not suspected during the initial processing of the crime scene. According to Eliopulos, investigators should consider contract murder if there are no indicators of other potential motives. Drug-related homicides might initially present as motiveless during the initial processing of the scene, but further examination of the evidence and cultivation of information from witnesses can direct the case. Considering that robbery-related homicides are "a very modus operandi-influenced event," Eliopulos says investigators should reconstruct the crime to discern discrepancies in the suspect's activities or MO that might have been altered through the evolution of improved techniques, as well as to determine if the decedent is the victim or perpetrator of the robbery. Eliopulos says that sexual homicides are recognizable due to the conditions of the decedent or the scene; for example, the victim might be unclothed or partially clothed, the genitalia might be exposed, the body might have been posed provocatively, the decedent might have foreign objects inserted into orifices, and the scene could demonstrate evidence of sexual activity ante-, peri-, or postmortem.

Eliopulos writes, "The crime scene becomes extremely important because the physical evidence may reveal behavioral traits of the murderer." Eliopulos adds that crimes that can be profiled include sadistic torture in sexual assaults, evisceration, postmortem slashing or cutting, mutilation murders, rapes, and ritualistic crimes. Serial murderers kill because they hear voices or see visions; they are compelled to kill a particular group of people such as homosexuals or prostitutes; they are hedonistic and enjoy killing to elicit a thrill; and they are control oriented. Eliopulos (2003) says the elements of profiling include victim typology, victim selection and procurement, type of weapon, type of assaults against the victim, tools of the crime, presence of evidence, disposal of the body, display of the remains, changes in MO as the crimes escalate, and postoffense behavior of the perpetrator.

In the article, "Evidence Dynamics: Locard's Exchange Principle and Crime Reconstruction," criminal profiling experts W. Jerry Chisum and Brent E. Turvey (2000) state, "Of all responsibilities shouldered by the forensic scientist, the reconstruction of the circumstances and behaviors involved in a crime is one of the most important." They add that it can be a powerful tool of corroboration of witness accounts, can provide an objective view that points to one theory over another, and can be used to investigate and establish the actions that occurred at the scene of a crime. Chisum and Turvey say, "Conclusions regarding the circumstances and behaviors elicited from the physical evidence related to a crime can infrequently be housed within the confines of absolute certainty. It is often an intensive process with imprecise results containing evidentiary holes, sequential gaps, and alternate possibilities." Although they do not suggest that crime reconstruction efforts "lack investigative or legal utility," they say its utility is more commonly found in "establishing the general circumstances of a crime, demonstrating links between victims, suspects, and offenders, corroboration of witness statements, providing investigative leads, and identifying potential suspects." They add quickly that on occasion, of far more investigatory and legal importance is what the physical evidence "excludes, fails to establish, or equivocates." Chisum and Turvey cite Dr. John Thornton (1997), who describes the mechanics of the logic that should be employed by forensic scientists when undertaking a forensic examination:

> Induction is a type of inference that proceeds from a set of specific observations to a generalization, called a premise. This premise is a working assumption, but it may not always be valid. A deduction, on the other hand, proceeds from a generalization to a specific case, and that is generally what happens in forensic practice. Providing that the premise is valid, the deduction will be valid. But knowing whether the premise is valid is the name of the game here; it is not difficult to be fooled into thinking that one's premises are valid when they are not.

Criminalist Dr. Richard Saferstein, retired chief forensic scientist from the New Jersey State Police Lab, also argues: "The physical evidence left behind at the crime scene plays a crucial role in reconstructing the events that took place surrounding the crime... The collection and documentation of physical evidence is the foundation of a reconstruction" (Saferstein, 1998).

Crime reconstruction, Chisum and Turvey say, involves examining the available physical evidence, those materials left at or removed from the scene, victim, or offender. These materials are used by the forensic scientist to establish contact between the suspect and victim or scene according to the principle proposed by Locard. These forensically established contacts are then considered in light of available and reliable witness, victim, and offender statements. From this, theories regarding the circumstances of the crime can be generated and falsified by logically applying the information of the established facts of the case. Left standing, ideally, will be legitimate, logical conclusions regarding the actions surrounding the commission of the crime. They point to the fictional character of Sherlock Holmes, the creation of author Sir Arthur Conan Doyle, who had remarked in the story *The Sign of Four*, "when you have eliminated the impossible, whatever remains, however improbable, must be the truth." Chisum and Turvey warn that investigators must be aware of the integrity of the physical evidence they are documenting and collecting, explaining that, "Even though a reliable chain of evidence may be established, physical evidence may have been altered prior to or during its collection and examination." They add, "Unless the integrity of the evidence can be reliably established, and legitimate evidentiary influences accounted for, the documentation of a chain of evidence, by itself, does not provide acceptable ground upon which to build reliable forensic conclusions." Chisum and Turvey say that the consideration of evidentiary influences, or what they call "evidence dynamics," is an essential part of the crime reconstruction process. Evidence dynamics refers to any influence that "changes, relocates, obscures, or obliterates physical evidence, regardless of intent. Evidence dynamics comes into play during the interval that begins as evidence is being transferred, and ends when the case is ultimately adjudicated." If a piece of evidence has been moved, changed, or obscured, the investigator must answer the questions of when and how. They add, "Forensic scientists can only include in their analyses those things for which evidence exists. However, if there is no reasonable suggestion of circumstances that could have influenced or obliterated evidence, then the examiner should not assume that they occurred."

According to Chisum and Turvey, evidence dynamics can include the following:

- Offender actions during the commission of their crime and the postoffense interval, including staging, precautionary acts, and ritualistic acts
- Victim actions prior to a crime that might result in artifacts that are mistaken for evidence, including defensive actions, such as struggling, fighting, and running, which can relocate transfer evidence, causing secondary transfer, or cleaning up a location or their person after an attack
- Witnesses' actions in the postoffense interval, including preserving victim dignity, as well as the deliberate theft of items from the scene on discovery of an incapacitated or deceased victim.
- Weather and climate that can impact the nature and quality of evidence that is left behind
- Decomposition, which, over time, can obscure, obliterate, or mimic evidence of injury to a body
- Fire, which can obscure physical evidence related to criminal activities
- Presence of law enforcement, crime scene technicians, or emergency first-responders within the crime scene, which can relocate evidence, obliterate patterns, cause transfers, and add artifact evidence to the scene

Chisum and Turvey demonstrate an example of a secondary transfer from a case in their files: The body of a preteen female was discovered on a couch in her home, where she lived with her mother and younger brother; she was wearing only a shirt and bra at the time. She was determined to have died of "asphyxia secondary to manual strangulation," and had a history of sexual abuse, "suggested by the absence of her hymen" and numerous anal scars, as well as a history of promiscuity. Sperm from one of her mother's lovers was found on her perineum. Chisum and Turvey observe, "Given the location and circumstances of the crime, the precise conditions of this exchange could not be reliably established." They suggest one possibility is that the suspect was engaged in some form of sexual activity with the victim, and that sperm transferred to her perineum as a result. However, the suspect and the victim's mother had sexual relations in the mother's bed, where the victim had been playing previously with her brother. There were also reports that the suspect and the victim's mother perhaps had sexual relations on the couch, where the victim would have been seated. Additionally, a review of the crime scene video shows several evidence technicians moving evidence around on the couch and other locations, and then touching the victim's body in multiple locations, examining her body as it is being photographed, with and without gloves. Chisum and Turvey add that given these circumstances and the victim's history, the following are potential evidence transfer relationships in this case: from the suspect to the victim during a forced sexual assault; from the suspect to the victim during a consensual (but unlawful) sexual encounter; from the couch to the victim's perineum; from the mother's bed to the victim's perineum; and from the scene technician's fingers to the victim's perineum.

Another example is that of a teenager who had been stabbed multiple times by rival gang members. He ran for help at a neighboring home but collapsed in the walkway. A photo of the scene taken prior to the arrival of the EMT team depicts a blood trail and the victim lying face down. Subsequent photos show several EMTs working on the body while it is in the supine position; in the course of emergency treatment, he had been rolled over onto the blood pool. It became impossible for blood stain pattern interpretation to be used to reconstruct the events leading to the death of the youth. Chisum and Turvey conclude, "The failure to consider evidence dynamics as a part of any crime reconstruction process has the potential to provide for misinterpretations of physical evidence, and inaccurate or incomplete crime reconstructions." They say that any subsequent use of the reconstruction for investigations, trial, or behavioral analysis would have a "diminished foundation and relevance, compounding the harm in legal, investigative and academic venues. It is the responsibility of the forensic scientist to perform reconstructions of the circumstances and behaviors involved in a crime with care, and to be aware of the possibility of evidence dynamics, in order that opinions regarding reconstruction of the crime reflect the most informed and accurate rendering of the evidence."

12.8 NURSES' CONTRIBUTIONS TO DEATH INVESTIGATION

Nurses working as death investigators for medical examiners and coroners are the eyes and ears of these professionals out in the field. They make significant contributions in the recognition, documentation, collection, and preservation of forensic evidence at crime scenes, as well as gather pertinent information at natural deaths.

12.8.1 Definitions Lacking

One hindrance to the advancement of nurses' functionality as death investigators is the lack of a clear definition of not only the role of a forensic nurse death investigator (FNDI), but that of a non-nurse death investigator (NNDI). Allert and Becker (2002), Lynch (2001), and Courson (2000) confirm this lack of a standard definition, making it difficult for the rest of the legal and scientific communities to differentiate between FNDIs and NNDIs. Vessier-Batchen (2003) says this void in definitions and lack of research on the death investigator's role has contributed to "an inability to link skills and knowledge used in death investigation with those used in nursing." Citing Allert and Becker (2002), Fulton (2003), and James and Nordby (2003), Vessier-Batchen (2003) states, "A composite definition states that the death investigator's role is to represent and advocate for the deceased. The investigator should possess scientific and experiental knowledge in order to make professional and accurate judgments on manner of death based on pre-death symptomology, history, post-mortem appearance, toxicology, and other diagnostic studies."

Arizona forensic nurse Mary Sullivan doesn't think that a distinction between nurse and NNDIs is needed:

> The death investigator role is well established already, and nurses bring to the position a wealth of information that enhances this role. That's not to say that nurses are necessarily better than other death investigators, because non-nurse investigators go through rigorous coursework, and if they don't cut the mustard with the medical examiner/coroner or with law enforcement, they are not going to be working, period. I simply think that nurses will approach medico-legal death investigation from a different angle, using their assessment and evaluation skills. Nurses can learn a lot from death investigators with non-medical backgrounds, and vice versa, and when working on a forensic medical team, it's all about how you fit into the picture, blending in and collaborating. Nurses can prove their worth by performing well, and demonstrating to their non-nurse colleagues their excellent job performance, their skills sets, and proof of how their nursing background can enhance that role.

12.8.2 Making a Case for Nurse Death Investigators

As death investigators, nurses pick up on death-scene subtleties, and many members of the forensic science community are not shy about praising their contributions to the medico-legal process. Mary Fran Ernst, a medico-legal death investigator for the St. Louis County Medical

Examiner's Office in St. Louis, as well as director of medico-legal education and a professor in the Division of Forensic Pathology at Saint Louis University School of Medicine, tells her students, "Dead people always come first." Ernst says:

> What is the dead person attempting to tell us? Dead people do talk to you; you just have to listen really carefully. Their bodies tell us what happened. The death investigator must be a medically knowledgeable person who anticipates the questions of the forensic pathologist who will perform the exam and autopsy. It might be the physical location of the body relative to the crime scene or the trace evidence on the clothing. We must know how the body got there; was it at the scene or brought to the scene? Was it moved? A death investigator is the first medical person with forensic training to be with the dead person so he or she must get as much information from the body as possible to try to establish time of death, what the medical condition of the person was before they died, and details about the incident that caused them to die.

Ernst believes forensic nurses make exceptional death investigators because they are quick to pick up on signs and symptoms related to medical conditions. "Not every jurisdiction has well-trained law enforcement, so death investigators must know how to do everything, to be sure the dead person gets the best treatment possible," Ernst says:

> Nurses make phenomenal death investigators because they know the terminology and the techniques. The law enforcement part is easy; the medical stuff is hardest, so nurses often have an advantage over some law enforcement. For a long time I had to convince a medical examiner that instead of more law enforcement at crime scenes, we need people like forensic nurses, people with medical backgrounds who take histories all the time and who excel at finding out what happened.

The subtleties of death investigation are what intrigue most nurse death investigators. "It's easy to do an investigation on a guy who has 16 gunshot wounds to his back," Ernst says. "That's a no-brainer. It's the subtle cases that are the most challenging and rewarding." Ernst recalls the time she was called to the scene of a decomposed dead body near a gun:

> The police officer says it looks like a homicide of one person, but as I drive to the scene I get more calls that there are more people, and by the time I get to the scene there are five bodies in what appears to be multiple shooting deaths. The bodies were left in an enclosed garage in the summer heat for three days so they were in the worst physical shape in which to find anything. A systematic examination revealed the bodies didn't have any gunshot wounds or any physical defects but they had cherry-red nail beds. These people were dark-skinned, so it was difficult, but a closer inspection of the evidence showed us that someone had left a car running in the garage. So what appeared to be a massive homicide by shooting turned out to be death by carbon monoxide poisoning. Without a thorough knowledge of toxicology, a small detail might have been overlooked.

Ernst recalls another case in which a police officer was killed when he responded to a burglar alarm in a shopping center:

> The officer had been beaten about the head with the butt of a revolver. He was lying face up but his right hand was underneath him, bent at the elbow. When I turned him over very carefully I saw he'd clenched his hand around a button that didn't match anything of his. The officer, knowing he was outnumbered five to one, knew he had to grab some kind of evidence to help us catch his killers. He was able to grab hold of one of his assailants and knew he had to hide that button. It was the one thing that tied one of the assailants to the crime and he was sent to the electric chair. It was another example of a subtle piece of evidence. In the same manner, nurses do the little things right. Just like documentation. There's nobody better at documentation than nurses, and in our business if you don't document it, it didn't happen.

Rae Wooten, BSN, RN, ABMDI, senior deputy coroner for Charleston County, South Carolina, says she first became aware of the need to validate death investigation as part of the nursing process in 2002, when a state board of nursing threatened not to renew the active licenses of nurses practicing as death investigators. The nursing board was unaware of the publication of the *Scope and Standards of Forensic Nursing Practice* by the ANA in 1992. "Nurses everywhere were seeking advice on how to get into death investigation, as they met resistance on many fronts; even some institutions of nursing education seemed not to be knowledgeable about forensic nursing," Wooten (2003) writes. "After lots of thought and some research, I have come to believe that part of the problem is the lack of a defined model that helps nurse death investigators clearly conceptualize what they do. As a consequence they have difficulty 'selling' themselves to others who have historically controlled death investigation. After all, if the nursing profession doesn't get it, how can we expect non-nurses to value what nurses have to offer?"

Wooten (2003) writes:

> What do we, as nurses, have to offer to death investigation? I believe that nurses, by virtue of their education, bring with them a tremendous knowledge base that is so suited to death investigation that it is difficult to imagine a better fit. Nurses are knowledgeable about normal anatomy and physiology, as well as deviations from normal. They are knowledgeable about pharmacology, grief and grieving, growth and development, interviewing and many

> more areas that are valuable to death investigation. This broad knowledge base is not typically found among those with criminal justice or law enforcement backgrounds or even among those non-nurse death investigators who frequently are employed by medical examiners.

Mary Sullivan advocates the constant pursuit of education and training by nurse death investigators:

> Forensic nursing is a relatively new specialty, and there is still much we need to know. We need to take our talents and knowledge as nurses and learn to apply it to medico-legal death investigation. There is still a lot of coursework and book smarts and street smarts that nurses need to incorporate into their nursing world. I think nurses can always learn more about what constitutes medico-legal significance and what to do with it. The nursing process encompasses assessment, planning, intervention and evaluation, so, for example, when it comes to medico-legal death investigation, nurses would then assess the crime scene, the situation, the victim, and then plan what you are going to do at the scene. Death investigation parallels clinical nursing practice beautifully. Forensic investigation protocols, such as stopping, looking around, getting organized, assembling your tools and your consulting specialists . . . that's exactly what nurses do in the everyday care of patients, so the cross-over is a smooth and natural one. Nursing intervention is an actionable item; at the crime scene, the nurse death investigator goes in and gets the evidence, whatever it is, then evaluates it. What's more, nurses have the unique ability to evaluate their techniques; they ask themselves, "Could I have investigated something from a different angle?" and then they do it. In all regards, the nursing process is a good way to live your life and do your job, whether clinical or medico-legal death investigation.

12.8.3 The IAFN Introduces Draft Standards for Forensic Nurse Death Investigators

In late 2004, the IAFN issued a draft of its Forensic Nurse Death Investigator Standards to its members for their review and comment. As of winter 2005, the standards had yet to be formalized and approved; however, the draft document provides a general sense of the direction the IAFN is taking in its efforts to guide this new and burgeoning nursing specialty. The draft standards were authored by Stacy A. Mitchell, MSN, RN, D-ABMDI; Teresa Royer, MSN, RN; and Angela Snow, MSN, RN; as well as reviewed by Jennifer Davies, BSN, RN, D-ABMDI; Donna Garbacz Bader, MSN, RN, D-ABMDI; Patti Hancock, RN; Alice Lloyd, RN; Virginia Lynch, MSN, RN; Constance Morrison, MSN, RN, JD; Bobbi Jo O'Neal, BSN, RN, F-ABMDI; and Rae Wooten, BSN, RN, D-ABMDI. The standards are meant to serve as a foundation for the FNDI and are not to supercede the authority and standards of the jurisdiction's medical examiner or coroner. The guidelines recommend that FNDIs be familiar with their state's scope of practice and local and state laws. The IAFN draft standards define an FNDI as

> a registered nurse who applies the nursing process to the subspecialty of death investigation in forensic nursing. The forensic nurse death investigator applies nursing practice to the scientific and medico-legal investigation of deaths across the life span; collaborates with interdisciplinary agencies to investigate deaths and identify trends of sudden and unexpected death and injury; conducts and/or participates in research; and promotes health and safety through community education.

The draft standards also define the APRN FNDI as "a registered nurse who holds a master's or doctorate degree with advanced specialized clinical knowledge in the forensic science arena. APRN is the umbrella term used to identify the advanced practice roles of the clinical nurse specialist and nurse practitioner." The IAFN suggests that the minimum qualifications to be an FNDI is status as an RN and documentation of continuing education or certificate training in medico-legal death investigation.

The draft standards delineate the responsibilities of the FNDI and the APRN FNDI separately, indicating a two-tier set of skills that historically has not existed. As envisioned by the IAFN Death Investigation Standards of Practice Task Force, the FNDI assesses the scene and decedent; documents the crime scene and decedent to aid in determining cause and manner of death; collects and preserves forensic evidence while maintaining the chain of custody; aids in positive identification of the decedent; notifies the next of kin; collaborates with legal and social agencies; queries to identify trends, coordinates plans to impact change, and evaluates outcomes; and provides education to health care providers, law enforcement, and members of the community. In addition to these aforementioned skills, the APRN FNDI initiates and interprets diagnostic tests and procedures, formulates a differential diagnosis regarding cause and manner of death, participates in the design and development of multidisciplinary and interdisciplinary processes, contributes to the development of organizational systems, facilitates utilization of systems and community resources to implement the plan, and synthesizes the results of the evaluation analyses to determine the impact of the plan.

In the draft standards, the IAFN attempts to define an FNDI's area of practice, commenting, "the forensic nurse death investigator is responsible for ensuring an objective, comprehensive, and scientific medico-legal death investigation while providing the utmost respect and dignity to the decedent, family, and identified support system. This responsibility is upheld by current evidence-based practices in the medico-legal death investigation through the professional nursing process of assessment, diagnosis, planning, implementation, and evaluation." The standards suggest that typical arenas of practice would include the medical examiner's or coroner's office, or the office of the justice of the peace. The draft standards state that "The practice of the FNDI can influence local, state, and federal legislation in areas of health care, legal and social reform. This responsibility is maintained by practicing the professional and ethical nursing process or assessment, diagnosis, implementation and evaluation."

The draft standards enumerate various forensic nursing interventions within the scope of practice of an FNDI, including: obtaining the initial death report and scene information; assessing and documenting observations at the scene; physically examining the decedent at the scene; collecting and preserving evidence on the decedent; interviewing the decedent's family and identified support system to obtain additional medical, surgical, and psychosocial history; assisting in the identification of the decedent and in taking control of unclaimed human remains; locating and notifying legal next of kin of the death in a timely, compassionate, and professional manner; obtaining medical records, police reports, and additional records and reports from other agencies; consulting with law enforcement and other agencies; and providing fact or expert testimony in an objective and professional manner. The IAFN draft standards for the FNDI, which advocate for a "holistic forensic nursing approach to the death scene," are based on several medico-legal principles, including Locard's Exchange Principle, as well as two other forensic concepts derived from Locard: the Four-Way Linkage Concept and the Transfer and Exchange Theory. The standards propose, "The FNDI actualizes the holistic forensic nursing approach when the concept of Transfer and Exchange Theory occurs between the death scene, physical evidence and objects, decedent, and potential suspect. The FNDI recognizes that this transfer and exchange occurs when anyone encounters the death scene, decedent, physical evidence and objects, and potential suspect."

The IAFN's draft standards explain that Locard's Exchange Principle involves four components: the death scene (where the FNDI assesses and documents every death scene in relation to the physical evidence and objects, decedent, and potential suspect), the decedent (where the FNDI examines the decedent and documents the findings in relation to the death scene, physical evidence and objects, and potential suspect), the physical evidence and objects (where the FNDI recognizes, documents, collects, and preserves physical evidence and objects relative to the death scene, decedent, and potential suspect while maintaining chain of custody), and the potential suspect (where the FNDI recognizes and upholds the theory of transfer and exchange of evidence in relation to the physical evidence and objects, death scene, and decedent). Henry Lee's (1994) Four-Way Linkage Concept includes the crime scene (death scene), victim (decedent), physical evidence and objects, and suspect (potential suspect). According to the IAFN's draft document, "the goal is to establish a link between all four of the components using the holistic forensic nursing approach for the accurate classification of cause and manner of death." The third concept used to establish the draft standards for FNDI is Gerberth's (1996) Transfer and Exchange Theory, which encompasses three principles: The perpetrator will take away traces of the victim and the scene; the victim will retain traces of the perpetrator and might leave traces of himself on the perpetrator; and the perpetrator will leave behind traces of himself at the scene.

The critical mass of the draft standards consists of seven proposed standards of care related to the nursing process and viewed through a forensic lens. The first proposed standard of care, assessment, is undertaken when the FNDI interviews individuals, investigates the scene, and conducts a physical examination of the decedent "to provide an accurate synopsis of the circumstances of death for the medical examiner/coroner." For comprehensive data collection to occur, the IAFN says, there must be "a collaborative and respectful relationship with legal, medical, and social agencies involved." In addition, there must be an established data-collection method that includes conducting a holistic forensic nursing assessment, recognizing and documenting physical evidence and objects, collecting and preserving data with appropriate equipment, and upholding the chain of custody and Fourth Amendment rights. Other components that facilitate data collection include a facility that allows for modifications of the data-collection process as needed; a concise, accurate, and appropriate record-keeping system; and a collection and storage system for the retrieval of data for law enforcement and other agencies.

The IAFN explains that the FNDI collects data in collaboration with other appropriate agencies in a timely manner; obtains data from sources such as legal, medical, and social agencies, decedent acquaintances, witnesses, scene investigation, and physical examination of the decedent; records data in a standardized, systematic, and concise format; and recognizes transcultural practices. In addition, the APRN FNDI initiates diagnostic tests and procedures relevant to the decedent's circumstances and interprets these tests and procedures.

According to the second proposed standard of care, diagnosis, the FNDI formulates diagnoses pertaining to forensic nursing issues from the holistic forensic nursing assessment, and provides for the application of nursing theory in the analysis of data collection from the holistic forensic nursing assessment.

According to the draft standards, the holistic forensic nursing assessment supports the diagnoses pertaining to forensic nursing issues; the diagnoses are validated with colleagues and the interdisciplinary team as appropriate; and are recorded in an accurate and systematic format. The FNDI also identifies nursing diagnoses based on the holistic forensic nursing assessment that are consistent with current accepted bodies of knowledge and valid research. Additionally, the APRN FNDI systematically compares and contrasts clinical findings with normal and abnormal variations and developmental events in formulating a differential diagnosis; utilizes complex data and information obtained during interview, examination, and diagnostic procedures in identifying diagnoses; and assists staff in developing and maintaining competency in the diagnostic process.

In the third proposed standard of care, outcomes identification, the IAFN says that the FNDI will identify expected individual outcomes based on the diagnoses of forensic issues in nursing related to the decedent, as "individualized outcomes provide direction for continuity of services and increased interdisciplinary collaborative efforts in the investigation of death." The IAFN document explains that outcomes are derived from the holistic forensic nursing assessment in collaboration with interdisciplinary agencies as appropriate. Within this framework, the FNDI will consider associated current scientific evidence, procedures, and clinical expertise when formulating expected outcomes; define expected outcomes in terms of the decedent, ethical considerations, environment, or situation with consideration of current scientific evidence; and involve other agencies and other departments when formulating outcomes. The APRN FNDI will identify expected outcomes that incorporate scientific evidence and are achievable through implementation of evidence-based practices; identify expected outcomes that incorporate cost and clinical effectiveness as well as continuity and consistency among providers; and support the use of clinical guidelines supported by outcomes.

In the fourth standard of care, planning, the FNDI will develop a comprehensive plan of action for each death scene to attain expected outcomes, based on and reflecting the holistic forensic nursing approach. Responsibilities include creating a plan of action that reflects current forensic nursing practice guided by theory and research, and enhances professional collaboration with inter-disciplinary agencies involved; as well as securing available resources for medico-legal death investigation. To this end, the FNDI will determine and prioritize the specific plan of action for each death scene based on the holistic forensic nursing approach, and document the plan of action in an accurate and systematic format. The APRN FNDI will identify assessment and diagnostic strategies, and interventions within the plan that reflect current evidence, including data, research, literature, and expert forensic nursing knowledge; participate in the design and development of multidisciplinary and interdisciplinary processes; contribute to the development and continuous improvement of organizational systems that support the planning process; and support the integration of clinical, human, and financial resources to enhance and complete the decision-making processes.

Regarding the fifth standard of care, implementation, the IAFN says that the FNDI implements the plan of action based on the holistic forensic nursing approach and the policies, procedures, and protocols of the facility to facilitate medico-legal death investigation. Within this framework, the IAFN explains that the plan of action recognizes that each death scene is unique, and that the plan of action should be implemented utilizing current forensic nursing practice, theory, and research. Therefore, the FNDI will implement the plan of action according to policies, procedures, and protocols of the facility; collaborate with colleagues and the interdisciplinary agencies to implement the plan of action as necessary; and document the implementation and all modifications from the plan of action as necessary. According to the IAFN, the APRN FNDI facilitates utilization of systems and community resources to implement the plan; supports collaboration with nursing colleagues and other disciplines to implement the plan; incorporates new knowledge and strategies to initiate change in nursing care practices if desired outcomes are not achieved; and fosters organizational systems that support implementation of the plan.

The sixth standard of care, evaluation, requires the FNDI to continuously assess data to evaluate and modify the plan of action to achieve the expected outcomes, as the "concurrent and retrospective evaluation of the plan of action is a continuous process to ensure accurate and systematic medico-legal death investigation," according to the draft standards. The FNDI will conduct ongoing, systematic evaluation of the diagnoses, outcomes, plan of action, and implementation for each medico-legal death investigation; pursue and disseminate new knowledge and research to provide accurate and systematic medico-legal death investigation; and systematically document the medico-legal death investigation process that can be used in the legal/judicial process. The APRN FNDI will evaluate the accuracy of the diagnosis and effectiveness of the interventions in relationship to the decedent's attainment of expected outcomes; synthesize the results of the evaluation analyses to determine the impact of the plan on the affected decedent(s), agencies, communities, and institutions; and use the results to make process or structural changes, including policy, procedure, or protocol documentation, as appropriate.

In the final standard of care, safety, the draft document suggests that the FNDI will practice safety principles, including physical well-being in and around the death scene to protect oneself and others. The IAFN comments,:

> The FNDI frequently responds to unknown hazardous environments and unknown persons. The initial responding law enforcement officer to the death scene identifies, prioritizes, and controls any dangerous situation(s) and/or

> person(s). Because there is often no prior health or behavioral data available, the safety must be insured to all participants in this process. Policies related to safety have implications for the FNDI, decedents, families, responding agencies, and community.

Within the aforementioned scenario, the FNDI will ensure that there is no immediate threat to self or other responding associates; if the scene involves a clandestine drug laboratory, biological weapons, radiological threats, or chemical threats, the appropriate personnel or agency must be contacted prior to entering the scene. Additionally, the FNDI is instructed to approach the scene in a manner designed to reduce the risk of harm to self while maximizing the safety of any and all people in the area; evaluate and maintain safety at all times; and notify supervisory personnel and make calls for assistance as necessary. Throughout the investigation of the crime scene, the FNDI is advised to observe Standard Precautions for the prevention of transmission of infectious diseases, as prescribed by the CDC.

A second significant component of the IAFN's draft standards for FNDIs is a set of three recommended standards of professional performance. The first proposed standard addresses quality assurance, wherein the FNDI "accurately and systematically evaluates the quality and effectiveness of the holistic forensic nursing approach." To this end, the IAFN suggests that the FNDI participates in evaluative processes and procedures in the agency; participates in professional development programs such as in-services, professional meetings, and formal education; disseminates new knowledge and research to colleagues; modifies practice based on new knowledge and professional evaluation; and participates in professional organizations. The APRN FNDI designs quality improvement initiatives, implements initiatives to evaluate the need for change, and evaluates the practice environment in relation to existing evidence, identifying opportunities for the generation and use of research.

The second proposed standard of professional performance is interdisciplinary collaboration with other professionals involved with medico-legal death investigation, including forensic scientists, forensic pathologists, and members of the criminal justice system. Within this directive, the FNDI should participate in facilitating open communication with the interdisciplinary members of the forensic team and document the results, as well as collaborate with others to generate positive outcomes through knowledge of the death. The draft standards say that the APRN FNDI should partner with other disciplines to enhance forensic care through interdisciplinary activities, such as education, consultation, management, technological development, or research opportunities.

The final proposed standard of performance is research, wherein the FNDI "contributes to the science of forensic nursing by recognizing, valuing, and utilizing research as critical to further forensic nursing practice," according to the IAFN, which adds that the FNDI is "responsible and accountable for the acquisition, analysis, and dissemination of knowledge and skills founded on valid research to promote forensic nursing. As the FNDI conducts and/or participates in sound research, innovative approaches to forensic nursing can be discovered and validated, thus improving practice."

The FNDI should identify trends in the community and professional environment necessitating research investigation; conduct or participate in research as appropriate to the FNDI's position, education, and practice; uphold the ethical and legal aspects of nursing research; and implement changes in practice based on valid research to improve forensic nursing practice. The IAFN explains that the APRN FNDI contributes to nursing knowledge by conducting or synthesizing research that discovers, examines, and evaluates knowledge, theories criteria, and creative approaches to improve forensic nursing practice; and formally disseminates research findings through presentations and publishing one's research.

The IAFN's draft standards are the first of their kind for nurse death investigators who have waited a long time for some type of formal instruction separate from the medico-legal death investigation guidelines established in 1998 for the general forensic investigator. Nurse death investigators now can have a set of guidelines more appropriate to their work and their nursing practice; however, some forensic nurses and nurse coroners are concerned about the attempt to establish a two-tier role that might pigeonhole FNDIs according to experience and education. In its draft standard, the IAFN states:

> By definition, the advanced practice registered nurse (APRN) holds a master's or doctorate degree with advanced specialized knowledge and skills in practice (AMA, 2004). According to the ANA, the APRN demonstrates "a greater depth and breadth of knowledge, a greater synthesis of data, increased complexity of skills and interventions, and significant role autonomy." The APRN is the umbrella term used by ANA to identify two advanced practice roles of clinical nurse specialist and nurse practitioner. The scope of practice and roles of each are distinguishable from the others, there is an overlapping of knowledge and skills within these roles.

Bobbi Jo O'Neal, a deputy coroner for the Charleston County Coroner's Office in South Carolina, was one of the reviewers of the draft standards, along with several forensic nurses from Houston, Texas. She comments, "Overall, I think that the standards are a good start. The problem with standards—and nursing standards in particular—is that it makes us try to put this specialty into the traditional nursing box, which it is not." O'Neal continues:

> My main concerns with the standards are with those that have been written for the advanced practice FDNI. To begin with there are very few of those in the country, if any. It is my opinion that we should not develop advanced standards yet, but others disagree. My concern is for those nurses who do not have a master's degree and plan to run for the political office of coroner. Based on the standards as they are written, those nonadvanced degree nurses would not be able to run an office and make decisions on their own. It may also make them vulnerable in the campaign process. This is a great set-up for state boards of nursing to tell nurses that they cannot represent themselves as a nurse while in political office because they are working outside their scope of practice. It has been stated that if the nurses were to win the election, that coroner law would prevail and the "coroner" could do those jobs, but they would not be able to do them as a "nurse."

O'Neal says she believes it is premature to develop advanced standards for a specialty in which there are only a handful of nurses. "It is my strong opinion that this is one specialty in which experience is much more important than nursing degrees, but again, I am a few of the vocal minority, and also one with the most experience." O'Neal cautions that when standards are reviewed by all of the IAFN's members, not just nurse death investigators, those nurses who do not practice specifically in the death investigation arena might make overly idealistic or unrealistic suggestions. Another dilemma is the country's patchwork quilt of medical examiner and coroner systems, which O'Neal says the proposed standards should take into account. "Just because a nurse working in an ME system has to practice in a certain way, doesn't mean that the nurse in the coroner's system does and vice versa," O'Neal explains. "The standards need to be based on not only nursing guidelines but state law enforcement guidelines as well. If we want nurses to represent themselves as nurses, then the standards need to flow with the laws of the state as well. The advanced FNDI standards could be very destructive to nonadvanced degree nurses in coroner states."

Arizona forensic nurse Mary Sullivan says she has only skimmed the draft standards and cannot comment fully on their content; however, as a general principle, Sullivan says:

> I think that if forensic nurses want to gain their advanced practice status, they should absolutely go for it. That requires extra skill sets, extra certification and training, and if you have it in you, definitely pursue it. But I do not think that all forensic nurses should have to be required to be an APRN to be considered a forensic nurse or a death investigator. There is a lot of talent, know-how out there, and a lot of nurses don't have the resources, time, or energy to pursue that credential, but they are damn good at what they do. I don't think forensic nurses or nurse death investigators should be required to be APRNs; if the powers-that-be begin to require that, I think we'll be shooting ourselves in the foot.

12.8.4 Death Investigation and the Nursing Process

Although it has been demonstrated in previous chapters that clinical forensic nursing is very much a part of the accepted scope of nursing practice, acceptance of death investigation by a nurse as a part of nursing practice has been slower in coming. Fulton (2003) writes, "Forensic nurse investigators utilize the nursing process; it is just applied differently and some of the steps are performed simultaneously with others. Assessment, planning, implementation and evaluation are components of every death investigation. These components are utilized to determine what is natural and what is not at a death scene." On entering the death scene, a nurse immediately begins to implement the nursing process with the first step of assessment, the investigation itself. The nurse collects information pertaining to the body, the immediate and surrounding environment in which it was found, and individuals and evidence at the scene. Assessment also extends to the decedent's next of kin, to determine if assistance is needed, and to collect observational data related to the victim. Planning occurs concurrently with assessment within the investigation, as contact with the family might be short-lived. Planning also includes how to proceed with the investigation and how and when to interact with the decedent's family. Implementation is reflected in the utilization of assessment data and creating a plan of action for the investigation. The evaluation process can be completed by a follow-up study of death rates to determine if intervention was successful. In the case of a child abuse death, evaluation would include reviewing the interview process to determine if future interviews could be improved. Finally, evaluation encompasses consideration as to whether the assessment, planning, and implementation stages of the investigation were accurate and comprehensive.

Wooten (2003) states:

> I believe that the nursing process approach to death investigation actually should be viewed as three separate components; one component related to the investigation of the death proper, a second related to the family and/or survivors and a third component related to the community or society. These components spiral and twist in such an interrelated and dynamic manner that, like a DNA helix, any change in one area impacts the whole. Additionally, these interrelated components exist within another framework that touches and impacts nursing and is conversely impacted by nursing. That framework is also composed of intertwining, evolving components to include medicine and health care, the law and other forensic entities and societal factors.

For Meliss Vessier-Batchen, MSN, RN, assistant professor at Charity School of Nursing at Delgado Community College and a doctoral student at Louisiana State University Health Sciences Center, death investigation involves a natural transferability of a nurse's skill sets and is a definite extension of the nursing process. She says that although the environment might have changed, basic principles do not. "Let's start with the similarities of planning," Vessier-Batchen says:

> When we as nurses take a report on a patient at the beginning of our shift, we must plan our day, from the initial assessment all the way to the end of the shift, unless the patient is discharged or otherwise. The planning process starts when we get a phone call, when we get paged, whenever our presence is required, whether it is in the hospital or at a death scene. When I get a call, I start planning by asking questions: Do we know what we have on our hands? Do we know how many people are involved? Do we know the circumstances? Do we have any witnesses? I try to get as much initial information as I can, and sometimes it isn't much. Normally, I don't speak to someone on the scene first, I'm speaking to a dispatcher; so I'm getting very limited information. As I drive to the scene, I am planning in my mind what I am going to do, where I am going to go, and how I am going to approach this scene.

Vessier-Batchen says the tools of the trade differ, too, but nurses need to have the right equipment for the job:

> When I make presentations on death investigation, a lot of times I ask nurses, "What do you carry onto the job when you start a shift?" They talk about their ink pens, their scissors, their hemastats, and their alcohol handrubs. I say, "I have a toolbox too, but in it I carry things like hip waders, galoshes, a rainsuit, and menthol petroleum jelly to put on the inside of a mask if I come across a decomposed body." So, my toolbox is much bigger and vastly different than what I used to carry as a bedside nurse in a traditional role. I make sure I have the right tools, and from there, I go to my assessment. As I am traveling to the scene, I am mentally preparing myself for what I will encounter. I approach my planning process with as much flexibility as I can because my planning might change at the scene. When I arrive, I begin to assess the scene. I park where I need to and I may walk up to a scene as opposed to driving directly to it. This gives me time to assess the safety of the scene, and assess the bigger picture of what I am facing. As I walk into the scene itself, I begin to assess what is where. Once I have surveyed the scene and I can go to straight to the decedent(s), I begin to assess on a more detailed level. Is this scene a motor vehicle accident? Does it appear to be a natural death, homicide, or suicide? I begin to look for evidence, being careful not to step on anything or contaminate the scene. I continue to make assessments all the way through the scene until I am assessing my decedent. I begin with a visual assessment, then a physical assessment. That's when the nursing process becomes particularly important. From the assessment phase I go into implementation of intervention. At the bedside, intervention means taking care of the patient. At a death scene, intervention is all about gathering impressions of the scene, collecting information from a medico-legal perspective. I might have to think about how this person got in this position; were they in this position in the beginning, and if not, where did they come from? Is there physical evidence I need to collect? Personal effects to collect and examine? As I begin my interventions, I am physically moving, touching, collecting things, all with proper documentation. The final evaluation comes when I am writing my summary, which essentially is my story. It's my depiction of everything I did, everything I saw, the pieces I can absolutely put together. As for the pieces I can't put together, I have to consider were they at the scene or introduced to the scene. Can I take anything at face value?

Vessier-Batchen recalls a death scene that taught her the value of letting the evidence speak for itself:

> At one of my scenes, there was a two-car accident with three fatalities. One of the passengers in the more mutilated car was thrown from the vehicle. State police asked if I thought he had been wearing a seatbelt. I said, "At this time, there is no way for me to be able to tell." It was undetermined, and that is what was printed in the paper. That was OK because it was the fact at the time—I could not determine if the passenger had been wearing a seatbelt. I took pictures of this decedent in order to make a positive ID, as he had no identification on his person. We had no viewing space for the mother to come in to identify the body, so I had to take pictures. When I went to the morgue to take these pictures, I noticed that as the body had cooled, bruising was evident over the right shoulder, down into the left hip area and across the lower abdomen; there was also one small spot of bruising on the chest. These bruises indicated injuries consistent with seatbelt usage. So, for my final evaluation, I can't say he definitely had a seatbelt on but I can say he has injuries consistent with seatbelt usage. I can say the bruises indicate the decedent probably had been seatbelted in, but I'm not saying he definitely did, because I don't know for certain. That's where some of my best nursing skills come into play, and probably one of the things that caught the attention of my supervisors at the medical examiner's office. It may not have been my assessment skills, my ability to pick up on medical aspects, or even the ability to ask medical-related questions that other investigators may not have thought of, but it definitely was my summaries that stood out. One of the things they noticed was that my wording was of a medico-legal nature, and comes, of course, from my nursing charting abilities.

Vessier-Batchen says that proper documentation in death investigation is aided by a nurse's indoctrination in proper charting:

> Because of many years of nursing charting, my death investigation summaries were as medico-legally sound as possible, as comprehensive and inclusive as possible. I make sure my wording is such that it's very clear, and that it doesn't imply things that I don't see at the scene. I am careful not to absolutely state things that may be implied, but to absolutely state those things at the scene that are visibly detectable. When I first started as a death investigator, the other investigators said, "Yeah, she's a nurse, no big deal," but it's really changed since then. The forensic pathologist is thrilled that nurses are expressing interest in coming into the office as reservists—not to take away from the investigators that have been there a long time, because they do their jobs well, it's just a different set of eyes and ears.

Minnesota legal nurse consultant and registered death investigator Melissa Becker, RN, D-ABMDI, feels strongly that death investigation is within the scope of practice of nursing "because it involves medical issues and how they relate to the death. A death investigation is more medical than law enforcement, unlike a burglary, computer crime, or ID theft, let's say." Becker says that nurses have a critical eye and a significant ability for detailed assessment, two skills that assist a nurse death investigator in obtaining a history of events leading up to the death, as well as conducting a review of the medical history for significant issues or clues. "Nurses' organizational skills are highly valuable, and their ability to see the big picture is very important, as law enforcement tends to have tunnel vision and jump to conclusions, often in the wrong direction," Becker notes. "Their understanding of a large body of medical information and disease processes allows them to identify pertinent medical issues and facts, and ignore other ones. For example, the smell of a GI bleed is not missed by an RN, but could be missed by a detective."

Becker, who started her own business, Resolve Medical Legal Consulting, in 1997, also has worked as a deputy coroner in Minnesota, so she has worked all angles of the medico-legal continuum. She says that the most important responsibility for nurse death investigators is to be able to "apply medical aspects to the scene." Becker explains:

> For an example of a true case, there was blood spatter around a naked body found in bed. I found scrub brushes in the groin and rectal area of the male, who had a towel over his penis. There was a lot of blood around his face; I named him *volcanus eruptus*, as he looked like a volcano with the crusted mound of blood outward from the mouth/face. Droplets of blood were circular, not angled at all, meaning that they came straight down. They did not smell like a GI bleed, and there was a medical history of AV malformation that was "clipped" three months prior. The police department immediately felt it was not suspicious, but I was not so sure. They opined that the blood was from his ruptured AV malformation, and when it ruptured, the blood poured out of his mouth. I knew this was not possible, as a head bleed does not come out of the mouth. This idea took a lot of convincing; due to the crusting of blood, we could not see the victim's neck region to rule out strangulation or other trauma. Due to the sexual nature of the body, the case could be a sexually mitigated death. The autopsy showed AV malformation did indeed rupture, causing death, but the blood was from the seizure he endured; he bit his tongue, so the blood spatter pattern was created when it flew out of his mouth upward and came straight down. The MD opined that the victim was probably masturbating and at climax, the AV malformation ruptured, thus triggering a seizure, where he bit his tongue and then died.

Becker explains that to best recognize forensic implications, "one must first have a full understanding of the nature of the death, including the events leading up to the death, as well as the medical history, and scene investigation." She continues:

> Then the nurse death investigator must analyze how all of these components interact. You cannot have one without the other three, or you will miss cases that are suspicious. You need to understand "normal" to be able to understand "abnormal." As for collecting and preserving evidence, one needs to work in collaboration with law enforcement to develop a team approach. If the investigator is also collecting all of the evidence, then there is room for tampering or mistakes, thus a team approach is best. It is important for nurses to take law enforcement-sponsored classes to understand the technical issues involved in skills such as forensic photography and forensic evidence collection.

Regarding a differentiation between nurse and NNDIs, Becker says:

> Again, I think this requires a team approach. I believe the person screening cases for the jurisdiction needs to be medically trained, as I have seen many suspicious, criminal, and questionable deaths missed by the police investigator who did not ask the correct questions to elicit the important information. However, law enforcement personnel are often better trained in some interview techniques than RNs are; therefore, the combination provides the best approach so that critical information is not missed. Currently, in most states, medico-legal death investigation is performed mostly by law enforcement or by nonmedically trained investigators. It is very difficult to get one's foot in the door because law enforcement is very slow to change. They are very territorial and mostly dominated by males. They have their own games and power/ego issues.

Becker adds that she found it difficult to enter the death investigation field, but made inroads through the public defender's office. "This required that I donate my time or reduce my fees so that I could show them how I could be cost-effective," she explains:

> The key to breaking into this field is to show them how you can be of value; for example, understanding the medical information, focusing on the important medical evidence, and letting go of other noncritical medical issues. The police will focus on words or the amount of blood when the real issue of importance is more subtle. I show how a nurse death investigator can make cases better by pointing out the medical evidence that cannot be disputed forensically.

Becker points to one of her cases of a woman who said she was assaulted by her boyfriend, who twisted her ankle until it popped. She went to the ER four hours later; the X-ray showed a fractured ankle with callus formation, and the boyfriend was charged with felony assault. "No one caught that callus formation cannot occur within four hours, thus the fracture was old, not new, and so there was no legitimate case." Becker also adds that in the case of a first-degree murder, no one looked at the angle of the bullet's path and how it did not match up with the events of the death. "There are many, many small details like this that nurse death investigators can point out to law enforcement, and prove their worth."

12.8.5 Acceptance of the Nurse Death Investigator

Vessier-Batchen says that it's like comparing apples and oranges; a nurse is not being elitist when he or she says a nurse's skills can greatly contribute to death investigation. It's simply that the nurse brings a whole different skill set to the job:

> Nurse death investigators don't want to take away from knowledge non-nurse investigators have, but to be recognized for the skills they bring to the table. In my experience, my nursing knowledge hasn't clashed with their experience. Most of my colleagues have been very accepting, very willing to show me what they know, as they have been there years longer than I have. The senior investigator has been there 10 years; she has no medical background but she is very good at her job. She was very accepting of me when I started attending death scenes and autopsies with her on a more regular basis. I would ask, "Does this look like this," or say, "I think this is what this may be," and she was open to what I had to ask and to offer. I like to think we can share our knowledge for the good of the team.

Vessier-Batchen says that ironically, she had more difficulty with clinicians once she crossed over to death investigation. "I had more trouble in hospitals than I did at death scenes," she recalls:

> One time I went into an ER for the purpose of investigation on the behalf of a patient who had a very lengthy history. He was brought to the hospital in full code and died, even though the nurses didn't do much to help him, and he was never revived. It wasn't likely he would have survived even though he was a younger person. I looked at a funny site on his side; evidently he had had heart surgery, with assorted various wounds and chest tubes associated with bypass surgery. I said to the nurse, "This looks like an old chest tube site that went bad and had been grafted." She said, "Oh no, his chest tubes would have been in the middle... that's really nothing." I said "Fine," but she was very rude, which I'm used to. When I talked to the wife, she said her husband had a lung collapse about three years ago and developed an infection at the chest-tube site. I asked her what they did at the time and she said, "Well, they put a patch or something over the site." "A graft?" I asked, and she said, "Yes, something like that, they had to put some new skin to patch it up." This nurse had no clue, talking to me like I was an idiot, and here I had recognized that this wound looked like something that should have been questioned. I didn't know for sure until the wife confirmed it. I get more trouble in the hospitals and from some of the paramedics than from the investigators with whom I work, and I'm not sure why that is. They get very testy with me and it may be because I'm more demanding. When I go into a hospital, I ask to see the charts. They'll say, "We don't have it." And I'll say, "Can I get it?" And then I proceed to read the chart. I had one nurse comment to me, "Nobody else does that." I said, "They don't get the chart?" and she answered, "Well, they get the chart but they don't stand there and read it so thoroughly." I said, "Do you have a problem with that?" and she shrugged, "I guess not." What I am doing is using my nursing background to scour the medical record for information, clues, a history. When I ask questions because the information I am looking for is not in the chart, they look at me like they want to throw me out the window. I guess I can be a little annoying to folks in the hospitals, but that is what my nursing has taught me.

12.8.5.1 Forensic Nurse Death Investigators: A Success Story

The Harris County (Texas) Medical Examiner Investigative Unit is home to this new breed of nurse death investigator (FNDI) and is setting new precedents for how forensic nurses can contribute to medico-legal death investigation. In April 2002, the office hired its first FNDI, Stacey Lasseter Mitchell, MSN, RN, SANE-A, D-ABMDI, an event that designated Harris County as the first medical examiner's office in Texas to incorporate the forensic nursing role into the medico-legal death investigation. The handful of forensic nurses join a dozen forensic investigators who are responsible for conducting death investigations by developing organized, concise, and accurate death reports in accordance with Texas law. The FNDIs provide coverage for evening and night shifts to increase investigative capacity and facilitate efficiencies within the office. They respond to hospital facilities to assess and document findings on certain medical examiner cases, and they also assist with a newly established forensic internship program. According to the Harris County Medical Examiner's Web site:

> The forensic nurse complements the forensic investigator, resulting in an improved investigative process while enhancing interaction among community agencies. The forensic nurse also provides a vital link between the investigative staff and the pathologist. With the advances in medicine, people are living longer and are prescribed multiple medications. The nurse has the knowledge base in which to interpret the often voluminous medical records in order to assist the pathologist.

FNDIs are impacting the death investigation process in Texas by conducting death scene investigations with emphasis on infant deaths, collecting evidence in cases of suspected sexual assault and child abuse, reviewing medical records and obtaining additional test results required by the pathologist, providing case management for complicated cases, and collaborating with organ and tissue procurement agencies to determine appropriate release of organs and tissue. The Harris County office acknowledges:

> Forensic nurses are specially trained to combine the forensic aspects of health care with practical nursing and apply that knowledge in the scientific death investigation of victims and/or perpetrators of violence, criminal activities, and traumatic accidents. The expertise of the forensic nurse is drawn from nursing science, forensic science, and criminal justice allowing them to better identify, collect, and document injuries and evidence. This often leads to plea bargains, thus eliminating victim testimony. These nurses do, however, testify as expert witnesses when cases are presented in court.

Nurse death investigators get the thumbs-up from Vincent DiMaio, MD, Chief Medical Examiner for Bexar County, which includes the city of San Antonio, Texas. "Forensic nurses excel as investigators for medical examiners," he says, adding that they also are very proficient at working natural-death cases due to their extensive medical backgrounds. "At least half of our cases are natural deaths," DiMaio reports:

> Many of my investigators are more oriented toward violent deaths, so they struggle with the medical complexities of natural deaths. But equally important, and in many ways more important, is the role forensic nurses can play in investigating suspicious injury and death in the hospital setting, and especially in the emergency room. If a patient comes in with nonlethal trauma, the only documentation you have is in the medical record. These records vary from mediocre to worthless when they are kept by physicians in most cases. They never locate the wounds, they don't know the correct forensic terminology . . . they don't care, which in a way is logical because they are there to treat, not to provide medico-legal records. I testified in a case in which an individual had been shot about two or three years ago. The doctors were long since gone, so I had to testify from what I saw in the medical records. I got on the stand and I said something to the effect of, "This man was shot six, seven, or eight times, in his upper and lower extremities, probably; he also had some wounds on the side of his chest." But I was not sure how the bullets entered and exited his body because the records were contradictory, and were obviously incorrect. Nobody in the ER is interested in documenting the trauma or the correct terminology. We typically see statements such as, "This person was stabbed; they have 32 lacerations." That's the wrong terminology. So, forensic nurses do a much better job of documenting injuries.
>
> A single gunshot wound is a really simple case. A natural disease case is the one that is going to tie me up for days. Medical records now are two feet thick. You have go through them carefully, and it's a hard job. Forensic nurses are more oriented to that task because of their medical expertise; they can pick up things that are medically wrong, while my nonmedical investigators can't. They may encounter an unfamiliar medical term, so they look it up in a medical dictionary and then they write it down. But they may not be able to make sense of it in context like nurses can.

12.8.6 Educating the Nurse Death Investigator

Vessier-Batchen and other nurses who work as death investigators say there are scant education and training opportunities besides these courses that cater to NNDIs. "The problem is that the road to get there is very bumpy and nasty," she says:

> The best thing I can tell nurses—if death investigation truly is their area of interest, is that they must begin to scope it out. Find out what system—medical examiner or coroner—is used in your jurisdiction. Find out if nurse investigators are even used in your area, and if so, what are the expectations of them? If nurses are not being used in the medico-legal system in your area, you may even have to contemplate moving in order to pursue your dream. The next thing to do is to examine your background and education. Have you been exposed to forensic principles in your education, either at a baccalaureate or at a graduate level? If your education did not include forensic principles, you will have to develop this interest on the outside. And for everyone, being credentialed with the American Board of Medical-legal Death Investigators

> (ABMDI) is essential. They require you to take a 40-hour course, and the two most notable courses in my book are St. Louis and Miami-Dade. Miami-Dade has just developed the same death investigation program but with a nursing component as the guiding force now, which is good; St. Louis probably isn't too far behind in this regard. Nurses have the foundation of knowledge in anatomy and physiology, pharmacology, and overall patho-physiology, but we need more, we need different, we need augmentation of the knowledge we already have, and these courses provide that. However, these programs are expensive; you're looking at a cost of $500 or $600 for the weeklong course, plus travel and room and board expenses. But it's a necessary investment in one's future.

The American Board of Medico-legal Death Investigators (ABMDI) is a national certification board that was established to promote the highest standards of practice for medico-legal death investigators. The organization certifies individuals who have demonstrated proven knowledge and skills necessary to perform medico-legal death investigations as set forth by the National Institute of Justice's report, *Death Investigation: A Guide for the Scene Investigator* (U.S. Department of Justice, 1999). The ABDMI was founded by veteran practicing medico-legal death investigators who were involved with the creation of the guidelines in this report. The ABMDI was developed to enhance and maintain professional standards by evaluating knowledge, competency, and skills of medico-legal death investigators based on examination. It administers objective and reliable examinations (both basic and advanced) in the field of medico-legal death investigation, and it recognizes qualified individuals who demonstrate mastery of basic and advanced skills and knowledge of medico-legal death investigation by granting certificates to individuals who have met all application requirements and successfully completed rigorous examination. Death investigators must be recertified by the ABDMI every five years according to established recertification criteria, including continuing education requirements to ensure that the individual is current in the field. The group encourages medico-legal death investigators to adhere to high standards of professional practice and ethical conduct when performing medico-legal death investigations, and it raises the level of professional competency in medico-legal death investigation by identifying appropriate training courses for professional development.

The ABMDI also sponsors a number of credible, reputable training opportunities for individuals seeking death investigation competencies. The Medico-Legal Death Investigator Course is offered several times a year at Saint Louis University School of Medicine in St. Louis. The Basic Training for the Medicolegal Death Investigator course is offered by the New Mexico Office of the Medical Investigator in Albuquerque. The Basic Training for the Medicolegal Death Investigator course is provided by Wayne State University in Dearborn, Michigan. The Forensic Medical Investigation and Workshop is held several times a year in Wichita, Kansas, and in Phoenix, Arizona. "From there, I think would-be nurse death investigators need to explore job opportunities," Vessier-Batchen says. "Not everybody can give free time away. However, if you can, give it away by finding an internship. Find someone you can volunteer with, which is what St. Tammany Parish does in the reservist program for death investigators. What reservists do is augment the staff by having a second investigator helping at a death scene, without having to lay out additional money. Plus, someone else learns the job and may be a potential investigator in the future."

Forensic pathologist Mary H. Dudley, MD, RN, profiled later in this chapter, says there is no greater priority for nurses than to secure a comprehensive educational background. Dudley advises nurses:

> Get as much education and training as you can so that you will be prepared for whatever comes your way. I always tell forensic nurses that building their résumé is a career-long endeavor. I also encourage them to seek education everywhere—certificate courses, conferences... they should attend as many seminars and training sessions as they can to build on their medico-legal skills. If they want to be death investigators, I tell them to take as many courses as they can, get involved with law enforcement and attend their training programs on gunshot wounds or blood spatter. There are so many new venues for education and training these days, and forensic nurses should take advantage of them. There is a tremendous need for forensic nurses, and increased interest in the area will drive it to be a viable specialty; for continued success in this field, nurses will need the most solid and ongoing education opportunities that they can find.

Dudley adds that clearly defined standards are lacking in the field, as nurses need better instruction in the standards that govern their practice, shape their education and training needs, and prepare them for performance on the job. "Nurses who want to be death investigators must be realistic about their ability to work in this field," Dudley adds:

> No education or training will absolutely guarantee them a job right out of school, although it will certainly help. It's the experience that matters in many jurisdictions, and nurses need hands-on experience. The other challenge is that most nurses working as death investigators are not going to be paid what they would if they were a nurse in an ICU, for example. So, if they decide they want to be a death investigator, nurses must be prepared to hang with the job until things change. They also must realize that they can do the work, but it will involve long, irregular hours and that the cases won't be clean or glamorous. They have to be OK with cases that are not pretty to look

at. But if they know what they are getting into and they decide that this is the job for them, they will need a top-notch education and credentials to get in the door. Lifelong learning is essential.

12.8.7 Attributes of a Good Investigator

"You just have to be nosy," asserts Vessier-Batchen:

> You have to know how to step on toes but while you are doing so, being able to smile, be reassuring and say, "It's OK." You need a certain amount of tact, but you also must know when to throw tact away and be assertive or almost aggressive in some instances, depending on the situation or the person with whom you are dealing. You must be a team player, but sometimes you'll witness other political battles that are not your own to fight. I am seeing more infighting between law enforcement agencies and coroners' offices because law enforcement agencies are fighting over who has to take the scene. We are standing there saying, "Guys, which one is it?" If the death scene happens to be in one little area in town not absolutely established as incorporated as city, county, or state, you have three or four agencies arguing over who writes up the scene. Politics is getting a little better, but we're not there just yet. But then again, you will have that anywhere you go, and the key to conflict resolution is communication. You must be able to communicate with individuals at all levels of education. One minute you may be talking to a sheriff's deputy who may be a college graduate or you are talking to a police officer deputy who got through high school and the police academy. Or you may be talking to a decedent's family member who has a third-grade education. Or maybe you are dealing with all of these people at the same time at the same scene, so you must be able to switch gears very quickly. This job is about being willing to stretch yourself in areas in which you didn't think you could stretch. And that includes knowing when to get assertive when you have to, or dealing with hysterical family members at a scene. It's about taking command and control of a scene but at the same time, being comforting to the decedent's family. As nurses, we are equipped to do both at the same time. Remember that many times, people are coping with a violent, unexpected, or traumatic death, and sometimes they aren't thinking properly or they don't have the capacity to function. If you are a nurse death investigator, your natural compassion spills onto the scene when you are dealing with survivors at the time of notification; that's just a nurse's personality.

An important piece of the death investigation puzzle is communication—conducting informational interviews of family members, friends, acquaintances and associates, as well as informing a decedent's next of kin in a competent yet compassionate manner. Nurses say they excel in this arena because of their advanced communication skills and display of sensitivity and empathy; however, there is a fine line between sympathy and objectivity. Charles (1999) writes, "The approach is tailored to this goal; the interview is for a very specific purpose, which is not intended to be therapeutic." Fulton (2003) argues, "Contrary to Charles' statement, nurses are equipped with the communication skills necessary to elicit the information from the next-of-kin and family of the deceased in a therapeutic manner."

There is little dispute that nurses can and do excel in the interviewing process, much like they would take a history from a living forensic patient. Fulton (2003) states, "In the midst of intensified interaction with family members, (death investigators) must develop a connection, collect information, and display an ability to move throughout the scene in a sympathetic manner." Fulton adds, "Forensic nurses are well equipped to perform these investigative and notification tasks with empathy, sensitivity, and compassion, as these characteristics are a part of nursing. Nurses utilize creativity and flexibility on a daily basis when tailoring nursing interventions to individual patient needs. Empathy, sensitivity and compassion are also key concepts of nursing practice."

Vessier-Batchen says that even though no laundry list of attributes of an FNDI is in the literature, she can readily tick off a number of characteristics she believes make the job easier: a curious nature; an eye for detail; the ability to discriminate and document pertinent information in an objective manner; a strong stomach; good coping skills, mechanisms, and techniques; solid education and training; inductive and deductive reasoning skills; an analytical, logical nature; extensive clinical experience; intuition; an ability to compartmentalize feelings; and maturity.

12.9 MEDICAL EXAMINERS AND CORONERS: CONTEXT FOR THE FORENSIC NURSE EXAMINER

An understanding of the current infrastructure, operations, and challenges to the medical examiner system can help nurses comprehend its needs and how they might be able to contribute to this system in the future. In 2003, a group of respected medical examiners stated in a report that impossible caseloads, underfunding, and a "culture of cutting corners" was threatening their ability to investigate death in a number of the more than 2,000 jurisdictions across the country. Because of a network of varying laws and regulations governing medical examiners and coroners, standards for death investigation vary widely from state to state. Twenty-three states and the District of Columbia require medical examiners to perform medico-legal investigations of death, whereas 10 states use the coroner system. Eighteen states use a combination of medical examiners and coroners. Medical examiners and coroners investigate all unnatural deaths, including murders, motor vehicle accidents, drug overdoses, and suicides.

Approximately 20 percent of the 2.4 million deaths in the United States each year are investigated by medical examiners and coroners, accounting for approximately 450,000 medico-legal death investigations annually. However, unless dramatic changes to the system are made, medical examiners warn, there will not be enough qualified professionals to handle the caseload. The most common placement for a medical examiner or coroner office is as a separate office of city, county, or state government; approximately 43 percent of the U.S. population is covered by this type of system placement. The second most common arrangement is having the medical examiner or coroner under a public safety or law enforcement office. The least common placement (14 percent of the U.S. population) is under a forensic laboratory or health department. Therefore, at a time of growing public health needs, few coroner or medical examiner offices have formal relationships with health departments.

The quality of a death investigation system is difficult to assess, but it can be measured with several indicators. One is accreditation by the National Association of Medical Examiners (NAME); just 42 of the nation's medical examiner offices, serving 23 percent of the population, have been accredited by NAME in recent years. Most of the population (77 percent) is served by offices lacking accreditation. Another indicator of quality is statutory requirements for training: About 36 percent of the U.S. population lives where minimal or no special training is required of those responsible for death investigations (Hanzlick, 1996). Requirements of medical examiners and coroners vary widely; medical examiners are medical doctors with advanced forensic pathology training, whereas coroners, often elected by local ballot, have vastly different skill levels and educational backgrounds. Most often, they do not have medical experience, according to Randy Hanzlick, MD, Chief Medical Examiner for Fulton County in Georgia. For example, in Georgia, the typical requirements for serving as a coroner are being a registered voter at least 25 years old, not having any felony convictions, having a high school diploma or the equivalent, and receiving annual training of one week.

The Institute of Medicine (IOM) Workshop on Medicolegal Death Investigation in the United States was convened in March 2003 at the request of NAME to discuss issues facing medical examiners. One such issue is the shortage of skilled, qualified personnel to serve as medical examinerss. Since 1959, only about 1,150 forensic pathologists have been board-certified. There are 41 training programs that can accept approximately 70 forensic residents each year, but many of those positions remain unfilled. The report issued from the workshop stated, "The shortage of skilled personnel contributes to the overall problem of inadequate death investigations in many jurisdictions. The problem is perpetuated by insufficient funding by local governments for operations and personnel." Discussion of the issues by medical examiners attending the workshop centered on related issues. Experts cited a lack of research by medical examiners, as well as a trend for researchers to use medical examiners' data without including the medical examiners as collaborators, stated Randy Hanzlick. In addition, lack of research stymies public health and precludes development of an evidence base for the field itself, according to Richard Bonnie. Regarding opportunities for growth, according to participants Marcella Fiero and Alan Trachtenberg, burgeoning interest by the public health and criminal justice communities creates new chances to promote medical examiner issues. Public health had ignored forensic pathology for years, they said, until it began to focus on violence as a public health issue. They added that the time was right for greater collaboration with public health and criminal justice, as long as the field expands its manpower through an infusion of funding and trainees. In terms of funding issues, participant Victor Weedn reported that user fees are used in some jurisdictions for select purposes, but they often have idiosyncratic purposes and so fail to promote standardization and comprehensiveness in data acquisition. A piecemeal approach to disease or injury however, is not a good way to garner resources, noted Kurt Nolte, and new forms of financing need to be cultivated for the field, according to Bonnie.

The IOM report made several recommendations for the improvement of the medico-legal death investigation system:

- Creating a referral-based medical examiner system. A local system would be best with regard to the need for communication, travel, and investigative response time, but it might be impossible because of an insufficient population or tax base. A referral-based medical examiner system could improve the function of coroner systems that do not have ready access to qualified pathologists and their services.
- Ensuring that death investigation systems are headed by trained and qualified medical professionals. The qualifications of those in charge of and working in death investigations must be raised at virtually all job levels in many areas of the United States. Inspection and accreditation of systems should eventually be required.
- Increasing the investment in personnel and facilities, and increasing medical examiner salaries and incomes. Current salaries are substandard and need to be higher to attract qualified people.

- Increasing the level of education, training, and qualifications of death investigators, and of modernization of facilities.
- Revisiting of the Model Postmortem Examinations Act of 1954 (Model legislation developed by the National Association of Counties to promote the shift from coroners to professional medical examiners trained and credentialed in medicine). Death investigation statutes in various states should be more uniform and modernized.

Although the subject of adding nurse death investigators to the team was not discussed in full at the workshop, participant Vincent DiMaio said that forensic nurses could be used to assist medical examiners and coroners in handling the increasing public interest in addressing nursing home deaths. The 2003 IOM report had covered some of the ground already tread by NAME. In 2001, the organization conducted an infrastructure study of medical examiner and coroner facilities; the survey was sent only to individual members of NAME (primarily medical examiners but also some coroners). Approximately 125 jurisdictions in 39 states replied to the survey. The jurisdictions covered a total of 175,000 deaths and 90,000 autopsies per year. The survey addressed issues relating to funding, workload, staffing, services, and facilities.

Overall, the survey revealed that systems were small, poorly funded, and housed in outdated facilities. According to the survey, there was wide variation in funding, ranging from $30,000 to $16 million per office. The average expenditure was $1 million to $2 million, translating to $1 to $2 per capita. Most offices spent $2,000 to $3,000 per autopsy; accredited offices spent more per capita than did nonaccredited offices. Findings on workload revealed even greater variation. The number of autopsies performed each year, on a per capita basis, varied by a factor of about 40. The average office performed 707 autopsies per year. More than half the offices were doing more than the NAME-recommended standard of 250 autopsies per pathologist. By that measure, most jurisdictions have heavy workloads. NAME bars accreditation if a pathologist performs more than 350 autopsies per year. The number of pathologists per office varied from one to 24, and 10 percent of the medical examiner slots were vacant. Of the 379 pathologists who replied, 80 percent were board-certified, but the questionnaire neglected to ask whether they were board-certified in anatomic pathology or in forensic pathology. Offices averaged 6.4 death investigators. Death investigators work with medical examiners and coroners to obtain and document information on reported deaths, conduct scene investigations, and participate in other parts of death investigations as directed by medical examiners or coroners. Only 37 percent of respondents had in-house toxicology laboratories, and 14 percent had in-house crime laboratories or DNA testing. The average toxicology expenditure was $50,000, including salaries. Many medical examiner facilities were a half-century old, but the average facility was 20 years old; many had inadequate space. Quality indicators revealed deficiencies. Although 83 percent had mass fatality plans, only 38 percent had bioterrorism plans. Slightly less than half of jurisdictions (43 percent) had both in-house toxicology facilities and death investigators; nonaccredited offices were far less likely than accredited offices to meet this quality measure.

Medical examiner and coroner systems need more funding to enhance quality with greater staffing, lower workloads, and modernized facilities. There are 41 forensic pathology training programs with full accreditation and three applications for new programs. The 41 programs sponsor a total of approximately 76 positions; thus, most carry fewer than two positions. Most programs are in the coroner or medical examiner office rather than under the institutional umbrella of a medical school. Among the core competencies required of trainees for accreditation is performance of at least 200 but not more than 300 autopsies per year. Those figures are lower than the former requirement of at least 250 but not more than 350 because of the increased complexity of cases and the greater number of tests to interpret. Manpower is a major concern to medical examiners. Since 1959, about 1,150 certificates have been awarded. In 2002, 34 forensic pathologists were newly certified. The failure rate on the American Board of Pathology examination in forensic pathology has been about 38 percent but this rate represents a disproportionate number of failures of candidates qualifying for the exam by experience rather than by formal fellowship training. Recent changes requiring all candidates for examination to have formal accredited training are expected to increase the pass rate while ensuring quality. A greater pass rate, however, cannot fulfill the demand for sufficient board-certified forensic pathologists for all medico-legal autopsies in the United States. More training programs and more trainees are needed.

Nowhere is the need for training more obvious than when the National Institute of Justice's death investigation guidelines, created in 1998, were tested on 100 coroners and deputy coroners in Indiana. Researchers from Occupational Research and Assessment, Inc. found that nearly 80 percent failed the examination. The results prompted Indiana to mandate training programs for death scene investigation; tests in other states revealed similar failure rates. Coroners with medical backgrounds (other than forensic pathologists) performed as inadequately as did coroners. The guidelines promulgated by the National Institute of Justice were the first such guidelines for death scene investigations. The publication was the culmination of a five-year process that had been triggered by a national needs-assessment survey: In 1994, 60 percent of medical examiners and coroners had reported their dissatisfaction with the level of investigative service that they received, either externally or internally.

12.9.1 Advantages and Disadvantages of the Medical Examiner and Coroner Systems

At the 2003 IOM workshop, medical examiner for Richmond, Virginia, Marcella Fierro, MD, explained that there are numerous advantages of instituting a medical examiner system, especially a statewide system. She added that the degree of centralization should be dictated by state geography, demographics, and ease of administration; but whether centralized or decentralized, medical examiner systems are highly desirable in comparison with coroner systems and mixed systems. Fierro explained that the major advantages of a statewide medical examiner system are the quality of death investigations and forensic pathology services and their independence from population size, county budget variation, and politics. Certification of death is accomplished by highly trained medical professionals who can integrate autopsy findings with those from the crime scene and the laboratory. These professionals have core competency in assessing immediate and earlier medical history, interviewing witnesses, and physical examination, she added. Other advantages of a statewide system are related to central administration, including statewide guidelines for case management and death scene investigation. Centralized administration can sustain the cost of central laboratories, and it can take advantage of economies of scale and purchasing power. Virginia's centralized administration devotes personnel to writing grants, which can be extremely time-consuming. A centralized medical examiner system also poses challenges, Fierro stated. It requires strong leadership, attention to state budget priorities and competition with other public health and criminal justice programs, and human resource management to ensure recruitment and retention of multiple types of professionals. She added that an ideal statewide system has a medical examiner system linked to a medical school and subspecialty pathologists, forensic science laboratories and scientists, and public health systems and laboratories; this proximity facilitates sharing of knowledge, system refinement, and access to new technologies.

In a similar vein, the 2003 IOM workshop heard from a Cincinnati forensic pathologist who was elected coroner, Carl Parrott, regarding the advantages and disadvantages of the coroner system. He explained that coroners are elected lay people who often do not have professional training, whereas medical examiners are appointed and have board certification in a medical specialty. The coroner system has advantages, but they are heavily outweighed by its disadvantages, he stated. The major advantages of the coroner system concern autonomy, access to power, and the ability to represent the will of the electorate. As an elected official, a coroner has the power to make decisions and has equal footing with other local elected officials; this situation places the coroner in a strong position to withstand political pressures imposed by other elected officials and to compete vigorously for the office's budget allocation. Being an elected official resonates with American political culture, he said, which views elected officials as the best representatives of a community's needs and values. Parrott pointed out two disadvantages of the coroner system, in that it is less likely to be medically proficient and that its structure can reflect patchwork legislative reaction to inadequacies, rather than intelligent design. Parrott characterized the coroner system as steeped in the vagaries of history rather than in a forward-looking, planned system that capitalizes on professional depth and knowledge. Coroner statutes are less specific about which types of cases are reported or investigated, and they tend to reflect the lowest common denominator in the qualifications of the office holder and the quality of investigations. He added that the coroner might be deficient in knowledge and might have conflicts of interest, especially when funeral directors, prosecutors, or sheriffs act as coroners. As elected officials, they cannot be dismissed for incompetence, except by the electorate after highly visible transgressions. Several coroners in Ohio are serving prison terms for Medicare fraud. Workshop participant Ellen Clark, of Reno, Nevada, proposed that the consensus conference could recommend national endorsement of the abolition of the coroner system and endorsement of the establishment of greater professionalism through a medical examiner system. Parrott and DiMaio suggested that the endurance of the coroner system is best explained by voter inertia, lack of awareness of the problem, and high capital expenditures for system startup. Parrott added that transformation in individual jurisdictions from a coroner to a medical examiner system will not solve the disparities within a state unless the commitment to reform is undertaken statewide through legislation. Hanzlick noted that is difficult for states to make such changes, because elected officials find it unpopular to promote removal of elected officials from office and state constitutional amendments might be required in some states even if a change might impact only one county.

12.9.2 The Value of Medical Expertise in Death Investigation

Vincent DiMaio, MD, Chief Medical Examiner for Bexar County in San Antonio, Texas, emphasized at the IOM workshop that medical expertise is crucial in death investigations, explaining that it commences with the examination of the body and evidence collection at the scene, and proceeds through the history, physical examination, laboratory tests, and diagnosis—similar to a medical doctor's treatment of a living patient. The goal, he added, is to provide objective evidence of cause, timing, and manner of death for adjudication by the criminal justice system. DiMaio illustrated the value of medical expertise in the screening process by explaining that in one county, for example, 8,000 cases are reported to the medical examiner's office, but only 2,000 are accepted. Screening must be handled in a scientifically defensible manner by people with medical training, knowledge, and objectivity, he explained, and the medical examiner's office is especially important in more subtle or complex cases of criminal activity, where there is the possibility of an undetected homicide. These cases, he added, are commonly not pursued by police or nonmedical coroners. Confronted with the death of a 30-year-old woman, who dies apparently of a heart attack, a lay coroner would most likely not do an autopsy, but a medical examiner would, given its medical implausibility, DiMaio explained. Similarly, many lay coroners do not autopsy burned bodies, but a medical examiner would investigate the possibility of homicide masked as an accident. In addition, the expertise of the medical examiner's office, supplemented by trained death investigators, can prove to be invaluable in the courtroom.

IOM workshop presenter David H. Kaye reported that one of the most important issues facing the legal system is the development of a credible and objective process to determine which deaths to investigate, how to investigate them, what constitutes a thorough investigation, and how to keep suspicious deaths and homicides from being overlooked. Accurate evidence from a death investigation should be used in court to convict the guilty and protect the innocent. A significant problem arises from the disparity in resources between criminal prosecution and defense, Kaye added, explaining that it is rare for defense counsel to undertake its own death investigation with the same resources as the prosecution. If the prosecution's coroner or medical examiner is negligent, biased, or inept, miscarriages of justice are inevitable. For example, Kaye recalled, a pathologist in Texas performed 450 autopsies a year for 40 Texas counties. Exhumations of some of the corpses revealed an absence of marks on the bodies, indicating that no autopsy had been performed. The system needs to be structured in such a way as to prevent miscarriages of justice or to capture them early in the process, Kaye concluded.

From a prosecutor's perspective, IOM workshop presenter Jeff Dusek said, the medical examiner's office is looked to for accuracy, promptness, and the ability to state opinions clearly in court. Accuracy must prevail as to the manner of death, the cause of death, and the time of death, he added. Dusek pointed to a high-profile child-abduction case that occurred in San Diego County, in which a suspect was charged even before the child's body was found. When the body was found several days later, the death investigation had to proceed quickly during the 10-day window before a preliminary hearing. The medical examiner, presented with a badly decomposed body, summoned the on-call forensic entomologist and dentist. The dentist was able to identify the victim and ruled that suffocation was the cause of death; some of the victim's teeth were missing, and the forensic dentist attributed that to their falling out from the pressure of suffocation. The case was successfully prosecuted on the basis of the quality of the medical examination. The only testimony that the jury requested be reread was that of the medical examiner and the entomologist. When asked why they concluded as they did, Dusek reported that the jurors responded, "The medical examiners were the objective fact finders in the case. We relied upon them."

Another important component to the efficiencies of the medical examiner system is the forensic laboratory. According to Susan Narveson, then-president of the American Society of Crime Lab Directors (ASCLD) and a presenter at the IOM workshop, the crime lab provides assistance in two key parts of medico-legal death investigations: personal identification and determination of cause of death. Factors that affect whether a medical examiner or coroner office takes full advantage of a crime laboratory, Narveson added, include its proximity and working relationships, knowledge of which laboratory services are available, the workload of the crime laboratory, and knowledge of the laboratory's requirements for sample collection, packaging, and preservation. Careful handling of specimens is important in guarding against contamination. The utility of the crime laboratory in death investigations, Narveson continued, can be improved by promoting effective partnerships with medical examiner and coroner offices; by encouraging discussion of the range, value, availability, and use of crime laboratory capabilities; and by supporting the development of procedures that maximize the contribution of the crime laboratory's expertise.

12.10 NURSES AS CORONERS

As the country continues a debate about the full adoption of a medical examiner system of death investigation, nurses would be wise to monitor any developments that might affect their prospects for employment. Currently, nurses are employed in some medical examiner offices across the country; however, it is only in the coroner system that nurses are making strides in the higher level positions in death investigation. Charleston, South Carolina employs several nurses. Susan Chewning, RN, BSN, is the elected coroner, and Rae Wooten, BSN, RN, D-ABMDI, serves as chief deputy coroner. Bobbi Jo O'Neal, RN, BSN, F-ABMDI, who serves as a deputy coroner, says that Chewning opened doors for nurses that had previously remained closed. In 1991, Chewning was working as a nurse in her local hospital's ER, when she first set her sights on the coroner's office. She observed how the previous coroner functioned in the community, and when she learned that person would not be running for reelection, Chewning decided to toss her hat in the ring. In the campaign for election, Chewning was the only candidate with a medical background, and she used that to her advantage when she was selling herself and her platform to the voters. She won the race, and more than a decade later, still serves a growing community of about 300,000 people.

Following in Chewning's and Wooten's footsteps in securing positions at the coroner's office is O'Neal, who joined the team in 1998. An ER nurse by training, O'Neal says she reached her goal of becoming a coroner through a calculated career path, aided by a little luck. "I wanted to work in the ER because I knew that would be a good entry into forensics," O'Neal explains. "I went through sexual assault nurse examiner training and coordinated a sexual assault response team, and I also worked on some projects with Susan Chewning, the coroner who then offered me the deputy coroner position. The coroner who ran for election was a nurse; had she not been a nurse I'm not sure others would have seen the value of having a nurse in office."

"I'm a Cinderella story," O'Neal adds, laughing. "Everything points to the fact that I am supposed to be doing this, because all of the doors just opened for me." O'Neal explains that she was still working in oncology nursing when a friend told her about a nurse who was serving as the county coroner:

> When I heard that, I thought to myself, "You've got to be kidding." I called her and she suggested I get some ER experience. I quit my job the next day and moved to the ER immediately. From my own experience, the first thing I would say to nurses who want to become death investigators or coroners, is that when people who have been there give you career direction, you must be willing to take those suggested steps. Here in the coroner's office, we get calls all the time from nurses who say, "I wish I could do what you're doing." And I'll say to them, "This is what I would do if I were you," and I tell them about my experiences. I ask them, "Where do you work now?" and they'll say, "Well, I work in general med-surg." And I'll say, "Put in your two-week notice. Go to the ER." They'll call me several months later and they tell me they are still working in general med-surg. If you really want to do this, you have to be enough of a risk taker to be willing to take that important first step. If not, I would question whether or not you should be in death investigation . . . there are many times, in cases we are investigating, that we have to be willing to step across the line to make a decision. So, if nurses are not willing to go for it and do the things that experienced people who have gone before them are suggesting, I can't do anything for them. It's not as if we're going to suggest they do crazy things; we're going to suggest strategies that work. If they are not willing to make some of those changes in their career, I'd question if they should be doing it at all.

O'Neal explains that death investigation is an area in which potential practitioners can't be timid or hesitant:

> You have to go after it yourself. I was lucky, because I was going into a coroner's office that had a nurse in it. She knew my skills, but she didn't know me. She said, "Go to the ER," and I went to the ER immediately. When she came to the ER to work a case, there I was. So now I have proved to her—just from that one action—that I am truly interested in getting into death investigation and forensics. She didn't hire me just because I was a nurse, as there are lots of nurses available. She hired me because she saw the initiative that I took.
>
> Susan really didn't expect a forensic background. She wanted a nurse who was reliable, and reasonable and teachable—you definitely have to be teachable. If you walk in and you think you know more than the people who are teaching you, you have the wrong attitude. In order to succeed, you must be willing to learn from the people who have gone before you. She wanted someone who she could trust; that's huge in this profession. She watched me go from working in the ER to working as a SANE; I was constantly learning. Even though I knew nothing about death investigation when I was hired, I was an open vessel, willing to learn and to follow. I also had enough initiative that if I didn't know the answer, I would ask. That's important because if you're not willing to tell people when you are unsure of something, then you are a scary, unreliable individual in their eyes. Susan would much rather I go to a scene and call someone, saying, "I really don't know about this," as opposed to saying "I know everything" and be mistaken, thus creating a huge mess because you are trying to be something that you are not.

When O'Neal first came to the coroner's office, she learned on the job, affording her the opportunity to experience things that one-dimensional textbooks couldn't touch:

> When I entered the coroner's office I did not take any death investigation courses, like the ones offered in St. Louis or Miami, but learned how things were done in the office. I learned about state laws, what our roles were, and I started doing natural deaths only. I didn't go to any suspicious death scenes initially, as I had to learn what was normal before trying to learn what is not normal. Eventually, I was allowed to respond to calls on my own. The process of being accompanied to being allowed to go solo probably only took a few months, which is very unusual. People who came to the office before me were working with others for months and months and months. For whatever reason, it just came natural to me.

When asked if she ever felt intimidated by the responsibility and the seriousness of the work, O'Neal responds:

> Absolutely. One of the first things we tell nurses who are starting in death investigation is, they really must understand their role, because if they don't, and they don't know which laws back them up, then you don't know what authority you have or don't have. So people can push you around and intimidate you. It took awhile for me to understand my role, my degree of authority, and that I have the right to make decisions. Until you know what your role is and until you get comfortable in that role, you will not be able to assume and project the authority that you do have.

O'Neal adds that nurses must walk a fine line between assertiveness and passiveness:

> When I first started, a lot of law enforcement officers would tell Susan, "Oh, that Bobbi Jo is so nice." That was simply me learning, trying to figure out who was who, and not rocking any boats until I had it figured out. The first time that I let it be known that I was upset, it got around real fast. It took a while for me to understand when I had the right to be upset and the right way to handle it in the law enforcement community.

Respect is a commodity that must be earned, O'Neal says, but it can be easily lost, too:

> Because most of them don't have training in forensics, coroners are typically not respected. This is not to say that individual coroner's offices are not respected, however. When Susan came into office, she had to earn respect. The same thing happened when I first started. Not that they didn't respect the title, it's just they didn't know me. I had to earn their trust and their respect. They had to learn that I am a team player, but then over time they also learned I am going to take the initiative and make decisions.

O'Neal adds, "There may be additional scrutiny of our office because the coroner system has received a bad rap." O'Neal points to the politics that can trip up appointed personnel versus elected personnel:

> We had a huge case in which it became very apparent that we need a coroner system and that this person needs to be elected. A young woman was shot in her boyfriend's home, who happened to be a police officer. It was investigated by a state police agency and they concluded that it was a suicide. There were lots of politics and players involved, as you can imagine. Had Susan been an appointed official, she probably would have been expected to go along with this finding without doing her own complete investigation.

O'Neal believes her status as a nurse is a significant asset, not a liability:

> What's interesting to me is that law enforcement doesn't always get it, but the public gets it. When we're talking to families of decedents or exhibiting at health fairs or interacting at other community events, members of the public generally say that having a nurse conduct death investigations makes sense. It doesn't however seem to make sense to certain members of the law enforcement community who have never seen this concept before. To them, we're just going against the grain, so it is hard for them to grasp. I think for the individuals who now know us and have worked with us, it makes a tremendous amount of sense. They see the value in different kinds of personnel investigating deaths, drawing upon their special skills wherever necessary. Other agencies have started to recognize the contributions we can make; for example, representatives from our ombudsman's office have come to us with pictures, asking us to take a look and give them some idea of what they are seeing, what we recommend they do, and we're talking to them from a medical standpoint. We have to prove ourselves continually. It goes back to, do we gain automatic respect just because we are here? No. We gain it by working with our colleagues and showing them we really have something important to offer to them.

O'Neal believes the best preparation for working in a coroner's office is hands-on training; hundreds of forensic nurses agree, judging by the popularity of the internship program offered by the Charleston County Coroner's Office. "I get so many e-mails about the internship I can't keep up with them," O'Neal reports:

> We've always had students in our office, whether it's undergraduate nursing students or the like. We started getting tons of requests from nurses through the IAFN because we were one of the only offices in the country made up predominantly of nurses. We hosted some of them and thought we should establish a formal program because nurses are caught in a classic catch-22 scenario; nobody will hire them because they don't have experience; they are not experienced because no one will hire them.

O'Neal adds that many nurses are pursuing their national certification through the ABMDI and they needed their skills checked off by a preceptor. "A lot of nurses couldn't get checked off so they couldn't take the test; they couldn't take the test because they couldn't get checked off," O'Neal continues:

> So we started a hands-on internship where students would be on call with us 24 hours a day and do whatever we are doing. If we are fingerprinting an unknown deceased, they are also fingerprinting. If we are knocking on a door at 3 a.m. to notify a decedent's next of kin, they are going to be right there with us. It's not a classroom experience. We never know what will come in; we've had weeks where we were begging for a case and weeks where we were so busy the interns couldn't believe it. We cover all

> the things a week-long, didactic course would, but we do it out in the field. Students will feel the rigor, talk about lividity, see interviews of family members; they will be right there with us.

O'Neal says response to the internship has been "overwhelming." She states:

> Last year we filled up in about two weeks. One week each month we host two interns at a time; we take 18 interns per year. Response has been huge because there is nowhere else for them to go to get practical experience. If we are going to encourage nurses and really believe forensic nurses are great in this role, which we do, then somebody has to train them. They have to network, but they can't get into the system for hands-on training because no one will let them in. We're hoping if we can get them in the door and teach them, encourage them to run for office, and get more nurses out there as coroners, everyone will benefit. For example, Patti Hancock, who is a recently elected cornoner in Washington state, is in a position where maybe she can hire another nurse. Many of them don't even know if this is something they want to do; we can show them the ropes.

2004 was the third year that the internship has been offered, and interest is going strong, she reports:

> The people coming through our door are extremely diverse. We have hosted everyone from the very proficient, accomplished nurse, with absolutely no forensic experience and who has never worked in the ER, to the SANE who has been doing examiner work for 20 years who wants to go to sexual homicide scenes. One recent intern was actually a domestic violence program coordinator in Ohio who is interested in running for office. We are seeing a diverse group. A couple of things we've observed is that when the two interns know each other, and come together, even if they are from different areas of the country, they seem to accomplish more when they return to their respective regions. It's because they have a built-in support system. Whereas if you are the lone ranger in your state, you return after the internship and you're still the lone ranger. You don't have a buddy to encourage each other when the going is slow or rough. A few interns who came not knowing each other have done well and are moving forward. It also depends on the person's drive to implement change.

O'Neal says it is common for interns to keep in touch with their office. "We encourage them to become the expert in their community," she adds, explaining that they can do this in a number of ways:

> They can write an article about forensics for their hospital newsletter. If they want to they send it to us and we will read it and help them with it. Most nurses have not published before, and as a result, they are hesitant to submit something they have written. While they are here, we try to talk to each one of them to figure out what they are trying to accomplish, why are they here... are they just here for a week of fun? Or do they really have something in mind that they want to accomplish? Do they see something in their hospital they are trying to change? One nurse who worked in a VA hospital wanted to make her facility more aware of domestic violence. We said, "Well, let's come up with a plan to do that." She said that she really didn't know to do, so my comment to her was, "Who knows more about domestic violence than you in your hospital?" She said "Nobody," so I replied, "You, then, are the expert at your facility, are you not?" She said, "I guess I am." I said to her, "Well, you are. Has anybody else been to a coroner's officer for a week and learned about domestic violence and death investigation? No. So you are the expert in your facility." We do a lot of coaching, and we need nurses who are willing to be coached, and willing to mentor others when they become established in their field. So what we said to her was, "OK, you have a hospital newsletter. Write an article, and if you don't know what to write about, write about your experience during the internship, use us if you have to. Trust me, we don't need the advertising, so don't do it for us, but if you don't know what else, write about what you did and what you learned. Pick a topic that affects your hospital and start writing about it, even if it's basic." We tell them to become their hospital's or their community's expert. And keep learning as you are doing it. If they are not doing anything, there is nothing to coach them on. Again, they have to take the first step, but we give them lots of ideas. That's one of the things we're good at is sitting down and brainstorming, saying, "Here's what I'd do—try this, try that." But if they are not willing to take action, we can't help them with that.

O'Neal suspects some nurses might come into the field or to the internship with false expectations and misconceived notions of the nature of the work:

> After nurses accompany us to homicide scenes, or knock on doors at 3 a.m. to notify a family member of a death, some step back and say, "Well, maybe this isn't for me after all, I'm not sure I can do that for a living." We also get those who have the *CSI* mindset; they want the big crimes, that serial murder case that's really interesting and on all the TV news channels. One of the places where we burst their bubble is we let them know those kinds of cases, the gunshot wounds, the homicides, other than the rare case, those are the easy cases. The hard cases are those where there isn't any kind of dramatic trauma. Some of the natural deaths can be more complicated than any traumatic-death that we work. Child deaths can be very complicated but they don't get the media attention that others get. I think a lot of nurses come in with expectations of big scenes, an expectation that is fostered by conferences where presenters show all of those big, sensational cases. They show cases such as an airplane crash or an arson fire that caused 50 deaths. Those cases are interesting, but they are rare. The cases where nurses' skills are

> really needed and really valuable are not in those cases necessarily. We always give the example, a man is lying on a train track and the train ran over him. A six-year-old can tell you why he died. A complicated case is that of 45-year-old decedent, with no trauma who doesn't have a drug or alcohol history that anyone is admitting to... those are the complicated cases where nurses' skills can really come into play.

O'Neal says that the daily grind of death investigation has taught her many things, including the realization that she is still human:

> That I still have emotions. That can be something death investigators can lose during this kind of demanding work. When you see so much bad stuff on a regular basis, sometimes it takes big cases to get through to your emotions. Like nurses in the ER... they get a bad rap for being cold and heartless; the reason many of them seem cold and heartless is because they have seen it all, not because they are cold and heartless people. They have seen bad cases come in, so when people come in with wimpy complaints, they can get abrupt; the same can happen here. One of the questions our interns ask all the time is, "Do you ever cry with the decedents' families?" They want to know if that is OK or not. We tell them that we cry with next of kin all of the time. I cry with some families more than others because you just have a closer relationship with them for whatever reason. I am glad that happens because it lets me know I still have a heart. Even though I have been doing this for a long time, I have not gotten so cynical that I can't see grieving people and grieve with them. Our interns seem relieved to know this. One case I vividly remember was of a 9-year-old who was killed in a traffic accident. I cried with that mom and dad when I was talking to them. I don't think that's a weakness on my part, it's merely human compassion.
>
> The cases that stretch my abilities are children's cases. Not the cases with obvious trauma, but the ones where there are no injuries. These cases stretch your ability to interview and to think. It takes time to become a good interviewer. Nurses interview well because they do it a lot; as a death investigation, it is the same type of interviewing, only with a different goal. Not everyone you interview is the same. It's important to learn how to interview and to learn from one case to another, and recognize where you have messed up and where you should have asked something different. The other thing we do with our interns, is we pull out the cases where we screwed up. It is a concern for us when teachers aren't willing to do that. If you know so much you are not willing to admit where you messed up—then you have a whole other issue of ego that can get in the way of job performance.

For nurses who want to land jobs in death investigation, O'Neal advises a thorough understanding of their state's system, and whether it falls under the medical examiner or coroner model. "Part of the problem nurses are having is that some states are under the ME system, an appointed position," O'Neal explains. O'Neal believes the elective process can be a good system and that nurses can use it to their advantage. "The public can choose who they want in office but the problem is the public can only choose between the people who run for the job," she says. O'Neal thinks it is incumbent on nurses to go after the job if that's what they truly want, instead of expecting someone to hand it to them:

> One of the problems nurses have is that they are used to taking that extra class, putting it on their résumé and thinking someone will want them just because of the coursework they have taken. In this world, that's not the case. It's all about networking. You have to get in the game and run for the position. The public will make the right choice. A forensic nurse in Washington State who ran for coroner was the only female and a nurse running against five male police officers. The public voted for her. It shows you the public recognizes the value in choosing a medical person.

That Washington nurse is Patti Hancock, RN, BSN, MSN, a forensic nurse specialist who captured the Stevens County coroner's seat in the November 2002 election. Hancock was running against five police officers in the September primary election; in the November election, she beat opponent Tony Harbolt with 51.16 percent of the vote to his 48.84 percent, a difference of 268 votes. She took office on January 20, 2003. Hancock knew that Washington State law dictated that when a county reaches a population of 40,000, a coroner must be elected. She says she was finishing her master's program when the population was about to hit the magical number, and was convinced she could make a successful bid for the office. Having politics in her family's bloodline didn't hurt, either. "My father was a state representative, and I have been active in politics during my youth as well as during most of my adult life. I knew this was a way in which I could use my master's-level education and also benefit my county."

Her unwavering sense of professional direction and rise to public office is in contrast to an earlier time when Hancock says she wasn't sure what she wanted for her life. "Twenty-eight years after I first became a nurse I went back to school for my BSN, and followed that with my MSN," Hancock explains. "When I went into the MSN program at Gonzaga University in Spokane, Washington, I wasn't sure exactly what I wanted to do. I knew for certain that I did not want to become a nurse practitioner, yet I didn't know what it was that I wanted. I took a class called Foray Into Forensics and I knew that this was something that I would like and I could use to help benefit the county in which I live."

Hancock says running her campaign wasn't easy, due to the strong presence of her law enforcement opponents, a sort of "home court" advantage she knew she had to overcome to win. "Running against five male police officers was no picnic," Hancock says:

> Our county is extremely large in area, about 70 miles wide and 150 miles long. Law enforcement is in every segment of the county, yet there are only two hospitals and three medical clinics in the entire county. So it was much easier for law enforcement to campaign for their fellow officers than for one nurse to campaign for herself. I was extremely lucky in the fact that because my father was a state representative in this county I was quite well known. My name recognition as well as my family's name recognition went a long way in helping me. I don't know how vindicated I feel but I do know that I have no intention of using law enforcement as my deputy coroners. My campaign was that it is a medical job and I plan on standing by that belief.

Hancock adds that her election to coroner will allow her to hire more nurses, an opportunity O'Neal believes is critical to the future success of nurse coroners everywhere. "(Success like Patti's) will absolutely elevate the profile of nurses as coroners," O'Neal says, adding that it gives nurses new opportunities to explain their role:

> People ask us all the time, "What exactly do you do?" When you explain it, and teach others that we really are doing nursing, just in a different setting. We cannot only investigate the deaths and represent the deceased, we can educate the community. In my jurisdiction, our community is so used to the way we run this office, they would demand that it continue to run this way. I don't think they would accept less. They are used to us as nurses doing educational programs, us taking it a step beyond, "Yeah, they're dead from a car accident." Nurse coroners are showing the community how we look out for the living and the dead.

Hancock feels strongly about the need for more nurses working as coroners due to their ability to approach death from a different perspective than law enforcement. "Nurses have the educational background to understand exactly what causes death and what happens to a body after death occurs," she says. "Death may be a criminal event, but it is always a medical event. Unlike law enforcement who look at the deceased and want to know, 'Who killed you?' nurses look a at a dead body and ask, 'Why are you dead?' If it is determined that the death was due to a criminal cause then it is law enforcement's job to determine who. Who better to determine the manner of death than medical personnel?"

Hancock says the foundation of her campaign for office was education. "I started out by trying to educate the public on exactly what a forensic nurse specialist is and then I went on to explain why nurses make great coroners." Education will be an ongoing theme for Hancock, both in her efforts to educate her constituents about medico-legal issues as well as in her own self-edification as she builds the coroner's office for Stevens County from scratch.

"If more nurses knew they could do the job, then I think more of them would become coroners," she says. "I am not sure that many nurses know about forensic nursing. Every talk I give since I became a forensic nurse specialist I start by educating nurses, doctors and lay people as to what a forensic nurse is." O'Neal and Hancock offer advice for forensic nurses who want to become coroners. "Nurses need to have either ER or ICU experience, something where they are seeing forensic cases," O'Neal says. "We get calls all the time where a med-surg nurse wants to get into forensics. I tell them you need to go where you will see forensic cases in action. They have to figure out their state's system, either coroner or ME; that's an important step because they must know if it is an elected or appointed position. If it's an elected office, run for office; if it's appointed, get to know the person currently in that position."

"I was very grateful that I had people like Bobbie Jo to talk with when I started," Hancock recalls. "Anyone running for the office of coroner should contact other coroners and pick their brains as to what works. Join groups before you run; join a political party and become an active member. Establish a name for yourself long before you throw your hat into the ring." O'Neal says the infiltration of nurses into the U.S. coroner's system will be a slow process, but believe it will take off eventually. "Houston recently hired their first nurse," O'Neal reports:

> She is not doing the kinds of things we are; she is more of an assistant to review medical records, but the office will get a sense that maybe they are missing the boat somewhere; I hear they are ready to hire a second nurse. Houston is a huge office, with 15 or 20 investigators, so the fact they recognize maybe they need another nurse in the office is encouraging. That ME will talk to a colleague and will say, "Our nurse is great, you need to have one." Word will spread and eventually nurses will get in everywhere. But for a while, nurses will have to go in kicking and screaming to get attention. We tell them to do some police or EMS ride-alongs to network and observe. Who goes to crime scenes first? They do. They will know the coroners and MEs. Start to network and figure out who makes decisions. Then get yourself in the door.

12.11 NURSES AS MEDICAL EXAMINERS

She is a widely respected medical examiner and forensic pathologist, but Mary H. Dudley, MD, MS, RN, also has the respect of the forensic nursing community for being a champion of nurses and a pioneer in forensic nursing education. "I don't think forensics was even something nurses thought about that much many years ago, as far as seeing the importance of recognizing injury, preserving evidence, and maintaining chain of custody," Dudley says. However, the majority of students in her twice-yearly medico-legal death investigation courses are nurses who want to broaden their skills. To understand her support for nurses, one must know her background, in which forensics and nursing are intertwined. Dudley received her diploma degree in nursing from the Hospital of the University of Pennsylvania and then picked up her bachelor's degree in nursing from Metro State University in Denver and her master's degree from the University of Colorado prior to going to medical school. Following medical school and residency abroad, she did a rotation in forensics that clinched her future as a medical examiner and forensic pathologist.

Along her complicated educational path of medical boards, rotations, and residencies, Dudley found herself teaching at Beth El University's School of Nursing in Colorado Springs, Colorado, helping the institution convert its diploma nursing program to BSN. She says right around that time, she first became acquainted with the concept of forensic nursing through her professional membership in the AAFS. A nurse introduced her to Virginia Lynch, who was conducting forensic nursing workshops with an emphasis on training SANEs. Dudley was approached by the school's dean who asked her to teach a forensic nursing course at Beth El. "At that point Virginia had a forensic nursing article published and interest in the specialty was growing," Dudley recalls. "I said, 'I'm a pathologist and a nurse, and I could probably do that."

A lack of college-level material on forensic nursing forced Dudley to craft the program herself, relying on her forensic knowledge from medical school and seeking the expertise of colleagues. A friend who was a psychologist, who in turn was married to an attorney, was interested in law enforcement and forensic psychology, and was instrumental in helping set up the Beth El forensic nursing program, Dudley says. The course offered instruction in introductory forensic nursing as well as criminalistics, investigation of injury, plus psychosocial and legal issues and a 60-hour clinical internship. Dudley says Lynch was a guest lecturer, and when Dudley passed her forensic pathology boards and accepted a position with the Maricopa County Medical Examiner's Office in Phoenix, she asked Lynch to teach her course. Dudley says she was eventually phased out of the program due to her need to commute between Arizona and Colorado, and decided to create her own medico-legal death investigation course, Forensic Medical Investigation, in 1996. The four-day course covers everything from an introduction to forensic investigation, to injury recognition, sudden natural and accidental deaths, to child fatalities and domestic homicide, plus a forensic skills internship.

Since 2000, Dudley has served as chief medical examiner, forensic pathologist, and district coroner for the Sedgwick County Regional Forensic Science Center in Wichita, Kansas. In her ongoing support of forensic nurses, Dudley reports she has hired her first forensic nurse to work in her office as a forensic photographer. "I think nurses are ideal in death investigation," Dudley says:

> When most people think of death investigation, they think about crime scene identification; yet crime scenes are a minor part. As much as 70 percent of cases referred to the ME's office are mainly natural deaths; the rest are motor vehicle accidents, suicides, and homicides. The police department's concern is the crime scene; they don't want someone without training coming into "their" crime scene and moving everything around. Death investigators don't want to do that either. They are there to be my eyes and ears, and to get the body out of the scene once they are able to process a path to it and bring it back so I can make a determination of cause of death. It's critical that at every scene, every time, certain things are done—photos taken, information gathered, and the scene secured. Nurses make excellent medico-legal death investigators because they have the science background. They just need to be cross-trained in criminalistics and legal issues to be expert witnesses.

Because crime scenes can be hospitals, Dudley says forensic nurses in a death investigator role have a big advantage:

> They can interface with physicians, they can find the medical histories on individuals; they can look at the medications at the scene and have an idea of why the person may have died. That may be difficult for someone from law enforcement. They may see Dilantin and not know what that was for; a nurse will know this person must have had a seizure disorder. That's why I have no hesitation about hiring nurses to work as death investigators.

Dudley encourages forensic nurses who want to become death investigators to get the necessary training through independent courses as well as through the ABMDI, which offers standardized certification. "They need 30 hours of classroom content and then they need to be checked off on their skills by a preceptor who is a medical examiner or another registered death investigator. They must sit for the four-hour registry exam, and then to actually be certified, they must have 4,000 hands-on hours working with the ME's office. This credential may be challenging for some nurses to obtain, but it's worth working toward."

She says the majority of the individuals who attend her courses seek to broaden their scope of knowledge and see forensics as a dynamic specialty. "Many of the nurses I see have gone as far as they can in nursing and they are disillusioned; they don't feel part of a team anymore," Dudley says. "In forensics, they are a big part of the team. When I presented my course in Colorado Springs, nurses said they loved it, calling it the most interesting and stimulating course they have ever taken. They are just like sponges, soaking up information. My advice to them if they want to get into the field is to get credentialed and registered and take as many courses as they can to establish themselves as experts and be ready when new opportunities present themselves."

Dudley admits it can be difficult to break into death investigation, especially because it has been traditionally a male-dominated field:

> There is a turf mentality until they are educated about how important it can be to have death investigators with special training to handle natural-death cases, which are not law enforcement's focus, on their team. Medical examiners need as much or more history when the case is a natural death, so we need investigators who can get that background information—and nurses are natural at it. We're not even at the tip of the iceberg yet as far as the potential of nurses in the field of death investigation.

Dudley's passion for the pursuit of forensic science propelled her from nursing into forensic pathology, and her storied career includes working as a medical examiner for Maricopa County, which encompasses the greater Phoenix, Arizona metropolis. Now in her fifth year in Wichita, Dudley says it's a different demographic, but the skills she developed early in her forensic pathology residency and cultivated on the job in various parts of the country continue to serve her well. "Not only does my job serve my interest in forensic pathology, but I also really enjoy being involved in the community through my work, research, and my teaching opportunities. I interact with numerous other agencies, and it keeps me on my toes." Dudley adds:

> We have a forensic advisory board that meets on a quarterly basis, with members from all agencies with whom we partner, such as the sheriff's office, coroners in other jurisdictions, the local medical school, sexual assault nurse examiners, funeral directors—it's a very diverse group. We discuss issues and make sure everyone is on the same page, and we work collaboratively. A multidisciplinary team approach really works well for us. We have to work with several other agencies and people to accomplish what we do, and working as a team is an efficient way to work. The way I communicate with county administrators is to give my boss a monthly report; he's the division head for public safety so he knows of our activities, plus we also meet with his division twice a month, communicating with him, for him to get the information up to another level of what we are doing at the forensic science center.

In her work as director of the Wichita forensic science center, not only does she handle her forensic caseload, but she juggles a full slate of administrative duties, including hammering out budgets and working with government representatives. Dudley says she attended academic study in public administration to better prepare herself for the rigors of the work, including leadership and conflict resolution. "I went through this mini master's degree in public administration and that really helped me learn about government and how it is different from the private sector," Dudley explains. "That coursework was very helpful, although I was in the job for two years before I figured out what we do in government," she says, laughing. "I have a dual role, not only being a forensic pathologist, but also an administrator, and I like the challenges inherent to each and how they apply to each other."

Dudley chuckles when she describes an average day on the job:

> I do cases, I do administrative tasks, and I teach. Sometimes I go to court. It's as simple as that. I enjoy the variety tremendously, and I wouldn't want to only have an administrative job. To be credible, you must be involved and hands-on in the field. I wouldn't want to be teaching and have to say to my students, "Well, 10 years ago I did an autopsy..." As I teach, I want to be able to say, "Last week I had an interesting case on this very subject" or "Today I had a case that showed this or that," so that what I teach is relevant and current to my students.

A sense of communication, integration, and synergy among multiple agencies and disciplines, comes into play, Dudley says, because her work affects so many other agencies and individuals. "I have a strong sense of purpose about my work because of its importance to the criminal justice system, as well as to the families of decedents. What we do will also affect other agencies that look at our data, examine our work, and use our information, such as law enforcement and the courts. I believe it is very important to do good work on behalf of the dead, as well as for the living."

Dudley feels equally strongly about serving as a neutral, unbiased resource for the criminal justice system:

> When I go to court, I do so as a neutral agency; I don't work under the sheriff's office or law enforcement or the county attorney, so I can go to court and tell the jury what the injuries were based on science, and be completely objective. I don't have any vested interests in the accused person being guilty or innocent; the court has my forensic findings and then it is up to the jury to make that decision. I have a strong sense of objectivity about what I do; I am not an advocate, as there are other agencies which serve as advocates for the victim. I use forensic science principles to determine my findings, and then the jury has to figure out whether they have the right bad guy or not. My work contributes to assurance that the proper medico-legal protocols were followed. I need to make sure things are done right, that we maintain proper chain of custody, that we properly and neutrally document injuries and maintain the evidence that will speak to the medico-legal issues

> involved. I must ensure that everything is done the same way each time so that no detail is missed, and that evidence is safeguarded properly.

Inevitably, Dudley deals with comparisons to how cases unfold on forensic television shows as compared with how cases are solved in real life:

> Often, the public formulates an unrealistic viewpoint of our work in forensic pathology, and we have to debunk myths occasionally. Others don't understand forensic science very well, for a number of reasons. We can't talk specifically about what we do, because of confidentiality issues. Plus, the general public has an opinion of what we do based on television. They watch *CSI* or *Forensic Files* and think it's real. These shows make it seem as if every case we have is a criminal case, but criminal cases only account for about 10 percent of the cases we see, with actual homicide as the manner of death. We see far more natural deaths, probably 70 percent, including suicides and accidents. On television, people see forensic practitioners solving cases in an hour, and that's just not reality.

In the real world, Dudley says, a much different timetable exists.

> Every day, I keep in the forefront of my mind that I have an obligation to get cases done in a timely fashion, even if I am doing other things. Our national standards say that homicide cases should be done within 60 days, and that other cases should be done within three months, with 95 percent of all cases done timely. When I first came to Wichita I said I wanted cases done in 45 days; I've been able to do that, although sometimes I must wait for toxicology reports to come back before I can wrap up a case. I actually get many cases done in two weeks because I have a monkey on my back that makes me say, "I will finish this no matter what." I expect everyone around me to do the same; while I hold them accountable, I realize not everyone can do that... but we're getting close. It's not as though I expect things of others that I can't do, so I lead by example.

Some years ago, Dudley's office found itself in the middle of a quadruple homicide, a rare occurrence that nonetheless tested the prowess of the department. It was a defining moment for Dudley and her staff, she recalls:

> It satisfies me when we can come together, do the job, and be recognized for our efforts. The week of the quadruple homicide, I had to really step up my game to handle all of the cases, because I had 11 homicides that week. That was off the scale, because usually we only have about 22 homicides a year. To avoid becoming overwhelmed, I paced myself, making sure that everything was done well, everything was done right the first time, and that I took care of my staff along the way, so that two years later, when the case went to court, everything went well without it looking that difficult, even though at the time, it was challenging.

When faced with an excessive workload, Dudley says she avoids burnout by "knowing what my limitations are. Knowing when to take some time off and rest is critical. I know how to not push myself beyond my ability, or I'm not good to anybody. Avoiding burnout means recognizing when it's time to say no graciously, so that I am always able to function well and not take out any stress on my staff." Finding the "zen" of forensic pathology might not always be possible, but Dudley says she strives for balance and understanding in her work, even if it means not pushing quite as hard as she would like to get something done. "I'm the kind of person who wants things done yesterday," she explains, adding:

> I always want to move forward without having to take any steps back, and I realize you can't expect other people to have the same goals or timetables you do; you must work within the system, and I've learned how to do that successfully. After all, when you interact with so many other departments and agencies, you work with people who all have different agendas. The secret is listening to them and trying to find a compromise whenever possible so that the other person also gets something out of it. Any change will initially be met with resistance so you have to take baby steps, and you must learn to be patient.

Dudley adds that one of the best parts about her work is her colleagues. "I love my staff, they are just wonderful people who are very capable, motivated, prompt, and fun-loving, and I am fortunate to work with them. I also really love my job, doing the day-to-day pathology and the challenges that arise from that, and also the teaching and research I am able to do. I also enjoy working in a field that is constantly changing and growing." To that end, Dudley says she supports the move toward an all-medical examiner system, as discussed earlier in this chapter. "I would advocate for legislation calling for an end to the outdated coroner system that exists today. I think it's important to establish an ME system county- or statewide, where the practitioners working in this field are trained as forensic pathologists and board certified. Also, I think that all death investigators should be properly trained and credentialed as well, including nurses who work as medico-legal death investigators." Dudley points to the system in New Mexico, where she spent time adding to her training and education, which employs as many as 135 trained death investigators statewide:

> In their system, the very minimal experience to be a death investigator requires a certain level of training and educational background. These investigators are working under a board-certified forensic pathologist who sets up the medico-legal protocols. I would like to see legislation

in every state mandating a system like this, and I think that this concept is forthcoming—it's just a matter of time. I think what will drive it is our response to bioterrorism. We're going to be missing clusters of fatalities if we don't have the proper referral program, and if the right questions during an investigation aren't asked.

There are a handful of principles and best practices to which Dudley adheres that might further explain her success and guide others wanting to follow in her footsteps. "I believe it's essential to be a team player and to work together," she emphasizes. "I also think it is important to provide leadership for my staff and others, to be accurate and objective in what I do as far as determining cause and manner of death, the core of my job as a forensic pathologist. It's vital to be efficient and have an adequate turnaround time on cases. Families can't wait three to five months for the autopsy report," she comments:

They need to know what happened to their loved one, and they need a death certificate on a timely basis. There are other reasons to work efficiently, as sometimes you have cases where you are subpoenaed within two weeks to go to court. It's critical to do a thorough job, but also to do it efficiently and timely so that you have the answers for people who need them. I also think it's important to do things well and fast, and also be nice to people. I think those are the underlying reasons for my success in this job.

Dudley adds that it is important to be involved in professional organizations serving the industry:

I am a member of the National Association of Medical Examiners (NAME), which establishes the accreditation process, so I feel we need to meet the national standards for our office. I'm on the committee setting standards for individual pathologists for autopsy practice. I think it's important to be active in national organizations which represent the field, and also to contribute to the field through research and teaching; that's why I try to present at the annual meetings of the American Academy of Forensic Science and NAME. It's essential to have an ethical practice, including maintaining confidentiality, having respect for the decedent, avoiding conflicts of interest, and being fair to the people with whom you work.

12.12 NURSES AS DEATH INVESTIGATORS AND LAW ENFORCEMENT OFFICERS

Attempting to expose the rest of that iceberg is Meliss Vessier-Batchen, the Louisiana forensic nurse who serves as a contracted death investigator. She is excited about the new state-of-the-art forensic science center that is slated to be constructed in the rapidly growing jurisdiction in which she serves, a facility that will better equip the investigators. A voter-approved tax will take the St. Tammany Parish's annual budget from significantly under $100,000 to $4 million a year. Vessier-Batchen says the new center will facilitate a number of processes that until now have been less than optimal. "Our morgue is almost completely at the other end of the parish, about 35 miles from the medical examiner's office, so we're constantly going back and forth," she says:

We really need new lab equipment, and the need is also great for space where next of kin can view decedents' bodies. Right now, our morgue space is donated by a long-term care facility. When we need to bring in people to view bodies, we have nowhere to do that. We either have to possibly breach confidentiality for other decedents and their families, or we take pictures and take them to the family. It's a mess, so we'd like a good viewing room. A decomp room would be wonderful, too, as we see a lot of decomposition of bodies due to our wet weather and densely wooded areas. Sometimes we can get some pretty messy stuff. A decomp room would really be helpful for doing autopsies and holding bodies. A lot of plans in the works, hopefully they will solidify and become a reality by the end of 2006.

Vessier-Batchen adds, "We are also at looking at building a SANE center in the forensic center so that we are not affiliating with one particular hospital. Although Charity Hospital has an unbelievable program, we sometimes would like to have it associated not with any particular hospital but bring the forensic nurses into the forensic center and operate from there."

Vessier-Batchen currently is the only nurse working as a reserve investigator, although she reports that several other nurses have signed up for the reserve list, riding shotgun with other investigators:

As the budget grows, they can hire more investigators, and they are definitely considering hiring on more nurses as death investigators. Up until now, the investigator's job description has been non-nursing, of course, and hasn't taken into account my nursing licensure and experience. However, I always keep my nursing skills in the forefront of my thoughts in anything I do for the medical examiner's office. I said to my senior investigator, "You know, with all of these nurses signing up for reservist positions, we need to consider rewriting a job description that would be more specific to nurses," and she said, "You're absolutely right." So we're in the process of developing a job description for those nurses who come into the role. I don't think there's any single, clear-cut, absolute way to define medico-legal death investigation for nurses, as it is still very much a play-it-by-ear, work-with-the-system, find-your-way-in and change-their-minds kind of thing.

Vessier-Batchen says that the relative ease or difficulty with which nurses break into the field depends frequently on the political makeup of any jurisdiction:

In seeing nurses aiming to reach multiple goals in forensic nursing, and practicing in everything from very urban areas to very rural populations, it really does depend on who you're dealing with. If you have a coroner or a medical examiner serving your county or state who is educated and forward-thinking, you stand a better chance of introducing new ideas, such as death investigation performed by nurses. But it can mean a lot of hard work to convince them to accept and integrate you and a new role into the system. If you are in an area served by a coroner who happens to run the hardware store or has a farm, and doesn't have a medical background, it can be even more difficult to enter the field. In northern Louisiana's parishes, there are coroners who own the funeral homes, which I think is a conflict of interest. Once you can get the ME's or coroner's attention, I think it's easy to introduce the advantage of nursing knowledge being merged into the role of death investigator. Many times, counties don't even have death investigators; the coroners have to do their own work—which is very interesting because if they have no medical background and training, I shudder to think how these investigations are conducted.

I believe that as nurses become more visible in this role, and begin to demonstrate—again, not from an elitist point of view but from a practical point of view—that we can bring a great deal of knowledge to the table and how well we really fit into the role, we will move forward. People may not accept us as readily, but then again, they may not fight us as hard as in the past. The onus is on us as forensic nurses to show them that nursing is a perfect fit with medico-legal death investigation. The two meld together so beautifully, so functionally, so easily. It's almost ludicrous not to take advantage of any nurses who would be interested in serving as death investigators.

Nancy Cabelus, MSN, RN, D-ABFN, has nearly had the nine lives of a feline. A slight exaggeration perhaps, but this Connecticut forensic nurse has served as an operating room tech, state trooper, and detective, and frequently serves as a forensic nursing educator. She has enjoyed an unusually rich and varied career path that has criss-crossed the medico-legal spectrum. "I started out as an OR technician holding a two-year associate's degree," Cabelus says:

When I started working in the OR, I really liked what I was doing but I felt as though I only got to see a little snippet of what really goes on in patient care. I liked watching the nurses at work because they seemed to be so knowledgeable, and they inspired me to go to nursing school. I worked as an OR tech during the night shift and went to school during the day. While I was doing all of this, I was dating a police officer who got me interested in law enforcement. My grandfather was a police officer and my uncle was a trooper, so there was an underlying interest in law enforcement. I thought, "I'll take the police academy admissions test and see how I do." I was among more than 4,000 other applicants. They accepted about 140 people, two classes of 70, from this list of 4,000. I got into the academy, not even sure if this was my life's purpose or not, and after six months there, I graduated. The whole time I was at the academy, I continued to work as a nurse in the ER in order to keep my nursing skills viable. I didn't want to let go of my nursing skills because I worked too hard to get them.

Cabelus discovered forensic nursing, quickly joining the IAFN and networking with other nurses. "I met Dr. Barbara Moynihan at the Pittsburgh IAFN conference, who told me she was writing a curriculum for a master's program at Quinnipiac University," Cabelus recalls:

She asked me if I had a bachelor's degree, and when I said yes, she said, "Terrific, with your law enforcement background, you'd be a perfect candidate for the program. I was very excited at the prospect, got on board with the program, and was in the first graduating class of 2002. To stay active within the IAFN, I joined the Connecticut chapter four years ago, and just got elected to the board of directors for the mother chapter. It was a quick acceleration into forensic nursing.

Cabelus says she was bitten hard by the forensic bug when at the academy, she studied under famed forensic scientist Dr. Henry Lee:

When I was a recruit, Dr. Lee frequently came to speak to us about the importance of forensic science. I thought to myself, "How am I ever going to go from being a highway patrol trooper to signing a warrant one day for murder... I knew I had to pay my dues and put in my five years as a trooper. I was invited to join the governor's security staff, where I served for four years, which was an extraordinary experience. When I finished that assignment, I then became a detective. I knew I needed additional specialized training, so I signed up for forensic science coursework. Dr. Lee was putting together a program with the University of New Haven, where a forensic science school exists. It's 1996, and while at a conference, I was introduced to Georgia Pasqualone, who was a nurse in the forensic science program because there was no forensic nursing program yet. She was among a handful of nurses who were going to school for a master's degree in forensic science, and they told me more about the IAFN. It was like a domino effect, with one event leading to the next.

Cabelus is the first to admit that her career path is unorthodox. She comments:

People ask me all of the time, "How do I do what you're doing? How do I do this without having to become a cop first?" I tell them it's been a lot of hard work, time and effort, and many people aren't in the position to expend that kind of energy because they are committed to family, raising children, other responsibilities and have established, full-time careers as nurses. You can't just drop everything and go to the police academy. People complain that there aren't any good jobs out there . . . well, you have to make your own path. That's what's great . . . there's so much out there, it's a big world. You can go any direction you want to get there, but there are a lot of people who are afraid to take that risk.

Cabelus acknowledges the obstacles over which she has had to leap to get where she is now:

Nursing puts you in a box, and then when you comply with all of the rules and regulations, they raise the bar even more, so you have to jump through more hoops to get to your destination. I find that characteristic of traditional nursing to be so frustrating. People say that nurses eat their young; well, police say the same thing, in that they don't nurture their junior troopers. They get thrown to the wolves to see which ones are survivors.

She recalls an experience that caused her fellow troopers to finally accept her as one of their own:

At the time, I was 26 and had been working highway patrol by myself for just a few months. I was working the midnight shift and had been busy all night doing various assignments. I finally had the chance to check my 66-mile patrol around sunrise. As I am pulling up to a vehicle that was pulled over to the side of the road, there's a White male standing there with a flashlight, waving at me. So I pulled over. Apparently he had been drinking that night with a girlfriend on a date. He took her home, then started for home himself. That's when he fell asleep, and the car hit the guard rail. There was minor front-end damage and a flat tire. The guy says to me, "Trooper, I just want to get home; this is my dad's car." The guy is only 24, and had indicated to me that he was a sheriff working in the courthouse. He wanted to become a trooper and we got to chatting about that. He said, "I am really concerned about this accident." I said, "I'll call a tow truck for you, and we'll just pretend this accident never happened. I'll call this in as a disabled motorist who needs a wrecker. I won't give you a ticket, you won't have an accident report, just handle the damage out of your own pocket with no points against your license." He said, "Wow, Trooper, you would do that for me? Thank you so much." I said, "I'll call the wrecker, but it will take a few minutes. I'm going to drive to the end of the road and make sure there's no one else stranded out here." So I make a sweep of my patrol, and in 10 minutes I'm back at his side. It's a cool October morning, so he sits in the car, telling me his life story, and how badly he wants to be a trooper. He had just taken a police agility test for a small department the day before. I knew he was armed, and he showed me his badge and a permit to carry this little snub-nosed .38. The wrecker arrived, and as I was looking in the rear-view mirror, the guy suddenly says, "Now this f------- a------ is going to tow my piece-of-shit car." His personality and demeanor had changed instantly. I said, "Wait a minute, buddy, he's here to help you, just as I am here to help you. Chill out, everything's going to be fine." I get out of the cruiser, and he gets out on his side, slamming the door and saying, "Well, you may as well call an ambulance too," and he puts his gun in his mouth and pulls the trigger. That quick, he's dead.

Now, I was riding along with another trooper up until about two weeks before this incident. At that point, the senior troopers wouldn't give me the time of day. I was very low on the totem pole. I walked into roll call the next day after this incident, and guess what, they addressed me as "Trooper Cabelus." I had earned the rank because I had witnessed a violent crime. They didn't know that as an OR nurse, I probably bagged and tagged more bodies than a lot of the senior troopers had, but they were thinking, "Now you've been christened because you had a brush with death." I think it's an example of eating your young.

Cabelus says that the skills she learned as a nurse had direct application to her work in law enforcement. "It was obvious to my supervisors that there was something different about the way I operated," she says. "They pulled me aside and said, 'There's something that sets you apart from the kid who graduated from the academy with you.' They noticed that I had people skills, documentation abilities—everything I did was a little different, and I attribute that to my nursing background." Cabelus explains that even her work as an operating technician and her understanding of the necessity to preserve the sterile field came in handy when she became a detective:

I knew sterile technique, and I knew that maintaining the sterile field and preventing cross-contamination would help protect the patient from getting an infection. At a crime scene, the same principles work . . . you prevent contamination of the scene by outside entities, and you prevent the mixing of any trace evidence. The same instinct kicks in, and you find yourself donning the same protective gear—the gloves, the masks, the foot covers—that you use in nursing, only now, you're using it before you go into the crime scene. My nursing skills helped me know instinctively how to protect the scene, being careful about where you step and how you move within the crime scene. I knew I had to be extra careful within a crime scene because you really only have one chance to process the evidence; you can't go back to it next week because your search warrant is only good for a period of time, and the evidence will deteriorate or disappear.

Death investigation goes to basic fundamentals of nursing: assessment, diagnosis, looking at the whole picture, and taking a holistic approach. We're used to treating live patients and it's really the same concepts, except that the person is deceased. We're still going to do a head-to-toe comprehensive examination and look for findings, only now instead of talking to doctors and nurses and lab technicians, you're talking to police and state's attorneys and other forensic practitioners on the team.

"Sometimes they see the value of clinical forensic skills, and other times, I don't know if they are being territorial or they just don't want to accept it because you do get some resistance," she adds:

> When the nurse death investigator role was introduced at the medical examiner's office, there was a little bit of chatter along the lines of "Oh really, why are they doing that? Why can't the pathologist do this?" They don't understand that the forensic pathologist has his or her own responsibilities and could use some support from a nurse who can go to crime scenes. At the ME's office there are some nurses, there are some investigators who have some medical experience or have taken forensic-related classes, while there are others who have done nothing to enhance their medico-legal knowledge, and these are usually police officers. The office will put nurses on probation for a year so they can see how they do as investigators, but they will take a police officer with no experience and not put them on probation and pay them $2 an hour more. It makes me want to pull out all of my hair at the thought.

Cabelus also notes similarities between the OR and the autopsy suite. "After working in the OR, it was an easy transition to the autopsy room," she says. "It was a similar environment. When I worked in the OR, most patients were under general anesthesia and they were out cold; you didn't have any verbal communication. When you are in the autopsy room there is no communicating with the dead person either, so it's the same kind of scenario. For me, the same principles of treating people with respect and dignity applied; I treat the dead the same way I would treat the living." Cabelus says she conducted about 250 hours of clinical practice in the medical examiner's office for her master's degree, in addition to her routine visits with the major crimes squad:

> I got to know everyone on a first name basis at the ME's office, and that was a tremendous help. Developing those relationships made it easier for me when I arrived at the major crimes because I already had all of the contacts I would need. Other detectives would get their autopsy or toxicology reports back and they'd come to me and say, "Hey Nancy, what does this mean?" Because of my medical background, I was frequently the go-to person.

Despite this, Cabelus says she felt the constant scrutiny of being a woman and a nurse in a male, nonmedical world:

> To this day I can still feel remnants of gender bias and prejudice. It's interesting because I am eligible to retire in about a year, after 20 years of service, and I still feel this bias. I think the sexual assault nurses have won over the cops, who finally recognize and appreciate their good work. But as for nurses as death investigators, there are still many cops who think, "Who are these people and why should we let them into the crime scene?" We're still being judged and probably will be for a long time.

When she first encounters a crime scene, Cabelus says she runs through her mental list of details to notice and document:

> Right away, I ask myself, "Where is the crime scene and what is its relationship to the physical properties of the house? Is it locked and has it been broken into? Is there sign of a struggle? Has furniture been overturned? Is there an obvious weapon? Is there a body? Is there a blood stain pattern and no body because the body has been dumped somewhere else? Do you have a murder on your hands?" You don't really know. You want to look at the body, the position of the body, the type of wounds, and what type of weapons would match up with those wounds; if there are no wounds, you have to ask yourself, could death or injury have been chemically induced? Or was it strangulation? There may or may not be neck trauma because it only takes four pounds of pressure to shut off the carotid artery; that's why people hang themselves so easily... doesn't take a whole lot of force. In a few moments there is no oxygen supply to the brain. It may not always be a violent scene, but as a death investigator, you are always looking for clues to help you narrow the focus of your investigation. You must rule out a lot of things before you can make a reasonable conclusion.
>
> You must conduct interviews and do a lot of tracking of leads; not all of your information is always at the crime scene. There are a lot of components, such as the crime scene, and the autopsy. You should always try to follow the same steps in every case every time, like the crime scene guidelines dictate, but it's not usually the same scenario every time. Sometimes you think you've seen it all, then there's a surprise for you. One of the tricks of the trade is to always be open minded; don't go into a scene thinking, "Oh, I have seen this before," because that's when you might miss something small yet invaluable.

Regarding evidence collection at a crime scene, Cabelus says that working as a team is essential. "It's critical to have that support, that extra back-up," she says:

> For example, if you are the primary photographer and you miss a shot or two, your backup photographer is going to follow the same steps in the protocol as the primary photographer and will have a whole different set of photos. Sometimes you have to draw from that second string of pictures. Sometimes both photographers will miss something that our videographer will pick up, or you're trying to sketch a map and you can't recall a detail and then you rely upon your photographer's work to fill in the blanks. Working together is essential in photo-documentation of the scene. When we first approach a crime scene, the video guy goes first, then the primary and secondary photographers, then the sketch map artist and the evidence collection person who selects what they

> want to have documented and collected. They will place the numbered cones at the scene, marking various pieces of evidence, and the put the numbers on and the photographers will come in and take the pictures. Then the sketch map person will sketch all this in with the numbers accordingly and create a key. It's very systematic, and you rely on your team members to carry their weight. Mind you, at these crime scenes, you get called out when you have had maybe 30 minutes of sleep and you're up for another day and a half. You get tired, you forget to do things. Teamwork is essential to do a thorough job.

Cabelus cautions that not every crime scene will yield its evidence easily, and sometimes, Mother Nature has other plans:

> You have to do the best you can in the circumstance in which you find yourself. If it's raining, for example, you use a tarp or do whatever you can to protect your crime scene. There was a case I had recently that involved a police officer who shot someone in the line of duty. Bullet casings went flying into the street, and we were intent on searching for them, even though it had been snowing. We found some of the projectiles but we were still looking for casings without much success. I said, "Let's go to Home Depot to get some salt so we can melt the snow and look for the casings using metal detectors." So we did, and we worked through the night. The shooting had occurred the night before, and now we were still working at deicing the street and sidewalk, waiting for the sun to come up. After all of this work, we found out that some little girl called up her friend and said, "There was a shooting outside of our house and my daddy found casings in the street and brought them into the house." So this other little girl tells her mommy and daddy what's going on and then they called the police, informing them that the evidence they were looking for is in the people's house. What would compel someone to do such a boneheaded thing, you have to wonder. But you never know what kind of a curveball a case will throw your way. In another situation, the scene of a fatal shooting was a car wash. It was pouring rain, and, of course, a car wash is pitched so that water goes down the drain, and we are standing there watching as the blood evidence and bullet casings were being washed down the drain. So we hurried to cover things up with whatever we had. It can really be awful if you encounter weather that can wreak havoc with your crime scene. So it's important to be prepared for any eventuality so that you can protect your crime scene above all else.

Sometimes, Cabelus says, the forensic nurse can be better prepared and better trained than law enforcement. "There was a forensic nurse in Connecticut who collected some evidence after a hit-and-run motor vehicle accident," Cabelus recalls:

> The victim had a lot of trace evidence in her clothing, and the nurse collected it, packaged it, and labeled it properly as she was taught. She called the police and said, "We have your evidence here," and they said, "What are we supposed to do with it?" Again, there is an assumption that the police are trained in forensic matters. This had occurred in a small police department that would normally rely upon the state police to help them, but they didn't even call us. Now they are up a creek with no paddle. They're thinking to themselves, "Should we get that evidence or tell the nurse to throw it away?" That's why we need unilateral forensic training so that the right hand knows what the left hand is doing; a lot of times it doesn't. You can't really point a finger at either discipline because sometimes both are wrong because they are just not trained.

As forensic nursing wrestles with a core curriculum (see chapter 15), Cabelus muses about her wish list for a solid educational offering for nurses. "Knowing what the standards are is key," Cabelus says. "Our standards of practice are outdated and I know they are being revised currently, but I think nurses need a set of guidelines to rely upon, to refer to, to adhere to." Cabelus explains that she wears an educator's hat when she teaches a forensic nursing specialist certificate course through the Florida Risk Management Institute:

> The first section is an introduction to forensic nursing, and it's eight hours; the second lecture is sexual assault, and again, that's eight hours; the two other segments are evidence collection and death investigation; there are people who leave these four lessons, or 32 hours of instruction including lunch, and they put "forensic nursing specialist" on their business cards. I make it clear that they are not a forensic nurse specialist with so little time spent on the coursework. We need to clear up that haziness as to who is and who is not a qualified, credentialed forensic nurse, and what requirements are necessary to attain that credential. There are so many quickie courses popping up, that I want prospective nurses to understand that they don't become forensic nurses overnight; it can take years of hard work and intense study and experience in the field. Many schools are simply pumping out business-card credentials. Those of us with a master's degree and 500 clinical hours under our belts, and who wrote papers and conducted research . . . those kinds of efforts certainly have more credibility than a 30-hour course. You're telling me that an RN can take a few classes and become a certified forensic nurse . . . it's ludicrous. I look back at how stretched I was, between taking night classes, working full time, getting called out to crime scenes in between everything else. There were only eight of us who graduated together in the first class of students at Quinnipiac, and some of those people weren't even working at the time they were going to school. I was working well beyond full time and doing all of this coursework and writing papers and doing research and it just doesn't seem fair to me that somebody could take a 40-hour class and suddenly be a certified forensic nurse. We don't want to adjust the standards to make it more difficult for the next

person, as we certainly want to encourage other nurses to follow in our footsteps, to make this profession more prolific, and to not turn anybody away, but yet we don't want to give them this little certificate to wave around . . . what kind of credibility is that? It doesn't prepare them for the rigors of the job, and it doesn't do any of us justice. I think many people are misled as to what is entailed to become a forensic nurse, so a core curriculum would help dispel the confusion. I tell people that if they want to be death investigators, to go down a certain path and don't go over here until you get to your goal, and it is a very confusing process for them simply because the path is not a straight and narrow one. If you are trying to sell somebody the role of the forensic nurse who has never heard of forensic nursing, it's pretty hard to do unless you have a good, broad curriculum or credential to say "Yes, I have the training and this is what I can offer you."

Armed with the right education, credentials, and experience, Cabelus believes there's no stopping a nurse who wants to work in death investigation:

It just makes so much sense. Death investigation is the perfect place for a nurse. But you have to be prepared to sell the idea and yourself to the medical examiner's or the coroner's office so they can see what a difference a forensic nurse death investigator can make. The problem is, a lot of the states don't have enough money in the budget to pay nurses' salaries. In Connecticut, there are a number of death investigation positions, and many offices are thrilled to take a nurse, but because their budgets are so tight, they can't pay what a nurse could make in a hospital. Unless that person is motivated to spend the money and invest in themselves and their education, medical examiner's and coroner's offices are going to have people with a patchwork quilt of various levels of education and capability. And that makes for a very stressful working environment. Some of the Quinnipiac University students are doing internships at these medical examiner's offices and they are recognizing such a void in forensic-related education in some of the nonmedical people they are shadowing. The nurse may know a whole lot more than someone who has been in law enforcement for 20 years and has been a death investigator for two. Overall, with time, I think the attitude toward nurse death investigators will improve. I mean, how could anyone *not* want a nurse?

That said, Cabelus cautions nurses who are would-be death investigators to not assume the red carpet will be rolled out for them automatically. "There's a certain amount of trailblazing that still needs to be done," Cabelus emphasizes:

You can't knock on the doors of a law enforcement agency or an ME's office without having a plan. You have to know specifically which skills you can offer them, and not just say, "Well, I'm thinking about this . . ." They are not career counselors. They are not going to say, "Oh, let's give it a try." They are not going to be that receptive; after all, why break the mold for a stranger walking in the door? But if you have a plan and explain to them what you can do and how you can do it, and what you can achieve, even if it's on a voluntary basis for a short while, and think about the future and maybe you could get a grant to keep it going . . . that's what will impress them. Without a solid plan of action, you're going to get shot right down.

Another pitfall for nurses, Cabelus says, is unrealistic expectations of the job of death investigator:

I think that Hollywood has both helped and hurt the field. The TV show *CSI* is not realistic but it certainly makes the work look attractive and sexy. In the classes I teach, I usually go around the room and ask people to introduce themselves and tell the group what first got them interested in forensic science. Nine times out of 10, they are either Patricia Cornwell fans or they love *CSI*. Yes, but none of that is real; they will realize that the first time they encounter a crime scene so horrific and traumatizing to look at, when they see dead children and mutilated people—the unmitigated results of violence. I recently watched an episode of *Cold Case* and it reminded me of a case I had worked two years ago where a woman was murdered in front of her little girl. For at least 24 hours, this child was in this apartment with her dead mother and the mother's dead boyfriend. She had to step over her mother's body and through the pool of blood to get to the refrigerator to get a pudding cup to eat because she was hungry. When I went to the crime scene I found two pudding cups on top in the garbage can; knowing that this is what this little girl endured for 24 hours . . . that's what Hollywood doesn't show you.

My students tell me, "I don't know how you do it." I don't want to stand there and tell them horror stories, but I will point to real cases to explain how evidence can solve a case, or where the CODIS system linked this person to six other rapes. I always try to illustrate the principles I am teaching with real-life examples and people are always amazed at the differences between what they see on TV and what I tell them is real from actual cases.

When asked what her work has taught her about herself, Cabelus pauses to reflect for a moment:

I once co-authored a paper on the psychological effects of violence on forensic nurses because it's something that people don't always think about. You have to put up a barrier around yourself to protect yourself from feeling the effects of the violence you encounter constantly. Sometimes it takes a toll on you and you don't realize it; sometimes it takes a couple of years before it kicks in. I was testifying in a murder case two months ago; it was a case that bothered me a great deal but I couldn't really figure out why. All of a sudden I realized that these two dead children were the same ages as my niece and nephew, with whom I spent the day in New York on the day these kids were murdered. I got home from New York, got off the train, and my pager was going off—I was summoned to the scene. I ended up in the autopsy room with all of the victims, a mother and two kids asleep in their beds, and it was disturbing. I just came off of a case I had the week before that was even worse, so it's like, "This is bad, but the one I had last week was worse. So I can get through this OK." But it still bothered me. That link, the fact that my niece and nephew were the same age as these kids sprawled out on this autopsy table with multiple stab wounds, and then hanging up their pajamas to dry in the evidence room with all the holes and the blood and it's like, "This is a tough one." As exciting as this kind of work appears, and as rewarding as it is, there's a lot of stuff going on in your head that you're not even paying attention to. I think it's essential for death investigators to have strong coping skills and healthy-living strategies, because there's no longevity in this field if you can't take care of yourself.

Cabelus says she especially enjoys the challenging cases that involve a team effort. She points to a child sex-abuse case she worked a number of years ago:

> As a detective, I have worked so many of those kinds of cases, and with my medical background, I knew what kind of evidence had to be collected; working with SANEs, I could go into hospitals and say, "I am a detective but I am also a forensic nurse so I understand your exams, how can I help you to get the information you need so we can work together on this?" In this one particular case, several children disclosed to the school counselor that they were being sexually abused at home; the counselor worked on this case with us and was very helpful in trying to get the information we needed. I worked on this case for a year, and it took me through many states. I followed this perpetrator from Florida to Georgia to Virginia to Rhode Island to Connecticut and he perped everywhere he went. He was a transient truck driver and would leave an area as soon as he knew the authorities were on to him. When I found him in Chicago I called him up and said, "Would you be willing to be interviewed and take a polygraph test?" He never thought I would actually come out to Illinois, so he said, "Sure," and there I was on his doorstep with a lot of police. I ended up taking him in with the help of the Illinois state troopers. There is usually very little money in the budget to be able to travel like that, but those few extra days I had in Chicago allowed me to gather circumstantial evidence to support what he was doing; I got a warrant, the judge signed it, and I had him extradited. He was eventually convicted and received a 20-year prison sentence. The school counselor who worked through the case with us was delighted in the outcome, and those children received the care they needed in the aftermath of the abuse. Working together with multiple disciplines makes it very rewarding.

In this way, Cabelus says, she can advocate for victims without becoming a victim advocate. Chapter 1 examined the advocacy versus science issue facing nurses; Cabelus adds that nurses working as death investigators must balance their desire for advocacy with science-based practice:

> You're a nurse first, and I think some of this is instilled in you forever, no matter what additional role you decide to take later in your career. I mean, we have to care for people, whether they are dead or alive; you can't just cut out that part and be the scientist. You have to take a step back and look at the whole picture. We have a duty to provide care and a duty to do no harm, and if not, then you have to stop being a nurse. So if you want to be an investigator, fine, go be an investigator. Sure, it's hard for me sometimes, because I am a nurse to the core. I am one year shy of retirement from the Connecticut State Police with 20 years of service; I won't be a police officer anymore but I'm going to continue to be a nurse forever. You find a way to balance being a nurse with your forensic duties.

Cabelus agrees that the "just-a-nurse" scourge is alive and well, but it is the job of the forensic nurse to disprove this disparaging comment:

> I think nurses still lead the pack in terms of professional respect, more so than any other discipline out there, even more so than doctors, according to recent studies. So nurses should take a lot of pride in their work. People believe that nurses are intelligent, too. They are credible, and they are held in high regard by the people who know not to get sucked into that just-a-nurse sentiment. That being said, there are still those who are surprised when a nurse responds to a crime scene. They'll quip, "Hey, nobody's sick here." It's an evolution, it's a process. My role didn't just happen; I tell people that they have to pay their dues, do their homework, and evolve into the next professional stage of their career.

Cabelus believes that mountains will have to be moved to take forensic nursing to the next level, but she's got her shovel ready and plans to move serious amounts of topsoil to make that happen. In 2004 she was elected to the board of the IAFN, and she says she has an ambitious agenda. "I want to see us actively educating, mentoring, and recruiting forensic nurses of all disciplines," Cabelus enthuses:

> We need to make sure the forensic nurse's role within police departments, protective agencies, courts, and throughout the criminal justice system is validated. How do you do that? You have to knock on doors and you have to show your face. I think we really need to emphasize the importance of networking with our forensic colleagues and getting to know people. Another agenda item is to address the fact that evidence collection procedures are not standardized in all states. Connecticut has a standardized collection process and recently the colonel of the state police appointed me to the state's standardization task force. We are tweaking our evidence collection kits and we're going to the state legislature and saying, "Hey,

this is what we need and this is what we want to do. And here is the data to support it."

12.13 FORENSIC NURSES AND DMORT DUTY

On the fateful day of September 11, 2001, the United States learned about its true capacity to respond to a mass disaster of epic proportions. As the twin towers of the World Trade Center in New York City were being reduced to rubble by terrorist-commandeered airplanes, local hospitals were being deluged with the injured, the dying, and the dead. For the first time in a very long time, the region's health care system was tested for its ability to triage and treat the victims of a catastrophic event. In the blink of an eye, first responders, nurses, physicians, and nearly every health care provider at local hospitals were transformed into forensic practitioners in what could be one of the most largest and significant medico-legal cases in American history. Having nurses serve on the front lines of triage is nothing new; military nurses and nurses in the Red Cross have been providing care and service for more than a century. Only now are these nurses learning of their heritage as forensic nurses, and the great need for medico-legal skills in times of war and mass disaster. In the future, in a continuing unstable and uncertain global political climate, health care providers with medico-legal sensibilities will serve in the forefront of their practice.

One of the most intriguing roles for a forensic nurse is that of a Disaster Mortuary Operational Response Team (DMORT) team member who responds to mass fatalities, such as terrorist attacks and plane crashes. Established in the 1980s as an adjunct of the National Funeral Directors Association, in the 1990s, DMORT was formally incorporated into the U.S. government's emergency response capability. DMORT teams are activated in the event of a natural disaster, terrorism event, or aviation or technological disaster, and its approximately 1,200 volunteer members hail from all aspects of the forensic and mortuary communities. They work under the jurisdiction of all local authorities or federal agencies. DMORT team members became highly visible during the terrorist attacks of 2001; DMORT teams were summoned to the site of the airplane crash by the coroner of Somerset, Pennsylvania. DMORT provides portable morgue units, computerized morgue management, and specialized protocols for victim identification and family assistance. Team members handle postmortem collection of DNA evidence, working in close collaboration with the Armed Forces DNA Identification Laboratory.

Joyce Williams, RN, BAN, a member of DMORT Region III who responded to the crash of United Flight 93 in September 2001, works as a forensic investigator for the Office of the Chief Medical Examiner for the state of Maryland. She says that DMORTs have evolved in the last decade and have been "instrumental in actively improving the mass fatality incident response in the United States."

Although the U.S. government has had a contingency plan for large-scale disasters since World War II, Williams explains that it wasn't until 1969 that Richard Nixon issued Executive Order 11490, assigning emergency preparedness functions to federal departments and agencies. She adds that the Robert T. Stafford Disaster Relief and Emergency Act (P.L. 93-288) provides for a comprehensive emergency management system to ensure a timely and coordinated response, and was designed to improve the haphazard response to mass fatality incidents by revising and broadening the scope of existing disaster plans.

The Stafford Act paved the way for the Federal Response Plan (FRP), which describes the basic mechanisms and structure by which the federal government mobilizes resources and conducts activities to augment state and local response efforts, Williams says. There are 12 emergency support functions (ESFs), lead by the U.S. Department of Health and Human Services, which leads, directs, coordinates, and integrates efforts to provide necessary medical and public health assistance during a disaster. They direct the activation of National Disaster Medical Services (NDMS), a partnership of federal agencies charged with providing for medical, mental health, and other human services to victims of national disasters. The Health and Human Service's Office of Emergency Preparedness (OEP) leads NDMS, and is joined by other federal agencies, including the Department of Defense, the Department of Veterans Affairs, and the Federal Emergency Management Agency (FEMA).

Williams points to the 1990 case where 87 people perished in a fire at a New York City social club. "The medical examiner was unprepared to provide for the dead along with their families and approached a group of funeral directors to assist," she says. "They were asked to fill a need—that of delivering the truth with compassion to the families of victims of these horrific tragedies. These volunteers . . . determined a location for the families to meet where information could be gathered to aid in the identification of the victims. Other agencies such as fire, police, and mental health were incorporated in these teams."

The local community had not been prepared for this type of mass disaster, and following an investigation by the OEP, a team of investigators identified the need to provide for the dead as well as the living, as well as the need for a multidisciplinary team to respond to events such as this. Following these determinations, DMORT was born in 1992. Four years later, DMORT was put to the test in the crash of TWA Flight 800 into ocean waters off of the coast of Long Island, New York. Williams says:

> Loved ones demanded better treatment of the victims with the interests of the victims placed ahead of the airlines.

They wanted expedient notification of victim identification, return of personal effects, access to information, counselors and a family assistance center on site. It was after this event that Congress became involved, along with the National Transportation Safety Board (NTSB), and passed the Aviation Disaster Family Assistance Act. Families now could expect certain things in the event of major aircraft incidents by coordinating with local, state, and airline authorities involved in investigating and managing a disaster. They are tasked with seven victim support tasks and victim identification by forensic and medical services.

DMORT teams had been forged into a cohesive unit of specialized citizens. They worked side by side, caring for the bodies of strangers often reduced to fragments. These forensic experts struggled to find meaning for the families who were grieving and in shock. All members are caregivers treating bodies with compassion and dignity as they are tasked with the identification and care of the victims.

12.14 INTEGRATING CLINICAL PRACTICE AND DEATH INVESTIGATION

Sometimes, forensic nurses are educators and death investigators who struggle to convince communities to make use of their skills. Frequently, these offers of assistance go unheeded. That's the situation in which Nebraska forensic nurse and educator Donna Garbascz Bader, MA, MSN, RN, D-ABMDI, finds herself. Bader is a faculty member at the College of Health Sciences Nursing who also practices as a staff nurse on a per diem basis. She is a registered death investigator, but the work is infrequent due to a complicated political scene. "At this time, local and state jurisdictions here are not progressive enough to appreciate the things that can be done by a forensic nurse," she says. Bader tries to work as much as she can with a local forensic pathologist, and she places great hope in being able to initiate a forensic science curriculum through one of the state colleges. However, much of what she does forensically is unpaid, indicative of the lack of value locals place on forensic nursing. "I think barriers exist, based on discrimination against nurses and females in general," Bader explains:

> I stay in touch with all of the law enforcement agencies and try to keep up my forensic-related skills, but no one ever calls. After calling a few times and getting no response, it feels like a waste of time. The other challenge is the stigma that exists in the Midwest. While some areas south of Nebraska, in Kansas and to the east and west, are becoming increasingly progressive by hiring a few forensic nurses, our state does not yet embrace forensic nursing or nurses working as death investigators. There is a negative impression of nurses in general that we can't seem to wipe out no matter what we do. The law enforcement community here in Lincoln can be sexist, believing that nurses could never be of any value to a medico-legal investigation. They see nurses as being females who take orders and do what the male doctors tell them to do, so in their minds there really isn't any correlation between nursing and forensic science or medico-legal investigation. It's very backward thinking. They think that if they hire nurses, we are going to boss them around or tell them how to do their jobs, so they shut us out.

Bader says she has attended autopsies at which she is treated rudely by members of law enforcement agencies because she is a nurse. "If I ask a question at the autopsy, they look at me as if to say, 'Why do you want to know?' Yet if a male student nurse attends an autopsy, they are treated differently. Suddenly it's like, 'Well, come join the police department; you'd be an asset, and we could work together.' It's not an isolated occurrence; it has happened every time there is a male in the group." Bader says she experiences professional isolation, in that she does not identify with the most known group of forensic nurses, SANEs, yet no other class of forensic nurse is recognized in her area. She says that there are not enough nurses to go around, thus preventing her facility from designating a nurse as solely having forensic responsibilities. In addition, nurses are struggling to be respected in their traditional nursing roles, let alone as something as progressive as a forensic nurse. "Nurses are not asked for their professional opinions beyond the basics of what are supposed to do," she says, adding, "They are not supposed to do anything else because they don't know anything else. I am not considered as a forensic nurse by my facility. I have attempted to get the position and the title formalized, but there is no need for this, nor are there monies to support it."

So instead of being able to practice as a forensic nurse daily, Bader says she must make do with whatever medico-legal work she can secure through the medical examiner. She is very much a self-made practitioner, paying for her own schooling:

> I can't ask people to open doors for me . . . I have to do it myself, and try to be recognized for what I know, not because of *who* I know. All the education that I've acquired and the courses I have taken have all been at my own expense, which I'll never complain about, because I see it as an investment in my career. I earned my credential as a death investigator, and just this past summer I took a course on skeletal remains recovery and investigation; I took a week off of work and paid for everything. It was an awesome experience. No one at work really cares about it, but I do, and I am good with that.

Bader says that at her facility, all forensic cases are instantly turned over to law enforcement, whether it is the police or the state patrol:

> When we get a gunshot wound in the ER it has to be reported, so law enforcement shows up in the blink of an

eye, and it's their case. They do the paperwork, the investigation, and the follow-up; as for the nurses, they are simply there for the police to point their finger at and say, "Make sure you chart everything," or "Don't do this," and "Don't do that," as if we already don't know that. They can't seem to understand how nurses can contribute to the investigation and evidence collection processes. They also don't seem to understand that we know the medical processes, what's normal and what's not. It's not a case of being better than the police, but merely contributing our nursing and medical expertise. Maybe it's all about egos, but we live with it. Still, law enforcement needs to have better understanding of and respect for the nurse and his or her medical knowledge and what this can bring to the forensic investigation unit.

It might be akin to beating one's head against the wall, but Bader tries to introduce the concepts of forensic nursing wherever and whenever she can:

I've tried to tell my colleagues about forensic nursing, but there's never time to talk about it to anybody for any length of time. I learned real early that the other nurses don't know what a forensic nurse does, and they really didn't understand forensic nursing until the medical examiner and I asked if we could present an in-service on the subject. So, we held an in-service called "Forensic Nursing in the ER," and more than 100 people showed up. However, that was the last time I was ever asked to do anything on forensic nursing.

Bader says that despite these attempts, a forensic protocol has not been established, and that the call-the-police-only mandate still rules the day. Frequently, she observes activities that break medico-legal protocol:

For example, in one situation, a patient was brought in from a crime scene and the evidence was in plastic bags. The police came up to me and, throwing his clothes at me, said, "Here are his clothes." I conducted my assessment, my patient care, and documented everything. When I was done, I asked the police officer who was there, "Is it OK if I take these clothes out of the plastic sacks and put them in paper bags?" and he said, "What do you want to do that for?" And I said, "The evidence will start to degrade if it remains in plastic." He simply said someone would be by to pick up the bags. So, I charted that I requested permission to remove the garments from the plastic bags to paper bags, and that the officer indicated "someone will be here to pick them up shortly." This was only two years ago, so you would think everyone would know by now that using plastic bags for evidence is not correct. But perhaps that is too much too assume.

There is a bright spot for Bader, in that she and a few SANEs are beginning to teach a baccalaureate-level, fourth-year, elective introductory forensic nursing course at her local school of nursing. They are developing the curriculum, using general forensic science texts plus a series of forensic nursing and medico-legal death investigation texts written by Wichita, Kansas-based forensic pathologist Mary Dudley, MD, RN. Bader says she has high hopes for the eventual success of the course. "The dean of students, the dean of curriculum, and the director of the school immediately told us that we had to put a limit on the class because they have already started getting calls about it; prospective students have already been inquiring about how they can be placed on a reserve list, it's so popular. They anticipate a very heavy demand for the class, and that's very exciting." Bader says the course will portray a realistic view of medico-legal death investigation and forensic nursing:

I am hoping that by the time these students are seniors, they will understand basic nursing principles, be able to think critically and process the information we will give them, and then apply it out in the real world. Everyone is fascinated by forensic science, yet we want them to understand there is very little, if any glamour involved. They must know that the visuals in the class will be very graphic, and may be hard to handle sometimes. If they can get past that and not leave the room to vomit, then we can get them to the investigative process. But in real life, they will be challenged by their first exposures to things like decomposed bodies left out in the elements . . . only then does the textbook material become real. *CSI* never truly captures the sights and smells that are at a crime scene. *CSI* doesn't really show you what a battered, assaulted person looks like . . . that's what we must prepare our students to encounter.

Bader chose to pursue her interest in forensic nursing because "it has been an interest of mine since I was in nursing school, and I always felt that medicine and law are related. In addition, the cause of human behavior has always been of interest to me." However, she wrestles with the fact that she has yet to be given a full opportunity to participate actively as a forensic investigator. To make this happen, Bader believes that "more acceptance from and confidence on the part of law enforcement officers would allow me to receive an increased amount of actual field experience." She adds, "Even though I am not able to be an active participant in forensic investigation, I am fortunate to at least be involved to some degree as an educator. I believe my work contributes to the medico-legal continuum currently by increasing awareness of the value of nursing education as it relates to forensic science." Bader believes there is a steep learning curve with which to reckon before forensic nursing will be accepted unilaterally:

People do not understand at all. Nurses in general do not understand the overall perception of forensic nursing, and law enforcement has limited knowledge and acceptance. How can this level of understanding be improved? Hopefully by an overall increase in their perception of nursing

> knowledge and the utilization of this knowledge as it applies to the critical-thinking process. This, in turn, can assist in a more complete investigation. Nursing knowledge of basic normal human anatomy, physiology and human behavior can complement other investigative techniques, however, law enforcement personnel cannot accept this one basic principle.

Bader believes new avenues for forensic nurses could open if the law enforcement community would be willing to discuss the issue. "It's extremely difficult to talk about this issue with any law enforcement directors or other law enforcement personnel. Basically, there is no support system, other than discussion among a few peers. Law enforcement is a male-dominated field, and the perception of nurses is that they are there to do what they are told by physicians, and essentially, they are not respected." Bader adds that barriers can be broken if

> Law enforcement, at the very least, would provide an opportunity to assess what a nurse with an additional education in forensic science can add to the field of forensic investigation. All we need is just one chance. Sooner or later, this part of the country will realize the significance for forensic nursing, and this specialty will become a major force in the field of nursing. It will prove to be an area of nursing that will be greatly valuable by law enforcement and those who are directly affected by a violent and/or fatal act that requires forensic investigation and family and community support. But before this can happen, I believe that the overall perception of nurses on all levels needs to improve.

Although she might win some battles and lose others, Bader says she is "honored and fortunate to at least try" to engage in the fight for forensic nursing. To those who are interested in breaking into the field Bader encourages them to "Be persistent." As for her hopes for the future of the field, Bader says, "Forensic nursing will absolutely become respected, but it's going to take effort and persistence on the part of individual nurses. And in general, nurses must do more to make their voices heard in regard to more truth in the current perception of nurses and nursing practice."

REFERENCES

Allert, L. J., & Becker, M. Death investigation: Nursing on the cutting edge. *Forensic Nurse.* September/October 2002.

Charles, L. L. Patterns of systemic interviewing in the investigation of a death: Using systemic family therapy concepts to illustrate how death investigators approach families in the aftermath of an unexpected death. *Fam Syst Health. 17,* 309, 1999.

Chisum, J. An introduction to crime reconstruction. In B. Turvey (Ed.). *Criminal Profiling: An Introduction to Behavioral Evidence Analysis.* London: Academic Press. 1999.

Chisum, W. J., & Turvey, B. Evidence dynamics: Locard's exchange principle and crime reconstruction. *J Behav Profil. 1,* 1, 2000.

Courson, S. *The Investigative Specialty of Forensic Nursing* (Pennsylvania State Nurses Association Career Series). 2000. Available at: http://www.psna.org/Career/forensic.htm.

Dudley, M. H. *Forensic Medical Investigation: A Comprehensive Review.* Wichita, KS: Dudley Publishing. 2002.

Dudley, M. H. *Forensic Medical Investigation: Forensic Nursing.* Wichita, KS: Dudley Publishing. 2003.

Eliopulos, L. *Death Investigator's Handbook: A Field Guide to Crime Scene Processing, Forensic Evaluations, and Investigative Techniques.* Boulder, CO: Paladin Enterprises. 2003.

Fisher, B. A. J. *Techniques of Crime Scene Investigation* (Sixth edition). Boca Raton, FL: CRC Press. 2000.

Forensic Focus 2003 Conference: A Medico-legal Forum for Nurses, Medical Examiners, Technologists, Investigators and Other Forensic Practitioners. Millennium Resort, Scottsdale, AZ, June 17–20, 2003.

Forensic Nursing Clinical Update: Death Investigation, Adverse Patient Events, and Evidence Collection in the Hospital Setting. Pointe South Mountain Resort, Phoenix, AZ, August 27–28, 2001.

Fulton, M. Forensic nurses as coroners and death investigators. *Forensic Nurse.* January/February, 2003.

Hanzlick, R. Coroner training needs: A numeric and geographic analysis. *JAMA. 276,* 21, 1775–1778, 1996.

Gerberth, V. J. *Practical homicide investigation.* (3rd ed.) Boca Raton, FL: CRC Press. 1996.

James, S. H., & Nordby, J. J., Eds. *Forensic Science: An Introduction to Scientific and Investigative Techniques.* Boca Raton, FL: CRC Press. 2003.

Lee, H. C., Ed. *Crime Scene Investigation.* Taoyuan, Taiwan: Central Police University Press. 1994.

Lee, H. C. *Henry Lee's Crime Scene Handbook.* New York: Academic Press. 2001.

Lynch, V. A. *Clinical Forensic Nursing: A New Perspective in Trauma and Medicolegal Investigation of Death.* Fort Collins, CO: Bearhawk Consulting Group. 2001.

Saferstein, R. *Introduction to criminalistics.* Upper Saddle River, NJ: Prentice Hall. 1998.

Saferstein, R. *Criminalistics: An Introduction to Forensic Science* (Seventh edition). Upper Saddle River, NJ: Prentice Hall. 2001.

Thornton, J. I. The general assumptions and rationale of forensic identification. In D. L. Faigman, D. H. Kaye, M. J. Saks, & J. Sanders, Eds. *Modern Scientific Evidence: The Law and Science of Expert Testimony* (Vol. 2). St. Paul, MN: West Publishing. 1997.

U.S. Department of Justice. *Death Investigation: A Guide for the Scene Investigator* (NCJ Publication No.167568). Washington, DC: National Institute of Justice. 1999.

Vessier-Batchen, M. Forensic nurse death investigators. *Mystery Magazine Web. 1,* 2, 2003.

Wooten, R. Applying the nursing process to death investigation. *Forensic Nurse*. November/December, 2003.

RECOMMENDED READINGS

Carter, J. M. Crisis in medico-legal death investigation. *J Natl Med Assoc. 94,* 1, 44–46, 2002.

Chewning, S. Nurses provide closure as death investigators. Nursing Spectrum. Available at: http://nsweb.nursing-spectrum.com/cfforms/GuestLecture/closure.cfm.

Cwiklik, C. An evaluation of the significance of transfers of debris: Criteria for association and exclusion. *J Foren Sci. 44,* 6, 1136–1150, 1999.

DeForest, P., Gaensslen, R. E., & Lee, H. C. *Forensic Science: An Introduction to Criminalistics.* New York: McGraw-Hill. 1983.

Flaherty, M. Secrets of the dead: Nurse death investigators hone their skills in forensic research. Nurseweek. 1999. Available at: http://www.nurseweek.com/features/99-2/death.html.

Hanzlick, R., & Combs, D. Medical examiner and coroner systems: History and trends. *JAMA. 279,* 11, 870–874, 1998.

Hanzlick, R., Combs, D., Parrish, R., & Ing, R. Death investigation in the United States, 1990: A survey of statutes, systems and educational requirements. *J Foren Sci. 38,* 3, 628–632, 1993.

Inman, K., & Rudin, N. *An Introduction to Forensic DNA Analysis.* New York: CRC Press. 1997.

James, S. H., & Eckert, W. G. *Interpretation of Bloodstain Evidence at Crime Scenes* (Second edition). Boca Raton, FL: CRC Press. 1998.

Lee, H. C., Ed. *Physical Evidence.* Enfield, CT: Magnani & McCormick. 1995.

Lee, H. C., & Tirnady, F. *Blood Evidence: How DNA Is Revolutionizing the Way We Solve Crimes.* Cambridge, MA: Perseus. 2003.

Smock, W. S. Forensic emergency medicine. In J. S. Olshaker, M. C. Jackson, & W. S. Smock, Eds. *Forensic Emergency Medicine.* Philadelphia: Lippincott Williams & Wilkins. 1999.

Standing Bear, Z. G. Forensic nursing and death investigation: Will the vision be co-opted? *J Psychosoc Nurs. 33,* 9, 59–64, 1995.

Taupin, J. M. Hair and fiber transfer in an abduction case: Evidence from different levels of trace evidence transfer. *J Foren Sci. 41,* 4, 697–699, 1996.

Thornton, J. I., & Kirk, P., Eds. *Crime Investigation* (2nd edition). New York: Wiley. 1974.

Turvey, B. *Criminal Profiling: An Introduction to Behavioral Evidence Analysis.* London: Academic Press. 1999.

Voelker, R. More expertise needed in death investigations. *JAMA. 273,* 15, 1164–1165, 1995.

13 Legal Nurse Consulting and Nursing Jurisprudence

CONTENTS

Legal nurse consultants (LNCs) have the opportunity to work on varying cases, ranging from medical malpractice and professional negligence, to personal injury cases, nursing home litigation, product liability, and forensic-related cases. The practice settings for LNCs vary, but all have the same principles in common: consultation and education, and performing liaison services among health care professionals, legal professionals, and any others involved where health care is at issue. Practice has expanded from medical malpractice, personal injury, and product liability to worker's compensation, risk management, and criminal law, just to name a few. An LNC might also single out a particular service not only for attorneys, but also for insurance companies, health care systems, or other independent consultants. Many have made a successful business specializing in a single service, such as medical research or locating expert witnesses. Other LNCs practice as life care planners, expert witnesses, crime scene investigators, licensing agency investigators, and government nurses.

13.1 THE LEGAL NURSE CONSULTANT

According to the American Association of Legal Nurse Consultants (AALNC), an LNC is a licensed RN who performs a critical analysis of health care facts and issues and their outcomes for the legal profession, health care professions, and others as appropriate. With a strong educational and experiential background, the LNC is qualified to assess adherence to standards of health care practice as it applies to the nursing and health care professions.

Meghan Persichino, RN, BSN, LNC, an independent LNC, says:

> Nurses who use their health professional experience and nursing knowledge to clarify health questions for an attorney do not practice law, nor do they fill any other legal role than that of health consultant for the case. An attorney may use a nurse for expert testimony in court, attendance at depositions and trials, or merely analyzing and researching health issues in the medical records. The function is decided by the LNC upon establishing his or her role.

She adds, "Before accepting a case for medical malpractice, negligence, personal injury, or other instances where health is involved, an attorney may ask a nurse to review the medical records and provide an opinion as to possible issues, and standard or substandard quality of care."

Persichino explains that LNCs are able to save the attorney invaluable time by "screening medical records for pertinent information, assessing the issues, providing a well-researched opinion, and even arranging the facts in a way that the physician would find most readable, should a medical expert need to be used." She continues, "The nurse serves as a knowledgeable liaison between the attorney and other medical experts. Many times, the nurse suggests the appropriate medical expert needed in a case review. This gives the attorney a better understanding of events and a more learned argument for him should he accept a case."

The LNC profession is growing, fueled by an increasingly litigious society, and the ever-increasing complexity of health care malpractice and negligence cases. The

AALNC, founded in 1989 and headquartered in Glenview, Illinois, has more than 4,000 members, and the Houston-based Medical-Legal Consulting Institute, Inc., claims to have trained more than 20,000 LNCs since it was founded in 1985 by Vickie Milazzo, RN, MSN, JD. Approximately half of the AALNC's members are in independent practice; about one quarter work in law firms; and another one quarter are employed in industry, government, HMOs, hospitals, or insurance companies. Many LNCs work part time when they are first getting started and then switch to full time once they have built a client base. Milazzo says fees range from $60 to $150 an hour for independent LNCs, and salaries for LNCs who work for employers are comparable to nursing salaries in a clinical setting. LNCs must be RNs, and Milazzo recommends that they have at least three years of nursing experience. They can become trained and certified in legal nurse consulting through the AALNC or other educational programs, such as Milazzo's institute.

The history of legal nurse consulting cannot be clearly delineated, according to Patricia W. Iyer, MSN, RN, LNCC, author *of Legal Nurse Consulting Principles and Practice* (2003), "since attorneys have sought nurses to answer questions for many years regarding medical-legal matters." Iyer adds, "Nurses' earliest and most common experiences in the legal arena have been as expert witnesses in nursing malpractice cases. As the courts began to recognize that nurses, rather than physicians, should define and evaluate the standard of nursing practice, nurses were sought to review cases and offer opinion testimony about nursing care." With the passage of time and the successful prosecution and defense of malpractice cases, Iyer adds, "The role of the expert nurse witness came to be recognized as an essential professional function. It was clear to both nurses and attorneys that nurses were uniquely qualified to aid attorneys in their medical-legal practices."

Iyer writes:

> Attorneys were searching for resources to help them understand medical records, medical literature, hospital policies and procedures, and medical testimony. Nurse consultants came to be valued as cost-effective alternatives to physician consultants, who were unavailable as a result of practice demands. Law firms began to employ nurses for their expertise. Attorneys began to value their input on a broader scope, not just medical and nursing negligence cases, but personal injury and criminal cases as well. Since then, the scope of practice of LNCs has considerably broadened from these areas.

13.2 THE TALES OF TWO LNCS

Connecticut nurse Prudence W. Schifley, RN, MA, CLNC, has blended a lifetime of nursing experience with her work as a certified LNC, specializing in child and elder abuse; psychiatry utilization review; and forensic, criminal, and paternity cases. She says that the desire to be a psychiatric nurse came to her when she was a youth after watching an old black-and-white film called *The Snakepit,* which depicted psychiatry and psychiatric hospitals. "It was at that point that I said to myself, 'I want to be a nurse so I can help people," Schifley recalls. "When I saw how horribly they were treated, and even though I knew it was a movie, I knew I had to become a nurse so that I could make a difference in psych patients' lives. And I think I have done that for more than 42 years."

Schifley added LNC work to her career at a time when she was dealing with her husband's illness and wanted to cut back on her hours at the hospital where she worked. "I wanted to be able to work per diem in the hospital and do something else that would afford me more flexible hours, and I thought that legal nurse consulting looked like a good field." Schifley attended training by Vickie Milazzo's Medical-Legal Consulting Institute, Inc. She says it was a "brutal" week of intense coursework, but at the end of those seven days, she emerged with a newfound need to succeed as an LNC. "I developed a burning desire to be able to say, 'I can do this,' and that I could do it as well as psych nursing, which I knew inside and out."

Schifley recalls her first case, laughing at the memory of a short-lived professional relationship. "I don't think the attorney for whom I did my first case liked what I did, because he paid me but he never called me back." She says that perhaps she had been too hasty, as the case had not yet gone to court. Schifley says she has been following it and observes:

> He had pooh-poohed some of the recommendations that I had made, but I noticed he is coming to terms with them more recently. He was a well-seasoned attorney with experience, and here I am, as green as grass; how in the world did I presume to tell him that, among other things, I thought he should not be using the treating physician as the expert witness in this case, that he needed someone else. So there were some things I recommended that he didn't like, but he didn't say anything to me.

Schifley wasn't going to give up on her career so easily, and began to make cold calls to attorney's offices to solicit LNC work, all the while recovering from the death of her husband in 2002 from full-organ failure caused by sepsis. "I made my first cold call to an attorney shortly after my husband died, and the attorney invited me to come into his office. That's the way I've gotten all my attorneys, believe it or not, from absolute cold calls." Coincidentally enough, the attorney discussed with Schifley a case of an older man who had died of sepsis and full-body organ failure. "Working on that case was cathartic for me," Schifley recalls. Since that initial case, Schifley has worked frequently with this attorney; she says that developing a bond with an attorney is one way to ensure repeat business.

Although not all attorneys are tough sells, Schifley says LNCs must work hard to prove their mettle to lawyers—and the occasional secretary working as a gatekeeper. "Some of them do not embrace us at all," she observes:

> In fact I once made a cold call to an attorney where I introduced myself to the receptionist, and wondered if the attorney had a moment to discuss how an LNC could assist him. The woman said, "We don't need any," and slammed down the phone in my ear. Many of them do not understand how LNCs can help them with cases. Most attorneys just want us to serve as experts and there are some of us who do not want to do that. I happen to be one who doesn't want to be an expert who testifies, as I am still working 40 hours a week. Any time I would have to take off for court would have to come out of my vacation time and I can't always get coverage. Right now I am very happy being a consulting expert and not a testifying expert.

Schifley says she believes some attorneys lack a basic understanding of the role of the LNC, and others might be biased based on misperceptions. "Some attorneys feel that their paralegals can do everything, and that they are able to interpret medical records and conduct research. Some of them have muddled through very well, while others have lost cases because of not having the complete understanding of the case or hiring the wrong experts. Some attorneys have gone so long over the years without needing the services of a legal nurse consultant, that they don't know what they are missing."

Schifley says that attorneys who think this way are missing out on the tremendous amount of expertise a nurse can bring to the table, as well as an increasing sense of authority. She explains:

> Nurses are advocates for the patient; they are the ones who have worked as the go-betweens of the doctors and the patients. Nurses are learning that they can speak up on behalf of the patient, even if it means not deferring to the physician. When I was in nursing school many years ago, when a doctor came to the nursing station, the nurse immediately stopped what she was doing and got up. She would say, "Here's a chair sir," "Let me get you the chart, sir," "Here's a pen, sir," "Is there anything I can help you with, sir?" Patients used to see their doctors as gods who could do no wrong and couldn't be questioned in any way for what they did and how they did it. Nursing has evolved since then; nurses are now supposed to be the eyes and ears of the doctor, and to report to the physician how that patient is doing. Nurses feel more comfortable, given this close contact with patients, in questioning what the physician does; not saying that the doctor has done anything wrong necessarily, but looking out for the patient and making sure that what the doctor did was what was intended. You could never do that years ago. As nursing has evolved, so has that role, and part of the oath we take is do no harm. If we see harm being done, and because nurses are caretakers, we need to speak up to see that things are rectified when necessary.

One such area of greater nurse involvement is in medical malpractice or professional negligence cases involving physicians and nurses. Iyer writes, "LNCs offer valuable informed assistance in the development of either the plaintiff or defense cases . . . The extensive education, analytical skills, and clinical experience of the seasoned LNC can contribute to business-like evaluation and informed assistance with professional negligence litigation." In these cases, the stakes are often very high, with professional reputations and licenses on the line. Iyer adds, "The LNC must perform a critical job in the face of powerful forces inherent in medical negligence work. The plaintiff may be profoundly injured, the family overwhelmed, and the amount of money at stake staggering." Making professional negligence a "tumultuous, demanding arena of LNC practice," Iyer writes, is everything from a prevailing social trend of viewing health care professionals as godlike deities and failing to participate in candid peer evaluation even in cases of gross negligence, to basing cases solely on jury appeal driven by the financial value of the plaintiff's injuries even when there has been no professional negligence. In these kinds of cases, Iyer says, LNCs must determine the following: Was there a duty for the defendant to provide care to the plaintiff? Was there a dereliction of that duty? Are there damages? Are the damages due to a direct result of the negligence of the provider?

In some cases, there might be adequate grounds to pursue a lawsuit, whereas in others, grounds might be entirely lacking, based on determinations made from the medical record and expert witness testimony. In cases of medical malpractice, Iyer says, the LNC must get used to determining negligence or causation, or lack thereof, and being able to deliver this kind of news to attorneys. Iyer writes:

> Many attorneys handling plaintiff claims are justifiably proud of their advocacy in the courtroom and believe that if they could "present their case in front of a jury," they would be able to make a great recovery. The attorney is and should be an advocate for the plaintiff's position. However, the LNC with unique knowledge and experience can often be most useful by playing the devil's advocate and reminding the attorney of the possible defenses he will face as the case moves forward . . . It will not be easy to remind an attorney that the child death case he is contemplating will require eight or 10 out-of-state depositions and three or four expensive, world-class experts to determine negligence and causation and could quite easily

cost more to pursue than the value of such a claim in his jurisdiction. Assuming this role takes assertiveness on the part of the LNC and may take some practice for the LNC to be comfortable. The LNC is uniquely qualified to fill this role and by doing so will elevate the profession of legal nurse consulting.

Much like nurses working in the ER, LNCs have many opportunities to work with forensic-related cases and the chance to hone their forensic antenna. Schifley says, "My forensic antenna is when my gut is telling me, 'Something is wrong here,' and I have to go and investigate it. I ask myself, 'What is my gut trying to tell me,' and I work through my intuition and what it may have to tell me regarding the facts or issues related to a case."

Like other subspecialties of forensic nursing, LNCs must be dedicated to lifelong learning. Schifley says, "I am constantly adding to the bulk of my knowledge," and urges others to do the same. Schifley's education took the circuitous, more scenic route. She graduated in 1963 from a nursing diploma program, and because her husband was in the military at the time, they were constantly roaming the globe. After settling back in the United States, Schifley found herself having to contend with three children at home, a mother-in-law suffering from the beginnings of Alzheimer's, and a mother with terminal cancer. She felt the walls beginning to close in on her. "I was feeling the effects of caretaker fatigue, and knew I wanted to go back to school," Schifley says. "I started at the associate's level and went all the way through with exception of three credits short of an associate's degree and certification in geriatrics. I said to heck with this, I am going on. Off I went to what is now called Eastern Connecticut State University; while they didn't offer anything in nursing they would accept everything from nursing school. I thought I'd get a degree in social work, and I did so in applied social relations." Schifley continues:

I did a year-long internship with the Department of Children and Families in Connecticut, working in protective services and doing child abuse investigations as well as conducting court studies for termination of parental rights. I loved every minute of it. I continued to work full time, and in 1978 or 1979, I earned my BA in applied social relations. I continued to work, not really knowing what I wanted to do next, and feeling a growing restlessness within me. I was working as the charge nurse on the psych unit; we didn't have a social worker there and that worked out very well for me because I was able to perform in a similar capacity—it was an ideal combination of nursing and social work. I was interested in pursuing a master's degree, so I started in a dual master's program in counseling and in nursing. I took some of the core courses for a master's in nursing but I thought to myself, "This going to take too long, I am getting too old, let's finish it up in counseling." By that time I was working as a case manager; I had developed a program for the chronically mentally ill to be able to work and live in the community independently. I truly found my niche, and continued in that program for 19 years.

When Schifley developed arthritis and could no longer walk up and down the stairs of the tenements she visited, she began conducting case utilization review and care management in the behavioral health unit of the hospital where she started her career initially—a job she holds still.

Working in legal nurse consulting and case management simultaneously is a plus, Schifley says, because it keeps her current in the health care process and health care policy. She says, "I think an LNC still needs to be clinically active because technology in nursing and medicine is changing so quickly. You must keep your foot in clinical somehow, and not just from reading and doing research; while these are vital components of the work, I think you must actually get out there and do it. In all good conscience, you have to remain clinically active and up to date."

Staying current in nursing is essential to the success of LNC work because of the LNC's scrutiny of the medical record and the ability to detect documentation that does not reflect proper clinical technique. It is the real-world experience, Schifley says, that enables LNCs to perform to their own high expectations. "The schools taught me nothing about legal nurse consulting... it's all real-world experience," Schifley confirms:

The only thing that prepared me for the field somewhat was the documentation courses that were drilled into our heads in nursing school. I'm not convinced that proper documentation is emphasized to nurses nowadays as it was back then, including what is appropriate and what is not appropriate to chart. I see so much generalization in charts these days; I look at medical record entries by the nurse, the social worker, and the doctor, and it's as if I'm looking at three different patients.

Clinicians must go back to the basic documentation lessons that taught you how to describe a patient's mental or physical state. You can say that the patient is depressed, the patient is delusional, the patient is agitated, but those are just descriptive words; clinicians must add "as evidenced by," such as "Patient is agitated as evidenced by..." or "Patient is delusional as evidenced by...." instead. You may know what you are talking about, and someone else may know what you are talking about, but the chart should make some sort of sense to anybody who picks up the chart, and show evidence of the behavior or the mood of the patient.

In forensic cases, Schifley adds, documentation becomes absolutely critical:

When clinicians are talking about bruising, for example, they must be very careful. The grading of bruising according to color and related to time is tricky; we now know not to base any conclusions about the timeline of the injury on a bruise's color. It is not sufficient to write, "Bruising on the arm." Clinicians must describe in detail where the bruise is on the body, and describe its size, color, and everything that they are seeing. When you are looking at a body, whether it's a living body or a dead body, the body is considered to be the crime scene in forensics. Clinicians must be as descriptive as possible so that their narrative tells the story, and the who, what, when, where, how, and why.

It's similar to when I am looking at a chart for the chief state's attorney's office, or for the Medicare fraud unit on elder abuse in nursing homes; much of the work has to do with wounds and decubiti. Because decubiti progress through the four stages so quickly, sometimes in a matter of days, I look for documentation of all the stages and see what is missing. Decubiti progress very quickly, especially in someone who is malnourished and dehydrated, so I look for charting of this progression. Whatever it is I am looking at in the medical record, whether it is an autopsy report or crime scene photos, I say to it, "OK, tell me what you are trying to tell me." I tell it, "Talk to me," and many times, what it is *not* saying is speaking as loud as what is visible in the record. In fact, sometimes it is speaking louder than what is visible. When I go over the medical records for the third time I am saying to myself, "What am I missing here?" "What is the record trying to tell me?" The medical record is an LNC's crime scene. It doesn't necessarily mean a crime was committed, because you can go through that chart and say there was nothing wrong done here. But that is as much a crime scene as a body is a crime scene or an accident is a crime scene; whatever your specialty area is, becomes your crime scene and your forensic area of expertise.

Schifley waxes philosophical about her work:

I see society at its worst but also at its best. I am ever the optimist, even when I am dealing with the most horrible things like intentional negligence or abuse. I am always optimistic that there is going to be a good outcome. I am optimistic that those who are responsible will in some way have to make amends. If I can make a difference for one patient, or if I have opened one person's eyes, or if I have affected one person in any way, then my purpose has been achieved. Justice will take care of itself. I believe that a case is only as good as the information that is collected and disseminated to the jury. It's up to the people doing the collection and the disseminating to do the best job they can, and for me to do the very best that I can on every case. If I do my best and a little bit more, then hopefully that will get disseminated to others so those coming along behind me will not have such a struggle as the ones of us who are just starting out.

Schifley explains that impeccable performance on the job will continue to uphold the good name that LNCs have created for themselves thus far:

When I walk into the chief state's attorney's office to meet with the team with whom I work, I am treated with so much respect for the knowledge that I bring to them in prosecuting these cases, both civil and criminal. My opinions are respected, and they are asked for. For example, the nurse attorney with whom I work is wonderful. We work as a team; she will ask me a question, which sets me off to find the answer, either within the chart or within independent research I do, or by finding someone who can help me understand the subject better. It's all about teamwork, working with investigators and attorneys and support staff to gain the best understanding of a case that we can. Each person, because of his or her expertise in a certain area, is an integral part of the team working on behalf of the client. Everybody's input makes case preparation complete. Each member has to do his or her job to the best of their abilities so the next person can do his or her job along the continuum. It's like a cog of a wheel; if one piece is not working well or is missing, then things don't go smoothly.

Collaboration is not reserved only for the legal team; Schifley emphasizes that LNCs in any community should work together to promote their specialty and assist each other with cases:

I belong to the Connecticut Council of LNCs, a grassroots group of about 16 or 17 people. We got together to do marketing because it can be so expensive. We pay annual dues and all of the money is pooled together to fund our marketing efforts. Not only do we market as a group of certified LNCs, we have a central access number, enabling any attorney to call in and be directed immediately to an LNC who specializes in sexual assault cases or pediatric cases, or whatever the need is.

Schifley explains that there is much camaraderie among LNCs in her area, fostering the ability to consult one another's expertise when necessary:

One of my colleagues called me up and said, "Can I run a case by you? There is something wrong here. The attorney wants to know is there a standard for someone who was having difficulty swallowing, and for the head of the bed to be kept up after eating." She told me that the patient had aspirated and died. While we were talking it came out that the patient really hadn't aspirated, but there was something else going on. The patient was on an antipsychotic medication that can cause diabetes; he had a blood sugar of 1,200, was having difficulty swallowing, and was not with-it in the head. Those were the only signs and symptoms that the attorney was looking at. I said to my colleague, "That patient was on a problematic medication and he was not being monitored." It took her forever to convince the attorney that the medication needed to be looked at, and the further we got into the record, it showed that the patient was sneaking food off of other people's plates, he was urinating on the floor all of the time, and the clinicians were putting it down in the medical record as simply inappropriate, bizarre, willful behavior because he had been told many times not to do those things. If you look at all of these signs . . . the guy is thirsty, he has increased hunger, he has polyurea . . . those are the clinical signs of diabetes. But do you think anybody did a check before he was put on this medication, or check his blood sugar while he was on it, or monitor his liver function? Absolutely not. Yet the attorney focused on the fact he aspirated because of the level of the head of the bed. The attorney was thrilled when my colleague went back with all this other information. It was a hard sell to begin with because he was so focused on a red herring, but the medical record told the truth about what had happened.

Despite the pressures of the work, Schifley reports that she tries to take the stress in stride, especially to avoid feelings of burnout experienced so frequently by many career nurses. The trick, according to Schifley, is recognizing when one needs a break—if the individual can tear himself or herself away from it long enough, that is. Schifley points to a particularly disturbing nursing home case she is working on and says, "There is something about this case that when I get working on it, I can't stop working on it. It's like not being able to stop eating potato chips—I just can't stop. It can be 2 a.m. and I'll still be working, getting completely caught up in the work." Schifley says she has created a comfortable workstation at home, fashioning a functional work space out of a lounge chair fitted with a desktop that spans the arms of the chair, courtesy of her son's carpentry abilities. From here, she works away contentedly, letting the facts of a case swirl around her as she digests the issues and maps out her strategies. Every once in a while, however, the cases are so nightmarish that she says she feels a welling up of anger and disgust from deep inside her:

When I get to a point where I am on overload, or if I can't help but get angry at what I am reading, or when I don't know whether I should be crying or vomiting over what I just read in the medical record—and that is how bad some of these cases are—I say to myself, "OK, I am to that point where I need to put my work down and step away for a while for a breather." Then I'll run as fast as I can to my grandchildren and my family because there's nothing more healing and grounding than that. It restores your soul to goodness. Then I come back refreshed and go at it for another eight to 10 hours. The case I am working on now has probably made the most impact on my life because it documents a case of inhumane cruelty to another person. I think it's unbelievable how doctors and nurses can allow things like this to happen.

We're all human, we all make mistakes. Some mistakes are so little that they have no bearing on the outcome of anything, but some mistakes are made that are huge, catastrophic mistakes. And sometimes bad things happen just because they happen, such as in surgery when there is a bad outcome. The cases that really bother me are those of intentional cruelty, the immense cruelty that was placed on defenseless elderly people who needed to be respected and loved and cared for. But I am always careful that my personal feelings never show and never overshadow my work. It's a fine line that all LNCs walk sometimes because as nurses, we care so much.

Half a dozen states to the south is recent Massachusetts transplant Constance A. Morrison, MS, CNS, MBA, JD, SANE, who is shaping the coordinator of the master's and postmaster's nurse practitioner in psychiatry program at East Tennessee State University (ETSU). Moving from the medical mecca of Boston to the Smoky Mountains was a cultural shift she took to very easily, and Morrison says she is enjoying the opportunity to craft a forensic-driven psych nursing program in a progressive environment. Says Morrison:

One of the reasons I came to ETSU is that the dean of the nursing school is very open to new and creative ideas in education. To have that environment and in a nursing educational institution to boot, was very enticing to me. There isn't an idea that I don't bring forth to the department and they say, "Why don't you go for it, investigate it." A new forensic center is being constructed at the medical school, and when I mentioned my interest to the dean, she said, "Why don't you call them up and take a tour?" It's been a wonderfully open environment.

Morrison's background in forensic nursing, coupled with her desire to develop a health care certificate program in forensics, provides her with the impetus to make forensic science an important component of her work at the university. She adds that ETSU has been very supportive of her desire to take a death investigation course, one of the elements not encompassed by her master's degrees in forensic science and forensic nursing, and that this kind of nurturing environment is ideal for fostering creative approaches to nursing curriculum. Morrison feels strongly that higher institutions must work hard to recruit and retain their high-caliber students:

One of the things I enjoy about being here is ETSU's support of their students. The school is constantly looking at ways to help students through technology, and it constantly asks itself, what can we do to foster the education of a student who wants to become a registered nurse? Or an RN who wants to get a nurse practitioner degree? Or an RN who wants to get a doctorate degree? The school has the same kind of caring and retention for its faculty as it does its students.

In this empowered environment, Morrison says, students are able to learn about the empowerment of their patients. "In psychiatry, we meet many of our people who have either fallen victim to violence or who are perpetrators of violence, and we, as nurses, have an obligation to care for all people," she says. "We don't make the distinction that this is a perpetrator or this is a victim. The distinction is, this is my patient. And all of our patients could be us, but by the grace of God, so my aim is to be sure that the students know that patients could be them or members of their family, that patients are ordinary people, except that the biochemistry in their brains has gone awry." Morrison continues, "When that happens, there is treatment for them, there is psychotherapy for them, there is psycho-pharmacology . . . it's the combination of both, along with a caring staff, that will make the difference."

Morrison says her role is to help the nurse role model this concept for other allied health care personnel, and in doing so, continue to fine-tune the nurse practitioner psychiatric program, which began in January 2005. She recalls:

> I remember when I was getting my nurse practitioner postmaster's certificate at the State University of New York, SUNY, and I had a wonderful preceptor who has turned into a longtime mentor and colleague. He said to me, "You know, as a nurse, you're all things to a person. You're the nurse, you're the psycho-pharmacologist, the psychotherapist, the social worker; you are talking about medications, looking into housing options, working on cognitive behavioral skills, so you're always going to be all things to all people." I've never forgotten that, and maybe that's why I believe that my passion, my mission, and my job are all rolled up into one. It's the same with forensic nursing, which intersects with psychiatric nursing; as the program progresses, I hope to introduce more of the principles of forensic psychiatric nursing into the curriculum.

Perhaps it's the work as a nurse attorney in her background that peeks out from time to time, but Morrison believes it is in the nursing student's best interest to have a firm grounding in the law:

> The word *forensic* means pertaining to the course of justice and pertaining to the law. All of our nurses will have a good understanding of the law. They will understand their state's nurse practice act, and they will understand the laws which govern their nursing practice. They will comprehend the basics of laws that govern patients for whom they care. Psychiatric nursing is one specialty to which forensic nursing is closely aligned, in terms of mentally ill offenders, incarcerated individuals, criminal personalities . . . psych nursing is one area where forensic nursing has a definite place and a comfortable fit.
>
> Nurses also must be very aware of mandated reporting per state law when it comes to child and elder abuse, so these are the principles we are teaching our nurses. In their psychiatric practice, they go into agencies and into the community and work with the mentally ill and there is a definite grounding in the respect for patients and their rights; it is the nurse's obligation to be that advocate for the patient. Unless the nurse understands the obligation she has, the contract she has with the people of her state to provide safe and legally responsible care. And that kind of care requires a background in psych, forensic nursing, law . . . making every nurse a forensic nurse in some regard.

Morrison says she shares this message with nurses so that they can embrace their heritage as forensic nurses:

> When I walk into a room full of nurses, I say to them, "My name is Constance Morrison; I am a forensic nurse and so are you." And they look at me and say, "No I'm not. What is she talking about?" You can see them lean over to the person next to them and you see the elbow nudge. And I say, "Let me tell you why everyone in this room is a forensic nurse." I tell them what forensic means, and that forensic nursing is more than just dead bodies. I say, "Why are you a forensic nurse?" and I proceed to tell them, "If you worked in the ER, you have probably seen your share of motor vehicle accidents. The police investigate, and your nurses' notes and medical records are probably going to end up in court at some time." Or I say, "OK, so you work on a med-surg unit where nobody has a bullet hole in them, and nobody got stabbed, but guess what, a man came in for treatment because he had an accident at work and your notes and his medical records are going to the worker's compensation board." That's why I talk to them very carefully about their documentation. Yes, it is for medical and clinical purposes, but it also has legal ramifications. I talk to them about how every time your medical record goes to someone who is involved in any legal aspect—civil or criminal—then you are a forensic nurse. If you are involved in transplants, that's a medico-legal case. If you are involved in the correctional system or psych nursing, or work in the ER, the OR, med-surg, acute care, critical care, your records have a good chance of showing up in a court of law some day. So that's why every nurse is a forensic nurse, and every nurse must be familiar with the law and how it impacts health care and nursing practice. I tell them, "So, you have been practicing forensic nursing for years and you don't even know it." And then I see the light bulbs over their heads light up—they suddenly get it, and they get on board with the concept. I also remind them that it's not just about sexual assault and domestic violence and child abuse—it's about the everyday living, and how we interact with and care for our patients in whatever situation they are in. It goes to the very core of nursing practice. I remind them, "The moment you set your pen to paper or you click a mouse, you are performing a legal aspect of nursing for the benefit of your patient. Therefore, you are all forensic nurses." We just need to get the word out, we just need to have people embrace it and we need to continue teaching it and I know that by the next century, we will get there.

Morrison shares a belief in the forensic antenna, and say it works equally well for psych nurses and nurse practitioners:

> What I tell everybody is, when they are in nursing school, they have these little nubs that grow on their head. They sometimes get a little itchy and they keep growing and all of a sudden, graduation day comes or pinning day comes and they get these fully formed antennas. With them they get this amazing sense of intuition, a gut feeling about when something might be wrong. It's when they are able to say to themselves, "Gee, I need to investigate this." Or, "I think something needs to be done here." The two groups of professionals who have these antennae are police officers and nurses. They can run with that kind of freedom of intuition. Nurses can go all the way with patient questioning and reading histories and talking to families. They have so many tools available to them, they can be inquisitive and they can do so because they have the best interests of patients at heart. Nurses see things and hear things and are able to investigate things that probably no one else can.

Getting to that point takes education and training, but it also takes stamina and belief in being able to steer one's own course in life. Like Prudence Schifley, Morrison took the more scenic, circuitous route, and gave herself time to find her own voice and her own unique calling:

> Because I was a lawyer for almost as many years as I was a nurse; I did take the circuitous route. I went to nursing school and got my LCN, my associate-degree RN, and my bachelor's degree, and then I pursued my MBA and JD. It was years later after I had been a lawyer that I went to get my postmaster's degree. I personally have never encountered any restraints on my pursuit of my education and my career. One of the things I always want to do is empower my students to be able to be vocal about their needs, to work on behalf of their beliefs, to let their voices be heard, and be able to pursue the education and interests that are right for them. I always tell them, "Don't let anybody step on your voice, because once they do, they are stepping on your patient." Nurses are far more visible and vocal, and there is renewed enthusiasm and hope for the profession. I once heard that one in every 50 votes is cast by a nurse; based on that statistic, that's a lot of power out there. We must have more education in the forensic arena so that nurses will have the competencies and the self-confidence to do great things.

13.3 THE SCOPE OF PRACTICE OF LNCS

According to the AALNC, the primary role of the legal nurse consultant is to "evaluate, analyze, and render informed opinions on the delivery of health care and the resulting outcomes." Parameters of practice can include the following:

- Facilitating communication and strategizing with the legal professional for successful resolution among parties
- Educating attorneys about the health-care-related facts and issues involved in the case
- Researching and integrating medical and nursing literature related to the issues of the case
- Reviewing, summarizing, and analyzing medical records to compare and correlate them to the allegations
- Assessing damages and causation relative to liability
- Identifying, locating, evaluating, and conferring with expert witnesses
- Interviewing witnesses and other parties in medically related cases under the supervision of an attorney
- Drafting legal documentation in medically related cases under the supervision of an attorney
- Developing collaborative case strategies
- Providing support during discovery, depositions, trial, and other legal proceedings
- Supporting the adjudication process

Standards of practice encompass assessment, analysis and issue identification, outcome identification, planning, implementation, and evaluation. The LNC is responsible for demonstrating high levels of quality of practice, performance, education, collegiality, ethics, collaboration, research, and resource management.

Iyer says that LNCs should be well versed in numerous aspects of law, nursing, and medicine, as well as issues relating to patient care, legal claims, and litigation. Iyer (2003) writes, "It is extremely important that the LNC be well read on such topics as managed care, case management, health care administrative concerns and issues, advanced practice issues, and health care policy. There are the legal 'hot' buttons that are being pressed in today's judicial arena." Iyer explains that LNCs will encounter practice issues involving civil law, criminal law, contract law, and tort law. Iyer defines civil law as "law that applies to the rights of individuals, whereas criminal law deals with offenses against the general public." She adds that "criminal law is created to provide guidance and protection to those injured by offense against society." In any criminal action, the level of proof required is "beyond a reasonable doubt," which Iyer says must be 51 percent or more; in medical malpractice claims (civil tort law), the proof is met by a "preponderance of the evidence." Iyer defines contract law as involving "agreements between parties, individuals, and entities." Tort law, Iyer adds, "encompasses negligence, personal injury, and medical malpractice claims. A tort is a wrongful act that is committed by someone or an entity that causes injury to another person or property." Whereas tort law remedies attempt to compensate in the form of a monetary award, criminal law seeks to fine or imprison an individual. Negligence is a significant component of tort law, defined as "a failure to act as an ordinary prudent person would do under similar circumstances." Iyer explains that four elements of negligence must be proved for a malpractice claim to have viability:

1. A duty must be owed to the patient (usually in the form of the provision of care and treatment).
2. There is a breach of duty or standard of care by the professional.
3. A causal connection must be evident between the breach of duty and the harm of damages that occurred to the plaintiff.
4. Damages or injuries must be sustained by the plaintiff.

Professional negligence is different from ordinary negligence because professionals are held to a different standard of care. Iyer writes, "When professionals are the subject or focus of a claim or lawsuit, the LNC must determine the appropriate professional standards of care that apply to the situation." Iyer explains that standard of care refers to what is accepted as "reasonable" under the circumstances. "The standard of care is that degree of skill, care, and judgment used by an ordinary prudent health care provider under similar circumstances," Iyer writes. Standards of care can be further defined through standard of care manuals from the ANA, or they can be as varied as state practice guidelines, material in textbooks, policies and procedures, equipment manuals, job descriptions, code regulations, and standards from organizations such as the JCAHO. According to Iyer, liability for health care providers can reside in diagnostic errors and issues related to treatment, communication, monitoring, supervision, medication, falls, restraints, and the like.

13.4 THE LNC AND THE MEDICAL RECORD

Iyer (2003) writes, "LNCs spend many hours reviewing, analyzing, and preparing medical records for litigation." She adds that these nurses should know what comprises a medical record to ascertain what might be missing from it. They should know whether a record is obtainable and how to procure it, and lastly, they should know basic rules of evidence that control the admissibility of the record in a court of law. Medical records are comprised of administrative data and clinical data, including everything from admission and discharge sheets, to diagnoses, consent forms, history and physical, physician's orders, progress notes, surgical reports, and nurses' notes. D'Andrea, D'Amico, and Davis (2003, as cited in Iyer, 2003) explain that "the primary role of the LNC is the evaluation, analysis, and rendering of informed opinions on the delivery of health care and the resulting outcomes. This is accomplished in part by reviewing, summarizing, and analyzing medical records and other pertinent health care and legal documents and comparing them to and correlating them with the allegations of the complaint." They emphasize that LNCs are particularly important to attorneys who are unable to review and interpret medical records. They add, "Small but highly significant details can be overlooked, with potentially disastrous results during discovery and at trial."

The LNC must first determine the allegations of the case and identify the disputed medico-legal issues; in doing so, the LNC collects data to support the systematic assessment of health care issues related to a claim. Once the allegations have been determined, it will become evident which medical records will be needed for a comprehensive evaluation of the case. In most states, before the medical record can be introduced into evidence, it must be complete, accurate, and authenticated, according to D'Andrea et al. (2003, as cited in Iyer, 2003). Specific types of medical records that should be considered for inclusion include heart monitor strips, radiographic films, videotapes or photographic documentation, EMS transport records, autopsy records, billing records, ER and OR logs, pharmaceutical and laboratory reports, EKG monitor strips, medical records dictation logs, and any other specialty records. In especially complex cases, the LNC might find it helpful to create an outline of important events during the initial review of the medical record, which will in turn guide the LNC through a more systematic review of the various components of a medical record, including the following:

- Face sheet and diagnostic related grouper (DRG)
- Consent forms
- Discharge summary and instructions
- History and physical examination
- Operative records and reports
- Anesthesia records
- Surgical pathology reports
- Reports related to consultations
- Physician progress notes
- Radiology reports
- Laboratory records
- Physician's orders
- Nurses' notes
- Nursing care plan
- Ongoing documentation

The LNC must also be aware of several challenges inherent to the review of medical records, including the detection of altered medical records, falsified entries, fabricated medical records, and concealment of medical records. According to D'Andrea et al. (2003, as cited in Iyer, 2003), "The plaintiff can use altered medical records to establish liability based upon the defendant's conscious wrongdoing. Juries do not respond favorably to intentional record alteration, and exposing such actions frequently leads to an award of punitive damages. Falsification of medical records can be the basis for both criminal indictment and civil liability for damages suffered."

A common alteration is a late entry; the LNC should secure a copy of the hospital's late-entry policy to facilitate determination if the late entry is valid. Falsified entries consist of entries that are back-dated or altered at a later date, and the LNC must scrutinize the rest of the medical record for supporting data to prove attempts at falsification. Fabrication of medical records involves inventing a set of circumstances in retrospect to justify the clinical outcome of a health care provider's actions. Fabrication can involve the rewriting or replacing of physician's or nurse's notes, most often seen in acute situations such as cardiac arrests or untimely deaths due to unrecognized problems, according to D'Andrea et al. (2003, as cited in Iyer, 2003). Omissions also constitute alteration of a medical record, as do illegible entries that contribute to negligence.

A critical component of the LNC's role is to assemble a summary of the medical records that conveys the most accurate and comprehensive view of the facts and issues related to the case. The summary can include an outline of the facts of the case or a short narrative of the issues involved, as well as a chronology of events and any pertinent charts, graphs, or diagrams to further explain the content of the medical record. "While there are many different LNC approaches and attorney preferences to medical record summaries," D'Andrea et al. write, "most attorneys want to read an analysis that not only gives a concise overview of the facts and issues, but also helps them to understand the bottom line quickly." They add:

> LNCs must overcome the temptation to tell the attorney/client what he or she wants to hear. Not only would this be unethical and dishonest, but it would do undeserved harm to other parties. Instead, a thorough and competent medical record analysis will list the strengths and weaknesses of the client's position. The medical record summary and analysis should always be followed with conclusions and recommendations to assist the attorney in determining how he or she wishes to proceed.

Forensic nurses should take a cue from the LNC when it comes to examining their own documentation in the health care setting. ER nurse Linda McCracken, RN, emphasizes:

> As a nurse, the minute you put your pen to paper, you must remember that this record could end up going to court. It is essentially your legal testimony, so nurses must get their documentation right. Nurses shouldn't chart forensically; they shouldn't use the word "alleged" or describe the patient as a "victim of domestic violence," because how do you know that this is definitely the case? Always chart exactly what the patient said, in their words.

One of the most critical aspects of nursing—proper documentation—is a concept introduced to students in the earliest exposure to nursing principles and practice and bears great importance in the medico-legal process. Nurses must chart in a comprehensive, detail-oriented manner. That's the theory, but in reality, timely and thorough charting frequently is low on the priority list for rushed health care providers. "Time and the overload of work nurses must do daily are factors affecting charting," acknowledges Jackie W. Palmer, RN, CEN, a consultant and lecturer on medico-legal issues. "We always must bear in mind that caring for the patient is the most important thing. Documentation truly does become secondary to patient-care priorities." Palmer agrees that the old adage, "If it wasn't documented, it didn't happen," is how the legal community views documentation, but says, "Healthcare professionals know that's not the case but that's the way it is looked at in court." Nurses must balance real-world clinical imperatives with legal imperatives, and it's a fine line forensic nurses must walk daily. "In our litigious society, documentation protects patients' well-being and nurses' livelihoods," Palmer says, adding that ironically, the charting methods health care facilities often impose on their nurses are an obstacle to that mission.

"One of the primary things that negatively impacts a nurse's charting is the very way in which facilities may require them to document patient care," Palmer adds. "A significant number of facilities utilize charting by exception, which is, from a legal viewpoint, the worst kind of charting because nurses never write down anything that's normal. It may be that what is normal is what is crucial to document," Palmer says:

> When I am reviewing a chart for an attorney, I get the records months or years after an adverse clinical event and I have to decipher what happened. Information may have been documented on multiple pieces of paper within that chart that I have to cross-reference to figure out the sequence of events at the time. In today's hospital setting, that documentation is not always done by the same individual. In specialty areas such as the ER and the ICU, most documentation is done by the nurse taking care of the patient. However, on some general-floor areas, the vast majority of the charting is done by nonnurses, the unlicensed assistive personnel who are the ones that take vital signs and get the patient up to walk, feed, or bathe. The RN may chart based upon his or her own observations, speaking to the patient or the family, or it may be nothing more than a chart check, depending on the RN's workload. On a large postsurgical floor, there may be 40-plus patients, two RNs, and all other staff are unlicensed.

According to Palmer, "Documentation becomes a nearly impossible task and that's where you can get into trouble." Palmer thinks that forensic training creates a heightened awareness of the medico-legal aspects of nurses' jobs and that forensic nurses might be better at charting, but not because of fear of litigation. "I don't teach nurses to chart because they may go to court; I teach them to chart because if they don't write it down, how is the next person taking care of that patient going to know what you did?" Palmer explains:

> In deposition, or on examination, an attorney may ask how the lack of charting a response to a breathing treatment in the ER days before the patient is discharged and subsequently dies at home is relevant to the outcome. The explanation is that nothing in nursing is done in a vacuum; it is a continuum of care. If it begins without adequate information, that is going to impact the rest of the patient's care. You can say, "I did that," but there's nothing to prove that you did if you don't write it down.

It might be hard to believe, but Palmer says thorough charting is not something that every clinician espouses. "I have been chastised by some of my peers and managers because they say I write too much," she says. "They are not going to make me chart any less than I do. If they have a problem with it, that's defensiveness on their part. They know they are not charting as much as I am and they're concerned that my amount of charting is going to make them look bad. That's not my problem, and I will do what I know is right. I teach my students to do it the right way, and after that, it is their choice." Palmer says nurses might have the willingness to chart, but lack of knowledge about what to chart keeps them from thorough documentation:

> We are all taught specific lingo; we think we know what it means but I have seen a significant number of incorrect terms documented. If you don't know the meaning of a term, don't use it. Another hazard in documentation is abbreviations. I see a lot of nurses using nonstandardized abbreviations, and even standardized terms don't mean the same thing from one facility to another. "SOB" is a classic—does it stand for "short of breath," "side of bed," or the other meaning? What if the SOB is SOB at the SOB? People tend to use shorthand that is not communicable across the continuum.

The need for clear and accurate charting becomes all the more important if a case goes to court. Palmer emphasizes that a pivotal factor for health care providers named as defendants is the ability to go back years after the fact and know what they meant when they wrote the notes in the chart:

> It can be 25 years after you cared for a patient that you have to look at your notes and figure out what you did. Attorneys hire consultants to look at nursing notes and they try to depose every named respondent if he or she can be found. If they can't be found, all you have is what they wrote. I grew up in an era of narrative charting as opposed to charting by exception and computerized checklist charting, and narrative charting gives you much more to go on.

Technology is revolutionizing the way nurses chart, but just how nurse-friendly the new computerized charting software is depends on how the system is set up, Palmer says:

> The only way to make it nurse-friendly is to have nurses directly involved in setting up the system. If it's set up by nonnursing personnel, it can be a nightmare. If it is set up by nurses, for the most part, it is fairly nurse-friendly but it seems there's always going to be a bug in the system somewhere. I have worked with several computerized charting systems so far and have found things I liked and disliked about all of them. Usually what I dislike is it didn't give me the opportunity to add something I thought was important. In that case there is supposed to be a place for the nurse to input narratives because a checkmark doesn't explain anything. I know that in many ways, checklists are a great boon; if I am doing a routine every-two-hour check on a patient and they are no different than they were two hours ago, that's great. But if they are different, then there has to be some mechanism in place for me to chart these differences and anything else I believe is pertinent.

Sometimes the best technology and the most thorough charting can't prevent one of the biggest enemies of documentation—tampering. "From a forensic standpoint, anything can be tampered with," Palmer says:

> Imagine the scenario of a chart where a crucial passage, critical to the legal case, is charted in a completely different tone and aspect from the rest of the chart. Something like that is an instant red flag even to the least experienced litigator. Everybody forgets to write things down and everybody makes mistakes, but there are appropriate mechanisms in place for dealing with that. If you forget to chart something, you are able to return to the record and amend it but you need to indicate that you have gone back at a later date and amended it. You don't go back and erase anything. You write, "Late entry," including the date and time you are making an amendment to the original record. If you make a mistake, you cross through it with one line, initial it and write the correct entry. Writing in the wrong chart can happen to anybody. Nursing can be chaotic and a lot of charting is retroactive, unfortunately. You can't always chart everything extemporaneously, although that is the goal.

One of the most important forensic implications of charting is objectivity in describing injuries, taking care not to diagnose but to detail what is observed from a clinical standpoint. "Everyone knows that a vast majority of what a nurse actually does at the bedside is of a diagnostic nature," Palmer acknowledges, emphasizing that this traditional modus operandi must take a back seat to objectivity:

> I know when I look at a patient who has a fire-engine red throat, has a temperature of 103, can't swallow and I can see their tonsils, they probably have tonsillitis secondary to a bacterial infection. I function with that understanding; however, what I chart is not tonsillitis. It's the color of the throat, the temperature they have, the complaints they have stated—not the interpretation of it. In forensic applications, that is particularly important when we look at wounds. I teach people how to identify bite marks but I constantly tell them you cannot write, "This is a bite mark." What you have to write is exactly what you see: an area that has bruising that is so many centimeters by so many centimeters, located at this anatomical location and is this color. Now, if the patient gives you a statement that corroborates what you see, the appropriate forensic term is, "is consistent with patient statement of." If a patient has a bite mark and they tell me they were bitten in that spot, I must describe in detail what I see and then I can say, "is consistent with patient statement he or she was bitten." You have to be really specific and that is difficult for many health care providers because it involves a lot more writing than they are used to and they are pressed for time. When I teach, I ask my students, "Who do you work for?" Your employer is the hospital but you are working for the patient.

Charleston County, South Carolina deputy coroner Bobbi Jo O'Neal says it can be beneficial for nurses to maintain a legal mindset at all times. She says that when she was working in the ER and specifically conducting a sexual assault evidentiary exam, going to court would be foremost in her mind as she performed the exam, but adds, "If I was just doing a regular ER case, medico-legal issues never really crossed my mind, which is interesting because now that I am in a coroner's role, I review a lot of ER records. Sometimes I've even had to read my own writing," she says, laughing. "A discharged patient may have died several years later and I happen to be investigating the case; I look back at the ER records and there are my nurse's notes in the medical record. At the time, I didn't think anything of it because I was simply doing my job, and we also did not have a forensic protocol about documenting injury, etcetera, although there were discussions that maybe we should." O'Neal adds:

> In hindsight, I can see where some of the things that are really important don't seem to get documented in the medical record, whether patients are in the ER or anywhere else in the hospital. These kinds of forgotten details can include documentation about the presence of family members or others at the patient's bedside; information like that can really help us down the road, especially with child cases such as Munchausen by proxy syndrome where we need to determine if the parents did or didn't come to the hospital or were in the room. Sometimes it not necessarily about the person, it's the surrounding environment that can be important. If someone is not asking that question, they may not recognize that we even want to know this information in the first place.

O'Neal says that she frequently sees inadequate documentation in the medical record:

> Many health care providers just don't document very much at all. It seems to be very short and sweet. They are not very good about documenting timeframes in the nurse's notes, so when you are trying to reconstruct timelines, it can be very difficult to create a proper chronology of events. And if they have a late entry, they need to indicate properly that it is a late entry. Forensic investigators love their timelines, and when entries don't match up, it will be questioned.

Regarding terminology, O'Neal advises nurses to take great care in how they phrase their findings:

> From an ER department perspective, I'm not sure we would want clinicians attempting to write forensically. If they are not absolutely certain as to what they are seeing, they need to say it in general terms. They should write what they see as opposed to trying to explain it. They need to remember that they would have to explain and defend these entries on the witness stand in court. An attorney would say, "Nurse so and so, you wrote such and such... are you an expert in this? Was it blunt-force trauma or was it a head injury?" They are not the ones who should be documenting it from a criminal or legal standpoint.

13.5 THE LNC AND FORENSIC CASES

It is in forensic-related and criminal law cases where the nurse is able to put to use his or her understanding of the intersection of medicine, nursing, and law. Criminal-case analysis performed by the LNC is most likely to encompass cases having to do with child abuse, elder abuse, domestic violence, sexual assault, driving under the influence, and death investigation. For each type of forensic case, Davis, Faugno, McMahon, and King (2003) describe the kinds of variables and questions the LNC should consider:

1. For child abuse cases:
    - The past and current medical history of the child.
    - Are acute injuries present?
    - Was a forensic interview administered to the child?
    - Is there a family history with CPS?
    - Who are the child care providers?
    - Are school records available?
    - Has the child exhibited changes in behavior?

2. For elder abuse cases:
   - What is the state of the elder's hygiene, nutrition, physical, and mental health?
   - Is the elder receiving sufficient personal care?
   - What are the elder's living arrangements?
   - On whom does the elder depend for care?
   - Is there evidence of any old or new injuries?
3. For domestic violence cases:
   - What are the victim's and the perpetrator's medical histories?
   - Are children involved, and what are their medical histories?
   - Have the children been removed from the home in the past?
   - Is there evidence of physical or sexual abuse of the children?
   - What were the findings of the victim's physical or mental injuries?
   - How much time has elapsed since the time of the injuries and when medical attention was sought?
   - What does the police report say?
4. For sexual assault cases:
   - What are the findings of all reports through the complete history of the investigation?
   - Did a forensic laboratory analyze the evidence of the rape kit?
   - Was the chain of custody followed properly?
   - What were the findings of the SANE/SART examination?
5. For driving under the influence cases:
   - Is there a previous history of DUI?
   - What are the preexisting and existing medical conditions?
   - Was evidence at the scene properly collected, documented, and preserved?
   - To what degree were narcotics or alcohol involved, based on toxicology reports?
6. For death investigation cases:
   - What are the mechanical aspects of the death, including motives, methods, wounds, crime scene reconstruction, cause, manner and time of death, and so on?

The LNC is responsible for reviewing the facts of a forensic case, and according to Davis et al., might be involved in the analysis of the following kinds of documents:

- Medical or forensic reports that assess the extent of the victim's injuries and determine if injuries are consistent with the timeframe and the history provided
- Autopsy reports that assess the extent of injuries; determine if injuries match the history; determine if preexisting injuries were present; determine whether wounds are entrance or exit wounds; identify the type of weapon used; determine whether the death was an accident, homicide, or suicide; and identify how much time elapsed between the injury and the time of death, and so on
- Police reports to assess the initial crime scene, identify witnesses, determine items removed from the scene, and so on
- Supplemental investigative reports
- Sexual assault reports to assess the presence or absence of injuries related to the history and timeframe
- Psychological testing reports to evaluate the competency of the accused to stand trial, and to assess the state of mind of the perpetrator and the victim at the time of the crime
- Forensic science reports to determine if the accused can be linked to the scene through trace or biological evidence

LNCs will also interview clients, witnesses, and potential experts to gather information about the crime, assist in obtaining experts and acting as a liaison between the experts and the attorney; perform research of the medical literature, and prepare transcription of medical records and chronologies of events. Davis et al. (2003) write, "Criminal law is the body of law by which all human conduct is judged." They emphasize that in criminal cases, the prosecution bears the burden of proof. They add, "In criminal law, the prosecutor is required to prove his case beyond a reasonable doubt in the eyes of the trier of fact." In criminal law, prosecutors and defense counsel alike depend on three types of evidence: testimonial evidence, physical evidence, and scientific evidence. Within these classifications are direct evidence, which is designed to establish a fact; and indirect evidence, which establishes a fact by reference. Although the latter type of evidence is competent, it must be viewed by the trier of fact to eliminate all other reasonable explanations. Davis et al. write, "Whether LNCs work for the defense or prosecution, they play a significant role in reviewing and analyzing the evidence to ensure that proper evidence collection protocols are followed as it relates to the medical issues of the case."

According to Davis et al. (2003), "Testimonial evidence is best defined as that evidence presented through the words of victims, witnesses and parties to a criminal case. This evidence amounts to the words of those who were present when a crime was committed, those who investigated the crime after it took place, or those who dispute the accused's involvement." Davis et al. define physical evidence as "objects or tangible items that are used to demonstrate or establish facts or elements of the crime charged." They also define scientific evidence as "that field of expertise in which physical objects and technology merge to establish facts or elements or to disprove facts or elements."

LNCs should be familiar with the Federal Rules of Evidence, which determine the admissibility of scientific evidence into a court of law. Of particular importance is Federal Rule of Evidence 702, which states, "If scientific, technical or other specialized knowledge will assist the trier of fact to understand the evidence or to determine a fact in issue, a witness qualified as an expert by knowledge, skill, experience, training or education may testify thereto in the form of an opinion or otherwise." The U.S. Supreme Cout case of *Daubert v. Merrell Dow Pharmaceuticals, Inc.* established a means for determining the reliability of expert scientific testimony and answered questions as to the proper standards for admissibility of expert testimony. Daubert supplanted a former test of admissibility known as *Frye v. United States*, where the rule of admissibility for expert testimony was delineated as requiring "general acceptance" of a technique in its respective scientific field before the technique in question would be considered to be admissible.

According to Davis et al. (2003), the Supreme Court created a gatekeeping function to "ensure that any and all scientific testimony or evidence admitted is not only relevant, but reliable." The Supreme Court suggested that courts should fulfill this gatekeeping role by determining if a technique had been submitted to peer review or publication, had been scrutinized for its known or potential rate of error, standards controlling the technique's operation, its refutability quotient, and whether the technique had gained acceptance in its scientific community. Another issue related to scientific evidence is the assurance of its chain of custody, which relates to the "handling of evidence from the time of retrieval up to testing and until presentation before the trier of fact." Davis et al. add, "The chain of custody is a requirement for admissibility because it substantiates reliability of the evidence by seeking to prevent altering or tampering with evidence." Finally, when presenting scientific evidence, the presenter is required to

> prove that the witness is qualified to render an expert opinion in the field for which the witness has been called. This requires the party calling the witness to show that the witness has knowledge, experience, and training that is sufficient to support his statements and conclusions… Only after a witness has been qualified as an expert will the court allow a witness to render opinion evidence; otherwise, witnesses are limited to factual testimony only.

13.6 THE FORENSIC NURSE GOES TO COURT

Forensic nurses believe that a day (or more) in court is an inherent part of their work as medico-legal professionals. They might serve as fact witnesses and in some cases, as expert witnesses, Morrison says. She explains:

> Almost anyone in this country can be a fact witness. If the nurse collected the evidence, then as a fact witness she is simply telling the court exactly how it happened: "I collected this information at such and such a time and this is how I did it." I do think we need to educate our nurses on how to testify in court properly because it is of vital importance to the administration of justice. Testifying in court appropriately, skillfully, and truthfully is a skill like anything else, and it's a skill we must have in our nursing skill sets. Regarding a nurse serving as an expert witness, like any other expert, the nurse must have the credentials in the area in which she is testifying. If she is a forensic death investigator, it will be to her credibility if she is able to say "Yes, I received my education at this particular school, I was trained under so and so, I took this forensic death investigator course and exam, and this is when I passed and since then this has been my experience." Well, if you are talking about a death, it sounds to me like this nurse has established her credibility. If you are talking about testifying as an expert witness on a sexual assault case, the sexual assault nurse examiner will reveal her credentials, her education, her advanced training, and her experience in performing sexual assault evidentiary examinations. Once a nurse has demonstrated certification, experience, and education, they are testifying to the truth of the matter as how they see it, and someone has taught them to have the strategies and the presence in court. That's what makes a great nurse expert witness.

Morrison says she believe it is every nurse's duty to perform well in a legal proceeding:

> As nurses, we have an obligation to testify as to whether or not the standard of care has been met. And we're talking the gamut of the nurse expert witness; whether we are a generalist, a SANE or death investigator… we nurses have worked hard to acquire the expertise, the education, and the certification, so for us not to testify as expert witnesses when we are able to, we are doing harm to the profession. Was the standard of care met or was it not? Who else is going to testify to our nursing standards? Who else is going to testify to our expertise? Personally, I don't want a physician testifying for me any more than I want to testify for a physician. So we have this obligation, once we acquire the education, certification, experience, and expertise in the field, we must go out there as experts.

Morrison says that case law supports the testimony of an RN to the standard of care for another RN in the case of malpractice or negligence, cases that LNCs are more than capable of handling. "There is definite case law in this country that permits the nurse expert witness to testify to the standard of care to be delivered by nurses," she emphasizes. Health care providers continually are at risk of legal proceedings when a patient brings an action against them on the grounds of inadequate standards of care, unprofessional behavior, or negligence and malpractice. Lynch (1997) writes, "The courts generally hold that nurses and physicians have different standards of care. Establishing the appropriate standard for nurses who practice in expanded roles brings not only a new independence but also new liabilities." She points to an appellate court ruling regarding the status of nurses whose opinion read, "Nurses are regarded as especially equipped to render professional services to patients when called on to do so rather than a workman. They are grouped with doctors and lawyers rather than with cooks and chambermaids."

As malpractice and negligence allegations abound, health care providers, especially nurses, must attempt to protect their credibility, but they must also understand the purpose of the legalities that confine them. Lynch says they must recognize that "the legal mechanism is designed primarily to protect the public from unsuitable or even dangerous physicians or nurses, as well as having a deterrent or punitive effect that will produce more stringent standards of care or require critical evaluation of current technique." In cases of malpractice or negligence, Lynch says forensic nurses' responsibilities are to the patient and to the health care professional against whom charges have been levied. Regarding a patient who might have suffered physical injury or emotional duress, Lynch writes, "It is often difficult to find our colleagues at fault when circumstances may be unclear and there are no witnesses to the incident except the parties involved. However, the patient who has been violated as a result of unacceptable standards of care or malicious behavior by a nurse or physician has the right to expect sanctions against the perpetrator." And regarding the health care provider, Lynch adds, "We have a responsibility to the health care professional against false charges by individuals seeking monetary compensation for fictitious disorders or injuries by blaming improper care or assault on the caretaker. It is imperative that the documentation and witnessing of such events be carefully recorded in order to provide a method of defense."

Regardless of whose rights are brought into question, Lynch emphasizes that it is the evidence, "proof that will confirm a plaintiff's accusation or a defendant's statement that is on trial." She adds, "Factual documentation, collection and preservation of evidence, as well as chain of custody will become a point of legal inquiry that may determine the outcome of the case."

A health care professional might face charges of malpractice or negligence. The failure to meet accepted standards of care where care administered to a patient is considered to be inadequate is negligence, whereas professional behavior that does not meet the level of quality expected of a health care professional is malpractice. Most legal proceedings having to do with negligence are within civil law; however, more serious charges canmay result in criminal law being invoked. Although criminal cases against nurses are rare, Lynch (1997) writes, "These cases generally thrust the profession of nursing into national and international headlines."

Many health care systems are just beginning to appreciate the many contributions a forensic nurse or an LNC can make to legal issues, specifically cases of alleged professional negligence or malpractice. Lynch (1997) writes:

> In conducting the affairs of a hospital, its officers and agents are liable for committing acts of negligence when the administrators fail to require or provide appropriate policy or provide qualified personnel to fulfill that policy. Recommendations for the inclusion of the role of the forensic nurse specialist would not only help to protect the patient's rights but also would serve the best interest of the health care institution and their employees against liability claims.

Lynch believes that, "Nurses educated in the forensic sciences can provide an improved relationship with the public and the judicial system by emphasizing the legal issues regarding patient care."

Forensic nurses from all over the country report varying degrees of proficiency in legal matters and their experience in formal civil or criminal court proceedings. Louisiana forensic nurse and death investigator Meliss Vessier-Batchen reports that she has not had much of an opportunity to testify in court, as her parish's forensic pathologist handles the bulk of court appearances. "Most of the cases we have that go to court concern testimony about evidence found at the time of autopsy," she says:

> I know the difference between serving as a fact witness and an expert witness, and I believe nurses excel in both kinds of testimony. Of course, the greater number of credentials a nurse has, as well as an advanced level of knowledge and experience, affects the amount of credibility that a nurse has and the amount of consideration as an expert witness they will generate. Many nurses can be a fact witness because they are essentially testifying to a fact that they saw or heard, or the evidence they collected, but when nurses get to the expert level, their opinions are sought and considered. The key to becoming an expert witness is to continue to seek out education and experience and advanced credentials, and don't be afraid to talk to anyone you can, other nurses, pathologists, investigators, to pick up new knowledge that will help you grow.

No stranger to the courtroom is Massachusetts forensic nurse consultant Georgia A. Pasqualone, MSFS, MSN, RN, CEN, DABFN, who balances her time between her work as a certified emergency nurse, a national and international lecturer, a death and crime scene investigator, a forensic photographer, and an LNC. This champion of the medicolegal process says she learned one of the most valuable lessons ever from one of her graduate school professors. Pasqualone was earning her first forensic master's degree in the crime scene investigation track at the University of New Haven, and a research project required her to radically adjust her way of thinking. It was an unexpected thought process that has stayed with her throughout her career. Pasqualone recalls:

> At the time of this project, the O.J. Simpson trial was all the rage. Our entire program dealt with trial issues and the investigative process. Because I was a nurse, my professor told me I was to deal with the medical evidence within the trial, such as the stomach contents, the DNA, the blood, etcetera. I said, "That's easy." He said, "But you are to research the medical evidence and present it to me as though you were preparing a brief for the defense." I stopped dead in my tracks. I was forced to think objectively about everything I had learned; everything is not as it seems, I cannot take everything at face value, and not every defendant is guilty. I could still tell the truth about that evidence but I had to present it as he had asked. I had to analyze what the defense and the prosecution did with the evidence and how Johnnie Cochran could have used it as a defense for his client. By being objective and letting the evidence speak for itself, you can get to the truth. However, many things were messed up in that case and that evidence, although it does not lie, could have been used and abused by the attorneys.

The continuum of the medico-legal process often includes building a case and taking it to trial—a component that makes even the bravest forensic nurse quake in his or her shoes. Pasqualone, a veteran of the courtroom, says stage fright is natural, but forensic professionals must keep their fears in check and focus on presenting the evidence. "You must have strength of conviction to get in front of a group of people and be able to speak your mind," Pasqualone says:

> Very little, besides ongoing experience, can prepare you to face judges and juries, as well as opposing attorneys who continuously badger you. They try to trip you up by saying things like, "Ms. Paqualone, you would say anything you could to protect your patient, wouldn't you?" That's a loaded question, so no matter what you say, yes or no, you are backed up against the wall. Then you start stuttering and you feel you have lost all credibility. All you ever wanted to do was get up there and tell the truth. Nurses shake in their boots at the thought of going to trial as a fact witness because they don't want to be subjected to that kind of humiliation. They get rattled and say things they never meant to say or maybe they say too much because they are trying to backpedal to get out of the hole they know they are falling into.

Pasqualone has survived her share of painful courtroom proceedings and shares with her students effective techniques to avoid being nailed to the wall by cross-examination:

> I give them examples of the times I fell flat on my face. I say, "This is what happened to me, and in retrospect, let's talk about how I got in this position and what to do to prevent this from happening to you." Forensic nurses have not had enough opportunity to be educated by other veteran forensic nurses; there aren't enough of us around yet. They haven't been taught how to act in a court of law—what you say to attorneys, how you behave, how you dress, how you present yourself and what you don't say.

Pasqualone recalls the first time she went to court:

> It was a hearing so my job description that day had not been delineated. I was going in as a fact witness because I was acting as a nurse investigator for a criminal defense attorney and I had interviewed witnesses and I knew what was going on with the case. The judge allowed me to testify as a fact witness but because I was also a nurse, he allowed me to give my opinions as they related to adolescent behavior and sexual child abuse. The assistant DA ripped me apart. It was the first time I had ever been to court to testify in that kind of capacity and I was reduced to rubble. The attorney I was working for said he couldn't even look at me on the stand because it was too horrible. At the end of the session, this attorney must have spent an hour with me in the back of the courtroom after everybody cleared out. He said, "You know she was paid to do that; it was nothing personal. You have to be more aware of and anticipate the hole they try to push you into. It has nothing to do with you as a nurse." I thought everybody loved a nurse because we are angels of mercy. But here's this woman pulling me apart and blowing holes into my testimony. The attorney pasted me all back together again like Humpty Dumpty and said, "When this is over, you will never do that again." He was right.

Pasqualone says nurses' outgoing, communicative nature often is the very characteristic that gets them into trouble. "Nurses do talk too much because we try to put our patients at ease," Pasqualone says emphatically, "It's a communication pattern among health care professionals. Nurses talk too much because they are very social, they want to educate. It gets us into trouble in court when it should be 'just the facts, ma'am.' Nurses need more classes on how they should conduct themselves in court, more mock trials and more nurses who have been to court should share information with other nurses."

Most forensic nurses who find themselves on the stand are fact witnesses, who go to court to tell the story, Pasqualone explains. "A patient comes into the ED and the nurse cares for him or her. Whatever transpires, whether the patient has injuries or has said something to the nurse, everything is documented. In court, the nurse is a fact witness to the way the patient presented his or her injuries, and a fact witness to the nursing notes, to the photo documentation, and to what they saw, heard and documented." Pasqualone says the number of nurses testifying as fact witnesses continues to grow, although the number of nurses considered knowledgeable enough to be expert witnesses is still small—a source of contention between doctors and nurses. "In the past, physicians have been the ones asked to testify as expert witnesses, even to nursing processes," Pasqualone says:

> Physicians have no business testifying about nursing; they don't know what we are all about. They haven't been to nursing school and they know nothing about what we do and how we care for patients. Attorneys are wising up. They are starting to call nurses as expert witnesses in fields where nurses have a great deal of experience. I have 33 years in critical care and emergency nursing so I think I am well equipped to have an opinion about nursing care and what nurses should or should not be doing. With my graduate studies in forensic science and forensic nursing, I feel I can have an opinion about patients that fall into my forensic categories. SANEs are entitled to have an opinion about what they see, how patients present, and all the psychosocial ramifications of rape trauma syndrome. Attorneys are realizing that nurses are doing more in their clinical practice that the physicians aren't privy to.

Pasqualone says a factor contributing to her first humiliating courtroom appearance was that the judge had never encountered a forensic nurse and was interested in her opinions. She cautions that the best of intentions can backfire and that forensic nurses must realize every word that comes out of their mouths has significant impact and can trap them. "I will never be backed into a corner like that again and all nurses must learn this valuable lesson," Pasqualone says. "After a horrible experience nurses must go into court knowing it's not personal; you expect a battle, realize they are going to try to discredit you and you can't get angry. They will try to find all the buttons to push. You just have to take a deep breath, try to outthink them, and try to find the most neutral answer that prevents you from going down that slippery slope."

Janet Barber, MSN, RN, observes:

> What is most important in a courtroom, and having been there on numerous occasions, I can say that most nurses have learned to defend themselves by rhetoric, and they frequently say too much. It's probably the downfall of many nurses who find themselves in the courtroom without first having any related experience. They either don't answer questions properly, or they do a lot of expository speaking, and that's the biggest pitfall. One of the lessons nurses must learn is that they should answer the question, nothing more, nothing less; if a yes or no answer will suffice, then just stop right there. Or you can simply say, "That has been my experience." But most nurses just can't let it go there. They get uncomfortable with any voids in conversation, so they start talking, and frequently they get themselves into a quagmire.

Nancy Cabelus says she has a very specific mindset when working her cases and when going to court:

> I think about the photographs I'm taking and the sketch map I'm creating at the scene, because I'm not the only one who is going to be looking at these things... they may go before a jury. I recently testified on two different homicide cases where my photographs, sketches, and evidence I collected were all introduced into the courtroom. A lot of these cases are three and four years old now, so you rely on photographs and documentation to refresh your memory and to paint an accurate picture for the jurors. I simply go into the courtroom as calmly as I can because I have reviewed my notes and documentation ahead of time.
>
> If you don't know the answer to a question, it might be right there in front of you, in a document or a photograph, so you say, "May I refresh my memory by looking at my report, or by the statement that I took, or may I look at my nurse's notes in a nursing situation." Take your time, and don't answer any question quickly—be sure to think about your answer, and be deliberate. Maintain good eye contact, especially with the jury. I love to look at the jurors and see their reaction to the information being presented, because they are the ones who really matter. They, more so than the prosecutor or the defense, are the ones who are interpreting your information. If you don't know or don't remember, just say you don't know or you don't remember, because if it's not quite the full truth or just sketchy details, the defense attorney will use that information against you. That's what they get paid to do... to discredit you. It's always music to my ears when the defense attorney says, "I have no further questions for this witness, your Honor." You think to yourself, "I did it!"

11.7 FORENSIC NURSES AND EXPERT TESTIMONY

An emerging area in clinical forensic practice is the use of nurse expert witnesses in courts of law. Lynch (1997) defines a nurse expert witness as "a nurse qualified by education, experience, occupation, present position, degrees held, publication, and professional organization membership that establish the credibility as an expert to give opinions as to whether the nursing care administered met the 'acceptable standard of care.'" She says that as an increasing number of nurses operate in new areas of practice, they are able to expand the arenas in which they are qualified to testify as expert witnesses. Lynch writes, "Nursing practice involves a distinct body of knowledge not found in the practice of any other profession. Today, nurses are expected to be the experts involved when the issue is standards of nursing care." Lynch outlines a number of circumstances included in nurse liability:

- Failure to adequately supervise patients

- Errors in administration of treatments and medications
- Failure to observe and report significant changes in the condition of the patient
- Failure to take an adequate patient history
- Failure to chart adequately and at the time
- Failure to intervene when necessary
- Failure to notify the physician
- Failure to question if something seems amiss

Issues of expert testimony have thrust nurse examiners to new heights of scrutiny. On June 20, 2001, the *CBS Evening News* aired an "Eye on America" segment on the testimony of SANEs that discussed recent controversies regarding three Virginia sexual assault cases and SANE testimony on the human sexual response. According to an account of the broadcast described by the IAFN, the segment included a visit to a SANE training session at the University of Pennsylvania taught by IAFN member Kathleen Brown, where nurses were shown discussing what should or should not be said during court testimony. CBS also interviewed James E. Starrs, a professor of law at George Washington University, and James G. Connell, a defense attorney. Reporter Jim Stewart explained to viewers that testimony by expert witnesses in court cases is a growing trend and that sexual assault examiners are "frontline health professionals summoned to the stand when the charge is rape."

The segment then showed Brown teaching at a training session. Brown told the nurses "You are the pioneers on this. There are no hard and fast rules." Stewart then described the work of SANEs as "arguably one of the most sensitive jobs in medicine." He said SANEs are nurses specifically trained to handle sexual assault cases and that they are "highly regarded" by lawmen. He added that SANEs are "the first to examine a woman alleging rape, the first to collect evidence, and the first to confront the ultimate question in such cases." CBS then showed Brown explaining that this ultimate question, whether or not a rape actually occurred, comes down to a "he said/she said" scenario. Stewart also noted the question often becomes complicated because victims know each other, and frequently drugs and alcohol are involved. He added that testimony of expert witnesses can be "enormously influential" in cases with jurors, and that "that is why most [SANEs] are very careful to testify only about what they saw, not about what they think." When SANEs do testify about what they think, legal controversies arise, according to Stewart.

The feature then explained that such a controversy occurred in three Virginia cases in which judges threw out the testimony of SANEs they believed "went too far." With more than 500 SANE programs in place in the United States today, Stewart said legal experts are realizing the importance of SANE testimony. The segment then included Starrs, who said that SANEs "cross the line when they go beyond what they've simply observed" to making conclusions on causes or implications of possible crime. CBS then described the case of a nurse from Inova Fairfax Hospital who testified that she could distinguish between consensual and nonconsensual sex. The nurse declined to discuss the case with CBS and was not featured in the report, but Stewart explained that she had cited the Masters and Johnson study on human sexual response to support her testimony. Connell explained that "virtually all" of the doctors who have studied human sexual response agree that "you simply cannot tell from an examination" whether sexual contact was consensual or nonconsensual.

The nurses in Brown's class told CBS that they are taught to "stick to the facts" when testifying, and nurses shown in the segment gave examples of what SANEs can and cannot say. One nurse said tissue response can be described, but further conclusions should not be made. Brown also explained that human sexual response does not always "kick in" during sexual contact, even in situations such as longtime marriages.

Stewart concluded the broadcast by saying that judges agree "no matter what he said or she said, jurors have a way of discerning the truth for themselves."

In a sexual assault case, *Commonwealth v. Johnson*, tried in the 19th Judicial Circuit of Virginia in November 2000, Judge Jane M. Roush ruled that Inova Fairfax Hospital nurse Suzanne Brown, RN, SANE, was an undisputed expert and permitted her to testify about injuries that she observed in a sexual assault victim, over the defense attorney's objection. The defendant was charged with two counts of rape and one count of sexual penetration. At a pretrial hearing, the commonwealth of Virginia indicated that Brown's testimony would be that she observed physical injuries to the genitalia of the complaining witness, and to a reasonable degree of medical certainty, physical injuries that are detectable by gross visualization are not present in women in whom the "human sexual response" has been triggered. The prosecutor offered expert testimony by Brown on the theory of human sexual response, specifically, that injuries that were visible without magnification indicated to the SANE that the sexual activity occurred without consent. The defense characterization of the SANE's opinion was that injuries detectable by gross visualization indicate a lack of human sexual response, which, in turn, demonstrates sexual intercourse without consent. Human sexual response, as described in the characterized opinion, is a group of automatic, immediate, and involuntary physical changes that women go through in anticipation of consensual sexual intercourse. When the human sexual response occurs, the labia engorge with blood and change structurally to avoid injury. Because this physical process does not occur in nonconsensual situations, injury is more likely to occur in a rape case than in a case of consensual sex. The defense argued that Brown's expert opinion was scientifically unreliable and therefore, inadmissible. Roush recognized Brown as an undisputed expert, ruled that her testimony was limited to factual observations about injuries observed, and permitted her to testify that any genital injuries were consistent with penetration or sexual intercourse.

Roush considered the defendant's objection that the nurse examiner's expert opinion was scientifically unreliable. The judge referred to various studies cited by the expert, including work by Laura Slaughter, MD, and Carl Brown, PhD, published in the *American Journal of Obstetrics & Gynecology*, which documented clinical findings in sexual assault victims. The court held after a careful review of those studies that none supported Brown's opinion that genital injuries detectable by gross visualization do not result from consensual sexual intercourse. The court concluded that because there is no support in the medical literature for Brown's opinions about human sexual response as it relates to genital injury, there was no sufficient foundation to warrant admission of the evidence and granted the defendant's motion to exclude Brown's testimony about the human sexual response. Johnson pleaded guilty to one count of rape.

According to a statement by the IAFN, "the ruling opened the eyes of the medical and legal communities to forensic nursing and drew attention to the valuable contribution that forensic nurses offer victims of sexual assault by providing sensitive care and serving as expert witnesses when cases go to trial. The news media quickly identified the case as a newsworthy controversy." The IAFN reported that the *Virginia Lawyers Weekly* ran a story on the decision on November 13, 2001, in which the reporter concentrated on the effect of the judge's ruling on the nature of the scientific basis for the human sexual response and the reliance on the medical literature by experts testifying at trial. According to the IAFN, although the article referred to the court's opinion to underscore the exclusion of testimony, *Lawyer's Weekly* did not include the portion of the judge's opinion that recognized Suzanne Brown as an undisputed expert and permitted expert testimony on the nature of injuries as being consistent with penetration or sexual intercourse. Likewise, on April 2, 2001, the IAFN reported, *The Washington Post* published an article focusing on the exclusion of opinion testimony by Brown based on the human sexual response but did not include the judge's explicit language on Brown's expert status and abilities. The *Post* interviewed George Washington University law professor James E. Starrs, who said that testimony by SANE nurses is "junk science" and that Roush's opinion was devastating to forensic nursing professionals. However, the jury, or in this case, the judicial analysis of the status of forensic nurse experts was still out. Subsequent to the publication of these articles, the Virginia Court of Appeals reviewed a similar issue in another case. In *Velasquez v. Commonwealth of Virginia*, a convicted sex offender argued that the trial court erred in allowing SANE Barbara Patt to testify as an expert witness. Velasquez argued on appeal that Patt impermissibly testified on the ultimate issue of fact when she stated that her findings were "inconsistent with consensual intercourse" and she lacked the expertise required to allow her to state "an expert medical opinion regarding the cause of the alleged victim's injury." The Virginia Appellate Court found, after reviewing her training and qualifications, that the trial judge properly qualified her to testify as "an expert in the diagnosis of a sexual assault" and the trial court properly qualified her as an expert. This was the most recent opinion of the Virginia Court of Appeals that found that SANEs are properly qualified as experts and can offer opinion testimony to assist the jury in understanding injuries sustained in sexual assaults. The Virginia appellate courts have upheld the testimony of forensic nurses who have offered testimony based on their professional expertise in six cases.

Kathy Bell, RN, SANE, director of forensic nursing services and SANE coordinator for the Tulsa (Oklahoma) Police Department and a former IAFN president, called *The Washington Post* article "important in the development of the profession of forensic nursing." Bell, who was instrumental in developing the Tulsa SANE program in Oklahoma in 1992, added, "SANEs have been qualifying as experts in criminal trials for over a decade. We have been awaiting recognition like the articles in the *Weekly* and the *Post* to draw attention to the extremely valuable services and care forensic nurses provide to the community."

The media interest in the recent Virginia cases is evidence of increasing public awareness in forensic issues. James A. Gilson, a former criminal prosecutor in New Jersey and a past IAFN president, said, "The investigation and prosecution of sexual assault cases in New Jersey has been significantly improved by the expert and sensitive care that forensic nurses provide our victims of sexual assault." Gilson added, "We now have over 15 appellate decisions throughout the country that uphold SANE expert testimony in sexual assault cases." Bell added, "Forensic nurses provide care to victims of interpersonal violence that is not otherwise available from existing systems. The medical profession, already overburdened by increasing responsibilities and decreasing resources, cannot prioritize the care of victims of violent crime the way forensic nurses can," said Bell. "Likewise, the legal profession and the criminal justice system have never been able to offer violent crime cases the level of care and intervention, including increasing the ability to provide expert witness testimony in criminal trials, offered now as a result of the services provided to victims by forensic nurses."

The Scope and Standards of Forensic Nursing Practice, as set forth by the ANA, provides that "the forensic nurse utilizes current knowledge of research in the forensic nursing practice" in Standard VII Research. Many nurses use medical research to support their practice outcomes and develop new questions about the care of patients in their respective specialties. IAFN supports accuracy in reporting research results and interpretations. The ANA social policy statement describes "the nature of nursing as complex and highly interactive, and asserts that society has historically understood nursing to be a noninvasive, nurturing discipline, focused more on creating the physiological, psychological, and socio-cultural environment in which the patient can gain or maintain health or heal." ANA's Scope of Nursing Practice states that the nurse field regulates itself by defining its practice base, providing for research and development of that practice base.

In the practice of forensic nursing, the SANE contributes to the development of science based on nursing theory and nursing practice outcomes. Within the practice, professional nurses are responsible and accountable for the acquisition, analysis, and dissemination of knowledge and skills in their respective areas of expertise. Through participation in the research process, innovative approaches can be discovered and tested.

The IAFN stated in a news release, "The recent appellate decisions around the country show that SANEs can be very credible witnesses in court as a result of extensive experience, expertise in conducting examinations, and education."

In the April 2, 2001 article in *The Washington Post*, "When Rape Is in Question, So Are Nurses' Answers; Lawyers Succeed in Limiting Expert Testimony," writer Tom Jackman explored the legal and evidentiary ramifications of the consent defense in sexual assault cases. He wrote, "Faced with a literal he-said, she-said, the prosecutors often turn to nurses specially trained in treating sexual assault, who testify on whether the woman's injuries could have come only from forced sex." He went on to describe the fact that in Virginia's Fairfax County, judges in three cases ruled that science does not support such testimony, and that a number of defense attorneys across the country are using the Fairfax rulings to mount a new offensive on nurses' testimony. Jackman reported that James G. Connell III, then a public defender in Fairfax, collected transcripts last year of SANE nurse testimony, then examined the scientific research that the nurses cited on the witness stand. Jackman quoted Connell as saying, "It turns out our SANE nurses here have taken their conclusions far beyond what the research says," Connell said. "It doesn't say anything like you can look at genital injury and tell whether a woman has been raped."

SANE Suzanne Brown planned to testify, as she had many times before, Jackman wrote, that the female body responds differently during consensual sex and during forced sex. If the sex is consensual, the body protects itself from injury. No such response occurs during forced sex. Therefore, Jackman quoted Brown as saying certain injuries show that sexual activity took place without consent. This kind of testimony had been crucial to several sexual assault prosecutions. Jackman reported, "Connell attacked that logic, not only with studies cited by Brown, but with others that contradicted those. Roush read them and concluded that 'nothing in the extensive medical literature submitted to the court . . . supports Ms. Brown's theory that she can distinguish nonconsensual from consensual sexual intercourse.'" Jackman said that none of the rulings resulted in an acquittal, so Fairfax prosecutors have not appealed them; however, he added, that hasn't stopped defense attorneys from calling Connell to secure copies of the scientific research and the judges' rulings. Jackman wrote, "While the significance of the rulings remains a subject of debate, there's little doubt that they have given defense attorneys a whole new avenue in sexual assault cases."

In Jackman's article, William B. Moffitt, past president of the National Association of Criminal Defense Lawyers, was quoted as saying, "I think the rulings are excellent and have probably done some good already. This kind of fuzzy science is frightening in a courtroom. If the courts give it the imprimatur of validity, jurors assume it's valid. Suddenly, there's some expertise on the subject of guilt: 'The defendant is guilty because I say so.'" Jackman also reported Andrew J. Kersey, an assistant commonwealth's attorney in Fairfax who handles sex crimes, as commenting, "I don't think it changes much in terms of how we present evidence from SANE nurses. It's up to the jury to determine whether a crime has been committed."

To his credit, Jackman interviewed Brown for his story, and reported that "Brown is adamant that the opinions she and other SANE nurses offer are accurate." He also reported that Brown said she wasn't fully prepared for the November hearing before Roush, and that she would have cited more supporting articles. She added that research shows "there are patterned injuries that are consistent with consensual or nonconsensual intercourse" and that the articles provided by Connell were "pulled out of context." Jackman also interviewed Storrs, also interviewed by CBS News, who told Jackman that nurses' testimony is "junk science." He added that Roush's ruling was "very carefully documented and a very devastating opinion to Suzanne Brown and her ilk."

Storrs told Jackman that Brown is "really a prosecutor's darling. She can do things doctors and medical examiners would not dare to do. There's no question that the defense bar is very much alert to what's going on." According to Jackman, Brown added that nurses "aren't making a medical diagnosis. We're making an opinion based on the evidence."

Forensic nurse examiner Cari Caruso, RN, SANE-A, says she thinks a forensic nurse's testimony in the Virginia cases might have been a case of trying to play judge and jury:

> It's not our place as nurses to decide if an assault happened or not. It's the jury's place to decide. If you use phrases such as something "being consistent with," or if you want to say things like "these injuries could be consistent with consensual intercourse, or nonconsensual intercourse," you're probably OK. But you cannot say, "I believe she was raped." That is taking the power away from the jury. There are other ways to phrase things, such as, "Yes, this could be consistent with this, but in my opinion I feel the victim's history was consistent with the injuries." The bottom line is that you can't take away the jury's power. I think the one thing that defense attorneys have learned is that if you put us up against a doctor, they have not had the experience that the forensic nurse has had, so they are getting smarter about hiring forensic nurses as expert and fact witnesses. What I remind the attorneys is that when the forensic nurse gets on the stand, she will tell you that "this could be consistent with consensual sex and could be consistent with nonconsensual sex," and she may, as an expert witness, say that "In this case I believe it's more likely to be nonconsensual." My place as a nurse is to say pretty much the same thing—that something could be consistent with consensual or nonconsensual sex, and depending on the injuries and on the circumstances. As a defense expert I get a whole lot more information than I would as the forensic nurse. I can look for consistencies or omissions and my job is to merely explain the document and reiterate, "I can't say if something is consensual or nonconsensual, but these injuries could be consistent with either."

In "Forensic Nursing, A Most Competent Practice," James Gilson (2000), RN, JD, expresses that in addition to offering an "unprecedented means of improving the community response to human abuse and interpersonal violence," forensic nurses can be "the single most important factor in . . . achieving successful prosecution of criminal cases." He explains that competent forensic nursing practice involves the analysis and application of specific evidentiary principles relating to hearsay and the admissibility of evidence at trial. He writes, "No less significant than the physical evidence collected during the forensic examination are the verbal statements offered by the victim during the history and physical exam, which can often form the evidentiary basis upon which a jury can determine a verdict." He points to nurses' ability to document statements made by adolescent and adult victims of violence at trial to improve the chances of prosecution as a critical component of forensic nursing practice. He adds, "Unfortunately, the premise that adult victims are not subject to similar dynamics results in cases being investigated and prosecuted based on the assumption that an adult victim of violent crime will testify competently at trial and establish the necessary elements of the crime to enable a conviction." Gilson states that the ability to document a victim's statements about the nature and cause of injuries, the identity of the offender, and the history of abuse provides an extremely important tool for the prosecutor in pursuing a conviction. "In many cases, the essential elements of crimes charged can only be established through the victim's testimony. Sexual violence and domestic violence are generally not witnessed events, so the proof may rest solely upon the victim's statements." Gilson emphasizes that forensic nurses are trained to key in on statements made by victims because they enable the courts to hold offenders accountable for their actions when these statements are introduced at trial. Gilson writes, "Regardless of the statements made to law enforcement officers and other individuals responding to a victim of violence, statements made to nurses and physicians can have special significance in a criminal trial." Gilson explains that the Confrontation Clause of the Sixth Amendment guarantees a criminal defendant the right to be confronted with the witnesses against him, and it might allow the defendant to exclude out-of-court declarations that are unreliable, where the declarant is not available to be cross-examined in court. Gilson adds that this provision reflects a preference for live testimony in lieu of out-of-court declarations wherever possible. Furthermore, if the victim is available to testify, but the prosecution instead offers his out-of-court declaration, Gilson says, the trial judge is more likely to find a confrontation violation when the victim is not available. Whether or not the victim is unavailable, his or her out-of-court declaration will not be allowed into evidence unless it contains "indicia of reliability." The Confrontation Clause of the Sixth Amendment, made applicable to the states through the Fourteenth Amendment, states, "In all criminal prosecutions, the accused shall enjoy the right . . . to be confronted with the witnesses against him." The Court further describes the basis of the exclusionary rule and the hearsay exceptions: "The central concern of the Confrontation Clause is to ensure the reliability of the evidence against a criminal defendant by subjecting it to rigorous testing in the context of an adversary proceeding before the trier of fact."

Gilson writes, "The combined effect of these elements of confrontation—physical presence, oath, cross-examination, and observation of demeanor by the trier of fact—serves the purposes of the Confrontation Clause by ensuring that evidence admitted against an accused is reliable and subject to the rigorous adversarial testing that is the norm of American criminal proceedings." Physical evidence as well as documented statements made by victims (or suspects under medical care) can be powerful tools used by prosecutors and defense attorneys in the courtroom, and these tools often serve as the basis for guilty pleas or convictions at trial. Gilson says that an important legal basis for the admissibility of victim statements can be found in states' nurse practice acts, which define the scope of nursing practice and the criteria for professional practice.

As was tested in the Virginia cases, "diagnosing and treating human responses to actual or potential physical and emotional health problems is an essential component of the practice and forms the basis for applying legal principles of the rules of evidence," Gilson adds. This diagnosis and treatment component, contained in many of the aforementioned nurse practice acts, should be considered by the forensic nurse as a standard of practice and applied as a basis for the use of evidence in the form of statements at trial. These state nursing standards, which apply to all nurses engaged in clinical practice irrespective of specialty, practice setting, or educational background, also establish legal criteria for the admissibility of out-of-court statements. According to ANA Standard II, "diagnosis" is established as a practice standard for nurses. It states that the nurse analyzes the assessment data in determining diagnoses that are derived from the assessment data, validated with the patient, family, and other health care providers, documented in a manner that facilitates the determination of expected outcomes and plan of care. In addition, the IAFN's Scope and Standards of Forensic Nursing Practice state that the forensic nurse will analyze the assessment data to determine a diagnosis pertaining to forensic issues in nursing, because the analysis of data provides the basis for planning timely and effective nursing interventions. It also states that diagnoses are based on identifiable data, and that the forensic nurse identifies those diagnoses that are consistent with the findings of other forensic health care, law enforcement, and judicial professionals that will facilitate a controlled pathway throughout to the judicial process. It also states that diagnoses of forensic assessments in nursing services are consistent with the accepted current bodies of knowledge, and that the forensic nurse analyzes evidence as appropriate to the area of practice. In addition, the IAFN standards define nursing as "the diagnosis and treatment of human responses to actual or potential health problems."

Gilson emphasizes:

> The IAFN standards of care provide that a forensic nurse perform an assessment and determine a diagnosis pertaining to forensic issues in nursing. The forensic nurse must identify expected individual outcomes based on the forensic diagnosis of the client and develop a comprehensive plan of action appropriate to forensic interventions. The standards require the forensic nurse to implement a plan of action based on forensic issues derived from assessment data and evaluate and modify the plan of action to achieve expected outcomes.

Essentially, the various standards of practice for nurses underscore the requirement that forensic nurses use diagnosis and treatment to function within this scope of practice. Gilson says that from a legal perspective, the existence of a patient–physician relationship and the application of medical diagnosis and treatment provide a chance to make admissible statements made by the victim during the course of treatment. Statements made under these circumstances can be admitted into evidence regardless of whether the victim is available to testify, he adds. The legal basis for the admissibility of statements made by a victim to a health care provider is found in the medical diagnosis exception to the hearsay rule. According to the Federal Rules of Evidence, hearsay is defined as "a statement, other than one made by the declarant while testifying at the trial or hearing, offered in evidence to prove the truth of the matter asserted." Statements considered to be inadmissible are judged by their lack of trustworthiness or reliability; however, verbal statements and nonverbal conduct made for purposes of medical diagnosis and treatment can be admissible in a criminal trial as an exception to the hearsay rule, according to Gilson. As well, statements regarding the cause of the injuries fall within this exception. Of considerable note to forensic nurses and other health care providers, the rules do not mandate that statements of this nature be made only to a physician to be considered an exception to the hearsay rule. Gilson says, "Statements made to the forensic nurse as part of a history and physical examination, therefore, become extremely important from a trial advocacy perspective because statements regarding the cause of injuries, including specific details of the assault and the identity of the offender, can be introduced through the forensic nurse examiner." Gilson adds that a forensic nurse's testimony can be of considerable value to a jury. "Statements made to a forensic nursing professional during the course of medical and nursing care, when introduced at trial can have added credibility and weight as perceived by a jury. When properly introduced, the jury can perceive an unbiased and independent witness with no interest in the outcome of the case."

Roger A. Canaff, JD, senior attorney with the National Center for Prosecution of Child Abuse of the American Prosecutors Research Institute, says that SANEs, working as part of a multidisciplinary team, can make significant contributions to evidence collection efforts in problematic child abuse cases. However, he cautions, there are numerous pitfalls that can trip up the examiners themselves and their medico-legal colleagues. In the white paper, "Pediatric Sexual Assault Nurse Examination: Challenges and Opportunities for MDTs in Child Sexual Abuse Cases," (2004a) Canaff enumerates the benefits of SANE programs, including their ability to provide care to child victims, which is far superior to the traditional ED, as well as their competent and consistent physical evidence collection. Most important, however, he says that SANEs can provide expert testimony about human anatomy and physical findings made during the examination. "The limits of this testimony continue to be debated, particularly with regard to the relationship, if any, between observed injury and the likelihood of consent. However, the basic question of whether SANEs can testify as experts in the field of sexual assault examination has been answered by many courts in the affirmative."

Canaff explains that in most states, the threshold for an expert is "simply someone who knows more about the subject than the trier of fact, and who can elucidate certain subjects for the sake of arriving at the truth." SANEs meet this criterion because they usually have at least 80 hours of training to become a pediatric-qualified SANE (40 hours SANE training with 40 hours additional pediatric training), and they hold a degree of RN or higher. Canaff advises that prosecutors facing challenges to SANE testimony on the basis of their expertise (i.e., the "she's not a doctor" challenge) should become familiar with their state guidelines on expert testimony, and should consult Federal Rule 702 for additional guidance. The absence of injury in pediatric or adult sexual assault cases is a big stumbling block for prosecutors and the juries they are attempting to persuade. Canaff writes, "Prosecutors may assume that, with their specialized knowledge of the ano-genital area, SANEs can usually detect and testify regarding injuries that support children's claims of abuse. Facts show, however, that most child sexual assault cases do not produce detectable injury." Canaff adds that the value of SANE expert testimony can lie in its ability to explain the absence of injury rather than its presence.

As discussed in chapter 6, experts say there are numerous reasons why injury might not present in a child sexual abuse case; factors include the type of abuse and the resiliency of the tissue. If, in a case, Canaff explains, a child complains of pain from slight digital penetration by the offender but there is no injury, the SANE can—in rebuttal—explain that the hymen in a prepubescent girl is tender to the touch, and even slight contact with the hymen or immediately surrounding tissue before puberty can cause discomfort. In the minds of many jurors, any pediatric or adolescent sexual assault case focuses on the disturbance of the hymen, which is thought by the layperson to be a sheet of tissue covering the vaginal opening, remaining unbroken until sexual intercourse occurs. In reality, the hymen is a ring of tissue surrounding the vaginal opening, not a seal that waits to be broken by intercourse. Physiological changes in the adolescent at the time of puberty make it possible for the child to have forced intercourse with little to no pain or no discernable injury to the hymen. Without complaints of pain or documentation of injury, the defense might suggest that sexual intercourse could not have occurred if the hymen is intact; Canaff says such a statement is irrelevant. SANEs also can clarify other misconceptions, such as hymenal injury to a prepubescent child through typical child play on a jungle gym and rough-housing, or through self-stimulation, based on correct anatomical information.

Although forensics nurse can be of immense value in the courtroom, Canaff says their testimony as expert witnesses must be scientific, unimpeachable, and utterly neutral. Specifically, Canaff says, a nurse cannot be seen as an advocate. Canaff says:

> It is of utmost importance for SANEs to be perceived by the court as neutral, scientific examiners. Although they are appropriate members of a SART, they are patient advocates, not victim advocates. SANEs should avoid referring to patients as "survivors," and even the term "victim" is not recommended. To a SANE, a suspected sexual assault victim is a patient, to be treated professionally and compassionately as the nursing role dictates. However, for the purposes of the examination, the SANE is an unattached, forensic professional.

Canaff says that prosecutors can develop SANEs as experts, and they should be treated as any other medical expert. Canaff writes, "Face to face pre-trial interviews, particularly when SANE methodology is new to the prosecutor, are crucial. Encourage SANEs to discuss their findings with the defense also; indeed, it is a mark of progress for a SANE program when defense attorneys seek their expertise." He cautions that SANEs must not become, or be perceived as in collusion with prosecutors and investigators. "This adherence to professionalism is crucial at all stages of the investigation and litigation process," Canaff emphasizes.

Alluding to the Virginia case of *Commonwealth v. Johnson* discussed earlier, Canaff says that SANEs can be admitted as experts to render opinions on human tissue and anatomy, as well as opinions on the possible cause of observed injuries to the ano-genital area in rape cases. "For instance, an expert may be able to opine that certain tears, bruises or redness to the vulva were caused by blunt-force trauma. In addition, experts can also render opinions as to why injury may not have been seen in a particular case; an expert's knowledge of the resiliency and elasticity of human tissue may help the jury to understand why no injury was observed even though a sexual assault was reported."

In "Limits and Lessons: The Expert Medical Opinion in Adolescent Sexual Abuse Cases," (2004b) Canaff explains that immense controversy has developed around the limits of medical expert testimony in consent-defense cases. "In such a case, observed injury to the vagina may be of interest to the prosecutor trying to corroborate the victim's claim that the sexual intercourse was nonconsensual," he writes. "In cases where the consent of the adolescent is at issue, relatively severe injuries observed to the vaginal area may give rise to the opinion that the intercourse was consistent with a nonconsensual act. It is this possible relationship between injury and the likelihood of consent that has generated so much controversy within the medical and legal communities." In this case, the judge found in the medical literature a basis for human sexual response and its relation to arousal, but did not find evidence directly linking consent, human sexual response, and the likelihood of injury. The SANE was allowed to testify as an expert as to certain matters, but not as to the relationship between injury to the victim and the likelihood of consent based on the phenomenon of human sexual response. According to Canaff, "This trial ruling sent shockwaves throughout the legal and forensic medical communities, and left many wondering how much expert testimony from SANEs was in jeopardy." Canaff says that the Johnson ruling should teach prosecutors two important things. First, prosecutors should not allow the defense to characterize a prosecution expert's opinion. Canaff explains, "the opinion prepared by the defense used language that in retrospect was too strong for scientific testimony ('injury detectable by gross visualization demonstrates sex without consent')." He adds that the word *demonstrates* is too inflexible for the "nonabsolute nature of medical testimony." In addition, Canaff says that a concept like human sexual response must be "framed carefully" to include all research and current, accurate medical thought. "Whatever the science allows, the point is that the expert herself, and not opposing counsel, should be the one articulating it to the tribunal," Canaff adds. The second point driven home to prosecutors, Canaff says, is the importance of pretrial preparation and communication between the prosecutor and the expert witness. Canaff writes, "In Johnston, the expert was not told in advance that a motion regarding the reliability of the underlying science was at issue. She was asked to appear to answer questions about her expertise, and did not have time to review the proffered opinion in advance." Canaff believes that a different result could have been achieved if the expert and the prosecutor would have been able to more carefully review the proffered opinion.

Canaff emphasizes that the Johnson case did not prevent SANE expert testimony altogether, conceivably a victory for the forensic nursing community, however the appellate-level case of *Commonwealth v. Velasquez* addressed earlier in this section answered many related questions about the limits of SANE testimony. Canaff explains that the Velasquez case touched on two important issues relevant to the limits of SANE testimony. "The defense asserted that, even if SANEs could be considered experts, they should not be allowed to render expert opinion about the possible cause of an observed injury. This, according to the defense, would constitute the making of a medical diagnosis, and thus lie beyond the scope of nursing practice." Canaff adds, "The case was appealed on the grounds that the SANE's testimony invaded the province of the jury by rendering testimony that spoke to the ultimate issue of the case." The Virginia Supreme Court ruled that SANEs do not practice medicine when they provide their opinions about the possible or probable cause of an observed injury. Canaff explains that no expert in Virginia can testify as to the ultimate issue in the case, but experts can express their opinion in terms of consistencies. "In this case, the SANE testified . . . that the injuries she observed were both 'consistent with nonconsensual sex' and 'inconsistent with consensual sex.'" The court said that when these responses are considered as a whole, they combined to "close the circle" and comment improperly on the ultimate issue. "From the language of the case, it appears that an opinion expressing the consistency of a certain injury with consensual sexual intercourse is permissible. However, an opinion expressed in such a way as to exclude all other possible causes of that injury is not," Canaff says.

13.8 PREPARATION FOR TRIAL AND PROFESSIONAL CONDUCT IN THE COURTROOM

Lynch (1997) writes, "Preparing for courtroom presentation must be carefully and deliberately designed. Although acting as a nurse expert witness is a stressful experience thoughtful and detailed preparation can build self-confidence and competence." She outlines ways nurses can best prepare themselves for the rigors of trial: Review the documentation involved in the case; be familiar with nursing standards of care, your state's nurse practice act, and other policies and procedures related to the case; and know the responsibilities of an expert witness and whether you meet the criteria. When testifying on the stand, Lynch recommends that nurses always tell the truth and that saying "I don't know" is always an acceptable answer; remain objective; answer all questions clearly and concisely without volunteering extra information; stay within the realm of nursing expertise; never respond to any question that is not understood; take time to compose a response; and remain calm and composed even under duress. Lynch adds, "Never get on the stand unless you have to; and when you are asked to consider a case as an expert witness, never accept the case unless you are prepared to go to court and testify."

A number of state bar associations offer a list of dos and don'ts of court testimony that can be applied to nurses testifying as fact or expert witnesses.

The Dos:

- A significant component of testimony is developing credibility with the judge and jury. Everything you say or do will be evaluated. It is important that you present yourself as a thoughtful, objective professional, that you communicate clearly and precisely, and that everything you say works to convince the court that you should be believed.
- Review the case file with the attorney before going to court. The court will need specific,

detailed information about the case. Your credibility as a witness will be enhanced if you have reviewed your case file and have a comprehensive understanding of the specifics of the facts and issues related to the case.

- Bring materials that will assist you in answering questions.
- Remain as objective as possible.
- Provide factual data from the nursing and medical literature to support your approach to the case, and be able to connect pertinent actual data, theory, and recommendations.
- Limit your conclusions and recommendations to what you can support with specific facts.
- Be conservative.
- Avoid jargon; explain nursing or medical concepts in layman's terms and illustrate with concrete examples.
- Be scrupulously honest.
- Listen carefully to the question asked, and answer only the question asked without offering additional information.
- If you do not understand a question, say so. If you need to, ask that the question be repeated.
- Take a moment to think about the question before answering. This will make you seem like a reasoned and thoughtful person, and could keep you from making a mistake.
- If you are asked to answer a question with just a "yes" or "no" and you cannot, say so.
- If you are asked a compound question (i.e., several questions in one) point out that there are several questions and that you cannot answer all with a single answer.
- If you do not know the answer to a question, say so.
- Stay focused on what you want to say, even during cross-examination.
- If there is something you want to say, find a way to insert the information you believe is important into your answers.

The Don'ts:

- Don't argue with any attorney.
- Don't appear to be defensive.
- Don't be surprised by cross-examination questions regarding current theories in your field of expertise; do your homework.
- Don't guess at an answer; you are on the stand to provide the facts.
- Don't be tempted to elaborate, as it is the opposing side's responsibility to get the answers they need.
- Don't become distracted; if your attention wanders, you could make mistakes.
- Don't respond to a question that you don't understand; ask to have it rephrased.
- Don't hesitate to request a break during a deposition, but do not ask for a break during trial.
- Don't forget to get a good night's sleep the day before the court proceeding, and to be alert and prepared for the courtroom experience.

The pretrial phase of case preparation should begin almost as soon as an indictment is filed. The prosecutor will consider his or her strategy, deciding which witnesses to call, and whether or not to call a medical expert or fact witness. If he or she can help the case by calling a medical witness, the prosecutor must decide whether the health care provider, or specifically, the nurse examiner, can be qualified as a medical expert. When evaluating a health care professional as a potential witness, the prosecutor will ask the individual to bring a copy of his or her curriculum vitae or résumé. If consulting on a particular case, the prosecutor might supply a subpoena for a medical record. The prosecutor will then review the medical record with the health care provider and ask him or her to explain each chart entry and abbreviation. The prosecutor will ask the potential witness to explain in detail the procedures he or she performed, as well as ask if the health care provider has an independent memory of the examination. If a prosecutor's trial strategy calls for the medical witness to be deemed an expert, the prosecutor will review the witness's curriculum vitae; inquire about articles he or she has published, whether the publications are peer reviewed, and the latest date of publication; and ask if he or she teaches, what subjects, and where. The health care provider's curriculum vitae will help determine in what field of expertise he or she might be qualified as an expert.

If the prosecutor decides to call the witness as an expert, or as a nurse, the witness should be given any relevant medical literature and studies pertaining to the facts at issue. The medical witness should read and digest the literature and be able to tell the prosecutor his or her opinion of the material. The prosecutor might also ask the medical witness for any relevant material he or she might have produced on the topic at hand. If the court allows the witness to testify as an expert, he or she might be able render an opinion based on the various studies in the medical literature. Depending on the health care provider's level of experience, a prosecutor might want to call the witness solely as a medical practitioner or nurse; that is, as a fact witness, not an expert. This type of witness also can provide powerful evidence at trial. Most important, the medical witness must be well prepared to withstand the rigors of courtroom proceedings. The prosecutor is advised to prepare every medical witness in the same manner, as if he or she has never testified before, to avoid misunderstandings. It also gives the prosecutor the opportunity to hear what the witness will testify to on the stand. The prosecutor must educate the medical witness about what he or she can or cannot say during testimony. The witness must use phrases such as "consistent with the type of conduct the victim reported," or other appropriate medico-legal language. The prosecutor will also explain that a medical or forensic witness cannot testify on the issue of consent or lack of consent in a sexual assault case, as this is in the purview of the jury. Although a medical expert cannot testify about consent or lack of consent, in some jurisdictions, testimony along the following lines has been deemed admissible: "Based on my education and experience as a sexual assault examiner, and due to the presence of multisite genital injuries in a patient reporting that he or she is the victim of sexual assault, his or her injuries are, in my opinion, consistent with his or her medical history." Although medical experts can render their opinion, they cannot determine consent or lack of consent based on injuries. The research does not support a claim that certain injuries occur only without consent. Further, the medical witness should never testify that a rape occurred, or that the victim was telling the truth; this will lead directly to a mistrial or to a reversal on appeal.

It is essential that prosecutors and witnesses prepare and educate each other prior to the commencement of trial. Experts say that medical witnesses are no different than other individuals called to testify in court. Witness preparation quells the witness's anxiety as well as the prosecutor's. Generally, a witness who is prepared will be more effective. The prosecutor should review with the medical witness the following aspects of trial: the elements of the crime that must be proved and how it should be accomplished through this witness's testimony, if applicable; reasons why the witness is testifying; the process of direct examination; the purpose of objections and what the witness should do in the event one of the attorneys objects; the process of cross-examination; and the purpose of redirect, as many witnesses believe that if on cross-examination they don't have an opportunity to answer a question fully, they have lost the opportunity to provide clarification.

Some aspects of witness preparation have special relevance to sexual assault trials. The prosecutor and the medical witness should educate each other about what they do in their respective roles, and their relevant medical and legal procedures. Prosecutors should not assume that because someone is a medical practitioner, they will be able to testify in a clear and concise manner, even if describing what they have done many times on the job. The prosecutor should construct questions that guide the witness through the procedures he or she performed. Prosecutors should explain to witnesses exactly what they are trying to accomplish with their testimony. This provides context and helps witnesses understand their role in the case. Many health care providers do not know legal terminology or understand its significance, but forensic nurses should be familiar with relevant legal phrases, such as, "within a degree of medical certainty" or "consistent with." The prosecutor will ask the medical witness to explain concepts, procedures, or terms that might not be easily understood by the jury using plain English whenever possible. When admitting evidence in a sexual assault case, many prosecutors consult the Federal Rules of Evidence relevant to expert witnesses. Federal Rule of Evidence 702, Testimony by Experts, provides:

> If scientific, technical, or other specialized knowledge will assist the trier of fact to understand the evidence or to determine a fact in issue, a witness qualified as an expert by knowledge, skill, experience, training or education, may testify thereto in the form of an opinion or otherwise if
>
> 1. The testimony is based upon sufficient facts or data,
> 2. The testimony is the product of reliable principles and methods, and
> 3. The witness has applied the principles and methods reliably to the facts of the case.

Before a medical witness can be deemed an expert in a given field, the proper foundation must be established. The witness should testify about his or her qualifications, which include, but are not limited to training and experience in a field of knowledge beyond that of an average layperson, and an explanation of this witness's area of expertise. The witness should explain field of expertise. The prosecutor must be clear in presenting the witness's qualifications as that of a health care provider whose main function is delivering medical care, not collecting evidence for the state. If a prosecutor attempts to qualify the health care provider as a forensic expert, the defense might have a compelling argument that the witness does not meet the requirements to be deemed an expert. If the medical witness does have training and experience in forensics, a prosecutor might consider asking the court to deem the witness an expert in the area of forensic science as well. Ruling on the qualifications of a medical expert is the same as for other experts.

After the witness's qualifications have been elicited and the witness is tendered to the court as an expert, the judge might ask whether the defense would like to *voir dire* the witness. Defense counsel can voir dire the witness on his or her qualifications before the court determines whether the witness has the qualifications to be deemed an expert. Some jurisdictions do not follow the practice of voir diring an expert prior to the court making its decision. If the health care provider is not deemed an expert, he or she can still testify as a fact witness who testifies to the facts at issue, but cannot render an opinion. After defense's voir dire, the attorney will either renew the objection to the witness being deemed an expert or withdraw it. The prosecutor will again move that the witness be deemed an expert in the relevant area of expertise. The judge will either accept or reject the witness as an expert. In some jurisdictions, the court is reluctant to give its imprimatur to the witness's testimony or rule on the witness's qualifications as an expert prior to hearing the actual opinion. In those jurisdictions, direct examination proceeds unless there is an objection; then the court will rule.

After the court has made its ruling regarding the expert status of the witness, the prosecutor will ask the witness to discuss the medical examination. If the victim was injured, the medical witness should have recorded all of the victim's injuries on the medical chart. Therefore, the prosecutor will shape a direct examination so that the witness refers to the medical chart and explains to the jury that the victim's entire body was the crime scene. The testimony should de-emphasize the genital injury. The witness's testimony should detail the injuries to other body parts that support the complainant's account of the facts. The prosecutor will elicit testimonial evidence of the complainant's demeanor or emotional state during the examination; for example, his or her nonresponsiveness, crying, flat effect, numbness, or anger. The prosecutor will use the medical chart and the medical witness's testimony to corroborate what the victim reported. The medical chart can provide independent corroboration of the complainant's recitation of the facts. For example, bruising to the upper arm corroborates the victim's account of the defendant grabbing her by the arm. If the victim had no injuries because she did not resist, the medical chart might corroborate this if she explained why she did not fight back; for example, documentation that the patient stated, "My children were in the next room and he said he would kill them if I did not do what he wanted." The prosecutor will ask if a follow-up examination was conducted, as it is not only useful evidence but discoverable to the defense. Several days later, the patient might present with pain and a bruised cervix. Photos taken with or without a colposcope are powerful evidence to present to the jury. If the complainant sought follow-up care, those records are also discoverable. All X-rays, dental exam records, diagrams, or other medical reports are also discoverable. If local law and the judge permit, the prosecutor will ask the medical expert to educate the jury. For example, an expert might testify about the medical literature showing that most sexual assault victims do not suffer visible genital injury. In many jurisdictions the expert can only be permitted to testify as to the facts of this particular case, or express an opinion about the examination performed on this victim, and cannot testify about what the studies and statistics report. A medical expert might be permitted to give a medical opinion as to whether the injuries the victim suffered were consistent with her account of the incident; for example, "The bruising to the victim's cervix is consistent with repeated exposure to blunt-force trauma." This statement, although it supports the victim's version of the attack, does not cross the line to the ultimate question of whether there was a rape.

During cross-examination, the prosecutor will consider what part of the case a defense attorney will attack, as the defense counsel will seek out the weakest aspects in every case to reveal and exploit them. To prepare for this inevitability, the prosecutor will—in pretrial meetings with the witness—review the witness's curriculum vitae, collect transcripts of trials in which the witness has testified, look for inconsistencies and weakness in the witness's testimony, and look for the areas that previous defense attorneys attacked and are likely to attack again. The prosecutor will read everything that the witness has written and the key treatises in the field about which the witness will testify. The medical witness must be prepared to be attacked on the stand by the defense counsel. The defense will most likely question the witness's qualifications. The defense attorney can attempt to minimize a nurse examiner's qualifications and impartiality in the eyes of the jury by saying, "You're just a nurse." The defense can also claim that a witness is an advocate who has the interest of the victim at heart and is therefore biased. The defense might also attempt to call into question the witness's familiarity with up-to-the-moment medical knowledge and techniques. For example, a defense attorney might point out that a medical witness who has 30 years of experience might be using techniques that are 30 years old.

To assist the medical witness in preparing for trial, the prosecutor must cross-examine the witness in advance. The witness should be ready to explain any point or inconsistency the defense attorney raises during cross-examination. If a prosecutor sees a potential problem with a potential mistake or an inconsistent statement, that issue should be brought out on the witness's direct examination; the prosecutor cannot let the jury hear this for the first time in cross-examination, as it could appear that the prosecution is hiding something. In preparing the witness, the prosecutor should also ask how the witness keeps current in his or her field, determining the research the witness might have published, or the medical techniques and procedures used or not used.

In a sexual assault case, there might be some questions about the chain of custody or the integrity of the samples in the rape kit. For example, there might be contamination or other compromise of evidence where a sample of biological evidence was stored in less than optimum conditions over a long period of time, as high temperature, humidity, and contaminants can all contribute to degradation of the sample. This degradation will affect the accuracy of the tests conducted on this sample. A medical witness must be prepared to testify whether or not evidence samples are in any way contaminated or compromised. The witness should also be prepared to explain to the jury how the test results would be affected. A medical witness should be willing to concede this point, but also be able to explain how the degradation of the sample impacted the test results. The jury should hear this testimony during the medical witness's direct examination, and the prosecutor should address the defense by bringing this information out on the direct and have the witness explain why the tests can still provide accurate information. In this scenario, it is important to remember the medical witness is not an expert in laboratory analysis, therefore, the medical witness should not do more than concede that the analysis might have been affected by the degradation of the samples. The laboratory technician should testify about the accuracy of the test results instead. It is critical to remember all evidence and every step, such as testing or storage, must be accounted for and documented.

It is critical for a prosecutor not to allow a medical witness to testify beyond the scope of his or her expertise. The witness should not overstate the statistics, exaggerate the numbers, or offer opinions not supported by the research. The witness is in the courtroom as a nod to his or her obvious expertise; however, a fatal flaw for a witness is exhibiting any of the following characteristics: arrogance, indifference, laziness, ineptitude, chauvinism, or partisanship. Experts say that a witness who is polite, prepared, and professional on the stand can only score points, making the defense attorney's job all the more difficult.

Former FBI agent Candice DeLong shares a few words of wisdom regarding surviving the court testimony process:

> Here's what nurses need to understand and what I learned once I got into law enforcement: It is the defense attorney's job not to see that justice is done, not to make sure the government proves its case and their client gets a fair trial; their job is to get the client off. Now obviously I am tongue-in-cheek here, but they really do want to get the client off the hook. They will attack you as the witness. It is their job to attempt to discredit every possible witness against their client. So if they are going to hire a doctor to say, "You are just a nurse," you will be able to say, "Well, I was the one who spent time with the patient, you didn't." When you get on the stand you are able to say something like, "This is what I observed: the patient was respiring 30 times a minute, the patient had cold and clammy skin, the patient refused to be touched, the patient had to be sedated for the vaginal exam, the patient's vagina is bruised and swollen, here's a picture." You state what you saw, what you heard, what you did. That said, forensic nurses might do well to get themselves some comprehensive education and training on how to testify properly to prepare themselves for the rigors of court. You are going to be torn apart by the defense attorney and if all they can say about you is that you're "just a nurse," then you know you probably have done a very good job on the stand. I advise nurses to be prepared, to do their homework and their legwork. Don't wilt just because you might take some heat on the stand. Be prepared, always be objective, be able to articulate your position clearly, because if you are weak on the stand, you are going to get creamed.

Barone and Ringholz (2003) emphasize the need for the nurse to combine his or her professional expertise with creative independent thinking to become an essential part of the litigation team. They write:

> Trial is the culmination of all the efforts put forth in developing a case. Depending on the nature of the case and its jurisdiction, the LNC and the trial team may have spent years working on a particular case. Thorough preparation is the key to a successful outcome. The attorney must be able to rely on the LNC to assist him or her in presenting the case in an organized fashion. The jury easily detects lack of preparedness in the trial team, and this will reflect on the team's competence. The ultimate outcome of the case will be influenced by how well and in what manner each side makes its presentation before the jury.

To satisfy the burden of proof in the case, evidence from the initial client intake, through discovery, and from experts is prepared for trial. All records must be in admissible form to be introduced as evidence during the trial. The legal team will determine which documents will be submitted as trial exhibits, and the LNC should establish the order in which the attorney will use each document. Physical evidence should be marked and identified on the exhibit list, and demonstrative evidence should be prepared in advance by the LNC. Demonstrative evidence refers to any evidence that allows the attorney to explain certain issues or facts to the jury in a way that facilitates their understanding of the concepts presented. Medical literature that will be referenced during the trial should be assembled by the LNC in an organized and easily accessible manner. This literature should follow the rules of admissibility and the LNC should be aware of major court decisions on what can be submitted.

Barone and Ringholz say that the nurse must be well versed in court proceedings. They write:

> The role of the LNC in a trial is as varied as the practice settings and specialization of nurses in the field. The common theme is anticipation—anticipation of testimony from witnesses for both the plaintiff and the defense. The LNC must be familiar with trial procedure and should be comfortable in the courtroom. This applies to all LNCs who have a role in the courtroom, whether as an expert witness or as a member of the trial team.

Nurses should be familiar with the various stages of a trial proceeding following jury selection. The opening statement is an argument to the jury within the rules of evidence and professional ethics; its purpose is to advise the jury of facts relied on and of issues involved, and to give jurors an overall picture of the pertinent facts of the case so that they will be able to understand the evidence. Barone and Ringholz advise, "The LNC should be able to analyze the opposing counsel's remarks and see whether any new theories may require a change in trial strategy, emphasis, or additional follow-up." The next step is the presentation of witnesses who explain the facts and issues of the case to the jury. Expert witnesses, who by reason of their experience, specialized training and education, and credentials, are capable of forming an accurate opinion. An expert witness is a witness who has been qualified as an expert in his or her field and is allowed to assist the jury in understanding complex or highly technical subject matter at the heart of the case. A fact witness presents testimony regarding the events of a particular situation that he or she witnessed.

Following the opening statements, the presentation of the case by the plaintiff begins, followed by the defendant's case. Examinations of each witness are conducted by both sides of the case, and the examination process consists of direct examination, cross-examination, and redirect examination, recross-examination, and rebuttal. Direct examination is conducted by the party who calls the witness. Cross-examination is conducted by the adverse party at the conclusion of direct testimony. Cross-examination can be followed by redirect examination to clarify or re-emphasize previous testimony. Rebuttal testimony is offered after the close of the defendant's case. Closing arguments are the summation of the testimony by the attorney for each party, and they are made by the attorneys to the court to summarize the evidence they believe they have established and the evidence they believe the opposing side has failed to establish. Jury deliberation ensues, and when a verdict has been reached, the jury returns to the courtroom and the verdict is read.

Barone and Ringholz (2003) comment, "The LNC's role, whether for the plaintiff or defense, should be a work of art providing an opportunity for the attorney to tell a story that will convince the jury which party should prevail."

13.9 THE FUTURE OF LEGAL NURSE CONSULTING AND NURSING JURISPRUDENCE

Prudence Schifley believes that there is much room for growth for forensic nurses who set their sights on a career in some form of nursing jurisprudence. "The law is ever evolving, and with these changes will come new opportunities for legal nurse consultants and nurse attorneys," she says. "As medicine evolves, the role of the LNC will evolve, too, because everything is becoming more complicated." Schifley believes that the trails blazed by nursing jurisprudence pioneers will continue to be heavily traveled by succeeding generations of nurses. She says that although the competition for work can be significant, she believes that persistent nurses will be able to foster lasting relationships with attorneys and legal teams. "Once you get your foot in the door and other attorneys see the impeccable work that you have done, additional work will come your way," Schifley says. She recalls a "no" that eventually turned into a "yes":

> I had called up an attorney and without even saying hello first he asked, "What are you selling?" and I said "Myself." At that point he didn't have any work for me and I asked if I could call him back, and he said, "Absolutely not." Six months later I called back and I said, "Do you have anything for me?" and he said, "How the hell are you?" I said, "I'm doing fine." And he said, "What can you do for me?" I replied, "I can make you the best damned abuse lawyer in the state of Connecticut," and he said, "You're hired, I've got a case for you." Sometimes the name of the game is persistence and belief in yourself.

REFERENCES

Barone, J., & Ringholz, J. Trial preparation. In P. W. Iyer, Ed. *Legal Nurse Consulting: Principles and Practice* (2nd edition). (pp. 953–968). Boca Raton, FL: CRC Press. 2003.

Canaff, R. A. Pediatric sexual assault nurse examination: Challenges and opportunities for MDTs in child sexual abuse cases. *NCPCA Update, 16*, 9, 2004a.

Canaff, R. A. Limits and lessons: The expert medical opinion in adolescent sexual abuse cases. *NCPCA Update, 17,* 3, 2004b.

Davis, D., Faugno, D., McMahon, J., & King, P. A. S. Evaluating forensics cases. In P. W. Iyer, Ed. *Legal nurse consulting: Principles and practice* (2nd edition). Boca Raton, FL: CRC Press. 2003.

Gilson, J. A. Forensic nursing: A most competent practice. *On the Edge,* Fall 2000.

Iyer, P. W., Ed. *Legal nurse consulting: Principles and practice* (2nd edition). Boca Raton, FL: CRC Press. 2003.

Lynch, V. A. *Clinical forensic nursing: A new perspective in trauma.* Ft. Collins, CO: Bearhawk Consulting Group. 1997.

14 DNA Evidence and Medico-Legal Issues

CONTENTS

Deoxyribonucleic acid (DNA) evidence is playing a larger role than ever before in criminal cases throughout the country, both to convict the guilty and to exonerate those wrongly accused or convicted. This increased role places greater importance on the ability of health care providers to understand the potential significance of DNA evidence in their patients' cases. DNA is pivotal in a number of cases and issues that forensic professionals will encounter, from suspectless cases and cold-case hits to the role of DNA evidence in acquaintance rapes.

14.1 DNA EVIDENCE COLLECTION

According to the International Association of Forensic Nurses (IAFN) (2003):

> In addition to treating the victims' emotional trauma and physical injuries, quality forensic care includes the careful and systematic collection and preservation of forensic evidence necessary to convict or exonerate accused perpetrators of interpersonal and sexual violence. Unfortunately, victims who survive an assault many times do not receive the complete investigative evaluation, including development of their kit. For some, the kit is never developed and the assailant goes unpunished.

The kit in question is the rape evidence analysis kit. It has been established that forensic nurses are competent collectors of evidence, and perhaps some of the most compelling evidence that they collect in medico-legal cases is DNA evidence. However, a vast majority of rape kits are relegated to the shelves of police lockers and storage closets at forensic laboratories because of lack of funds, limited resources, and an overwhelming volume of DNA evidence that must be analyzed for not only sexual assault cases, but in cases involving homicide and other violent crimes. At the time of writing, approximately 500,000 pieces of evidence have yet to be analyzed, much less used in the prosecution of a perpetrator. For the last several years, this significant backlog has garnered growing attention from the media, from crime victims, and from lawmakers who are struggling to increase the capacity of a limited number of public forensic laboratories. IAFN past president Patricia M. Speck, MSN, APRN, BC, FAAN, SANE-A, has remarked, "Victims and suspects have to wait for justice with no assurance it is coming. Today, in theory, we don't need a suspect but we still can't get the kit developed because the labs can't handle it."

On its Web site, the IAFN points to four problems victims of sexual assault face with DNA and other evidence:

- Health care professionals receive no information about forensic issues in their basic medical and nursing education and enter the workforce at a deficit.
- Many health care facilities have incentive to clean up, patch up, and send sexual assault victims home as soon as possible. "Cleaning up" sexual assault victims inherently destroys DNA, the very evidence that could otherwise be used by the law enforcement system to apprehend the offender.
- In those health care facilities where some care is taken to collect forensic evidence, it is often gathered by individuals who are not trained in handling forensic specimens. When brought to court, this evidence is often inadmissible.
- In health care facilities where forensic evidence is routinely collected by a qualified SANE, the evidence might still sit on a shelf for years while a perpetrator of the crime is free to rape again and again.

It is this last point that concerns members of the entire medico-legal community, who say that the power of the most important crime-fighting tool of the century, DNA, cannot be unleashed if it is sitting in a small box on a high shelf, untouched, unanalyzed, and awaiting the end of many states' statutes of limitations. Many more boxes of evidence are thrown out in short-sighted jurisdictions, and with these parcels go the hopes of victims across the country.

A better understanding of DNA and its role in the medico-legal and criminal justice processes is essential for forensic nurses of all subspecialties. DNA is the building block for the human body, with DNA present in everything from blood and saliva to skin tissue, hair, and bone. DNA is a powerful investigative tool because, with the exception of identical twins, no two people have the same DNA. Therefore, DNA evidence collected from a crime scene can be linked to a suspect or can eliminate a suspect from suspicion. During a sexual assault, for example, biological evidence such as hair, skin cells, semen, or blood can be deposited on the victim's body or on other objects at the crime scene. Properly collected DNA can be compared with known samples to place a suspect at the scene of the crime. In addition, if no suspect exists, a DNA profile from crime scene evidence can be entered into the FBI's Combined DNA Index System (CODIS) database to identify a suspect anywhere in the United States or to link serial crimes to each other. In 1982, California was the first state to begin requiring blood samples from certain sex offenders. Although DNA was not specifically mentioned in the statute, and although the basis for modern forensic DNA analysis was not introduced until 1985, California's identification of the utility of collecting blood samples from a specified group of known offenders was groundbreaking at the time. In 1988, Colorado became the first state to specify through statute the requirement for DNA samples from certain offenders, and in 1990, Virginia became the first state to enact a law requiring DNA from all convicted felons. In 1991, the FBI established guidelines for states on sex offender DNA database laws and began developing the concept of a computer software program that would operate similar to the national criminal fingerprint database (IAFIS). In 1994, this DNA database program was officially created in statute by Congress through the DNA Identification Act and was formally named CODIS. Today, every state has a DNA database statute that allows collection of DNA from specified offenders. All 50 states require DNA from sex offenders and murderers, and 46 states require DNA from all violent felony convictions (including assault and battery and robbery). Over the past several years, a growing number of states have been expanding their databases to include nonviolent felony convictions; 45 states require DNA from burglary convictions, 36 states require DNA from certain drug convictions, and 31 states require DNA from all felony convictions. (These figures are current through July 2003.) According to the FBI CODIS program office, there were 1,321,854 offender DNA profiles in NDIS as of April 2003. Additionally, 41 state CODIS laboratories reported 463,209 offender samples that were expected to be part of the laboratory backlog by June 30, 2003. CODIS uses two indexes to generate investigative leads in crimes that contain biological evidence. The forensic index contains DNA profiles from biological evidence left at crime scenes, and the offender index contains DNA profiles of individuals convicted of violent crime. CODIS enables federal, state, and local forensic crime laboratories to work together, between jurisdictions and across state lines, to solve crimes.

The effective use of DNA as evidence might also require the collection and analysis of elimination samples to determine the exact source of the DNA. Elimination samples can be taken from anyone who had lawful access to the crime scene and might have left biological material. When investigating a rape case, for example, it might be necessary to obtain an elimination sample from everyone who had consensual intercourse with the victim within 72 hours of the alleged assault to account for all of the DNA found on the victim or at the crime scene. Comparing DNA profiles from the evidence with elimination samples can help clarify the results.

The monograph *Understanding DNA Evidence: A Guide for Victim Service Providers*, produced by the National Institute of Justice and the Office for Victims of Crime (2001), reviews for nurse examiners and other medical personnel the important tenets of identifying, collecting, transporting, and storing DNA evidence. Above all else, it is essential to remember that if DNA evidence is not initially identified at the crime scene or on the victim, it might not be collected, or it might become contaminated or degraded. To avoid contamination of evidence that could contain DNA, always take the following precautions: wear gloves and change them often; use disposable instruments or clean and disinfect them thoroughly before and after handling each sample; avoid touching the area where you believe DNA might exist; avoid talking, sneezing, and coughing over evidence; avoid touching your face, nose, and mouth when collecting and packaging evidence; air-dry evidence thoroughly before packaging; and put evidence into new paper bags or envelopes, not into plastic bags. To assist in the evidence collection process, victims of sexual assault should not change clothes, shower, or wash any part of their body after the assault, as evidence such as semen, saliva, and skin cells can be found on clothing or bedding, under fingernails, or in the vaginal, anal, or mouth region. Evidence on or inside a victim's body should be collected by a SANE or other qualified professional. A medical examination should be conducted immediately after the assault to treat any injuries, test for STDs, and collect forensic evidence, such as fingernail scrapings and hair. Typically, the vaginal cavity, mouth, anus, or other parts of the body that might have come into contact with the assailant are examined. The examiner should also take a reference sample of blood or saliva from the victim to serve as a control standard. Reference samples of the victim's head and pubic hair might also be collected if hair analysis is required. A control standard is used to compare known DNA from the victim with that of other DNA evidence found at the crime scene to determine possible suspects. Given the sensitive nature of DNA evidence, the National Institute of Justice monograph emphasizes that examiners should always contact crime laboratory personnel or evidence technicians when procedural collection questions arise. Because only a few cells are needed for a useful DNA sample, the following list from the National Institute of Justice identifies some areas at the crime scene or on the victim that might contain DNA evidence:

- Bite mark or area licked: saliva
- Fingernail scrapings: blood or skin cells
- Inside or outside surface of used condom: semen or skin cells
- Blankets, sheets, pillows, or other bed linens: semen, sweat, hair, or saliva
- Clothing, including undergarments worn during and after the assault: hair, semen, blood, or sweat
- Hat, bandanna, or mask: sweat, skin cells, hair, or saliva
- Tissue, washcloth, or similar item: saliva, semen, hair, skin cells, or blood
- Cigarette butt, toothpick, chewing gum, or rim of bottle, can, or glass: saliva
- Dental floss: semen, skin cells, or saliva
- Tape or ligature: skin cells, saliva, or hair

DNA evidence can become contaminated when DNA from another source is mixed with DNA relevant to the case. For this reason, investigators and laboratory personnel should always wear disposable gloves, use clean instruments, and avoid touching other objects, including their own body, when handling evidence. Environmental factors, such as heat and humidity, can also accelerate the degradation of DNA. For example, wet or moist evidence that is packaged in plastic will provide a growth environment for bacteria that can destroy DNA evidence. Therefore, biological evidence should be thoroughly air-dried, packaged in paper, and properly labeled. Handled in this manner, DNA can be stored for years without risk of extensive degradation, even at room temperature. When transporting and storing evidence that could contain DNA, it is important to keep the evidence dry and at room temperature. Once the evidence has been secured in paper bags or envelopes, it should be sealed, labeled, and transported in a way that ensures proper identification of where it was found and proper chain of custody. Never place evidence that migh contain DNA in plastic bags because they retain damaging moisture. Direct sunlight and warmer conditions also can be harmful to DNA, so avoid keeping evidence in places that can get hot, such as a room or police car without air conditioning.

According to *What Every Law Enforcement Officer Should Know About DNA Evidence* from the National Institute of Justice of the U.S. Department of Justice (2004):

> Investigators with a fundamental knowledge of how to identify, preserve, and collect DNA evidence properly can solve cases in ways previously seen only on television. Evidence invisible to the naked eye can be the key to solving a residential burglary, sexual assault, or child's murder. It also can be the evidence that links different crime scenes to each other in a small town, within a single state, or even across the nation. The saliva on the stamp of a stalker's threatening letter or the skin cells shed on a ligature of a strangled victim can be compared with a suspect's blood or saliva sample. Similarly, DNA collected from the perspiration on a baseball cap discarded by a rapist at one crime scene can be compared with DNA in the saliva swabbed from the bite mark on a different rape victim.

DNA evidence can be collected from virtually anywhere, and has helped solve many cases when imaginative investigators collected evidence from nontraditional sources. One homicide was solved when the suspect's DNA, taken from saliva in a dental impression mold, matched the DNA swabbed from a bite mark on the victim. In another case, a masked rapist was convicted of forced oral copulation when his victim's DNA matched DNA swabbed from the suspect's penis six hours after the crime. Numerous cases have been solved by DNA analysis of saliva on cigarette butts, postage stamps, and the area around the mouth opening on ski masks. DNA analysis of a single hair (without the root) found deep in the victim's throat provided a critical piece of evidence used in a capital murder conviction. According to the National Institute of Justice report, because extremely small samples of DNA can be used as evidence, greater attention to contamination issues is necessary when identifying, collecting, and preserving DNA evidence. DNA evidence can be contaminated when DNA from another source gets mixed with DNA relevant to the case. This can happen when someone sneezes or coughs over the evidence or touches his or her mouth, nose, or other part of the face and then touches the area that might contain the DNA to be tested. Because a new DNA technology called polymerase chain reaction (PCR) replicates or copies DNA in the evidence sample, the introduction of contaminants or other unintended DNA to an evidence sample can be problematic. With such minute samples of DNA being copied, extra care must be taken to prevent contamination. If a sample of DNA is submitted for testing, the PCR process will copy whatever DNA is present in the sample; it cannot distinguish between a suspect's DNA and DNA from another source.

Forensic nurses should be familiar with the basics of DNA testing. According to the National Institute of Justice monograph, the most common form of DNA analysis is PCR. PCR has allowed investigators to successfully analyze evidence samples of limited quality and quantity. The PCR process makes millions of copies of very small amounts of DNA, which enables the laboratory to generate a DNA profile, which can be compared with the DNA profile from a suspect. A statistic is then generated to reflect how often one would expect to find this particular DNA profile in the general population. Three types of results can occur in DNA testing: inclusion, exclusion, and inconclusive. It is important that forensic professionals understand the meaning of these terms and be able to explain their implications. The National Institute of Justice (2001) establishes these three definitions:

- Inclusion: When the DNA profile of a victim or suspect is consistent with the DNA profile from the crime scene evidence, the individual is included as the possible source of that evidence. However, the strength of inclusion depends on the number of loci (locations on the DNA strand) examined and how common or rare the resulting DNA profile is in the general population.
- Exclusion: When the DNA profile from a victim or suspect is inconsistent with the DNA profile generated from the crime scene evidence, the individual is excluded as the donor of the evidence. However, exclusion does not imply innocence. In a rape case, for example, a perpetrator wearing a condom could be excluded as a suspect because no semen was found at the crime scene, but evidence found elsewhere at the crime scene might include that same person as a suspect.
- Inconclusive: Inconclusive results indicate that DNA testing could neither include nor exclude an individual as the source of biological evidence. Inconclusive results can occur for many reasons. For example, the quality or quantity of DNA might be insufficient to produce interpretable results, or the evidentiary sample might contain a mixture of DNA from several individuals (e.g., a sample taken from a victim of a gang rape).

As with all DNA testing results, additional testing might be needed and findings should be interpreted in the context of other evidence in the case. According to the National Institute of Justice monograph:

> Advanced DNA technology, such as PCR, makes it possible to obtain conclusive results in cases in which previous testing might have been inconclusive. This can result in the identification of suspects in previously unsolvable cases or the exoneration of those wrongfully convicted. It is important to realize that while testing or retesting may exonerate an individual, exclusionary results may not necessarily prove actual innocence. Prosecutors, defense counsel, the court, and law enforcement should confer on the need for testing on a case-by-case basis.

According to Hogan and Swinton (2003), DNA evidence has catapulted criminal justice into a new era, and has equipped prosecutors with an immensely powerful tool for determining the identity of persons who commit crime. There are few techniques in the history of forensic science that have been more thoroughly scrutinized and validated than forensic DNA testing. Although DNA is no longer the unchartered waters that it used to be, experts in forensic science and criminal justice agree that developing specific policies for utilizing DNA evidence can help prosecutors and law enforcement officials establish priorities and avoid pitfalls in the adjudicatory process.

14.2 DNA EVIDENCE POLICY CONSIDERATIONS

In November 2003, the American Prosecutors Research Institute (APRI), the nonprofit research, training, and technical assistance affiliate of the National District Attorneys

Association, assembled more than 200 prosecutors, law enforcement officers, DNA analysts, SANEs, and other criminal justice community members for a two-and-a-half-day conference. Participants discussed and evaluated different approaches regarding DNA evidence and the maximization of both resources and probative value, and identified recurrent issues and potential policy responses. These key points were compiled into a monograph, *DNA Evidence Policy Considerations for the Prosecutor* (APRI, 2004), which also proposed several promising policy ideas that jurisdictions can implement or modify to fit their unique needs and capabilities.

The policies created by consensus share two common denominators: They are sensitive to the specific needs of different jurisdictions, with their differing populations, caseloads, and resources; and they involve the participation of law enforcement agencies, SANEs, prosecutors' offices, and labs. The monograph states, "Without their participation and cooperation, success of these policies is unlikely. However, the cooperative development of appropriate policies with regard to the identification, collection, development, discovery and use of DNA evidence will allow for the elimination of backlog, expeditious case management and successful prosecutions; in short, achieving the full potential that DNA evidence has to offer." Experts agree it is essential to develop policies that establish a triage system of the appropriateness of the use of DNA evidence in new cases, suspectless cases, and collaterally attacked closed cases, as well as to develop policies that address the way that relevant agencies will respond to defense discovery requests. New cases are defined as those cases in which the offense has been newly detected but the perpetrator has not yet been charged.

Participants of the APRI conference identified two issues that would most benefit from policy development: early case evaluation and discovery. Timely evidentiary review improves the management of current cases containing biological evidence and caseloads. The APRI monograph explains that certain cases, such as child sexual abuse or homicide, have historically used multidisciplinary evidence reviews, citing increased communication and early analysis as producing stronger rebuttal to whatever defense is proffered. The monograph adds:

> In evaluating every case, prosecutors, police and forensic scientists or criminalists should determine what evidence is probative of the defendant's guilt. This evidentiary or case review should be a collaborative process. By reviewing cases as soon as possible after a crime has been discovered, the panel can identify which pieces of evidence are amenable to DNA testing, which have the most probative value, and/or which should be tested first. The case review panel must also identify potential defenses, which will help determine the appropriate testing to better challenge untrue defenses.

For example, DNA testing might be relevant in murder cases in which the anticipated defense is the justified use of deadly force to corroborate the physical evidence or eyewitnesses, or in a sexual assault case to corroborate the victim's account that there were two assailants involved in the offense, or to compare the location of the DNA mixtures with the victim's account of the offense. This kind of case review also documents why certain items of evidence were, or were not, tested; experts say that avoiding unnecessary testing of evidence reduces the laboratories' caseloads and frees up those resources for more appropriate use.

The APRI monograph suggests the following guidelines for multidisciplinary case review:

- Prosecutor responsibilities include designating which agencies will participate in the evidence reviewing team; designating an "on-call" prosecutor who would either respond to crime scenes or be available by telephone on a 24-hour basis for homicide, sexual assault, or other cases; and assigning responsibility to a specific prosecutor for notifying the laboratory and police when a case is either abandoned or closed.
- Laboratory responsibilities include assigning a specific staff member to participate in multidisciplinary case reviews that might occur prior to evidence testing; immediately notifying police and prosecutors if sample consumption or exhaustion is anticipated; immediately notifying police and prosecutors if there is a CODIS match or cold hit.
- Police responsibilities include assigning an officer to participate in collective case or evidence review prior to any testing; immediately notifying prosecutors if a chain of custody issue is either anticipated or created; and immediately notifying prosecutors and the laboratory if information of a CODIS match or cold hit is received.

DNA evidence is extremely important in solving suspectless cases, which are often old, unsolved cases, usually referred to as cold cases. They might have remained unsolved because DNA evidence analysis was not available when the crime was committed, or the crime scene evidence was tested but failed to yield a suspect match. There is a difference between cold cases and cold hits, according to the APRI monograph. Cold cases are suspectless cases often solved through DNA cold hits. *Cold* refers to the suspectless nature of the case, regardless of its age. *Hits* refer to any match of crime-scene DNA to a DNA profile of a known human being, usually from a DNA database. A cold hit can occur in a case of any age.

Forensic DNA evidence databanks rely on software that constantly compares profiles from crime scenes to profiles developed from individuals. As soon as crime-scene DNA data from a case of any age is entered into the database, the software rapidly searches for a match. Until there is a hit, the evidence samples remain in storage. As a result, one of the biggest problems plaguing the justice community is the backlog of untested evidence. Aggressively reviewing old unsolved cases can address some of the backlog issues. At a minimum, the APRI monograph asserts, cold case review policies should establish a triage system for reviewing cases, submitting existing DNA data into the databases, and initiating DNA testing of untested evidence samples; and address the logistics of implementing the triage system. One of the initial steps in addressing the backlog issue should be identifying which and how many cases have remaining and available biological evidence. Several questions must be answered: Will all unsolved cases be reviewed, or only those in which there is reason to believe a serial rapist was involved? Is viability of a prosecution the determinative factor for testing? Should cases only be tested when all necessary witnesses are available and cooperative, or should all unsolved cases with biological evidence be tested regardless of the viability of the prosecution? Does the forensic laboratory have the availability, resources, and personnel to test backlog or cold-case evidence, or will the testing have to be outsourced?

Some of the answers to these questions depend on location, the APRI monograph states. For example, jurisdictions that have long-standing SANE programs are likely to have a larger number of cases with preserved biological evidence. Those jurisdictions might want to review sexual assault cases before reviewing homicides or burglaries. Similarly, jurisdictions with established databanks are likely to benefit from early identification of likely serial criminals. The question of who will review the cases must be answered. Whereas some jurisdictions have used retired police officers, other jurisdictions have used officers to review unsolved cases while supplementing the case review committees with a couple of prosecutors. An increasing number of government entities have earmarked funds for the outsourcing of cases to private-sector laboratories.

One of the more successful programs in the country is the Solving Unsolved Cases program in Alameda County, California. Whenever a truly suspectless case involving biological sexual assault evidence arises, the investigator contacts the deputy district attorney to schedule a review of the case. A copy of the entire investigation is provided at that time and the file is maintained by the district attorney's office. When formulating policies to address suspectless cases, certain responsibilities are shared by prosecutors, police, and labs, including participating in the development of triage decisions and assigning case-review responsibilities to specific members of the multidisciplinary team, at specific locations, by certain deadlines. In addition, prosecutors have a responsibility to review each case after initial case review by the multidisciplinary team, to anticipate potential defenses, and to plan appropriate responses. Police responsibilities under this program include determining the number of cases with remaining biological evidence, and determining if material witnesses or victims are available. The forensic laboratories are responsible for estimating the number of cases that can be tested within established time frames.

Cold-hit policies address the most appropriate laboratory, law enforcement, and prosecution responses to the notification of a hit. The solving of a cold case is often a newsworthy event, which raises several important issues. If the proper agencies do not act expeditiously, the victims, survivors, witnesses, and suspects will learn of the identification of the suspect from the news media. The consequences can be disastrous. Victims or witnesses might not know that they have a right not to speak to reporters, or they might not be able to communicate their refusal in a way that does not constitute a comment on the case. Witnesses' remarks could be taken out of context, or their statements might come back to them in cross-examination by a defense attorney. Victims deserve personalized attention, with sensitivity to their possible trauma and access to someone who can answer their questions. Properly preparing a victim for a likely media event can prevent these damaging outcomes. Potential sources of leaks extend beyond the evaluating team. To the extent possible, the team should elicit the cooperation of magistrates who issue search warrants or arrest warrants. No single agency should be precluded from celebrating the identification of a criminal, but all should wait until the case has been prepared.

As part of the follow-up investigation after the notification of a hit, a confirmation DNA sample must be acquired from the identified suspect. There are three ways a confirmation sample can be obtained legally: through consent, search warrant, or abandonment. Prosecutors might prefer one approach to another because there could be ramifications with a jury; therefore, the method to be used should be discussed beforehand. It is also beneficial for prosecutors to participate in drafting consent forms and search warrants, to avoid suppression issues. Finally, the method used to obtain the confirmation sample is often intertwined with whether damaging offender statements can be obtained. The following language from a cold hit protocol developed by Alameda County might be helpful: A computer-generated cold hit is meant to begin the investigation, rather than represent the end of the investigation. There are substantial legal considerations to be made about the case as a whole, some of which involve the form of legal admissibility of evidence derived from the cold hit. Offenders' statements are always an important piece of evidence; although not always apparent, they are often affirmative admissions. Furthermore, depending on the crime committed, an offender's statements might be crucial to overcoming an untrue defense, such as victim consent in sexual assault cases. For example, when an offender gives a statement denying having any contact with the victim, let alone raping her, DNA evidence connecting this offender to the victim can be quite powerful. Similarly, an offender statement describing the crime in a way that is inconsistent with the physical evidence (e.g., a defendant states that a struggle occurred at a specific location but all the blood—verified by DNA evidence—belonging to victim and offender is found at a different location altogether) can be devastating to the defense.

A consistent cold hit policy can maximize the power of DNA as forensic evidence. Investigators working under such a policy should know why they should obtain a sample consensually and how to obtain incriminating suspect statements in the process. They should be prepared to interview the suspect about all known allegations, because the very nature of DNA databanks promotes identification of repeat offenders. Furthermore, agencies that have developed cold hit policies might be able to prevent the media or corrections officers from informing the defendant that he or she has been "matched." Finally, the use of proactive unsolved case policies, together with reactive cold hit policies, will bring justice for the sometimes-forgotten victims as well as the unprosecuted criminals.

The identification and resolution of more than one crime committed by an offender has several obvious benefits, including filing the appropriate charges for prosecution, leverage for plea agreements, use of other crimes or bad act evidence, or enhancement of punishment at sentencing hearings. Collaterally attacked closed cases are cases in which the defendant has been convicted of an offense and seeks to collaterally attack his or her conviction. Prosecutorial policies that address postconviction relief enhance public trust in the integrity of the legal system. A proactive search for potentially problematic cases, testing or retesting in cases when the results would be consequential, and publication of the results are all essential to reinforcing public confidence. Generally, both the trial prosecutor and the elected or appointed prosecutor should be involved in deciding whether to set aside a conviction based on exclusionary DNA results. Jurisdictions vary in who they select to review closed cases: law enforcement officers, law students, or senior prosecutors. Some jurisdictions have included defense lawyers in limited roles. Others have defined a limited role for advocates who meet with the victims throughout the process. A few jurisdictions have established precedent conditions for cases to be included in a review: The conviction occurred before a certain date, and the defendant must have maintained his or her assertion of mistaken or wrongful identification. For example, the Ramsey County (Minnesota) Attorney's Office initiated a review of past crimes against persons that were prosecuted in 1994 or earlier. They further defined the scope of the review by requiring that biological evidence must still be available, the defendant had consistently maintained his or her innocence based on mistaken or wrongful identification, and current DNA technology could provide exonerating evidence. An important consideration is the role the convicted offenders should play. After all, they are the best situated to know of actual misidentification. In Oregon, letters were written inviting eligible defendants to apply for postconviction testing, explaining strict deadlines and the rules to the testing process. The defendants' responses, or lack thereof, were integral to the decision-making process.

Once prosecutors, police, and labs have developed noncrisis working relationships and established appropriate policies, they can make mutually satisfactory decisions to prioritize the allocation of resources. Should remaining evidence in old unsolved cases be reviewed before all other cases, or should postconviction cases, perhaps smaller in number, be reviewed first? If old, unsolved cases are to be reviewed first, should only cases with suspects merit evidence review before testing? These difficult decisions can be made with deliberation and forethought through a comprehensive review of available resources; coordination among law enforcement, laboratory analysts, and prosecutors; and implementation of policies for guidance. According to the APRI monograph:

> Backlog elimination is imperative, as an increasing number of states are taking DNA samples from all convicted felons. The aforementioned policies, when combined, can make significant progress toward reducing the backlog. For example, because "pre-DNA" post-conviction and cold cases generally occur in manageable numbers, it may be prudent to review, test and resolve them promptly. Prosecutors have been reactive for too long in their use of forensic DNA evidence. When prosecutors are proactive, they can help the labs eliminate backlog and remain current in casework. In doing so, they will enhance public confidence in our criminal justice system.

As of this writing, 31 states have passed legislation authorizing the taking of DNA samples from all persons convicted of any felony: Alabama, Alaska, Arizona, Arkansas, Colorado, Connecticut, Delaware, Florida, Georgia, Illinois, Iowa, Kansas, Louisiana, Maryland, Massachusetts, Michigan, Minnesota, Mississippi, Montana, New Jersey, New Mexico, North Carolina, Oregon, South Dakota, Tennessee, Texas, Utah, Virginia, Washington, Wisconsin, and Wyoming.

14.3 JOHN DOE CASES

In the article, "Newest Suspect in Rapes: The DNA," which appeared in the June 20, 2004 issue of *The Boston*

Globe, writer Suzanne Smalley (2004) reported on the advent of using "John Doe" DNA indictments, where prosecutors bring charges—even when the perpetrator is unknown—against the DNA profile from the evidence gathered. Smalley explained that the approach originated in Milwaukee in 1999 and spread to counties in Texas, California, and New York. In April 2003, Congress approved legislation allowing prosecutors to bring John Doe DNA indictments for federal sex offenses. Smalley writes, "It is expected to expand further as states grow their DNA databases, which will allow the DNA profiles to be regularly checked against criminals whose DNA is entered in the databank." She added that this new technique is "setting off concern among civil libertarians and defense lawyers, who argue that DNA indictments are nothing more than a clever device to evade existing statute of limitations laws, which require a prosecutor to bring charges against someone within a reasonable period of time after a crime has occurred, so a solid defense can be mounted." Smalley reported that defense attorneys worry that rape cases could now be brought several decades after the crime, "which will leave the accused unable to mount a strong defense, because alibi witnesses and memory can grow fuzzy, and other evidence can get stale." She quoted Barry Steinhardt, director of the American Civil Liberties Union Technology and Liberty project, as saying, "The problem with having a trial 20 years after the fact is that the only evidence available may be the DNA evidence."

In August 2003, New York City Mayor Michael Bloomberg announced the city's John Doe Indictment Project, an effort endowed with a $350,000 grant from the U.S. Department of Justice. Under this program, hundreds of rape cases at least nine years old are anticipated to be reviewed. Smalley reported that so far, the Manhattan District Attorney's office has indicted 17 John Doe DNA profiles involving 21 victims but has not apprehended any suspects. Faring a little better has been Milwaukee. Smalley reported that of the 15 John Does indicted by prosecutors since 1999, six have been matched through the DNA database. Of the six, four were already in jail and one is missing; another was apprehended after the match was made.

14.4 HARNESSING THE POWER OF DNA

There is no question that the biggest development of all in the prosecution of criminal cases is the advent of DNA. According to the National Institute of Justice (National Commission on the Future of DNA Evidence, 1999):

> The development of DNA profiling has revolutionized 20th century forensic science as well as the criminal justice system. It frequently enables prosecutors to conclusively establish the guilt of a defendant, particularly in sexual assault and homicide cases where an offender is most likely to leave his genetic signature—trace and biological evidence. DNA evidence is even more likely to exonerate a wrongly accused suspect than to identify a guilty one. This helps prosecutors to avoid unjust prosecutions that may carry high human, financial and political costs.

More than a decade after its introduction, DNA profiling is still only selectively used. The costs of DNA testing remain high, and processing backlogs are in the tens of thousands. This can be expected to change, however, as research develops less costly and time-consuming DNA evidence collection and profiling methods. Currently, every state is in the process of implementing a DNA database of individuals convicted of certain crimes such as rape, child abuse, and murder. Their DNA profiles are entered into CODIS, against which DNA evidence from crime scenes can be compared.

Writing in the white paper, "Forensic DNA," former police sergeant-turned-educator and consultant Joanne Archambault (2000) remarks:

> Advances in technology have made DNA testing an established part of the sexual assault investigation and subsequent prosecution. Traditional serology identity testing for blood, saliva, and semen, are now virtually obsolete. In 1996, there were more than 17,000 cases involving forensic DNA in the United States alone, yet the potential for DNA is far greater than its current use, due to current budget limitations in testing DNA evidence and the systems used to collect and access DNA information.

Since the mid- to late-1990s, there have been a number of attempts to harness the power of DNA testing to exonerate individuals wrongfully convicted of rape and homicide. In 1998, former U.S. Attorney General Janet Reno created the National Commission on the Future of DNA Evidence, which was tasked with submitting to the attorney general recommendations to ensure more effective use of DNA as a crime-fighting tool and foster its use throughout the criminal justice system. Archambault notes, "To date, law enforcement's role has been limited because DNA technology developed primarily as a prosecutorial weapon, not an investigative tool. DNA evidence has been used primarily to confirm the identity of someone already under suspicion."

In the United Kingdom, DNA was first applied in a mass testing of more than 4,500 individuals in a case in which no one had yet been charged. In the United States, Archambault explains, DNA testing has been conducted primarily in cases of sexual assault involving biological evidence. In the United Kingdom, the majority of DNA database matches involve burglaries, with the evidence tested consisting of blood found at the sites of forced entry.

The human body offers a plethora of DNA sources, including saliva, skin cells, bone, teeth, tissue, urine, feces, vomit, and other bodily substances discovered at crime scenes. Forensic nurses should know where to swab the victim's body for these potential sources of the perpetrator's DNA. Archambault writes, "A suspect's saliva may be found on a sexual assault victim's bra, put on after the suspect has licked or sucked on a victim's breasts. It can also be found in chewing gum, cigarette butts, envelopes and drinking cups. Fingernail scrapings or swabs from a suspect's hands might corroborate digital penetration of the victim's genitals. The potential for DNA evidence is almost unlimited." Unfortunately, she adds, appropriate DNA evidence is often not collected from the crime scene, or not analyzed by crime laboratories due to limited resources. She points to an FBI survey that revealed of all rapes, less than 10 percent had evidence submitted to crime laboratories. As a result of the limited resources in crime laboratories, in only 6 percent of the 250,000 rape cases was the recovered DNA tested, leaving a backlog of several hundred thousand cases awaiting processing.

Forensic examiner Cari Caruso, RN, SANE-A, recognizes the overwhelming backlog of sexual assault evidence kits as well as the resulting delay in the kits' processing by law enforcement. "In forensic television shows, we see evidence being analyzed instantly," Caruso says:

> So I think that is a little misleading for the public as well as clinicians who have unrealistic expectations. We do need to address the backlog because there are sexual assault kits sitting on shelves. In reality, if studies are demonstrating that the majority of individuals are sexually assaulted by someone they know, and the cases boil down to the fact that he says it was consensual and she says it wasn't consensual, there is no need to analyze those kits. The fact is, we know who the accuser is and we know who the accused is, so we are not looking for DNA. The issue is when we have an unknown assailant, and we need as much evidence to go on as possible. If we have 1,000 rape kits on the shelves, and 95 percent of those kits represent cases of known assailants and consent/nonconsent, it's the other 5 percent of cases whose DNA evidence we need to concentrate on. That's where we need to put our analysis time, energy, and resources, not with the cases where we have a known offender. Of course, at the time we collect the evidence, we don't know what the victim is going to say, so we must always collect evidence in every case.

Caruso also would like to see some kind of presumptive test for semen in the sexual assault evidence kit:

> It would be helpful to have the option of some kind of presumptive testing for the cases that might be iffy, where the victim doesn't remember much of what happened or if anything happened. Presumptive testing might be able to tell us if we have a case to investigate. Or maybe it is a possible drug-facilitated sexual assault and the victim blacked out; if some sort of quick test could be done, we can find out if we need to be looking for sperm of not, and of course, there may be many reasons why there may not be semen in any case.

Archambault writes, "In reality, this is only the tip of the iceberg. Many law enforcement agencies have not been properly trained to recognize and collect potential DNA evidence. In addition, the DNA molecule is long-lived and likely to be detectable for many years in bones or body fluid meaning that old cases can now be solved and possibly prosecuted using current forensic technology." She explains that investigators must be able to re-evaluate these cases and identify those that lend themselves to DNA testing. Archambault adds that many medical personnel, including forensic nurses, are startled to learn that few cases are actually analyzed for forensic evidence. She writes, "Attention to the number of DNA reference samples that have been collected from sex offenders and typed has led most of us to believe that the problem has been solved." She points to the sheer volume of evidence found in the average case:

> Processing a pure sample such as blood or a saliva swab is only a small part of the DNA process. Evidence from the scene, sheets, rape kits, and numerous items of clothing, must still be screened for potential DNA evidence. One sheet or shirt may contain numerous stains. Once a stain is detected, it must be extracted for DNA comparison. This continues to be a time-consuming and costly process. But, until the evidence from the scene can be analyzed, there will be nothing to compare with any database, no matter how many offender DNA profiles the database contains.

Archambault describes the real-world challenges facing police departments and forensic laboratories in addressing the mounting pile of evidence requiring processing:

> The San Diego Police Department started their DNA lab in 1992. Once DNA work began, it became the standard. Serology, a much less time-consuming process, ceased to exist. In our case, sexual assault investigations account for 70 percent of the DNA work performed by our lab, another 10 percent comes from homicide and 20 percent from the rest of the department, such as domestic violence and child abuse. Patrol officers are taught to impound everything they believe might be associated with the crime scene. It is therefore not uncommon to have 10 or more large, grocery-type bags of evidence impounded in the property room (i.e., sheets, blankets, sofa cushions, clothing, and rape kits). Detectives are rarely taught about the process used to analyze crime scene evidence or how different criminalistic disciplines, such as trace, latents, and biology might be assigned to analyze evidence submitted to crime laboratories. In the past, San Diego Police Department Sex Crimes detectives submitted their lab

requests as soon as possible, believing it would give them a better chance of having the evidence analyzed. The "old" lab service request simply had the victim's name, the date of the request and the case number. Detectives would write one line on the request, "Analyze all evidence for trace and semen." Neither detectives nor their supervisors really understood the process set in motion as a result of this request. Forensic scientists have been able to identify the source of trace evidence on the basis of its general appearance and structural features, but unlike DNA, it has rarely been possible to determine the source definitively. In San Diego, the section of the lab responsible for screening evidence for trace evidence was not backlogged. Thousands of lab hours were therefore wasted, screening evidence for trace that was most likely never going to be used. Detectives and their supervisors, however, had no idea this was happening.

Archambault adds that analysis for trace evidence will continue to be used in isolated situations. She says:

As an example, DNA and trace might be found in a specific sexual assault. Once a criminalist determines that DNA is present, we know it will be used to confirm the identity of an assailant. If additional sexual assaults are identified and believed to be related because of a similar modus operandi, suspect description or geographical area, evidence collected in those cases may not contain relevant biological material that can be DNA typed. For example, it is not uncommon for sex offenders to begin to use condoms once their assaults escalate, to protect themselves from sexually transmitted diseases and HIV. In these cases, trace evidence might be used to link the cases to the same suspect based on the totality of the investigation.

Several years after DNA became the standard in San Diego, we had a nightmare on our hands. Due to limited resources, only a small number of cases could be analyzed for DNA. Cases were only assigned to a criminalist when a court date was approaching. Often times, the case could not even be analyzed before the scheduled trial date. Judges and defense attorneys routinely registered complaints. Detectives, prosecutors and victims were left frustrated. Sadly, DNA evidence was rarely used to solve a case. The cases assigned for DNA work were those already issued or charged by the prosecutor, meaning that there was most likely some other type of corroborative evidence and the DNA evidence only made the case stronger. Our freezers were full of rape kits and in fact, we had to buy more freezers to store all the kits. Many of the kits were disposed of after the statute of limitations expired without ever being analyzed. Those of us working in the field of sexual assault, recognize how difficult it is for a sexual assault victim to go through a forensic examination following an assault. Sexual Assault Response Teams (SARTs) have been formed across the country to provide more victim sensitive services. In addition to the cost of the exam ($200 to $700 per exam depending on the jurisdiction) generally incurred by law enforcement, it is a tragedy to think that victims are being subjected to further trauma believing that the evidence collected will make a difference, when the majority of the kits and evidence across the county are never analyzed.

Archambault explains that until new technology makes analysis quick and more cost-effective, forensic laboratories must have resources sufficient to test the evidence submitted to them and law enforcement must learn to use these precious resources wisely. She says that to accomplish this goal, San Diego Police Department Sex Crimes detectives and supervisors met with the DNA section supervisor:

New lab service requests and a preliminary rape case information form were created to help detectives focus on what was being requested and why. They also provide criminalists with directional tools, based on the history of the victim and the nature of the assault, which item of evidence will most likely contain potential evidence. Detectives must ask the sexual assault survivor if they had consensual sex within 96 hours prior to the time the biological samples are collected. If so, reference samples, from all consensual partners, should be collected before submitting a DNA request to the crime laboratory. Questions need to be asked about the type of sexual activity involved in the assault (i.e., fellatio, cunnilingus, if a condom was used and whether the suspect ejaculated and where).

Additional issues of DNA evidence analysis, with regard to consent issues and the implications of non-stranger assaults, are discussed later in this chapter.

14.5 ADDRESSING THE DNA BACKLOG

While speaking before the U.S. Senate Judiciary Committee Subcommittee on Crime and Drugs on May 14, 2002, Susan Herman, then executive director of the National Center for Victims of Crime, testified to the importance of the then-titled DNA Sexual Assault Justice Act of 2002, explaining that the legislation would make significant improvements to the collection and processing of DNA evidence, "bringing relief to countless victims of sexual assault and other crimes." While acknowledging the solving of cold cases using DNA from crime scenes and rape kits that are matched to DNA profiles in databanks, Herman pointed to hundreds of thousands of DNA samples culled from rape kits, crime scenes, and offenders that remain untested. She stated:

We know from the experience of state DNA databanks that processing the backlog of existing rape kits and offender samples would close potentially thousands of cases, bringing perpetrators to justice and bringing relief to victims. In addition, numerous studies of convicted rapists have found that many such offenders committed multiple assaults, ranging from an average of seven to 20 sexual assaults per offender. Thus, the earlier, successful identification and prosecution of sex offenders that would be possible with the processing of DNA evidence would likely prevent additional assaults.

The National Center also applauds the bill's creation of a grant program to improve the responses to and investigation of sexual assault cases, through sexual assault examiner programs and training, law enforcement training, and forensic equipment. Sexual assault nurse examiners are trained to perform rape exams in a way that not only preserves the evidence of the assault, but minimizes the trauma to the victims. Similarly, training of law enforcement personnel can also increase their sensitivity to the needs of sexual assault victims, as well as improve the collection of evidence. Therefore, this grant program will not only improve the quality and reliability of the evidence collected, but minimize the additional suffering of sexual assault victims. In turn, the improved treatment of victims may increase their willingness to participate in the investigation and prosecution of the case. The bill would also permit the use of so-called "John Doe" warrants, permitting the filing of an indictment describing the accused as a person with a particular DNA profile. The use of such warrants can serve to avert the expiration of the statute of limitations in cases where an offender is unknown by anything other than the DNA profile contained in the evidence collected. While the National Center supports this provision, we urge Congress to go further, and eliminate the criminal statute of limitations for serious sex offenses. At least 19 states have no statute of limitations for the prosecution of serious sex offenses. At least 12 more have extended their criminal statutes of limitation for sex offenses where there is DNA evidence. Because sex offenders pose a continuing danger to society, and because of the terrible and lifelong impact of sexual assault on victims, there should be no limitation on the prosecution of such crimes.

Following closely on Herman's heels, on May 29, 2002, the office of Senator Maria Cantwell, in conjunction with the Washington State Office of Crime Victims Advocacy, Smith Alling Lane, P.S. Forensic Laboratory Services Bureau, Washington State Patrol, the IAFN, the SANEs of St. Peters Hospital, and the Washington Coalition of Sexual Assault Programs, released "A Report on the Potential for Apprehending Rapists in Washington State Using DNA Analysis." This report details an opportunity to apprehend and convict more rapists in the state of Washington through the use of DNA evidence, especially in suspectless rape cases. The report stated:

Across the country, local hospitals and police offices are filled with forensic evidence from rapes that have not been analyzed for DNA, often because there are no obvious suspects and to date resources simply have not permitted testing of all rape kits. Additionally, many DNA crime scene samples cannot be analyzed due to poor collection or handling of the evidence. No one is certain just how many untested samples are in this backlog as the samples are spread throughout the case files and evidence rooms of local police stations across the country. However, in jurisdictions that have aggressively worked to first get samples tested, and second to cross check the samples against expanding linked state databases of convicted felons' DNA profiles, results have been dramatic. Particularly in cases of rape where no suspect existed, rates of apprehension have been as high as 25 percent.

The report endeavored to estimate the size of the backlog in Washington State, and to propose solutions for eliminating the state backlog and apprehending more rapists. The report discovered that a significant discrepancy exists between the number of victims undergoing rape examinations to collect evidence and filing charges in Washington State, and the number of cases in which samples were sent to the state crime lab for testing. The report stated, "In the past five years, 17,115 cases of forcible rape have been reported to law enforcement, while DNA samples have only been sent to the lab for testing in 4,165 cases. That means that in the past five years alone at least 12,950 women in Washington state have submitted to humiliating and traumatic exams for the collection of evidence that has not been analyzed to help solve their rape." Additionally, in the two years since the Washington State lab began performing DNA analysis on evidence gathered in rape cases where police had no known suspect, 348 analyses were performed and cross-checked against the Washington State felon database. Of those 348 samples, 28 samples, or 8 percent resulted in a match, and a rape was solved. If this 8 percent number is applied to the 12,950 cases in which DNA analysis has not been performed, 1,036 of the rapes that have occurred in Washington State in the last five years could be solved, according to the report. Based on the experience of other states, the report added, Washington state's 8 percent "cold-hit" rate is likely to increase as the state's new law to expand the criminal database to include all convicted felons took effect on July 1, 2002, and the number of felons in the database increased. The report also found that the number of rapes after which women undergo an initial physical examination but do not file charges is also likely to increase if more hospitals are able to implement programs taking advantage of trained SANEs, as this program helps to increase both the likelihood that a testable DNA sample of forensic evidence will be preserved, and that a victim will file charges.

The Washington report recommended increased funding of DNA testing on the estimated 12,950 samples collected, but not tested, throughout Washington State over the past five years, and the increased funding of additional SANE programs in Washington State and throughout the country to increase the number of cases in which trained forensic examiners perform the evidence collection and provide simultaneous compassionate care to victims. These recommendations were included in the Debbie Smith Act, Cantwell's bill to eliminate the rape evidence kit backlog. The report also reviewed the importance of DNA evidence in solving suspectless rape cases. In March 1989, Virginia resident Debbie Smith was raped by a stranger in the woods behind her home. As her attacker placed his gun to her head, he told her that she should not tell anyone because he knew where she lived and could return to kill her. At the urging of her husband, Smith went immediately to the hospital after the assault, and although samples of the assailant's DNA were collected during a physical examination, due to funding constraints, local law enforcement was not able to analyze these samples at the time. More than six years later, when funding became available, Smith's assailant's DNA profile was entered into the Virginia DNA databank and was found to match the DNA of a current prison inmate. He was convicted of the rape and was sentenced to two life terms plus 25 years.

The I-5 Rapist, the case of Jeffrey Paul McKechnie, is another example of a suspectless case solved by DNA evidence. In Olympia, Washington, Nancy Young-Diaz was called to the ER of St. Peter Hospital to perform her duties as a SANE one evening in 1997. A frightened and physically shaken woman walked into the ER that same evening, and within minutes, she was ushered into a private room with Young-Diaz and other members of the all-female SANE staff. The victim said that while she was home alone, waiting for her husband to return, an intruder forced his way into the residence and proceeded to bound and rape her at gunpoint. After the initial interview, Young-Diaz performed a full physical examination and collected DNA evidence. The evidence Young-Diaz gathered was intrinsic to the conviction of the victim's attacker. When the assailant's profile was entered into the state felon databank, it was found to match the already convicted serial rapist Jeffrey Paul McKechnie, known as the I-5 rapist. McKechnie is responsible for raping at least nine women in Washington State.

A third case illustrates the pivotal use of DNA in suspectless cases. In Seattle in February 1997, a 21-year-old woman was assaulted when a man grabbed her and forced her down into a loading dock area. He put his shirt over her head, punched her several times, and proceeded to rape her. Evidence from this case was received at the Seattle Crime Laboratory in 1997 and DNA samples were analyzed. The DNA profile was run against the RFLP Felon Database but no matches were found. In August 2001, after the implementation of the new STR/DNA technology, a new DNA profile was run against the new STR Felon Database. This time a match was found, and a suspect was apprehended more than four years after the crime was committed. These cases highlight the fact that Washington State's sexual assault rates are higher than the national average. According to a study released by the Washington State Office of Crime Victims Advocacy (OCVA) in December 2001, 23 percent of Washington women report having been victims of rape, and 38 percent of Washington State women report being sexually assaulted at some point in their lives. This statewide study, the first on the subject, was conducted by the Harborview Center for Sexual Assault and Traumatic Stress at the request of the OCVA. The national average is 13 percent.

According to a September 1999 survey conducted for the Attorney General's National Commission on the Future of DNA Evidence, an estimated 150,000 rape kits are awaiting analysis in the United States; however, the process of collecting and analyzing DNA evidence makes determining the actual number of unanalyzed samples difficult. Rape evidence is collected both at crime scenes and through physical examinations of victims at hospitals. If a woman does not decide to report her assault to law enforcement, local hospitals usually keep collected DNA evidence on file at the hospital for several years. If a woman does file charges with local law enforcement, DNA evidence samples from the hospital will be transferred to the local police station. At that point, resources permitting, evidence samples will hopefully be sent to a crime laboratory for analysis. Because rape evidence samples are distributed between hospitals, local police stations, and crime laboratories, the true rape evidence kit backlog is uncertain; recent media reports have estimated the national backlog of rape kits to be as high as 500,000.

Although media attention has focused on the rape kits sitting on storage shelves, much of the rape evidence that must be examined is sitting in police property lockers or labs in the form of bed linens, clothing, or abandoned property from a crime scene. Funding must be allocated to trained investigators who can analyze these items and collect valuable DNA samples from them.

Just as the national backlog is uncertain, the Cantwell report stated that the number of unanalyzed rape evidence samples in Washington State is unknown. However, what is clear is the large discrepancy between the number of rape victims who undergo physical evidentiary examinations and file charges with local law enforcement, and the number of rape evidence samples sent to the state crime laboratory for analysis. In the past five years, 17,115 cases of forcible rape have been reported to law enforcement, but DNA samples have only been sent to the lab for testing in 4,165 cases. This discrepancy—12,950 cases—represents the best possible estimate of the backlog of rape evidence kits currently sitting in cold case files in police stations throughout the state. While this figure represents the best estimate of the rape evidence kit backlog in Washington State for the past five years, this estimate presumes that testable DNA samples have been preserved in all 12,950 cases. In fact, many of these samples are probably not testable due to poor collection or handling of the DNA evidence. Additionally, many victims choose not to follow their case through to judgment even after initially reporting their assault to law enforcement. In these cases, law enforcement might choose not to preserve the evidence kits. The Cantwell report stated:

> It should be noted that the Washington State Patrol Crime Lab has done a commendable job processing the evidence received at the lab, analyzing well over 90 percent of the kits it receives. Including 2001 and 2002 figures to date, the Washington State Patrol Crime Lab has received 5,606 total cases since 1999, 5,263 of which police had identified a viable suspect. Of these 5,263 suspect cases, only 300 have not yet been analyzed.

The Cantwell report summarized a course of action that would help resolve the current rape evidence analysis backlog. The report advocated nationwide formation of SANE programs, which provide communities with nurses trained specifically in how to collect and handle forensic evidence, as well as how to treat the physical and emotional needs of sexual assault victims. The report explained that SANE programs can provide multiple benefits, including theses: speeding up the evidentiary examination process by reducing the time victims have to wait in a hospital's ED and the time it takes to complete the examination; increasing the quality of the examination because an experienced SANE is adept at identifying physical trauma and psychological needs and ensuring that victims receive appropriate medical care; and uncovering important evidence, as SANE staff have increased knowledge of what evidence to look for and how to document injuries and other forensic evidence, thereby ensuring a more thorough and effective criminal investigation. The report pushes for the speedier analysis of rape evidence kits to encourage greater rates of victim reporting. In her testimony before the Senate Judiciary Committee on May 14, 2002, Debbie Smith stated that she would be "much more (likely)" to submit to the invasive physical examination and evidentiary collection process and report a sexual assault to law enforcement if she knew that there was an extensive, efficient system in the United States that could analyze DNA information in a timely fashion and match it to the profile of convicted criminals. The Cantwell report stated:

> Women who have the courage to come forward and report a sexual assault deserve the peace of mind of knowing the information they provide will be analyzed and checked against a database of convicted felons in a timely fashion. In order to guarantee this peace of mind, state and federal governments must make analyzing all outstanding DNA evidence, including no-suspect cases, a national priority. As Ms. Smith's comments indicate, increasing the efficiency of this process could very likely encourage other rape victims to come forward and report a sexual assault. Increasing the rate of reporting will increase the number of sexual offenders we prevent from assaulting again.

The report also supported further streamlined function of CODIS. Although many states were already operating searchable databanks of convicted violent felons, it was not until 1994 that Congress granted the FBI authority to establish a national DNA index for law enforcement purposes with the passage of The DNA Identification Act. In October 1998, the FBI's National DNA Index System (NDIS) became operational. CODIS is implemented as a distributed database with three hierarchical levels: local, state, and national. Local law enforcement and state law enforcement can enter searchable DNA information on convicted offenders into LDIS and SDIS, respectively. Information from these two systems can be uploaded into NDIS, the highest level in the CODIS hierarchy. This enables the laboratories participating in the CODIS program to exchange and compare DNA profiles on a national level. The tiered approach allows state and local agencies to operate their databases according to their specific legislative or legal requirements. The Convicted Offender index contains DNA profiles of convicted felons; however, the federal government and each state independently decide what offenses qualify for entrance into the databank. The Forensic index contains DNA profiles developed from crime scene evidence, including rape evidence kits. CODIS does not store criminal history information, case-related information, Social Security numbers, or dates of birth, and therefore does not raise major privacy concerns. CODIS also holds the key to identifying offenders in previously suspectless cases, the Cantwell report emphasized. CODIS utilizes computer software to automatically search these indexes for matching DNA profiles. Matches made among profiles in the Forensic index can link crime scenes together, possibly identifying serial offenders. Based on a match, police can coordinate separate investigations and share leads developed independently.

According to a study by the National Institute of Justice, the average rapist commits eight to 12 sexual assaults, meaning that if law enforcement could immediately apprehend the rapist after the first offense, a minimum of seven women would be saved from the trauma of sexual assault. CODIS technology has also given new hope to solving suspectless cases, or cases without suspects, witnesses, or any other clues. Prior to the introduction of this technology, rape victims who reported their assault by a stranger to local law enforcement and even furnished DNA evidence were often told there was very little chance of apprehending the assailant. With CODIS, DNA samples from suspectless cases can be tested, and often yield a match that points to the sexual assailant.

Finally, the Cantwell report advocated the expansion of criminal databases. In 1990, Virginia expanded its database to include all convicted felons. This expansion dramatically increased their rate of cold-hits, with estimates ranging as high as 25 to 40 percent. Other states were inspired to follow suit and, as of publication, 21 states have expanded their databases to include all convicted felons. These rates are a sharp contrast to the current situation in Washington State, where the Washington State Patrol Crime Lab reports a cold-hit rate of 8 percent. However, in March 2001, the Washington state legislature passed legislation to expand the state database to include all adults and juveniles convicted of any felony, plus misdemeanor stalking, harassment, or communicating with a minor for immoral purposes. The law became effective on July 1, 2002, and retroactively applies to all incarcerated convicted felons. This new law is expected to increase the number of felon samples submitted each month from 300 to 2,250.

A number of members of the forensic science community have spent countless hours of their time at personal expense to educate lawmakers about the urgency of resolving the DNA analysis backlog. Paul Ferrara, PhD, director of the Virginia Division of Forensic Science and a member of former Attorney General John Ashcroft's Working Group on DNA Laboratory Analysis Backlog Reduction, was one of a handful of influential forensic science and criminal justice experts who made their case for greater funding in front of the Subcommittee on Crime, Terrorism and Homeland Security of the Senate Judiciary Committee in July 2003. "For all of (DNA's) promise, our forensic science laboratories today face a crisis of increasing demands and reduced resources that threatens the full potential of this marvelous technology," Ferrara emphasized in his testimony. "Physical evidence that potentially can quickly establish the identity and guilt or innocence of a suspect languishes in a police property room or in forensic laboratory evidence storage for months or years waiting until a highly trained and qualified analyst even opens the evidence containers." Ferrara pointed to a number of cases in which incomplete or delayed forensic analysis and implementation severely impacted open cases, and said that the successful use of DNA technology and databanks—particularly in the critical early stages of a criminal investigation—depended on the presence of a sophisticated and secure data processing system that allows searching of DNA profiles within a state or locality, and across states, localities, and the FBI; the maintenance of large databases of DNA profiles from persons previously arrested or convicted for certain crimes; and having the capacity to process all crime scene evidence from all types of criminal cases and develop any foreign DNA profiles present.

Ferrara believes he and many of his colleagues who testified were able to make an impact on the lawmakers in whose hands so much rests—or at least to direct their attention to deficits not addressed by previous legislation and funding under the Paul Coverdell National Forensic Sciences Act of 2000. "After testifying, I talked to several members of the Virginia delegation who were really excited and proud of what Virginia has achieved with its cold hits, but it might be their own parochial pleasure at seeing Virginia's success as opposed to really grasping the issue," Ferrara says. "They seemed to take the issue to heart and were upset by the backlog situation." At the time of Ferrara's testimony, according to the National Institute of Justice, the current backlog of samples from rape and homicide cases was approximately 350,000. Estimates of the backlog of convicted offender samples is between 200,000 and 300,000, with between 500,000 and 1 million samples that are required under law but not yet collected. In the Department of Justice (2003) report, "Advancing Justice Through DNA Technology," it is hoped that analysis and placement of sample profiles into the CODIS database can dramatically enhance the chances that potential crime victims will be spared the violence of repeat offenders.

A second issue is that of diminished capacity of forensic laboratories to analyze and process DNA samples in a timely fashion due to limited equipment resources, outdated information systems, lack of qualified personnel, and overwhelming caseloads. "Certainly there is attention being brought to bear on this issue," Ferrara says. "There's been a lot of talk about the 'CSI effect,' the misrepresentation of the speed with which labs can process evidence. The average guy on the street thinks investigations are run just like CSI portrays them, and we know that's not true. I am approaching a 2,000-case backlog that keeps building even though my resources have remained constant. We're working on striving to increase productivity without people, essentially." A third issue is the need for advanced training of forensic scientists and lab personnel to maximize the use of DNA technology. These issues are addressed in greater detailer later in this chapter.

With the two main thrusts of the initiative—the DNA database expansion and the DNA backlog—being equally important, which issue will be resolved first? "I think the DNA database will get caught up or at least we'll be able to make serious inroads as funding becomes available," Ferrara says:

> There's a cottage industry of private labs lining up who have the capacity and the wherewithal to run a large number of convicted offender samples. This is a resource the public labs can and should use to reduce the rape-kit backlog so they can focus attention on crime-scene evidence. It's this crime-scene evidence backlog that I see nagging for some time. As DNA training, education and awareness continues, more and more evidence that can be collected will be collected. In Virginia we've seen an almost 90 percent increase in DNA work in the last three

> years. We think that's a result of the awareness of what we can do and what kind of cases to which the technology is applicable. That continues to grow faster than the lab's capacity to do it. We constantly ponder what case to do next and how to prioritize cases because as the backlog increases, the impact of it will come back and bite us—there will be the cases that don't get done.

Although automation is the wave of the future and has its place, Ferrara believes robotics can never truly replace the human element, especially when it comes to the gist of the process: expert interpretation of the results. "Robotics will be important but it can't help the front end and back end of any DNA case, meaning the evaluation of physical evidence for the presence of some meaningful biological fluid," he adds. "Robotics can do extractions, and such but when the results come in, it's back to the analyst who must record and interpret the results, come to conclusions, write reports, do the statistical analysis, do the review and all of the quality steps and make sense of all the data. I just don't know how we're going to solve that problem in the short term." That brings Ferrara back to outsourcing:

> I was asked by a senator if I thought a private lab would play an important role and I said, "Absolutely." The success of our databank in Virginia wouldn't have been possible without the involvement of a private lab. Some states are choosing to do convicted offender samples in-house and outsource rape kits. Of all the different types of crime-scene evidence, the rape-kit swabs are amenable to a private lab running them and seeing if there is foreign DNA present. I would assume the full work-up of that case will still fall back to the local lab as well as all of the follow-up and full confirmation, but at least it affords a quicker initial assessment of what you have in a case.

Ferrara says quicker turnaround of violent-crime cases such as rape can be of extraordinary benefit to victims who wait in fear while evidence sits on a shelf.

> The idea of developing a DNA profile of a sperm donor who is not a consensual sex partner of the victim means a profile is searchable very quickly, so I think there will be more privatization of rape-kit processing. Rape-kit evidence sits for nine to 18 months or more and victims wait for some word on their cases. They are going to get very frustrated and will start making some noise, which is a good thing because we always close the barn door after the horse has escaped. In rape cases, instead of a six- to nine-month turnaround, it ought to be six to nine days. I don't know how we're ever going to get to that because we are buried with evidence and resources remain the same due to budget problems.

With the President's DNA Initiative calling for almost $1 billion in funding over five years, Ferrara thinks it's a solid start—but the need is almost indefatigable. "It will be enough money to start the ball rolling; the problem is, I don't know if the impact will be felt for a number of years," he observes:

> Some of this stuff gets down to bricks and mortar, which is going to take time. And where are the new DNA examiners going to come from? Who is going to train them? That takes time. I'm afraid there will be an expectation for this tremendous improvement overnight and that's not going to happen. Bush's initiative will be a great benefit in the long run. Is it going to do everything? No, but it will be able to fund most of what the states can do right now. Initially, you're looking at money for equipment, supplies and training, but it doesn't create new buildings, big labs and new people overnight. I suspect in five years, we'll be in better shape than we are now, hopefully doing two to three times as many cases as we are doing now.

Still, the avalanche of evidence mounts. "We are up to almost 1,500 cold hits and a lot of that is due to submission of evidence in cases that would never have been considered prior," Ferrara says. "I am digging in my heels and saying to investigators, 'No, we are not going to use DNA technology to help you with a misdemeanor drug case.' We're going to concentrate on felony cases. Among our 2,000 cases are rape cases and a lot of breaking and entering (B&E), but you do the rape cases first. The difference is B&E cases usually consist of one or two samples—a little bit of blood on a piece of glass. You don't have a differential extraction, you don't have multiple donors, etc. Rape cases are a lot more complicated; you have several known samples and a wide variety of potential probative samples. Another issue is that if we don't analyze every piece of evidence that comes in, the defense is going to ask why. So we're not being afforded the opportunity to unilaterally say, 'Look, this was a vaginal rape, we looked at the vaginal swab, developed a foreign profile, ran it, and got this hit. We didn't bother looking at the bed clothing, the underpants, oral swabs or other samples.' So the defense says, 'Maybe my guy was there but it was consensual, or maybe he didn't murder her because there was somebody else there.' I have some cases with up to several hundred samples in each, which means dozens of rape cases could have been done in that time instead. These are the elements working against us in terms of catching up. In some ways you don't want to discourage the complete collection of samples in all types of crimes, but we're at the stage where casework volume is exploding." This is due in part to Virginia's success with its violent offender arrestee law, where DNA samples are taken from offenders at the time of arrest. "We now have experience with this arrestee law, and we made 36 hits so far, including nine rapes and four homicides out of about 5,400 persons arrested for violent felonies. The kicker we have had to remove a third of them because those people have been dismissed or found not guilty, which blows me away. These are arrests for violent felonies and to think such a large chunk is being pleaded down to misdemeanors. That's why these misdemeanor property crimes are gateway-type crimes. There's a good chance these guys are violent offenders but yet to be convicted of it."

14.6 MAKING A CASE FOR DNA

There are a number of eye-opening cases that demonstrate the justification of requiring DNA samples from arrestees and convicted felons throughout the country. Here is a sampling of cases from the 2003 *National Forensic DNA Study Report*, prepared by the Division of Governmental Studies and Services of Washington State University and Smith Alling Lane, PS. A case in California illustrates the need for states to collect DNA from all convicted felons to prevent repeat offenders from striking again. In the Alameda County area, a series of 12 sexual assaults occurred in 1997 in a two-month period, all of which were attributed to the same unidentified suspect. The offender wore a ski mask in all the attacks, often robbed his victims, and in many instances attacked two women on the same day. This rapist struck quickly and frequently, as his first five detected attacks occurred during a period of 10 days. Due to the extremely violent nature of the offenses and other similarities linking the attacks, it is reasonable to expect that DNA analysis would be expedited in these cases, as is often done when a serial offender is at large in a community. A latent fingerprint found at the scene of the 12th attack was linked to a former high school track and field coach who had an extensive criminal record. This individual was formally charged and convicted in six of the cases, and is currently serving a 59-year-to-life imprisonment sentence. The perpetrator's criminal record included 21 prior arrests, most of which were felony charges ranging from murder to interfering with a police officer. Although most of the offenses occurred prior to the introduction of DNA databases, the man's last brush with justice was a 1993 parole violation for a 1989 felony burglary conviction; the offender was discovered to be in possession of weapons and spent another 16 months in prison. DNA evidence from the first rape in 1997 could have been matched to the offender by the time of the sixth attack (occurring 11 days after the first attack) if the state had required DNA from all convicted felons, thereby preventing six rapes. In another California case in 1998, a woman was raped in Ventura County. A DNA profile from the criminal evidence was uploaded to the DNA database, but no match was made. Two additional rapes that occurred four months apart in 2002 were subsequently matched to the 1998 case, and new testing of a 1993 case was also eventually linked to the same unknown offender. The offender became a suspect in these crimes after being identified in another case. He provided a DNA sample that linked him to the four rapes. He is currently awaiting trial. The suspected rapist had a prior conviction for felony drug possession in 1990. If the state statute had required DNA from all convicted felons, including felony drug possession, and if the 1993 rape case had been submitted for DNA testing in a timely manner, at least three rapes could have been prevented.

In Massachusetts in late 1997, a woman was found raped and murdered in her home in Springfield. In early 1998, another three women were found raped and murdered—one in her home, two others in alleys. All four murders were linked through DNA, and due to the unique positioning of the bodies, which became the offender's "signature." Following the fourth murder, a voluntary DNA sample was collected from a person who had become a suspect in the case; within a few weeks, that suspect was tied to the crimes through a DNA match. The suspect's criminal record included two prior felony convictions in 1996—one for larceny and the other for breaking and entering, for which he was sentenced to community supervision. If Massachusetts had required a DNA sample for either of the 1996 nonviolent felony convictions, a DNA match could have been obtained after the first rape and murder, thereby preventing the subsequent three rapes and murders.

In Missouri, between 1988 and 1997, an unidentified masked man was beating and raping women in areas of Missouri and across the Mississippi River in Illinois. Because many of the 29 or more attacks happened in south St. Louis, the media dubbed the attacker the South Side rapist. DNA linked at least 13 of the cases together, but the police were unable to identify a perpetrator. In October 1998 St. Louis City Police were called when a man was seen breaking into a house. A van registered to a person known to the police was reported leaving the scene of the break-in. This person's appearance matched a physical description of the South Side rapist and police asked for a DNA sample. The suspect voluntarily agreed to have his mouth swabbed. Several weeks later the DNA results were returned and positively identified the suspect as the South Side rapist, who by that time had disappeared. He was arrested several months later in Albuquerque, New Mexico after a worried mother found his hotel number in her daughter's belongings. The suspect ultimately confessed to raping at least 100 women since his late teens. Sometime in 1991 the suspect was convicted of felony burglary, for which he served a sentence in state prison. Prosecutors indicate that there were a minimum of 10 rapes occurring after this conviction that are attributable to the suspect. If the state had required a DNA sample from this perpetrator after the burglary conviction, the suspect could have been linked to serial rapes occurring prior to his conviction, thereby preventing at least 10 additional rapes.

Also in the Missouri and Illinois area, from April 2001 through May 2002, police began finding the bodies of women who had been raped and murdered in the St. Louis and western Illinois area. Investigators recovered semen from the victims' bodies that was sent for crime laboratory analysis. The DNA profiles from the semen recovered from the victims all matched. A person known to the police became a suspect in the crimes after he wrote an anonymous letter to a local newspaper. An Internet-generated map enclosed with the letter led to some computer forensics that eventually identified the specific computer that downloaded the map. The suspect was ultimately arrested in June 2002 when police found videotapes of himself killing and torturing his victims. On the videotape, the suspect states that he had just committed "murder No. 17." Police have conclusively linked 12 victims to this offender thus far, and believe the number could be as high as 20. This individual committed suicide shortly after his arrest. In March 1988, this offender committed a series of five robberies and was sentenced to 15 years for robbery and armed criminal action. In June 1994, he was paroled after serving five years and three months of his sentence. Missouri does not require DNA from convicted robbers, and this offender was released without submitting a DNA sample for the state database. With a DNA sample in the database, this offender could have been identified as the killer of the first victim long before a minimum of 11 additional women lost their lives.

In Kentucky in 1998, a female attendant at a gas station was raped. In this case, DNA was collected but was not tested. Approximately 10 days later, another female gas station attendant was raped, and over the next three years an additional seven rapes were committed by the same repeat offender. Investigators identified a suspect in the last rape in August 2002 after he used the victim's ATM card. In 2003, DNA testing finally linked the man to the first two rapes in 1998, and other evidence linked the remaining cases to one another. The suspect was a known sex offender in Kentucky who had committed 12 documented rapes as a juvenile. His first rape committed as an adult occurred within a month of his release from juvenile detention facilities. Kentucky did not require DNA from juvenile offenders adjudicated delinquent of sex crimes at the time of the suspect's juvenile sentences. If the state had required DNA from juveniles adjudicated delinquent of felonies, at least seven rapes could have been prevented. Moreover, in 2002, the requirement was not made retroactive to encompass persons on probation or parole. Had it not been for good police work, this rapist could still be a threat to public safety today.

Also in Kentucky, from June 1997 through October 2000, six rapes and several attempted rapes took place in the Louisville area. In addition to DNA evidence that linked these rapes to one another, the rapist frequently used a flashlight to blind his victims, thus earning him the nickname the flashlight rapist. In November 2000 a suspect was arrested and subsequently convicted on numerous burglary charges in Louisville. A sex-crimes detective began to suspect the man was the flashlight rapist and obtained a warrant for a DNA sample. The DNA analysis positively identified the man as the flashlight rapist, and he later pleaded guilty to the crimes. The flashlight rapist had been previously convicted on felonious burglary charges in 1991 in Florida, which did not at that time require DNA from all convicted felons. Had DNA been required, at least five rapes could have been prevented. Moreover, although Kentucky altered its law to require DNA for burglary convictions in 2002, the provision was not made retroactive to include probationers or parolees and the implementation date of the law was delayed. Thus the 2000 burglary conviction in Kentucky might also have slipped through the cracks and allowed the crimes to remain unsolved if not for good investigative work.

In Louisiana, between September 2001 and March 200, five women were raped and murdered in the Baton Rouge area. All five crimes were linked to the same unidentified perpetrator through DNA testing. In May 2003, a volunteered DNA sample collected from a mass sampling of potential suspects resulted in the identification of a suspect. Subsequent to this match, at least one additional murder has been tied through DNA to the suspect, and more than 20 additional cases are being reviewed for possible connections to the suspect in question. The suspect had a 1993 conviction on felony burglary charges arising from an attack on a 74-year-old man. If his DNA sample had been collected and entered into the database, at least four deaths could have been prevented. The suspect also had prior convictions for beating up his girlfriend in a bar and trying to run over a sheriff's deputy at a roadblock. Finally, in New York, in August 1993, a young woman was raped in the Bronx in what was to be the first of up to 51 rapes attributed to the same offender over a five-year period. The perpetrator was dubbed the Bronx rapist by the media. A person known to the police became a suspect when he was identified in a transaction involving a victim's jewelry at a pawn shop. He was arrested and subsequent DNA testing linked him to several of the rapes. He has been convicted on 14 counts of rape in the Bronx, six counts of sexual abuse, 19 counts of robbery, and two counts of criminal possession of a weapon. He has been sentenced to two life sentences. This offender had a prior conviction in 1989 for felony robbery and assault, for which he received a seven-year sentence. If New York had begun requiring DNA from all convicted felons in 1990 this offender would have been in the DNA database prior to the first rape in 1993, and at least 13 rapes could have been prevented. Moreover, when New York's database was established in 1994, an inclusion of all convicted felons and retroactive application to persons previously convicted but still under supervision would have captured this offender's DNA sample much earlier in the investigation.

14.7 THE JUSTICE FOR ALL ACT OF 2004

The stranger's hand clamps itself around her mouth before she has a chance to scream.

Someone will be sexually assaulted in the United States every two minutes, according to the U.S. Department of Justice.

She feels the sharp point of a knife at her ribs and her blood runs cold.

This translates to 30 sexual assaults per hour, 720 per day, and 262,800 per year.

She knows that in an instant, her life has changed forever.

She represents one in three women who will be sexually assaulted in their lifetimes.

"She" is someone's wife, mother, sister, girlfriend, or daughter. She is among the thousands of victims whose offenders might never be caught because of a rape kit processing backlog. While technology is revolutionizing the ability to identify and convict rapists and other violent offenders, a lack of funding, time, and trained personnel conspire against the swift processing of DNA evidence. Until, perhaps, now. Although the promise of DNA technology has long been understood in the lab and in the courtroom, it has only been recently that lawmakers are recognizing DNA's impact on criminal investigations and criminal justice, and endeavoring to empower the entities that can harness and use the power DNA affords in the solving of rapes, homicides, and other violent crimes. On October 30, 2004, President George W. Bush signed into law a piece of legislation, the Justice for All Act, that had had been circulating in the House of Representatives and in the Senate for a few years. Although it has had many names and many bipartisan supporters, it had fallen victim to political maneuvering, as bills are wont to do on Capitol Hill. However, persistence on the part of the bill's various sponsors and supporters paid off, and the crucial piece of legislation was on its way through the appropriations process. The law provides funding to analyze the DNA evidence from approximately 221,000 open rape and murder cases, which could lead to solving as many as 67,000 of these cases, according to a statement by the National Center for Victims of Crime, the RAINN. "It will result in thousands of rapists being locked up. Because of this expected result, and the tens of thousands of future rapes that will likely be prevented by locking up 'professional rapists,' we consider this to be the most important anti-rape legislation Congress has ever considered."

The bill had garnered numerous bipartisan supporters, including Senators Orrin Hatch, Patrick Leahy, Joseph Biden, and Jon Kyl and Representatives James Sensenbrenner, William Delahunt, Carolyn Maloney, Mark Green, and Jerry Nadler. Also lending their voices to the fight for the bill were rape-victims-turned-advocates Debbie Smith and Kellie Greene. Specifically, the Justice for All Act of 2004, which incorporates the Advancing Justice Through DNA Technology Act and the Debbie Smith Bill, creates the Debbie Smith DNA Backlog Grant Program and authorizes $755 million over five years for grants to states and local authorities to eliminate the backlog of untested rape evidence kits; authorizes grants to state sexual assault coalitions for programs under the Violence Against Women Act and expands VAWA to provide legal assistance for victims of dating violence; provides grants for training law enforcement, judges, and medical personnel on the use of DNA analysis in sexual assault cases; provides funding to expand local and state witness assistance programs and crime victim notification programs; and extends enhanced rights to crime victims. According to U.S. Representative Carolyn B. Maloney, President Bush signed the bill into law just as police in New York State made their first arrest based on an indictment of a DNA sample of a suspect in a sexual assault case from 1996. On October 6, 2004, the House of Representatives overwhelmingly passed H.R. 5107 by a vote of 393–14, and the Senate unanimously passed the legislation three days later. A portion of this legislation, which will bring long overdue justice to rape victims and their families, had passed the House of Representatives overwhelmingly (357–67) on November 5, 2003, as H.R. 3214, the Advancing Justice Through DNA Technology Act. The Advancing Justice Through DNA Technology Act of 2003 contained legislation, The Debbie Smith Act, introduced by Maloney and Representative Mark Green (R-WI), that would provide the necessary funding for processing the backlog of DNA evidence, for training SAFEs, for training prosecutors and law enforcement in using and gathering DNA evidence, and for establishing a national standard for the collection of DNA evidence. H.R. 5107 also contains provisions guaranteeing that crime victims have certain rights, and The Innocence Protection Act, which will ensure that federal and state inmates have access to DNA testing.

"I am very proud of all the hard work that led to this bill being signed into law," Maloney says. "This is a great day for all the victims and survivors of sexual assault. I want to thank Debbie Smith for her courage and dedication on this critical issue. She truly is an inspiration to us all. With the 'Justice for All Act,' we will get rapists off the streets and put them in prison where they belong." Maloney authored the original Debbie Smith Act after Debbie Smith testified before the House Government Reform Committee in June 2001 about using DNA evidence to solve rape cases. Says Maloney, "Debbie Smith was raped near her home in 1989. For six and a half years, Debbie lived in fear that her attacker would return to kill her. Only on the day that her husband told her that the man who had raped Debbie, who had been identified because of DNA evidence, already was in prison, was Debbie able to live without fear."

H.R. 2874, The Debbie Smith Act, which was introduced in the 107th Congress, garnered 160 bipartisan cosponsors and would have authorized $410 million over three years for processing the backlog of DNA evidence and for training SANEs. H.R. 1046, introduced in the 108th Congress, expands on the original legislation by authorizing funding for training law enforcement and prosecutors in the handling of DNA evidence and by authorizing the issuance of "John Doe" indictments in federal sexual assault cases. This legislation was encompassed into H.R. 3214, the Advancing Justice Through DNA Technology Act. Originally called the Rape Kit Analysis Backlog Elimination Act, introduced to the House as H.R. 3961 by Jerrold Nadler (D-NY), and introduced to the Senate as SB 2318 by Senator Hillary Clinton (D-NY), the bills sought to clarify that grants authorized under the existing DNA Analysis Backlog Act of 2000 could be used to expedite processing of the large numbers of rape kits waiting to be analyzed and their results entered into the nationwide CODIS database.

Although some cold cases are being solved as DNA samples are matched to DNA profiles in databases, hundreds of thousands of DNA samples from rape kits, offenders and crime scenes remain untested due to inadequate funding. The Debbie Smith Act endeavored to provide the necessary additional funding for laboratories to process this backlogged DNA evidence. A companion bill to the Debbie Smith Act, Senate Bill 2055, was introduced by Senator Maria Cantwell (D-WA). Cantwell testified on using DNA evidence to combat crime before the Judiciary Subcommittee on Crime and Drugs. She stated:

> Debbie Smith's experience is testimony to the power of DNA evidence. It would have been impossible to solve a no-suspect case like Debbie's without the use of DNA evidence. It took six years for the forensic evidence sample taken at the time of her rape to be cross-checked against the Virginia database of convicted felons. But, when the comparison was made, her attacker was found and he was sentenced to two life terms plus 25 years. Debbie put her own experience with DNA testing to good use. By talking openly about her own rape, I believe she is partially responsible for the increase that we are seeing in the reporting of rape.
>
> If women have the courage to come forward and report a sexual assault, and to submit to a physical examination and evidence gathering, we owe them an absolute guarantee that at a minimum that sample will be analyzed and checked against databases of known sexual offenders and violent felons.

In her testimony, Cantwell called on lawmakers to support the establishment of a greater number of SANE programs. In 2003, the services of SANEs were offered to victims in about 10 percent of U.S. counties. There are an estimated 330 established SANE programs and another several hundred fledgling programs in the country today; this is a small number considering there are more than 6,000 hospitals and 3,066 counties in the United States. "Women who are raped also deserve to receive respectful treatment by people trained to collect and preserve forensic evidence," Cantwell said. "That is what the SANE does."

14.8 DEBBIE SMITH'S STORY

Debbie Smith's ordeal began on May 3, 1989. She was performing routine household chores while her husband Rob, then a police lieutenant, was asleep after working the night shift and then appearing in court. After going outside briefly, Smith left the kitchen door unlocked for a few minutes, planning to return to take out the trash. A masked stranger entered the home, overtook her, and dragged her to a wooded area behind the house where he blindfolded, robbed, and raped her repeatedly. He said that if she told anyone, he knew where she lived and would come back. When Smith was freed, she awakened her husband, told him what happened and begged him to let her take a shower to try to wash away the pain caused by her perpetrator. Rob Smith's law enforcement instincts kicked in and he prevented Debbie from making a mistake that allowed many rapists to go free—washing crucial trace evidence down the drain. "Had I taken a shower, I probably would have ruined any chance of finding my attacker," Debbie says. "I was crying and telling him I had to get rid of all traces of my attacker to feel better. If Rob had not stopped me, there wouldn't have been any evidence, my attacker might not have been identified, and I might still be living in fear. He knew if we were going to catch the rapist, we had to preserve trace evidence."

It wasn't until July 26, 1995, that a scientist in the Virginia crime laboratory made a cold hit, identifying Debbie's attacker from a DNA match to a man serving time for felony bad check writing. For the first time since her attack, Debbie knew her assailant couldn't return to hurt her or her two children. A backlog of rape kits forced Debbie and Rob Smith to wait six years before the identity of her attacker could be discovered. Says Rob:

> Virginia is usually slow-moving, but we actually lead the country in DNA usage. We had 180,000 samples in our database. In the first three months of this year we had 40 hits per month; in April we had 64; that's more than a lot of states are getting in a year. Other states are working to catch up with us. Our case occurred in 1989 when our lab was just starting to work with DNA. In the early 1990s

> Virginia passed legislation to allow blood samples to be taken from convicted felons to create DNA profiles.
>
> There was a serial rapist 25 or 30 miles from here who was attacking little girls at bus stops. He left enough evidence at a scene to procure a DNA sample. Police got a hit from a guy convicted of another felony. They were able to clear a dozen rapes because he was in prison for writing bad checks.

The man who raped Debbie also was already serving time for robbery and abduction. When Debbie visited the evidence storage room of the Virginia crime lab, she says she nearly broke down when she saw the large number of unprocessed rape kits. "It broke my heart," Debbie says, her voice wavering with emotion:

> I looked at all of those kits on the shelves and I thought, "These aren't just boxes, these are people's lives." Sometimes I feel guilty that I was able to find out who my perpetrator was while other victims continue to wait. The worst of it is that a timely DNA match can prevent other people from being hurt by the same assailant. The average rapist will rape eight to 12 times until he is caught. That's a lot of lives impacted, especially when the rapist also affects the lives of your loved ones.

Debbie also knew the pain her husband was feeling. "I've finally been able to come to terms with what happened to Debbie," Rob says, but he admits that it was a long journey to some small peace of mind. "I had to deal with being a police officer whose wife was raped. We have a certain mindset we think we have to uphold; policemen don't cry and nothing bothers us. At the time, my focus was on getting Debbie through the ordeal. I pushed my own feelings into the background but found out later it was a mistake. I have since dealt with the enormous feelings of guilt about not being able to protect my wife."

Debbie says watching her family suffer along with her prompted her to want to speak out about the attack. However, she says it wasn't without misgivings. "(Speaking out) was and sometimes continues to be very much out of my comfort zone. I knew I had to put myself on the line for something this important."

Debbie says she was being interviewed by a local reporter regarding the one-year anniversary of the rape and the fact no suspect had been found. When the reporter asked her if she could use Debbie's name in the story, Debbie decided it was the moment when she could take a stand on behalf of all rape victims:

> We talked it over with our children because I knew going public could cause them some problems. I told them I wanted to do it; if this can happen to me then it can happen to anybody. It was hard to go public for many reasons. It meant opening myself up to people who might not understand why I was speaking up about the rape. I didn't want anyone to think I was doing this for publicity's sake; I was doing this for women everywhere. We as rape victims can't allow our attackers to be left on the streets, preying on others. I didn't want this to happen to me, but now I can try to keep it from happening to anyone else.

Debbie says her experience in the ER of the local hospital was a good example of the lasting impressions a rape creates on the victim and why change in who works with sexual assault victims is needed. "The emergency staff could not have been nicer to me," Debbie explains:

> The problem was that they didn't know that there was a better way. I was not mistreated, but from my viewpoint, it was humiliating. I was taken to a room in which people were constantly coming in and out from everywhere. I was so confused, trying to figure out what was going on. Three nurses and a doctor were helping me. They were going in and out, asking questions then leaving. A lot of the questions sounded the same, so I thought they were trying to make me stumble in my answers. With each question, they needed slightly different information, but to me it sounded like they didn't believe me.
>
> They asked me to remove all of my clothing, which became evidence, and they gave me a gown to put on. I had to leave the room I was in and walk through the main part of the ER while trying to hold my gown together. There were no other patients there, but I had to walk past other ER staff to get to the other side where an OB/GYN table was. They were just standing there, looking at me. I know they were as shocked as I was that this happened, but I felt like I was on display. I was asked to lie down and put my feet in the stirrups. I waited and waited, lying there exposed. Finally the doctor comes in and started combing, swabbing, and plucking. The whole time I was thinking, "Please let it be over, let me go home." What I went through at the hospital was almost as devastating as the actual rape; I was afraid they didn't believe me. What I know now about SANE programs in hospitals, I think how much better they are for rape victims. It would have been so much easier to deal with just one person, and that the person examining me and collecting evidence was a female instead of a male. I mean, this crime happened at the hands of a man. A SANE would have made my experience at the hospital so much better.

Debbie knew she had to get a SANE program launched at her community hospital. "We initially approached hospital administration and evidently that was the wrong thing to do," Debbie recalls:

> They're not bad people, it's just that the bottom line is all they tend to think about. On paper, I don't think a SANE program looked cost effective to them at first. I got to know the victims' witness assistant in our court system when my case went to trial. She heard about my experience at the hospital and it devastated her. She talked to

> the hospital's auxiliary board and to the volunteer coordinator and got us a hearing. I addressed the board members and later learned it was the first time in history they had voted unanimously on anything. Their only questions were, "How many nurses do we need and how much money does it take to get a SANE program started?"

"We have the highest regard for forensic nurses," Rob Smith says:

> The hospital experience wasn't pleasant for Debbie, but it would have been more endurable for her if a SANE nurse had attended to her. The people who worked on her knew me and by virtue of that they gave Debbie the kid-glove treatment. Still, having a SANE would have been better. I think SANE programs should be part of all health care delivery. Debbie didn't give the outward appearance of being physically injured—there were no cuts or bruises. But some ER staff wouldn't understand the emotional depth of the pain rape victims go through.

Rob Smith believes forensic nurses are key players in the effort to document evidence needed to catch perpetrators or provide expert testimony in court:

> I had a case recently involving a 16-year-old male youth sodomizing his 2-year-old nephew. The exam revealed scarring that had been going on for some time. We had nothing but circumstantial evidence—his grandmother walked into the room at the same time he was walking out, zipping up his pants. And the child's diaper was off. In my mind that's enough, but in court, that's insufficient evidence. The defense brought in the ER doctor and the child's family physician to support the defendant. The SANE testified and her analysis of the physical evidence convinced the judge that the youth was guilty. The judge said the forensic nurse had done a better job of presenting the evidence. My advice to SANE nurses is: continue your training and education and keep doing what you're doing. They are doing all the right things to help police officers.

"I would love to see the day SANE programs are mandatory in every community," Debbie says. "The first reaction a rape victims gets from people has a lot to do with the way she begins to process everything. I cannot think of a better way to help a rape victim than for a SANE to be his or her first contact."

In 2000, the Department of Justice addressed the DNA backlog by providing funding to states to help process these samples. Then Attorney General John Ashcroft said that to date, more than 347,000 convicted-offender DNA profiles and nearly 8,000 suspectless cases have been analyzed under the DNA Backlog Reduction Program. This analysis identified 610 offenders and produced 193 forensic hits in cases not known to be related and committed by the same offender. He reported that states participating in the program achieved a 19 percent average hit rate among suspectless cases. A number of states have been successful in matching DNA samples to criminals and other crimes; Virginia had a 48 percent hit rate and Kansas a 28 percent hit rate. When North Carolina analyzed 154 cases under the federal program, it had 25 hits—50 percent of which were rape cases. To expedite the backlog, Ashcroft asked the FBI to redesign the infrastructure of its CODIS system to increase the system's capacity from 1.5 million to 50 million DNA profiles, reduce the search time for matching DNA profiles from two hours to just seconds, increase the frequency with which search requests are performed against the national database from weekly to instantly, and reduce the system server sites from 181 to one to reduce state costs.

In 2003, Rob and Debbie Smith said they were encouraged by the strong bipartisan support H.R. 2874 had received, and Debbie had launched an ambitious letter-writing campaign. She wrote a handwritten note to every member of the House and Senate, even though it would have been far more efficient to send a computerized form letter. In an interview in 2003, Debbie commented, "If it's handwritten it will show them how important an issue it is to me. A form letter is too impersonal, and besides, rape is a very personal, intimate crime. It's a slow process, and hopefully the legislation will be passed before I get through my list. My goal is to write 10 letters a day so that I can finish in two months." At the time, policymakers were equally forthright about the importance of the backlog issue. "DNA evidence is our best weapon to fight rapists, but it's not being used effectively," said Carolyn Maloney:

> The failure to process DNA evidence quickly and correctly has left thousands of victims without justice. For example, in New York City alone, we have the potential to resolve 16,000 unsolved rape cases if we could just process the 18-month backlog of DNA evidence. Only six of more than 60 hospitals in New York City have adequate programs to collect DNA evidence. Ninety-five percent of rape survivors never see a professionally trained examiner. The consequences are an American scandal: in one in five cases where DNA evidence is collected by untrained examiners, the evidence is inadmissible in court.

When Maloney approached Congressman Mark Green, a member of the House Judiciary Committee and the House Crime Subcommittee, about supporting the Debbie Smith Act, he jumped at the chance. When interviewed in 2003, Green had commented, "Carolyn came to me because of my interest in helping victims. I get approached by a lot of people about a lot of bills, like we all do, but reading Debbie's story and then having the chance to meet her ... I was sold. You can't help but be moved by what she went through and her willingness to turn her terrible tragedy into something positive." Green believed the backlog of unprocessed rape kits is a travesty politicians can—and must—fix quickly:

> The only way we're going to win this battle is if we utilize the DNA technology we have. We want to make sure the states have the human and financial resources they need to fulfill the promise of this technology. The promise of this DNA technology is that it will catch the bad guys and free the innocent and that's what unites us. Every time we imprison someone falsely, that means there's another bad guy who is still out there. The frightening reality is that sex offenders have a much greater recidivism rate. I don't believe any of us should rest easy as long as any sex offender is out there because he'll do it again.

Green pointed to sexual assault statistics and said they can be so horrifying:

> At first you don't believe them. We've seen incredible statistics about how often pedophiles strike. When I was elected to the Wisconsin State Assembly, I wanted to double-check to make sure the numbers weren't missing a decimal point. When you realize how often sexual assaults occur, you realize how unbelievable the scope of the problem is. It is unacceptable. I want the bill to put bad guys away and keep the streets safe. I like this legislation because it empowers law enforcement and health officials by giving them the tools and resources they need.

14.9 THE PROVISIONS OF THE JUSTICE FOR ALL ACT OF 2004

The Justice for All Act of 2004 enhances protections for victims of federal crimes, increases federal resources available to state and local governments to combat crimes with DNA technology, and provides safeguards to prevent wrongful convictions and executions. Title I of the bill is the Scott Campbell, Stephanie Roper, Wendy Preston, Louarna Gillis, and Nila Lynn Crime Victims' Rights Act. The provisions of this title establish enhanced and enforceable rights for crime victims in the federal criminal justice system, and authorize grants to help states implement and enforce their own victims' rights laws. Titles II and III of the bill establish the Debbie Smith DNA Backlog Grant Program, which authorizes $755 million over five years to address the DNA backlog crisis in the nation's crime labs, and also authorize more than $500 million in new grant programs to reduce other forensic science backlogs, train criminal justice and medical personnel in the use of DNA evidence, and promote the use of DNA technology to identify missing persons. Title IV of the bill, the Innocence Protection Act, provides access to postconviction DNA testing in federal cases, helps states improve the quality of legal representation in capital cases, and increases compensation in federal cases of wrongful conviction. It also establishes the Kirk Bloodsworth Post-Conviction DNA Testing Program, which authorizes $25 million over five years to defray the costs of postconviction DNA testing. The Scott Campbell, Stephanie Roper, Wendy Preston, Louarna Gillis, and Nila Lynn Crime Victims' Rights Act establishes enhanced rights for victims of federal crimes, including the right to be reasonably protected from the accused; the right to reasonable, accurate, and timely notice of certain proceedings and events; the right not to be excluded from certain proceedings; the right to be reasonably heard at certain proceedings and to confer with the attorney for the government in the case; the right to full and timely restitution; the right to proceedings free from unreasonable delay; and the right to be treated with fairness and with respect for the victim's dignity and privacy. It also authorizes grants to assist state and local authorities in implementing and enforcing crime victims' rights laws, including grants to develop and implement state-of-the-art systems for notifying crime victims of important dates and developments relating to the criminal proceedings at issue in a timely and efficient manner.

The Debbie Smith Act of 2004 reauthorizes and expands the DNA Analysis Backlog Elimination Act of 2000, increasing the authorized funding levels for the DNA Analysis Backlog Elimination Program to $151 million annually for the next five years, as proposed in the President's DNA initiative. Subsection (a) names the Backlog Elimination Act grant program in honor of Debbie Smith, a rape survivor and leader in promoting the use of the DNA technology to solve crimes. In addition, subsection (a) amends the eligibility provisions to add "units of local government" as potential grantees, so that federal resources can meet local needs more quickly.

Subsection (b) provides a single annual authorization for the program, and modifies existing program objectives by adding the collection of DNA samples from convicted offenders as a specific program purpose and ensuring that DNA testing and analysis of samples from crime scenes are carried out in a timely manner. Subsection (b) further provides for the disbursement of grant funds by the Attorney General in conformity with a formula that maximizes the effective use of DNA technology to solve crimes and protect public safety, and addresses areas where significant backlogs exist. A minimum grant amount of 0.50 percent is to be awarded to each state, and a specified percentage of remaining funds will be awarded to conduct DNA analyses of samples from casework. Conversion of the Backlog Elimination Act grant program into a formula grant program will ensure that funds will be fairly distributed among all eligible jurisdictions. It is expected that the factors given weight in the formula will include the magnitude and nature of the DNA backlogs and current DNA work demands in the jurisdictions that seek funding; deficits in public laboratory capacity for the timely and efficient analysis of DNA samples in these jurisdictions, and cost requirements for remedying these deficits; and the ability of these jurisdictions to use the funds to increase DNA analysis and public laboratory capacity for such analysis. It is further expected that the formula will target funding on the use of DNA analysis to solve the most serious violent crimes, including rapes and murders, the solution of which through DNA testing promises the greatest return in promoting public safety. Subsection (b) also reserves no more than 1 percent of the grant amounts to assist state and local crime labs to become accredited, and to undergo regular external audits, to ensure that such labs fully comply with federal quality assurance standards. If an external audit of a crime lab funded by this Act identifies measures to remedy deficiencies with respect to the lab's compliance with FBI standards, such remediation must be implemented as soon as practicable. Finally, subsection (b) provides that DNA backlog grants can be used for non-DNA forensic science backlogs if the state has no significant DNA backlog or lab improvement needs relating to DNA processing. Currently, CODIS, the national database of DNA identification information that a state chooses to collect, is limited to analyses of DNA samples from convicted offenders, crime scenes, unidentified human remains, and missing persons. The Debbie Smith Act also expands CODIS to allow the inclusion of virtually any DNA information that a state chooses to collect, with two exceptions: DNA profiles of arrestees who have not been charged in an indictment or information, and DNA samples that are voluntarily submitted solely for elimination purposes. It also provides new authority for state and local law enforcement to perform "keyboard searches" of CODIS; using this tool, law enforcement can attempt to match DNA analyses of samples taken from crime suspects against the analyses in CODIS without permanently uploading information into the system. In addition, this section provides for the collection, analysis, and inclusion in CODIS of DNA samples from all convicted federal felony offenders—another significant expansion of the national database.

In addition, the Debbie Smith Act provides that, in a case where DNA testing implicates an identified person in the commission of a felony, except for a felony offense under chapter 109A, no statute of limitations would preclude prosecution of the offense until a time period equal to the statute of limitations has elapsed from the date of identification of the perpetrator. The Debbie Smith Act also amends the VAWA to include legal assistance for victims of "dating violence," defined as violence committed by a person who is or has been in a romantic or intimate relationship with the victim; and where the existence of such a relationship is determined based on consideration of its length and its type, and on the frequency of interaction between the persons involved. Finally, the Debbie Smith Act clarifies that grants can be made through vouchers and contracts to private for-profit laboratories to assist in collection of DNA samples from offenders and processing of crime scene DNA evidence.

The DNA Sexual Assault Justice Act of 2004 requires that eligible state and local government public crime labs are accredited and undergo external audits, not less than once every two years, to demonstrate compliance with federal standards established by the FBI. It authorizes grants to provide training, technical assistance, education, and information relating to the identification, collection, preservation, analysis, and use of DNA samples and DNA evidence by law enforcement personnel and other first responders who collect or examine crime scene evidence; court officers, including prosecutors, defense lawyers, and judges; forensic science professionals; and corrections personnel. The grant program is authorized through 2009 at $12.5 million per year. Of significance, the DNA Sexual Assault Justice Act of 2004 authorizes grants to provide training, technical assistance, education, and information relating to the identification, collection, preservation, analysis and use of DNA samples and DNA evidence by medical personnel and other personnel, including doctors, medical examiners, coroners, nurses, victim service providers, and other medical professionals, including existing sexual assault examination programs (SANE, SAFE, and SART). The grant program is authorized through 2009 at $30 million per year. Additionally, it authorizes grants for research and development to improve forensic DNA technology, including funding of demonstration projects involving law enforcement agencies and criminal justice participants to evaluate the use of forensic DNA technology. The grant program is authorized through 2009 at $15 million per year.

This act directs the Attorney General to appoint a National Forensic Science Commission, composed of members from the forensic science and criminal justice communities, which will be responsible for examining various issues, including maximizing the use of forensic sciences to solve crimes and protect public safety; increasing the number of qualified forensic scientists; disseminating best practices concerning the collection and analyses of forensic evidence; and assessing federal, state, and local privacy protection laws and practices relating to access to, or use of, stored DNA samples and analyses. The grant program is authorized through 2009 at $500,000 per year. It authorizes $42.1 million per year through 2009 for FBI DNA programs and activities, including nuclear DNA analysis, mitochondrial DNA analysis, regional mitochondrial DNA laboratories, CODIS, the Federal Convicted Offender DNA Program, and DNA research and development. The act authorizes $2 million per year through 2009 for grants to promote the use of forensic DNA technology to identify missing persons and unidentified human remains, and it modifies the existing criminal provision for unauthorized disclosure of DNA information to include unauthorized "use" of such information, and increases the potential fine to $100,000 for each criminal offense.

Of great interest to the crime lab, the act expands the Paul Coverdell Forensic Sciences Improvement Grant Program, thus permitting funds to be used to eliminate a backlog in the analysis of forensic science evidence, including ballistics examination, latent prints, and toxicology, and extends authorization of appropriations for 2007, 2008, and 2009, at $20 million a year. Current authorizations are $128,067,000 for 2004, $56,733,000 for 2005, and $42,067,000 for 2006. This section further amends the program to require any state applying for funds to certify that it has a process in place to conduct independent external investigations into any allegations of serious negligence or misconduct affecting the integrity of forensic results.

The Innocence Protection Act of 2004 is a multipronged effort to exonerate the innocent through DNA testing. It has several provisions, including the following:

- Establishes rules and procedures governing applications for DNA testing by inmates in the federal system.
- Prohibits the destruction of DNA evidence in a federal criminal case while a defendant remains incarcerated, with certain exceptions. The government can destroy DNA evidence if the defendant waived the right to DNA testing, if the defendant was notified after his or her conviction became final that the evidence might be destroyed and did not file a motion for testing, if a court has denied a motion for testing, or if the evidence has already been tested and the results included the defendant as the source. If the evidence is large or bulky, the government can remove and preserve a representative sample. Intentional violations of these evidence-retention provisions to prevent evidence from being tested or used in court are punishable by a term of imprisonment. Nothing in this section supersedes any law requiring that evidence be preserved.
- Authorizes $5 million a year in grants through 2009 to help states defray the costs of postconviction DNA testing.
- Authorizes a grant program, to be administered by the Attorney General, to improve the quality of legal representation provided to indigent defendants in state capital cases.
- Increases the maximum amount of damages that the U.S. Court of Federal Claims can award against the United States in cases of unjust imprisonment from a flat $5,000 to $50,000 per year in noncapital cases, and $100,000 per year in capital cases.
- Expresses the sense of Congress that states should provide reasonable compensation to any person found to have been unjustly convicted of an offense against the state and sentenced to death.

14.10 THE REST OF THE STORY

In an interview just a few weeks after the signing of the Justice for All Act in the fall of 2004, Rob and Debbie Smith basked in the glow of a mission completed. They reported feeling ecstatic that the hard work of so many individuals has paid off. "It's like you've waited all year for the biggest Christmas present of your life and you finally get to open it, but it took four years," Rob Smith says. He recalls the long road leading to this victory:

> It was the last day of the Congressional session. We had done some calling and writing and lobbying efforts before then, including attending the next-to-the-last Judiciary Committee hearing of the session. We were told it would get out of committee and onto the floor, so we went to Washington, and it didn't happen. We were just heartbroken. Senator Leahy came over to speak with us and try to console us. It was so hard for Debbie because we just didn't know what was going to happen. Congress had a quorum that had been held together for two hours; the Republicans who were against a part of the bill argued and argued over different amendments. By the time they got ready to vote, there was no quorum. So it disbanded and it was very upsetting to us. At that point, Senator Leahy made a promise to Debbie that he would get this bill passed.

Rob explains that at the time, he and Debbie were traveling on a lecture circuit:

> When they finally got it out of committee, we were somewhere in Wyoming. The bill made it out of committee, so that was good, but we were down to the last few weeks of Congress, and we were just holding our breaths and praying and hoping for the best. On the last day of Congress, Debbie was babysitting our youngest grandson and was doing chores at home when the phone rang. It was a senator calling her personally. The senator informed her that Senator Leahy was log-jamming the bill. The amendment he had proposed to be included in the legislation had been honed down more than he wanted, so he was going to stop everything. Well, this particular senator told Debbie that if Congress didn't pass the bill today, it may never ever pass.
>
> I think that was maybe a pep talk to get her to take immediate action. I thought we still could have started the legislation over again, but regardless, it was very disturbing to her to hear it may never come to fruition. That

particular senator, whom I have to leave nameless, told her to call Senator Leahy's office and apply some pressure; he said to call everyone and anyone we knew to put pressure on Congress. When Debbie called, one of Leahy's staffers told her that the senator was on a plane coming back from Vermont. Debbie said, "I don't care where he is or what he's doing, all I want him to do is keep the promise he made to me personally." The senator who initiated the first call called later that evening and said, "Debbie, it worked. Your phone call got through to him. I just got a call from Leahy's staffer who said 'Did you sic Debbie Smith on us?'" They agreed to extend Congress to the next day, as they were haggling over several other bills anyway.

The next day we were on a plane to San Francisco for a conference. When we landed in Dallas to change planes, the phone rang. It was Senator Leahy himself. He said, "Debbie, I passed your bill for you." It was like cloud nine after that, because three different senators and three different members of the House called Debbie personally to congratulate her. In the weeks since, it's been a tremendous ride, but it's been especially overwhelming for Debbie because the word got out that it was her phone call that broke the logjam. Everybody is heaping all this praise and attention on her and of course, we both feel this has been a nationwide effort among so very many people to get this through Congress, and she felt uncomfortable getting so much of the focus. But that's the nature of the way things happened... whoever made that call would have gotten the attention. Of course, I don't know if anyone else would have gotten through to the senators like she did because of the interaction they had in the past. It was an overwhelming, joyous week for both of us.

Rob reports that he and Debbie had stayed busy on the lecture circuit while the bill had been snaking its way slowly through Congress, because they were focusing on advocating for forensic nursing and for victims' rights. "It was a rollercoaster ride," he adds:

We stayed busy year-round, going to a dozen different conferences this year, not counting all the trips to Washington, DC to deal with the bill. A majority of the conferences were attended by SANEs, and the heart of this bill addresses their training needs. Debbie is such a big fan of that program, not having had the luxury of the use of it during her case. She sees the immense value of it and her wish is to have every rape victim have access to a SANE program no matter where they are in the country. She would get pumped up from each conference, especially from all of the forensic nurses who would tell her, "You are the first person to even say the word SANE in Congress and get us some attention." That was a mutual thing—she is pumping them up by her actions and then their reaction to her actions was pumping her back up. Groups like RAINN were constantly calling us or e-mailing us, keeping us posted on the bill's progress, and that was important because we were brand new at this and didn't know what we were doing. We depended on people like them with the background and expertise of dealing with congressional issues to help us get through it.

Both Rob and Debbie say they learned a great deal about how democracy works, including the give-and-take that accompanies political maneuvering. "I was wondering how anything gets done in Washington," Rob says:

It was a game of, if you do this for me I will do that for you... it was a lot of stuff you don't see or don't know about that goes on in Washington. A lot of things were happening and no one from the different congressional offices would inform us. In fact, one time Debbie was quoted by a newspaper as saying that things weren't getting done fast enough. She got a call from one of the staffers saying, "But Senator or Congressman so-and-so has been doing this and this and this behind the scenes." Well, that doesn't tell us anything. As far as our perspective at the time, nothing seemed to be happening. That misunderstanding encouraged lawmakers to keep us more in the loop. We thought, Debbie didn't ask for her name to be put on this piece of legislation, but it's there, and if her name is on it, don't you think that's who the media will call and question, so don't you think you should keep her informed? The last thing we ever wanted to do was antagonize any member of the House or Senate.

In fact, Rob says, treating Congress members and their staffs well was part of the plan:

We knew that legislators would take our call or open the door for us rather than sneak out the back door if we were civil and helpful. We plan on advocating for other issues after this one, so we want that door readily opened. We want them to say, "Oh good, Debbie and Rob are here." Not, "Oh my God, they're back." The legislative process is more complicated than what the average citizen could ever imagine. The process was a real eye opener for us.

Once indoctrinated into the Beltway, Rob Smith says that he and Debbie were fascinated by the efforts undertaken by lawmakers to get the bill passed:

Orrin Hatch had really championed the cause. We even had an occasion to get on a private jet with Senator Hatch. A private corporation was flying him down to Atlanta for a fundraising luncheon, and we just happened to be in Atlanta with that very corporation in order to make a presentation. They mentioned they were flying him down and I said I'd love for Debbie to have a few minutes to talk with the senator. The CEO of this corporation looked at me and said, "You want it? Consider it done. You just be at Dulles airport and I'll get Debbie 15 minutes with him." So she took her 15 minutes and Senator Hatch carried it on, asking questions for much longer, and he promised Debbie he'd make sure it would happen. He was genuinely interested in the issue, and he really took to

Debbie personally. Those personal times we've had with some of the members of Congress helped to solidify their interest in the bill, because when you put a face to something like this, it's harder to forget it.

Debbie says that many of the lawmakers needed an education about the rape kit backlog. "I know some of them were very surprised at the numbers of kits that were sitting there on shelves, and I think that maybe some of them were even a little naive as to what it meant to have those kits still sitting there," she says:

The kits connected them to a victim. I think a lot of people have the idea that once you get over the rape, it's easier to recover day by day, but that's not the case. Because that's when fear starts setting in, especially if the perpetrator hasn't been caught. Your mind starts racing, wondering where he is and thinking, is he still following you and watching you? I don't think Congress members understood the aftermath of this crime and the significance of unanalyzed rape kits sitting in a police storage locker.

Debbie adds that she was encouraged by the questions lawmakers were asking of her during testimony in front of Congress:

One of the things they didn't know was what a SANE was. They really had no idea. I was naive enough to think I was the only one who hadn't heard of it. In my very first subcommittee hearing I used the term; I just kept using the acronym SANE instead of saying sexual assault nurse examiner, and that was one of the first questions asked: "What is this SANE you are talking about?" They wanted to know what the nurse did, and I was able to tell them, "I truly believe with all my heart that a SANE is the missing link between the victim and getting the victim to report the rape." I know that when my husband was still working as a police officer, several times he was able to convince a victim to report the crime or have evidence collected because he said he could take them to a hospital that had a SANE. I know it can be a decision-maker.

As a former police officer—Smith retired several years ago—Rob found it difficult to sit on his hands while rapes went unsolved. "Being a police officer and wanting to solve crimes, I want every possible crime-solving tool we can get at our disposal. To put DNA out there as a science that is available yet unavailable due to funding constraints, it's like taking the handcuffs out of my holder and putting them on me instead of on the criminal. It was like, 'Here they are, but I am just going to dangle them in front of you—you can't use them.'"

Debbie reports that she receives effusive thanks from forensic nurses since the passing of the bill that could significantly boost appropriations for training of medical personnel:

What I hear from them constantly is "Thank you." They keep me going. Anyone who would choose to deal with this subject and to help people who have experienced violence and are willing to give of their time to do it, they are just very special people from the start. I hear from people who agree that we really need to do something about getting more health care institutions to have SANEs and SART teams, as opposed to making the victim go from agency to agency, and relating the same story over and over again to several different people. States with SANEs and SARTs realize how important it is to work together for the good of the victim. If victim advocates and law enforcement and health care providers aren't working together or communicating with each other, that places a big stress on the victim.

Debbie hopes the passing of the 2004 legislation will serve as a greater mandate for SANEs' presence in health care institutions. "I'm hoping it will create more opportunities for forensic nurses. I know that the bottom line for a lot of hospitals is money. But this grant program will provide the funds for training and I know there are other grant programs to go through to get the equipment. If nothing else, it will help to foster awareness and make the hospitals which are resisting SANE/SART programs realize how important they are."

Rob Smith believes SANEs are playing an extremely important role in not only the collection of evidence, but in testifying about the evidence in a court of law. "Even before we got involved with this legislation, I was involved in a case that still seems very vivid to me," Rob says:

It was a case of 2-year-old boy who was being sodomized by a 17-year-old relative. The older boy's callousness was shocking; I conducted the interview with him and this teenager took no responsibility for it. He had no concern that he was even hurting this small boy. The pediatric SANE found scarring; the family said nothing had been happening, yet it was apparent that the abuse had been happening for some time. The grandmother walked into the room when the older boy had the diaper off the little boy; the older boy was zipping up his pants at the time. It was mostly circumstantial, but when we got into court, the defense brought in the ER doctor who didn't have a whole lot to say about it. The family pediatrician didn't help our side of the case, but then we brought in the SANE, and when it was all said and done, when the judge rendered his decision, he said, "I listened to both sides, and this nurse has educated me more than anybody else. I am compelled to find him guilty." It was a major victory and convinced me that what the SANES are doing is important. ER physicians get sidetracked with heart attack victims, while the SANEs are going to be more attentive and less distracted in their duties. They are devoted to whatever time it takes to do the evidentiary exam. To me, it's the only way to go. We are getting better evidence documented, collected, and preserved because these nurses are better trained than other medical professionals.

> Therefore, our odds are increasing with each rape kit that we are going to get solid evidence to go on.

Forensic nurses are looking to the provisions of the Justice for All Act with mixed feelings of hope and uncertainty. Forensic nurse examiner Cari Caruso is among those who are cautious about legislation that overpromises and underdelivers, and says she is concerned about lingering misperceptions about DNA and unrealistic expectations.

Caruso comments, "I think we can legislate ourselves to death, and the way legislation comes out in the end isn't exactly how we intended it to be in the beginning, so I am always wary of these kinds of things." She refers to a controversial California initiative that would require mandatory collection of DNA samples of all arrestees and says many people simply don't understand the intentions of DNA legislation. "They don't understand that the identifying parts of the DNA that we use forensically are not the parts that determine what a person's health history is," she says:

> So there is a lot of science that people won't understand. I don't see a big difference between taking someone's fingerprints upon arrest and taking someone's DNA, although there is a lot of opposition to it based on privacy concerns. I don't think it's understood that DNA is just a newer form of fingerprints; there was a time when fingerprint technology was controversial, too. Some of these legislative issues piggyback on others and get tweaked enough to become less meaningful.

Colorado forensic nurse Valerie Sievers is concerned about continued funding of victims' services, but is hopeful that forensic nursing programs will finally receive an infusion of cash. "I think it will be a good thing, even if the money is centralized, so that forensic laboratories get the resources they need to help support nurses' evidence collection efforts. I think it would be great if there was going to be a glut of money that would foster continued financial support of forensic nurse training and the training of other medical personnel regarding forensic protocol. We'll have to wait and see."

California forensic examiner Diana Faugno comments:

> I would be very pleased to see some of these forensic nursing programs funded so that nurses can become even more educated and apply their newfound knowledge to their jobs, forensic or not. The Justice for All Act has certainly raised awareness of forensic nursing issues, and that has real value. But how much these lawmakers truly understand the issues is up for debate. We just finished up a trial here in San Diego, a case from 1997. The perpetrator was released from prison in 1992, and you know what kind of DNA we were doing back then. Eventually, serology caught up with DNA, and in 2002, there was another sexual assault. We got a cold hit, and it was this same perpetrator. But for five years he was out on the streets and God knows what he has done in that time. Cases like these illustrate why it's so important to address the backlog.

14.11 THE BELEAGUERED FORENSIC LABORATORY

In December 2003, the *National Forensic DNA Study Report*, a joint effort between the Division of Governmental Studies and Services of Washington State University and Smith Alling Lane, PS, was released through a grant from the National Institute of Justice and the U.S. Department of Justice. The report, authored by Nicholas P. Lovrich, PhD, Michael J. Gaffney, JD, Travis C. Pratt, PhD, Charles L. Johnson, MA, Christopher H. Asplen, JD, Lisa H. Hurst, and Timothy M. Schellberg, JD, discussed solutions to increasing burdens on forensic laboratories' DNA analysis capabilities. They write:

> Cases that previously may have been unsolvable have been transformed into solvable cases where viable suspects can be identified and arrested or removed from suspect lists. While this new technology enhances the opportunity for the criminal justice system to do justice in more cases of suspected wrong-doing, it also creates an added need for law enforcement agencies to review old cases for potential biological evidence that should be sent to a crime laboratory for testing.

To better understand the dimensions of the backlog problem, the authors of the report asked themselves these questions: How big is the case backlog? How did it grow so large? What is the capacity of the evidence collection, storage, analysis, and retrieval system to reduce that backlog and provide timely information for the criminal justice system? For the answers to these queries, the authors relied on data produced by a national survey of local and state forensic laboratories and local law enforcement agencies, as well as extensive interviews of prosecutors, investigators, and laboratory administrators. For the first time, an attempt was made to determine the number of criminal cases that might benefit from DNA analysis, to discover law enforcement and laboratories' capacities for dealing with cases involving DNA, and to identify significant issues relating to the expansion of the use of DNA forensic analysis in criminal cases.

The authors of the report describe the backlog of unsolved rapes and homicides in the United States as "massive." The survey found that the number of rape and homicide cases with possible biological evidence that local law enforcement agencies have not submitted to a laboratory for analysis is more than 221,000, including approximately 52,000 homicide cases and about 169,000 rape cases. The number of property crime cases with possible biological evidence that local law enforcement agencies have not submitted to a laboratory for analysis is more than 264,000. Additionally, the number of unanalyzed DNA cases reported by state and local crime laboratories is more than 57,000. The total number of crime cases with possible biological evidence either still in the possession of local law enforcement or backlogged at forensic laboratories is approximately 542,700.

The report states:

> A significant proportion of law enforcement agencies continue to misunderstand the potential benefits of DNA testing. While these figures address the first question as to the approximate size of the case backlog, the second question remains regarding how the backlog came to grow so large. The answer to this question is quite complicated, and the phenomenon of a substantial growth in criminal case backlogs involves a variety of factors, some of which are vexing and difficult to manage. However, a series of questions posed to local law enforcement agencies and forensic laboratories reveal several interesting patterns of response which, when considered collectively, begin to provide an accurate picture of how the backlogs tend to develop and why they continue to exist.

Regarding reasons why cases with DNA evidence have not been submitted to the laboratory:

- 50.8 percent of responding local law enforcement agencies indicated that forensic DNA was not considered a tool for crime investigations.
- 31.4 percent responded that no suspect had been identified.
- 9.2 percent indicated that the prosecution had not requested testing.
- 10.2 percent responded that a suspect had been identified, but not yet charged.
- 23.6 percent of responding agencies suggested that DNA evidence from unsolved cases was not submitted for reasons relating to poor funding.
- 9.4 percent indicate a lack of funding for DNA analysis.
- 10.4 percent indicate inability of laboratories to produce timely results.
- 3.8 percent indicate crime laboratory is not processing requests for DNA testing.

The National Institute of Justice report characterizes state and local crime laboratories as being "overworked, understaffed, and insufficiently funded." In many jurisdictions, processing times at crime laboratories pose significant delays. The report found that state laboratories take an average of 23.9 weeks to process an unnamed suspect rape kit, and local laboratories average 30.0 weeks for such tests. The cost for testing these rape kits was estimated at $1,100 per case, and does not account for many overhead costs. Both state and local laboratories indicated that personnel needs were among the most significant concerns for their DNA programs. Specifically, most laboratories said they need supplemental funding for additional DNA staff; several laboratories indicated that their priority concern was for additional funding to augment current salaries to avoid the loss of skilled personnel to other prospective employers. A strong need was also reported for reagents (chemicals used in DNA analysis) and for technical equipment used for DNA analysis. The report also found that although the need for the expansion of mitochondrial DNA testing is substantial, the need for the more common nuclear DNA testing is even more pressing. Forensic laboratories reported 2,999 cases over the last 12 months that could have benefited from mitochondrial testing.

What makes legislation like the Justice for All Act so important is the relatively little attention that has been paid to the funding of labs in the past. The report states, "The role of the federal government in funding forensic DNA analysis has been, up to this point, important but rather minimal." Most laboratories also reported that although federal funding has played an important role in assisting with backlogged DNA cases, the proportion of their overall DNA budgets funded through federal sources is minimal. The survey of laboratories found that 20.5 percent of state crime laboratories receive 50 percent or more of their funding from federal sources; that figure is only 4.5 percent for local laboratories.

The benefits derived from DNA analysis are unquestionable. The authors stated:

> Armed with a better understanding of the (backlog) problem, policy makers subsequently ask for a definition of the expected benefits of devoting limited resources to the solution. Although this report does not attempt a comprehensive, econometrically-derived cost–benefit analysis, the report includes case studies on "preventable" crimes through strong DNA programs, along with an overview of DNA database successes. Forensic DNA databases are important tools in solving a variety of crimes, committed by a variety of criminals.

The analysis of DNA database hits presented in the National Institute of Justice report provides a breakdown of 4,092 DNA database hits in 38 states. The majority of database hits have linked repeat offenders to violent crimes. In fact, for several years the Virginia Division of Forensic Science has reported that more than 80 percent of the hits on the state's DNA database would have been missed if the database had been limited to only violent offenders. Most states, however, have only recently begun to require DNA testing for nonviolent offenders for placement on their DNA database. Similarly, several laboratories will not process DNA evidence from property crimes if it is sent to the laboratory for analysis. There are numerous crimes that are potentially preventable through better, more efficient use of forensic DNA analysis, the report states. The authors say that a review of specific cases in 19 states reveals more than 100 serious crimes that could have been prevented through either the inclusion of all convicted felons in the database or shorter DNA analysis processing times. The report adds, "The cost and the offsetting benefits associated with DNA testing present several questions relating to return on investment which merit further study."

In February 2005, the U.S. Department of Justice's Office of Justice Programs and the Bureau of Justice Statistics released the report, *Census of Publicly Funded Forensic Crime Laboratories: 50 Largest Crime Labs, 2002*, which painted a more detailed picture of the state of forensic laboratories across the country. According to the Department of Justice report, the 50 largest publicly funded forensic crime laboratories in the United States employed more than 4,300 full-time equivalent (FTE) personnel in 2002 and had total budgets exceeding $266.6 million. These labs received more than 994,000 new cases, including more than 1.2 million requests for forensic services during calendar year 2002. The report defined a *case* as evidence submitted from a single criminal investigation, and might include multiple requests for forensic services. For example, one case might include a request for biology screening and a request for latent prints. A case or request is defined as backlogged if it is in the laboratory and remains unreported for a period of 30 days or more. The requests represented about half of all requests for forensic services handled by publicly funded laboratories nationally. These labs ended 2002 with more than 93,000 backlogged cases, including about 270,000 requests for forensic services—more than twice the backlog at the beginning of the year. The backlog increased in all categories of forensic services. Large laboratories estimated that about 930 additional FTEs would have been needed to achieve a 30-day turnaround for all 2002 requests for forensic services. Based on starting salaries for analysts or examiners in the large laboratories, the estimated cost of the additional FTEs exceeds $36.2 million. Most of the large laboratories indicated that resources beyond personnel increases would also have been needed to achieve a 30-day turnaround on all 2002 requests, including equipment, supplies, and space requirements, plus funds for overtime, travel, and training. Among those labs providing detailed cost estimates, additional equipment accounted for about $18.3 million.

In terms of backlogged requests, the 50 largest labs surveyed began 2002 with approximately 117,000 backlogged requests for forensic services. These labs received an additional 1.2 million requests during 2002 and completed nearly 1.1 million requests. The total estimated backlog at year end, about 270,000 requests, represents an increase of nearly 154,000 requests, or 132 percent, from the beginning of the year, according to the report. Dividing the estimated backlogged requests by those completed results in a ratio that describes backlog growth relative to the laboratories' current capacity to process requests; overall, for every four requests completed by these large laboratories, there was one outstanding request at year end. Eighty percent of the estimated 270,000 backlogged requests for forensic services in these large laboratories was attributable to requests for controlled substances (50 percent), latent prints (19 percent), and DNA analysis (11 percent). About 136,000 requests were attributable to analysis of controlled substances. For every three such requests completed in 2002, approximately one request was outstanding at year end. The backlog included about 51,000 requests for latent print services, or about one fifth of the total. For every two latent print requests completed in 2002, approximately one request was outstanding at year end. The backlog included about 31,000 requests for DNA analysis. Although these requests comprised about one tenth of the total backlog, they had the greatest backlog relative to labs' current capacity to process requests: For every one DNA analysis request completed in 2002, an estimated 1.7 requests were outstanding at year end.

The survey asked directors of forensic laboratories to report their performance expectations for one FTE examiner per year in each category of forensic services. Overall, examiners in the largest labs processed requests at or above 90 percent of the expected average in all but two categories: biology screening (82 percent) and DNA analysis (78 percent). Examiners performing biology screening were expected to process an average of 166 requests per year; they actually processed 136 requests per year, or about 82 percent of the expected average. Examiners performing DNA analysis were expected to process an average of 69 requests per year; they actually processed 54 requests per year, or about 78 percent of the expected average. Overall, the largest laboratories estimated that an additional 931 FTEs would be needed to achieve a 30-day turnaround on all requests for forensic services received in 2002 at an estimated total cost of more than $36.2 million. A little more than half of the needed FTEs were in the areas of controlled substances (10 percent), latent prints (17 percent), and DNA analysis (25 percent).

In a conversation prior to the passage of the Justice for All Act, Ferrara noted, "It's getting better, but we have a long way to go." Ferrara has testified before the Crime Subcommittee of the House Judiciary Committee regarding various pieces of legislation that would ease the DNA backlog. He says he was pleased about the first federal appropriation of $15 million to help reduce this growing workload. "In the last several years, the National Institute of Justice has received federal funding to continue administering grants aimed at reducing the rape-kit processing backlog," he says:

> I think we are on the right track but it's going to take more than just throwing money at the problem. You need funding but you also need trained law enforcement and forensic nurses. We foresee an explosion in potential evidence being submitted to forensic laboratories. In rape cases, we would like to think they will be reported at a higher frequency and evidence will be collected properly and promptly and analyzed expeditiously. We anticipate that in other types of crimes like homicides, the police are recognizing, collecting, and preserving more pieces of evidence. It's a good and a bad place to be. We already have backlog problems; if we train even more first responders and law enforcement, it means more evidence coming in. So the answer to the capacity problem is training more forensic scientists who are capable of DNA analysis. It's a cradle-to-grave kind of need; the cradle begins at the crime scene or with the victim and if that first step fails us, our grandiose science becomes useless.

"The capacity issue is not going to be solved easily," Ferrara predicts, although he says legislation like the Debbie Smith Act will provide short-term relief in the form of increased funds for specialized training of forensic professionals such as nurses and crime lab scientists. "We did 37 DNA cases in 1989; in 2001 we did more than 1,800 cases," Ferrara says. "As more labs do more cases, you get better statistical data. I've seen the number of DNA laboratories go from single digits to 120; I think that number will need to double in coming years. In 1989 we passed the first DNA database bill in the country and in 1990 we started collecting DNA samples from all felons. To date, there are less than 30 states that do so. Are we making progress as fast as I'd like? No. But I also know how much time, effort, personnel, and training it takes." Ferrara says he struggles with the dilemma of assigning priority to large numbers of cases, both existing and new, in his lab. "Which case do we do next?" Ferrara ponders:

> Do you do first in or first out? If I have a capacity of doing 100 cases a month—and that's pretty damn good—and I have 200 cases a month coming in, you can see the need for prioritization. Most labs will consider a priority the cases where the police have a suspect and a known DNA sample, or they have the guy under arrest and need to analyze DNA samples expeditiously. Obviously, those cases take priority, but the reality for many labs with limited capacity is cases with no known suspect are at the bottom of the priority list—even though that is exactly the kind of case the DNA databanks are designed for. Those are the kinds of cases that encourage rape victims who don't know who the perpetrator is to report them. They at least have a reasonable expectation their sample will get analyzed and a good chance of getting a match.

Ferrara says he is sometimes haunted by the memories of cases that fell through the prioritization cracks. In his testimony before the Subcommittee on Crime in 2000, Ferrara related the case of Jemma Saunders:

> Police suspected a man named Christopher Banks in the rape and stabbing of a woman in Virginia Beach, Virginia. Until they could get DNA test results from us, they could only hold Banks on a shoplifting charge. They considered Banks a serious threat and asked us for an expedited analysis before his hearing on the shoplifting charge. At the time some 1,000 other DNA cases were already in the queue. We don't get the case done before Banks was released on the shoplifting charge. Eleven days later, Banks raped and killed 22-year old Jemma Saunders in Norfolk. When we finally got to the Virginia Beach evidence, our DNA analysis established that Banks had committed the Virginia Beach rape and stabbing. Had we done that analysis in even two months, Jemma Saunders would be alive today.

Ferrara says because property crimes often are precursors to violent crimes, his lab will work property crimes as quickly as they can. "We prioritize those cases because we know that today's burglar is often tomorrow's rapist," Ferrara emphasizes. "A lot of breaking-and-entering cases may be some kind of stalking or souvenir-hunting activity by an offender. The Banks case exemplifies why backlogs are unconscionable. I don't know if there will ever be a time when cases are turned around in 30 days or in 10 days, but I think we need to reach a point when as a case comes in, work is started immediately."

Ferrara reports his lab analyzed 258 cases in July 2002 and those completed had been in the lab an average of 150 days:

> To me, that's too long; to others, that would be great. We have 38 DNA examiners, and they can only do about six to eight cases a month on average. But if 38 examiners do an average of seven cases, that's 266 cases per month. We received 334 cases in July. You see the problem with trying to keep up. Fortunately, I don't have 10,000 unworked rape kits going back 5 or 10 years, and luckily Virginia doesn't have a statute of limitations. If that sample is properly collected and preserved, which our samples are, even if it takes us a number of years, and it has, we will eventually get our guy. In January 2003 we began taking DNA samples upon arrest. The beauty of it is, a sample goes to the databank upon arrest, so instead of waiting months or years before the case is adjudicated, he's convicted and you find out he's the guy that committed several other rapes.

That's good news for rape victims whose lives come to a grinding halt while they await the processing of their rape kit and wait for the day when their attacker is identified through DNA sampling. "Studies suggest the average rapist commits 8 to 12 rapes," Ferrara says. "I've seen a figure from the Bureau of Justice that the societal cost of a rape is as high as $86,000. If you get a good sample after the first rape and are able to catch him after the second, you have saved hundreds of thousands of dollars. But most importantly, you have prevented as many as 10 more women from being victimized. That's what makes it all worthwhile."

Ferrara says he is optimistic about the funding that will eventually come down the federal pipeline from the provisions of the Justice for All Act of 2004:

> I don't know how long it is going to take before the money starts flowing. In the past, it's been a very slow process for federal funding to come through. The federal government is pumping money into a whole slate of different areas, which has got to benefit the laboratory community in terms of increased capacity. The one thing it can't do is deliver instant personnel to the labs. I was disappointed in that the government chose not to fund institutions committed to training new forensic scientists. They're throwing money at a problem, and I realize that is the way we tend to want to solve problems, and then we expect some sort of immediate results. Well, if it takes me a year to train a DNA examiner and I have calculated that I need to double my staff, where am I going to get 40 new forensic DNA examiners in one fell swoop? None of this federal money really goes to that kind of need. It can't give me positions to hire these people and it can't pay their salaries; however, labs will receive funding for new equipment, and you can also get labs accredited; there is money for upgrading labs and lab information management systems, reducing backlogs, and outsourcing work, but it misses the mark in terms of addressing education and training of new forensic scientists, which is pretty critical, I think.
>
> I have five new DNA examiners in the Virginia Institute of Forensic Science and Medicine who graduate in September of next year; I'll have positions for them so I'll hire them, and then I'll have five more examiners. That's a small incremental step which isn't going to meet the 111 percent increase in DNA cases that I have seen in the last three years. There's no shortage of people trying to get into the Institute for training; the difficulty is the capacity of the institute. We just can't handle any more than what we already have in operation currently; we have 19 fellows in DNA, firearms, latent fingerprints, and controlled substances, and that's about all we can handle with our existing funding and faculty. But we need to do 10 times that. There is no shortage of students, however. What I have seen is a tremendous proliferation of undergraduate- and graduate-level academic programs in forensic science, so there's a tremendous interest on the part of young people in getting into forensic science; they are fascinated by it. The difficulty is that there are not enough places for them to go after graduation. They will find it difficult to get jobs because state and local governments never seem to get the number of positions they need to cope with the level of forensic services needed.

Ferrara explains that his laboratory is working at its maximum capacity, and then some. "We're at our busiest ever," he says. "We have more than 2,000 DNA cases backlogged right now and that number is growing. The volume of evidence in any given case has exploded, as have the number of cases. And the better trained the police are, the more evidence they collect, labs like mine will be forced to make difficult decisions." Ferrara explains that recently, his lab has been forced to not process what he calls "touch" evidence on any cases other than violent crimes:

> If, for example, the case involves possession of a firearm, we're not going to swab the handle of the gun and try to identify that person for what is not a violent felony. If it's a rape or murder case, however, that's different. If better evidence is not found, and if touch evidence is involved in the case, then we'll do it. But because our resources are stretched thin, we had to make a hard decision like this, one which has been met with alacrity, to say the very least, by user agencies such as the police. They understand our reasoning, but that doesn't mean they like it. We've already said we're not going to do DNA analysis in drug possession cases to establish possession. It's a very frustrating situation because arguably, when you have a technology like DNA available, how do you justify not using it? We'll continue to do property crimes and cases like that because we think it's very worthwhile; we have resisted the temptation to say "OK, let's just do rape and homicide cases and not these other cases." I think that would be a terrible mistake but I can see where it could become necessary in order to get the rape and murder cases out the door. We triage cases, of course, but there are so many rape cases.

Ferrara sounds weary, as a professional who has seen it all in his 34 years of duty, including the steady torrent of violent cases that beg to be solved quickly. "It's common to have a profile, run it through the first time, and you don't make a hit; but just today we had a case where a guy just got caught on a property crime, his DNA sample was entered into the database, and we made him on a rape case." Ferrara believes that until the backlog is significantly reduced or eradicated, forensic laboratories must continue to stand firm on selecting for analysis items of evidence with the most probative value, even as the gigantic tide of collected items comes rushing in:

> I'm not as worried about forensic nurses and examiners contributing to the backlog because there is a limited universe of samples these nurses collect. They should, however, re-examine plucking of head and pubic hairs for microscopic comparison because they are of questionable value. The examiners should continue to comb for any foreign hairs, but I question the collection of large numbers of hairs from victims. What we do is go right to the most probative evidence first, which in the case of a sexual assault, a vaginal rape, we go right to a vaginal swab.

> Regarding all of the other evidence collected in rape kits; if we can show positive results on the most probative piece of evidence, that vaginal swab, then what we have tried to do is say, "OK, stop there, don't analyze the sheets, the pillow cases, the clothing, and all of the other sundry items in a case. However, in saying that, I must emphasize that the collection of these items is still important because there are cases where you come up blank on what you thought were the most probative pieces of evidence. When that happens, you go to other evidence, such as a breast swab, which may yield a saliva sample. The perpetrator forced the victim to douche but didn't think about his saliva left on her breasts when he licked them. Maybe the lab won't analyze this swab, but I would much rather the forensic examiner collect it and we not use it. The problem arises now where we get prosecutors to buy into what we're doing and being content with just the vaginal swab evidence, but then the defense comes along and says "Wait a minute, my client admits he had consensual intercourse with the victim but she was fine when he left; someone else must have murdered her," or "Someone else must have raped her and didn't ejaculate." The defense will get a court order for the forensic lab to examine and analyze all the other items of evidence in the case, looking for some other foreign profile, to support the weak scenario they want to propose. The judges are not refusing those orders for evidence, so that stuff comes back into the lab.

Ferrara explains that a case usually consists of a finite number of items of evidence, perhaps 10 to 20 items per case that must be examined. The bigger problem for labs, he says, is when law enforcement collects hundreds of pieces of evidence from a crime scene. "There is almost no limit to what they can collect," he says. And it all ends up at the lab, in many cases. "Fundamentally, you can't really collect too much evidence, but even as I say that, labs are struggling to keep up with its workloads. I would rather have the evidence at my disposal, because if you don't collect it you can't go back to the crime scene again. But we can opt not to examine everything, again, relying on the most probative pieces of evidence to save time and resources. And if the courts order us to test everything, well, then, I guess, so be it."

Ferrara says it is possible for jurisdictions, with the help of forensic examiners, to take a fresh look at what's in their rape kits to perhaps streamline the collection process. "We all have our own kits, and we know the kinds of samples we like to collect," Ferrara acknowledges. "It might be prudent to look at some ways to refine the contents of kits. For example, a known sample from a victim doesn't have to be a blood draw if there is no oral sodomy involved; if I can get a buccal swab, then I don't need blood from the victim. The only time we would need it is when there was oral sodomy involved and we need the mouth rinse." Ferrara says the forensic examiner can glean much-needed information from the victim that will help guide the collection of the kinds of pertinent, probative evidence that forensic laboratories need:

> The kinds of questions asked, and the specific, detailed information from the victim is extremely critical—what did the perpetrator do exactly, where was the victim touched, did the perpetrator ejaculate, and where . . . these are critical pieces of information. We've seen cases where the perpetrator forced the victim to perform oral sex and then washed out the victim's mouth. They're all aware of DNA analysis now, so they are being a lot smarter, if you can call a perpetrator that.

He recalls a case in which the forensic examiner's good thinking resulted in evidence that clinched the case:

> We had a case where a 9-year-old girl was digitally penetrated by an uncle. The forensic examiner asked the little girl if he touched her anywhere else, and she replied that sucked on her ear. She was wearing earrings at the time of the assault, so the earrings went to the lab as evidence and we got the guy. The breast swabs are a good example of good alternate sources of DNA. There are numerous cases where perpetrators force the victim to douche or they wear a condom and think they're home free, and it's been the breast swabs primarily that have resulted in the hits.

Ferrara says hair is a problematic sample that most labs are choosing not to analyze; he adds:

> We go after nuclear DNA first and foremost, and it's only in 100 cases a year out of several thousand that we get down to a foreign hair as being the only probative piece of evidence we have. In that case, you're going to mitochondrial DNA on the hair if there is any hair root. As for collecting large quantities of head or pubic hair from the victim, I'm not sure how valuable that is. Failing oral, vaginal or anal swabs, then the next best samples are seminal fluid or vaginal drainage in underwear. Then after that, you get into hair samples, and it's not that useful that often. It's difficult to say skip certain samples because we must satisfy forensic needs, yet we must find ways to manage our caseloads. It's a fine line we walk.

14.12 FORENSIC LABORATORIES PARTNER WITH FORENSIC NURSES

"Thoroughness starts with the forensic nurse," Ferrara says. "We have our DNA people spend a lot of time with forensic nurses, teaching and working with these people because we realize, garbage in, garbage out. They are the first responders to victims, and they are the ones who can help crime lab personnel get the most accurate, untainted samples possible." Recognizing that a crime lab can't work in a vacuum and must depend on the frontline professionals who have the closest contact with victims, the

Virginia lab has a reputation for its extensive outreach to forensic professionals desiring training. "We have worked with medical examiners on refining DNA sample collection, trained forensic nurses, and worked with personnel from numerous law enforcement agencies," Ferrara confirms. "The payoff is palpable. There's nothing I can tell forensic nurses about evidence collection and preservation they don't already know," Ferrara continues. "It's important for forensic labs to make the efforts of forensic nurses worthwhile by analyzing them promptly. If you are going to take the sample, damn it, run them. If forensic nurses are doing their jobs well, and yet they think, 'Here I am taking samples and it will be years before we see results,' i''s pretty disheartening, not only for the victim, but for that forensic nurse."

Ferrara says his lab has worked closely with forensic nurses and acknowledges their help many years ago in developing the rape kit the lab currently uses. Ferrara says forensic nurses' input has shaped the contents of the extensive rape kit on which other states have modeled their own. "While we can address the technical side of what DNA samples we want and need, we are not in the best position to know how to make this as painless as possible to the victim; the forensic nurses do," Ferrara emphasizes. "Our nurses do a wonderful job of getting samples." This knowledge, coupled with evolving technology and new procedures, ensures that rape kits are supplying the kinds of evidence needed to make DNA matches.

The challenge for forensic scientists is looking for new sources of DNA when offenders try to cover their tracks. "Once an unknown rapist's DNA sample is in the databank and they know a match could be made, they try to protect themselves from leaving any biological material," Ferrara says. "I don't see how they can do that. Locard's Exchange Principle says that in any crime, the victim and the perpetrator exchange DNA material. In the case of a rape, there can be no more intimate exchange of trace evidence than this. It works to our advantage. The perpetrator can force his victim to douche or bathe, but there are still many possibilities for the collection of trace evidence, such as skin fragments under fingernails or traces of saliva."

14.12.1 Rape-Kit Standardization

There is much discussion currently regarding the standardization of sexual assault evidence kits (SAEKs), commonly referred to as rape kits. The national protocol discussed in chapter 6 is one effort to unite SANEs in their practice, and other organizations such as the IAFN continue to seek ways to standardize the contents of these kits. Parnis and Du Mont (2002) examined the practices relating to the standardization and processing of the SAEK. Despite the presumed scientific objectivity of this protocol, the researchers reported that their survey of sexual assault nurses, physicians, police, and forensic scientists revealed that discretionary practices frequently pervaded the evidentiary process. They argue that there must be greater awareness of the shaping of medico-legal evidence, and given the diverse characteristics of sexual assaults and of the health care needs of sexually assaulted women, the researchers also suggest that it might be unreasonable to apply a single standard model of a rape kit. According to Arndt (1988), in 1987, California became the first state to standardize its sexual assault protocol statewide. To date, there is still significant variation in the type of evidence collected and how it is collected. According to Ledray (2001), essential steps of the evidentiary exam include the following:

- Obtain written consent.
- Obtain an assault history, including orifices where violence was used or penetration occurred and by what; forms of violence used and where.
- Obtain pertinent medical information, including allergies, current pregnancy status, and menstrual cycle.
- Conduct a physical exam for trauma and areas of tenderness.
- Examine involved orifices for trauma and to collect sperm and seminal fluid.
- Collect any foreign matter present.
- Comb the pubic hair for foreign hair and matter.
- Complete fingernail scrapings; collect the survivor's blood for type and DNA screen.
- Collect saliva for secretor status.
- Collect torn or stained clothing.

The areas of variation in these protocols include the amount of documentation, prophylactic treatment for STDs versus culturing, what clothing is saved as evidence (all vs. only torn or soiled clothing), if head and pubic hairs are plucked and how many, and the collection of additional blood specimens for drug and alcohol analysis.

Currently, most national, state, and institutional protocols recommend that evidentiary exams be completed within 72 hours after a sexual assault (Frank, 1996; Ledray, 1999). Post-72-hour exams are, however, sometimes conducted in cases when there are injuries that can be documented or when the victim has not changed clothes or showered and evidence might still be available for collection. Ledray (2001) explains that SANEs look for evidence to confirm recent sexual contact, to show force or coercion was used, to help identify the suspect, and to corroborate the survivor's story. A few programs still collect a vaginal normal saline aspirate (Osborn & Neff, 1989), and some pluck 15 to 20 head hairs and pubic hairs (Osborn & Neff, 1989), or cut hairs rather than plucking, as many laboratories do not analyze the root (Neff, 1989). Ledray adds that most experts today, however, do not recommend collection of vaginal aspirates or head or pubic hair evidence in the ED, because if hair evidence is needed from the victim it is retrievable at a later date in time. Some state crime laboratories still request this evidence, however, and it is essential that the forensic examiner is aware of the local standards.

Linda Ledray, RN, PhD, LP, FAAN, who literally wrote the book on sexual assault, comments:

> I support standardization of rape evidence kits as long as the protocol allows me to do—or not do—the things I want, and as long as it's not saying to pull pubic hairs, pull head hairs, or do STD testing. Conversely, I think other nurses will support standardization as long as it includes pulling head hairs and pulling pubic hairs. So there is going to be some difficulty in standardizing these kits across the country because jurisdictions vary. I think we all have components of our evidence kits which we like, as well as things we don't like about kits. We came up with a national protocol, which I wasn't sure would be possible, given so many differences in state and regional protocols across the country. For example, in Tennessee, I believe the protocol is to do kits up to 96 hours after an assault. That's problematic, but it's also problematic if you only do it up to 72 hours after an assault, because then, the defense attorney will say it is missing exculpatory evidence, and I think that's inappropriate. I suspect that people started to build protocols based on outliers from research, which is a bad way to determine any protocol. To date, any of the cases where they found evidence beyond 72 hours, in fact probably closer to 36 hours, have been outliers in research. I think that it's well-meaning but misguided clinicians who are changing the protocol based on that. If you talk to prosecutors, all we're doing now is collecting a lot more negative evidence; it's making the process more expensive because they are doing exams for a longer period of time after an assault.

Diana Faugno, RN, BSN, CPN, SANE, observes:

> Standardization certainly makes the examiner's life a little easier. And mistakes are less likely to happen because the examiner is familiar with the kit. For example, I deal with 16 different law enforcement agencies, and if they all had different evidence kits, I'd be crazed. Whether or not this country can agree on a standardized kit remains to be seen, but I doubt it. I just want the best tools I can get to do my job, and if there's a better swab out there, then give it to me.

However, Faugno hopes that nurses' preferences for certain medical supplies or for supplies that facilitate evidentiary examinations will be heeded by manufacturers:

> We are not the crime lab, and we are not the end user in some cases, so we are akin to the middleman. Even though we use the supplies in the kits every day, and we see manufacturers and vendors at conferences, these vendors typically listen more to other entities who are footing the bill for the kits. Will forensic nurses' clinical preferences ever be considered? I think so, sure. I know that's happening, but it's a slow recognition in the business world.

When it comes to working with forensic laboratories to determine the best supplies and protocols for SAEKs, Faugno says nurses should defer to their expertise:

> Each jurisdiction varies in what its authorities want in their kits and how they want to process them. Our crime lab is very specific about what it wants, too. For example, we used to do wet-mount slides to look for motile sperm, but they don't want us doing that anymore, unless motility is an issue in the case. That's fine by me, because we're not the experts. We also used to do the little saliva wafer, and we don't do that anymore. A lot of kits don't require drawing blood, just the buccal swabs, and things have become much more streamlined because of it. I know that the lab's DNA people and the trace people are using different sets of cards; our crime lab is not so much into reference samples, such as hair, unless it's matted or has foreign debris in it. They give us some leeway to use our critical thinking skills when we do the kit. Today we are doing more swabbing than we were five years ago because of DNA. If a perpetrator puts his hand over a victim's nose and mouth, we will swab those areas and it's possible that we will get his DNA. When we interview the victim, we try to get the finer details that guide us as to where to swab. It's a very individual approach to the kits and to the evidence collection process.

Cari Caruso believes forensic nurses rely upon established standards and guidelines, as well as on advice from local experts:

> I pay close attention to what various crime labs want. For example, the Los Angeles crime lab just wants swabs for certain things, but the sheriff's crime lab wants swabs and slides. Most of my evidence goes to the sheriff's crime lab, so obviously I am going to make sure the evidence I submit is to their liking. I also ask them for feedback about what we can do to improve our evidence collection and preservation, and also to find out what's new. So I believe we're never going to be able to universalize collection of evidence so that everyone is doing exactly the same thing. Actually, I think this is a good thing because it allows nurses to be unrestricted in our critical thinking skills and in our evidence collection.

Caruso says that building relationships with law enforcement not only helps to guide her evidence collection techniques, but also improves her job performance as a forensic nurse:

> When I first started going to the crime lab to pick up my sexual assault kits, I met with a few of the senior criminalists. They were so happy to meet a forensic nurse, and

> I was eager to speak with them so that I could understand what happens to my kits when they reach the lab for analysis. It was a relationship that sprang out of my initial curiosity. Now, when I am training new nurses, we take a field trip down to the crime lab and we see what happens to the evidence we collect.

Caruso says she frequently takes advantage of training by local law enforcement's forensic laboratories, and considers the lab to be an essential part of a medico-legal triumvirate. "Any multidisciplinary team includes the district attorney, law enforcement and the crime lab, and the forensic medical practitioners," Caruso explains:

> The crime lab can help us with little details that make everyone's job easier. I also pick up from them information as to how others do their kits. I was picking one crime lab person's brain and she said, "I love your kits." That really made me happy, so I asked her what she liked about them. She said that they were always carefully done, in contrast to others that were sloppy. She said that for example, one nurse smeared biological evidence all over the slide, while I make a little circle in the middle of a slide that a cover slip can cover. She said, "Your slides take 20 minutes to look at, but when you haphazardly smear stuff all over the slide, it takes me an hour and 20 minutes to look at it." Those are the little intricacies that the crime labs pick up on that I want to know.

Sometimes, Caruso says, forensic nurses get caught between ever-changing protocols issued by their local jurisdictions. She explains:

> When I first started sexual assault examinations, we were taking four internal vaginal swabs, and then it was changed to two, and then it went back to four again, the reason being that defense attorneys want their own swabs to analyze and if we have four of them, that's enough for everyone. Those are the little things I want to be privy to, and know what the crime lab wants and needs so that I can help them do the best job possible. For example, someone from the lab told me that the last priority for analysis and testing is hair, and that's good to know. I always send the lab a "love note" with the evidence, in which I tell them what we collected and where we collected it on the victim's body so they can arrange the evidence in order of priority. They won't really know if we have neglected to collect something, but it's better to collect too much evidence than not enough. Someone asked me recently, "If you don't know what happened to that person, how do you know what to collect?" I said if that is the case, then I collect everything, and part of that is having a vivid imagination. As an experienced examiner in the real world, you know what perpetrators can do to their victims, and that can help direct us in our evidence collection. We are able to think through an assault and ask the kinds of questions that will help us find the evidence. My interviews are very thorough and pointed so that I can get as complete a history as I can, but if I'm not able to get a history, then I use my imagination to try to collect whatever it is I think may be of value.

Sharon Crowley, MN, RN, says the challenges to standardization include numerous interpretations even within a standardized kit. "Even if we are able to decide upon a standardized kit, within the state of California, different agencies would demand their own variations," she notes:

> Each jurisdiction would probably object, saying, "We don't want to do it that way, we're going to do it this way." I don't think that will change, nor do I think it should change. I don't believe that just because there is a standardized kit, everyone will use it. If the criminalists want it their way, they will change it or ignore certain aspects of the kit, and I think that's fine. Any evidence kit must work for the community in which it is used. The way Los Angeles County does it is very different from the way Santa Cruz County or Santa Clara County does it, even so far as referenced standards within the evidence kit. Since 1987, California has had a medico-legal protocol which allows jurisdictions to change certain portions of it, as long as professionals in that jurisdiction do it consistently and at the very least, have agreed to disagree. I don't think it will be any different on a national level. There are certain things I disagree with scientifically, and I don't know if all the research is in on certain aspects of forensic protocol associated with the evidentiary exam and the kits.

Like Caruso, Crowley is a strong proponent of forensic nurses working closely with forensic laboratories. "It should be a collaborative effort," she emphasizes:

> Santa Cruz has a much smaller number of rapes than Los Angeles County, so if their crime lab has to deal with 10,000 kits a year, their needs are very different from a pure physical storage capacity. In that sense, everyone has to collaborate to determine which evidence is most probative. From the very inception of my forensic nursing career, I have always considered the forensic laboratory as an integral part of the team. The other important consideration is that, while I may know a lot about certain scientific aspects of my work, if something is not in my area of expertise, I need to collaborate and get the buy-in of the crime lab or of law enforcement. It scares me when nurses, for example, take it upon themselves to presume they know absolutely everything about DNA evidence collection and have not consulted with expert criminalists. It's important to check in regularly with the experts you respect; in turn, you may be able to educate them, because they are not experts in nursing or medical practice. So it has to be collaborative practice, and sometimes it can make or break a case.

Crowley says that nurses must use their best judgment when evaluating evidence collection protocol:

> One area which is touchy is the controversy over the collection of head hairs and pubic hairs. Or the fear of overcollecting . . . I have talked to criminalists whom I really respect, so if it is a problem in your region, nurses should do the same. I think it may come down to if everything is in the kit then I have to analyze everything, and if it's not scientifically necessary, then it's like adding a lot of commas after a word—if they are not needed, let's look at it. I think it's something that needs a lot of quality control and input from a lot of people. I can't dictate if what I do is impacting the job of other people—it's essential they give their input. Because most of the time it's not an issue of I don't want to analyze it, if there is valid reasons, I need to look at my practice and go, well, it isn't just the science, we have to look at the practicality.

Crowley adds that evidence collection is dictated by a number of factors, including information from the victim interview, science, protocol, and even the nurse's past experience:

> Good protocol should be based on a wide variety of principles and variables, including what has worked best in the past, based on experience and on science. It also should be predicated on what might be needed in the future, for technologies we don't have yet. It's dictated by what works, by the frameworks of the protocol, and by the boundaries of the jurisdiction. I think there is give and take within protocol; the most important consideration is that it be under regular evaluation. What worked 10 years ago may not be working today. We're in a field where it must bear up under courtroom scrutiny. Nurses must ask themselves in everything that they do, "If I do or don't do something, is that going to be acceptable in court?"

Although some forensic nurses are calling for the standardization of rape kits, Ferrara believes a cookie-cutter approach isn't necessary. "I don't understand standardization. Certainly we don't have to all use the same rape kit. Fundamentally, I'd like standardization in terms of the completeness of the kit, but each state has its own laws, analytical techniques, and procedures that would make standardization difficult." Ferrara says he has not heard of any problems associated with the quality or the completeness of the sampling performed in Virginia, but believes aiming for complete and thorough collection and preservation of trace evidence is a given. A complete narrative from the victim, documented by the forensic nurse, is another critical element of the information and evidence collection process:

> Was the victim sodomized, are we looking at vaginal rape? Was there oral sodomy? What was the nature of the act? The answers to these kinds of questions help scientists know what sample offers the most promise, especially since our lab faces a large volume of samples and our rape kit contains 20-plus types of samples that can be taken. For example, we start with a vaginal swab, find a foreign DNA profile and go from there. There's certain information we like to have, and our rape kit is designed to get that.

Another challenge to the standardization of rape kits, Ferrara says, is the variation between how the samples in the kits are actually analyzed. "What the proponents of standardization of kits are thinking is that if all the samples, such as a cotton swab, are standardized, it makes it easy for a high-volume lab to treat a large number of samples by doing one simple motion of cutting off the end of a swab tip and analyzing that," Ferrara comments:

> But this leaves no room for labs to explore new efficiencies. Our lab is going to automate our analyses; we are developing a unique buccal swab that consists of a piece of blotter paper that goes inside the cheek and gum and then we'll punch a little hole out of that and use that as our sample. If someone suddenly said everyone is only going to use traditional buccal swab samples, that shoots down our new process, so what is the point? The important thing is that rape kits contain all the fundamental elements of sampling as well as directions and forms to elicit important details about the crime from the victim.

Caruso says she is opposed to the micromanagement of rape kit collection that attempts at standardization can achieve:

> I don't write a policy every time I sneeze, but that's the way things are going with rape kits and talk about standardization. People are saying, "I don't do fingernail scrapings, I do swabbing," or "We still pluck hairs." I have a global way that we collect evidence but I don't have to have everything my way, step by step by step. I think evidence collection is unique to each nurse and that it is part of the clinical style the nurse needs to develop. She must consider the right way to do things and improve on this system, so when my nurses are getting their training, I don't expect them to do everything as I do it. They have seen me do everything exactly like I do it; when they move into their own area of practice, they can choose their own order of collection—as long as they don't omit something and as long as they do impeccable, complete evidence collection and don't miss any of the details, then they should have their own style. I can't regulate that they do this or this first, or in a certain way, like proponents of standardization are suggesting. I've noticed that not only in nursing but almost in everything, as soon as an entity or occupation starts to grow, there is this need for increased regulation. I think that takes away the creativity we depended on in the beginning to make forensic nurse examinations successful.

Linda Ledray says one thing she perceives as problematic is that

> forensic laboratory personnel are still trying to drive the evidence collection, and in many cases, they are driving what is analyzed, causing fights between law enforcement and prosecutors who think they are the ones who should be making the decisions. The lab personnel figure that since they are doing it, they can make the decisions. I think the lab isn't trusting the trained forensic nurse to make some of the important decisions as to what evidence they send to them; I think some labs are still going by the old standards of "collect everything because we don't trust you to sort through it." A lot of people are collecting who don't know how to sort through the preponderance of evidence. I think that goes to show why the whole system—nursing, law enforcement, prosecutors, and the forensic laboratory—has to work together.

No matter the strategy to eliminate or mitigate the DNA backlog, Ferrara says the major obstacle is the very nature of forensic science: exacting, precise, and laborious. "Short-term solutions like outsourcing DNA samples for analysis to private labs are good," he says:

> It's a valuable use of commercial labs to run convicted-felon samples and it has been shown that these private labs can be very effective in running large numbers of rape kits. I don't know how we are ever going to automate the laborious process of searching things like clothing, carpeting, or car seats for traces of blood, seminal fluid, perspiration, or saliva; finding it, isolating it, then making sense of the data when it comes back for analysis. The forensic examiner must often elucidate mixtures of samples, and in rape cases, mixtures are a fact of life. It takes a lot of time and a lot of skill. We have all the technology we need, but we need increased manpower to put this technology to work.

Barry A. J. Fisher, director of the Los Angeles County Sheriff's Department forensic laboratory, comments, "You can have the most capable forensic nurses in a hospital, collecting fantastic evidence that gets handed off to the police and is sent to the crime labs, but if the labs don't have the wherewithal to do the work, all of that effort, as good as it was, has been for naught."

Fisher, speaking at a recent forensic nursing conference, shared with nurses ways they can make the most of sexual assault evidence. He emphasized that the key to any successful investigation and prosecution is collaboration between forensic nurses and the crime lab. "For the investigative process to work, the recognition that each element of the criminal justice and health care system is important; no single piece is more important than the other," he said, explaining that a chain is only as strong as its weakest link. He said that evidence, especially DNA evidence, collected from victims of a sexual assault by forensic examiners, is key to proving that an assault occurred, the nature of the assault, and the identity of the perpetrator. He added, "Observations and actions taken during examination will assist the investigation and prosecution of the crime in a variety of ways. Competent, well-trained forensic nurses are essential to the effort." Fisher explained that sexual assault evidence can establish key elements of the crime, including vaginal, anal, or oral penetration, and nonconsensual intercourse; can prove the identity of the rapist; can demonstrate the location of the assault; and can connect a rape with other sexual assaults. Effective evidence collection, he said, includes following prescribed evidence collection protocols and using a standard sexual assault evidence kit, taking detailed notes, asking the victim what occurred and looking for clues to corroborate the information, asking about oral and rectal penetration, and considering collecting toxicology specimens for alcohol and drugs. He reminded forensic nurses that if they are stumped, they should pick up the phone and call a local crime lab for assistance. He explained. "Most people think of DNA testing in sexual assault cases. While DNA is a powerful forensic tool, there are many other items of physical evidence that crime labs can examine to identify perpetrators and help in prosecuting a case." For example, in nonreported rapes or incest resulting in pregnancy, the fetal material from a therapeutic abortion is a source of DNA, and DNA testing has successfully confirmed the identity of the father-rapist. In another instance, a sexual assault victim's hand was cut while reaching for a knife. The suspect tore off the bottom of his undershirt and gave it to the victim to use as a bandage. The bandage was subsequently compared to the torn undershirt, linking the suspect to the rape. Fisher added that forensic nurses should look to their local forensic laboratories to help them stay up to date on current technology that might affect how evidence is collected and analyzed, including using buccal swabs instead of collecting blood specimens, or employing lab automation systems to help address the sexual assault evidence backlogs. Fisher says that above all, nurses should remain realistic about labs' capabilities:

> The public has let themselves be drawn into what they see on television, which doesn't mirror reality in most cases. The truth is, most crime labs can do phenomenal work on an individual case basis, so if there is a hot case we need to work on, we can marshal incredible resources and get it done well. For example, the Los Angeles County Sheriff's Department was helpful with a local investigation where a serial rapist responsible for as many as 30 rapes was identified. We've worked on this case with the police for years; when the person was arrested we turned the evidence around in a weekend with people working around the clock. But as good as that effort was, we can't do that on every case because there are not enough resources. What is the public willing to fund? And how do we get policymakers at the state and federal level to deal with these backlog issues?

Fisher is quick to answer his own questions:

The first order of the day is education. We must inform politicians about the consequences of us not being able to do what needs to be done. There are serial rapists out there who are still working their trade because crime labs haven't been able to get to the evidence in time to catch them before they strike again. People are being assaulted and murdered because the impressive arsenal of science and technology that we have is not being used in our crime labs.

Something is broken and we need to fix it. (The DNA analysis backlog) is an offensive situation because it places public safety and welfare in jeopardy. It says maybe we'll get to the evidence the second time around. Crime lab personnel are dedicated people but they can't make things happen because policymakers aren't making the right decisions. Because of resource challenges we face significant backlogs. We are trying to grow our capacity but it's almost like a bottomless pit; the more success we have through cold hits, it still points to other cases that need attention, too.

Fisher also doesn't mince words when it comes to his support for forensic nurses. "Forensic nurses fill an important role, in hospitals and other settings, where a trained medical practitioner who has the understanding of what it is to collect and preserve evidence is needed," he says:

Forensic nurses know how to handle medico-legal issues no one else wants to. I used to lecture, some 25 years ago, to ER physicians; the vast majority of them weren't terribly interested in getting involved in sexual assault or abuse cases because it took them out of the ER and into court. Forensic nurses are a highly capable group of individuals who came along at the right time. They deserve the utmost respect of the rest of the criminal justice system and the support of those of us in the trenches with them.

Fisher says forensic nurses can help by developing relationships with the forensic science crime labs that process and analyze the evidence they collect. Fisher is troubled by the fact there is usually no way for the crime lab to provide feedback about the type and quality of the trace evidence collected by forensic nurses and he advocates more communication between the two parties:

A forensic nurse does the examination, collects the evidence, sends it to the lab and the lab doesn't have the mechanism to say, "You've done a great job" or "You're missing the mark." If that kind of dialogue could be developed, that would be beneficial to everyone involved in the criminal justice process. Unlike other groups just focused in one discipline, the American Academy of Forensic Science is unique because it brings all the people whose first name is "forensic." My advice to nurses is to get this kind of cross-pollenization by interacting with all kinds of professionals in the forensic science community. It's important for all of us to interact and understand our commonalities. How forensic nurses deal with physical evidence, DNA evidence, trace evidence is something we need to know, and the ability to kick around ideas is a valuable thing.

14.13 ISSUES OF CONSENT AND DNA EVIDENCE

When it comes to DNA evidence, forensic nurses can find themselves at the heart of a complicated issue having to do with consent in sexual assault cases, and the court's expectation of the discovery of not only DNA evidence, but of injuries consistent with forced sex. It can be a murky area, but an increasing number of nurses, law enforcement professionals, and prosecutors are exploring to cast some light on this controversial set of intermingled issues.

14.13.1 Sexual Assault: Stranger Versus Known Assailants

Nationally, approximately 70 percent to 80 percent of sexual assaults involve persons known to the victim. Most of the defendants in these cases will claim the sexual assault was consensual. Archambault (2000) writes:

We live in a society that quickly blames victims of sexual assault depending on her lifestyle, the circumstances of the assault and her perceived credibility. Sexual assault suspects know this and many stranger attacks will also result in a consent defense. Whenever possible, a preliminary statement should be obtained from the suspect as soon as possible. We rejoice when the suspect denies engaging in sexual contact with the victim because in those cases, we are provided with an opportunity to use the wonderful world of forensic technology. However, in those cases where the suspect admits that he had sex with the victim, but the act was consensual, detectives and prosecutors need to evaluate the need for forensic DNA. There are cases where the prosecutor will want to have DNA work completed. However, in some cases, depending on the crime lab's workload, law enforcement might ask the prosecutor to send the work out themselves.

Archambault adds, "In a consent defense case, detectives might not submit a lab request for DNA, however, depending on whether there was force and whether the victim suffered an injury resulting in bleeding, the detective might submit a lab request to detect blood, to corroborate the use of force." She explains that the criminalist must determine if the victim or suspect bled during the assault and from what areas of the body, whether during emergency treatment the victim or suspect received a blood transfusion that might interfere with the DNA results, and whether clothing was collected from the scene. Archambault says, "In most assaults, all or part of the victim's clothing is removed during the assault. This clothing should be identified since it could contain pre-ejaculate fluids, saliva stains, or trace evidence. Clothing is often times used to wipe the genitals following a sex act. It is also critically important to identify and collect any clothing put on after the assault, especially those pieces of clothing worn closest to the genital structures." She says that crime scene investigators realize that based on the information provided by the victim, they might be able to determine which items of clothing or bedding are most likely to have seminal fluid stains from the suspect. Archambault adds, "Remember, the purpose of these questions is to reduce the time-consuming process of screening large amounts of evidence."

If the assault occurred in the suspect's own bed, Archambault explains, the presence of his own seminal fluid is irrelevant; however, the victim's epithelial cells would at least place her in the suspect's bed in the case of a denial. Investigators should determine if any type of consensual sex act took place on the bedding since the last time it was washed. If so, reference samples should be obtained from any consenting partner before submitting the evidence for DNA analysis. "If the victim and suspect are involved in an intimate relationship and they engaged in consensual sex prior to the sexual assault in question, any analysis would be a waste of valuable crime laboratory resources," Archambault notes. In cases involving more than one suspect or cases where consenting partners must be eliminated, all reference samples should be submitted for analysis and comparison at the same time. Archambault explains that this procedure allows the forensic laboratory to manage its caseloads more efficiently, and facilitates an increased number of cases that can be screened and typed. Once the preliminary rape case information has been completed and reference samples collected, the investigator submits the lab service request, prioritizing those items of DNA evidence he or she wants examined depending on the type of investigation and the history of the assault obtained from the victim. The item listed should be specific, such as "victim's panties" or "vaginal swabs," not, "check victim's clothing" or "rape kit," Archambault advises.

14.13.2 Reporting, Investigation, and Prosecution of Nonstranger Sexual Assault Cases

Rape victims are significantly more likely to report their attack to the police than they were just a few years ago, according to the 2002 NCVS, released by the U.S. Department of Justice's Bureau of Justice Statistics. The percentage of all rapes and sexual assaults that were reported to police rose to 53.7 percent, up from less than 30 percent in 1999, the report found. Although this increase should be interpreted cautiously, given the small sample size, it does continue a trend that began in 2000. From 2000 to 2002, an average of 46.8 percent of rape victims reported the attack to police, up from an average of 30.8 percent from 1993 to 1995. The report also showed that the total number of rapes and sexual assaults in the United States continued its record decline. In 2002, there were 247,730 rapes and sexual assaults against victims age 12 and older. This is a slight decline from the 2001 total of 248,250, and a massive decline from the 1993 total of 485,000. There was one rape or sexual assault every 2 minutes last year, about the same as in 2001.Of this total of about 248,000 sexual crimes in 2002, about 87,000 were completed rapes, 70,000 were attempted rapes, and 91,000 were sexual assaults. The annual NCVS study is based on interviews with 76,050 Americans. Children 11 and younger are not interviewed, so crimes against them are not included in NCVS totals. NCVS is considered the most comprehensive and trustworthy source of crime statistics in the country (as a measure of crime against people 12 and older). Unlike the FBI's Universal Crime Reports, NCVS includes crimes whether or not they were reported to police.

Experts believe two trends are largely responsible for the tremendous decline in sexual violence over the last decade. "First, tough-on-crime policies of recent years, including longer sentences, three-strikes laws and mandatory minimums, mean fewer criminals overall are on the streets. Because rapists commit many kinds of crimes, and because all kinds of criminals commit rape, locking up an armed robber or drug dealer will often prevent future sexual assaults," says Scott Berkowitz, president and founder of RAINN. "The second trend is generational. Rape victims are overwhelmingly young—80 percent are under 30 years old. This generation has grown up knowing that 'no means no,' and young women today are both more careful about entering into potentially dangerous situations and more willing to forcefully express their own desires," Berkowitz continued. "This generational shift, combined with increased media attention and a greater societal openness about the issue, are likely the key factors in the increased willingness to report to police." Separately, RAINN reported that calls to the National Sexual Assault Hotline were up by 27 percent, to more than 10,000 per month, further evidence of the effects of increased media attention. The report also found that 69 percent of victims were attacked by a nonstranger (57 percent friend or acquaintance, 10 percent intimate, 2 percent other relative) and 28 percent by a stranger.

In a July 23, 2004 article in *The Los Angeles Times*, writer Cynthia Daniels reports that despite numerous strides made in the prosecution of rape cases, juries remain skeptical and often want evidence of verbal protest or physical resistance. Daniels pointed to several recent cases in southern California that illustrate the typical scenario in which consent plays a role in nonstranger sexual assaults. A 21-year-old University of California at Santa Barbara student was raped by her boyfriend and the district attorney decided not to prosecute because he felt he could not prove the crime occurred. In another case, a jury of nine women and three men delivered not-guilty verdicts on several charges and deadlocked on others against three high school students accused of raping a college freshman in her dorm room during a campus tour. Following the trial, Daniels reported, several jurors said the woman's testimony lacked credibility. A judge later dismissed charges against two of the three men, but prosecutors said they planned to retry the third suspect. In a case in Orange County, Daniels reported, jurors could not decide whether three teenagers sexually assaulted a 16-year-old girl who was allegedly knocked out by drugs and alcohol. The defense portrayed the girl as "a deceitful would-be porn actress who was merely pretending to be unconscious." The district attorney plans to retry the defendants.

Daniels wrote that in the past 35 years, California law has evolved to favor victims, in that attorneys can no longer use a victim's manner of dress as a defense, nor can the defense force the victim to undergo a psychiatric test to analyze his or her state of mind. Also eradicated is legislation that required a victim to have actively resisted during the assault. "Yet, despite these changes, law enforcement officials and prosecutors acknowledge that jurors are often skeptical in rape cases," Daniels wrote. She quoted Nancy O'Malley, chief assistant district attorney for Alameda County and chairwoman of the sexual assault committee of the California District Attorneys Association, as stating, "It is a challenge, there is no question. With some prospective jurors, you're dealing with a different dynamic. We have to continually reinforce the idea that this is not about sex; it's a crime of violence, power and control." Daniels explains:

> Prosecutors know that to convict rapists, they need to have not only a victim willing to testify, but also corroboration—physical evidence backing up the accusations, and expert testimony. Experts say the burden is on sexual assault victims from beginning to end. They are expected to report the crime . . . and to reveal intensely private matters when they testify. Still at the center of most rape prosecutions is the question of consent. Experts say jurors often expect sexual assault victims to fight their attackers and vocally resist submission.

There are inherent challenges to the investigation and prosecution of nonstranger sexual assault cases, not usually encountered in other violent crimes, asserts Joanne Archambault, a former police sergeant with the San Diego Police Department and an independent consultant. In a 2001 white paper, "Responding to Non-Stranger Sexual Assault," co-authored with Suzanne Lindsay, PhD, Archambault writes, "Sexual assault is one of the few crimes reported to law enforcement that requires intense scrutiny into the believability of the victim's description of events." She adds, "Further, it is probably the only reported crime in which the suspect can successfully defend himself by claiming that the victim consented to the crime." Archambault and Lindsay add that other significant factors that come into play in these kinds of cases include the context of the assault, the age and the perceived character of the victim, the prior relationship of the victim and the perpetrator, and the perception of criminal justice practitioners about what constitutes a "real" sexual assault.

Understanding the potential success or failure of an investigation and prosecution of a sexual assault case, and that of a nonstranger sexual assault case in particular, requires a look at underlying misperceptions and stereotypes. Many consider a sexual assault to be a violent and unprovoked attack by a stranger on a defenseless and unsuspecting victim, Archambault and Lindsay say. "Our understanding of this crime as one perpetrated by an unknown and violent stranger influences (even without conscious intent) our attempts to investigate and evaluate sexual assaults," they write. In truth, a significant number of sexual assaults are perpetrated not by an unknown suspect, but by someone known—to a varying degree—by the victim.

LeBeau (1988) examined sexual assaults reported to the San Diego Police Department between 1972 and 1976, and in four out of five years, stranger assailants were described in 70 percent or more of the reported cases. In a more recent study of sexual assaults, Archambault and Lindsay (2001) found that from 1992 to 1996, just 17 percent to 31 percent of sexual assaults reported to the San Diego Police Department involved stranger assailants. Archambault believes that investigators and examiners must change their thinking when it comes to separating stranger from nonstranger sexual assaults, and the first step is not being taken in by stereotypes. LeBeau theorized, "Assaults by strangers allow victims to see themselves as classic victims conforming to the popular conceptions of the crime." Archambault points to a 1995 article in a publication of the International Association of Chiefs of Police that stated, "Generally, the actions and the appearance of a legitimate rape victim leave little doubt that a crime has been committed. Under such circumstances, the victim is highly agitated, emotionally distraught, often in a state of hysteria and may have sustained injuries, cuts, bruises or wounds. The victim's clothing is often ripped or torn off as evidence that it was forcibly removed and if the rape occurred outdoors, the victim is generally thrown to the ground and her outer garments stained or soiled." Comments Archambault, "Experienced sexual assault investigators and rape crisis advocates know this description is the furthest point from the truth in most sexual assaults."

Archambault and Lindsay believe a number of factors are responsible for the increase in the number of nonstranger sexual assaults, including a groundswell of victim-advocacy activity that prompted rape reform of laws that were unnecessarily harsh on victims. Common elements in these new rape laws included the provisions that the victim no longer had to prove evidence of resistance for the assault to be considered a crime, the victim was no longer required to reveal prior sexual history with partners other than the suspect, corroborative witnesses were no longer required, and mandates were established for standardized, timely, victim-centric responses to sexual assault. Other factors included the establishment of SANE/SART programs, the creation of better funded victim advocacy programs and crisis centers, and the launch of the women's movement, which empowered women's rights pertaining to the investigation and prosecution of sexual violence. The implications of nonstranger sexual assault cases for investigators and examiners are numerous, Archambault and Lindsay assert. They write, "The dynamics of nonstranger sexual assault are very different from stranger sexual assault and are not well understood. This is important for law enforcement because the crime of sexual assault cannot be prevented or even investigated appropriately until the true dynamics of the assault are understood."

The comprehension of nonstranger sexual assault can be influenced by beliefs that sexual assaults committed by nonstrangers are less traumatic than those perpetrated by strangers. The literature says otherwise. Gidycz and Koss (1991) write, "Acquaintance rape is different from stranger rapes and other types of victimizations in that it presents a unique challenge to a woman's belief system." Katz (1991) says that women who are raped by nonstranger assailants were more traumatized and took longer to recover than women raped by strangers. Victims of nonstranger assaults might experience a feeling of responsibility for the assault, and might be more harshly judged by their peers, the community, the judicial system—and even by the responding officer, Archambault and Lindsay say.

Reporting of this kind of crime is affected. "Many of these crimes still go unreported, and very few of those reported ever see successful prosecution," Archambault and Lindsay write. "In many cases, the victim recognizes the difficulty in pursuing prosecution and she chooses to suspend the investigation." Lindsay (1998) reported that only 35 percent of victims of nonstranger sexual assault reported the crime to law enforcement within 24 hours of the assault, and 23 percent waited more than a week to report. Thirty percent of victims of acquaintance rape waited up to a month to report. As such, late reporting reduces the likelihood that a victim will receive a sexual assault evidentiary examination, and it also reduces the likelihood that the report will be believed, Archambault says. She adds that serial rapists, many of whom prey on younger siblings, girlfriends, neighborhood children, and acquaintances, determine that it is easy to get away with rape and then escalate their behavior. In "Serial Rapists and Their Victims: Reenactment and Repetition," Ann Burgess and colleagues (1988) report on a study of 41 serial rapists responsible for 837 known rapes and 401 attempted rapes. Most of the rapes were never reported.

In the 2001 white paper, "Dynamics of Sexual Assault," Archambault says that stranger cases are black and white, "therefore relieving all of us from having to sort through 'he said, she said' testimony, and in the end, make difficult decisions about truth, innocence, and guilt." However, in nonstranger cases, investigators and examiners might still be applying some of the same rules to evidence collection, keying in on classic forms of evidence such as hair and fibers, biological evidence, fingerprints, and so on, that are used to identify a stranger assailant. Instead, Archambault says that investigators should be thinking about ways to overcome the consent defense used in most cases of nonstranger sexual assault, including obtaining photographs of the victim's external injuries, documenting complaints of pain, identifying and interviewing the first person to whom the victim disclosed the assault, scene evidence that might support accounts of a struggle, and so on. Archambault says that most police officers receive instruction in the law and sensitivity training, but the two elements "lack any common bridge and officers aren't quite sure how to apply instruction in rape trauma syndrome to what they believe they are seeing," she writes. "Society, officers, judges and juries have definite expectations about the way rape victims should behave. Non-stranger rape is particularly misunderstood, often perceived as nothing more than 'bad sex.'" Archambault adds, "It's common for officers and jurors to state that the victim wasn't believed because she 'just didn't act like a rape victim.'" Demographic and age factors play a significant role in acquaintance rapes, according to various studies, and Archambault says that the complex dynamics of an acquaintance sexual assault could explain why these cases "do not typically demonstrate the same type of evidence as might be expected in stranger assaults." She adds, "It is important for the investigator to recognize that a victim assaulted by an acquaintance may present very differently than one assaulted by a stranger, and that the expected evidence may be very different." For example, victims assaulted by strangers were more likely to sustain injury than those assaulted by acquaintances (60 percent vs. 49 percent), Archambault reports. "Victim presentation and the evidence expected as a result of a stranger assault should not be viewed as the gold standard for assessing whether or not a crime was actually committed," she writes.

Health care providers should be aware that nonstrangers perpetrate a number of sexual crimes. According to the Bureau of Justice Statistics of the U.S. Department of Justice 2002 NCVS 40 percent of sexual assault victims knew their assailants. Archambault and Faugno (2001) examined cases reported to the San Diego Police Department Sex Crimes Unit to determine prevalent factors that could be used to educate the public to reduce their risk of sexual assault. One significant factor that they identified was that seven out of 10 sexual assaults reported were perpetrated by nonstrangers. Archambault and Faugno scrutinized evidence collection in these cases and discovered that forensic examiners were focusing on the genitalia, and trace evidence, such as hairs, fibers, fingerprints, and biological evidence such as blood and semen for DNA analysis. This evidence, however, can be refuted when the nonstranger assailant or even the stranger perpetrator claims that the victim consented to having sex. The burden for the prosecution, then, shifts to proving that the act was not consensual, instead of attempting to prove that sexual contact occurred. Archambault and Faugno write:

> Given the fact that a jury must presume a suspect innocent until proved guilty, a one-on-one assault with no other corroborating evidence is difficult to prove to a jury beyond a reasonable doubt. As a result, most sex offenders are never prosecuted or held accountable for their violent assaults. Any evidence, no matter how seemingly insignificant, can be used to tip a balanced scale in favor of the victim or the suspect. Police, prosecutors and SANEs/forensic medical examiners must be trained to look for any evidence that can be used to overcome a consent defense.

Archambault and Faugno encourage the forensic examiner to look at the evidence in a new light. For example, they say, instead of identifying a suspect, the presence of blood could corroborate an injury that occurred to the suspect or to the victim during the assault. Similarly, although hair can identify a suspect, hair can be examined to determine if it has been pulled out of a person's head during a struggle. They emphasize the value of photographs of genital injuries captured by a colposcope because they can be easily viewed and understood by a jury. They also advise forensic examiners to carefully document the presence of external, nongenital injuries such as bruises, abrasions, or scratches. Although forensic examiners have been taught not to overhandle the victim's articles of clothing so as not to disturb potential trace evidence, Archambault and Faugno say that many professionals have not properly assessed clothing in sexual assault cases. They say that trace evidence is rarely used in sexual assault cases, and that some examiners fail to carefully examine clothing for the kind of evidence that can be used to corroborate many nonstranger sexual assaults, such as rips, stretched-out elastic, missing buttons, blood, and dirt stains, for fear of compromising fragile trace evidence. The situation is compounded, they add, by evidence that is usually left in police storage lockers or freezers until a crime lab service request is initiated by a detective or a prosecutor. They write, "As a result of inadequate investigations and prosecution of nonstranger sexual assaults and the shortage of crime lab resources, most rape kits and the clothing impounded with them, are never looked at by anyone." Archambault and Faugno point to a survey conducted by the FBI that discovered of all rapes, less than 10 percent had evidence submitted to crime laboratories. Due to limited resources in crime laboratories, in just 6 percent of the 250,000 rape cases investigated the recovered DNA was tested. They add, "The reality is that there could be many hundreds of thousands of sexual assault kits and other items of evidence, such as clothing and bedding that should be analyzed."

The FBI statistic referring to rape does not include all forms of sexual assault or evidence that might have been collected from a crime scene. Archambault and Faugno emphasize that many members of law enforcement have not been trained in the proper recognition and collection of DNA evidence, with the end result that detectives and prosecutors are making decisions about whether to move forward with a case based on the preliminary investigation, the investigative follow-up, and the forensic examiner's written documentation. "As a result," Archambault and Faugno write, "we must ensure that the victim and suspect's clothing, if available, is carefully examined and any visible signs corroborating the use of force by the suspect or resistance by the victim, is carefully documented." This includes recovering, impounding, and preserving the victim's clothes worn during the assault, or donned immediately after the assault. Forensic examiners should indicate where signs of force might be detected by analysts in the crime laboratory, based on the victim's history of the sexual assault. Archambault and Faugno have described a clothing documentation form, created by the San Diego County SART to assist in documentation of critical pieces of evidence such as clothing. The form is helpful to examiners and to law enforcement because it provides clear documentation of clothing and its condition, improves communication between law enforcement and the examiner as to the location of additional clothing or evidence and the status of that information, helps corroborate the use of force or resistance by the victim, and saves the examiner time by checking the item of clothing instead of writing out time-consuming clothing descriptions. Archambault and Faugno write, "Clearly the SANE/forensic examiner must be aware of the evidence needed in a sexual assault where consent is the likely issue. Proper identification and documentation of evidence can be a significant factor in facilitating case investigation and prosecution."

Dr. Kimberly A. Lonsway, research director at the National Center for Women and Policing, alludes to the varying statutory definitions of sex crimes by state, and says they can be more readily understood by analyzing their elements. She adds that investigators can frame their investigative strategy based on the defense that is most likely to be raised. In the 2001 monograph, *Successfully Investigating Acquaintance Sexual Assault: A National*

Training Manual for Law Enforcement (National Center for Women and Policing, 2001), Lonsway explains that in most states, the foremost decision to be made in a case is whether sexual penetration or sexual contact has occurred. Although definitions vary, states generally recognize a distinction between penetration, such as intercourse, fellatio, and sodomy, and other variations of sexual activity (short of penetration), such as fondling. Some states refer to sexual penetration as sexual assault, whereas cases involving sexual contact are called sexual abuse, and some jurisdictions characterize sexual offenses as first or second degree, depending on whether penetration or contact occurred. Regardless of these kinds of definitions, Lonsway says most states differentiate crimes involving sexual penetration versus contact, so the investigator must recognize this distinction to identify the type of offense that has been committed. Although a case of sexual violence might include multiple offenses that involve a combination of contact and penetration, each charge must be made independently. To prosecute a sex crime, the state must first establish that the alleged sexual activity took place. If the assault involves sexual contact, the prosecution must prove that it took place between the assailant and the victim; similarly, if the assault involves sexual penetration, the state must prove this occurred as well. Lonsway says sexual activity provides the grounds for a defense strategy of denial; in other words, if the suspect denies that the sexual activity took place, and if he can create reasonable doubt to that effect, he will be acquitted. "For this reason," Lonsway writes, "any investigative strategy must first focus on establishing whether or not the sexual activity took place."

Forensic examiners know that sexual activity has been historically documented by seminal fluid that has been collected from the body or from the clothing of the victim. Spermicides or lubricants can also indicate sexual activity. Additional biological evidence has been collected by forensic examiners who swab any areas of the victim's body that were kissed, sucked, or bitten by the suspect, directed by the patient's history or an examiner's suspicions. A forensic evidentiary examination of the suspect can identify evidence of transfer from the victim's body, such as vaginal fluid or cells, hairs, and other trace evidence, as well as the aforementioned spermicides or lubricants, which are suggestive of sexual contact if a match is found between materials present on the victim's and suspect's bodies, per Locard's Exchange Principle discussed in chapter 12. Transfer can also occur in cases of multiple offenders; for example, seminal fluid from the first suspect might be found on the body of the second suspect if they penetrated the victim consecutively. Lonsway writes, "It is imperative that investigators conduct forensic examinations of the suspect(s) involved in a sexual assault offense. Although this exam is often overlooked, it can be crucial for identifying and documenting evidence of sexual contact between the victim and suspect."

"I remember people saying that we should not be asking a victim of sexual assault about their consenting sexual partners unless we find something in the evidentiary examination," says Archambault:

> That is absolutely ludicrous. We should probably be asking about consensual activity that may have occurred at least three weeks prior to the assault. It's not a matter of being offensive or invasive, it's a matter of explaining to the victim that the biological contribution of any of those sexual partners could show up as evidence. Especially in an age where so many people are engaging in casual sex. The other thing to consider is, if it takes two years for the rape kit to be looked at, chances are you have to go find the guy because he and the victim are no longer dating, and he doesn't cooperate in providing a DNA elimination sample. People think that rape shield laws will protect the victim from having to answer questions about his or her sexual activity; that is absurd when we are arguing that these injuries are consistent with sexual assault. You don't get to have it both ways. It's a lack of training on what it is you are arguing here—improper diagnosis, for example. We do better now, but for example, how many times have cops and prosecutors asked nurses if the victim was raped and the nurse saying yes—that's an improper diagnosis. I think the nurses were putting too much emphasis on what they were seeing. What I have trained on for years is that nurses should not be saying whether there is evidence. They can comment on whether there's visible injury, and they can comment on the collection of evidence, but they are not criminalists and they should not be stating whether there is or is not evidence.
>
> Nurses are doing a great job of collecting the evidence and maintaining the chain of custody, but we are not seeing these cases moving forward. So we have to ask ourselves, what do we, as a team, need to do differently now? Why do we think we have to disprove these cases? A lot of times, sex-crime cases are approached as not founded until proven, versus being founded until not proven to have happened. I think because in most sex crimes, we know who the offender is. Cops think, well if you know who the offender is, and you have a crime, then you should be seeing it move forward, and, of course, we know in sex crime cases, that's not true. The burden is so much higher in these cases because of the social views of sex crimes and women.

As a side note, as with all Crime Index offenses, reports of forcible rape are sometimes considered to be "unfounded" by law enforcement, and they are then excluded from the crime count. The rate of unfounded cases is notably higher for rape than for any other index crime. In 1995, 8 percent of forcible rapes were determined by law enforcement to be unfounded, compared with 2 percent of all other index crimes (Federal Bureau of Investigations, 1996). Some individuals in the criminal justice system might assume that all unfounded cases are false reports, deceitfully reported, and baseless. However, this is not necessarily the case. Reported rape cases are actually classified by police as unfounded for a variety of reasons, including the police are unable to locate the victim, the victim decides not to follow through with prosecution, the victim repeatedly changes the account of the rape, the victim recants, no assailant can be identified, or the police believe no rape occurred. According to Linda Ledray, there are also a variety of other situations that impede or prevent completion of the investigation and in which the case can be classified as unfounded. "Unfortunately, not everyone distinguishes between 'changing the story' and recalling additional data, or telling different aspects of the same story, or distinguishing between an untrue allegation and a victim who is so fearful of the assailant that she recants her story out of fear for her life or the life of her family," she says. Ledray adds that the primary reason victims give for not wanting to report is fear of the assailant, whose parting words in 76 percent of the cases were, "If you tell anyone... (or report to the police), I'll come back and kill you."

The second step of the investigatory process is when the investigator determines whether sexual penetration or contact was committed using force or threat, Lonsway explains, or whether the situation was one in which no force is required for sexual activity to constitute a criminal offense. If force is involved in sexual penetration or contact, many believe that a sexual assault has been committed. Lonsway emphasizes that the variable some states do not include in this simple equation is any reference to the presence or absence of consent by the victim. Lonsway writes, "Although some states retain language that the sexual act must be 'against the will' of the victim, most states have recognized that nonconsent is implied by the presence of force or threat." Put simply, if the suspect employs force or threat, it is assumed that the victim does not consent to the sexual activity in question. "Despite this general recognition that sexual activity is illegal when committed using force or threat, there remains no clear standard as to what constitutes such a situation. Rather, the presence of force or threat must be determined by considering the entire context surrounding the event," Lonsway writes. Investigators should consider the following:

- Was physical violence or a weapon used?
- Were physical or verbal threats made?
- What were the surrounding circumstances that made the victim believe that real or implied threats would be carried out?
- Was there a discrepancy in the physical size and strength of the individuals involved?
- Were the individuals isolated from others?
- What was the victim thinking and feeling at the time of the event?
- Were there multiple suspects involved or others present during the assault?

Absent a clear standard for force or threat, investigators must consider the context of the situation, taking into account the victim's perception of events (including a woman's degree of fear or intimidation contrasted with that of a man's). Lonsway explains that some states assert that the victim's behavior cannot be used to make this determination, specifically, that physical resistance by the victim can be used as evidence that force or threat was present in a sexual situation. However, Lonsway adds, the lack of physical resistance cannot be used as proof of consent. When confronted by a sex crime, a suspect can deny the alleged offense, but if the sexual activity is proved and it is alleged to have taken place under threat or force, he can employ a defense of identity. This defense is used traditionally in cases in which the suspect is a stranger to the victim. A second defense is the consent defense, whereby the suspect claims that he and the victim know each other to some degree. "This is the defense that usually stipulates that the sexual activity took place, but argues that it did not involve force or threat," Lonsway writes.

To complicate matters further, some sexual assault cases can shift from an identity defense to a consent defense. Lonsway explains, "If the suspect originally raises an identity defense (i.e., 'You've got the wrong guy') but the prosecution can prove that sex actually took place between the suspect and victim, he may switch his story to assert a consent defense (i.e., 'She wanted it')." If a suspect raises an identity defense, Lonsway says the investigation should focus on the following:

- A complete physical description of the suspect from the victim or from witnesses
- Biological and trace evidence collected from the victim's body and clothing
- Biological and trace evidence collected from the suspect's body and clothing
- Any evidence linking the suspect to the victim or crime scene

Lonsway emphasizes that in an identity defense, it is important to first determine whether the suspect denies engaging in sexual activity with the victim. If the suspect does deny the sexual activity, the aforementioned evidence will be useful in challenging this denial. If the suspect is charged with multiple crimes it is crucial for examiners and investigators to collect data and evidence linking the incidents. For example, if the offender used a specific behavioral pattern for committing the offenses, it is vital to demonstrate that the same pattern was exhibited in the cases being linked. Lonsway says the suspect will likely focus on the following factors to support an identity defense:

- Factors that limited the victim's ability to see or hear the offender during the assault
- Factors that could have potentially biased the police identification procedures
- Limitations of the forensic examiner and police evidence collection or analysis
- Failure to pursue investigative leads that might point to an alternative suspect

"The investigation must therefore be conducted with meticulous care and documentation for all evidence collection and analysis," Lonsway emphasizes. All steps must be taken to ensure that the victim is not intentionally or unintentionally led in any particular direction during the investigation, and investigators must be open to the possibility that the suspect is innocent, she adds. "All investigative leads must be pursued to identify potential suspects, and evidence gathered to rule them in or out of consideration."

Archambault acknowledges adversarial situations exist between law enforcement and nurses, but says that far more common is collusion between cops and health care providers that can make a mockery of an unbiased investigation. "I have often seen the police and the medical people in collusion, and it's disturbing," she confirms. "In fact, the relationships between some cops and nurses are so strong, and because they like each other and want to get along, cops will tell the nurse, 'Oh, this is a bullshit case, I don't believe her,' and the nurse will substantiate that opinion based on the cop's impression versus the evidence."

Some experts believe that the science of sexual assault investigation is the best way to overcome a consent defense, a mechanism that is being adopted by an increasing number of suspects and their defense counsel. When a defense of consent is raised, experts say that the investigation should focus primarily on evidence to establish that consent was absent and force or threat was present, including the following:

- Evidence of physical or verbal resistance on the part of the victim
- Evidence of genital or nongenital injury
- A detailed account of the victim's thoughts and feelings during the assault
- Information regarding the suspect's size and strength in comparison with the victim's
- Information regarding the environment in which the assault took place, to document the degree of isolation, and so on
- Information regarding the victim's postassault behavior, including posttraumatic stress
- Any other evidence to corroborate the victim's account Anything that is inconsistent with the character of a consensual sexual act
- Information that demonstrates consistencies between the victim's and suspect's descriptions of events

Evidence of injury or physical resistance on the part of the victim can establish that force or threat was present in the situation, but the absence of injury or resistance cannot be used as proof of consent. Lonsway says that in a consent case, the issues at trial will likely focus on the victim's and suspect's behavior, both parties' perception of events, and on challenges to the victim's credibility. There are circumstances, Lonsway adds, in which sexual activity is criminal absent force or threat, including situations where the victim is legally viewed as unable to consent, either due to age or some type of incapacitation, such as disability, lack of consciousness, or drug use. In this case, the investigation is limited to denying the sexual activity, disputing the status of the victim that renders them unable to consent, or claiming that the suspect did not know and could not reasonably have known about the status of the victim, according to Lonsway. She adds that there might be cases in which the investigator or prosecutor prefers to charge the suspect with forcible sexual assault instead of (or in addition to) the offense, in which no force is required. For instance, Lonsway explains that if the victim and suspect are of particular ages that are recognized by state law as constituting statutory rape, the investigator has only to establish sexual activity, the ages of the victim and the suspect, and the suspect's knowledge of the victim's age. Force or threat do not need to be proven because the circumstance is one in which no force is required to constitute an offense.

However, if force or threat was present in the situation, the investigator or prosecutor can charge the suspect with forcible rather than statutory rape because the former charge carries a higher penalty. In these cases, evidence is needed to prove force or threat to overcome a traditional consent defense. An unconscious or incapacitated victim cannot legally consent to sexual activity, experts say, so that sexual penetration or contact constitutes sexual assault. A suspect can deny that the sexual activity occurred, or that the victim was unconscious. Force is not an issue because the victim's lack of consciousness equates with an inability to legally consent to sexual activity. Complicating the issue is the lack of a clear legal standard for incapacitation, so the issue quickly becomes contentious between the prosecution and the defense, Lonsway points out. Based on the victim's account, toxicology report, and interviews with witnesses, it is possible to demonstrate that the victim was so incapacitated that she could not legally consent to sexual activity, she adds, so in these cases, the defense is likely to focus on denying that the victim was incapacitated to the degree alleged by the prosecution. The defense might also argue that the suspect was intoxicated, and so it becomes important to demonstrate who was in control of the situation. In any of these cases, the defense will also need to argue, however, that not only could the victim consent to sexual activity, but she did consent to the acts in question, Lonsway says. Thus, even in cases in which the prosecution has framed the case as one involving an incapacitated victim, the defense is likely to challenge this characterization and raise a more traditional consent defense. She writes, "When a consent defense is raised, the victim's intoxication is usually used as a means of challenging the victim's credibility." There are also no clear legal standards to determine when a victim's disability affects cognition or communication that can render an individual unable to consent.

Lonsway adds that a determination must first be made to decide whether the individual is capable of understanding and giving consent to sexual activity. If a victim is determined to be unable to consent, Lonsway asserts that whether or not sexual activity took place is the only element that remains to be established. Force is not an issue here because the victim is not legally recognized as able to consent to sexual activity. Evidence establishing that sexual activity occurred addresses one element of each offense; other elements are met with evidence documenting the presence of force or threat, the incapacitation or age of the victim, and so on. Investigators must determine the purpose for each piece of evidence to make most effective use of it. The primary purposes for evidence are as follows:

- Proving an element of the offense
- Connecting the suspect with a particular person or place
- Reconstructing or corroborating the victim's account of events
- Reconstructing or corroborating the suspect's account of events

Associative evidence essentially connects one person either to a particular location or crime scene, or to another individual. An example of this is biological DNA evidence that is discovered at the crime scene that can establish that the suspect was in that location at some point. Blood, semen, or other bodily fluids collected from the victim's body can similarly connect the suspect with the victim. This type of evidence is traditionally considered to be identification evidence, which is one aspect of associative evidence. In addition, trace evidence such as hair, fibers, and other debris can be used to connect one person with another person or place, even though it might not be used to identify an individual with any degree of certainty. Reconstructive or corroborative evidence can help jurors visualize the events of the crime, and can also be used to demonstrate consistency with the victim's or the suspect's account of events. Investigators should be familiar with statutory requirements that constitute an attempt offense: an intent to commit a criminal offense and a substantial step toward committing that act. The investigator should consider the context of the circumstance and take into account a number of factors regarding the victim, suspect, and situation. When establishing intent, the victim should be asked the following questions:

- What did the victim think the suspect was going to do? This might be based on prior contact with the suspect, including such behaviors as battering or stalking.
- What did the suspect say? Statements made by the suspect are often key in communicating his intent.
- What did the suspect do? For example, did he tear at the victim's clothing, or begin removing his own?
- What was the suspect's physical appearance? For example, were his pants unzipped, or his penis exposed? Did he have an obvious erection?
- Does the suspect's behavior match that of other crimes in the area, such that they could potentially be attributed to the same person?
- If the suspect is in custody, does he have any prior criminal history?

An area of great contention is the number of false rape reports that are filed. Archambault says that she hears a number of police officers say they rarely investigate valid complaints, but instead dismiss allegations of rape due to believing the reports are false. Influencing factors include an uncooperative victim, the involvement of drugs or alcohol, or late reporting. "Some of the perception can be explained by looking at the training often provided to law enforcement officers," she writes in "So How Many Rape Reports are False?" Archambault says officers are taught that any of the following can be indicators of a false report:

- Delayed report.
- Report made to a person or entity other than law enforcement.
- The victim is indifferent to injuries or seems to experience a lack of pain.
- The victim is extremely vague about details of the assault or is extremely detailed.
- The victim attempts to steer away from unsafe details in the description of the assault, such as location of the offense or suspect description.

Archambault says that studies provide the rate of false reporting of sexual assault as ranging from 0 percent to 98 percent, accounting for differences in definitions and different ways of determining a complaint to be false. She writes, "The truth is that the data they are citing doesn't actually exist. In fact, we have no knowledge of what percentage of sexual assaults is false on a national level." She explains that a number of complaints of forcible rape are determined to be unfounded in crime index reporting vehicles, and that much of the data is confusing in its presentation. She writes, "I have found that investigators unfound a case if the investigation doesn't produce evidence to corroborate or substantiate the allegation. I believe this practice is in error; however, one can see that absent guidelines, a variety of different interpretations are possible." She adds that investigators are using different standards for clearing their caseloads. Archambault suggests that investigators consider the following points regarding sexual assault cases:

- Sexual assault victims will most likely be acquainted with the suspect(s) in some way.
- The victim rarely expected intimacy and the stereotype of date rape rarely applies.
- Suspects rarely use weapons (short of shame and embarrassment).
- Victims normally delay hours, days, weeks, or months in reporting their assault, and many never disclose to anyone.
- Victims rarely report to law enforcement or authorities first.
- Few victims are injured to the point that emergency medical attention is required.
- Alcohol and drug use is involved in a high percentage of sexual assaults.
- Victims lie about the circumstances of the sexual assault because they feel their actions might have contributed to the assault, or they won't be believed.
- Professionals responding to sexual assault must reassure the victim that he or she will not be judged and that the complaint will be taken seriously.

Archambault, a 23-year veteran and former sergeant with the San Diego Police Department, who now works as an independent consultant and trainer, started her career on the streets as a young officer working with gangs. It was a rough indoctrination to the force ("It was safer for me on the streets with the gang members than in my own unit," she says) and after a year and a half, she transferred to the child abuse unit. "I wanted to go to a unit like child abuse, not because I knew anything about the cases, but because it was a female-dominated field. It was a very nurturing place to go, where I interacted with female doctors and social workers... supportive people. Going from a negative environment to a positive environment, I thrived. And I loved the work," she recalls. "I did that for three years, but found the work really takes its toll."

When Archambault rotated to the sex crimes unit, she found satisfying work that also challenged her beliefs about these kinds of crimes:

> When I went to sex crimes, I was overwhelmed. I thought I was going to investigate stranger cases, because that's what everyone thinks of when they think of sex crimes. Instead, I saw all of these nonstranger cases, and the dynamics were the same as what I saw in child abuse cases. I got hooked by the work, and began doing some training in child sexual abuse. At the time, the only people teaching child abuse were social workers. As well, police officers, some prosecutors and even judges in those days didn't see child abuse as a criminal problem, they saw it more as a social issue. They relegated these cases to family court, not criminal court. I didn't agree with that; I think people who abuse children should be put in jail. So I created the first curriculum for child abuse investigation from a criminal perspective at the police academy. That was the initial direction of my training services, and it kept growing from there.

On retirement from the San Diego Police Department, Archambault founded and serves as training director for her consulting business, Sexual Assault Training & Investigations (SATI). "No one else was doing it, so I decided I'd better do it. It was a calling. I feel so strongly that we need to do better at our responses to victims and our investigations." Archambault provides training to law enforcement, criminal justice, and forensic professionals throughout the country. She doesn't hesitate when it comes to saying what she thinks about the state of investigations and general awareness:

> I am very disappointed with the whole sexual assault movement. Sexual assault has always been around, it's always going to be around... as uncomfortable as domestic violence is, you can't run from it because it's visible. You have broken bones, you have dead bodies. We get those once in a while in sexual assault cases, but it's still a hidden crime, and it's still a very uncomfortable crime for people to talk about. That's one of the reasons why we haven't made as many strides as we have in domestic violence cases. Law enforcement agencies have been sued successfully in domestic violence cases, but we haven't seen them sued for ineffectively responding to sexual assault cases. We have serial offenders out there because police didn't believe a victim when she came forward.

Archambault says that having recently returned from the 10th anniversary celebration of the VAWA in Washington, DC, in the fall of 2004, she finds it ironic that so much effort in awareness at the conceptual level has resulted in so little traction in real life:

> It was an incredible experience, but the event reinforced my belief I am doing the right thing, because sexual assault was a very small part of the event's focus; it was overshadowed by domestic violence. We've made great strides but I also feel like we're stuck, too. For example, we're still preaching to people about why SART programs are good, and why they need them in their communities, but we've become stuck because we're not seeing these cases prosecuted like they should be. We have the DNA technology, so we are doing better on stranger cases; we have the President's DNA Initiative, so now finally we are getting the rape-kit backlog addressed. But I don't see society making strides in changing the way we view women and our distrust of rape reports. People still think, "If a woman is drinking, she deserved what she got." And that's where these cases get stuck. I think we have a lot more work to do when educating people.

Archambault adds that fingers are pointed in the wrong directions:

> People say, "Educate law enforcement and prosecutors!" but these people aren't on juries. I consulted on some grand jury training for a law enforcement agency in Texas recently, and one of the sergeants sent me an e-mail telling me about one of the grand jurors talking about how in the Bible, a woman must submit to her husband any time he wants sex, so there is no such thing as marital rape. It shows us how far we have to go to educate about things like nonstranger sexual assault.

Archambault believes that issues like nonstranger sexual assault cases, and the specific kinds of evidence that are needed in these cases, bring to light the need for discussion and training on professional boundaries. Although she believes in a coordinated approach like the SART program, Archambault says it is necessary to keep medico-legal practitioners focused on their specific duties. For example, she believes that advocacy is best left to advocates, not police officers or nurses. (This topic is discussed at greater length in chapter 2.) As Robert Frost once described in his poem "Mending Wall," "Good fences make good neighbors."

> Science is science and good police work is good police work. I don't think forensic nurses or police officers should be advocates. I do a lot of training on boundaries, and I tell students the same thing. I do believe that I have advocated for victims of crime every day of my career, but I am not an advocate . . . that's why we have professional, specially trained victim's advocates. As a police officer, I stay in my role as an investigator; as an advocate, you stay in that role, and as a forensic examiner, you stay in that role, especially since forensic examiners are supposed to be a neutral party. When you become an advocate, you are not neutral.
>
> I think turf wars are happening and I think people are crossing over boundaries. To say that a nurse should be an advocate is a huge mistake. A nurse is supposed to be a nurse, a cop is supposed to be a cop, and an advocate is supposed to be an advocate. It's not that nurses and cops can't advocate, but we're not professional advocates—our specific role is not to advocate. Advocacy is having one professional whose sole purpose is working for the victim, being there for the victim no matter what the victim said or did. The advocate is not going to judge that person. The nurse, however, does judge that person. When you are doing a medical exam, and I don't mean judge in a negative way, but you are saying that these injuries are consistent or inconsistent with what happened in the assault, so you are making a conclusion, you are forming an opinion, and so do the police and the prosecutors and the jury. The advocate's job is not to form any conclusion. There's a huge difference there.
>
> In my early days of child abuse investigation, if the victim was under the age of 12, we would have a licensed clinical social worker do the forensic interview. That was a county protocol. The cop is trying to establish a lack of consent, which really isn't necessary in child abuse cases, or at the very least, trying to ascertain the context of the situation. In one such case, the investigator was watching the interview and he wanted the interviewer to ask the child if he screamed. It was a fair question because the detective was trying to establish if there were witnesses; it wasn't that there was a doubt in his mind, because it's not a consent-defense crime. The social worker refused to ask the question because she felt it would be putting the child on the spot or trying to judge that child. It's an example of the need for cross-training and educating individuals about other professionals' intentions and the reasons behind them.

Archambault adds that getting on the same page requires use of a common language that spans medical, legal, and advocacy platforms:

> Language is crucial because the cops talk in cop talk and the medical people talk in medical talk and the legal people talk in legal talk, and no one understands each other. I don't think it's done by accident sometimes, because it's a clever way to maintain territories. It also allows professionals to keep their distance. Nurses squirm at legalese and cops don't have a clue about the posterior forchette. That's not good enough because that cop needs to understand what the impact of the clinical findings are in the case, and the nurse needs to know what happens in court. What it's telling me is that they're not talking to each other.

Many issues intermingle in this regard; coming on the heels of these boundary and collaboration issues, Archambault says, are the topics of medical reporting and the payment for rape kit analyses:

I believe in medical-mandated reporting and a lot of people don't. I believe that the community has a right to know when a felony has occurred. Just because you, as a medical practitioner, have someone come in with a gunshot wound and you report it, it doesn't mean I, as a police officer, get to hook that person up to a torture chamber to get information from that person. So, when a rape victim comes in for treatment to a medical facility, I cannot arrest the person for not talking to me, and so I think there is great confusion there. A lot of people are saying, no medical mandated reporting; I am concerned about the states that don't have medical mandated reporting or the states that don't require law enforcement to pay for the evidentiary exam. You see, I believe when you are doing a forensic exam, it is clearly an act of the criminal justice process, because there is hope that we will be able to use the evidence in a criminal court of law to help an investigation. Because of that, I believe that the forensic exam should be paid for by law enforcement. I believe that the whole backlog issue and the lack of communication and coordination happened because we're not operating as a team. How could the backlog be a surprise to so many people if they were, in fact, communicating with each other? That's impossible. What I see going on in a lot of places is practitioners think the forensic exam is the whole investigation and the truth is, the forensic exam is most often a very small part of that investigation. It's not the medical people's jobs to make or break the case. They should simply be a neutral party, an arm of the investigation . . . they are acting as an agent.

This is why reporting is so important: If you are not clear that this is a criminal justice investigation, it gets ugly. The moment the victim says he or she is not going to report, it's a medical examination; but if they say they want to have evidence collected, it's now a criminal justice and law enforcement response, and the victim gets to choose if she cooperates or not. A lot of problems happen because we have such divided opinions in this country about roles. I think that our failure to see the forensic exam process as a true criminal justice exercise allows law enforcement to not do their job. Cops respond to traffic accidents, which are civil cases unless DUI is involved. The police do not bill people for their accident reports. Yet many states are still billing victims of sexual assault, even though the VAWA says they are not supposed to. I think we need to be clear that this is a criminal justice process, that the exam should be paid for by law enforcement, that the nurse examiner collects the evidence and is an arm of that investigation, and that the only reason she is doing it is because it is an intimate exam and cops shouldn't be doing it. Then, roles are clear and people are held accountable for doing their jobs. I believe that in many cases, forensic examiners have overstepped their boundaries. The ones who do this are workaholics and they take great pride in what they do. In their defense, though, the reason they have done it is that they are so dedicated and they care. On the one hand I say, don't overstep your boundaries and on the other hand, they are the only ones out there knocking down the doors.

Archambault recalls a conversation she had with a forensic nurse on this very topic:

Pat Speck and I got into this debate about payment for kits and who should determine what goes into them. I said that law enforcement should be providing these kits and the contents and analysis should be dictated by the crime labs that are analyzing the evidence. Pat said, "They are not going to tell me what to do until they pay for them," and I said, "My point exactly." They should be paid for by law enforcement because this is an arm of the investigation. If we put the burden on law enforcement where it belongs, I think we would see standardization of rape kits and processing. And the labs should be dictating those kits based on science and ability and equipment. I sense that what forensic nurses are saying is, "If I am paying for it, it's going to go my way." That's interesting to me because they shouldn't be paying for it in the first place, and you have just lost the scope of this while thing: It's about the victim and it's about the crime lab processing the evidence.

Archambault believes that many forensic practitioners have the investigative process backward, and this can lead to detrimental turf wars:

Because so many jurisdictions are unhappy with the police, rather than hold them accountable, they just exclude them in the investigatory process. I often see medical practitioners and advocates actually attempting to dissuade the victim from reporting to the police. They'll tell the victim, "We don't need the police because I can do the interview, I'll collect the evidence, and you can make up your mind later." When I see that, it worries me very much. A lot of the people I deal with can't appropriately explain what an investigation should look like and I think people should be held accountable. You certainly don't exclude people.

Some programs are acting as though there is going to be only one interview of the victim and the forensic examiner is going to do it because he or she is trained and victim-sensitive. I would hope they would understand that the first interview should never be looked at as a complete interview. The victim must have time to digest the crime that occurred, and then of course, we will want to ask follow-up questions as the investigation unfolds.

There are legitimate reasons for their feelings, but I think their response is inappropriate. There was a SART program in Georgia whose nurses were actually going to quit doing the exams. The nurses felt that they were telling victims to do certain things and then the police were using the information against them; the nurses felt they were being misused or the response by law enforcement was putting them in unethical situations. They felt they had lied to the victim, such as in the case of a drug-facilitated sexual assault, where the victim says to the nurse, "Yes, I was drinking," and the nurse puts it in the report—which

> they should, of course—but then it's used by the police to discredit the victim. That's just one example I have heard about police bad behavior, but then again, I have seen just as many medical people mess up. Everyone must assume accountability.

Archambault bristles at the suggestion by some health care providers that police shouldn't be a significant part of the medico-legal process:

> The SART program was sold to people as a way to get police officers back onto the street and as a way to reduce the number of interviews for the victim, and I think that's ridiculous. The investigator is still going to want to interview the victim and the police should be reinterviewing the victim as the investigation develops, for clarification. Rather than telling the victim, "We're all going to sit down here and interview you together to reduce the number of interviews and trauma," what we really need to do is say, "Look, this is what we are doing now, this is my role now. But you'll be interviewed by a detective who will pick up your case and stay with it until the end. And the DA will want to talk to you, and it will feel like a lot of different people are asking you questions, but this is why we're doing it: to work your case successfully."

Because police officers and ER nurses share the role of being first responders, Archambault says their relationship can be one of mutual respect, trust, and understanding. Archambault recalls her experiences as a patrol officer: "Patrol officers were very close with ER folks. In San Diego, all of the trauma hospitals had report-writing rooms for us, where they would keep coffee and sandwiches for us. They loved to have us in their EDs because they were dealing with the same clientele we were dealing with. We always had great relationships with ER folks, and with our SART people, too." However, if an adversarial relationship between law enforcement and health care personnel develops, Archambault says it's essential to recognize, re-establish, and respect boundaries. "If you have a training issue, then you need to deal with that. Sometimes I hear from cops, 'Why didn't the nurse just tell me what the problem was?' People must feel safe enough to give others on the team feedback. I think that honest communication sometimes doesn't take place." She continues:

> One of the things I hear all the time from forensic practitioners and advocates is, "Go to the police academy to train the cops," and I say right back, "You need to be trained on what the cops need from you, and how we can work together." Cross-training and awareness on the part of all parties is critical. For example, a nurse called me up one day and said, "I have this great idea. I am going to write a grant so we can get an evidence van and we can respond to crime scenes for the police. I said, "Do you not realize I already have six of those vans? I have a whole crime lab that responds to scenes."

Archambault points to another example of the right hand not knowing what the left hand is doing:

> Many nurses have no idea we were not able to get our rape kits done immediately, or how the kits got processed. I was conducting training recently with a group of new forensic nurses and they had no idea what happened to the kits after they were collected. They thought that they went straight to a crime lab and technicians started looking at the evidence. They didn't understand about police property rooms and dry storage lockers, or about how cases are worked up, and that is so important to their understanding of the process.
>
> They need to understand that while the victim is hearing about the wonders of DNA from them, the cop is saying, "How the hell do I get my DNA done?" The police officers are thinking to themselves, "It's nice to hear about President Bush's DNA Initiative, but I don't have access to speedy analysis." So, making all of these scenarios real to people like forensic nurses is important. If you have created a protocol that can't be worked in real life, then you have to go back and change it. I think a lot of our protocols are written from the concept and not from practice. Like the idea of SART—I see some nurses treating police officers as transport officers. They will transport the victim, drop them off and go back out in the field, answer radio calls, and then when the medical people are done, they will pick up the kit and go away. That kind of thinking reflects a lack of education about how complex a sexual assault investigation is and how much work is done by all parties. Anyone who thinks that cop should go out and answer radio calls doesn't understand that there is a lengthy investigation in front of that officer. That's just the preliminary investigation, not counting the follow-up that will be done. I think it has allowed law enforcement to do the lousy job they have done in many instances; by saying that specially trained nurses are going to take care of everything, and by them telling the cops, "You guys can go away and do what you do best—go out and arrest people"—that doesn't make any sense. I don't try to tell nurses how to do the exams and I think there are still a lot of people who don't think the cops are doing a really great job. I think forensic nurses are some of the most dedicated, obsessive-compulsive people I have ever met. They're fascinating to me.

Although investigators and nurses and other members of the medico-legal team will undoubtedly continue to face these boundary issues, one thing they have in common is the desire to see cases investigated and prosecuted successfully. When they are not, the result can have a chilling effect on professionals' efforts on behalf of the victim.

"The right thing to do is to conduct a thorough investigation and don't go out and arrest someone until you have made a solid case to support the arrest, and hopefully you'll be able to hold him in," Archambault says:

> Instead, what happens in a lot of cases is that the victim reports, the police go out and make an arrest, but they don't do a thorough investigation and the guy is kicked out of the system and nothing ever happens. We really want to slow down the investigation and do a thorough job; there's no reason to rush unless he is a serial predator. These guys don't go anywhere—they are arrogant, and they think they are going to get away with it and most often they do. The common ground that medico-legal professionals have is they feel their work is wasted.

Archambault says she spends an extraordinary amount of time reminding law enforcement and health care professionals about the value of their contributions in a case:

> I am always reminding people that their work is never wasted when you can effectively respond to a victim of sexual violence. You can't consider what happens in the outcome as a measurement of success. You have to focus on the fact that you treated this person with respect, giving them your time, doing the best job you could do. I tell people to stay in the moment. It shouldn't be their job to worry about what the jury does or what the judge does. If we all just focused on doing our part of the process the best we can do it, we'd see a lot more of these cases moving forward. It's what's referred to as downstream orientation. I think domestic violence investigators have made advancements because they don't face what we face in the sexual violence field—most domestic violence cases are prosecuted as misdemeanors, and juries don't have problems with misdemeanors; but in a sex-crimes case, you are looking at a minimum of four, six, eight years of prison or life terms; these are big sentences, and we are talking prison. There's no middle ground. You can't take a rape and drop it to a misdemeanor. I remember sitting in San Diego Assistant City Attorney Gael Strack's strangulation class and I told her this is great stuff, but my question is, why are you prosecuting it as a misdemeanor? We're talking attempted homicide here! This is assault with a deadly weapon at the least. She said, of course, but she can't get the DAs to prosecute as a felony. That's where I think we are not real with ourselves here. We say we have done a really good job educating people on strangulation—they have it down, but why are we prosecuting it as a misdemeanor? So I don't think our courts have changed that much. Not to say we don't have lots of good prosecutors out there doing really great work, like we have with the forensic examiners, but I think we have to do more community education. Those prosecutors are doing the same things the cops and nurses are doing, and that's downstream orientation; they are asking themselves, "Why waste the effort?" Some people say "Why put additional trauma on the victim?" If the victim wants her day in court, she deserves it, is my opinion, and it should be her decision. Outcomes often stop at the arrest. We need to know what happened to the arrest, and what happened to every sexual assault case that is reported.
>
> Professionals will burn out if a victim's inability to participate in an investigation is taken personally or the investigation is viewed as a waste of time. Investigators should always be commended for conducting a comprehensive, evidence-based investigation. A thorough investigation may exonerate an innocent person rather than leaving doubts in the minds of others. I think this reflects the criminal justice system at its best.

REFERENCES

American Prosecutors Research Institute. *DNA Evidence Policy Considerations for the Prosecutor.* Alexandria, VA. September 2004

Archambault, J. So how many rape reports are false? SATI, Inc. Available at: www.mysati.com.

Archambault, J. Forensic DNA. Proceedings report, National Non-Stranger Sexual Assault Symposium, September 15–17, 1999. 122–126, September 2000.

Archambault, J. Dynamics of sexual assault. SATI, Inc. Available at: www.mysati.com. 2001.

Archambault, J., & Faugno, D. K. Overcoming a consent defense to sexual assault. *J Emerg Nurs. 27,* 204–208, 2001.

Archambault, J., & Lindsay, S. Responding to non-stranger sexual assault. In M. Reuland, C. Brito, & L. Carroll, Eds. *Solving Crime and Disorder Problems: Current Issues, Police Strategies and Organizational Tactics.* Washington, DC: Police Executive Research Forum. 2001.

Ardnt, S. Nurses help Santa Cruz sexual assault survivors. *California Nurse.* October 1988.

Burgess, A. W., Hazelwood, R. R., Roukos, F. E., Hartman, C. R., & Burgess, A. G. Serial rapists and their victims: Reenactment and repetition. *Annals New York Academy of Sciences, 528,* 277–295, 1988.

Daniels, C. Despite gains, prosecution of rape still a tough task. *Los Angeles Times.* July 23, 2004.

Division of Governmental Studies and Services, Washington State University. National forensic DNA study report. Pullman, WA. Available at http://www.ojp.usdoj.gov/nij/pdf/dna-studyreport-final.pdf. 2003.

Federal Bureau of Investigations, Criminal Justice Information Services Division. *Crime in the United States—1996.* Clarksburg, WV. 1996.

Frank, C. The new way to catch rapists. *Redbook.* December, pp. 61–65, 1996.

Gidycz, C. A., & Koss, M. P. The effects of acquaintance rape on the female victim. In L. Bechhofer & A. Parrot, Eds. *Acquaintance Rape: The Hidden Crime* (pp. 270–283). New York: Wiley. 1991.

Hogan, S., & Swinton, S. Meeting defense challenges to DNA evidence. *American Prosecutors Research Institute, Silent Witness. 8,* 1, 2003.

International Association of Forensic Nurses. Statement of the IAFN on DNA and sexual assault. Available at: www.iafn.org/news/dna-sa-statement.pdf. October 8, 2003.

Katz, B. L. The psychological impact of stranger vs. non-stranger rape on victims' recovery. In L. Bechhofer & A. Parrot, Eds. *Acquaintance Rape: The Hidden Crime* (pp. 251–269). New York: Wiley. 1991.

LeBeau, J. Statute revision and the reporting of rape. *SSR, 72,* 3, 201–207, 1988.

Ledray, L. E. *Sexual Assault Nurse Examiner (SANE) Development and Operation Guide* (NCJ 170609). Washington, DC: U.S. Department of Justice, Office for Victims of Crime. 1999.

Ledray, L. E. Evidence collection and care of the sexual assault survivor. *Violence Against Women.* August 2001.

Lindsay, S. *An Epidemiologic Study of the Influence of Victim Age and Relationship to the Suspect on the Results of Evidentiary Examinations and Law Enforcement Outcomes in Cases of Reported Sexual Assault.* San Diego, CA: University of California, San Diego. 1998.

National Center for Women and Policing. Successfully Investigating Acquaintance Sexual Assault: A National Training Manual for Law Enforcement. 2001. Available at: http://www.womenandpolicing.org.

National Commission on the Future of DNA Evidence. *Postconviction DNA Testing: Recommendations for Handling Requests* (NCJ 177626). Washington, DC: U.S. Department of Justice, National Institute of Justice. 1999.

National Institute of Justice, Office for Victims of Crime. Understanding DNA Evidence: A Guide for Victim Service Providers. 2001. Available at: http://www.ojp.usdoj.gov/ovc/publications/bulletins/dna_4_2001/welcome.html.

Neff, J. A. Editor's notes. *J Emer. Nursing, 15,* 3, 1989.

Office of Senator Maria Cantwell. A repost on the potential for apprehending rapists in Washington state using DNA analysis. Olympia, WA: May 29, 2002.

Osborn, M., & Neff, J. Patient care guidelines: Evidentiary examination in sexual assault. *J Emerg Nurs. 15,* 3, 1989.

Parnis, D., & Du Mont, J. Examining the standardized application of rape kits: An exploratory study of post-sexual assault professional practices. *Health Care Women Int. 23,* 8, 846–853, 2002.

Smalley, S. Newest suspect in rapes: The DNA. *Boston Globe.* June 20, 2004.

U.S. Department of Justice. *Advancing justice through DNA technology.* Washington, DC. March 2003.

U.S. Department of Justice, National Institute of Justice. What Every Law Enforcement Officer Should Know About DNA Evidence. Available at: http://www.ncjrs.org/nij/DNAbro/intro.html. 2004.

U.S. Department of Justice, Office of Justice Programs, Bureau of Justice Statistics. *Census of publicly funded forensic crime laboratories, 2002.* Washington, DC. February 2005.

RECOMMENDED READINGS

Connors, E., Lundregan, T., Miller, N., & McEwen, T. *Convicted by Juries, Exonerated by Science: Case Studies in the Use of DNA Evidence to Establish Innocence After Trial* (Research Report. NCJ 161258). Washington, DC: U.S. Department of Justice, National Institute of Justice. 1996.

Du Mont, J., & Parnis, D. Sexual assault and legal resolution: Querying the medical collection of forensic evidence. *Medicine and Law. 19,* 4, 779–792, 2000.

Du Mont, J., & Parnis, D. Constructing bodily evidence through sexual assault evidence kits. *Griffith Law Review. 10,* 1, 63–77, 2001.

Hammond, H. A., & Caskey, C. T. *Automated DNA Typing: Method of the Future?* (Research Preview NCJ 184373). Washington, DC: U.S. Department of Justice, National Institute of Justice. 1997.

Inman, K., & Rudin, N. *An Introduction to Forensic DNA Analysis.* Boca Raton, FL: CRC Press. 1997.

Jones, J. S., Wynn, B. N., Kroeze, B., Dunnuck, C., & Rossman, L. Comparison of sexual assaults by strangers versus known assailants in a community-based population. *Am J Emerg Med. 22,* 6, 454–459, 2004.

McKenna, J. A., Cecil, J. S., & Coukos, P. A reference guide on forensic DNA evidence. In *Reference Manual on Scientific Evidence.* Washington, DC: Federal Judicial Center. 1994.

National Research Council. *DNA Technology in Forensic Science.* Washington, DC: National Academy Press. 1992.

National Research Council. *The Evaluation of Forensic DNA Evidence.* Washington, DC: National Academy Press, 1996.

U.S. Department of Justice, Federal Bureau of Investigation. *Handbook of Forensic Services: Evidence Examinations.* Washington, DC: FBI. 1999.

Weedn, V. W., & Hicks, J. W. *The Unrealized Potential of DNA Testing: Research in Action* (NCJ 170596). Washington, DC: U.S. Department of Justice, National Institute of Justice. 1998.

15 Professional Issues: Forensic Nursing Education and Training

CONTENTS

The last two decades have witnessed the birth and growth of a number of important forensic nursing specialties, an overall maturing process within the field, and an increase in the number of individuals calling this vocation their own. As forensic nursing grows in its clinical significance and its contributions to the medico-legal community, and as it attracts new legions of practitioners, it must do so within a more structured framework.

For all of its accomplishments and contributions to nursing practice, forensic nursing is crippled by the lack of a comprehensive core curriculum, a road map with which these practitioners—both novice and veteran—can navigate swiftly and assuredly the varied topography of this unique nursing specialty. Lynch (1995) states:

> The traditional lack of comprehensive forensic instruction in schools of nursing has contributed significantly to the current situation in which there are large numbers of hospitals in which cases of liability-related injuries and deaths are inadequately and improperly investigated and treated. This is evident from recent headlines in the news media and has resulted in increased awareness of the need for the application of forensic science to the investigation of trauma associated with violence. In clinical cases as well as in the community arena, the subtle indications of pernicious human behavior require an investigation of the kind and depth necessary in an increasingly complex society.

15.1 THE CURRENT STATE OF HEALTH CARE EDUCATION AND TRAINING

Forensic nursing is not alone in its quest for a meaningful, relevant, practical core curriculum; much of the health care field is attempting to update or redefine their scopes and standards of practice, or, at the very least, in some way better respond to victims of violence and medico-legal cases that present to health care institutions. According to the 1999 report to Congress by the Agency for Healthcare Research and Quality (AHRQ) and U.S. Department of Health and Human Services, *Medical Examination and Treatment for Victims of Sexual Assault: Evidence-Based Clinical Practice and Provider Training*, "There appear to be few university-based, academic training programs for health professionals that include curricula to develop clinical skills for performing forensic or medical evidentiary examinations. However, a handful of degree-granting programs in medicine and nursing are known to exist, and a small number of colleges and universities have recently added coursework to existing programs in nursing and medicine." Since 2000, a number of new forensic nursing degree and certificate programs have been created, and are discussed later in this chapter. (It should also be noted that while many studies and reports on the topic of health care provider education do not specifically refer to forensic nursing and/or medico-legal training, they do discuss the topic of IPV. In many cases, it might be appropriate to substitute the term *medico-legal issues* for references to IPV.) According to some experts, however, the first step in addressing education and training issues might be to convince the majority of health care providers that IPV is not simply a social issue, but an issue with significant health-care-related components that requires attention from nursing school curricula. The Institute of Medicine (IOM, 2002) report, *Confronting Chronic Neglect: The Education and Training of Health Professionals on Family Violence* states, "Family violence, although of ancient origins, is newly recognized as a substantial concern for the public health and health care systems. For many in health care, it is perceived more easily as a social or legal problem." C. Everett Koop, a former U.S. Surgeon General, had stated more than a decade ago, "Identifying violence as a public health issue is a relatively new idea. Traditionally, when confronted by the circumstances of violence, health professionals have deferred to the criminal justice system . . . (now) the professionals of medicine, nursing, and the health-related social services must come forward and recognize violence as their issue."

According to the IOM (2002) report, "Progress appears to have been made on health professionals' recognition of family violence as a health issue." It points to the 1991 guidelines published by the ANA to help nurses identify and treat intimate partner violence, as well as similar guidelines issued in 1992 by the AMA. A shift in perspectives was documented in a 1995 survey of OB/GYN physicians in which 86 percent said they believed that intimate partner violence was a medical problem. (Parsons, Zaccaro, Wells, & Stovall, 1995). Moore, Zaccaro, and Parsons (1998) found that 5 percent of public health nurses, 4 percent of private-office nurses, and 3 percent of hospital nurses agreed with the statement that IPV is not a medical problem. On an even more promising note, Woodtli and Breslin (1997) found that in a survey of 107 nursing educators at all levels, 100 percent agreed that all nursing students should be taught the signs of abuse across a patient's life span. Eighty-six percent of respondents said that this content should be integrated throughout the curriculum, but just one third said that resources to do so were available. It is interesting to note that although many clinicians acknowledge that IPV is an important health problem to address in the patient population, it is not an issue they encounter, according to research conducted by Sugg and Inui (1992) and Reid and Glasser (1997).

Forensic practitioners know that human bite marks and injuries to the teeth and jaws can be a sign of domestic or sexual violence; however, dental professionals who are in a position to help make professional determinations of abuse frequently are the ones who believe IPV is not a health issue. Tilden et al. (1994) surveyed dentists, dental hygienists, physicians, nurses, psychologists, and social workers and asked them to respond to the statement, "Professionals in my discipline have as much responsibility to deal with problems of family violence as they do to deal with clinical problems." In the study, 98 percent of psychologists, 97 percent of social workers, 87 percent of nurses, and 85 percent of physicians agreed, but 47 percent of dentists and 46 percent of dental hygienists disagreed.

As nursing struggles to raise awareness of IPV and create a curriculum for its forensic specialty, it is of no comfort to learn that physicians also are struggling with proper training of forensic aspects of practice. The 2002 IOM report identified only seven pediatric medicine fellowship programs affiliated with medical schools in the United States that include one to two years of training on child abuse and neglect or child forensics. They also noted a few medical and nursing schools that offer one- to four-month elective courses or other clinical rotations related to child abuse or domestic violence. However, the degree to which the courses build clinical skills related to medical evidentiary examinations is unknown.

Referring to curricula on family violence in general, the report concluded generally that the content is incomplete, instruction time is generally minimal, the content and teaching methods vary, and the issue is not well integrated throughout the educational experience. In addition, studies indicate that health professionals and students in the health professions often perceive curricula on family violence to be inadequate or ineffective.

The IOM report also paints a discouraging picture of the current state of health care training. It comments, "Health professional curriculum development occurs in an environment of competing needs in which diverse curricular objectives must be sorted and prioritized." It says that adding any "new" topics, such as IPV or medico-legal principles, to an already-bursting curriculum could require a reduction of content elsewhere. The report adds, "Despite the increasing belief that family violence is an important issue for health care, training efforts on family violence may be perceived as displacing other more established educational topics long considered necessary to prepare health care professionals for clinical practice."

Citing research by Fox (1993) and Wilkinson and Forlini (1999), the IOM report states that the U.S. health care system "is suited to handle physical illnesses and injuries that used to be the predominant causes of morbidity and mortality, but it is not so well prepared to handle complex health issues with social underpinnings that are in the legitimate purview of health care and of public health." The IOM report characterizes IPV as "a complex, multifactorial problem that extends beyond these traditional focuses of medicine to social and ethical issues." The report explains that treating an acute injury per se does not require an investigation of the cause of the injury, and symptoms of family violence "can be treated without identification of the underlying cause, leaving the patient at risk for subsequent episodes." The IOM report cites research by Mashta (2000) that reflects on physicians' reluctance to commit precious clinical time toward learning how to evaluate a "frustrating and often incurable situation, especially when there are other, more pressing treatable issues that can be addressed." A critical issue is that even when they document a physical injury, clinicians tend to record facts such as injury location, without sufficient context, including the circumstances surrounding the event, according to the IOM report.

Hence, the need for education and training of all health care providers about medico-legal issues is critical; however, the amount of time allotted to IPV education has been minimal, according to the IOM report. Tilden et al. (1994) reported that 33 percent of allied health care providers, including nurses, had received no education about child or elder abuse, or IPV, during their formal education and training. A lack of training on the parts of doctors can be used as evidence of the need for nurses trained in medico-legal issues; a survey of 705 academic emergency physicians indicated that just one quarter of them could recall receiving any training about elder abuse during their residencies, just 20 percent reviewed the topic during continuing education, and only 31 percent said they had a written protocol for the reporting of elder abuse at their facility (IOM, 2002; Jones, Veenstra, Seamon, & Krohmer, 1997).

An eye-opening finding in the IOM report was the presence of institutional culture and norms that pervaded institutions of higher learning. The report stated that revisions to health care curricula can encounter barriers in the form of inertia or resistance to change, dynamics of power, need for leadership, professional socialization, multidisciplinary collaboration, and marginalization. "Studies suggest that faculty resistance to change is a major barrier to curricular reform, as the drive to maintain the status quo often overrides the desire to make educational innovations," the report suggests. The report acknowledges that even when curricular changes are made, there is the tendency to drift back to previous patterns; many educators also believe that the time-worn basic principles should not be replaced with or challenged by more progressive content dictated by current trends. "Moreover," the report states, "establishing programs is more challenging if the topic is not embraced by academic leaders or widely recognized by the faculty. Unless there is an internal mandate from an influential institutional leader or an external mandate from an accrediting body or legislative authority, curricular innovation may be difficult to achieve."

Forensic nursing leaders also face the challenge of impressing on health care providers the importance of overcoming hesitation about invading a patient's privacy by conducting medico-legal inquiry—another barrier to education noted by the IOM report. The report cites studies by Kurz and Stark (1998) that have found that health care professionals have expressed discomfort with intervening in situations they view as private matters and might demonstrate these reservations when teaching or supervising students. Kurz and Stark and Bograd say that although most clinicians sincerely want to help, they are uncomfortable doing so because they believe that inquiry, investigation, and intervention in cases of IPV invades their patients' personal affairs. Citing Sugg and Inui (1992), the IOM report reveals that open-ended interviews of primary-care physicians regarding attitudes about IPV suggest that concerns about privacy were the most frequently identified barriers to identification and intervention. The nursing literature also delves into this topic. McGrath et al. (1997) found in a survey of nurses, physicians, and social workers that 63 percent cited personal discomfort and 57 percent cited concern about privacy as barriers to effective responses to IPV.

Training and education of health care providers also is challenged by the need for multidisciplinary collaboration, because intervention in abusive situations requires the involvement of the health, social, and legal systems. What is taught might not be reinforced in clinical situations, the IOM report says, pointing to Tilden et al. (1994), who found that nurses were more than twice as likely as any other health care providers to handle the situation alone when confronted with a potential medico-legal situation.

There are several other barriers to the education of health care providers. The IOM report also examines the pattern of a charismatic educator who might be able to make great inroads in introducing material on IPV, but if this individual leaves the institution, curriculum could revert back to its prior incarnation. "The presence and efforts of a singular faculty leader paradoxically can be an impediment to curricular innovation," the report observes. "That leader may single-handedly take responsibility for family violence curricula or extracurricular activities. However, once the leader moves on to other pursuits, the programs generally wither due to insufficient institutional commitment." Also, societal norms can influence students who might otherwise consider pursuing the study of IPV as it relates to health care. The report adds, "Students may make their career choices, in part, based on others' perceptions of particular fields" or to avoid marginalization by others.

To better shape a curriculum for health care providers, educators should be aware of certain professional issues, as cited by the IOM report:

- Many health care providers feel they lack sufficient time to adequately assist victims of abuse (Sugg & Inui, 1992).
- Primary care providers are frustrated by what they perceive as an "extra" social responsibility, and that they could quickly become overwhelmed

in caring for "nonmedical" issues (Sugg & Inui, 1992).

- Health care providers have expressed concern regarding their inadequate preparation, uncertainty how to proceed if maltreatment is disclosed, and frustration with the inability to ensure positive outcomes for victims (Reid & Glasser, 1997).
- Receiving continued education on IPV has been associated with increased screening for abuse (Carbonell, Chez, & Hassler, 1995).

In addition to these challenges for students, Guze (1995) found that incentives for health professionals to participate in teaching appear inadequate. Cohen et al. (1997) reported that health care providers, including physicians, who treat victims of violence, believe that such work "garners little respect from their peers and will not result in prestigious research grants and other support necessary for promotion and tenure."

Personal issues might also serve as barriers to the education and training of health care providers, according to the IOM (2002) report. The personal values or biases that health care professionals hold might tempt them to form conclusions and assumptions about their patients based on socioeconomic status and lifestyle choices that might not be validated by the evidence. The report states, "In some cases, for example, close identification by a health professional with a patient's lifestyle or socioeconomic class produces an assumption that no violence is occurring, whereas distinct differences in lifestyle and class produce expectations of violence." The report also explains that "some personal values regarding family violence and difficulty in addressing it may stem from personal experiences with victimization." Ellis (1999) found that 57.5 percent of nurses in an urban trauma center reported experiences with family violence, and that feelings of vulnerability related to personal experiences with abuse can pose challenges to the training of health care professionals. However, the report clarified, studies of nurses and physicians have found no significant association between having a personal history of violence and reported screening behavior for IPV (Moore et al., 1998; Parsons et al., 1995; Rodriguez, Bauer, McLoughlin, & Grumbach, 1999). Saunders and Kindy (1993) found that having personally known a victim of violence has been positively associated with an improved response to abuse. As inconclusive as the impact of personal experiences of violence might be on health care providers, some evidence suggests that vicarious traumatization occurs among health care providers when they encounter victims of violence and take their histories (McCann & Pearlman, 1990; Neumann & Gamble, 1995; Talbot, Manton, & Dunn, 1992).

The IOM (2002) report made the following conclusions about the current state of professional training on family violence:

- Although family violence is understood to be widespread across the United States and to have significant health consequences, its full effects on society and the health care system have not been adequately studied or documented.
- Variation in the definitions, data sources, and methods used in research on family violence has resulted in inconsistent and unclear evidence about its magnitude and severity, as well as its effects on the health care system and society.
- Curricula on family violence for health professionals do exist, but the content is incomplete, instruction time is generally minimal, the content and teaching methods vary, and the issue is not well integrated throughout educational experience. Moreover, studies indicate that health professionals and students in the health professions often perceive curricula on family violence to be inadequate and ineffective.
- Evaluation of the effects of training has received insufficient attention. Few studies investigate whether curricula on family violence are having the desired impact on the delivery of health care to family violence victims. When evaluations are done, they often do not utilize the experimental designs necessary to provide an adequate understanding of effects.
- In addition to effective training on family violence, a supportive environment appears to be critically important to producing desirable outcomes.
- Core competencies for health professional training on family violence can be developed and tested based on similarities in the content of current training programs. The important content areas include identification, assessment, and documentation of abuse and neglect; interventions to ensure victim safety; recognition of culture and values as factors affecting family violence; the understanding of applicable legal and forensic responsibilities; and prevention.
- Existing education theories about behavior change suggest useful teaching methods and approaches to planning interventions for health care professionals tailored to the issue of family violence. These approaches include ways of changing behavior and practice in health care delivery systems, the use of techniques to address

professionals' biases toward victims, and the use of health care outcome measurement.
- Challenges to developing, implementing, and sustaining training programs for health professionals on family violence include the nature of accreditation, licensure, and certification; characteristics of health professional organizations; views of stakeholders' groups; attitudes of individual health care providers; and the existence of mandatory reporting laws and education requirements.

Funding for research, education development and testing, and curricular evaluation on family violence is fragmented, and information about funding sources is not systematically available. No consistent federal sources of support for education research on family violence appear to exist.

The *Confronting Chronic Neglect* report (IOM, 2002) made the following recommendations:

1. The Secretary of Health and Human Services should be responsible for establishing new multidisciplinary education and research centers with the goal of advancing scholarship and practice in family violence. These centers should be charged with conducting research on the magnitude and impact of family violence on society and the health care system, conducting research on training, and addressing concerns regarding the lack of compatibility in current research. The ultimate goal of these centers will be to develop training programs based on sound scientific evidence that prepare health professionals to respond to family violence.
2. Health professional organizations and health professional educators, including faculty in academic health centers, should develop and provide guidance to their members, constituents, institutions, and other stakeholders. This guidance should address competency areas for health professional curricula on family violence, effective strategies to teach about family violence, approaches to overcoming barriers to training on family violence, and approaches to promoting and sustaining behavior changes by health care providers.
3. Health care delivery systems and training settings, particularly academic health care centers and federally qualified health clinics and community health centers, should assume greater responsibility for developing, testing, and evaluating innovative training models or programs.
4. Federal agencies and other financiers of education programs should create expectations and provide support for the evaluation of curricula on family violence for health care professionals. Curricula must be evaluated to determine their impact on the practices of health care providers and their effects on victims of violence. Evaluation must employ rigorous methods to ensure accurate, reliable, and useful results.

The report did acknowledge that nursing curricula are not altogether devoid of information on IPV-related issues. Woodtli and Breslin (1996) reported that 100 percent of 298 schools queried about their curricula indicated that they presented violence-related content in their programs; however, just 53 percent felt that this content was adequately addressed. Tilden et al. (1994) paint a different picture by showing that just one third of more than 1,500 practicing clinicians in six disciplines, including nursing, said they had received no instruction in family violence. The report adds, "Attention to IPV in the literature on nursing research and practice appears to be increasing, accompanied by professional association and curriculum development. Curriculum content on IPV has increased with official nursing organization attention to the issue," including from the ENA, ANA, and others.

15.1.1 The Most Visible Forensic Nursing Education: SANE Training

Not surprisingly, the subspecialty of forensic nursing that continues to be the most visible, sexual assault examination, also tends to be the discipline that has received the most attention to its curriculum needs. Interestingly, much of the discussion of forensic nursing education and training is still couched in terms of sexual assault and does not mention other forensic nursing disciplines, including death investigation, corrections nursing, psychiatric forensic nursing, and so on. Albeit quaint in its seemingly naive "discovery" of this branch of forensic nursing, the aforementioned AHRQ report to Congress does highlight the field in general by remarking, "The nursing profession is moving to develop new academic programs which train students to perform evidentiary examinations for victims of sexual assault, child abuse, elder abuse and domestic violence." It continues to explain that a handful of colleges and universities offer graduate, undergraduate, or certificate programs in forensic nursing. The report states, "The newest program was developed through the nursing and law schools at Duquesne University in Pittsburgh, Pa., which offers both a master's of science in nursing (forensic nursing) or a post-master's certificate in forensic nursing."

The report explains to the uninformed and the uninitiated that, "A training program that is still growing rapidly and bringing substantial change to the field is the sexual assault nurse examiner (SANE) program." It explains further:

> The growth of these programs across the country has established forensic nurses as the dominant provider of medical evidentiary examinations in many communities. SANE programs are often integrated into a Sexual Assault Response Team (SART) model for the delivery of emergency medical care to survivors of sexual assault. Within a local community, SARTs bring together providers, law enforcement, prosecution, and victim advocacy and public health organizations to promote more coordinated, comprehensive, effective, and efficient care. In addition to its multidisciplinary focus, the SART model features use of specially trained forensic nurses who conduct evidentiary exams, most often with the supervision of a physician medical director.

The AHRQ report further explains that the basic SANE program is available to trained RNs, and offers certification as a nurse examiner on completion of classroom and clinical training. Typically, programs require 40 or more hours of classroom instruction, along with clinical training and subsequent continuing education.

Sharon Crowley, MN, RN, acknowledges the high visibility of SANEs in the field, but says she is concerned about the depth of the average training sessions offered to prospective examiners. "I took the SANE preparation course and was surprised that there was no material on genital trauma during the entire four-hour presentation," she says:

> I took this course, not because I was interested in becoming certified, but because I wanted to see what things SANEs were being taught these days. Isn't the evaluation of genital trauma something we are supposed to be experts in? Yet the subject wasn't discussed, other than a recommendation to look at a few books on the topic. I didn't take the test, so I don't know if the exam had addressed genital trauma, but if the course didn't even cover it . . . it's worrisome that an important subject like that is not being covered in a basic curriculum. A curriculum means nothing unless it continually evolves and addresses new thought in the field.

Cari Caruso, RN, SANE-A, reports that she received comprehensive examiner training, but that not all courses are equal, adding:

> As far as SANE courses go, I think that mine was the best course ever, and I hope other courses measure up to it. Mine was five days long, with 40 hours of training, plus a 40-hour preceptorship, which I had to complete before I earned my certificate of completion. Nowadays, they are leaving preceptorships up to the students. I am concerned that not all SANE courses across the United States demonstrate the same degree of rigorous coursework and training.

The AHRQ report also explains that "many programs offered on sexual assault or domestic violence provide students with an overview of issues related to violence and abuse, but few are intended to teach skills related to evidentiary examinations and therefore most lack technical content related to forensic evidence collection. The emphasis tends to be on screening, management, and referral of victims to social service organizations; however, the programs vary in this regard." For example, the AHRQ report points to the VAWA of 2000, which amended the Stop Violence Against Women Formula Grants Program, administered by the U.S. Department of Justice to add a purpose area for training of sexual assault forensic medical examiners in the collection and preservation of evidence, provision of expert testimony, treatment of trauma, and prevention related to sexual assault.

The report commented:

> In general, however, the lack of detailed material on sexual assault and training on performing medical evidentiary examinations in programs on family violence is somewhat puzzling, given that rape is a common component of family violence. Most sexual assaults are perpetrated by husbands, boyfriends and other current or former intimate partners. Yet, a review of materials on family violence will reveal that rape, child molestation, or other sexual assault is seldom mentioned in screening or management of patients who are victims of family violence. Rather, coursework tends to focus on physical assault, broken arms, bruises, concussions, strangulation, and the like, and future safety planning and community resources. Evidence collection skills tend to be limited to a mention of the usefulness of taking notes on victim statements and use of a body map or photograph to document injuries.

Aside from the issue of whether the content related to sexual assault and evidentiary examination is adequate, the AHRQ report noted that "many of the programs offered do not appear to be solidly constructed," and added, "There are few scientific underpinnings to support the content, instructional methodologies, or extent of education now being provided in these training programs . . . Curricula content is incomplete, instruction time is generally minimal, the content and teaching methods vary and the issue is not well integrated throughout their educational experiences."

The report recommends that core competencies for health professional training on family violence be developed and tested, and concludes that the core competencies needed include the identification, assessment, and documentation of abuse and neglect. They point to the limited evidence base in family violence generally. Additional barriers to development of improved academic training programs include a lack of interest among faculty, competing pressures for curriculum time, and the limited availability of developmental resources.

15.1.2 Clinical Practice Guidelines: Tools for Practitioners

Professional organizations or quality improvement bodies develop clinical guidelines, professional standards, and practice protocols to help guide practitioners toward improved health outcomes. They are distinct from educational programs that are part of a formal academic training program. According to the AHRQ report, "The development of guidelines and protocols has grown in recent years as evidence-based medicine has become a dominant force in the way medicine is practiced." The report added:

> At the heart of evidence-based practice is the systematic review of a body of research which can evaluate what clinical practices work best, for whom, and at what cost. It is only possible, however, if there is a body of rigorous study to support conclusions. In the case of medical evidentiary examinations, the necessary evidence base is sparse. In reality, most medical care is not solely based on evidence from carefully designed studies, and variations in practice are common. Much medicine derives from experience and common wisdom handed down; where clear evidence is not available, practitioners rely on experience-based clinical judgment. However, in the last two decades or so, the movement to evidence-based practice has brought about further improvements in the outcomes of care provided, and works to conserve resources by eliminating unnecessary or ineffective health care services.

In general, the report said that lack of research on the outcomes and effectiveness of the components of the evidentiary examination process

> can be expected to hamper efforts to improve existing training programs and establish effective practice protocols. A well-written guideline presents a synthesis of the available scientific evidence on a topic relevant to clinical practice. Ideally, the synthesis is presented in a structured format that facilitates the ability of providers and patients to make decisions about health care services to be provided. To be viewed as solid and reliable guidance, the guideline must be based on a systematic literature search and review of existing scientific evidence published in peer-reviewed journals.

15.1.3 Guidelines for Performing Medical Evidentiary Examinations

Although a number of states and locations have adopted protocols or clinical guidelines for conducting medical evidentiary or forensic examinations related to sexual assault and child abuse, few are based on systematic reviews of the literature, nor have they been compared or tested in terms of outcomes for patients and the purposes of criminal justice, according to the AHRQ report. The largest national repository of clinical guidelines is the National Guideline Clearinghouse (NGC; www.ngc.gov), an Internet-based, collaborative public resource that is sponsored by AHRQ in partnership with the AMA and the American Association of Health Plans (AAHP). It accepts science-based clinical care guidelines developed under the auspices of medical specialty associations, professional societies, government agencies, public or private organizations, and integrated health care organizations and plans. The science that supports those guidelines that are accepted varies according to the topic and the available research base, but each is evaluated by the NGC to assess whether development of the guideline was based on a rigorous scientific process. As of late 2002, approximately six guidelines in the NGC referenced forensic or medical evidentiary examination; two are specifically intended to guide examiners in how to conduct such examinations: "Practice Parameters for the Forensic Evaluation of Children and Adolescents Who May Have Been Physically or Sexually Abused," issued by the AACAP, and "Practice Parameters for Child Custody Evaluation," issued by the AACAP. The other guidelines are less specific about procedures related to performing evidentiary examinations, but describe key elements in a general way: "National Guideline for the Management of Adult Victims of Sexual Assault" by the Association for Genitourinary Medicine and Medical Society for the Study of Venereal Diseases, "Care of the Adolescent Sexual Assault Victim" by the AAP Committee on Adolescence, "Practice Guideline for Psychiatric Evaluation of Adults" by the American Psychiatric Association, and "Domestic Violence" by the Institute for Clinical Systems Improvement.

15.1.4 Professional Policies and Standards

In addition to guidelines, specialty-specific professional organizations and accrediting bodies often develop clinical protocols, training materials, professional standards, and policy statements to assist their members. Many organizations have policies and protocols related to identification, treatment, and or reporting of family violence, but few are specific in terms of the mandate of this report: training of health professionals to perform medical evidentiary examinations. Among the organizations that appear to have developed materials or policies that are specifically related to sexual assault, child molestation, or medical evidentiary examinations are the following:

- American Academy of Pediatrics (AAP). The AAP's Committee on Child Abuse and Neglect (COCAN) has developed an excellent series of practice guidelines, policy statements, and technical bulletins that focus on the physical, sexual, and mental abuse and neglect of children and adolescents. The journal *Pediatrics* published a guideline in 1999 outlining the basic skills needed when examining a child for possible abuse, including details on taking history, performing a physical examination, recording data, and treatment. The AAP recommends that pediatric residency training programs and continuing medical education programs incorporate education on family violence and child abuse. Resources developed by AAP include guidelines and teaching materials related to care for the adolescent sexual assault victim, CD-ROM courses on child abuse and other self-teaching materials, and technical information on oral and dental aspects related to child abuse and neglect, a joint product of the AAP and the American Academy of Pediatric Dentistry.

- American Association of Critical Care Nurses (AACN). The AACN recommends that schools of nursing ensure there is a curriculum with content related to domestic violence across the life span. They also recommend that students be provided opportunities to practice in clinical settings to learn screening, assessment, and caring for victims of violence. It is unclear whether training related to caring for victims of sexual assault is encompassed by this policy statement.
- American College of Emergency Physicians (ACEP). The ACEP has actively sought to develop policies and protocols related to sexual assault that will be helpful to frontline health care providers. In 1997, the ACEP and more than a dozen partner organizations worked collaboratively to develop a handbook on the evaluation and management of sexually assaulted patients. The handbook addresses the medical and emotional needs of the patient, as well as the forensic requirements of the criminal justice system. The effort involved more than a dozen public and private health and law enforcement organizations, including the American College of Obstetricians and Gynecologists (ACOG), the American Medical Association (AMA), Centers for Disease Control and Prevention (CDC), the FBI, the International Association of Chiefs of Police, the Emergency Nurses Association (ENA), International Association of Forensic Nurses (IAFN), and the American Society of Crime Laboratory Directors. Advocacy organizations included the National Alliance of Sexual Assault Coalitions, the National Network of Children's Advocacy Center, and STOP Violence Against Women. Although there were areas of disagreement among the participants, the resulting document, the *Evaluation and Management of the Sexually Assaulted or Sexually Abused Patient* (ACEP, 1999), provides a basic protocol for conducting medical evidentiary examinations of adult, pediatric, and adolescent patients. It also includes technical assistance tools such as information on how to develop a coordinated community response plan, a guide to development and operation of a SANE program, and a list of key organizations in the field. The materials developed included a guide to federal grant programs related to domestic violence, sexual assault, and stalking. Most of the federal grant programs at the time were applicable to development of community sexual assault prevention programs, and training for law enforcement and social services personnel. Among the programs are grants to states to provide limited compensation for the medical expenses of sexual assault and other victims of crime. There was no federal assistance for development of curricula, training, or forensic capabilities associated with evidentiary examinations. The ACEP Board of Directors recommended in 1997 that EDs have written protocols on the recognition and treatment of elder abuse, which include appropriately educated staff and referral mechanisms. Notably, the ACEP opposes mandatory reporting of elder abuse and neglect, but encourages voluntary referrals. Other policy statements seek to educate providers about recognition of child abuse and family violence.
- American College of Obstetricians and Gynecologists (ACOG). ACOG has mounted a sustained effort to educate their membership about the identification and management of intimate partner violence and sexual assault among patients. They publish materials designed to promote effective screening and management of patients, including a slide lecture presentation, available in hard copy and CD-ROM, to be used in training residents, fellows, medical students, and other health care providers (http://www.cdc.gov/nccdphp/drh/violence/ipdvp.htm), and offer related continuing education sessions in conjunction with their annual meeting. ACOG also maintains updated information on its Web site. A technical bulletin for members provides practical direction related to the incidence of sexual assault, use of assessment kits, conduct of a medical evaluation, legal concerns, patient counseling, and follow-up treatment.
- American Dental Association (ADA). The ADA recommends development of educational programs for training dental providers on how to

recognize and report abuse and neglect of children, women, elders, people with developmental disabilities, physically challenged, and others who might be the object of abuse or neglect. It also seeks educational collaborations with other professional organizations, including the AMA and the APA.

- American Medical Association (AMA). The AMA publishes and offers for sale a series of diagnostic and treatment guidelines that address the basics of a patient interview and examination, as well as documentation, legal issues, testimony, and trends in treatment and prevention. Specific guidelines are available on child physical abuse and neglect, child sexual abuse, domestic violence, and sexual assault. The guideline on elder abuse is less specific but also includes a discussion of ethical and legal issues around detection and reporting. The organizational visibility of family violence was raised significantly in 2000, when the AMA House of Delegates approved a resolution calling for a committee of representatives from the National Advisory Council on Violence and Abuse and its Committee on Medical Education to identify the knowledge and skills needed by physicians to identify and respond to violence and abuse, to identify where in medical education these skills could be included, and to investigate continuing education needs. The resolution also called on the AMA to advocate for hospital and community support of violence survivor programs, as well as for equitable coverage and reimbursement for all health and mental health related to family violence.
- American Professional Society on the Abuse of Children (APSAC). APSAC has five data-based guidelines on key areas of practice related to child maltreatment. The guidelines were developed by expert task forces, and then reviewed by other experts, legal counsel, and APSAC leadership. The guidelines address psychological evaluation of suspected sexual abuse in children, descriptive terminology in child sexual abuse in medical evaluations, use of anatomical dolls in child sexual abuse assessments, photographic documentation of child abuse, and psychological evaluation of suspected psychological maltreatment of children and adolescents APSAC also offers weeklong forensic interview training clinics with both classroom and clinic-based sessions. Topics include forensic interviewing techniques, legal issues, and other practical skills needed for both investigative and therapeutic purposes. The training targets mental health professionals, as well as professionals in CPS, law enforcement, social services, medicine, and law. The guidelines have not been systematically tested or compared in terms of how well they support the dual purposes of a medical evidentiary examination: providing medical care and collecting evidence for use in prosecution.
- American Psychological Association (APA). The APA has developed a guide on the education and training of psychologists on issues of child abuse and neglect that is designed to facilitate development of semester-long courses. The association has developed educational materials for graduate-level programs as well.
- American Society of Testing Materials (ASTM). The ASTM has a standard guide for sexual assault investigation, examination, and evidence collection that calls for using trained forensic examiners in the setting of a multidisciplinary team. The ASTM guide requires facilities to have written procedures for providing information on the treatment plan, evidentiary and medical examinations, documentation and evidence collection, transmittal of evidence, and the chain of custody and postexamination procedures. Agencies conducting child sexual assault investigations are required to develop special protocols appropriate for the examination of children.
- Joint Commission on Accreditation of Healthcare Organizations (JCAHO). The JCAHO is a nonprofit entity that evaluates and accredits more than 17,000 hospitals, health care networks, home care, and other health care organizations in the United States. Its guidelines require that hospital organizations have observable, objective criteria for identifying victims of physical assault, rape or other sexual assault, domestic abuse, and abuse of elders and children. In addition, the hospital is required to have a staff education plan and to maintain a list of organizations that provide or arrange for assessment and care of alleged or suspected victims of abuse and neglect, to aid in making appropriate referrals. JCAHO specifies that medical assessment of abuse victims must be conducted with the consent of the patient; meet legal responsibility for the collection, retention, assessment, and safe keeping of evidentiary material; and include the notification and release of information to the proper authority when legally required.

15.1.5 Recommendations for Evidence-Based Practice

The AHRQ makes several broad recommendations for the further consolidation and enhancement of evidence-based practice. The first recommendation is to promote cross-collaboration to enhance research, education, and practice. The agency says that efforts to improve the quality and outcomes of medical evidentiary examinations, for example, "could be facilitated by consolidating and enhancing the existing knowledge base through the promotion of cross-collaboration and communication among the various disciplinary and organizational entities involved in education, research, and practice." These efforts, according to the AHRQ, are hindered by "a lack of a coherent body of research in the field"; specifically, a comprehensive evidence base to provide an integrated framework for what is taught to students and providers. The AHRQ adds that this problem is related to all forms of violence, but is particularly acute for the evidence base related to sexual assault. There are several contributing factors. Support for research available from federal, state, foundation, or private industry sources is "sparse and fragmented," according to the AHRQ. It states:

> Thus, sexual assault as a field does not represent a viable career path for many academic clinicians who might otherwise be attracted to it. In addition, there is limited demand for teaching faculty who are expert in sexual assault. There are few courses, and little prestige connected with this expertise within the academic setting. This, combined with meager research funding, has created a dearth of experienced researchers and university-based clinical faculty with the skills needed to advance the field. For many, work in the field of sexual assault is as much a personal cause as it is an academic pursuit. Further, greater collaboration and communication is needed among researchers and practitioners in order to integrate, consolidate, and enhance the baseline descriptive information available on issues related to quality, outcomes, cost and access to medical evidentiary examinations and related treatment services.

To improve education and training programs, the AHRQ advises educators to consider the following questions:

- Who is currently performing medical evidentiary examinations for victims of rape and other sexual assaults? How are they trained? What services do they provide? What are the variations in practice, and in the related quality, effectiveness, and outcomes of care?
- What is the experience of victims, including the types of settings where they receive care, waiting times, and access to services? To what extent are special provisions made for children who are sexually molested?
- What are the immediate and long-term costs associated with sexual assault, including the cost to providers and the health care system of an involvement with legal proceedings?

The AHRQ also examined the relationship among the services that are provided; the training received by providers; and the outcomes, costs, and effectiveness of care. "Decisions about when and under what circumstances an evidentiary examination should be performed continue to be controversial, as is the issue of who decides," the AHRQ report states:

> Sometimes the decision is based on the believability of the victim and/or the likelihood of prosecution, as assessed by the law enforcement officer on the scene. In addition, technological innovations are changing the practice of forensic science. The time frame during which useable evidence can be recovered is being extended and new techniques are improving the range and reliability of other testing. The assessment of under what circumstances examinations should be undertaken is further complicated by the fact that examination results are frequently not actually used in criminal proceedings. Arrests may not be possible or assailants may plead guilty, although examination results may increase the likelihood of a guilty plea.

The AHRQ also examined health care provider training and preparedness as it relates to its usefulness in subsequent legal proceedings of evidence from evidentiary examinations. The agency observes:

> A few studies seem to indicate that evidentiary examinations do not strongly influence the outcomes of court proceedings, but that outcomes tend to turn on factors such as the credibility of the victim and the demeanor of the accused. Other studies show a selective impact (i.e., that parts of the examination are useful). Still others conclude that examination results provide pivotal information for prosecutors. In particular, DNA results are often key, resulting in the conviction or confession of some accused persons, but also conclusively exonerating other suspects.

Because evidentiary examinations are emotionally difficult for most patients to undergo, as well as costly, further study is needed on questions such as these:

- When are evidentiary exams indicated? How is the decision about whether an evidentiary exam is conducted affected by the judgments of police and prosecutors?
- What contributes to their effectiveness both in terms of meeting patient care needs and leading to successful prosecutions?
- How are services best organized and delivered?

- What are the costs and effectiveness of different models of care?
- What is the impact of enhanced training on practice and outcomes?

A variety of strategies have been recommended by experts in the field to consolidate, integrate, and enhance the infrastructure for collaboration and communication in research and training on issues related to the examination and treatment of sexual assault. The IOM report on training for health professionals in family violence recommends development of multidisciplinary education and research centers that would be charged initially with conducting research to do the following:

- Understand the magnitude and impact of family violence on society and the health care system.
- Evaluate existing training curricula and educational approaches.
- Expand scientific research on the magnitude of health effects and effectiveness of interventions for family violence.

The vision is that, over time, such centers would develop training programs based on scientific evidence, and work with others to test, evaluate, and disseminate education and training programs. They might also provide training directly and undertake a range of other activities to advance the field. The idea of creating centers of excellence to focus on work in a specific field has been used in many areas with considerable success. It is an approach that, perhaps as part of centers with a more general focus on women's health or family violence, could be useful for advancing the training and care provided to victims of sexual assault. Support for such centers could come from a variety of sources including existing federal programs, states (which already support educational programs in state schools of medicine, dentistry and nursing), and private foundations. The California Medical Training Center at the University of California, Davis (UC Davis) is an example of a comprehensive program created by a state. A research and educational focus on examination and treatment of sexual assault could also be built into other current multidisciplinary programs with a women's health or family violence focus funded by federal agencies such as the Department of Health and Human Services, the Department of Justice, and the Department of Defense.

The AHRQ says that there are few existing opportunities for individuals to advance their skills in the field of sexual assault examination and treatment, but adds, "such opportunities could be enhanced by modifying or supplementing existing fellowship and training programs at the state or federal level, and encourage additional foundation support for such training. For example, there are existing research fellowships—public and private—that tend to focus on disease-specific topics, that could be opened to persons interested in the field of sexual assault."

A second recommendation by the AHRQ is to encourage federal, state, and community involvement in the development, standardization, and dissemination of evidence-based training materials and protocols. The Department of Justice has played an active role in refinement and dissemination of SANE programs, so there is precedence for the federal government to encourage development of specialized curricula and training programs through its role as coordinator. When legislative authority and funds are available, it can also provide financial support for forensic-related special projects. As well, under the VAWA of 2000, the U.S. Attorney General is required to develop national recommendations for a protocol for sexual assault forensic examinations, and a number of states are developing practice protocols and standardized evidence collection kits and forms. The exercise of developing national recommendations will require a comparison of protocol components, with the goal of identifying optimum approaches agreed on by practitioners in the field. The AHRQ says that a useful follow-on project would be to compare and test alternative models, and to convene a group of national experts to establish a research agenda that targets areas of uncertainty. In partnership with state, federal, and professional organizations, community organizations can also contribute by providing training and awareness building for health care organizations.

A third recommendation by the AHRQ is to encourage access to evidence-based training and education through the use of distance learning and other medical technologies. The AHRQ elaborates further:

> A relatively untapped resource is the use of federal and state distance learning facilities associated with colleges, universities, federal facilities, and law enforcement to provide rural and small town hospitals and professionals with relevant training programs over time. Studies show that one-time continuing education programs are likely to have little impact, but consistent reinforcement and interaction with peers can change practice. Problems with the compatibility of live video training hookups may place limits on what can be done, though the possibilities have not yet been explored in a systematic way across the country. These programs need to be assessed, and a source of funding identified. Since it is not feasible for every physician and every nurse to acquire and maintain skill levels in an area as complex and changing as forensic medicine, other approaches are needed to assure skills are available to sexual assault patients in rural and small towns by fostering regional capabilities and training.

The AHRQ is pushing for improvement in the organization and delivery of care for victims of sexual assault and other forms of violence, and advocates for better coordination at the community and state levels among law enforcement, social service organizations, specially trained health care providers, state and local public health agencies, mental health providers, and community advocates. The agency backs SART programs:

> advocated by many and adopted in an increasing number of communities, and brings together police, prosecutors, nurses, physicians, hospital administrators, public health agencies, mental health providers, and victim advocates to collaborate on a sustained basis in providing coordinated care to sexual assault victims. A more coordinated approach can help minimize burdens for the victim associated with long waits at the hospital, repetitive police and medical interviews, poorly trained or inexperienced providers, inappropriate or inadequate facilities, and uncoordinated treatment and follow-up services. Coordination is thought to help overcome fragmentation of resources and offer improved efficiency and effectiveness in the delivery of needed services to sexual assault victims. Community organizations can play an important role in contributing to the viability of coordinated community response efforts, by providing services as well as training and awareness-building activities.

The AHRQ also encourages greater investment in the facilities and equipment that forensic practitioners so desperately need. It comments:

> There have been quantum leaps in the sophistication of camera and examination equipment and tests and testing procedures. This has led to sharp disparities in the quality and accessibility of services from city to city, state to state, and between urban and rural areas. At the same time, there has been little investment in upgrading crime labs that process evidentiary material, and in the training for health and law enforcement personnel in the use of technical advances. Many of the improvements available have great potential for extending consultation services to rural and isolated areas. For instance, in the Sonoma Valley, a rural area of California, a local hospital has purchased digital cameras and colposcopes that link directly to medical consultants at the UC Davis California Training Center. It is possible for nurse examiners to show consultants images of victims, and then discuss interpretation and follow-up with university-based experts. Consultants can then also provide expert testimony on issues as needed, and more consultations can be offered because the need for travel time is less.

The AHRQ has picked up on forensic professionals' concern about the use of digital cameras related to the difficulty of detecting alterations. The agency observes:

Digital cameras are appealing because images can be transmitted quickly to law enforcement and technical consultants. The image clarity is also greater, especially in poor light conditions and for persons of dark complexion. They enable the kind of distance consultation described above. However, some jurisdictions prohibit use of images from digital cameras as evidence. Hospitals and forensic investigative teams should explore this issue before investing in equipment and training. In addition to the security issues, diffusion is also hampered by the initial high cost of equipment and training.

15.2 FORENSIC NURSES SPEAK OUT ON THEIR EDUCATION AND TRAINING NEEDS

No matter the specialty, forensic nurses agree that a number of critical issues related to education, training, and professional development go unresolved. These issues include the lack of a core curriculum, lagging development of forensic nursing-centric programs, lack of standardization of coursework, lack of clearly defined career paths, and friction between groups of nurses pushing for different levels of credentials with which to practice forensic nursing. There is growing debate focused on whether baccalaureate, graduate, or postgraduate education is sufficient, as well as differing opinions on whether a degree in forensic nursing or forensic science better prepares students for the rigors of the work. Sharon Crowley comments:

> I think that dividing into opposing camps is an unfortunate development. I believe that as nurses, we need to learn everything we can in order to do our jobs, and everything else is secondary. Personally, I don't care where I get the education and training, as long as I get it, and as long as it is relevant. I don't feel strongly that I have to get a certain degree in a certain area of the field in order to be the most prepared. If I want to be a chemist and I'm sure a bachelor's degree in chemistry will fill the requirement, that's what I need to get; however, I don't know if that's true in nursing. We have always had to get our basic requirements and kind of fly by the seat of our pants and find various educational offerings that fill our needs after that. There has never been a graduate-degree program that filled all the needs for every nursing job that might come up; mine certainly didn't. I've always had to be creative in my quest for education and training.
>
> I think you have to find a program to address your personal needs. There are the basics, such as learning how to think critically and how to do basic research, which form the foundation. But quibbling over what kinds of degrees and from which schools and in which disciplines, well, I think that is stupid and self-defeating.

She advocates for an education that provides students with a broad perspective:

> Nurses need a firm foundation in all of the disciplines. Then they need to be the kind of individuals who can be self-motivated and think on their feet and continue their specific training. It's ongoing; as a nurse you must be a lifelong student. The education and training needed to stay

current in our field is never going to end because it's too specialized... and it's only going to get more so.

On the other hand, I don't want to see people come out of school without training in traditional nursing concepts, such as caring for people. We can't lose that human touch that has made nursing such a special springboard for forensic science. Nursing is so unique and of all the people who deal with forensics, we are the only ones who can provide both the gift of human intervention and science. No other participant in the medico-legal community does both, so we are fortunate to have this responsibility. However, that means we must ensure that our education and training keeps pace with the times and scientific development in our field.

Constance Morrison acknowledges that although forensic nursing might still be in its infancy curriculum-wise:

That's frequently the way it is with disciplines which are on the cutting edge and require time to establish formal education and credentialing parameters. We have a ways to go, but I think we are making many important strides across the nation. I can point to a number of excellent schools, including Quinnipiac University in Connecticut, Fitchburg State College in Massachusetts, Gonzaga University in Washington State, and Beth-El in Colorado; in addition, there are a number of highly recognized and accredited online programs like Kaplan which offer certificate programs in forensic nursing. I think that forensic nursing, and the need for education and training opportunities, is catching on. Could the delivery of education programs be faster? Yes, but nursing has been a profession for a couple hundred years and forensic nursing has really only been recognized since the 1990s, so we're right on the cusp. Sure forensic nursing has caught on in England, but how long has England been around? If you look at it, we are in our birth stage here in the United States, as is our curriculum. I think we have come a long way for being so new. Are we moving fast enough? Well, probably not, but we are moving, which is the important thing right now. We're certainly not standing still.

One of the most pressing concerns cited by forensic nurses is a growing number of courses that overpromise and underdeliver on their curriculum and employment prospects on completion of courses. "There are suddenly a lot of forensic nursing programs popping up everywhere," observes Meliss Vessier-Batchen:

I think potential students should be aware that not all of these courses are good, and not all of them are bad, but that they should invest the time to investigate the coursework and the school that is offering it, whether it's a degree program or a certificate program. They should determine if the school is accredited, and examine its reputation, as well as look at the costs and the demands on your time—these are the things many people don't consider, especially when it comes to online courses. Online courses require a very disciplined, very structured type of personality and a lot of people don't realize this kind of program is not for them until they have sunk money into it and are not getting what they need. Nurses must consider whether or not they will have sufficient job opportunities when they get out of school, and realize that no school can guarantee a job.

Also concerned about fly-by-night programs is Janet Barber, who notes:

The biggest disservice being done to forensic nurses are by institutions which offer educational programs in which the student pays considerable sums of money for courses that are virtually worthless. There are a lot of forensic nursing or forensic science programs out there now, and I tell students that when they sign up for a program, they must look at who has been in the program, who is teaching it, and what credentials they have. They must also look at the fair market value of what they are getting for the tuition dollars they are spending. They must ask the school, "What am I going to have at the end of this program and what is it going to enable me to do that I can't do right now?" Frequently, nurses do not know the difference between getting a certificate and being certified, and there is a big difference. I think there should be a disclaimer attached to these courses that somehow says, "Even though the university is granting you, at the end of this course, a certificate in forensic nursing, this certificate only says you have taken these courses; it does not prepare you for any kind of licensure or certification, and it doesn't guarantee that you are going to get a job." Nurses need to know that any course is not a guaranteed meal ticket. I don't want any student to sign up for a program and then say, "I got my certificate in forensic nursing so I can instantly get a job as a forensic nurse." That's not going to happen. What's really heartbreaking is that many nurses go to great lengths to earn various credentials and then they find out those credentials are worthless. It is important up front to explain to students which courses lead to degrees, and which courses are orientation courses which help them to identify what they want to do in life or which nursing specialty they may want to pursue. If a student tells me they really want to be a death investigator, the first thing I say is, "This course is a beginning course to whet your appetite; now I am going to refer you to a course where you can get a legitimate credential which will help you to get a job." Students must be able to discern the difference between a course that introduces them to forensic nursing, and a course that will actually improve their skills. Some educational programs don't make that distinction as clearly as they should, so nurses should investigate these courses so they aren't disappointed by false expectations. I don't want some poor soul to spend a couple hundred dollars on a three-hour course, expecting to come out on the other side with a piece of paper that

> they will take to their local hospital and say, "I want to be your forensic nurse and here is my credential."

Cari Caruso agrees that a number of forensic nursing certificate programs have cropped up lately, and says there is nothing wrong with this kind of entrepreneurship, except that she expects truth in advertising:

> I'm not so much as suspicious of these online programs as I am hopeful that they will truly teach students what they need to know about forensic nursing, and that they will provide specific, focused education. I hope people are not going in blindly, getting forensic degrees or certificates willy-nilly. I do want to say that I believe there is no education that will ever hurt you. I think it is important to attend as many seminars and programs and classes as possible to keep your skills fresh and current. Education is extremely meaningful to forensic nurses; the more relevant material they can learn and absorb . . . it's going to be nothing but helpful to them. I think it comes down to nurses investigating their education options and making wise choices.

Linda Ledray also expresses concern about programs that create forensic nurses overnight:

> My fear is that there is going to be a lot of marginal forensic nursing programs developing. One organization, which offers a two-and-a-half day course, says "Pass a test and be certified as a forensic nurse." That's the type of thing people are afraid will happen within forensic nursing. So a forensic nursing core curriculum is one attempt to try to forestall that. It's disappointing that some programs are only in it to make money, not provide adequate training.

Another issue of concern is nurses being willing to go the distance for the sake of their own personal and professional edification. Nurses must realize that much of their education will be an investment in themselves and their future, and they must be willing to foot the bill for their training. Cari Caruso reflects on her training to be a SANE:

> Years ago, there weren't very many classes to attend. It was the first time I ever spent that much money, and the first time I ever went far away for a class. But I thought of it as an important investment in myself and in my future. Now, when I hear nurses complain that their hospital won't pay for their classes, I think to myself, "This is your thing . . . if you want this, you go and get it." Maybe it's paying one's dues, but I think it made me work harder and be more dedicated because it did come out of my own pocket.

Paying one's dues is not always monetary; Caruso says nurses must understand what they are getting into when they pursue the field of forensic nursing. "There were a few nurses who worked for me who decided this line of work wasn't for them," she says:

> They didn't like the pager going off at three in the morning, and they didn't like the idea of being on call. I admit it took some adjustment. I used to try to plan my life around my on-call time, and now, I'm essentially always on call, so my life has to go on despite my hectic schedule. There was a time I would say to myself, "I am on call, so I won't go to the supermarket because I don't want to get caught with a cart full of groceries if I have to leave." Now, I just have to go ahead and do my thing. If I get called, that's the priority. One of the by-products of the job is how you feel about it; you either love it or you don't. At a recent presentation I was making, someone asked me how I deal with the feelings of burnout on the job. I replied, "I don't get burnout." I have great relationships with my staff, with law enforcement and the crime labs, and I have a very good person at home; plus, I set boundaries between my work and my personal life, and that helps to continually renew my enthusiasm for my work and enthusiasm for lifelong learning.

Some nurses say the forensic nursing curriculum should address issues related to the degree of self-knowledge, self-motivation, and self-discipline that forensic nursing exacts from its practitioners, as well as time spent on occupational forecasts for the various specialties. "As a Southern California regional representative for the International Association of Forensic Nurses (IAFN), I receive many phone calls from people who want to know about forensic nursing," Caruso says:

> The first thing I do is probe for their motivations, and what specifically in forensic nursing that they want to accomplish. Many people see the field as a blanket that covers everything, so they don't know about the various specialties. The other day, I received a letter from someone wanting to know what kind of job they would be able to get if they took an online forensic nursing course. To these people I say that you must figure out what you like in life, and then apply that to a forensic nursing specialty. Do you like psychiatry? Then maybe forensic psych nursing is for you. Do you want to work in corrections? Death investigation? Many people aren't sure. I recently received a call from a man who wanted to be a forensic nurse but he didn't know what he wanted to do specifically. I was trying to draw it out of him when I asked, "What are you doing now?" He told me he was a psych nurse, so I said, "OK, now we're getting somewhere." I asked him if he was interested in psych nursing in a forensic capacity, explaining to him that there were a lot of nurses who dealt with victims and perpetrators, and I put him in touch with Colleen Love. I told him that people like Colleen can tell you about educational requirements and about the work itself, but only you can determine if a certain forensic nursing specialty is right for you. Many people are waiting for a sudden revelation or epiphany that tells them what

> to do, and that may never come without doing one's homework in the field. People will say, "I want to be a forensic nurse, where is my job?" They have unrealistic expectations about the field, and don't realize that so many forensic nurses are self-made, self-directed.

Forensic nursing educator Yvonne D. McKoy, PhD, RN, CS, DABFN, assistant professor in the department of nursing at Xavier University in Cincinnati, Ohio, believes that the need to prepare students "in developing knowledge and skills in assessment, care, treatment and documentation of forensic concepts in each nursing program is paramount. It is important that clinical faculty assign patients that will provide learning opportunities that will assist students in sharpening their skills and understanding of forensic cases throughout their nursing education." McKoy advocates for a collaborative approach by institutions of higher learning, explaining:

> Forensic nursing interfaces with medicine, law, criminal justice, forensic science and public health. Forensic nursing has evolved from the public health framework and includes coursework related to medico-legal issues, criminal justice, psychopathology, investigational techniques and family issues involving violence. Consequently, a qualified multidisciplinary faculty of nurses, attorneys, physicians, forensic preceptors, criminologists, law enforcement officers, psychiatrists, psychologists, and forensic pathologists are involved to provide educational opportunities and expert supervision.

McKoy acknowledges a dearth of forensic nursing programs:

> As roles of the forensic nurse are clarified, many nurses have recognized the need for specialized training and in-depth understanding of various sciences and disciplines. Even though there is a need for more educational institutions to develop and implement programs that provide understanding of forensic protocols, direct patient care training, legal proceedings, and administrative functions, they often are not widely available. Formal programs that are needed to provide quality courses to prepare nurses in this advanced specialty are just beginning to move beyond the infancy stage. Presently, only a few colleges of nursing throughout the country offer graduate education and courses that include investigation of injury and death, courtroom proceedings, criminalistics, and advanced practice in dealing with victims and perpetrators. Other approaches that offer forensic nursing courses may be obtained through distance education, the Internet, internship programs, securing mentors and attending conferences and workshops.

She explains that to better prepare for the rigors of the field, forensic nurses require curricula that reach beyond traditional nursing concepts and provide solutions to modern-day problems of IPV, trauma, terrorism, and other medico-legal situations that demand progressive solutions and critical thinking skills:

> The essence of forensic nursing is to be able to provide patients, victims, survivors, and perpetrators with competent nursing care. It is crucial that the forensic nurse provides critical, calculated, and creative thinking interwoven into practical clinical experiences. If forensic nurses are to provide effective responses to the growing incidence and extent of violence and trauma resulting from criminal and interpersonal violence, the education and clinical practice of nurses in this subspecialty must also reflect additional and unique preparation that is beyond that of more traditional nursing roles. The accountability and responsibility of forensic nurses brings this new specialist in contact with a wider range of professionals. Training must include experiences that will prepare nurses to provide continuity of care of victims from areas such as an emergency room and/or crime scene to courts of law and may include continued follow-up in the home or other facility.

> Forensic nurses are demonstrating a wider range and quality of services than ever before. Forensic nurses must have an understanding of nursing theory and concepts, advanced clinical skills, understanding of the legal and judicial system, skilled in substantive and procedural concepts and trained to communicate with diverse populations. Forensic nurses must also practice within the guidelines of the standards of care. These standards are used on a daily basis in all aspects of nursing care and together are the yardstick that the legal system uses to measure the actions of a nurse in a malpractice suit.

McKoy is enthusiastic about the opportunity to improve on existing curricula to satisfy the fast-growing, diverse needs of all forensic nursing specialties. It might also include redefining the classroom experience to encompass a crime scene—the forensic nurse's new arena for professional edification. "The educational preparation of forensic nurses is challenging and provides an opportunity to reconceptualize traditional teaching," she says:

> Educators play vital roles in the preparation of forensic nurses in developing high-level cognitive skills and mental processes including thoughtful analyses, strategic planning, observation, decision-making, monitoring, and evaluation. Teaching forensic nursing requires a general knowledge in the use of special equipment, media creativity, ability to maintain a high level of interaction in the classroom, as well as onsite instruction at the scene of a crime. It is important that a climate conducive to innovative instructional techniques is employed early, since the classroom may be at the crime scene.

Just as the curriculum must change to meet the unique needs of forensic nursing students, so too must educators evolve in their thinking and instructional approaches. McKoy says:

> Teaching in less familiar ways will be necessary since students will learn to collaborate with lawyers, coroners, and investigators. Faculty must be willing to redefine their role as the chief dispensers of knowledge and reframe their role in order to provide optimum learning experiences for student. Faculty must be willing to facilitate rather than orchestrate what and how information is acquired. The days where the teacher is the "sage of the stage" are gone, and being replaced by teachers who are have insight into the idea of facilitating discovery learning for students. Consequently, faculty members who guide students in forensic courses are able to enhance each student's individual development and understanding of forensic concepts and at the same time provide a rich environment for the emergence of other useful skills such as research. As more nurses enter this exciting subspecialty, nursing programs will be challenged to integrate more forensic concepts and advanced courses into the curriculum. Bold new ideas and better ways to educate forensic nurses will ensue from continued collaboration and exploration of approaches between nursing faculty and other disciplines. This will provide a forum for increased support of forensic nursing programs and potential growth of this unique and much-needed subspecialty.

Educator Barbara Moynihan, RN, PhD, APRN, assistant professor of nursing at Quinnipiac University in Connecticut, is prominent in the forensic nursing education world. Many individuals in this first generation of forensic nursing have trained under Moynihan, and they say that she continues to be a leader in thought and vision for the field. In addition to teaching and clinical work, Moynihan maintains a private practice in psychotherapy. "Many of my referrals come in as a result of my background in areas of victimization, post-traumatic stress disorder, interpersonal violence, sexual abuse, incest, and trauma/emergency nursing. These experiences placed me in the arena of multidisciplinary collaboration, a concept that continues to enhance and enrich my practice in the classroom as well as in the clinical arena." Moynihan is involved in law enforcement training, created a victimology program while at Yale New Haven Hospital, and a community-based sexual assault crisis service. She also assisted with the development of the Greater New Haven Task Force on Domestic Violence. "All of this experience helped me learn about how to best assist those who have been traumatized and victimized. This broad-based knowledge and experience enhances the education of students and colleagues who are entering the forensic nursing arena or who require consultation and guidance."

Collaboration is key, Moynihan emphasizes, whether it is among educators, nurses, or colleagues in the medico-legal community:

> As the field evolves and there is increased multidisciplinary collaboration, I think that professional barriers and turf issues are much less frequently encountered. As forensic nursing becomes less of an anomaly, other clinicians and forensic practitioners are beginning to recognize the value of working together. And that is good for the growth of this evolving area of nursing specialization.
>
> I don't think forensic nurses have as many barriers to practic as previously, but I do think we have to continue to explain and validate our work. Those of us who are educators, and those who have been in the field a long time know that we've been working in forensic nursing since we hit the ground running when we graduated from nursing school. I think that instead of calling it a new area of nursing practice, we should call it an underdeveloped area of nursing practice. We know so much more now than we did back then. We didn't know about preserving evidence; in the emergency room we would cut through clothes and throw them on the floor, perhaps losing valuable evidence in the process. We didn't realize the importance of forensic science as an extension of care for that patient. Life-saving measures take priority, no question about that, but nurses must understand how connecting the dots is important for their patient, whether that person is a victim or a perpetrator. And as educators, we play an important role in helping connect those dots for our students.

Moynihan believes that the visibility of the field will increase when a greater body of forensic-nursing-related research is amassed, and as nurses pursue more elevated levels of education:

> The more we educate the community, the more seminars we participate in, the more articles and textbooks we publish, and the more we are visible, the sooner people will begin to understand what we do and the contributions we make to health care and to the medico-legal community. As the practice of forensic nursing advances, the demand for advice and consultation from these experts will increase. A greater recognition of the specialty of death investigation, as a respected and critical role, is an example of the gains this venue of practice (forensic nursing) has made. There is a greater understanding that the word *forensic* means simply "pertaining to the law" and involves the living forensic patient as well as the deceased. People tend to resist anything which is new and somewhat novel as a venue of practice, whether they are nurses or physicians. With the continued focus on the education of students and the community, the value of forensic nursing will be realized and sought after.

Like Cari Caruso, Moynihan believes that forensic nurses must articulate a vision for their career path to secure the most appropriate education and prepare them for the real-world application of their education to nursing practice. "If nurses want to get into forensic practice, they have to be self-directed," Moynihan comments:

> They must find the specialty that will fulfill them, and in many cases, create their own positions and convince others of their worth. As nurses, we have to take charge of our careers. We must ask ourselves, "Do I want to tread ground where there isn't a path yet?" "Do I want to be someone who helps create that path?" Even as the field grows and evolves and increases in its visibility, its practitioners must be prepared to explore new territory. Some were skeptical regarding a future in forensic nursing, but this has changed; others saw the forensic nurse only as the sexual assault nurse examiner—a vital role—while others could not contemplate nurses dealing with the dead as well as the living. The challenge is preparing and educating nurses for what lies ahead, especially in these troubled times.

Some educators point to the urgent need to grow and groom new nurses to combat the escalating shortfall of nurses in the future. "We must continue to face an acute nursing shortage," Moynihan confirms:

> There are many novel forensic science programs which are attracting nurses as well as nonnurses. There may be some people who are attracted to the overall field of nursing because of forensic nursing; I think that most people are attracted to nursing because of the appeal of the nursing profession. Once they are in nursing school and they begin to hear about specialties such as forensic nursing, they may be drawn to this area of specialization. We have to be very careful that nurses don't forget they are nurses first. Nursing practice has been expanded to include forensic practice and to examine every situation through a forensic lens. However, we can't lose sight of the fact they need a solid grounding in basic nursing principles, to complete and enhance their assessment and intervention more holistically and to then focus on forensic issues, which broadens the scope of nursing practice.

Moynihan emphasizes that forensic practice follows the core and advanced core of nursing education:

> Students must be grounded in nursing practice before they specialize, but I also think they should have at least some kind of forensic thread running throughout their nursing education. First, the nursing groundwork is laid, and then they expand on those skills through specialization. Students who enter our master's degree program often have a background in trauma, emergency department, or critical care nursing, and are ready to explore the forensic track.

Moynihan explains that she is currently teaching a class of 20 students in an accelerated program for individuals who already have degrees, but whose desire is to become nurses:

> They are in a perfect position to learn that in every area of nursing, there is the possibility of a forensic issue, whether you are working with women, children, the elderly, the chronically ill ... the possibility of a forensic issue may exist.

When asked her opinion about the state of the forensic nursing curriculum nationwide, Moynihan observes:

> I think we are doing very well. Now that forensic nursing is becoming a familiar specialty—or at least less unfamiliar than it has been in the past—we can continue to address the curriculum. Various members of the IAFN have been meeting frequently to develop a core curriculum for forensic nursing. In doing so, we are looking with new knowledge at the scope of practice; the American Nurses Association (ANA) and the IAFN developed the scope of practice in 1995, so we are updating it to match the sophistication of forensic nursing practice now. There also will be a credentialing examination that will be developed with the new curriculum. As a new area of practice evolves, there are many considerations to explore, examining new dimensions of the field and targeting areas that need further development.
>
> In any area of nursing, what you need first is a foundation, and then you can build on that foundation. We're building on a model that has traditionally held up over the years: First and foremost is basic nursing knowledge, then an area of specialization. We are taking a broad range of issues and then delving into the specialty forensic core, exploring methods to identify the forensic client, and developing the ability to recognize forensic issues, and then how to connect the dots.

That essential foundation lays the groundwork for continuing education and lifelong learning which is so critical to the success of a specialty such as forensic nursing, considered to be on the cutting edge of nursing practice. "Continual enhancement of our knowledge is important," Moynihan concurs:

> An increasing number of educational doors are opening up to us, and there are increasing opportunities available to expand one's forensic knowledge. Attendance at conferences and seminars are venues for advancing and increasing knowledge and skills in any area of interest and specialization; this is of particular importance in this new and exciting field of nursing practice. This specialty requires that a nurse think about forensic-related issues consistently. A solid foundation is the building block for excellence in practice.

Adjunct professor Joyce Williams, RN, who currently teaches an introduction to forensic science course at Shepherd University Community Technical College, says she has an extensive, ambitious agenda for her students because she feels she has so much ground to cover in a very short amount of time. She explains that the first half of the course covers criminalistics, and in the second half she covers "everything else they have never been taught before," she says:

> I am cramming stuff into the curriculum right and left because there is just so much information they need to have. And yes, I will be introducing them to forensic nursing concepts. The course is hands-on, with opportunities to explore a crime scene van so they can become familiar with the tools of the trade, as well as activities such as a bite mark lab... I truly believe that students must have the opportunity to get their hands on the tools we use every day to make their studies as relevant to real-world practice as possible.

Regarding the general state of forensic nursing curriculum nationwide, Williams says:

> I don't think nursing schools are exposing their students to enough forensic science principles and concepts about forensic nursing and forensic cases. Some programs only offer forensic nursing instruction at a graduate level, and I believe these principles should be introduced at the undergraduate level as well. Whether it's undergraduate, graduate, or doctorate level, I don't believe there are enough forensic nursing programs with a concentration in forensic science, but there are a few programs offering master's degrees and doctorate degrees in forensic nursing. I think so many curricula are still missing some essential forensic nursing components.
>
> For example, a colleague of mine in Chicago says that many operating room nurses have no concept of what to do with forensic evidence when they encounter it—that is, if they can recognize it for what it is. I find that to be a sad commentary on the state of education and training for nurses. OR nurses, like ER nurses, should know about evidence recognition, collection and preservation, and the chain of custody. Yet they are not learning this in nursing school. In the mid-1990s when the Joint Commission on Accreditation of Healthcare Organizations said that health care facilities must screen for forensic cases, that gave us hope for a strong mandate for forensic nursing, but I can say from experience that they don't do that. Having worked in the emergency room for 14 years, I know that most nurses were not trained to inquire in potential forensic cases whether or not a patient was a victim of violence. Nurses must know how to recognize signs of abuse, how to collect and preserve evidence properly, how to recognize patterns of injuries, and how to do forensic photography... all of these are essential topics that should be addressed in a basic nursing curriculum. I think that most nursing schools miss a significant body of forensic knowledge which should be taught. We must consider an overhaul of our nursing curricula so that forensic principles and practice can be integrated.

15.3 CORE COMPETENCIES AND A CORE CURRICULUM FOR FORENSIC NURSING

A core competency is an area of knowledge, skills, and attitudes that health care professionals must possess to provide effective health care to patients. Until now, there has been no critical mass of information regarding core competencies applied to forensic nursing, nor any reliable yardstick with which forensic nurses could measure their progress through a forensic nursing curriculum. Nurses who have been fortunate to live near the handful of universities and colleges with established forensic nursing programs have fared better than their colleagues who not only face logistics issues, but are distanced or removed from guidance regarding suggested coursework, training regimens, and career paths. Many nurses stumble across forensic nursing and are intrigued about this specialty, but are unsure of the education required; others remain adrift in a sea of confusing choices, with no clear educational and vocational direction.

At its ninth annual meeting in September 2001, the board of directors of the IAFN produced a resolution on forensic nursing education that called for the development and implementation of comprehensive information at all levels of forensic nursing education. They recommended the development of a forensic nursing core curriculum as well as working with accreditation entities to implement forensic nursing information into the current nursing curriculum. In June 2004, then president Patricia Speck had requested IAFN members to stay after the final Graduate Core Curriculum Committee meeting to begin the process of revising its *Forensic Nursing Scope and Standards of Practice* to fit the ANA framework. According to correspondence by Speck to IAFN members, the goals of the IAFN Scope and Standards of Practice Task Force were to review ANA documents and to customize these statements to apply to forensic nursing internationally. In September 2004, the IAFN's advanced practice forensic nursing core curriculum was submitted to its membership for review. A memo from Speck explained that the core curriculum task force had convened to develop "competencies and essential content that would provide the foundation for graduate programs with a major in advanced practice forensic nursing." Speck added that the draft of the curriculum, including working definitions of forensic nursing from IAFN and other professional sources, was used to "define advanced practice nursing, identify the attributes of advanced practice nursing and expand the concept of advanced practice forensic nursing." She added, "This effort reflects many individuals who volunteered their time and effort to the identification of resources and organization of data, the debate over essential content and the consensus regarding core competencies." Describing the draft as a "culmination of over a year's work" and "a definitive document representing the best distillation of ideas and information available for our review at this point in time," Speck reported that the curriculum "reflects the input of practitioners, educators, administrators and researchers. It is a document that will evolve as graduate programs in advanced practice forensic nursing refine the educational process used to prepare nurses involved in advanced practice, education, policy-making, administration, and research." The task force that created the draft core curriculum emphasizes that "jurisdictional and community standards for advanced practice nursing will dictate how the core curriculum is used," and that "changes in accreditation standards and certification/licensing criteria will impact the content and application of this document," thus requiring a "mechanism for periodic review and amendment." The task force also explained that every academic institution "has the responsibility to organize the core content and achieve the core competencies in academic models consistent with their philosophy, mission and parent institution." The IAFN opened the draft core curriculum document to review by its members through November 30, 2004, and will send the document to the ANA for its review. Following the receipt of their recommended changes, the draft document will be resubmitted. According to Speck, "Our goal is to complete the project within the year... In my opinion, this will be the most important document for all IAFN members."

The following is drawn from the draft of the IAFN's Advanced Practice Core Curriculum for Forensic Nursing:

- Competency No. 1: The advanced practice forensic nurse will develop, promote and implement protocols and systems responding to victims of trauma, injury, accidents, violence, abuse, and other forms of victimization. According to the draft curriculum, the following content is proposed to support this competency: differentiation of disease and injury; forensic applications of basic and medical sciences; applications in forensic populations (including advanced pathophysiology, pharmacology, and physical and health assessment); concepts relevant to forensic nursing practice (including human response to injury through accident, trauma, crime, victimization, violence, and abuse); violence as a public health problem; public health/community health models; and other concepts, such as survivorship, manipulation, and boundary violations; forensic theories of criminology, forensic psychiatry, forensic mental health, and perpetrator theory; evidence collection and processing; advanced documentation and interviewing (including crime scenes, accident scenes, sites of trauma or violence, and situations of victimization); systems involved in serving the health care needs of individuals, families, and communities as they respond to accident, injury, violence, trauma, crime, or other victimization (including justice systems, forensic science applications and roles, legal and ethical expectations, and boundaries of practice); techniques of self-awareness and self-reflection necessary for objective and effective advanced practice forensic nursing.
- Competency No. 2: The advanced practice forensic nurse will impact research and policy affecting human responses to violence, injury, trauma, accidents, abuse, and victimization. According to the draft curriculum, the following content is proposed to support this competency: definitions of health in forensic settings; goals for forensic nursing (including the prevention and reduction of violence, crime, trauma, and other forms of victimizations among individuals, groups, and communities; and the promotion of values of caring in forensic settings); forensic-sensitive variables representing characteristics of forensic clients and systems; forensic roles and applications in nursing and health care; forensic issues such as interpersonal violence, trauma, injury, and accidents; interdisciplinary collaboration models; interaction of justice, political, and social systems with health care delivery systems; empirical evidence on which to base advanced practice forensic nursing applications, including research and best practices; effective communication of forensic issues with other professional communities; and factors affecting the credibility and recognition of advanced practice forensic nursing.
- Competency No. 3: Advanced practice forensic nurses will develop and supervise systems of care for complex health problems related to accidents trauma, crime, victimization, violence, and abuse. According to the draft curriculum, the following content is proposed to support this competency: organizational behavior applied to forensic settings and systems; forensic issues and practices in health care systems; leadership roles and skill sets applied to forensic cases and settings; health policy and related financial, jurisdictional, ethical, and political issues impacting forensic nursing and forensic patients; public health models applied to forensic populations; and evidence-based practice models applied to forensic nursing.
- Competency No. 4: The advanced practice forensic nurse will educate others in the concepts and practice of forensic nursing and

> forensic health. According to the draft curriculum, the following content is proposed to support this competency: levels of forensic nursing roles, based on academic preparation, skill sets, competencies, credentialing, and societal need; teaching/learning strategies and educational goals related to forensic nursing as applied to forensic patients, other health care professionals, lawmakers, and the public; the history of forensic nursing; evolution of the specialty and its various subspecialties; organizations that cultivate and credential forensic nursing; and application of accreditation or other credentialing standards to forensic nursing academic programs.

Although recognizing that the IAFN core curriculum is still in its draft form, some nurses are expressing discontent or concern with its content, particularly its leanings toward advanced practice status. Louisiana nurse Meliss Vessier-Batchen comments:

> I love the IAFN, but it wants to frame the curriculum within the context of having a nurse practitioner background. It's the same story with the death investigation certification exam which they are drawing up currently; to quality you must be a nurse practitioner. I'm not an NP, but I do have 15 years of nursing experience. I have a master's degree and I am pursuing my doctoral degree, I have three years of experience in death investigation, and almost 11 years of teaching experience, so I don't want to go back and get my NP. But will that shut me out of the death investigation certification process? Now that the core curriculum is pushing for NP status, too, I think that's a problem. I don't mind it being a clinical nurse specialist status, but not NP, and that's where I am at odds with many of my colleagues.

Vessier-Batchen muses further:

> Only three more classes stand between me and an NP, and that would forever exclude me from getting the IAFN's death investigation certification . . . that bothers me. I understand that the IAFN wants to ensure a high level of proficiency, but I feel that it will exclude a lot of nurses who don't want to pursue an NP status. In concept, I agree with the core curriculum content because it is time for some kind of educational standardization so that all forensic nurses can get on the same page. A core curriculum is the only way you can really measure quality, and establish a solid reputation as a specialty. So, I think that the core curriculum is an absolute necessity, but I disagree with the NP status expectation. We have to do something soon to pull together this specialty, and to give nurses the educational guidance they need. Without it, we have not been jelling as a team, and we have no way of evaluating or guiding forensic nursing students. We have no way to gauge the quality of the forensic nursing programs out there, especially now that they have been springing up everywhere. Students pay all of this money, go through the program, and then say, "I can't find a job." There has to be a better way.

Vessier-Batchen says that the core curriculum must establish a solid foundation on which a graduate education is built. "That's when you begin to develop the deeper concepts of nursing specialty practice. The core curriculum must also support the practicum hours that a nurse needs. I think that all of the disciplines that feed into forensic nursing science need to be covered in the core curriculum, encompassing all concepts, theories, philosophies, and foundations that are built into the program."

Cari Caruso says she identifies with nurses who debate with themselves about pursuing higher levels of education. "I get excited every now and again when I think about going for a more advanced degree and then I beat myself down again and wonder what it's going to get me," she says. "I could have more credibility with a degree, but then I think, well, I have a lot of credibility now. Degrees are costly, and I wonder if you are any further ahead when all is said and done, and then I relax about the whole issue until the next time that I start thinking about it again." Caruso continues:

> Those nurses who are particularly ambitious, they are our leaders. They are the ones up on the podium addressing the rest of us, and breaking through the barriers with their credentials, and I totally respect that. There is a lot of discussion right now about moving from diploma nursing programs toward BSNs and MSNs, and that trend may have to do with younger nurses pursuing higher levels of education than older nurses. One of the nurses who works with me also is a nurse midwife; she says there are many parallels between midwives and forensic nurses in regard to the struggle of being recognized and gaining professional credentials. It's not that there is no merit to an associate's degree; after all, I am the worker bee, I am the one who has tried to find as much education I can to make it possible to do the things I wanted to do. The fact is, if there were no merit to associate degrees, then schools would stop providing them. There's a big difference in the coursework for someone like me who graduated in 1974 and someone who graduated in 2004. So maybe I will keep on keeping on until the day when not having an advanced degree prevents me from achieving my goals. However, I am doing everything I can to encourage other nurses to get all of these wonderful degrees because they will be our leaders in the future and define the credibility of us as a whole.

Janet Barber believes that eventually, all generic nursing curricula will contain fundamental principles of forensic sciences, but that nurses who intend to specialize in forensic nursing will need a graduate degree, or credentials as an advanced practice nurse at the very least. Barber comments:

> There are people who have been practicing as forensic nurses for many years in specialties such as sexual asssss-sault and death investigation who are not AP nurses. There are numbers of talented individuals who have achieved a great reputation in their field and I think that is imperative that such nurses are not left behind feeling disenfranchised and illegitimate until they earn a graduate degree or advanced-practice credentials. After all, these are the founding members of IAFN. I can tell you that most of these people are so busy doing what they do best every day, and that they don't have time to stop and get credentials they don't need to have for continuing to do what they are already doing very, very well. I think that IAFN's intent to limit certification for forensic nursing to APNs and graduate prepared nurses is going to alienate a significant portion of our forensic nurse population and make them feel like second-class citizens.
>
> I think to have a goal that by 2015 or 2020, or whatever number you pull out of a hat, that the entry point into forensic nursing should be at the graduate-degree level, either a graduate degree in forensic science or forensic nursing or a graduate degree in a nursing specialty with an emphasis in forensic science—is not wrong to do. However, what I do think is wrong is to suddenly say, "IAFN is not going to give you any further credentials. We no longer choose to legitimize the work that you have been and are doing." Think of the impact of that notion in the courtrooms!

Linda Ledray comments:

> Much more work needs to be done to ensure the presence of forensic nursing knowledge in every nursing curriculum nationwide. Nurses must have at least basic forensic principles in every bachelor's program and in every physician's program as well, but the universities still are not getting it and that must change soon. It would be terrific to have more graduate programs in forensic nursing, but I can't see that happening until forensic nursing is in all of the undergraduate programs. We are far from meeting the need. It's the same concept as the Joint Commission that should be requiring that every hospital and every level-one trauma center have a forensic nurse; I think it's appalling that they haven't because they are really missing the boat.

Valerie Sievers says she hopes the core curriculum for forensic nursing is driven by the desire to improve education, not by politics:

> There are many people who are rooted in university systems working on the core curriculum who haven't had recent real-world experience. It is also my hope that the core curriculum is not developed by people with political agendas, but rather that it is shaped by those who envision a more holistic approach. I think that the overall concept of a core curriculum is a great idea, and hopefully, it will apply to all specialties of practice.
>
> In Colorado, if you want to sit for the SANE curriculum, you must have a minimum of three years of current nursing experience and you must be currently practicing in emergency nursing, labor and delivery, acute care, pediatrics, or ICU, so that you have been working in an area where you are accustomed to the changing conditions of patients. I know some health care employers will take nurses right out of school who maybe haven't even taken a blood pressure on their own. Forensic nursing practice involves a lot of critical thinking and decision making, so I think the experiential piece is very important. I don't think you have to have a master's degree to provide care for forensic patients, however. If we limit forensic practice to those with master's degrees or higher levels of education, there are going to be a lot fewer forensic nurses available to care for patients

Sievers says she does see the value of preparing nurses for forensic practice early in their education:

> If we educate nurses in their beginning nursing education, I think that's going to prepare them for the rigors of the work and they won't have to wait until they achieve 10 years of experience in order to realize, "Gee, we're not doing a great justice to victims of violence by requiring extremely advanced levels of education." If new nurses can at least have their eyes opened to forensic practice before they go out into the real world and decide what specialty they want to be in, and if we can give them that forensic foundation, that will make them more astute, and their forensic antennas will grow that much earlier.

Diana Faugno agrees that there is much work to be done to hone a more responsive nursing curriculum steeped in forensic principles:

> We certainly have come a long way, but regarding our nursing curriculum, on a scale of 1 to 10, we are at a 2, so we have a long way to go. On my wish list for a national forensic nursing curriculum are universities which offer a master's degree in forensic nursing; I don't want a master's degree in forensic science. And I want it to be easy for students to find the right education they need to grow as forensic nurses. I would like to see some component of forensic practice in basic nursing school curricula. I would also like to see SANE training or child and elder abuse training all fold into some university and become a certificate program, and you take that as you move up the ladder to get your master's degree.
>
> Change to the current nursing curriculum has to come from the top because it doesn't work from the bottom up. If the deans of universities and the curriculum writers don't believe in change, then it will never happen.

Nancy Cabelus says she would like to see more formal, accredited forensic nursing programs established:

> It's great to hear an excited 18-year-old say, "I want to be a forensic nurse," but it's difficult when you look around and say, "That's nice, but where are we going to send you to school?" because there is no school. It's really a sad commentary that there are still so few forensic nursing programs. We are turning away promising nursing students every fall because we have no teachers. The commissioner of education in our state reported recently that most new degrees are in business and that almost no one is going into nursing because there are no programs and no teachers available, and that is feeding the nursing—and forensic nursing—shortage.
>
> By adjusting the current nursing curriculum and making it more interesting and relevant, we could attract more nurses and hopefully more educators. And while we're at it, every nursing school ought to have a forensic nursing 101 course in the first semester because nursing students need exposure to forensic principles immediately. At the very least, they need guest lectures from forensic experts.

Barber says she wants forensic nurses to understand that it is not just about collecting as many credentials behind one's name as possible; nurses must be able to put into practice adeptly the material they study and the skills they learn. One critical proving ground is the courtroom, where knowledge on paper will only get nurses so far.

> Many nurses become consumed with assembling numerous letters behind their names, and this can complicate issues in the courtroom. There is a very big risk of putting too much behind your name, because if you are in court to testify, the expectations about what you bring into that setting can be enormous. If you have all these credentials—and especially if most of them are just pieces of paper—it gives the other side more reasons to attack you. For example, if nurses have four or five organizational titles behind their names, like the American Board of Forensic Examiners, the AAFS, and the IAFN, then the defense attorney can take each one of these designations and can begin to chink holes in your armor, by asking, "Do you know when this organization was started? Do you know how many members are in the group? Do you read their journal?" And if you say no, then it sounds as if you are not really involved in this organization, and that may leave you vulnerable to having the rest of your credentials, education, and experience questioned. All you really need is your education, your basic licensure, and maybe one or two other credentials that show you have some standing in your specialty. On the stand, nurses will be asked about their credentials, and if they do not have mastery in their fields represented by all of those credentials, their expertise may be questioned. Sometimes the more credentials that you have, the more they are brought into question. Many nurses have credentials in more than one field; they may be a critical care nurse, a certified emergency nurse, a certified infection control practitioner; whatever they are, they don't have to use every credential in every instance. I think it is advisable that they select those from their dossiers which apply to the field in which they are engaged at the time. If you're in the courtroom as an expert witness in a pediatric sexual assault case, I don't care if you are an AACN or a CIC, what I really want to know is if you are a certified sexual assault examiner specializing in pediatric cases. If nurses just can't help themselves and have to collect all of these credentials, they should ensure that in certain forums they only use the ones that are the most relevant. Nurses will continue to gather these credentials, however, because there is more opportunity to get them.
>
> Credentials tell others, "I have the right education and the right indoctrination to do what I am doing." In terms of gaining legitimacy, any time there is a new specialty, it seems there is a quest to see how many groups of letters you can compile behind one's name, but to me, it becomes a little ridiculous when you start having alphabet soup behind your name. Noting a basic academic degree and one or two professional designations is fine. I don't have any quarrel with people who want to designate themselves as being a fellow of an academy or having a graduate degree or PhD, but we don't need to know every certification, every licensure, every advanced practice credential that they have. To me, if you are an MD or a PhD, it stands to reason that you have arrived. I think we struggle too hard to differentiate ourselves from our peers, and I'm not sure that's so necessary.

So who are nurses trying to impress? "I think many nurses are trying to impress one another," Barber quips, adding that job performance is the most important validation of one's education and career standing. "Your performance is what is going to distinguish you from your peers, not the letters behind you name," she emphasizes. "What really matters is your professional abilities, your conduct on the job, your research, your presentations, your teaching experiences, your ability to mentor, your activities in the field and what you are able to do on behalf of your patients. That's what brings recognition and respect in the field, not necessarily long lists of letters and licensures." Barber also believes nurses must invest some thought into their prospective career paths to better determine an appropriate course of education and professional training:

> One's educational and vocational career path is frequently determined by the forensic specialty in which you want to work. For example, if you are going to be a death investigator, I think you need a bona fide course and a preceptorship in death investigation. I think that the IAFN and other forensic organizations need to establish suggested education paths for certain forensic careers, and what the minimum educational requirements ought to be. I don't think anyone should be in death investigation

> without an internship, and you shouldn't be a sexual assault nurse if you don't have the basic skills.

Barber points to a trend she thinks might be jeopardizing the development of core competencies:

> Many educational institutions don't have the faculty with which to teach all of these nursing skills and to validate all of these clinical skills, so instead, they provide students with a list of competencies that they will have to carry with them into their career and have them validated on the job. At some time before you get your credentials to go out and practice on real people, someone will have to observe your skills and make sure you know how to perform exams correctly. The course itself may not be obligated to teach you these skills and validate them. It's similar to the scenario of a medical student who willlearn at least some of the basics about brain surgery during basic education but not everyone who completes medical school will actually perform brain surgery. However, if a doctor does decide to do brain surgery, there is extensive training and someone will have to verify the candidate's requisite knowledge and skills.

Barber, a lifelong educator, has evaluated many curricula in her day, and she says she has reservations about the proposed framework for IAFN's core curriculum:

> The whole idea of a core curriculum is to create a structure upon which you lay the building blocks for practice. It contains precise information about knowledge, skills, attitudes and values essential to specialty practice. It does not leave you with a feeling of being lost in a wilderness, surrounded by lofty words that confuse rather than elucidate the essential elements of the forensic nursing discipline.
>
> I think the proposed core curriculum leaves educators begging for somebody to step forward and create "flesh for the bones" that will help them in designing courses of study. A core curriculum should define clearly what a forensic nurse must know to be able to do their jobs successfully, as well as define what tools they need, what resources they need, and where to find the information and materials they need. Educators are trying desperately to prepare themselves to teach forensic nursing content, but they just don't know quite how to do it in a real-world context... we need a core curriculum that will give them the answers they need for the sake of their students.

Nurses might have to wait months or even a few more years for a core curriculum, but they know a solid curriculum when they see one. And although the wish lists for a perfect forensic nursing curriculum differ among nurses currently practicing in the field, there are a number of key components that are common threads. These include the following:

- Nursing science concepts related to forensic nursing practice, research, education, and administration
- Nursing leadership skills and concepts, including understanding and influencing institutional behavior, developing an organizational culture, and exploring theories of communication, motivation, and conflict resolution.
- Nursing research skills, including development of research inquiry, search of the medical literature, creation of hypotheses and theories, testing those theories, and calculating and presenting data
- Introduction to forensic science within health care settings
- Criminal law principles and practices, including evidence documentation, collection and preservation, death investigation, and crime-scene investigation
- Forensic science principles within the framework of forensic nursing practice, including clinical forensic skills such as injury patterns
- Medico-legal issues and investigation techniques
- Scientific foundations for forensic nursing
- IPV
- Forensic mental health
- Working with vulnerable populations
- Legal and ethical issues
- Courtroom testimony and nursing jurisprudence
- Forensic photography in the health care setting
- A practicum in forensic nursing that allows the student to develop critical skills under the preceptorship of a forensic nursing expert

Lynch (1995) writes:

> With increasing focus on the forensic aspects of trauma, schools of nursing are responding with formal and informal arrangements for education and clinical experiences that incorporate forensic science, death investigation, criminal law, court procedures, and testimony, as well as an exploration of new roles, new responsibilities, and new occupational opportunities for nurses in these violent times. Professional knowledge that qualifies nurses to undertake medico-legal work continues to expand the boundaries of nursing beyond tradition.

Meliss Vessier-Batchen, RN, MSN, an assistant professor with Charity School of Nursing/Delgado Community College and a doctoral student at Louisiana State University Health Sciences Center, says that the forensic nursing specialty is a continually evolving education arena. In the 2005 white paper, "Envisioning Forensic Nursing Science Education," Vessier-Batchen explains that this untraditional role requires unique and specialized education and training. "New programs are being developed nationally and internationally," she writes. "The focus of the curricula and the quality of the program are important considerations as programs are examined, as well as the type of employment being sought and use of the educational experience." She advises prospective students considering an educational program to ask themselves whether the program addresses the interests of the generic, nondegreed student, and which type of program—classroom or online—would be most suitable to the individual's learning style.

When it comes to evaluating undergraduate programs, Vessier-Batchen advises nurses to consider which specific forensic nursing role they would like to pursue, and to contact a prospective employer regarding the competencies they believe would be most critical to a position. Vessier-Batchen writes, "It is important to know what that potential employer requires as part of the requirements of a forensic position." Vessier-Batchen says most undergraduate programs do not offer forensic nursing science as the focus, but might offer electives that introduce the concepts of forensic nursing science. She writes, "There may be programs available for the generic student allowing focus in the forensic nursing science arena within the baccalaureate degree program, but to date, I have not identified any program that specifically awards a BSN with a focus in the forensic nursing sciences." Vessier-Batchen adds that some programs offer postbaccalaureate certification in forensic nursing science, and a few even provide busy nurses with accelerated courses designed to "allow maximum course work in compressed time blocks," she says.

Many nurses are taking advantage of online instruction for postbaccalaureate certification in forensic nursing. Vessier-Batchen writes, "Online options are becoming more abundant as schools seize the opportunity to increase enrollment and meet the demands of working students." She says that students should evaluate online programs as carefully as they would traditional classroom learning programs, scrutinizing the online program's levels of credentialing and academic standing. "There are some very positive aspects to the online courses, such as being accessible from any distance, flexibility in accessing and completing course work, student independence, and scheduling which allows many students to continue full-time employment, if necessary," she writes, adding that potential negatives of virtual learning programs include the lack of live group interaction, the loss of immediate responses and feedback, the need for much self-discipline and structured behaviors, and the loss of face-to-face encounters with the faculty.

At the graduate level, nurses seeking graduate-level courses in forensic nursing science have many options and programs available to them. Whether the nurse is searching for a master's program or certification in forensic nursing science, it should be remembered that any program that addresses a newer and ever-developing academic field such as forensic nursing science should be examined cautiously to ensure that the program is reputable and the information is usable. The student must examine multiple components of any academic pathway, including reputation and quality of the program, cost-effectiveness, and time commitment.

Graduate programs are designed to educate the student using a more advanced and specific curriculum content. Therefore, the nursing student pursuing a forensic nursing science program should have a clear understanding of the roles available in forensic nursing and what each of those roles demands of its participants. The graduate student should list education and employment goals using these goals to find a program that best fits his or her objectives and the potential employers' requirements. The program should contain the advanced components and concepts of nursing including philosophy, theory, advanced skill development, and research, but should also include applicable content specific to the forensic nursing environment, presenting a rounded approach to the forensic nursing roles. A practicum or internship component is crucial in completing the educational experience. This course allows the student to apply the knowledge garnered through didactic work and create a potential employment opportunity in the forensic arena, while demonstrating the advantages of nurses working in these roles.

The decision of using online versus real-time classroom programs at the graduate level should be the student's choice. It would be best to find a program that optimally fits the student's learning style, time constraints, financial abilities, and ultimate employment role. The usual cautions are always applicable. Scrutinize the program's reputation, validity, and overall satisfaction rate among students. There are many ways to do this. The Internet can do more than assist a student in finding a program; it can also help students to assess the program.

As interest in forensic nursing science roles continues to grow, nurses and nursing students should know as much as possible about their options in choosing a role and the education needed to fulfill the responsibilities of that role. A thorough examination of the choices available and the requirements of available positions is an excellent beginning. The use of forensic nurses in the geographic area should also be investigated.

Specific objectives and goals for the application of the knowledge and the resulting degree or certification should be developed. Any need for additional academic courses and requirements for employment in the forensic areas should also be considered.

Forensic nursing science is igniting new interest in nursing. It has sparked many nurses to reinvest in continued education. The diversity of roles and the educational opportunities available have again created swells of students enrolling in local and distance programs (American Nurses Association, 2003). Television has played a key role in promoting the forensic discipline and nursing has embraced the potential. The quality and usefulness of an educational experience are paramount in supporting the growth of forensic nursing science in a positive and expanding practice arena.

15.4 OPPORTUNITIES FOR EDUCATION AND TRAINING

Although no list is comprehensive due to the constant addition and subtraction of programs and curricula, the following is a list of forensic nursing education and training opportunities in the United States at the time of writing.

California

American Forensic Nurses
http://www.amrn.com

University of California, Riverside Extension
Forensic nursing certificate program (online)
http://www.ucrextension.net/certificates/forensic-nurse.html

Colorado

Beth-El College of Nursing, University of Colorado
Colorado Springs, Colorado
http://web.uccs.edu/bethel/
Graduate Certificate in Forensic Nursing
http://web.uccs.edu/bethel/grad_cert_programs.htm

Connecticut

Quinnipiac University
Hamden, Connecticut
http://www.quinnipiac.edu
Master of science in forensic nursing
http://www.quinnipiac.edu/x1338.xml

Idaho

Canyon College
Caldwell, Idaho
Online forensic nursing certificate program
http://www.canyoncollege.edu/forensicnur.htm

Louisiana

Louisiana State University Health Sciences Center (LSUHSC)
New Orleans, Louisiana
http://www.lsuhsc.edu
Introduction to forensic nursing
http://www.nursingsport.lsuhsc.edu/
http://nursing.lsuhsc.edu/ContinuingEducation/Programs/Spring/Forensics2.cfm

Maryland

Johns Hopkins University School of Nursing
Baltimore, Maryland
http://www.jhu.edu
Masters of science in nursing; clinical nurse specialist, forensic nursing http://www.son.jhmi.edu/academic_programs/masters/hlthsys/forensics.asp

Massachusetts

Fitchburg State College
Fitchburg, Massachusetts
http://www.fsc.edu
Masters of science in forensic nursing
http://www.fsc.edu/nursing/grad/index.html
Forensic nursing certificate program
http://www.fsc.edu/catalog/Grad/forensicnursing.html

New Jersey

Monmouth University
West Long Branch, New Jersey
http://www.monmouth.edu
Masters of science in forensic nursing
http://www.monmouth.edu/academics/registrar /msnforensic02.asp
Forensic nursing certificate
http://www.monmouth.edu/academics/schools/graduate/programs/fngc.asp

New York

Kaplan College
New York, New York
http://www.kaplancollege.edu
Forensic nursing certificate program (online)
http://www.elearners.com/program/4038.htm

Ohio

University of Cleveland State
Cleveland, Ohio
http://www.csuohio.edu/nursing
Masters of science in nursing, forensic populations
http://www.csuohio.edu/nursing/Forensic %20graduate %20bulletin.pdf

University of Cincinnati
College of Nursing
Cincinnati, Ohio
http://nursing.uc.educ
Advanced Concepts in Forensic Nursing
http://nursing.uc.edu/ProfessionDevelop/ForensicNursing.html

Xavier University
Cincinnati, Ohio
http://www.xu.edu
Master of science in nursing with forensics concentration
http://www.xu.edu/MSN/forensics/forensics.html

Oklahoma

University of Central Oklahoma
Edmond, Oklahoma
http://www.ucok.edu
Master of science in forensic sciences
http://204.154.117.68/nursing/msin.htm
http://nurse.ucok.edu:8080/MSForensic.jsp

Pennsylvania

Duquesne University
Pittsburgh, Pennsylvania
http://www.nursing.duq.edu
Masters of forensic nursing (online)
http://www.nursing.duq.edu/gradMsnForen.html
http://www.forensics.duq.edu/academicprograms%20folder/nursingmasters.html

University of Scranton
Scranton, Pennsylvania
http://matrix.scranton.edu
Nursing 444 Forensic Health Care of Victims

University of Pennsylvania, School of Nursing
Philadelphia, Pennsylvania
http://www.nursing.upenn.edu/
Minor in forensic nursing/forensic science, forensic mental health nursing, victimology

Tennessee

Vanderbilt University School of Nursing
Nashville, Tennessee
http://www.vanderbilt.edu/
Masters of science in nursing program, forensic nursing
http://www.mc.vanderbilt.edu/nursing/msn/forensic.html

University of Tennessee
Health Science Centre
Memphis, Tennessee
http://www.utmem.edu/
MSD PhD Forensic Focus DNSc
http://www.utmem.edu/nursing/dnsc/forensic/

Washington

Gonzaga University
Spokane, Washington
http://www.gonzaga.edu
Masters of science in nursing, with option of forensic/corrections

University of Washington
Seattle, Washington
Advanced practice forensic nurse specialist
38-credit course of study leading to a master of nursing (MN) degree http://www.son.washington.edu/eo/apfns/

REFERENCES

Agency for Healthcare Research and Quality. A report to Congress: Medical examination and treatment for victims of sexual assault: Evidence-based clinical practice and provider training. Rockville, MD: 2003.

American College of Emergency Physicians. Evaluation and management of the sexually assaulted or sexually abused patient. Dallas, TX. Available at: www.acep.org. June 1999.

American Nurses Association. Nursing school enrollment up 16.6 percent. Nursing Insider. December 2003. Available at: http://www.nursingworld.org/news/nws12_03.htm.

Carbonell, J., Chez, R., & Hassler, R. Florida physician and nurse education and practice related to domestic violence. *Women's Health Issues. 5,* 203–207, 1995.

Cohen, B.J., Levin, R. F., Bashoff, M. L., Ellis, E., Condie, V., & Gelfand, G. Educators' responses to changes in the health care system. *J NY State Nurses Assoc. 28,* 2, 4–7, 1997.

Ellis, J. M. Barriers to effective screening for domestic violence by registered nurses in the emergency department. *Crit Care Nurs Q. 22,* 1, 27–41, 1999.

Fox, D. M. *Power and Illness: The Failure and Future of American Health Policy.* Berkeley: University of California Press. 1993.

Guze, P. A. Cultivating curricular reform. *Academic Medicine. 70,* 11, 971–973, 1995.

Institute of Medicine. *Confronting Chronic Neglect: The Education and Training of Health Professionals on Family Violence.* Washington, DC: National Academies Press. 2002.

Jones, J. S., Veenstra, T. R., Seamon, J. P., & Krohmer, J. Elder mistreatment: National survey of emergency physicians. *Ann Emerg Med. 30,* 4, 473–479, 1997.

Kurz, D., & Stark, E. Not-so-benign neglect. In K. Yllo & M. Bograd, Eds. *Feminist Perspectives on Wife Abuse* (pp. 249–265). Newbury Park, CA: Sage. 1988.

Lynch, V. A. Clinical forensic nursing: A new perspective in the management of crime victims from trauma to trial. *Crit Care Nurs Clinics North America. 7,* 3, 489–507, 1995.

Mashta, O. Mental health experts should offer training to GPs. *British Medical J. 320,* 7229, 208, 2000.

McCann, I., & Pearlman, L. Vicarious traumatization: A framework for understanding the psychological effects of working with victims. *J Trauma Stress. 3,* 131–149, 1990.

McGrath, M. E., Bettacchi, A., Duffy, S. J., Peipert, J. F., Becker, B. M., & St. Angelo, L. Violence against women: Provider barriers to intervention in emergency departments. *Acad Emerg Med. 4,* 4, 297–300, 1997.

Moore, M. L., Zaccaro, D., & Parsons, L. H. Attitudes and practices of registered nurses toward women who have experienced abuse/domestic violence. *J Obstet. Gynecol Neonat Nurs. 27,* 2, 175–182, 1998.

Neumann, D., & Gamble, S. Issues in the professional development of psychotherapists: Counter transference and vicarious traumatization in the new trauma therapist. *Psychotherapy. 32,* 341–347, 1995.

Parsons, L. H., Zaccaro, D., Wells, B., & Stovall, T. G. Methods of and attitudes toward screening obstetrics and gynecology patients for domestic violence. *Am J Obstet Gynecol. 173,* 2, 381–386, 1995.

Reid, S. A., & Glasser, M. Primary care physicians' recognition of and attitudes toward domestic violence. *Acad Med. 72,* 1, 51–53, 1997.

Rodriguez, M. A., Bauer, H. M., McLoughlin, E., & Grumbach, K. Screening and intervention for intimate partner abuse: Practices and attitudes of primary care physicians. *J Am Med J. 282,* 5, 468–474, 1999.

Saunders, D., & Kindy, J. Predictors of physicians' responses to woman abuse: The role of gender, background and brief training. *J Gen Intern Med. 8,* 606–609, 1993.

Sugg, N. K., & Inui, T. Primary care physicians' response to domestic violence: Opening Pandora's box. *JAMA. 267,* 23, 3157–3160, 1992.

Talbot, A., Manton, M., & Dunn, P. Debriefing the debriefers: An intervention strategy to assist psychologists after a crisis. *J Trauma Stress. 5,* 45–62, 1992.

Tilden, V. P., Schmidt, T. A., Limandri, B. J., Chiodo, G. T., Garland, M. J., & Loveless, P. A. Factors that influence clinicians' assessment and management of family violence. *Am J Public Health. 84,* 4, 628–633, 1994.

Vessier-Batchen, M. Envisioning forensic nursing science education. Mystery Magazine Web. 2005. Available at: http://lifeloom.com/II3VessierBatchen.htm.

Wilkinson, A., & Forlini, J. Medicaring: Quality end-of life care. *J Health Law Policy. 2,* 501–530, 1999.

Woodtli, M. A., & Breslin, E. T. Violence-related content in the nursing curriculum: A national study. *J Nurs Educ. 35,* 8, 367–374, 1996.

Woodtli, M. A., & Breslin, E. T. Violence and the nursing curriculum: Nurse educators speak out. *Nursing Healthcare Perspectives, 18,* 5, 252–259, 1997.

RECOMMENDED READINGS

Biehler, J. L., Apolo, J., & Burton, L. Views of pediatric emergency fellows and fellowship directors concerning training experiences in child abuse and neglect. *Ped Emerg Care. 12,* 5, 365–369, 1996.

Blumenthal, D., & Meyer, G. S. Academic health centers in a changing environment. *Health Affairs. 15,* 201–215, 1996.

Bolin, L., & Elliott, B. Physician detection of family violence: Do buttons worn by doctors generate conversations about domestic abuse? *Minn Med. 79,* 6, 42–55, 1996.

Brandt, E. N., Jr. Education and research in adult family violence: A perspective. *Acad Med. 70,* 11, 968–997, 1995.

Brandt, E. N., Jr. Curricular principles for health professions education about family violence. *Acad Med. 72,* 1 (Suppl.), S51–S58, 1997.

Bullock, K. Domestic violence training at an inner-city hospital found helpful. *J Emerg Nurs. 23,* 4, 299–300, 1997.

Bullock, K. Child abuse: The physician's role in alleviating a growing problem. *Am Fam Physician. 61,* 2977–2980, 2000.

Campinha-Bacote, J. Cultural diversity in nursing education: Issues and concerns. *J Nurs Educ. 37,* 1, 3–4, 1998.

Campinha-Bacote, J. A model and instrument for addressing cultural competence in health care. *J Nurs Educ. 38,* 5, 20320–20327, 1999.

Centers for Disease Control and Prevention. Education about adult domestic violence in U.S. and Canadian medical schools, 1987–88. *MMWR. 38,* 2, 17–19, 1989.

Cheung, K. F., Stevenson, K. M., & Leung, P. Competency-based evaluation of case-management skills in child sexual abuse intervention. *Child Welfare. 70,* 4, 425–435, 1991.

Courson, S. The investigative specialty of forensic nursing (Pennsylvania State Nurses Association Career Series). 2000. Available at: http://www.psna.org/Career/forensic.htm.

Davis, D., O'Brien, M. A., Freemantle, N., Wolf, F. M., Mazmanian, P., & Taylor-Vaisey, A. Impact of formal continuing medical education: Do conferences, workshops, rounds, and other traditional continuing education activities change physician behavior or health care outcomes? *JAMA. 282,* 9, 867–874, 1999.

Davis, D. A., Thomson, M. A., Oxman, A. D., & Haynes, R. B. Evidence for the effectiveness of CME: A review of 50 randomized controlled trials. *JAMA. 268,* 9, 1111–1117, 1992.

Department of Health and Human Services. *Surgeon General's Workshop on Violence and Public Health.* Washington, DC: Health Resources and Services Administration. 1986.

Ernst, A. A., Houry, D., Nick, T. G., & Weiss, S. J. Domestic violence awareness and prevalence in a first-year medical school class. *Acad Emerg Med. 5,* 1, 64–68, 1998.

Ernst, A. A., Houry, D., Weiss, S. J., & Szerlip, H. Domestic violence awareness in a medical school class: 2-year follow-up. *South Med J. 93,* 8, 772–776, 2000.

Estabrooks, C. A. Will evidence-based nursing practice make practice perfect? *Can J Nurs Research. 30,* 1, 15–36, 1998.

Family Violence Education. Family violence education in medical school-based residency programs: Virginia, 1995. *MMWR. 45,* 31, 669–671, 1996.

Ferren, A., & Mussell K. Leading curriculum renewal. In A. Lucas, Ed. *Leading Academic Change* (pp. 246–274). San Francisco: Jossey-Bass. 2000.

Ferris, L. E. Canadian family physicians' and general practitioners' perceptions of their effectiveness in identifying and treating wife abuse. *Med Care. 32,* 12, 1163–1172, 1994.

Ferris, L. E., & Tudiver, F. Family physicians' approach to wife abuse: A study of Ontario, Canada, practices. *Fam Med. 24,* 4, 276–282, 1992.

Flaherty, M. Secrets of the dead: Nurse death investigators hone their skills in forensic research. Nurseweek. February 1999. Available at: http://www.nurseweek.com/features/99-2/death.html.

Ganley, A. L. *Improving the Healthcare Response to Domestic Violence: A Trainer's Manual for Healthcare Providers.* San Francisco: Family Violence Prevention Fund. 1998.

Gerbert, B., Caspers, N., Bronstone, A., Moe, J., & Abercrombie, P. A qualitative analysis of how physicians with expertise in domestic violence approach the identification of victims. *Ann Intern Med. 131,* 8, 578–584, 1999.

Geyman, J. P. Evidence-based medicine in primary care: An overview. *J Am Board Fam Pract. 11,* 1, 46–56, 1998.

Humphris, D. A framework to evaluate the role of nurse specialists. *Profess Nurse. 14,* 6, 377–379, 1999.

Institute of Medicine. *Crossing the quality chasm: A new health system for the 21st century.* Washington, DC: National Academy Press. 2001.

Knight, R. A., & Remington, P. L. Training internal medicine residents to screen for domestic violence. *J Women's Health Gender Based Med. 9,* 2, 167–174, 2000.

Kripke, E. N., Steele, G., O'Brien, M. K., & Novack, D. H. Domestic violence training program for residents. *J Gen Intern Med. 13,* 12, 839–841, 1998.

Larkin, G. L., Rolniak, S., Hyman, K. B., MacLeod, B. A., & Savage, R. Effect of an administrative intervention on rates of screening for domestic violence in an urban emergency department. *Am J Public Health. 90,* 9, 1444–1448, 2000.

Lynch, V. *Clinical Forensic Nursing: A New Perspective in Trauma and Medico-Legal Investigation of Death.* Fort Collins, CO: Bearhawk Consulting Group. 2001.

McMurray, D. W., & Dunlop, M. E. The collaborative aspects of online learning: A pilot study. 2000. Available at: http://ultibase.rmit.edu.au/Articles/online/mcmurry1.htm.

Moore, D., Jr. Needs assessment in the new health care environment: Combining discrepancy analysis and outcomes to create more effective CME. *J Contin Ed Health Profess. 18,* 133–141, 1998.

Morey, A. The growth of for-profit higher education. *J Teacher Educ. 52,* 4, 300, 2001.

Osattin, A., & Short, L. *Intimate Partner Violence and Sexual Assault: A Guide to Training Materials and Programs for Health Care Providers.* Atlanta, GA: Centers for Disease Control and Prevention, National Center for Injury Prevention and Control. 1998.

Palusci, V. J., & McHugh, M. T. Interdisciplinary training in the evaluation of child sexual abuse. *Child Abuse Negl. 19,* 9, 1031–1038, 1995.

Roberts, G. L., Raphael, B., Lawrence, J. M., O'Toole, B., & O'Brien, D. Impact of an education program about domestic violence on nurses and doctors in an Australian emergency department. *J Emerg. Nurs. 23,* 3, 220–227, 1997.

St. Germain, D. K., & Vessier-Batchen, M. A different venue. *Advance for Nurses. 2,* 8, 16–18, 2004.

Standing Bear, Z. G. Forensic nursing and death investigation: Will the vision be co-opted? *J Psycho Nurs. 33,* 9, 59–64, 1995.

Woodtli, M. A. Domestic violence and the nursing curriculum: Tuning in and tuning up. *J Nurs Educ. 39,* 4, 173–182, 2000.

16 Professional Issues: Forensic Nurses as Entrepreneurs

CONTENTS

Many forensic nurses have grown tired of bumping their heads on glass ceilings, trying to convince hospital administrators of their worth, or attempting to thrive in an environment that is hostile to their instincts, passions, and contributions. Others want to pursue their practice outside of an institution or health care system to achieve greater prestige, financial security, or independence. There are many factors underlying a nurse's decision to go off on his or her own; however, the common thread seems to be the desire to do what they do best on their own terms.

16.1 THE SANE

Cari Caruso, RN, SANE-A, an independent SANE in California and proprietor of Forensic Nurse Professionals, Inc., says that forensic nurses can't simply sit back and expect their careers to come to them; they must invest the time and effort required to secure employment, whether it is in a hospital or as an independent consultant. "Some of the younger nurses especially get into the field and say, 'OK, I'm here, where's my job?' We're still pushing our way into health care and it's not always as easy as that," Caruso comments. "To succeed as a forensic nurse you must get off your duff and work toward what you want to achieve in your career because no one is going to hand it to you. You have to fend for yourself." Caruso says she first entertained thoughts of becoming an entrepreneur and providing evidentiary examinations independently of the local hospitals when a detective suggested she start her own business. "I laughed at him, and when I quit laughing I started looking into it," she says. "I thought it might be an interesting, challenging career move, so I sought the support of some of the police stations I had been serving, and they were there for me. It was really exciting and really scary to go off on my own, but I've never had a better time in my life and I've never regretted it." Caruso says she "stumbled" onto forensic nursing, adding, "Sexual assaults and molestations would come into the ER and everybody would run the other way... except me." She says she found forensic cases to be "exciting and interesting," and that she liked the "ability to apply nursing to other venues and collaborate with law enforcement and the legal system." She says that years of experience in other nursing specialties such as emergency nursing, pediatrics, women's health, and gastroenterology helped to prepare her for the rigors of her work "I believed I was well prepared for forensic nursing since I had been doing exams for about three years prior to my SANE training," Caruso says:

> Forensic nursing was in its infancy and we grew up together. Even so, I had never heard of doing forensic exams in my 15 years of nursing, before my introduction to forensic nursing in 1990. I always had an interest in investigation and crime solving, but I never imagined that I would be a part of it some day. When I got my first taste of forensic work, I was totally committed. I very much enjoy contributing to the law enforcement investigation, providing services, and serving as a resource for information and education. I believe my work is an extension of the nursing role into the legal system. The medical and legal fields have their own language and procedures and my work can help bridge the gap. It has changed the ways that nurses and law enforcement interact. Now, there is more of a partnership instead of a great divide.

Having made significant inroads as a forensic practitioner, Caruso says there is still constant work to be done to foster and maintain important relationships in the medico-legal community:

> Communication and understanding that working together is better than not working together is essential. There is still some resistance in certain areas but I believe the goals are the same... to maximize the care of the patient, which includes any issues that may involve litigation. We are

> getting there, however. Those who have experienced the work of the forensic nurse have a great deal of respect for us, as well as the realization that the forensic nurse can be a major factor in their processes. Nurses who are not forensic nurses see someone who can handle the issues that they are not prepared to handle (such as sexual assault, interpersonal violence, evidence collection, photography, and going to court) and would otherwise take up a great deal of their time if they had to do it. Some may see it (or used to see it) it as invading their territory, such as physicians, who see the forensic nurse as having a great deal of education in matters in which they only had minimal exposure. Nevertheless, physicians didn't like to do the time-consuming exams and didn't like going to court. Now that we have taken on that role, most physicians are grateful. Exposure to the forensic nurse's skills and talents will take time, but continuing to educate people will eventually allow us to prevail.

Lynch (1995) states, "A contemporary role in forensic nursing that is being recognized as a new occupational opportunity is that of independent contractor in forensic services." As one of the first forensic nurses in Los Angeles County to offer independent services outside of a hospital setting, Caruso knows a thing or two about persistence. "I have encountered some barriers but have managed to run a successful business for over a year. It is a new concept and, like all new things, takes time to get used to. I have the support of police departments and have realized tremendous benefits to this approach," she says. Caruso adds that she has a terrific support system in place:

> With IAFN validating the practice and having so many forensic nurses to call upon for support, that presence is certainly felt. As far as support at home, I have more than anyone could ask for. From the moment I started in forensic nursing I have received nothing but the best of support from home. I know of many nurses who had problems at home when they had to leave the house at dinnertime or the middle of the night and didn't receive encouragement, as I have. It helps enormously when my partner shares the pride in what I do and realizes that there is a level of importance in my work.

She says she doesn't experience burnout, even under the duress of working as an entrepreneur. "I do offer presentations on preventing burnout for various groups. I explain the difference between burnout and vicarious trauma and discuss the boundaries that should be maintained to prevent it. There hasn't been much written about those of us in this particular field and I hope to relay a healthy, positive attitude for all who work with victims of violence. We need to stay strong so people don't leave the field."

In regard to the future of forensic nursing, Caruso says, "Expanding services and creating innovative roles will always be on the horizon. I think that they will have a hard time looking back and wonder what they did before there were forensic nursing roles. It is going to be like wondering how we survived without computers." She adds that she is proud to be among the first generation of forensic nurses. "I have always seen myself as an ambassador for forensic nursing and now, a bit bold and daring to push the envelope a little further in creating a new environment. I like the independence, autonomy, and self-motivation involved in my work, as well the opportunities for collaboration, and the ability to educate, create, find solutions, and assist patients."

Caruso says she looked to other nurses who had done the same thing and were operating quite successfully:

> I started looking around and discovered that there are quite a few forensic entrepreneurs who can serve as role models. For me, one of them was Melinda Waddell Wheeler, a very creative entrepreneur who has six or seven sites at which she offers examiner services. She contracts with nurses through the local hospital, where the local sexual assault program is housed. I took it one step further. I am not associated with a hospital, which did cause some heads to turn. Many people asked, "How can you do that?" The answer, of course, was before I did something like that, I spent months researching this kind of practice and making sure it was within the scope and standards of practice, not only with the California board of nursing but also with the IAFN's scope and standards. I am not providing any medical care or making diagnoses other than nursing diagnoses; my service is the collection of evidence from the individual. It does involve some assessment, but nothing beyond the scope of practice.

Lynch (1995) states, "A private facility permits victims and law enforcement officers to circumvent the hospital emergency department, thus avoiding the hassles and delays often encountered in that setting." She explains that most emergency personnel lack the time, equipment, or training to gather evidence necessary for a consultation, and that physicians and ED staff, who are faced with increasing numbers of acute medical problems, are spared the additional burden of a lengthy evaluation and continuing responsibility of litigation associated with forensic cases. As well, law enforcement officers are out of circulation for a shorter period and can usually avoid the hospital emergency altogether. Lynch adds, "A private facility provides timely and sensitive examinations, which decrease the stress and humiliation of the experience for the victim. Thus, this comprehensive method contributes not only to the efficiency and effectiveness of forensic science but also encourages victims to report sexual offenses with confidence that they will be accorded justice through a thorough and empathic system."

Caruso explains that some hospitals will refer victims of sexual assault to her, but her primary source of referrals is local law enforcement agencies. "They will receive a report of a sexual assault and they will contact me," she says. "We will all meet here at my center to do the forensic exam. If a patient is unable to be moved from the hospital, then I will do an in-hospital exam, but those are far less frequent in occurrence." She says that she operates her center much the same as other centers, with a standardized evidentiary examination at the core of her services. "I try to keep up to date on changing trends so that I can perform as standard and accurate of an evidentiary examination as I can. I communicate with the regional crime labs to ensure that I am collecting the kind of evidence that they want and which is most probative." Caruso says her contracted-services business model might not be the norm in all regions, but it provides a swift, efficient response to victims. "Judging by the comments I receive from patients, they like this kind of service," she says:

One of the primary comments that I hear most is that because I am not in a hospital environment, and because my center has a private entry, the patient is assured greater levels of privacy and confidentiality. When a patient walks into a hospital accompanied by a law enforcement officer, all eyes are upon them. Even though protocol dictates that these patients are to be taken away from the general ER population and environment as soon as possible, even for a few moments, I'm sure the victim feels that everyone—other patients and staff—are looking at him or her and wondering if he or she is a criminal or a victim of sexual assault. I have heard this from patients and from law enforcement. I give my patients a patient-satisfaction survey and I tell them not to fill it out until they feel comfortable in doing so. It gives us an idea of how we are doing. Not everyone turns them in, but the ones who do comment that they feel more at ease being away from a bustling ER, and having more personal interaction with our nurses. I think that elevates their comfort level.

At the same time that she is serving her patient population, Caruso says she realizes she is building bridges with the law enforcement community, a critical relationship in the care of and service to sexual assault victims:

> It's all about breaking down barriers and establishing good communication for the benefit of patients. As a rule, it's not the detectives who bring patients to my center, it's the patrol officers. All I have to tell them is to sit down and relax and I will take care of everything for them, and when they leave the center, they will have a sexual assault evidence kit and a report in their hands, including a narrative that will be e-mailed or faxed to the detective the next day. These officers are part of the interview process so that they feel included; instead of them handing over the case to the nurse, they are participating in the case with the nurse. Of course, they are not present for the physical exam, although sometimes I do have a patient who has bonded with the female officer and so I will let her into the exam room. It's all about making law enforcement know that this is a collaboration.

Caruso says she no longer worries about being respected in the community because she has worked hard to win her colleagues' respect and trust of her expertise:

> I think lack of validation of nurses by law enforcement is a shame, and I hear other nurses describing a less-than-ideal relationship with the police. Even when I am not working a particular case—for example, I do not take pediatric cases—I will get calls from a police officer who wants my opinion on something. When that started happening several years ago, I thought, "Wow, they must think I know something at last!" When you are known as an authority in your region, it's fulfilling, and when you can help others solve a problem, it's tremendously rewarding. After all these years, I still get excited about doing cases. My patients and local law enforcement know that the relationship they have with me isn't going to end when the patient leaves my center. Instead of simply saying, "Let's collect the evidence and you're out of here," I want to make sure that patients have a safe place to go; I ask a lot of questions about their home life, and their well-being, so I can form a whole picture of this person and determine what kind of referrals and follow-up they might need. Even though there's a process within the evidentiary exam that you go through which remains the same on every patient, there's never anything that is exactly the same for every patient because you must treat them as individuals. You have to think about where they came from, what their life is like, and if you can do some education on prevention or risk assessment. You treat them not as if you are simply performing a task for law enforcement but because you care about what is happening to them.

Whether a center is hospital-based or operated independently by forensic nurse entrepreneurs, the most common challenge is keeping its doors open. "There is so much more recognition of SANE programs and buy-in from the community and from state and federal entities," Sharon Crowley observes:

> But on the individual level, it is still hard, and many nurses struggle to make ends meet. I see start-up programs still having to work very hard for equipment and to cover operational costs, and nurses are still often vastly underpaid for the services they perform. From personal experience, it's the same old nightmare of trying to obtain funding, whether it's for research or for operations; unless you have significant financial backing, it can be tough. Most nurses don't have backgrounds in business, and I think it's unfortunate that they don't have more of a focus on financial and business issues related to health care provision. I would strongly recommend that nurses become better trained in how to run a business enterprise. Whether they work for someone else or work independently, it would be invaluable experience. Ideas and talent aren't enough without the business skills that entrepreneurs need. You have to have business savvy to bring in the money and market your services to stay viable and

make a difference for forensic patients you serve. Nurses have a hard time with that traditionally; they want to make people feel better, but it's difficult for them to also look after the bottom line... and that is such an important responsibility.

Regarding independent centers and programs, Crowley notes:

Having consulted and conducted training for both hospital-based and independent models of business, I think there are advantages and disadvantages. In today's economy, there is certainly more safety in numbers, but conversely, if you are affiliated with a large agency you're going to be subjected to their budgetary controls. But like any other small business, if you are going out on your own, you have the same kinds of limitations. It takes an especially strong person and a very good businessperson to be able to supply goods and services at the same level as a hospital but to do it independently. A lot of people do go off on their own because of their frustrations with working within the hospital system. Nurses must decide what they can live with and what they can't within each environment. Within the hospital environment, even with all its potential faults, there are many benefits; you have more access to the traditional model of health care delivery, and you have access to a lot of resources and existing protocols—there is security in that. However, when you go out on your own, you constantly have to watch the bottom line. You can't provide anything to patients if you don't stay afloat financially. Sometimes that becomes such a detriment it is hard to provide your services. Going out on one's own can be a 24/7 proposition and that can get old after a while. Still, you have a certain amount of freedom and independence. Nurses have to do some soul-searching and decide what is best for them.

Crowley says she believes that new opportunities will come to nurses who keep looking for them:

The patient population we serve is growing, and whether you are out on your own or associated with a hospital, you will find the right opportunities to serve them. If there are capable people who can provide a high-level service at a reasonable cost, then that health care delivery model will work. But as science grows in leaps and bounds, people who specialize or who work independently will have to be more creative in how they provide their services.

Caruso advises:

Don't wait for someone to hand it to you. You must make your own way and prepare intensely, with a full-time education base, for what most likely will be a part-time job. The independence starts with the education. If the initial training is good it will continue to meet the needs of the patients and practitioners alike. But the education does not stop there... one must be actively involved to ascertain the latest in technology and techniques that are applied to our work everyday. There must be a connection with our peers for the dissemination of information to be a continuous flow.

Forensic nursing is intense, in-depth work that requires critical thinking and problem solving. It's not for everybody. The most common misperception is that the work is glamorous and easy, like the TV shows. Well, just wait until your pager goes off at 3 a.m. and we'll see how glamorous it is. Sometimes, that is the single element that separates the boys from the men, so to speak, or I should say the girls from the women, although there are male forensic nurses, and good ones, too.

16.2 THE LEGAL NURSE CONSULTANT

Texan Gail Lindsey, RN, BSN, decided to hang out her own shingle as an LNC because the work seemed challenging, interesting, and rewarding. However, it was her background in death investigation and forensics that not only bolstered her legal work, but provided a compelling way to first pursue her interest in the medico-legal process. Lindsey was working as a faculty associate at a health science center school of nursing in Lubbock, Texas, on the fateful day that she discovered the application of forensic science to nursing. When Lindsey realized that she needed some additional continuing education units for her nursing license, she scouted out the possibilities. By chance she happened on a flier posted at the health science center promoting a workshop being presented by Virginia Lynch, one of the pioneers of forensic nursing. "I saw that she was going to be discussing the collection of evidence and I thought it sounded fascinating," Lindsey recalls. "I went to the workshop, and throughout Virginia's entire presentation, I was dumbfounded and astounded by the content. I met with her afterward and that's how I got started in forensic nursing. After learning more, I got my foot in the door with the medical examiner's office."

Lindsey explains that her forensic nursing coursework required her to undertake a 150-hour internship with a forensic practitioner, so she located the medical examiner in Lubbock, and persuaded him to talk to her:

I simply went into the office and talked to him. He had heard about forensic nurses, and he said to me, "Have you thought about doing sexual assault examination, because Lubbock needs a program like that." He had worked in Amarillo, a city that had a well-established sexual assault nurse examiner program. He said, "Would you be interested in doing something like that?" and I said, "Maybe. But can I get my 150 hours first?" He was willing to serve as my preceptor and he was extremely nice. My entire experience was very good, as everyone had been very receptive to my presence.

Perhaps, Lindsey says, it might have had a little something to do with her job performance, and some well-placed junk food didn't hurt, either. "I took doughnuts every time I went to the ME's office. I confess that I just played to their egos quite a bit and remembered where my place was, and asked a lot of questions. They were wonderful teachers, and I think that by my being a nurse and a faculty associate, it helped validate my presence." Lindsey emphasizes that the ME's office was very supportive of either realm of practice for a nurse, whether it was sexual assault or death investigation. "Once I got in there, they probably said to themselves. 'Hey she's not dumb or lazy after all,' or whatever stigma they have attached to nurses. My problem was with the director of the local rape crisis center. Maybe she was feeling threatened because she was not a nurse, but I had no reception from her whatsoever." Lindsey also recalls being rebuffed by a nurse practitioner with whom she had shared her ideas. "I had shared with her what I wanted to do, and she was not very helpful. I think she might have been kind of threatened, too. Funny enough, these people were female, which makes their actions a bit surprising."

Around this time, Lindsey says, various staff members in the ME's office had asked if she had heard about legal nurse consulting. "I immediately started doing some research on that. They were thinking that a few people might go into business together and do this on the side. They wanted me to do the legwork, get it organized, and put it together, and they would consult on some of the cases if they were needed. And that's how I got started in the legal nurse consulting business." Lindsey says that she had observed a great deal of opportunity for LNC business in not only a litigious society, but in a town filled with lawyers. "I thought to myself, there are a lot of lawsuits out there, there are a lot of attorneys in this town, and a few people are practicing as LNCs already. I got the feeling they were being protective of their territory, but I knew there was room in this town for more than two LNCs." At the time of the launch of her business, Lindsey was still employed by the ME's office. "I was still working for the ME at the time I started my legal nurse consulting practice. I could review these cases in the evenings, as long as it wasn't a conflict of interest. The ME didn't have a problem with it; in fact, he was a very good sounding board for me."

Lindsey started working from her home to keep overhead costs as low as possible. "I was fortunate then and still am to be in a position where financially, I was able to make the leap to start my own business," she notes, "because it is a very big commitment. I tried to keep my expenses as minimal as I could and just work from home in an extra room." She emphasizes that structure is important when launching a home-based business in particular. "What I found out about myself was, I need a formal setting and a place to go to do my work, or I am not going to get anything done. That's the way I was in nursing school, too, thinking that I wasn't going to study until I absolutely had to," she says, chuckling. "In all honesty, it's probably better for me to have an office to go to; even now I will catch myself vacuuming or dusting rather than working on cases!"

Most of Lindsey's clients are located in Lubbock, Texas, she says, adding:

> I have not marketed to the San Antonio market yet. That's another weakness of mine—marketing—you see that in a lot of LNCs and in a lot of women in general—a reluctance to ask for business. But you must knock on doors, you must get out there and sell yourself because of the competition. Work is like an ebb and flow. There are days when you'll get three or four referrals and other days when you will have a dry spell. When it comes to marketing, I have a letter of introduction and brochures that I send out to potential client attorneys. I also went to the expense of having professional business cards made, and I try to hand them out at various functions at law schools or lawyers' associations where I might be speaking or attending or both. The key is to show up somewhere, get your foot in the door, and start talking as fast as you can. Be sure to reach out to the young attorneys coming up before they even pass the bar; talk to them about what an LNC does. I am such a firm believer in using what your community has to offer—law schools, professional groups, business networking functions and the like.
>
> You have to get out there and network, and carry those business cards, and force yourself to meet people. The more you meet people, the more your phone is going to ring and the more comfortable you are going to be at it.

Lindsey adds that more so than almost anything, credentials frequently mean the difference between securing work and walking away empty-handed:

> It's much more so in a city such as San Antonio than in a smaller place like Lubbock. A BSN is really something in Lubbock, but in San Antonio, a BSN is not that big of a deal. So you have to differentiate yourself by your credentials, by your experience and your knowledge. In my case, I do that with my forensic ties and medico-legal abilities. There are so many more nurses with master's degrees in the region, so you have to find other ways to compete. It's the same with attorneys. The larger firms have more experience and business is conducted on a much more professional level at these kinds of firms. Attorneys in Lubbock are professional, but they don't have the resources or 20 partners in a firm due to the city's smaller population. It's a different ball game when looking for work.

Regarding her interaction with attorneys, Lindsey says most now have a good understanding of what an LNC can do in terms of reviewing medical records and advising on cases. "The larger firms usually have a nurse on board, so they are familiar with LNCs. I think, however, that they are still trying to separate the paralegal from the LNC in their minds. They can get by with paying a paralegal less money, and not having to pay as much as they should be paying a nurse. That's a challenge to our livelihoods."

Lindsey says she enjoys her work because of the opportunity to learn and grow with every case. "You will learn something new with every case you take," she promises. "If you are open to what you are investigating, you will learn an incredible amount about the way the human mind works, and about human behavior and how people interact in both civil and criminal cases. I'm astounded at some of the things people do and what they try to pull off." She says she also is intrigued by the differences in an attorney's perspective versus that of a health care provider. "In some personal-injury cases, you see what's going on in the health care system and what kind of health care the plaintiff is receiving. Then you look at the case from an attorney's point of view and you think, gosh, you ought to be suing the doctor instead of the health care institution."

Lindsey's background in death investigation is a rich resource from which she draws almost daily:

> Because of my experience with medico-legal investigations and assisting at autopsies at the medical examiner's office, I was fortunate to see things that were never talked about in nursing school. You can look at pictures of pathology in textbooks all you want, but it's not until you come face to face with injury and death, or when you get to the actual hands-on practice of pathology, does it hit home. Of course, at a death scene, as a nurse, it's too late for you to do anything to help that patient, but there are other ways you can do something. My background and contact with various forensic professionals has taught me so much, and it's an incredible asset to know about physiology and mechanisms of death firsthand.
>
> I no longer am active in death investigation, however, I still keep in touch with the pathologists and the investigators. They are good sounding boards for some of my LNC cases, and if there is something I can't figure out, I can get their opinion if they are willing to share it. I try not to bother them; to me, some of this stuff is very complex but to them it is very simple, and they can explain it to me.

Lindsey credits her nursing education and experience for the success she has in evaluating medical records for attorneys:

> The legal nurse consulting work sprung from my forensic background; I don't know that without that early exposure, that I would have gone into legal nurse consulting. But the two components work well together. When I was working for the ME, part of my job responsibilities was to go through the medical records and quickly determine what I saw in there for the pathologist. Of course, they will take a look at them when they finish the autopsy anyway, but I was able to give them a fast heads-up as to the decedent's history or anything I see that might be relevant to the case. In that way, I could help put the pieces of the puzzle together.

In legal nurse consulting, it might be the same puzzle, but the pieces are different, Lindsey says:

> The work varies according to which side you are on in court. As a nurse, you will be able to look at a case from both sides. As an advocate for the patient, you have to be nonjudgmental and objective, and look at both sides of the story in order to better assist your attorney. In any case, the attorney will try to develop a theory early, and their theory and your theory may not be the same. So it's interesting to see how the case develops based on their theory and your theory, and you simply try to ask, "Isn't my theory also a possibility?" The answer to that will depend on whether or not the attorney is open-minded and receptive. It's your job to educate the attorneys. Some of them are very versed in medical jargon; those who have been doing it for a long time know quite a lot. If they just do back-injury cases, then they will undoubtedly know the spine very well and have been educated about it from their stable of experts. But they don't know it from a nurse's perspective, which is a whole different ball game because a nurse looks at it not just from the checkbook perspective, she looks at it as a holistic case.

Sometimes, Lindsey says:

> Being a nurse, it's tempting to always identify with the patient. There have been some cases where I am constructing a chronology of events and I see his or her health care deteriorating and I think, "They are going to kill him or her before this is all over." I may even be working the defense side but I am still worried about the plaintiff and what's happening physically, mentally, and emotionally. But you must always focus on what you are there to do and to be professional and effective at all times.

Lindsey says the process of launching a business has been a journey into discovery about who she is and what is important to her. She advises:

> If legal nurse consulting is something you have decided that you are going to, then you must commit 100 percent to the effort. Be prepared to treat it like any other job, something you are going to do 8 to 5 (or sometimes much longer) everyday. Give it a certain amount of predetermined time and set that goal for yourself. If you don't meet it, then re-evaluate the situation to see if it's really not what you want to do or where you should be in life. But take the first steps, instead of just trudging along, thinking about your own business, and not doing anything about it.

Lindsey recalls that she didn't encounter much difficulty making the transition from faculty associate to independent businesswoman. "I suppose I already had the mindset that I needed," she says. "I didn't have that difficult of a time making the transition, but for nurses that depend on their income, it is a very serious consideration. I was very fortunate to have a safety net. It can be very scary to leave a secure job, but the payoffs can be terrific."

She believes the future of legal nurse consulting is a good one, and thinks the climate is still right for nurses to become entrepreneurs. "In Texas, at least, there is talk about caps on some of the damages awarded in court, but no matter what happens there, I think there will be a need for legal nurse consultants and other forensic practitioners. There are many underserved areas in Texas that need expertise, and attorneys are working where there still aren't any LNCs. If that is something someone wants to do, I certainly think there will be an opportunity out there."

16.3 THE EDUCATOR

Californian Faye Battiste-Otto, RN, has a unique take on entrepreneurship. As president and CEO of Palm Springs-based American Forensic Nurses, Inc. (AFN), Battiste-Otto is a savvy businesswoman, but she also draws on years of experience as a nurse in the trenches, and as one of the pioneers of forensic nursing when she helped a small band of fellow visionaries found the IAFN. In fact, in 1996, she was awarded the Pioneer Award in Forensic Nursing, presented annually by the IAFN. She has been a guest speaker at several forensic-community functions, including the IAFN's third annual scientific assembly, where she presented the paper, "Patterns of Injury in Sexual Assault Victims" based on an analysis of approximately 300 examinations. She also presented at the AAFS annual meeting, and in 1996, she addressed the Pacific Northwest Forensic Medicine Conference by speaking on "The Male Suspect Examination in Sexual Assault Cases." She also organized a two-day seminar, "Typology of the Sexual Offender and Medical Legal Examination of the Adolescent Victim of Abuse," at the Sheriff's Department of San Bernardino County (California). In 1998, she was a contributor to the publication *Scope and Standards of Forensic Nursing Standards,* produced by the ANA and the IAFN.

Battiste-Otto's taste for forensics was cultivated early in her career, while she was working as supervising nurse in the ED of Desert Regional Hospital in Palm Springs. "I had the opportunity to observe law enforcement officers and their in-custody and frequently unruly DUI/drug suspects having to wait for a nurse to collect blood samples, which removed the officer from his primary-duty assignment for long periods of time and potentially created a risk to those in the emergency department," she recalls. "The thought occurred to me that if a private RN were permitted to perform the blood withdrawals at jail facilities, law enforcement would benefit financially by reason of eliminating officer downtime, occasioned by suspect transportation to and from a hospital facility and the frequently experienced delays at such facilities. This thinking generated the initial purpose of AFN." She continues:

> Initially in 1983, I persuaded the Riverside County Sheriff's Department, Indio area, to try my concept, and subsequently, the Palm Springs Police Department followed. The sheriff was very satisfied with both AFN's service and cost savings. The program was so effective, upon his election, he instituted AFN's services throughout Riverside County. This recognition ultimately led to AFN's expansion of its forensic services to numerous law enforcement agencies in Riverside, San Bernardino, Los Angeles, and San Diego counties.

While Battiste-Otto was associated with the Desert Regional Hospital and JFK Hospital in Indio, California, located in southern California's high desert, she also observed the examination and limited forensic evaluation of victims of sexual assault:

> These victims frequently were assigned low priority, in most instances because staff physicians did not wish to become prosecutorial witnesses in the event the assailant was caught and scheduled for trial. This, and the availability of training for and professional recognition of sexual assault nurse examiners (SANEs), led me to further expand the forensic services of AFN by creating the first privately owned and operated sexual assault examination center.

This led Battiste-Otto to open a number of examination facilities in Riverside, San Bernardino, and Los Angeles counties. "Again, this was satisfying a community need while at the same time it was a tremendous cost-saving service for those involved in the administration of justice and law enforcement. This area of endeavor also included the forensic examination of sexual assault suspects."

As the forensic services offered by AFN increased, Battiste-Otto obtained a provider license to offer continuing education units for RNs. She developed a 40-hour course leading to certification as a SANE, and then instituted in-house training programs in a variety of forensic evaluations. She also produced a sexual assault training video and program reference guide that have been distributed worldwide to hospitals and law enforcement agencies. When it was time to differentiate herself from her competitors, Battiste-Otto says the greatest challenge came from separating herself from former colleagues. She explains:

> Essentially, AFN's competition has been from those formerly associated with it, which, likely inspired by my entrepreneurial efforts, sought to venture forth with their

> own service organization. This is always a threat to an entrepreneur, but I recognized this as the type of event that makes America the great country it is, and could be successfully overcome by AFN pursuing its mission of providing the best service available.

Battiste-Otto believes that nurses need quality, real-world training opportunities. "Most hospital physicians will readily agree that the best source of information concerning the status of their patients is that he/she is trained to be an observer and ultimately acquire practice in this field. A forensic nurse must expand and take advantage of training courses, nursing programs (which should include forensics in their curriculum), together with acquiring practical experience in those areas." In crafting a curriculum that would meet the needs of nurses everywhere, Battiste-Otto also tailored her products and services to the specific needs of the larger medico-legal community:

> Initially, the development of those services offered by AFN mirror my originating concept; however, additional services were provided based on the needs of law enforcement, such as sexual assault victim examinations, sexual assault suspect examinations, blood specimen collection in instances of law enforcement officer shootings, DNA evidence collection, and urine specimen collections. Additionally, my association with the IAFN and its members has been a constant source of information in the formulization of forensic services AFN can offer both the public and private sectors.

Although any seasoned professional can make a job look easy, Battiste-Otto acknowledges that starting her own business was an adventure that challenged every aspect of her capacities for business. "It was indeed a challenge to create AFN," she confirms:

> To do so successfully, I had to devote all of my time and energy to its creation and the sale of its services in the absence of the comfort and financial awards afforded by a full-time nursing position. Moreover, my education, and experience, was in the field of nursing and I had no formal schooling in the fields of business administration, finance, and human resources. However, my husband encouraged me by commenting that many leaders of corporate America lacked such schooling, and that they, like me, were doers, not academicians. Fortunately, and like those leaders, and as AFN grew I surrounded myself with a support staff knowledgeable in those areas of business where I was lacking.

Battiste-Otto cautions, however:

> Those in the manufacturing or service industries, regardless of the superiority of their product or their service, will never achieve success unless the consuming public is made aware. AFN is, and was, no different, and in the absence of effective sales, would not have succeeded. From the sales standpoint, AFN's most challenging effort was persuading cost-conscience law enforcement of the financial benefits in using the services AFN provided; that continues today as a principle challenge.

Although so much of her work is done in the business realm, Battiste-Otto says she hasn't strayed from continuous work on clinical skills. "I maintain my nursing clinical skills through several avenues," she says. "First, AFN owns and operates a senior assisted-living facility, and the medical issues of its residents present an opportunity to sustain my basic nursing techniques. In addition, AFN has a Web site, and through it, I work in conjunction with University of California-Riverside by offering a number of courses in forensics, authored by registered nurses who are acknowledged leaders in the field of forensic nursing." It is through this particular venture that Battiste-Otto believes she can help bolster the current quality of forensic nursing training and education:

> In my view, the availability of forensic nursing education, on balance with other fields offering specialized techniques is, unfortunately, minimal if not nearly nonexistent. I am trying to correct this neglected area of academia through AFN's Web site and AFN's course materials offered in partnership with UC-Riverside. Other areas of forensics, not specifically structured for nurses, have fared better in terms of both subject matter and availability, and nurses are limited to acquiring specialized forensic skills through these sources. Hopefully, the IAFN, working in unison with other forensic organizations, will improve upon this situation.

Despite the various inherent challenges, the joys of entrepreneurship are not lost on Battiste-Otto. "I could say that the best part is being my own boss, however, and while acknowledging some truth in that response, I would supplement it by responding that my joy in being an entrepreneur is the success I have achieved financially and the sharing of that success with all of those who work at AFN." In advising others who are interested in becoming entrepreneurs, Battiste-Otto says that adherence to principles such as pride in professionalism, persistence, honesty, integrity, and commitment to quality service will go far in carrying any venture. Battiste-Otto believes the future portends well for forensic nursing opportunities in the public and private sectors:

> As the field of forensic technology, education, and specialties expands, it will provide ever-increasing opportunities to entrepreneurs in the field of forensics, either as specialists or as leaders of organizations dedicated to that field. As a founder of the IAFN, and witnessing its phenomenal membership growth, together with the ever-increasing technology and education in the field of forensics, I would believe that the future of forensic nursing is unlimited.

REFERENCES

Lynch, V. A. Clinical forensic nursing: A new perspective in the management of crime victims from trauma to trial. Adapted from Critical Care Nursing Clinics of North America. September 1995.

17 The Future of Forensic Nursing

Forensic nursing is a blank slate on which future generations of forensic nurses will describe its significant contributions to the medico-legal community. For so many reasons, it is impossible to predict the precise course this specialty will take; however, its current practitioners say the importance of forensic nursing will continue to grow as it infiltrates and influences all aspects of health care, medicine, and forensic science. Sixteen previous chapters have presented and discussed the important issues, opportunities, and challenges facing forensic nursing, as it leaves its infancy as a nursing specialty. Moving into its adolescence, forensic nursing must continue its ardent championship of forensic patients, its tight embrace of scientific practice, and its contributions to the ever-evolving health care industry.

Working from its established foundation, forensic nursing must now address issues related to job opportunities, program funding, education and training needs, professional development mandates, and an ongoing quest for an understanding of and respect for the specialty by medical, health care, and forensic science colleagues and lay persons alike. Flying under the radar is no longer acceptable to many forensic nurses, who are now striving toward greater recognition of their medico-legal contributions.

Acceptance and acknowledgment can be achieved, according to Mary Sullivan, by an uncompromising belief in the value of forensic nursing:

> We, as forensic nurses, must believe in ourselves, and that belief must be unshakable. As our colleagues become more informed about what we do, and as nurses continue to grow increasingly confident of their abilities and their contributions, our profile will be raised and our work will be better understood. Although it will not happen overnight, it will happen. It is simply a matter of continuing to raise awareness about forensic nursing. This will certainly happen when forensic nursing principles are gradually incorporated into clinical practice for nurses, doctors, and anyone else who comes in contact with forensic patient populations.
>
> My personal hope is that someday there will be a forensic nurse in every patient-care area on every shift, every day, whether it is the ER, the OR, the ICU, med-surg, inpatient psych; anywhere there is a forensic patient being cared for, there should be someone with the knowledge and skills to handle medico-legal situations. This kind of role would open up so many opportunities for nurses in clinics, hospitals, nursing homes; if every facility which cared for human beings had someone with a forensic nursing background and training, there would be a wonderful wave of job opportunities.

A significant challenge for forensic nurses will be convincing potential employers of the contributions they can make to their facilities. Georgia Pasqualone says that although her hospital is exceedingly supportive of nurses, she recognizes that not every practitioner might be so lucky to have unwavering professional backing:

> There are so many hospitals that barely have enough staff to take care of the patients they have, let alone take a few more minutes to preserve forensic evidence or establish and protect a crime scene in the clinical setting. It's one of the major problems that exist in our health care system today. My advice to these nurses is to persist, because one of these days, a case is going to fall into their laps that might be high profile. If they pay attention to what they are doing, they can help prove someone's innocence or guilt because they recognized some piece of evidence for what it was. For example, the nurse may have detected suspicious injuries and took the initiative to report them and to photograph them. One of my goals is to get a complete photo-documentation policy established at my hospital. We see plenty of women who come into the ED who say they fell down the stairs or walked into a door because they are not going to say their husbands or boyfriends beat them up. If we consistently photo-document these injuries and place the photographs into the medical record, one of these days there will be enough evidence to go to court and this woman, being at the end of her rope, will decide to press charges. And that's when a forensic nurse's medico-legal contributions will prove his or her value.
>
> Nurses must persist in taking cases like these to their nursing managers or to their vice presidents of nursing and say, "We must have a heightened awareness of forensic issues and be alert to potential forensic patients." Ideally, there should be two or three forensic nurse consultants at every hospital who can pay attention to these kinds

of details, especially when staffing is less than optimal. A designated forensic nurse can also assist other nurses, or forensic nursing responsibilities can be incorporated into their existing role, which will make a lot of facility bean counters very happy. There may not be a lot of money to pay someone an additional salary to work as a forensic nurse, but there are many creative ways that the position of forensic nurse consultant can be added. The job has no boundaries except those of a nurse's own imagination.

In their quest for professional respect, forensic nurses must continue to demonstrate the exemplary clinical performance they have come to expect from themselves and from others. "The more professional we are as individuals and a collective body, the greater chance our voices will be heard and our work will be recognized," says Linda McCracken. "Victims will speak out, sharing their experiences and their gratitude for the nurses who helped them. And our medical and forensic colleagues will see the consistency and professionalism of our work, and our credibility will continue to increase."

Nurses must be self-motivated when pursuing a career in forensics. "Don't hold your breath, waiting for people to roll out the red carpet for you," cautions Sullivan. "It's a lot of hard work to break into the field and no one will do it for you. You must be self-directed and be able to make a case for whatever you want to do in the forensic nursing field."

"Nurses must be the commanders of their own careers," concurs Sharon Crowley:

They may have to beat their heads against some walls, but they will eventually be recognized. Professional and personal success in this field is still going to depend on someone being highly directed to achieve his or her goals, and even once they get a foot in the door, they must be prepared to prove themselves. Forensic nurses must be flexible and creative in their search for work, as in most health care facilities, a forensic nursing position is seen as a luxury, not a necessity. I think that prestigious teaching facilities will have the greatest ability to create new opportunities for forensic nurses. Many hospitals are struggling to survive, and we may still be seen as a luxury even though it is a luxury they cannot afford to be without. It will take a self-directed person to show these facilities that they are the ones who can fulfill the facility's medico-legal needs better than anyone else.

Forensic nurses of all specialties suggest that prospective and fledgling nurses should consider the following points when pursuing a career in this specialty:

- Understand thoroughly the heritage of forensic nursing and the application of forensic principles to nursing and medical practice; be prepared to demonstrate to prospective employers how forensic nursing can improve the provision of medico-legal services in a health care setting.
- Get as much formal training and education as possible from accredited sources and institutions, attend conferences and seminars, and stay on top of continuing education opportunities.
- Share forensic principles with colleagues and administrators to further underscore the importance of forensic nursing. If these principles and protocols are already established at a health care facility, ensure that all medical personnel know and follow them; if not, pursue sources of information and formulate a plan of implementation.
- Become your facility's resident expert on forensic principles and practices.
- Be proactive about your career: Propose new opportunities, pursue an internship, seek a mentor, or network with like-minded individuals.
- Be a role model or mentor if you are already established in your field.
- Grow in your practice, and teach others along the way. Reach out to those following behind you to guarantee continued viability of the field.

"Now that forensic nursing isn't quite the obscure, unsung entity it used to be in the days before official recognition by the American Academy of Forensic Science (AAFS) and the American Nurses Association (ANA), practitioners of this unique nursing specialty can rest on their laurels, right?" says Faye Battiste-Otto:

Wrong! Nurses have seen forensic nursing grow from a tiny seed of an idea to a discipline finally coming into its own. It's not so much a quest for validation anymore as it is the pursuit of respect from other members of health care and medicine. Forensic pathologists, law enforcement investigators, and members of the legal community have been quicker to support forensic nursing because it augments and contributes to the medico-legal process. Other physicians, clinicians, and even some nurses continue to be puzzled by forensic nursing's insistence on fundamental tenets of evidentiary examinations, chains of custody, evidence collection, preservation and documentation, and its bigger purpose in a court of law.

We still have a long way to go. I think that with increased education and research, we will eventually gain the respect we deserve. The problem is, the community is not sure what forensic nursing is. They are afraid of it. When I started my business years ago, people said, "You are involved in forensic science so you must be involved with dead people." They did not know about living forensic patients.

Virginia Lynch adds that some of the greatest opposition has come from nursing itself. "It was such a foreign concept to nursing," she says:

> Understanding came first from forensic pathologists and forensic scientists, then from law enforcement, and finally nursing. But once nursing recognized the value of what I was trying to do, they embraced it wholeheartedly. It was such a strange evolution because generally, medicine is the last to be the first to support nursing; however, forensic pathologists were the only specialists in the entire history of medicine that didn't have their own nursing specialists. Pediatricians had pediatric nurses; oncologists had oncology nurses; critical care physicians had critical care nurses; and even neurosurgeons wouldn't consider going into surgery without their skilled surgical nurses. But the forensic pathologist only had nonmedical police officers to assist them.

Lynch credits Dr. Thomas Noguchi as being one of the first to recognize a specific role for nurses in forensic science:

> Dr. Noguchi was the famed coroner in L.A. who autopsied John Belushi, Natalie Wood, and Marilyn Monroe, among other high-profile cases. Almost 20 years ago, when I introduced forensic nursing at the AAFS, he told me he had always believed that a nurse would be the ideal clinician to work with families of sudden infant death syndrome. He felt that police officers and traditional death investigators didn't have the psychosocial skills necessary to communicate with families who were so emotionally traumatized.

Lynch says there were many others who saw and believed in the value of nurses in forensic pathology:

> The very first was Dr. John Butt from Canada as long as 35 years ago. At that time he did a five-year study to see who made the best death scene investigator. He used paramedics, lab techs, police officers, and registered nurses, and came to the conclusion it was the registered nurse who made the best death scene investigator. Among their greatest skills cited was their ability to communicate, their psychosocial intervention. The chief forensic pathologist in Dallas, Dr. Charles Petty, opened the door of the Southwestern Institute of Forensic Science for me as a nursing student. He allowed me free reign to study in all of the departments of the Institute, not even knowing at that time what I would do with it. And, of course, it was Dr. Patrick Besant-Matthews who took me through my first autopsy there... who today still is one of the greatest champions of forensic nursing. Dr. Nizam Peerwani gave me my first job as a medical examiner's investigator, the job that led me to realize what nurses needed to know and were capable of doing.

Forensic nursing is sometimes an uneven landscape, its broad stretches of smooth terrain punctuated by hidden pitfalls and sheer cliffs. Traversing this path, sojourners will encounter not only the need for professional recognition; they face education and training challenges, barriers to employment, and perhaps most significantly, fighting for the right to call themselves forensic nurses. Lynch says it's a matter of semantics, really, because nurses have already been serving in this capacity for a hundred years. "Many nurses were already working in a variety of forensic roles, but no one called it forensic nursing," she explains:

> Nurses had long been working with the criminally insane, the suspects, and the accused who were remanded while waiting to stand trial. Nurses had just started doing rape exams in the mid-1970s, about the same time as nurses in death investigation. Nurses had been managing forensic cases in the ED but no one called them forensic cases, and SANEs weren't referred to as forensic nurses at that time.
>
> When we talk about the evolution of forensic nursing, it wasn't that these nurses were not practicing in forensic roles; they just didn't know they were. I will never forget when Cindy Peternelj-Taylor, who teaches at the University of Saskatoon in Canada, wrote to me after my first article was published and thanked me. What she said has always stayed with me. She said, "What you have done is give us an identity. We've always known we were doing something very unique, very special, but you have given it a name." I based the development of forensic nursing categories on the categories of specialists in the AAFS. You didn't have to have a medical degree to be a death investigator, yet nurses were not accepted for membership at that time because they were nurses. But as a death investigator I had become a member and had established a foundation on which to project forensic nursing. It was from that platform that I began to insidiously interject forensic nursing from a wide range of perspectives—sexual assault, death investigation, psychosocial intervention, and all of the existing areas. Academy members like Dr. Michael Baden and Dr. Patrick Besant-Matthews supported me and have remained strong defenders of forensic nursing.

Lynch and Battiste-Otto are among many who believe a strong forensic nursing curriculum is essential to the future growth of the field and the edification of its practitioners. "As a result of my interest in the forensic sciences as an undergraduate nursing student working with rape victims, I began to realize that the knowledge I was gaining through forensic science was something that every nurse should know," says Lynch, director of the Forensic Nursing and Forensic Health Science program at Beth-El College of Nursing at the University of Colorado. "As I became a death investigator, I realized the valuable contributions of forensic science to our work, not just to nurses as death investigators, but to every nurse. They weren't teaching this information in nursing school. Some of the things most basic but critical to nursing practice, such as the difference between a cut and a laceration, weren't being taught and could have serious legal implications."

Lynch points to a Florida case as an example:

> A nurse had repeatedly documented multiple lacerations throughout the patient's chart. The defense attorney reviewed the chart and asked the judge to dismiss the charges against his client. He said, "My client was carrying a knife and a knife cannot inflict a laceration; my client wasn't carrying a baseball bat or a club." Every nurse should know the difference between a cut and a laceration and yet doctors and nurses outside the forensic arena continue to misdocument the term *laceration*.

Lynch relates another example:

> The most frequently overlooked sign of abuse is the human bite mark, yet this is not taught in traditional nursing education. Wouldn't you assume that if we were expected to identify crime victims, to collect evidence, and report these cases to law enforcement, that the single most overlooked sign of abuse should be taught in schools of nursing? Nurses need to know the human bite mark is also commonly associated with sexual assault; or the fact that cardiac arrest is not a cause of death. The most basic concepts that every nurse should know appeared to be recognized only in forensic science.

The gap between nursing practice and forensic science was much wider in the early days than it is now, and Lynch decided to address it:

> When I wrote my master's degree program in forensic nursing I wanted a combination of nursing science, forensic science, and criminal justice that would bridge the gap between health care and the law. I was in the right place at the right time and the right person who made it happen was Dr. Sam Hughes. He was the graduate dean at the University of Texas at Arlington School of Nursing; I don't know whether it was because he was a man or because he was a military nurse, but he immediately understood my vision of forensic nursing. Unfortunately, he died my first semester and the new graduate dean didn't understand the concept of a forensic specialist in nursing. But what Dr. Hughes did was to open the door to forensic education in nursing and from that point it has evolved into one of the most sought after courses by nurses in the U.S. and today worldwide.

Exactly why many are skittish about using the word *forensic* is a mystery, but some forensic nurses are serious about calling a spade a spade. "There was a dean of nursing in Georgia who told me I could teach my course if I would eliminate the word *forensic*," Lynch recalls:

> I said I couldn't do that. I had developed this field based on the definition of the word forensic as a companion role to forensic medicine; she simply didn't understand what the word forensic means. And understanding this term has been a difficulty among nurses. You have to educate people about the meaning of the word as it pertains to the law. Forensic medicine has long been a respected component of public health; today forensic nursing holds the same status with health care and the law.

Even the bastion of health care, JCAHO, couldn't bring itself to use the "F" word in the early days. Says Lynch:

> The Joint Commission, without even knowing it, laid a platform for the acceptance of forensic nursing when it stated as early as 1992 that every ED "shall have on staff an individual skilled in the identification of crime victims and the collection and preservation of evidence." They didn't say a nurse, but they didn't say a doctor. It has taken until this year for JCAHO to use the term forensic nurse or forensic case. And it was the word forensic that was the greatest obstacle with nursing.

It's a matter of claiming something that has always been theirs, Lynch adds:

> Nurses have always been expected to care for crime victims. They were always required to collect evidence, only they called it specimens. Nurses could just as easily be subpoenaed to court without any preparation then as now. Any nurse could. Finally they realized what forensic cases were, and yes, nurses were dealing with them on a daily basis but without specialized knowledge. I don't think we are any different than any other new discipline in nursing ever was. Nurse practitioners had a tremendous obstacle to overcome, especially with physicians. Every nursing discipline has had to go through this developmental phase. I am not discouraged in any regard. I believe we have unlimited potential and that the future is ours. I believe one day every hospital, every trauma center will be required to have on staff a forensic nurse examiner. They will become the liaison between the hospital and police and courts of law and families. It is a position that is just beginning to evolve. What I find so exciting and interesting is that it is the nurses themselves who understand the role better than hospital administrators or other officials because it is the nurses who have had to deal with victims, with the police, with evidence, and with the criticisms that came from police when nurses didn't understand their responsibilities to the law and legal agencies. They were often viewed by police as obstructing justice.

Battiste-Otto acknowledges the snail's pace of the development of training and education resources for aspiring forensic nurses, and in the meantime, education occurs on the mentoring level:

> We are very willing to share our expertise and knowledge but we are so small that it takes a lot of time for education to move forward. There are a few master's degree programs out there and they can be expensive; nursing is a profession in which until recently, nurses didn't earn a lot of money. Offering courses from reputable schools and making them affordable will help registered nurses become involved in forensic nursing. That is a lot to ask of universities, but the future of forensic nursing depends on it.

There currently is no official certification as a "forensic nurse" in the United States, except for SANE certification. It is a source of frustration for established and new nurses alike, but the pioneers say that will come all in good time. "We are coming into our own and it is just a matter of time that today's obstacles will no longer exist," Lynch says:

> We are working as hard and as fast as we can to get the credentials nurses want and need. As more schools of nursing provide the education, the sooner we will realize this goal. Certification is secondary to the education and experience, but when we talk about lack of standardization and lack of education or credentials—it will all come in good time. Nurses have always provided these services. Whether they have a forensic education or forensic certification, nurses in every hospital in every city will still be required to care for crime victims; certification is a matter of making it official. Before there was an Emergency Nurses Association or before there was certification for psychiatric nurses, nurses were still working in those areas and it took time to establish their credentials.
>
> I remember some years ago attending the ANA conference in Washington, DC, when they featured the evolution of psychiatric nursing. It was the most amazing thing to hear some of the 90-year-old nurses that helped establish it talk about what they went through. I don't see that we are having greater difficulties than that group of pioneering nurses. It takes patience and it takes time. The enthusiasm of nurses in forensic practice is overriding the time that it's taking to get these credentials. They want it now, and I want them to have it now. But it doesn't mean they can't work as a forensic nurse until we have credentialing in areas other than sexual assault examination.
>
> I realize these credentials are extremely important when they go to court, but guess what: Nurses were going to court long before forensic nursing existed, and by having a forensic education, we can still be better expert witnesses, better fact witnesses, better clinicians, because we are nurses. We are taught as nurses to observe closely and document what we see and what we do. We are keen observers, excellent at documenting minute details, and are fantastic caretakers of those who need us most. No one does it better than nurses. Forensic nursing is making tremendous inroads into the future of health and justice.

To make these inroads, forensic nurses need stamina. "They also need a great deal of persistence," Battiste-Otto adds:

> Doors close in your face constantly; as an entrepreneur, doors closed in my face for three years, but I didn't give up because I had a story to tell, a mission to complete and I wanted to make a little bit of difference in the world of forensic science. Honesty, integrity, and forthrightness are of the utmost importance. If you have all of these qualities and don't give up, you can succeed out there.

Despite the challenges, forensic nurses remain upbeat about the future. "I would love to see every hospital have on its staff a clinical forensic nurse specialist," Battiste-Otto says, "one who can deal with medico-legal issues. I think we may get there but it's a slow process. There is so much happening, we have not even hit the tip of the iceberg yet."

"We have arrived," Lynch declares. "Forensic nursing is an entity whose time has come, in spite of all obstacles and negativity of those who did not share this vision. Forensic nursing is here to stay."

Pasqualone has contemplated the future of forensic nursing and observes:

> The general public is still oblivious to what we do and what we have the potential of doing. The populace is still under the impression that our role is limited to caring for sick people and giving shots. The scope of practice of a forensic nurse reaches beyond the patients we have traditionally cared for in the hospital. Judges, police officers, detectives, attorneys, school superintendents, medical examiners, coroners, physicians, and psychiatrists, to name only a few, are on a priority list for education and enlightenment regarding our emerging specialty.

She says the onus is on forensic nurses to educate others about their specialty:

> Forensic nurses struggle with marketing issues which could be more easily resolved if the disciplines with which we collaborate received an information blitz regarding the skills and knowledge we can provide. Nurses need to speak out for themselves. There are no jobs in the classified section with a pink neon sign that points to forensic nursing positions. These positions exist but need to be persuaded, coaxed, and groomed into the public eye. I realize that economics play a tremendous role in curbing the expansion of forensic nursing; however, the cliché of one step at a time seems to fit here. My dear friend and colleague, Janet Barber, states that the military "gets it," and more people need to get it. Clients who have benefited from a forensic nurse on the case get it. Attorneys who have had a forensic nurse in their office get it. Hospitals that have produced Joint Commission-approved policies and procedures written by a forensic nurse get it. Schools that have forensically educated nurses on staff get it. But

> the need is tremendous. The knowledge deficit is still daunting. Nursing has always been about repairing the wrongs done to patients. Forensic nursing goes much farther than that. Forensic nursing must acknowledge the magnitude of preventing these wrongs in the first place, and collaborating with other disciplines in order to mitigate and adjudicate the wrong that has been committed. Go market yourselves to those who need a forensic nurse by their side. If you do what you love, everything else will fall into place.

Connie Morrison believes forensic nursing is poised for greatness in the very near future, provided nurses receive the education and training that will prepare them for the challenges ahead. "Forensic nursing is a dynamic, powerful movement that is sweeping the country. Do I think it's moving fast enough? No. But I think there are enough of us out there to keep the momentum going forward. I also believe that it won't be long before more forensic nursing positions will be created because the demand for them will increase, and health care facilities will see these nurses' valuable contributions."

Bell and Benak (2001) state:

> There is strong support of forensic nursing from those who recognize the amount of knowledge required, to go beyond the traditional treatment of crime victims and fill a greater role through forensic expertise in health care. There is a need to understand what the term forensic means to different practitioners, so deficiencies can be identified and addressed through nursing education. Life is dramatic, and traumatizing circumstances remain unique to each individual; forensic nursing is the healthcare response to violence. Better prepared to meet the demands of the 21st century, nurses everywhere continue to improve the quality of the living as they contribute to the decline of violence through their professional practice.

Recognizing the need to blaze trails for succeeding generations, Linda McCracken says:

> I learned everything that I know about forensic nursing the hard way, but I'm trying to make it so other nurses don't have to go through the struggles I went through. I have put all of my energies into clinical forensics in the emergency setting and believe that ED nurses are in a prime place to practice forensic nursing in the future. Everything that we do as forensic nurses today will impact future generations of forensic nurses, and perhaps we have planted the seeds that will bloom and grow.

Lynch (1995) has stated that challenges for nurses in the clinical arena provide unique opportunities to make valuable contributions to forensic practice as they manage issues commonly encountered in the investigation of trauma. She predicts, "As we enter the next decade of nursing practice, forensic nursing will be well established. With the increasing emphasis on the forensic nursing paradigm as one strategic step to break the pattern of cyclical, interpersonal violence, it is perceived that forensic nursing will become equally important to other standard specialties." Like many nurses, Lynch embraces the hope that health care facilities around the globe will understand the need for a forensic nursing specialist to deal with the numerous medico-legal cases that will only grow in number and scope in the future. She also points to new roles and responsibilities that will enhance and expand the scope of forensic nursing, including death investigation, postmortem sexual assault examination, and mass disaster response, to name a few.

More than anything else, forensic nurses can be assured of the perpetuity of their work. As Lynch says:

> The loss of human life and function due to violence constitutes a phenomenon that affects millions of patients annually. Society demands an investigation of trauma associated with criminal activity. No longer is it acceptable for health care professionals to operate in isolation of forensic philosophies and principles. It is assumed that the individuals responsible for the performance of the examination of forensic victims have the necessary basic education, experience, and skills. Health care professionals involved in the initial response to these victims, either at the scene or in the emergency department, are faced with unique problems as social changes require continual reevaluation of standards and professional responsibility.
>
> As we enter a new era of nursing practice, forensic nursing is recognized as the most significant contemporary phase of nursing education, practice, and research as we prepare for critical issues in health care in the 21st century. Increasingly, nurses have an expanded role to play in the investigation of trauma, deaths, and crimes. In areas of the country where no medical examiner system exists and the clinical forensic physician has not yet been established, the forensic nurse may be the only medico-legal professional available and may be called upon by a variety of legal agencies to consult in cases of child abuse, sexual assault, elder abuse, and suspicious deaths. It must be emphasized that the objectives of the forensic nurse are not necessarily the same as those of law enforcement personnel but parallel them in a common perspective from a multidisciplinary approach. The nurse, physician, police, attorneys, and social services, therefore, should work together as a team and combine expertise to observe, document, and record all pertinent findings and ensure the acquisition and retention of all specimens in cooperation with the wider network of experts necessary to the resolution of the case in question.

Forensic nurses provide a continuity of care from birth to death, and from the crime to the courtroom. Lynch explains:

> The forensic nursing role has been expressly designed to provide solutions to some of the most urgent concerns in our society. Forensic nursing focuses on the areas in which medicine, nursing, and human behavior interface with the law. Existing problems are great and multifaceted and call for new solutions. The application of forensic science to contemporary nursing practice reveals a wider role in the investigation of crime and the legal process that contributes to public health and safety. The responsibility of the forensic nurse is to provide continuity of care from the health care institution or the crime scene to courts of law . . . from trauma to trial.

In the white paper, "Forensic Nursing: A Prestigious History, A Promising Future," Lynch (2001) writes:

> Forensic nursing is one example of an innovative expansion of the role nurses will fill in the arena of public health and safety in the 21st century . . . With the development of graduate and undergraduate education programs, role development in forensic nursing in the U.S. and abroad is recognized as one important component in anti-violence strategies . . . Advances in forensic and nursing science has brought this new discipline to the forefront as one of the top areas for nursing development in the 21st century.

REFERENCES

Bell, K., & Benak, L. D. Forensic nursing: The fastest growing discipline of nursing for the 21st century. Available online at: www.iafn.org. 2001.

Lynch, V. A. Clinical forensic nursing: A new perspective in the management of crime victims from trauma to trial. *Crit Care Nurs Clinics North America. 7,* 3, 489–507, 1995.

Lynch, V. A. Forensic nursing: A prestigious history, a promising future. Presented at the Fundamentals of Forensic Nursing seminar at the International Association of Forensic Nurses conference, Orlando, FL, October 2001.

RECCOMMENDED READING

Barber, J. Frontiers and challenges in critical care. *Crit Care Nurs Q. 14,* 2, 1991.

Index

F

N

T